BREWER'S DICTIONARY OF NAMES

Adrian Room

CASSELL

Cassell
Villiers House, 41/47 Strand
London WC2N 5JE

387 Park Avenue South
New York, NY 10016-8810 USA

First published 1992

British Library Cataloguing-in-Publication Data
A catalogue entry for this book is available
from the British Library.

Library of Congress Cataloging-in-Publication Data
available from the Library of Congress

ISBN 0-304-34077-4

Printed and bound in Great Britain by Mackays of Chatham, plc.

INTRODUCTION

'What's the use of their having names,' the Gnat said, 'if they won't answer to them?'
'No use to *them*,' said Alice; 'but it's useful to the people that name them, I suppose. If not, why do things have names at all?'

Lewis Carroll, *Through the Looking-Glass*, 1871.

What's in a name? Or perhaps one should ask, what *is* a name?

For most people, and certainly for the purposes of this dictionary, a name is a word or phrase, spelled with a capital letter, that denotes a *special individual representative of a larger group or sub-group*.

In some cases, the named object is unique, such as *Mount Everest*. That is, Mount Everest is the only mountain to bear this name. In many cases, however, the named object, animate or inanimate, shares the name with others. There are hundreds of men named *John* and thousands of women named *Mary*. But each of them is an individual, and has been given a name as a 'label' to denote his or her individuality.

Table is not a name, but simply a word that indicates what the object is. There are thousands of tables, of all shapes and sizes. But *Round Table* (with its capital letters) *is* a name, denoting the special individual table that was that of King Arthur and his Knights.

Put another way, if I say 'I'll fetch a table', you'll expect me to return not just with a piece of furniture but one that probably has a flat top and four legs. And if I say 'I'll call the dog in', you'll almost certainly see a smallish domestic animal with a hairy coat, four legs and a possibly wagging tail. You may also not be surprised to hear a bark. But if I say 'I'll get Sam', you are much less sure who (or even what) will appear. Sam may be male (Samuel) or female (Samantha), young or old. Sam may even be a cat or a dog. Yet *Sam* is a name that clearly indicates its bearer's special individuality. *Table* does not do that, even if I say 'I'll fetch *the* table'. The word does not imply uniqueness, even if the definite article *the* indicates that you have a particular table in mind, or that it is the only one in the room.

The function of declaring an object's intrinsic individuality is thus the most important that a name has, even when the same name is borne by others.

The capital letters that many languages use for names act as 'flags' to denote their special status. They are found not only for established, traditional names, but also for a wide range of 'nonce' titles. The administrative and political structures of most countries produce hundreds of names of this type, from a *Council of Ministers* to a *Department of Employment*, from a *Court of Session* to *NATO*.

Names like these, formed from standard words, are easy to understand and are relatively self-explanatory, once we make due allowance for the officialese. They do not feature widely in this dictionary, since their meanings are mostly obvious and their origins transparent. (In a sense, too, they are really more titles than names as such.)

iii

When it comes to the origin of what might be called a 'real' name, however, such as that of a person or a place, the etymology is not so straightforward.

If one compares common nouns (such as *colonel*) with proper nouns (such as *Colin*), one finds that most common nouns have evolved from an original form or sense that is directly linked to the nature or function of the designated object. The common noun *town*, for example, has evolved in English from Old English *tūn*, meaning 'enclosure'. The sense-development went something like this: 'enclosure', 'enclosure round a dwelling', 'group of dwellings on an enclosed piece of land', 'inhabited place consisting of several houses and other buildings'. *Colonel*, similarly, evolved from Old Italian *colonnello*, 'column of soldiers'. The colonel came to be the officer in charge of such a column.

The proper noun *Oxford*, however, although indicating 'town' and (as a name) implying this particular town's unique status, originated from an Old English phrase that means 'ford where oxen cross', not in itself an indication of a place of habitation. Similarly *Jonathan*, while implying 'man' or 'boy' and indicating the named person's individuality, evolved from a Hebrew expression that literally means 'God has given'.

It is the frequently unexpected origins of names that adds to their special status and that enhances popular interest in them. Who knows what hides behind a name such as *Chile* or *Connecticut, David* or *Diana*?

This new dictionary reveals the origins of a wide selection of familiar names, from personal names to place-names, brand names to astronomical names. It includes a broad selection of names of animals, mythological and literary characters, sports teams, languages, nationalities, political parties and pop and rock groups. It takes in the names of holidays and festivals, of schools and colleges, of battles and revolutions, and of well-known individual buildings such as clubs, hospitals, country houses, museums and theatres. It includes the origins of the names of famous individual persons, from *Caesar* to *Sophocles, Homer* to *Ho Chi Minh*. Names of well-known fictional characters are also represented, such as Shakespeare's *Desdemona* and *Hamlet* and, at a lighter and later level, Rudyard Kipling's *Mowgli* and A.A. Milne's *Winnie-the-Pooh*. Equally present are the titles of literary works and musical compositions, such as *Lavengro* and *Lohengrin*.

It will be seen that there is a high proportion of place-names. This is because the names of countries, cities and regions in all parts of the world are familiar to us from the media. We have all heard of *Maryland, Melanesia, Morocco* and *Munich*, even if (to be honest) we are sometimes not too sure of their exact geographical location. Coverage of place-names is thus worldwide in scope in the dictionary, and is the fullest category to be represented.

Place-names are important not simply because of their inherent ubiquity. Many place-names have come to fulfil other functions. Several surnames, for instance, derive directly from place-names. To take simply the second letter of the alphabet, and in the English-speaking world alone, we thus have people surnamed *Bainbridge* and *Batsford, Bedford* and *Bingham, Boycott* and *Buchanan*. Place-names have also been adopted as commercial names. Familiar examples are *Ascot, Basildon Bond, Columbia, Granada, Hitachi, Longines, Scania* and *Vauxhall*.

Place-names, too, are notable for their immense historic range, from the near-primeval to the very recent. *London* is such an ancient name that its origin is still uncertain. *Leningrad*, on the other hand, came into existence only in the 20th century. But although personal names have a similar lengthy history, and have likewise engendered many commercial names, their representation in the book is more modest. This is because they are normally familiar only in a person's native language, which in the case of most readers will be English. Their coverage is therefore restricted to those found mostly in the English-speaking world. Even so, some well-known non-English personal names are included, such as *Ahmed* and *Muhammad, Igor* and *Olga*.

Place-names and personal names are almost certainly the two most familiar categories of name. There are other kinds, however, and at this point it would be helpful to say something about them, since each has its showing in the dictionary. Let us begin with place-names and personal names themselves.

1 PLACE-NAMES

The universality of place-names inevitably involves a whole host of different languages. Even in a single country, many place-names will have evolved from a language that is no longer spoken. This usually means an 'Old' language, such as Old English in Britain, Old French in France, Old High German in Germany, and so on. Many non-European countries, however, have more or less transparent place-names. Most place-names of China and Japan can be literally translated and so be instantly meaningful. *Peking* (or *Beijing*, as we are now recommended to call it) means 'northern capital', for instance, while *Tokyo* means 'eastern capital'.

Newer states and countries frequently have names transferred from older ones, imported by colonists and settlers. The former British Empire scattered a veritable diaspora of British names in many parts of the globe, notably North America, South Africa, Australia and New Zealand. Sometimes the new place-names were not transferred from places but from people, whether as surname, first name or aristocratic title. A good example is *New York*, named not directly for the English city of York but for the Duke of York. Names involving a double transfer of this type (place to person to place) are not infrequent.

As with history in general, the further back one goes with place-names, the more complex and obscure can their source become. Many of Britain's own place-names are not Old English in origin but Celtic. These are the oldest names, those of the original inhabitants of the islands before the arrival of the Romans in the 1st century AD, the Angles and Saxons in the 5th century, the Scandinavians in the 9th century, and the Normans in the 11th century. Each of these peoples left place-names in their own language, with one people frequently adopting an existing name and adapting it to their own tongue. The Romans, for example, took Celtic *lindo*, 'pool', latinized it as *Lindum*, then added their own word *colonia* to give what would eventually become modern *Lincoln*. As it was the Anglo-Saxons, however, who provided the nucleus of the language that all English speakers speak today, it is frequently their names that are more readily meaningful. But by no means always! We are not all that far wrong if we see the germ of 'new town' in the place-name *Newton*. On the other hand, we have veered far off course if we see *Harrogate* as 'harrow gate', or *Swansea* as 'sea with swans'.

These last two names offer good examples of 'folk etymology', of the desire to make meaningful a name that has become meaningless. This happens in languages other than English. The name *Niger* is not related to Latin *niger*, 'black', however appropriate such a meaning may seem for an African river. Nor does *Colombo*, the capital of Sri Lanka, derive its name from Columbus.

Many countries and regions of the world have gained their names from the people who originally inhabited them, or who may still do so. *France*, for example, is named for the Franks, and *Turkey* for the Turks. But equally well-known lands may have taken their name from a single person. Examples are *America*, *Colombia* and *Saudi Arabia*. Others are named for natural features: *Brazil*, *Cameroon*, *Iceland*. Other names again are purely geographical: *Japan* means 'land of the rising sun', that is, 'land of the east'. *Australia* means 'southern land'.

In short, diversity is all, especially in those countries where there has been a succession of inhabitants or invaders. Like the Celtic names in Britain, it is the oldest, indigenous names that are often the hardest to interpret. This means the Indian names in North America, the Aboriginal names in Australia, and the Maori names in New Zealand, to say nothing of names given by vanished or departed tribes. Several German place-names are Slavic in origin. Examples are *Dresden*, *Leipzig* and *Chemnitz*. But the Slavs have long gone from the territory of what in the 20th century became for 41 years the German Democratic Republic, or East Germany.

As is perhaps to be expected, classical languages lie behind a number of well-known place-names of the world. Examples are the Latin and Greek that gave the *Arctic*, *Antarctic*, *Atlantic* and *Mediterranean*. More interesting, perhaps, and often more controversial, are the 'colour' names: *Black Sea*, *Red Sea*, *White Sea*. The *Yellow River* may get its colour from its waters, but in what sense is the *Black Sea* black and the *Red Sea* red?

The names of rivers are almost everywhere the oldest place-names in a country. They are therefore frequently the most obscure. Very often, the name of a river turns out to mean simply 'river'. *Avon* is a good example. What sort of a name is that? The answer is that there is no need to name a river which everyone knows. We simply use the word itself, as in, 'Isn't the river running high this morning?' Eventually, one people's word for 'river' becomes another people's name for it. This happened with *Avon*, from a Celtic word that gave modern Welsh *afon* and Irish *abha*. River names, too, run in 'families'. In Britain it is likely that the names of the *Thames*, *Taff*, *Tamar* and *Teviot* are related, while Britain's *Don* is a twin to Russia's *Don* and they are both cousins of Europe's *Danube*.

Place-names are also subject to change. Not only do they alter in form and spelling over the years, but this political power or that may deliberately change the name of a place, even that of a whole country. Thus *Cambridge* evolved by gradual and fairly natural processes to its present spelling from *Grantacaestir*, so recorded in the Venerable Bede's 8th-century *History of the English Church and People*. It was thus in essence *Grantchester*, now the name of a village near Cambridge. (To compound the confusion, the village's name has a different origin.) Then the Soviet authorities gave the world *Leningrad* for *St Petersburg* and *Gorky* for *Nizhny Novgorod*. These particular cities have now reverted to their original names, but there are still several that have not.

Place-names can thus pose special difficulties, and are not all as straightforward as England's *Newcastle* or Australia's *Great Dividing Range*. (Even here one is right to seek further detail: when was Newcastle 'new', and what exactly does the great range divide?)

The reader will find that many place-name entries mention the particular languages from which the name has evolved. Some names are fairly obvious and familiar, but others are inevitably more esoteric. *Occitan* and even *Old High German* are examples. In such cases, or where there is doubt, the reader is recommended to turn to consult p xx, where a concise guide to language names is given.

2 PERSONAL NAMES

Personal names are broadly of two types: first names and surnames. Each designates a particular individual, although surnames, by their very nature, run in families, so that they designate individuals who are known to be related. Many people, in many countries, also bear 'middle' or extra names. These are brought into use mainly on formal occasions, such as the identification of a particular individual, or the signature of an official document.

Naming systems vary in different parts of the world. They have also been subject to change over the centuries, so that the type or number of names that an individual bears today may well differ from those borne by his or her ancestors.

As a general rule, one name per person was originally enough. Why have more? This was certainly the rule for the Ancient Greeks. A boy or girl was given a name at birth, and if and when the girl married she kept this name.

The names themselves were meaningful and were frequently theophoric, that is, they incorporated the name of a god. Examples are *Apollodoros*, 'gift of Apollo', *Heracles*, 'glory of Hera', *Diogenes*, 'born of Zeus'. Many names were simply propitious, evoking fame and success for the bearer. Names of this type include *Megacles*, 'of great fame', *Helene*, 'bright', *Sophocles*, 'famous in wisdom'. The first son in a family was usually named after his grandfather, and the first daughter after her grandmother.

The Romans, too, initially had just one name, so that *Romulus* and *Remus* had no further names. Soon, however, and under Etruscan influence, the Romans developed a well-defined system under which each person had first two, then finally three, names, such as *Marcus Tullius Cicero* or *Gaius Sempronius Gracchus*.

Since the technical terms for such names are used in this dictionary, it would be helpful to describe and illustrate them here.

The first name was the *praenomen*. This was a personal name, and the equivalent of what we would now call a first name, given name, forename or Christian name. There were in fact relatively few such names, and they were so well known that they were conventionally written in abbreviated form, often simply by their first letter. They were: *Appius* (*App.*), *Aulus* (*A.*), *Caeso* (*C.*), *Decimus* (*D.*), *Gaius* (*G.*), *Gnaeus* (*Gn.*), *Lucius* (*L.*), *Marcus* (*M.*),

Manius (*M'*.), *Mamercus* (*Mam.*), *Numerius* (*N.*), *Publius* (*P.*), *Quintus* (*Q.*), *Servius* (*Ser.*), *Sextus* (*Sex.*), *Spurius* (*Sp.*), *Tiberius* (*Ti.*) and *Titus* (*T.*). Three of these are 'number' names: *Decimus*, 'tenth', *Quintus*, 'fifth' and *Sextus*, 'sixth'.

The second name was the *nomen*, that of a person's *gens* or 'clan'. This was not so much a family name as that of a *group* of families, who had descended in the male line from a single ancestor. *Nomina* can often be recognized by the ending *-ius*. Familiar examples are *Antonius, Aurelius, Claudius, Cornelius, Horatius, Julius* and *Lucius*.

These are all male names, of course. Women also originally bore *praenomina* and *nomina*, but, at least in the upper classes, came to abandon the *praenomen* and instead used the *nomen* alone with a feminine ending. They were thus *Antonia, Claudia, Cornelia, Julia*, and so on, names which are familiar today.

A later, third name was the *cognomen* or nickname. This was often a hereditary name. It was similar to a *nomen*, but originated from a meaningful nickname given to an ancestor. Such nicknames often described physical characteristics, not always flatteringly. They include *Barbatus*, 'bearded', *Cincinnatus*, 'curly', *Crassus*, 'fat', *Flavius*, 'yellow' (*i.e.* fair-haired), *Longus*, 'tall', *Naso*, 'nosy' (*i.e.* having a prominent nose) and *Sulla*, 'red-headed'. Some names of this type are familiar from well-known Roman writers, such as *Cicero*, 'bean' and *Tacitus*, 'silent'. The *cognomen* was thus the virtual equivalent of the modern surname.

Occasionally a Roman would also have a fourth name. This was an *agnomen*, or additional *cognomen*. A familiar example is that of Publius Cornelius Scipio *Africanus*, whose *agnomen* relates to his successful battles in *Africa*.

Later, this neat system broke down, so that people reverted to having a single name. The triple-name system at least formed the basis for that found in many western countries today. Most Americans still have a first name, middle name and surname, and for Russians the three names are almost invariably personal name, patronymic (derived from that of the person's father) and surname. Bearers of just two names, first name and surname, have similarly inherited the original Roman naming formula.

Although, as cited above, some modern female first names are specifically Roman in origin, most of the best-known names, male and female, are not so much classical as biblical.

The Bible has provided many of today's popular names, several of them adopted by English Puritans in the 16th and 17th centuries. Familiar names of Old Testament origin thus include *Abigail, Abraham, Adam, Benjamin, Daniel, David, Deborah, Esther, Eve, Hannah* (which gave *Ann*), *Isaac, Jacob, Jeremiah* (giving *Jeremy*), *Jonathan, Joseph, Judith, Michael, Miriam* (giving *Mary*), *Moses, Naomi, Rachel, Rebecca, Ruth, Samuel, Sarah* and *Simeon* (giving *Simon*). Most of these are still specifically favoured today by Jewish families, but Christians and non-Jews generally have also readily adopted such names as *David* and *Rachel*. The Apocrypha famously gave *Susanna* (the *Susan* of today).

The most common first names of all in the English-speaking world, however, are among those found in the New Testament: *Andrew, Bartholomew, Elizabeth, James, John, Luke, Mark, Martha, Mary, Matthew, Paul, Peter, Philip, Simon, Stephen, Thomas, Timothy*. Many of these are the names of apostles, and are particularly popular.

Most Old Testament names are Hebrew in origin, and can be interpreted literally. Their original sense usually expresses a religious sentiment, and may even include the word for, or name of, God, respectively *el* and *yāh*. *Daniel* thus means 'God is my judge', and *Jeremiah* means 'appointed by Yah', that is, by Jehovah.

New Testament names may be classical in origin, such as *Andrew*, from the Greek for 'man', or *Mark*, from Roman *Marcus*, of uncertain origin (perhaps ultimately related to *Mars*). *John* and *Mary*, two of the most common of all names, are both Hebrew in origin, respectively meaning 'God is gracious' and (perhaps) 'fertile'. *Barnabas*, however, is Aramaic in origin.

It goes without saying that most of these biblical names are equally popular in languages other than English. *John* and *Mary* have their familiar equivalents in French *Jean* and *Marie*, Italian *Giovanni* and *Maria*, and Russian *Ivan* and *Mariya*.

Sometimes an English name will have non-English equivalents that have been adopted by English speakers to a greater or lesser degree. Thus *Sean* (or *Shaun*), the Irish form of *John*, is fairly widely found, while Italian *Maria* and Irish *Moira* (originally *Móire*) are forms of *Mary* that have found equal favour.

Early Christian saints and martyrs have similarly given popular first names. They include *Adrian, Agnes, Anthony* (giving *Tony*), *Barbara, Catherine, Christopher, Dorothy, George, Helen, Lucy, Margaret, Martin, Nicholas, Patrick* and *Ursula*. The fact that some of the saints may not even have existed, such as *Barbara* and *Catherine*, has not in the least affected the popularity of their names.

A large number of saints' names are classical in origin.

In medieval times several names of Germanic origin were imported to Britain, in many cases by the Normans. They include several familiar 'royal' names, such as *Albert, Charles, Edward, Henry, Richard, Robert* and *William. Arthur*, however, is of Celtic origin.

The Victorian age saw the rise of a number of flower names for women. They include *Daisy, Iris, Lily, May, Pansy, Rose* and *Violet*. Many of these have now fallen from favour, their blossom faded.

The most recent first names of all are those that have been promoted by popular literature and the media. Examples include *Charlene, Darren, Jason, Kim, Kylie, Samantha* and *Tracy*. A few such names are actually very old. *Jason*, for instance, is first known from Greek mythology. But many new names are genuinely new creations or at any rate adaptations. *Kylie*, for example, appears to be a blend of *Kyle* and *Kelly*.

Kyle and *Kelly* both originated as surnames, which themselves frequently serve as first names. Examples are *Beverley, Clifford, Douglas, Dudley, Graham, Keith, Kimberley, Leslie, Shirley* and *Stanley*. Of these ten typical surnames-turned-male-first-names, four have in turn become adopted for female use: *Beverley, Kimberley, Leslie* and *Shirley* (sometimes with a slight modification of spelling, as *Beverly* or *Lesley*). This appears to have happened through the association of the final *-ley* or *-lie* with existing female names ending in *-y*, such as *Amy, Audrey, Betty, Dorothy, Emily, Judy, Lily, Lucy, Mary, Molly, Nancy, Peggy, Sally*.

Many of these last names originated as shortened 'pet' forms from a longer original, giving another source of first names. *Betty* is a derivative of *Elizabeth*, for example, and *Sally* of *Sarah*. It was *Margaret* that gave *Peggy*, and *Mary* that produced *Molly*.

Unlike surnames, first names are capable of producing an almost limitless number of derivatives like this, both variants and diminutives. *Margaret*, for example, has produced a variant form *Marjorie* as well as diminutives *Maggie* and *Peggy*, among others. *Elizabeth* has variants *Elspeth* and *Isabel* as well as 'pet' forms *Elsie, Bessie, Betty, Libby, Lisa* and *Lizzie*. These in turn have short forms such as *Bess, Bet* and *Liz*. Male names have produced similar regular 'pet' forms, such as *Jim* from *James* and *Mike* from *Michael*. In fact just about any regular first name can produce a pet form by a reproduction of its stressed syllable: not only *Pete* and *Chris* from *Peter* and *Christopher*, but even *Shirl* from *Shirley* and *Wend* from *Wendy*.

The dictionary concentrates on the most familiar first names and derivatives, especially where the latter are noticeably different from the parent form, such as *Sally* from *Sarah* or *Bob* from *Robert*.

English surnames broadly divide into four types: those that represent an ancestor's *given name* (that is, his or her individual personal name), those that originated in a *place-name*, showing where a person lived, those that derive from an *occupation*, and those that were originally descriptive *nicknames*.

One of the most familiar types of surname is the one that ends in *-s* or *-son*, indicating a relationship with an identically named father. Examples are *Adams* ('son of *Adam*'), *Edmunds, Mathieson* ('son of *Matthew*'), *Robertson, Thompson* ('son of *Thomas*') and *Williams*. A first name can in fact produce a number of derivative surnames. *Peter* has generated not only *Peters* and *Peterson* but also *Parkinson, Pearce* and *Perkins*. Some personal names now function dually as first names and surnames, with no indication of 'son of' for the latter. Familiar examples are *Adam, Bartholomew, Denis, Gilbert, John, Martin, Nicholas, Richard* and *Thomas*.

Common place-names that have given surnames include *Newton, Norton, Easton, Weston* and *Sutton*, to name merely a handful. Indeed, just about every place-name on a map of Britain will have produced a surname at some time, so long as the place-name itself dates from pre-Conquest times. Even county names are found, so that there are people surnamed *Cornwall, Derbyshire* and *Wiltshire*. The 1989 Leicester Telephone Directory has over 80 people named *Lester* in it, many of them actually living in Leicester. The 1990 Peterborough Telephone Directory, on the other hand, has no one named *Peterborough*. The place-name evolved only in the 14th century, too late to serve as a surname.

Many people bear a surname that is that of a now long-abandoned occupation: *Archer, Bowman, Bowyer, Cartwright, Chapman, Fletcher, Parker, Sawyer, Stringer, Walker*. All medieval life is there, but hardly contemporary society. Five of these names relate to bows and arrows, for example: *Archer* and *Bowman* were competent marksmen, *Bowyer* made the bows, *Fletcher* made the arrows, and *Stringer* made the strings for the bows. Some occupations still survive, such as *Taylor* and *Thatcher*, but more are obsolete, or obsolescent, than current.

Descriptive nicknames relate either to a person's physical characteristics, or to some moral or abstract quality. *Long* was a tall man, and *Snow* a white-haired one. *Keen* was brave, but *Bragg* was boastful. Names of this type can mislead. *Coward* was not a coward, but a *cowherd*. *Best* looked after *beasts*, or in some way resembled one in character. *Lemon* was a *lover* (the words are not related, however).

3 MYTHOLOGICAL NAMES

Mythology and folklore have given many familiar names to the world, whether of people (fictional characters) or places (equally fictional).

The best-known such names are those of classical mythology, with origins that are usually in Greek or Latin. It is necessary to specify 'usually' because several apparently Greek or Latin names are actually pre-Greek or pre-Latin. They have been adapted to one or other of these classical languages, however, and have in many cases acquired a meaning appropriate for the person or place that bears it.

A famous example is the name of *Aphrodite*, the Greek goddess of love. This has come to be traditionally derived from Greek *aphros*, 'foam', referring to her birth from the foam of the sea (as depicted in Botticelli's famous painting, popularly known as *Venus on the Half-Shell*).

But her name is probably pre-Greek, and almost certainly has its origin in that of the Semitic fertility goddess *Ashtoreth*, herself identified with the Phoenician goddess *Astarte* and the Babylonian goddess *Ishtar*.

All we can do in this dictionary is to give the traditional interpretation of a mythological name like this, and point to an earlier origin if that seems more likely. Sometimes the original name is so ancient that its meaning may be unknown. But at least the reader will find entries for most if not all the legendary Greeks and Romans, such as *Achilles, Apollo, Ajax, Alexander, Castor* and *Pollux, Cupid, Icarus, Jason, Mars, Oedipus, Penelope, Sisyphus* and *Venus* (Aphrodite's Roman counterpart). Some of these, it will be noted, have given personal first names that are still popular today, such as *Alexander* and *Penelope*.

Greek and Roman mythology may be the most familiar in the western world, but of course there are other mythologies, which will also be represented here. Among the most important are those of Egypt, Mesopotamia and, nearer home, Scandinavia. Although these are to most of us more obscure than the people and places of classical mythology, they have nevertheless produced some names that many will recognize. Well-known Egyptian gods and goddesses, for instance, include *Amon, Aten* (the sun disk), *Hathor, Horus, Isis, Osiris, Pharaoh* (strictly speaking a royal title), *Ptah, Ra* (the sun god) and *Thoth* (the moon god). Some of these may be more familiar from the Bible.

Names from Mesopotamian mythology that will be known to some include *Gilgamesh, Marduk* and *Tammuz*.

Norse mythology, however, is perhaps the best-known after that of Greece and Rome. This is the world of *Asgard, Fafnir, Freya, Frigg, Loki, Odin, Ragnarok, Sigurd, Thor, Valhalla* and the *Valkyries*. It is also the land of *Yggdrasil*, the world tree, whose name has in modern times attracted cryptic crossword setters. Many characters of Norse mythology, too, have their Germanic counterparts, often with similar names. The god *Odin* thus has his equivalent in *Woden*, who gave the name of *Wednesday*, while *Sigurd* has his near namesake in *Siegfried*.

Further afield are the figures of Hinduism, the gods and goddesses of India, such as

Brahma, Buddha, Devi, Hanuman, Indra, Lakshmi, Siva and *Vishnu.* They, too, have their origins and etymologies.

So what of Britain itself? There are perhaps three main mythologies that most people will acknowledge as familiar. First there is the Arthurian cycle, with names that are perennially popular: *Arthur* himself, *Avalon, Camelot, Excalibur, Galahad, Gawain, Guinevere, Lancelot, Merlin, Percival, Tristram, Uther Pendragon* and the Lady of *Shalott.* Almost all these are of Celtic origin, although some have come to be interpreted through the medium of French retelling. In Victorian times they were promoted by the poems of Tennyson, especially his *Idylls of the King.*

Next there are the names of the *Mabinogion,* the Welsh tales also based on old Celtic legends. The names are fewer, but include *Geraint, Peredur* and *Taliesin.*

Finally, and most famous of all, there are the figures of *Robin Hood, Little John, Friar Tuck* and *Maid Marian.* Their deeds and personalities may have been sentimentalized and trivialized over the years, but their names remain as fresh as ever.

4 BIBLICAL NAMES

Reference has already been made to biblical names in the context of modern first names. But there are also names of people and places in the Bible that are equally well known, and that require an etymology.

There are basically four types of biblical name that deserve consideration: names of individual characters, names of peoples and tribes, names of places, and names of actual books or sections of the Bible.

Names of characters are legion, and include, apart from those already mentioned, and allotting a single alphabetical letter to each: *Abel, Boaz, Cain, Dan, Elijah, Felix, Gabriel, Herod, Isaiah, Jesus, Kezia, Laban, Methuselah, Nehemiah, Obadiah, Pontius Pilate, Jeroboam, Saul, Tobit, Uriah* and *Zebedee.* Tribal or other group names that merit explanation include the *Hittites, Levites, Nazarites, Pharisees, Sadducees* and *Samaritans.*

Biblical place-names that are well known include *Babylon, Bethesda, Bethlehem, Caesarea, Capernaum, Damascus, Ephesus, Galilee, Gethsemane, Golgotha, Israel, Jerusalem, Laodicea, Mizpah, Nazareth, Palestine, Shiloh, Sinai, Tyre* and *Zion.* Many of these remain as important place-names today. *Damascus,* for example, is the capital of Syria, and *Jerusalem* is the capital of *Israel.* Nor should one forget the purely spiritual places, such as *Eden, Gehenna* and *Paradise.*

Some names of biblical books present little difficulty, since they are based on (or actually consist of) personal names or place-names. This notably applies to the titles of the prophetical books of the Old Testament (*Isaiah, Jeremiah, Ezekiel* and so on), of the four gospels similarly (*Matthew, Mark, Luke, John*), and of the Epistles of St Paul to the inhabitants of various regions and cities (*Romans, Corinthians, Galatians* and the like).

On the other hand, the titles of some biblical books seek an etymology, especially when they have remained in a non-English language, as is the case in the Authorized Version. They include, in particular, *Genesis, Exodus, Leviticus, Deuteronomy, Ecclesiastes* and *Ecclesiasticus,* this last in the Apocrypha. But even English titles such as *Numbers, Chronicles, Lamentations, Acts* and *Revelation* could do with an explanation. Who or what is *numbered* in the first of these, for example, and what is *revealed* in the last?

Names for sections or versions of the Bible can also be usefully glossed. They include such titles as *Pentateuch, Septuagint, Vulgate* and *Apocrypha.* Even *Old Testament, New Testament* and *Bible* itself deserve their individual entries.

5 ASTRONOMICAL NAMES

There is a significant overlap here with mythological names. Many famous names from Greek and Roman mythology have found their way into the heavens, notably in those of all but one of the nine planets: *Mercury, Venus, Mars, Jupiter, Saturn, Uranus, Neptune, Pluto.* The sole exception is *Earth.*

Apart from the planets, several constellations and individual stars have well-known names. One has only to think of the 12 zodiacal constellations (*Aquarius, Aries, Sagittarius* and others) as well as *Orion, Ursa Major, Cassiopeia* and similar constellations outside the zodiac. Even the most somnolent stargazer, too, will know of *Aldebaran, Algol, Betelgeuse, Procyon, Sirius* and *Vega* as the names of individual stars.

All names of planets and zodiacal constellations are Latin or Greek in origin. Most names of individual stars, on the other hand, are Arabic. Whatever their language, an etymology can be helpful, even where it coincides with that of a mythological character.

The dictionary contains a selection of familiar astronomical names. In general, however, it does not include the less important names, such as those of satellites of the planets, of minor planets (asteroids), or of features on the Moon or other celestial bodies.

6 NATIONALITIES AND LANGUAGES

The origin of the name of a country or region is very often the origin of the name of its indigenous inhabitants. Thus the meaning of the name of *Finland* intrinsically involves the meaning of the name of the *Finns*, and the etymology of the name of *Arabia* is the etymology of the name *Arab*.

The same identity frequently applies between a people and their language. To learn the origin of language names such as *Danish, Polish, Swedish* and *Turkish* one needs to study the origins of the names of the *Danes, Poles, Swedes* and *Turks*, together with those of their countries: *Denmark, Poland, Sweden* and *Turkey*. Sometimes one has a language name with no related ethnic name: *Romany* is not spoken by the Romans but by *Gypsies*, and *Sanskrit* is a language used by *Indians*. Again, some language names relate to the names of their speakers but not to that of their country. *Dutch* is spoken by the *Dutch* in the *Netherlands* (or *Holland*). Anomalies like these make the history of a linguistic or ethnic name particularly interesting.

The formation of language names is not identical in English. The familiar *-ish* suffix, for example, as found for *Danish, English, Swedish* and *Turkish*, can assume a different form, as for *French* and *Welsh*. Where names of this type differ radically from the norm they will often have their individual entries in the dictionary, if only to explain why, for example, the language of the Isle of Man is *Manx* rather than 'Mannish'.

Also included are the names of defunct languages, such as *Oscan* and *Etruscan*, as well as the names of artificial languages, such as *Esperanto, Ido* and *Volapük*. There are similarly names of extinct peoples and races, such as those of the *Franks, Gauls* and *Picts*. They have their entries, too, as do some of the best-known national designations and nicknames, such as *Kaffir, Negro* and *Yankee*. Many of these are now offensive, of course, but they are still names with a history, and so deserve their place here.

7 TIME AND CALENDAR NAMES

The dictionary includes the origins of the English names of the days of the week and months of the year. The names of the months in the French Revolutionary (Republican) calendar are also familiar to many, so here therefore are *Brumaire, Germinal* and their fellows. Also to be found are the best-known names of the Jewish and Muslim calendars, such as *Nisan* and *Ramadan*.

Apart from the days of the week and months of the year, many calendar names are those of religious seasons and festivals, whether observed on a single day or over a longer period. Some of the festivals are very ancient, and of pagan origin. Others are much more recent. Either way, they certainly have their place in the dictionary. The reader will therefore find entries for the following Christian festivals and occasions, among others: *Advent, All Saints Day, All Souls Day, Annunciation, Ascension, Ash Wednesday, Candlemas, Christmas, Corpus Christi, Easter, Ember Days, Epiphany, Good Friday, Hallowe'en, Lady Day, Lammas, Lent, Low Sunday, Maundy Thursday, Michaelmas, Mothering Sunday* (and *Mother's Day*), *Palm Sunday, Pentecost, Sabbath, Septuagesima, Shrove Tuesday, Thanksgiving Day* and *Whit Sun-*

day. Well-known Jewish fasts and festivals include *Rosh Hashanah, Passover, Purim, Shavuot, Sukkoth* and *Yom Kippur*.

There are also several 'day names' that are not directly religious in origin. They also have their place, and include *Boxing Day, Flag Day, Hock Tuesday, Labor Day* (and *Labour Day*), *Oakapple Day, Plough Monday, Primrose Day, Remembrance Sunday* and *Veterans Day*.

8 RELIGIOUS NAMES

Apart from the specifically biblical names already mentioned, there are also a number of well-known religious names that require representation in the dictionary. They are chiefly those of established world religions and of churches, sects or groups within a particular religion.

Names involving world religions include *Christian, Hindu, Islam, Jew, Muslim* and *Shinto*. Names of churches, sects and groupings within Christianity include *Baptist, Catholic, Congregational, Jehovah's Witnesses, Methodism, Mormon, Nonconformist, Orthodox Church, Oxford Group, Plymouth Brethren, Presbyterian, Puritan, Quaker, Salvation Army, Seventh Day Adventist* and *Wee Frees*. The Church of England itself has its *High Church* and *Low Church*.

The names of the sacred scriptures and religious writings of non-Christian religions also belong here. They include the Jewish *Gemara, Masora, Mishna, Talmud* and *Torah*, the *Koran* of Islam, the *Rig-Veda, Upanishad* and *Veda* of Hinduism, and the *Avesta* and *Zend-Avesta* of Zoroastrianism.

Equally, the names of the gods or deities of the major religions have their place in the dictionary. They include *Ahura Mazda, Allah, Brahma, Elohim, Jehovah, Krishna,* and *Yahweh*.

The borderline between, say, *Vishnu* as Hindu deity and *Vishnu* as mythological figure is very fine. A similarly blurred distinction exists between *Buddha* as religious leader and teacher and *Buddha* as divinity. Both find their places in dictionaries of mythology, as indeed does *Christ*. Whatever their divine or worldly status, however, their names (or titles) are of interest and importance, and they thus merit their individual entries here.

9 LITERARY NAMES

Literary names involve the titles of fictional works (and some non-fictional) and the names of fictional characters.

There is scope here for a book in itself, so that the selection of literary names in the present dictionary is relatively restricted.

Even so, it includes the origins of some of the more baffling or ambiguous literary titles, such as Samuel Butler's *Erewhon*, Spenser's *Faerie Queene*, Thomas Moore's *Lalla Rookh*, George Borrow's *Lavengro*, Herman Melville's *Moby-Dick*, Conrad's *Nostromo*, Borrow's *Romany Rye*, Omar Khayyám's *Rubáiyát*, Thomas More's *Utopia*, Thackeray's *Vanity Fair* and Emily Brontë's *Wuthering Heights*.

A similar selection of fictional characters has been drawn from a wide range of literature, from classical works to children's fiction. They embrace both people and animals, and include, among others, *Ayesha, Bagheera, Cinderella, Frankenstein, Gargantua, Gunga Din, Hiawatha, Ivanhoe, Mephistopheles, Minnehaha, Mowgli, Pantagruel, Quasimodo, Rob Roy, Rumpelstiltskin, Stalky, Struwwelpeter, Tarka, Tartuffe, Tarzan* and *Winnie-the-Pooh*.

Shakespearian names to feature include *Ariel, Autolycus, Banquo, Caliban, Cordelia, Cymbeline, Desdemona, Falstaff, Hamlet, Holofernes, Imogen, Macbeth, Miranda, Oberon, Othello, Portia, Prospero, Puck, Romeo, Titania* and *Yorick*. Some of these, such as *Imogen* amd *Miranda*, have been adopted as regular first names, so belong both here and to the category of first names already considered above.

Names of fictional peoples or beings are likewise represented, such as the *Houyhnhnms* and *Yahoos* from Swift's *Gulliver's Travels*. Similarly, from the same work, the fictional place-names *Brobdingnag, Laputa* and (of course) *Lilliput* also have their respective entries.

10 NAMES FROM HISTORY

School history books have long been traditional repositories of wars and battles, plots and treaties, and many of their names stick firmly in the mind all one's life. For this reason alone the inclusion of such names in the dictionary is valid.

The more straightforward names are those of wars and battles. Wars are frequently named for their cause (*War of the Spanish Succession*), national, regional or partisan involvement (*Boer War, Civil War, Wars of the Roses*) or length (*Hundred Years War, Thirty Years War*). Battles are usually named for their site or approximate location (*Battle of Agincourt, Battle of Hastings, Battle of Waterloo*). In dealing with battles one is thus usually dealing with place-names.

Names of plots, mutinies, treaties, laws and parliaments vary considerably. Even so, many of them are familiar, such as the *Addled Parliament, Boston Tea Party, Boxer Rebellion, Cabal, Commonwealth, Corn Laws, Danelaw, Field of the Cloth of Gold, Gadsden Purchase, Grand Remonstrance, Jameson Raid, Long Parliament, Magna Carta, Reformation, Restoration, Rump Parliament, South Sea Bubble* and *Triple Alliance*. They are all represented here, and their names explained.

Also in the book are the names of famous historic characters, some of them almost legendary, such as *Attila, Boudicca (Boadicea), Caesar, Genghis Khan, Godiva, Hengist* (and *Horsa*), *Hereward the Wake, Joan of Arc, Tamerlane*, the Venerable *Bede* and *Vercingetorix*. Historical nicknames such as those of the *Black Prince* and Henry *Hotspur* belong to this group.

Names of military, loyalist and other groupings also feature, such as the *Cavaliers, Chartists, Fenians, Golden Horde, Huguenots, Jacobites, Lollards, Luddites* and *Roundheads*.

Some such names overlap with those familiar from religion or politics, of course, since history is not neatly limited to particular causes or categories. Religious names were mentioned earlier. Political ones now follow.

11 POLITICAL NAMES

The names of political parties and groupings tie in closely with a nation's history. Many parties that were formed in historic times, and in particular circumstances, are still current today.

There are two types of name that can be grouped as 'political'. The first type are those of the established political parties that a country has. The second are the parties, groupings and factions that have arisen to oppose an established party, or to promote a particular cause. Many such organizations are unofficial. Some are even criminal, or at least outlawed. Whatever their background, they are almost all well known and deserve their due entries.

Names of established political parties include *Conservative, Democrat, Fianna Fáil, Green, Labour, Liberal, Plaid Cymru, Republican, Tory* and *Whig*.

Names of 'counter-groups' and reforming parties, some of which have gained significant power in their time, include *Bolshevik, Fabian, Fascist, Ku Klux Klan, Menshevik, Militant Tendency, Nazi, Orangeman* and *Sinn Féin*.

Along with the names of political parties should be included the names and titles of parliamentary offices and titles, as well as those of the parliaments or councils of foreign countries. Among such names are *Black Rod, Cortes, Dáil Éireann, Knesset, Reichstag, Sanhedrin, Senate* and *Taoiseach*.

12 EDUCATIONAL NAMES

The field of education is large enough to have its own distinct category of names, centring on those of individual universities, colleges and schools.

Many universities are named after the town or city in which they are located and in which they were founded. As such, they excite no special interest, since the name involved is a place-name. Some universities, however, such as the privately endowed ones in the United States, are named for their founder or for a prominent benefactor. These have their individual entries here, and include *Brown, Brunel, Cornell, Harvard, Heriot-Watt, Johns Hopkins, Laval,* the *Sorbonne, Vassar, Wilberforce, William and Mary* and *Yale.*

Other universities have 'distinctive' names of some kind which merit their inclusion. Examples are *City University, Open University* and the *Queen's University of Belfast.*

Oxford and Cambridge Universities have some 70 colleges between them, many with well-known names. Among the most familiar are Oxford's *All Souls, Balliol, Christ Church, Lady Margaret Hall, Magdalen, New College, Somerville, Trinity* and *Worcester,* and Cambridge's *Christ's, Clare, Emmanuel, Girton, Jesus, King's, Magdalene, Queens', Sidney Sussex* and *Trinity.* Other universities also have individually named colleges, such as London's *Birkbeck, King's* and *Royal Holloway* (now combined with *Bedford*).

Here too belong the familiar military colleges, such as *Sandhurst, Welbeck* and *West Point.*

Britain's public (independent) schools, like her universities, can be named either after the town of their location or for a founder or benefactor. The former have brought fame to place-names such as *Eton, Harrow* and *Rugby.* It is the latter, however, that have the more distinctive names. Schools named for individual founders or benefactors include *Blundell's, Colston's, George Heriot's, Gresham's, Lady Eleanor Holles, Latymer Upper, Perse* and *Whitgift.* There are several schools with 'royal' names of this type, named for a particular king or queen, such as *King Edward's* or *Queen Elizabeth's.* Others are simply *King's School,* and the dictionary interprets these by naming the king in question. Other foundations again bear the name of a guild or company, such as *Haberdashers' Aske's* and *Merchant Taylors'.*

Some schools have names of a religious origin, such as *Charterhouse* or *Christ's Hospital.* Schools that obviously belong to this group are those with saints' names, such as *St Edmund's* and *St Edward's.* A small selection of these is given, with the aim of explaining why the school was named for the particular saint.

There are so many girls' schools with saints' names that it has unfortunately been necessary to limit their representation. Even so, some are duly entered, as are several schools with original or unusual names, such as *Eothen, La Retraite, Moira House, Queenswood* and *Red Maids'.*

Some schools, such as *Bedales,* have moved since their foundation, but have kept the name of the place where they were established, even when originally that of a house. They are also worthy of mention.

Well-known youth organizations can also be regarded as having educational names, and likewise have their entries. They include *Brownies, Cub Scouts, Girl Guides* and *Boy Scouts.*

13 NAMES OF BUILDINGS

Universities, colleges and schools are not the only buildings to have interesting names. Other types of building with names worthy of inclusion here are churches, hospitals, country houses, theatres, museums, hotels, railway stations and the many different kinds of 'ancient monument' and historic edifice that are a constant draw to tourists.

Churches, as is to be expected, almost always bear a religious name, usually a dedication to a particular saint or deity. The point of interest here is not so much the dedication itself, but why a particular church should bear the dedication it does. Why is London's *St Paul's Cathedral,* for example, dedicated to this particular saint and not, say, St Peter? Do some saints' names have a special significance as a dedicatory name? The answer is that in some cases they do.

Britain's earliest church dedications are to *St Peter and St Paul, St Mary, St Michael* and *St Lawrence,* respectively representing the two apostles, the Virgin, the archangel, and the 3rd-century deacon and martyr of Rome. Churches dedicated to *St Peter* alone frequently imply an allusion to the saint's status as first bishop of Rome and to the literal meaning of his name as 'rock'. Several English cathedrals are dedicated to him, including those at York, Lichfield and Worcester. Churches dedicated to *St Martin,* on the other hand, are frequently found in an outlying or remote district of a community. As bishop of Tours in the 4th century, St Martin is known to have made a special point of granting the outlying parts of his diocese a personal 'visitation', often on foot or by boat.

At the same time, there is little doubt that many church dedications are more or less conventional. Hundreds are dedicated to *St John* or *St Mary* or *All Saints*, with no specific allusion or attribution intended. Only the most famous or distinctive churches and cathedrals will have their entries here, therefore.

Like churches, many hospitals are also of religious foundation, and similarly bear saints' names. One has only to think of London's *St Bartholomew's* and *St Thomas's*. Others, like schools and colleges, are named for their founder or benefactor, such as *Guy's* in London or *Addenbrooke's* in Cambridge. But again, also like colleges, many hospitals are named simply for a town or city, so that their identity and individuality blends with that of their particular location.

With country houses ('stately homes') one has a much wider field in every sense of the word. Again like schools and colleges, many such homes and houses are named for their locality, whose own name is thus preserved in theirs. *Broadlands*, the former Hampshire home of Lord Palmerston and Earl Mountbatten, is thus simply named for its 'broad lands', with its locality name transparent for once, and meaning what it says. Even so, some country houses bear interesting names. *Anglesey Abbey* in Cambridgeshire, for example, has no connection with Anglesey, North Wales, while *Boscobel House*, in Shropshire, has a name of Italian origin. On the other hand *Abbotsford*, the home of Sir Walter Scott near Melrose, Scotland, and *Alton Towers*, the now popular amusement park in Staffordshire, both have original names designed specifically for them. *Blenheim Palace* similarly has a unique name, that of a battle.

Several country houses are therefore duly represented in the dictionary, especially when their names are noteworthy or unexpected.

Theatres may have interesting names. Like other buildings, they are frequently named for their location, whether town or street. London's *Haymarket* and *St Martin's* theatres are named for the respective streets in or near which they are situated. But others are named for their founders, such as *Albery* and *Wyndham's*, while several have a name indicating royal patronage, such as *Her Majesty's* or *Theatre Royal*. In some instances, however, the royal patronage is only apparent, so that the name is merely commendatory, not historic. The *Duke of York's* theatre has a name of this type. A few theatres have generally commendatory names, such as *Ambassadors* or *Criterion*. Others take their names from former famous theatres, such as the *Globe*. London's *Old Vic* derives its name from a nickname, while the former *Round House* took its name from that of the building in which it was established.

There are several theatres named *Theatre Royal* in the English-speaking world, and the dictionary provides a historic survey of them in a single entry under this heading.

Cinemas can have distinctive names, even when duplicated in a chain or group, such as *Odeon*. One innovative name is that of London's *Minema*. Sometimes a cinema retains the name of a former theatre, as is the case with London's *Dominion*.

Museums and art galleries, where not named for their location, are frequently named for their founders, patrons or benefactors. Well-known examples include London's *Courtauld Institute Galleries*, *Tate Gallery* and *Victoria and Albert Museum*, Oxford's *Ashmolean*, and Cambridge's *Fitzwilliam*.

Hotels may also be named for their founders or owners, such as London's *Brown's Hotel* and *Ritz* or New York's famous *Waldorf-Astoria*. 'Owner' here may equally be 'landowner', as for London's *Grosvenor House Hotel*. Oxford's well-known *Randolph Hotel* takes its name from the owner of a former nearby art gallery.

Railway stations are usually named for their locality, or for a nearby prominent building or structure. London's *Waterloo*, for example, was named for its location by Waterloo Bridge over the Thames, while *Liverpool Street Station* is named for a nearby street. Such names can be misleading, and suggest that the station has trains running to the place it names. But no trains run from Liverpool Street to Liverpool!

'Ancient monument' is a rather general term for any old or historic building or structure that has come to be regarded as 'heritage', in the sense that it is in some way unique and serves as a visible memorial to a country's past. In the United Kingdom this means anything from a castle to a cromlech, and includes such famous and diverse places as the *Antonine Wall*, *Fountains Abbey*, the *Giant's Causeway*, *Hadrian's Wall*, *Skara Brae*, *Stonehenge* and the *Tower of London*. All these names have their respective entries, as do those of many similar places.

Other well-known buildings and locations, not all of them 'ancient monuments', include the *Albert Hall, Buckingham Palace, Chequers, Cleopatra's Needle, Jarlshof, Leeds Castle, Pentagon, Somerset House, White House* and *Woburn Abbey*. They also have their entries.

A sort of halfway house between regular place-names and names of buildings are the names of streets and roads. These can range from Roman roads such as *Ermine Street* and *Icknield Way* to the familiar streets of major cities, such as London's, *Piccadilly, Regent Street* and *Trafalgar Square*, the Paris *Champs Élysées*, Berlin's *Unter den Linden*, Moscow's *Red Square*, Peking's *Tiananmen Square* and New York's *Broadway* and *Times Square*. These are all internationally familiar names, so clearly deserve their individual entries.

14 COMMERCIAL NAMES

As consumers, we can hardly fail to be aware of commercial names, those of the advertisers who know that *they* have the goods or services that *we* are certain to need.

Commercial names are basically of two types: those based on the name of a company's founder or a product's inventor, and those that have been artificially devised. Many stores are named for their founders, such as *Boots, Marks & Spencer* and *Woolworths*. These happen to be chain stores, but individual shops or stores frequently have names of this type, such as London's *Selfridges* or New York's *Macys*.

Inside the stores will be found a wide range of goods and products. They, too, often bear the name of their original manufacturer, such as *Barratts* shoes or *Pears* soap. Such names are especially prominent in food and drink products: one need only mention *Armour* canned meat, *Cadburys* chocolate, *Heineken* lager, *Keillers* marmalade, *Lyons* ice cream, *Martell* brandy, and *Smiths* potato crisps.

Two distinctive areas of commercial names are cars and publishers. The names of cars are among the most widely known and most vigorously promoted that there are in the media, and include such familiar and popular names and marques as *Audi, Austin, Chrysler, Daimler, Ferrari, Ford, Lancia, Maserati, Porsche, Renault, Rolls-Royce* and *Toyota*. Cars that are not named for their original manufacturer are in the minority, and include *Jaguar, Lotus* and *Vauxhall*, among others.

Publishers are not as widely promoted as cars, but many of their names will be familiar enough. They usually represent the founder of the firm, and include *Bartholomew, Batsford, Cape, Cassell, Chambers, Dent, Gollancz, Harper & Row, Harrap, Heinemann, Hutchinson, Methuen, Mills & Boon, Routledge* and *Warne*.

On the other hand there are several well-known commercial names that do *not* derive from a personal name. They can range over the whole spectrum of goods, products and services, and include such familiar names as (allowing one only for each letter of the alphabet) *Anadin, Bovril, Coca-Cola, Dettol, Elastoplast, Flora, Grape Nuts, Hovis, Indesit, Jeep, Kodak, Lec, Minolta, Nikon, Ovaltine, Polaroid, Quaker Oats, Rentokil, Sony, Toshiba, Uhu, Velcro, Wimpy, Xerox, Yorkie* and *Zubes*.

The field of commercial names is so vast that even a separate book devoted to them could not hope to cover half the number that currently exist. However, many of the best-known ones will be found in the present dictionary, whether their origin is in personal names or invented words. Entries for the former identify the named person, and for the latter give the etymology, wherever possible. (Some names are near random, and defy a conventional analysis. But meaningful speculation can provide clues.)

15 MUSICAL NAMES

Just as books have literary titles, so do musical compositions also have their names. In classical music, the most common title for a piece of music is a factual designation such as *Piano Sonata in A, Op 101* or *Symphony No 1 in C minor, Op 5*. But many well-known compositions have acquired a name or nickname, such as Beethoven's *Eroica Symphony* or Chopin's *Raindrop Prelude*. This is quite apart from the formal titles of operas, cantatas and other instrumental works, such as Richard Strauss's opera *Der Rosenkavalier* or Prokofiev's symphonic poem *Peter and the Wolf*.

As with fictional titles, there are simply too many musical names to include here anything like the whole range. Even so, the names of some operas, operettas and other orchestral works are represented. Greater prominence, however, is given to the names that came to be popularly attached to well-known works, such as the two already quoted.

Such names tend to relate to the work in popularly expressive or vaguely evocative terms, as if to make the compositions themselves more approachable. It is thus easier, in one's home, to 'put on the *Pastoral*' rather than sit down for a serious session with Beethoven's *Symphony No 6 in F major, Op 68* (1808). It has to be said, however, that this particular name was one given by the composer himself, as also was that of the *Eroica* already mentioned. Most such names, though, were given by someone other than the composer, or arose from a public billing of a new work as a 'promotion' for it.

All the most familiar classical composers have works with such names. Bach has his *French Suites*, *Goldberg Variations* and *Wedge Fugue*, Beethoven his famous *Moonlight Sonata*. Handel has *The Harmonious Blacksmith* and Chopin the *Minute Waltz*. It is perhaps Haydn who is the doyen of nicknamed compositions, simply because he wrote so many symphonies. They include the *Farewell Symphony*, *London Symphony* and *Surprise Symphony*, as well a veritable ménage in *The Bear*, *The Clock*, *The Hen*, *The Hunt*, *The Philosopher* and *The Schoolmaster*. (These names are sometimes known in their French or German forms, as *L'Ours*, *Die Uhr*, *La Poule*, *La Chasse*, and so on.)

Mendelssohn has given the world the popular *Spring Song* and *The Bee's Wedding*, the latter not to be confused with *The Flight of the Bumble Bee* by Rimsky-Korsakov. Mozart has several nicknamed symphonies to his credit, including the *Haffner*, *Linz*, *Paris*, *Prague* and *Jupiter*, three of which were named for the cities where they were first performed. Other well-known named compositions include Purcell's *Bell Anthem*, Dvořák's *New World Symphony* (its original subtitle), and Schubert's *Unfinished Symphony*.

Musical names also involve the names of orchestras and other groups. Some such names, such as the *London Symphony Orchestra* or *Vienna Philharmonic*, are virtually self-explanatory. There are other names, however, that can benefit from a derivation, such as the *Hallé Orchestra* or *Boston Pops*. A selection of the best-known orchestra and musical group names is included in the dictionary, as are names of leading ballet and opera companies.

Names of pop and rock groups, on the other hand, are mostly *not* self-explanatory. Even the apparently prosaic, such as the *Beach Boys*, *Beatles*, *Commodores*, *Drifters*, *Monkees*, *Pretenders*, *Rolling Stones*, *Supremes* and *Temptations* can hide a more subtle origin or reference.

Many pop groups are named for one or more of their members, however allusively, such as the *Bee Gees*, *Carpenters*, *Fleetwood Mac*, *Jackson Five* and *Osmonds*. But here, as frequently elsewhere, all may not be so straightforward. The *Doobie Brothers* contained no member of that name, nor did the *Smiths* or the *Thompson Twins*.

Some pop group names are apparently meaningless. Others are plain surreal, despite their formation from standard English words. An origin is therefore required, and in most cases is provided, for such names as *Black Sabbath*, *Boomtown Rats*, *Deep Purple*, *Dire Straits*, *Electric Light Orchestra*, *Genesis*, *Girlschool*, *Grateful Dead*, *Guns N' Roses*, *Hot Chocolate*, *Human League*, *Humble Pie*, *Iron Maiden*, *Lovin' Spoonful*, *Madness*, *New Order*, *Pretty Things*, *Psychedelic Furs*, *Sex Pistols*, *Small Faces*, *Spooky Tooth*, *Talking Heads*, *Tears for Fears*, *10cc*, *Ten Years After* and *Yes*. A sort of sub-subgroup here is formed by names consisting of a monosyllabic word preceded by *The*, such as *The Clash*, *The Cream*, *The Cure*, *The Damned*, *The Doors*, *The Kinks*, *The Move*, *The Who* and even *The The*.

These also have their origins, as do names that clearly contain a proper name of some kind, such as *Creedence Clearwater Revival*, *Fairport Convention*, *Jefferson Airplane*, *Jethro Tull*, *Pink Floyd*, *Spandau Ballet*, *Thin Lizzy*.

Some groups have based their names on book titles, such as *The Doors* (above), *Manhattan Transfer*, *Soft Machine*, *Supertramp* and *Velvet Underground*. Then there are the groups with creatively original names, in non-standard English (or even not in English at all), such as *Bananarama*, *Depeche Mode*, *Duran Duran*, *Led Zeppelin*, *Lynyrd Skynyrd*, *Moby Grape*, *Procol Harum*, *REO Speedwagon*, *Shakatak*, *Sha Na Na*, *Showaddywaddy* and *Ultravox*.

They are given their origins in the dictionary, as far as they are known, together with many more popular musical names of similar type. Some, by their very nature, contain allusions to 'sex and drugs and rock and roll', but at least they preserve us from the po-faced.

16 SPORTS NAMES

The names of sports teams and sporting awards can have origins that are hard to establish. The dictionary does its best, however, to demystify many such names, including those of popular football clubs such as *Arsenal, Aston Villa, Celtic, Charlton Athletic, Crewe Alexandra, Crystal Palace, Heart of Midlothian, Hibernian, Manchester United, Nottingham Forest, Plymouth Argyle, Queen's Park Rangers, Sheffield Wednesday, Tottenham Hotspur* and *West Bromwich Albion*. Names of continental European clubs are also represented, such as *AC Milan, Ajax, Benfica, Borussia, Dynamo Moscow, Fiorentina, Juventus* and *Sampdoria*.

Names of sporting awards usually pass to the contest for which the award is named. Examples are the *Admiral's Cup* in yachting and the *Ladies' Plate* in rowing at the Henley Regatta. This makes it all the more desirable to know who the admiral is and the ladies were!

Some of the best-known sporting contests and awards are those in horse racing, and in particular the five Classic races: *Derby, Oaks, One Thousand Guineas, St Leger, Two Thousand Guineas*. (These are now commercially sponsored, so that their names are officially the *Ever Ready Derby, Gold Seal Oaks* and, incongruously, *General Accident One Thousand Guineas*.) The United States, meanwhile, has its 'Triple Crown' of *Belmont Stakes, Kentucky Derby* and *Preakness Stakes*. France has her *Prix de l'Arc de Triomphe*. Other well-known horse races in Britain include the *Cambridgeshire Handicap, Cesarewitch, Gimcrack Stakes, Goodwood Cup, Grand National* and *Lincoln Handicap*. Famous rowing races, on the other hand, include Oxford's *Torpids*, Cambridge's *Mays*, and London's *Doggett's Coat and Badge*.

Ascot is a place-name made famous by its horse racing. Other such names are show-jumping's *Badminton*, motor racing's *Silverstone*, rugby's *Twickenham*, football's *Wembley* and tennis's *Wimbledon*. In some cases, however, it is the ground that has the famous name, such as cricket's *The Oval* and polo's *Cowdray Park*. Football club grounds are also represented. The most famous place-name-based sporting contest, however, is undoubtedly the *Olympic Games*.

17 ANIMAL NAMES

Animals also have their place in the world of names. Here we are concerned not so much with the names of individual animals, such as *Pegasus*, the winged horse of classical mythology, or *Bucephalus*, the steed of Alexander the Great, although they do feature, but the names of breeds.

Breed names can be straightforwardly descriptive, such as (for dogs) *terrier* and *retriever*, which hardly merit capital letters, or more allusive, such as (again for dogs) *Chihuahua, Great Dane, Rottweiler* and *Sealyham*. In fact almost all breed names of this type are derived from place-names. Even so, they merit some kind of origin and etymology, so that the most familiar ones will be found here. Examples of horse breed names in the dictionary are *Lipizzaner* and *Percheron*, while *Aberdeen Angus* cattle and *Leghorn* and *Rhode Island Red* poultry are likewise entered.

18 OTHER NAMES

It is obviously possible to categorize and subcategorize names almost indefinitely. Some of the most important categories have been outlined above. This does not, of course, encompass the whole range of names that exist. As well as names of books and musical compositions, for example, there are titles of well-known works of art. Leonardo da Vinci's *Mona Lisa* is perhaps the most famous portrait in the world, with its name equally familiar as *La Gioconda*, especially to non-English speakers. The names can cause problems of interpretation, however, if only because for English speakers they are of foreign origin. They therefore qualify for inclusion here.

Street and road names have already been mentioned. There are also well-known names of railway lines, if only the routes of the London Underground, such as the *Bakerloo Line*, *Circle Line*, *District Line*, *Jubilee Line* and *Metropolitan Line*. Some of these names grew out of the original railway companies that built and ran them. Others relate to the route itself or to the occasion of its construction. Mainline trains can themselves have familiar names, such as the *Cornish Riviera* or *Golden Hind*. The latter was named for a famous ship, and they similarly have their place in the book. Another familiar ship name is that of the *Ark Royal*. Well-known aircraft, too, must also be represented. *Concorde* is an obvious example.

In short, whatever its category and origin, any well-known name is an immediate candidate for inclusion in this dictionary. If a name is *not* found in the pages that follow, however, it may well be because its origin remains obscure or unknown, so that little can usefully be said about it apart from its actual identification. On the other hand, it may well be that a name has been deliberately omitted from one or other of the categories mentioned for lack of space. (Not quite all the names mentioned above appear, for instance, although the vast majority do.) If there are any genuinely glaring omissions, however, the author would appreciate notification. He can be contacted c/o the publisher at the address on the reverse of the title page.

The inclusion of the name of Dr Ebenezer Cobham Brewer (1810–1897) in the title of the present work is not simply a general compliment to the famous 'miscellaneous writer' and compiler of reference books, although it is also that. The book will readily be seen not only to be in the tradition of Dr Brewer's lastingly popular *Dictionary of Phrase and Fable*, first published in 1870 and revised and updated in many editions since, but also to follow closely in the steps of other works of his, such as *The Reader's Handbook*, first published in 1880, whose aim was to elucidate (as the book's subtitle put it) 'Allusions, References, Plots and Stories'.

According to its own subtitle, Dr Brewer's *Dictionary* had the specific aim of 'Giving the Derivation, Source, or Origin of Common Phrases, Allusions and Words that have a Tale to Tell'. With due modification, the present book might be said to approach names similarly. Every name has a derivation, a source and a 'tale to tell', even if in some cases the precise origin remains disputed. However, considerable advances have been made in linguistics and related disciplines in the hundred years that have elapsed since Dr Brewer's heyday, and not least in the field of onomastics, or name studies, as will be immediately obvious to any reader who compares Dr Brewer's original work with its present successor.

The book is also in the 'Brewer tradition' in that it shares with the *Dictionary* and the *Handbook* the aim of covering as wide a spectrum of its particular field as possible. It contains entries not only for the familiar names of people and places, but for many other types of names, from astronomical bodies to pop groups. Its range is thus universal and catholic, and if Dr Brewer were able to peruse its pages now, a century on, he might well express the keen regret that he never, despite his longevity and prolificacy, produced anything quite like it.

Adrian Room (personal name)
Stamford, Lincolnshire (place-name)
November 1991 (calendar name)

LANGUAGE GUIDE

As already mentioned, the dictionary entries frequently refer to particular languages, especially when tracing the origins of place-names. Many language names can be confusing or even misleading. It is thus helpful to distinguish between *Amharic* and *Aramaic*, *Low German* and *Low Latin* (where *Low* has a different sense in each). A guide is therefore given below to several of the languages that will be encountered. If a language name is not listed here, however, it may well be entered in the dictionary in its own right. The descriptions provided are of the briefest and simplest, and do not pretend to be linguistically comprehensive.

Afrikaans The form of Dutch spoken in South Africa.

Akkadian The extinct Semitic language spoken in Mesopotamia from about 3000 to 1000 BC. The two varieties of Akkadian are Assyrian and Babylonian.

Amharic The official language of Ethiopia. It is a Semitic language written with the aid of a special syllabary (set of symbols) which, unusually for a Semitic language, reads from left to right.

Anglo-Saxon An alternative name for Old English. In this book the term is used not for the language but for the historic West Germanic peoples (Angles, Saxons and Jutes) who settled in Britain from the 5th century and who came to speak the unified language.

Arabic The Semitic language that remains today the official language of many countries of the Middle East, including Algeria, Libya, Egypt, Saudi Arabia, Syria, Jordan, Lebanon and Iraq (but not Iran).

Aramaic An ancient Semitic language that is known chiefly from its use for certain parts of the Bible (in the books of *Daniel* and *Esdras*). It is still spoken in parts of Syria and Lebanon.

Attic The chief literary dialect of classical Greek, regarded as specially elegant. As its name indicates, it was spoken in Attica, with Athens as its capital.

Avestan The oldest recorded language of the Iranian branch of the Indoeuropean family, in which the sacred books of Zoroastrianism were written.

Basque The language of the Basques, the people who live round the western end of the Pyrenees in southwest France and northwest Spain. The influence of the language was at one time much more widespread than it is today. Basque belongs to no known language group.

Berber A group of languages spoken throughout North Africa. They vary widely in their sound systems but have a similar grammar and vocabulary and are written in the Arabic script.

Breton The Celtic language spoken in Brittany, northwest France. It is very similar to Cornish.

Catalan The language of Catalonia, northeast Spain, that is quite closely related to Spanish and Provençal.

Celtic The branch of the Indoeuropean family of languages that includes modern Scottish Gaelic, Irish, Welsh and Breton, and that formerly included Gaulish. Cornish and Manx are two minor Celtic languages of Britain. They have effectively become extinct but are being revived and promoted by regional enthusiasts.

Coptic A Hamitic language descended from ancient Egyptian. It remained as a spoken language until about 1600 but is now extinct except in the use of the Coptic Church, the ancient Christian Church of Egypt.

Cornish The Celtic language spoken in Cornwall until about 1800. It is quite close to Breton.

Doric The dialect of classical Greek spoken by the Dorians, who invaded Greece in about 1100 BC and who settled in the Peloponnese.

Dravidian The family of languages spoken in the south of India and what is now Sri Lanka. Its main representatives are Tamil, Telugu, Kannada and Malayalam. These languages are not related to those in any other family, although it is thought that they must have been spoken over a much wider area at some time in the past.

Finno-Ugrian The family of non-Indoeuropean languages that includes Finnish, Hungarian and Estonian. ('Ugrian' essentially means Hungarian.)

Flemish The Germanic language spoken in Belgium that is virtually (but not quite) identical with Dutch.

Gaulish The extinct Celtic language of Gaul, that is, of the geographical region that today corresponds to northern Italy, France, Belgium, a part of Germany and the southern Netherlands. It died out in about the 5th century AD. Many words of Gaulish known to us today are to a large extent hypothetical, so that their exact original form is uncertain. Masculine nouns are traditionally written with a final -*o*, feminine with an -*a*, and neuter with a -*u*.

Germanic The branch of the Indoeuropean family of languages that includes modern German, English, Dutch, Norwegian, Swedish, Danish and Icelandic, and that formerly included Gothic.

Gothic An ancient Germanic language, spoken by the Goths, who originated in Scandinavia and settled south of the Baltic in about the 1st century AD. They then moved south to Ukraine and, as the *Ostrogoths* and *Visigoths* (*see dictionary*), invaded various parts of the Roman Empire from the 3rd to the 5th century. Their language is known almost entirely from their 4th-century translation of the Bible. By the 6th or 7th century Gothic was extinct.

Hamitic A group of north African languages related to Semitic.

Hebrew The ancient Semitic language of the Hebrews, in which most of the Old Testament was written. It has been revived in modern times as the official language of Israel.

Hindi The language of the Indic branch of Indoeuropean languages spoken in north central India. The name is also used for a recent literary form of Hindustani.

Hindustani The dialect of Hindi spoken in Delhi, India, used as a *lingua franca* throughout India.

Hittite The extinct Indoeuropean language of the Hittite empire, in Asia Minor (Anatolia), spoken from about 3000 to 2000 BC. It has been deciphered from cuneiform inscriptions.

Illyrian The extinct language spoken many centuries BC along the eastern coast of the Adriatic and believed by some to have been an ancestor of Albanian.

Indian Any language spoken by the American Indians. The particular language will usually be specified (which is why no names of American Indian languages are included in this listing).

Indoeuropean The family of languages that includes English and many other extinct and current languages of Europe and India, including Latin, Greek and Sanskrit. Two leading European languages that are *not* Indoeuropean are Finnish and Hungarian. All the Romance languages such as French, Spanish and Italian are, however, as are the Slavonic languages such as Russian, Polish and Czech.

Iranian The modern language of Iran, known also as Persian. It is Indoeuropean in origin, but uses the Arabic alphabet. The term is also used in linguistics for the branch of Indoeuropean languages that includes it (as in the entry for *Pashto* below).

Irish The Celtic language of Ireland, known also as Irish Gaelic or Erse. It is close to the Gaelic spoken in Scotland.

Italic The branch of Indoeuropean languages that includes many of the ancient languages of Italy, such as Latin, and the modern Romance languages which replaced them, such as French and Italian.

Late Latin The form of written Latin in use from the 3rd to the 7th centuries.

Ligurian The extinct language spoken by the Ligurians, in northwest Italy. It is believed to have been an Indoeuropean language and may have held an intermediate position between the Celtic and Italic languages.

Low German A language of northern Germany (where the terrain is *lower* than in the south), spoken in rural areas. It is closer to Dutch than to standard German.

Low Latin Any form or dialect of Latin that differs from the classical language, such as Vulgar Latin or Medieval Latin.

Lydian The extinct Indoeuropean language spoken in Lydia, in western Asia Minor (Anatolia).

Macedonian The name is used both for the extinct language of ancient Macedonia (in what is now Greece, Bulgaria and Yugoslavia) and for the modern Slavonic language spoken in the Macedonia of today, in what was southern Yugoslavia.

Malay The language spoken in Malaysia and Indonesia.

Malayalam The Dravidian language related to Tamil that is spoken in southwest India, where it is the state language of Kerala.

Medieval Latin The form of Latin used throughout Europe during the Middle Ages, *i.e.* in *medieval* times.

Middle English The form of English current from about 1100 to 1450, that is, in the *Middle* Ages or medieval times.

New Latin The form of Latin used since the Renaissance, *i.e.* since roughly the 16th century, especially for scientific terminology.

Norman French The medieval Norman and English dialect of Old French, spoken by the Normans in England after their invasion of 1066.

Occitan A medieval language spoken in the south of France and including Provençal. Its name is directly related to that of *Languedoc* (*see dictionary*).

Old Church Slavonic The oldest recorded Slavonic language. The Bible was translated into it in the 9th century, and it remains the liturgical language of the Orthodox Church in Slavic countries such as Russia and Bulgaria.

Old English The early form of the English language from the 5th century to about 1100. It is also known as *Anglo-Saxon* (*see above*).

Old French The form of French in use from about the 9th century to about 1400.

Old German A general term for a former form of German that included Old High German.

Old High German The form of German spoken in southern Germany (where the terrain is *higher*) before about 1200. This later became High German and spread to being the standard German of today.

Old Icelandic The dialect of Old Norse that was current in Iceland up to about 1600.

Old Norse The language spoken in Scandinavia in medieval times, from about 700 to about 1350. The Vikings (Danes, Norwegians and Swedes) introduced it to Britain in the 9th century, where it remains today in a number of place-names, especially in northern, central and eastern England.

Oscan The extinct language spoken in ancient southern Italy.

Pashto The Iranian language that since 1936 has been the official language of Afghanistan. It is written in a modified form of Arabic.

Pelasgian An ancient non-Indoeuropean language spoken in Greece and the Balkans before the arrival of the Greeks.

Phoenician The extinct language of the Phoenicians, an ancient Semitic people of northwest Syria.

Phrygian The ancient language of Phrygia, in west central Asia Minor. It was probably related to Greek.

Pictish The language spoken by the Picts, who from the 1st to the 4th centuries AD inhabited what is now northeast Scotland. It was subsequently replaced by Gaelic. It has been reconstructed chiefly from place-names, but its relation to any other language remains uncertain.

proto-Indoeuropean The prehistoric unrecorded language that was the forerunner of all Indoeuropean languages.

Punic The language spoken by the Carthaginians as a late form of Phoenician.

Romance The family of languages derived from Latin that includes modern French, Spanish, Portuguese, Italian, Romanian and Romansch.

Romansch The dialects spoken in eastern Switzerland and part of Italy, recognized as an official language from 1938. As its name implies, it is a Romance language.

Sanskrit The ancient mother tongue of the Indoeuropean languages, long in use in India as a literary language and current today among Hindus for religious purposes. India's modern languages of Hindi, Bengali, Punjabi, Urdu and Singhalese effectively derive from it.

Semitic The branch of Afro-Asiatic languages that includes Arabic, Hebrew, Aramaic, Amharic and such extinct languages as Akkadian and Phoenician.

Serbo-Croat The Slavonic language that is one of the official languages of Yugoslavia. The Croats write Serbo-Croat in the Roman script (*i.e.* as for English), the Serbs in Cyrillic (as for Russian). Serbian and Croatian are two Serbo-Croat dialects spoken respectively (as their names indicate) in Serbia and Croatia.

Singhalese The Indic language of the Indoeuropean family that is spoken today in Sri Lanka.

Slavic An alternative term for *Slavonic*, used fairly widely in this dictionary. Where *Slavonic* is used the reference will usually be specifically to the family of languages that includes Russian, Polish and Czech, and that is in many cases written in the Cyrillic alphabet. *Slavic*, on the other hand, frequently refers to the people who speak these languages.

Sogdian The almost extinct Iranian language spoken in central Asia, especially in the region centring on Samarkand.

Sumerian The extinct language spoken in southern Mesopotamia from about 3000 to 2000 BC. It is related to no other known language.

Syriac The dialect of Aramaic spoken in Syria until about AD 1200 and still in use among certain Eastern churches.

Tamil The Dravidian language spoken in southern India and Sri Lanka. It is the state language of Tamil Nadu.

Telugu A Dravidian language spoken in southeast India, where it is the state language of Andhra Pradesh.

Thracian The extinct language spoken in Thrace (modern Greece and Bulgaria), and believed to be related to Phrygian.

Tokharian An extinct Indoeuropean language spoken in the north of East (Chinese) Turkestan between the 5th and the 10th centuries AD.

Tuareg A dialect of Berber spoken in the Sahara.

Turkic The family of languages that includes Turkish, Turkmen, Kirgiz, Tatar and others, spoken in Turkey itself and across parts of central Asia to as far as northeast China.

Urdu An official language of Pakistan, spoken also in India. It is close to Hindi, but uses an Arabic alphabet.

Vedic The classical form of Sanskrit used by the Vedas in the sacred writings of Hinduism.

Vogul The Finno-Ugrian language spoken in western Siberia and in parts of northeast Europe.

Votyak The Finno-Ugrian language spoken in west central Russia, between the Volga and the Urals.

Vulgar Latin A term for any of the dialects of Latin other than classical Latin. It is this form of Latin that developed into the Romance languages (French, Spanish and Italian are the best known).

Yiddish The Germanic language spoken as a vernacular by Jews in Europe. It is usually written in the Hebrew alphabet.

Zyrian The Finno-Ugrian language spoken by the Komi people in northwest Russia.

THE WRITTEN FORM OF FOREIGN LANGUAGES

The reader of English is fortunate in having a straightforward Roman alphabet, with an entire absence of accents, except in foreign words that have been imported into English.

This same Roman alphabet (so called as it was the one adopted by the Romans for writing Latin) is also found as the basis for many other languages, especially those of western Europe such as French and German.

However, some languages have a completely different alphabet, such as Greek or Cyrillic (the latter used for Russian), while a number of languages such as Chinese and Japanese have no alphabet as such at all.

Again, while many languages other than English use the Roman alphabet, many have accents that need to be taken into account. They are particularly familiar from French. Unfortunately, they are frequently regarded as superfluous or at best unnecessarily 'fussy' to English speakers, who tend to omit them. They should not be ignored, however, as they form an essential and integral part of the language, however tiresome they may seem. They therefore appear in the words that require them in this dictionary.

While it is reasonable to expect the reader to cope with such niceties in a Roman alphabet, however, it is almost certainly *un*reasonable to ask a dictionary user to handle non-English alphabets or writing systems. Words from languages that do not use the Roman alphabet, therefore, are transliterated into words that do. They will at least then be readable.

A few words should now be said about accents and non-Roman alphabets.

ACCENTS AND ALPHABETS

Accents, perhaps more accurately known as diacritics, are the signs placed above or below a letter to indicate that it has a different pronunciation, that it is stressed, that it has a special tone, or for some other reason.

Most languages of western Europe have accents, although some languages, such as French, have them more frequently than others, such as Italian and German. Even English has preserved the accents on imported words such as *café* and *protégé*. As mentioned, therefore, the reader should expect to find them where they occur.

When it comes to the written form of the classical languages of Greek and Latin, there are certain conventions regarding diacritics. Greek, for example, when written in the Greek alphabet, involves a rather fearsome array of aspirates and accents. When transliterating Greek words into the Roman alphabet, however, these can be dispensed with, and the so called 'rough breathing' and 'smooth breathing' can be rendered respectively by the Roman letter *h* and by omission. In the Greek alphabet, on the other hand, it is necessary to distinguish between short *o* (omicron) and long *o* (omega), and also between short *e* (epsilon) and long *e* (eta). This is done by writing the long vowel with a macron (bar) over it. Thus Greek *onos*, pronounced roughly 'on us', means 'ass', 'donkey', but *ōnos*, pronounced something like 'onus', means 'price', 'payment'. Similarly *meros*, with *e* as in 'merry', means 'part', 'share', but *mēros*, with *e* as in 'mere', means 'thigh'.

Latin should properly be written with this same sign (the macron) over its long vowels, such as *mēnsa*, 'table' or *amō*, 'I love'. There is thus a difference between *liber*, 'book' and *līber*, 'free'. Most Latin dictionaries and school primers rightly include the macron. Extracts from Latin prose or verse usually omit it, however, and it is normally ignored when reading Latin. For the sake of simplicity, it is therefore omitted here, and does not appear, for example, on the *i* of *Pontus Euxinus*, the Latin name of the Black Sea.

Old English words *are* printed with the macron where necessary, however, if only because to English speakers its value will be more readily appreciated. It can appear on any vowel, and so differentiates *god*, 'god' from *gōd*, 'good'. These are pronounced respectively 'god' and 'goad'. When the macron appears on *y* the resulting sound is like a lengthened *u* in French *tu*, or as the *ü* in German *grün*.

Apart from the vowels as in modern English, Old English also has the digraph *æ*. This is pronounced as in modern *cat*, but when appearing with a macron is like the vowel sound in modern *care*. Old English *æt* thus means 'at', but *ǣt* means 'eatables', 'food'. Diacritics also appear in Old Norse, for example in *vik*, 'bay'.

It should be noted that in Chinese the 'accents' denote tones, not vowel length. Chinese has four tones, with a different sign for each. A macron denotes a high level tone, as in *bō*, 'turn'; an acute denotes a rising tone, as in *bó*, 'rich'; a breve (like a semicircle) denotes a slight fall followed by an immediate rise, as in *bŏ*, 'lame'; and a grave indicates a falling tone, as in *bò*, 'thumb'. The form of the 'accents' thus more or less represents the tone in musical terms. (It should be added that the four vocables here can have meanings other than those given.)

In Arabic the sign ' , similar to an apostrophe, transliterates the first letter of the alphabet, known as *aleph*, pronounced as a glottal stop (as in English Cockney *la'er* for *later*). Its converse, ʿ , similar to an inverted apostrophe, transliterates the 16th letter of the alphabet, known as *ʿain* (a word that begins with it). It is now silent.

A circumflex accent over a consonant (as distinct from a vowel) indicates a particular pronunciation. Thus a Hebrew or Arabic *ĥ* represents a sound close to the final *ch* of Scottish *loch*. The letter *ŝ*, similarly, is pronounced like *sh* in *ash*. The Hebrew *shwa*, a faint indistinct vowel sound like the *e* in English *mother*, is represented by a superscript (raised) small letter *e*, thus: 'ᵉ'. It occurs between two consonants at the beginning of a word to make it easier to pronounce them. It should perhaps be added that the macron found on Hebrew vowels does not necessarily denote vowel length but indicates a full letter, not just a so called vowel point (representing a vowel sound before or after a consonant). An example is the Hebrew name *Yᵉmīmāh*, 'Jemima', which has a *shwa* for its first vowel and macrons on its other two vowels.

Very occasionally Greek or Cyrillic letters are used by way of illustration. It should always be clear which letters are referred to.

Some languages have no capital letters, or even no actual letters as such at all. Proper names transliterated from such languages, for example Chinese, will therefore begin with a small letter. The Chinese name of Peking is thus *běijīng*, with a small *b*.

When all is said and done, however, such exotic signs and symbols can be for the most part happily ignored, since their presence or absence does not affect the stated meaning of a name. John and Mary are still John and Mary when in the nude, although normally one expects to see them clothed.

FORM OF ENTRIES

I have tried wherever possible to keep entries reasonably consistent, despite the different types of name that they treat. Many entries, especially for place-names, begin with a brief descriptive phrase or sentence, defining the name. This is chiefly to avoid ambiguity, but also because the definition of a name, and the identity of a particular place-name, may actually have a bearing on its origin. It is thus significant that *Inverness* is a Scottish place-name, even that it is the name of a town at the mouth of a river. The dating or period of a name can also be relevant, as certainly is its language of origin.

I have also aimed to give the best-known or most popular version of a name, the one we think of first, even where it may not in fact be the correct form or even, of a place-name, the formal current form. In some cases, where the difference is slight, the entry may actually appear under that name, as for *Mafeking* (not *Mafikeng*). In others, especially where it is more radical, there will be a cross-reference, for example from *Burma* to *Myanmar*. (These are actually one and the same name, but the marked difference in spelling suggests a dissimilarity.)

The dictionary is mainly, of course, a dictionary of origins. It is also, however, a sort of universal encyclopedia. Put another way, it is possible to look a name up for its definition only. To know that *Inverness* is a coastal town in northern Scotland at the mouth of the river Ness may be all that some readers require. The fact that the dictionary also gives the *origin* of the name could, for such a reader, even be irrelevant. That the one is accompanied by the other could be seen as a bonus. Even so, it is a necessary accompaniment, since it is as well to establish the definition of a particular name before going into its history and origin. A dictionary of place-name origins will normally tell you *something* about the place, even if only its geographical location.

Some entries are inevitably longer than others. Several entries are quite short, since there is little further to be said. A few entries are lengthy, and may include quotations from other sources or texts. These are designed to help rather than hinder, and to add to the general treatment of a name. If some such quotations are also entertaining, so much the better. (Indeed, if the dictionary as a whole is seen as a sort of 'browser's paradise' I shall feel my labour has not entirely been in vain!)

Many reference books (although not that many dictionaries) contain a bibliography. Obviously, I have consulted dozens of books and sources in the course of compiling this particular work. But I have not included a separate bibliography for several reasons. First, it would be inordinately lengthy. Second, it could never be comprehensive, and so might seem unduly selective. Third, it would contain the titles of books, journals and articles which the average reader might well find difficulty in tracking down. Fourth, many of the books consulted were (inevitably) in a language other than English, and the dictionary is aimed primarily at the general reader, who is unlikely to be a specialized linguist. Even so, some entries do contain specific references to works that provided this or that piece of information, and quotations are almost always given chapter and verse – quite literally, when they come from the Bible.

Finally, a disclaimer. While I have tried to give the origins of the names as accurately as possible, it is very probable that some etymologies are tentative or speculative. This is not through the indulgence of personal whimsy. It is simply because the origins of several names are still uncertain. Even *London* remains a mystery, and cannot be conclusively traced back to a reliable source or etymology. In such cases, I have aimed to say as much, and the wording should make it clear that the stated origin remains uncertain, obscure or frankly unknown. At the same time, I hope I have avoided the more colourful derivations that can still be found in some popular books of name origins, especially in the fields of first names and place-names. The temptation to concoct an etymology at all costs is clearly great where the true source remains annoyingly uncertain. It is nice and neat to derive *Catherine* from Greek *katharos*, 'pure', or *Leicester* from Latin *legionis castra*, 'camp of the legion'. Such popular etymologies are in fact nothing new, and several of the personal name interpretations given in the Bible are similarly suspect or even downright wrong. The resemblance of a name to a particular word was often enough for the writer to conclude that the name actually *was* that word, and that it meant whatever the word meant.

The reader should be aware of the insidious lure of such literary licence, therefore, and be reminded that all that glitters is not necessarily gold!

ACKNOWLEDGMENTS

I am particularly indebted to the following, who provided information on specific subjects or individual names.

Jean Birchenough, Librarian, Crewe Library, Crewe; Professor C.N.L. Brooke, Professor of Ecclesiastical History, Gonville and Caius College, Cambridge; Christopher Butler, Assistant Archivist, Corpus Christi College, Oxford; Anthony Camp, Director, Society of Genealogists, London; Mrs M. Crane, Headmistress, Clarendon School, Bedford; Margaret Claydon, Headmistress, Saint Felix School, Southwold; Professor Richard Coates, Professor of Linguistics, University of Sussex; Mrs Anne Darlow, Headmistress, Sir William Perkins's School, Chertsey; Barbara Dixon, Records Department, National Rifle Association, Bisley; J.R. Elliott, Area Librarian, Central Library, Plymouth; Enid Essame, Potters Bar; Darrell J. Farrant, Headmaster, Abbotsholme School, Uttoxeter; Mrs Hilary Fender, Headmistress, Godolphin School, Salisbury; R.S. Goddard, Secretary, Henley Royal Regatta, Henley-on-Thames; C.J.T. Gould, Headmaster, Badminton School, Bristol; Mrs Clare Hopkins, Archivist, Trinity College, Oxford; C.R. Humphrey-Smith, Principal, The Institute of Heraldic and Genealogical Studies, Canterbury; Jean Lambert, Fellow Librarian, Hughes Hall, Cambridge; Mary Laney, Librarian, Reference & Information Services, Brighton Reference Library; J.K. Maddison, Local Studies Officer, Smethwick Library; E.F. Mills, College Archivist, Jesus College, Cambridge; R.R. Milne, Sub-Librarian, Trinity College Library, Cambridge; Chantal Morel, Librarian, Institut Français, London; Elizabeth Murray, London; Felicity O'Mahony, Assistant Librarian, Manuscripts Department, Trinity College Library, Dublin; Malcolm S. Oxley, Second Master, St Edward's School, Oxford; Mrs Pamela Parsonson, Headmistress, Francis Holland School, London; Dr Sandra Raban, Trinity Hall, Cambridge; Miss D.C. Raine, Headmistress, Eothen School, Caterham; Jane M. Renfrew, Lucy Cavendish College, Cambridge; Miss Daphne Ridge, Cambridge; Miss Margaret Rudland, Head Mistress, The Godolphin and Latymer School, London; Miss C. Sibbit, Headmistress, The Alice Ottley School, Worcester; Mrs S.M. Simmons, Reference Librarian, Malvern Library, Malvern; F.H. Stubbings, Hon Keeper of Rare Books, The Library, Emmanuel College, Cambridge; Conrad Swan, Esquire, York Herald of Arms and Registrar of the College of Arms, London; David Sykes, Bedales Memorial Library, Bedales School, Petersfield; Maria Twist, Local Studies Department, Central Library, Birmingham; Mrs Enid Wayman, Deputy Headmistress, Moira House School, Eastbourne; David Williamson, Co-Editor, Debrett's Peerage Limited, London.

For valuable assistance in the processing of a computerized text equally acceptable to printer and publisher, I am greatly indebted to Shaun Tyas. As a publisher himself he not only knows what is required at the crucial stage when an author hands over his completed work but, equally importantly, he has the necessary equipment and expertise to produce it.

A

Aachen The city and spa in western Germany has a name that refers to its springs, deriving from Old High German *aha*, 'water'. The French name of Aachen is *Aix-la-Chapelle*, with the second part of the name (added to differentiate the town from AIX-EN-PROVENCE and AIX-LES-BAINS) referring to the church in which the emperor Charlemagne is buried.

Aarhus The city and port in Denmark has a name (also spelled *Århus*) which is that of the river on which it stands. The river's name itself means 'river mouth', from Old Danish *å* or *aa*, 'river' and *os*, 'mouth' (*cp.* OSLO), referring to the point where it flows into *Aarhus Bay* and so into the Kattegat.

Aaron In the Old Testament, the name is that of the son of Levi and elder brother of Moses who was the first high priest of the Israelites. It represents Hebrew *Aharōn*, perhaps meaning 'bright'.

Abadan The port in southwest Iran, famous for its oil, is named for *Abbad ibn al-Husayn*, the Arab holy man who founded the city in the 8th or 9th century. It is a coincidence that the place-name happens to contain the Iranian word, *ābād*, which occurs as the final element of many eastern place-names to mean 'habitation', such as HYDERABAD in India and ISLAMABAD in Pakistan.

Abaddon The name occurs just once in the Bible: 'And they had a king over them, which is the angel of the bottomless pit, whose name in the Hebrew tongue is Abaddon, but in the Greek tongue hath his name Apollyon' (*Revelation* 9.11). The Hebrew behind the name is *'abaddōn*, 'destruction', from *'abad*, 'he perished'. As the text points out, the Greek name APOLLO has an identical sense. The name primarily occurs in the Old Testament to refer to the dwelling place of the dead, otherwise hell. It is always translated, however, as in: 'Hell is naked before him, and destruction hath no covering' (*Job* 26.6); 'Destruction and death say, We have heard the fame thereof with our ears' (28.22); 'For it is a fire that consumeth to destruction' (31.12); 'Hell and destruction are before the LORD' (*Proverbs* 15.11). Milton adopted the New Testament personification of the name for the 'bottomless pit' itself in *Paradise Lost* (1671): 'In all her gates Abaddon rues/Thy bold attempt' (IV, 624).

Abba The famous Swedish pop quartet of the 1970s took their name, suggesting musical notes, from the initials of their first names: *A*gnetha Faltskog, *B*jorn Ulvaeus, *B*enny Andersson and *A*nni-Frid Lyngstad. They first performed in public in 1971 and adopted the name the following year.

Abbasids The name of the dynasty of Caliphs who ruled at Baghdad after the massacre of the Umayyads in AD 750 is derived from that of *Abbas*, Muhammad's uncle, whose family worked to gain control of the empire. His own name, properly *'Abbās*, is common among Muslims and is the Arabic word for 'sullen'. Severity was regarded as a desirable quality for male Arabs.

Abbeville The town near Amiens in northern France has a name that means 'abbot's village'. It originated in the 9th century as a dependency of the *abbots* of St Riquier.

Abbey National Building Society The society arose as the result of a merger in 1944 between two existing societies. The first of these, the *Abbey Road* Building Society, had been founded in 1849 in Abbey Road, northwest London. Abbey Road is itself named after the former Kilburn Priory. It also gave the name of the Beatles' album *Abbey Road* (1969), as the group's early singles were recorded in EMI's studio here.

Abbey Theatre Ireland's national theatre takes its name from *Abbey* Street, Dublin, where it opened in 1904 on the site of the New Princess Theatre of Varieties. Abbey Street itself is named after the 12th-century Cistercian foundation of St Mary's Abbey, of which only the chapter house remains today.

Abbotsford The name is that of the fine house by the river Tweed near Melrose, Scotland, which was the home of Sir Walter Scott. It was originally a small farm called *Clarty Hole* ('dirty hole') when Scott bought it in 1811. On extending the house, however, Scott gave it a new name, referring both to the *Abbot* of Melrose Abbey, who previously owned the land here, and to the nearby *ford* across the Tweed.

Abbotsholme School The Derbyshire public school was founded in 1889 and takes its name from its locality, near the Staffordshire border. On 19th-century maps this appears as *Abbots or Monks Clownholm*. The *abbot* was presumably that of nearby Rocester. *Holme* here probably means 'water meadow' (Old English *hamm*), from the site of the school by the river Dove. The *Clowne* is a small stream.

Abbott The name arose as a nickname for a person employed in the house of an abbot, or who was thought to resemble an abbot in some way, possibly through excessive piety or at least show of piety.

ABC The British rock group, formed in Sheffield in 1980, took a straightforward, memorable name, chosen because 'the first three letters of the alphabet are known the world over'.

Abdullah The name of the father of Muhammad, the founder of Islam, is properly *'Abd-Allāh*, Arabic for 'servant of Allah', that is, of God. The name is one of the most common in the Muslim world, and has been borne by many famous Islamic leaders since. One of the most recent was Abdullah, king of Jordan, assassinated in 1951.

Abednego The biblical name is perhaps the most familiar of those of the three young companions of Daniel who were saved from the 'burning fiery furnace' of King Nebuchadnezzar. In origin it is probably a distortion of the Aramaic theophoric name *Abed-Nabu*, 'servant of *Nabu*', the latter being a god of writing and wisdom whose name is also seen in that of NE-BUCHADNEZZAR himself. Abednego's original name was AZARIAH. *See also* SHADRACH.

Abegg Variations Schumann's Opus 1 for Piano (1829–30) is dedicated to his friend Meta *Abegg*, and its theme comprises the four notes based on her name, A-B-E-G-G. The B is in the German notation, so corresponds to English B flat.

Abel The name is that of the second son of Adam and Eve in the Bible, killed in a quarrel by his brother Cain. It perhaps represents Hebrew *Hebel*, literally 'breath', implying vanity, but could also come from Assyrian *aplu*, 'son'.

Aberdeen The city and port in northeast Scotland has a name of Celtic origin, meaning 'mouth of the *Don*'. The modern city stands on the river Dee, but it developed from a settlement at the mouth of the Don, which enters the sea in the present district of Old Aberdeen. Celtic *aber*, 'mouth', is found as the first element of the names of other coastal towns in Scotland and Wales, such as ABERYSTWYTH. *See also* ARBROATH.

Aberdeen Angus The famous breed of black, polled cattle derives its name from *Aberdeenshire* and *Angus*, the two former adjacent counties in northeast Scotland (now in the Grampian region) where the cattle were originally raised.

Aberystwyth The well-known Welsh resort and university town, on Cardigan Bay, has a Celtic name that means 'mouth of the *Ystwyth*'. Today the town is at the mouth of the Rheidol, but its original site was in the valley of the Ystwyth, which now flows into the sea to the south. The relationship between name and topography is thus similar to that at ABERDEEN. The river's name means 'winding'.

Abidjan The former Ivory Coast (now Côte d'Ivoire) capital was founded in 1903. When the first French colonists arrived here, they met some women and asked them where they were. The women, misunderstanding the question, replied '*T'chan m'bi djan*', 'Coming from cutting leaves' in their native language. The Frenchmen noted the name, and gave it to the town.

Abigail In the Bible, the name is that of the second wife and 'handmaid' (as she regarded herself) of King David. It represents Hebrew *Abīgayil*, literally 'father rejoices' (that is, at the birth of his daughter). It became a stock name for a maid in a number of Elizabethan plays, and for some time was a nickname for a lady's maid in general.

Abimelech The name occurs for two Old Testament characters: the king of Gerar who takes Sarah for himself after Abraham introduces her as his sister, and the son of Gideon who murders his 70 brothers and proclaims himself king of Shechem. It is Hebrew in origin, and represents *Abimelek*, 'my father is king'. Hebrew *melek*, 'king' occurs in many other biblical names, such as MOLOCH and MELCHIZEDEK.

Abingdon The name of the Oxfordshire (formerly Berkshire) town means '*Æbba*'s hill', with the latter half of the name representing Old English *dūn*, 'hill' (modern 'down'). The hill in question is probably the higher ground to the north of the town.

Abner In the Bible, the name is that of the cousin of Saul who was the commander of his army. It derives from Hebrew *Abnēr*, 'Father (*i.e.* God) is light'. Today the name is popularly associated with Li'l *Abner*, the hero of Al Capp's cartoon strip.

Abominable Snowman The existence of the hairy, bearlike creature of this name in the Himalayas has not yet been conclusively proved. Its name is a translation of the creature's Tibetan nickname, *Metohkangmi*, from *metoh*, 'foul' and *kangmi*, 'snowman'. The creature is also known as the YETI.

Abraham In his important place in the Bible as first of the patriarchs and father of the Hebrew nation, *Abraham* has a name that represents Hebrew *Abrāham*. This is explained in the Old Testament as follows: 'Neither shall thy name any more be called Abram, but thy name shall be Abraham; for a father of many nations have I made thee'. But the meaning 'father of many' does not tally with the Hebrew form of the name, which is probably simply an orthographical alteration of *Abram*, itself meaning 'father on high'. The name itself is very ancient, however, and has been discovered

in the form '*a-bu-ra-mu* in Mesopotamian hieroglyphics dating from the second half of the third millennium BC. One of the best-known promoters of the name in modern times was the American president *Abraham* Lincoln (1809–65).

Abraxas The 2nd-century god of the Gnostics, the source of divine emanations and lord of heavens, has a name formed from the seven Greek letters alpha (A), beta (B), rho (P), alpha (A), xi (Ξ), alpha (A), sigma (Σ). Each of these has a corresponding numerical value, as follows: 1 + 2 + 100 + 1 + 60 + 1 + 200. This totals 365, the number of days in a year (the 'fullness of world time') and also the number of heavens in Gnostic cosmology (the 'fullness of world space'), while the seven letters of the name represent the mystic figure 7 with its own connotations of summary. The name itself is thought to have given the magic word *abracadabra*.

Abruzzi The mountainous region of south central Italy had the Late Latin name of *Aprutium*. The exact origin of this is uncertain, although it may be related to Latin *aper*, genitive *apri*, 'boar', or possibly to *abruptus*, 'steep'. The mountains are the highest and most rugged in the Apennines.

Absalom The name of the favourite son of King David in the Old Testament derives from Hebrew *Abŝālōm*, meaning 'father of peace' (*cp.* SALEM). In Dryden's allegorical poem *Absalom and Achitophel* (1681), Absalom represents the Duke of Monmouth, the illegitimate son of Charles II.

Abu Bakr The name of Muhammad's closest adviser and companion, father of his wife Ayesha, and his successor as first caliph, means 'father of *Bakr*', with the latter name, common among male Muslims, meaning 'young camel'. The Muslim title for Abu Bakr is *Aṣ-Ṣiddīq*, 'the upright'. Abu (from Arabic *ab*, 'father') in names of this type should not be understood literally. It implies that the bearer of such a name is the metaphorical father or 'owner' of what is mentioned in the word that follows. Abu Bakr was thus regarded as possessing the qualities implied by 'young camel'.

Abu Dhabi The constituent emirate of the United Arab Emirates has a name that

3

means 'father of *Ẓabī*', the latter male personal name deriving from Arabic *ẓab*, 'gazelle'. The sheikhdom grew up around the settlement of *Abu Zabi*, now the capital of the Emirates as a whole.

Abu Hassan The name is that of the rich merchant of Baghdad in *The Arabian Nights* who is granted his wish to be 'caliph for a day'. It means 'father of *Hassan*', the latter being one of the most popular male Muslim names, with the literal sense of 'good', 'handsome'.

Abu Simbel The former village in southern Egypt is famous for its two temples built by Rameses II, with four huge statues of Rameses himself in front. Its name means 'father of *Sunbul*', the latter being a Muslim male name meaning 'hyacinth'. The temples were moved to higher ground in 1966 before the area behind the Aswan Dam was flooded.

Abyssinia The former name of Ethiopia is said to derive from an Amharic root *hbŝ*, meaning 'mixed', referring to the mixed black and white races who at one time inhabited this part of Africa. Some Amharic scholars doubt this origin, however.

Acadia The name is that of the former French colony in eastern Canada, corresponding to the present Maritime Provinces. It is a native one, from the Indian word *akadi* meaning 'fertile land'. It happens to suggest ARCADIA, a suitable name for a newly discovered 'paradise'.

Acapulco The port and resort in southwest Mexico has a name that is Aztec in origin and that is said to mean 'conquered city' or 'destroyed city'.

Accra The capital of Ghana derives its name from the local African word *n'kran*, 'ant'. This was the nickname used by the native forest dwellers for the Nigerian tribesmen who settled here in the 16th century.

Accrington The Lancashire town has a name that probably meant 'acorn farm' originally, from Old English *æcern*, 'acorn' and *tūn*, 'farm' (modern 'town'). Accrington was formerly on the edge of Rossendale Forest, and acorns from there would have been used as 'mast' for feeding pigs.

Aceldama In the Bible, the name is that of the place near Jerusalem that was bought with the 30 pieces of silver paid to Judas for betraying Jesus. In *Matthew* 27.8 and *Acts* 1.19 it is interpreted as 'field of blood', alluding to this act of treachery, and thus perhaps represents Aramaic *haqal-demā*, from *haqal*, 'field' and *demā*, 'blood'. But the second word may originally have been Aramaic *demah*, 'sleep', so that the meaning is 'field of sleep', otherwise metaphorically 'cemetery'. This tallies with *Matthew* 27.7, which describes the place as a 'potter's field, to bury strangers in'.

Achates The name of the faithful companion of Aeneas in Virgil's *Aeneid* represents the Greek word *akhatēs*, 'agate'. This could symbolize steadfast loyalty, but Achates was equally the name of the river in Sicily where the mineral was first found.

Achernar The name of the brightest star in the constellation Eridanus represents Arabic *āhir an-nahr*, 'end of the river'. This refers to the star's location in Eridanus, which 'flows down' to it.

Acheron In classical mythology, the name is that of one of the rivers in Hades over which the souls of the dead were ferried by Charon. Its name is said to derive from the Greek phrase *o akhea rheōn*, 'the river of woe', with the second word related to English *ache*.

Acheson The name is a mainly Northern Ireland variant of ATKINSON, so like it means 'son of little ADAM'.

Achilles The famous Greek hero has a name that was explained by ancient writers as deriving from Greek *a-*, 'without' and *kheilea*, 'lips', since as a child Achilles had never been suckled. But it is possible that the name is really based on Greek *akhos*, 'pain', 'distress', referring to the grief and anguish that Achilles caused in his wrathful deeds.

Acis The lover of the nymph Galatea in Greek mythology has a name that has not been satisfactorily explained. It may somehow relate to Greek *akros*, 'top', 'extreme' or to Latin *acus*, 'needle', although the precise implication of these senses is not clear.

Ackroyd The name derives from a place-name, so originally applied to a person who lived in a clearing in an oak wood, from Old English *āc*, 'oak' and *rod*, 'clearing'.

AC Milan The popular Italian football club was founded in Milan in 1899 by an Englishman, Alfred Edwards, as the *Milan Cricket and Football Club*. The English form of 'Milan', instead of Italian *Milano*, thus tells of the club's English roots. In 1906 it changed its name to *Milan FC* (for 'Football Club'), but in 1938 was ordered by Mussolini to adopt an Italian form of this, *AC Milano*, the initials standing for *Associazione Calcio*, 'Football Association'. After the war the club reverted to English *Milan*, but kept the Italian *AC*.

Aconcagua The mountain in western Argentina, the highest in the Andes, has an Indian (Araucan) name derived from that of the river that rises in its foothills. The river's own name derives from *konka*, 'sheaf of straw' and *hue*, 'place abundant in', referring to the fertility of its valley as it flows towards the Pacific.

Acre The city and port in northern Israel, captured and recaptured many times in the Crusades, has a name that may derive from a Hebrew word meaning 'enclosed', referring to its location on the Bay of Haifa. It is mentioned twice in the Bible, once as *Accho* (*Judges* 1.31) and again as *Ptolemais* (*Acts* 21.7). The latter name comes from the Egyptian king *Ptolemy* II Philadelphus who conquered it in the 3rd century BC.

Acrilan The patent acrylic fibre or fabric has a name that was created in America in 1950 as the result of a contest, two conditions being that the name should have three syllables and should not end in *-on* (like *nylon*). The first half of the name links with *acrylic*, while the latter suggests Latin *lana*, 'wool'.

Acropolis The name of the famous citadel of Athens on which the Parthenon stands is self-descriptive, meaning simply 'citadel', literally 'top town', from Greek *akros*, 'top', 'highest' and *polis*, 'city'. *Cp.* AKRON.

Actaeon In Greek mythology, the name is that of the hunter who, as a punishment for accidentally seeing Artemis bathing naked, was turned into a stag and killed by his own hounds. His name is traditionally derived from Greek *akteon*, 'one must

lead', from *agō*, 'I lead', 'I go', referring to one prominent in the chase.

Acton The district of west London has a name found elsewhere in Britain that means 'oak-tree farm', from Old English *āc*, 'oak' and *tūn*, 'farm', 'settlement'.

Acts of the Apostles, The The name of the New Testament book summarizes its subject, the active expansion of the early Christian church. In the original Greek the title of the book was *Praxeis*, 'Acts' or *Praxeis apostolōn*, 'Acts of Apostles'. In a sense '*The* Acts of *the* Apostles' is a misnomer, since the book contains a detailed account of only two apostles, Peter and Paul.

ACT UP The name is that of the lesbian and gay pressure group originating in the United States with the aim of forcing government agencies and public bodies to take more direct action to counter the spread of AIDS and support people with HIV. In the manner of many pressure groups, the name is a punning acronym, in this case standing for *A*ids *C*oalition *T*o *U*nleash *P*ower. The group has gained a reputation for its angry and imaginative public protests, or 'zaps', and since 1989 has had its equivalent in Britain. *See also* OUTRAGE.

Ada The name gained independent use from the first part of a German name such as *Adelheid* (which gave ADELAIDE), where it has the meaning 'noble'. It may have been influenced by the slightly different name *Adah*, which occurs in the Bible (*Genesis* 4.19) as that of the first woman mentioned after Eve, and which comes from a Hebrew word meaning 'ornament'.

Ada The high-level computer programming language, widely used in military systems, takes its name from *Ada*, Lady Lovelace (1815–1852), Byron's daughter, who was personal assistant to Charles Babbage, inventor of a calculating machine, and who herself wrote the first computer program.

Adam The name is famous in the Bible as that of the first man, and is traditionally derived from Hebrew *Ādām*, 'of red earth', this being the colour of the 'dust of the ground' from which God formed him (*Genesis* 2.7). But recent scholars have suggested that the names of *Adam* and the ultimately meaning simply 'valley'. If so, Adam was simply a 'valley dweller' or 'man of the plains'. *See also* ADEN.

Adam and the Ants The well-known British rock band was formed in 1977 by *Adam Ant* (real name Stuart Leslie Goddard), who adopted his new surname as a collective name for the group of four he sang with. His stage name, suggesting 'adamant', has a connotation of strength.

Adastral House The government building in Theobalds Road, London, was erected in 1950 and in 1955 became the headquarters of the Air Ministry (now part of the Ministry of Defence). It takes its name from the Latin motto of the Royal Air Force, *Per ardua ad astra*, 'Through difficulties to the stars', itself the motto of the Mulvany family.

Addenbrooke's Hospital The well-known Cambridge teaching hospital takes its name from John *Addenbrooke*, a Cambridge doctor who died aged only 39 in 1719 bequeathing about £4000 'to erect and maintain a small physical hospital'. The old hospital buildings remain in Trumpington Street, but the main Addenbrooke's is now in new buildings to the south of the city.

Addis Ababa The capital of Ethiopia has an Amharic name meaning 'new flower', from *ǎddis*, 'new' and *ǎbǎba*, 'flower'. This was the auspicious name given it by Empress Taitu, wife of Emperor Menelik II, when in 1887 she persuaded him to build a new capital near the hot springs at the centre of the country in place of its predecessor, Entoto, which had been located on a cold, exposed site.

Addison The name means 'son of *Addie*', this being a diminutive of the first name ADAM.

Addled Parliament The nickname was that given to the second parliament of James I, from April to June, 1614. It passed no acts, so like an infertile egg was deemed to be 'addled'.

Adela Like ADA, Adela developed from the German name *Adelheid* (modern ADELAIDE), so like it means 'noble'. William the Conqueror's daughter *Adela* married Stephen, Count of Blois, and their third son, Stephen, became king of England in 1135.

Adelaide The well-known Australian city and capital of South Australia was founded in 1837 and named in honour of Queen ADELAIDE, wife of William IV. The Queen had requested that her name should be given to the new city, and she bequeathed part of her library to it.

Adelaide The name is a French version of an Old German name that is now *Adelheid*, meaning 'nobility' and implying a person of noble birth. It was popularized by Queen *Adelaide* (1792–1849), wife of William IV of England. A directly related name is ALICE.

Adélie Land The region of eastern Antarctica was discovered in 1840 by the French explorer Jules-Sébastien-César Dumont d'Urville, who named it for his wife, *Adélie*.

Adelphi The London buildings of this name off the Strand were erected as an elegant residential complex in 1768 by the four Scottish architect brothers John, Robert, James and William Adam, who gave their work a name based on Greek *adelphoi*, 'brothers'. The original Adelphi was demolished in 1936 to be replaced by a grandiose block of offices.

Adelphi Theatre The theatre in the Strand, London, takes its name from the nearby ADELPHI buildings. The original theatre opened in 1806 as the *Non Pareil*, becoming the *Adelphi Theatre* in 1819 and the *Theatre Royal, Adelphi* in 1829. The present theatre is the fourth of the name on the site.

Aden The main port and capital of Yemen has a name that probably derives from the Akkadian word *edinnu*, meaning 'plain'. Some scholars, however, relate it more directly to the name of the biblical Garden of EDEN, to which the personal name ADAM may also be akin.

Adidas The make of sportswear takes its name from Adolf ('*Adi*') *Das*sler (1900–1978) who founded his business near Nürnberg, Germany in 1948. His footwear first appeared at the 1952 Olympic Games, Helsinki.

Adirondacks The mountain range in New York State is named after an Indian

(Algonquian) tribe. The original meaning of the name has, however, been lost.

Admetus The name of the king of Thessaly in Greek mythology is traditionally derived from Greek *admētos*, 'untamed'.

Admiral's Cup The famous racing trophy is awarded to the winner of a biennial international competition among teams of three sailing yachts each. The contest comprises four separate races, two short and two long, the final one being the Fastnet Cup. The trophy was established in 1957 by the Royal Ocean Racing Club, and is so named because it is presented to the winner by the *Admiral* of this club.

Admiralty Arch The triumphal arch at the top of The Mall, London, was built in 1910 as part of the national memorial to Queen Victoria, who had died nine years earlier. It takes its name from the nearby *Admiralty*, now housing the navy department of the Ministry of Defence.

Admiralty Islands The islands, in the southwest Pacific, were so named in 1767 by the British navigator Philip Carteret in honour of the *Admiralty*, who had financed his expedition. The archipelago was discovered by the Dutch in 1616, who named the group *The Twenty-One Islands*, although there are actually rather fewer than this. They should not be confused with the AMIRANTE ISLANDS.

Adolph The name represents the Old German name *Adalwolf*, meaning 'noble wolf' (*cp.* ADELAIDE). The modern German spelling of the name is *Adolf*, familiar from *Adolf* Hitler (1889–1945), who caused a sharp decline in its popularity.

Adonis In Greek mythology, the name is that of the beautiful youth who was the favourite of Aphrodite and Persephone. His name derives from the Phoenician *adonī*, 'my lord', a title of the god Tammuz. This also gave one of the Hebrew names of God, *Adonai*.

Adrastus In Greek mythology, the name is that of the king of Argos who led the Seven against Thebes. It represents Greek *adrastos*, 'not running away', an appropriate name for a warrior prince.

Adrian The name goes back to Latin *Adrianus* (*Hadrianus*), the adjective used for an inhabitant of the city and port of *Adria* (on the ADRIATIC) in northern Italy. The only English pope, born Nicholas Breakspear (d. 1159), was *Adrian* IV.

Adriatic The sea takes its name from the Venetian port of *Adria*, which also gave the personal name ADRIAN. The city's name probably comes from the Illyrian word *adur*, 'water', 'sea', although today the port is more than 12 miles (20 km) inland.

Adullamites The name is that of a group of English politicians who withdrew from the Liberal Party in 1866. It derives from the fortified cave of *Adullam* mentioned in the Bible (1 *Samuel* 22.1) to which David and others fled from King Saul.

Advent In the Christian calendar, the name is that of the season before Christmas when the *advent* (coming) of Christ is commemorated, both as his birth in the past and as his second coming in the future. It is celebrated from *Advent* Sunday (the one nearest to 30 November) to Christmas Day (25 December). Since the season is concerned with the coming of Christ, *Advent* Sunday, in the Western Church, is the beginning of the Christian year.

Advocates' Library The name for the National Library of Scotland, in Edinburgh, derives from the fact that it was founded in 1689 by Sir George Mackenzie, king's *advocate*, and that it was presented to the nation in 1924 by the Faculty of *Advocates*. Advocates in Scotland are the approximate equivalent of barristers elsewhere in Britain.

Aegean The sea between Greece and Turkey is traditionally named after the mythical Athenian king AEGEUS who is said to have thrown himself into it on learning, mistakenly, that his son Theseus was dead. The name has popularly been linked with Greek *aix*, genitive *aigos*, 'goat'. It may well date back to pre-Hellenic times, however, and represent a word *aiges* meaning 'tides', 'waves'.

Aegeus The Athenian king and father of Theseus has a name that is closely bound to that of the AEGEAN, and that therefore has the same Greek or (more likely) pre-Greek origin.

Aegir In Scandinavian mythology, the name is that of the god of the sea. It represents Old Norse *ǽgir*, 'sea', related to the Old English word *ēagor*, 'flood' which may have given *eagre* as a term for a tidal bore.

Aelita The name is that of the heroine of the early Soviet science fiction novel of the same title by Alexei Tolstoy, published in 1922. She is the princess of the planet Mars, and her name was devised by the author from Greek *aēr*, 'air' and *lithos*, 'stone'. It was adopted for first name use as one of the innovative names that were fashionable in Soviet society in the heady years following the Revolution.

Aeneas The famous Trojan prince who was the son of Anchises and Aphrodite has a name that is traditionally derived from Greek *aineō*, 'I praise'. His praiseworthy deeds are told in the AENEID.

Aeneid The name is that of the epic Latin poem by Virgil that relates the adventures of AENEAS after the fall of Troy. The *-id* suffix means 'of', 'pertaining to'.

Aeolian Hall The former London concert hall, in New Bond Street, opened in 1904 with a name suggesting music from the *Aeolian* harp or in the *Aeolian* mode. The name was popular in other musical contexts in Victorian times, as for the *Aeolian* Company that manufactured player-pianos. The ultimate source of the name is with AEOLUS, the god of winds. The Aeolian Hall was taken over by the BBC in 1941 as a recording studio and closed in 1975.

Aeolus The name, that of the god of the winds in Greek mythology, is almost certainly pre-Greek in origin. It may have developed from Phoenician *aol*, 'tempest'.

Aer Lingus The Irish state airline, founded in 1936, has a name that represents Irish *aer loingeas*, 'air fleet'.

Aeroflot The Russian airline was founded in 1923 as *Dobrolyot*, an abbreviation of its full title, *Vserossiyskoye obshchestvo dobrovol'nogo vozdushnogo flota*, 'All-Russian Company of the Voluntary Air Fleet', with the second half of *polyot*, 'flight'. This was changed to *Aeroflot*, 'air fleet', in 1930.

Aertex The cellular cotton fabric, popular for shirts and blouses, was invented in 1888 and was so named for its light, *airy* *tex*ture.

Aeschylus The great Greek dramatist of the 6th and 5th centuries BC has a name that literally means 'shameful', 'ugly', from Greek *aiskhos*, 'shame', 'ugliness'. The meaning does not relate specifically to Aeschylus, but must have originally been applied as a nickname for an ugly person.

Aesculapius The Roman god of medicine was the equivalent of the Greek god *Asclepius*, whose name is difficult to explain. It may relate to Greek *skallō*, 'I stir up', referring to the skill of the surgeon.

Aesir In Norse mythology, the name is that of the chief gods, who dwell in ASGARD. The word is the plural of *áss*, 'god'. This was derived by the medieval Icelandic poet Snorri Sturluson from ASIA, but that is simply a typical example of the 'learned' etymology of his time. It in fact derives from a common Germanic word for 'god' found as the initial *Os-* in personal names such as OSBERT and OSWALD.

Aesop The Greek author of the famous fables has a name that has been literally interpreted as 'burnt-faced', from Greek *aithō*, 'I burn' and *ōps*, 'face', otherwise 'dark-skinned', 'negroid' (as for ETHIOPIA). But the biographical background to the writer is so diffuse and uncertain that the relevance of the name cannot be positively established.

Afghanistan The central Asian republic derives its name from its native inhabitants, the *Afghanis*, with the latter part of the name representing Old Persian *stān*, 'country' (ultimately related to English 'stand'). The people's own name comes from *Afghana*, a Persian word that may be the name of one of their ancestors. For other names in *-stan*, *cp.* PAKISTAN, TURKESTAN.

Africa The Roman name *Africa* related only to a small part of the present continent, corresponding to modern Tunisia. The name itself probably comes from Arabic *'afar*, 'dust', 'earth', referring to the deserts that predominate here. This would at first have been a tribal name, 'people of the dusty land', which subsequently became that of the region and eventually of the whole continent.

Afrikaans The name is that of one of the two official languages of South Africa, closely related to Dutch and Flemish. It is the Dutch word for 'African', describing the modified form of Dutch spoken by Dutch and other European settlers who came to South Africa in the 17th century before the British. It was formerly known as *Cape Dutch*. Speakers of Afrikaans are known as *Afrikaners*.

Aga The well-known make of cooking stove and range takes its name from that of its original Swedish manufacturers, the *Svenska Aktienbolaget Gasackumulator*, 'Swedish Gas Accumulator Company', with *Aga* an acronym formed from the initial letters of the latter two words.

Agadir The name of the port in southwest Morocco represents Tuareg *agādir*, 'wall', 'embankment', referring to the natural slope on which the old town was built above the modern port and harbour.

Agag The name of the Amalekite king, spared by Saul but killed by Samuel, is of Hebrew origin but uncertain meaning. It has been associated by some with the name of GOG AND MAGOG.

Aga Khan The hereditary title is that of the head of the Ismaili Islamic sect. Both words are of Turkish origin, with *aga* meaning 'lord', 'master' and *khan* a contraction of *khāqān*, 'ruler'. The first Muslim head to bear the title, Aga Khan I (1800–1881), was born Hasan ʿAlī Shāh. The present *Aga Khan* (IV), Prince Karim, became spiritual leader of the Ismaili Muslims in 1957 at the age of 20 on the death of his grandfather.

Agamemnon In Greek mythology, the name was that of the king of Mycenae who led the Greeks at the siege of Troy. His name, appropriately, means 'very resolute', from Greek *agan*, 'very' and *menos*, 'purpose', 'resolve'.

Agate The name originally denoted a person who lived by a gate, from Middle English *a*, 'at', 'on' and *gate*. *Cp.* AGUTTER.

Agatha The name represents Greek *agathos*, 'good', and was first widely adopted from the 3rd-century virgin martyr St *Agatha*. In recent times the name has become familiar from that of the popular detective writer *Agatha* Christie (1890–1976).

Agfa The photographic products brand name is an acronym of the name of the original German manufacturing company founded near Berlin in 1867, *Aktiengesellschaft für Anilinfabrikation*, 'Dye Manufacturing Company'. In 1964 Agfa merged with the Belgian company *Gevaert*, named after its founder, Lieven *Gevaert*, a calcium paper manufacturer, to form *Agfa-Gevaert*.

Agincourt, Battle of The famous battle of 1415 in which Henry V and his longbowmen won a decisive victory over the French takes its name from the village in northern France near where it was fought. The name itself means 'Aizo's homestead'. The modern French name of the village is *Azincourt*.

Agnes The name comes from the Greek word *hagnos*, 'pure', 'chaste', but has become popularly associated with Latin *agnus*, 'lamb'. This link has been reinforced by pictures of the 4th-century virgin martyr St *Agnes* holding a lamb, as well as by the concept of Jesus, pure and sinless, as 'Lamb of God'.

Agnew The name arose either as a nickname for a meek person, from Old French *agneau*, 'lamb', or perhaps originally applied to someone who had come from *Agneaux*, in northern France.

Agni The name of the Hindu god of fire actually means 'fire', from Sanskrit *agni*, to which are related Latin *ignis* and so English *ignite*. Agni is one of the three chief deities of the Vedas, and his name occurs more often in the *Rig-Veda* than any other except that of Indra.

Agra The city in northern India is mentioned in the *Mahabharata* as *Agrabana*, a name said to mean 'paradise'. Ptolemy referred to it in the 2nd century AD as *Agara*.

Agricola The 1st-century AD Roman general and governor of Britain had the full name Gnaeus Julius *Agricola*. The name was thus a *cognomen*, or nickname, deriving from the identical Latin word meaning 'farmer'.

Agrigento The ancient town in Sicily, southern Italy, has a name ultimately going back to Greek *Akragas*, traditionally said to refer to *Akragante*, daughter of Zeus, who built it. But as so often in such instances her name was almost certainly devised to explain that of the original Greek city.

Agrippa The name of the 1st-century BC Roman general is traditionally linked with Latin *aeger*, 'sick', 'painful', as if one born in pain, or able to inflict pain on others.

Aguascalientes The Mexican city, capital of the state of the same name, has a name representing Spanish *aguas calientes*, 'hot waters', referring to the many thermal springs here.

Agulhas, Cape The southernmost cape in South Africa, and therefore in Africa as a whole, has a name representing Portuguese *agulha*, 'needle'. The reference is said to be to the magnetic needle of a compass, which shows no deviation here but points due north.

Agutter The name originally denoted a person who lived by a water channel, from Middle English *a*, 'at', 'on' (as in *aground*) and *gutter*. A similar name is AGATE.

A-Ha The Norwegian rock trio, formed in 1982, owe their name to their keyboardist, Magne ('Mags') Furuholmen, who selected a title that was readily memorable and also familiar as an expression of recognition or discovery in many languages.

Ahasuerus The king of ancient Persia and husband of Esther, who features throughout the Old Testament Book of *Esther*, is generally identified with XERXES. His name thus has the same origin.

Ahithophel In the Old Testament, the name is that of a member of King David's council who conspired with Absalom against the king and who hanged himself when his advice was disregarded (2 *Samuel* 15.12–17.23). His name is spelled *Achitophel* in the Vulgate (Latin version of the Bible) and in Miles Coverdale's translation. It is said to be Hebrew for 'brother of folly', *i.e.* foolishness.

Ahmadabad The city of western India, famous for its mosque, has a name meaning '*Ahmad*'s town', from the Arabic personal name *Ahmad* (*see* AHMED) and Hindi *ābād*, 'inhabited', a word of Iranian origin (*cp*. ABADAN and towns with similar endings, such as ALLAHABAD, HYDERABAD). The city was founded in 1411 by Sultan *Ahmad*

Shah. The name is also spelled *Ahmedabad*.

Ahmed The name is familiar as that of the prince in the *Arabian Nights* who marries the fairy Peri-Banou. It is a regular Muslim name and represents Arabic *ahmad*, 'more commendable', from *hamida*, 'to praise'. *Cp*. MUHAMMAD, which is derived from the same source.

Ahura Mazda The alternative name for the creative deity ORMAZD in Zoroastrianism means literally 'wise spirit', from Avestan *ahura*, 'spirit' and *mazdā*, 'wise'. *See also* MAZDA.

Aïda The name is familiar from Verdi's opera of 1871, where it is that of the heroine. She is an Ethiopian princess who is captured as a slavegirl in ancient Egypt. The libretto of the opera was based on a story by the French writer Camille du Locle, published three years earlier. The princess's name appears to represent Arabic *'Aidā*, 'benefit', 'reward', while at the same time suggesting French *aider*, 'to save', and Greek *aidōs*, 'modesty', 'reverence'.

Ainslie The Scottish name appears to derive from a place-name, although no such place has been identified.

Ainsworth The name comes from that of a place so called, such as *Ainsworth* west of Bury, near Manchester. This in turn means '*Ægen*'s enclosure'.

Aintree The Liverpool racecourse, famous as the scene of the Grand National, is named after the district where it is located. The name itself means 'one tree', probably referring to a lone tree formerly here, and is Scandinavian in origin.

Airdrieonians The Scottish football club, based in *Airdrie*, near Glasgow, was formed in that town in 1878, originally with the name *Excelsior* Football Club. They adopted their present name in 1881, denoting residents of *Airdrie* and based on similar 'native' names, such as *Caledonian*.

Airedale The breed of terrier takes its name from its place of origin, the dale or valley of the river *Aire* in Yorkshire.

Aix-en-Provence The first word and main name of the town and spa in southeast

France has the same origin as that of *Aix-la-Chapelle*, otherwise AACHEN, so refers to its springs and means 'waters', from Latin *aqua*, ablative plural *aquis*. The city, which was the medieval capital of Provence, was founded in 123 BC by the Roman proconsul Sextius Calvinus, and was then known as *Aquae Sextiae*.

Aix-les-Bains The town and spa in eastern France has a name which, as with AACHEN and AIX-EN-PROVENCE, refers to its springs. The second part of the name relates to the sulphur *baths* here, known since Roman times.

Ajaccio The capital of Corsica has a name that probably comes from Low Latin *adjacium*, 'stop', 'resting place', referring to its location on the Mediterranean coast. In mythology, its name has been linked with that of AJAX.

Ajax The name of the famous warrior of Greek mythology is the Latin form of Greek *Aias*. It traditionally derives from Greek *aiētos*, 'eagle', referring to the one seen by the hero's father, Telamon, when Heracles (Hercules) prayed to Zeus to give his friend a brave son. Sophocles, however, related the name to Greek *aiazō*, 'I wail', 'I cry "ah"', prophetically referring to Ajax' death by suicide.

Ajax The internationally renowned Dutch football team was founded in 1900 and took the name of the great Greek warrior AJAX.

Akela The name is that of the leader of the wolf pack in Kipling's *Jungle Books* (1894, 1895). It represents the Hindi word for 'lone', 'solitary', so that Akela is 'Lone Wolf', as Kipling also actually calls him. The word has been adopted to designate the adult leader of a pack of Cub Scouts (formerly *Wolf* Cubs).

Akhenaten The king of ancient Egypt, famous for introducing the worship of ATEN, has a name that means 'he who serves the *Aten*'. His original name, however, was AMENHOTEP (*which see*).

Akron The city in Ohio is 1200 feet (370 m) above sea level, at the confluence of two rivers, and when it was founded in 1825 it was given a Greek name referring to its location, from *akron*, 'tip', 'summit'. *Cp.* ACROPOLIS.

Alabama The American state takes its name from the river that flows through it. This in turn is a Choctaw tribal name, either from *alibamo*, 'we stay here', or *alba-ayamule*, 'we clear a path through the forest'.

Aladdin The famous hero of the *Arabian Nights*, with his magic lamp, has a name that is a corruption of Arabic *'Alā'ad-Dīn*, 'excellence of the faith'. The first part of this is also found in the name of ALI BABA.

Alamo The name is that of the fort in San Antonio, Texas, where in 1836 about 200 volunteers, fighting for Texan independence, were massacred by a huge force of Mexican troops. It represents the Spanish word for 'cottonwood', a tree that grew where water could be found.

Alan The name is probably Celtic in origin, perhaps with a meaning 'handsome', related to Irish *alainn* which has this sense. In Wales, where it is still popular (often in the form *Alun*) it is associated with the name of the river *Alun*.

Alasdair *See* ALISTAIR.

Alaska The American state has an Eskimo name, representing *alakshak*, 'great land'. This was spelled *Alyaskat* on the first Russian maps of the region. Russia sold Alaska to the United States in 1867.

Alastor Shelley's visionary poem, published in 1816, has a title borrowed from Greek *alastōr*, the name of the Avenging Deity, literally 'he who does not forget', from *a-*, 'not' and *lanthanomai*, 'I forget'. When the poet is not satisfied by worldly love and human affection, the Spirit pursues him to his death.

Albacete The city in southeast Spain has a name that represents Arabic *al-basīṭa*, 'the plain', from *al*, 'the' and a word based on *basaṭa*, 'to stretch', 'to extend'. The city is in the historic La Mancha region.

Albania The Balkan republic has a very old name, perhaps deriving from a pre-Celtic word *alb*, 'hill' (*cp.* ALPS) or an Indoeuropean root *albh*, 'white' (*cp.* ALBION). The Albanian name for the country is *Shqipëria*, 'land of eagles'.

Albany The ancient poetic name for Scotland probably has the same origin as that of ALBION.

Albany The state capital of New York was named in 1664 in honour of the duke of the same title who was the brother of Charles II and who in 1685 became James II.

Albany The apartment block of this name off Sackville Street, London, was originally built in 1770 for Lord Melbourne and was named *Melbourne House*. It was acquired in 1791 by Frederick, Duke of York and ALBANY, and when sold in 1802 was converted into 'residential chambers for bachelor gentlemen' and renamed after his second title.

Albert The name is of Germanic origin, and in Old English was *Æthelbeorht*. This represents *adal*, 'noble' (as for ADELAIDE) and *beorht*, 'bright', so overall has a sense such as 'nobly famous'. It became popular in English-speaking countries when in 1840 Queen Victoria married Prince *Albert*. (He was German, and his original name was *Albrecht*.)

Alberta The Canadian province was formed in 1882 and was named in honour of Princess Louise Caroline *Alberta* (1848–1939), fourth daughter of Queen Victoria and wife of the Governor General, John Douglas Sutherland Campbell, Marquess of Lorne. Since the Princess was named after her father, Prince ALBERT, the name of the province can equally be regarded as a tribute to the Queen's late husband.

Albert Hall London's famous concert hall, properly the *Royal Albert Hall*, was built in 1867–71 and was named in memory of Prince *Albert*, husband of Queen Victoria, who had died in 1861. The original idea for a 'Hall of Arts and Sciences' here had been that of Prince Albert himself. Facing the Albert Hall, in Kensington Gardens, stands the *Albert Memorial*, erected in 1863–76.

Albertville The French town in Savoy, the site of the 1992 Winter Olympics, takes its name from Charles *Albert* of Savoy (1798–1849), king of Sardinia-Piedmont, who created it in its present form in 1835 by combining the village of L'Hôpital with the small town of Conflans.

Albery Theatre The London theatre, in St Martin's Lane, opened in 1903 as the *New Theatre*, after the street opposite, *New Row*. In 1973 it was given its present name, in memory of its manager and director Sir Bronson James *Albery* (1881–1971).

Albi The town in southern France takes its name from the Roman personal name *Albius*, perhaps deriving from Latin *albus*, 'white'.

Albion The ancient and poetic name of Britain, and individually of England and Scotland, probably derives from an Indoeuropean root word *albh*, 'white'. This itself gave Latin *albus*, with the same meaning, and traditionally relates to the famous white cliffs of Dover, the first natural feature seen by many visitors to Britain when crossing the English Channel. Some scholars, however, consider that 'white' refers to the Celts or original 'Ancient Britons'.

Albion Rovers The Scottish football club, based in Coatbridge, near Glasgow, was formed in that town in 1882 and adopted the poetic name of Scotland, ALBION. *Cp.* STIRLING ALBION.

Al Borak In Muslim mythology, the name is that of the steed on which Muhammad made his 'night flight' from Mecca to Jerusalem. It is Arabic in origin, meaning 'the shining one', related to modern *bark*, 'lightning' (*cp.* HAMILCAR BARCA). The mount is traditionally described as a white horse, in size between a mule and an ass, with a long back, long ears, and white wings on his legs to enable him to leap well.

Albuquerque The city in New Mexico was founded in 1706 and named for the viceroy of Mexico, the Spanish administrator Francisco Fernandez de la Cueva, Duque de *Alburquerque* (1617–1676). The place-name has omitted the first *r* of his title by confusion with the famous Portuguese soldier Afonso de *Albuquerque* (1453–1515). The Portuguese surname is Spanish in origin, from the place-name mentioned. Its own meaning is 'white oak', from Latin *albus*, 'white' and *quercus*, 'oak'.

Alcaeus The 7th-century BC Greek poet has a name that means 'mighty one', from Greek *alkē*, 'force', 'power'.

Alcatraz The former United States federal prison takes its name from the island on which it was located in San Francisco Bay, California. The island, now called Yerba Buena Island, was so named from the Spanish word for 'pelican', as these birds were numerous there. The prison closed in 1963. *Yerba Buena*, literally 'good herb', is the name of the sweet-scented herb that grows on the island.

Alcázar The name applies to one of a number of Moorish palaces in Spain, especially that at Seville which became a royal palace. It represents Arabic *al-qaṣr*, 'the castle', a word that itself derives from Latin *castra*, 'encampment'.

Alcestis In Greek mythology, the name is that of the wife of king Admetus of Thessaly. It has been interpreted as 'strong home', from Greek *alkē*, 'power', 'might' and *hestia*, 'house', 'home'. Alcestis was thus the 'power of the home', otherwise essentially 'housewife' in the original English sense of the word as 'mistress of the household'.

Alcibiades The 5th-century BC Athenian statesman and general has a somewhat tautologous name that means 'strong force', or 'mighty might', from *alkē* and *bia*, both meaning 'strength', 'force', 'might'.

Alcmene The name of the mother of Hercules by Zeus in Greek mythology appears to mean 'force of strength', and is thus tautologous, like the name of ALCIBIADES. The elements of the name are *alkē* and *menos*, both meaning 'force', 'strength'. But this would be appropriate for the mother of Hercules: where else did the famous hero gain his strength if not from his mother and father?

Alcock *See* COX.

Alcyone In Greek mythology, the name is that of the daughter of Aeolus and wife of Ceyx who drowned herself in the sea on finding the body of her husband washed up on the seashore. Taking pity on her, the gods turned both of them into kingfishers. A related story tells how Aeolus, as commander of the winds, sent calm weather to still the seas in winter when it was believed that kingfishers hatched their eggs by incubating them on the surface of the sea. Hence *halcyon* as a poetic name for the kingfisher and *halcyon days* as a term for a time of happiness and prosperity. In the light of both accounts Alcyone's name is traditionally derived from Greek *hals*, 'sea', 'salt' and *kuō*, 'I brood', 'I am pregnant'. In astronomy, *Alcyone* is the brightest star in the Pleiades.

Aldebaran The binary star is the brightest in the constellation Taurus. Its name represents Arabic *ad-dabarān*, actually written *al-dabarān*, 'the follower', since it appears to follow the Pleiades, in the same constellation.

Alderney The name of the third largest of the Channel Islands is probably Scandinavian in origin, from an unrecorded word *aurin*, 'gravel' and the commonly found *ey*, 'island' (as also for GUERNSEY and JERSEY). The Romans knew it as *Riduna*, while its French name, closer to the original, is *Aurigny*.

Aldershot The Hampshire town, a noted military centre since the mid-19th century, takes its name from Old English *alor*, 'alder' and *scēat*, 'corner of land' (literally 'shoot'). Alder trees would thus have grown on an area of land here, perhaps one in a bend of the little river Blackwater.

Alderton The surname comes from any of the places so called, such as the Northamptonshire village near Towcester or the one in Wiltshire near Malmesbury. The place-name itself means either 'alder enclosure' or '*Ealdhere*'s settlement'.

Aldgate The street and district of east central London has a name popularly understood as 'old gate' but much more likely to be 'ale gate', referring to a gate here where medieval travellers could claim their 'dole' (a drink of ale). The original name of the gate was *Eastgate*.

Aldous Made famous by the writer *Aldous* Huxley (1894–1963), the name represents the first element of a former Old English name such as *Ealdwine*, modern *Aldwin*, where *eald* means 'old'.

Aldwych The London street and district have a name that originally meant 'old dwelling', from Old English *eald*, 'old' and *wīc*, 'farm', 'dwelling'.

Aldwych Theatre The well-known London theatre, famous for its farces, was opened in 1905 and named for its location in ALDWYCH.

Alethea The name properly represents Greek *alētheia*, 'truth', although it is now sometimes associated with ALTHEA, a different name. Maria *Aletea* was the young daughter of Philip III of Spain offered in marriage to Charles I of England in 1623.

Alexander The well-known name, familiar in mythology as the second name of Paris, son of King Priam, and famous in history as that of *Alexander* the Great, means 'defender of men', from Greek *alexein*, 'to defend' and *anēr*, genitive *andros*, 'man'.

Alexandra The name is the feminine form of ALEXANDER, first in use in England from the 13th century, but popular as a royal name from the 19th century. Royal bearers of the name include: Queen *Alexandra* (1844–1925), the Danish wife of Edward VII; the Empress *Alexandra* of Russia (1872–1918), granddaughter of Queen Victoria and wife of Tsar Nicholas II; Princess *Alexandra* (1891–1959), who married Prince Arthur of Connaught; Princess *Alexandra* (1936–), who married Angus Ogilvy and who is now Lady Ogilvy.

Alexandra Palace The prominent building on Muswell Hill, north London, was opened in 1863 as a rival exhibition centre to the Crystal Palace and was named in honour of Princess ALEXANDRA, who that year had come to England and who married the future king Edward VII. The nickname of the building is the ALLY PALLY.

Alexandra Rose Day The day is a 'flag day' in June when paper roses are sold to raise funds for voluntary organizations that care for the sick and disabled. The charity of the same name was inaugurated in 1913 by Queen ALEXANDRA, widow of Edward VII, to mark what she described as 'the fiftieth anniversary of my coming to this beloved country'. The rose is the national flower of England. (*Rose* was not one of the queen's own six names.)

Alexandria The ancient Egyptian port takes its name from *Alexander* the Great, who founded it in 332 BC, following his capture of Egypt.

Alfa Romeo The first half of the car's name is a near acronym for the title of the Italian company that first manufactured it in 1910, *Società Anonima Lombarda Fabbrica Automobili*, 'Lombardy Automobile Works Company'. It also suggests Italian *alfa*, 'alpha', as the first letter of the Greek alphabet. The second half is the surname of the man who became the firm's manager in 1914, Nicola *Romeo* (1876–1938).

Alfred The modern name represents Old English *Ælfrǣd*, from *ælf*, 'elf' and *rǣd*, 'counsel', 'rule', that is, an 'elf in counsel', or a good adviser. *Alfred* the Great is one of the most famous bearers of the name in history. Its modern pet form, *Fred*, lacks much of the status of the original, however.

Algarve The former kingdom of southern Portugal has a name representing Arabic *al-ğarb*, 'the west', referring to its location in former Arabian territory as a whole. The region is usually referred to in English as *the* Algarve, as if translating the first part of the original Arabic name.

Algeciras The port and resort in southwest Spain derives its name from Arabic *al-jazīra al-ḥaḍrā*̔, 'the green island', from *al*, 'the', *jazīra*, 'island' and *ḥaḍrā*̔, feminine of *aḥḍar*, 'green'. When the Arabs landed in Spain in 711 they were struck by the greenness of the landscape, by contrast with their own dry and barren land.

Algeria The North African country takes its name from ALGIERS, the town selected to be its capital in 1830, when Algeria was a French colony.

Algernon The name is Norman French in origin, from *als gernons*, 'with whiskers'. This was originally a nickname, applied to such aristocratic English families as the Howards and Percys, who subsequently adopted it. It is now rare, but retains its aristocratic association.

Algiers The capital of Algeria has an Arabic name, from *al-jazā̔ir*, 'the islands', from *al*, 'the' and *jazā̔ir*, the plural of *jazīra*, 'island'. The reference is to the four islands that formerly lay off the coast here, but that were joined to the mainland from 1525.

Algol The name is that of the second brightest star in the constellation Perseus, and the first known eclipsing binary. Its name represents Arabic *al-ğūl*, 'the demon', referring to its sinister 'winking'. In classical times it was seen as depicting the eye in the severed head of the Gorgon Medusa, which Perseus held in his hand after he had slain her. The Arabic word behind the name gave English *ghoul* as a term for an evil spirit.

Algol The well-known computer language was devised in 1958 and has a name that is an acronym of *algo*rithmic *l*anguage, or *algo*rithmic *o*riented *l*anguage, this being a set of 'step-by-step' computational procedures used for mathematical and scientific purposes.

Algonquian The name of the North American Indian people and that of the languages they speak may derive from a native Micmac word *algoomeaking*, meaning 'at the place where fish are speared', with *algoom* the word for 'spear fish'.

Alhambra The citadel and palace in Granada, Spain, was built for the Moorish kings in the 13th and 14th centuries. Its name comes from Arabic *al-hamrā'*, 'the red', referring either to the red colour of the sun-dried bricks from which it was made, or to Muhammad Ben *al Ahmar*, its original builder. In London, the *Alhambra* was a famous theatre and music-hall in a Moorish-style building in Leicester Square, on the site of the present-day Odeon cinema.

Ali Baba The *Arabian Nights* hero, who uses the magic words 'open sesame' to steal the treasure from the cave abandoned by the Forty Thieves, has a name that means simply 'Father *Ali*'. *Baba* is a word for 'father' related to Arabic *ab* and ultimately akin to English *papa*. The name *Ali* means 'sublime', 'elevated'. Historically, Ali was the son-in-law of the prophet Muhammad, and husband of his daughter Fatima.

Alicante The port in southeast Spain has a name that evolved, under Arabic influence, from its Roman name of *Lucentum*. This is probably a word of Iberian origin, but has been derived by some scholars from Greek *akra leuka*, 'high and bright', with reference to its seaside location. It may be no coincidence that the coast here has come to be known as the COSTA BLANCA.

Alice The name is a French version of the German *Adelheid*, like ADELAIDE, but much 'smoother'. It therefore also means 'nobility'. The name was greatly popularized by the little girl heroine of Lewis Carroll's books, which were written for a real Alice, *Alice* Liddell, daughter of the Dean of Christ Church, Oxford.

Alice Ottley School The girls' public school in Worcester was founded in 1883 as the *Worcester High School for Girls*, with *Alice Ottley* as Headmistress. Miss Ottley retired in 1912 and died on the day her successor took office. To commemorate her, the school changed its name to *The Alice Ottley School* in 1914.

Alice Springs The town in central Australia is named for Lady *Alice* Todd, wife of Sir Charles Heavitree Todd, Postmaster General of South Australia. The name originally applied to some *springs* used as a watering place by engineers erecting an overland telegraph line here, with Lady Alice responsible for its construction. The name was then adopted for the telegraph station that opened in 1871 and subsequently passed to the town. When the town was gazetted in 1888, however, it was originally called *Stuart*, for the Scottish-born explorer John McDouall *Stuart*, and it did not gain its present name until 1933.

Alison The name evolved as a French diminutive form of ALICE. In Britain it came to be regarded as a typically Scottish name from the 19th century.

Alistair The name is simply a Gaelic form of ALEXANDER. The preferred Scottish spelling of the name is *Alasdair*.

Alitalia The Italian national airline has a name that is an abbreviation of its full title on being formed in 1946, *Aerolinee Italiane Internazionali*, 'International Italian Airlines', from the first and fifth letters of the first word and the first six of the second, which mean 'Italy' in their own right.

Alka-Seltzer The name of the analgesic preparation indicates that it is *alka*line, and so antacid, and that it effervesces in solution like *Seltzer* water. The latter is a na-

15

turally effervescent water from the mineral springs at Nieder *Selters*, near Wiesbaden, Germany.

Allah The Muslim name of God comes from Arabic *al-ilah*, 'the god', meaning *'the* god', the only one, otherwise 'God'.

Allahabad The city of northern India, a centre of religious pilgrimage, has a Hindi name of Arabic origin meaning 'city of ALLAH', *i.e.* 'city of God'. The name was given in 1583 by the Indian emperor Akbar.

All Blacks The New Zealand international rugby union team are so named for their *all-black* strip (shirt, shorts, socks). The name dates from 1905, when the All Blacks made their first British tour, winning all games but one.

Allegheny Mountains The mountain range in the Appalachians has a name that derives from Delaware Indian *alleghany*, itself of uncertain origin. A meaning 'endless mountains' has been suggested.

Allegro, L' Milton's poem of 1632 has an Italian title meaning 'The Cheerful One'. It is a pastoral idyll, celebrating a mood of gaiety, and contrasting with the author's earlier *Il Penseroso*. In music, *allegro* is a standard term to indicate that a piece or movement has a quick tempo. It is sometimes used as a title, for example Elgar's *Introduction and Allegro for Strings* (1905).

Allen The name developed from the first name that is now usually spelled ALAN, so has the same meaning, itself obscure.

Alleyn's School The public school in Dulwich, southeast London, was part of the foundation of 1619 known as *Alleyn's College of God's Gift*. This contains the name of its founder, the Elizabethan actor Edward *Alleyn* (1566–1626), who the same year founded and endowed Dulwich College itself as the *College of God's Gift*.

Allhallows The name is a less common alternative to ALL SAINTS DAY, so has the same meaning, with *hallow* a former word for 'saint' (directly related to modern *holy*). The name is mostly familiar today from the church dedication *All Hallows*, similarly corresponding to *All Saints*.

All Hallows School The public school for girls near Bungay, Suffolk, was founded in 1864 by the Community of *All Hallows* to provide an education within the framework of the Church of England. The school is located next to the mother house of the Anglican community of nuns for whom it is named.

All Saints Day The day, 1 November, is that in the Christian calendar when the faithful celebrate all those saints who have no special day of their own. It was formerly known as ALLHALLOWS. The following day is ALL SOULS DAY.

All Souls College The Oxford college has the full name of *College of All Souls of the Faithful Departed*. It was founded in 1438 by Henry Chichele, Archbishop of Canterbury, with Henry VI as co-founder, and included a chantry where the fellows should pray for the *souls* of those killed in the Hundred Years War with France. It is unique in being the only British college with no students.

All Souls Day The day, 2 November, is that in the Christian calendar when, especially in the Roman Catholic Church, the faithful pray that the suffering of *all souls* in purgatory may be mitigated. It follows ALL SAINTS DAY.

Ally Pally The name is the affectionate nickname of the ALEXANDRA PALACE, London, devised for its friendly, rhyming suggestion of 'pal'.

Ally Sloper The name is that of an amusing character who appeared in a series of humorous publications in the 19th century. He had a bulbous nose and a receding forehead and was notorious for his dishonest or inept practices. He first appeared in the pages of *Judy* magazine in 1867. His surname indicates his shifty nature, as someone who 'slopes off' when there is trouble.

Alma The small river in the Crimea, famous as the scene of the English and French defeat of the Russians in 1854 during the Crimean War, has a name deriving from the Turkic *alma*, 'apple'. The river flows through a fertile fruit-producing region. *Cp.* ALMA-ATA.

Alma-Ata The capital of Kazakhstan has a name that represents Kazakh *Almaty*, traditionally interpreted as 'father of apples', from *alma*, 'apple' (*cp.* ALMA) and *ata*, 'father'. Recent research has shown, however, that the name has been distorted from an original form *Almalyk*, meaning simply 'abundant in apples'. The town arose from a fort founded in 1854, and from 1885 to 1921 was known as *Verny*, 'true', 'faithful', implying a stronghold that would not yield to an enemy.

Almagest Ptolemy's famous work on astronomy, written in the 2nd century AD, has a name that derives from Arabic *al-majisti*. This is a combination of Arabic *al*, 'the' and Greek *megistē*, 'greatest', meaning that it was the greatest systematic treatise of its kind.

Almeida Theatre The small theatre in Islington, north London, arose from a former Victorian Literary Institute and takes its name from the short street in which it stands. The street itself is named commemoratively for the Battle of *Almeida* (1811), from the Portuguese fortified settlement captured by the British and Portuguese in the Peninsular War.

Almería The port in southern Spain derives its name from Arabic *al-mir'aya*, 'the watch tower', from *al*, 'the' and *mir'aya*, 'mirror', 'watch tower', ultimately from *ra'ā*, 'to see'.

Alpha Centauri The name is the astronomical designation, or catalogue description, of the binary star that is the brightest in the constellation CENTAURUS. It means simply 'Alpha of Centaurus', with this Greek letter normally used for the brightest star in a constellation. Its companion is PROXIMA CENTAURI.

Alps The well-known mountain range has a name that is almost certainly pre-Celtic and possibly Ligurian, based on the same pre-Celtic root word, *alb*, meaning 'height', that perhaps gave the name of ALBANIA.

Alsace The region of eastern France has a name that has different possible origins. It may come from the Gaulish word *alisa*, 'cliff', since the cliffs of the Vosges here would have impressed the Gauls when they came from southern Germany. On the other hand, it may derive from a similar Gaulish word, *aliso*, 'alder', as these trees are common here. Some scholars also link the name with that of the river *Ill*, which runs through Alsace.

Altai Mountains The mountains of central Asia may derive their name from Mongolian *alt*, 'gold', although this metal was discovered here only in the early 19th century.

Altair The name is that of the brightest star in the constellation Aquila. It derives from Arabic *aṭ-ṭā'ir*, actually written *al-ṭā'ir*, 'the bird', a description originally applied to the whole constellation.

Althea The name represents the Greek name *Althaia*, which itself derives from the verb *althainein*, 'to heal'. In Greek mythology, Althaia was the mother of the hunter Meleager. The name was also the Greek word for the marshmallow plant, which has healing properties.

Alton Towers The popular amusement park near Stoke-on-Trent, Staffordshire, takes its name from the 19th-century Gothic mansion, now a ruined shell, around which it developed after the First World War. The house was built by Charles, fifteenth Earl of Talbot, on land owned by the Talbot family since the 15th century. He originally called it *Alton Abbey*, despite lack of any religious connection. On his death in 1827 the house passed to his nephew, John, the sixteenth earl, who in 1831 enlarged it with towers and turrets and renamed it *Alton Towers*. *Alton* is the name of the nearby village, itself meaning '*Ælfa*'s settlement'.

Altrincham The former Cheshire town, now a district of Greater Manchester, was originally the equivalent of *Aldringham*, meaning 'place of *Aldhere*'s people'. The soft *g* of this became the *ch* of the present spelling.

Alun *See* ALAN.

Alvin The name is Old English in origin, representing either *Ælfwine* or *Æthelwine*. The first comprises the words *ælf*, 'elf' (as for Alfred) and *wine*, 'friend', the second *æthel*, 'noble' and *wine*. The name has always been more popular in the United States than in Britain.

Alvis The car of this name was first manufactured in 1920. It is said to be a name that is simply easy to pronounce, but could perhaps combine the first two letters of a word such as 'aluminium' with the Latin word *vis*, 'power'.

Amabel *See* ANNABEL.

Amadeus String Quartet The well-known chamber music group, formed in 1947, was named after the composer whose works formed an important part of its repertoire, Wolfgang *Amadeus* Mozart. It was disbanded in 1987. Friends of the quartet affectionately referred to its members as 'the Wolf Gang'.

Amalthea The nymph (or goat) in classical mythology who brought up the infant Zeus on goat's milk has a name of disputed origin. It may derive from Greek *amaltheuein*, 'to nourish'.

Amanda The name is the feminine form of the saint's name *Amandus*, Latin for 'fit to be loved'. It was first popularized in literature by Amanda, the young wife of Loveless in two 17th-century plays, Colley Cibber's *Love's Last Shift*, and *The Relapse*, its sequel by Sir John Vanbrugh. Her name thus punningly contrasts with that of her husband: she is 'loved', while he is 'unloved' (although *Loveless* was a nickname for a philanderer). *See also* ST-AMAND-MONTROND.

Amaryllis The name, used for a typical country girl by classical writers such as Virgil and Ovid, is traditionally interpreted as 'clear stream', from the Greek verb *amarussō*, 'I sparkle'.

Amazon The famous South American river has a native (Tupi or Guarani) name meaning 'wave', referring to the notorious bore in its lower reaches. When Spanish explorers came here in the 16th century, they related the name to the AMAZONS of classical times, especially since the native tribesmen were beardless and graceful, like the legendary women warriors.

Amazons The legendary women warriors have a name that is traditionally derived from Greek *a-*, 'without' and *mazos*, 'breast', since when being trained to ride, hunt and fight, their girl children are said to have had the right breast burnt off, to free their arm when drawing the bow. But the name probably derives from some ancient Iranian word simply meaning 'warrior'. *See also* AMAZON.

Ambassadors Theatre The London theatre, in West Street, off Shaftesbury Avenue, was opened in 1913. It appears to have been given a purely prestigious name, although ambassadorial crests appear as decorations on the building and were part of the original design.

Amboise The town in northwest central France has a name that may derive either from Gaulish *ambe*, 'river', referring to the Loire, on which it stands, or from a Gaulish personal name *Ambatius*. *See also* AMIENS.

Ambrose The name ultimately comes from Greek *ambrosios*, 'immortal'. Hence the word *ambrosia* for the food of the gods, who were immortal. The name became familiar from the 4th-century Roman saint who reinforced the secular power of the early church and wrote many hymns.

Amelia The name is sometimes associated with the Roman clan name *Aemilius*, but is more meaningfully derived from an Old German name such as *Amalberga*, where *amal* means 'hard-working', 'industrious'. Princess *Amelia* (1783–1810) was the youngest daughter of George III.

Amélie-les-Bains-Palalda The spa town in extreme southeast France, near the border with Spain, was originally known simply as *Les Bains*, 'the springs'. In 1840 it was renamed for Marie-*Amélie* of Bourbon (1782–1866), wife of king Louis Philippe. *Palalda* derives ultimately from Latin *palatium*, 'palace' with the Roman personal name *Danus*.

Amenhotep The name was that of four kings of ancient Egypt. The best known was *Amenhotep* IV, who reigned in the 14th century BC. His name means 'AMON is satisfied', referring to the god also known as *Amen*. In the sixth year of his reign, however, Amenhotep broke away from the worship of Amon, and changed his name to AKHENATEN (*which see*), as whom he is often known today.

America Columbus discovered America in 1492, but its name did not appear before

1507, when the German cartographer Martin Waldseemüller placed it on a map of South America. He derived it from the latinized forename, *Americus*, of the Florentine (Italian) explorer *Amerigo* Vespucci, who had accompanied Columbus. Amerigo itself corresponds to English *Henry* (*cp.* modern Italian *Enrico*). The Chinese name for America is *mĕizhōu*, which literally means 'beautiful continent'. However, *mĕi* does not actually have this sense in the name as it is simply a phonetic rendering of *America* (or rather of its stressed syllable).

America's Cup The international yachting trophy was first offered in 1851 by the Royal Yacht Squadron of Great Britain for a race round the Isle of Wight. It was then known as the *Hundred Guinea Cup*. The race was won by the New York schooner *America*, and the trophy subsequently became known by this name. Since 1857 it has been presented by the New York Yacht Club to the winner of the race that is now sailed at Newport, Rhode Island.

Amery The surname represents the Old German name *Amalric*, where *amal* means 'industrious' (as for AMELIA) and *rīc* means 'power'. The name came into English through French, which explains its 'smoothed' form.

Amharic The name of the language of Ethiopia derives from that of the former kingdom of *Amhara*, now a province of Ethiopia. The place-name is itself of uncertain origin but may contain a root word meaning 'noble'.

Amiens The name of the cathedral city in northern France, known to the Romans as *Ambianum*, derives from the *Ambiani*, a Gaulish people. Their own name comes from Gaulish *ambe*, 'river', probably seen also in the name of AMBOISE, on the Loire. Amiens is on the Somme, and its Celtic name in pre-Roman times was *Samarobriva*, 'Somme bridge'.

Amirante Islands The island group in the Indian Ocean, a dependency of the Seychelles, has a name of Portuguese origin, from *ilhas do almirante*, 'admiral's islands'. The name was given in honour of Vasco da Gama, who discovered the islands in 1502. They should not be confused with the ADMIRALTY ISLANDS.

Amman The Jordanian capital has a name that pays tribute to *Ammon*, the ancestor of the ancient Semitic people known as the *Ammonites*. In the Old Testament his own name is related to that of their city of origin, referred to as 'Rabbath of the children of Ammon' (*Deuteronomy* 3.11), which itself amounts to little more than 'city of the Ammonites'. The name also occurs for the biblical character who was the son of Lot by his incestuous relationship with his younger daughter: 'And the younger, she also bare a son, and called his name Benammi: the same is the father of the children of Ammon unto this day' (*Genesis* 19.38). This could mean 'son of his uncle', from Arabic *ben*, 'son' and *'amm*, 'paternal uncle'. The name would refer to the relationship in the same way that the name of MOAB does, as that of the son of Lot by his elder daughter. On the other hand it could mean simply 'son of the people', with the second part representing Arabic *'am*, 'people'.

Ammonites *See* AMMAN.

Amoco The petrol is named after the abbreviated name of its original producer, the *American Oil Company*, who in 1925 merged with its present distributor, Standard Oil of Indiana.

Amon The name, also spelled *Amen* or *Amun*, is that of the Theban god of life and fertility who was identified by the Egyptians with the national sun god Amen-Ra. His name means 'concealed', 'hidden'. *See also* AMENHOTEP, TUTANKHAMEN.

Amoretti The series of sonnets by Spenser, printed in 1595, has a title that is the Italian word for 'little loves'. The sonnets are believed to represent the poet's courtship of Elizabeth Boyle, whom he married.

Amos The name of the biblical prophet, and that of the Old Testament book called after him, represents Hebrew *Āmōs*, meaning literally 'borne', that is, by God. The name is now more popular among Americans than in British use, as for example in the popular American radio show of the 1920s to 1940s, *Amos n' Andy*, featuring two blackface clowns.

Amphitrite In Greek mythology, the name is that of the sea goddess who was the wife of Poseidon and mother of Triton. Its origin is uncertain, although it has been interpreted by some scholars as 'wearing away all round', from Greek *amphi*, 'about', 'around' and *truō*, 'I wear out'. This origin equates the name exactly with that of AMPHITRYON. It makes sense, however, to think of a sea goddess as a 'corroder'.

Amphitryon The name of the grandson of Perseus and husband of Alcmene suggests Greek *amphi*, 'on both sides', 'around' and *truō*, 'I distress', 'I harass'. Amphitryon caused much suffering to those close to him, even accidentally killing his uncle Electryon, so the name seems apt.

Ampleforth The Roman Catholic public school for boys, in North Yorkshire, was originally founded by English Benedictine monks at Dieulouard (appropriately, 'God-Preserve'), near Nancy, France, in 1608. The school transferred to England at the time of the French Revolution and eventually settled at the village of *Ampleforth*, near Thirsk, in 1802. The village's own name probably means 'dock ford', from Old English *ampre*, 'dock', 'sorrel' and *ford*, 'ford'.

Amritsar The city in northern India, in Punjab, has a name deriving from Sanskrit *amrta*, 'immortal' and *saras*, 'lake', 'pool'. The actual 'lake of immortality' is the sacred pool round which the town was founded in 1577. The Golden Temple that stands on an island in the pool is the principal holy place of the Sikhs.

Amsterdam The name of the Dutch capital means literally '*Amstel* dam', referring to the dyke or barrage that was originally built across the river Amstel here. Similar names are those of ROTTERDAM and EDAM, among several others.

Amstrad The computer and electronics company has a name based on that of its founder, Alan Michael Sugar (1947–), who in 1968 set out to exploit gaps in the consumer market. The name he devised was adopted from his original business name, *A.M.S. Trading*, the first three letters being his initials.

Amu Darya The river of central Asia has a name of Uzbek origin, from *amu*, 'long' and *dario*, 'river', a self-descriptive name for a river whose length is approximately 1500 miles (2400 km). It forms most of the boundary between Afghanistan and Tajikistan.

Amur The river in northeast Asia, where it forms the border between Manchuria and Russia, has a name that probably represents Mongolian *amar*, 'calm', 'peace'. On the other hand the Mongolians themselves know it as *har mörön*, 'black river', and the name could have evolved from this.

Amy The name comes from Old French *amee*, modern *aimé*, 'beloved', so is similar to AMANDA. In Daniel Defoe's romance *Roxana* (1724), *Amy* is Roxana's faithful maid, and in Dickens' *Little Dorrit* (1857) *Amy* Dorrit is the central character.

Anabaptists *See* BAPTISTS.

Anabasis The name is that of Xenophon's account of the expedition made by Cyrus the Younger into Asia against his brother, King Artaxerxes II. The Greek word literally means 'going up', as the expedition was made inland from the coast.

Anacreon The Greek lyric poet of the 6th century BC has a name that means basically 'ruler', from *kreiōn* with the 'strengthening' particle *ana-*.

Anadin The analgesic tablets were invented in the United States in 1918 and were originally known as *Anacin*. This name may have been based on '*anal*gesic' and '*cincho*na', the latter being the tree that yields quinine, as a fever-reducing, pain-relieving compound. The product was introduced to Britain in 1931, but had to be sold under a slightly modified name, as *Anacine* already existed in the Trade Mark Register.

Anaglypta The trade name for a type of embossed wallpaper derives from Greek *anagluptos*, meaning literally 'carved outwards', that is, embossed.

Ananda The name of the first cousin of the Buddha and one of his chief disciples represents Sanskrit *ānanda*, 'joy'.

Ananias In the New Testament, the name is that of a Jewish Christian of Jerusalem who was struck dead for lying. The name is the Greek form of HANANIAH. *Cp. also* HANNAH.

Anastasia The name is the feminine form of the Greek name *Anastasios*, from *anastasis*, 'awakening', 'resurrection', and was given by early Christians to their children to symbolize a 'rebirth'. It became familiar from the Russian princess *Anastasia* (1901–1918), youngest daughter of Tsar Nicholas II, said by some to have survived the royal family's massacre after the Revolution, almost as if enacting her name.

Anatolia The name is used for Asia Minor, and derives directly from Greek *anatolē*, 'sunrise', 'east', since the region is in the eastern part of the continent, approximating to modern Turkey in Asia.

Anaxagoras The 5th-century BC Greek philosopher has a name that means 'master of the assembly', from *anax*, 'lord', 'master' and *agora*, 'assembly', 'market-place'.

Anchises The Trojan prince who was the father of Aeneas by Aphrodite in Greek mythology has a name that has been interpreted as 'near to Isis', from Greek *ankhi*, 'near' and the name of the Egyptian goddess. The implication seems to be that Aphrodite and Isis had a certain identity as fertility goddesses. But this particular explanation is purely speculative, and the true origin of the name has not been determined.

Anchorage The largest city in Alaska has a self-descriptive name referring to its role as a port. It was founded in 1914 as the headquarters of the Alaska Railroad to Fairbanks.

Ancona The port in central Italy was founded by Greeks from Syracuse in the 4th century BC and derives its name from Greek *ankōn*, 'bend', 'elbow', referring to the curving coastline here.

Andalusia The region of southern Spain takes its name from its original native inhabitants, the VANDALS.

Andaman Islands The islands, in the Bay of Bengal, have a Hindi or Bengali name that ultimately derives from Sanskrit *hanumant*, the name of HANUMAN, king of the monkeys in the *Ramayana*, the Sanskrit epic poem.

Anderlecht The Belgian football club was founded in 1908 and takes its name from the suburb of Brussels in which it has its home ground, southwest of the city centre.

Anderson The name, common in Scotland, means 'son of ANDREW'. *Cp.* ANDREWS.

Andes The South American mountain chain has a name of Quechua origin, although its precise meaning is uncertain. It may come from *andi*, 'peak', 'crest', or *anti*, 'east'. The latter, however, would seem unlikely as the Andes are in the west of the continent. Another possible source is the word *anta*, 'copper', as this mineral is found here.

Andhaka The demon son of Kasyapa and Diti in Hindu mythology, with his thousand heads and thousand arms, has a name that represents the Sanskrit word for 'blind'. He was so called from his stumbling gait, like that of a blind man, although his sight was perfectly normal.

Andhra Pradesh The Indian state, in the Deccan, has a name that means 'Telugu state', from Telugu *andhramu*, 'Telugu' and *prades*, 'state', itself from Sanskrit *pradeśa*, 'place', 'region'. *Cp.* HIMACHAL PRADESH.

Andorra The name of the Pyrenean principality probably derives from a native (Navarrese) word *andurrial*, meaning 'shrub-covered land'.

Andover The name of the Hampshire town was originally that of the river, now the *Anton*, on which it lies. It is of Celtic origin, meaning 'ash stream', from *onno*, 'ash-tree' and *dubro*, 'water'. The latter word also lies behind the name of DOVER. The present river name arose from a misreading of the name *Trisantona* in a text by Tacitus, although that name actually referred to a river *Trent* (as the famous Yorkshire one) or *Tarrant*.

Andrew The name, familiar from the Bible as that of one of the twelve apostles, now the patron saint of Scotland, ultimately goes back to Greek *anēr*, genitive *andros*, 'man', so means 'manly', 'brave'. The final *-ew* probably arose under the influence of the name MATTHEW, that of another apostle.

Andrews The name means 'son of ANDREW'. *Cp.* ANDERSON.

Andrex The toilet tissue was originally manufactured in 1945 by a small firm in St *Andrews* Road, Walthamstow, London, and was at first called *Androll*, after the street. The name was changed to *Andrex* in 1954. The suffix *-ex* in brand names often implies 'out' (from Latin) and a cleaning process, as for KLEENEX.

Androcles In Roman legend, the name is that of the slave whose life was spared in the arena by a lion from whose paw he had earlier extracted a thorn. It is of Greek origin, from *anēr*, genitive *andros*, 'man' (as for ANDREW) and *kleos*, 'glory' (as for CLEOPATRA).

Andromache In Greek mythology the name is that of the wife of Hector. It derives from Greek *anēr*, genitive *andros*, 'man' and *makhē*, 'battle'. Andromache's whole life was a 'battle against men', for her father, seven brothers and husband were all killed by Achilles, and she later lost her baby son and second husband, Neoptolemus.

Andromeda The name, in Greek mythology, is that of the daughter of Cassiopeia and wife of Perseus. It represents Greek *anēr*, genitive *andros*, 'man' and *medōn*, 'ruler', 'guardian', implying one fit to rule men.

Andromeda The name is that of a familiar constellation in the northern hemisphere, lying between Cassiopeia and Pegasus. The latter respectively represent the mother and husband of ANDROMEDA in classical mythology. Certain stars were seen by ancient astrologers as marking prominent points on Andromeda's figure: Alpheratz is her head, Mirach her waist, and Almach her foot.

Angara The well-known Siberian river has a name that may derive from Evenki words *ang* meaning 'water' and *gara* meaning 'going', referring to the river's course as it flows out of Lake Baikal towards the Yenisei.

Angela The name is the feminine form of the now rare male name *Angel*. It means what it says and implies an 'angelic' nature or appearance. It has been popular among English-speakers from the 18th century,

and came to be regarded as that of a typical schoolgirl, possibly promoted by the actual name of *Angela* Brazil (1868–1947), a noted writer of English schoolgirl stories.

Angelica The name is Italian in origin, ultimately from Latin *angelicus*, 'angelic'. It is now generally regarded by English speakers as a diminutive of ANGELA, however, and has been in select use since the 19th century.

Angers *See* ANJOU.

Angevin *See* ANJOU.

Angharad The Welsh name comprises *an*, an intensifying particle, and *câr*, 'love', so means 'much loved'. It is still borne mainly by Welsh women, such as the actress *Angharad* Rees (1949–   ).

Angkor Wat The famous 12th-century Cambodian temple takes its name from the region here in the northwest of the country known as *Angkor*, ultimately from Sanskrit *nagara*, 'city'. *Wat* represents Cambodian *vot*, the word for a pagoda or any Buddhist shrine.

Angles The Germanic people, who gave their name to ENGLAND, took their own name from their region of origin, *Angeln*, in what is now Schleswig-Holstein, northern Germany, just south of the border with Denmark. The place-name in turn probably refers to the region's 'angular' contours or outline, although some derive it from the 'angled' shape of the hooks used by fishermen there (by *anglers*, in fact).

Anglesey The Welsh island has a name that has long been popularly linked with the ANGLES. But, as with other islands round the Welsh coast, the name is more likely to be Old Norse in origin, coming either from *ǫngull*, 'angle' and *ey*, 'island', referring to its 'angular' coastline, or from a personal name, so that it was '*Ongull*'s island'.

Anglesey Abbey The early 17th-century manor house in Cambridgeshire was built on the site of a medieval *abbey*. It takes its name from the locality, probably meaning 'island of the ANGLES', implying an area of raised land here that was occupied by the Angles as a kind of enclave among people of some other origin. It is not certain, however, who the other people were. The name is thus not connected with that of ANGLESEY in North Wales.

Angola The African country is named for *N'gola*, the title of the native ruler here in the 16th century, when the land was colonized by the Portuguese.

Angostura The name (from its foundation in 1764 until 1846) was that of the Venezuelan city now known as CIUDAD BOLÍVAR. It represents Spanish *angostura*, 'strait', 'narrows', referring to the location of the town in a narrowing of the river Orinoco.

Anguilla The West Indies island was so named by Columbus when he discovered it in 1493. The name is the Spanish word for 'eel', and probably refers to the island's long shape.

Angus The essentially Scottish name represents the Gaelic *Aonghus*, 'unique choice', from *aon*, 'one' and *ghus*, 'choice'. Angus was originally the name of a Celtic god.

Anhui The province of eastern China has a name deriving from *ān*, 'peace', 'calm' and *huī*, 'excellence', 'splendour'. The two parts of the name represent the first elements of the names of two of the province's largest cities, *An*king, the former capital (to 1949), and *Hui*chou. The name is sometimes spelled *Anhwei*.

Animals, The The British pop group formed in Newcastle in 1962 when lead singer Eric Burdon joined the Allan Price Combo, a band of four named after their keyboard player. The new group were soon referred to by their local fans as 'the animals', for their rowdy stage act, and adopted the name the following year. At the same time, the name echoes that of the *Allan Price Combo* itself, and happens to be formed from letters in the name.

Anita The name is a Spanish diminutive of ANN. Among English speakers it has been more popular among Americans than Britons. One well-known bearer was the American writer *Anita* Loos (1893–1981).

Anjou The former French province has a name equating to that of *Angers*, one of its oldest cities. This represents *Andecavi*, the Roman name of the tribe here, from Gaulish *ande*, 'greater' and *cavi*, 'allies'. The Gaulish name of Angers is unknown. The Romans called it *Juliomagus*, 'Julius

(Caesar)'s market'. The name also lies behind that of the *Angevins*, the Plantagenet kings of England in the 12th and 13th centuries who were descended from Geoffrey, Count of *Anjou*.

Ankara The capital of Turkey perhaps derives its name from the same Indoeuropean root element *ang*, meaning 'bend', that lies behind that of ANCONA. This would refer to its place of origin in a winding gorge. It is not likely that the name relates to *anchor* (in some language), as if referring to a place where a tribe came to settle or 'anchored', although this is the traditional explanation of the name.

Ann The name is the English form of the biblical name HANNAH, so like it means 'grace'. It was popularized generally in Europe by the figure of St *Anne*, as the mother of the Virgin Mary, although she is not named in the Bible. The spelling *Anne*, now equally popular, arose through French influence.

Annaba The port in northeast Algeria has a name that has evolved from the original Arabic *madīnat al-'unnāb*, 'town of the jujube' (a spiny tree with dark red edible fruits). The city's former French name was *Bône*, from its ancient name of HIPPO (*which see*).

Annabel The name probably arose as an alteration of the rarish name *Amabel*. This derives from Latin *amabilis*, 'lovable', so is similar to AMANDA in origin. The final *-bel* of *Annabel* is now felt to be related to the French word for 'beautiful'. The mother of James I of Scotland was *Annabella* Drummond (1350–1402).

Annam The former kingdom and empire, now part of Vietnam, has a Vietnamese name meaning 'peace of the south', from *an*, 'peace' and *nam*, 'south'. The ancient Chinese name for the kingdom was *Nam Viet*, the same as for modern VIETNAM.

Anna Perenna In Roman mythology, the goddess of the coming new year has a name that means 'lasting year', from Latin *annus*, 'year' and *perennis*, 'everlasting', 'permanent'.

Annapolis The state capital of Maryland was settled in 1649 by Puritans under the original name of *Providence*. In 1694, when it became the capital, the settlement was renamed for Princess *Anne*, who as Queen Anne gave it a charter in 1708. Greek *polis* means 'town'.

Annapurna The name of the Himalayan massif, in Nepal, is that of a Hindu goddess, deriving from Sanskrit *anna*, 'food' and *pūrṇa*, 'abundant'. The mountains here were seen as favourable to agriculture in the valleys below.

Ann Arbor The Michigan city was founded in 1824 by two settlers, John Allen and Elisha W. Rumsey, who named it for their wives, both called ANN.

Anne *See* ANN.

Annecy The city and resort in eastern France takes its name from the Germanic personal name *Anerik*.

Annunciation In the Christian church, the name is that of the occasion when the angel Gabriel *announced* to the Virgin Mary that she would bear a son, Jesus, as told in the New Testament (*Luke* 1.26–38). *Annunciation* Day, also known as LADY DAY, is celebrated in the Christian calendar on 25 March. On 25 December, exactly nine months later, Christmas Day marks the birth of Jesus to Mary.

Antalya The port in southwest Turkey derives its name from *Attalus* II, king of Pergamum, who founded it in the 2nd century BC.

Antananarivo The name of the capital of Madagascar means 'city of a thousand', from Malagasy *an-*, a prefix denoting a place-name, *tanàna*, 'town', and *arivo*, 'thousand'. The name refers to the great number of inhabitants. During the French colonial period, the city was known as *Tananarive*, a modification of this.

Antarctic The continent surrounding the South Pole has a classical name, from Greek *anti*, 'opposite' and *arktikos*, 'Arctic', referring to its position, exactly opposite the ARCTIC around the North Pole.

Antares The star is the brightest in the constellation Scorpius. It is a variable binary star whose main component is a red giant. This accounts for its name, meaning 'rival to Mars', from Greek *anti-*, 'opposing' and *Ares*, the Greek equivalent to Mars. The

planet Mars is also famous for its reddish-orange colour.

Anthea The name is the feminine of Greek *antheios*, 'flowery', from *anthos*, 'flower', occurring in mythology as a byname of the Greek goddess Hera. Robert Herrick's poem 'To Anthea' (1648) gave the name some popularity, but it was only in the mid-20th century that it really became fashionable in English-speaking countries.

Anthony The name goes back to the Roman clan name *Antonius*, whose own meaning is uncertain. It may ultimately be of Etruscan origin. The spelling with *th* probably developed in an attempt to associate the name with Greek *anthos*, 'flower'. Mark *Antony*, the Roman general who served under Caesar, is one of the earliest and most famous bearers of the name.

Antibes The port and resort in southeast France has a name that is a corruption of Greek *Antipolis*, 'opposite the town'. Antibes is on the Mediterranean coast, and faces Nice across the Baie des Anges.

Anticosti The island in eastern Canada, in the Gulf of St Lawrence, is popularly said to have a name representing Spanish *ante*, 'before' and *costa*, 'coast'. However, it is more likely to be an Indian name in origin. A meaning 'hunting ground of the bear' has been suggested.

Antigone The name is familiar in Greek mythology as that of the daughter of Oedipus and of Jocasta, the mother of Oedipus. Her birth was thus incestuous, as her name implies. It derives from Greek *anti-*, 'against' and *gonos*, 'child', 'birth', so that she had a 'contrary birth', one 'against motherhood'.

Antigua The island in the West Indies was discovered by Columbus in 1493 and named by him after the church of Santa Maria *la Antigua* (St Mary the Ancient) in Seville.

Antilles The name of the West Indies island group was originally given in 1474 by the Florentine (Italian) cartographer Paolo Toscanelli to a hypothetical island here. Later, after the islands' discovery by Columbus, the name was given to the group as a whole. It has been popularly derived from Latin *ante*, 'before' and *illas*, 'islands', as islands off the coast of America, but its true origin probably lies in an older language. Some scholars link the name with that of the ATLANTIC.

Antioch The name is that of many ancient towns in the Middle East, but is particularly associated with the ancient biblical city in Syria, now *Antakya*, Turkey. This was founded in about 300 BC by the Macedonian general Seleucus Nicator, and he named it for his father, *Antiochus*. The other towns, founded by Seleucus' successors, were given the same name. The personal name is traditionally derived from Greek *anti*, 'equal to' and *okhos*, 'carriage', 'chariot', implying a swift person, one who could run quickly.

Antipodes The uninhabited South Pacific islands, southwest of (and belonging to) New Zealand, have a Greek name meaning 'opposite the feet', from *anti*, 'opposite' and *pous*, genitive *podos*, 'foot'. This refers to their location, which is diametrically opposite to that of Greenwich. (The longitude of Greenwich is 0°, and that of the Antipodes 180°.)

Antofagasta The port in northern Chile derives its name from Quechua *anta*, 'copper' and *pakakta*, the accusative case of *pakak*, 'hidden'. The name implies a place that guards an underground supply of copper. The city still exports copper from its mines today as one of its major industries.

Antonia The name is the feminine form of ANTHONY. It caught on among English speakers only from the 20th century, but was in continental European use much earlier. Its French diminutive, *Antoinette*, became well-known through Marie-*Antoinette* (1755–93), the ill-fated queen of France, who with her husband Louis XVI was guillotined in the Revolution.

Antonine Wall The famous defence work was built by the Romans in the mid-2nd century BC across what is now southern Scotland, from the river Clyde in the west to the Firth of Forth in the east. It is named after the Roman emperor who ordered its construction, *Antoninus* Pius, the adopted son and successor of Hadrian, who had earlier ordered the building of HADRIAN'S WALL.

Antony *See* ANTHONY.

Antrim The county of Northern Ireland has a name that literally means 'one house', from Irish *aon*, 'one' and *treabh*, 'house', 'family'. This could originally have applied to a place that was simply a solitary farm, and which gradually gave its name to the surrounding region.

Antseranana The port in northern Madagascar has a Malagasy name that means 'the port', from *an-*, the prefix denoting a place-name (as for ANTANANARIVO), and *serànana*, 'port'. The town's former name was *Diego-Suárez*, a combination of the names of *Diego* Dias, the Portuguese captain who discovered the island in 1500, and Hernán *Suárez*, the Spanish admiral who landed here in 1506.

Antwerp The Belgian port has a name of Germanic origin, from *anda*, 'at' and *werpum*, 'wharf', referring to its location on the river Scheldt. A popular legend tells how a Roman warrior cut off the hand (*hand*) of a giant here only to throw (*werpen*) it into the river.

Anyang The town in eastern China has a name from Chinese *ān*, 'peaceful' and *yáng*, 'light' or 'sun'. The word *yáng* is the same as that for the male principle in Taoism, the counterpart of *yin*.

Apache The name of the North American Indian race is descriptive of their belligerent nature, and derives from Indian (Yuman) *apa*, 'man', *ahwa*, 'battle', and the plural suffix *-tche*.

Apeldoorn The town in the central Netherlands has a name that means 'apple tree', from Dutch *apel*, 'apple' and *door*, a former word for 'tree' (the present word is *boom*).

Apennines The famous Italian mountain chain has a name based on Celtic *penn*, 'hill', found in England in the name of the PENNINES and in names of towns in Celtic regions, such as PENZANCE in Cornwall and PENMAENMAWR in Wales.

Aphrodite The name of the Greek goddess of love and beauty is traditionally derived from Greek *aphros*, 'foam', as she was born from the foam of the sea. But her name is almost certainly of pre-Greek origin, and is probably related to that of the Phoenician fertility goddess ASTARTE, identified with ASHTORETH of the Hebrews, mentioned in the Bible.

Apis The ancient Egyptian fertility god with a bull's head, closely linked with OSIRIS, has a name that means 'hidden', 'concealed'.

Apocalypse The alternative name for the Book of *Revelation* in the New Testament is simply the Greek word *apokalupsis*, 'revelation'. The name subsequently came to be used as a general word for any cataclysmic event, such as those described in that book.

Apocrypha The name is used for the 14 biblical books that were included as an appendix to the Old Testament in the Septuagint (the Greek version of the Old Testament) and the Vulgate (the Latin version of the Bible) but that were not accepted by the Jews. They are not normally included in Protestant versions of the Bible. Their name is the Greek word for 'hidden (writings)', since they were withheld from general publication because of doubts about their authenticity.

Apollinaris The sparkling mineral water takes its name from that of the spring where it was discovered near Bad Neuenahr, south of Bonn, Germany, in the mid-19th century. The spring itself was named after a nearby chapel, presumably having some pagan association with APOLLO. The water has long been colloquially known as 'Polly'.

Apollo The great god of the Greeks and Romans, the god of light, poetry, healing, music and prophecy, has a name that is traditionally derived from *apolluein*, 'to destroy', so that he was Apollo the Destroyer. But Apollo's attributes are almost all good and positive, and this interpretation appears to have little validity. It may have arisen, as often, simply as an attempt to make an obscure name meaningful. *See also* ABADDON.

Apollo Theatre The London theatre, in Shaftesbury Avenue, was opened in 1901 with a name derived from the Greek god APOLLO. This was regarded as appropriate for a theatre that would stage mainly musicals, as Apollo was the god of music (among other things).

Appalachians The mountains in eastern North America take their name from a now extinct Indian tribe, the *Apalachee*, who lived in what is now northwest Florida. Their own name comes from the Indian (perhaps Hitchiti) word *apalatchi*, meaning 'people on the other side'.

Appaloosa The American breed of saddle horse, well known for its spotted rump and striped hooves, probably derives its name from the tribe that originally raised it. These were the *Palouse* Indians of northwest America. Their own name means 'grassy expanse', from an Indian name translated into French. (*Cp.* modern French *pelouse*, 'lawn'.)

Appassionata The name of Beethoven's Piano Sonata No 23 in F minor (1804–5) was given by his publisher. It is the Italian word for 'impassioned', and aptly describes the mood of passionate despair in which the composer wrote it, and which is reflected in the music. Beethoven himself often used the direction *appassionato* ('passionately') in his works.

Appenzell The town in northeast Switzerland has a name that represents its Roman name of *Abbatis cella*, 'abbot's cell'. *Cp.* ABBEVILLE.

Appian Way Also known as the *Via Appia*, the name is that of the Roman road in Italy which runs south from Rome to Capua and then on to Brindisi. It was the first great Roman road, and is named after its initiator in the 3rd century BC, the Roman censor *Appius* Claudius Caecus.

Apple The well-known make of home computer was given its name by the American engineer Steven Jobs who first marketed it in California in 1977. It was partly inspired by memories of a pleasant summer he had spent working in the orchards of Oregon. But it was also designed to be 'user-friendly', as distinct from the baffling technical terminology that made computers a closed book to many potential customers.

April The fourth month of the year has a name that is popularly derived from Latin *aperire*, 'to open', since this is the time when plants flower and trees come into bud. But the name is more likely to derive from that of APHRODITE, the Greek goddess of love and beauty, or from some earlier goddess whose name came to give hers in turn.

April The girl's name is that of the month, one of the most attractive of the year, implying youth and flowering. Its French form, *Avril*, is linked with the name *Averil*, but that name is of different origin, evolving from the Old English name *Everild*, from *eofor*, 'boar' and *hild*, 'battle'.

Apsley House The last house in Piccadilly, London, with the prestigious address 'No 1, London', was long famous as the residence of the Duke of Wellington. It is named after Baron *Apsley*, for whom it was built in 1771–8.

Apurimac The river in southern Peru is said to have a name that represents Quechua *apu rimak*, meaning 'the speaking lord', from *apu*, 'lord', 'wealthy one' and *rima*, 'to speak' (*cp.* LIMA).

Aqaba The port in southwest Jordan derives its name from a Hebrew root word meaning 'heel'. *Cp.* the name of JACOB.

Aquarius The name of the constellation between Pisces and Capricorn in the southern hemisphere is the Latin word traditionally translated into English as 'The Water Carrier'. The outline of the constellation was seen as the figure of a man pouring water from a jar, with the jar itself represented by the four stars Gamma, Eta, Zeta and Pi Aquarii. In astrology, Aquarius is the 11th sign of the zodiac.

Aquascutum The make of rainwear combines the Latin words *aqua*, 'water' and *scutum*, 'shield'. The descriptive name was first used in 1853 for a chemically treated rain-repellent fabric patented two years earlier by a London cloth manufacturer.

Aquila The name is that of a constellation in the Milky Way on the celestial equator. It is Latin for 'The Eagle', with this bird represented by the outline of its stars. The name is echoed in that of its brightest star, ALTAIR, otherwise Alpha Aquilae. Aquila is close to another bird-named constellation, Cygnus.

Aquinas, Thomas The noted Christian philosopher and saint takes his name from the Italian town of *Aquino*, on the road from Rome to Naples, near which he was born in 1224 or 1225. The town's own name derives from Latin *aqua*, 'water'.

Aquitaine The former Roman province in southwest France borders the Atlantic, and its name refers to this location, deriving from Latin *aqua*, 'water' and a suffix that probably means simply 'land'.

Arabella The fashionable name may have evolved from Latin *orabilis*, 'one who can be entreated', as *Orabilis* was a doublet for some women called *Arabella*. But it has certainly been influenced by names such as ANNABEL and ISABEL. Pope dedicated his poem *The Rape of the Lock* (1712) to *Arabella* Fermor, on whom the poem's heroine Belinda is directly based.

Arabia The name of the Middle Eastern country derives from the *Arabs* whose native land it is. Their own name is traditionally interpreted as 'tent-dweller', implying a nomadic people. The Bible states 'neither shall the Arabian pitch tent' (*Isaiah* 13.20), although the Hebrew word *'aravī* translated as 'Arabian' here seems to refer to any inhabitant of the desert. The name could also relate to Arabic *ḡarb*, 'west', as in the ALGARVE and MAGHREB.

Arabian Nights, The The full name of the popular collection of stories in Arabic is *Arabian Nights Entertainments*, while its alternative name is familiar as *The Thousand and One Nights*. The 'Nights' are those in which the supposed narrator, Scheherazade, aims to postpone her own execution by telling her husband, Schahriah, a succession of entertaining stories, breaking off each one at a point that excites his curiosity and makes him want to hear more the following evening, rather in the manner of a modern TV 'soap'. The Arabic name for the tales is *alf laylah wa laylah*, literally 'thousand nights and (a) night'. The figure of 1001 is now taken literally, but was originally intended simply to indicate a large number.

Arafura Sea The sea between Australia and New Guinea perhaps takes its name from that of the *Alifuru*, the people who live in the Moluccas here. Their own name may represent the local word *halefuru*, 'uninhabited (region)', referring to the general condition of the islands.

Aragon The region of northeast Spain was formerly the kingdom that gave the title of Catherine of *Aragon*, first wife of Henry VIII. It comes from the name of a river here, which itself is based on the Indoeuropean root word *ar*, 'water', found in the names of several rivers of western Europe. Others are the AYR in Scotland, *Eure* in France and ARNO in Italy.

Araldite The patent adhesive was developed by Aero Research Ltd at Duxford, near Cambridge, in the 1930s. The product was always referred to as 'ARL', from the company initials, and this gave the name *Araldite*. The suffix *-ite* is common for manufactured substances, such as ebonite, cordite or vulcanite.

Aral Sea The large lake between Kazakhstan and Uzbekistan probably takes its name from a Kirgiz or Kazakh word *aral*, meaning 'island'. The designation is apt, since the Aral Sea contains over 1000 islands.

Aramaic The ancient language of the Middle East was originally that spoken in *Aram*, the biblical name for Syria. This occurs in *Genesis* 10.22 as the name of one of the sons of Shem, and is the Hebrew word for 'height'.

Aran Islands The island group in Galway Bay off the west coast of Ireland has a name that derives from Irish *ára*, 'kidney'. This refers to the kidney-shaped contour of the three islands, which are individually named Inishmore ('great island'), Inishman ('middle island') and Inisheer ('eastern island').

Ararat The volcanic mountain in eastern Turkey, said to be the resting place of Noah's Ark after the Flood, was originally known as *Urartu*, from the name of an ancient Assyrian kingdom. The root word behind the name may be pre-Indoeuropean *ar*, 'mountain'. The Turkish name for Ararat, however, is *Ağrı dağı*, 'mountain of sorrow', said to refer to a Georgian village that was buried when the volcano erupted in 1840. Where the English Bible story of Noah's Ark has 'upon the mountains of Ararat' (*Genesis* 8.4), the Vulgate (Latin version of the Bible) has *super montes Armeniae*, 'on the mountains of Armenia'.

Arbor Day The name is that of an annual day when trees are planted in the United States, from Latin *arbor*, 'tree'. The day was first observed in Nebraska in 1872.

Arbroath The Scottish town, famous for its 'Arbroath smokies', or smoked haddock, has a name that means 'mouth of the Brothock', this being the stream on which it stands. The initial *Ar-* is thus the same as the *Aber-* of other towns such as ABERDEEN. The full form of the name comes in Southey's poem *The Inchcape Rock* (1802):

And then they knew the perilous rock,
And blest the Abbot of Aberbrothok.

Arbuthnot The name is of Scottish origin, representing the village now spelled *Arbuthnott*, south of Aberdeen. Its own name means 'confluence of the *Buthnot*', this being a small stream here.

Arcadia Geographically, the name is that of a district of Greece, in the central Peloponnese. In literature, however, where it is also known poetically as *Arcady*, it is an idealized rural setting. The name is traditionally derived from that of *Arcas*, son of Zeus, who was king of Arcadia in Greek mythology, and who was turned into a bear, the Greek for which is *arktos*.

Arc de Triomphe Construction of the famous 'triumphal arch' in Paris, at the upper end of the Champs Elysées, was decreed by Napoleon Bonaparte in 1806 to commemorate his victories in the Napoleonic Wars. The arch was completed and inaugurated in 1836. It has many sculptures symbolizing victories and bears the names of 386 French generals. Below it is the Tomb of the Unknown Soldier.

Archangel The town and port on the river Dvina in northwest Russia was so named in 1613 for its 12th-century monastery, dedicated to St Michael the *Archangel*. It was founded by Ivan IV in 1584, the year of his death, as *Novokholmogory*, 'New Kholmogory', after a village on the same river. The Russian form of the name is *Arkhangel'sk*.

Archduke Trio Beethoven's Trio in B flat for piano, violin and cello (1810–11) is so called because it was dedicated to Archduke Rudolph of Austria, one of the composer's piano pupils.

Archer The name was formerly an occupational name for a bowman, as is the modern name BOWMAN itself.

Archibald The name derives, through French, from Old German *Erkanbald*, comprising *erkan*, 'real', 'true' and *bald*, 'brave'. It has long been a popular name in Scotland, but has also come to be regarded as a typically 'aristocratic' name generally in Britain.

Archimedes The famous Greek mathematician and physicist has a name that appropriately means 'outstanding mind', from the Greek prefix *arkhi-*, 'ruling', representing *arkhein*, 'to rule', and *mēdea*, 'cunning', 'craft'.

Arctic The name of the regions of the North Pole comes from Greek *arktos*, 'bear'. This refers not to the polar bears found there but to the constellation of the Great Bear, under which the Arctic lies. *Cp*. ANT-ARCTIC.

Arcturus The name is that of the brightest star in the constellation BOÖTES. It derives from Greek *arktouros*, from *arktos*, 'bear' and *ouros*, 'guard'. It is thus the 'bear-keeper' to the nearby constellation of Ursa Major, the 'great bear'.

Arden The Forest of *Arden* once covered much of the Midlands in England, and is now commemorated in one or two place-names, such as the village of Henley-in-*Arden*, Warwickshire. As for the ARDENNES, the origin lies in a Celtic root word *ardu*, 'high', referring to the relatively high ground here. The name is particularly associated with Shakespeare, who was born in Warwickshire, whose mother's maiden name was Mary *Arden*, and who set *As You Like It* in the Forest of *Arden*. The *Arden Shakespeare* (*New Arden* from 1951) is a standard edition of his works, with one volume for each play.

Ardennes The wooded plateau of northeast France and southeast Belgium has a Gaulish name, probably based on *ardu*, 'high', or deriving from the two words *ar duenn*, 'land of forests'. The Forest of ARDEN in England has a similar name.

Areopagitica Milton's plea for a free press and free discussion, published in 1644, takes its name from the Greek AREOPAGUS, the hill in Athens where the members of the highest judicial council met.

Areopagus The hill in Athens, west of the Acropolis, has a name that is a contraction of Greek *Areios pagos*, 'hill of ARES'. According to legend it was so named because it was the place where the gods had tried and acquitted Ares on a charge of murdering Halirrhothios, Poseidon's son, who had raped Ares' daughter here.

Arequipa The city in southern Peru derives its name from Aymara *ari*, 'peak' and Quechua *qipa*, 'behind'. The town is thus 'behind the summit', describing its location at the foot of the dormant volcano El Misti.

Ares The Greek god of war, whose Roman counterpart was Mars, has a name that has been appropriately linked with both *anēr* 'man' and *aretē*, 'excellence', 'manhood'.

Arethusa In classical mythology, the name is that of the wood nymph whom Artemis changed into a spring so that she could escape from the river god Alpheus. Her name is perhaps based on Greek *aretē*, 'goodness', 'excellence'.

Argenteuil The suburb of Paris had the Roman name of *Argentogilum*. This derives from the Gaulish personal name *Argantius*, itself comprising *arganto*, 'silver' and *iala*, 'clearing', 'village', otherwise 'dweller in the bright place'.

Argentina Spanish explorers in southern South America in the early 16th century bartered goods for the silver ornaments worn by the natives, not realizing that the silver was not obtained locally. It was this metal, however, which gave the present republic its name, from Spanish *argento*, 'silver'. *See also* PLATA.

Argo The name of the ship on which the ARGONAUTS sailed with Jason in search of the Golden Fleece is traditionally said to have derived either from its builder, *Argus*, or from the place where it was built, *Argos*. Cicero claimed that the name referred to the *Argives*, the Greeks from Argos who sailed in it, while Ptolemy said that Heracles had built the ship and named it for *Argo*, son of Jason. The basic word behind the name was probably simply Greek *argos*, 'bright', 'swift'.

Argonaut The *Argonauts* were the Greek heroes who sailed with Jason in search of the Golden Fleece. Their name comes from that of the ARGO, Jason's ship, and Greek *nautēs*, 'sailor'.

Argos The ancient city in southeast Greece probably derives its name from Greek *argos*, 'white', 'shining', although some derive it from a pre-Hellenic word *arge*, 'land', 'plain'.

Argus The giant with a hundred eyes who guarded the heifer Io has a name that may simply derive from Greek *argos*, 'bright', referring to his shining eyes. After he was killed by Hermes his eyes were transformed into a peacock's tail.

Argyll The former Scottish county has a name that means 'land of the Gaels'. The Gaels were originally an Irish people who came to settle as a Scots kingdom in what was Pictish territory in the 5th century.

Ariadne The name is famous in mythology as that of the daughter of King Minos who gave Theseus a ball of thread to help him find his way out of the Minotaur's labyrinth. It is traditionally derived from the Greek intensive suffix *ari-* and *hagnos*, 'pure' (as for AGNES), so that she was 'very pure'.

Ariel In the Bible, the name is that of one of the companions of Ezra sent to bring ministers for the house of God (*Ezra* 8.16, 17). It is also a symbolic name for Jerusalem (*Isaiah* 29.1, 2). It probably comes from Hebrew *Arī`ēl*, 'lion of God', although the interpretation 'hearth of the altar', from Hebrew *Har`el* would suit Jerusalem better to express its sacred character. In Shakespeare's *The Tempest* (1612), Ariel is described in the *Dramatis Personae* as 'an Ayrie spirit', so that his name is related to *air*.

Aries The name is that of a constellation in the northern hemisphere between Taurus and Pisces. It is known in English as 'The Ram', a translation of the Latin word. The particular ram represented is the one in classical mythology whose golden fleece was sought by Jason and the Argonauts.

The stars of the constellation appear to depict a ram turning its head as if to admire its own fleece.

Arimathea The biblical town is mentioned in all four gospels as the one from which a certain Joseph came to bury the body of Jesus. The name is not known in any text outside the Bible, however, so that its location, and even its identity, is problematical. According to some scholars, the name of Joseph of *Arimathea* is simply an untranslated rendering of Hebrew *yōsef hŏr-hammetīm*, 'Joseph of the hole of the dead', otherwise simply 'Joseph the grave-digger'.

Aristarchus In Greek history, the name is that of a 3rd-century BC astronomer (*Aristarchus* of Samos) and a 2nd-century BC scholar (*Aristarchus* of Samothrace), among others. It comes from Greek *aristos*, 'best' and *arkhein*, 'to rule', so means 'best ruler'.

Aristides The name of the well-known Athenian general of the 6th and 5th centuries BC is based on the Greek root word *aristos*, 'best', as for ARISTOPHANES and ARISTOTLE.

Aristophanes The name of the 5th-century BC Greek comic dramatist means literally 'showing best', from Greek *aristos*, 'best' and *phainein*, 'to show'. This is a coincidentally appropriate name for one of the greatest writers of classical times.

Aristotle As for ARISTIDES, the famous Greek philosopher of the 4th century BC has a name based on *aristos*, 'best'. The Greeks usually applied this word to people with an implied sense 'bravest' or 'noblest'.

Arizona The name of the American state has been popularly derived from Spanish *arida zona*, 'dry region'. This, however, is probably a modification of the original Indian (Papago) name *Arizonac*, from the words *ali*, 'small' and *shonak*, 'place of the spring'. The name was that of a village with a small stream near silver mines in the south of the present state.

Arkansas The southern American state takes its name from that of the Indian *Arkansea* tribe here. The French wrote their name with a final plural *s*, so that the name falsely suggested a link with KANSAS. The name is still pronounced without the *s*, however, in the French manner. The meaning of the tribal name is unknown.

Ark Royal The name *Ark* was early adopted for ships of various kinds, with reference to Noah's *Ark*. The first *Ark Royal* was a ship of 1587 that was originally called the *Ark Ralegh*. It was renamed *Ark Royal* on being taken over from Sir Walter *Ralegh*, but was then somewhat unexpectedly renamed *Anne Royal*, for the queen of James I, in 1608. In the 20th century the *Ark Royal* has been the name of a seaplane carrier and two aircraft carriers. The order of the words is French, by contrast with ship names beginning *Royal*, such as *Royal Oak* and *Royal Sovereign*.

Arkwright The name is a former occupational name for a person who made *arks*, otherwise chests. Similar names are CART WRIGHT, WAINWRIGHT and WRIGHT itself.

Arles The city in southeast France has a name that probably derives from the Indoeuropean root element *ar*, 'water', 'river', referring to its location in the wide delta of the river Rhône.

Arlington National Cemetery The American national burial ground and patriotic shrine in Virginia, on the Potomac opposite Washington, takes its name from its location of *Arlington*. The central feature of the site is the estate of George Washington Parke Custis, adopted son of George Washington. He named it for Henry Bennet, first Earl of *Arlington* (1618–1685), who shared Charles II's grant of the colony of Virginia with Lord Thomas Culpepper. The earl's own title comes from *Harlington*, Middlesex (now a district of Hillingdon, Greater London).

Armada *See* SPANISH ARMADA.

Armageddon The name is used in the Bible (*Revelation* 16.16) for the final battle at the end of the world, that between good and evil. It derives from Hebrew *har megiddōn*, 'hill of *Megiddo*'. Megiddo was a fortified city in northern Palestine that was the site of several Old Testament battles, for example that described in 2 *Kings* 23.29. As a general word, *armageddon* now refers to any great catastrophe or scene of destruction, such as the First World War.

Armagh The Irish county and town have a name that means either 'height of *Macha*', from Irish *árd*, 'height' and the personal name Macha, or 'height of the plain', from *árd* and *machaire*, 'plain'. Macha was a goddess in Irish mythology.

Armagnac The former region of southwest France takes its name from that of a family here, whose original name may have been related, even if remotely, to that of ARMENIA. Armagnac is now familiar as a type of dry brandy that came from this region.

Armalite The automatic rifle is named after its manufacturers, the *Armalite* Division of the Fairchild Engine and Airplane Company. The name is doubtless a blend of *arm* and *light*, as it is a lightweight weapon.

Armenia The origin of the name of the former Soviet republic is uncertain. It is traditionally derived from one *Armenak*, said to have been the original ancestor of all present Armenians. Modern scholars, however, derive it from *Nairi*, 'land of rivers', the ancient name of a mountainous region of the country. The place-name is first recorded in a rock inscription dated AD 521 near the Iranian city of Bakhtaran (formerly Kermanshah).

Armitage The name formerly applied to a person who lived by a *hermitage*, so that it is directly related to this word.

Armorica The ancient name of Brittany is Gaulish in origin, from *are*, 'on', 'at' and *mor*, 'sea', describing the maritime location of the region.

Armstrong The name arose as a nickname for a physically powerful person, one whose *arm* was *strong*.

Army and Navy Club The London club, founded in 1837, is for officers of the British Army and the Royal Navy and Marines. It was originally planned to be the *Army Club*, for army officers only, but when the Duke of Wellington became its first patron he did so on the condition that it was also open to navy and marine officers.

Army and Navy Stores The famous London store, in Victoria Street, was opened in 1871 by a group of army and navy officers as a cooperative establishment where officers and men and their families could buy goods at a discount, at prices lower than in the West End. There are now other stores outside London.

Arnhem The city in the eastern Netherlands, famous as a Second World War battle site, had the Roman name of *Arenacum*. This represents Latin *arena*, 'sand' to which has been added Germanic *heim*, 'homestead', denoting the location of the original settlement on the banks of the Rhine.

Arno The name of the Italian river derives from the Indoeuropean root word *ar* meaning simply 'river', 'water'. It also lies behind other river names such as those of ARAGON and AYR.

Arnold The name came into English, through French, from the Old German name *Arnwald*, deriving from *arn*, 'eagle' and *waltan*, 'to rule'. The name is now more common as a surname.

Arnold School The Blackpool public school dates from 1896, when a class of just eight boys was formed in a house in Bright Street, Blackpool. In 1903 the expanding school moved to its present site in Lytham Road, and was named *Arnold School* after a previous school located in what is the Senior Boarding House. The earlier school may have been named after Thomas *Arnold* (1795–1842), the famous headmaster of Rugby School.

Arras The town in northern France takes its name from the *Atrebates*, the Gaulish people who lived in the province of ARTOIS, of which it was the capital. *See* the latter name for the origin.

Arsenal The famous English football club was founded in 1886 in Woolwich, then in northwest Kent, with a ground on Plumstead Common. They were known as *Royal Arsenal*, from their proximity to the government arms foundry here of that name. In 1891 they changed their name to *Woolwich Arsenal*, as the arms factory did, and after playing at various different grounds moved in 1913 to their present home stadium at Highbury, north London, abbreviating their name soon after to *Arsenal*.

Artaxerxes The western spelling of the name of the 5th-century BC king of Persia represents Old Persian *Artakhshathra*, meaning 'great king'. Artaxerxes was the son of XERXES, the previous king.

Art Deco The style of interior decoration, popular in the 1930s, has a name that is an abbreviation of French *art décoratif*, 'decorative art', itself a term adopted from the title of the *Exposition des arts décoratifs*, 'Decorative Arts Exhibition', held in Paris in 1925.

Artemis The name is that of the Roman goddess of the hunt and the moon who was the counterpart of the Greek goddess Diana. Her name is probably pre-Greek in origin, but has been traditionally linked with either Greek *artemia*, 'safety', referring to the purity and rightness of her virginity, or *arktos*, 'bear', with reference to hunting.

Artex The commercial name for the type of coating for walls and ceilings is a blend of *art* and *texture*, the latter referring to the coating's textured finish.

Arthur The name is of uncertain ultimate origin, but has been linked with Celtic *art*, 'bear', related to Greek *arktos* with the same meaning (as for the ARCTIC). Above all else the name is associated with the semi-legendary King *Arthur*, who led the Celts against the Saxons in the 6th century.

Art Nouveau The style of art and architecture of the late 19th and early 20th century had a French name meaning 'new art', referring to its deliberately innovative nature, with long, sinuous lines and stylized forms. In Germany it was known as *Jugendstil*, 'youth style', in Austria as *Sezessionstil*, 'secession style' (as promoted by young artists who had *seceded* from mainstream art), in Italy as *Stile floreale*, 'floral style' or *Stile Liberty*, 'Liberty style' (*see* LIBERTY), in Spain as *Modernismo*, 'modernism' and in Russia as *stil' "modern"*, 'modern style' (from French *moderne*).

Art of Noise, The The British rock trio, formed in 1984, were given their name by Paul Morley of ZTT Records, who adopted it from an Italian futurist manifesto. It was appropriate for the band's initial aim to produce instrumental music only, not vocal, in a near anonymous guise.

Artois The name of the former province of northern France represents that of its original Gaulish inhabitants, the *Atrebates*, whose own name means simply 'inhabitants', from *trebu*, 'tribe'. *Cp.* ARRAS.

Arundel The name of the West Sussex town does not derive from French *hirondelle*, 'swallow', as popularly supposed, despite the fact that this bird appears on the Arundel coat of arms. It comes from Old English *hārhūne dell*, 'hoarhound valley', denoting the plant that at one time must have grown by the river Arun here. The river takes its name from the town. It was originally known as the *Tarrant* (preserved in *Tarrant* Street in the town), a name of identical origin to that of the TRENT. *See also* ANDOVER.

Aryan The name is sometimes used for speakers of Indoeuropean languages, or for their ethnic type, and was also adopted by the Nazis to apply to a superior race of non-Jewish, Nordic people. It derives from Sanskrit *ārya*, 'noble', perhaps itself based on the root element *ar*, 'mountain', as for ARARAT and IRAN.

Asa In the Bible, the name is that of a king of Judah who abolishes many idols. It represents Hebrew *Āsā*, meaning 'healer'.

Asaph The name of the well-known Welsh saint is ultimately of biblical origin (1 *Chronicles* 16.5 and elsewhere), from Hebrew *Āsāph*, 'collector'. In modern times it has been made familiar by the American astronomer *Asaph* Hall (1829–1907), who in 1877 discovered the two satellites of Mars, Deimos and Phobos.

Ascension Day In the Christian calendar, the name is that of the 40th day (always a Thursday) after Easter that celebrates the occasion when Jesus *ascended* to heaven, as told in the Bible (*Acts* 1.9). The period of 40 days was that during which Jesus appeared to the disciples after the Resurrection (*Acts* 1.3). In Roman Catholic countries Ascension Day is usually a public holiday, but not in mainly Protestant Britain.

Ascension Island The South Atlantic island was discovered on ASCENSION DAY, Thursday 1 June 1508, by the Portuguese explorer João da Nova, and was named after the religious festival.

Ascot The famous annual horse race meeting, officially *Royal Ascot*, is named after the former village near Windsor, Berkshire, where it is held. The place-name itself, found elsewhere in England, means simply 'eastern cottage'. The original settlement here may have been so named because it lay to the east of Easthampstead, now a district of Bracknell.

Asgard In Scandinavian mythology, the name is that of the dwelling place of the gods, the AESIR, corresponding to the Greek Mount Olympus. Its name derives from Old Norse *Ásgarthr*, from *áss*, 'god' and *garthr*, 'enclosure' (related to English *garth*, *yard* and *garden*).

Ashanti The name of the African people and their language in central Ghana means 'people united for war' in their own tongue. The name is also that of an administrative region, representing the former native kingdom that was suppressed by the British in 1900 after the four Ashanti Wars.

Ashburton Shield The shooting challenge award was first made in 1861 by the 3rd Baron *Ashburton*, who donated £140 for a shield to be competed for at Bisley by teams from public schools. Three schools entered that year, Eton, Harrow and Rugby, the last of these being the winners.

Ash Can School The name is that of the group of American painters who in the early years of the 20th century depicted life in the slums and tenements of New York. It refers to the sordid aspect of their subject, *ash can* being the American equivalent of the British *dustbin*. The group were also known as *The Eight*, from their number.

Asher In the Old Testament, the name is that of the son of Jacob by Zilpah, Leah's maid, who became the ancestor of one of the 12 tribes of Egypt. It is popularly derived from Hebrew *āŝēr*, 'happy', a meaning alluded to in the account of his birth: 'And Leah said, Happy am I, for the daughters will call me blessed: and she called his name Asher' (*Genesis* 30.13). This sense of Asher's name is to be compared with that of his brother, GAD, 'fortunate'.

Ashes, The The familiar name is that of the symbolic prize in the cricket Test Matches between England and Australia. When Australia won a sensational victory in 1882, the *Sporting Times* published the following mock obituary: 'In Affectionate Remembrance of English Cricket Which died at the Oval on 29th August, 1882. Deeply lamented by a large circle of sorrowing friends and acquaintances. R.I.P. N.B. – The body will be cremated and the ashes taken to Australia.' The ashes of a burnt cricket stump were subsequently placed in an urn and given to the English team when it next won.

Ashkenazi The name is that used for a Jew of northern and central Europe, in particular Germany and Poland, as opposed to a SEPHARDI. It derives from the name of *Ashkenaz*, son of Gomer (*Genesis* 10.3, 1 *Chronicles* 1.6, *Jeremiah* 51.27), a descendant of Noah through Japheth, who was identified with the ancient Ascanians of Phrygia and subsequently with the Germans.

Ashmolean Museum The Oxford University museum and library of ancient history, fine arts and archaeology is named for the donator of its original collection in 1677, the antiquarian Elias *Ashmole* (1617–1692).

Ashtoreth The name, mentioned more than once in the Bible (1 *Samuel* 21.10, 1 *Kings* 11.5, 2 *Kings* 23.13), is that of an ancient Semitic fertility goddess. It has been identified with the names of ISHTAR and ASTARTE, and so with that of APHRODITE, the Greek counterpart of Venus.

Ashur *See* ASSYRIA.

Ashurbanipal The 7th-century BC king of Assyria, who built the fine palace and library at Nineveh, has a name representing Assyrian *Aš-ur-bani-pal*, 'the god *Assur* creates the son'. *See also* ASSYRIA.

Ash Wednesday The name is that of the first day of Lent in the Christian calendar. It is so called from the custom of marking a cross on the foreheads of the faithful, as a sign of penitence, with the *ashes* of the palm branches that had been kept in the home from the previous year's celebration of Palm Sunday.

Asia There are many theories to account for the name of the continent. It may represent Assyrian *asū*, 'to rise', meaning 'land of the rising sun', otherwise an eastern land as opposed to Europe, to the west. Sanskrit *usā*, another possible source, means 'dawn', so has the same basic sense.

Aslan The great lion who is one of the central figures in C.S. Lewis's *Narnia* books for children has a name that is simply the Turkish word for 'lion'. Lewis is said to have found it while reading the *Arabian Nights*.

Asmodeus The prince of the demons in Jewish demonology has a name that ultimately comes from Avestan *Aēsma-daēva*, 'spirit of anger'. He is referred to in the Apocrypha as 'the evil spirit' (*Tobit* 3.8,17) and he is sometimes identified with *Aeshma*, one of the seven demons of Parseeism.

Asnières The suburb of Paris, known in full as *Asnières-sur-Seine*, has a name that ultimately derives from Latin *asinus*, 'ass', 'donkey'. The place was one where donkeys were bred or kept.

Aspasia The name of the noted 5th-century BC Greek intellectual who was the mistress of Pericles comes from Greek *aspasia*, 'welcome', 'desired'.

Aspinall A person with this name would originally have come from *Aspinwall*, now in the parish of Ormskirk, Lancashire. The name itself comprises Old English *æspe*, 'aspen', 'trembling poplar' and *wælle*, 'spring', 'stream'.

Aspro The patent form of aspirin acquired its name as a combination of 'Nicholas' and '*pro*duct'. The former was the surname of the Australian chemist, George *Nicholas*, who first produced his brand of aspirin in 1915. The name also, of course, suggests '*aspirin*' itself.

Asquith Familiar from Britain's prime minister and Liberal Party leader, Herbert Henry *Asquith* (1852–1928), the surname represents the place-name *Askwith*, that of a village in North Yorkshire, itself Scandinavian in origin and meaning 'ash wood'.

Assam The state of northeastern India has a name that is probably tribal in origin, from the *Ahamiya* who invaded the region in the 13th century. They spoke *Ahom*, a Tibetan-Burmese language, and its name in turn may represent Thai *ahom*, 'invincible'. Some authorities, however, claim a Sanskrit origin, from the prefix *a-*, 'without' and *sama*, 'same', in other words, 'without equal'.

Assassins The name was that of a secret sect of Muslims who at the time of the Crusades (11th–14th centuries) murdered their Christian victims, usually under the influence of the drug hashish. Their name means 'hashish eaters' or 'hashish smokers', from Arabic *ḥaŝŝāŝīn*, the plural of *ḥaŝŝāŝ*, 'taker of hashish', itself from *ḥaŝŝīŝ*, 'hashish'. The name gave the standard word *assassin* for the murderer of a politician or other important person. The historic *Assassins* were organized by the Syrian grand master Rashid ad-Din as-Sinan, the legendary 'Old Man of the Mountain', from his castle at Alamut in Persia (modern Iran). (His nickname is a mistranslation of Arabic *ŝayh al-jabal*, literally 'chief of the mountain'.)

Assisi Famous as the birthplace of St Francis, the town in central Italy has a name that is probably Umbrian in origin. Its meaning is obscure.

Assumption In the Christian calendar, the name is that of the day, observed by Roman Catholics on 15 August, that commemorates the taking up or *assumption* of the Virgin Mary into heaven at the end of her earthly life. *See also* LADY DAY.

Assur *See* ASSYRIA.

Assyria The origin of the name of the ancient kingdom of Mesopotamia is the same as that of its chief city, *Assur* (*Ashur*). This in turn represents the name of the god of the Assyrians, and probably derives from Assyrian *sar*, 'prince'. In the Bible, *Assur* is cited as one of the sons of Shem (*Genesis* 10.22). *See also* SARDANAPALUS and the (unrelated) name of SYRIA.

Astarte The name is that of a fertility goddess worshipped by the Phoenicians. It has been identified with that of the goddess ASHTORETH of the Hebrews and that of ISHTAR of the Babylonians and Assyrians. It therefore also relates to the name of APHRODITE, the Greek goddess who was the counterpart to the Roman Venus.

Asterix The hero of the children's cartoon stories by the French writer René Goscinny and illustrator Albert Uderzo is a Gaul, and has a mock Gaulish name ending in *-rix*, like that of the Gallic chieftain VERCINGETORIX. The first part of his name suggests Greek *astēr*, 'star', doubtless as he is the 'star' of the stories.

Astolat The name of the town mentioned in Arthurian legend, popularly identified with Guildford, is probably of Celtic or pre-Celtic origin, and is the *Shalott* of Tennyson's famous poem 'The Lady of Shalott' (1832), in which 'The Lady' corresponds to Elaine, the 'Lily Maid of Astolat' in the earlier Arthurian romances. Tennyson based the subject for his poem on a medieval Italian novelette, *Donna di Scalotta*. In Thomas Malory's *Le Morte D'Arthur* (late 15th century) the name was spelled *Ascolet*. When Caxton printed this work in 1485, however, he misread the *c* as a *t*. It thus appeared as *Astolat*, and has traditionally remained in this spelling ever since. The actual meaning of the name is obscure.

Aston Martin The car was first manufactured in 1932 by Lionel *Martin*, who as a racing driver had won several races on the course at *Aston* Clinton, near Aylesbury, Buckinghamshire. Its name is thus a combination of his own and the scene of his successes.

Aston University The Birmingham university, founded in 1966, and formerly a College of Advanced Technology, takes its name from the district of *Aston* in which it is located.

Aston Villa The well-known Birmingham football club was founded in 1874 by members of the *Villa Cross* Wesleyan Chapel cricket club. Villa Cross itself was a road junction in a residential district of southern Aston and was so named for its *villas*, or newly built private houses. The club's original ground was in the Aston Lower Grounds amusement park, near Villa Cross. In 1876 it moved to another ground in Perry Barr, then back to Aston Lower Grounds in 1897. The latter ground was subsequently developed with a new stadium and was renamed *Villa Park*.

Astor Famous from the rich Anglo-American family founded by the financier John Jacob *Astor* (1763–1848), the surname was originally a nickname for someone resembling a bird of prey in some way, from Old Provençal *astur*, 'goshawk'. *See also* ASTORIA.

Astoria Familiar from various cinemas and theatres in the English-speaking world, and from hotels outside it, the prestigious name ultimately derives from the wealthy ASTOR family. London's *Astoria* cinema, in Charing Cross Road, opened in 1927 but in 1977 was converted to a theatre. *See also* WALDORF-ASTORIA.

Astrakhan The Russian city, famous for its furs, has a name said to represent Turkish *hacı tarhan*, from *hacı*, 'hajji' (the term for a Muslim who has made a pilgrimage to Mecca) and *tarhan*, 'untaxed', from *tarh*, 'tax'. Astrakhan was founded by a hajji, and its religious repute gained it exemption from local taxes.

Astrid The name is of Scandinavian origin, from the Old Norse name *Astrithr*, itself from *áss*, 'god' and *frithr*, 'fair', so overall meaning 'divinely beautiful'. It is now familiar as a royal name, notably of Princess *Astrid* (1932–   ), daughter of King Olav V of Norway, and Queen *Astrid* (1905–1935), wife of King Leopold III of Belgium.

Astrophel The name is that by which Sir Philip Sidney identifies himself in his sequence of songs and sonnets *Astrophel and Stella* (1582), with Stella representing Penelope Rich, the woman he loved. His name comes from Greek *astron*, 'star' and *philos*, 'loving', said to have been devised by abbreviating 'Philip Sidney' as 'Phil. Sid.', interpreting this as Greek *philos* and Latin *sidus*, 'star', then translating the latter to its Greek equivalent. Whatever the case, the name relates specifically to STELLA, itself the commoner Latin word for 'star'.

Asturias The name of the coastal region and former kingdom of northwest Spain derives from Basque *asta*, 'rock' and *ur*, 'water', describing its maritime topography.

Aswad The Rastafarian reggae band, formed in London in 1975 by three young blacks, took the Arabic word for 'black' as their name.

Aswan The famous dam on the Nile in Egypt takes its name from the ancient city where it was originally built in 1902. (It was rebuilt as the *Aswan High Dam* four miles (6 km) upstream in 1971.) The city's name represents Arabic *aswān*, a form of its Egyptian name *Suānit*, meaning 'market'. The name is in the Bible as *Syene* (*Ezekiel* 29.7).

Atacama The desert region along the west coast of South America derives its name from that of a local tribe here. Their own name is said to represent Quechua *takama*, 'black duck', perhaps their totemic animal.

Atalanta The name of the mythical maiden who agreed to marry any man who could beat her in a running race may have been formed from the Greek prefix *a-*, 'not' and *talantos*, 'balance', since she was unevenly matched in such a race. In the event she was beaten by Hippomenes when she stopped to pick up three golden apples that he had purposely dropped.

Ate The name of the Greek goddess who blinded men so that they would perform guilty deeds is simply *atē*, the word for 'folly', 'rashness'.

Aten The name, also spelled *Aton*, is that of the god of ancient Egypt who was the personification of the disk of the sun. His name means simply 'disk'. The Egyptian king AMENHOTEP IV changed his name to AKHENATEN and built the city of *Akhetaten* ('horizon of *Aten*'), now *Tell el-Amarna*, as a centre for the worship of *Aten*.

Athanasius The name is that of the 3rd-century saint and patriarch of Alexandria who is said to have composed the Athanasian Creed, the well-known Christian affirmation of faith in the Western Church. His name comes from Greek *athanatos*, 'immortal'.

Athelstan The name is familiar in English history as that of the 10th-century king of Wessex and Mercia who extended his kingdom to cover much of England. It comes from Old English *æthele*, 'noble' and *stān*, 'stone'.

Athenaeum London's élite literary and intellectual club was originally known as *The Society* when it opened in 1824. In 1830 it was renamed after the *Athenaeum* in Rome, the academy of learning founded by the emperor Hadrian in the 2nd century AD, itself with a Latin name formed from Greek *Athēnaion*, 'temple of ATHENE'.

Athene The Greek goddess of wisdom has a name that may derive from Greek *a-*, 'not' and *thuntos*, 'mortal', so that she is the 'immortal one'. An alternative derivation takes the name from *a-* and *tithēnē*, 'nurse', as she was born without being nursed by a mother. Her name is probably pre-Greek in origin, however. Either way, it is inextricably linked with that of ATHENS, of which she was the goddess protectress.

Athens The Greek capital and ancient city-state is popularly regarded as deriving its name from the goddess ATHENE, whose great temple there was the PARTHENON. But the city's name is almost certainly older than her own, and is thus pre-Greek and of unknown origin.

Athos, Mount The Greek mountain, renowned for its many Greek Orthodox monasteries, has a descriptive name, from Greek *thoos*, 'sharp', 'pointed', referring to its marble peak. The Greek Church also know it as *Hagion Oros*, 'Holy Mountain'.

Atkinson The name means 'son of Atkin', with the latter a diminutive of ADAM. The surname is fairly common in Scotland, and equates to its mainly Northern Ireland counterpart, ACHESON.

Atlanta The state capital of Georgia was given its name on gaining city status in 1845 by J.E. Thomson, a railway builder, with reference to its location at the terminus of the Western & *Atlantic* Railroad. Its original name, when founded in 1837, was actually *Terminus* itself.

Atlantic The great ocean bears the name of both ATLAS and ATLANTIS, and it is hard to say which of the two is the precise origin. The name is first found in the 5th century BC in the writings of Herodotus, who tells of a 'sea beyond the Pillars of Hercules (*i.e.* the Straits of Gibraltar) called Atlantis'.

Atlantic Richfield The leading American oil company developed from a merger in 1966 between two existing companies, *Atlantic* Refining Company, founded as Atlantic Petroleum Storage Company in 1866, and *Richfield* Oil, a smaller company that aimed to strike oil in a 'rich field' off the west coast. The company, based in Los Angeles, markets petrol under the name *Arco*, an acronym of *A*tlantic *R*ichfield *Co*mpany.

Atlantis The name is that of the ancient legendary land said to have sunk beneath the ATLANTIC Ocean west of southern Spain. It is directly related to that of both the ocean and the giant ATLAS.

Atlas The Greek giant, forced to bear the sky on his shoulders as a punishment for rebelling aginst Zeus, has a name that may represent Greek *athlos*, 'struggle' (as in modern English *athlete*). On the other hand, it may well derive from ATLANTIS, since in some accounts this was the land where Atlas stood when holding up the sky. Later, he was associated with the ATLAS MOUNTAINS of northwest Africa.

Atlas Mountains The mountains take their name from the mythological giant who held up the sky, since that is what they themselves appear to do. In late mythology, ATLAS is said to be the king of this region of northwest Africa, which is also not too far from the location of the supposed submerged land of ATLANTIS.

Aton *See* ATEN.

Atropos *See* FATES.

Attic The name is that of the chief literary language of classical Greece, spoken in *Attica*, the territory of ATHENS. Hence its name, from Latin *Atticus*, 'of Athens'.

Atticus The Roman scholar and patron of the arts, who lived in the 1st century BC, was long a resident of ATHENS. Hence his name, from Latin *Atticus*, 'of Athens'. In literature, *Atticus* was the character under which Pope satirized Addison in the 18th century, alluding to his wit and intellect. The name has been adopted by, or applied to, many other writers, including that of a regular columnist in the *Sunday Times*.

Attila The famous (or infamous) 5th-century king of the Huns, the 'Scourge of God' who laid waste much of the Roman Empire, has a name of Gothic origin. Gothic *atta* means 'father', and *attila* is its diminutive, 'little father'. Although the Goths were the people the Huns defeated and drove west, some Goths must have regarded Attila not so much as a fierce tyrant but as a good master, who provided loot, so gave him a 'paternal' name accordingly.

Auberon The name is of Norman French origin, in turn from a Germanic name whose composition remains uncertain. It may be related to the name AUBREY. *See also* OBERON.

Aubrey The name came into English as a French spelling of the Old German name *Alberic*. The Old English form of this was *Ælfric*, from *ælf*, 'elf' (as for ALFRED) and *rīce*, 'strong', 'powerful'.

Auckland New Zealand's chief port, in North Island, was founded in 1840 as capital of the British colonial government and was named after George Eden, Earl of *Auckland* (1784–1849), First Lord of the Admiralty, later Governor General of India. The Earl inherited the title from his father, who was born at Windlestone Hall near Bishop *Auckland*, Co Durham.

Audi The car of this name was first manufactured in 1909 by Dr August Horch, of Zwickau, Germany, originally under his surname. For legal reasons, he subsequently translated this (*horch* is the German for 'hear') into its Latin equivalent.

Audrey The name is a 'smoothed-down' version of *Etheldreda*, itself of Old English origin, meaning 'noble strength'. It became familiar from the 7th-century queen of Northumbria, St *Audrey*, whose name gave the modern English word *tawdry*, originally applied to the cheap necklaces like those she is said to have worn when young.

Augsburg The city in southern Germany has the Roman name *Augusta Vindelicorum*. This refers to the Roman emperor *Augustus*, who founded it in 14 BC, and to the *Vindelici*, the people who lived here. German *burg*, 'fort' was added to the first part of this name, which was eventually reduced to the first syllable.

August The eighth month is named after the title adopted by the Roman emperor AUGUSTUS. It was originally called *Sextilis*, 'sixth', since it was the sixth month from March, when the year began. (Hence SEPTEMBER, 'seventh month', and the three that numerically follow.)

Augusta The name is the feminine form of AUGUSTUS or AUGUSTINE. In Roman times, *Augusta*, meaning 'venerable', was the title given to the wives of emperors who themselves had assumed the title *Augustus*.

Augusta The name is found for more than one American town. *Augusta*, Georgia, was founded in 1735 and named for Princess *Augusta* (1719–1772), the future mother (in 1738) of George III. *Augusta*, the state capital of Maine, was so named in 1797, probably (though not certainly) for Pamela *Augusta* Dearborn, daughter of the American Revolutionary officer Henry Dearborn (1751–1829), who was locally prominent.

Augustine The name is a derivative of AUGUSTUS, and was popularized by two saints. The first St *Augustine* (of Hippo) was famous for his *Confessions*, a spiritual autobiography written in about 400. The second was the Roman monk sent to Britain in the late 6th century to convert the Anglo-Saxons to Christianity.

Augustinians The various religious orders of this name base their rules on that of their founder, St AUGUSTINE of Hippo. One such order is the AUSTIN FRIARS.

Augustus The name comes from the title, from Latin *augustus*, 'venerable', adopted by many Roman emperors. The best known, the first emperor of Rome, was originally Gaius Octavianus. After his adoption by Julius Caesar, he then became Gaius Julius Caesar Octavianus. Finally, in 27 BC, he adopted the title *Augustus*.

Auld Lang Syne The familiar farewell or parting song takes its name from the words that Burns adopted in the late 18th century from an existing traditional Scottish song. The words of the refrain mean literally 'old long since', that is, times past, the 'good old days'.

Aurelius The 2nd-century AD Roman emperor Marcus *Aurelius* Antoninus had a Roman clan name that probably derived from Latin *aureolus*, 'golden', with the implied sense 'fine', 'excellent'.

Auriga The constellation of this name lies in the northern hemisphere between Ursa Major and Orion, and the Latin word is usually translated into English as 'The Charioteer'. No particular charioteer in mythology seems to be represented, and the outline of the stars in Auriga does not even depict a chariot, but simply its driver, a young man holding a whip.

Aurora The name of the Roman goddess of the dawn is actually the Latin word for 'dawn'. Her Greek counterpart is *Eōs*, a name with the same meaning.

Austen Famous from the novelist Jane *Austen* (1775–1817), the surname is simply a variant spelling of AUSTIN. As a first name it became well-known through the British statesman Sir *Austen* Chamberlain (1863–1937) (although it was originally his middle name, not his first, which was Joseph).

Austerlitz, Battle of The battle was the one of 1805 in which Napoleon defeated the Austrians and Russians and brought the Holy Roman Empire to an end. The town, now in central Czechoslovakia, has a name that evolved from its medieval name of *Nuzedliz*, meaning 'new village'. Its Czech name is *Slavkov*, as if emphasizing its SLAV allegiance rather than its German past.

Austin The state capital of Texas was founded in 1839 and named for its founder, the Texan pioneer Stephen F. *Austin* (1793–1836).

Austin The first name was adopted from the surname, which itself arose as a given name in medieval times, as a spoken form of AUGUSTINE. It thus has the same origin as that name.

Austin The well-known make of car was first manufactured in 1905 by Herbert *Austin*, later first Baron Austin (1866–1941), and is named after him. Austin had earlier been involved with the company that gave the name of the Wolseley car.

Austin Friars The Austin Friars take their title from the founder of their order, St AUGUSTINE of Hippo, whose name appears in its medieval form of AUSTIN. Their full title is *Order of the Hermit Friars of Saint Augustine*.

Austin Reed The firm of men's tailors and outfitters is named after its Berkshire-born founder, *Austin Reed* (1873–1954), who opened his first tailor's shop in Fenchurch Street, London, in 1900. The present chairman of the company, Barry Reed (1931–), is the grandson of the founder.

Australasia The name is now used compositely for Australia, New Zealand and the islands of the southwest Pacific. It was originally devised in the mid-18th century as a combination of the Latin word for 'southern', *australis* (the basis of the name of AUSTRALIA), and ASIA, to apply to lands, many still then undiscovered, that lay south of Asia.

Australia Since at least the 2nd century AD, stories had told of a *terra australis incognita*, 'unknown southern land', that was believed to exist in the southern hemisphere. Australia was sighted by the Spanish in the early 17th century, and later that century explored by the Dutch, who called the land *New Holland*. Finally, in the early 19th century, the continent was circumnavigated by the English explorer Matthew Flinders, who gave it the original name of *Terra Australis* (no longer *incognita*). This was soon abbreviated to the form in which we know it today.

Austria The name of the European country is a shortened form of the Medieval Latin name, *Marchia austriaca*, 'eastern borderland', so called as it was in the eastern extreme of Charlemagne's former empire. Confusingly, the Latin name suggests 'south' (as with AUSTRALIA) rather than 'east', but this is because it represented the Old German name, *Ōstarrīhi* (modern German *Österreich*), 'eastern kingdom', not classical Latin *australis*, 'southern'.

Autolycus The roguish 'snapper-up of unconsidered trifles' in Shakespeare's *The Winter's Tale* is named after the son of Hermes in Greek mythology who was a celebrated cattle thief. The name represents Greek *autos*, 'self', 'very' and *lukos*, 'wolf'.

Auvergne The region of south central France takes its name from the *Arverni*, the Gaulish people who once lived here.

Their own name is of disputed origin. It may represent *are*, 'at' and *verno*, 'alder', so that they lived by an alder wood, or else *ar*, 'excellent' and *verno*, 'warrior', describing them as fine fighters.

Aux Deux Magots The famous Paris café has a name that means 'at (the sign of) the two magots', a *magot* being a macaque, or Barbary ape, at one time popular in Paris as a pet. The ape's own name comes from that of *Magog* (*see* GOG AND MAGOG). The animal name was transferred to the term for a small oriental figure of porcelain or ivory, representing a grotesque obese person.

Auxerre The town in central France derives its name from a combination of the Gaulish personal name *Autesio* and *duru*, 'door', 'house', 'fort'.

Ava The name is probably a development from *Eva*, itself a form of EVE. It is now popularly associated with Latin *avis*, 'bird', however. It was promoted by the Italo-American film actress *Ava* Gardner (1922–1990).

Avalokiteshvara The name of one of the main Bodhisattvas (divine beings) in Buddhist mythology represents Sanskrit *avalokita-īśvara*, meaning 'god who looks down'.

Avalon In Celtic mythology, the name is that of an island paradise in the western seas. It is more familiar, however, from Arthurian legend, as the place where Arthur was taken to die when he was mortally wounded. The name is traditionally derived from the Celtic word that gave modern Irish *abhall* and Welsh *afal*, 'apple', to which *apple* is itself related. An alternative explanation, however, relates the name to that of *Avalloc*, who is said to have ruled it with his daughters. Avalon has come to be identified with Glastonbury, the Somerset town that is popularly regarded as Arthur's burial place. This came about because Avalon had itself come to be associated with the paradisal 'Glass Island' of Celtic legend. The identity gave a false link with *Ineswytrin*, the Welsh name of Glastonbury that was recorded in the early 7th century and translated by the 12th-century Welsh chronicler Caradog as 'island of glass', from words corresponding to modern Welsh *ynys*, 'island' and *gwydrin*, 'glass'. *See* GLASTONBURY itself for the real origin.

Aveline *See* EVELYN.

Aventine The name is that of one of the seven hills on which Rome was built. It derives from the *Aven*, one of the rivers of Latium.

Avenue of the Americas The name is the official one given to New York's Sixth Avenue in the 1940s to honour the countries of Latin America. It remains official, however, and is never used in everyday speech.

Averil *See* APRIL.

Avernus, Lake The Italian lake, near Naples, lies in the crater of an extinct volcano. Because of its forbidding appearance and emissions of vapours it was regarded in classical times as the mouth of Hell. Hence its name, from Greek *a-*, 'without' and *ornis*, 'bird', from the belief that the vapours killed birds flying over it. Its Italian name is *Lago d'Averno*.

Avesta The collection of sacred writings of Zoroastrianism has a name that in the Middle Persian language, Pahlavi, means 'original text'. The Avesta together with its commentary is known as the ZEND-AVESTA.

Avicenna The traditional western rendering of the name of the 11th-century Arab philosopher and physician represents his Arabic name, *Abū ibn Sīnā*, 'Abu son of Sina'.

Avignon The city in southeast France, with its famous medieval bridge, now destroyed, bases its name on the proto-Indoeuropean root word *ab* meaning 'water'. The city is on the river Rhône.

Avila The city in central Spain has a name that is said to be a contraction of *Albicella*, from Latin *alba cella*, 'white cell'. However, the original settlement here predates Roman times, and the name may be Phoenician in origin.

Avon The common British river name (and that of a modern county) comes from the Celtic word *abonā*, meaning merely 'river'. The name would originally have been simply a reference to a local river, just as we would say 'We walked by the river'.

There is no need to give the name of a river when it is clear which one is meant.

Avon The famous 'Avon lady', as a door-to-door cosmetics seller, owes her name to David McConnell, the American founder of the original manufacturers, the California Perfume Company. McConnell was a Shakespeare lover, and his own birthplace, Suffern-on-the-Ramapo, New York, suggested 'Stratford-on-Avon', where Shakespeare was born. He therefore chose 'Avon' for its prestigious literary connotations. The company was founded in 1886, when the first 'Avon lady', Mrs P.F.E. Albee, began selling the 'Little Dot' perfume set in New York.

Avril *See* APRIL.

Ayer The surname was originally a nickname for a person who was the heir to a title or a fortune, from Middle English *eir*, 'heir'. In Scotland, however, the name could denote a person who came from AYR.

Ayers Rock The spectacular mountain in the centre of Australia, where it is the world's largest monolith, was named in 1873 for Sir Henry *Ayers* (1821–1897), prime minister of South Australia.

Ayesha This was the name, more accurately spelt *Aisha*, of the third and favourite wife of Muhammad. It represents Arabic *'Ā'iśa*, 'flourishing', from the verb *'āśa*, 'to live'. The spelling *Ayesha* was popularized by Rider Haggard for the heroine of his novel *She* (1887) and for the title of its sequel (1905).

Aylesbury The Buckinghamshire town has an Old English name meaning '*Ægel*'s fort'. The same personal name is found in other English place-names, such as *Aylesford*, Kent and *Aylestone*, Leicestershire.

Aylmer Now more common as a surname, *Aylmer* represents the Old English name *Æthelmær*, from *æthele*, 'noble' (as for ATHELSTAN) and *mære*, 'famed'. Its more common equivalent is ELMER.

Aylward The surname derives from the Germanic name *Æthelweard*, itself consisting of *adal*, 'noble' and *ward*, 'guard', 'protection'.

Ayr The name of the Scottish town and former county is that of the river on which the town stands, from a pre-Celtic word *ar* meaning simply 'water'. The same word lies behind continental European names such as ARAGON in Spain and ARNO in Italy.

Ayutthaya The city and former capital of Thailand, in the south of the country, adopted its name from that of another ancient city, whose location remains unknown. Its own name represents Sanskrit *ayodhya*, 'unconquerable', from *a-*, 'not' and *yodhya*, 'that can be conquered', from *yudh*, 'to conquer'. The city is often referred to as *Krung Kau*, 'former capital'.

Azariah The name is that of around two dozen different men in the Old Testament, including a king of Judah and one of the three companions of Daniel. (The latter is given the new name ABEDNEGO when taken into the service of king Nebuchadnezzar.) It represents Hebrew *'Azaryāh*, 'helped by Yah', *i.e.* by Jehovah.

Azazel In Muslim demonology, the name is that of the prince of demons who was cast out of Heaven for refusing to worship Adam. In the Greek and Latin versions of the Bible, it was wrongly interpreted as 'scapegoat' (Latin *caper emissarius*). Its origin is in Hebrew *'ăzāz'ēl*, which the Bible translators (especially Tyndale) apparently misunderstood as *'ēz 'ōzēl*, 'goat that departs'. The confusion is understandable, as the passage that mentions the name actually involves a goat. Two goats participated in the ritual of the Day of Atonement (Yom Kippur), with the high priest casting lots upon each: 'one lot for the Lord, and the other lot for the scapegoat' (*Leviticus* 16.8). The goat on which the lot fell 'for the Lord' (*i.e.* the 'good' goat) was then offered as a sacrifice, while the other, symbolically bearing the sins of the people (as the 'bad' goat), was led out into the wilderness, the abode of *Azazel*, where it was released. In the Revised Version of the Bible the proper name *Azazel* replaces the word *scapegoat* in the verse quoted.

Azerbaijan The name of the former Soviet republic may ultimately derive, through Persian, from Greek *Atropatene*, from the personal name *Atropatis*, that of the general who proclaimed the independence of this land in the time of Alexander the Great. But other authorities prefer an origin in a local word *azer*, 'fire' and Iranian *baykān*, 'guardian', referring to the former temples of fire worshippers here.

Azores The North Atlantic island group was discovered by the Portuguese in 1492 and named for the abundance of goshawks here, from *açor*, plural *açores*, the Portuguese word for this bird.

Azov, Sea of The sea to the north of the Black Sea is probably named after the town of *Azov*, near the mouth of the Don at its eastern end. This in turn may be from Turkish *azak*, 'low'. It is popularly explained as deriving from *Azum* or *Azuf*, the name of a Polovtsian prince killed when the town was captured in 1067.

Azrael In Jewish and Muslim angelology the name is that of the angel who separates the soul from the body at death. It has been equated with that of *Azarel* and *Azriel* in the Bible, so like them probably derives from the Hebrew meaning 'help of God' or 'helped by God'.

Aztec The Indian people of Mexico came from a land that they called *Aztlán*, whose name bears a remarkable similarity to that of ATLANTIS. However, it is more likely to derive from the Indian (Nahuatl) words *aztatl*, 'heron' and *tlan*, 'near', so that they originally lived 'near the herons'. It is not certain where this was.

B

Baader-Meinhof Gang The name was popularly applied to the *Rote Armee Fraktion* ('Red Army Faction'), a group of West German guerrillas who in the late 1960s pledged themselves to overthrow capitalist society. It derives from the surnames of their leaders, Andreas *Baader* (1953–1977) and Ulrike *Meinhof* (1934–1976). Both committed suicide, Meinhof when in prison, Baader when under sentence of life imprisonment.

Baal The name is not only that of the sun god of Phoenician mythology but that of several Semitic fertility gods. It is simply the Hebrew word *ba'l* meaning 'lord', 'master'. Baal is mentioned several times in the Bible (especially in 1 and 2 *Kings*), and his name also occurs as an element in the names of other pagan gods, such as BEELZEBUB and JERUBBAAL. *Cp.* BEL.

Baalbek The ancient Syrian city, important in Phoenician and Roman times, is now a town in Lebanon. Its name represents Arabic *ba'labakk*, with *ba'l* being either the word for 'lord', 'master' or, more likely, the name of the Phoenician sun god, BAAL, and *bakk* probably meaning 'city'. The city was a centre of the worship of Baal, and was renamed by the Greeks as HELIOPOLIS, 'city of the sun'.

Ba'ath The *Ba'ath* Party is a socialist party founded in Syria in 1953 with the aim of uniting all Arab countries in the Middle East. It has been in power in Syria since 1963 and in Iraq since 1968. Its name derives from Arabic *baaî*, 'rebirth'.

Babar The elephant in the children's books by the French writer and artist Jean de Brunhoff, the first of which appeared in 1931, appears to be named somewhat perversely from Turkish *bābar*, 'lion'. More plausibly, the author borrowed the name from that of the famous 16th-century Mogul ruler in India, whose byname it was. However, *Babar* was an African elephant, not an Indian one, so this too is perverse!

Baba Yaga The ogress of Russian folklore has a name that means 'evil woman', 'witch', from Russian *baba*, 'old woman' and a word *yaga* that is probably related to Old Icelandic *ekki*, 'pain', 'grief' and Old English *inca*, 'question', 'doubt', 'grievance'.

Babel Now a standard word meaning 'confusion', 'hubbub', *Babel* occurs in the Bible as the Hebrew name of BABYLON. This name, properly *bavel*, itself represents Akkadian *Bāb-īlu*, 'gate of God', from *bābu*, 'gate' and *īlu*, 'god' (*cp.* BETHEL). The famous 'Tower of Babel' mentioned in the Bible is said to have been so called 'because the Lord did there confound the language of all the earth' (*Genesis* 11.9), but the writer of Genesis appears to have himself confused Hebrew *bavel* with *balol*, meaning 'to mingle', 'to cause confusion'. The Greek translators of the Septuagint (the Greek version of the Old Testament) made the same mistake, rendering this word as *sunkhusis*, 'mixture', 'confusion'. Despite the similarity, *Babel* and English *babble* are not related, the latter being simply an imitative word for confused or incoherent speech.

Bab el Mandeb The strait between the Red Sea and the Indian Ocean has an Arabic name, from *bāb al-mandab*, 'gate of the tears', from *bāb*, 'gate' (*cp.* BABEL and BABYLON), *al*, 'the' and *mandab*, 'tears', 'lamentations', the plural of *nadaba*, 'to weep'.

Babycham The proprietary brand of perry won many awards when it was first marketed in 1949, so that it was a 'baby champ'. This phrase was subsequently reinterpreted as 'baby chamois', and a stylized young chamois was devised to

43

advertise the drink pictorially. The name itself also happens to suggest 'champagne', of course.

Babylon The famous ancient city, once the capital of Babylonia, and now a site in Iraq 55 miles (88 km) south of Baghdad, has a name that is similar to that of the biblical BABEL. It thus derives from Akkadian *Bāb-ilān*, 'gate of the gods', from *bābu*, 'gate' and *ilān*, 'gods'. *See also* ZERUBBA-BEL.

Bacardi The brand of rum takes its name from the *Bacardi* family of distillers, active in Spain from the 17th century. The particular association is with Facundo *Bacardi* (1892–1932), who distilled rum in Cuba after the business moved there from Spain in 1862.

Bacchus The Roman god of wine, corresponding to the Greek Dionysus, has a name that is the Latin form of the Lydian name *Bakis*, which was both the epithet for Dionysos, his Greek equivalent, and the original of the Greek name for him, *Bakkhos*. It probably had no meaning as such, but simply represented a cry of joy at a Bacchanalian feast. The traditional corresponding Greek cry of this kind was *euoi*, rendered in Latin as *evoe!* An equivalent cry in modern times is the Scottish highland dancer's *hooch*, readily adopted in a bibulous setting.

Backhouse The name would have originally been that of a person who lived or worked at a bakehouse, or bakery.

Backs, The The collective name for the gardens of many Cambridge colleges relates to their location between the *backs* of the college and the river Cam. The term does not seem to be older than the 19th century.

Bacon The name originally applied to a person who sold cured pork, otherwise bacon.

Bactria The former region of central Asia, at present represented by the territory of Afghanistan, Pakistan and the former Soviet Central Asia, takes its name from the village that is now called *Balkh*, near Wazirabad in Afghanistan. The village name in turn is that of the river here, and is probably Persian in origin.

Badajoz The Spanish city, on the border with Portugal, has a name that derives from Arabic *badâhus*. This is not an Arabic word itself, however, and probably represents a name in some other language. Latin *battalia*, 'battle' or *Pax Augusta*, 'peace of Augustus' (*i.e.* the Roman emperor) have been proposed as the origin, though neither suggestion is very convincing.

Baden The former state of southwest Germany has a name that simply means 'baths', referring to the natural springs found here. It is now part of Baden-Württemberg. *Cp.* BADEN-BADEN and Britain's BATH.

Baden-Baden The spa town in southwest Germany, in the Black Forest, has a name that refers both to its own natural springs (German *Baden*, literally 'baths') and those of the district of *Baden*-Württemberg, formerly the state of BADEN, in which it is located. At the same time the name indicates that it is the *Baden* town of the name, as distinct from any other Baden with springs elsewhere in Germany. *See also* WÜRTTEMBERG.

Badminton School The Bristol public school for girls was founded in 1858 in *Badminton House*, a private house in Worcester Terrace, Clifton, and was originally known as *Badminton House School*. In 1921 it moved to larger premises in Westbury-on-Trym and simplified its name to *Badminton School*. The house was doubtless named for the famous *Badminton House* not far from Bristol, built in the village of Great *Badminton* in the 17th century for the Duke of Beaufort. The place-name itself means 'Beadumund's farmstead'. It was Badminton House that gave the name of the sport of *badminton*, where it is said to have been first played in about 1873. Appropriately, it is today one of those played at Badminton School.

Baffin Bay The inlet of the Atlantic between Greenland and Baffin Island, in the Canadian Arctic Archipelago, takes its name, as does the island, from the English explorer William *Baffin* (1584–1622), who carried out research here in 1614 in his quest for the Northwest Passage.

Bagamoyo The coastal town in Tanzania, north of Dar es-Salaam, has a name that has been derived from Swahili *bwaga-moyo*, translated as 'lay down the burden of your heart'. The name is said to have been given by caravan porters from the interior on reaching their destination.

Baghdad The historic city and capital of Iraq has an ancient pre-Islamic name that probably means 'gift of God', with *Bagh* related to Russian *bog*, 'god' and *dād* indirectly related to English *donor*. Marco Polo spelled the name *Baudac*. Another early spelling, *Baldac*, lies behind the name of the English town of BALDOCK, and the city also gave the name of the silk brocade now known as *baldachin* or *baldaquin*.

Bagheera The name of the black panther in Kipling's *Jungle Books* (1894, 1895) is based on Hindustani *bāgh*, 'tiger', of which it is, according to the author, 'a sort of diminutive'. The usual Hindustani word for 'panther' (or 'leopard') is *chītā* (English *cheetah*).

Baha'i The name is that of the Muslim 'splinter group' religion whose adherents hold that all religions are valid and that all scriptures are sacred. It derives from that of its founder, the Persian religious leader and former Shiite Muslim, Mīrzā Husayn ʿAli Allah (1817–1892), known as *Bahā*, 'glory of God'. Members of the faith are thus his followers.

Bahamas The Atlantic island group is popularly said to have a name that derives from Spanish *baja mar*, 'low sea', referring to the shallowness of the water here. It is more likely, however, that the present name represents the local name *Guanahani*, itself of uncertain origin.

Bahía Blanca The port in eastern Argentina takes its name from the bay at the head of which it stands. The bay in turn has a Spanish name meaning 'white bay', describing its light-coloured sands.

Bahrain The island group in the Persian Gulf has an Arabic name, representing *al-baḥrayn*, 'the two seas', from Arabic *al*, 'the' and *baḥrayn*, the dual form of *baḥr*, 'sea'. Bahrain lies in the middle of a bay on the southern coast of the Gulf, so that its 'two seas' lie respectively east and west of it.

Baia-Mare The town in northwest Romania has a name that literally translates as 'big bath', from Romanian *baie*, 'bath' and *mare*, 'big' (from Latin *magnus*). However, the reference is not to baths but to mines, and the city is noted for its lead and zinc smelting plants. This sense is confirmed by the town's Hungarian name, *Nagybánya*, from *nagy*, 'big' and *bánya*, 'mine'. The misinterpretation came about through confusion of the Hungarian word for 'mine' with the Romanian word for 'bath'.

Baikal The Russian lake is the largest freshwater lake in Asia and the deepest in the world. Its name is of Turkic origin, representing *bol*, 'rich' and *göl*, 'lake', referring to its abundance of fish, and especially sturgeon, which yield caviar.

Baile Átha Cliath The Irish name of DUBLIN means 'town of the hurdle ford'. Dublin is on the river Liffey, and the name refers to the woven withy-hurdles that were used to ford it in early times. The name is pronounced approximately 'Bla*cleeoo*'.

Bailey A person of the name would originally have been a steward or domestic official in a household, or else someone who lived by the outer wall of a castle. The first sense gave the English word *bailiff*, while *bailey* is a regular architectural term for the outermost wall or court of a castle. *See also* OLD BAILEY.

Bainbridge The surname derives from a place of this name in Yorkshire, a village on the river *Bain* near Hawes.

Baires *See* BUENOS AIRES.

Bakelite The patent thermosetting resin, the first synthetic plastic, takes its name from its inventor in 1909, the Belgian-born American chemist Leo *Baekeland* (1863–1944), with the suffix *-ite* denoting a commercial product. The name happens to suggest 'baked' and 'light', which is fortuitous for a substance made from a resin that sets solid when heated and that is lightweight as a finished product.

Baker The name means what it says, and would have originally applied to someone who baked bread, especially in the kitchen of a large house or castle. *Cp.* BAXTER.

Bakerloo Line The original name of the London Underground line, opened in 1906, was the *Baker Street and Waterloo Railway*. This was shortened to *Bakerloo*, combining parts of both names, by an *Evening News* journalist, and despite some protests was the name officially adopted by the railway company itself.

Baker Street The well-known London street was built on the estate of the Portman family in the mid-18th century and named for its builder, William *Baker*.

Baku The capital of Azerbaijan has a name that may derive from Old Persian *badkuba*, 'windward', referring to its exposed location on the west coast of the Caspian Sea.

Balaam In the Old Testament, the name is that of the soothsayer who was summoned by Balak, king of Moab, to curse the Israelites but who blessed them instead, on being reproached by his ass. His name represents Hebrew *Bilěam*, popularly interpreted as meaning 'destroyer of the people'.

Balaclava, Battle of The battle was an inconclusive engagement of the Crimean War in 1854 that included the ill-advised Charge of the Light Brigade, or attack of the British cavalry against Russian entrenched artillery. The town of *Balaclava*, near Sebastopol, Ukraine, has a name that has been derived from Turkish *balık*, 'fish' and *yuva*, 'nest', which would certainly be appropriate for this area of the Black Sea, which yields rich hauls of fish. But the second word of this derivation could hardly lead to the place-name in its present form, and like many places along this part of the coast the origin may actually be Greek, perhaps from a name such as *Palakion*, with the Turks interpreting this in their own way.

Balaton The large lake in western Hungary may have a name that is Slavic in origin, related to Russian *boloto*, 'marsh', 'swamp'. Although it is the largest lake in Europe, it is shallow in many places, with a maximum depth of only 35 feet.

Balboa The Panamanian port, at the Pacific end of the Panama Canal, takes its name from the Spanish explorer Vasco Núñez de *Balboa* (1475–1519), who sighted the Pacific 'standing on a peak in Darien' in 1513.

Balder The name is that of the best and wisest of the gods in Norse mythology, the favourite son of Odin (Woden) and Frigg. It represents the Norse name *Baldr*, related to Old English *bealdor*, 'lord', 'master', 'hero', from which modern English *bold* derives.

Baldock Unexpectedly, the Hertfordshire town has a name that derives from that of BAGHDAD. This came about when the town was founded in the 12th century by Knights Templars, who in their aim to preserve Christian shrines in the Middle East were familiar with the Arabian city under its medieval name of *Baldac*.

Baldwin The surname derives from a Germanic personal name comprising *bald*, 'bold' and *wine*, 'friend'. *Baldwin* of Boulogne was the first Christian king of Jerusalem in the 12th century. Baldwin is sometimes given as an English first name today.

Balearic Islands The Mediterranean group of islands, belonging to Spain, has a name that probably goes back to pre-Indoeuropean *bal*, 'shining', 'white', describing the islands' appearance. Some authorities, however, trace the name to a Phoenician word ultimately related to English *ballistics*, meaning 'island of slingers', referring to the way in which the inhabitants fought the Romans in the 2nd century BC by slinging stones at them.

Balfour The Scottish surname derives from one of the places so called in Scotland. The name itself means 'farm pasture', from Gaelic *baile*, 'house', 'farm' and *pór*, 'grass', 'pasture' (*cp*. Welsh *pawr*, 'grass').

Balkans The *Balkan* Peninsula, between the Adriatic, Aegean and Black Seas, has a name that probably goes back to Turkic *balkan*, 'mountain'. This would have referred to the highest mountain in the Balkan range, now Botev Peak, in Bulgaria.

Ball The surname originated as a nickname for a squat, dumpy person, or perhaps in some cases for someone who was bald. (The English word *bald* means literally 'balled', that is, someone having a round, ball-like patch on his head.) The name could also have denoted a person who lived by a round hill, for which the former word was also *ball*.

Balliol College The Oxford college takes its name from its founder in 1263, John de *Balliol* (d. 1269). His own name comes from one of the places called *Bailleul* in northern France, with the place-name itself probably deriving from Old French *baille*, 'fortification', from which English *bailey* evolved as a term for a castle's outer wall.

Balmoral The royal residence near Braemar, Scotland, takes its name from its locality. The name itself means 'homestead in the big clearing', comprising Gaelic *baile*, 'homestead' and *mór*, 'big' with British (Celtic) *ial*, 'clearing'. The same name, with the same meaning, exists elsewhere in Celtic regions, for example near Belfast in Northern Ireland.

Baloo The name of the 'sleepy brown bear' in Kipling's *Jungle Books* (1894, 1895) is simply the Hindustani word for 'bear', *bhālu*.

Balthazar The name is traditionally that of one of the Magi or Three Wise Men who brought gifts to the infant Jesus. The other two are CASPAR and MELCHIOR, although none of them is actually named in the Bible. The name itself is Akkadian in origin, from *Bēl-šarra-uzur*, 'may Bel protect the king', BEL being the god of the earth. Another form of the name does occur in the Bible, however, for *Belshazzar*, described in the Book of *Daniel* as the king of Babylon and son of Nebuchadnezzar (5.1,2). In point of fact the historical Belshazzar was the son of Nabonidus and never had the title of king. Even so, his name has exactly the same origin as that of Balthazar. When Daniel himself enters the service of King Nebuchadnezzar, his name is changed to *Belteshazzar*, 'protect the life of the king'.

Baltic The name of the northern sea and of the republics of Estonia, Latvia and Lithuania that lie on its shore is of uncertain origin. It may derive from a Lithuanian or Lettish word meaning 'white' (as for ALBION), or from a Slavic word meaning 'marsh' (as perhaps for Lake BALATON), or from a Danish word related to English *belt*. The last of these would refer to the strait formed by the Skagerrak and Kattegat, between Sweden and Denmark, at the southwestern end of the sea.

Baltimore The well-known city in Maryland takes its name from Cecilius Calvert, second Baron *Baltimore* (1605–1675), who in 1632 received the charter that granted him the possession of Maryland. The city was founded in 1729. Lord Baltimore's own title derives from the small port of this name in southern Ireland where the Calverts had their family seat. Its own name represents Irish *Baile na Tighe Mór*, 'townland of the big house'.

Baluchistan The region of southern Asia, in Iran and Pakistan, has an Urdu name meaning '*Baluchi* country', with the final *-stan* as for AFGHANISTAN. The Baluchi were the original inhabitants, with their own name coming from Urdu *balūĉ*, 'peak', as they were mountain dwellers.

Bamako The capital of Mali, West Africa, has a name that is said to represent Bambara *Bamma-ko*, 'behind *Bamma*', the latter being a personal name. Other sources, however, derive the name from *bamma-ko*, 'the crocodile affair', alluding to the custom, now happily defunct, of offering a live victim to the crocodiles of the Niger every year.

Bambi The popular Walt Disney cartoon film (1942) on the life of a deer was based on the book of the same name (1923) by the German author Felix Salten. The name of the deer is based on Italian *bambino*, 'baby'.

Bananarama The British all-girl vocal pop trio formed in London in 1981. That year they released their first single, a Caribbean tribal dance number called 'Aie A Mwana'. This suggested that they should call themselves *The Bananas*. They rejected the name, however, as being too unoriginal, and instead combined *Bananas* with the title of the Roxy Music hit 'Pyjamarama' (1973) to produce *Bananarama*.

Banat The historic region of east central Europe has a name based on Serbian *ban*, 'lord', referring to its governor in historic times.

Bancroft The name originally denoted a person who lived by a 'bean croft', or field where beans were grown.

Bancroft's School The public school at Woodford Green, Essex, takes its name from its founder in 1727, Francis *Bancroft*, who bequeathed his personal estate to the Worshipful Company of Drapers in London to endow almshouses for 24 old men, with a chapel and schoolroom for 100 poor boys and two dwelling-houses for masters. The school was originally at Mile End, but in 1884 transferred to Woodford Green.

Band, The The name is that of the most influential American rock group of the late 1960s and early 1970s. They made their solo debut in 1968 and gained their name when working as a backing band for Bob Dylan.

Band-Aid The proprietary surgical dressing, the American equivalent of ELASTOPLAST, is manufactured by the medical products company Johnson & Johnson. The idea for a 'home dressing' of this sort was put forward in 1920 by a newly married company employee, whose young wife kept cutting and burning herself in the kitchen. That same year, the company marketed its first Band-Aid dressings, with their name self-descriptive for a *band*age that was an *aid* in the home, and that was in the form of a *band* of adhesive surgical dressing.

Band Aid The charity project launched by the pop musician Bob Geldof in 1982 to raise funds for famine victims in Ethiopia was given a self-descriptive name, referring to the grouping of various pop musicians to form a *band* that would provide *aid* for the needy. At the same time the name was a direct echo of the commercial BAND-AID adhesive plaster.

Bandar-Log The name of the Monkey-People in Kipling's *Jungle Books* (1894, 1895) represents Hindustani *bandar*, 'monkey' and *log*, 'people'.

Bandar Seri Begawan The name of the capital of Brunei, formerly known as *Brunei Town*, was given it by Hassanal Bolkiah, Sultan of Brunei, in honour of his father, Sir Omar Ali Saifuddin (´Uma ´Ali Saif-ud-Din) (1918–1986), who abdicated in 1967 in favour of his son. *Bandar* is the Malay word for 'port', and *Seri Begawan* was the honorary title of the abdicating sultan, meaning 'illustrious', 'blessed'.

Bandoola The title of the book by Lieutenant-Colonel J.H. Williams, published in 1953, was the name of the elephant who was its subject. The book itself describes the animal's work on the construction of the Burma Road during the Second World War. The elephant was named for the Burmese general Maha *Bandula* (d. 1825), killed by the British in the first Anglo-Burmese War. Three years earlier Williams had published his popular *Elephant Bill*, the story of his work training elephants in Burma for use in war. The title of this was the nickname given to Williams himself.

B & Q The familiar 'do-it-yourself' furniture centres are named from the initials of Richard *B*lock and David *Q*uayle, who opened their first such centre in Southampton in 1969.

Bandung The city in southwest Java, Indonesia, has a name representing Malay *bandong*, 'embankment'.

Bangalore The city in southern India, west of Madras, has a name that is basically the same as that of BENGAL and BANGLADESH. Although some distance south of present Bengal, Bangalore arose in a region formerly inhabited by Bengali speakers.

Bangkok The name of the capital of Thailand means 'region of olive trees', from Thai *bāng*, 'region' and *kok*, 'olive tree'. The native name of Bangkok, however, is *Krung Thep*, 'city of angels', from Thai *krung*, 'city', 'capital' and *theph*, 'angel'. This name had been applied descriptively to the former capital, *Ayutthaya*. An alternative name is *Phra Nakhon*, from *phra*, 'god', 'lord', an honorific title, and *nakhon*, 'city'. The official abbreviated (*sic*) Thai name of Bangkok is as follows: *krungtheph-phramahanakhon bowonratanakosin mahintharayuthaya mahadilokphiphobnobpharad radchataniburirom udomsantisug*. The lengthy full name can be rendered in English as follows: 'city of gods, the great city, the residence of the Emerald Buddha, the impregnable city (of Ayutthaya) of the god Indra, the grand capital of the world endowed with nine precious gems, the happy city abounding in enormous royal palaces which resemble the heavenly abode wherein dwell the reincarnated gods, a city given by Indra and built by Vishnukarm'.

Bangladesh The Asian country is surrounded on three sides by India and bounded to the south by the Bay of Bengal. Its name is Bengali for 'Bengali country', from *bāṅglā*, 'Bengali' and *deś*, 'country'. *Cp.* BENGAL.

Bangles, The The American folk-rock band, formed as an all-girl group in Los Angeles in 1981, initially performed as *The Supersonic Bangs*. They then shortened this name to *The Bangs*, but were obliged to alter it to *The Bangles* the following year on learning that a New Jersey group was already recording as *The Bangs*.

Bangor The town in North Wales arose as a monastic establishent and has a name directly derived from Welsh *bangor*, a term for the upper row of rods in a wattle fence, and hence the enclosure of a monastery. The town of *Bangor* in Northern Ireland arose as a daughter foundation of the Welsh monastery, and is named after it.

Bangui The capital of the Central African Republic has a name of local (Bobangui) origin meaning 'the rapids'. The town was founded in 1889 beside the highest rapids of the river UBANGI.

Banjul The capital of Gambia, western Africa, has a native name that arose from a misunderstanding. When the first Portuguese colonists discovered this part of Africa in the 15th century, they asked local people what it was called. The inhabitants took the question to be 'What are you making?' and replied *'Bangjulo'*, 'rope matting'. The Portuguese duly transcribed this as the name of the region.

Banks A person of this name would have been someone living by a hillside or river bank. The final *-s* does not necessarily denote a plural, but more probably a possessive, as if a 'bank's' dweller.

Banks Island The island of northern Canada, in the Northwest Territories, was so named in honour of the British naturalist Sir Joseph *Banks* (1743–1820), President of the Royal Society and a member of Cook's voyage round the world on board the *Endeavour*.

Bannockburn, Battle of The famous battle, in which the Scots under Robert the Bruce defeated the English under Edward II in 1314, takes its name from the stream

near Stirling where it took place, the *Bannock Burn*. The stream name itself means 'white stream', from the Celtic words *ban oc*. There is no connection between the name and the type of oatmeal cake known as a 'bannock'.

Banquo The name of the Scottish general whose ghost haunts Macbeth in Shakespeare's play is probably of Celtic origin, from Gaelic *bàn-chu*, 'white dog'. But he is not a historical character, and Shakespeare seems to have chosen his name for its association with *banquet*, since it is in the banquet scene that he appears.

Bantu The *Bantu* languages, spoken widely in Africa south of the Sahara, have a name that means 'the men', 'the people', as the plural of *muntu*. The root word *ntu*, 'man', takes the prefix *mu-* in the singular, *ba-* in the plural. The name was adopted for the family of languages in 1862 by the German-South African philologist Wilhelm Bleek.

Baptists The religious sect originated in the 17th century as a group of English Protestant Dissenters who had taken refuge in the Netherlands. The name refers to their practice of baptizing believers by total immersion, unlike the more symbolic sprinkling of water on the forehead adopted by most western Christian churches. They were originally known by their opponents as *Anabaptists*, literally 'those who baptize again', since most of their converts were adults who had already been conventionally baptized as children.

Barabbas In the Bible, the name is familiar as that of the criminal, doubtless a rebel leader, whom the Jewish crowd persuaded Pontius Pilate to set free so that the punishment due to him would be inflicted on Jesus instead. In origin it is Aramaic for 'son of the father', from *bar*, 'son' and *abbā*, 'father'.

Barbados The Caribbean island has a Spanish name meaning 'bearded', from *barbados*, plural of *barbado*. The name was given by 16th-century Spanish explorers for the beard-like leaves or trails of moss on the fig trees that grew abundantly here.

Barbara The name ultimately goes back to the feminine form of Greek *barbaros*, 'foreign', so means 'foreign woman'. It became familiar from stories about St *Barbara*, said to have been murdered by her father, who was then struck dead by lightning. But she may well never have existed.

Barbarians The rugby union touring club was formed in Bradford in 1890 and was so named for its 'invasion' of the territory of existing northern rugby clubs. The club are popularly known as the *Baa-Baas*, a name that belies their often aggressive style of play.

Barbarossa The title or nickname, Italian for 'red beard', was that given the 12th-century Holy Roman emperor Frederick I, who subsequently became a legendary hero and symbol of unity for the Germans. In the Second World War, Operation *Barbarossa* was the German code name for the plan to invade the Soviet Union in 1941. (There may also have been a more subtle allusion to 'singeing the beard' of the 'Reds', or Communists.)

Barbary Coast The name is that of the Mediterranean coast of North Africa inhabited by BERBERS. The people's own name was assimilated to Greek *barbaros*, 'foreign', 'ignorant', a term applied to those who spoke a different language and who therefore 'babbled' or were 'barbarians'.

Barber The surname is self-explanatory, and was originally used for a person who was a barber. In medieval times this would have been not just someone who cut hair and shaved beards but who also pulled teeth and carried out rather basic surgery, including phlebotomy (blood-letting). The red stripe on the barber's pole still found outside some men's hairdressers is said to refer to the latter practice.

Barbican The London *Barbican* in its present form is a group of high-rise apartment blocks grouped round the *Barbican* Centre, a large building opened in 1982 as a major cultural and exhibition complex. The location is just outside the historic City of London, and takes its name from a former street here that was itself named for a watch-tower in the city walls. The word *barbican* derives from medieval Latin *barbacana*, itself of unknown origin. A proposed ultimate origin in Arabic *bāb*, 'gate' (*cp*. BABYLON) has yet to be supported.

The fact that Latin *barba cana* means 'grey beard' is purely coincidental!

Barbizon School The name is that of a group of French painters of landscapes in the 1840s, including Rousseau, Corot and Millet. They took it from *Barbizon*, the village near Paris where they regularly met. The village name itself represents a Roman personal name, *Barbatius*, 'bearded one'.

Barbour The fashionable jackets take their name from John *Barbour* (1849–1918), a South Shields draper who began selling 'wet weather wear' to visiting seamen in this north of England port in the 1890s.

Barcelona The famous Spanish city is said to take its name from the Carthaginian general Hamilcar *Barca*, its traditional founder in the 3rd century BC. *See* HAMILCAR BARCA for the meaning of his name.

Barclays Bank The British bank was founded by John Freame in Lombard Street, London in 1692. It takes its name from James *Barclay*, who joined the business as a partner in 1736 and who went on to marry Freame's sister.

Barebones Parliament The parliament summoned by Oliver Cromwell in 1653 to replace the Rump Parliament was nicknamed for one of its leading members, Praise-God *Barbon* (1596–1679).

Barents Sea The sea of the Arctic Ocean, north of northwest Russia, is named for Willem *Barents* (or *Barentsz*) (1550–1597), the Dutch explorer who sought a northern passage here between the Atlantic and the Pacific.

Bari The port in southeast Italy has a name deriving from Latin and Greek *baris*, a word of Egyptian origin meaning 'boat'.

Barker The surname originally described a person who tanned leather, using tree-bark in the process.

Barmecide The name is familiar in literature from the prince in the *Arabian Nights* who serves empty plates to beggars, claiming that they are full of sumptuous food. The *Barmecides* or *Barmekids* were a priestly family of Persian origin descended from a *Barmak*, a high priest in the Buddhist temple at Nawbahar. His title represents

Arabic *barmok*, 'high priest'. A 'Barmecide feast' is now an expression for an imaginary banquet.

Barnabas The biblical name derives from Aramaic *barnĕbhŭʾāh*, literally 'son of consolation'. In the New Testament, Barnabas is one of the apostles, and a companion of St Paul.

Barnard College The college of Columbia University, New York, was founded in 1889 and became part of the university in 1900 as a liberal arts college for women, with Columbia College the corresponding college for men. It is named for the American educator and commissioner of education Henry *Barnard* (1811–1900).

Barnardos The voluntary organization that runs homes, schools and other centres for orphans and deprived children, including those with physical and mental handicaps, takes its name from its founder in 1867, the British philanthropist Thomas John *Barnardo* (1845–1905). The organization was formerly known as *Dr Barnardo's Homes* although Barnardo was not medically qualified.

Barnes The district of Richmond, Greater London, has a name that means what it says, referring to a settlement that arose by a *barn* or barns. The earliest records of the name are in the singular, as in the Domesday Book, where the place appears as *Berne*.

Barnsley The Yorkshire town has a name that means '*Beorn*'s clearing'. It is not known who Beorn was, but his name was probably a short form of a longer name such as *Beornwulf*, comprising Old English *beorn*, 'man', 'warrior' and *wulf*, 'wolf'. *Cp.* BERMONDSEY.

Baroda The city in western India has a name representing Sanskrit *vaṭodar*, from *vaṭa*, 'banyan' (a kind of large fig tree). Since 1976 the city has been known as *Vadodara*, a spelling more accurately reflecting the Sanskrit original.

Barrett The surname is either a form of BERNARD or else arose as a nickname for a deceitful or quarrelsome person, from a former English word *barat* to which modern *barter* is related.

Barry The name is an English form of the Irish name *Barra*, a short form of *Fionnbarr*, 'fair-headed'.

Barsac The sweet white wine takes its name from the French town of *Barsac* in the Gironde, its place of origin. The town's own name derives from a Gaulish personal name, *Barcios*.

Bartholomew The name is Aramaic in origin, meaning 'son of *Talmai*', and is familiar in the Bible as that of one of the 12 apostles. Some biblical scholars identify Bartholomew with Nathaniel, so that it is simply a byname describing his parentage. There are characters named Talmai in the Old Testament, but not in the New.

Baruch In the Bible, the name is that of a disciple of the prophet Jeremiah. His name is Hebrew, meaning 'blessed', so corresponds to BENEDICT. The book of *Baruch* in the Apocrypha is attributed in the text to this same man.

Basel The Roman name of the well-known Swiss city was *Basilia*, from the Greek *basileia*, 'royal' (which also gave the personal name BASIL). The town was founded in 44 AD, originally with the Roman name *Robur*, from Latin *roburetum*, 'oak grove'. It was renamed *Basel* in 374, when it became the fortress of the Roman emperor Valentinian I. The French form of the name is *Bâle*, and an older form of this, *Basle*, is still sometimes used in English.

BASIC The computer-programming language, developed in 1964, has an acronymic name standing for '*B*eginner's *A*ll-purpose *S*ymbolic *I*nstruction *C*ode'. The language is relatively easy to learn, or 'basic', as the acronym implies.

Basic English The name is that of a simplified form of English devised by the English scholar C.K. Ogden in the 1920s and 1930s as an international auxiliary language. Although it is genuinely 'basic', with a vocabulary of only 850 words, its name is also designed as an acronym for '*B*ritish, *A*merican, *S*cientific, *I*nternational, *C*ommercial'.

Basil The name is Greek in origin, from *basileios*, 'royal', a word that also gave English *basilica*. It was popularized by St *Basil* the Great, the 4th-century theologian who

51

is regarded as one of the Fathers of the Orthodox Church. St Basil's Cathedral is one of the best known in Moscow.

Basildon Bond The brand of stationery, manufactured by DRG, was first produced in 1911 by a firm taken over in 1918 by John Dickinson (the 'D' of *DRG*). The name was adopted from that of *Basildon*, a village near Pangbourne, Berkshire, since this was felt to alliterate well with *bond*, as a term for a superior type of strong white paper.

Basingstoke The *-stoke* of the name of the Hampshire town represents Old English *stoc*, meaning 'place', but implying a place that was dependent on another. Basingstoke's name thus shows that it was originally dependent on *Basing*, now a much smaller place and an eastern extension of Basingstoke itself, although originally a separate village. Its own name means 'people of *Basa*', the Anglo-Saxon who would have held the land here.

Basque The people who inhabit a region of the western Pyrenees in northern Spain and southern France have a name that comes from Basque *euskara* or *eskuara*. This contains a basic root *sk* which is believed to relate to sea-dwelling peoples or sailors, and which is also found in the name of the *Etruscan* people (*see* ETRURIA). The Roman name for the Basque Country was *Vasconia*, with the same origin.

Basra Iraq's principal port, in the Shatt-al Arab delta, has an Arabic name, from *al-baṣrah*, 'the soft', with reference to the soft soil here. The name is said by some to have given the English word *alabaster*, although *Alabastron*, an Egyptian town, also has this claim.

Bass The well-known make of beer takes its name from William *Bass* (1717–1787), a carrier of Burton-on-Trent, who in 1777 turned his hand to brewing the beer that he had formerly been transporting, at the same time transferring his carrier business to Pickfords.

Basse-Terre The capital of Guadeloupe, in the West Indies, has a French name meaning 'low land'. This refers to its location below the dormant volcano of Soufrière. The name is also that of the whole island on which the capital lies, with Guade-loupe's other main island, its twin to the east, being *Grande Terre*, 'great land'. The island of *Basse Terre* is actually the more mountainous of the two.

Bastille The notorious fortress in Paris was used for centuries as a state prison until it was stormed and destroyed by the mob in the Revolution of 1789. Its name is an alteration of Provençal *bastide*, in turn from Old French *bastir*, 'to build', to which English *bastion* is related. It was thus originally simply a 'building'.

Basutoland *See* LESOTHO.

Batavia The ancient district of the Netherlands, on an island at the mouth of the Rhine, takes its name from the *Batavi*, the people who inhabited it. Their own name may derive from Old German *bata*, 'better'. It was this *Batavia* that gave the former name (until 1949) of JAKARTA.

Bateman's The house at Burwash, Sussex, the former home of Rudyard Kipling, takes its name from the owner of a local forge for whom it was originally built in 1634.

Bates The name means 'son of *Bate*', this being a diminutive of BARTHOLOMEW.

Bath The historic English city has a name that refers directly to its Roman *baths*, famous for their warm springs. The Roman name of Bath was first *Aquae Calidae*, 'warm waters', then *Aquae Sulis*, 'waters of Sulis', the latter being the name of a pagan god. A former Anglo-Saxon name for Bath was *Akemanchester*, still found in the Roman road *Akeman Street*, which leads to Bath. This probably evolved from *Aquae*, but came to be popularly understood as 'aching man's town', for the rheumatic sufferers who went to Bath for treatment in the waters.

Bath, Order of the The British order of knighthood, believed to have been founded in the early 15th century, in the reign of Henry IV, is so named from the symbolic bathing required of new knights before the award was conferred.

Bath Oliver The type of unsweetened biscuit takes its name from William *Oliver* (1695–1764), a physician at BATH who is said to have invented it, presumably for its nutritional or dietetic properties.

Bathsheba The name is familiar in the Bible as that of the wife of Uriah who commits adultery with King David and subsequently marries him. It is Hebrew in origin, meaning either 'seventh daughter' or 'daughter of the oath' (*cp.* BEERSHEBA). Despite her transgression, Bathsheba's name was adopted by some English Puritans in the 17th century by virtue of the fact that she was 'very beautiful to look upon' (2 *Samuel* 11.2).

Baton Rouge The state capital of Louisiana has a name that is French for 'red stick'. This may have originally been the name of an Indian chief. An alternative account, however, tells how 17th-century French colonists set up a red pole here, like an Indian totem pole, to mark the boundary between their territory and that of the native Indians.

Batsford The surname derives from a place of this name in Gloucestershire, a village near Moreton-in-Marsh. The place-name itself means '*Bæcci*'s slope', with the second part of the name (from Old English *ōra*) influenced by the word *ford*.

Battenberg This was the original name of the *Mountbattens*, the British branch of the family founded by Prince Alexander of Hesse, who in 1851 morganatically married a Polish countess, Julia Therese von Haucke. The long extinct title of the medieval countship of *Battenberg*, taken from the German village of this name near Marburg, in Hessen, was then revived for her. In 1917, as a response to anti-German sentiment, the British Battenbergs changed their name to Mountbatten, a half translation of the original name, which may mean 'water-meadow hill'. The kind of cake known as *Battenberg* appears to be named directly from the village.

Battersea Although the district of London lies by the south bank of the Thames, its name has nothing to do with 'sea'. It was originally '*Beaduric*'s island', with this personal name and its possessive *s* followed by Old English *ēg*, 'island'. The 'island' would have been higher land by marshy ground here. BERMONDSEY has a similar name.

Battle The Sussex town was founded by William the Conqueror, who named it to mark his victory in the *Battle* of Hastings (1066). This was actually fought here at Senlac, some distance from Hastings itself.

Battle Symphony Beethoven's Op 91 (1813) is a piece of programme music designed to represent Wellington's defeat of Napoleon's troops at Vitoria, Spain, that same year. It includes the well-known melodies of *Rule, Britannia!*, *Malbrouck s'en va-t-en guerre* (more familiar as the almost identical 'For he's a jolly good fellow'), and *God Save the King*. Beethoven dedicated his composition to the Prince Regent.

Batumi The city in Georgia is a major Black Sea port. Its name is said to derive from that of the river *Bathus* in Colchis (the ancient country here). The river's own name is Greek and means 'deep', a word that could equally apply to the gulf of the Black Sea on which Batumi itself stands.

Bat Yam The coastal city in Israel, a suburb of Tel Aviv, has a name that represents Hebrew *bat yam*, 'daughter of the sea', from *bat*, 'daughter' (*cp.* Arabic *bint*) and *yam*, 'sea' (*cp.* EL FAIYÛM).

Bauhaus The German school of architecture and design was founded in 1919 by the architect Walter Gropius. Its name is not a regular German word, but was formed by inverting the two halves of *Hausbau*, 'building of a house' so that the word meant 'house of building', in other words a school of architecture.

Baule The name of the native inhabitants of Côte d'Ivoire (formerly Ivory Coast) means 'the child is dead', from Baule *ba*, 'child' and *uli*, 'he has died'. The story goes that when the people first came to settle here, from eastern Africa, their queen, who led them, had to sacrifice one of her children in order to cross a river.

Bavaria The German administrative region is named for the *Boii*, a Celtic tribe who formerly lived here, with the latter part of the name representing Germanic *warjan*, 'to defend' (related to English *warrior*). The German name for Bavaria is *Bayern*, with the same origin. *Cp.* BOHEMIA.

Baxter The surname was originally the feminine form of *baker*, with the suffix the same as that in the still feminine *spinster*.

Bayard The name was that of the legendary magic horse given by Charlemagne to Rinaldo, the eldest and most important of the noblemen known as the 'Four Sons of Aymon'. The horse's name is French for 'bay'.

Bay City Rollers The Scottish pop group, formed in 1969, are said to have created their name when a pin stuck at random into a map of the United States by their manager, Tam Paton, landed on *Bay City*, Utah. *Rollers*, while obviously referring to rock 'n' roll, emphasized that the group differed from the already established ROLLING STONES.

Bayeux Tapestry The famous tapestry, depicting and describing the invasion of England by William the Conqueror, takes its name from the northern French town where it was probably woven and where it has been on display since the 15th century. The name of the town itself derives from the Celtic people known as the *Baiocasses* or *Badiocasses*, based on the Celtic word *badio*, 'victory'. By coincidence Bayeux was the first town in western Europe to be liberated by the Allies at the end of the Second World War.

Bayonne The port in southwest France has a name that derives from Low Latin *baia*, 'bay' and Basque *on*, 'good'. It was this town that gave the name of the *bayonet*, said to have been first made here in the early 17th century.

Bayreuth The German town, in BAVARIA, has a name deriving from Old German *Baierrute*, from *Baier*, 'Bavarian' and *riuti*, 'to clear', meaning 'place cleared by the Bavarians'. The town is famous for its opera festivals. These arose from the Festival Theatre set up by Wagner, who lived here in a house named *Wahnfried*, 'illusion of peace'.

Beach Boys The American pop group took a name to reflect the leisurely 'sun, sand and surf' lifestyle of California, where it was formed in 1961.

Beach-la-Mar The name of the English-based creole language spoken in Vanuatu and Fiji is a corruption of French *bêche-de-mer*, 'trepang'. This sea cucumber is a major local trading commodity, and Beach-la-Mar is essentially a language for trading and negotiation between different races. The French word has been distorted so as to suggest English *beach*.

Beachy Head The name of the famous chalk headland on the Sussex coast seems to suggest a beach. But it is actually a corruption of French *beau chef*, 'beautiful headland', to which English *head* was tautologically added when the first part of the name was no longer understood. The name was given by the Normans, who must have regarded the white headland as an excellent landmark when crossing the English Channel.

Beaker Folk The name is used of the prehistoric people, thought to be of Iberian origin, who spread over Europe in the 2nd millennium BC. It relates to the distinctive earthenware *beakers* found among their remains.

Beamish The surname is Norman in origin, denoting a person from either *Beaumais* or *Beaumetz* in northern France, the former near Caen, the latter near Arras. The name itself means 'beautiful dwelling', and gave the name of the Durham village of *Beamish*, near Stanley. Some bearers of the name could equally have come from there.

Beard A person with this surname would have had a distinctive beard, unlike most people, who in much of Europe were clean-shaven in medieval times, except in Jewish communities.

Bear Symphony Haydn's Symphony No 82 in C major (1786) is so nicknamed either because the theme of the finale suggests the performance of a bear leader or because the 'growling' theme of the same movement evokes the the sound of a bear.

Beat Generation The name is that of the *beatniks* of the 1950s and 1960s, who rejected the social and political conventions of their time in favour of communal living, drugs, and a general anarchic approach to life. Their leaders included the American writer Jack Kerouac, who is credited with inventing the name. In an interview, however, he linked the term *beat* specifically with 'beatitude' rather than 'beat up', since he held that the movement had a religious basis.

Beatles The famous British pop group, formed in Liverpool in 1959, evolved a name that was obviously based on *beat* in its musical sense but that equally evoked associations with the BEAT GENERATION, then at its height. At the same time it developed from an earlier name, the *Silver Beatles*, that is said to have been inspired by the *Crickets* (*see* HOLLIES), a group formed three years previously.

Beaton The name is of Norman origin, denoting a person originally from *Béthune* in northeast France. The place-name itself derives from the Germanic personal name *Betto*.

Beatrice In literature, the name is famous as that of Dante's beloved, who guides him through Paradise in the *Divine Comedy*. It derives from Latin *beatrix*, 'she who makes happy', from *beatus*, 'happy', 'blessed'. Some authorities trace the Latin name back to an earlier *viatrix*, 'voyager', as if describing someone on her journey through life, especially as a Christian. This would be equally appropriate for Dante's Beatrice.

Beaufort Sea The sea, in the Arctic Ocean north of Alaska, is named for the British admiral Sir Francis *Beaufort* (1774–1857), hydrographer to the Royal Navy. He also gave his name to the *Beaufort* Scale for measuring wind speeds, which he devised.

Beaujolais Famous for its red wine, the region of Burgundy, in France, takes its name from the small town of *Beaujeu*. The Roman name of the town was *Bellojocum*, from *bellus*, 'beautiful' and *jugum*, 'mountain', but with the latter word altered as if from *jocus*, 'joke'.

Beaumont The surname is a Norman one, denoting someone from one of a number of places so called in northern France. The name itself means 'beautiful hill'. There are one or two places in England called *Beaumont*, with the same meaning, and the surname could equally derive from one of these.

Beauvais The city of northern France, with the tallest cathedral in the country, has a name that derives from the *Bellovaci*, the Gaulish tribe who once inhabited the region. Its Roman name was *Caesaromagus*,

'Caesar's market', a name also given by the Romans to CHELMSFORD in England.

Becher's Brook The formidable Grand National jump is named for Captain Martin Henry *Becher* (1797–1864), a noted rider of his day, who with his horse fell here in the first Grand National in 1839.

Bechuanaland *See* BOTSWANA.

Beckenham The Kent town is not named for its becks or beeches, as sometimes suggested, but has a name that means '*Beohha*'s village', the latter part of the name being Old English *hām*.

Bedales The public school near Petersfield, Hampshire, famous as the first coeducational boarding school, takes its name from the large Victorian house near Haywards Heath, Sussex, in which it was originally founded in 1893 by J.H. Badley. The house was named for land nearby, itself at one time belonging to a *beadle*. The name of the school thus only coincidentally suggests that of its founder.

Bede, Venerable The great 8th-century English theologian and historian has a name that in Old English was *Bēda*, deriving from *bedu*, 'asking', 'prayer'. (The word gave modern English *bid* and *bead*. Beads were originally used for counting prayers before their adoption as ornaments.) The name was more than appropriate for Bede, who entered the local monastery in what is now Sunderland at the age of seven, and who spent his whole life as a priest and teacher. His title of *Venerable* may have been taken from the Latin couplet on the stand that supports his shrine in Durham Cathedral: *Haec sunt in fossa/Bedae venerabilis ossa* ('These bones in the grave are of the worthy Bede').

Bedford The English town has a name that means '*Bēda*'s ford'. It is not known who Bēda was, but he has the same name as the Venerable BEDE. For a town at an important road and river crossing, it is strange that Bedford never acquired a more 'urban' name, ending for example in *-ton* or *-ham*.

Bedford College The college of London University was founded in 1849 to give women a liberal education, and took its name from its original site in *Bedford*

Square. It moved to Regent's Park in 1913 (*see* REGENT'S COLLEGE) and in 1984 merged with the ROYAL HOLLOWAY COLLEGE to become *Royal Holloway and Bedford New College*, a name that presumably will be abbreviated in due course.

Bedlam The name was that of the oldest mental hospital in Europe, opened in London in the 14th century. It arose as a corruption of the full name, the *Bethlehem Royal Hospital*, so called as it had developed from the priory founded a century earlier for the sisters and brethren of the order of the Star of *Bethlehem*. The word *bedlam* later entered the language as a colloquial term to mean 'uproar', 'noisy confusion', with reference to the disturbed behaviour of the inhabitants. The hospital still exists, now as the *Bethlem Royal Hospital* in Beckenham, Kent.

Bedlington The breed of terrier, with its short body, long legs, and curly hair, takes its name from the town of *Bedlington*, Northumberland, where it was developed in the early 19th century.

Bedouin The nomadic people of Arabia and North Africa have an Arabic name, from *badāwīn*, the plural of *badāwī*, 'desert-dweller', from the root word *badw*, 'desert'.

Beecham The surname is an English spelling of the Norman name *Beauchamp*, used for a person who had come from a place so called in northern France. The name itself means 'beautiful field'.

Beecham's Pills The proprietary remedy took its name from Thomas *Beecham* (1820–1907), a chemist who began selling his famous pills in Wigan, Lancashire in 1850. His grandson was Sir Thomas *Beecham* (1879–1961), the well-known orchestral conductor.

Beefeaters The colloquial name of the Yeoman Warders of the Tower of London means what it says, with *beefeater* a historic nickname for a well-fed servant. A popular etymology derives the name from a spurious French word *buffetier*, said to relate to *buffet*, 'sideboard'. But no such word exists, and this is an attempt to find a learned explanation for a sense that is actually straightforward.

Beefsteak Club The London club, established in 1876, arose from the *Beef-Steak Society* that was founded in 1735 so that 24 men of noble birth could meet weekly for a beef-steak dinner.

Bee Gees, The The British-born pop trio, comprising Barry Gibb and his twin brothers Maurice and Robin, emigrated to Australia with their parents in 1958. They are said to have received their name from the initials of *B*ill *G*ates, who discovered them there when they were singing to raise cash by a speedway track. At the same time, and more probably, the initials stood simply for '*B*rothers *G*ibb'. They returned to England in 1967.

Beelzebub The name of the god of the Philistines (2 *Kings* 1.2) was interpreted by St Jerome in the 4th century as meaning 'lord of the flies', from Hebrew *ba'al zĕbhŭbh*, and this has remained the traditionally accepted origin to the present time, when it was popularized in its biblical sense by the title of William Golding's novel *Lord of the Flies* (1954). In this particular interpretation, the name doubtless indicated that the god was believed to offer protection from fly-borne diseases. In the New Testament, too, Beelzebub is referred to more generally as the 'prince of the devils' (*Mark* 3.22) and the name came to be adopted for that of the Devil himself. In recent years, however, other origins have been proposed for the name. They include a corruption of Greek *diabolos*, 'devil', so that *Beelzebub* means 'BAAL the devil', and a derivation in the Hebrew verb *zabal*, 'to drive out unclean spirits', in which case *Beelzebub* means 'lord of the filth' rather than 'lord of the flies'. No doubt the actual meaning is something of a blend of all three senses.

Beersheba The Israeli city has a Hebrew name meaning either 'well of the oath' or 'well of the seven', from *be'er*, 'well' (as for BEIRUT) and either *šavóaʿ* , 'to swear' or *šévaʿ* , 'seven', as for BATHSHEBA. Both interpretations are alluded to in the Bible. The Old Testament tells of an oath and a covenant between Abraham and Abimelech regarding a well, 'therefore the name of the city is Beersheba unto this day' (*Genesis* 26.33). But a parallel account, referring to the same covenant, has Abraham giving Abimelech seven lambs (*Genesis* 21.28).

Bee's Wedding, The The fanciful nickname of Mendelssohn's SONGS WITHOUT WORDS No 34 in C Major (1845) for piano derives from the 'busy' nature of the music, which equally suggests undulating 'buzzing' to some. The piece is also known as *Spinnerlied* ('Spinning Song').

Beijing The official name of the capital of China, still better known as PEKING, derives from Chinese *bĕi*, 'north' and *jīng*, 'capital', so that it is the 'northern capital', as distinct from NANKING, the 'southern capital'. It has been the capital continuously from 1421 except for the period from 1928 to 1949, when Nanking was the capital. It was then known as *Peiping*, from Chinese *bĕi*, 'north' and *píng*, 'peace', so that it was 'peace of the north'. It had also borne this name much earlier, from 1368 to 1416, under the first Ming dynasty. Before that, in the 13th century, it was *Khanbalik*, 'city of the khan', a name recorded by Marco Polo as *Cambaluc*.

Beira The name of the port in eastern Mozambique was given by Portuguese colonists for their own native province of *Beira*, in central Portugal. The name itself means 'riverside', from Portuguese *ribeira*, 'river'. The Portuguese province is crossed by the Douro, Tagus, Mondego and many other rivers. The Mozambiquan port is on the Mozambique Channel at the mouth of two smallish rivers.

Beirut The Lebanese capital has a Hebrew name that means 'the wells', from *beʾrōt*, the plural of *bᵉʾer*, 'well' (*cp.* BEERSHEBA). Before Roman times, wells were the only source of water in this region.

Bejaia The name of the seaport in northeast Algeria is possibly a corruption of Arabic *baqāyā*, 'survivors', as the plural of *baqayya*. The French form of the name is *Bougie*, and the town's manufacture and export of wax and candles gave *bougie* as the standard French word for 'candle'.

Bejam The familiar freezer centres have a name that represents the family of the man who introduced them in 1968. He was John Apthorp (1935–), so that *B* is for *B*rian his brother, *e* is for *E*ric his father, *ja* is for *J*ohn *A*pthorp himself, and *m* is for both

*M*ildred his mother and *M*arion his sister. A genuine family business, therefore.

Bekaa The name of the valley in central Lebanon derives from Arabic *al-biqāʿ*, 'the lands', from *al*, 'the' and *biqāʿ*, the plural of *buqʿa*, 'earth', 'land', 'field', 'country'.

Bel In Assyrian and Babylonian mythology, *Bel* is the god of the world. He is mentioned in the Bible, and is named in one of the books of the Apocrypha, *Bel and the Dragon*. In origin, his name is the same as that of BAAL, so means 'master', 'lord'. His name also appears in those of BALTHAZAR and BEELZEBUB.

Belarus *See* BYELORUSSIA.

Belém The Brazilian port arose in 1616 as a fortified settlement that came to have the Portuguese name *Nossa Senhora de Belém do Grão Pará*, 'Our Lady of Bethlehem of the Great Pará', and derives its present name as a shortening of this. The *Pará* is the river on which it stands, and its name is today also sometimes used for the city.

Belfast The capital of Northern Ireland has an Irish name, *Béal Feirste*, meaning 'ford-mouth of the sandbank'. The sandbank is the one that formerly existed at the point where the river Farset (itself named for the sandbank) joined the Lagan, just below Queen's Bridge. At low tide the river could be forded here. The ford fell out of use only when Long Bridge was built over the Lagan.

Belfort The fortress town in eastern France has a name that translates as 'fine fort'. The ancient castle stands on a rocky site between the Vosges and Jura mountains with a panoramic view over the surrounding historic *Territoire de Belfort*.

Belgium The European country takes its name from the *Belgae*, the people who inhabited Gaul in Roman times. Their own name may derive either from Gaulish *volca*, 'swift', 'active', or from an Indoeuropean root *bhelgh* meaning 'swell in anger', referring to the belligerent nature of the tribe. The same root word also probably gave English *bellow*, *bellows*, *belly* and *billow*, and perhaps originally Latin *bellum*, 'war'.

Belgorod The Ukrainian town north of Kharkov has a name that means 'white city', from Russian *belyy*, 'white' and *gorod*, 'town', 'city'. The name is found elsewhere in Russia and in Slavic countries generally (*see* BELGOROD-DNESTROVSKY and BEL-GRADE). A 'white' city may be named as much for the colour of its buildings as for its location by a river. For further considerations of the particular sense, *see* BYELORUSSIA.

Belgorod-Dnestrovsky The Ukrainian port has a basic name meaning 'white city' (*see* BELGOROD), with *Dnestrovsky* referring to the location of this particular Belgorod on the river DNIESTER. The city formerly belonged to Moldavia, when it had the equivalent name of *Cetatea albă*, 'the white city', from Romanian *cetate*, 'city', with the feminine definite article suffix -*a*, and *albă*, 'white', the feminine of *alb*. In 1484 it was conquered by the Turks, who named it identically *Akkerman*, from Turkish *ak*, 'white' and *kerman*, 'fort'. The city kept this name until as recently as 1944. *Cp*. the name of INKERMAN.

Belgrade The capital of Serbia, and formerly of Yugoslavia as a whole, has a Serbian name meaning 'white city', from *beo*, 'white' (related to the name of ALBION) and *grad*, 'city' (as in VOLGOGRAD). The original 'white city' was the stone fortress built by the Celts here in the 4th century BC.

Belgravia The prestigious district of London takes its name from *Belgrave* Square, in turn named for the estate of *Belgrave* in Cheshire. This belonged to the Dukes of Westminster, who owned much of modern Belgravia. The Cheshire place has a name that was originally recorded in the Domesday Book as *Merdegrave*. This was taken to be French for 'dung grove', so was changed to *Belgrave*, 'beautiful grove', as a pleasanter name. But it actually derives from Old English *mearth*, 'marten' (the weasel-like animal), so was really quite inoffensive.

Belial The name is one of those of the Devil, mentioned in the Bible (*Deuteronomy* 13.13 and elsewhere) and also appearing in Milton's *Paradise Lost*, where *Belial* is a fallen angel who 'could make the worse appear the better reason'. It is of Hebrew origin, from *belīaʿal*, 'worthless', from *belīy*, 'without' and *yaʿal*, 'worth'.

Belinda The name is of uncertain origin, although it has popularly been associated with French *belle*, 'beautiful' and Spanish *linda*, 'pretty'. More recently it has been directly linked with LINDA itself. Some authorities claim a Germanic source for the name, such as *lind*, 'lime tree' or *lindi*, 'snake', but there is no evidence to support either of these. It was a popular name in 17th-century literature, and is that of the heroine of Pope's *Rape of the Lock* (1714).

Belize The country in Central America, with its former capital of the same name, was originally named HONDURAS by Spanish colonists. It takes its present name from the river *Belize* that flows through it, to enter the sea at *Belize City*. The river name is probably Indian in origin, but is claimed by some to be a corruption of the surname of Peter *Wallace*, an English pirate who settled here in the 17th century.

Bell A person with this surname could originally have been either a bellringer or a maker of bells (bellfounder), or someone living by an actual bell, such as one in a bell-tower serving as a town's bell to call people to a public meeting. In some cases the name may have described a good-looking person, from Old French *bel*, 'handsome'.

Bell Anthem Purcell's verse anthem *Rejoice in the Lord Alway* (1682) is so nicknamed for the 'pealing' passages of the instrumental introduction.

Belle Isle The Canadian island at the entrance to the strait named for it, between Labrador and Newfoundland, has a French name meaning simply 'beautiful island'. The name is found elsewhere, for example for the French island of *Belle-Ile* in the Bay of Biscay, off the coast of Brittany, and in Britain for *Belle Isle*, in Lake Windermere. The Breton name of the French island is different, however. It is *ar Gerveur*, 'the big town', from *ar*, 'the', *kêr*, 'town', a word that becomes *gêr* after the definite article (as a feminine noun), and *meur*, 'big' (which similarly becomes *veur* after a feminine). The name may seem surprising for an island, but it currently has over 1000 inhabitants. The English island was originally known simply as *The Holme*, *i.e.* 'the island'. In 1781, however, it was

58

purchased by one Isabella Curwen, who renamed it (perhaps so as to reflect her own name).

Bellerophon In Greek mythology, Bellerophon was a hero of Corinth who performed many deeds with the aid of his horse Pegasus. One of these was to kill the tyrant Bellerus. His name thus means 'slayer of *Bellerus*', with the last part of his name representing Greek *phonē*, 'murder'. In another interpretation, however, his name is seen as meaning 'dart bearer', from *belos*, 'dart' and *pherein*, 'to bear'.

Belle Sauvage, La The historic inn on Ludgate Hill, London, was originally the *Bell Inn* (or *Bell on the Hoop Inn*) owned by a man named *Savage*. This 'Savage's Bell Inn' was then metamorphosed and reinterpreted as the more colourful *La Belle Sauvage*, 'the beautiful wild woman'. The site later became the headquarters of the publishing house Cassell, who favoured the latter interpretation and depicted an Amazonian-type huntress as their colophon. The building no longer exists.

Belmont Stakes The famous American horse race takes its name from *Belmont* Park, near New York, where it was first run in 1867.

Belmopan The capital of Belize, founded in 1970, has a name that is a blend of *Belize* itself, as the name of the former capital, destroyed by Hurricane 'Hattie' in 1961, and *Mopan*, the river on which it lies.

Belo Horizonte The Brazilian city has a Portuguese descriptive name meaning 'beautiful horizon'. The 'beautiful horizon' is the Serro do Curral, a hilly ridge that surrounds the plateau on which Belo Horizonte was built in 1897 as Brazil's first planned modern city, modelled on Washington.

Bel Paese The mild, creamy Italian cheese has a name that is simply the Italian for 'beautiful country'. The name is a proprietary one in Italy.

Beltane The name is the Celtic one for May Day (1 May), the beginning of summer, when sacrificial bonfires were lit. It represents Scottish Gaelic *Bealltainn*, a name of uncertain origin, but perhaps meaning 'bright fire', although erroneously connected with BAAL.

Belvoir The famous English hunt takes its name from its base, *Belvoir* Castle, on the edge of the Vale of *Beauvoir* near Grantham, Lincolnshire. The name itself is of Norman origin and aptly means 'beautiful valley'.

Benares *See* VARANASI.

Bendix The familiar make of washing machine, and the launderettes that installed them, take their name from the American inventor and industrialist Vincent *Bendix* (1882–1945). His main involvement was with automobile and aircraft technology, and the washing machines that popularized his name were introduced only as a sideline.

Benedict The name is directly of Latin origin, from *benedictus*, 'blessed'. Not surprisingly, it has been adopted by several popes. It was originally made famous by St *Benedict*, who founded the BENEDICTINES.

Benedictines The name of the Roman Catholic order of monks and nuns derives from that of St BENEDICT, who founded it in Italy in the 6th century. St Augustine brought the order to England, and several Oxford and Cambridge colleges were founded by Benedictine monks. The liqueur called *benedictine* is so named since it was developed at the Benedictine monastery at Fécamp, in France.

Benelux The name is that of the customs union of *Be*lgium, the *Ne*therlands and *Lux*embourg, and derives from the first syllables of the names of these countries. *Benelux* was formed in 1944 as a precursor of the European Economic Community. The name itself happens to suggest 'good luxury' or 'good light' in Latin and other European languages.

Benetton The fashion stores take their name from Giuliana *Benetton* (1938–), an Italian truck driver's daughter, who on the death of her father worked as a young girl sewing sweaters for a textile manufacturer in Treviso, near Venice. She began making garments at home on a knitting machine, and in 1955 founded her own business, which gradually built up into the major knitwear business it is today.

Benevento The city in southern Italy has a name of Roman origin meaning 'fair wind', from Latin *bene*, 'well' and *ventum*, 'wind'. The actual original name of the town was *Maleventum*. The first part of this is of pre-Indoeuropean origin and means 'height'. However, it was taken to mean 'bad', from Latin *male*, 'badly', 'ill'. The name was therefore changed to its more propitious supposed opposite.

Benfica The official title of the well-known Portuguese football club is *Sport Lisboa e Benfica*, which derives from a merger in 1908 between Grup Sport Lisboa, founded in Lisbon in 1904, and Sport Clube de *Benfica*, formed as an athletics and cycling club in 1906. The latter took its name from the western district of Lisbon where it arose.

Bengal The name of the former province of eastern India is of the same origin as that of its neighbour, BANGLADESH. It is that of its native inhabitants, the *Bengalis*, whose own name is said to derive from their original ancestor, a chief named *Banga*. The province name gave the English word *bungalow*, from Hindi *banglā*, 'belonging to Bengal', referring to the simple, single-storeyed houses that are still found here.

Benghazi The Libyan port has an Arabic name meaning 'sons of the conqueror', from *banī*, plural of *ibn*, 'son', and *ğāzī*, 'conqueror'. *Bani Ghazi* is itself the name of a locally venerated marabout (holy man) whose tomb lies to the north of the city. The Greek name of Benghazi was *Hesperides* or *Euhesperides*, for the Islands of the Blessed in Greek mythology, or the maidens who guarded the golden apples there. Later, the city took the additional name *Berenice*, either for the wife of Ptolemy III or for the daughter of Salome and niece of Herod (or perhaps as a compliment to both).

Benin The name of the west African state, formerly known as DAHOMEY, is that of a historic kingdom here, and comes from its indigenous inhabitants, the *Bini*, now more closely linked with southern Nigeria (hence the name of *Benin* City in that country). Their own name may be related to Arabic *banī*, 'sons'.

Benjamin The name is famous in the Bible as that of the youngest son of Jacob. It represents Hebrew *Binyāmīn*, literally 'son of the right hand', that is, a favourite son. The biblical Benjamin had originally been named *Benoni*, 'son of sorrow', as his mother Rachel died in giving birth to him. Jacob did not wish him to have such an ill-omened name, however, and called him *Benjamin* instead (*Genesis* 35.18).

Bennett The surname is a form of the personal name BENEDICT. *Cp.* BENTINCK.

Ben Nevis Britain's highest mountain, in Scotland, takes its name from a nearby river, the *Nevis*. Gaelic *beinn* means 'mountain' and is found in many Scottish mountain names. The river's name represents Gaelic *nemess*, 'spiteful', referring to its evil repute in local folklore. Popular etymology, however, derives the name of Ben Nevis from Gaelic *Beinn-nimh-bhathais*, 'mountain with its brow in the clouds'. But this, alas, is poetry rather than prosaic pedantry.

Benson & Hedges The cigarette manufacturers and cricket match sponsors originated in the persons of Richard *Benson* and William *Hedges*, who opened a tobacconist's shop in Old Bond Street, London, in 1873.

Bentalls The well-known department store in Kingston-upon-Thames, Surrey, takes its name from its founder in 1867, the draper Frank *Bentall* (1843–1923).

Bentinck The name is a Dutch form of the personal name BENEDICT. *Cp.* BENNETT.

Bentley The prestigious make of car derives its name from that of Walter Owen *Bentley* (1888–1971), a racing-car driver who turned to making car engines, then cars themselves. The first model bearing his name underwent its road trials in London in 1920.

Benzedrine The proprietary type of amphetamine derives its name from two of its constituents, *benz*yl-methyl-carbinamine and eph*edrine*, the latter being a drug used to alleviate asthma, hay fever and the like.

Beowulf The famous Old English poem, surviving in a 10th-century manuscript but perhaps written much earlier, is named for its hero, *Beowulf*. His own name is said by some to mean 'bee wolf', from Old English *bēo*, 'bee' and *wulf*, 'wolf', this being a euphemism for 'bear' (*cp*. Russian *medved'*, 'bear', literally 'honey eater'). Others, however, see the derivation in an original name *Beadowulf*, from Old English *beado*, a form of *beadu*, 'war', and *wulf*, so that he is a 'war wolf', an appropriate name for a warrior hero.

Beppo The poem by Byron, published in 1818, has as its central character an Italian named *Beppo*. His name is a pet form of *Giuseppe*, the equivalent of English JOSEPH.

Berber The north African people, who gave their name to the BARBARY COAST, have a name that remains of disputed origin. It is popularly derived from Greek *barbaros*, 'foreign', 'different', which gave English *barbarian*. The true source almost certainly lies elsewhere. One ingenious derivation is from Germanic *ber*, 'bear' and Indoeuropean *bher*, 'to bear', so that the people are 'bearers of the bear', supposedly a reference to the astronomical Great Bear. But that seems equally unlikely.

Berenice The name of the daughter of Herod Agrippa, mentioned in the Bible as *Bernice* (*Acts* 25.13), is probably a form of the Greek name *Pherenike*, 'bringer of victory', from *pherein*, 'to bring' and *nikē*, 'victory'.

Bergamo The city in northern Italy takes its name from a Celtic or Ligurian root word *berg*, 'mountain' (as in Germanic languages). The town lies in the foothills of the Alps.

Bergen The port in southwest Norway derives its name from Old Norwegian *Björgvin*, from *björg*, 'mountain' and *vin*, 'pasture'.

Bergerac The French town, in the Dordogne, has a name that means '*Bracarius*' place', with this Gallo-Roman personal name in turn meaning 'maker of breeches'. The name is associated with the 17th-century French writer Cyrano de *Bergerac*, the hero of a classic play by Rostand. But he did not come from here. He was born in Paris, and took his name (or title) from the land owned by his father in another place called *Bergerac*, southwest of Paris. The popular British television series *Bergerac*, first shown in 1981, is not even set in France but in the Channel Islands, and is named for its central character, the Jersey detective Jim *Bergerac*.

Bering Sea The *Bering* Sea and *Bering* Strait, between Alaska and Siberia, are both named for the Danish explorer Vitus *Bering* (1681–1741), who entered the service of Peter the Great of Russia in 1724 and who was the first European to sight Alaska.

Berkeley The Californian city takes its name from the Irish philosopher George *Berkeley* (1685–1753). His name was selected as appropriate for the campus site that opened in 1873 for the new University of California, created as a merger between the existing University and the earlier College of California founded in Oakland in 1853, the centennial year of Berkeley's death.

Berkshire The English county is unusual in having a name that does not derive from one of its important towns, as Oxfordshire does from Oxford, for example. The first part of its name represents *Berroc*, the ancient name of a wood. The wood was in turn probably named after the hill on which it lay, since *Berroc* almost certainly comes from the Celtic root word *barro*, meaning 'hill', as for the Scottish town of *Barrhead*. Local research has established that the hill in question was probably one near Hungerford.

Berlin The German capital has an ancient name that is ultimately of uncertain origin. The city coat-of-arms shows a bear, as if the name derived from German *Bär* or even *Bärlein*, 'bear cub'. But this is simply folk etymology at work. *Cp*. BERN.

Bermondsey The district of London, by the Thames, has a name that means '*Beornmund*'s island', with the 'island' not one in the river but simply an area of higher ground beside the marshy banks of the Thames. A short form of the personal name occurs in the name of *Barnsley*.

Bermuda The name of the British colony, in the northwest Atlantic, bears tribute to the Spanish explorer Juan *Bermúdez*, who visited the islands in 1515. He originally called them 'Devil Islands', perhaps for reasons associated much later with the famous Bermuda Triangle.

Bermuda Race The major ocean-going yacht race is held every two years, alternating with the Fastnet Cup, over a course from Newport, Rhode Island to BERMUDA and back.

Bern As with BERLIN, the name of Switzerland's capital is popularly associated with the German word *Bär*, 'bear', in this case because the Helvetii, the Celtic people who lived here in the 1st century BC, are said to have worshipped a she-bear. But this is probably a fanciful account, even though Bern's city coat-of-arms shows a bear. A more likely origin for the name is in an Indoeuropean root word *ber*, meaning 'marshy place'. Some authorities have linked the name with that of VERONA, as if Bern were a northern equivalent of that Italian city.

Bernard The name is of Germanic origin, comprising *ber*, 'bear' and *hard*, 'hardy', so meaning someone strong and brave. There were several famous churchmen of the name, the best known being the *Bernard* who gave the name of the ST BERNARD breed of dog.

Berry The former province of central France had the Roman name *Bituricus*, from the Gaulish people known as the *Bituriges*. Their own name means 'kings of the world', from Gaulish *bitu*, 'world' and *rix*, 'king'. The name sounds unduly grand, but merely stressed that they were the masters of their own 'world' or territory.

Bertha The name derives from Germanic *beraht*, 'bright', 'famous'. *See* BIG BERTHA for a historic nickname based on it.

Bertram The name comprised the Germanic words *beraht*, 'bright', 'famous' and *hramn*, 'raven'. The raven symbolized wisdom in Germanic mythology, so the name overall denotes someone who is both famous and learned.

Berwick-upon-Tweed The Northumberland town, close to the Scottish border, has a name found elsewhere in England. It means 'barley farm', from Old English *berewīc*. The name of the river Tweed was added to distinguish this Berwick from the others.

Beryl The name is one of those derived from precious stones that came into fashion for women at the end of the 19th century. Beryl itself is best known in its green transparent variety, the *emerald*. This has not itself given an English name, but ESMERALDA exists as a Spanish equivalent. Names of this type were favoured because precious stones are worn as ornaments, and the best type of name should be both functional and 'decorative'. Moreover, a name derived from a jewel implies that its bearer is likewise 'precious'. *Jade* and *Ruby* are also 'jewel names', while GEMMA has the basic sense.

Besançon The French town, the capital of Franche-Comté, has a name that contains an Indoeuropean root word *ves*, 'mountain', as perhaps for the VOSGES mountains. Besançon lies in eastern France below the Jura mountains.

Bessarabia The territory of southeast Europe, annexed by Russia in 1812, and now divided between Moldavia and Ukraine, has a name that is nothing to do with *Arabia*. It probably derives from the dynastic name *Basarab*, that of the princes of Walachia, itself based on Turkish *basar*, a derivative of the verb *bas*, 'to oppress', and related to the Turkish noun *basın*, 'press'.

Best The surname does not mean what it seems to mean, but comes from the former English word *beste*, modern *beast*, meaning someone who looks after animals, as a herdsman, or who was thought to resemble an animal in some way, either physically or in character or behaviour.

Betamax The commercial video system was developed by the Japanese company Sony in the 1970s. Its name derives from Japanese *betabeta*, 'all over', and *max* as a short form of English *maximum*. The suggestion of *beta* as the second letter of the Greek alphabet is thus only coincidental, although the manufacturers were aware of this interpretation. The attribute 'all over' refers to the fact that the whole area of the videotape could be used for recording, unlike earlier tapes, which had guard bands and empty spaces. The system long competed with *VHS* ('Video Home System'), and eventually lost out to it for most home videos.

Betelgeuse The name, also spelled *Betelgeux*, is that of the brightest star, a variable red supergiant, in the constellation Orion. It traditionally derives, in a French spelling, from Arabic *bāṭ al-jawzāʾ* , 'armpit of the giant', that is, of Orion. Some astronomers, however, take the name instead from Arabic *yad al-jawzāʾ* , 'hand of the giant' or even *mankib al-jawzāʾ* , 'shoulder of the giant', depending on how the star is perceived in the outline of Orion in the sky.

Bethany The biblical village near Jerusalem, the home of Lazarus and the place where Jesus stayed in the week before the Crucifixion, has an Aramaic and Hebrew name that means 'house of poverty', from *bēt*, 'house of', construct state (*see below*) of *báyit*, 'house', and *ʿanya*, 'poverty'. The Hebrew word for 'house', *báyit*, gave the name of *beth*, the second letter of the Hebrew alphabet, which is shaped like a house. This in turn gave the name of the Greek second letter *beta*, which lies behind English *alphabet*. In Semitic languages, the *construct state* is the state in which one noun depends on another, where in Indoeuropean languages the second noun would be in the genitive case. In the name of *Bethany*, as in those (below) of BETHEL, BETHESDA, BETHLEHEM, BETHPHAGE and BETHSAIDA, *bēt*, 'house of' is in the construct state of *báyit*. For other examples, *see* PENIEL and RAMAT GAN.

Bethel In the Bible, the name is that of the place on the river Jordan where the dream of Jacob occurs (*Genesis* 28.19). It is Hebrew for 'house of God', from *bēt*, 'house of' and *el*, 'God' (which also lies behind the name of ALLAH). The name was adopted in the 19th century for various Nonconformist chapels, and the Welsh villages so called are thus named for their chapel. *See also* BETHESDA.

Bethesda In the Bible, the name is that of the pool in Jerusalem said to have healing powers (*John* 5.2). It is Aramaic for 'house of grace', from *bēt*, 'house of' and *ẖesdā*, 'grace'. The Vulgate (Latin translation of the Bible) misrenders the name as BETHSAIDA, but that is a different place (*which see*). The North Wales town of *Bethesda* is so called because it arose round its Calvinistic Methodist chapel, which was set up in 1820 and named for the biblical pool.

Bethlehem The famous biblical town, the traditional birthplace of Jesus, now an Israeli-occupied city on the river Jordan, has a Hebrew name that means 'house of bread', from *bēt*, 'house of' and *léhem*, 'bread'. The reference is to the fertility of the plain surrounding Bethlehem. The city of *Bethlehem*, Pennsylvania, was founded by Moravian missionaries in 1741 and took the name of the biblical town from its occurrence in a Christmas hymn that they sang (as in the later English carol 'O little town of Bethlehem').

Bethpage The town in New York State is named for the biblical town of BETHPHAGE. It is so called because it arose between settlements originally known as Jericho and Jerusalem, just as its biblical nearnamesake is situated halfway between Bethany and the top of the Mount of Olives.

Bethphage The biblical town near Jerusalem has an Aramaic name meaning 'house of figs', from *bēt*, 'house of' and *pagga*, 'fig' (the Aramaic and English words are related). *See also* BETHPAGE.

Bethsaida The biblical village, now a ruined town in northern Israel, has a Hebrew name meaning 'house of food', from *bēt*, 'house of' and *tseyda(r)*, 'hunting', 'food'. The village was located near the northeast shore of the Sea of Galilee (Lake Tiberias), so that the 'hunting' would have been fishing and the food itself the fish.

Betty The popular name originated in the 18th century as a pet form of ELIZABETH, based on the last syllable of this name.

Betws-y-Coed The Welsh village, with its picturesque waterfalls, has a name that means 'chapel in the woods' from Welsh *betws* (pronounced 'betoos'), 'chapel', *y*, 'the' and *coed*, 'wood'. The Welsh word *betwys* is a borrowing of Old English *bedhūs*, literally 'bead-house', *i.e.* prayer-house.

Beulah The biblical name for the land of Israel (*Isaiah* 62.4) in Hebrew in origin and means 'married woman'.

Bevan The name means 'son of *Evan*', the Welsh equivalent of JOHN. *Bevin* means the same. The initial *B-* represents Welsh *ap* or *ab*, 'son'. *Cp.* EVANS.

Beverly Hills The residential district of Los Angeles, California, famous as the home of Hollywood film stars, was originally *Beverly* until 1911, when the present name was adopted. Its basic name was suggested from a newspaper report in 1907 that President Taft was spending some time at a place called *Beverly Farms*.

B-52's, The The American pop group, formed in 1976, took their name from the Southern nickname for the *bee*hive hairstyle adopted by its two female members. The hairstyle in turn was called after the huge American B-52 bomber, perhaps with added reference to height and 'impact'. The aircraft itself was so designated since it was manufactured by BOEING in 1952.

Bhagavadgita The sacred Hindu text of unknown authorship, dating from the 2nd century BC and incorporated into the *Mahabharata*, has a name of Sanskrit origin meaning 'song of the *Bhagavat*'. The latter is a title of the supreme deity and means 'blessed one'. In the *Bhagavadgita* it is the title of Krishna.

Bharat The Hindi name for INDIA represents Sanskrit *bhārata*, the name of an ancient hero of India. His own name is based on the root element *bhṛ*, 'carrying', 'supporting', itself related to English *bear*. This same name lies behind that of the epic Sanskrit poem known as the MAHABHARATA.

Bhopal The city in central India has a name said to derive from Sanskrit *bhūpāla*, 'king', 'prince', from a root element related to English *be*. Some authorities, however, take the name from *Bhoj*, that of the city's founder in the 11th century, to which Hindi *pāl*, 'embankment' has been added. *Bhoj* is said to have built the latter himself.

Bhubaneswar The ancient city in eastern India has a name deriving from Sanskrit *bhuvana*, 'universe' and *īśvara*, 'supreme deity'.

Bhutan The Asian state has a Hindi name that comes from Sanskrit *bhoṭa*, the name of TIBET, and *anta*, 'end'. This describes the location of Bhutan at the southern extremity of Tibet. The native Tibetan name of Bhutan is *Druk Yul*, 'land of the dragon'.

Biafra The region of eastern Nigeria takes its name from the Bight of *Biafra*, on which it lies on the delta of the river Niger. The name of the bight is a European rendering of the tribal name *Mafra*.

Białystok The city in eastern Poland has a name meaning 'white river', from Polish *biały*, 'white' and *stok*, 'river', 'confluence'. The direct source of the name is that of the river *Biała* on which the city stands.

Biarritz The well-known seaside resort and spa town in southwest France, near the Spanish border, has a Basque name meaning either 'place of two rocks' or 'place of two oaks', from *bi*, 'two' and *harri*, 'rock' or *haritz*, 'oak'. The Basque name of Biarritz is *Miarritze*.

Bible The *Bible* derives its name from Late Latin *biblia*, a feminine singular noun that was earlier a neuter plural and that was in turn borrowed from Greek *ta biblia*, 'the books', that is, the canonical books that form the Bible, otherwise the 'Scriptures'. The Greek word was a plural of *biblion*, grammatically a diminutive of *biblos*, 'papyrus', 'paper', but that had lost its diminutive sense and was the standard word for 'book'. An actual reference to the Bible comes in the Apocrypha, where the original Greek for 'the holy books of scripture' (1 *Maccabees* 12.9) was *ta biblia ta hagia*.

Bic The popular make of ballpoint pen takes its name from the French brothers who first manufactured it near Paris after the Second World War, Marcel and Gonzalve *Bich*.

Bifrost In Scandinavian mythology, the name of the rainbow bridge linking Asgard (the realm of the gods) with earth means 'shaking path', from Icelandic *bifa*, 'to shake' and *rost*, 'path'.

Big Ben The popular name for the bell in the clock tower of the Houses of Parliament, London, and also for the clock and tower themselves, probably derives from the name of *Benjamin* Hall, Commissioner of Works at the time the bell was cast in 1858. Outside Victoria Station stands *Little Ben*, a miniature version of the clock tower, only 30 feet high.

Big Bertha The nickname for the German howitzers in use at the start of the First World War derived from *Bertha* Krupp (1886–1957), great-granddaughter of Friedrich Krupp (1787–1826), founder of the famous steel works at Essen that bore his name. Control of the works devolved to Bertha Krupp on her father's death in 1902, when she was still only 16, but subsequently passed to her husband after her marriage in 1906. In fact the howitzers were not made by the Krupp Works at all, but by the Škoda Works in Pilsen.

Biggleswade The Bedfordshire town has a name that means '*Biccel*'s ford'. The word that means 'ford' is not as for *Oxford*, for example, but is the Old English word *wæd*, denoting a place where people and animals can 'wade' or walk across a stream or river. Biggleswade is on the river Ivel.

Bihar The Indian state and town (not its capital) have a Hindi name deriving from Sanskrit *vihāra*, 'monastery'. The town was formerly surrounded by Buddhist monasteries.

Bikini Famous as the site of American atom bomb tests from 1946 to 1963, the atoll in the Marshall Islands is named *Pikinni* in the native language. According to one authority, this represents *pik*, 'surface' and *ni*, 'coconut', but the explanation is probably conjectural. The island gave the name of the *bikini*, the two-piece swimsuit that came into fashion at the time of the first atomic tests, and that apparently was so nicknamed for its 'explosive' effect. Later, the *bi-* of this was interpreted as 'two', for the two parts of the costume, so that a one-piece (topless) swimsuit was a *monokini*.

Bilbao The name of the Spanish port, on the Bay of Biscay, is a corruption of its Roman name of *Bellum Vadum*, 'beautiful ford', referring to that over the river Nervión, at the mouth of which it lies.

Bill The well-known name arose as a pet form of WILLIAM in the 19th century. It is based on the first syllable of the full name, with the initial *W* becoming *B* as happens in some languages for corresponding words. The Irish word for English *wall*, for example, is *balla*. It may even have

been the Irish nickname 'King Billy' for William of Orange that led to the regular name Bill.

Billy Bunter The name is that of the fat, bespectacled boy in the stories by Frank Richards about Greyfriars School in the *Magnet* children's paper from 1908 to 1940. Richards may have based his name on the rare word *bunt*, meaning something round or swollen, or adapted the nickname 'Baby Bunting' as applied to a plump baby.

Bingerville The seaport town in the Côte d'Ivoire (formerly Ivory Coast) takes its name from the French naval officer and explorer, Captain Louis-Gustave *Binger* (1856–1936), the Ivory Coast's first governor (from 1893). The name has a French pronunciation, akin to *lingerie*, not an English one.

Bingham A person of this name would originally have come from the Nottinghamshire village of *Bingham*, near Nottingham. The place-name may mean 'settlement of Binna's people'.

Birch The surname originally described someone who lived by a birch tree or in a birch wood.

Bird A person with this surname would at one time have been so nicknamed for some actual or fancied resemblance to a bird. In a few cases the person could have been a bird catcher.

Birds Eye The well-known make of frozen foods takes its name from the American businessman and inventor Clarence *Birdseye* (1886–1956), who pioneered food refrigeration processes and who in 1923 founded the company that bears his name, originally Birdseye Seafoods, Inc.

Bir Hacheim The Libyan village, the scene of much fighting in the Second World War, is centred on an oasis. Its name refers to this, and represents Arabic *bi'r hakīm*, 'well of the wise man', from *bi'r*, 'well' (*cp.* BEIRUT) and *hakīm*, 'wise man', 'sage'.

Birkbeck College The London University college is named for one of its founders in 1823, the physician, philanthropist and educator, Dr George *Birkbeck* (1776–1841). Its original name was the *London Mechanics' Institution*, and it was the first college of education in England to provide classes for people at work in the day. In 1866 it was renamed the *Birkbeck Literary and Scientific Institution*, and in 1907 it gained its present name.

Birmingham The name of Britain's second largest city could be that of any small village. It means 'settlement of *Beorma*'s people'. It is not known who Beorma was, but his name is a shortened form of the Old English name *Beornmund*, literally 'man-guardian', which itself gave the name of London's BERMONDSEY.

Biro The well-known make of ballpoint pen owes its name to the Hungarian engineer generally credited with its invention in 1938, László József *Biró* (1899–1985).

Birobidzhan The Siberian city, capital of the Jewish Autonomous Region, has a name of Yiddish origin representing those of two rivers here, the *Biro* and the *Bidzhan*.

Biscay, Bay of The name of the familiar bay between France and Spain is Basque in origin, representing *bizkar*, 'mountain country', referring to the Pyrenees, off the coast of which it lies.

Bishkek The capital of Kirgizia was founded in 1878 on the site of the former fortress of *Pishpek*, with a name of unknown origin. In 1926 it was renamed *Frunze*, for the Communist military leader Mikhail *Frunze* (1885–1925), who was born here. In 1991 the city reverted to its former name, but with a corrected spelling *Bishkek*.

Bishop The surname arose to describe a person who either worked in a bishop's household, or who was stately or pompous like a bishop. In some instances the name would have been given to someone elected a 'boy bishop' on St Nicholas' Day.

Bishop Rock The rock west of the Scilly Isles, famous for its lighthouse, has a name that may allude to its shape. The name was recorded in a document of 1302 as *Maenenescop'*, the first part of which represents Cornish *men*, 'stone'. A group name for the rock with its smaller surrounding rocks is *Bishop and Clerks*, *i.e.* the bishop with his clergy.

Bismarck Archipelago The island group in the southwestern Pacific is a former German protectorate and takes its name from the German chancellor Otto von *Bismarck*

(1815–1898). The same man gave the name of the American city of *Bismarck*, state capital of North Dakota, which was adopted in recognition of his financial contribution towards the construction of the railway. The chancellor's own name derives from that of his family's ancestral estate near Altmark in Magdeburg, formerly recorded as *Biscopesmark*, 'bishop's boundary', from its location on the edge of an episcopal see. (*Cp.* MARCHES.)

Bisto The well-known gravy powder was first marketed in 1910 and was given a name that could be arbitrary. It has been explained as an anagrammatic acronym for '*Browns, Seasons, Thickens In One*'. Appropriately enough, it also happens to suggest French (now also English) *bistro*, as well as Italian *bistecca*, 'beef-steak'.

Bizerta The Tunisian port has an Arabic name that is a corruption of Low Latin *Hippo Zarytus*, itself a distortion of classical Latin *Hippo Diarrhytus*. This represents Greek *hippōn*, 'stable' and *diarrutos*, 'flowing through' (the source also of English *diarrhoea*), denoting a halting place for horses that was crossed by a stream. Bizerta is on the Mediterranean at the mouth of a channel from Lake *Bizerte*, and was originally a Phoenician outpost before becoming a Carthaginian town and Roman colony. *Cp.* HIPPO.

Black The common surname arose as a descriptive name for a dark-haired or dark-skinned person. Paradoxically, it was also used to describe a fair-haired or pale-skinned person, since Old English *blæc*, with a short vowel, meant 'black', while *blāc*, with a long vowel, meant 'white' (*cp.* modern English *bleak* and *bleach*). This means that it is impossible to tell whether the ancestors of a person named Black were dark or fair. *See also* BLAKE.

Black & Decker The familiar make of power tools derives from the two American engineers S. Duncan *Black* and Alonzo G. *Decker*, who built up their business from the portable electric drill they invented in Baltimore, Maryland, in 1916.

Black and Tans The specially recruited police force sent to Ireland in 1921 by the British government to combat the Sinn Féin nationalists was so nicknamed from the khaki uniform and black belt worn by its members. The name was suggested by the Irish *Black and Tans* hunt in Munster.

Blackburn Rovers The well-known football club was formed in 1875 as *Blackburn Grammar School* Football Club, since players were members of this school. They spent much of their first season without a home ground, so within a matter of weeks renamed themselves as *Blackburn Rovers* to indicate this. They retained the name even when, in 1890, they settled at Ewood Park, their third home ground and the one they occupy today.

Black Country The central industrial area of England, based roughly on Birmingham, was formerly so nicknamed for its grimy factories, blackened by the dense, soot-laden smoke from their chimneys. Today, under anti-pollution laws, the name is no longer appropriate.

Black Death The name is a relatively modern one for the epidemic of bubonic plague that ravaged much of Europe in the 14th century. The reason for the particular colour is not clear, although black has long been traditionally associated with death.

Blackfoot The Indian people, now mainly in Saskatchewan, Canada, derive their name from the black moccasins that they habitually wear.

Black Forest The mountainous region of forest in western Germany consists predominantly of pine trees, and these give the overall dark colour for which it is named. The Roman name for the forest was *Silva Nigra*, and the German name is *Schwarzwald*, both meaning the same.

Blackfriars The area of east central London is named for the Dominican Order of Preachers who settled here in 1221 and who were popularly known as the *Black Friars* from the colour of their habit. Blackfriars Bridge, over the Thames, leads to the area. The pulpit-like structures of the present bridge are a visual allusion to the historic origin of the name.

Black Hole of Calcutta The name, or nickname, was given to the incident in Anglo-Indian history when in 1759 the Nawab of Bengal confined 146 British prisoners overnight in the cell at Fort William,

Calcutta. Only a few survived. The adjective 'black' can be taken both literally, referring to the dark cell, and metaphorically, as a grim event. At the same time *black hole* was long in general army use as a term for the punishment cell or guard room in a barracks.

Black Mountains The range in South Wales is so named because the mountains appear dark when seen from the southern or eastern side.

Black Muslims The self-descriptive name is that of an American religious and political organization of black people, formed in 1931 to preach a form of Islam and to establish a new black nation.

Black Panthers The name is that of the militant organization of black people formed in America in 1965 with the aim of ending the political dominance of whites. They adopted a black panther as their party emblem.

Blackpool The well-known Lancashire resort takes its name from a pool of water formerly here, about half a mile from the sea. By the end of the 18th century the surrounding area had been turned into meadowland, and the stream that flowed from the pool became the town's main sewer. The 'black' colour of the pool arose from its peaty water.

Black Prince The nickname was that given to Edward, prince of Wales (1330–1376), son of Edward III, who wore black armour in battle. *See also* PRINCES RISBOROUGH.

Black Rod The name is that of the officer of the House of Lords who has the main duty of summoning the Commons at the opening (and also proroguing) of parliament. His full title of *Gentleman Usher of the Black Rod* refers to his staff of office, a *black rod* with a gold lion on top.

Black Sabbath The British heavy metal group, formed in 1967, took their name from one of their early songs. The song's own name was a reference to the keen interest shown by one of the group's members, Terry 'Geezer' Butler, in the stories of the 'black magic' crime novelist Dennis Wheatley.

Black Sea The European sea, with Russia on its northern shore and Turkey on its southern, has a name that probably describes its appearance during stormy weather. In bright sunny weather it is as blue as any other sea. The sea is noted for its storms, and the Old Persian word used to describe it was *ahŝaēna*, 'dark'. This word was adopted without being translated by the Greeks, who called it the *Pontos Axeinos*, *pontos* meaning 'sea'. But *Axeinos* came to be understood as *Axenos*, 'inhospitable', so that it was the 'Inhospitable Sea'. Later, perhaps out of superstition, the Greeks altered this ill-omened name to *Pontos Euxenos*, 'Hospitable Sea', and this name was traditionally rendered in English, without being translated, as *Euxine Sea*. Another theory claims that the Black Sea is so named because some Asiatic languages use colour words for the four points of the compass. The Black Sea would thus be the 'North Sea', just as the RED SEA, according to this concept, would be the 'South Sea' and the WHITE SEA the 'West Sea'. Support for this is lent by the fact that the modern Turkish name for the Mediterranean is *Akdeniz*, 'White Sea' (although this may be an attempt to give a meaning to *Ege denizi*, the Turkish name for the *Aegean Sea*, as an arm of the Mediterranean).

Black Watch The name is that of the Royal Highland Regiment in the British Army, so called from the dark colours of its tartan. 'Watch' has its former sense of 'guard'.

Blagoveshchensk The Siberian city, a port on the river Amur in southeast Russia, was founded as a military post in 1856. Two years later the Church of the Annunciation was built. The town is named after it, from Russian *Blagoveshchenie*, 'Annunciation', a direct translation of Greek *euangelismos*, 'a bringing of good tidings'.

Blake The surname is a form of BLACK, so would originally have meant 'dark' or 'fair', depending on the precise Old English word of origin.

Blaue Reiter, Der The group of German Expressionist painters, formed in Munich in 1912, adopted this name, meaning 'The Blue Rider', from a book on aesthetics co-authored by two of their leading members, Kandinsky and Marc, and that was itself named after a painting by Kandinsky.

Blaupunkt The German electronics company, founded in 1925, has a name that consists of the German words for 'blue dot'. It originated in the blue dot that was used as a 'quality symbol' by engineers of the founding company, Ideal, to denote their most technically advanced earphones.

Blefuscu The name occurs in Swift's *Gulliver's Travels* (1726) for an island separated from LILLIPUT by a narrow channel. It is generally taken to represent France. The name has been 'decoded' to mean 'bluff as you', which seems not altogether appropriate, while a derivation from French *bref*, 'short' and Latin *oscus*, 'filthy' has also been suggested, again, not particularly convincingly.

Blenheim, Battle of The famous battle takes its name from the Bavarian village where, in 1704, the Anglo-Austrian forces under the Duke of Marlborough and Prince Eugène of Savoy defeated the French and Bavarian armies in the War of the Spanish Succession. The German name of the village is *Blindheim*, and the German name of the battle is *die Schlacht bei Höchstädt*. The latter word comes from the full name of the village, which is now *Blindheim-Höchstädt*.

Blenheim Palace The mansion near Woodstock, Oxfordshire, was built in the early 18th century for the Duke of Marlborough as a gift from Queen Anne to commemorate his victory at the Battle of BLENHEIM, in 1704. The house was thus named after the battle.

Blighty The nickname for Britain, popular among British troops serving overseas in the First World War, derives from Hindi *bilāyatī*, 'foreign', adopted from Arabic *wilāyat*, 'country'. The name itself originated in the Indian army.

Blitz The colloquial name for the series of air-raids on London in 1940 was taken from the *Blitzkrieg* or 'lightning war' that the Germans conducted elsewhere in Europe at the start of the Second World War. The ready British acceptance of the foreign word may have been aided by its subconscious association with *blizzard*.

Bloemfontein The South African city has a name that can literally be understood as 'fountain of flowers', from Afrikaans *bloem*, 'flower' and *fontein*, 'fountain'. But the name could equally pay tribute to the local farmer on whose land the town arose, one Jan *Bloem*.

Blondie The American pop group, formed in New York in 1974, took its name from the vivid blonde hair of its sole female member, Deborah Harry, which contrasted sharply with the dark hair of its five male members. The name came to be particularly identified with Harry herself, although she never actually adopted it as a performing name.

Bloodless Revolution The name is an alternative one for the GLORIOUS REVOLUTION, and refers to the fact that no lives were lost in the coup which overthrew James II.

Bloody Mary The nickname of Queen Mary I was given her by Protestants and refers to the persecutions that she authorized, in which many lives were lost.

Bloomsbury The district of London, noted for its literary associations, derives its name from the *burg* or manor house held by the Anglo-Norman family of *de Blémunt*, who probably came from *Blémont*, near Poitiers in northern France.

Bluebeard The name is that of the villain in the *Contes de ma mère l'Oye* or *Mother Goose Tales* (1697) by Charles Perrault. It was originally *Barbe-Bleue*, from the blue-grey colour of his beard. The tales are thought to have been based on the evil deeds of the French marshal Gilles de Rais in the 15th century, who fought with the English against Joan of Arc but later kidnapped and murdered over a hundred children, for which he was hanged. In the folktale, the subjects of his murders became his disobedient wives.

Bluebell Railway The private railway between Sheffield Park and Horsted Keynes, Sussex, formerly familiar as the *Bluebell Line*, is so named because at one time the guard stopped the train in the country to allow passengers to pick bluebells by the track.

Bluecoat School The name is an alternative one for CHRIST'S HOSPITAL, referring to the blue coats originally worn by the charity boys and now still worn by both boys and girls on special occasions. The school provides the uniform free.

Blue Cross The charity organization, which provides veterinary treatment for pets whose owners cannot afford it, was founded in 1897 and took a name that was complementary to that of the RED CROSS, just as pets are complementary to humans.

Blue Mountains The Australian mountains, part of the Great Divide, take their name from the bluish haze visible over them in clear weather. The colour is at least partly attributable to the dense eucalyptus forests that traverse the mountains.

Blue Peter The popular children's television programme, first broadcast in 1958, takes its name from the naval term for the signalling flag that is hoisted when a ship is about to sail. The flag is blue with a white rectangle. *Peter* is said to be a corruption of *repeater*, as the flag was originally used to indicate that a message had not been understood and should be repeated.

Blue River *See* YANGTZE.

Blundell's School The boys' public school at Tiverton, Devon, takes its name from its founder in 1604, Peter *Blundell*, a local clothier.

Blunt The surname could originally have been a nickname for a stupid or 'thick' person, but could equally have applied to a fair-haired person, deriving from an Old French word that gave modern *blond*.

BMW The make of car has a name that is an abbreviation of that of its German manufacturing company, *Bayerische Motoren-Werke*, 'Bavarian Motor Works', founded in Munich in 1916, originally to construct aircraft.

Boabdil The name of the last Moorish king of Granada, reigning in the 15th century, is a corruption of his original name, *Abu Abdullah*, 'father of ABDULLAH'. His name probably gave that of Captain *Bobadil*, the braggart and coward in Ben Jonson's play *Every Man in his Humour* (1598).

Boadicea *See* BOUDICCA.

Boanerges In the Bible, the nickname is that given by Jesus to James and John: 'And he surnamed them Boanerges, which is, The sons of thunder' (*Mark* 3.17). The name is Hebrew in origin, from *b'nēy regeŝ*, literally 'sons of tumult'. The two disciples were so called since they wanted to 'command fire to come down from heaven' (*Luke* 9.54) to punish the Samaritans for not recognizing Jesus as the Lord. The name came to be applied to any vociferous orator, one who 'thunders'. The spelling of the name has developed under Greek influence. Oddly, it can be interpreted direct from Greek as 'thunder worker', from *boaō*, 'I roar', 'I thunder' and *ergon*, 'work'.

Boaz In the Bible, the name is that of the husband of Ruth and great-grandfather of King David. It is of Hebrew origin but uncertain meaning. An interpretation 'swiftness' has been suggested.

Bob The name is a pet form of ROBERT, derived from the first half of this name. The initial *R* changed to other letters to produce similar pet forms in medieval times, among them *Dob*, *Hob* and *Nob*.

Bodhisattva In Buddhism, the title is that given to a divine being, a future Buddha, who although worthy of entering nirvana remains on the human level to help others to salvation. The name is Sanskrit, and means 'essence of enlightenment', from *bodhi*, 'enlightenment' (*cp.* BUDDHA) and *sattva*, 'essence'.

Bodleian The principal library of Oxford University was founded by Duke Humphrey in 1455, but takes its present name from Sir Thomas *Bodley* (1545–1613), who restored and reopened it in 1602. *See also* BODLEY HEAD.

Bodley Head The British publishing house was founded in 1887 by two Devon men, Elkin Mathews and John Lane, the latter being the uncle of Allen Lane who founded Penguin Books. The name represents the sign that they hung outside their London shop, that of the *head* of Sir Thomas *Bodley*, who like themselves was a booklover from Devon. Sir Thomas also gave his name to the BODLEIAN Library at Oxford.

Bodmin The Cornish town has a Cornish name, from *bod*, 'house' and *meneghi*, a derivative of *managh*, 'monk', referring to the monastery said to have been founded here in the 10th century by King Athelstan.

Body The name would originally have been a nickname for a stout or fat person. In some instances, however, it could have derived from Old English *boda*, 'messenger' (to which modern English *bode* is related).

Boeing The well-known American aircraft take their name from William Edward *Boeing* (1881–1956), who founded the Pacific Aero Products Company in 1916. The following year it was renamed after him as the Boeing Airplane Company. The firm became a major manufacturer of military and commercial aircraft, producing such famous models as the B-17 Flying Fortress, B-29 Superfortress and B-52 Stratofortress. *See also* B-52'S.

Boers The name is that of the Dutch settlers, or descendants of Dutch settlers, who were in South Africa from the early 18th century. Their name is Dutch (and Afrikaans) for 'farmer', and related to English *boor*. The *Boer* War is named for the two major conflicts between the Boers and the British in South Africa between 1880 and 1902.

Boğasköy The village in Turkey that is the site of the ancient Hittite capital of Hattuša has a name meaning 'village of the pass', from Turkish *boğaz*, 'pass', 'gorge' and *köy*, 'village'.

Bognor Regis The Sussex coastal resort has a name that means '*Bucge*'s bank', from the Old English personal name *Bucge*, that of a woman, and *ōra*, 'bank', 'edge'. The latter word may not refer to the shore but to the low hills that lie inland from Bognor. The second part of the name, Latin for 'of the king', relates to George V, who convalesced at Craigwell House near Bognor in 1929.

Bogomils The religious sect that arose in Bulgaria in the 10th century is said to have taken its name from that of its founder, the priest *Bogomil*. His own name means 'dear to God', from Old Russian or Bulgarian *bog*, 'God' and *mil*, 'dear'.

Bogotá The Colombian capital was founded on 6 August 1538, the Feast of the Transfiguration. The Spanish name for the festival is *Santa Fé*, literally 'Holy Faith', and this was the city's original name. Later it became *Santa Fé de Bogotá*, the latter word probably being the name of *Bagotta*, an Indian chieftain here.

Bohemia The former central European kingdom takes its name from its historic inhabitants, the *Boii*, whose own name comes from Indoeuropean *bhoi*, 'battle', so that they were 'warriors'. The second part of the name represents Indoeuropean *haimoz*, 'home', giving an overall meaning 'home of the Boii'. The use of 'Bohemian' to mean 'Gypsy', and later applied to an unconventional person, derives from the fact that Gypsies were at one time thought to come from Bohemia. *See also* GYPSY itself.

Boise The state capital of Idaho was named in the early 19th century by French-Canadian trappers. The name represents French *boisé*, 'wooded', referring to the tree-lined river that shaded travellers crossing the arid Snake River Plain. The city thus stands on the river of the same name. The name is pronounced as if 'Boysie'.

Bolivia The South American state takes its name from the nationalist leader Simón *Bolívar* (1783–1830), who fought the Spanish colonial forces in many South American countries, including his native Venezuela. On his liberation of Upper Peru in 1825, that country changed its name to *Bolivia* in his honour.

Bollinger The well-known champagne takes its name from a German vintner, Joseph *Bollinger*, who in 1829 married the daughter of the French vineyard owner for whom he worked, Amiral le comte de Villermont (1762–1840). In 1854 Bollinger took French citizenship and changed his name to Jacques Bollinger de Villermont.

Bologna The name of the city in northern Italy may either derive from Gaulish *bona*, as for BONN, or else from the people known as the *Boii*, who gave the name of BOHEMIA. *See also* BOULOGNE.

Bols The brand of liqueur takes its name from the Dutchman, Lucas *Bols*, who founded his gin-making business in Schiedam in 1575. The company went on to specialize in making *genever*, or Dutch gin, also known as hollands or schnapps. The last of the Bols family died in 1815.

Bolshevik The *Bolsheviks* were the members of the Russian Social Democratic Party who took Lenin's side in the split after the party congress of 1903, and who subsequently seized power in the Revolution of 1917 and became the Communist Party. They were in the majority, as opposed to the MENSHEVIKS, and their name derives from Russian *bol'she*, 'more'. *Cp.* BOLSHOI THEATRE.

Bolshoi Theatre The well-known Moscow theatre has a name that means 'big theatre'. It was founded in 1776 by a group of actors in a private house, but in 1780 moved to a building on Petrovka Street, and took the name *Petrovsky*. The premises were destroyed by fire in 1805, but were rebuilt in 1824 as a larger theatre, known as the *Bolshoy Petrovsky*. This in turn burned down in 1853, and when the new theatre opened in 1856, it was known simply as the *Bolshoy*. English traditionally adopts the French spelling of the name.

Bolton The town near Manchester has a name that is found elsewhere in the north of England. It derives from the Old English words *bōthl*, 'building' and *tūn*, 'settlement', meaning overall 'village with buildings', that is, the main residential part of a settlement, as distinct from outlying farms.

Bolton Wanderers The well-known football club was formed in 1874 as *Christ Church Football Club*, since their ground belonged to this church. A disagreement with the vicar, however, led them to break away, and in 1877 they renamed themselves *Bolton Wanderers*, the latter word referring to the fact that they now had no home ground. They found a ground (at Pikes Lane) in 1881, but kept their name, even when in 1895 they finally moved to their present ground, Burnden Park.

Bomba 'King *Bomba*' was the nickname of the tyrannical king of the Two Sicilies Ferdinand II (1810–1859), given him for his heavy *bombardment* of Messina in 1848. (The word is the Italian for 'bomb'.) It was probably this name that gave that of '*Bomba* the Jungle Boy', the Tarzan-like hero of the popular American stories of the 1920s, with a subsequent movie of 1949, in which Bomba was played by Johnny Sheffield. The original Italian nickname for the king, *Re Bomba*, may have been at least partly suggested by his royal title of *Il Borbone*, 'the Bourbon'.

Bombay *See* MUMBAI.

Bond The common surname was originally the word for a peasant farmer, who was 'bound' to a lord. His status was not as lowly as that of a serf. The Old English word behind the name also gave *husband*, as someone who was originally a house-holder, 'bound' to his house.

Bond Street London's well-known street, with its high-quality shops and stores, takes its name from Sir Thomas *Bond*, a member of the consortium who built it in the late 17th century. The street is properly *Old Bond Street*, to be distinguished from *New Bond Street*, built as its northern continuation in the first quarter of the 18th century.

Boney M The West Indian pop group, formed in West Germany in 1976, were given their name by their songwriter and producer Frank Farian, who based it on an Australian television detective series, *Boney*, showing in Germany at the time. The 'M' is either arbitrary or a reference to the names of three of the group's four members, *M*arcia Barrett, Liz *M*itchell and *M*aizie Williams.

Boniface The name, that of nine popes, is the English form of Late Latin *Bonifatius*, from *bonum*, 'good' and *fatum*, 'fate', a propitious name for a newborn child. In medieval times the name came to be interpreted rather differently as 'doing good', from *bonum* and *facere*, 'to do'. The 8th-century English Benedictine monk St *Boniface*, who brought Christianity to Germany, had the original name of *Wynfrith*, representing Old English *wynn*, 'joy' and *frith*, 'peace', an equally propitious name.

Bon Jovi The American rock band was formed in Sayreville, New Jersey, in 1983 and took its name from the assumed name of its lead singer, Jon *Bon Jovi* (original name, John Bongiovi).

Bonn The German city that was the capital of West Germany derives its name from Gaulish *bona*, 'foundation', 'fortress', 'city'. *Cp.* BOLOGNA and BOULOGNE.

Bonnie and Clyde The well-known pair of American criminals, familiar from the film of the same name (1967), had the full names of *Bonnie* Parker (1911–1934) and *Clyde* Barrow (1900–1934). They carried out a series of bank robberies in Texas and elsewhere in the early 1930s when Clyde, a car thief, teamed up with the daughter of his intended victim. They were killed in a police ambush.

Bonzo The common dog's name was invented by Captain Bruce S. Ingram, editor of *The Sketch*, for a comic-looking puppy that featured in his paper in a series of drawings by G.E. Studdy in the 1920s. The name appears to be arbitrary, but may have been influenced by the popular contemporary Australian colloquialism *bonzer* meaning 'excellent', 'very good'.

Bonzo Dog Doo-Dah Band, The The British pop group, formed in London in 1965, were originally the *Bonzo Dog Dada Band*, formed whimsically from the common dog's name BONZO and a vague reference to the DADA nihilistic art movement of the early 20th century. 'Doo-Dah' is a meaningless repeated phrase in the popular plantation song 'Camptown Races', as well as a general word for any object.

Boodle's The fashionable London club was founded in 1762 and named after its first proprietor, Edward *Boodle* (1722–1772).

Booker Prize The famous annual literary prize for fiction is named after its sponsors, *Booker* plc, formerly *Booker* McConnell, who first financed it in 1969. It is currently worth £20,000.

Book of Common Prayer The service book of the Church of England is so named since it is designed for use for public worship by a congregation, as distinct from private prayer by an individual.

Book of the Dead The name is that of an ancient Egyptian book of incantations, prayers and exorcisms which was buried with the dead to serve as a guide on their journey through the underworld. It is sometimes known as the *Egyptian Bible*.

Boomtown Rats, The The British new wave group, formed in Ireland by Bob Geldof in 1975, originally as the *Nightlife Thugs*, took their name from the film *Bound for Glory* (1976). This was based on the travels through Texas in 1936 of the

American folksinger Woody Guthrie, and included the 'Boomtown Rats' as a group of newcomers to the Oklahoma oil fields in Guthrie's home area.

Boon The surname is either a variant of *Bone*, from a Norman nickname meaning 'good' (as modern French *bon*), or else applied to a person who had come from *Bohon*, near Cherbourg in northern France.

Boötes The constellation of the northern hemisphere represents a herdsman driving a bear (Ursa Major) round a pole. Hence its name, which is the Greek word for 'herdsman', 'ploughman', from *bous*, 'cow', 'ox'. The constellation's brightest star has the related name ARCTURUS.

Booth The name would originally have been used for someone who lived in a small hut or bothy, or for a person who was a cowherd or shepherd.

Boots The British pharmacy chain takes its name from its founder, Jesse *Boot* (1850–1931), a Nottingham chemist who took over his father's shop, trading in medicinal herbs, in 1863. He built up a business in the sale of patent medicines and the manufacture of drugs, so that by his death he had over 1000 shops nationwide.

Bophuthatswana The 'independent' black national state, within the territory of South Africa, has a Tswana name, from *bo-*, a prefix for abstract nouns, *phutha*, 'to gather', and *tswana*, the name of the TSWANA people. Overall the sense is thus 'place where the Tswana gather'. *See also* BOTSWANA.

Bordeaux The French city and port had the Roman name *Burdigala*, which comprises two Aquitanian words, *burd* and *gala*, both of uncertain meaning. They may represent the name of a tribe once here. Popular etymology explains the name as meaning 'by the water's edge', from French *au bord des eaux*. But, as usual, this is fancy at work!

Borders The name is officially that of a region of southeast Scotland, so called since it is located by the border with England. The term 'the Borders' has long been in use to describe the district that straddles the English-Scottish border, roughly along the Cheviot Hills, and the term almost

certainly originated in Scotland, since to the Scots *the* border would have been the only one, that with England. The abbreviation *N.B.* meaning 'north of the border' was for some time in unofficial use as a postal term for 'Scotland'.

Boris The Russian name is probably not of Russian origin, but originated from a Tatar word meaning 'small'. It was taken to be a pet form of a longer Russian name such as *Borislav*, however, where the first half of the name represents Slavic *bor*, 'battle', 'struggle'.

Borneo The large Pacific island has a name that is a Portuguese alteration of BRUNEI, located on it.

Bornholm The name of the Danish island, in the Baltic Sea, was originally *Burgundarholm*, from Old Danish *Burgundar*, 'Burgundians' (*see* BURGUNDY) and *holm*, 'island'. It was from Bornholm that the Burgundians emigrated to France in the 5th century AD.

Borstal The term 'borstal' was originally used for what are now known as young offender institutions. It derives from the former prison for young offenders at *Borstal* near Rochester, Kent, where the first detention centre for young offenders was opened in 1908. Rather curiously, the place-name actually means 'security place', from Old English *borg*, 'security', 'bail' (modern *borrow*) and *steall*, 'place' (modern *stall*). The name would have been used for a safe place of refuge in battle, and *borstal* itself came to be used as a local dialect word for a narrow sunken path up the side of a hill, in which a person could feel 'secure'.

Borussia The German football club, based in Dortmund, has a name which is the Roman name of PRUSSIA, in which their home city was originally located (from 1815).

Boscobel House The 17th-century country house near Shifnal, Shropshire, is famous as the place where Charles II took refuge in an oak tree after his defeat at the Battle of Worcester. The name derives from Italian *bosco bello*, 'beautiful wood', describing its sylvan setting.

Bosnia-Herzegovina The former constituent republic of Yugoslavia, independent since 1991, has a name representing the two provinces that united under Austria-Hungary in 1878, *Herzegovina* having itself been formed as an independent duchy in the 15th century from the southern part of the original Bosnia. *Bosnia* takes its name from the river *Bosna*, itself perhaps from an Indoeuropean root word *bhog* meaning 'current'. *Herzegovina* has a name denoting its original status as a duchy, from Old Serbian *herceg*, 'duke', followed by the possessive ending *-ov*, in turn followed by the suffix *-ina*, meaning 'country', 'territory'. *Herceg* (which gave modern German *Herzog*) was the title taken in 1448 by the local ruler Stjepan Vukčić, and it was he who demarcated his territory from that of Bosnia.

Bosporus The name, also spelled *Bosphorus*, is that of the strait joining the Black Sea with the Sea of Marmara. It is traditionally derived from Greek *bous*, 'ox' and *poros*, 'passage', 'ford', so that essentially it is the same as OXFORD. In Greek mythology, the strait is the one that Io swam across after she had been changed by Zeus into a heifer. (*See* IO.) The Turkish name of the Bosporus is *Karadeniz Boğazı*, 'Black Sea strait', from *Karadeniz*, 'Black Sea' and *boğaz*, 'strait'.

Boston The state capital of Massachusetts takes its name from the English port of *Boston*, Lincolnshire, the home of many of its original Puritan settlers. The English *Boston* has a name that is popularly interpreted as 'St Botolph's stone', St Botolph being the local saint to whom Boston's main church, the 'Boston Stump', is dedicated, and the 'stone' being the one where he preached. But historical evidence is lacking to establish the identity of this particular saint.

Boston Pops Orchestra The American orchestra, drawn from members of the regular Boston Symphony Orchestra, gave the first of an annual series of light music concerts in 1885. From 1900 the concerts were known as 'Pops', for the popular works that were played, and the name was transferred to the orchestra itself.

Boston Tea Party The name came to be ironically given to an incident in 1773 when American colonists, disguised as Red Indians, threw a cargo of tea into Boston harbour as a protest against the newly imposed British tax on tea. It was one of the events that led to the War of American Independence (American Revolution).

Bosworth, Battle of The battle, also known as the *Battle of Bosworth Field*, was the one of 1485 that ended the Wars of the Roses, in which Richard III was killed and Henry Tudor was crowned king as Henry VII. Bosworth Field is south of *Market Bosworth*, Leicestershire, and the town took its name from the site. The name itself means '*Bār*'s village', from an Old English personal name and the word *worth*, denoting an enclosure or homestead.

Botany Bay The inlet on the east coast of Australia is so named from the many unfamiliar botanical species found there in 1770 by Captain Cook. In his diary entry for 6 May that year Cook wrote: 'The great quantity of New Plants &ca. Mr. Banks and Dr. Solander found in this place occasioned my giving it the name of Botany Bay'.

Botswana The republic of southern Africa is named for its indigenous inhabitants, the Tswana, from *bo-*, the prefix for abstract nouns, and TSWANA, the people themselves. It was formerly known as *Bechuanaland*, the first part of this being an English corruption of *Botswana*.

Boudicca The queen of the Iceni, still popularly known as *Boadicea*, the Latin form of her name, is famous in history for leading a revolt of the native Britons against the Romans in the 1st century AD. Her name means 'victor' (which in the event she was not), from a Celtic root word that gave modern Irish *buaidh*, 'victory' and Welsh *buddugwr*, 'victor'.

Bougainville The name of the largest of the Solomon Islands, in the western Pacific, derives from that of the French navigator Louis Antoine de *Bougainville* (1729–1811), who discovered it in 1768. *See also* FALKLAND ISLANDS.

Boulogne The French town, on the English Channel, derives its name from Gaulish *bona*, 'foundation', 'fortress', as for BOLOGNA. It seems unlikely that the Roman emperor Constantine named Boulogne directly for the Italian city, as has been claimed. *See also* Bois de BOULOGNE.

Boulogne, Bois de The famous Paris park, to the west of the city centre, takes its name from the village (now suburb) of *Boulogne*-Billancourt, towards which it extends. The village, formerly named *Boulogne-sur-Seine*, is so called as it was founded by pilgrims from the coastal resort of BOULOGNE. The full name of the latter, to be distinguished from it, is *Boulogne-sur-Mer*.

Bourbon The French royal house takes its name from the former province of *Bourbonnais*, central France, itself with a name deriving from that of *Borbo* or *Borvo*, a Celtic god associated with warm springs. The god's name is in turn formed from Gaulish *borvo*, 'foam', 'froth', probably related to Greek *borboros*, 'mud', 'mire'. The type of American whiskey known as *Bourbon* takes its name from *Bourbon* county, Kentucky, where it was first made. The county was named for the French royal family at the time of the American Revolution, when there was a keen interest in things French.

Bournemouth The well-known Dorset coastal resort has a purely descriptive name meaning 'mouth of the *Bourne*'. The Bourne is the little river that flows through the Pleasure Gardens into the English Channel here. Its own name means simply 'stream', like Scottish *burn*.

Bournville The make of Cadbury's chocolate takes its name from the purpose-built factory and estate near Birmingham where it was first produced in the 1880s. The first part of the name is that of the *Bourn* Brook here. The latter half was chosen for its French associations, since French chocolate was highly regarded at that time.

Bovril The concentrated essence of beef was so named in 1887 from a combination of Latin *bos*, genitive *bovis*, 'ox', and *vril*, an artificial word occurring in Lord Lytton's novel *The Coming Race* (1871). In the latter, it is a type of mysterious force, and is presumably itself derived from Latin *virilis* or English *virile*:

> These people consider that in vril they have arrived at the unity in natural energic agencies, which has been conjectured by many philosophers.
>
> Chapter 7.

Bow Bells A person born within the sound of *Bow Bells* is traditionally said to be a true Cockney. The bells are those of the church of St Mary-le-Bow, in Cheapside, London. The church's own name does not relate to *Bow*, the district of east London, so named for an arched bridge over the river Lea here, but refers to the curved arches of the Norman crypt over which the church itself stands. *See also* MARYLEBONE.

Bowen The name is Welsh, meaning 'son of OWEN'. The initial *B* of the name represents Welsh *ap* or *ab*, 'son of'.

Bowery, The The name is that of a street and section of Lower Manhattan in New York. The street follows a road that led to the *bouwerie* (farm) of the Governor, Peter Stuyvesant. Hence its name.

Bow Group The title is that of an influential society of younger members of the Conservative Party. They take their name from the place where they first met in 1951, the *Bow* and Bromley Club, in southeast London.

Bowman The name is occupational and means what it says, describing a person who was a good shot with a bow and arrow. It thus corresponds to ARCHER. *Cp.* BOWYER.

Bow Street The name is used for the chief London Metropolitan police court, near the former Covent Garden. The street itself is so named for its curve, like that of a *bow*.

Bowyer The name was an occupational one for a person who made *bows*, as distinct from a BOWMAN, who was an ARCHER.

Boxer Rebellion The name refers to the tragic incidents of 1899 and 1900 in which Chinese nationalists besieged the foreign legations in Peking (Beijing) and murdered European missionaries and hundreds of Chinese Christian converts. The nationalists originally belonged to the secret religious organization known in Chinese as *yìhéquán*, 'righteous harmonious fist', from *yì*, 'righteous', *hé*, 'harmonious' and *quán*, 'fist', 'boxing'. New members vowed that they would not 'be avaricious, be debauched, disobey parents' rules, disobey existing laws', and that they would 'destroy foreigners, kill corrupt officials'. Rebel members of the organization subsequently became known as the *yihéqún*, 'righteous harmonious group', with *qún*, 'group', 'crowd' a modification of *quán*, 'fist'. It was these rebels who were involved in the insurrection. Because 'fist' had formed part of the original name, however, they were (incorrectly) known as *Boxers*.

Boxing Day The public holiday on 26 December, the day after Christmas Day, is so named because it was formerly the custom to give 'Christmas *boxes*', that is, gifts of money, to tradespeople, postmen, errand boys, servants and the like. The custom seems to date back to the late 18th or even early 19th century, and is associated with this particular day since on Christmas Day itself most of the people who received the gift would have been kept busy.

Boycott A person of this name would have come from one of the places so called, now very small hamlets mostly in the Midlands. The name itself means '*Boia*'s cottage'. It was the retired army captain Charles *Boycott* (1832–1897), a land agent in Co Mayo, Ireland, who gave the word *boycott* to the language as a result of his tenants' refusal to deal with him in an attempt to get their rents reduced. The word actually arose in the autumn of 1880 to describe the action taken by the Irish Land League against those who incurred its wrath:

> The people of New Pallas have resolved to 'Boycott' them and refused to supply them with food or drink.
> *The Times*, 20 November 1880.

Boyne The river in Northern Ireland, well-kown from the *Battle of the Boyne* that was fought on its banks in 1690, with William III of England defeating the deposed James II, takes its name from Irish *bo bhán*, 'white cow'. The reference is not to a literal animal but to the traditional symbol of good fortune in Irish folklore.

Boy Scouts The original name of the *Scouts*, the youth movement founded by Robert Baden-Powell in 1908, was inspired by the military *scouts* who carried out reconnoitring in time of combat. Baden-Powell used the word in this sense in his own writings prior to the formation of his movement: 'Without special training a man cannot have a thorough confidence in himself as a scout'

(*The Matabele Campaign*, 1896). *Cp.* the quotation under GIRL GUIDES.

Brabançonne, La The Belgian national anthem was composed in 1830 and takes its name from the former Netherlands duchy of BRABANT, where the revolt of the French-speaking population that year led to the formation of Belgium as an independent state. The Flemish population of Belgium did not accept *La Brabançonne* as their national anthem until 1951.

Brabant The province of central Belgium has a name of Old High German origin, from *bracha*, 'new land' and *bant*, 'region'. The present province was formerly *South Brabant*, and in Dutch hands until 1830. *North Brabant* is now a province of the Netherlands. It has kept the name even though geographically it is in the south of the country.

Bradford There are many places of the name in England, with the industrial city near Leeds the best known. The name means simply 'broad ford', and in the case of the Yorkshire town would probably have denoted a ford over what is now the small Bradford Beck, in the city centre. This particular *Bradford* is unusual in being a city that is not on a river of any size.

Bradman The name was originally a nickname for a 'broad man', otherwise a well-built person.

Braemar The Scottish village, not far from Balmoral in Grampian, is famous for its annual Highland Games, the *Braemar Gathering*. The place-name means 'upper part of *Marr*', from Gaelic *braigh*, 'upper' and a personal name.

Bragg The surname arose as a nickname for a cheerful or lively person, from a former English word *bragge* to which the modern verb *brag* meaning 'boast' is related.

Braggadochio The name is that of the boaster or *braggart* in Spenser's *Faerie Queene* (1590, 1596). The poet probably derived the name from a combination of English *braggart* and the Italian augmentative suffix *-occio*, often implying plumpness (as in *bamboccio*, 'fat child'). The name has since become generic for a braggart or for boastful talk.

Bragi In Scandinavian mythology, the name is that of the son of Odin who was the god of poetry and music. It probably derives from Icelandic *bragr*, 'poet', 'best'.

Brahma In Hinduism, the name is that of the creator of the cosmos, forming with Vishnu and Siva the Trimurti, or three aspects of the absolute spirit. It is Sanskrit in origin, from *brahman*, 'praise', 'prayer'.

Brahmaputra The great Asian river, a tributary of the Ganges, has a name that literally means 'son of Brahma', from Hindi BRAHMA, the Hindu god, and *putra*, 'son'.

Brandenburg The former Prussian province and East German city are traditionally said to have a name of Slavic origin, from *Branibor*, literally 'defence forest'. Others, however, have derived the name from a Germanic original meaning 'burnt city', with words corresponding to modern German *Brand*, 'burning' and *Burg*, 'fortress', 'city'. The name may actually be of Celtic origin, and relate to a personal name such as *Brando*.

Brandenburg Concertos The six concertos by Bach, composed between 1711 and 1720, were dedicated to Christian Ludwig, Margrave of *Brandenburg*, and so are named for him.

Brandenburg Gate The well-known Berlin gateway, at the western end of Unter den Linden, and formerly the entrance to East Berlin from West Berlin, is so named as it led out of Berlin to the road to BRANDENBURG.

Brands Hatch The famous motor-racing circuit near Gravesend, Kent, has a name that literally means 'brink gate', referring to a gate or 'hatch' that leads to land on a slope, a 'brink'. Brands Hatch is actually located on a fairly steep slope.

Brandywine, Battle of The battle was that of 1777 in the War of American Independence (American Revolution) in which the British, under Howe, defeated the Americans, under Washington. It takes its name from the place where it occurred, *Brandywine* Creek in Pennsylvania. The name of the creek probably arose as a folk interpretation of the name of a landowner here, one Andrew *Braindwine*.

Branston Pickle The popular pickle, made by Crosse & Blackwell, takes its name from the village of *Branston*, near Burton-upon-Trent, Staffordshire, where it was first made in 1920.

Brasenose College The Oxford college takes its name from a bronze knocker on the main gate of the original *Brasenose Hall* in medieval times. The knocker was taken to Stamford in the 14th century when an academic group went there to set up a more tranquil site for university studies than turbulent Oxford. It remained there on Brasenose House until 1890, when the college bought it back. Brasenose College itself was founded in 1509, when in the absence of the original 'brazen nose' a new knocker was made in the form of a human face and fastened to the main gate.

Brasilia The capital of Brazil (from 1960) has a name that is simply the New Latin name of BRAZIL itself.

Braşov The city in central Romania has a name representing Hungarian *Brassó*, which itself may be a form of the Turkish name *Borašugh*, 'clean water', although this interpretation is disputed. It has also borne the German name *Kronstadt*, 'crown town'. From 1950 to 1960 the city was known as *Oraşul Stalin*, 'the town of Stalin', from Romanian *oraş*, 'town' with the suffix *-ul*, 'the', and the name of the famous Soviet leader.

Bratislava The capital of Slovakia, in eastern Europe, takes its name from that of a former Slav colony that was itself probably named for its head or founder. The Polish city of WROCŁAW has a name of identical origin.

Brazil The name of the South American country derives from that of the *brazil* tree, found widely here, and valued for its red dye wood. (It is not the same tree as the one that yields Brazil nuts, although as its name implies that also grows in Brazil.)

Brazzaville The capital of the Congo Republic takes its name from the French explorer Pierre Savorgnan de *Brazza* (1852–1905) who founded it in 1883. He was born an Italian count, and his own name derives from the Adriatic island of *Brazza*, now known as *Brač* and belonging to Croatia. He became a French citizen in 1874.

Brecon Beacons The mountain range in South Wales takes its name from the nearby town of *Brecon*. The peaks are called 'beacons' because they were used as sites for signal fires in medieval times, as hills and mountains were elsewhere in Britain. *Brecon* itself derives its name from the personal name *Brychan*, that of a 5th-century Welsh prince. The Welsh name of the town is *Aberhonddu*, 'mouth of the Honddu', the latter being the name of the river that joins the Usk where Brecon stands.

Breda The city in the southern Netherlands has a name that represents Old Dutch *brede*, 'broad' (modern Dutch *breed*) and *a*, 'river'. Breda lies at the junction of the rivers Merk and Aa, the latter name meaning simply 'river' and identical to the second element of the city's name.

Bregenz The resort in western Austria derives its name from Celtic *briga*, 'height', referring to its location on the shore of Lake Constance at the foot of the Pfänder Mountain. *Cp.* BREST (in Brittany) and BRIE.

Bremen The German city has a name that goes back to Old High German *brem*, 'marshland', a word to which modern English *brim* is related. Bremen is a port in low-lying land on the river Weser, whose own name is also 'watery' in origin.

Bremerhaven The German port, at the mouth of the river Weser, has a name simply meaning 'port for BREMEN', since the latter is 43 miles (69 km) inland. The former name of Bremerhaven was *Wesermünde*, 'mouth of the *Weser*'.

Brenda The name may derive from a Scandinavian word *brand*, 'burning', perhaps with reference to a 'flaming sword'. Despite the similarity, it is almost certainly not related to BRENDAN.

Brendan This is an English form of the Irish name *Bréanainn*, based on a Celtic word meaning 'prince'. (*Cp.* Welsh *brenin*, 'king'.) It was made famous by the 6th-century Irish saint, *Brendan* the Voyager, said to have been the first European to have landed in America.

Breslau *See* WROCŁAW.

Brest The port in Brittany, northwest France, has a Celtic name representing *bre*, 'hill', with this word in turn from Gaulish *briga* of identical meaning. Brest lies on two hills divided by the river Penfeld. *Cp.* BREGENZ and BRIE.

Brest The town in Byelorussia, on the Polish border, takes its name from Slavic *berest*, 'elm', a tree found widely here. It was formerly (until 1921) known as *Brest-Litovsk*, the latter part of which means 'Lithuanian'. The town passed to Lithuania in the early 14th century.

Brett The surname originally applied to someone who was a *Breton*, from *Brittany*. In some cases it could have been a nickname for a dull or slow person, as the Bretons had a reputation for stupidity.

Brewer The name arose as an occupational one for a person who brewed beer or ale.

Brian The name is probably of Celtic origin, from a root word *brig* meaning 'high', to which Scottish *brae* as a word for 'hill' is related. *Brian* has always been a popular name in Ireland, thanks to *Brian* Boru, a famous 10th-century high king.

Bridewell The name was that of a notorious house of correction for vagrants in Blackfriars, London. It took its name from the well dedicated to St *Bride* (BRIDGET) that was originally on the territory of the royal palace built here in the early 16th century for Henry VIII. The buildings were destroyed in 1863. *Bridewell* came to be a general word for any house of correction or prison.

Bridge The name originally described someone who lived by a bridge or who kept a bridge as a toll collector. The name *Bridges* has the same meaning, and did not necessarily denote a plural. *Cp.* BANKS in this respect.

Bridge of Sighs The name is that of a covered bridge in Venice that led from the Doge's palace to the state prison. The bridge was the route by which prisoners under sentence of death were led to their fate, and the name poetically but grimly relates to this. The name is also that of a bridge resembling it at St John's College, Cambridge, leading over the river Cam.

Bridgeport The Connecticut city, on Long Island Sound, has a name that dates from 1800 and that commemorates the opening of the first drawbridge over the Pequonnock River here.

Bridget The name is an English form of the Irish name *Brighid*, of uncertain origin. It is probably not derived from Irish *brigh*, 'force', since that word has a long vowel (pronounced roughly 'bree'), while *Bridget* has a short one. St *Bridget*, also known as St *Bride*, was the 6th-century founder of a church and monastery at Kildare. She is now a patron saint of Ireland.

Bridgetown The capital of Barbados takes its name from the bridge built here by Carlisle Bay when the town was founded in the early 17th century.

Bridgwater The Somerset town has a somewhat misleading name, referring not to a bridge over water but to '*Walter*'s bridge', the personal name being that of the Norman owner of the bridge, *Walter de Dowai*. Even so, the bridge of the name does cross the water of the river Parrett.

Brie The well-known type of soft French cheese derives its name from the region of *Brie* east of Paris. The ground rises here, as is indicated by the name, which derives from Gaulish *briga*, 'hill', 'height'. *Cp.* BREGENZ and BREST (in Brittany).

Briggs The name originally denoted someone who lived by a *bridge*, or who was a bridge keeper.

Bright The name would originally have been given as a nickname for a person who was fair or attractive.

Brighton The name of the well-known English resort, in East Sussex, has evolved from Old English *Beorhthelms tūn*, '*Beorhthelm*'s farm'. It is not known who the farm owner was, but his name translates as 'bright helmet', implying a famous warrior. Brighton was known as *Brighthelmstone* as recently as the 19th century.

Brighton and Hove Albion The Sussex football club was founded in 1900 as *Brighton and Hove Rangers*. It gained its present name when it turned professional in 1901. Rather than being adopted from the already existing WEST BROMWICH

ALBION, it appears that the name refers to the *Albion* Hotel, Queen's Road, Brighton, where the club members held their committee meetings.

Brindisi The Italian port takes its name from an Illyrian word *brento* or *bretto*, meaning 'deer'. These animals must have been numerous here at one time.

Brisbane The capital of Queensland, Australia, is named for Sir Thomas Makdougall *Brisbane* (1773–1860), the Scottish general who was governor of New South Wales (then a larger region than now) from 1821 to 1825. Brisbane was named when the former convict settlement there became a town in 1834.

Bristol The famous West of England port has a name that is basically the equivalent of *Bridgestow*, meaning 'place with a bridge'. The bridge referred to may have been where Bristol Bridge is now, crossing the Floating Harbour. The final *l* of the name derives from a local pronunciation where this letter is added to words ending in a vowel sound, so that the name *Monica* is pronounced 'Monical', for example. Bristol gave its name to the *Bristol Channel*, on which it stands. *Cp.* the surname BRISTOW.

Bristow The name originally applied to someone who came from BRISTOL.

Britain The name of the country comes from that of her people, the *Britons*. Their own name was recorded by the Greeks in the 4th century BC as *Prittanoi*, explained as meaning literally 'figured folk', 'tattooed people', referring to their habit of decorating their bodies, as the Ancient Britons did with woad. *See also* PICTS and *cp.* BRITTANY.

Britannia The Roman name of BRITAIN is in use for various applications in modern times. It is that of the figure of a woman with a shield and a trident on the reverse of certain coins of the realm, a personification of Britain, the name of the Royal Yacht, and that of the college for officer cadets of the Royal Navy at Dartmouth, in full *Britannia Royal Naval College*, formerly HMS *Britannia*.

British Columbia The Canadian province was established as a British crown colony in 1858, and the name was officially proclaimed that year. It derives from that of the river *Columbia*, which was itself named by the American captain Robert Gray for his ship *Columbia*, in turn named for Christopher *Columbus*. It was originally planned to name the province *New Caledonia*, after the Roman name of Scotland, but this was rejected in favour of *British Columbia*, apparently by Queen Victoria herself, in order to avoid confusion with the French island of that name.

Brittany The region of northwest France, called *Bretagne* in French, has a name that directly relates to that of BRITAIN. It arose in the 5th century when Britons living in southern Britain fled across the English Channel to this part of France to escape the invading Germanic tribes of Angles, Saxons and Jutes. *See also* GREAT BRITAIN.

BRM The make of British Grand Prix racing cars derives from the initials of both *British Racing Motors*, who produced them, and Peter *Berthon* and *Raymond Mays*, who originally designed them in the 1930s.

Brno The city in the southeastern Czech Lands, known to the Germans as *Brünn*, has a name that may derive from Old Czech *brn*, 'clay', referring to the damp, muddy location here, or less probably from German *Brunnen*, 'spring'.

Broadbent The surname derives from a place so called, a hamlet near Oldham, Lancashire. The name itself means 'broad bent', the latter being a type of grass.

Broadmoor Well-known as a hospital for mentally disturbed criminal offenders, near Crowthorne, Berkshire, the name is self-descriptive, referring to the expanse of open land where the original *Broadmoor Asylum* was built in 1873.

Broads The *Broads*, or *Norfolk Broads*, are a group of about 12 lakes in Norfolk and Suffolk, famous for their bird life and boating amenities. The name describes the wider waters of the lakes, by contrast with the 'narrow' waters of the rivers and other channels that join them.

Broadstairs The Kent coastal resort has a name that means what it says, referring to a 'broad stairway' that was cut in the cliffside to give access to the sea some time in the 15th century.

Broadway The major avenue in New York, famous for its theatres in the section nicknamed 'the Great White Way', has a self-descriptive name as a wide thoroughfare, by contrast with a road of standard width. The name is not unique to this street, and the English town of *Broadway*, near Evesham, Hereford and Worcester, has a name dating from at least the 10th century. Other villages of the name exist elsewhere in Britain.

Brobdingnag The country of giants in Jonathan Swift's famous novel *Gulliver's Travels* (1726), visited by Gulliver after his 'voyage to Lilliput', has a name that appears to be as arbitrary as that of its capital, *Lorbrulgrud*, although the latter is (satirically) said by Swift to mean 'Pride of the Universe'. It is, however, possible to detect a form of Old English *gigant*, 'giant' in the name, with the initial *Brob*-suggesting Welsh *bro*, 'land', 'region'. In a mock introductory letter to 'his Cousin Sympson', Gulliver states that the name should have been spelled 'Brobdingrag' but was misprinted. It has also been suggested that this could be a near-anagram of 'grand big noble'!

Brodie The Scottish surname derives from *Brodie* Castle, near Forres, now in Grampian. The place-name itself probably comes from Gaelic *brothach*, 'muddy'.

Brogan This is an English form of the Irish name *Ó Brógáin*, 'descendant of *Brógán*', the latter personal name perhaps deriving from Irish *bróg*, 'shoe' (*cp*. English *brogues*).

Broken Hill The Australian town, in western New South Wales, was so named in 1883 when minerals such as lead, zinc and silver were extracted from the land here, and the 'hill' was 'broken'. The Zambian town of *Kabwe* formerly had the same name for the same reason.

Bromberg *See* BYDGOSCSZ.

Bronx, The The New York borough derives its name from the Dutch immigrant farmer Jonas *Bronck*, who had a farm here just north of Manhattan Island. People came to speak of going to 'the Broncks', and the name then developed into its present spelling. The definite article remains as part of the name.

Brook A person of this name would have originally lived near a brook or stream.

Brooke Bond The make of tea derives its name from that of Arthur *Brooke*, a Manchester tea merchant who set up his retail business in 1869. The second half of the name was chosen simply for its alliterative and prestigious associations, and there was no Mr *Bond* behind the business.

Brooklands The motor-racing circuit near Weybridge, Surrey, took its name from *Brookland* Farm, which was absorbed into the complex when it was built in 1907 as a test ground for early makes of motor car. The farm took its name from the low-lying marshland and streams by the river Wey here. The circuit was long disused, but was reopened in 1991.

Brooklyn The New York City borough was founded in 1636 by the Dutch farmer Joris Jensen de Rapelje, who named it after his native village of *Breukelen*, near Amsterdam. This was subsequently anglicized to *Brooklyn*, as if named for a brook.

Brooks's The London club, favoured by Conservatives, was founded in 1764 and takes its name from its proprietor from 1778, William *Brooks*, a wine merchant and moneylender.

Bros The British pop trio, formed in 1980, took its name from its twin brother members Matt and Luke Goss, at the same time rhyming with their surname and developing from the group's original name, *Gloss*.

Brough The surname applies to someone who came from any of the places so called, most of them in the north of England. The name itself means 'fortress', from Old English *burh* (modern English *borough*).

Brown The very common surname would originally have been a nickname for someone with brown hair or brown skin, especially a person who was conspicuous among fair-haired or pale-skinned people.

Brownie The make of Kodak camera has a name that was taken by Kodak's founder, George Eastman, from the little humanoid creatures who appeared in the books and poems of the American writer and illustrator Palmer Cox. These 'Brownies' were helpful and efficient, as Eastman wished the camera to be. *Cp.* BROWNIES.

Brownies The *Brownie Guides* derive their name from the elf-like beings in the stories by Juliana Horatia Ewing, *The Brownies, and other tales* (1870). Although these original Brownies were two brothers, they were industrious in the home, and this, together with their name, appealed to Robert Baden-Powell when he founded the Brownies as a junior branch of the Girl Guides in 1918. The girls wear a brown uniform to reinforce the association. *See also* BROWN OWL.

Browning The surname basically means 'son of BROWN', that is, a descendant of a person nicknamed for his brown hair or skin.

Brown Owl The title adopted for the leader of a pack of BROWNIES derives from the Old Owl in the stories by Mrs Ewing that gave the name of the Brownies themselves. In these, the Old Owl shows the brothers what to do as 'Brownies'. The name is no longer in official use and the leader's title is now usually *Brownie Guider*.

Brown's Hotel The fashionable London hotel is named for James *Brown*, a former manservant, who opened it in 1837.

Brown University The American university was founded by Baptists in Providence, Rhode Island in 1764 and was originally called *Rhode Island College*. In 1804 it was given its present name, for the businessman who was instrumental in locating it, Nicholas *Brown* (1729–1791).

Bruce The first name was adopted from the Scottish surname, famous as that of Robert the *Bruce*, the 14th-century king of Scotland. The name itself is probably Norman in origin, from some place in France that has not been positively identified.

Brücke, Die The German Expressionist art movement, flourishing in the early years of the 20th century, has a name translating as 'The Bridge'. It was given by a member of the group, the student of architecture Karl Schmidt-Rottluff, who explained that one of the aims of *Die Brücke* was 'to conduct toward it all the revolutionary and fermenting elements'.

Bruges The city in northwest Belgium has a name that represents Flemish *brug*, 'bridge', referring either to the many bridges over the canals here or to the fact that the town arose by a particular bridge. Its Dutch name is *Brugge*. *See also* ZEEBRUGGE.

Bruin The traditional name for a bear is found in the medieval French fables known as the *Roman de Renart*, in which the chief character is Reynard the Fox. It represents Dutch *bruin*, 'brown'.

Brumaire The second month of the French Revolutionary calendar, corresponding to the period 23 October to 21 November, has a name deriving from French *brume*, 'mist'.

Brunei The former sultanate on the north coast of BORNEO, to which it gave its name, has a Hindi name that probably derives ultimately from Sanskrit *bhūmi*, 'land', 'region'.

Brunel University The university, at Uxbridge, Middlesex, is noted for its engineering studies and links with industry. It is named for the engineer Isambard Kingdom *Brunel* (1769–1849), whose Great Western Railway passed through Acton, where the university was founded as a college of advanced technology in 1957. It received its charter in 1966.

Brunhild The legendary queen of Germanic and Scandinavian mythology, who in the *Nibelungenlied* was won for King Gunther by Siegfried, has a name that represents either Icelandic *Brynhildr* or Middle High German *Brünhilt*. It combines Germanic *brun*, 'armour', 'protection' and *hild*, 'battle', implying overall 'battle in a protected place'. The name is familiar as that of *Brünnhilde*, the Valkyrie in Wagner's opera cycle *The Ring of the Nibelung* (1876).

Brünn *See* BRNO.

Brunswick The city in central Germany, with the native name of *Braunschweig*, has a name that means '*Bruno*'s settlement', from *Bruno*, the son of the Saxon duke Liutolf, who founded it in 861, and Old

High German *wīch*, 'village', found also in many English place-names, such as NORWICH and GREENWICH.

Brussels The Belgian capital has a name of Germanic origin, from *broca*, 'marsh' and *sali*, 'room', 'building', the latter word borrowed from Latin *cella*, 'room', 'granary' (English *cell* and *cellar*). Brussels is low-lying, and arose in the 6th century as a fortress on a small island in the river Senne, a tributary of the Scheldt.

Brutus Famous as the Roman statesman who plotted with Cassius to kill Julius Caesar, *Brutus* has a name that derives from the identical Latin word meaning 'heavy', 'dull', 'stupid', in which in turn gave English *brute*. This was a Roman *nomen* or clan name, not a first name.

Bryanston The public school near Blandford, Dorset, founded in 1928, takes its name from the parish in which it is located, itself meaning '*Brian*'s estate'. One *Brian* de Insula held the manor here in the 13th century.

Bryant The name derives from the personal name BRIAN, with a final (and extraneous) -*t* added at some stage.

Bryant & May The well-known make of safety matches is named for the partnership of William *Bryant* (1804–1874) and Francis *May* (1803–1885), set up in London in 1839, originally as general merchants, with matches only a sideline. They first produced safety matches in 1861.

Bryher The name of the smallest of the five populated islands of the Scilly Isles derives from a conjectural Cornish word *bre*, 'hill', with the plural ending -*yer*. It thus means 'hills', and could refer to the highest part of the single island that the Scillies once were.

Brylcreem The patent hair dressing by the Beecham Group has a name that is a stylized blend of '*brill*iantine' and '*cream*'. *Brylcreem* was first marketed by the County Chemical Company in 1928. During the early years of the Second World War, a nickname for smart young Royal Air Force officers was 'the Brylcreem Boys', from an advertisement depicting such an officer who had dressed his hair with Bryl-creem.

Bryn Mawr College The American college was founded in 1880 and takes its name from the residential community of *Bryn Mawr*, Pennsylvania, in which it is located. The place-name itself was adopted from the South Wales town and means 'big hill'.

Brythonic The name of the southern group of Celtic languages, comprising Welsh, Cornish and Breton, derives from Welsh *Brithon*, 'Briton'. *See also* BRITAIN, BRIT-TANY.

Bucephalus The name of Alexander the Great's favourite horse is Greek in origin, as *Boukephalos*, 'bull head', from *bous*, 'ox', 'bullock' and *kephalē*, 'head'. The name was an epithet of horses generally, and referred to the fact that they were branded with a bull's head.

Buchan The Scottish name derives from any of the districts so called, themselves probably so named as they were pasture lands for cows, from Gaelic *baogh*, 'cow'.

Buchanan The Scottish name comes from *Buchanan* Castle, near Loch Lomond, so named as it was originally the 'canon's house', from Gaelic *buth*, 'house' (*cp.* English *bothy*) and *chanain*, 'of the canon'.

Bucharest The Romanian capital is tradition-ally said to take its name from a shepherd called *Bucur*, who is supposed to have founded it in 1457. But there was almost certainly a settlement here before this. Its original name may, even so, be a personal name, perhaps that of a landowner. A deri-vation from Romanian *a bucura*, 'to rejoice' seems unlikely.

Buckingham The town in the county of the same name has a name that is best under-stood as meaning 'land in the bend of a river belonging to *Bucca*'s people'. *Bucca* is the personal name that forms the first part of the name. The *-ing-* represents the people who were associated with him, and the *-ham* derives from Old English *hamm*, a term for 'hemmed-in' land, in this case enclosed in a river bend. Buckingham is in a bend of the river Ouse.

Buckingham Palace The London home of the British sovereign takes its name from the title of John Sheffield, first Duke of

Buckingham (1648–1721), for whom it was originally built (as *Buckingham House*) in 1703, the year that he was created duke. It became a palace after it was bought by George III in 1762.

Buck's Club The London club opened in 1919 and took its name from Captain Herbert *Buckmaster*, a Household Cavalry officer, who with fellow officers had the idea of starting such a club while they were at the front in the First World War.

Bucks Fizz The British pop group, formed in 1981 with the express purpose of repre-senting Britain in the Eurovision Song Con-test, which they won, took their name from the upper-class nickname for a cock-tail composed of champagne and orange juice. This was a 'fizz' said to have been invented by the first barman at BUCK'S CLUB, London.

Budapest The Hungarian capital was formed in 1872 from the merger of two separate towns, *Buda*, on the right bank of the Danube, and *Pest*, on the left bank. *Buda*'s name is said to derive from that of its founder, *Buda* or *Bleda*, a brother of Atti-la, although it is more likely to relate to some word meaning simply 'water'. *Pest* (pronounced 'Pesht') comes from a Slavic word *pešt*, 'furnace', 'oven', probably re-ferring to a natural cave, as for PÉCS, another Hungarian town.

Budd The surname was originally a nickname for a squat or dumpy person, presumably fancied to resemble a thick bud on a branch.

Buddha The founder of Buddhism, who died in 483 BC, had the personal name *Siddhārtha Gautama*, the former word being his personal name, from the Sanskrit for 'one whose aim is accomplished'. *Buddha* was therefore his title, as 'Messiah' was for Christ. It is the Sanskrit word for 'enlightened one', literally 'awakened one', from *budh*, 'to awake', 'to perceive', a term already in religious use for a person who had achieved a state of perfect enlightenment or knowledge. Another of his titles was *Sakyamuni*, relat-ing to the *Sakya* warrior tribe into which he was born. (The literal sense of the Sanskrit title is 'Sakya sage'.) Buddha was thus only the latest in a series of buddhas, and he should correctly be referred to as 'the Buddha' for this reason.

Budweiser The name of the familiar brand of beer comes from that of *Budweis*, the German name of the Czech town, now *České Budějovice*, where it was first brewed. But *Budweiser* is an American beer, and developed from the recipe 'poached' from the Czech brewery by a former employee, Adolphus Busch, who emigrated to America and in 1876 opened his own brewery in St Louis. The original Czech beer is still produced in the Czech Lands, however, where it is known as *Budvar* lager.

Buenos Aires The Argentine capital has a Spanish name meaning literally 'good breezes'. This is all that remains of the original name of the port, which was *Nuestra Señora Santa Maria de los Buenos Aires*, 'Our Lady St Mary of the Favourable Winds'. The Virgin Mary was venerated in Spain as the patron saint of sailors. The town of Buenos Aires, as distinct from the port, was founded on 23 May 1536, Trinity Sunday, and originally named *Ciudad de la Santisima Trinidad*, 'City of the Most Holy Trinity'. Today the briefer name is sometimes abbreviated further to *Baires*.

Buffalo The origin of the name of the city in New York State is disputed, but it probably derives from the name of an Indian chief who lived by the creek now known as Buffalo Creek.

Buffalo Springfield The American folk-rock group, formed in Los Angeles in 1965, took their name from that seen on a steamroller working on road repairs.

Bugatti The make of car takes its name from the Italian automobile designer Ettore *Bugatti* (1881–1947), who first produced models of his own manufacture at Molsheim, near Strasbourg, in 1909.

Buick The name behind the car is that of David Dunbar *Buick* (1855–1929), a Scottish-born American engineer who produced his first models in Detroit in 1903.

Bulawayo The city in Zimbabwe has a name of Ndebele origin, from *bulawa*, 'massacre', with the locative suffix *-yo*. The 'place of the massacre' was a fort here burned by a Matebele chief in 1893 when the town was founded.

Bulgaria The name of the eastern European country has been explained as deriving from Turkic *bulga*, 'mixed', referring to the mixed race that the Bulgarians represent. This seems likely, since the Bulgarians are believed to have originated as a Turkic tribe of Central Asia, and travelled west of the Volga to integrate with the Slavs of the Black Sea coast. It was the Bulgarians who (via Old French *bougre*) gave modern English *bugger*, the origin lying in the condemnation of Eastern Orthodox Bulgarians as heretics in the 11th century. Only subsequently did the word come to mean 'sodomite' when it was applied to later heretics.

Bulge, Battle of the The name is that of the last German offensive on the western front in the Second World War, when in 1944 Hitler attempted to push the Allies back from the Ardennes. The name was taken from Winston Churchill's description of the resistance that he (mistakenly) thought was being offered to the Germans in this region in 1940 just before the collapse of the Anglo-French forces. The 'bulge' was the salient or wedge that the Germans drove into Allied lines. The name has subsequently been humorously adopted for a person's attempt to diet or lose weight.

Bull A person of this name would have been so called because of his burly or aggressive, bull-like appearance. In some cases the name could also have been given to someone who kept bulls.

Bundestag The name is that of the legislative assembly in Germany (and formerly in West Germany) which is elected by the nation as a whole and which in turn elects the federal chancellor. Its literal meaning is 'Federation Diet'. *Cp.* REICHSTAG.

Bunker Hill, Battle of The battle was the first significant engagement of the American War of Independence, in 1775, when the colonists, although defeated, proved that they could take a firm stand against British soldiers. The battle was actually fought on nearby Breed's Hill, not Bunker Hill. The latter, near Boston, was probably named for George *Bunker*, an early settler. There are other places of the name in America, mostly named after the battle.

Bunting The surname arose as a nickname for a person who was thought to resemble the bird in some way, perhaps because he was small and plump. *Cp.* BILLY BUNTER.

Burberry The well-known make of raincoat is named for Thomas *Burberry* (1835–1926), an English draper who started business in Basingstoke, Hampshire in 1856.

Burgas The port in southeast Bulgaria derives its name from Turkish *burgaz*, 'fort', a dialect word that itself originated from Greek *purgos*, 'tower'. *Cp.* BURGOS.

Burgenland The province of eastern Austria has a name that means 'land of castles', from German *Burgen*, the plural of *Burg*, 'castle', and *Land*, 'land'. It is so called from three castles that today are actually outside the province, over the border in Hungary.

Burgess The name was originally a title given to a person who was a townsman ('burger') and who doubtless had special municipal rights, perhaps as a freeman of the town. *Cp.* BURKE.

Burghley House The Elizabethan mansion near Stamford, Lincolnshire, built by William Cecil, first Lord Burghley, and the home of the elder line of Cecils (Marquesses of Exeter) ever since, takes its name from the location here, probably regarded as the 'borough lea', otherwise the cleared woodland by Stamford. *Burley House* near Oakham, only 12 miles (19 km) away, has a name of parallel origin.

Burgos The Spanish city, capital of the former kingdom of Castile, has a name of Germanic origin, from *burg*, 'fortress'. The reference is the fort built here in the 9th century as a defence against Arab invaders.

Burgundy The former French kingdom takes its name from the *Burgundi*, a Germanic tribe who settled here in the 4th or 5th century, many of them coming from BORNHOLM. Their own name may go back to a Gothic word *baurgjans*, meaning 'fort dwellers', that is, people who lived in a well defended region.

Burke The name represents Old English *burh*, 'fortress', 'town', so denoting someone who lived by a fort or who was a townsman. All medieval towns of any size would have had a fort for defensive purposes.

Burke's Peerage This is the short name of the *Genealogical and Heraldic History of the Peerage, Baronetage, and Knightage of the United Kingdom*, first issued by the Irish genealogist John *Burke* in 1826.

Burkina Faso The African state, formerly (until 1984) Upper Volta, has a native name meaning 'land of the worthy men', from *burkina*, 'worthy' and *faso*, 'land', literally 'father village', from Dyula *fa*, 'father' and *so*, 'village'.

Burlington House The well-known building in Piccadilly, London, the home of the Royal Academy and formerly housing the Royal Society, is named for Richard Boyle, first Earl of *Burlington* (1612–1697), who bought it in 1667 when it was still only partially built. The earl's title comes from *Bridlington* in Yorkshire. The name of this North Sea coastal resort was popularly corrupted to *Burlington* in the 17th century, reflecting the local pronunciation. It appears as such in the first edition of the *Encyclopaedia Britannica* (1771):

> BURLINGTON, a sea-port town in the East Riding of Yorkshire, situated on the German ocean, about thirty-seven miles north-east of York.

Burma *See* MYANMAR.

Burns The Scottish or north of England name was used for a person who lived by a stream, thus corresponding to BROOK. The ancestors of the famous Scottish poet Robert Burns were actually named Campbell, but they came from Burnhouse, near Loch Etive, and were subsequently known as the 'Campbells of Burness', from this name. When he was 27, Robert Burns and his brother decided to adopt the surname *Burns* as a form of this.

Burrell Collection The famous Glasgow art gallery is named for Sir William *Burrell* (1861–1958), the Scottish shipping magnate who founded it in 1944.

Burrows The surname described someone who lived by a hill or barrow (tumulus).

Burtons The well-known clothing chain takes its name from Montague *Burton* (1885–1952), the adopted English name of a Lithuanian emigrant to Britain who first set up as a draper in Chesterfield, Derbyshire in 1904.

Burundi The name of the central African country derives from that of its inhabitants, the *Barundi*, with *Ba-* the prefix for the people, and *Bu-* that for the country.

Bury St Edmunds The Suffolk town has a basic name found fairly commonly in England, with *Bury* representing Old English *burh*, 'fort', 'town' (modern *borough*). The latter half of the name relates to *St Edmund*, who was killed by the Vikings in 869 and came to be revered as a saint and martyr. His remains were interred at Bury, and a small monastery was set up there to safeguard them. The place was at that time called *Beadriceswyrth*, or '*Beaduric*'s enclosure'. In the 11th century, when a larger Benedictine monastery had been built, and the place had become a noted religious centre, this early name was replaced by the present one, to commemorate him. Bury St Edmunds is in the administrative district of *St Edmundsbury*, which is the same name with elements in a different order.

Bush The surname would have originally been used for a person who lived by a thicket of bushes.

Bush House The London building that houses the overseas broadcasting services of the BBC is named for the American, Irving T. *Bush*, who planned it as a trade centre when it opened in 1935.

Bushmen The name of the indigenous people of southern Africa refers to their place of origin and habitation, the *bush*, that is, the extensive uncultivated area covered with trees and shrubs. English *Bushman* is a translation of Afrikaans *boschjesman*. The name is also that of the Khoisan languages that they speak.

Busiris The ancient Egyptian city takes its name from Egyptian *Per-Ūsīr*, 'house of Osiris', from *per*, 'house' and *Osīr*, 'OSIRIS', the Egyptian god who ruled the underworld. There were other shrines of Osiris that also bore the name.

Butcher The surname is an occupational one, for a butcher or slaughterer.

Butler The name originally applied to a person who was a wine steward, and whose status would have been that of the senior servant in a medieval household. The name itself is directly related to the Old French word that gave English *bottle*.

Butlins The well-known English holiday camps take their name from Sir William ('Billy') *Butlin* (1899–1980), who opened the first one on the site of a former sugar-beet field near Skegness, Lincolnshire, on Easter Saturday, 11 April 1936.

Buttermere The lake in the Lake District has a name that means what it says, 'butter lake', referring to the rich pastureland by the lake where cows produced good milk for making butter.

Byblos The ancient city of Phoenicia, now the coastal village of *Jubayl* in Lebanon, north of Beirut, and also familiar as the biblical city of *Gebal* (*Ezekiel* 27.9), has a name of Phoenician origin meaning 'hill'. The town was famous for its exporting of *papyrus*, which was thus named after it. Hence Greek *biblion*, 'paper', 'book', and so ultimately BIBLE. Hence also, via *papyrus*, English *paper*.

Bydgoscsz The city in northern Poland, known to the Germans as *Bromberg*, derives its name from an Indoeuropean root word *bredahe*, meaning 'marsh', 'swamp'. The town is near the confluence of the rivers Brda and Vistula. The name is pronounced approximately '*Bid*goshch'.

Byelorussia The republic in central Europe, still sometimes known as *White Russia*, has a name that indeed translates thus (*cp.* BELGRADE). However, the reason for the colour is uncertain. The chief theories put forward to explain the name are as follows: 1. the indigenous population are mostly fair-haired with light grey eyes and a national dress that is predominantly white; 2. the sands that cover a large part of the region are very pale; 3. the Byelorussians have never been subdued by the Tatars, so they are 'white', *i.e.* free; 4. the territory is to the west of 'mainstream' Russia, and 'white' can mean 'west' in some place-names (*cp.* BLACK SEA, RED SEA, WHITE SEA). But the name may simply have arisen by contrast with 'Black Russia', a neighbouring region of uncertain geographical parameters. The republic's official native name is *Belarus*.

Byrds, The The innovative American folk-rock group, formed in Los Angeles in 1964, has a name that was a deliberate alteration of *birds*. It was suggested by their guitarist Roger McGuinn, who wished to write and play music that would soar and fly, lifting both performer and listener 'up and away' from the constant sounds and stresses of life.

Byron The surname, that of the famous English poet Lord *Byron*, comes from Old English *bȳrum*, meaning 'at the cattle sheds', from the basic word *bȳre*, 'byre'. A person of the name would either have lived by the cowsheds or worked there, as a cowman.

Byzantium The ancient Greek city, capital of the Byzantine Empire, later CONSTANTINOPLE, then the ISTANBUL of today, is said to derive its name from its Greek founder in the 7th century BC, *Buzas* of Megara.

C

Cabal The name was used for the group of ministers of Charles II who governed from 1667 to 1673. They were a *cabal* in the sense of being an inner group with a common policy, and so derived their name from the Hebrew word *qabbālāh*, meaning 'tradition', literally 'what is received', that gave this English word. But by coincidence the ministers' initials also gave the name, viz. *C*lifford, *A*shley, *B*uckingham, *A*rlington, *L*auderdale. The committee they formed was in fact the precursor of the Cabinet of today.

Cáceres The city in western Spain was founded in 74 BC by the Roman consul Quintus *Caecilius* Metellus, and is named for him.

Cadburys The well-known make of chocolate is named for John *Cadbury* (1801–1889), a tea dealer and coffee roaster who set up his business in Birmingham in 1824 and who first made cocoa and chocolate there in 1831.

Cadillac The car of the name was first manufactured in Detroit in 1903 and took the name of the city's founder in 1701, the Frenchman Antoine de la Mothe, Sieur de *Cadillac* (1658–1730). His own title comes from the small town of *Cadillac* in southwest France, itself derived from a Gaulish personal name *Cadilus*.

Cádiz The port in southwest Spain has a name deriving from Phoenician *gadir*, 'fort'. This originally applied not to the town or even its fort but to the rock on which the latter was built. Pliny claimed it was part of Atlantis.

Cadmus In Greek mythology, the name is that of the Phoenician prince who killed a dragon and planted its teeth. From these there sprang a host of warriors who fought among themselves until only five remained to join Cadmus and to found Thebes. His name is itself of Phoenician origin and means 'eastern'.

Caedmon The earliest-known English poet, who lived in the 7th century, has a name that cannot be satisfactorily explained in English. It is probably Celtic in origin, and is perhaps an adaptation of *Catumanus*, based on *catu*, 'battle'.

Caelian The name of one of the Seven Hills of Rome derives from that of the Etruscan chief, known to the Romans as *Caelius*, who based his headquarters here. It was formerly also known as *Querquetulanus*, from Latin *quercus*, 'oak', trees that were once abundant here.

Caen The city of northern France has a Gaulish name meaning 'battlefield', from *catu*, 'battle' and *mago*, 'field', 'plain'. The strategic site of the Normandy town on the river Orne has long made it a focus of military interest, and in the Second World War it was one of the main objects of the Allied invasion.

Caerleon The historic town in South Wales near Newport has a name that is half Welsh and half Latin, meaning 'fort of the legion', from Welsh *caer*, 'fort' (as for CAERNARFON) and Latin *legio*, genitive *legionis*, 'legion'. The town is the site of a Roman camp that was the station of the Second Legion, who moved here from Gloucester (which they knew as *Glevum*) in AD 75. The Roman name of Caerleon was *Isca legionis*. The first word of this represents the Roman name of the river Usk, on which the town stands. *See also* CAMELOT.

Caernarfon The port and resort in northwest Wales has a Celtic name meaning 'fort in *Arfon*', from Welsh *caer*, 'fort' and *Arfon*. The latter is the name of the district here whose own name means 'opposite Anglesey', from Welsh *ar Fôn*, with *ar* meaning 'over' and *Fôn* the mutated form of *Môn*, the Welsh name of Anglesey.

Caerphilly The creamy white cheese takes its name from the Welsh town where it originated. The town itself has a name meaning '*Ffili*'s fort', from Welsh *caer*, 'fort' and the personal name. It is not known who Ffili was.

Caesar The name of Julius *Caesar* is traditionally said to derive from the fact that he or one of his ancestors was born *a caeso matris utere*, 'from the incised womb of his mother', in other words, by *caesarian* section. The tradition has no historical basis, however, and the true source of the name is in Latin *caesaries*, 'head of hair'. This would have originally applied not to Julius Caesar but as a nickname for Iulus, son of Aeneas, the first member of the Roman patrician family to bear the name. In modern times *Caesar* has given the title *Kaiser* for German emperors and that of *tsar* for Russian rulers.

Caesarea The name is that of various ancient towns and cities of Phrygia, Bithynia, Palestine, Syria and elsewhere. They are all named for one or other of the Roman emperors CAESAR, not necessarily Julius Caesar. The *Caesarea* that was the capital of Roman Palestine, mentioned in the Bible, and now known as *Horbat Qesari* (Hebrew for 'ruins of Caesarea'), is named for Herod's patron, the emperor Augustus *Caesar*.

Café Royal The well-known London restaurant, noted for its French cuisine, owes its French name to its French founder in 1865, the Parisian wine merchant Daniel Thévenon. It has no specific connection with royalty, although royalty has dined there. The establishment did contain a café, however, in the late 19th century.

Caiaphas The name of the high priest during the trial of Jesus is of uncertain origin. A source in Babylonian *qêpu*, 'watchman' has been suggested.

Cain In the Old Testament, the name is that of the first son of Adam and Eve who gained notoriety by killing his brother Abel. It is interpreted in the Bible as 'I have gotten' (*Genesis* 4.1) but is more likely to be a Greek or Latin form of Hebrew *qayīn*, 'smith', that is, 'blacksmith'.

Cairngorms The Scottish mountain group takes its name from its highest peak, *Cairn Gorm*, whose Gaelic name means 'blue rock', from *carn*, 'rock' and *gorm*, 'blue'. The name should correctly be pronounced 'Cairn*gorm*', with the stress on the second syllable, since it is the colour that is emphasized.

Cairns The port in Queensland, northeast Australia, takes its name from Sir William Wellington *Cairns* (1828–1888), the British governor-general of Queensland for two years from 1875. The town was founded in 1873 as a government customs collection point.

Cairo The Egyptian capital has a name that derives from Arabic *al-qāhira*, 'the fort', in turn from *al-qāhir*, 'the victorious'. The latter was an epithet of the planet Mars, which was in the ascendant at the precise time when construction of the new city began, on Tuesday ('Mars-day') 6 July 969. The name was given in 972. The earlier Egyptian name of the town was *Khere-ohe* or *Kheri-aha*, 'place of combat', referring to the battle between the gods Horus and Seth that was said to have taken place here. The settlement was captured in 641 by a general of the caliph Omar I, who founded a new town on the site by the name of *Fostat* or *Fustat*, in Arabic *fuṣtāt*. This means 'military camp' and derives from Latin *fossatum*, 'entrenched', from the verb *fodere*, 'to dig'.

Caithness The former Scottish county has a name meaning 'headland of the *Cat* people', with Old Norse *nes*, 'promontory' added to the Celtic tribal name. It is not known why the people had this particular name.

Caius College The Cambridge college, in full *Gonville and Caius College*, is named for the English physician John *Caius* (1510–1573). His own college was *Gonville Hall*, named after the English cleric Edmund *Gonville* (d. 1351) who had founded it in 1349. In 1557 Caius expanded the college, named it *Gonville and Caius*, gave it a generous endowment, and in 1559 became its master. The name is pronounced as if 'Keys'.

Cajun The name is used for a native of Louisiana, descended from French immigrants, for the dialect of French that they speak, and for their distinctive music. The original French colonists had settled in ACADIA, and the name is a corruption of *Acadian*. *Cp. Injun* as a corruption of *Indian*.

Cakebread The name applied to a baker who specialized in fancy breads. The word *cake* was used in medieval times for a loaf of bread made from fine flour.

Calabria The southern region of Italy has a name derived from that of the race of people who once lived here, from a pre-Indoeuropean root word *kalabra* or *galabra*, 'rock'. *Cp.* CALAIS.

Calais The French port takes its name from the *Caleti*, the Gaulish people who inhabited this region. Their own name may come either from a pre-Indoeuropean root *kal*, 'rock' or from a later Celtic word *cul*, 'channel', referring to the English Channel, on which Calais lies.

Calatayud The ancient town in northeast Spain has a name of Arabic origin, representing *qal'at ayyūb*, 'fort of Ayyub', from *qal'a*, 'fort' and *ayyūb*, 'Ayyub', the name of a Moorish prince, and of identical origin to that of the biblical JOB. The town was founded in the 8th century and is noted for its ruins of Moorish forts.

Calcutta India's largest city, the capital of West Bengal and from 1833 to 1912 capital of the country as a whole, has a name that derives from that of KALI, the Hindu goddess of the dead. Calcutta was only a small village when a trading post was set up here in 1690 by the East India Company.

Calcutta Cup The trophy for the annual rugby football match between England and Scotland was originally the cup belonging to the CALCUTTA Football Club. When the latter wound up in 1878, they presented it to the Rugby Football Union.

Caldicott The name derives from any of the places so called, with the place-name itself meaning literally 'cold cottage'.

Caleb In the Old Testament, the name is that of one of the 12 scouts sent out by Moses to reconnoitre the Promised Land. It derives from Hebrew *kālēb*, 'dog', probably implying boldness.

Caledonia The historic name of Scotland derives from its inhabitants, the *Caledones*. The origin of their own name is uncertain. A source in Celtic *kal*, 'hard' has been suggested, with a figurative application for hardy people. The name is familiar today from the *Caledonian* Canal, which extends across Scotland from the North Sea to the Atlantic.

Caledonian Club The London club was founded in 1891 as a meeting place for Scottish gentlemen in London. Hence its name. *See* CALEDONIA.

Caledonian Market The London antique dealers' market, held every Friday in Bermondsey Street, takes its name from the *Caledonian* Road where it was originally held as a cattle market in the 19th century. The road takes its name from the former *Caledonian* Asylum that was established here in 1815, at the end of the Napoleonic Wars, for the children of Scottish servicemen who had been killed or wounded in battle. The road also happens to run due north out of central London as if leading to Scotland, *i.e.* CALEDONIA.

Calgary The Canadian city, in Alberta, was so named in 1876 by Colonel James Macleod (1836–1894) of the Royal Canadian Mounted Police, after his native village of *Calgary*, on the Isle of Mull, Scotland.

Caliban The name of the misshapen monster in Shakespeare's *The Tempest* (1612) probably derives from *Carib* or *cannibal*, or a blend of both, which is etymologically justifiable. Some scholars, however, have seen the name as another blend: that of the biblical CAIN and ABEL. *See also* CARIBBEAN.

California The precise origin of the name of the American state remains uncertain. There are two leading theories to account for it: either that it was given by the Spanish conqueror of Mexico, Hernán Cortés, for a mythical Greek island reigned over by a queen named *Caliphia*, or that it evolved from Spanish *caliente fornalla*, 'hot furnace', alluding to the great heat of the sun here. In all probability the latter explanation arose as an attempt to explain the former.

Caligula The 1st-century AD Roman emperor, noted for his cruelty, had the original name *Gaius Caesar*. He was given the nickname *Caligula*, meaning 'little boots', by his father's soldiers when he was a young boy running around camp. The name is a diminutive of Latin *caligae*, the term used for soldiers' boots, ultimately related to Latin *calx*, 'heel'.

Calke Abbey The 18th-century country house near Ashby de la Zouch, Derbyshire, was built on the site of a former *abbey*. It takes its name from the nearby village of *Calke*, whose own name derives from Old English *calc*, 'chalk', referring to the soil here.

Callaghan The name is an English form of the Irish name *Ó Ceallacháin*, meaning 'descendant of *Ceallachán*'. The personal name here is a diminutive of *Ceallach*, 'strife'.

Callanetics The system of exercise involving frequent small muscular movements takes its name from its American inventor, the fitness expert *Callan* Pinckney (1939–). The name also happens to suggest *callisthenics*, as another system of light exercises designed to produce general fitness (itself from the Greek meaning literally 'beautiful strength'). Pinckney first developed her system in the early 1970s, but the name was widely popularized by her book *Callanetics* published in the United States in 1984 and in Britain in 1989.

Callimachus The Greek poet, noted for his hymns and epigrams, has an appropriate name meaning 'battle of beauty', from *kallos*, 'beauty' and *makhē*, 'battle', 'contest'. A battle is not necessarily a military affair, but can be an agreeable contest, as a 'battle of wits'.

Calliope In Greek mythology the name is that of the muse of poetry and mother of Orpheus. It derives from Greek *kallos*, 'beauty' and either *ops*, 'voice' or *ōps*, 'face'. The former would be more appropriate; the latter by no means to her disadvantage.

Callisto The name is that of the Greek nymph loved by Zeus and changed by Hera into a bear. Zeus then set her in the sky as the constellation Ursa Major. It derives

from Greek *kallistos*, 'most beautiful', the superlative of *kalos*, 'beautiful'.

Calor Gas The proprietary type of bottled butane gas takes its name from Latin *calor*, 'heat'. It was first marketed in 1936.

Calvados The region of Normandy takes its name from that of a group of rocks here, whose own name may represent Latin *caballi dorsum*, 'horse's back' or *calvum dorsum*, 'bald back'. It is hardly likely that the name derives from the *Salvador*, a ship of the Spanish Armada wrecked off the coast here, although this origin has also been proposed by some. The cider brandy called *calvados* takes its name from this region, where it is distilled from locally grown apples.

Calvary The name of the place outside Jerusalem where Jesus was crucified derives from Late Latin *Calvaria*. This was a translation of Greek *kranion*, 'skull', itself a translation of Aramaic *gulgulta*. The latter gave the alternative name of GOLGOTHA.

Calvinist The extreme Protestant Reformist sect takes its name from the doctrines propounded by the French theologian Jean *Cauvin* or *Chauvin* (1509–1564), whose latinized name was *Calvinus*.

Calypso Homer's *Odyssey* tells how the sea nymph of this name detained Odysseus for seven years on the island of Ogygia. The meaning is 'hider', with reference to this, from Greek *ekalupse*, 'concealed'. The modern *calypso* as a type of West Indian ballad probably derives from her name, although the precise reference is not clear. They are both of island origin, however.

Camargue The region of southern France has a name of uncertain origin. It was first recorded in 869 as *Camaria*. It could possibly be related to Spanish *comarca*, 'country', 'region', although one authority derives it from Provençal *camp marca*, 'frontier field'.

Camberwell The district of south London has a name that appears to mean 'spring at the crane stream', from Old English *cran*, 'crane', *burna*, 'stream', and *wella*, 'spring', 'well'.

Cambodia The country of southeast Asia derives its name from *Kambu*, that of a

91

legendary ancestor of the Cambodians. His union with the nymph Mera is said to have given birth to the people.

Cambrai The town of northern France derives its name from the personal name *Camarus*, itself apparently from Latin *cammarus*, 'crayfish', 'prawn', a word of Greek origin. *Cp.* CAMEROON.

Cambria The Medieval Latin name for Wales, familiar from the *Cambrian* Mountains of today, derives from the Welsh people's name for themselves, the *Cymry*, literally 'fellow countrymen'. *Cp.* CUMBRIA.

Cambridge The famous university town is *not* named for its bridge over the river *Cam*, although that is indeed the name of the river here. The name was recorded in the 8th century as *Grantacaestir*, *i.e.* 'Grantchester', meaning 'Roman fort on the river *Granta*', from the river name and Old English *ceaster*, 'camp', itself ultimately from Latin *castra* with the same meaning. Over the centuries, and mainly through Norman influence, the first part of the name was altered to *Cam* while the second was replaced by *-bridge*. However, the alternative name of *Granta* remains for the river, and is that of the university students' magazine. If the name had not changed, it would be the same as that of the village of GRANTCHESTER, only two miles away. The river *Cam* thus takes its name from that of the city, not the other way round. *Cambridge*, Massachusetts, was named after the English city for its historic connections: the American city is the seat of Harvard University, whose founder, John Harvard, an English-born Puritan minister, had attended *Cambridge* University.

Cambridge Circus The London road junction is so named for George, Duke of *Cambridge* (1819–1904), cousin of Queen Victoria, who in 1887 opened the Charing Cross Road that now passes through it. London's OXFORD CIRCUS is better known, however.

Cambridgeshire The last annual flat race of the season is run at Newmarket, *Cambridgeshire*, and takes its name from that of the county.

Cambridge Theatre The London theatre, opened in 1930, takes its name from its location on the corner of Earlham Street and CAMBRIDGE CIRCUS.

Camden Place The 16th-century mansion in Chislehurst, Kent (now Greater London), takes its name from the antiquarian and historian William *Camden* (1551–1623), who spent the last years of his life here. Sir Charles Pratt, first Earl *Camden* (1719–1794), lived later at the house and took his title from it, passing the name in turn to London's *Camden Town* when this district was laid out in 1791 on his land there. Camden Place is now the headquarters of Chislehurst Golf Club.

Camelot The famous name is that of the town where King Arthur had his legendary court and palace, and where the Round Table was. It has been variously identified with Winchester in Hampshire, CAERLEON in South Wales, and places with similar names such as *Camelford* in Cornwall, *Cadbury* Castle and Queen *Camel* in Somerset, and even *Camelon* near Falkirk in Scotland. The origin of the name is as uncertain as its location. Treated purely as a place-name, it could be based on a Celtic word related to Welsh *cant*, 'circle', 'rim', 'edge'. This is topographically appropriate for Cadbury Castle. The Arthurian scholar R.S. Loomis, editor of *Arthurian Literature in the Middle Ages* (1959), suggests that the name may be a blend of CAERLEON and AVALON. But this does not explain the final *-t*.

Camembert The soft cheese takes its name from the village of *Camembert* in northwest France. The village name itself derives from Latin *campus*, 'field' and the personal name *Manberht* (meaning 'famous man'), so that it was '*Manberht*'s field'. The cheese is said to have been first produced here in the 18th century by one Marie Harel (1761–1818).

Cameron As a Scottish Highland name, *Cameron* developed from a nickname meaning 'crooked nose', from Gaelic *cam*, 'bent' and *sròn*, 'nose'. As a Lowland name, however, it usually derives from one of the places so called, in this case probably meaning 'crooked hill'.

Cameroon The country of central Africa takes its name from the river that runs through it. This was named *Rio dos Camarões*, 'river of prawns' by 16th-century Portuguese explorers who were impressed by the abundance of these creatures in its waters. The name gradually altered to its present form.

Camilla The name is a feminine form of the Roman clan name *Camillus*, of uncertain origin. In modern times it has been popularly associated with the flower name *camellia*, although that actually derives from the surname of Georg Josef *Kamel*, the Moravian Jesuit missionary who introduced it to Europe in the 18th century. The name was promoted by the heroine of Fanny Burney's novel *Camilla* (1796), who also gave the name of the author's house, *Camilla Cottage*, near Mickleham, Surrey, which she built partly on proceeds from its sales. The hamlet here is now called *Camilla Lacey*, after the nearby country house of POLESDEN LACEY.

Camino Real The name, Spanish for 'royal highway', was originally that of the road which in the 16th century connected the Spanish cities of Gijón, León and Madrid. The name was also given to a coastal highway built in California during the Spanish period (16th to 19th century). Tennessee Williams adopted the name for an experimental play of 1953.

Camorra The Italian secret society formed in about 1820 by criminals in Naples probably takes its name from Spanish *camorra*, 'quarrel'.

Campania The region of southern Italy has a name that straightforwardly means 'plain', from Latin *campus*. Bronze bells from this region were first in Christian use in about the 6th century, hence *campanile* as a word for a bell-tower, and *campanology* as the art of bell-ringing.

Campari The Italian aperitif originated from the Dutch-style bitters first produced in Novara, near Milan, by Gaspare *Campari* in the mid 19th century. It evolved into the present distinctive brand of the name under his son Davide Campari, who promoted his bitters worldwide in the 1890s.

Campbell The Scottish name arose as a nickname meaning 'crooked mouth', from Gaelic *cam*, 'bent' and *beul*, 'mouth'.

Campbell College The Belfast public school was founded in 1894 in accordance with the will of Henry James *Campbell*, of Craigavad, Co Down, with the aim of providing a school in Ireland that could be run on the same lines as the public schools of England and Scotland.

Camp David The official country residence of American presidents, in the Appalachian Mountains, was originally named *Shangri-La* by F.D. Roosevelt. When Dwight D. Eisenhower was elected president in 1953, however, he renamed it after his young grandson, *David* Eisenhower (who in 1968 married Julie Nixon, daughter of former president Richard M. Nixon). *David* was also the president's own middle name.

Campeche The port in southeast Mexico derives its name from Maya *kam*, 'grass snake' and *peque*, 'tick' (the small parasitic insect), as both these creatures are found there.

Camperdown, Battle of The British naval victory over the Dutch in 1797 took place near the village of this name (Dutch *Kamperduin*) on the northwest Netherlands coast. The name itself means 'field hill'.

Campion The name means 'champion', and originally applied to a person appointed in medieval times to settle a 'wager of battle' such as a duel.

Campion Hall The private college at Oxford for Jesuits was founded in 1896 as an annexe of St John's College and was at first called *Clarke's Hall*. In 1918 it was renamed for the Jesuit martyr Edmund *Campion* (1540–1581), who had studied at St John's.

Cana The biblical village near Nazareth, also known as *Cana of Galilee*, has a name ultimately of Hebrew origin, representing either *qen*, 'nest' or *qanō*, 'to envy'. The Hebrew word for 'zealot', *qannā* or *qanna'ī*, has a similar origin. This is probably why Simon the Canaanite was really 'Simon the Zealot' rather than 'Simon of Cana' (or CANAAN).

Canaan The former name of Israel, before its conquest by the Hebrews, is of Hebrew origin, representing *qɛná'an*, the meaning of which is unknown. In the Old Testament (*Genesis* 9.18) *Canaan* is the son of Shem and grandson of Noah.

Canada The North American country has an indigenous Indian name, from Huron or Iroquois *kanata*, meaning simply 'camp', 'village'. When sailing up the St Lawrence in 1536, the French explorer Jacques Cartier noticed that the Indians referred to their settlements as *kanata*, and the French assumed that this was the name of the entire country. Proposed artificial names for the confederation established in 1867 included *Albertsland*, *Albionora*, *Borealia*, *Britannia*, *Cabotia*, *Efisga* (from the initials of *E*ngland, *F*rance, *I*reland, *S*cotland, *G*ermany, *A*boriginal lands), *Norland*, *Superior*, *Transatlantia* and *Victorialand*. Fortunately for posterity none of these prevailed, and on 1 July 1867 'the provinces of Canada, Nova Scotia, and New Brunswick' became 'one Dominion under the name of Canada'.

Canada Day The annual Canadian holiday, on 1 July, marks the anniversary of the day when in 1867 Canada became the first British colony to receive dominion status. It was formerly known as *Dominion Day*.

Canaries The Spanish Atlantic island group was known to the Romans as *Canariae insulae*, based on Latin *canis*, 'dog', for the large wild dogs which, according to Pliny, they had found there. Canary songbirds are thus named for the islands, not the islands for the birds.

Canaveral, Cape The Florida peninsula has a name of Spanish origin meaning 'cane-brake', with reference to the abundance of this plant discovered here by Spanish explorers in the 16th century. In 1964 Cape Canaveral was renamed *Cape Kennedy* as a tribute to President John F. *Kennedy*, assassinated the previous year. In 1974, however, the former name was readopted.

Canberra Australia's capital probably has a name of Aboriginal origin, from *nganbirra*, 'meeting-place'. Despite its rather unpropitious location, Canberra was chosen as capital in 1913 when the two largest settlements, Melbourne and Sydney, were both

rivals for the honour and neither could be advantageously selected over the other.

Cancer The constellation in the northern hemisphere and sign of the zodiac has the English name of 'The Crab', since its stars seem to delineate the crab that attacked Hercules in Greek mythology. The claws of Cancer are represented by the two stars Alpha Cancri and Beta Cancri. The *Tropic of Cancer* is so called since at the time of the summer solstice the sun originally reached its most northerly point in the sky when it was in this sign. Today, however, due to the precession of the equinoxes, it is actually in Gemini at this time.

C and A The clothing chain takes its name from the initials of its founders, the Dutch brothers *C*lemens and *A*ugust Brenninkmeeijer, who opened a general store in Holland in 1841. The store uses another form of the name for its trade name *Canda*.

Candace This was the hereditary name of a number of queens of Ethiopia, one of whom is mentioned in the Bible (*Acts* 8.27). The Greek form of the name was *Kandakē*, of unknown and almost certainly non-Greek origin.

Candia The Italian name for the port of Heraklion, Crete, and also for the island of Crete as a whole, derives from the Venetian form of the Arabic original name, *al-ḥandaq*, 'the ditch'.

Candida The name derives from Late Latin *candidus*, 'white', 'shining', with an implication of purity and beauty.

Candlemas In the Christian calendar, and especially among Roman Catholics, the name is that of the Feast of the Purification of the Virgin Mary and the Presentation of Christ in the Temple, on 2 February, the day when *candles* are blessed as symbolic of the coming of Jesus as a 'light to lighten the Gentiles' (*Luke* 2.32).

Canis Major The constellation in the southern hemisphere, close to Orion, and in English sometimes known as the Greater Dog, is so named since, together with CANIS MINOR, the Lesser Dog, it represents the dogs who followed Orion in Greek mythology. Canis Major, moreover, contains SIRIUS, the DOG STAR, the brightest star in the sky.

Canis Minor The small constellation in the northern hemisphere, close to Orion, and in English sometimes known as the Lesser Dog, is so named since, with CANIS MAJOR, the Greater Dog, it represents the dogs who followed Orion in Greek mythology. It contains the star PROCYON.

Canned Heat The American electric blues group, formed in Los Angeles in 1966, took their name from the song 'Canned Heat Blues' recorded in 1928 by the Mississippi bluesman Tommy Johnson.

Cannes The city of southern France has a name of pre-Indoeuropean origin, from *kan*, 'height'. The old part of the town lies at the foot of low hills.

Cannock Chase The district of Staffordshire takes its name from the town of *Cannock* (itself from Old English *cnocc*, 'hill') to which 'Chase' has been added. Cannock Chase was formerly an enclosed royal hunting ground.

Cannon Street The London street, with the railway station of the same name, was originally the much longer *Candelwrichstrete*, literally 'candlewright street', that is, a street where candlemakers or chandlers lived and worked. The present, shorter name doubtless developed by false association with *canon* or *cannon* (probably the former rather than the latter).

Canon The Japanese make of camera takes its name from that of *Kannon*, the Buddhist goddess of compassion and mercy known to the Chinese as *Kuan-yin*. The camera name was originally *Kwannon* when the firm was founded in 1933, but in 1947 this was altered to *Canon*, a name more acceptable to a western market.

Canopus The name of the second brightest star in the sky, in the constellation *Carina* ('The Keel'), originally *Argo Navis* ('The Ship Argo'), appropriately takes its name from the mythological pilot of Menelaus, king of Sparta.

Cantabrian Mountains The mountain chain along the north coast of Spain takes its name from a Mediterranean root word *kanto*, 'rock', 'stone', which also lies be-

hind the name of the French department of CANTAL.

Cantal The department of south central France derives its name from the Mediterranean root word *kanto*, 'stone', 'rock'. The same origin lies behind the French girls' name *Chantal*.

Canterbury The name of the famous cathedral city in Kent means 'fortified place of the men of KENT'. The middle -*er*- of the name represents Old English -*ware*, 'dwellers', while the final -*bury* is Old English *burh*, 'fort'. The Roman name of Canterbury was *Durovernum*, 'walled town by the alder marsh'.

Canton The well-known city and port in southeast China has a name that is a europeanized form of the name of the province of GUANGDONG, of which it is the capital. The Chinese name of the city is *Guangzhou*, from *guǎng*, 'wide' and *zhōu*, 'region'.

Canuck The colloquial nickname for a Canadian, and in particular a French Canadian, is of uncertain origin but is probably a fanciful elaboration of the first syllable of *Canadian* itself.

Canute The name of the famous 11th-century Danish king of England is now normally spelled more accurately *Cnut* or *Knut*. In the original Old Norse it was *Knútr*, meaning literally 'knot', as a nickname for a small, squat 'knotted' man. The English form *Canute* developed under French influence: cp. French *canif* and English *knife*, both with the same basic meaning.

Cape Cod The long sandy peninsula in Massachusetts takes its name from the codfish that abound off its shores.

Cape Horn The southernmost point of South America was rounded in 1616 by the Dutch navigator Willem Schouten, who named it for his native town of *Hoorn*. This name itself means 'horn', so is coincidentally appropriate for a headland.

Cape of Good Hope The extremity of southern Africa was so named optimistically by King John II of Portugal after it was rounded by Vasco da Gama in 1497. The specific 'good hope' was that of reaching India by this route. The cape had been dis-

95

covered ten years earlier by Bartolomeu Dias, who called it *Cabo Tormentoso*, 'cape of storms', for the rough seas here, where the waters of the Atlantic meet those of the Indian Ocean.

Capernaum The biblical town by Lake Galilee (Sea of Tiberias) has a name of Hebrew origin meaning 'village of NAHUM', from *kefar*, 'village' and *nahūm*, 'Nahum'. the name of the prophet. The French word *capharnaüm*, from the French form of the town's name, is used to mean 'glory hole', 'junk room', with reference to a biblical passage: 'And again he (*i.e.* Jesus) entered into Capernaum [...]. And straightway many were gathered together, insomuch that there was no room to receive them, no, not so much as about the door' (*Mark* 2.1,2).

Cape Town The South African city derives its name from the CAPE OF GOOD HOPE, on which it is located, in Cape Province.

Cape Verde The Atlantic island republic takes its name from the cape to the west of which it lies. The cape was named *Cabo Verde*, 'green cape', by Portuguese explorers here in the 15th century, with reference to the greenness of the palm trees by contrast to the barren, sandy coast.

Cape Wrath The headland on the northwest Scottish coast has an apparently apt name for the stormy seas encountered here. It actually derives, however, from Old Norse *hvarf*, 'turning point', since the cape marks the point where ships would alter course to follow the coastline, veering south to enter The Minch, for example, if sailing west.

Cape York *See* YORK, CAPE.

Capital Radio London's independent radio station, founded in 1973, has a name that reflects its location in the British *capital* and that perhaps also suggests its professionalism, providing a *capital* service. The station could not use *London* in its title as this would have caused confusion with the BBC's *Radio London*, founded in 1970, as well as with the rival independent *London Broadcasting Company* (LBC), also set up in 1973.

Capitol The temple in Rome took its name from the *Capitoline* Hill on which it stood, together with the temple of Jupiter. The hill in turn derives its name from Latin *caput Oli*, 'head of *Olus*', this being the name of the mythological giant *Olus*, whose skull is said to have been discovered here. The *Capitol* that is the meeting-place of the Congress of the United States in Washington DC was opened for the first Congress in 1800 and is named after the Roman citadel. The similarity between 'Capitol' and 'capital' is thus fortuitous, even though Washington DC is the capital of the United States. The name is also found for the statehouse in other American state capitals or former state capitals, the oldest being that at Williamsburg, the earlier capital (from 1699 to 1780) of Virginia.

Cappadocia The ancient region of Asia Minor takes its name from that of its inhabitants. Their name in turn derives from Assyrian *Katpa Tuka*, '*Tuka*'s side', with *katpa* related to Hebrew *katef*, 'side', 'shoulder'.

Capri The Italian island has a name of uncertain origin, associated variously with Greek *kapros*, 'boar', Latin *capra*, 'goat' and Etruscan *capra* 'land of burial-places'.

Capricorn The sign of the zodiac and faint constellation in the southern hemisphere, also known as *Capricornus*, and sometimes in English as 'The Goat' or 'The Sea Goat', takes its name from the outline of a goat with a fish tail discerned in it. The *Tropic of Capricorn* was formerly the southernmost point below the equator reached by the sun at the time of the winter solstice. Now, however, due to the precession of the equinoxes, the sun is actually in Sagittarius at this time.

Capua The city in southern Italy is said to derive its name from its founder in the 9th century, one *Capys*.

Capuchin The strict order of Franciscan friars takes its name from the *capuche* (large hood or cowl) that the friars wear. The word itself derives from Italian *cappuccio*, 'hood', to which English *cape* is related. *See also* LITTLE RED RIDING HOOD.

Caracalla The 3rd-century Roman emperor Aurelius Antoninus was given his nickname from the long, hooded Gaulish cloak that he introduced.

Caracas The Venezuelan capital was founded in 1570 as *Santiago de León de Caracas*, 'St James of León of Caracas'. The last word of this is the name of an indigenous Indian people, itself of uncertain origin.

Caractacus The name is famous as that of the British chieftain who rebelled against Roman rule in the 1st century AD. Its more accurate form is *Caradoc*, Welsh *Caradog*, based on the root word *cār*, 'love', to which Latin *carus* and French *cher*, 'dear' are related.

Carbonari The Italian secret political society was formed in about 1811 by refugees living in the mountains of the Abruzzi. They took their name from the *carbonari*, the 'charcoal burners' who also lived here. Their chief aim was the unification of Italy.

Carcassonne The city of southwest France has a name of pre-Indoeuropean origin, based on the root words *kar*, 'rock', 'stone' and *kasser*, 'oak'.

Cardew The name is of Cornish origin, deriving from a place-name which itself means 'black fort', from Cornish *ker*, 'fort' and *du*, 'black'.

Cardiff The capital city of Wales has a name that is an anglicization of its Welsh name, *Caerdydd*, 'fort on the *Taff*', from Welsh *caer*, 'fort' and the name of the river on which Cardiff stands, itself probably simply meaning 'water', and of the same root origin as the name of the THAMES. The district of Cardiff known as LLANDAFF has a similar name.

Cardigan The name of the town and port in western Wales derives from *Ceredigion*, '*Ceredig*'s land', the historic name of Cardiganshire that is today an administrative district of Dyfed. Ceredig was one of the sons of the 5th-century ruler Cunedda, whose own name gave that of GWYNEDD. It is unusual for a town to take its name from its surrounding territory like this, rather than the other way round.

Carew The Welsh name derives from a place so called, whose own name means 'hill fort', from Welsh *caer*, 'fort' and *rhiw*, 'hill'.

Carey The name usually derives from a place-name, itself probably meaning 'pleasant stream', from the Celtic root element *car*, 'love'.

Carfax The name of the crossroads in the centre of Oxford, at the meeting point of the four roads from the former North, South, East and West Gates, is a corruption of Latin *quadrifurcus*, 'four-forked'. There was at one time a similar *Carfax* at Exeter, Devon, and there is still one at Horsham, West Sussex.

Caria The ancient division of Asia Minor has a name based on the pre-Indoeuropean root word *kar* or *kal*, 'stone', 'rock', 'mountain', which also lies behind English *cairn* and names such as CARCASSONNE and CARINTHIA. Caria has many mountains.

Caribbean The sea takes its name from an old name of the island group here known as the Lesser Antilles, one English version of which was the *Caribbees*. This in turn represents the indigenous people on the islands, the *Caribs*, whose own name ultimately derives from an Arawak word *kalinago* or *kalino*, meaning 'brave men'. The Spanish name of the islands, *Caribale*, gave modern English *cannibal*, from the West Indian people's alleged habit of killing and eating their captives.

Carinthia The Austrian province derives its name from its native inhabitants, in turn based on the pre-Indoeuropean root word *kar*, 'stone', 'rock', since they were mountain dwellers. The German name of Carinthia is *Kärnten*. *Cp*. CARIA.

Carling The name behind the well-known 'Black Label' beer is that of the Canadian Thomas *Carling*, who founded his brewery in Ontario in 1840.

Carlisle The town of northwest England has a name representing Celtic *cair*, 'fort', together with the name of the Roman fort itself, *Luguvalium*. The latter derives from a Celtic personal name, *Luguvallos*, meaning 'strong as *Lugus*', from the name of a Celtic god. The name is a reminder of the extensive territory occupied by the Britons, which included almost the whole of western Britain south of the present border with Scotland.

Carlow The Irish county has a name that represents Irish *Ceatharlach*, 'four lakes'. There is no sign of the lakes now, though at one time they may have been at the point where the rivers Burren and Burrow meet.

Carlsberg The well-known Danish brand of lager takes its name from the brewery near Copenhagen where it was first produced in 1847. The brewery's own name is a combination of that of *Carl*, the young son of its founder, Jacob Jacobsen (d. 1887), and Danish *berg*, 'hill'.

Carlton Club The famous London club, with its Tory tradition, was founded in 1832 in *Carlton House* Terrace, and takes its name from this street. Carlton House, which gave the name of the street, was built in the early 18th century for Henry Boyle, Lord *Carleton* (d. 1725), who took his title from *Carleton* near Pontefract, West Yorkshire. The Carlton Club is now in St James's Street. *Cp.* JUNIOR CARLTON CLUB.

Carmagnole, La The French Revolutionary song and dance took its name from the *carmagnole*, the costume worn by many Revolutionaries, with a distinctive short jacket. The costume was probably adopted from that worn in *Carmagnola*, northern Italy.

Carmarthen The Welsh town has a name that represents Celtic *cair*, 'fort' and the personal name *Myrddin*, itself probably meaning 'seaside fort', as also in the town's Roman name of *Maridunum* or *Moridunum*. The name is thus something of a tautology, with 'fort' included twice. Carmarthen is only ten miles (16 km) from the sea. A distorted form of the British name gave that of the legendary magician MERLIN.

Carmel The mountain in Israel, featuring in the Bible as the place where Elijah summoned Israel to choose between God and Baal and as the place of retreat for Elijah and Elisha (1 and 2 *Kings*), has a Hebrew name, from *karmel*, 'garden', 'fertile field'. The mountain gave the name of the CARMELITE order.

Carmelite The order of mendicant friars takes its name from Mount CARMEL, where it was founded in the 12th century. The corresponding order of Carmelite nuns adopted the title on their own foundation in the 15th century.

Carmen The name is a Spanish form of CARMEL, altered by association with Latin *carmen*, 'song'. The latter interpretation has been enforced by the heroine of Bizet's opera *Carmen* (1875), although this was actually based on Mérimée's novel of the same name (1845).

Carmichael The name is Scottish in origin, and derives from the place so called near Thankerton, formerly in Lanarkshire. The place-name itself means '*Michael*'s fort', with Gaelic *ker*, 'fort' followed by the personal name.

Carmina Burana The scenic cantata by Carl Orff, first performed in 1937, is a setting of a Latin text based on 13th-century poems (on 'wine, women and song') found in the Benedictine monastery of *Beuron*, western Germany. The name thus means 'Songs of Beuron'.

Carnac The village in Brittany, northwest France, noted for its many megalithic monuments, has the Breton name *Karnag*, probably based on *karn*, 'tumulus' (English *cairn*), with a Latin place-name suffix *-acum*.

Carnegie The Scottish name derives from the place so called near Arbroath, formerly in Angus. The place-name itself means 'fort at the gap', from Gaelic *cathair an eige*.

Carnegie Hall The famous concert hall in New York, opened in 1891, takes its name from the American steel manufacturer and philanthropist who endowed it, Andrew *Carnegie* (1835–1919).

Carniola The mountainous region of northwest Slovenia, known in Slovene as *Kranj*, takes its name from the *Carni*, the people who originally lived here. Their own name is probably based on the pre-Indoeuropean root element *kar*, 'rock', as for CARIA.

Carolina The two American states of North and South *Carolina* were originally a single territory, named by French colonists *Caroline*, in honour of Charles IX of France, whose Latin name was *Carolus*. This name then fell into disuse, and when Charles I of England granted the territory to the English colonist Robert Heath in 1629 it was under the name *Carolana*. In 1663 Charles II regranted the region to nine proprietors under the name *Carolina*, which was as applicable to him as it had been to his father. The distinction between North and South Carolina became official in 1710.

Caroline The name arose as a French form of Latin (or Italian) *Carolina*, a feminine diminutive of *Carolus* (CHARLES).

Carolines The Pacific islands were named the *Islas Carolinas* by the Spanish in 1686 in honour of their king, *Charles* II. When originally discovered in 1528, the islands were known as the *Islas de los Barbudos*, 'islands of the bearded ones', with reference to the bearded Polynesians who formed the indigenous population.

Carpathians The mountain range of southeast Europe has a name that is possibly based on Indoeuropean *ger*, 'to turn', referring to a peak or crest where a mountain slope forms an angle or 'turns'.

Carpentaria, Gulf of The inlet of the Arafura Sea, in northern Australia, was named in 1623 by the Dutch navigator Jan Carstensz for the governor-general of the Dutch East Indies, Pieter de *Carpentier* (1588–1659).

Carpenter The name means what it says, and denotes a person who worked in wood as a carpenter.

Carr When not a variant of KERR, the name often represents the Irish name *Ó Carra*, 'descendant of *Carra*', the latter personal name meaning 'spear'.

Carrara The town in northwest Italy takes its name from Low Latin *quadraria*, 'quarry', with reference to the local quarries that provide the famous Carrara marble.

Carreras The brand of cigarettes is named for José Joaquim *Carreras*, a Spanish nobleman's son, who in 1843 opened a shop in London selling tobacco, cigars and snuff.

Carruthers The Scottish name derives from a place so called near Ecclefechan, formerly in Dumfriesshire. The place-name in turn means '*Ruther*'s fort', from Gaelic *ker*, 'fort' and a personal name that probably means 'red king'.

Carson City The state capital of Nevada, founded in 1858, took its name in honour of the frontiersman and trapper Kit *Carson* (1809–1868), famous in the southwest, where Carson City is itself situated.

Cartagena The port in southeast Spain was founded in the 3rd century BC by the Carthaginian general Hasdrubal. It later became known to the Romans as *Carthago Nova*, 'new CARTHAGE', and its present name evolved from this. Both cities are on the Mediterranean.

Carter The name is a straightforward occupational one, for a carter, a person who transported goods and merchandise.

Carthage The name of the historic city of North Africa is of Phoenician origin, from *qart ḥadaš*, 'new town', an accurate description when the city was founded in the 8th century BC. *See also* CARTAGENA.

Carthusian The austere monastic order takes its name from *Carthusia*, the medieval Latin name of CHARTREUSE, near Grenoble, in southern France, where it was founded by St Bruno in 1084.

Cartier The prestigious make of watches and jewellery is named for Louis-François *Cartier* (1819–1904), who opened a 'fantasy jewellery' business in Paris in 1847.

Cartwright The name originally meant 'cartmaker', just as *wheelwright* means 'wheelmaker'. *See also* WAINWRIGHT.

Carver The name formerly applied either to someone who carved wood or sculpted stone, or to a ploughman. In the latter case the origin is ultimately in Latin *carruca*, 'plough', 'cart'.

Casablanca The port in northwest Morocco has a Spanish name meaning 'white city', translating its earlier name *Casa Branca*, given by the Portuguese in 1515 to the town they founded on the site of the former village of Anfa. Many of the city's houses are still white today.

Casanova The general name for a compulsive womanizer derives from a specific one in the person of the Italian adventurer and rake, Giovanni Jacopo *Casanova* (1725–1798). His own name means nothing more suggestive than 'new house'.

Cascade Range The chain of mountains in North America, a continuation of the Sierra

Nevada range, was so named in 1820 after the waterfalls or *cascades* on the Columbia River, which crosses it in a deep gorge near the Washington-Oregon border.

Caspar The name is traditionally that of one of the Magi (Three Wise Men) who brought gifts to the infant Jesus, the others being Balthazar and Melchior. They are not named in the Bible, however. The name itself is a Dutch form of JASPER.

Caspian Sea The great saltwater lake between Russia and Iran, the largest inland sea in the world, takes its name from the people known to the Romans as the *Caspii* who lived on its shores and who originated from a region of the Caucasus. Their name may mean 'white', but an association with the biblical name CUSH is also possible.

Cassandra In Greek mythology, the name is that of the prophetess daughter of Priam and Hecuba whose prophecies were fated never to be believed. Her name has been interpreted as 'entangler of men', from Greek *kassuō*, 'I concoct a plot' and *anēr*, genitive *andros*, 'man'. The reference may be to her prophecies themselves.

Cassell The London publishing house is named for John *Cassell* (1817–1865), who began his career by issuing temperance literature in London in 1848.

Cassidy The name is of Irish origin, and represents *Ó Caiside*, 'descendant of *Caiside*'. The personal name derives from *cas*, 'curly'.

Cassiopeia In Greek mythology, the name is that of the wife of Cepheus and mother of Andromeda. It has been explained as meaning 'cassia juice', with the latter part of the name representing Greek *opos*, 'juice'. This interpretation may have been intended to denote her 'oriental' connections, since her father, Arabus, had an Arabic name and her husband, Cepheus, was king of Joppa. In astronomy, the name is that of a conspicuous constellation in the northern hemisphere near the Pole Star. Its distinctive 'W' shape represents Cassiopeia seated in a chair and holding up her arms in supplication. The constellation's Arabic name is thus *az-zāt al-kursī*, 'the lady in the chair'. *See also* SCHEDAR.

Cassius The Roman clan name is famous through the Roman general who led the conspiracy against Julius Caesar. It is of uncertain origin, but may be related to Latin *cassus*, 'hollow', 'empty'.

Castel Gandolfo The former papal palace near Rome, now the Pope's summer residence, takes its name from a historic *castle* here that belonged to the ducal *Gandolfi* family in the 12th century.

Castile The former kingdom of Spain, originally part of León, is famous for its castles. Hence its name, representing Low Latin *castilla*, from classical Latin *castella*, itself the plural of *castellum*, 'castle'. Not for nothing is 'castles in Spain' an expression for a pipe dream or unrealistic ambition. (The term derives from the French *faire des châteaux en Espagne*, a vain hope for the French in medieval times, when they had no hold in Moorish Spain, even though it was their neighbouring country.)

Castle A person of this name would originally have been someone who worked as a servant in a castle.

Castle Combe The picturesque Wiltshire village has a name that denotes its location, by a *coomb* (valley) of the former *castle* here. The original castle was destroyed by the Danes in the 9th century, and even the Norman replacement has not survived.

Castle Howard The impressive baroque mansion near Malton, Yorkshire was built in the 1730s for the *Howard* family to replace Henderskelfe Castle, which had been destroyed by fire in 1693. It was Charles Howard, third Earl of Carlisle, who requested Vanbrugh to design the present house. Castle Howard is not of course a 'castle' in the medieval sense of being a fortified residence.

Castor The name is familiar in classical mythology as that of the twin of POLLUX. It appears to represent Latin *castor*, 'beaver'. The relevance of this is obscure, and it may be more meaningful to derive his name from Greek *kosmeō*, 'I arrange', 'I adorn', especially if Castor is seen as symbolizing the day, while Pollux represents the night.

Castrol The brand of motor oil has *castor oil* as its base and was named for this constituent in 1909 in place of its original name of *Wakefield Motor Oil*, when first marketed in 1906.

Catalan The people and language of northeast Spain have a name that may be related to Gaulish *catu*, 'battle'.

Catalonia The region of northeast Spain takes its name from its indigenous CATALAN people.

Catania The name of the Sicilian port is of disputed origin. It may represent a local word meaning 'bowl', referring to the location of the town among hills. Some authorities derive it from Phoenician *qaton*, 'little', that is, by comparison with Syracuse.

Catanzaro The city in southern Italy had the Byzantine Greek name of *Katantzarion*, which may represent Greek *kata*, 'on', 'near' and Arabic *anjār*, 'terrace'. The town is at an altitude of 1050 feet (320 m) overlooking the Gulf of Squillace, an inlet of the Ionian Sea.

Cathay Marco Polo's name for CHINA derives from the *Khitan*, a semi-nomadic Mongol people who conquered northern China in the 10th century AD and held it for the next 200 years. The name survives in the modern Russian name for China, *Kitay*.

Catherine The name, famous as that of the saint who was tortured on a spiked wheel (a 'Catherine wheel'), is of uncertain origin, but has been popularly linked with Greek *katharos*, 'pure'. This interpretation led to the spelling of the name as *Katharine*, as one of its many variants and diminutives, including the popular KATE (*which see*).

Catholic The *Catholic* or *Roman Catholic* Church has a name that declares it to represent the entire body of Christians worldwide. The name derives from Greek *katholikos*, 'universal'.

Cato The Roman statesman and writer of the 3rd and 2nd centuries BC has a name that originated as a *cognomen* or nickname, his full name being Marcus Porcius *Cato*. It represents Latin *catus*, 'sharp', which in a favourable sense could mean 'shrewd' and in an unfavourable, 'cunning'.

Catskill Mountains The mountain range in New York State, famous as a resort, has a name of Dutch origin meaning '*Kat's stream*', with Dutch *kil*, 'stream' following the personal name. In popular etymology the name is associated with wildcats found here.

Catullus The 1st-century BC Roman poet has a name, in full Gaius Valerius *Catullus*, that originated as a *cognomen* or nickname, from Latin *catulus*, 'puppy'.

Caucasus The mountains in southwest Russia between the Black and Caspian Seas probably derive their name from a Pelasgian word *kau* meaning simply 'mountain'. Pliny proposed a Scythian origin for the name, from a word meaning 'snow-white'.

Caudebec The name is that of two small towns in northern France, near Rouen, *Caudebec*-en-Caux and (the larger) *Caudebec*-lès-Elbeuf. The name is Old Norse, from *kald*, 'cold' and *bekkr*, 'stream'. The towns are in Normandy, settled by the Norsemen. Hence the origin of the name, which has its exact counterpart in the English village of *Caldbeck* near Wigton, Cumbria.

Caudillo, El The title assumed by General Franco as supreme head of the Spanish state means 'the leader', from Late Latin *capitellum*, the diminutive of *caput*, 'head'. It is thus the Spanish equivalent of German FÜHRER and Italian DUCE.

Cavalier The name was that of the supporters of Charles I in the English Civil War. It was originally a derogatory nickname for the group, who were seen as belligerent, swashbuckling knights and courtiers. It was adopted by them, however, and subsequently passed to the court party at the Restoration. The Cavaliers' own contemptuous name for their opponents was ROUNDHEADS. The adjective *cavalier* has retained something of its disapprobatory use to mean 'offhand', 'haughty'. Its literal meaning is 'horseman'.

Cavan The Irish county takes its name from the town of *Cavan*, whose own name represents Irish *An Cabhán*. The town lies in a hollow, above which rises a round, grassy hill. Irish *cabhán* can mean either 'hollow' or 'hill', the one being an inversion of the other.

Cave The name originally applied either to someone from *Cave*, near Market Weighton, now in Humberside, or to a person in charge of the cellar in a large house. The place-name probably refers to a river, so does not mean 'cave' but comes from Old English *cāf*, 'swift'. The occupational name is of French origin, from *cave*, 'cellar'. In some cases, however, the person could have literally been a cave-dweller, with the name also from French *cave* but in its original sense.

Cavendish The name is a place-name in origin, from *Cavendish* near Long Melford in Suffolk. The name means '*Cāfna*'s field', with Old English *edisc*, 'enclosure' added to a personal name that itself means 'bold'.

Cavendish Laboratory The Cambridge University physics laboratory was founded in 1874 and named for the noted physicist Henry *Cavendish* (1731–1810), a Cambridge man.

Caxton Hall The former well-known London registry office was opened in 1878 as the Westminster City Hall and takes its name from *Caxton* Street, in which it stands. The street itself is named for the famous printer William *Caxton*, who set up his press here in the 1470s.

Cayenne The capital of FRENCH GUIANA has a name that is a French form of that of GUYANA. Its origin and meaning are thus the same.

Cayman Islands The British island group in the West Indies takes its name from the abundance of caimans (alligator-like reptiles) found there.

Cecil The name was originally the surname of a noble English family, famous from the 16th century. (The first of the name was William *Cecil*, Lord Burghley, chief adviser to Queen Elizabeth. *See* BURGHLEY HOUSE.) The surname in turn is apparently an altered form, through Welsh, of Latin *Sextus*, 'sixth', with the spelling influenced by *Caecilius*. *See also* CECILY.

Cecily The name derives from Latin *Caecilia*, a feminine form of *Caecilius*, in turn from *caecus*, 'blind'.

Cedric The name appears to have been invented by Walter Scott for the character *Cedric* of Rotherwood in his novel *Ivanhoe* (1819). It may have been a respelling of (or even error for) *Cerdic*, itself of uncertain origin but perhaps a form of the Celtic name that gave English CARACTACUS.

Cedron *See* KEDRON.

Ceefax The teletext service of the BBC has a name that denotes its basic function, to enable the viewer to 'see facts'. *Cp.* ORACLE.

Celia The name is the feminine form of the Roman name *Caelius*. This is of uncertain origin, but may be related to Latin *caelum*, 'heaven', 'sky'.

Cellophane The brand of filmy wrapping material is made from regenerated *cellulose* which is transparent or dia*phan*ous. Its name duly reflects the substance and its quality.

Celt The name of the historic Indoeuropean people of western Europe, familiar in Britain as the forerunners of the Irish, Welsh and Scots, perhaps derives from a Gaulish root word *gal* or *gala*, meaning 'brave', 'strong', 'famous'. *Cp.* GAELIC, GAUL.

Celtic The famous Glasgow football club was founded in 1887 by a group of Irish Roman Catholic priests to raise money for a local children's charity. The name originally considered was *Glasgow Hibernian*, to match that of HIBERNIAN, who were originally *Edinburgh Hibernian*. The name *The Celtic Football and Athletic Club* was then proposed by one of the priests to denote the club's Irish origins, and was duly adopted. The club's ground, named after them, is *Celtic Park*. The club still has strong Roman Catholic support today, especially in matches with Protestant Rangers.

Celtic Sea The name was adopted by oil industry workers for the area of sea between Wales, Ireland and Cornwall, England, in order to avoid nationalist significance. It thus relates solely to the common Celtic heritage of these otherwise disparate lands.

Cenotaph The memorial to the dead of both World Wars that stands in the middle of Whitehall, London, was erected in 1920 and has a Greek name meaning 'empty tomb', from *kenos*, 'empty' and *taphos*, 'tomb' . This refers to the fact that it is a memorial only, and that the dead it commemorates are buried elsewhere. The word was in general use earlier for a memorial of this type.

Centaurus The constellation in the southern hemisphere contains stars that form the outline of a *centaur*, the creature of Greek mythology that had the head, arms and upper body of a man but the lower body and legs of a horse. Some have taken Centaurus to represent Chiron, the wise centaur who was the tutor of many Greek heroes, and who was set in the sky after accidentally being hit by an arrow from Hercules. The word itself is of unknown origin. It is almost certainly not related to Greek *tauros*, 'bull'.

Central African Republic The country of central Africa has a name that refers to its central location in the continent as a whole. It was formerly the French colony *Ubangi-Shari*. Rather unusually, the colonial name was a native one, whereas that of the modern independent state is European. For many other African countries the converse applies.

Central Line The London Underground line, opened in 1900, was so named as it was originally intended to be a purely local service linking important *centres* in the city. Later, however, it was extended both westwards and eastwards, so that only a portion of its route remains in central London. It was the Central Line that was the original 'Twopenny Tube', running between Bank and Shepherd's Bush.

Central Park The large park in New York City is named for its central, midtown location in Manhattan. It was laid out and landscaped in 1857.

Centre Point The 33-storey office block, built in 1965, is named for its prominent position in central London, where it stands at the junction of Oxford Street, Tottenham Court Road, New Oxford Street and Charing Cross Road. It is not the central point of London from which distances are traditionally measured, however, as that is Charing Cross.

Cephalonia The Greek island, in the Ionian Sea, has a name based on Greek *kephalē*, 'head', in the sense 'mountain', referring to its topography.

Cepheus The faint constellation of the northern hemisphere is named for the mythical king of Ethiopia who was the father of Andromeda and husband of Cassiopeia, whose respective constellations adjoin it. Cepheus himself can be discerned in his royal robes, with his head represented by the three stars Delta, Epsilon and Zeta Cephei, which form a triangle. His own name is of uncertain origin, but has been linked with Greek *kaiō*, 'I burn'.

Cerberus The name of the three-headed dog that guarded the entrance to Hades in Greek mythology has been derived from Greek *Ker berethrou*, literally '*Ker* of the pit'. *Ker* was a female spirit of death resembling one of the Furies. The true origin of his name, however, may not be in Greek at all.

Ceres The Roman goddess of agriculture, who gave English the word *cereal*, has a name that may derive from the root element of Latin *creare*, 'to create'.

Cesarewitch The annual flat race, run at Newmarket, takes its name from the Russian *tsesarevich* Alexander (1818–1881), the future Alexander II, who was present at the inaugural race in 1839. The Russian title was that of the tsar's eldest son and heir to the throne.

Cévennes The mountain range of south central France, on the edge of the Massif Central, has a name that is probably originated from a pre-Celtic root word *kem* or *kam*, meaning 'rounded height'. *Cp.* CHAMONIX.

Ceylon The historic name of SRI LANKA ultimately derives from Sanskrit *simha*, 'lion', either applied metaphorically to a 'lionlike' race of inhabitants, the *Singhalese*, or suggesting that there were actually lions on the island at one time. There are none today.

Chablis The white Burgundy wine takes its name from the small town in central France where it is produced. The town's own name is said to derive from Late Latin *capulum*, 'halter', perhaps referring to ropes used for winching floating timber from the river Serein here.

Chad The republic of central Africa takes its name from Lake *Chad*, in turn deriving from Arabic *tŝād*, from a local word meaning 'large expanse of water', in other words, 'lake'.

Chadwick The name derives from any of the places so called in England, such as *Chadwick* Green near Billinge in Merseyside. The place-name means '*Ceadda*'s farm'. The personal name is the same as that of St *Chad*.

Chalcis The ancient Greek city, on the island of Euboea, has a name deriving from Greek *khalkos*, 'copper', 'brass', from the historic bronze workings in the region.

Chaldea The ancient region of Babylonia has a name that derives from its native people, the *Chaldeans* or *Chaldees*. Their own name is of uncertain origin, but could come from an Assyrian root meaning 'conquer'. This appears to be supported by the biblical description of the Chaldeans as a 'bitter and hasty nation' who are 'terrible and dreadful' (*Habakkuk* 1.6,7). The eponymous ancestor of the Chaldeans is generally regarded as being *Chesed*, one of the 12 sons of Nahor mentioned in *Genesis* 22.22.

Châlons-sur-Marne The city in northeast France takes its name from the *Catalauni*, the people who once inhabited the region. Their own name probably represents Gaulish *catu*, 'battle' and *vellauno*, 'best', implying their prowess as warriors. The name of the river MARNE is added to distinguish this town from others with similar names (but not necessarily identical origins), such as the smaller *Chalonnes-sur-Loire* and the larger *Chalon-sur-Saône*. The latter's name may derive from a Ligurian root word *cab*, 'height'.

Chamberlain A person of this name would originally have been an official in charge of the private rooms (chambers) of his master. Later, the name became a title, as did similar names such as STEWART. *Cp.* CHAMBERS.

Chamber of Horrors The name appears to have originated with the section of MADAME TUSSAUD'S waxworks exhibition,

London, that depicts famous criminals at their work. The phrase is clearly a literal translation of French *Chambre des Horreurs*, 'Horror Room'.

Chambers The name formerly applied to a person employed in the living quarters (chambers) of his master, rather than in the public rooms of a manor house. It thus denoted a more humble position than that of CHAMBERLAIN.

Chambers The publishers of the well-known *English Dictionary* take their name from the Scots brothers William *Chambers* (1800–1883) and Robert *Chambers* (1802–1871), who set up their business in Edinburgh in 1820.

Chambéry The city in southeast France had the Medieval Latin name of *Camberacium*. This derives from Gaulish *cambo*, 'bend', 'curve', with the Latin place-name suffix *-acum*. Chambéry lies on a bend in the valley of the river Leysse, between the massifs of Beauges and La Grande Chartreuse.

Chambord The village in north central France, famous for its château, derives its name from Gaulish *cambo*, 'bend', referring to its location on a bend of the small river Cosson, a tributary of the Loire. *Cp.* CHAMBÉRY.

Chambourcy The brand of yoghurt owes its origins to Jacques Benoit, a French doctor's son from Marseille, who first made yoghurt as a refugee in Austria in the Second World War. After the war, he and his brother André started selling yoghurt in Marseille. In 1948 they moved to the village of *Chambourcy*, west of Paris, and set up their business in a dairy farm that they purchased there. The present company thus dates its foundation from this year.

Chamonix The famous mountain resort in southeast France, in the Alps at the foot of Mont Blanc, has a name deriving from a pre-Celtic, perhaps Ligurian root word *kam*, meaning 'rounded height'. *Cp.* CÉVENNES.

Champagne The well-known region of northeast France takes its name from Latin *campus*, 'plain'. *Cp.* CAMPANIA, Italy. The name has gained worldwide fame through its association with *champagne*, which comes from the many vineyards in the former province. The prestigious wine has thus promoted the place-name round the world, so that the word has its equivalents in Russian *shampanskoye*, Hindi *šāmpīn*, Japanese *shampen* and Chinese *xiāngbīng-jiǔ* (*jiǔ* meaning 'wine'), to cite just four leading languages.

Champ-de-Mars The prominent park in Paris, between the Ecole Militaire and the Seine, was laid out in 1765 as a parade ground for this military training establishment. Hence its name, 'Field of Mars', referring to the Roman god of war. The name was taken from that of the *Campus Martius* in Rome, the exercise-ground for Roman armies between the Capitol and the Tiber. Other cities have their own 'Field of Mars' for similar reasons, such as the *Marsovo Pole* laid out by Peter the Great in the 18th century in St Petersburg.

Champlain, Lake The lake, on the Canadian-American border, takes its name from the French explorer and founder of Quebec, Samuel de *Champlain* (1567–1635).

Champs Elysées The major boulevard in central Paris, extending from the Place de la Concorde to the Arc de Triomphe, has a name that translates as *Elysian Fields* (*see* ELYSIUM). The avenue was laid out in the 17th century, but was not named until later.

Chanctonbury Ring The site is that of an Iron Age fort on the northern edge of the South Downs, near Worthing, Sussex. The 'ring' is the circle of stones here. The main part of the name derives from that of nearby *Chancton*, 'farm of *Ceawa*'s people', to which Old English *burh*, 'fort' has been added.

Chandernagore The port in eastern India, on the river Hooghly, has a name that means 'moon town', from Hindi *čaṅdra*, 'moon' and *nagar*, 'town'. The name relates to a former cult of the Moon here.

Chandigarh The city in northern India, where it is the capital of the Punjab and Haryana, derives its name from Hindi *čaṅḍi*, the name of a Hindu goddess, itself from Sanskrit *čaṇḍa*, 'cruel', 'violent', and *garh*, 'fort'.

Chandler The surname is an occupational one, denoting a maker and seller of candles.

Chanel The well-known perfume is named for the French dress designer Gabrielle ('Coco') *Chanel* (1883–1971) who opened a couture house in Paris after the First World War and introduced a range of new fashions and jewellery. The famous 'Chanel No 5' perfume was first sold in 1920.

Changchun The city in northeast China, the capital of Jilin province, derives its name from Chinese *cháng*, 'long' and *chūn*, 'spring' (the season). *Cp.* CHANGSHA.

Changsha The port in southeast China, the capital of Hunan province, has a name that represents Chinese *cháng*, 'long' (*cp.* CHANGCHUN) and *shā*, 'sand'.

Chantal *See* CANTAL.

Chantilly The town in northern France had the Medieval Latin name of *Chantiloium*, representing the Gallo-Roman personal name *Cantilius*, with the Latin place-name suffix -*acum*.

Chao Phraya The river in northern Thailand derives its name from Thai *chao*, 'king', 'royal', 'sacred' and *phraya*, 'general', 'chief', an honorific term.

Chaplin The name was originally that of a clergyman, from the Old French word *chapelain* that gave modern English *chaplain*.

Chapman The name originally described a person who was a merchant or trader, from the Old English word *cēap*, 'barter', 'trade' that gave the place-names CHEAPSIDE and CHIPPING CAMPDEN and modern English *cheap*.

Chappell The name would originally have applied to someone who lived near a chapel, or who worked in one.

Charente The river and department in west central France derive their name from proto-Indoeuropean *karantono*, 'sandy', from *karanto*, 'sand'.

Charge of the Light Brigade, The The name is that of the disastrous incident of the Crimean War when in 1852 the British Light Brigade of cavalry charged against Russian entrenched artillery at Balaclava, sustaining heavy losses.

Chari The river in north central Africa has a native name meaning simply 'river'. It gave its name to the latter half of *Ubangi-Shari*, the former name of the Central African Republic, in which it rises.

Charing Cross Romantics like to derive the name of this district of central London from French *chère reine*, 'dear queen', said to be the endearing tribute made by Edward I to his wife, Queen Eleanor. The true meaning of the name, however, is 'cross at the place by the bend', from Old English *cierring*, 'turn', 'bend' and modern 'cross'. The 'bend' was probably that in the road here from London to the West of England. The cross marked the final resting-place of the coffin of Queen Eleanor on its route from Lincoln to London following her death in 1290 at Harby in Nottinghamshire. A similar 'Eleanor cross' was erected at each of the 11 previous resting points: Lincoln, Grantham, Stamford, Geddington (near Kettering), Northampton, Stony Stratford, Woburn, Dunstable, St Albans, Waltham (now Waltham Cross), West Cheap (now Cheapside). Only three of the original crosses survive, at Geddington, Northampton and Waltham Cross.

Charing Cross Hospital The well-known London hospital, in Fulham Palace Road, originally opened in 1818 near the Haymarket Theatre as the *West London Infirmary and Dispensary*. In 1823 it moved to Villiers Street and in 1827 adopted its present name, for its location at CHARING CROSS. In 1973 it moved to its new site in west London, some five miles away, but retained its former name.

Charlemagne The famous Holy Roman Emperor has a name that is simply a French form of his Latin name, *Carolus Magnus*, 'Charles the Great'.

Charleroi The Belgian town arose on the site of a village originally named *Charnoy*. In 1666 it was renamed *Charleroi* by the Spanish governor-general of the Low Countries, the Marquess de Castel Rodrigo, in honour of his king, *Charles* II. The new name thus reflects the old while having a specific personal reference.

Charles The name ultimately derives from a Germanic word, meaning 'free man', that gave Old English *ceorl*, 'man', which is itself the source of modern *churl* and *churlish*, though originally lacking the present derogatory sense. *See also* CHARLEMAGNE.

Charleston There are two famous American towns of the name. *Charleston*, state capital of West Virginia, was named by George Clendenin, who founded it in 1794, for his father, *Charles* Clendenin. The port of *Charleston*, South Carolina, was founded in 1670 and named for *Charles* I of England. The dance named the *charleston* originated in the 1920s in the latter town.

Charleville-Mézières The name is that of the city formed in 1966 on the river Meuse in northeast France through the amalgamation of the two towns mentioned and some smaller communes. *Charleville* was so named in 1606 for *Charles* de Gonzague, who rebuilt it. *Mézières* derives its name from Latin *maceria*, 'masonry', 'enclosing wall'. The same word lies behind the English name *Makerfield*, as for Ashton-in-Makerfield, near Manchester.

Charlotte The name is a French feminine diminutive of CHARLES, popularized in England by Queen *Charlotte* (1744–1818), wife of George III.

Charlotte The largest city in North Carolina was settled in the mid-18th century and named for Princess *Charlotte* (1744–1818), the future wife (from 1761) of George III.

Charlotte Amalie The capital of the Virgin Islands of the United States was established as a Danish colony in 1672 and named for *Charlotte Amalia*, Queen of Denmark. The name was changed to *St Thomas* in 1921, but reverted to its original in 1936.

Charlottenburg The district of Berlin, Germany takes its name from Sophia *Charlotte* (1668–1705), the second wife of Frederick the Great of Prussia.

Charlottetown The capital of Prince Edward Island, Canada, was founded in about 1720 as a French settlement named *Port la Joie*. When the island passed to the British in 1763 it was renamed *Charlottetown*, for Queen *Charlotte* (1744–1818), wife (from 1761) of George III. The island itself was still *St John's Island* at this time, and did not receive its present name until 1798.

Charlton Athletic The London football club takes its name from the district of *Charlton* in the southeast of the city in which it was founded in 1905.

Charmian Historically the name arose as a diminutive of Greek *kharma*, 'delight'. In modern times, however, it has been associated with *charm*, a word of different origin (from Latin *carmen*, 'song').

Charon The name of the ferryman who brought the dead over the river Styx (or Acheron) to Hades has been derived from Greek *khara*, 'bright' and *ops*, 'eye', so that he was the 'bright-eyed one'.

Charterhouse The well-known public school for boys was founded in 1611 on the site of a former CARTHUSIAN monastery in what is still called *Charterhouse* Square, by the Barbican in the City of London. In 1872 the school moved to its present location at Godalming in Surrey. The name *Charterhouse* for a Carthusian monastery arose as a folk etymology of CHARTREUSE, the French village where the order was founded in the 11th century. Present and past members of Charterhouse School are known as *Carthusians*.

Chartist The name is that of the British working-class political reformers who were active from 1838 to 1848. They took their name from the *People's Charter*, the document that stated their main aims.

Chartres The city of northern France takes its name from the *Carnutes*, a Gaulish people for whom Chartres was a sacred place. The people's own name is based on the pre-Indoeuropean root element *kar*, meaning 'stone', 'rock'. Cp. CARIA.

Chartreuse The French village, in full *St-Pierre-de-Chartreuse*, near Grenoble, probably takes its name from the *Caturiges*, an Alpine race who inhabited the region. Their own name derives from Gaulish *catu*, 'battle' and *riges*, plural of *rix*, 'king', so that they were 'kings of battle', or first-rank warriors. The place-name gave not only that of the green or yellow liqueur but the title of the CARTHUSIAN monastic order and, through them, that of CHARTERHOUSE School. The liqueur is actually produced at

the Carthusian monastery, itself known as *La Grande Chartreuse* from its location in the heart of the mountains of this name north of Grenoble.

Chartwell The country house that was the home of Sir Winston Churchill near Westerham, Kent, takes its name from the locality here, regarded by the Anglo-Saxons as a 'spring in rough ground', from Old English *ceart*, 'rough ground' and *wella*, 'spring', 'well'. There are several other places named *Chart* in Kent, such as *Chart* Corner near Maidstone, Great *Chart* near Ashford, and *Chartham* near Canterbury.

Charybdis In Greek mythology, the name is that of the ship-devouring monster who lay on the Italian coast opposite Scylla on the coast of Sicily. The site of her operations has been identified as a whirlpool at the northern end of the Strait of Messina. Her name may be based on Greek *rhoibdeō*, 'I gulp', itself related to *rhoibdos*, 'rushing'.

Chase Manhattan Bank The American bank was created in 1955 as a merger between the Bank of *Manhattan*, founded in 1799, and the *Chase* National Bank of the City of New York. The latter, founded in 1877, took its name from Salmon Portland *Chase* (1808–1873), who originated the United States banking system in 1863.

Châteauroux The city in central France is named for its medieval *château* (castle), built in the 10th century by *Raoul* le Large, prince of Déols.

Château-Thierry The name of the town in north central France means '*Thierry*'s castle'. The castle (*château*) was built in 718 by Charles Martel, grandfather of Charlemagne, as a royal residence for the Merovingian king *Thierry* IV (701–737) (sometimes known as *Theuderic*). At the time of the French Revolution the name was temporarily changed to *Egalité-sur-Marne*, after Louis Philippe Joseph, duc d'Orléans, known as Philippe *Egalité* ('Philip Equality'), who supported the Revolution and voted for the death of Louis XVI, his cousin. In 1793, however, he was himself executed when his son, the future king Louis-Philippe, defected to the Austrians.

Chatham The town in Kent, formerly famous for its royal dockyard, has a name that means 'settlement by a wood', from the Celtic root element *ceto*, 'wood' (seen also in the names of BETWS-Y-COED and LICHFIELD) and Old English *hām*, 'settlement'. The country to the south of Chatham is still well wooded.

Chatham Islands The New Zealand island group was discovered in 1791 by Lieutenant William R. Broughton, who named it for his ship, the *Chatham*, herself named after her home port of CHATHAM, England.

Chatsworth House The mansion near Bakewell in Derbyshire, the seat of the dukes of Devonshire, was built in the late 17th and early 18th century and is named for its locality, which in turn has a name meaning '*Ceatt*'s enclosure', from the Anglo-Saxon personal name and Old English *worth*, 'enclosure'. The personal name has been recorded only in place-names, and is also found for *Chattisham*, the village near Hadleigh, Suffolk.

Chattanooga The city in Tennessee probably takes its name from the Indian (Creek) name for what is now Lookout Mountain. The name itself is said to mean 'rock rising to a point'.

Chaucer The famous literary name was originally that of a person who made leggings, from Old French *chausses*, 'footwear', 'leggings', a word that gave modern French *chaussures*, 'shoes' and *chaussettes*, 'socks'.

Chaux-de-Fonds, La The town in western Switzerland perhaps derives the first word of its name from a pre-Indoeuropean root word *calma* meaning 'bare height' (*cp.* CARIA). The name as a whole is sometimes explained by a reference to two former fountains or springs here, one of which froze in winter while the other did not. The first was known as *Font Froide*, 'cold spring', while the second was *Chaude Font*, 'warm spring'. But this is probably just a traveller's tale.

Cheapside The name is now that of the London street that runs east from St Paul's Cathedral towards the Bank of England. It originally related to that of a more extensive area, the former main market of medieval London. The name itself reflects this origin, deriving from Old English *cēap*, 'market' (eventually giving modern English

cheap). The 'side' denotes that the street, when built, ran along one side of the market. Many street names here have preserved medieval trades and crafts, such as *Bread Street, Milk Street, Poultry*.

Checkpoint Charlie The name was long familiar as the most notorious of the official crossing-points between East and West Berlin. It was at the junction of Friedrichstrasse and Kochstrasse in the American sector and was so named from the NATO phonetic code for the letter 'C'. It was therefore designated as the third in order. The first two crossing-points were Checkpoint Alpha, at Helmstedt-Marienborn, and Checkpoint Bravo, at Dreilinden-Drewitz. Checkpoint Charlie was the only crossing-point in the Berlin Wall to be open 24 hours a day. It was dismantled in 1990.

Cheddar The well-known cheese originally came from the region of the Somerset town that bears its name. The town's own name derives from Old English *ceod*, 'bag', 'pouch', probably referring to the famous caves here in *Cheddar* Gorge, with their stalagmites and stalactites.

Cheju The volcanic island southwest of Korea and the province of South Korea derive its name from Korean *che*, 'end' and *chu*, 'region', 'province', referring to their location. The second half of the name is directly related to Chinese *zhōu* found in *Guangzhou*, the Chinese name of CANTON.

Chelmsford The Essex city has a name that means '*Cēolmǣr*'s ford', the latter being over the river here, the *Chelmer*, itself named for the town. The personal name means 'ship fame'.

Chelsea The district of southwest central London has a name that means 'chalk landing place', from Old English *cealc*, 'chalk' and *hȳth*, 'landing place'. The latter part of the name has been distorted to suggest 'sea', as for BATTERSEA and BERMONDSEY. The name as a whole denotes a point on the Thames where chalk was unloaded.

Cheltenham The Gloucestershire town has a name of uncertain origin. It certainly ends in Old English *hamm*, 'river meadow', describing the site of the original settlement here by the river *Chelt* (whose own name derives from that of the town). The first part of the name has been linked to that of the CHILTERNS, with perhaps a basic sense 'hill' for both. In the case of Cheltenham, the reference would be to Cleeve Hill, which overlooks the town to the northwest.

Chelyabinsk The city in western Russia derives its name from Bashkir *cheliab*, 'bucket', alluding to the depression in which the town is situated.

Chemnitz The city in eastern Germany has a name of Slavic origin, from the root word *kamy* (Russian *kamen'*), 'stone'. From 1953 to 1990 the city was known as *Karl-Marx-Stadt*.

Chepstow The South Wales town near Newport has an English name meaning 'market place', from Old English *cēap*, 'market' (as for CHEAPSIDE) and *stōw*, 'place'. Chepstow was thus a trading centre. Its Welsh name is *Cas-Gwent*, 'castle in GWENT'.

Chequers The country residence of the British prime minister, near Princes Risborough, Buckinghamshire, has the full name *Chequers Court*. The present house was built on the site of a 13th-century one owned by Laurence de *Scaccario*, whose own surname probably meant that he was an official of the medieval Court of *Exchequer*, the court of law that dealt with matters of revenue. *Scaccario* was thus translated as *Exchequer* (or its medieval equivalent) and shortened to *Chequers*. Chequers was presented to the nation by Lord Lee of Fareham in 1921 'as a place of rest and recreation for her prime ministers for ever'. The financial association of the historic name is coincidentally appropriate for the prime-ministerial residence, since the Prime Minister is also First Lord of the Treasury. For a similar serendipity, *see* DOWNING STREET.

Cherbourg. The Roman name of the port in northwest France was *Coriallum* or *Coriovallum*, comprising Gaulish *corio*, 'army' and Latin *vallum*, 'fortification'. The present name appears to derive from a Germanic translation of this, from *hari*, 'army' and *burg*, 'fort', so that a hypothetical *Hariburg* eventually became the *Cherbourg* of today. On English soil this could have given a name such as *Harbury* or *Herbury*.

Chernobyl The site of the Soviet nuclear disaster of 1986, in what is now Ukraine, is said to take its name from a plant here known in Russian as *chernobylnik*. This is mugwort, botanically *Artemisia vulgaris*.

Cherokee The Indian people of North America were originally cave-dwellers in the southern Appalachian mountains. Their name derives from their habitat, and represents native *chilukki*, 'caves'.

Chersonese, The The name was applied in ancient geography to several peninsulas in Europe, notably the one that is now known as the Crimea, where it gave the name of the present Ukrainian port of *Kherson*. It represents a combination of Greek *khersos*, 'dry land' and *nēsos*, 'island', denoting an 'island' that was attached to dry land.

Cheryl The relatively modern name appears to be a blend of *Cherry* and BERYL.

Chesapeake Bay The largest inlet of the Atlantic, in the eastern United States seaboard, has an indigenous Indian name, either from Delaware *kcheseipogg*, 'great salt water' or Algonquian *chesipoc*, 'to the big river'. The only certain element is the initial *che*, meaning 'big'.

Cheshire The English county takes its name from the city of CHESTER, its chief town. It is thus really 'Chestershire', and the county name actually appears in this form in a document of 1326.

Chester The city and port in northwest England has a name representing Old English *ceaster*, 'Roman fort', ultimately from Latin *castra*, 'camp'. Unlike names such as MANCHESTER and WINCHESTER, the initial element has disappeared. The Venerable Bede, however, referred to Chester in the 8th century as *Legacæstir*, the first part of which represents Latin *legionum*, 'of the legions'. The actual Roman name of the station here was *Deva*, derived from the river DEE on which Chester stands. *See also* CHESHIRE.

Chesterfield The Derbyshire town has a straightforward descriptive name meaning 'fort in a field', from Old English *ceaster*, the term for a Roman fort, and *feld*, 'field', more in the sense 'open land' than the modern field. A Roman fort has recently been found at Chesterfield, but its original name is unknown.

Cheviots The hills on the English border with Scotland have a name of unknown origin. The range as a whole takes its name from a single mountain here, *The Cheviot*, whose name was recorded in the 12th century as *Chiuiet*. The name may be related to that of CHEVY CHASE.

Chevrolet The car takes its name from the Swiss-born American racing-car driver Louis *Chevrolet* (1879–1941), who founded the motor manufacturing company that bears his name in 1911.

Chevy Chase, Battle of The battle was that of 1388 in which the Scots defeated Henry Percy ('Hotspur') at Otterburn, north of Hexham. *Chevy Chase*, in Northumberland, where it took place, derives its name from a hill here, whose own name may relate to that of the CHEVIOTS, only 15 miles (24 km) from Otterburn. The 'Chase' was a former hunting ground here. *The Ballad of Chevy Chase* is the title of an old English ballad. The American film actor Cornelius Crane Chase (1943–   ) adopted the name 'Chevy Chase' as his pseudonym, taking it from *Chevy Chase*, the suburb of Washington DC. This was itself named for the ballad.

Cheyenne The North American Indian people take their name from a native (Dakota) word *shaia*, 'talkers', implying a tribe who speak a language that is unintelligible to others. When the state of Wyoming was created in 1868 the name *Cheyenne* was proposed for it, but was rejected. It was, however, adopted for the city that is the state capital.

Chiba The city in the island of Honshu, in central Japan, derives its name from Japanese *chi*, 'thousand' and *ha*, 'leaf', 'foliage'.

Chicago The famous American city, in Illinois, has an Algonquian name probably meaning 'garlic place', referring to the garlic or wild onions originally growing in the meadows here by Lake Michigan. The name was first applied to the river, then to the town that was built by it in the early 19th century.

Chicago The American rock group took its name from the city of CHICAGO where it was formed in 1967.

Chichester The Sussex town and cathedral city has a name meaning '*Cissa*'s fort', with Old English *ceaster*, 'Roman fort' added to the name of *Cissa*, one of the three sons of Ælle, the first king of the South Saxons (who gave their name to SUSSEX) in the 6th century.

Chihuahua The breed of dog takes its name from the Mexican town of *Chihuahua* where it originated. The town's own name is of Indian origin meaning 'dry', 'sandy'.

Chil The name of *Chil* the kite in Kipling's *Jungle Books* (1894, 1895) actually means 'kite' in Hindustani. Presumably the native name is onomatopoeic, referring to the bird's shrill, thin cry. Kipling said it should be pronounced 'Cheel'.

Child A person of this name would have come to be so called either because he was unusually young, or youthful, or because he was a young man of noble birth. For the latter sense *see* CHILDE HAROLD.

Childe Harold The name is that of the central character in Byron's poem *Childe Harold's Pilgrimage* (1812–18), describing his travels and experiences as he journeys through Europe. *Childe* is in effect a title for a young man of noble birth, and was applied in medieval times to a young noble awaiting knighthood. The same title is found for *Childe Roland* in Scottish legend and in Browning's poem *Childe Roland to the Dark Tower Came* (1855).

Children's Hour The popular early evening BBC radio programme for children, broadcast from 1922 to 1964, took its title from the poem of the same name by Longfellow. This describes the regular early evening visit of the poet's three young daughters to their father, with an opening verse:

> Between the dark and the daylight,
>   When the night is beginning to lower,
> Comes a pause in the day's occupations
>   That is known as the Children's Hour.
>   'The Children's Hour', in *Birds of Passage*, 1860.

Chile The South American country has a name of uncertain origin, deriving possibly from an Indian word meaning either 'land's end' or 'cold', 'winter'. The latter sense is only coincidentally suggestive of English *chilly*.

Chi-Lites The American soul group were formed in Chicago as the *Hi-Lites* in 1960. On discovering a rival band of the same name, they added an initial *C* for CHICAGO.

Chilterns The well-known hills, in southern central England, have a name of pre-Celtic origin perhaps meaning simply 'hill', found also in the name of CHELTENHAM. The name is not related to CELT.

Chimborazo The extinct volcano in Ecuador takes its name from that of the river *Chimbo* here, itself from Quechua *chimpa*, 'opposite', to which Peruvian *rasu*, 'snow' has been added. The river is thus 'opposite' the volcano, which is permanently snow-capped.

Chimkent The city in Kazakhstan has a name that represents Kazakh *chim*, 'turf' and *kent*, 'town'. The implication is that the town was built on a grassy site.

China The name of the famous oriental country is traditionally derived from that of the *qín* or *Ts'in* dynasty, which reigned from 221 to 206 BC. But the name of the territory here was already recorded as *Tsinstan* in the 4th century BC, at the time when Alexander the Great was conquering Persia and India. The Brahmans, too, had long referred to the Chinese by the Sanskrit name *čina*. The true source of the name thus appears to be in that of the central province of SHAANXI or *Shensi*, with capital *Shian*, around which the present country gradually arose. It was therefore the country that gave the name of the dynasty, not the other way round. The Chinese name for China is either *zhōngguó*, 'middle kingdom' or *zhōnghuá*, 'middle flower'. *See also* CATHAY.

Chindits The name is that of the group of Allied forces fighting behind the Japanese lines in Burma in the Second World War under the command of Orde Wingate. It derives from Burmese *chinthé*, the fabulous lionlike creature that guards Burmese pagodas and that they took as their badge. The adoption of this particular name may have been at least partly influenced by that of the *Chindwin*, the river of northern Burma.

Chink The derogatory name for the Chinese probably derives from *Chinese* itself, with *chink* perhaps also referring to the characteristic narrow shape of Chinese eyes.

Chinon The town in northwest France, known to the Romans as *Cainum*, derives its name from the Latin personal name *Catinus*, perhaps representing *catinus*, 'bowl', 'pot'.

Chinook The North American Indian people of the Pacific coast near the Columbia River have a native name that is more accurately *tsinúk*. Its meaning is unknown.

Chios The name of the Greek island in the Aegean Sea is of uncertain origin. It has been derived by some authorities from Greek *khiōn*, 'snow', referring to the snow that shines brightly on the island's mountains in winter. The Turkish name for Chios is *Sakız adası*, 'island of mastic'.

Chippewa The North American Indian people living in a region to the west of Lake Superior have a native name that means 'puckered', referring to the puckered seams in their moccasins. Their name is a corruption of OJIBWA, which thus has an identical meaning.

Chipping Campden The Gloucestershire town has a name whose first word represents Old English *cēping*, 'market place', from *ceap*, 'market' as in CHEAPSIDE. The second word of the name means 'valley enclosure', from Old English *camp*, 'enclosure' and *denu*, 'valley'. The place would originally have been simply *Campden*, but *Chipping* was added when it acquired an important local market. The same thing happened with other towns of the name, such as *Chipping Norton*, Oxfordshire, *Chipping Ongar*, Essex, and *Chipping Sodbury*, Avon. *Cp.* MARKET HARBOROUGH.

Chiquito The tribe of South American Indians in Bolivia has a name representing Spanish *chiquito*, 'little one'. It was given them by Spanish explorers who were struck by the very low doorways of the people's thatched huts, and who consequently (but erroneously) supposed that the inhabitants must be small. In fact the Indians were of normal height, but entered their huts on hands and knees instead of walking in upright.

Chiron The name of the wise and kind centaur of Greek mythology is *Kheirōn* in Greek, referring to his skill as a surgeon (Greek *kheirourgos*). The latter Greek word literally means 'hand worker'.

Chiswick The district of west London, on the left bank of the Thames, has a name that means 'cheese farm', from Old English *cēse*, 'cheese' and *wīc*, 'dairy farm'. The name has its exact northern counterpart in KESWICK.

Chita The city in southeast central Russia takes its name from the river on which it lies. The river's own name represents the Evenki word *chita*, 'mud', 'clay'.

Chittagong The Bangladeshi port has a name deriving from Hindi *ĉiṭṭāgāṅv*, 'white village', from *ĉiṭṭā*, 'white' and *gāṅv*, 'village'.

Chloe The name, familiar in literature as that of the lover and wife of Daphnis, is of Greek origin, meaning 'young green shoot', from a root word *khlōros*, 'green', seen in modern English *chlorine*, a greenish-yellow gas.

Choctaw The Indian people of North America are popularly said to derive their name from Spanish *chato*, 'flat', with reference to the tribal custom of compressing the heads of their babies. But the true source of the name is likely to be indigenous. Its precise meaning is unknown.

Cholmondeley The surname derives from a place in Cheshire that gave the name of *Cholmondeley* Castle, near Whitchurch. It means 'Cēolmund's wood', with Old English *lēah*, 'wood', 'clearing' added to a personal name that itself means 'ship protection'. The name is traditionally pronounced 'Chumley'.

Chomolangma The Tibetan name of Mount EVEREST means 'mother-goddess of the world', from *ĉomo*, 'goddess' (literally 'highest one'), *lang* (literally 'elephant', symbolic of the world), and *ma*, 'mother'.

Choral Symphony The popular name of Beethoven's Ninth Symphony (1823–4) refers to the last movement, which has a setting of Schiller's *Ode to Joy* for chorus and soloists.

Christ The name is the title of Jesus, from Greek *khristos*, 'anointed one', itself translating the Hebrew term that gave his other title, MESSIAH. Jesus presented himself (and was presented) as the one whom God had anointed, and the Bible contains many references to this, for example: 'He hath anointed me to preach the gospel to the poor' (*Luke* 4.18), 'Thy holy child Jesus, whom thou hast anointed' (*Acts* 4.27). The 'title' aspect of the name is reinforced by references to 'the Christ'. Because of the Crucifixion and the cross as the chief Christian symbol, the name *Christ* has also become closely associated with the word *cross*, so that English *criss-cross* is not a mere reduplication (like *mish-mash* or *zigzag*) but represents an original *Christ's cross*. In some languages the name even gave the word, so that Russian *krest*, 'cross' evolved from Old High German *krist*, 'Christ'. The sense development here was thus 'Christ' to 'cross on which Christ was crucified' to 'cross'. *See also* XMAS.

Christadelphian The name is that of a Christian millenarian sect founded in the United States in about 1848. It derives from a combination of Greek *Khristos*, 'CHRIST' and *adelphos*, 'brother'. *Cp.* ADELPHI, PHILADELPHIA.

Christchurch The city in South Island, New Zealand was founded in 1851 by John Godley, of the Anglican Canterbury Association, and he named it for his Oxford college, CHRIST CHURCH. The name is doubly apt for what was originally a model Church of England settlement, since Canterbury is the seat of the Church of England and the cathedral there is *Christ Church*.

Christ Church The Oxford college, founded in 1546, was originally known as *Cardinal's College*, after Cardinal Wolsey, who had begun it in 1525. In the year stated, however, Henry VIII designated the former priory church here as *Christ Church* Cathedral and as the chapel of the college. It therefore takes its name from this. *Cp.* TRINITY COLLEGE, Oxford, Henry's other great foundation.

Christian The name means 'follower of CHRIST', and occurs in the Bible itself in this sense: 'And the disciples were called Christians first in Antioch' (*Acts* 11.26).

Christians, The The Liverpool vocal quartet, formed in 1984, took their name from three of their members, the brothers Garry, Russell and Roger Christian. Ten years before, the three had appeared as the soul trio Natural High on the TV talent show *Opportunity Knocks*.

Christies The famous London auctioneers take their name from James *Christie* (1730–1803), who held his first sale in Pall Mall in 1766.

Christine The name is a French form of *Christina*, itself a simplified spelling of *Christiana*, the feminine equivalent of the Latin name *Christianus*, all of which imply 'CHRISTIAN'.

Christmas The popular Christian festival, in celebration of the birth of Christ, has a name that literally means 'CHRIST's mass', from Old English *Cristes mæsse*. 'Mass' here implies a celebration of the eucharist, in this case one in specific honour of Christ. The date of 25 December for Christmas was fixed by the western church as being exactly nine months after 25 March, the Feast of the ANNUNCIATION. *See also* NOEL, XMAS, YULE.

Christmas Island The island in the Indian Ocean south of Java, ceded in 1958 to Australia, was named by the Dutch captain Willem Mynors, who sighted it on *Christmas* Day 1653. It was already known to earlier European navigators, however. It should not be confused with the former *Christmas Island* in Polynesia that is now called KIRITIMATI.

Christopher The origin of the name lies in Greek *Khristophoros*. This means 'bearer of CHRIST', from *Khristos*, 'Christ' and *pherein*, 'to bear'. The meaning of the name was originally metaphorical, for someone who 'bore Christ' in his heart. Later, it gave rise to a legend about St *Christopher*, who literally carried the infant Christ over a river, and who came to be regarded as the patron saint of travellers. Equally, the name is sometimes understood as 'borne by Christ', in the sense of one who is sustained by his Christian faith.

Christ's College The Cambridge college was originally founded as *God's House* in 1436. It was refounded under its present name, for its dedication to Christ, in 1505.

Christ's Hospital The public school now at Horsham, West Sussex, popularly known as the BLUECOAT SCHOOL, was founded in the City of London in 1552 for the education of poor children. Its name derives from the dedication of the original hospital to Christ. *Hospital* here has a special sense denoting a charitable institution devoted to the upbringing of children. It is found in the names of one or two other schools of this period, such as *Queen Elizabeth's Hospital*, Bristol, founded in 1590.

Chronicles The two historical books of the Old Testament, 1 and 2 *Chronicles*, are so called since they *chronicle* the history of Israel from the time of Adam to the activity of the prophets Ezra and Nehemiah after the Babylonian Exile (6th century BC). The English name is a rendering of the original Hebrew title, *Divrai hayyamīm*, meaning 'events of the days' and implying a journal or diary. The Greek title of *Chronicles* in the Septuagint is *Paraleipomena*, literally 'things left out', that is, the books that are supplementary to the four books of *Samuel* and *Kings*, and that supply what is omitted from their own history. The Latin title follows the Greek, and is *Paraleipomenon*, meaning 'of the omitted things', with *liber*, 'book', understood.

Chrysler The car owes its name to the American engineer Walter Percy *Chrysler* (1875–1940), who first manufactured it in 1924.

Chrysostom The 4th-century Greek patriarch and archbishop of Constantinople St John *Chrysostom* was a noted preacher and expositor of the Bible. Hence his Greek surname, which translates as 'golden-mouthed', from *khrusos*, 'gold' and *stoma*, 'mouth'. The Russian Orthodox Church knows him as *Ioann Zlatoust* with the same meaning, from Old Church Slavonic *zlato*, 'gold' and *ousta*, 'mouth'. *See also* ZLATOUST.

Chubb The well-known safe locks owe their name to Charles *Chubb* (1772–1845), who first manufactured locks in Wolverhampton in 1830 and who patented his first safe five years later.

Chukchi The name of the people of the *Chuckchi* Peninsula, in northeast Siberia, is a Russian alteration of *chetko*, their own name for themselves, meaning simply 'people', 'men'.

Church The name would originally have applied to a person who lived by a church, rather than someone who was specifically a churchman.

Churcher's College The public school at Petersfield, Hampshire, was founded in 1722 by Richard *Churcher* (1659–1723), a local man, for boys to be taught English, mathematics and navigation in preparation for a career with the East India Company, in which he had himself been employed. The terms of his will were modified by Act of Parliament in 1744 to allow a more general education.

Churchill The name derives from any of the places so called, such as the village near Worcester or that near Stourbridge. The place-name means what it says, and describes a hill with a church on it (as frequently still found).

Churchill There are two rivers of the name in Canada. One, rising in Labrador, and flowing into the Atlantic, was formerly known as the *Hamilton*. In 1965 it was renamed for Sir Winston *Churchill* by J.R. Smallwood, prime minister of Labrador, who had attended Churchill's funeral in London that year and who proposed the change 'to honour Churchill's name'. The other, rising in Saskatchewan and flowing into Hudson Bay, was named for John *Churchill*, first Duke of Marlborough (1650–1722), governor of the Hudson's Bay Company for six years from 1685. Sir Winston was a direct descendant of the Duke of Marlborough.

Churchill College The Cambridge college was founded in 1960 as a memorial to Sir Winston *Churchill* (1874–1965) and is named for him.

Cicero The 2nd-century BC Roman orator and writer had the full name Marcus Tullius *Cicero*. His name was thus a *cognomen* or nickname. It derives from Latin *cicer*, genitive *ciceris*, 'chick-pea', denoting

some physical characteristic, such as a wart, that must have been borne by an ancestor. Until the early 19th century he was usually referred to in English as *Tully*.

Cid, El The Spanish title of the 11th-century soldier and hero of the wars against the Moors derives from Arabic *sayyid*, 'master', 'lord', so can be translated as 'The Master'. His real name was Rodrigo Díaz de Vivar.

Cincinnati The city in Ohio was so named in 1790 by General Arthur St Clair (1736–1818) in honour of the recently formed Society of the *Cincinnati*, a hereditary order itself named for the Roman general CINCINNATUS, regarded as a model of soldierly simplicity and ability, and symbolizing republican values. The town's original name, when founded in 1788, had been *Losantiville*, a compilation of *L*, the initial of *Licking Creek*, *os*, Latin for 'mouth', *anti*, Greek for 'opposite', and French *ville*, 'town', so that it was 'town opposite the mouth of Licking Creek', the latter being the river here.

Cincinnatus The legendary Roman general of the 5th century BC had the full name Lucius Quinctius *Cincinnatus*. His name is thus a *cognomen*, or nickname, deriving from Latin *cincinnus*, 'lock of hair'. The name has been popularly associated with *natus*, 'born', as if meaning overall 'born hairy'.

Cinderella The fairy tale heroine, beautiful but obliged to be a household drudge, was known as *Cendrillon* in the original *Mother Goose Tales* of 1697 by the French writer Perrault. This means 'Little Cinders', as a diminutive of French *cendres*, 'cinders', 'ashes', with reference to her habit of sitting among the cinders in the chimney corner when her work was done. Her original nickname in the story, however, was *Cucendron*, 'Cinder Bottom', from French *cul*, 'bottom' and *cendres*, but the younger of her stepsisters, who was 'not so horrid as the elder', changed this to a pleasanter *Cendrillon*. Sitting among the cinders may have meant dirty clothes but it would also have meant keeping warm. Cinderella was not the only one to warm herself thus: another was 'Little Polly Flinders' of the familiar English nursery rhyme.

Cinna The 1st-century BC Roman patrician, whose full name was Lucius Cornelius *Cinna*, had a *cognomen* or nickname that may have derived from Latin *cinis*, 'ashes', perhaps originally referring to a grey-haired person.

Cinque Ports The ports of Hastings, Romney, Hythe, Dover and Sandwich, in southeast England, are collectively known by a name that derives from Old French *cink porz*, 'five ports'. The five were granted special privileges in return for providing men and ships for the navy, although such privileges were revoked in the late 17th century. Further minor ports were added later to the original five. The title 'Warden of the Cinque Ports' has existed since medieval times, and is currently held by Queen Elizabeth the Queen Mother (from 1978).

Cinzano The brand of aperitif takes its name from two Italian brothers, Carlo Stefano and Giovanni Giacomo *Cinzano*, who set up a distilling business near Turin in 1757. The vermouth of the name was first exported in 1860.

Circassia The region of Russia that lies on the northeast coast of the Black Sea is named for its indigenous people, known in Russian as *cherkesy*. This is said to represent an Ossetian word *čarkas* meaning 'eagle'. The Circassians' name for themselves is *Adygei*, from the Abkhazian word *adi*, 'water', so that they are the 'water dwellers', living by the Black Sea.

Circe The enchantress who in Greek mythology turned the followers of Odysseus into pigs has a name that is usually derived from Greek *kirkos*, 'circle', referring to the round island of Aeaea that was her territory.

Circle Line The London Underground line has a self-descriptive name referring to the railway's continuous circular route. The first section of the line opened in 1868 as part of the plans to construct an 'inner circle' that would link the two ends of the METROPOLITAN LINE.

Cirencester The Gloucestershire town has a name that denotes its origin by a Roman fort (Old English *ceaster*, ultimately from Latin *castra*, 'camp'). The first part of the name represents *Corinium*, that of the Ro-man station here. Its meaning, however, remains obscure.

Ciskei The Bantu homeland in South Africa has a name that means 'this side of the *Kei*', from Latin *cis*, 'on this side' and the name of the river that flows into the sea east of it. *Cp.* TRANSKEI.

Cistercian The strict Benedictine order of monks and nuns takes its name from *Cistercium*, the Medieval Latin name of the French village of *Cîteaux*, near Dijon, where it was founded in 1098. The place-name itself derives from Old French *cistel*, 'reed', a plant that grew widely here.

Citroën The French car takes its name from André-Gustave *Citroën* (1878–1935), who began mass production of it in Paris in 1919.

City of London School The London public school for boys was founded in 1834 by the Corporation of London and is endowed with an annual sum towards its maintenance from estates bequeathed in 1441 for educational purposes under the will of John Carpenter, town clerk of the *City of London*. Its original site was in Cheapside, but in 1883 it moved to the Victoria Embankment and in 1986 to new premises in Queen Victoria Street. The *City of London School for Girls*, its sister foundation, was established in 1894 by the Corporation of London in accordance with the will of 1881 of William Ward, which directed 'that the School shall correspond, as near as may be, to "The City of London School [for Boys]"'. The school originally opened in Carmelite Street, near the Guildhall School of Music, but in 1973 moved to new buildings in the Barbican.

City University The London university was founded in 1966 and developed out of the *Northampton Polytechnic* that was founded in 1896 and that was named from its site in *Northampton* Square. It remains there today, but acquired its new name, referring to its location in the *City* of London, on gaining university status.

Ciudad Bolívar The port in eastern Venezuela has a name meaning 'city of *Bolívar*', the latter being the South American liberator who gave the name of BOLIVIA. From its foundation in 1764 until 1846 it was known as ANGOSTURA.

Ciudad Guayana The port complex in northeast Venezuela has a name meaning 'Guayana City', deriving from the historic region of northeast South America that is more familiar from the modern states of GUYANA (*which see* for the origin of the basic name) and FRENCH GUIANA. The complex was founded in 1961 and incorporates the historic Spanish settlement of Santo Tomé de Guayana ('St Thomas of Guayana').

Ciudad Juárez The city in northern Mexico was founded in the latter part of the 17th century and for over 200 years was known as *El Paso del Norte*, 'the pass of the north'. In 1888 it was renamed for the Mexican president Benito Pablo *Juárez García* (1808–1872), who made his headquarters here in 1865 during the struggle against the French.

Ciudad Real The town in south central Spain was founded in the mid-13th century by King Alfonso X as *Villa Real*, 'royal town'. In 1420 it was granted the status of a city (Spanish *ciudad*) and given its present name.

Ciudad Victoria The city in east central Mexico was founded in 1750 and in 1825 named for the first president of Mexico, Guadalupe *Victoria* (1789–1843), whose real name was Manuel Félix Fernández.

Civil War A *civil war* is not one between civilians (in the sense non-military people) but one fought between opposing factions of fellow-*citizens* within a single nation. Major civil wars have been the *English Civil War* of 1642 to 1651 between the Royalists (supporters of Charles I) and the Parliamentarians, the *American Civil War* of 1861 to 1865 between the North and the South, the *Russian Civil War* of 1918 to 1920 between the anti-Bolsheviks ('Whites') and the Bolsheviks (Communists), and the *Spanish Civil War* of 1936 to 1939 between insurgent nationalists (under General Franco) and the republican government.

Civitavecchia The historic city and port on the Tyrrhenian Sea in central Italy was founded by the Romans in the 2nd century but destroyed by the Saracens in 828. The inhabitants fled and settled elsewhere, but subsequently returned to the 'old city', Medieval Latin *civitas vetus*, modern Italian *città vecchia*.

Clackmannan The Scottish town and former county have a name that literally means 'stone of *Manau*', the latter being a district name. The stone (Gaelic *clach*) is an ancient glacial rock in the middle of the town, where it stands next to the Town Cross and the Tolbooth.

Clannad The Irish folk group, formed in 1976, at first sang only in Irish. Their name derives from Irish *clann a Dobhair*, 'family from Dore', *i.e.* Gweedore, Co Donegal, where teenage Maíre Brennan, her brothers and uncles, first sang in a pub.

Clare The Irish county has a name deriving from Gaelic *clar*, 'board', 'plank', applied figuratively to describe a flat district. The English town of *Clare* in Suffolk also has a name of Celtic origin, but from a word probably related to modern Welsh *claer*, 'clear', 'bright', 'shining', doubtless referring to the river Stour on which the town stands. The Medieval Latin form of the latter place-name, *Clarentia*, gave the royal title and personal name CLARENCE.

Clare The name is a form of earlier *Clara*, which itself represents the feminine form of Latin *clarus*, 'clear', 'bright', that is, 'famous'.

Clare College The Cambridge college was originally founded in 1326 as *University Hall*. It takes its present name from Elizabeth de CLARE, Lady de Burgh (1291–1360), who refounded it in 1359. *See also* CLARE HALL, CLARENCE.

Clare Hall The Cambridge college was founded in 1966 by CLARE COLLEGE as a separate graduate institution of the university, and is named after it.

Claremont Park The Palladian mansion near Esher, Surrey, now a girls' school, was built by Vanbrugh in the early 18th century. It takes its name from a subsequent owner, Thomas Pelham-Holles, Earl of *Clare* (1693–1768). His original name for it was *Clare Mont*, referring to the hill on which the house stands. In the year of Pelham-Holles's death, Claremont was bought by Robert Clive, Baron Clive of Plassey ('Clive of India').

Clarence The name derives from the royal title, that of the Dukes of *Clarence*. The first bearer of the title was Lionel of Antwerp (1338–1368), third son of Edward III, who was betrothed to Elizabeth, daughter of William de Burgh, when he was only three. She, barely nine years old herself, was the heiress of CLARE in Suffolk, so that on her succession to the title in 1360, following the death of her grandmother, Elizabeth of Clare, founder of CLARE COLLEGE, he became (in 1362) *Dux Clarentiae*, 'Duke of Clarence'. The first name use of the title was promoted by the last Duke of *Clarence*, Albert Victor (1864–1892), elder son of the Prince of Wales, the future Edward VII.

Clarence House The London residence of Queen Elizabeth the Queen Mother takes its name from the Duke of CLARENCE, the future king William IV, for whom it was built in 1825.

Clarendon Press The academic imprint of the Oxford University Press takes its name from the *Clarendon* Building, Oxford, built for the Press in 1711 and partly paid for from the profits of its publication of Lord *Clarendon's The True Historical Narrative of the Rebellion and Civil Wars in England* (1702–4). Edward Hyde, 1st Earl of *Clarendon* (1609–1674), a noted benefactor of Oxford University, took his title from lands near Salisbury, Wiltshire, now *Clarendon* Park, containing *Clarendon* House and the ruins of the medieval *Clarendon* Palace, that he had inherited from his father, who came from Dinton, only 12 miles (19 km) away. The place-name itself probably means 'clover hill'.

Clarendon School The girls' public school was founded in 1898 in *Clarendon* House in Malvern, Worcestershire, moving to Abergele, North Wales, in 1948 and to its present location, Haynes Park, near Bedford, in 1976. The original private house was presumably given a generally prestigious name, associated with the Earls of *Clarendon* (*see* CLARENDON PRESS).

Claridge's The prestigious hotel in London's West End takes its name from William *Claridge*, a butler in a noble household, who had saved enough to buy the small hotel that it originally was in the mid-19th century.

Clark A person of this name would originally have been either a scribe or secretary or else a member of a religious order, otherwise a *cleric*. Clerks came to be so called since in medieval times it was the clerics who were virtually the only people able to read and write.

Clarks The well-known make of shoe is named for Cyrus *Clark* (1801–1866), who with his brother James *Clark* (1811–1906) set up a tanning, rug- and slipper-making business in Street, Somerset in 1833. By 1840 they were manufacturing footwear alone.

Clash, The The British punk group, formed in 1976, chose as their name a word that frequently occurred in the headlines of the tabloid press and that reflected their aggressive approach to life through their music.

Classical Symphony Prokofiev's Symphony No 1 in D Major (1916–17) is so named as it was written in the manner of Haydn, so is deliberately 'classical' in style.

Claud The name, also spelled *Claude*, derives from the Roman *nomen* or clan name *Claudius*, itself from the *cognomen* or nickname *Claudus*, from the identical Latin word meaning 'lame', 'crippled'.

Claudia The name is the feminine form of the Latin name *Claudius* that gave CLAUD, *which see* for its meaning.

Cleethorpes The town and North Sea resort near Grimsby has a name that means '*Clee* hamlets', the latter half of the name representing Old Norse *thorp*, 'farm', 'hamlet'. *Clee* means 'clayey place'.

Clement The name means what it says, 'clement', 'merciful', although deriving from the Latin name *Clemens*, genitive *Clementis*, not direct from the English.

Cleopatra The name is famous as that of the beautiful queen of Egypt who was successively the mistress of Julius Caesar and Mark Antony. It means 'father's glory', from Greek *kleos*, 'glory' and *patēr*, 'father'.

Cleopatra's Needle The ancient granite obelisk on the Victoria Embankment,

London, was brought to England from Alexandria, Egypt, in 1878. It was originally erected in Heliopolis, Egypt, in about 1475 BC and is so named as it was said, on very doubtful grounds, to have have been a memorial to a son born to Julius Caesar by CLEOPATRA. A similar obelisk was set up in Central Park, New York, in 1880.

Clerkenwell The district of London has a name that means, as it implies, 'well of the clerks'. The 'clerks' would have been students from a religious foundation here, and doubtless the 'well' was the place where they regularly met.

Clermont-Ferrand The city in southern central France owes its dual name to the union of the two towns of *Clermont* and *Montferrand* in 1630. *Clermont* has a name that means 'clear mountain', that is, one easily discernible from a distance. *Montferrand* means *'Ferrand*'s mountain', from a personal name denoting a man with 'iron-grey' hair. *Montferrand* lost its first syllable in order to avoid repetition when it was paired with *Clermont*.

Cleveland The city in Ohio was so named in 1796 for Moses *Cleaveland* (1754–1806), of the Connecticut Land Company, who had laid it out. In 1832 the middle *a* of his name was dropped to make the name simpler.

Cleveland The county of northeast England takes its name from the *Cleveland* Hills here, their own name meaning literally 'cliff land', describing a hilly district. The county was formed only in 1974, but the name dates from at least the early 12th century.

Clifford The first name has been adopted from the surname, which itself has been taken from a place-name, itself comprising Old English *clif*, 'cliff', 'bank' and *ford*, 'ford'. There are many 'fords by a bank' in England, and the personal name could have come from any of them.

Clio The muse of history in Greek mythology has a name that comes from Greek *kleos*, 'fame', 'glory'.

Clive The name comes from the surname, itself originally a place-name, such as that of the village of *Clive* near Wem in Shropshire. The place-name represents Old English *clif*, 'cliff', 'hill-slope'. The first name may have been boosted by '*Clive* of India', otherwise Robert Clive, Baron Clive of Plassey (1725–1775), famous for strengthening British control in India.

Cliveden The 17th-century country house near Taplow, Buckinghamshire takes its name from its locality. This describes it as a valley (Old English *denu*) by a hill-slope (Old English *clif*, modern *cliff*). The hill in question is an escarpment by the Thames, over which there is a fine view from the house (now a hotel) and its grounds.

Clonmel The county town of Co Tipperary, Ireland has a name that represents Irish *Cluain Meala*. This means 'meadow of honey', from Irish *cluain*, 'meadow' and *mil*, genitive *meala*, 'honey'. The name probably related to a meadow where wild bees nested, rather than to one with beehives.

Close The name was originally used either to describe someone who lived by an *enclosure* of some sort, such as a farmyard in the country or a courtyard in a town, or as a nickname for some who was secretive and kept things *close*.

Clotho *See* FATES.

Clough The name would originally have applied to a person who lived by a steep slope, the Old English word for which was *clōh*.

Clovis The name of the 6th-century king of the Franks is a latinized form of the Germanic name *Chlodwig* that itself gave *Louis* (*see* LEWIS).

Cluj The city in northwest Romania had the Medieval Latin name of *Castrum Clus*. The latter word represents Latin *clusum*, 'closed', referring to the location of the town, which is encircled by hills.

Cluniac The name of the Reformed Benedictine order derives from the place of its foundation in 910, the French town of *Cluny*, in east central France. The town's own name represents the Latin personal name *Clunius*, perhaps itself from *clunis*, 'buttock'. *See also* CLUNY MUSEUM.

Cluny Museum The well-known Paris museum of medieval art and artefacts opened in 1844 in the *Hôtel de Cluny*, the former

Paris residence of the CLUNIAC Benedictine abbots.

Clwyd The Welsh county, in the north of the principality, takes its name from the river here, whose own name basically means 'hurdle' (Welsh *clwyd*), perhaps because hurdles were used to ford it or to make a causeway over it in historic times. If so, the name has a parallel in that of BAILE ÁTHA CLIATH, the Irish name of Dublin.

Clyde The well-known Scottish river has a name meaning 'cleansing one', from a conjectural Celtic root element *clouta*, which lies behind Latin *cloaca*, 'sewer'.

Clydesdale The breed of heavy, powerful carthorse takes its name from its region of origin, the Scottish county of Lanarkshire, in the valley of the river CLYDE.

Clytemnestra The wife (and murderer) of Agamemnon in Greek mythology has a name that means 'famous bride', from Greek *klutos*, 'famous' and *mnēsteira*, 'bride'. Bride she may have been, but more infamous than famous.

Cnidus The ancient Greek city, famous for its school of medicine, has a name that may derive from *knizō*, 'I scrape', 'I tease', alluding to the temple of Aphrodite here, as an object of worship that 'inflamed'.

Cnut *See* CANUTE.

Coates The name originally applied to a person who lived in a humble dwelling or *cot*, the equivalent of the later modest *cottage*, by comparison with the larger and more comfortable *house*. In some cases the person may have come from a place so called, such as the village of *Coates* near Whittlesey, Cambridgeshire, here in the plural meaning 'cottages'.

Cóbh The port in Co Cork, southern Ireland, has a name that is an Irish spelling of English *cove*. The reference is to Cork Harbour. From 1849 to 1922 the town was known as *Queenstown*, in honour of *Queen* Victoria, who paid an official visit here in the former year.

COBOL The name of the computer programming language designed for general use is an acronym of '*co*mmon *b*usiness *o*riented *l*anguage'.

Coca-Cola The popular aerated drink has a name that was created in 1886 to refer to two of its constituents, extracts from *coca* leaves and from the *cola* nut. Coca leaves yield (and gave the name of) *cocaine*, a form of which was originally present in the product. *See also* COKE.

Cochin The port of southwest India has a Tamil name that may represent an original word *koñcam*, 'little', referring to the small river where the town was originally built.

Cochin China The former French colony of Indochina, now part of Vietnam, has a name that arose as a Portuguese corruption of its local name *Ko-chen*, of uncertain meaning, to which *China* was added in order to distinguish it from the Indian port of COCHIN.

Cochrane The Scottish name derives from a place so called near Glasgow, itself perhaps based on a Celtic word meaning 'red' to which modern Welsh *coch* is related in the same sense.

Cockaigne In medieval legend the name was that of an imaginary land of luxury and idleness, with food and drink for the asking. It is generally held to derive from a Germanic word related to modern English *cake*, referring to the small cakes with which the houses in the land were built. Others, however, see it as related to English *cook*, with reference to the readily available food. Either way, it has been humorously (or erroneously) connected with COCKNEY, as if London were a 'land of Cockaigne'.

Cockney The traditional name for a Londoner, especially one born within the sound of Bow Bells, has its origin in Middle English *cockeney*. This literally means 'cock's egg', and was the term for a hen's egg that was small or misshapen in some way. On an analogy with this, the phrase came to be used as a derogatory nickname for a townsman, who led a 'soft' life by comparison with the 'hard' life of country folk. A person born or living in London was an obvious townsman, with distinctive manners and speech, so the name finally gained its specific reference.

Cocos Islands The islands in the Indian Ocean, southwest of Java, take their name from their many *coco*nut trees. They are

119

still sometimes known by their alternative name of *Keeling Islands*, from the name of the English captain, William *Keeling*, who discovered them in 1609.

Cognac The town in southwest France, famous for its brandy, had the Medieval Latin name of *Comniacum*. This represents the personal name *Comnius* followed by the suffix, *-acum*, that means 'territory'.

Cohen The Jewish name represents the Hebrew word *kohen*, meaning 'priest'. Jewish priests are traditionally regarded as belonging to a distinctive caste descended from Aaron, brother of Moses. It does not necessarily follow, however, that all Jews named Cohen belong to this caste.

Coimbra The city in central Portugal has a name based on the two Celtic words *cun*, 'height' and *briga*, 'fort'. The original 'fort on the height' was some 8 miles (13 km) to the southwest of the present town, at the location now named *Condeixa*.

Cointreau The orange-flavoured liqueur takes its name from Adolphe and Edouard *Cointreau*, who first made liqueurs in Angers, France, in 1849. The family did not register their surname for the distinctive brand until after the First World War, however.

Coke The alternative name for COCA-COLA arose as a popular nickname before the First World War. When it came to be used of other, similar drinks, the Coca-Cola Company registered it in 1920 as their exclusive property. It so happens that *coke* is also a slang word for *cocaine*, which was originally present in the product through the *coca* leaves that provided one of its constituents.

Colchester The ancient Essex town has the familiar *-chester* that shows it to have been a Roman station, from Old English *ceaster*, 'Roman camp', itself ultimately from Latin *castra*. The first part of the name represents that of the river *Colne* on which it stands, with the river's own name meaning simply 'water' and of Celtic origin. The actual Roman name of the encampment here was *Camulodunum*, meaning 'Camulos' fort', after *Camulos*, a Celtic war-god.

Cole The name is either a pet form of NICHOLAS or else arose as a nickname to describe a dark-skinned person, the colour of *charcoal*.

Coleman In several cases the name has evolved from a form of the name made famous by St *Columba*, the 6th-century Irish missionary who founded the monastery at Iona, and whose own name derives from Latin *columba*, 'dove'. In other instances it may simply have been an occupational name for someone who burnt charcoal or who gathered coal. In the latter case, it is thus similar to COLLIER.

Colfe's School The London public school for boys takes its name from the Rev Abraham *Colfe* (1580–1657), vicar of Lewisham, who in 1652 refounded a grammar school that had originated as a chantry school in Lewisham in the 15th century.

Colgate The make of soap and toothpaste takes its name from William *Colgate* (1783–1857), an Englishman from Kent who was taken to America as a child and who opened a soap and candles factory in New York in 1806.

Colin The name represents a diminutive form of the medieval name *Col*, itself a short form of NICHOLAS.

Coliseum The name was taken up generally in the 19th century for theatres and places of entertainment as an adoption of the Late Latin form of COLOSSEUM. The London theatre of the name, also known as the *London Coliseum*, opened in 1904 in St Martin's Lane and was apparently so called from the start, even at the planning stage. Its designers seem to have associated the name with both *colossal* and *column*, as the building is an unusually large and imposing one, with columns a prominent feature of its façade and roof decoration.

Colleen The name, regarded as typically Irish, represents Irish *cailín*, 'girl'. However, it is not actually used as a first name in Ireland itself. Some now see it as a female equivalent to COLIN.

Collier The name was originally an occupational one for a person who burnt charcoal or who sold coal. *Cp.* COLEMAN.

Collins The name means 'son of COLIN'.

Colmans The well-known make of mustard ultimately derives its name from Jeremiah

Colman, a Norfolk flour miller who in 1814 set up a watermill near Norwich to grind mustard. He took his nephew James *Colman* into partnership in 1823 and James in turn took his son Jeremiah James *Colman* as his own partner in 1850. It was the last two men that gave the firm its original name of J. and J. *Colman* Ltd.

Cologne The famous German city takes its present name from the first word of its Roman name, *Colonia Agrippensis*, 'colony of Agrippina'. The latter was the mother of Nero, in honour of whom the emperor Claudius named the colony of retired soldiers that he founded in the 1st century AD. The perfume known as *eau de Cologne* was first made in the early 18th century by Giovanni Maria Farina, an Italian who had settled in Cologne. The French name fortuitously suggests 'odour Cologne' to an English ear.

Colombia The country of South America was so named, on its administrative reorganization in 1863, in honour of Christopher *Columbus*, the famous discoverer of America (but not the first!). An earlier name of Colombia had been *Nueva Granada*, 'New Granada', given by Spanish colonists for GRANADA in the 16th century.

Colombo The capital of Sri Lanka has a name of Singhalese origin that derives from an Arabic original *kalambū*. The meaning of this is not known. The name has sometimes been wrongly associated with that of Christopher *Columbus*, although the famous navigator was never here. Even so, 16th-century Portuguese settlers in Ceylon must have been pleased to discover that the name of the chief port happened to suggest that of the explorer of the New World a century before them, especially as he had made his original base in Portugal.

Colón The Panamanian port, at the Caribbean entrance to the Panama Canal, was founded in 1850 and originally named *Aspinwall*, for William Henry *Aspinwall* (1807–1885), American promoter of the Panama Railway. In 1890 it was given its present name, the Spanish for the surname of Christopher *Columbus*. Its suburb, the twin port of *Cristóbal*, in the Canal Zone, bears his Spanish Christian name.

Colorado The American state is named for its river, in turn with a name representing Spanish *colorado*, 'coloured', 'reddened'. The reference is to the reddish hue of its waters as a result of the clay washed down from the cañons through which it passes.

Colosseum The name of the great amphitheatre at Rome, built in the 1st century AD, derived from a *colossus* or huge statue of Nero that stood near it. The name came to be adopted for various European theatres in modern times. It was also the name of a huge rotunda that stood for half a century in Regent's Park, London in Victorian times. *See also* COLISEUM, COLOSSUS OF RHODES.

Colossians The book of the New Testament that has the full title *The Epistle of Paul the Apostle to the Colossians* contains St Paul's address to the people of *Colossae*, an ancient city in southwest Phrygia in Asia Minor.

Colossus of Rhodes The name was that of giant bronze statue of Apollo that stood on the island of Rhodes in the 3rd century BC and that was one of the Seven Wonders of the World. The Greek word *kolossos* was used of any great statue, and the Latin form of this, *colossus*, gave the English word *colossal* to refer to anything huge. *See also* COLISEUM, COLOSSEUM.

Colston's School The Bristol public school for boys takes its name from its founder in 1710, the noted local benefactor Edward *Colston* (1636–1721).

Columbia The river of northwest America, the state capital of South Carolina, and the District of *Columbia* that is coextensive with the American federal capital, Washington, all take their name from Christopher *Columbus*. The river was so named in 1792 by the American sea captain Robert Gray who explored it in his ship *Columbia*. *Columbia*, South Carolina, was settled in about 1700 and founded as capital in 1786. The District of Columbia was formed in 1791. *See also* BRITISH COLUMBIA, COLOMBIA, COLÓN, COLUMBUS.

Columbia The famous American record label owes its name to the Maryland, Delaware and District of COLUMBIA franchise set up in 1889 under the North American Phonograph Company which leased and serviced graphophones (a type of dictation machine). The name is now used by CBS in America and by EMI in the rest of the world.

Columbia University The well-known American university was founded in New York in 1754 as *King's College*. It closed during the War of American Independence (American Revolution) but reopened in 1784 as *Columbia College*, so named for Christopher *Columbus*. Other schools were added, and the whole academic establishment was renamed *Columbia University* in 1912. *Columbia College* remains as the liberal arts college for men, however, with BARNARD COLLEGE its counterpart for women.

Columbine The name was originally that of the stock servant girl in the Italian *commedia dell' arte*. Later it was that of the sweetheart of Harlequin, especially in English pantomime. It derives from the feminine form of Italian *colombina*, 'dove-like', from *colomba*, 'dove'.

Columbus Both the state capital of Ohio and the city of Georgia were named for Christopher *Columbus*, the former in 1812, the latter in 1828.

Colwyn Bay The popular North Wales coastal town and resort arose only in the mid-19th century, adding *Bay* to be distinguished from the original village of *Colwyn* to the east, now known as *Old Colwyn*. The name itself is that of the little stream here, and is the Welsh word for 'puppy', alluding to its small size.

Comanche The name of the North American Indian people, and that of their language, derives from their native word *kaumonses*, 'bald-headed ones', from their custom of shaving their heads.

Comedy Theatre The London theatre, in Panton Street, off the Haymarket, opened in 1881 as the *Royal Comedy Theatre*. The theatre was intended to be the home of comic opera and was therefore given an appropriate name. The initial *Royal* of the name, apparently included without warrant, was dropped in 1884.

Commodores The American soul group, formed in 1968, are said to have picked their name at random from a dictionary.

They point out that they were nearly called the *Commodes*.

Commonwealth The name is familiar in two main contexts, historical and geographical. The former is the name of the republic that existed in Britain from 1649 to 1660, when Oliver Cromwell and his son Richard were successively Lord Protector of the Commonwealth. The name for this period (curiously similar to Cromwell's own surname) literally means 'common wealth', implying both public good or welfare and a state in which the *wealth* is held in *common* by the people. In its geographical sense, the name (formerly in full *British Commonwealth of Nations*) came to apply to those countries that had mostly been dominions or colonies in the British Empire.

Como, Lake The lake of northwest Italy is named for the city of *Como* at its southwest end. The city has a name of Celtic origin meaning 'valley', from a word to which modern Welsh *cwm* and English *coomb* are related.

Comoros The island republic, in the Indian Ocean off the northwest coast of Madagascar, has a name that represents Arabic *qamar*, 'moon'. This was the Arabs' name for the Magellanic Clouds which indicated the south, and which they transferred to all the islands in the southern latitudes here, including Madagascar. Some scholars also link the name with that of the mythical *Mountains of the Moon*, which were said to be situated somewhere in equatorial Africa, not all that far from the Comoros.

Compiègne The name of the city of northern France evolved from its Latin name of *Compendium*, meaning 'short cut'. This referred to the Roman route (if not road) that ran across the river Oise here between Beauvais and Soissons.

Compton Wynyates The famous Tudor country house near Shipston-on-Stour, Warwickshire, has a name that overall means 'valley estate with a windy pass', from Old English *cumb*, 'valley', *tūn*, 'estate', and *wind-geat*, literally 'wind-gate'. The house is in a valley surrounded by low hills. The name is thus much older than the house, and describes its location. *Compton* is a common place-name, and

Wynyates was added in medieval times to distinguish this particular Compton from others.

Conakry The capital of Guinea derives its name from a local word *konakri* meaning 'over the water', referring to the location of the town on a peninsula which is equally visible from north or south.

Concertgebouw The Amsterdam concert hall, famous for its *Concertgebouw Orchestra*, has a name that is simply the Dutch word for 'concert building'.

Conciergerie The former prison of the Palais de Justice, in Paris, where many noted persons were incarcerated at the time of the Revolution, was originally a royal palace, and is so called since it was originally the home of the *concierge*, the high-ranking official who was the custodian of the palace.

Concord The state capital of New Hampshire was founded in 1725 and at first named *Pennycook*, from an Algonquian word meaning 'descent'. In 1763 it was renamed *Concord*, after another town of the name in Massachusetts, itself probably so called to mark a peaceful settlement between two warring factions, or else simply as a general commendation. There are several places of the name in the United States.

Concorde The famous supersonic airliner, which made its first flight in 1969, was of joint Anglo-French construction and was given a name that was meaningful in both English and French to reflect this collaboration. To the French, the name has added associations expressed by the name of the Place de la CONCORDE in Paris.

Concorde, Place de la The famous Paris square was laid out in the mid-18th century and was originally named *Place Louis XV*, in honour of the king. In 1790, at the time of the Revolution, the square was renamed *Place de la Révolution*. As such, it was the scene of many executions by guillotine, including that of Louis XVI in 1793. In 1795, after the Revolution, it was given its present name, 'Concord Square'. It reverted temporarily to a royal title with the restoration of the monarchy in the early 19th century, but regained its present name for good in 1830.

Condom The historic town in southwest France had the Roman name of *Condomum*, representing the Gaulish personal name *Condus* and *mago*, 'field', 'market'.

Coney Island The island off the southern shore of Long Island, New York, famous for its amusement park, has a name which refers to the rabbits that formerly bred here, from Dutch *konijn*, 'rabbit'.

Confucius The well-known Chinese philosopher has a latinized form of his original Chinese name, which was *kŏng fū-zī*, 'Kong the master' (literally 'man's son', from *fū*, 'man' and *zī*, 'son'). The name was probably given its Latin form by Jesuit missionaries.

Congo The African state takes its name from the river that flows through it. The river name is of Bantu origin, meaning simply 'mountain', with reference to the local topography.

Congregational Church The evangelical Protestant church is so named since each *congregation* is self-governing and maintains bonds of faith with other congregations. In Britain most churches in the Congregational Church merged with the United Reformed Church in 1972.

Congress The bicameral federative legislature of the United States consists of the House of Representatives and the Senate, and is so named as it is the body where members of these two chambers meet (in the Capitol, Washington DC), *congress* meaning 'meeting', literally 'walking together'. It is significant that the major American legislative terms or names are Latin in origin (*Representatives*, *Senate*, *Congress*), suggesting a Roman exemplar or at least inspiration. *See also* CAPITOL.

Congreve The name comes from the place so called near Penkridge, Staffordshire. The place-name itself means 'grove valley', from Old English *cumb*, 'valley' and *græfe*, 'grove'.

Connacht The Irish province takes its name from the *Connachta* tribe who once lived in this part of Ireland. Their own name is traditionally derived from a legendary hero *Conn*, said to have founded Connacht as the first kingdom of Ireland. The name is still sometimes spelled *Connaught*.

Connaught Hotel The London West End hotel had the earlier name of *Coburg Hotel*, from the German royal title of *Saxe-Coburg* that had been borne by Prince Albert, consort of Queen Victoria. At the outbreak of the First World War, in deference to anti-German sentiment, the name was changed from *Coburg* to *Connaught*. This was not only another aristocratic name but one that was similar enough to enable the hotel to retain its monogram. The royal family itself similarly changed its name from *Saxe-Coburg-Gotha* to WINDSOR.

Connaught Rooms London's largest permanent banqueting hall, in Great Queen Street, was originally founded in 1775 as a masonic hall and was named for the Duke of *Connaught*, who was Grand Master of the Freemasons.

Connecticut The American state takes its name from the river of the same name, in turn deriving from an Indian word *kuenihtekot*, 'long river'. The middle *c* of the name, which is not pronounced, was probably added by false association with English *connect*.

Connemara The breed of Irish pony takes its name from the western, coastal region of Co Galway where it arose. The region's own name means 'sea district of *Conmac*'s people'. *Conmac* was the son of the Ulster warrior Fergus McRoy who married the legendary Queen Maeve.

Connolly The Irish name represents an original name *Ó Conghalaigh*, 'descendant of *Conghalach*', the latter personal name meaning 'valiant'.

Conrad The name is of Germanic origin, and comprises the words *kuon*, 'bold' and *rad*, 'counsel'.

Conservative The British political party developed from the TORY Party in the 1830s, and adopted a name that indicated its aim to *conserve* cherished political and ecclesiastical institutions, unlike some earlier Tories, who had been reactionary.

Constable The name originally applied to the law officer of a parish, the *constable* of today. It could also be used as a medieval title for certain other officers, such as a person of authority in a household or even in the army. The literal meaning is 'officer of the stable', from Late Latin *comes stabuli*.

Constable The British publishing house is named for Archibald *Constable* (1774–1827), a Scottish stationer and bookseller who set up his business in Edinburgh in 1795.

Constance The name is a French form of the Late Latin name *Constantia*, itself meaning 'constancy' and having a masculine equivalent *Constantius*. *See also* Lake CONSTANCE.

Constance, Lake The European lake takes its name from the German town of *Constance (Konstanz)* that stands on its shore. The town was founded by the Roman emperor *Constantius* Chlorus in the early 4th century, and is named after him.

Constanţa The port and resort in southeast Romania takes its name from the Roman emperor *Constantine* the Great, who rebuilt the town in the early 4th century and named it after himself. *Cp.* CONSTANTINOPLE.

Constantine The walled city in northeast Algeria takes its name from the Roman emperor *Constantine* the Great, who rebuilt it in AD 311. His own name derived from a basic Latin name *Constans*, 'constant'. *Cp.* the female name CONSTANCE.

Constantinople The historic name of ISTANBUL is of Greek origin, meaning 'city of *Constantine*', from *Konstantinos*, 'CONSTANTINE' and *polis*, 'city'. The Roman emperor *Constantine* the Great made the city of BYZANTIUM his capital and renamed it for himself in AD 330. The Russian name of Constantinople was *Tsargrad*, 'city of the emperor'.

Constitution Hill The well-known London avenue, leading from Green Park to Buckingham Palace, has a name that remains of uncertain origin. It is popularly said to relate to the daily *constitutional* walk that Charles II took here, although the origin may perhaps be in something more obviously political or parliamentary.

Continent The name is that generally used in Britain for mainland Europe, as distinct from the British Isles. Geographically, linguistically, culturally and in other ways, the *Continent* is regarded as being sufficiently distinctive to deserve a separate designation. An alternative name is *Europe*, although politically and economically Britain already belongs to this particular continent.

Conway Hall The hall in Red Lion Square, London is now used for various kinds of public functions. It was built in 1929 as the home of the South Place Ethical Society, and named for the Society's pastor in the 19th century, the American clergyman Moncure D. *Conway* (1832–1907).

Cook The name means what it says, and was applied to a person who cooked in a household, or who sold cooked meats.

Cook Islands The Pacific islands, belonging to New Zealand, take their name from the famous English navigator Captain James *Cook* (1728–1779), who discovered them in 1773. Various other places also bear his name, such as Mount *Cook* in South Island, New Zealand, and *Cook* Strait, between North and South Islands, New Zealand.

Cooper The name originally applied to a person who made and repaired wooden vessels such as barrels and tubs. The commonness of the surname shows that this was an important occupation in medieval times.

Copenhagen The Danish capital has a name that means 'merchants' port', from Danish *køber*, 'merchant' (literally 'buyer') and *havn*, 'port', 'harbour'. Copenhagen remains Denmark's leading commercial city today.

Copt The Christians of Egypt, who form the *Coptic* Church, have a name deriving from Arabic *qubt*, itself a form of Greek *Aiguptos*, 'Egyptian'.

Coral Sea The Pacific sea, northeast of Australia, has a self-descriptive name alluding to its many coral reefs.

Corbett The name originated as a nickname meaning 'little crow', from Norman French *corbet*, a diminutive of *corb* (modern French *corbeau*). This could have applied to a small, dark person.

Corcoran Gallery of Art The art gallery in Washington DC, with its noted collection of American paintings, was founded in 1859 through provisions made by the banker William W. *Corcoran* (1798–1888).

Cordelia The name is familiar as that of King Lear's daughter in Shakespeare's play. Scholars are not agreed on its origin. The traditional explanation is that the name combines Latin (and poetic Italian) *cor*, 'heart' with the name *Delia* as a typical Elizabethan literary anagram of *ideal*. But other theories see the name as representing Latin *cor de illa*, 'from her heart', as a joint anagram of *cord* and *a lie* (implying Cordelia's breaking of her bond to her father), and even as a form of *Coeur de Lion*, the byname of King Richard I. Earlier accounts of the Lear story have her name as *Cordella* or *Cordeilla*. The second of these exactly matches the spelling of the second interpretation quoted.

Cordilleras The mountain ranges on the western side of North and South America take their name from Old Spanish *cordilla*, 'cord', 'small rope', since they run down the continents like a continuous cord.

Córdoba The Spanish city, formerly the centre of Moorish Spain, has a name that may derive from Phoenician *qorteb*, 'oil press'. The Argentine city of the same name was founded in 1573 by the conquistador Jerónimo Luis de Cabrera, who named it after *Córdoba* in Spain, his wife's birthplace.

Corfu The island in the Ionian Sea has a name that represents Byzantine Greek *stous korphous*, 'of the teats', with reference to the twin mountain peaks here. The Greek name of the island is *Kerkyra*, derived from a European root word *kerk*, 'bend', perhaps referring to the winding coastline.

Corinth The historic Greek city, in Greek *Korinthos*, derives its name from the Pelasgian word *kar*, 'point', 'peak', referring to its location on the Isthmus of Corinth. The *-nthos* of the name is not Indo-european in origin but represents an unidentified Mediterranean language.

Corinthians The two New Testament books have the full names of *The First and Second Epistles of Paul the Apostle to the Corinthians*, and are addressed to Christians living in and around CORINTH.

Coriolanus The legendary 5th-century BC Roman general who is the subject of Shakespeare's tragedy (1608) derives his name from the Italian city of *Corioli*, which he conquered in about 493 BC.

Cork The city in southwest Ireland has the Irish name *Corcaigh*, representing *corcach*, 'marsh'. Cork was founded on marshland in the 7th century, and its streets were intersected by muddy streams as recently as the 18th century.

Cornelius The name is that of a Roman clan, and is perhaps related to Latin *cornu*, 'horn'.

Cornell University The American university was founded at Ithaca, New York, in 1865 and takes its name from Ezra *Cornell* (1807–1874), the businessman who contributed heavily to its endowment.

Corn Laws The laws introduced in Britain in 1804 to protect farmers against foreign competition imposed a heavy duty on imported *corn*, hence their name.

Cornwall The name of the English county is based on a tribal name, that of the *Cornovii*, who lived here in early times. Their name means 'horn people', from a word related to Latin *cornu*, 'horn' and ultimately to English *horn* itself. The reference is to the long peninsula or 'horn' that Cornwall is. The Anglo-Saxons added Old English *wealh*, 'foreigner' to this, implying a people who spoke a Celtic language, unlike themselves. *Cp.* WALES.

Cornwell The surname could have originally applied either to someone who came from CORNWALL or to a person from *Cornwell*, near Chipping Norton, Oxfordshire. The latter place-name means 'crane stream'.

Coromandel Coast The name of the southeast coast of India is a corruption of Sanskrit *ĉolamāndala*, literally 'circle of *Chola*', indicating its ownership by an early ruling dynasty. The Portuguese changed the original first *l* to *r*, the Italians then rendered the *ch* as *c*, and finally the French altered the ending to give the present form of the name. The *Coromandel* Peninsula, in North Island, New Zealand, was so named in the early 1800s after a visiting naval vessel.

Coronation Mass The nickname of Mozart's Mass in C, K 317 (1779), is said to refer to its composition for the annual crowning of a statue of the Virgin Mary in a church near Salzburg.

Corpus Christi In the Christian church, and in particular among Roman Catholics, the name is that of the festival in honour of the Real Presence of Christ in the consecrated bread and wine of the eucharist, observed on the Thursday after Trinity Sunday. The name is Latin for 'Body of Christ'.

Corpus Christi College The Oxford college was founded in 1517 by Bishop Richard Foxe and was apparently so named for his devotion to the Eucharist, as venerated in the festival of CORPUS CHRISTI. Evidence for this as the origin, rather than the festival itself, is found in the dedication to Foxe of a religious work by Bishop John Fisher, *De Veritate Corporis et Sanguinis Christi in Eucharistia* ('Of the Truth of the Body and Blood of Christ in the Eucharist') (1527): 'Quum libuit, ob devotionem animi quam peculiariter ad Eucharistiae sacramentum habes et habuisti semper, insignire Collegium ipsum titulo nominis ejusdem' ('Since it has pleased [you] to call the college itself by the title of the same name, on account of the devotion of soul that you so particularly have, and have always had, for the sacrament of the Eucharist'). *Corpus Christi College*, Cambridge, however, takes its name from the two Cambridge guilds of *Corpus Christi* and the Virgin Mary, whose members founded it in 1352.

Corsica The French island, in the Mediterranean, has a name of uncertain origin. A source in Phoenician *horsi*, 'wooded' has been proposed, since the Phoenicians built their boats from pinewood of Corsican origin.

Cortes The national assembly of Spain and formerly of Portugal has a name that means literally 'courts', from the plural of *corte*, 'court'. The assembly dates back to at least the 13th century.

Cortina The popular make of *Ford* car takes its name from the Olympic resort of CORTINA D'AMPEZZO, with its due associations of speed and sport.

Cortina d'Ampezzo The Italian town, site of the 1956 Winter Olympics, takes its name from Italian *cortina*, 'little court', with the town itself located in the *val d'Ampezzo*. The latter name derives from Italian dialect *in pezzo*, 'in the piece', that is, in the area of land here.

Corunna The city of northwest Spain, known in Spanish as *La Coruña*, has a name that may derive from Latin *columna*, 'column', referring to the Tower of Hercules, the Roman lighthouse still in use off the coast here.

Corybantes The wild attendants of the goddess Cybele in Greek mythology have a name that is probably of Phrygian origin, perhaps with a meaning of 'whirlers'.

Corydon The name of the stock shepherd or rustic character in pastoral literature probably derives from Greek *korudos*, 'crested lark'.

Cossack The Russian race, famous as warrior peasants, has a name of Turkic origin meaning simply 'nomad'. *See also* KAZAKHSTAN.

Costa Blanca The 'White Coast' lies between Valencia and Alicante, in southeast Spain. The name of the latter town may account for the particular colour (*see* ALICANTE).

Costa Brava The 'Wild Coast' is that of Catalonia, northeast Spain. The coastline is rugged here.

Costa del Sol The coast of southern Spain has a name translating 'Sun Coast', a commercial title designed to attract tourists, like many of the names below, including those with *Côte*. For a Slavic counterpart, *see* SLĂNCHEV BREG.

Costa Dorada The 'Golden Coast' lies between Barcelona and Valencia, eastern Spain, and is popular for its sunny, golden sands.

Costa Rica The Central American state has a Spanish name translating as 'Rich Coast'. This is not a touristic name, but one given in 1502 by Columbus, with reference to its abundance of vegetation and water. He also named it *Costa del Oro*, 'Gold Coast', perhaps referring to the gold ornaments worn by the indigenous population.

Costa Smeralda The 'Emerald Coast' is an Italian name designed to attract tourists to the northeast coast of Sardinia. The colour is that of the bright green vegetation here.

Costa Verde The 'Green Coast' is that between the French frontier and Corunna (La Coruña), Spain, so named for its verdure and fertility.

Costello The Irish name comes from an original name *Mac Oisdealbhaigh*, 'son of *Oisdealbhach*', the latter personal name meaning 'fawn-like'. In some cases, however, the name is of Norman origin, not Irish, denoting a person who lived by a slope or river bank, from Old French *coste* (modern *côte*), 'side', 'bank'.

Côte d'Argent France's 'Silver Coast' extends south from the Gironde to the Spanish border. The name is a touristic one, like most of those below.

Côte d'Azur The 'Azure Coast' is better known to the British as the 'French Riviera', and is the Mediterranean coastline of the south of France extending approximately from Cannes to Menton. The colour is that of the sea and sky. *See also* RIVIERA.

Côte d'Ivoire The West African country is still sometimes known by its English name of IVORY COAST, although this was officially changed to its French equivalent in 1986. The trade in ivory was initiated by Portuguese colonists here in the 16th century.

Côte d'Or The department of Burgundy, France, famous for its rich vineyards, has a name that translates as 'golden slope' (not 'golden coast'), referring to the range of hills here above the valley of the Saône.

Côtes du Nord The French department has a geographically descriptive name meaning 'northern coasts', referring to its location on the north coast of Brittany, by the English Channel.

Côte Sauvage The 'Wild Coast' is a name sometimes used for the Quiberon peninsula, Brittany, northwest France.

Côte Vermeille The 'Vermilion Coast' is a name sometimes applied to a small stretch of coast in southeast France, north of the border with Spain. The sand is dark red here.

Cotonou The chief port of Benin has a name of native origin, properly *Ku Tonu*, from *ku*, 'dead person' and *tonu*, 'lagoon'. A local legend tells how the souls of the dead were borne down the river Ouémé into the sea. The legend doubtless arose from the fact that the trees round the lagoon here are reddish, and were thought to be stained with the blood of the dead.

Cotopaxi The active volcano, in Ecuador, has a name of Quechua origin, from *kotto*, 'mountain' and *paksi*, 'shining'.

Cotswolds The range of Gloucestershire hills has a name that means '*Cōd*'s weald', referring to the high open ground here that belonged to an Anglo-Saxon named *Cōd* (pronounced 'Code'). The Cotswold village of *Cutsdean*, near Winchcombe, is probably named after the same man, with its *dean* the valley of the river Windrush.

Cottesloe Theatre The smallest of the three theatres that together form the Royal National Theatre, London, opened in 1977 and is named for Sir John Fremantle, the fourth Baron *Cottesloe* (1900–   ), first chairman of the South Bank Theatre Board, which was responsible for the building.

Coty The well-known make of toiletries takes its name from that of Corsican-born François *Coty* (1874–1934), who by 1900 had become established in Paris as a successful manufacturer of perfumes.

County Hall The impressive building on the South Bank of the Thames, London, was built in 1922 as the headquarters of the former London *County* Council, the forerunner of the Greater London Council, which occupied it in its turn. When the latter was abolished in 1986 County Hall was vacated and put up for private sale.

Courbevoie The industrial suburb in northwest Paris derives its name from Latin *Curva Via*, 'curved way'. The reference is to the Roman road from Paris to Rouen, which altered course from west to north here.

Court The surname could have one of two origins. It either denoted a person who lived and worked in a manorial *court*, that is, the private residence of the lord of the manor, or someone who was short or small, from Old French *curt* (modern French *court*) in this sense.

Courtauld Institute Galleries The well-known London art gallery, originally in Woburn Square but from 1990 in Somerset House, takes its name from Samuel *Courtauld*, direct descendant of the founder of COURTAULDS, who gave a portion of his art collection to the Courtauld Institute of Art, part of London University, at the time of the Institute's foundation in 1931, and bequeathed the rest on his death in 1947.

Courtaulds The famous textile company owes its origins to Samuel *Courtauld* (1793–1881), who set up as a silk throwster in Essex in 1816. The resultant firm began manufacturing viscose in 1904, the year it regards as that of its foundation.

Courtenay The name originally denoted someone who came from one of the places called *Courtenay* in Normandy, this name in turn deriving from a Roman personal name *Curtenus*, 'short'. In some instances the name may have arisen as a nickname for a snub-nosed person, from Old French *curt* (modern French *court*), 'short' and *nes* (modern *nez*), 'nose'.

Courtrai The town in western Belgium was known to the Romans as *Cortracum* or *Curtracum*, a name that is of Celtic origin meaning 'enclosure'.

Courvoisier The cognac is named for the French wine merchant Emanuel *Courvoisier*, who is said to have selected the blend for Napoleon on the latter's abdication in 1815.

Coutts The Scottish name originally denoted a person from *Cults*, now a suburb of Aberdeen. The place-name itself means 'woods', from Gaelic *coillte* to which English plural *s* has been added.

Coutts Bank The prestigious London bank takes its name from James *Coutts*, who became a partner of the business in 1755 when he married the niece of George Campbell, the son of John Campbell, its founder in 1692. The present chairman of the bank, the appropriately named Sir David Money-Coutts (1931–   ), is James Coutts's great-great-great-great-grandson.

Covent Garden The alternative name of the Royal Opera House, London, derives from the region in which it is located. This was originally the *convent garden* of Westminster Abbey, which later became famous for its fruit and vegetable market (not necessarily developing out of the original convent orchard here). The market moved to New Covent Garden in Vauxhall, over two miles away, in 1974. *See also* THEATRE ROYAL.

Coventry The English city has a name that means '*Cofa*'s tree'. It is not known who *Cofa* was, nor is the site of his 'tree' known. It probably served as an assembly point or marker of some kind.

Cowan The Scottish name, also spelled *Cowen*, is common enough but remains of uncertain origin. In some cases, however, it may be a form of *McEwan*, 'son of Ewan' (a Gaelic equivalent of EUGENE).

Coward The name originally denoted a person who was a *cowherd*, so is not related to modern *coward*. The latter word ultimately derives from Latin *cauda*, 'tail', as if the person concerned was like a dog with its tail between its legs.

Cowdray Park The name of the famous polo ground refers to its location in the *park* of *Cowdray* House, the 16th-century seat that was almost entirely destroyed by fire in 1793, so that the present house is relatively modern. The house takes its name from the location, whose own name means 'hazel grove' (*see* COWDREY).

Cowdrey The name derives from a placename, either *Cowdray* in Sussex (*see also* COWDRAY PARK) or a place called *Coudrai* or *Coudray* in Normandy. The origin of all these place-names is in Old French *coudraie*, 'hazel grove', based on *coudre*, 'hazel'.

Cowes The Isle of Wight resort, famous for its yachting events, especially in *Cowes* Week, has a name that derives from two sandbanks off the mouth of the river Medina here. They were called 'the Cows', as if the main island was the 'bull', rather in the manner that the Calf of Man is a small island off the Isle of Man. The name was then transferred from the banks to the settlement on the shore.

Cow Gum The brand of adhesive takes its name from Peter Brusey *Cow* (1815–1890), who set up his original business to make waterproof garments at Deptford, London, in 1851.

Cowley The name derives from any of the places so called, such as *Cowley* near Oxford. The place-name means either 'cow clearing', from Old English *cū*, 'cow' and *lēah*, 'wood', 'clearing', or '*Cufa*'s clearing', from a personal name.

Cox The name represents a former English word *coke*, here with a possessive *-s*, which was added to almost any diminutive personal name to make a pet name, such as *Alcock* (added to *Al* from *Alan*, *Alexander* and the like), or *Hancock* (added to *Han*, from *Johan*, that is, JOHN).

Craig The Scottish name denoted a person who originally lived near a steep rock or *crag*.

Crankshaw The name formerly applied to a person who came from the place that is now *Cranshaw* Hall, near Warrington in Lancashire. Its original meaning is 'crane wood', from Old English *cran*, 'crane' and *sceaga*, 'grove', 'wood'.

Craven Cottage The home ground of Fulham Football Club, on the east bank of the Thames in southwest London, takes its name from a former hunting lodge and house that had been built in 1780 by the sixth Earl of *Craven*. The original Craven Cottage, burnt down in 1888, stood in what is now the middle of the football pitch.

Crawford The name would have originally applied to a person from any of the places so called in Britain, such as *Crawford* near Skelmersdale in Lancashire or *Crawford* near Abington in Scotland. The name itself means 'crow ford'.

Crawley The West Sussex town, designated a New Town in 1947, has a name meaning 'crows' wood', from Old English *crāwe*, 'crow' and *lēah*, 'wood'. The name is of course not unique to this particular Crawley.

Cream, The The British rock group, formed in 1966, regarded themselves as the best, so chose a name accordingly.

Creation Mass Haydn's Mass No 13 in B flat major (1801) is so named as it contains a quotation from his own oratorio *The Creation* (1796–8).

Crécy, Battle of The village of northern France was the scene of the first decisive battle of the Hundred Years War, in which Edward III of England gained a victory over Philip VI of Valois in 1346. The place-name itself derives from the Gaulish personal name *Crixsius*.

Cree The North American Indian people and their language have a name that is a shortened form of their Canadian French name *Christinaux*. This probably derives from Algonquian *kiristino*, of uncertain meaning.

Creedence Clearwater Revival The American rock group, formed initially among high school friends in 1959, adopted their permanent name only in 1967. *Creedence* was said to be the name of a friend, *Clearwater* was from a beer commercial, and *Revival* was a 'statement of intent'.

Creighton The name is Scottish in origin, and denoted a person who came from *Crichton*, near Pathhead, southeast of Edinburgh. The place-name probably means 'boundary farm', from a combination of Gaelic *crioch*, 'border' and Old English *tūn*, 'farm'.

Cremona The Italian city takes its name from the *Cenomani*, the Celtic tribe who also gave the name of LE MANS.

Creole The name used for a descendant of European settlers in the West Indies or Spanish America, and for the language spoken by such a person, probably represents Portuguese *crioulo*, itself from *criar*, 'to raise', ultimately from Latin *creare*, 'to create'.

Creon The mythical king of Corinth has a Greek name that means 'prince'. His daughter, *Creusa*, bears the feminine form of this, meaning 'princess'. Cp. CRESSIDA.

Cressida Familiar as the lover of Troilus, Cressida has a name that may derive from Greek *kreissōn*, 'stronger', 'mightier', denoting a superior person. She was, after all, the daughter of a Trojan priest. Her name is thus related to the many mythical heroines called *Creusa*. Cp. CREON.

Crete The Greek Mediterranean island is traditionally said to derive its name from *Krus*, the mythical ancestor of the Cretans. The name is probably tribal in origin.

Crewe The Cheshire town is near enough to the Welsh border to have a Welsh name. It represents Welsh *cryw*, 'creel'. A creel is literally a fish basket, but here it came to acquire the sense 'stepping stones', probably because such stones would have been laid alongside a wickerwork fence or 'basket' placed across a river to catch fish. The stepping stones would have been over one of the many small streams here.

Crewe Alexandra The well-known Cheshire football club was formed in CREWE in 1876. It took its name from Princess *Alexandra*, who with her husband, the Prince of Wales (the future Edward VII), paid an official visit to Crewe that year on the occasion of the opening of Queen's Park, named for the Prince's mother, Queen Victoria.

Cricklewood The northwest district of London has a name that seems to mean what it says, and that originally applied to a 'crickled wood', that is, a wood with a 'crimped' or uneven edge. The wood in question would have been a western extension of the present Hampstead Heath.

Crimea The Black Sea peninsula, in southern Ukraine, has a name of uncertain origin that has been derived by some from Greek *krēmnos*, 'escarpment', 'steep bank'. Others see a link in Mongolian *herem*, 'strength', which may have given the name of the KREMLIN.

Crimplene The synthetic material, similar to TERYLENE, is like it manufactured by ICI and is so named from its 'crimpled' appearance. By coincidence there is a small stream named *Crimple* Beck at ICI Fibres' headquarters near Harrogate, Yorkshire.

Cripplegate The former London gate, in the north wall of the City, is believed to take its name from the *crypel* or narrow passage that was here (through which it was necessary to *creep*). The name became popularly associated with the miraculous cures of *cripples* here, however, perhaps through biblical associations. The name is preserved in that of *Cripplegate* Street.

Crispin The name derives from the Latin name *Crispinus*, itself from the nickname *Crispus*, 'curly', applied to someone with curly hair.

Criterion Theatre The London theatre, at Piccadilly Circus, was opened in 1874 as an addition to a large restaurant of the same name that had been built on the site the previous year. For the restaurant the name implied a high standard of cuisine and service. It had the same association for the theatre, with the additional implication that its plays would be well received by a theatre *critic*.

Croatia The republic in what was formerly northern Yugoslavia may have a name related to Russian *khrebet*, 'mountain chain', referring to the mountains by the Adriatic coast. The name gave the English word *cravat*, since neckties of this type were worn by Croats in the French army during the Thirty Years War.

Crockett The Scottish name would originally have been given as a nickname for someone with curly hair, from Old French *croquet*, a diminutive of *croque*, 'curl'.

Crockford A person with this name would originally have come from the place now known as *Crockford* Bridge, in Chertsey, Surrey. The name probably means 'pot ford', from Old English *croc*, 'pot' and *ford*. This may have been a place with a pot-shaped hollow in the ground by the Thames here, rather than one where pots or potsherds were found.

Crockford The annual directory of the clergy of the Church of England, in full known as *Crockford's Clerical Directory*, is named for John *Crockford*, who first published it in 1857.

Croesus The 6th-century BC king of Lydia, famous for his great wealth, has a name which, like that of CRESSIDA, may derive from Greek *kreissōn*, 'stronger', 'mightier', implying a ruler. *Cp.* CREON.

Cro-Magnon The cave of this name, in the Dordogne, is famous as the place where the remains of Cro-Magnon man were discovered in 1866. The name itself derives from a local word *cro*, 'cave', 'grotto' and the Roman personal name *Magnio*, genitive *Magnionis*.

Cromwell The surname derives from a place so called, such as *Cromwell* near Newark-on-Trent, Nottinghamshire. The place is named for its 'crooked stream', from Old English *crumb*, 'bent' and *wella*, 'stream', 'spring' (modern English *well*).

Cross The name originally applied to a person who lived by a stone cross, often one by a roadside or in a market square, or to someone who lived at a crossroads.

Crosville The Cheshire-based bus company was founded in 1906 and takes its name from its founders, George *Cros*land Taylor, a mill owner's son, and Georges *Ville*, a French motor engineer from Paris. The first *Crosville* bus service operated in 1910 between Chester and Ellesmere Port.

Crown Imperial William Walton's popular march is so named since it was composed for the coronation of George VI in 1937. A *crown imperial* is properly the crown of an emperor, as distinct from that of a king. Goerge VI was both, however, as Emperor of India and King of the United Kingdom, so the title is justified.

Crowther The name originally described a person who played on the *crowd*, a medieval bowed stringed instrument known in Welsh as the *crwth*.

Croydon The former Surrey town, now part of Greater London, has a name that means 'saffron valley', from Old English *croh*, 'saffron' (to which modern *crocus* is related) and *denu*, 'valley'. The valley is that of the river Wandle, which rises near here. Saffron was a herb used for dyeing and medicinal purposes in ancient times. For a similar name, *cp.* SAFFRON WALDEN.

Crozier A person of this name would originally have had the job of carrying a *cross* or a bishop's *crozier* in church processions.

Crucible Theatre The well-known Sheffield theatre opened in 1971 on the site of the former Playhouse. Sheffield has long been famous for its steel, and the theatre is named for the *crucible* process of steel production which was invented here by Benjamin Huntsman in 1742. The building, with its semi-circular shape and steeply-rising banks of seats, also suggests an actual crucible as well as a metaphorical theatrical 'melting pot'.

Cruft's The famous dog show, organized annually by the Kennel Club, takes its name from Charles *Cruft* (1852–1938), who held his first such show in London in 1886.

Cryer The name originally applied to a person who was a town *crier*, that is, who made public announcements in a loud voice.

Crystal Palace The huge building originally erected in Hyde Park, London, for the Great Exhibition of 1851 was so nicknamed for its large quantity of glass. After the Exhibition it was moved south to Sydenham, and the name *Crystal Palace* subsequently spread to the surrounding district. It was adopted by *Crystal Palace* Football Club, founded here in 1905, although the club moved further south again to Selhurst Park in 1924. Crystal Palace itself was destroyed by fire in 1936. The building caught the public imagination, however, and there are now plans to build a new *Crystal Palace* on the Sydenham site as a grand leisure complex with bowling alley, hotel and night club.

Crystals, The The American black 'girl group', formed in 1961, took their name from that of *Crystal* Bates, daughter of their first songwriter, Leroy Bates.

Cuba The island state, in the Caribbean, has an Indian name of unknown origin. A possible sense 'region' has been suggested, but the language that gave the name is extinct and this is merely a conjecture.

Cubism The early 20th-century art movement, with its revolutionary geometrical forms, is said to have been given its name by a member (name unknown) of the Hanging Committee of the *Salon des Indépendants* in Paris in 1908. On seeing a painting by Georges Braque being carried into the hall he exclaimed, *'Encores des cubes! assez de cubisme!'* ('More cubes! Enough cubism!'). A journalist picked up the remark and printed it, with the result that Braque and his fellow artists accepted the nickname and began calling themselves 'cubists'.

Cub Scout The *Cub Scouts*, or *Cubs*, were originally *Wolf Cubs* when introduced by Baden-Powell as a junior branch of the Boy Scouts (now Scouts) in 1916. Their name was inspired by Kipling's *Jungle Books* (1894, 1895) in which the boy Mowgli, the central character, is a human 'man cub' adopted by a family of wolves.

Cuchulain The great hero of Irish legend had the original name *Setanta*, perhaps linking him to the British tribe *Setantii*. He obtained his present name by replacing, as guard, the hound of *Culan* that he had killed, so that he was *cú Chúlainn*, 'Culan's hound'. The historicity of Cuchulain is disputed, although certain historical characters appear in the stories connected with him.

Cuenca The town in central Spain derives its name from Medieval Latin *concha*, 'shell', which gave modern Spanish *cuenca*, 'bowl'. The town is on a hill site surrounded by mountains above the confluence of two rivers. The city of *Cuenca* in southwest Ecuador also lies in a 'basin' among mountains.

Cuff The name would originally have been used for a seller of gloves, or as a nickname for a person who wore fine gloves. Modern English *cuff* originally meant 'glove'.

Culford School The public school, at Bury St Edmunds, Suffolk, was founded in 1881 and takes its name from its location in *Culford* Hall, an 18th-century country house that was formerly the seat of Earl Cadogan. The house's own name is that of the locality here, originally '*Cūla*'s ford'.

Cullen The Scottish name is that of a person from the place so called near Buckie, formerly in Banffshire. It means 'little corner', from Gaelic *cùilan*, a diminutive of *cùil*. As an Irish name, *Cullen* could derive either from *Ó Cuilinn*, 'descendant of *Cuileann*' (a personal name meaning 'holly') or from *Ó Coileáin*, 'descendant of *Coileán*' (a personal name meaning 'puppy'). In a few instances it could apply to someone from COLOGNE.

Culloden, Battle of The battle was that of 1746 in which the army of Prince Charles Edward Stuart (the 'Young Pretender') was destroyed by the Duke of Cumberland. *Culloden* Moor, where it took place, near Inverness, has a name that may derive from Gaelic *cul lodain*, 'back of the little pool', referring to a particular location in the vicinity.

Culpepper The name was an occupational one for a person who was a herbalist or spicer, who 'culled peppers', in fact.

Cult, The The British new wave group, formed in 1982, had the original name *Southern Death Cult*, taken from a newspaper headline. They later shortened this to the *Cult*.

Culture Club The British rock group was formed in 1981 by Boy George and some musician friends from the underground London *club* scene. They aimed to play *cult* music, so chose a name that reflected their origins and ambitions. The name also echoes the *country club* of fashionable American society.

Culzean Castle The 18th-century Gothic Revival mansion on the coast southwest of Ayr, Scotland, takes its name from the locality. The name probably represents Gaelic *cùil*, 'corner' and either *sian*, 'storm' or perhaps more likely *eun*, 'bird'. The name was recorded in 1636 as *Cullen*, and today is pronounced approximately 'Co*lane*'.

Cumae The ancient Greek colony in Italy, on the coast west of Naples, may derive its name from Greek *kuma*, 'wave', 'billow'.

Cumberland Hotel The London hotel, at Marble Arch, stands on the corner of Great *Cumberland* Place, and takes its name from it. The street was in turn named for *Cumberland* Gate in Hyde Park opposite, itself so called in honour of Prince William, Duke of *Cumberland*, brother of George III and victor at the Battle of Culloden in 1746.

Cumbernauld The New Town near Glasgow has an old name, representing Gaelic *comar-an-allt*, 'meeting of the streams', otherwise 'confluence'. A stream still flows through the original village of *Cumbernauld* here to join another nearby.

Cumbria The English county, corresponding roughly to the former *Cumberland*, has a historic name referring to the *Cymry*. This was the name, meaning 'fellow countrymen', that the Britons used for themselves, and that is today the Welsh name for the Welsh.

Cunliffe The surname derives from the place so called near Rishton in Lancashire. The place-name literally means 'cunt cliff', that is, a slope with a crack in it.

Cunningham As a Scottish name, *Cunningham* derives from the place so called near Kilmarnock, itself of uncertain origin. As an Irish name, it represents *Ó Cuinneagáin*, 'descendant of *Cuinneagán*', this personal name being a diminutive of *Conn*, 'leader'.

Cupid The Roman god of love, familiar as the figure of a winged boy with bow and arrows, takes his name from Latin *cupido*, 'desire', to which modern English *cupidity* is related.

Curaçao The Caribbean island was discovered by the Spanish in 1499 and originally named *Isla de los Gigantes*, 'island of giants', for the tall Indian inhabitants. The story then goes that a group of Spanish sailors suffering from malaria were later abandoned on the island, but were subsequently discovered completely cured. The island was thus renamed *Curación*, 'cure', which under Portuguese influence became *Curaçao*. But the truth is probably much more prosaic, and the name is doubtless a distortion of some Indian name.

Cure, The The British pop group originally called themselves *The Easy Cure*, a stock phrase, when they formed in 1976, but subsequently shortened this to *The Cure*.

Curragh, The The plain near Kildare that has become world famous as the home of Irish horse racing takes its name from Irish *An Currach*, meaning simply 'the racecourse'.

Currys The electrical and electronic goods stores take their name from their founder, Henry *Curry* (1850–1916), a Leicester man who began his career making and selling bicycles, mangles and fireguards in the 1880s.

Curtis The name arose as a nickname with two possible senses. One would have been given to an ultra-refined person, from Old French *curteis*, 'accomplished', as if living at *court*. The other would have applied to a short person, or one who wore short stockings, otherwise a 'curt hose'.

Curtis Cup The women's golf contest, held biennially between Britain and the United States in each country alternately, takes its name from the American golfers who donated the cup, Harriet and Margaret *Curtis*, winners of the US women's amateur championships in the early 1900s. The trophy was first awarded in 1932.

Curzon The name could either be a diminutive of COURT or else have denoted a person from the place now called Notre-Dame-de-*Courson* near Caen in northern France. Its own name derives from a personal name *Curtius*, 'short'.

Cush In the Old Testament, the name is that of the son of Ham and brother of Canaan and also that of the country of his supposed descendants, in what is now Sudan and Ethiopia. It is said to derive from an Ethiopian word meaning 'dark-faced', 'swarthy'.

Cussons The well-known make of soap is named for Alexander Tom *Cusson* (1875–1951) who set up as a chemist in Swinton, near Manchester in 1895. The famous 'Imperial Leather' brand was first manufactured in 1937, and was named for a leather-scented perfume said to have been devised in the 18th century for the Russian imperial family.

Cuthbert The name comprises the two Old English words *cūth*, 'known' and *beorht*, 'bright', that is, 'famous'. The two halves of the name thus express basically the same concept.

Cutler The name is occupational, denoting a person who made knives, from a word that gave modern French *couteau*, 'knife' and English *cutlery*.

Cutty Sark The historic merchant clipper of 1869, now at Greenwich, London, takes her name from the witch (the 'winsome wench') in Burns's poem *Tam o' Shanter* (1791), who wore only a *cutty sark*, 'short shift', otherwise a shirt or smock that, in the words of the poem, was 'in longitude tho' sorely scanty'. The name is also that of a brand of whisky, derived from the ship name.

Cyclades The group of islands in the southern Aegean forms a ring round Delos.

Hence their name, from Greek *kuklos*, 'circle'.

Cyclops The *Cyclopes*, encountered by Odysseus, were a race of giants with only a single eye in the middle of their forehead. Their name derives from Greek *kuklōps*, 'round eye', from *kuklos*, 'circle' and *ōps*, 'eye'. Odysseus and his companions were trapped in a cave by the Cyclops Polyphemus.

Cygnus The constellation in the northern hemisphere has a name translating as 'The Swan'. In ancient times the configuration of its stars was seen as representing a swan flying down the Milky Way, in which it is located. It is not clear whether it was regarded as a particular swan of classical mythology, although it could be the one that Zeus turned into when he visited Leda, wife of King Tyndareus of Sparta. The result of their union was the heavenly twin Pollux.

Cymbeline Shakespeare's play (1610) has as its central character, at least nominally, the 1st-century AD British king who was the father of CARACTACUS. His name is more accurately rendered as *Cunobelinus*, itself based on a Celtic root word meaning 'chief'.

Cynewulf The 9th-century Northumbrian poet has an Anglo-Saxon name that means 'royal wolf', from Old English *cyning*, 'king' and *wulf*, 'wolf'.

Cynopolis The ancient city of Egypt has a Greek name meaning 'dog city', from *kuōn*, genitive *kunos*, 'dog' and *polis*, 'city'. The city was the site of the main temple of the 'dog god' Anubis, a human figure with the head of a dog or jackal.

Cynoscephalae The two hills near Larissa, northeast Greece, are so named because of their resemblance to dogs' heads, from Greek *kuōn*, genitive *kunos*, 'dog' and *kephalē*, 'head'.

Cynthia In Greek mythology, *Cynthia* was a byname of Artemis, who was said to have been born on Mount *Kynthos*, on the island of Delos. The mountain name itself is of pre-Greek and uncertain origin.

Cyprus The Mediterranean island has the Greek name *Kupros*, probably representing Sumerian *kabar* or *gabar*, 'copper', 'bronze'. Copper mines were famous here in historic times, and the English word for the metal derives ultimately from the island name. The *cypress* tree is also named after the island.

Cyrene The ancient Greek city of northern Africa, near the coast of Cyrenaica, is said to derive its name from the nymph *Cyrene* of Greek mythology. Her own name relates to *kurios*, 'lord'.

Cyril The name is of Greek origin, ultimately from *kurios*, 'lord'.

Cyrillic The Slavonic alphabet now used for Russian, Bulgarian and the Serbian dialect of Serbo-Croat takes its name from the alphabet based on Greek that was devised in the 9th century by St CYRIL and his brother St Methodius for the translation of the Bible and church texts.

Cyrus The name is that of several kings of Persia, and is famous from one of them, *Cyrus* the Great, who lived in the 6th century BC. The ultimate source of the name is unknown, but it came to be associated with Greek *kurios*, 'lord', as for CYRIL.

Czechoslovakia The name of the eastern European country, a single state from 1918 to 1992, combines those of its two main peoples, the *Czechs* and the *Slovaks*. The Czechs may take their name from an ancestral chieftain, although some derive it from Czech *četa*, 'army'. The Slovaks have a name of the same origin as that of the SLAV race to which they belong. *See also* YUGOSLAVIA.

Częstochowa The city in southern Poland has a name that appears to represent Polish *częstikoł*, 'palisade', with reference to the enclosure that at one time protected the city from invasion.

D

Dacca *See* DHAKA.

Dachau The town in southern Germany, notorious as the site of a former Nazi concentration camp, derives its name from Old High German *daha*, 'clay'.

Dacia The ancient region that corresponds roughly to modern Romania takes its name from Phrygian Greek *daos*, 'wolf', referring not to the wild beast but to the predatory native population.

Dacron The American name for TERYLENE is almost certainly of arbitrary origin. Even so, the initial *D* happens to suggest the name of *D*u Pont, its manufacturers, and also that of the state of *D*elaware, where Du Pont has its headquarters. The final *-on* was doubtless selected to blend with 'nyl*on*'.

Dada The name of the nihilistic art movement of the early 20th century derives from French *dada*, a child's word for 'hobbyhorse'. According to one account the name was selected by the process of inserting a paper knife into a French-German dictionary, and was seized on by the group as being suitably nonsensical and 'anti-aesthetic'.

Daedalus In Greek mythology, the name is that of the inventor who built the labyrinth for Minos and made wings for himself and his son Icarus to flee their imprisonment. It is traditionally derived from Greek *daidalos*, 'cunningly wrought', which seems appropriate enough.

Dagenham The name of the London district means '*Dæcca*'s homestead', with the personal name followed by Old English *hām*, 'village'.

Dagestan The Russian republic, in the eastern Caucasus, has a name meaning 'mountain country', from Turkish *daǧ*, 'mountain' and Old Persian *stān*, 'country' (as for AFGHANISTAN).

Dagon The West Semitic god, subsequently also god of the Philistines, represented as half man, half fish, is mentioned more than once in the Old Testament (*e.g. Judges* 16.23–24, 1 *Samuel* 5.2–7). He has a Hebrew and Ugaritic name explained by some authorities as meaning 'grain', referring to the fact that he was the god of crop fertility and legendary inventor of the plough. Another derivation, however, takes the name from the diminutive of *dāg*, 'fish', so that he is the 'little fish'. *Cp.* the river TAGUS.

Dahomey The former name of BENIN represents the historic kingdom of *Dan Homé*, usually interpreted as meaning 'on the stomach of Dan'. This is taken as referring to the palace of King Aho, said to have been built on the site where his rival Dan was buried. One school of thought, however, sees the name as a corruption of *Agbomi*, 'inside the fort', from *agbo*, literally 'buffalo', so 'strength', 'rampart' and *mi*, 'inside'.

Dáil Éireann The name of the lower chamber of the Irish parliament, often shortened to 'the *Dáil*', derives from the words for 'assembly of Ireland', from *dáil*, 'assembly' and *Éireann*, the genitive of *Éire*, 'Ireland'.

Daimler The car takes its name from the German engineer Gottlieb *Daimler* (1834–1900), who founded the Daimler Motor Company in 1890. The first British Daimlers were those built in Coventry in 1897.

Daiquiri The brand of rum is said to take its name from a beach in southeast Cuba where American troops landed in 1898 in the Spanish-American War and where they were regaled by grateful patriots with local rum.

Dairen The name is that of the port of northeast China now usually known as *Talien*, and forming part of the conurbation of LÜDA. It represents the Japanese pronunciation of Chinese *dàlián*, from *dà*, 'big' and *lián*, 'to connect'.

Daisy The name derives from the familiar flower, itself so called because it is the 'day's eye', that is, it discloses its yellow centre, resembling the sun, in the morning, and covers it again with its white petals in the evening. The name seems to have evolved as a form of MARGARET, by punning reference to French *marguerite*, 'daisy'. *See also* MAISIE.

Dakar The capital of Senegal has a name of Wolof origin, from *n'dakar*, 'tamarind tree'. When early European explorers asked local people for the name of the place that is now known as Dakar, the Africans thought they were being asked about a prominent tamarind tree on the coast here and gave its native name.

Dakota The former American territory, now divided into the states of North and South Dakota, takes its name from an Indian word *dakota* or *lakota*, meaning 'friends'. This was the name of a tribe here that had formed an alliance with the Sioux.

DAKS The make of menswear by *DAKS*-Simpson is said to be a blend of *dad* and *slacks*, and to have been originally designed for the trousers made by the firm in the 1930s.

Dalai Lama The title of the chief lama and ruler of Tibet was first held by Bsod-nams-rgya-mtsho (1543–1588), who was given it by the Mongol chief Altan Khan. The first word of the title is the English form of Mongolian *tal-le*, 'ocean', corresponding to the two final elements *rgya-mtsho* of his Tibetan name, which are themselves borne by all rulers of Tibet. The title in either language implies breadth and depth of wisdom. *Lama* itself is the western form of Tibetan *blam-ma*, 'superior one', a further title that was originally used to translate Sanskrit *guru*, 'venerable'.

Dale A person of this name would originally have lived in a *dale* or valley.

Dalecarnia The region in west central Sweden has the Swedish name of *Dalarna*. This means 'the valleys', from Swedish *dalar*, the plural of *dal*, 'valley' (English *dale*), and *-na*, the definite article ('the').

Dalek The robot-like creatures of the popular children's television series *Dr Who*, first broadcast in the 1960s, probably have an arbitrary name, although an article in *Radio Times* (30 December 1971) claimed that their creator, Terry Nation, had devised the name from the title of an encyclopedia volume containing entries *DAL-LEK*. In 1973, however, Nation denied that this was the source.

Dalgleish The Scottish name derives from a place so called near Selkirk, itself meaning 'green field', from Gaelic *dail*, 'field' and *glas*, 'green'.

Dallas The well-known Texas city, first settled in 1841 and laid out in 1846, is named for George M. *Dallas* (1792–1864), Vice President of the United States from 1845 to 1849.

Dalmatia The coastal region of Croatia (formerly Yugoslavia) derives its name from the Indoeuropean root word *dhal*, meaning 'young animal', perhaps with reference to its mountain pastures. The church vestment known as a *dalmatic* is named for Dalmatia, since it was originally woven from wool from there.

Dalmatian The distinctively spotted breed of dog is named for its first known home, DALMATIA. The exact period and place of its breeding there are not known.

Dalrymple The Scottish name derives from the village so called near Ayr. The place-name itself is said to derive from Gaelic *dail chruim puill*, 'field of the crooked stream'.

Dalton A person so named would have originally come from one of the places so called, such as the villages named *Dalton* in Yorkshire. The name itself means 'valley settlement', from Old English *dæl*, 'dale' and *tūn*, 'settlement'.

Dalziel The Scottish name comes from the place so called between Motherwell and

137

Wishaw, in the Clyde valley. The name itself probably derives from Gaelic *dail*, 'field' and *geal*, 'white'. The *z* in the name was not originally a modern *z* at all, but a medieval letter rather like it that had the sound of *y*. This gave the regular pronunciation of the name as 'Dee-yell' or 'Da-yell'.

Damaraland The region of central Namibia derives its name from the *Damara*, the people who live here. Their own name is of uncertain origin. It may represent a native word meaning either 'child' or 'rich'. It seems unlikely to come from *damar*, the coniferous tree of southeast Asia that yields a dark resin (the word itself being Malay for 'resin'), although some authorities claim that Dutch colonists could have so named the African people from their dark-coloured skin. It is even less likely to derive, as some claim, from the biblical character *Damaris* (*Acts* 17.34), a female Christian convert, with the name supposedly applied to the Africans when they were similarly converted. The Damara people's own name for themselves is *Herero*, said to mean 'to be merry'.

Damart The make of thermal clothing was first produced in Lyon, France, after the Second World War in the Rue *Damart*ine, and takes its name from this street.

Damascus The Syrian capital has a name of unknown origin, with the western spelling representing Arabic *dimasq̂*. The colloquial Arabic name of the city is *aŝ-ŝam*, which can also be used for SYRIA itself and which may have been responsible for the link sometimes made between the country's name and that of ASSYRIA. The type of linen known as *damask* was originally made in Damascus.

Dam Busters The nickname was given to the special RAF squadron that in May 1943 carried out bombing raids on the Sorpe, Ede and Moehne dams in Germany to flood the Ruhr valley and so disrupt German industry. Their exploits were re-created and popularized in the film *The Dam Busters* (1954).

Dame Allan's School The public school for boys, in Newcastle upon Tyne, was founded in 1705 by Dame Eleanor *Allan*, who in her lifetime executed a deed of gift

bequeathing a farm at Wallsend to trustees for a school to be set up. The school has been on its present site since 1935.

Damned, The The British punk rock group, formed in 1976, chose a name that was suggested by the Dracula-style fancy dress worn by the band's lead singer, Dave Vanian.

Damocles In classical legend the name is that of the courtier forced by Dionysius, tyrant of Syracuse, to sit under a sword suspended by a single hair in order to demonstrate that being a king was not the happy condition Damocles claimed it was. His name has been traditionally interpreted as 'glory of *Damon*', from Greek *Damōn*, the name of the loyal friend of Pythias in Greek legend, and *kleos*, 'glory'.

Dan In the Old Testament, the name is that of the fourth son of Jacob and the tribe descended from him. It derives from the Hebrew root *din*, 'to judge'. *Cp.* DANIEL.

Danaë The mother of Perseus by Zeus has a name that has been traditionally derived from the same Hebrew source that gave the biblical name of DINAH, so has the same meaning.

Dandie Dinmont The breed of terrier is named after Andrew ('*Dandie*') *Dinmont*, a character in Walter Scott's novel *Guy Mannering* (1815) who owned three pairs of dogs of this type, each dog in each pair respectively named Mustard and Pepper.

Dando The name is Norman in origin, and was first used for a person who was *de Aunou*, or 'from Aunou'. Aunou, near Alençon in northwest France, has a name that itself means 'alder grove'. One person or family of this name is commemorated in that of the West Country village of Compton *Dando*, near Bath.

Danelaw The name of the historic area of northern and eastern England that was settled by the Vikings in the 9th century is self-descriptive, defining it as a region where the *law* and customs of the *Danes* prevailed.

Danes The native inhabitants of DENMARK have a name that has been derived from Old High German *tanar*, 'sandbank', but that has also been linked by some with German *Tanne*, 'fir'. They are thus either the 'sandbank dwellers' or the 'forest people'. The former seems more likely, in view of the topography of Denmark, with its many miles of coast and islands.

Dangerfield The name is of Norman origin and denotes someone who was *de Angerville*, or 'from Angerville'. There are several places of this name in Normandy, with the name itself deriving from a Scandinavian personal name to mean '*Ásgeirr*'s settlement'.

Daniel The name is biblical in origin, from Hebrew *Dāni'el*, 'God is my judge'. It is familiar as that of the prophet whose story is told in the Old Testament book named for him. When Daniel is deported to the court of king Nebuchadnezzar, together with Hananiah, Azariah and Mishael, he is given the name *Belteshazzar* (*Daniel* 1.7), from Akkadian *Beli.-shar-uzur*, 'protect the life of the king'. (*Cp.* BELSHAZZAR, Nebuchadnezzar's son, for whom Daniel interprets 'the writing on the wall' in the same book.) Shakespeare puns on Daniel's name in *The Merchant of Venice* when Shylock exclaims to Portia, in her disguise as a judge named Balthazar (*i.e.* Belshazzar), 'A Daniel come to judgment!' The reference is to the apocryphal *History of Susannah*, in which Daniel passes judgment on the two elders who had accused Susannah of adultery when they were unable to seduce her.

Danube The well-known river of central Europe has a name that may derive from Sarmatian *dānu-avi*, 'river of sheep', with the first element of this seen also in the name of the river DON.

Danzig *See* GDAŃSK.

Daphne The name represents Greek *daphnē*, 'laurel', and in Greek mythology was that of a nymph changed into a laurel by her father to enable her to escape the unwelcome attentions of Apollo.

Daphnis In classical legend, the name is that of the Sicilian shepherd who was regarded as the inventor of pastoral poetry. As for DAPHNE, his name is usually derived from the Greek word for 'laurel', either because he was born in a laurel grove or because his mother abandoned him in one when he was a baby. In later literature, his name is romantically linked with that of Chloë ('green').

Dardanelles The strait between the Aegean Sea and the Sea of Marmara has a name that either gave or derives from that of *Dardanus*, the ancestor of the kings of Troy in classical mythology. The ancient city of Troy lies just south of the Dardanelles. In classical times the strait was known as the HELLESPONT.

Dar es Salaam The former capital of Tanzania has a name of Arabic origin, from *dār as-salām*, 'house of peace', from *dār*, 'house', *al* (here *as* before *s*), 'the', and *salām*, 'peace' (*cp.* SALEM). This may have originally applied to the palace of the Sultan of Zanzibar, Seyyid Majid, who founded the town in 1866, or have more generally related to the town as a place where merchants could buy and sell freely. The name is sometimes interpreted as 'haven of peace', as if from Hindi *bandar*, 'harbour', 'port', although no early records contain this word and it is unlikely that *Bandar*, stressed on the first syllable, would have reduced to *Dar*.

Darius The name is familiar as that of various kings of Persia, in particular *Darius* the Great, who extended the Persian empire but who was defeated at the Battle of Marathon in 490 BC. His name derives from Old Persian *Dārayavahush*, literally 'he who is rich'.

Darjeeling The name of the town of northeast India derives from Tibetan *dojeling*, 'diamond island', from *doje*, 'diamond' and *ling*, 'island'. The reference is to the form of Buddhism known as Vajrayāna (literally 'vehicle of the diamond'), otherwise Tantric Buddhism.

Dark Ages The name is used of the premedieval historical period that extends from about the 5th to the 10th century, or sometimes even for that of the MIDDLE AGES itself, which was formerly regarded as being 'unenlightened'.

Darling The Australian river was named in 1829 by the explorer Charles Sturt for Sir Ralph *Darling* (1775–1858), governor of New South Wales from 1825 to 1831.

Darling The surname means what it says, and denotes a person who was originally regarded as 'beloved', or more literally a 'little dear'.

Darlington The Durham town has a name meaning 'settlement of *Dēornōth*'s people', with the *n* of the personal name becoming *l* under Norman influence. It is not known who *Dēornōth* was but his name means 'animal plunder'.

Darmstadt The city in central Germany was originally known as *Darmundenstadt*, from a personal name that was a shortened form of *Darmundolf*. The similarity of the second element of the name to German *Mund*, 'mouth' subsequently suggested a 'town at the mouth of the *Darm*', but the name of the river Darm on which the city now stands was not recorded before 1759.

Darren The name is a recent one, and may have been adapted from a surname such as *Darrell*. One of the earliest bearers of the name was the American film actor *Darren McGavin* (1922–), but it was popularized by a character in the 1960s television comedy *Bewitched*.

Dartford The Kent town is on the river *Darent*, and its name refers to a *ford* formerly over it here.

Dartmoor The upland region of Devon takes its name from the river *Dart* which rises here and which enters the sea just below DARTMOUTH.

Dartmouth As its name implies, the Devon port and resort is located near the *mouth* of the river *Dart*, which rises on DARTMOOR. The river's own name means 'oak stream', from the Celtic word that also gave the name of the DERWENT.

Dartmouth College The American higher education establishment was founded in Hanover, New Jersey in 1769 and took its name from William Legge, second Earl of *Dartmouth* (1731–1801), president of the trustees of the college's English funds.

Darwin The harbour (Port *Darwin*) of this port of northern Australia was discovered in 1839 and was named for the famous naturalist Charles *Darwin* (1809–1882), who had visited the coast here three years earlier. The town was founded in 1869 and was at first named *Palmerston*, in honour of the British prime minister Viscount Palmerston (1784–1865). In 1911, how-ever, control of the Northern Territory was transferred from South Australia to that of the Commonwealth of Australia, and a reversion was made to the original name.

Darwin College The Cambridge college was founded in 1964 as the university's first graduate college, and was built as an extension of Newnham Grange, the family home of Sir George *Darwin* (1845–1912), son of the famous scientist Charles *Darwin* (1809–1882).

Dasht-i-Kavir The salt desert in central Iran has a name that represents Iranian *daŝte kavīr*, 'salt desert', from *daŝt*, 'rocky plain' and *kavīr*, 'salt marsh'. Cp. DASHT-I-LUT.

Dasht-i-Lut The desert plateau in east central Iran takes its name from Iranian *daŝte lūt*, 'barren plain', from *daŝt*, 'rocky plain' and *lūt* 'barren desert'. Cp. DASHT-I-KAVIR.

Datsun The make of Japanese car was first produced in 1913 and took its name from the initials of the three financial backers of the manufacturing company, Kenjiro *D*en, Rokuro *A*oyama, and Meitaro *T*akeuchi. The original name of the car was thus *DAT*. This then became *Datson*, intended to mean 'son of DAT'. However, *son* was too close to the Japanese word for 'loss' (*cp.* SONY), so the spelling was modified to *Datsun*. In 1931, before this final name change, the firm was taken over by the company that three years later itself became NISSAN, and in the early 1980s a policy decision was taken to standardize all *Datsun* cars under this name.

Daugavpils The Latvian city has a name that means 'palace of the western Dvina', from *Daugava*, 'western DVINA' and *pils*, 'palace'. The town was founded in 1278 with the German name of *Dünaburg*, 'fort on the Dvina'.

Dauntsey's School The Wiltshire public school, near Devizes, takes its name from its founder in 1542, the London alderman William *Dauntsey* of the Mercers Company. It opened on its present site in 1895 as an agricultural college.

Dauphiné The former province of southeast France has a name that derives from what was originally the personal name *Dauphin*, 'dolphin'. This was adopted by Guigues IV, comte d'Albon, in the 12th century, to distinguish his descendants, with the dolphin becoming the family's heraldic symbol. Land in this part of France belonged to the family, and was named after them in the 13th century. In 1349 *Dauphiné* was sold to the future Charles V of France, and he established the practice whereby the kings of France ceded the territory to their heir apparent. Hence the adoption of *Dauphin* as the title of the heir apparent to the French crown from 1350 to 1830.

David The biblical name, familiar from King *David*, is of Hebrew origin, from *Dāwīd*, 'dear one', 'beloved'.

David & Charles The West Country publishers, famous for their books on railways, take their name from their founders in 1960, *David* St John Thomas (1929–) and *Charles* Hadfield (1909–). The firm's first premises were in rooms at the railway station in Newton Abbot, Devon, and the company remains based in that town today.

Davies Both this name and its alternative spelling of *Davis* mean 'son of DAVID'. *Davies* is typically the Welsh form of the name, and *Davis* the English. The Scottish equivalent is *Davidson*.

Davis Cup The annual international men's tennis championship is named for its trophy, which was donated in 1900 by the American tennis player and subsequent civic leader, Dwight F. *Davis* (1879–1945). The formal name of the award is the *International Lawn Tennis Challenge Trophy*.

Davis Strait The strait between Baffin Island, Canada and Greenland takes its name from the English navigator John *Davis* (1550–1605), who discovered it in 1585 when searching for a Northwest Passage (from the Atlantic to the Pacific).

Davos The name of the Swiss mountain resort derives from Romansch *davo*, 'behind'. The reference is to the valley in which Davos lies. This turns to the north behind the town and so shelters it from the wind.

Dawson The former capital of the Yukon, Canada, was founded in the Klondike gold rush of 1896 and named for the Canadian explorer George M. *Dawson* (1849–1901).

Dax The town and spa of southwest France has a name that is really *d'Ax*, with the latter word representing Latin *aqua*, 'water'. (*Cp.* AIX-LES-BAINS.) The reference is to the hot saline springs here.

Day-Glo The brand of fluorescent paint and colouring materials originated in Cleveland, Ohio, in the 1950s. It was so named because the colours are four or five times brighter than conventional colours, so have the unusual quality of appearing to *glow* in *day*light.

Dayton The Ohio city was founded in 1796 and takes its name from one of its founders, the Revolutionary army captain and member of the House of Representatives Jonathan *Dayton* (1760–1824).

Daytona Beach The city and Atlantic resort in northeast Florida takes its name from Mathias *Day*, who founded it in 1870. His surname was suffixed with the common *-ton* meaning 'town' and the *-a* that ends many American town names.

D-Day The name is that of the day, 6 June 1944, when the Allied invasion of Europe began. The initial *D* simply stands for *day*, and the phrase was already in military use as a code name for the start of any operation. A field order of the Allied Expeditionary Force dated 7 September 1918 began: 'The First Army will attack at H-Hour on D-Day with the object of forcing the evacuation of St. Mihiel salient.' The exact hour and day would have been known to those concerned.

Dead Heart, the The name for the remote interior of Australia, although obviously self-descriptive, is said to have been adopted from the title of the book *The Dead Heart of Australia* by the British geologist John Walter Gregory, published in 1906. The term was apparently in use before this, however, and according to some sources was introduced by the geologist John Simpson in 1901.

Dead Kennedys The American punk band, formed in San Francisco in 1978, chose a name that was designed to shock and outrage, like that of the SEX PISTOLS in Britain. It referred to the assassination of President John F. Kennedy in 1963 and that of his brother, Senator Robert F. Kennedy, in 1968.

Dead March in Saul, The The name is popularly used for the funeral march from Handel's oratorio *Saul* (1739), traditionally played at state funerals, especially military ones. The oratorio itself has as its subject the biblical Saul who was first king of the Hebrews and who fell in battle against the Philistines (1 *Samuel* 31). Dickens mentions the title in one of his novels: 'That's the Dead March in Saul. They bury soldiers to it' (*Bleak House*, 1852).

Dead Sea The lake (rather than sea) between Israel and Jordan is so named because it contains no living organisms as a result of its very high salinity. The name was first recorded in Greek as *nekrē thalassa*, then in Latin as *Mare Mortuum*. In the Bible, the Dead Sea is referred to as 'the salt sea' (*Genesis* 14.3 and elsewhere), as a translation of Hebrew *yam hammélah*. Its Arabic name is either *al-bahr al-mayyit*, 'the dead sea' or *bahr lūt*, 'sea of Lot', the latter alluding to Lot's wife, who was changed into a pillar of salt here (*Genesis* 19.26).

Dead Sea Scrolls The name is used for the ancient manuscripts in Hebrew and Aramaic found in caves at the northern end of the DEAD SEA between 1947 and 1956. According to radiocarbon tests made in 1991, most of the Scrolls date to the last two centuries BC, so that they are the earliest extant manuscripts of the Old Testament and Apocrypha.

Deal The Kent resort has a name that represents Old English *dæl*, 'valley', modern English *dale*. This seems an unlikely description of modern Deal, where the land is flat. There has doubtless been a change in the topography, however, which has flattened a former hollow here.

Dean A person of this name either originally lived in a valley (Old English *denu*, modern English *dean*), or was regarded as resembling a dean in some way, or was actually the servant of a dean, that is, of the official who was the head of a chapter of canons in a cathedral.

Dean, Forest of *See* FOREST OF DEAN.

Dean Close School The Cheltenham public school was founded in 1886 and was named commemoratively for Dr Francis *Close* (1797–1882), Rector of Cheltenham from 1826 to 1856, and subsequently *Dean* of Carlisle.

Dearborn The Michigan city, settled in 1795, was named in 1833 for the American Revolutionary hero Henry *Dearborn* (1751–1829).

Death A person of this name was probably so nicknamed in medieval times because he played the figure of Death in a play or pageant, or because he was sad or sickly. Some modern bearers of the name respell it as *De'Ath* in an attempt to avoid the unpleasant associations. This could even be a genuine name for someone who was *de Ath*, or 'from Ath', as there is a place of this name in Belgium.

Death Valley The desert valley in eastern California and western Nevada is the lowest, hottest and driest region of America. Its name relates to the extreme conditions experienced by a party of immigrants when crossing it in 1849, with some fatalities.

Deauville The town and resort of northwest France has a name that means 'town of the damp plain', from French *d'*, 'of', Germanic *auwa*, 'damp plain' (itself based on *aha*, 'water'), and Latin *villa*, 'settlement', 'town'.

Debenhams The well-known chain store developed from the draper's shop in London which originally opened in 1778 but which in 1813 was run as a partnership by Thomas Clark and William *Debenham*. The shop duly developed into *Debenham* and Freebody, one of London's most prestigious stores, closing only in 1981.

Deborah The name is biblical in origin, borne by Rebecca's nurse and by a woman prophet who led the Israelites to victory over the Canaanites. Her name is Hebrew, from *Debōrāh*, 'bee'. The connotation is as much of sweetness (for the bee's honey) as of diligence. *Cp.* her Greek equivalent, MELISSA.

Debrecen The city in eastern Hungary has a name that may represent the Slavic root word *debr* (related to English *deep*) meaning 'ravine', 'escarpment'. The name is pronounced approximately 'Debretsen'.

Debrett The name is the short title of *Debrett's Peerage, Baronetage, Knightage and Companionage*, listing the British aristocracy, and first published in 1802 by John *Debrett* (1750–1822).

Decadents The name for the French Symbolist poets of the late 19th century was first applied to the group in the collection of parodies by Gabriel Vicaire and Henri Beauclair entitled *Les Déliquescences d'Adoré Floupette* (1885). The epithet was taken up by *Le Figaro* in its issue of 22 September 1885 ('Le décadent n'a pas d'idées. Il n'en veut pas. Il aime mieux les mots.') and was readily accepted by the early Symbolist poet Paul Verlaine, who subsequently contributed to the magazine *Le Décadent* (1886–9).

Decalogue The name is an academic one for the *Ten Commandments*, from Greek *deka*, 'ten' and *logos*, 'word'.

Decameron The title of 100 witty tales by the Italian writer Boccaccio, published between 1348 and 1353, refers to the ten days (Greek *deka*, 'ten' and *hēmera*, 'day') taken by its ten storytellers, seven women and three men, as they flee from the plague in Florence. *Cp.* HEPTAMERON.

Decapolis The name is Greek for 'ten towns', and applies to a region of ancient Palestine where a league of cities of this number existed in the 1st century BC. The most important town of the ten was DAMASCUS.

Decatur The city in Illinois, founded in 1829, is named for the American naval hero Stephen *Decatur* (1779–1820), killed in a duel.

DECCA The source of the name of the British record company remains uncertain, and it may have been arbitrary. It was originally that of a portable gramophone manufactured in 1913. It has popularly been seen as representing the musical notes D-E-C-C-A.

Deccan The name of the southern peninsula of India derives from the Hindi word *dakkin*, simply meaning 'south', itself from Sanskrit *dakṣiṇa*, 'right' (as opposed to left). When facing the rising sun the south is at one's right hand. *Cp.* YEMEN, involving a similar notion.

December The name of the 12th and last month of the year derives from Latin *decem*, 'ten', since in the early Roman

calendar, in which the year began in March, it was the tenth month.

Decembrist The name is used in Russian history for the revolutionaries who led an unsuccessful uprising against Tsar Nicholas I in *December* 1825. They did so in Senate Square, St Petersburg, renamed *Decembrist* Square in 1925 after them. The name translates Russian *dekabrist*.

Decorated The 14th-century style of architecture is so named for the *decoration* found characteristically in church windows, typically in geometrical patterns or (later) wavy lines.

Dee The well-known river name is of Celtic origin and represents *deva*, 'goddess'. Rivers were often personified or deified in Celtic times in this manner.

Deep Purple The British heavy metal rock group, formed in 1968, modelled themselves on the American group *Vanilla Fudge*, and chose a name to contrast with this.

Defender of the Faith The title, in Latin *Fidei Defensor*, is that conferred on Henry VIII by Pope Leo X in 1521 in recognition of the king's attack on Luther's doctrines. It has been retained by subsequent British sovereigns, and appears in abbreviated form as *F.D.* on British coins.

Defenestration of Prague The name refers to the incident of 1618 in Prague when Protestants of the Bohemian National Council threw two Roman Catholic members out of the window of the Hradčany Castle. A similar ejection had occurred in 1419, when city councillors had been pushed from the window of the New Town Hall in a popular uprising. The word itself derives from Latin *de fenestra*, 'out of the window'.

Def Leppard The British heavy rock group, formed in 1977, adopted a name that was a deliberate spelling alteration of the whimsical name *Deaf Leopard* proposed by the band's lead singer, Joe Elliott. It is possible the revised spelling may have been at least subconsciously suggested by that of LED ZEPPELIN.

Deir al-Bahri The ancient Egyptian temple site, on the west bank of the Nile near Thebes, has a name representing Arabic *dayr al-baḥrī*, 'monastery of the river', from *dayr*, 'monastery' and *baḥrī*, the adjectival form of *baḥr*, 'sea', 'river' (*cp.* BAHRAIN). The temple was occupied by monks early in the Christian era.

Deirdre The Irish name was made famous by a tragic heroine of Celtic legend, often referred to as *'Deirdre* of the Sorrows'. The name itself is of uncertain origin, but has been related to Celtic *derdriu*, 'angry' or Gaelic *deoirid*, 'broken-hearted', 'sorrow-struck'.

Delaware The American river, bay and state all take their name from Thomas West, Lord *de la Warr* (1577–1618), the English soldier and colonist who was appointed governor of Virginia in 1610.

Delft The town in the southwest Netherlands takes its name from Old Dutch *delf*, 'ditch', 'canal' (to which English *delve* is related). Delft is on the Schie Canal.

Delhi The name of the Indian city is of unknown origin, although Hindi *dehlī*, 'threshold' has been suggested. This would refer to the location of Delhi on a 'threshold' between the Indus and the Ganges. The city is now divided into *Old Delhi*, a walled city reconstructed in 1639 on the original site, and *New Delhi*, to the south, chosen in 1911 as the capital to replace Calcutta.

Delia *See* CORDELIA.

Delilah The name is familiar in the Old Testament as that of Samson's mistress, who tricks him into revealing the secret of his strength (his hair) and then betrays him to the Philistines. It is traditionally derived from Hebrew *Delīlāh*, 'delight', with the similarity of the English and Hebrew words purely coincidental. Some scholars, however, relate it to Hebrew *lāila*, 'night', as opposed to the name of Samson, which means 'sun'. Others trace it back to Arabic *dalla*, 'to tease', 'to flirt'. As 'delight', *Delilah* could be a shortened theophoric name, *i.e.* one derived from a god, but with the god's own name not actually mentioned. An example of a full such name is *Dalil Ishtar*, 'delight of *Ishtar*' (the Babylonian and Assyrian goddess of love and war).

Delos The uninhabited Greek island, in the Cyclades, has a name deriving directly

from Greek *dēlos*, 'clear', 'visible', from its prominence.

Delphi The ancient Greek city has a name that represents Greek *delphis*, 'dolphin'. In Greek mythology, Apollo assumed the form of a dolphin (symbolic of water and transformation) when he founded his shrine or oracle here on the slopes of Mount Parnassus.

Demavend, Mount The volcanic peak in northern Iran has a Sanskrit name, from *himavant*, 'snowy mountain' (*cp.* HIMALAYAS).

Demelza The name is that of the heroine of the 'Poldark' novels by Winston Graham, set in 18th-century Cornwall. It was widely popularized by the television series *Poldark* of 1976–7 based on the books. It is not a Cornish personal name, however, but a place-name adopted by Graham for first name use, that of a location in the parish of St Wenn, near St Columb Major. The name itself is probably based on Cornish *dyn*, 'fort' together with an obscure personal name.

Demeter The name of the Greek goddess of fertility and protector of marriage and women probably derives from *dē*, a variant of *gē*, 'earth' and *mētēr*, 'mother', so that she is the 'earth mother'. Her name thus complements that of ZEUS (JUPITER), the 'sky father'.

Demetrius The Latin name derives from that of DEMETER, the goddess of fertility and protector of marriage. The Russian name *Dmitry* is of the same origin.

Democrat The name can apply to a member of any democratic (usually left-wing) political party, but is specially associated with the *Democratic* Party of the United States. The party had its origins in a group of 1792 who adopted the name *Democratic-Republican* to emphasize their anti-monarchic stance. It then used various titles until it finally settled as the *Democratic* Party in the 1830s. The basic name means 'people's power', from Greek *dēmos*, 'people' and *kratos*, 'power'.

Democritus The 4th-century BC Greek philosopher has a name that literally translates as 'people's choice', from Greek *dēmos*, 'people' and *kritos*, 'chosen', 'choice'.

Demosthenes The name of the 4th-century BC Athenian statesman and orator can be literally translated as 'people's strength', from Greek *dēmos*, 'people' and *sthenos*, 'strength', 'power'.

Demotic The name for the spoken form of modern Greek, as distinct from the literary form, derives from Greek *dēmotikos*, 'of the people', from *dēmos*, 'people'. *Cp.* KATHAREVUSA.

Dempster The name originally denoted a person who was a *deemster*, or judge, especially one in Scotland. Strictly speaking the *-ster* suffix denotes a female, as originally for BAXTER and WEBSTER (*see* WEBB), but the sex distinction had been lost even in medieval times.

Denbigh The name of the town and former county of North Wales means 'little fortress', from Welsh *din*, 'fortress' and *bych*, a variant form of *bach*, 'little'. The original fortress would have been where the ruins of the 12th-century castle now lie, on Castle Hill to the south of the town.

Dendera The ancient city of Upper Egypt, on the left bank of the Nile, has a name that has evolved through Coptic and Greek from *Iunit Tentōre*, itself a corruption of the original name *Iunit ta Netert*, 'Iunit of the goddess'. *Iunit* is based on Egyptian *iun*, 'column', while *ta Netert*, from *netert*, 'goddess', was added to distinguish this city from another of the same name, now usually known as *On* or HELIOPOLIS. The goddess in question was Hathor, the goddess of creation.

Deneb The name of the brightest star in the constellation Cygnus derives from Arabic *dhanab*, 'tail'. This stands for the full name *dhanab ad-dajāja*, 'tail of the hen', referring to the position of the star on the tail of the bird delineated in the constellation. (To the Arabs this was a hen, but in the western classical world a swan.)

Denis The name, also spelled *Dennis*, derives from the Greek name DIONYSUS, so has the same basic meaning.

Denman The name originally denoted a person who lived in a valley or *dean*. *Cp.* DEAN.

Denmark The country of northern Europe takes its name from its inhabitants, the DANES, whose border territory (Danish *mark*, English *march*) it is. *Cp.* MARCHES.

Dennis *See* DENIS.

Dent The London publishers had the full name of J.M. Dent & Sons Ltd until they were acquired by WEIDENFELD AND NICOLSON in 1987. This represents the founder, Joseph Malaby *Dent* (1849–1926), who set up his business as a publisher in London in 1888. *See also* EVERYMAN'S LIBRARY.

Denver The state capital of Colorado was founded in 1858 as a gold-mining centre named *Auraria*, 'golden'. The following year it was renamed in honour of General James W. *Denver* (1817–1892), governor of the territory at the time.

Depeche Mode The British pop group, formed in 1980, chose a name that is clearly French but of uncertain precise origin. It could mean 'by telegram' in telegraphese, but is more reliably said to have been seen in a fashion magazine, where it would have been a style name (properly *dépêche mode*) meaning 'despatch fashion'.

Derby The English city originally had the Old English name of *Northworthy*, 'northern enclosure'. When the Danes settled here in the 9th century, they renamed the settlement as 'deer village', from Old Norse *djúr*, 'deer' and *bý*, 'village'.

Derby The famous annual flat race at Epsom Downs, Surrey, is named after the twelfth Earl of DERBY (d. 1834) who founded it in 1780.

Derek The name represents an English form of the Germanic name *Theodoric*, which also gave TERRY. The meaning is thus the same as for that name.

Dermot The name is an English form of the Irish name *Di\'harmait*, said to mean 'free from envy', from Gaelic *di-*, 'not' (like English *dis-*) and *farmat*, 'envy'.

Derry The name is an alternative for the Northern Ireland city of LONDONDERRY, *which see* for the meaning.

Derwent There are several rivers of the name in England. The meaning is 'oak river', from the Celtic root word *deruenta* that also gave the names of the *Darent* at DARTFORD and the *Dart* on DARTMOOR and at DARTMOUTH. All these names testify to the many oak forests formerly in Britain. *See also* LONDONDERRY.

Descartes The small town south of Tours, west central France, was originally known as *La Haye-en-Touraine*. It is the birthplace of the famous philosopher René *Descartes* (1596–1650), and to commemorate him the town's name was changed to *La Haye-Descartes* in 1802. In 1967 this was officially shortened to *Descartes*. Descartes' family itself originated from a hamlet called *Les Cartes*. The philosopher's name was latinized as *Renatus Cartesius*, and the latter word gave the adjective *Cartesian* to apply to his philosophy or mathematical system.

Desdemona The tragic wife of Othello in Shakespeare's play has a name that probably derives from Greek *dusdaimōn*, 'ill-fated'.

Desert Orchid The famous racehorse, four-times champion of the King George VI Chase (1986, 1988, 1989, 1990) and winner of other major races, was foaled in 1979. His sire (father) was Grey Mirage and his dam (mother) Flower Child. Racehorses are frequently given names based on those of their parents. With the names of these particular parents in mind, the horse's owner originally thought of *Desert Air*, with special reference to Thomas Gray's poem, *Elegy Written in a Country Churchyard*, which has the lines:

Full many a flower is born to blush unseen,
And waste its sweetness on the desert air.

The name would thus come directly from this, with 'desert' evoking the sire's name and the first line having the 'flower' that was in the dam's name. However, this name was not acceptable to Weatherbys, publishers of registered names of horses for the Jockey Club, since a horse named *Desert Heir* already existed, and this could cause confusion, especially from the point of view of a commentator if both horses happened to be in the same race. Instead, the name *Desert Orchid* was proposed, keeping the first word of the name but with the second coming from *Grey Orchid*,

that of the horse's grandmother. Thus the popular *Dessie* got his name!

Desert Rats The nickname was that of the British 7th Armoured Division when serving in the North African campaign of 1941–2, and derived from their symbol, that of a jerboa. The name (and symbol) continued in use subsequently for the 7th Armoured Brigade, and was popularized when this force was again in action in the Middle East during the Gulf War of 1991.

Des Moines The state capital of Iowa is named from the *Rivière des Moines*, the French name of the river on which it arose. This is traditionally interpreted as 'river of monks', referring to French Trappist monks who settled here. It is more likely to be a name of Indian origin, however, recorded in a text of 1673 as *Moinguena*. The meaning of this is unknown.

Desmond The name is of Irish origin, and originally denoted someone who came from *Deas-Mhumhan*, the Irish name for 'south Munster'. Its spelling has been influenced by ESMOND, a quite different name.

De Stijl The group of Dutch abstract artists of the 1920s, led by Mondrian, took as their name the Dutch words for 'the style'. *De Stijl* (1917–32) was also the name of the periodical with which they were associated.

Detroit The Michigan city was founded by French colonists in 1701 as *Fort Pontchartrain du Détroit*. The last word of this, French for 'strait', referred to the narrow sound between Lake St Clair and Lake Erie on which the fort was built. The fort was in turn named for the Comte de *Pontchartrain*, the minister of state to Louis XIV who was the patron of the main founder, Antoine de la Mothe, sieur de Cadillac (1658–1730).

Dettol The well-known brand of antiseptic and disinfectant was first marketed in the 1930s, when the name '*Disinfectol*' was considered for it. This name was regarded as placing too much emphasis on the product's disinfectant properties, however, at the expense of its value as an antiseptic. The proposed name was therefore modified to *Dettol*, which was also felt to have a more medicinal flavour.

Deucalion In Greek mythology the name is that of the son of Prometheus, who with his wife Clymene was the only survivor on earth of a flood sent by Zeus. It is appropriately based on Greek *deuō*, 'I wet'.

Deuteronomy The Old Testament book has a name that literally means 'second law', from Greek *deuteros*, 'second' and *nomos*, 'law'. This derives from the phrase *to deuteronomion touto*, 'this second law', occuring in the Septuagint (the Greek version of the Old Testament) as a mistranslation of Hebrew *miśnēh hattōrāh hazzōth*, 'a copy or duplicate of this law', which in the Vulgate (the Latin version) is *Deuteronomium legis hujus* and in the Authorized Version is 'a copy of this law' (*Deuteronomy* 17.18). 'Copy' is a better definition of the book, as it is basically an address by Moses to the Israelites in which he repeats the law to them before they enter the Promised Land. The Greek name has thus remained untranslated in English. The Hebrew name of the book is *Devarim*, 'words', from its opening words: 'These be the words which Moses spake unto all Israel' (*Deuteronomy* 1.1).

Deutsch The London publishing house of Andre Deutsch take their name from their founder in 1951, André *Deutsch* (1917–   ).

Deux-Sèvres The department of western France has a name meaning 'two Sèvres', referring to the two rivers that both rise here, the SÈVRE Nantaise and the *Sèvre* Niortaise.

Devanagari The name of the syllabic script in which Sanskrit, Hindi and other modern Indian languages are written means 'alphabet of the gods', from Sanskrit *deva*, 'god' and *nagari*, 'alphabet' (literally 'of the city').

Devereux The name has a Norman origin, denoting a person *de Évreux*, or 'from Évreux'. Évreux is now a sizeable town west of Paris.

Devi The Hindu goddess who is the wife of Siva has a name that represents the Sanskrit word for 'goddess'.

Devil's Trill Sonata The violin sonata in G minor by Tartini (1714) is so named for the long trill in the last of its four movements. The story is that Tartini dreamed he had lent the Devil his violin, who played a beautiful solo piece on it. On waking up, the composer tried to play the same piece, but failed, so composed the sonata instead.

Devizes The name of the Wiltshire town derives from Old French *devises*, 'boundaries', itself from Latin *divisae*, 'divisions'. Devizes is at the boundary between two former hundreds, that of Potterne, held by the king, and that of Cannings, held by the bishops of Salisbury. The boundaries of the two passed through the former Devizes Castle.

Devo The American rock band, formed in 1972 in Akron, Ohio, took their name from the video *The Truth About De-Evolution*, an award winner at the 1975 Ann Arbor Film Festival. The group saw their own music as 'de-evolving' or 'falling apart'.

Devon The English county takes its name from the *Dumnonii*, the Celtic people who once lived here, their own name either meaning 'deep ones', in the sense 'valley dwellers', or deriving from that of their god, *Dumnonos*.

Dexedrine The stimulant drug is a preparation of *dex*amphetamine sulphate, and the name is based on the first part of this, with the rest modelled on BENZEDRINE.

Dexy's Midnight Runners The British rock group, formed in Birmingham in 1978, chose a name that was based on the slang term for the pep pill DEXEDRINE, although the band themselves claimed to observe a code of 'no drink or drugs'.

Dhaka The capital of Bangladesh derives its name from Hindi *ḍhākā*, from *ḍhāk*, 'dhak', a local tree (*Butea frondosa*) whose flowers yield a yellow dye known as butea gum or Bengal kino. The name formerly had the conventional English spelling *Dacca*.

Dhanvantari The physician of the gods in Hindu mythology has a name that derives from Sanskrit, meaning 'moving in an arc'. He was probably originally equated with the sun, which daily 'arcs' across the sky.

Dhaulagiri The mountain in west central Nepal has a Hindi name meaning 'white mountain', from Sanskrit *dhavala*, 'white' and *giri*, 'mountain'.

Dhritarashtra In Hindu mythology, the name is that of the eldest son of Vyasa, the legendary wise man and recluse. It is Sanskrit in origin and means '(he) whose kingdom is firm'.

Diabelli Variations The name is that of Beethoven's piano variations on a waltz by Diabelli, composed between 1819 and 1823. The Austrian music publisher Anton *Diabelli* (1781–1858) had commissioned 50 composers to write one variation each on his waltz theme, including Schubert and the young Liszt, who was then only 11 years old. Beethoven's contribution developed into 33 variations, however, and is one of his major piano works.

Diana The name is famous in Roman mythology as that of the goddess of the moon and of hunting. It is almost certainly of literally 'divine' origin, and contains the same root element as that in both DIONYSUS and JUPITER.

Diaspora The term used for the dispersion of the Jews after the Babylonian and Roman conquests of Palestine derives from the Greek word for 'scattering', from the verb *diaspeirein*, 'to disperse'.

Dick The name is a short form of RICHARD, corresponding to *Rick*. The substitution of *D* for *R* is said to derive from the efforts of the English to pronounce the trilled French *r* in Norman times.

Dickson The name means 'son of DICK', and therefore is an equivalent of RICHARDS or *Richardson*. The spelling variant *Dixon* is of the same origin.

Dido The name is that of the mythical princess of Tyre who founded Carthage and became its queen. It is said to be of Phoenician origin and to mean 'bold', 'resolute'. This could relate to her suicide by stabbing herself on her funeral pyre when she was abandoned by her lover Aeneas. The story is told by Virgil.

Dieppe The Channel port and resort in northern France has a name that basically equates to English *deep*, referring to the depth of the water at the mouth of the river Arques here.

Dijon The city of eastern France has a name deriving from Latin *Divio*, genitive *Divionis*, representing the personal name *Di-*

vius, itself meaning 'divine', 'godly'. *Cp.* DINAN.

Dikson The Russian Arctic port, on the estuary of the Yenisei, takes its name from that originally given in 1875 by the Swedish Arctic explorer Baron Nordenskiöld to a deep inlet on what is now known as *Dikson* Island, about a mile (1.5 km) off the coast here. Nordenskiöld gave the name in honour of the financier of his expedition, the Scottish-born Swede Oskar *Dikson*.

Dillons The bookshop chain takes its name from Miss Una *Dillon*, who in 1936 opened a small bookshop near London University to gain its custom. In 1956 it became the official university bookshop, and from the 1980s opened branches elsewhere in the country.

Dimbleby A person of this name would originally have come from *Dembleby*, a village near Sleaford in Lincolnshire. The village name itself perhaps means 'stream farm', from a Scandinavian word that gave the north of England dialect word *dimble* meaning 'dell', 'dingle'.

Dimitrovgrad The town in southern Bulgaria was given its name on its foundation in 1947 in honour of the Bulgarian Communist and prime minister Georgi *Dimitrov* (1882–1949).

Dinah The name is biblical, as that of Jacob's daughter by Leah, and derives from Hebrew *Dīnāh*, 'revenged'. Dinah was raped by Shechem but was avenged by her brothers Simeon and Levi. Today the name is popularly associated with DIANA, although that has quite a different origin.

Dinan The city of northwestern France has a name originating from Gaulish *divo*, 'holy' and *nanto*, 'valley'. Dinan lies in the valley of the river Rance.

Dinard The town in Brittany, northwest France, has a Breton name deriving from *din*, 'hill' and perhaps *arzh*, 'bear', the latter denoting its northern location (*cp.* ARCTIC).

Dinka The people of southern Sudan, and the language they speak, have a name that derives from their native word *jieng*, 'people'.

Diocletian The 3rd-century AD Roman emperor had the full name Gaius Aurelius Valerius *Diocletianus*. He was initially known as *Diocles*, from the Greek meaning 'glory of Zeus'. He then added *Valerius*, after the name of his daughter, *Valeria*, and finally took the *nomen* (clan name) *Aurelius*. *Gaius* was his *praenomen* (forename).

Diogenes The Greek philosopher, famous for rejecting social conventions and for advocating a simple life, has a name that means 'born of Zeus'.

Diomedes In Greek mythology, the name is that of a king of Argos and suitor of Helen who fought with the Greeks at Troy. It probably means 'divine ruler', from Greek *dio-*, 'of the gods' and *mēdon*, 'ruler'.

Dionysus The name of the Greek god of wine, also spelled *Dionysos*, means 'divine one of *Nysa*', from Greek *dio-*, 'of the gods' and *Nysa*, the city where he was raised. The historic name *Dionysius* is of the same origin, and the Greek name is also the source of modern English (and French) DENIS.

Dioscuri The Greek name for Castor and Pollux, taken together, means 'sons of Zeus', from *Dios*, genitive of *Zeus*, and *kouros*, 'son', literally 'boy'.

Directory The name, in French *Directoire*, is that of the government of the French Republic from 1795 to 1799. It was so called as it had an executive of five *directors*.

Dire Straits The British rock group, formed in 1977, chose a name that reflected the initial financial plight of its members.

Dis The name of the Roman god of the underworld is a contraction of Latin *dives*, 'rich', itself a translation of the name of his Greek counterpart PLUTO. *See also* DIVES.

Diss The small Norfolk town has a name that is a development of Old English *dīc*, 'ditch', with the final *ch* sound softened to *s* under Norman influence. There must have been a ditch or dyke near here in ancient times.

Dissonance Quartet Mozart's string quartet in C, K 465 (1785), is so named for the unexpected use of discords in its introduction.

District Line The London Underground line takes its name from the *Metropolitan District Railway Company* that was established to raise the necessary funds to complete the CIRCLE LINE by extending the METROPOLITAN LINE. It was thus closely connected with the Metropolitan Railway and was expected to merge with it. The two fell out, however, so that the District ran its own trains from 1871, having completed the section of the Circle Line from South Kensington to Westminster Bridge in 1868.

Diti The name of the goddess of Hindu mythology, the daughter of Dakshi and wife of Kashyapa, represents Sanskrit *Dīti*, 'constraint', 'limitation'.

Dives The name of the rich man in the biblical parable of *Dives* and Lazarus (*Luke* 16.19–31) is not really a proper name at all, but simply the Latin word *dives*, 'rich man', which occurs in the Vulgate (the Latin translation of the Bible). The name does not occur in the Authorized Version, which refers to him simply as 'a certain rich man' (*Luke* 16.19).

Dixieland The distinctive type of jazz originated in New Orleans. The city had come to be nicknamed *Dixie* for the 10-dollar bills issued there before 1860, as these had *dix*, French for 'ten' printed on them. The name *Dixieland* was then taken up to apply to the southern states as a whole.

Dixons The camera and electrical goods stores developed from a small photographic studio opened in Edgware, London in 1937. The founder was Charles Kalms, who called his business *Dixons* after a former Southend department store in preference to giving it his own rather unusual name.

Djibouti The republic of East Africa takes its name from its capital, whose own name is said to derive from an Afar word *gabouri*, 'plate'. The reference is to a plate woven from doum palm fibres and raised on a pedestal for ceremonial purposes.

Dneprodzerzhinsk The Ukrainian city derives the first part of its name from the DNIEPER, on which it lies. The remainder of the name represents that of the Russian revolutionary and Communist Party leader Feliks *Dzerzhinsky* (1877–1926). The town's earlier name was *Kamenskoye*, from Russian *kamen'*, 'rock'.

Dnepropetrovsk The Ukrainian city is on the DNIEPER, and the first part of its name derives from this. The rest represents the name of the Soviet Communist Party official Grigory *Petrovsky* (1878–1958), who worked in the city's factories and became a revolutionary leader there. The name was given in 1928. The town was founded in 1783 as *Yekaterinoslav*, in honour of Catherine the Great. From 1796 to 1802 it was known as NOVOROSSIYSK, a name now in use for another city.

Dnieper The major Russian river is said to derive its name from Avestan *dānu*, 'river' (*cp.* DON, DANUBE) and *apara*, 'far', meaning a river that was remote. *See also* DNIESTER.

Dniester The Russian river probably takes its name from Avestan *dānu*, 'river' (*cp.* DON, DANUBE) and *nazdyō*, 'near', meaning a river that was relatively close. There may have been an implicit contrast between the Dniester and the DNIEPER when considered from a region to the west of the Black Sea, into which both rivers flow: the former would be 'near' and the latter 'far'.

Doberman The German breed of working dog, also known as *Doberman pinscher*, takes its name from the man who developed it, Louis *Dobermann*, a night watchman and dogpound guard in Apolda, eastern Germany, who is said to have generated the breed from a bitch named *Schnupp* ('shooting star') in 1890. *Pinscher* was the name of a type of terrier from *Pinzgau*, a district in Austria.

Docetism The name is that of an early Christian heresy that the earthly body and life of Christ were not real but only apparent. It derives from Greek *dokein*, 'to seem'.

Dr Feelgood The British rhythm 'n' blues revival band, formed in 1971, took their name from the 1962 American hit 'Doctor Feel-Good' by bluesman Piano Red, which he had himself recorded as *Dr Feelgood and The Interns*.

Dr Hook The American rock group, formed in New Jersey in 1968, took a name that was visually prompted by the piratical appearance of singer Ray Sawyer, who wore an eye patch after losing an eye in a car accident. *Captain Hook* is the one-armed pirate captain in J.M. Barrie's play *Peter Pan* (1904).

Dodd The surname was originally a personal nickname, perhaps meaning 'plump', 'stout'.

Dodecanese The island group, in the southeastern Aegean Sea, has a name that means 'twelve islands', from Greek *dō-deka*, 'twelve' and *nēsos*, 'island'. The twelve are: Astypalia, Kalymnos, Karpathos, Kasos, Khalkē, Kos, Leros, Lipsos, Nisyros, Patmos, Symē, Telos.

Dodge City The Kansas city takes its name from the American soldier Richard I. *Dodge* (1827–1895), who was commander of Fort Dodge when the city was founded in 1864.

Dodsworth The name would originally have applied to a person from *Dodworth*, now a colliery town near Barnsley in South Yorkshire. The town's own name means 'Dodd's enclosure', from a personal name that gave the modern English surname DODD.

Dogger Bank The extensive submerged sandbank in the North Sea takes its name from the *doggers*, or Dutch fishing vessels, that worked here.

Doggett's Coat and Badge The prize for the annual watermen's sculling race on the Thames at London takes its name from its founder in 1715 in honour of the accession of George I, the actor Thomas *Doggett* (d. 1721). The original prize was a red *coat* with a large silver *badge* on the arm.

Dogs, Isle of No definitive origin has yet been offered to account for this familiar London name. It is that of the peninsula of land (rather than actual island) that is formed by a bend in the Thames and that is now the site of the London Docklands development. It may not even relate to dogs: a corruption of *Isle of Ducks* has been suggested. It is tempting to see it as *Isle of Docks*, given that in the early 16th century *dock* had the basic sense 'bed in which a ship lies low in the water'. The name has not been found earlier than 1593 (as *Isle of Doges Ferm*). Whatever the reference, the name is probably purely descriptive.

Dog Star The English name for SIRIUS relates to its being the brightest star in the constellation CANIS MAJOR. The name 'dog days' for the hottest period of summer refers to the Roman belief that the great heat at this time was caused by the Sun and Sirius rising together. The Roman name for this period, *caniculares dies*, gave modern French *canicule*, 'heatwave', and Russian *kanikuly*, 'vacation', 'school holidays', a time traditionally associated with the warm days of summer.

Dolgellau The town in northwest Wales has a name representing Welsh *dôl*, 'loop' and *cellau*, the plural of *cell*, 'cell'. The name as a whole points to monastic *cells* that were once here in a *loop* of the river Aran.

Dollar Academy The Scottish public school, founded in 1818, takes its name from the town of *Dollar* where it is located. The town's own name probably derives from Celtic *dol*, 'field' and *ar*, 'ploughed land', so that it arose as a place 'by a ploughed field'.

Dolomites The mountain range in northeast Italy takes its name from the French geologist Déodat de Gratet de *Dolomieu* (1750–1801), who discovered the important mineral *dolomite* here, also named after him. His own name comes from his birthplace, the village of *Dolomieu* near Grenoble in southeast France.

Dolores The name is of Spanish origin, from the title of the Virgin Mary, *María de los Dolores*, 'Mary of the Sorrows'. The name is thus understandably popular among Roman Catholics. According to the Roman Breviary the 'Seven Sorrows' of Mary are: 1. the prophecy of Simeon (that a sword would pierce her soul); 2. the flight into Egypt; 3. the loss of the Holy Child (in Jerusalem); 4. the meeting with the Lord on the road to Calvary; 5. the Crucifixion (when she stood at the foot of the Cross); 6. the Deposition (taking down of Christ from the Cross); 7. the Entombment (burial of Christ).

Domesday Book The record of the survey of England carried out by William the Con-

queror in 1086 is so called since it was regarded as a final and irrevocable authority. There was therefore no appeal against it, any more than there was against *Doomsday*, the day of the Last Judgment.

Dominica The West Indies republic (not to be confused with the DOMINICAN REPUBLIC) is on a volcanic island that was discovered by Christopher Columbus on Sunday 3 November 1493, and named by him after this day, in Spanish *Domingo*, from Latin *dominica dies*, 'Lord's day'.

Dominican The Roman Catholic order of preaching friars, also known as BLACK-FRIARS, takes its name from its founder in 1215, the Spanish priest St *Dominic*.

Dominican Republic The West Indies republic (not to be confused with DOMINICA) occupies the eastern half of the island of Hispaniola. Its name is a latinized form of Spanish *Santo Domingo*, 'Holy Sunday', which it was given in 1697 with reference to its original discovery by Spanish explorers on a Sunday in 1496.

Dominion Day *See* CANADA DAY.

Domrémy-la-Pucelle The village in northeast France is famous as the birthplace of Joan of Arc. The first word of the name evolved from its Roman name of *Dompnum Remigius*, itself from Latin *domnus*, a form of *dominus*, 'lord' and *Remigius*, the name of a famous 6th-century bishop, known in French as *Rémi*, who also gave the name of REIMS. The last part of the name represents the nickname of Joan, French *pucelle* meaning 'maid', 'virgin'. For more about her place of origin *see* JOAN OF ARC.

Don The famous Russian river has a name that probably ultimately derives from Avestan *dānu*, 'river', 'water'. The English river *Don* has a name of similar origin, from a Celtic word of identical meaning. *Cp.* DANUBE, DNIEPER and DNIESTER.

Donald The name is an English form of the Scottish name *Domhnall*, literally 'world rule', from Celtic *dubno*, 'world' and *val*, 'rule'. The final *d* of the English name probably arose under the influence of a name such as RONALD.

Donbass The name of the industrial region of Russia and Ukraine is an abbreviation of Russian *Donetsky ugol'nyy basseyn*, 'coal basin of the *Donets'*, in which it is located. The river has a name of the same basic origin as that of the DON. *See also* DONETSK.

Doncaster The Yorkshire town has a name that declares it to have been a former Roman station (Old English *ceaster*, ultimately from Latin *castra*, 'camp') on the river DON. The Roman fort here was itself named *Danum*, after the river.

Donegal The Irish county is named for the town here, whose Irish name is *Dún na nGall*, 'fort of the foreigners', from *dún*, 'fort' and *gall*, 'foreigner', 'stranger' (*cp.* GALLOWAY). The 'foreigners' were the Danes, who took possession of a primitive fort here in the 10th century.

Donetsk The city in Ukraine is the main industrial centre of the DONBASS, and takes its name from the full Russian phrase that gave this abbreviated form. Its original name when founded in 1862 was *Yuzovka*, *i.e.* 'Hughesovka', for the Welsh entrepreneur John *Hughes* who established the first ironworks here. From 1924 until 1961 it was known as *Stalino*.

Donmar Warehouse Theatre The London 'fringe' theatre, in Covent Garden, was opened in 1960 in a former warehouse for ripening bananas and was known simply as *The Warehouse*. The name of *Donmar* was then added to refer to its original purchasers, *Don*ald Albery and his friend, the ballerina *Mar*got Fonteyn. Donald Albery was the son of Bronson James Albery, who gave his name to the ALBERY THEATRE. The Donmar Warehouse closed in 1991.

Donna The name is simply the Italian word for 'lady'. *Cp.* MADONNA.

Donohue The Irish name was originally *Ó Donnchadha*, meaning 'descendant of *Donnchadh*'. The latter personal name means literally 'brown battle', so has the same origin as the name DUNCAN.

Donovan The name is an English form of the Irish name *Ó Donndubháin*, meaning 'descendant of *Donndubhán*. This personal name means literally 'brown black', from Gaelic *donn*, 'brown' and *dubh*, 'black'. The name would have been used for a swarthy or dark-haired person. *Cp.* the names DUNN and DUFF.

Don Quixote The hero of Cervantes' novel *Don Quixote de la Mancha* (1605, 1615) is called Alonso *Quijano* at the start of the story, as an elderly country gentleman who lives in the province of La Mancha. On reading romances of chivalry, however, he believes that he is called on to right the wrongs of the world and changes his name to *Quijote* and is knighted by an innkeeper as *Don Quijote* (*i.e.* Don Quixote). In converting the Spanish surname *Quijano* to *Quijote* the hero has adopted the ordinary word for 'thigh-piece'. (English *cuisse* as a term for the same piece of armour is directly related, although borrowed from the French word for 'thigh'.) *Don* is the Spanish title for a nobleman, from Latin *dominus*, 'lord'. The hero's name gave English *quixotic* as a word to mean 'impractically unrealistic'.

Doobie Brothers The American rock group, formed in 1970 in San José, California, took their name from *doobie*, the Californian slang term for a marijuana cigarette.

Doors, The The American rock group, formed in Los Angeles in 1965, took their name from Aldous Huxley's book about his experience of the drug mescaline, *The Doors of Perception* (1954). Huxley himself took the title of his book from words by William Blake: 'If the doors of perception were cleansed everything would appear as it is, infinite' (*The Marriage of Heaven and Hell: A Memorable Fancy*, 1790).

Dora The name is a short form of a name such as *Theodora*. See DOROTHY.

Dorcas In the New Testament, the name is used simply to 'explain' the name TABITHA: 'Now there was at Joppa a certain disciple named Tabitha, which by interpretation is called Dorcas' (*Acts* 9.36). It derives from Greek *dorkas*, 'doe', 'gazelle'.

Dorchester The county town of DORSET has a name probably based on a Celtic word meaning 'fist' to which modern Welsh *dwrn* in this sense is related. The reference could have been to a place covered in fist-sized stones, or even to fist-fights that were held here. The remainder of the name represents Old English *ceaster*, from Latin *castra*, 'camp', showing that there was a Roman fort here.

Dorchester Hotel The top-class hotel in Park Lane, London, was built in 1931 on the site of the historic *Dorchester* House which had itself been built in 1751 and which was given its name when the landowner, Joseph Damer, became Earl of *Dorchester* in 1792.

Dordogne The name of the river and tourist region of southwest France derives ultimately from an Indoeuropean root word *dur* or *dor*, 'current', 'river' and *anun*, 'deep'.

Dordrecht The port in the southwest Netherlands derives its name from *Thyre*, a former river name, and Old Dutch *drecht*, 'channel'. Dordrecht stands at the place where four rivers meet.

Doreen The name is a form of DORA with the ending *-een* that is an Irish diminutive in origin and that is found in other names, such as MAUREEN.

Dorian The name of the Hellenic race derives from that of their mythical ancestor, *Dōros*, whose own name may be related to Greek *dōron*, 'gift'. The Dorians in turn gave the name of *Doris*, their homeland, as well as the English adjective *Doric*. See *also* the personal name DORIS.

Dorian The name is familiar from Oscar Wilde's story *The Portrait of Dorian Gray* (1891). Wilde seems to have taken the name from the DORIAN race of Greek-speaking people.

Doris The name derives from the Greek word for 'DORIAN woman'.

Dorking The Surrey town has a name meaning 'place of *Deorc*'s people'. The ending *-ing* in names like this usually means 'people of' following a personal name.

Dormobile The make of camper was originally designed as a vehicle for people to sleep in when travelling. Hence its name, which is a blend of '*dorm*itory' (or Latin *dormire*, 'to sleep') and 'auto*mobile*' (or simply '*mobile*').

Dorneywood The country house that is the official residence of the foreign secretary, near Burnham Beeches, Buckinghamshire, takes its name from the *wood* here named *Dorney*. The wood name is said to derive from Old English *dora*, 'humble-bee' (here in the genitive plural, *dorena*) and *ēg*,

'island', in the sense of raised land among streams.

Dorothy The name is Greek in origin, and means 'gift of God', from *dōron*, 'gift' and *theos*, 'god'. The present form of the name developed from the earlier *Dorothea*, which itself had a counterpart in the name *Theodora*, with the two parts of the name reversed.

Dorothy Perkins The fashion stores are so called after the type of rose, which was itself named for the daughter of George H. *Perkins*, founder of the American rose nursery of Jackson and Perkins. The rose name was adopted for the particular breed of rambling rose in 1901.

Dorset The English county has a name meaning '*Dorn* settlers', with *Dorn*, the basic original name of DORCHESTER, now the county town, followed by Old English *sǣte*, 'settlers'. *Cp.* the names of SOMERSET and GRANTCHESTER.

Dortmund The name of the German city looks as if it denotes a town at the *mouth* (German *Mund*) of a river 'Dort'. But Dortmund is not on a river at all, only a canal, and its name must have some other origin. It was recorded in the 9th century as *Throtmenni*, apparently from a Germanic word *thrut*, 'throat', referring to some natural feature here, and a second element of obscure meaning.

Douai The city in northern France, famous as a centre of exiled English Roman Catholics from the 16th century, derives its name from the Gaulish personal name *Dous*. The name is found for the *Douay* Bible, the English translation of the Bible from the Vulgate carried out by Roman Catholic scholars at Douai in 1610, and also for *Douai School*, the Roman Catholic public school for boys near Reading, originally founded by Benedictines in Paris in 1615 but then dispersed until refounded at *Douai* in 1818, eventually moving to England in 1903.

Douala The chief port and largest city of Cameroon is so called after the Bantu people of the same name. Their own name probably derives from one of their early ancestors. The town was so named in 1907, having earlier been called *Kamerun*,

153

a legacy of the region's history as a German protectorate from 1884.

Douarnenez The town in Brittany, northwest France has a name that means 'St *Tutuarn*'s island', with the saint's name followed by Breton *enez*, 'island'. St Tutuarn founded a monastery on a small island off the coast here.

Doubleday The American publishers are named for their founder in 1897, Frank Nelson *Doubleday* (1862–1934), originally in partnership with Samuel Sidney McClure (1857–1959), the founder of *McClure's Magazine*. The partnership lasted only three years, however.

Dougal The name is an English form of the Scottish name *Dubhghall*, literally 'dark stranger', from Gaelic *dubh*, 'black', 'dark' and *gall*, 'stranger', 'foreigner'. The name is believed to have been originally applied to the dark-haired Danes in Scotland, as distinct from the blond Norwegians and Icelanders.

Doughty The name means what it says, and would originally have been a nickname for a strong or brave person, such as a warrior.

Douglas The capital of the Isle of Man has a name that means 'black stream', from Celtic root words represented by Gaelic *dubh*, 'black' and *glas*, 'stream'. Douglas stands at the confluence of the small rivers Doo and Glass, which appear to have taken their names from it.

Douglas The first name was adopted from the Scottish surname, itself said to have derived from some place in southern Scotland where the family lived, with the place-name itself meaning 'black stream', as for DOUGLAS, Isle of Man.

Doukhobor The name is that of a member of the Russian peasant Christian sect, founded in the late 18th century, who through persecution emigrated to Canada in the 1890s. They believe in direct personal revelation or 'inner light', and their name literally means 'spirit wrestlers', from Russian *dukh*, 'spirit' and *borets*, 'wrestler'.

Doulton The familiar make of pottery is named for Sir Henry *Doulton* (1820–1897)

who began producing his distinctive stoneware in London in the 1850s.

Douro The river of Spain and Portugal derives its name from an Indoeuropean root word *dur* or *dor*, 'water', 'river'. The same element lies behind the name of the DORDOGNE, among other places.

Dove Cottage The former home of the poet Wordsworth at Grasmere in the Lake District was originally an inn called the *Dove and Olive Bough*. Hence the name of the house. The inn's name ultimately goes back to the biblical story about the dove that returned to Noah's Ark with an olive branch (*Genesis* 8.11). Wordsworth and his sister lived at the cottage from 1799 to 1807.

Dover The well-known port on the English Channel, in Kent, takes its name from a Celtic word meaning 'water' to which modern Welsh *dwfr* in the same sense is directly related. The reference is not to the sea but to the streams that enter the English Channel here. One of these is called the *Dour*. Across the Atlantic, the state capital of Delaware was identically so named in 1683 by William Penn for the English town.

Down The county of Northern Ireland takes its name from the fort (Irish *dún*) that gave the name of its county town, DOWNPATRICK.

Down House The house near Sevenoaks, Kent, famous as the former home of Charles Darwin, takes its name from the village of *Downe* in which it is located. The origin is in Old English *dūn*, 'hill' (modern *down*). The ground rises to over 500 feet (150 m) south of the village, whose name is spelled *Down* on the 1819 Ordnance Survey map.

Downing College The Cambridge college was founded in 1800 under the will of Sir George *Downing* (1684–1749), and is named for him. Sir George was the grandson of the identically named Sir George Downing for whom DOWNING STREET is named.

Downing Street The London street that contains the official residences of the prime minister (No 10) and the chancellor of the exchequer (No 11) takes its name from the soldier and diplomat Sir George *Downing* (1623–1684) who built it on its prestigious site opposite the royal palace of Whitehall. By coincidence Downing was First Secretary of the Treasury Commission, and one of the main titles of the prime minister is First Lord of the Treasury. (For a parallel to this, *see* CHEQUERS.)

Downpatrick The county town of Co DOWN, Northern Ireland, has a name that means 'St *Patrick*'s fort'. The original fort (Irish *dún*) probably stood where St Patrick's Cathedral is today. The personal name was added to the basic name in the 12th century, when relics said to be those of the saint were discovered here.

Downs, The The roadstead of this name off the southeast coast of Kent is protected by the Goodwin Sands but is so called since it lies opposite the eastern end of the South *Downs*.

Downside The Roman Catholic public school for boys, near Bath, was founded at DOUAI in 1606. At the time of the French Revolution it transferred to England, and came to its present site in 1814. The name is that of the locality here, denoting a place by the *side* of a *down* or hill (Old English *dūn*). It is simply a coincidence that the school's name resembles that of its French place of origin.

Draco The 7th-century BC Athenian statesman was notorious for drawing up laws that prescribed death for almost every offence. Aptly enough his name is the word for 'dragon' (Greek *drakōn*, Latin *draco*). It gave modern English *draconian* as a synonym for 'harsh'.

Dracula The sinister count-turned-vampire who is the central character of Bram Stoker's novel of 1897 named for him has a fairly complex history. He evolved from a character in an anonymous story published in Nürnberg in 1499, the opening words of which were, in translation: 'Here begins a very cruel frightening story about a wild bloodthirsty man Prince Dracula.' This Dracula in turn was based on a contemporary real tyrant, one Vlad Țepeș, who succeeded to the Walachian throne in 1456. His cruel deeds and punishments were widely known in Transylvania. The name *Dracula* represents Romanian *drac*-

ul, 'the dragon', from *drac*, 'dragon' and the suffix *-ul* denoting the definite article after masculine nouns ending in a consonant. This was the title Țepeș had inherited from his father, who in 1441 had been received into the Order of the *Dragon* in Nürnberg.

Drake The name originated as a nickname, either describing a person who in some way suggested a snake or *dragon*, or denoting a person who was thought to be like a *duck*, either in appearance or habits.

Drakensberg The mountain range of southern Africa has a name meaning 'dragon mountain', from Middle Dutch *drake*, 'dragon' and *berg*, 'mountain'. The mountains are wild and dangerous, as a dragon is traditionally supposed to be.

Drake Passage The strait between southern South America and the South Shetland Islands derives its name from the famous circumnavigator Sir Francis *Drake* (1540–1596). Drake actually sailed from the Atlantic to the Pacific by passing through the Strait of Magellan, further north, but his ship, the *Golden Hind*, was blown back into the northern regions of the passage by a storm, so in that sense he was familiar with its waters.

Dragon School The well-known Oxford preparatory school was founded (as the *Oxford Preparatory School*) in 1877 and seems to have acquired its name by way of a nickname. Its first pupils were familiar with St George and the *Dragon* on the coinage of the day and with the name of the Rev H.B. *George*, a member of the school council. The boys called themselves 'the Dragons' and wore improvised dragon badges on caps and hatbands. The name was not officially adopted until 1921, however.

Dralon The acrylic fibre fabric is especially suitable for upholstery, and has a name that appears to reflect this use, from '*dra*pery' and the ending of 'ny*lon*'. The fabric is of German origin, however, so that its name may actually derive from German *Draht*, 'wire', 'thread', referring to the manufacturing process.

Dramamine The proprietary make of travel-sickness tablets derives its name as a contraction of its chief constituent, *d*iphenhyd*ramine* theoclate, with an added extra syllable.

Drambuie The Scottish liqueur has a name of Gaelic origin, either from *dram buidheach*, 'satisfying drink' or *dram buidhe*, 'golden drink'. It is said that the original recipe for the liqueur was given to the Mackinnon family by 'Bonnie Prince Charlie' as a reward for giving him refuge when he was defeated by the English in 1746.

Draper The name is a straightforward occupational one, denoting a person who made and sold cloth.

Dravidian The family of languages of southern and central India has a name that identifies one of them, deriving from Sanskrit and Hindi *draviḍa*, an alteration of Tamil *tamiḷ*, 'TAMIL'. The name is also used of the aboriginal people who speak these languages.

Drenthe The province of the northeast Netherlands has a name that derives from Germanic *thrija-hantja*, 'three lands', from *thrija*, 'three' (modern Dutch *drie*) and *hantja*, 'land'.

Dresden The city in southeast Germany has a name of Slavic origin, from *drenzga*, 'forest'. The name shows that the Slavic races of neighbouring Poland and Czechoslovakia at one time extended as far west as this part of Germany.

Drew The surname can have a number of origins. It may have been a short form of ANDREW, or have derived from the personal name *Drogo*, of uncertain meaning (perhaps 'carrier'), or have been a nickname for a beloved one (from Old French *dru*, 'favourite'), or else have denoted a person who was *de Rieu* ('from Rieu') or who lived in *Dreux*. The last two places are in the north of France.

Drinkwater The name means more or less what it says, and originated as a nickname for a person who was poor and so could only *drink* cheap ale that was as weak as *water*.

Drogheda The port in northeast Ireland, near the mouth of the river Boyne, has a name that represents Irish *Droichead Átha*, 'bridge of the ford'. There was a bridge

over the river here as early as the 12th century.

Droitwich A place-name ending in *-wich* derives this element from Old English *wīc*, a word, itself from Latin *vicus*, that usually denotes a special place of some kind, in particular one with a commercial activity such as dairy farming. In the case of Droitwich, it denotes salt workings, as also at NANTWICH and NORTHWICH. The town has long been known for its saline springs, and its Roman name of *Salinae* also refers to the saltworks. The first part of the name represents Old English *drit*, 'dirt', 'mud', so that overall Droitwich, near Worcester, has a name meaning 'muddy place with saltworks'.

Drôme The department of southeast France takes its name from the river that flows through it. Its own name represents the proto-Indoeuropean root element *drawa* or *dorava*, meaning 'current', itself related to the root word *dor*, 'river', found for the DOURO and the DORDOGNE.

Druid The name for the ancient order of priests in Celtic lands, especially Gaul, Britain and Ireland, derives from a Celtic root word meaning 'magician', of which modern Irish and Gaelic *draoi*, with the same meaning, are the equivalent. The word has also been connected with Greek *drus*, 'oak', since it is known that the historic Druids regarded this tree as sacred and that they performed religious ceremonies in oak groves. In modern times the name has been adopted by movements who aim to revive druidism, and who often claim to descend from the original priests. The best-known and oldest such organization is the secret benefit society founded in London in 1781 as the *United Ancient Order of Druids*, which has lodges called *groves* to reflect the former practices. Modern druids have also come to be associated with the Welsh *eisteddfodau*, and have been popularly promoted in the media by their gatherings at Stonehenge on Midsummer Day to greet the rising of the sun.

Drummond The Scottish name denotes a person who came from any of the places so called, such as *Drummond Hill* near Loch Tay or what is now the village of

Drymen near Balloch. The place-name itself derives from Gaelic *druim*, 'ridge'.

Drumroll Symphony Haydn's Symphony No 103 in E flat major (1795) is so nicknamed because it opens with a roll on the kettledrums.

Drury Lane The London street, famous for its theatres, takes its name from the land-owner here in about 1500, Sir Robert *Drury*. His home, Drury House, was a noted building here for almost 200 years.

Druze The name is that of a religious sect of Syria and Lebanon that has much in common with the Muslims. It derives from the name of its founder, the 11th-century Muslim leader, Muhammad ibn Ismail ad-*Darazi*. The latter part of his name (actually that of his father) means 'Ismail the tailor'.

Dublin The name of the Irish capital means 'black pool', from Irish *dubh*, 'black' and *linn*, 'pool'. The reference is to the dark waters of the river Liffey on which Dublin stands. By coincidence, the name exactly echoes that of BLACKPOOL, the English port across the Irish Sea from Dublin. The present official Irish name of Dublin is BAILE ÁTHA CLIATH, which also relates to the Liffey, but more historically than geographically.

Dubonnet The French aperitif takes its name from Joseph *Dubonnet*, who first produced it in Paris in 1846.

Dubrovnik The port in southern Croatia, on the Adriatic, has a name meaning 'oak forest' from a Slavic root word that gave Russian *dub*, 'oak', which is itself related to the Celtic word for the tree that gave Welsh *derw* and that lies behind the name of the DERWENT and other rivers. The city's Italian name is *Ragusa*, from the name of the small island of *Lausa* here. Its own name is of uncertain origin.

Duce, Il The title, meaning 'the leader', was that assumed by Mussolini as leader of Fascist Italy. *Cp*. El CAUDILLO for Franco, and Der FÜHRER for Hitler.

Duchess Theatre The London West End theatre, in Catherine Street, off the Strand, opened in 1929 and appears to have been given a generally prestigious name that may have been intended to com-plement that of the DUKE OF YORK'S THEATRE not far away in St Martin's Lane.

Duff The Scottish name originated as a nickname for a swarthy or dark-haired person, from Gaelic *dubh*, 'black'.

Dugi Otok The Croatian island in the Adriatic, off the coast of Dalmatia, has a Croat name meaning 'long island', from *dug*, 'long' and *otok*, 'island'. The island's Italian name, *Isola Longa*, has the same sense. The island is 27 miles (43 km) long.

Duisburg The town of northwest Germany may have a name that means '*Diu*'s fort', from the name of a god that is also found in English TUESDAY and that is directly related to that of ZEUS.

Duke The name originally denoted either a person who was full of 'airs and graces', like a *duke*, or someone who worked in a duke's household.

Duke of York's Theatre The London theatre, in St Martin's Lane, was opened in 1892 under the original name of *Trafalgar Square Theatre*. In 1895 it shortened its name to the *Trafalgar Theatre* and that same year adopted its present name, in honour of the then *Duke of York*, the future king George V. A request for permission to use the name brought the following reply from the Duke's Treasurer:

> I am desired to inform you that HRH the Duke of York has no objection to the Tra-falgar Theatre being called The Duke of York's Theatre but to say that this permis-sion gives no authority for the use of the word Royal in connexion with the theatre nor may any reference be made such as 'By permission of HRH the Duke of York.'

Dukeries The area of Nottinghamshire, in the northern part of Sherwood Forest, takes its name from the grand mansions and estates built here by seven *dukes* after the Dissolution of the Monasteries.

Dulwich The district of southeast London has a name meaning 'dill marsh', from Old English *dile*, 'dill' and *wisce*, 'marshy meadow' (preserved in the Sussex dialect word *wish*). The *-wich* of the name is thus not the same as in NORWICH or WOOLWICH. Dill is a herb that has long been cultivated for medicinal use.

Dumbarton The town in western Scotland is centred round the historic Rock of Dumbarton, a stronghold since ancient times. The town's name refers to this, and means 'fort of the Britons', from Gaelic *dùn*, 'fort' and *Breatann*, 'of the Britons'. The reference is to the occupation of the fort by the British from the 5th century. The Britons themselves called their fortress here *Alclut*, meaning 'fort by the CLYDE'.

Dumbarton Oaks The mansion in Georgetown, Washington DC, is famous as the scene of conferences held in 1944 with the aim of setting up the United Nations. The house was built in 1801 on an estate that was named for DUMBARTON in Scotland. The *Oaks* are those in its grounds.

Dumbo The name of the baby elephant in the popular Walt Disney cartoon, released in 1941, was undoubtedly based on JUMBO, but with the implication that he was *dumb* in the American sense of being not very clever (although he discovered that he could use his ears to fly).

Dumfries The town in southern Scotland has a name of Gaelic origin, from *dùn*, 'fort' and *preas*, 'copse'. This can overall be understood as 'wooded stronghold'. The fort was probably in the oldest part of the town, now known as Mid Steeple.

Dunaújváros The town in west central Hungary was founded on the river DANUBE in 1950 and has a name that literally means 'Danube new town', from Hungarian *Duna*, 'Danube', *új*, 'new' and *város*, 'town'. The name is pronounced approximately 'Doona-*ooee*-varosh'. Its original name (until 1962) was *Sztálinváros*, 'Stalin's town'.

Dunbar The port and resort in southeast Scotland has a name that means 'fort on the height', from Gaelic *dùn*, 'fort' and *barr*, 'height'. The 'height' is the rocky headland above the harbour where the ruins of Dunbar Castle now stand.

Duncan The name is an English form of the Scottish name *Donnchadh*, meaning literally 'brown battle', from Gaelic *donn*, 'brown' and *cath*, 'battle'. The name would originally have applied to a swarthy or dark-haired warrior. The English form of the name has taken a final *n* by confusing

the second word with Gaelic *ceann*, 'head'. *See also* DONOHUE.

Dunciad, The The mock-heroic satire by Pope, first published anonymously in 1728, has a name based on that of the ILIAD, implying that it is an 'epic for dunces'.

Dundee The port in eastern Scotland is on the Tay, and its name is popularly regarded as meaning 'fort on the Tay' for this reason, with the river name giving the *-dee* of the town's name. But it is more likely to mean '*Daig*'s fort', from Gaelic *dùn*, 'fort' and the personal name *Daig*. The fort would have stood where the former Dundee Castle was. It is not known who Daig was, but his name may have meant 'fire' (Gaelic *daig*).

Dunedin The port in South Island, New Zealand was founded in 1848 by Scottish Presbyterian settlers who originally wanted to name their settlement 'New EDINBURGH'. Sir William Chambers, mayor of Edinburgh, instead suggested they name their colony *Dunedin*, after the historic name of Edinburgh. This was, moreover, a purely Celtic name and therefore appropriate for a place of Scottish foundation.

Dunfermline The historic city in eastern Scotland has a name of uncertain origin. There is no doubt that the first syllable represents Gaelic *dùn*, 'fort'. The remainder of the name, however, has so far defied any meaningful interpretation.

Dungeness The Kent headland, famous for its nuclear power stations and its bird sanctuary, takes its name from nearby *Denge* Marsh (with *ness* meaning 'headland'). The marsh's own name means 'valley district', from Old English *denu*, 'valley' and *gē*, 'district'. *Cp.* ELY and SURREY.

Dunhill The well-known tobaccos and pipes take their name from Alfred *Dunhill* (1872–1959), a London man who at first made harness and motorists' accessories but who then opened a tobacconist's shop in Duke Street where in 1907 he began specializing as a tobacco blender. In 1910 he sold his first pipe, made to his own specifications.

Dunkirk The port and city on the Strait of Dover in northeast France has a name meaning 'dune church', from Middle Dutch *dune*, 'dune' and *kerke*, 'church', referring to the church of St Eloi that was built on the dunes here by the sea in the 7th century. The French form of the name is *Dunkerque*.

Dún Laoghaire The Irish port and suburb of Dublin has an Irish name that means 'fort of *Laoghaire*'. It is not certain who Laoghaire was. According to some accounts he was a high king of Ireland and a disciple of St Patrick. From 1821 to 1921 the port was known as *Kingstown*, after George IV, who passed through it on his return to England from Dublin in the former year. The name is pronounced approximately 'Dunleary' and was actually spelled as such before 1821.

Dunlop The make of tyre takes its name not from the company founder but from the inventor of a new kind of pneumatic tyre in 1888, the Scotsman John Boyd *Dunlop* (1840–1921). The actual founder of the manufacturing company in 1896 was Harvey du Cros (1846–1918), who had earlier worked with Dunlop and who wished to continue the association that had developed between Dunlop's name and his invention.

Dunn The name is Scottish, Irish or English in origin, but with the same meaning, denoting a dark-haired or swarthy person, from Gaelic *donn* or Old English *dunn*, 'brown', 'dark'. As a Scottish name it could also have applied to someone from *Dun*, near Brechin in the former county of Angus. This name represents Gaelic *dùn*, 'fort'.

Dunn The menswear stores are named for George Arthur *Dunn* (1865–1939), a Birmingham man who opened his first hat shop in London in 1887.

Dunsinane The hill in central Scotland, in the Sidlaw Hills, has a ruined fort at its summit that is popularly regarded as being Macbeth's castle. The name of the hill probably means 'hill of the teat', from Gaelic *dùn*, 'hill' and *sineachan*, 'of the teat', from *sine*, 'teat', 'nipple', referring to its conical peak.

Dunstable The Bedfordshire town has a name meaning '*Dunna*'s post', with the personal name followed by Old English *sta-*

pol, 'post', 'pillar' (modern *staple*). The post in question was probably a waymark since Dunstable stands at the intersection of Watling Street and the Icknield Way.

Dunstan The name represents the Old English words *dunn*, 'dark' and *stān*, 'stone', as applied to a swarthy or dark-haired warrior, who was 'hard as stone'.

Dunwoodie The Scottish surname denotes a person from the place now known as *Dinwoodie*, near Lockerbie. The meaning of the place-name is uncertain.

Duracell The make of long-life battery has a name indicating its particular property, that of being a *dura*ble *cell*. It was introduced on the market in the mid-1970s by the American company Dart Industries.

Duran Duran The British pop group, formed in Birmingham in 1978, played their first gig at Barbarella's club there, and took their name from the mad professor *Durand-Durand* in the spoof science-fiction movie *Barbarella* (1967), starring Jane Fonda as Barbarella and Milo O'Shea as Durand-Durand.

Durban The port and city in Natal, South Africa takes its name from Sir Benjamin *D'Urban* (1777–1849), governor of Cape Colony at the time of the town's foundation in 1824. It was originally called *Port Natal*, after its province, but was then renamed for the governor, at first in the spelling *D'Urban*, but simplified to *Durban* in about 1870. Sir Benjamin's own name has the basic sense 'town', appropriately enough.

Durex The well-known brand of condom is said to derive its name from the first letters of '*du*rability, *re*liability, *ex*cellence', although its first part seems to suggest '*dura*ble' alone. The final -*ex* is simply a commercial suffix, as for KLEENEX. In Australia, *Durex* is the brand name of a make of adhesive tape similar to SELLOTAPE.

Durga The name of the wife of Siva in Hindu mythology is Sanskrit in origin and means essentially 'inaccessible', from *dus-*, the pejorative ('bad') prefix, and *ga*, 'mobile'.

Durgapur The city in northeast India has a name that means 'town of DURGA', with the name of the goddess followed by Sanskrit *pur*, 'town'.

Durham The English city and county has a name that is a combination of Old English *dūn*, 'hill' and Old Norse *holmr*, 'island'. Durham is on a hill in a bend of the river Wear, the hill being the 'island'. The name might have evolved to something like *Dunham* if it had not been modified under Norman influence. The original spelling of the name is preserved in the Latin abbreviation *Dunelm* (from *Dunelmensis*, 'of Durham') for the signature of the bishop of Durham.

Durrës The name of the port in western Albania evolved from Latin *Dyrrhachium* and Greek *Durrakhion*. A meaning 'dangerous cliffs' has been proposed for the origin.

Duryodhana In Hindu mythology, the name is that of the eldest son of King Dhritarashtra, featuring as a warrior prince in the *Mahabharata*. It derives from Sanskrit and means '(he) with whom it is hard to fight'.

Dushanbe The capital of Tajikistan has a name deriving from Tajik *duśanbe*, 'Monday', this word itself coming from *du*, 'two' and *śanbe*, 'Saturday', *i.e.* a day that is two days after Saturday. The reference is to a regular Monday market. From 1929 to 1961 the city was known as *Stalinabad*, 'Stalin's town'.

Düsseldorf The name of the city in western Germany means '*Düssel* village', from the river on which the town is located. The river name itself has an Indoeuropean base *dur* or *dor*, 'current', 'river', as for the DORDOGNE. The German word for 'village', *Dorf*, corresponds to the *thorp* in English names such as SCUNTHORPE.

Dust Bowl The region of the south central United States acquired its name when it was denuded of topsoil by wind erosion during the droughts of the mid-1930s.

Dutch The name of the people of the Netherlands derives from that of their language, which itself comes from a Germanic root word meaning 'popular', 'national', referring to a tongue spoken by ordinary people, as against the learned Latin of the church. It is directly related to the modern German word *Deutsch*, 'German', and 'Dutch' was used in English in the 15th and 16th centuries in the same sense as we now use 'German'. The language spoken in the Netherlands was thus 'Low Dutch', while 'High Dutch' was spoken in what is now Germany. ('Low' and 'High' relate to the physical terrain: see NETHERLANDS.)

Dvina The name is that of two lengthy European rivers: the Northern *Dvina*, in northwest Russia, and the Western *Dvina*, further south in Byelorussia and Latvia. The basic name may derive either from Finnish *vieno*, 'gentle', referring to its slow current, or Estonian *väin*, 'channel', referring to one of its many narrow stretches. The Western Dvina gave the name of the Latvian city of DAUGAVPILS, which lies on it.

Dwight The first name was adopted from the surname, which itself may ultimately derive from a feminine form of the Greek name DIONYSUS, and so be indirectly related to DENIS. The name is popular in the United States, where it is familiar from President *Dwight* D. Eisenhower (1890–1969).

Dyfed The county of southwest Wales has a historic name derived from that of the *Demetae*, a people who inhabited this part of Wales during the Roman occupation. The meaning of their name is unknown.

Dylan The name is Welsh in origin, and is that of a legendary god of the sea. Its precise origin is uncertain, but it was popularized by the Welsh poet *Dylan* Thomas (1914–1953).

Dymock The name originally applied to a person from the place so called near Newent in Gloucestershire. The meaning of the place-name is probably 'fort of pigs', from Celtic *din*, 'fort' and *moch*, 'pigs'.

Dynamo Moscow The well-known Russian football club was formed in 1923 after absorbing the Orekhovo Sports Club, itself founded in 1887 at Orekhovo-Zuyevo, outside Moscow, by British mill owners named Charnock. It acquired the name *Dynamo* when it was sponsored by the Electrical Trades Union. Its Moscow stadium of the same name was built in 1928.

Dzerzhinsk The industrial city in central Russia was so named in 1929 to commemorate the Communist leader Feliks *Dzerzhinsky* (1877–1926). Its earlier name was *Rastyapino*, of uncertain origin.

Dzhambul The city in Kazakhstan was so named in 1938 for the Kazakh folk poet *Dzhambul* Dzhabayev (1846–1945) (*sic*). The poet was himself named for a mountain near his birthplace in this region. The town's earlier name was *Auliye-Ata*, from Uzbek *auliye*, 'holy' and *ata*, 'father'.

Dzungaria The region of western China derives its name from Mongolian *züün*, 'left' and *gar*, 'hand', describing its geographical location from the point of view of someone facing north in China or Mongolia.

E

Eade The surname is a short form of the personal name EDITH.

Ealing The borough of west London has a name that means 'place of *Gilla*'s people', this despite popular attempts to associate the name with *eel*, all the more for its proximity to the Thames.

Earls Court The district of southwest London takes its name from a former manor house or *court* which was owned by the *earls* of Oxford until the 16th century. The house itself stood on the site between Barkston Gardens and Bramham Gardens, almost opposite the present Earls Court Underground station.

Early English The name for the style of English Gothic architecture, as exemplified in Salisbury Cathedral, appears to have been introduced in the late 18th century. It was presumably adopted from the term sometimes used to describe the form of English spoken in late medieval times.

Earth, Wind and Fire The black American soul band, formed in 1969, were given their name, suggesting the four ancient elements earth, air, water and fire, by their singer and drummer Maurice White, who was interested in Egyptology and astrology.

East Anglia The name of the region of eastern England that includes Norfolk, Suffolk, and parts of adjacent counties is a somewhat artificial latinization of the Old English name *Eastengle*, 'East Angles', given to the inhabitants of the former Anglo-Saxon kingdom here. This was 'east' by contrast with the kingdom of the Middle Angles, who occupied what is now basically the East Midlands.

Eastbourne The popular East Sussex resort has a name that literally means 'eastern stream', by contrast with another place on a 'western stream'. The latter is in fact the village of *Westbourne*, some 50 miles (80 km) to the west, near the border with Hampshire. The stream in question in Eastbourne is the one that rises near St Mary's Church.

Easter The major festival of the Christian church, celebrating the Resurrection of Christ, has a name of pagan origin, unlike that of the other great festival, CHRISTMAS. It derives from the name of the Germanic goddess *Eostre*, whose festival was celebrated at the vernal equinox. Her own name is related to modern English *east*, showing that she was the goddess of the dawn and the sunrise. The name is not inappropriate for a festival commemorating the rising from the dead of Christ (the 'light of the world') at his Resurrection.

Easter Island The South Pacific island was first reached by Dutch navigators on *Easter* Sunday (or possibly Monday) 1722, and is named for that day.

East London The port in Cape Province, South Africa was so named after LONDON, England, to the *east* of which it lies on the south*east* coast of South Africa.

Ebbw Vale The Welsh town, formerly famous for its coal and steel, has a half-Welsh, half-English name, referring to its location in the *valley* of the river *Ebbw*. The river's name may mean 'horse river', from a Celtic word to which modern Welsh *ebol*, 'colt' is related. Horses may have worked here, had a drinking pool here, or simply had a regular crossing place here.

Ebenezer The name is biblical, but was originally not that of a person. *Ebenezer* was both the place where the Philistines defeated the Israelites (1 *Samuel* 4.1) and the memorial set up by Samuel to mark the spot where the Israelites took their revenge (1 *Samuel* 7.12). The name itself means 'stone of help', from Hebrew *eben-*

ha'ezer. The Puritans adopted the name as a Christian name, either because they mistook it as a personal name, or because they felt its literal meaning was favourable.

Ebor Handicap The well-known horse race, founded in 1843, is run annually at York, whose Roman name was *Eboracum. Ebor* is also the official signature of the Archbishop of York, where it is the Latin abbreviation of *Eboracensis*, 'of York'. *See also* YORK itself.

Ebro The Spanish river has a name that probably derives from a root word meaning simply 'river', such as Indoeuropean *var* or Celtic *iber* (*cp.* IBERIA).

Ecbatana The ancient city in Iran, formerly the capital of the Medes, has a name that ultimately goes back to the personal name *Agbatas*, of uncertain origin, but perhaps related to the Arabic name AHMED. Today the city is known as *Hamadān*, a form of its earlier name.

Ecclefechan The town in southwest Scotland has a Celtic name meaning 'little church'. The first half of the name relates to Latin (from Greek) *ecclesia*, 'church', as does that of ECCLES. The second half of the name has an equivalent in modern Welsh *bach*, 'little'.

Eccles The Midlands town has a name that simply means 'church', from a Celtic word that itself derived from Latin *ecclesia*, 'church', in turn from Greek *ekklēsia*, 'assembly'. There would have been a pre-Anglo-Saxon community or church here. *Cp.* ECCLEFECHAN.

Ecclesiastes The book of the Old Testament has a title that is a Greek translation of its Hebrew name, *Qōhéleth*, 'ecclesiast', literally 'assembler' (*i.e.* of the congregation), but traditionally rendered 'preacher'. The full title of the book is thus *Ecclesiastes; or, The Preacher* and the opening verse runs: 'The words of the Preacher, the son of David, king in Jerusalem' (*Ecclesiastes* 1.1). This description can only refer to Solomon, although the Aramaic content and style of the book date it at least 600 years later, to the 3rd century BC.

Ecclesiasticus The book of the Apocrypha has the alternative title *The Wisdom of Jesus the Son of Sirach.* The latter is the name of its author in about 190 BC, one Jesus ben Sirach, who was probably a scribe. The main title represents Latin *Liber ecclesiasticus*, 'ecclesiastical book', otherwise 'church book', so named from its practical use as a book of instruction in the church. The name of the book is similar to that of ECCLESIASTES, with which it should not be confused, although both are books of 'wisdom'.

Echo In Greek mythology, the name is that of the nymph who when spurned by Narcissus pined away until only her voice was left. It is simply the Greek word *ēkhō*, 'echo', itself related to *ēkhē*, 'sound'. In other words, the nymph was an echo personified.

Echo and the Bunnymen The British post-punk rock band, formed in Liverpool in 1977, adopted a name that was based on *Echo*, their nickname for their drum machine. *Bunnymen*, perhaps inspired by *bunny girl*, suggests someone who talks or 'rabbits' a lot. The band soon 'fired' Echo and took on a real live drummer, Pete de Freitas.

Eclogues The title of Virgil's pastoral poems, also known as the *Bucolics*, derives from Greek *eklogē*, 'choice', 'selection', implying a poem that has been 'selected' from a larger work. In the plural, as here, the term simply applies to a set of poems, not necessarily ones that had earlier appeared elsewhere.

Ecuador The South American country has a name that is the Spanish word for 'equator', since the equator runs across it, a little to the north of its capital, QUITO, whose name was that of the country as a whole until 1830. In many European languages the name of Ecuador and the word for 'equator' are one and the same, for example French *Equateur* and *équateur*. *Cp.* EQUATORIAL GUINEA.

Edam The town in the northwest Netherlands, famous for its cheese, grew up by a *dam* across the river *Ye* here. The river name itself represents Old Dutch *e*, 'river'. *Cp.* AMSTERDAM and ROTTERDAM.

Edda The name is that of two medieval collections of Old Norse poems and myths, known respectively as the *Poetic Edda* or *Elder Edda* and the *Prose Edda* or *Young-*

er Edda. The basic name *Edda* is of uncertain meaning. It has been linked with Old Norse *ódhr*, 'poetry', 'metre' and also with *Edda*, the name of the great-grandmother in the Old Norse poem *Rigsthul*.

Eddystone Lighthouse The present lighthouse on the *Eddystone* Rocks south of Plymouth is the fourth to be built there since the 17th century. The name of the rocks themselves is self-descriptive, referring to the sea currents that swirl round them.

Eden The biblical Garden of *Eden* has a name that probably means simply 'plain', from a Sumerian word *edin* in this sense. The Jews interpreted the name as meaning 'delightful', from Hebrew *'éden*. This sense is reflected in the Vulgate, where the name is translated by Latin *Paradisum voluptatis*, 'paradise of delight'. *See also* ADAM, PARADISE.

Edessa The ancient city of northern Mesopotamia, now the Turkish town of *Urfa*, was so named in the time of the Seleucids (4th to 1st century BC) after the identically named city in western Macedonia, Greece. It had earlier had the Syriac name of *Urhai*, and this gave the Turkish city's modern name.

Edgar The name is Old English in origin, from *ēad*, 'prosperity' and *gār*, 'spear', implying a successful warrior. The name was popularized by the 10th-century king *Edgar*.

Edgbaston The well-known cricket ground takes its name from the district of Birmingham where it is located. The name itself means '*Ecgbeald*'s farm'.

Edge Hill, Battle of The battle was the indecisive first one of the Civil War, in 1642, between Charles I and the Parliamentarians. It took place on the Warwickshire hill ridge of the name, not far from Banbury, with the name itself simply denoting an escarpment, a 'hill with an edge'.

Edgware Early records of the name of this northern district of London show it to have have had the meaning '*Ecgi*'s weir'. It is not known who Ecgi was, but the weir would probably have been a fishing enclo-

sure in what is now the small stream called Edgware Brook.

Edict of Nantes The edict was the law promulgated by Henry IV that granted religious and civil liberties to the Protestants of France. He did so on 30 April 1598 in the city of NANTES, in northwest France. The edict was revoked by Louis XIV in 1685.

Edinburgh The name of the Scottish capital is usually interpreted as 'castle of *Edwin*', the latter being the 7th-century king of Northumbria who is said to have built the original fort here on the site of the present medieval Edinburgh Castle. But the name was recorded before his time, as *Eidyn* in about AD 600, so cannot refer to him. The true origin is probably in a Celtic phrase meaning 'fort on a slope', the 'fort' being Gaelic *dùn*. To this, Old English *burh*, also meaning 'fort', was added when the original sense had been lost. *See also* DUNEDIN.

Edirne The Turkish city evolved its name as a 'smoothed-down' form of Greek *Adrianopolis*, 'Hadrian's city', for the Roman emperor *Hadrian* who rebuilt it in about AD 125. This same emperor gave the name of HADRIAN'S WALL in Britain.

Edith The name is somewhat similar to EDGAR, since it derives from Old English *ēad*, 'prosperity' and *gȳth*, 'strife', implying a person successful in battle. It was borne by St *Edith* (962–984), daughter of King Edgar, following the Anglo-Saxon custom whereby children were given the same name element as that of their father.

Edmonds The name means 'son of *Edmond*', the French spelling of EDMUND. *Edmondson* means the same.

Edmonton The capital of Alberta, Canada, was so named in 1877 after *Fort Edmonton*, originally built some 20 miles (32 km) from the present town in 1795. The fort was destroyed by the Indians in 1807 and rebuilt the following year on the site of today's city. It was then given its name by William Tomison after *Edmonton* near London (now in Greater London), as a compliment to his secretary, John Peter Prudens, a clerk of the Hudson's Bay Company, who had been born there.

Edmund The Old English name derives from *ēad*, 'prosperity' and *mund*, 'protector'. This implies a person who will be a successful defender in battle and win profitable victories. Of all the early saints of the name, the best-known is the 9th-century king of East Anglia who gave the name of BURY ST EDMUNDS.

Edmund Ironside The nickname of Edmund II (d. 1016), king of England, alludes to his bravery in battle, and is recorded in the *Anglo-Saxon Chronicle*. He was the son of ETHELRED THE UNREADY. *Ironside* was also a derisive nickname given Cromwell by the Royalists. It subsequently passed to his soldiers.

Edna In the Old Testament, the name is that of the mother of Sarah. It probably derives from Hebrew *'ēdnāh*, 'rejuvenation', although some have associated it with the Garden of EDEN, in which case it may mean 'delight'. Many bearers of the name in modern times have been given it as an English form of the Irish name *Eithne*, meaning 'kernel', implying that the person is the best or most valuable in a family.

Edo The former name of TOKYO (to 1868) meant 'gate of the bay', from Japanese *e*, 'bay' and *to*, 'door', 'gate'. This can be understood as 'estuary', and refers to the location of Tokyo at the point where the river Sumida enters Tokyo Bay. For another name relating to this same bay, *see* YOKOHAMA, now part of the urban agglomeration of which Tokyo is the centre.

Edward The Old English name derives from *ēad*, 'prosperity' and *weard*, 'guard', implying a person who is a good guardian of what he owns, and that he has something worth guarding in the first place. The name has been borne by many English kings and royal persons, from *Edward* the Confessor in the 11th century down to Prince *Edward* (1964–   ) in present times.

Edward, Lake The large lake of central Africa, between Uganda and Zaïre, was discovered by Stanley in 1888 and named as a compliment to *Edward*, Prince of Wales, the future Edward VII (1841–1910). He was the son of Queen VICTORIA, whose name was given to Africa's largest lake.

Edwards The name means 'son of EDWARD'. *Edwardson* has the same meaning more obviously.

Edwin The name is Old English in origin, representing *ēad*, 'prosperity' and *wine*, 'friend', suggesting a good ally and capable protector. A noted bearer of the name is the 7th-century king of Northumbria, popularly but erroneously associated with the name of EDINBURGH.

Eeyore The name of the old grey donkey of A.A. Milne's *Winnie the Pooh* books represents the traditional *hee-haw* braying of an ass.

Effie *See* EUPHEMIA.

Egbert The Old English name derives from *ecg*, 'edge' (*i.e.* of a sword) and *beorht*, 'famous' (literally 'bright'), implying a skilled warrior, famed for his victories. *Egbert*, king of Wessex in the 9th century, was the first overall ruler of England.

Egypt The country of northeast Africa was a region known to the Romans as *Ægyptus* and to the Greeks as *Aiguptos*. Both these represent Egyptian *hūt-kā-ptah*, 'temple of the soul of Ptah', from *hūt*, 'temple', *kā*, 'soul' and PTAH, the famous god. This was actually a name of the city of Memphis, which the Greeks adopted for the country as a whole. The Egyptian name of Egypt was *Kemet*, meaning 'black country', probably with reference to the dark skin of the ancient Egyptians. This name was itself borrowed from the biblical name of HAM, son of Noah. The Arabic name of Egypt is *misr*, adopted from that of *Misraim*, one of Ham's sons, so a grandson of Noah. His name in turn comes from Assyrian *misir*, 'fort', which gave the modern Greek name of Cairo, *Misiri*.

Eifel The mountainous massif of western Germany has a name of uncertain origin. It has been explained as representing a form of *Hochfeld*, 'high field', as deriving from Old High German *eiver* (modern German *Eifer*, 'eagerness' (although in what sense is not clear), and of being an alteration of Greek *Euphalia*, as if from *eu*, 'good' and *-phalia* as in WESTPHALIA. Whatever the case, the name gave that of the famous designer of the EIFFEL TOWER.

Eiffel Tower The well-known French landmark, a symbol of Paris and of France itself, was erected for the Paris Exposition of 1889, a centennial commemoration of the French Revolution. The tower is named for its designer, the French engineer Alexandre-Gustave *Eiffel* (1832–1923).

Eights Week The rowing races held in the summer term at Oxford University are so named for the college *eights* (boats with crews of eight) that take part.

Eilat The port that is Israel's only outlet to the Red Sea has a name deriving from Hebrew *elōn*, 'oak'.

Eileen The name is an English spelling of Irish *Eibhlín*, itself derived from the Norman name *Aveline*. This was probably of Germanic origin, but its ultimate meaning remains uncertain.

Eindhoven The name of the city in the southeast Netherlands has evolved from Old Dutch *eind*, 'end' and *hoven*, 'property'. It was thus originally a 'property at the end' (of Woensel, now a district of Eindhoven itself).

Eire The name is the Irish word for IRE-LAND, *which see* for the origin.

Eisenach The industrial city in central Germany has the appropriate name of 'iron place', from a Germanic word that gave modern German *Eisen*, 'iron', referring to the iron deposits known to be here in Roman times. The Austrian town of *Eisenstadt* has a similar name, 'iron town', while *Eisenhüttenstadt*, near Frankfurt an der Oder in eastern Germany, was formed round a metallurgical complex in 1961 and has a name meaning 'ironworks town'.

Eithne *See* EDNA.

Elaine The name developed as a variant of HELEN, so has the same meaning and origin as that name. In Arthurian legend, it was the name of the woman who fell in love with Sir Lancelot, and it was popularized by Tennyson in his *Idylls of the King* (1859):

> Elaine the fair, Elaine the loveable,
> Elaine, the lily maid of Astolat.

Tennyson must have been aware of the origin of the name, as his *Elaine the fair* directly echoes, in person as well as in name, the famous 'fair Helen' of classical mythology.

El Aiún The coastal city of Morocco, formerly the capital of Spanish Sahara, has a name representing Arabic *al-ʿayūn*, 'the springs', from *al*, 'the' and *ʿayūn*, the plural of *ʿayn*, 'spring'.

Elastoplast The brand name for the adhesive surgical dressing is virtually self-descriptive, as an *elastic plaster*. The dressings were originally marketed in the late 1920s as *Elastic Adhesive Bandages*.

Elba The Italian island, Napoleon's first place of exile, takes its name from the *Ilates*, a Ligurian people whose own name is of uncertain origin. The Greek name of Elba is *Aithalia*, from *aithalos*, 'soot', referring to the pollution (even then) of metalworks here in classical times.

Elbe The central European river, flowing through the Czech Lands and Germany, has a name that probably means either 'river' or 'white', in the latter case from the Indoeuropean root word *albh* that also gave ALBION.

Elche The ancient city in southern Spain was known to the Romans as *Illici* and to the Greeks as *Heliki*. It has been suggested that the origin of the name lies in an Iberian root element *al*, meaning 'salt'.

Elder The name means what it says, and would originally have been given as a nickname to denote the *elder* of two identically named people. *Cp.* OLD and contrast YOUNG.

Eldorado The fabled land of South America, said to be rich in treasure and eagerly sought by 16th-century Spanish explorers, has a name that is Spanish *el dorado*, 'the golden one'. According to some accounts, the name was originally that of a local ruler here who was said to coat his naked body with gold dust during festivals then plunge into a lake or river to wash the dust off. The geographical region traditionally associated with this legend is usually given as that of Bogotá, Colombia, although the land of Eldorado was said to be in the valleys of the Amazon or Orinoco.

Eleanor The name has long been associated with HELEN, but is probably of Germanic origin, based on the root word *ali*, 'foreign'. It was introduced to England in the 12th century by *Eleanor* of Aquitaine, the French wife of Henry II.

Electra The unfortunate daughter of Agamemnon and Clytemnestra, who prevailed on her brother Orestes to avenge their father's death by killing his murderers, the equally tragic Clytemnestra and her lover Aegisthus, has despite it all a propitious name, from Greek *ēlektron*, 'amber', literally 'shining', 'radiant' (from which English *electric* also derives). The relevance of the name in Electra's case is still disputed.

Electric Light Orchestra The British pop group, formed in 1971, began by playing classically influenced music in a band that included orchestral instruments such as cellos. The name refers to their electric instruments, while also punning on 'electric light' and 'light orchestra'.

Electric Prunes The American psychedelic rock group, formed in Seattle in 1965, chose a surreal name that encapsulated the psychedelic values of the time.

Elephant and Castle The traffic junction in southeast London takes its name from an 18th-century tavern here, whose own name derives from the crest of the Cutlers' Company that shows an *elephant* with a howdah resembling a small *castle* on its back, the connection being the use of ivory for making knife-handles. The name is not thus a corruption of *Infanta of Castile*, as popularly stated (and doggedly defended by some). The name is found for pubs today elsewhere in the country.

Elephantine The ancient Egyptian city on the island of the same name in the river Nile, opposite Aswan, has a Greek name representing *elephantinos*, 'of ivory', from *elephas*, 'elephant', 'ivory', translating the Egyptian name *Ābū*, 'elephant'. The Greek word for 'elephant' is a curiosity, since it comprises two parts that each independently mean 'elephant'. The *el-* is a Hamitic root element, which gave words for 'elephant' in Semitic languages such as Hebrew *pīl*, Arabic *fīl* and hence Turkish *fil*, among others. The *-ephas* represents Egyptian *ābū*, which is found in Sanskrit and Hindi *ibha*, Coptic *ebu*, and Latin *ebur*, 'ivory', with English *ivory* also related. The modern name of the island is *Jazirat Aswan*, 'Aswan Island'. *Elephantine* is pronounced either 'Elephantiny', rhyming with *tiny*, or 'Elephanteeny', rhyming with *teeny*.

Eleusis The ancient Greek city that is famous as the site of the Eleusinian mysteries (the religious festival held here in classical times) has a name that probably derives from Greek *eleusis*, 'arrival', 'coming', in the sense of a place where people gathered. *Cp.* ELYSIUM.

El Faiyûm The historic city in northern Egypt has a Coptic name, deriving from *Fiom*, 'the lake', with the initial *F* representing the definite article, and *iom* meaning 'sea', 'lake'. The city lies in the bed of the ancient Lake Moeris, and is famous for its archaeological finds. The *El* of the name is the Arabic definite article ('the'), added when the original name was no longer meaningful.

Elgin The cathedral city in northeast Scotland has a name meaning somewhat unexpectedly 'little Ireland', from *Ealg*, one of the early Gaelic names for Ireland, and the diminutive ending *-in*. The name would have denoted a colony here of Scots who had immigrated from Ireland. *See also* ELGIN MARBLES.

Elgin Marbles The Elgin Marbles are not marbles from ELGIN but an assortment of unique 5th-century BC Greek sculptures brought from the Parthenon in Athens to England by Thomas Bruce, seventh Earl of *Elgin* (1766–1841) in the early years of the 19th century. They are now in the British Museum. His first shipment was lost at sea.

Eli Familiar in the Old Testament as the priest and judge who raised the future prophet Samuel, *Eli* has a name that derives from Hebrew *'Ēlī*, 'high'.

Elijah The famous Israelite prophet, whose deeds are told in 1 and 2 *Kings*, derives his name from Hebrew *Ēlīyāhū*, literally 'my God is Yah', *i.e.* Jehovah, the personal name of God.

Elisha The Old Testament prophet who was the successor to Elijah has a name that represents Hebrew *Elīŝā*, 'God is salvation'.

Elizabeth The name is of biblical origin, and in the New Testament is that of the mother of John the Baptist. Its origin is in Hebrew *Elīšeba*, 'my God gave the oath'. In the Authorized Version of the Bible, Elizabeth's name is spelled with an *s*. It is famous not only for being a royal name (of two reigning queens, as well as the mother of the second Elizabeth) but for having a whole range of diminutives. Some of the best-known are *Bessie, Betty, Elsa, Libby, Lisa, Liz, Liza*.

Elizabeth There are various towns and cities of the name in the English-speaking world. That in New Jersey is named for the wife of Sir George Carteret, who founded the city in 1664. That in South Australia, near Adelaide, was planned as a satellite town for the latter city in 1955 and named for Queen *Elizabeth* II. The American city was known as *Elizabethtown* until 1740.

Elizabeth College The Guernsey public school for boys was founded in 1563 by Queen *Elizabeth* I and is named for her.

Elizabeth Garrett Anderson Hospital The London hospital in Euston Road, one of only three in England run exclusively by and for women, was originally founded in Seymour Place in 1866 as the *St Mary's Dispensary for Women and Children* by *Elizabeth Garrett Anderson* (1836–1917), the first woman in England to qualify in medicine. It was moved to its present site in 1888 and renamed for its founder on her death. Dr Anderson retained her maiden name of *Garrett* after her marriage.

Elizabeth Restaurant The well-known Oxford restaurant opened as a tea house soon after the Second World War and took its name from a subsequent manageress, *Elizabeth* Woods, who opened a restaurant on the first floor.

Ellen The name originated as a variant of HELEN, though it has now come to be adopted in its own right.

Ellesmere Island The Canadian island in the Arctic Ocean, in the Northwest Territories, was discovered by William Baffin (of BAFFIN BAY) in 1616, but was not named until 1852. It was then given the name of Francis Egerton (originally Leveson-Gower), first Earl of *Ellesmere* (1800–1857), whose own title came from *Ellesmere*, Shropshire.

Elliott The name is either a diminutive of ELLIS or evolved from a former Old English personal name *Elyat*, meaning 'noble battle'. The name is spelled in various ways, with both single and double *l* and *t* in different combinations.

Ellis The surname derives from a medieval personal name which was itself a pet form of ELIJAH.

Ellis Island The island in Upper New York Bay that was the reception centre for European immigrants arriving in America from 1892 to 1943 takes its name from Samuel *Ellis*, who owned it in the 1770s. It is now a National Historic Site.

Elmer More common in America than Britain, the name was adopted from the surname, which in turn was originally an Old English personal name, from *æthele*, 'noble' and *mære*, 'famous', an entirely propitious combination.

Elne The historic town near Perpignan in southern France was originally known as *Illiberis*, from Aquitanian *ili*, 'town' and *beri*, 'new'. In the early 4th century AD it was refounded by Constantine the Great as *Castrum Helenae*, 'Helen's fort', after the emperor's mother, *Helena*. This gradually evolved to the present name.

Elohim The word is used in the Hebrew text of the Bible as a name for God, and is usually translated simply as *God* in the English Bible, for example: 'In the beginning God [*elohim*] created the heaven and the earth' (*Genesis* 1.1). It is grammatically the plural form of the Hebrew word *eloha*, 'god', but is treated as a singular, the plural conveying uniqueness. *See also* JEHOVAH.

El Paso The city in Texas lies at the foot of Mount Franklin below a pass where the Rio Grande emerges from the Rockies. The original site was thus in 1598 given the Spanish name of *El Paso del Norte*, 'the pass of the north'. The name was later shortened to *El Paso*. The present city was not laid out until 1859, however.

El Salvador The name of the country in Central America is Spanish for 'the saviour', this being the title of Christ regarded as saving mankind from sin. It was originally given in 1524 by Spanish colonists to the fort situated where the country's capital, SAN SALVADOR, is now, and spread from there to the whole territory.

Elsa *See* ELIZABETH.

Elsan The proprietary type of portable toilet takes its name from the initials of its inventor in 1924, the chemical manufacturer *E*phraim *L*ouis Jackson, together with the first syllable of '*san*itation'.

Elsinore The Danish port, famous as the scene of Shakespeare's *Hamlet*, has the Danish name *Helsingør*. This probably represents a tribal name followed by Old Norwegian *ör*, 'tongue of land'.

Elton The name derives from any of the places so called, such as the village near Stockton-on-Tees or that near Birmingham. The place-name itself is usually based on the Old English personal name *Ella* or *Elli*.

Ely The cathedral town northeast of Cambridge has a name that means 'eel district', from Old English *æl*, 'eel' and *gē*, 'district' (*cp*. SURREY). The district would have been an administrative region in Anglo-Saxon times. The name was later associated with Old English *īeg*, 'island', appropriately enough for a town on an 'island' of land in the Fens. But it is the eels that gave the original name.

Elysium The name for the dwelling-place of the blessed after death in Greek mythology derives from Greek *eleusis*, 'arrival', 'coming', as the designation of a place where people gather. *Cp*. ELEUSIS. An alternative name for Elysium is *Elysian Fields*. *See also* CHAMPS ELYSÉES.

Emanuel School The London public school for boys originated from *Emanuel* Hospital, founded in Westminster by the will of Anne Sackville, Lady Dacre in 1594. In 1883 it moved to its present site on the edge of Wandsworth Common when it took over the disused premises of the Royal Victoria Patriotic Fund Orphanage. For the dedication, *see* EMMANUEL.

Ember Days In the Christian church, especially among Roman Catholics and Anglicans, the name is used of the groups of three days each of prayer and fasting, falling on the Wednesday, Friday and Saturday after the first Sunday in Lent, Holy

Cross Day (14 September), and St Lucia's Day (13 December). By false association with ASH WEDNESDAY and the prayer and fasting of Lent, the name has been linked with *embers*. However, it actually derives from Old English *ymbrene*, 'circuit', literally 'running round', referring to the regular occurrence of the days round the year.

Emilia-Romagna The first part of the name of the region of north central Italy derives from the Via *Aemilia* here, the Roman road that was built in the 2nd century BC under the consulate of Marcus *Aemilius* Lepidus. The second half of the name relates to the fact that in the 8th century five cities here, till then under Lombard rule, passed to the pope of *Rome*. Until 1948 the region was simply known as *Emilia*.

Emily The name has come to be associated with AMELIA, but unlike that name originated as the feminine form of the Roman *nomen* (clan name) *Aemilius*, itself probably from *aemilius*, 'rival'.

Emma The name, made famous by Jane Austen's heroine (1816), is of Germanic origin and arose from the first part of a name such as *Ermintrude*, where the element *ermen* means 'entire'.

Emmanuel The name is used in the Bible for the promised Messiah, with the spelling *Immanuel* in the Old Testament, and *Emmanuel* in the New. The derivation is in Hebrew *'Immānūēl*, literally 'with us (is) God', or as the New Testament more elegantly explains it: 'And they shall call his name Emmanuel, which being interpreted is, God with us' (*Matthew* 1.23). *See also* EMMANUEL COLLEGE.

Emmanuel College The Cambridge college was founded by Sir Walter Mildmay in 1584 for the education of Protestant preachers, its name being chosen by the founder. The scriptural name, with its meaning of 'God with us', was widely adopted by Protestants and Puritans in a number of contexts, including those that were not in themselves overtly religious, such as the headings of books or records. Shakespeare refers to this use in *Henry VI, Part 2* (1590) when the Clerk of Chatham is brought before Jack Cade:

> CADE Come hither, sirrah, I must examine thee: What is thy name?

CLERK Emmanuel.
DICK They use to write it on the top of letters: 'twill go hard with you.

Emmaus The town of ancient Palestine, on the road to which Jesus appeared after his Resurrection to two of his disciples (*Luke* 24.13), has a name of Aramaic origin, from *ḥammat*, 'hot spring'. (*Cp*. HAM, son of Noah.) Its name today is *'Imwas*, in the part of Jordan occupied by Israel.

Emmy The name is that of the gold-plated statuette awarded to a deserving television programme or performer by the American Academy of Television Arts and Sciences. It is said to be an alteration of *Immy*, a colloquial term for an *im*age orthicon tube in a television camera, but could equally have evolved from 'Acad*emy*'. It also happens to suggest the personal name EMMA. Its British equivalent is the BAFTA award made by the British Academy of Film and Television Arts.

Empedocles The name of the 5th-century BC Greek philosopher, who held that the world is composed of the four elements air, fire, earth and water, has the meaning 'eternal glory', from Greek *empedos*, 'steadfast', 'lasting' and *kleos*, 'report', 'fame', 'repute'. However, according to legend Empedocles committed suicide by throwing himself into Mount Etna in an attempt to convince followers of his divinity. His name could thus be seen as the cause of his ruin through his endeavour to embody it. Matthew Arnold pondered on the import of his act in his famous poem *Empedocles on Etna* (1852).

Emperor Concerto The nickname for Beethoven's Piano Concerto No 5 in E flat major (1809) is perhaps intended to compliment Napoleon, who had crowned himself emperor five years before. But Beethoven himself would not have so named it (*see* EROICA SYMPHONY), and the name is not used in continental Europe. It may simply have been regarded as generally appropriate for a 'majestic' work, which was in the event the composer's final piano concerto.

Emperor Quartet Haydn's String Quartet in C major Op 76 No 3 (1797) is so named because the slow movement is a set of variations on the tune he wrote for the EMPEROR'S HYMN.

Emperor's Hymn The former Austrian national anthem is so named because it was composed by Haydn in 1797 for the Holy Roman *Emperor* Francis, the future Francis II of Austria, with the commission for the work specifying that the anthem should rival *God Save the King*. The composer based the melody on that of a Croatian folksong. The hymn (with different words) later became the German national anthem, *Deutschland über Alles*, and is familiar in the English-speaking world as the hymn tune usually known as *Austria*, with words beginning 'Glorious things of thee are spoken'. *See also* EMPEROR QUARTET.

Empire State Building The famous New York skyscraper was built in 1931 and named for New York State, popularly known as the *Empire State* for its leading position in population, wealth and commercial enterprise.

Ems The river of western Germany has a name that probably represents a Germanic root word *ame*, meaning 'current', 'river'. The spa town of *Ems* or *Bad Ems*, near Koblenz, has a name of identical origin. It is not on the *Ems*, however, but the *Lahn*.

Ena The name is an English form of Irish *Eithne*, which also gave EDNA (*which see* for the origin).

Encaenia The annual commemoration of founders and benefactors at Oxford University, held in June, takes its name from the Latin form of Greek *enkainia*, 'feast of dedication', comprising *en*, 'in' and *kainos*, 'new'. The commemoration is part of the annual degree ceremony, and specifically refers to the *dedication* of the Sheldonian Theatre in 1669, when the degree ceremony was transferred there from the University Church of St Mary the Virgin.

Enceladus The name of the giant who rebelled against the gods (and was killed by a stone thrown at him by Athena) appears to derive from Greek *egkeleusma*, 'encouragement'.

Enderby Land The region of Antarctica, in the Australian Antarctic Territory, was discovered in 1831 by the English navigator John Briscoe. He named it after the whaling firm of Samuel *Enderby* & Sons, who had financed his expedition and who owned the ship, the *Tula*, on which he undertook it.

Endor The town of ancient Palestine, famous for the biblical 'witch of Endor' sought by Saul (1 *Samuel* 28.7), has a Hebrew name, from *'ēn-dōr*, 'spring of time'. *Cp.* EN-GEDI.

Endymion The name of the handsome youth loved by the moon goddess Selene, who visited him every night, is traditionally derived from Greek *enduō*, 'I enter', referring to Selene's seduction of her loved one, and of his answering love for her.

Engadine The upper part of the valley of the river Inn in Switzerland has a name that may represent Romansch *en cò d'Oen*, 'at the head of the Inn'.

En-gedi The village of ancient Palestine, mentioned in the Old Testament (*Joshua* 15.62), has a name that represents Hebrew *'ēn-gedī*, 'spring of the kid'. *Cp.* EN-DOR.

Engels The Russian city on the river Volga opposite Saratov was so named in 1931 in honour of Friedrich *Engels* (1820–1895), the German socialist leader and colleague of Karl Marx. It was founded in 1747, and was originally known as *Pokrovka* (after 1914 *Pokrovsk*), after its church, which was dedicated to the Protection of the Virgin (Russian *Pokrov*, literally 'covering').

England The largest country of the British Isles has a name that derives from that of the ANGLES, who came from what is now northern Germany to settle here in the 5th and 6th centuries AD. The origin can be seen even more clearly in some of the foreign names for England, such as French *Angleterre*, literally 'Angle-land'.

English The name of the inhabitants of ENGLAND (and sometimes, loosely, of Britain as a whole), together with their language, derives from that of the Germanic people who gave the land its own name, the ANGLES. The final *-ish* developed as a suffix denoting an adjective, and is found in the name of many peoples and their languages, such as Ir*ish*, Dan*ish*, Span*ish* and Swed*ish*. Other forms of it occur in the names Fren*ch*, Dut*ch*, Scot*ch*, Wel*sh* and even Man*x*. *England* and *English* are unique in being the only words in English

to have an *e* pronounced as *i* in a stressed position.

English Channel The sea passage between England and France is named distinctively by each country. To the British, it is the *English* Channel or simply the *Channel*. To the French it is *La Manche*, literally 'the sleeve', for its shape, with the 'cuff' as the Strait of Dover, or *Pas de Calais*, as the French call it. (Somewhat confusingly the French name for LA MANCHA, the plateau of central Spain, is also *La Manche*, although that name has quite a different origin.) The English name has a classical precedent from the Romans, who called it *Oceanus Britannicus*. The Strait of Dover was known to them as *fretum Britannicum*, 'strait of Britain', although the word after *fretum* could equally be *Caletanum*, 'of Calais', *Gallicum*, 'of Gaul', or *Morinorum*, 'of the Morini' (a people of Belgic Gaul who lived by the North Sea).

English Suites The six keyboard suites by Bach, composed in about 1715, are said to be so named since they were specially composed 'for the English'.

Enid The name is generally regarded as being of Celtic origin, but its exact meaning is still uncertain. It has been linked with Welsh *enaid*, 'soul'. In the Arthurian romances, *Enid* is the patient wife of Geraint.

Enigma Variations Elgar's popular orchestral work, first performed in 1899, has a name that is (perhaps deliberately) an *enigma* itself. It is properly the name of the theme on which the variations are based, and may be a pun on the composer's own name, of which it is a sort of free 'variation'. *See also* NIMROD.

Enlightenment, The The name of the 18th-century movement that challenged existing political, moral, religious and other beliefs was a translation of its German name, *Aufklärung*. The name implies the shedding of a new *light* on traditional doctrines and values.

Enniskillen The town in Co Fermanagh, Northern Ireland, has a name that represents Irish *Inis Ceithleann*, 'Cethlenn's island', referring to its location on an island in the river Erne. The British Army regiment known as the *Inniskilling* Fusiliers take their name from the town. They were raised in 1689 for the express purpose of defending it on behalf of the Protestant king William of Orange against the Catholic forces of James II.

Enoch The biblical name is that of the son of Cain and father of the long-lived Methuselah. It derives from Hebrew *Hānōkh*, probably meaning 'enlightened'.

Enschede The city in the eastern Netherlands has a name that represents Old Dutch *Aneschedhe*, from *ane*, 'at', 'on' and *schedhe* (modern German *Scheide*), 'boundary', 'border'. Enschede is close to the frontier with Germany.

Entre-Deux-Mers The name, French for 'between two seas', is that of the wine-growing region between two *rivers*, the Dordogne and the Garonne, in southern France.

Eothen The full title of A.W. Kinglake's popular account of his adventures is *Eothen, or, Traces of Travel Brought Home from the Near East* (1844). The first word represents Greek *ēōthen*, 'from dawn', that is, 'from the east', deriving from *ēōs*, 'dawn', with the particle *-then*, added to nouns to denote motion from a place.

Eothen School The public day school for girls in Caterham, Surrey, was founded in 1892 and appears to have been named for Kinglake's book EOTHEN. The school was established at a time when there was a keen interest in the provision of educational opportunities for girls, and the name may thus, in view of its original Greek meaning, have been given symbolically to refer to the 'dawn' of women's education.

Epaminondas The Greek Theban statesman and general of the 4th century BC has a name that appears to derive from an ancestor named *Epamnon*, itself probably based on Greek *epamuntōr*, 'helper', 'defender'.

Épernay The town in northeast France, on the river Marne, was known to the Romans as *Sparnacum*, and the present name is a development of this. The Roman name is based on Gaulish *eperno*, 'thorn'.

Ephesus The ancient town of Asia Minor has a name that may derive from Greek *ephoros*, 'overseer', 'ruler', with reference to its importance as a religious centre and to the fact that it was specifically 'a worshipper of the great goddess Diana' (*Acts* 19.35). It was to the inhabitants of Ephesus that St Paul addressed his Epistle to the *Ephesians*.

Ephraim In the Old Testament, the name is that of one of the sons of Joseph. It derives from Hebrew *Ephrayim*, 'very fruitful', and is so explained in the Old Testament: 'And the name of the second called he Ephraim: for God hath caused me to be fruitful in the land of my affliction' (*Genesis* 41.52).

Ephrata The former name of Bethlehem, mentioned in the Bible (*Genesis* 35.16), is Hebrew in origin with a sense identical to that of the personal name EPHRAIM. It thus means 'fruitful'. *Cp.* BETHLEHEM itself, which has a similar meaning.

Epicurus The 3rd-century BC Greek philosopher, who held that the highest good is pleasure, has a name that represents Greek *epikouros*, 'helper', 'ally'. His name gave modern English *epicure* as a term for a gourmet (as distinct from a gourmand).

Epidaurus The ancient port in Greece, in the northeast Peloponnese, has a name that may represent Greek *epidasus*, 'rather bushy', from *epi*, 'on' and *dasus*, 'thick', 'dense'. The reference would be to the vegetation here.

Epigoni In Greek mythology, the name is used collectively for the sons of the Seven against Thebes who avenged their fathers by destroying Thebes. It means simply 'descendants', from Greek *epigonos*, literally 'born after'.

Epiphany The Christian festival, celebrated on 6 January, is in the Western Church that of the manifestation of Christ to the Magi (the 'Three Wise Men'), and in the Eastern Church that of the baptism of Christ. The former is told in *Matthew* 2.11, the latter in *Matthew* 3.16. Either way the name derives from Greek *epiphaneia*, 'appearing'. *See also* TIFFANY.

Epipsychidion The autobiographical poem by Shelley, published in 1821, has a Greek title that appears to mean 'soul above (my soul)', from *epi-*, 'on', 'above', 'near' and *psukhē*, 'soul', in other words 'beloved', 'soul of my soul'. The poem is devoted to the poet's search for abstract beauty in the earthly form of his various wives and mistresses. At the same time, the title may have been a punning reference to the *epithalamium* that was the conventional marriage song. *See* EPITHALAMION.

Epirus The region of both ancient and modern Greece takes its name from Greek *ēpeiros*, 'mainland', as opposed to the country's large island territory.

Episcopalian The name is used for a member of an *episcopal* church, such as the Episcopal Church of Scotland or the Protestant Episcopal Church of the USA, which unlike many other Protestant churches are governed by bishops (Greek *episkopos*). These two particular churches are autonomous branches of the Anglican Communion.

Epithalamion Spenser's poem of 1595 is a marriage song or bridal hymn, and has a Greek name that is short for *to epithalamion melos*, 'the nuptial song', with *epithalamios* literally meaning 'upon the bridal chamber', from *epi-*, 'upon', 'at' and *thalamos*, 'bedroom'. In classical literature, an *epithalamium* was a conventional poem or song written to celebrate a marriage. In Spenser's case the marriage was to Elizabeth Boyle in 1594. *Cp.* PROTHALAMION, his later poem.

Epping Forest The Essex forest, or what remains of it, takes its name from *Epping*, which in turn has a name meaning 'people of the lookout place', from Old English *yppe*, 'lookout place' (to which modern English *up* is related) and the *-ing* suffix meaning 'people'. The actual 'lookout place' may have been the ancient hill-fort here called Ambersbury Banks, actually in Epping Forest by the B1398 road.

Epsom The Surrey town was formerly famous for its 'salts' from the saline spring here and is popularly associated with the annual Derby horse race. Its name means '*Ebbe*'s homestead', with the personal name followed by Old English *hām*, 'homestead', now represented by the last two letters of the name.

Equatorial Guinea The republic of West Africa, formerly known as *Spanish Guinea*, has a name that indicates its location near

(but not quite on) the *equator* in the extensive region long known as GUINEA. *Cp.* ECUADOR.

Erasmus The basic word behind the name is Greek *erān*, 'to love'. (*Cp.* EROS.) The name is famous from the great Dutch humanist scholar, Desiderius *Erasmus* (1466–1536). He was the illegitimate son of Margaret, a doctor's daughter, and Roger Gerard, a priest, and his original name was *Gerard Gerards*, 'Gerard son of Gerard'. But he was a 'love child', and his adopted name reflects this in both Latin and Greek, from Latin *desiderare*, 'to desire', 'to long for' and Greek *erasmios*, 'beloved'. He was thus the 'longed for loved one'. But there was at that time in any case a fashion for renamings of this type, when a meaningful name would be translated into its classical equivalent, and it is possible that Erasmus thought that *Gerard* meant something like 'loving', so that he 'translated' it accordingly.

Erato The name of the Greek muse of love poetry means simply 'lovely', as one might expect, from Greek *eratos*, related to the name of EROS.

Eratosthenes The name of the 3rd-century BC Greek mathematician and astronomer can be interpreted to mean either 'strength of ERATO' or, more directly, 'lovely strength', either way based on *eratos*, 'lovely' (*cp.* ERASMUS) and *sthenos*, 'strength', 'power'.

Erebus In Greek mythology, the name is that of the god of darkness and son of Chaos. It derives from Phoenician *'ereb*, 'evening', 'west'. *Cp.* MAGHREB.

Erebus, Mount The volcano on Ross Island, Antarctica, was named by the British explorer Sir James Ross after one of the ships of his expedition, the EREBUS. The particular classical name is appropriate for a volcano, with its hidden 'darkness'. A second ship, the *Terror*, gave the name of another volcano here.

Erechtheus The king of Athens, who sacrificed his daughter Chthonia because the oracle at Delphi said this was the only way to win the war against the Eleusinians, has a name that appears to relate to that of his daughter, and to be a shortened form of *Erechthothonios*, literally 'earthshaker', from Greek *erekhthō*, 'I rend', 'I break' and *khthōn*, 'earth'. 'Earthshaker' was also one of the names of Poseidon (or Neptune) in his capacity as a bringer of earthquakes. In the case of Erechtheus, however, it was not the earth he 'broke' but his daughter, Chthonia ('of the earth').

Erewhon Samuel Butler's satirical novel of 1872 has a name that is an anagram of *nowhere*. This was a dig at the title of Thomas More's UTOPIA (1516), which has the same meaning. The name is a near reversal of *nowhere*, and characters in the novel have names that are true reversals, such as *Yram*, the jailer's beautiful daughter, and *Senoj Nosnibor*, with whom the narrator, Higgs, lodges. Higgs finally marries Nosnibor's daughter *Arowhena*, whose name is a near-anagram of *Erewhon* itself, with the feminine ending *-a*.

Erfurt The city in central Germany derives its name from Old High German *erp*, 'dark' and *ford*, 'ford'. Erfurt is on the river Gera.

Eric The name is Scandinavian in origin, from Old Norse *einn*, 'one' and *ríkr*, 'ruler', in other words 'monarch'. Not surprisingly, the name has been popular (in the spelling *Erik*) for kings of Norway, Sweden and Denmark. Two famous 10th-century bearers of the name are *Eric* the Red, who explored and named Greenland, and *Eric* Bloodaxe, who killed seven of his eight brothers to secure the throne (hence his nickname).

Eridanus The name is that of a long, winding constellation in the southern hemisphere extending from Orion to Hydrus. It is traditionally linked with that of the river *Eridanus* in classical mythology, into which Phaethon fell after his attempt to drive the chariot of his father Helios, the god of the sun. The river's name has itself been equated with that of ACHERNAR, the constellation's brightest star.

Erie, Lake The lake between the United States and Canada takes its name from that of an Indian people here. Their own name means 'long tail', probably referring to the panther or puma, their original totemic animal.

Erin *See* IRELAND.

Erinyes The older Greek name for the EUMENIDES, or Furies, is of uncertain origin and meaning. There may be a link with the prefix *eri-* used to strengthen the sense of a word, so that they were 'very' something. The singular form of the name is *Erinys*.

Eritrea The province of northern Ethiopia borders the Red Sea. Its name alludes to this location, as it derives from Greek *eruthros*, 'red'. *See also* RED SEA itself.

Erlking, The Schubert's famous song of 1816, in German *Der Erlkönig*, was a setting to music of Goethe's poem of the same name, published in 1782. In German folklore, the erlking was the king of the elves who lived in the Black Forest and lured children to their deaths. Although now understood as meaning 'elf-king', German *Erlkönig* really means 'king of the alders', from German *Erle*, 'alder'. The name arose as a mistranslation by Goethe's fellow poet, Johann Gottfried von Herder, of Danish *ellerkonge*, 'elf-king', which he confused with *elverkonge*, 'alder-king'. The misrendering appeared in his *Stimmen der Völker in Liedern* ('Voices of the Peoples in Songs', 1778). The true German word for 'elf-king' is thus *Elfenkönig*.

Ermine Street The well-known Roman road, running through London from the south of England to the north, takes its name from the *Earningas*, the people through whose territory it passed. Their own name means 'people of *Earna*', but they are commemorated in the name of no known settlement, unlike the people who gave the name of WATLING STREET. Some sources mistakenly derive the name from that of the 1st-century AD German national hero *Arminius*.

Erne, Lough The large lake in Northern Ireland takes its name from a people known as the *Erni* or *Ernai*, who were said to live here at a time before the lake existed. The meaning of their own name is unknown.

Ernest The name is Germanic in origin, and means what it says, implying someone who is serious or *earnest*, especially in battle.

Eroica Symphony The popular name of Beethoven's Third Symphony (1803–04) derives from its full original title when published, *Sinfonia eroica, composta per festiggiare il Sovvenire di un grand Uomo* ('Heroic symphony, composed to celebrate the memory of a great man'). The 'great man' was Napoleon, and Beethoven had originally planned to name the work *Bonaparte*, but did not do so on learning that Napoleon had betrayed the democratic cause by crowning himself emperor in 1804. *Cp.* EMPEROR CONCERTO.

Eros The name of the Greek god of love is simply the word for 'love' itself, and specifically sexual desire. Hence English *erotic*. The statue popularly known as *Eros* at Piccadilly Circus, London was actually intended to represent the Angel of Christian Charity, and its official name is the *Shaftesbury Memorial Fountain*. But the winged figure with a bow certainly suggests the boy Cupid, and the statue is a well-known meeting-place for young lovers. It was long famous, too, for its flower girls, selling posies for sweethearts.

Erse The name is an alternative for the GAELIC language, and especially for Irish Gaelic. It relates specifically to the latter, since it derives from Lowland Scots *Erisch*, 'Irish'. Irish Gaelic is traditionally regarded as the literary form of Gaelic. *See also* IRELAND.

Erskine The Scottish name derives from a place-name, that of what is now the town of *Erskine* near Renfrew. The town's name is almost certainly Celtic in origin, but its meaning remains obscure.

Erzgebirge The mountains between Germany and the Czech Lands have a German name meaning 'ore mountains', referring to their mineral wealth. Minerals and metals found naturally here include gold, silver, lead, copper, tungsten (wolfram) and pitchblende.

Erzurum The historic city in eastern Turkey has a name that represents Arabic *arḍ ar-rūm*, 'land of Rome', that is, of the Byzantine Christians. It arose from a Byzantine fortress that fell to the Arabs in the 8th century.

Esau Famous in the Bible as the elder twin brother of Jacob, to whom he sold his birthright, *Esau* has a name that derives from Hebrew *'Ēsāw*, 'hairy'. The reference is to Esau's appearance at birth: 'And the first came out red, all over like an hairy garment; and they called his name Esau' (*Genesis* 25.25).

Esbjerg The port in southwest Denmark may have a name that evolved from an earlier *Eskebjerg*, 'ash-tree hill' or 'ash-tree rock', from Old Norse *eski*, 'ash-tree place' and *berg*, 'hill' or *bjarg*, 'rock'.

Escorial The village of central Spain is famous for its 16th-century architectural complex, comprising a monastery, palace and college built by Philip II. Its name does not refer to this, however, but is the Spanish word for 'slag-heap', 'dump', relating to the refuse and workings of mines formerly here.

Esdras The two books of the Apocrypha, 1 and 2 *Esdras*, are respectively known to biblical scholars as *Greek Ezra* and *Ezra Apocalypse*, the first to distinguish it from the biblical book of *Ezra*, written in Hebrew, the second to denote the nature and content of the book, which is a series of visions to the seer Salathiel-*Ezra*. Either way, the origin of the name *Esdras* is exactly the same as that of EZRA.

Esher The Surrey town has a name that means literally 'ash share', from Old English *æsc*, 'ash' and *scearu*, 'share'. This denotes a district of ash-trees.

Eskimo The name of the people of Greenland and northern Canada, and that of their language, derives from a local Indian word *eskimantsik*, literally 'eaters of raw meat', from *eski*, 'raw' and *mants*, 'he eats'. The Eskimos' own name for themselves is INUIT (*which see*). Their name for Europeans is *Qavdlunat*, 'the big eyebrows'.

Eskişehir The city of west central Turkey has a name that means 'ancient city', from Turkish *eski*, 'ancient' and *şehir*, 'town'. The reference is to the nearby ancient Phrygian city of *Dorylaeum*, now in ruins.

Esmeralda '"Why do they call you La Esmeralda?" asked the poet. [...] She drew from her bosom a sort of small oblong bag [...]; it was covered with green silk, and had in the centre a large boss of green glass, in imitation of an emerald. "Perhaps it's on account of that," said she.' Thus the Gypsy dancer *Esmeralda* explains the origin of her name (the Spanish word for *emerald*) to Pierre Gringoire, in Victor Hugo's *The Hunchback of Notre-Dame* (1831). It was this particular novel that promoted the name generally.

Esmond The name is Old English in origin, comprising *ēst*, 'grace', 'beauty' and *mund*, 'protection'.

Esperanto The name of the well-known artificial language derives from the pseudonym, *Dr Esperanto*, of its creator in 1887, the Polish oculist and philologist Ludwik Zamenhof (1859–1917). His pseudonym is Esperanto for 'hoping one', perhaps at least partly punning on his surname, as German *hoffen* means 'to hope'.

Essen The city in western Germany, the leading industrial centre of the Ruhr, has a name that ultimately derives from the Indoeuropean root element *as*, 'burning', 'dry', also lying behind English *ardent* and *arid*. The reference was probably literal, to a 'burnt' or arid region.

Essenes The name of the religious sect that flourished in Palestine in the 1st centuries BC and AD, and to whom the DEAD SEA SCROLLS have been attributed, is presumably of Hebrew or Aramaic origin, but the precise meaning is uncertain. Suggested origins include Syriac *chase*, plural *chasēn*, 'pious', Hebrew *hāsā*, 'to be silent', or Hebrew *hitsōnim*, 'outsiders', the latter said to be a name used by the Pharisees to refer to their position *outside* orthodox Judaism. The name does not occur in the Bible.

Essex The county of southeast England takes its name from the *East Saxons*, whose kingdom here in the 7th century included not only the present county but also that of Middlesex and much of Hertfordshire.

Esso The well-known brand of petrol has a name that stands for the initials of the *S*tandard *O*il Company, originally founded in the USA in 1870 by J.D. Rockefeller.

Esther The name is familiar in the Bible as that of the young and beautiful Jewish orphan who becomes the wife of the Persian king Ahasuerus and who has a book of the Old Testament named after her. She originally had the Hebrew name *Hadassah*, 'myrtle' (*Esther* 2.7), and *Esther* is said to be a form of this. There are some scholars, however, who derive it from the Persian name *Ishtar*, that of the Babylonian goddess of love and fertility, itself probably meaning 'star'. In the latter respect, *see also* STELLA.

Estonia The Baltic republic takes its name from its indigenous population, the *Estonians*. Their own name may mean 'waterside dwellers', from a Baltic word *aueist*. It is not likely to be related to *east* (German *Est*), despite the appropriateness of this for its location.

Estremadura The region of western Spain and province of Portugal are so named as they are the 'extremity of the DOURO', that is, the territory farthest from this river.

Etchells The name derives from one of the minor places so called, mostly in the north of England. The place-name means 'land added to an estate', from Old English *ēcan*, 'to increase'.

Ethel The Germanic name is the short form of a name such as *Ethelberta* or *Etheldred*, where the first element means 'noble'.

Ethelred the Unready The well-known 10th- and 11th-century king of England has a name deriving from Old English *æthele*, 'noble' and *ræd*, 'counsel', so that in theory he was a good adviser. He himself was poorly advised, however, so that he lacked *ræd* or counsel and acted purely through motives of expediency. The nickname thus puns on his personal name, and did not originally imply that he was 'not ready' or ill-prepared.

Ethiopia The name of the state of northeast Africa represents the Greek word for its native inhabitants. This was *aithiops*, 'burnt appearance', from *aithō*, 'I burn' and *opsis*, 'aspect', 'appearance'. The reference was to their dark skins. The indigenous name for the country is ABYSSINIA. The biblical name for Ethiopia is *Cush*, which in *Genesis* 10.6 is given as the name of one of the sons of Ham, so a grandson of Noah.

Etna The famous volcano, in Sicily, probably derives its name from Phoenician *attūnā*, 'furnace', rather than Greek *aithō*, 'I burn', despite the similarity of sense. The Sicilian name for Etna is *Mongibello*, probably representing Italian *monte bello*, 'beautiful mountain', influenced by Arabic *jabal*, 'mountain'.

Eton The Berkshire town, with its famous public school, lies on the Thames, as its name implies. It derives from Old English *ēg*, 'island' and *tūn*, 'farm'. 'Island' in this sense implies higher land by a river, as is the case with Eton. Many places named *Eaton* have the same origin, although in several instances the first part of the name may derive not from the word for 'island' but from Old English *ēa*, 'river'. Often only early records of the name and a careful study of the topography of the place will show if it is a 'river farm', well watered by a river or streams, or an 'island farm', on raised ground by water.

Etruria The ancient country of central Italy has a name of uncertain origin, but one that is known to equate with that of modern TUSCANY. It also gave English *Etruscan*. The *sc* of these names is found in other western European names of countries and peoples, such as BASQUE, and may ultimately mean 'water'. In the case of Etruria, this could be a reference to the rivers Arno and Tiber, between which it lies.

Euboea The largest island after Crete in the Greek archipelago has a name that means 'rich in cattle', from Greek *eu*, 'well', 'rich' and *bous*, 'ox', 'cow'.

Euclid The name of the famous Greek mathematician means 'well-famed', from Greek *eu*, 'well' and *kleos*, 'fame'.

Eugene The name has the propitious sense 'noble', literally 'well-born', from Greek *eu*, 'well' and *genos*, 'race', 'descent'. *Eugenics* is the study of improving the quality of human life.

Eumenides The Greek name for the Furies, the three avenging goddesses, literally means 'benevolent ones', and was intended euphemistically in order to placate them.

Eunice The name is of Greek origin, meaning 'good victory', from *eu* 'well', 'good' and *nikē*, 'victory'.

Euphemia The Greek name implies a person who is a good orator, from *eu*, 'well' and *phēnai*, 'to speak'. Characters called *Effie* in Victorian novels were so named as a pet form of *Euphemia*.

Euphrates The river of western Asia has a Greek-looking name that is probably not actually of Greek origin. It may derive from Akkadian *ur*, 'river' and *at*, 'father', so that it is the 'father of rivers', so named for its size, or similarly from *u*, 'very' and *pratu*, 'wide'. The Euphrates is mentioned in the Bible as one of the four rivers of Eden, the other three being the Pison, Gihon and Hiddekel (*Genesis* 2.11–14).

Euphrosyne The name of one of the three Graces derives from the Greek word for 'cheery', 'merry', literally 'well minded', from *eu*, 'well' and *phroneō*, 'I think', 'I am disposed'.

Euphues The title of John Lyly's prose romance, remembered today for its peculiarly florid style (*euphuism*), represents the Greek word for 'graceful', literally 'well-grown', from *eu*, 'good' and *phuē*, 'growth'. The full title of the work, in two parts, is *Euphues: The Anatomy of Wit* (1578) and *Euphues and His England* (1580).

Eurasia The name for the continents of *Eur*ope and *Asia* is a blend of both their names. It seems to have first appeared in a German textbook, *Handbuch der Geographie*, published in 1858.

Eure *See* ARAGON.

Eureka The town and port in northwest California was settled in 1850 and named for the state motto, adopted the previous year. The motto was taken from the famous exclamation by Archimedes (Greek *heurēka*, 'I have found (it)') on realizing, while bathing, that the volume of a solid could be calculated by measuring the water displaced when it was immersed. American pioneers used the word to name places where they had discovered gold (as particularly in California) or where a settlement could be favourably made, for example one with a good supply of water.

Euripides The name of the well-known Greek tragedian of the 5th century BC is said to derive from that of the *Euripus*, a narrow strait between Euboea and the Greek mainland, either because he was born near there or because he was inconstant, like its tides, which the ancient Greeks held to occur seven times a day.

177

Euroclydon The name is that of a north or northeast wind in the Middle East, mentioned in the Bible as causing the shipwreck of St Paul: 'a tempestuous wind, called Euroclydon' (*Acts* 27.14). As it stands it derives from Greek *Eurus*, the name of the east wind, itself from *euros*, 'breadth' (*cp*. EUROPE), and *kludōn*, 'wave', 'billow'. But the second part of the name is more likely to represent an unrecorded word *akulōn*, 'north wind', in turn from Latin *aquilo*. The name was given to a Herefordshire country house and estate built in the 1860s on the windy hills near the Gloucestershire border by one Thomas Brain, a rich (and classically minded) coal-owner from the Forest of Dean.

Europe The name of the continent remains of uncertain origin. It has been traditionally linked with that of *Europa*, the Phoenician princess of Greek mythology, and also with Greek *euros*, 'breadth', as if a 'broad' region. But it is almost certainly pre-Greek, and may derive from Phoenician *'ereb*, 'evening', 'west', otherwise 'land of the setting sun', as distinct from ASIA, 'land of the rising sun'. *See also* MAGHREB.

Eurydice The dryad who married Orpheus, and who was sought by him in Hades after her death, has a name that was borne by other characters in Greek mythology and that literally means 'wide justice', from *eurus*, 'wide' and *dikē*, 'order', 'right'. The name thus amounts basically to 'queen', and is more a title than a personal name.

Eurythmics The British (more exactly Anglo-Scottish) pop duo, formed in 1977, adopted their name (in 1980) from the term for the 'rhythmic gymnastics' devised in the early 20th century by the Swiss musician Emile Jaques-Dalcroze as a form of music and movement for children.

Eustace The name appears to mean 'fruitful', 'bountiful', from Greek *eu*, 'good' and *stakhus*, 'ear of corn', as if implying that the person would reap a good harvest.

Euston The district of London, with its well-known railway terminus, takes its name from the earls of *Euston* who owned the land here. Their own title comes from the village of *Euston* near Thetford, Suffolk, its name meaning '*Eof*'s village'. *Cp*. EVESHAM.

Euterpe The name of the muse of lyric poetry and music means 'delightful', 'charming', from Greek *eu*, 'good', 'well' and *terpō*, 'I delight'.

Evans The Welsh name means 'son of *Evan*', this being the Welsh equivalent of JOHN. The name is thus the same as both BEVAN and JOHNSON.

Eve Famous as the first woman in the Bible, the wife of Adam, *Eve* has a name that is generally regarded as representing Hebrew *Havvāh*, 'life'. Adam first named 'every living creature', otherwise the animals (*Genesis* 2.19), then 'called his wife's name Eve; because she was the mother of all living' (*Genesis* 3.20).

Evelyn The name, now used more for girls than boys, derives from the surname, which itself was apparently adopted (and adapted) from the Norman female personal name *Aveline*. The ultimate meaning of this is uncertain (*see* EILEEN).

Evenki The Tungus people of eastern Siberia have a name that probably means simply 'people'.

Everard Although in modern times the first name may have derived from the identical surname, it was originally a given name in its own right, from Old English *eofor*, 'boar' and *heard*, 'hardy', 'brave', so overall means 'brave as a boar'. (*Cp*. modern 'strong as an ox'.)

Everest, Mount The famous mountain in Nepal, the highest in the world, was so named in 1865 for Sir George *Everest* (1790–1866), the British surveyor-general of India. He may have had more to do with maps than mountains, but in a sense the name is coincidentally appropriate for an abiding peak that 'ever rests'. Its Tibetan name is CHOMOLANGMA.

Everglades The expanse of swampy land and rivers in southern Florida has a name that is less straightforward than it might seem. *Glade* here has its southern sense of 'marshy area'. *Ever* appears to have a spatial sense instead of its usual temporal one, denoting a region that is extensive or even metaphorically 'endless'. The overall meaning is thus probably descriptive, 'extensive area of marshland'.

Everyman Cinema The well-known repertory cinema in Hampstead, northwest London, specializing in old and foreign films, was formerly the *Everyman Theatre*, opening in 1919 and named for Ben Jonson's comedy *Every Man in His Humour* (1598). The theatre became a cinema in 1933.

Everyman's Library The popular standard edition of masterpieces of world literature was founded in 1906 by the publisher J. M. Dent (*see* DENT) and first edited by Ernest Rhys (1859–1946). Rhys has described how the name of the series was arrived at:

> Good titles, like good lyrics, drop from heaven. The finding of one, attractive and explicit, was the puzzle. We discussed a score of likely names for the series, but not one was quite convincing. Then, when we had begun to despair of the search, one day on my way through Garrick Street to the publisher's office in Bedford Street, the lines of the old play: 'Everyman, I will go with thee and be thy guide, In thy most need to go by thy side' came into my head. Here, unexpectedly, was the waiting word, *Everyman's Library*.

> Quoted by Bernard Levin in *The Times Saturday Review*, 21 September 1991.

The quotation, which appears in the front pages of all volumes in the series, including the non-fiction reference works, is from the anonymous 15th-century morality play *Everyman* itself, in which the lines are spoken by Knowledge. The 1000th *Everyman* volume (Aristotle's *Metaphysics*) was published in 1976.

Everything But The Girl The British pop duo, formed in Hull in 1982, took their name from that of a local secondhand furniture store. The name is potentially misleading, as one of the two is female.

Evesham The town near Worcester is in a bend of the river Avon, as its name indicates, since the *-ham* represents Old English *hamm*, 'riverside land' (literally 'hemmed-in land'), rather than *hām*, meaning simply 'homestead'. The first part of the town's name is the Old English personal name *Eof*, as for EUSTON.

Évian-les-Bains The town and spa in eastern France, on Lake Geneva, had the medieval name of *Aygueani*, deriving from Latin *aquianum*, from *aqua*, 'water'. The reference is to the mineral springs here, whose water is bottled for export worldwide.

Évreux The industrial town in northwest France takes its name from the *Eburovices*, the Gaulish people who once inhabited the region. Their own name derives from Gaulish *eburo*, 'yew', a tree that probably had a totemic significance. *Cp.* YORK.

Ewan The Scottish name is a form of the Gaelic personal name *Eògann*, at one time popularly equated with English JOHN but now believed to be a development from EUGENE. The spelling *Ewen* also exists.

Ewer The name was originally an occupational one for someone who carried water, and ultimately derived from Latin *aqua*, 'water', as did the directly related word *ewer* for what is now a large jug or pitcher.

Excalibur King Arthur's magic sword, which he alone could free from the stone, so proving his right to become king, has a name of complex origin. The medieval chronicler Geoffrey of Monmouth, in his *Historia Regum Britanniae* (*c.* 1136), calls the sword *Caliburnus*, as if from Latin *chalybs*, 'steel' (from Greek *khalubs*). This name then became *Escalibor* in French accounts of the Arthurian romances. The actual origin is probably in a Welsh name that was itself related to Irish *Caladbolg*, also the name of a legendary sword. The Irish name in turn represents *caladh*, 'hard', 'firm' and *bolgr*, 'belly', with 'hard belly' having a metaphorical sense of 'voracious'. The sword was thus one that would 'eat up' those it attacked. Its name is sometimes subconsciously confused with EXCELSIOR.

Excelsior The common brand name, especially in American use, is simply the Latin word for 'higher'. In a commercial sense this implies 'better', 'of a higher standard'. The word was popularized by Longfellow's poem of the name, written in 1842, about

> A youth who bore, 'mid snow and ice,
> A banner with the strange device,
> Excelsior!

The word had already been adopted in 1778 as the official motto of New York State, accompanied by a rising sun. Hence the nickname *The Excelsior State*. The motto is traditionally translated as 'Ever Upward', although strictly speaking the Latin word is an adjective, not an adverb. The same goes for Longfellow's use of it. According to a biography of Longfellow by his brother Samuel, published in 1886, the poet was unaware of the grammatical slip, and when it was pointed out, claimed that it might well have been an adjective extracted from a sentence such as *Scopus meus excelsior est*, 'My sword is higher'. But this looks like a rather lame attempt to justify an obvious solecism!

Exeter The Devon city takes its name from the river *Exe* on which it lies. The present name represents what might otherwise have been 'Exchester', since the latter half of the name derives from Old English *ceaster*, the term for a Roman station, from Latin *castra*, 'camp'. The Roman name of the settlement here was *Isca Dumnoniorum*, with the first word representing the river name (itself meaning simply 'water') and the second being the name of the *Dumnonii*, the people who gave the name of DEVON.

Exeter College The Oxford college takes its name from the title of its founder in 1314, Walter de Stapeldon, bishop of EXETER. The bishop was a Devon man, and the college still has strong links with the West Country, while the bishop of Exeter is the college visitor (official arbiter, though now only nominally). *Cp.* LINCOLN COLLEGE.

Exmoor The high moorland area in Somerset and Devon, officially known as *Exmoor Forest*, takes its name from the river *Exe* that rises on it. For the meaning of the river's name, *see* EXETER.

Exocet The name of the missile, launched from ship, submarine or aircraft to travel fast but low over the water, is the French word *exocet*, 'flying fish', itself from Greek *exō*, 'outside' and *koitē*, 'lair', 'den'. This is represented in the New Latin scientific name for the fish, *Exocoetus volitans*. The missiles are actually made by a French company.

Exodus The second book of the Old Testament has a name that is the (untranslated) Latin form of its Greek title in the Septuagint, which was *Exodos*, literally 'going out'. The reference is to the deliverance of the Israelites from bondage in Egypt and their safe passage through the Red Sea to the Promised Land. The Hebrew name of the book is *Ŝemot*, 'names', from its opening words: 'Now these are the names' (*Exodus* 1.1).

Eyre, Lake The salt lake in South Australia is named for the British colonial administrator Edward John *Eyre* (1815–1901), who discovered it in 1840. He may have known that his own name originally meant 'heir', so that the lake would be his 'heritage'.

Ezekiel The well-known prophet, with an Old Testament book named for him, has a name that derives from Hebrew *Yehezqēl*, 'may God strengthen'. The sense of the name is alluded to in the book: 'Behold, I have made thy face strong against their faces, and thy forehead strong against their foreheads' (*Ezekiel* 3.8).

Ezra The Old Testament prophet, with a book named for him, has a name that represents Hebrew *'Ezrā*, 'help', implying that he operated with the help of God.

F

Faber and Faber The London publisher takes its name from Geoffrey *Faber* (1889–1961), who founded the firm of Faber and Gwyer in 1925. In 1929 the company was reconstituted as *Faber and Faber*. There was no second Faber, and the repetition of the name was a purely commercial device.

Fabian The name is Latin in origin, from the Roman clan name *Fabius*, itself probably deriving from *faba*, 'bean'.

Fabian Society The association of British socialists was founded in 1884 and advocates the establishment of democratic socialism by gradual means. The name is a reference to the Roman general and statesman *Fabius* Maximus, nicknamed *Cunctator* ('delayer'), who adopted a policy of gradually wearing out the enemy in battle by delaying tactics. The Fabian Society recommends a similar cautious advance, as distinct from the more immediate kind of revolution normally associated with socialism.

Fablon The proprietary name is that of a brand of adhesive-backed plastic material for lining shelves, drawers and the like. It presumably represents a blend of '*fab*ric' and 'ny*lon*'.

Faces, The The British rock group was formed in 1969 from the former SMALL FACES after singer and guitarist Steve Marriott left to form HUMBLE PIE.

Faenza The city in northern Italy derives its name from Latin *faventia*, 'silence', 'meditation', presumably alluding to its peaceful location. It became famous for its majolica earthenware or *faïence*, the latter word coming from the name.

Faerie Queene, The Spenser's famous poetic work, with the first three books published in 1590 and the second three in 1596, does not have a title that refers to a 'fairy queen' in the modern sense but to a 'queen of fairyland'. The word *fairy* (from Old French *faerie*) originally meant 'land of fays', a *fay* being an individual fairy. Spenser revived the medieval word as the name of the complex allegorical world described in his work, which has no 'fairies' in the popular sense. When the Introduction to Book II refers to the 'lond of Faery' it thus means 'land (that has the name) of Fairy'. The *Faerie Queene* herself is Gloriana, a blend of the abstract concept of Glory and a concrete evocation of Queen Elizabeth.

Faeroes The north Atlantic island group has a name representing Faeroese *Føroyar*, 'islands of sheep', from *før*, 'sheep' and *oy*, 'island', plural *oyar*. Sheep are still plentiful here. *Cp.* FAIR ISLE.

Fafnir In Scandinavian mythology, the name is that of a son of the giant Hreidmar who gains possession of the treasure originally owned by Andvari, which he guards in the guise of a dragon. He is killed by Sigurd (more familiar as Siegfried), who in turn becomes the owner of the treasure. Fafnir's name means 'smith', from an Old Norse word related to Latin *faber* in the same sense.

Fairbanks The Alaskan city was founded in 1902 during a gold strike and takes its name from Charles W. *Fairbanks* (1852–1918), a senator from Indiana who led a commission to settle the Alaska boundary dispute.

Fairclough The name derives from a place so called, itself meaning 'beautiful ravine', ultimately from Old English *fæger*, 'fair', 'beautiful' and *clōh*, 'ravine'.

Fairfax The name originated as a nickname for someone with beautiful long hair, from Old English *fæger*, 'fair', 'beautiful' and *feax*, 'hair'. *Fax* was a word for *hair* in

181

English down to the 16th century. *Cp.*
HALIFAX.

Fair Isle The first word of the Shetland
island name represents Old Norse *faar*,
'sheep', since these animals graze freely
here. Hence the familiar *Fair Isle* knitwear, made from their wool. *Cp.* the
identical name of the FAEROES.

Fairport Convention The British folk-rock
band was formed in 1967 and named after
the house, *Fairport*, in which its guitarist
Simon Nicol lived in Muswell Hill, London.

Faisalabad The city of northeast Pakistan
has a name that amounts to '*Faisal*'s
town', with Iranian *ābād*, 'inhabited place'
following the personal name, that of King
Faisal (1905–1975) of Saudi Arabia, who
was widely respected in Pakistan. The city
acquired the name only in the year of King
Faisal's death. Earlier it had been *Lyallpur*,
after Sir James *Lyall*, who laid it out in the
1890s, with *pur* the Hindi word for 'town'.
The personal name *Faisal* derives from
Arabic *fahṣal*, 'judge' (literally 'separator',
from *faṣala*, 'to separate').

Faith The name refers to the Christian
virtue, as traditionally coupled with Hope
and Charity. It was popular among Puritans
in the 17th century.

Faith No More The American rock group,
formed in Los Angeles in 1980, are said to
have taken their name from that of a greyhound on whom they had placed a bet.

Falkirk The town in central-Scotland has a
name that translates as 'speckled church',
from Old English *fāg*, 'variegated' and *cirice*, 'church'. The reference is to the original church here, which must have been
built of mottled stone.

Falkland Islands The South Atlantic island
group, invaded by Argentina in 1982 but
recaptured by the British, was so named in
1690 by Captain John Strong for Anthony
Cary, fifth Viscount *Falkland* (1656–1694),
who as Treasurer of the Navy had financed
Strong's expedition. Cary's own title came
from *Falkland*, Scotland. Strong had originally given the name just to Falkland
Sound, between the two main islands, and
the name *Falkland's Islands* is first recorded only in 1765, when the British
admiral John Byron took possession of the
group. The islands' original name was *Davis Land*, for their discoverer in 1592, John
Davis. In 1594 they were *Hawkins Mai-
denland*, so named by Sir Richard *Hawkins*
in honour of Queen Elizabeth, the Virgin
Queen. The Spanish name for the islands
is *Malvinas*, short for *Islas Malvinas*, from
French *Malouins*, the name for the inhabitants of ST MALO, who attempted to colonize them in 1764 under the French navigator Louis-Antoine de Bougainville (who
gave his name to BOUGAINVILLE, the
largest of the Solomon Islands).

Falmouth The Cornish port obviously takes
its name from its position at the *mouth* of
the river *Fal*. The meaning of the river's
name is unknown. Names beginning with *F*
are rare in Celtic languages, so the name
either originally began with another letter
or is not Cornish. It may be pre-Celtic.

Falstaff The famous comic character, the fat
and bibulous knight of Shakespeare's plays,
is known to be based on the 15th-century
Protestant martyr Sir John Oldcastle, but
his name is based on that of his contemporary, the soldier Sir John *Fastolfe*.
Moreover, the Falstaff in *Henry VI, Part 1*
is a cowardly soldier based on the real
Fastolfe, and he is usually referred to as
Fastolfe for this reason, to distinguish him
from the comic character. Shakespeare had
originally used Sir John Oldcastle's name
for the comic knight in *Henry IV*, but
changed it to *Falstaff* out of deference to
Oldcastle's descendants. Some commenta-
tors see a pun on SHAKESPEARE's own
name and that of Falstaff, as if a man with
'shaking spear' had become one with a 'falling staff'. Such a pun would be in the best
(or worst) Elizabethan literary tradition of
sexual innuendo.

Famagusta The historic city and port in
eastern Cyprus has a name that has
evolved from Phoenician *ḥamat*, 'fort'.
Under the Romans this became *Fama
Augusta*, as if 'fame of Augustus', while to
the Greeks it was *Ammokhōstos*, as if from
ammos, 'sand' and *khōstos*, 'heaped up',
otherwise 'sand-dune'.

Farewell, Cape The southern extremity of
Greenland is so named as it was the point
of departure of the English explorer John
Davis when in 1586 he set sail on a voyage
of discovery to Canada. The northern

extremity of South Island, New Zealand, has the same name, but in this case it was the departure point of Captain Cook in 1770 when he set sail for the east coast of Australia.

Farewell Symphony Haydn's Symphony No 45 in F minor (1722) is so named since in the work's adagio finale the orchestra players gradually leave until only two violins are left. Haydn's aim was to persuade his employer, Prince Nikolaus, not to detain the court musicians unduly at the prince's summer residence at Esterháza but to let them return to their families at Eisenstadt. It is said the prince took the hint.

Farmer The name is an occupational one, not so much for a farmer in the modern sense as for a tax-*farmer*, that is, a person who collected taxes and paid a *firm* or fixed sum for the proceeds. Present-day farmers originally rented land in this way for cultivation.

Farnborough The Hampshire town has a name that means 'fern hill', from Old English *fearn*, 'fern' and *beorg*, 'hill'. There is no obvious hill here now, but the reference is probably to the lowish one that has Farnborough Park at its southern end, north of the town centre. The name of *Faringdon*, the small town in Oxfordshire, has exactly the same meaning. There, however, the hill and the ferns are more obviously evident.

Farquhar The Scottish name derives from the Gaelic personal name *Fearchar*, meaning 'dear man'.

Farrar The name is an occupational one for a smith, who worked in iron, the former word for whom was *ferrer*, from Latin *ferrum*, 'iron'. *Cp*. the related occupation of *farrier*, someone who shoes horses.

Farsi The name of the language of modern Iran derives from *Fars*, the native name of PERSIA, to which it is directly related. The native name itself represents Iranian *fārs*, formerly *pārs* but with the *p* changing to *f* under Arabic influence. Its ultimate origin is in Old Persian *parsi*, 'pure'. *See also* PARSEE.

Fascist The reactionary political movement associated with Mussolini in Italy takes its name from Italian *fascio*, 'political group', itself from Latin *fascis*, 'bundle'. In ancient Rome the *fasces* ('bundles') were a symbol of penal power in the form of a bundle of birch rods containing an axe with its head projecting. This same symbol was adopted by the Fascists in 1919.

Fastnet Race The *Fastnet Cup* is a yachting trophy awarded to the winner of the race sailed from Ryde, Isle of Wight to (and round) the *Fastnet Rock*, off the southwest coast of Ireland, and back. The race is held every two years, alternating with the BERMUDA RACE, and counts towards the ADMIRAL'S CUP. The Fastnet Rock itself has a name of Scandinavian origin, meaning 'strong headland', from Old Norse *fastr*, 'fast', 'firm' and *nes*, 'headland' (English *ness*).

Fates The *Fates* (ultimately from Latin *fari*, 'to speak') were the three mythological goddesses of fate, at first identified separately as the Greek *Moirai* (from *moira*, 'part', 'portion', 'lot') and Roman *Parcae* (from Latin *parere*, 'to bring forth', rather than *parcere*, 'to spare', as sometimes explained), but later assimilated to three identical figures. The Greek *Moirai* seem to have evolved from a single goddess *Moira*. In their three individual persons, they were represented as three old women spinning, respectively named *Clotho* (*Klōthō*), 'spinner', who held the distaff of life, *Lachesis*, 'apportioner', who drew off the thread, and *Atropos*, 'inflexible' (literally 'unturnable'), who cut the thread short. The *Parcae* had the respective names *Nona*, 'ninth', referring to the nine months of human gestation, regarded by the Romans as premature, *Decuma*, 'tenth', for a full ten months' gestation, and *Morta*, 'dead', implying a stillbirth.

Fatima The familiar Muslim name derives from Arabic *fāṭima*, 'weaner', denoting a woman who weans a baby or who abstains from forbidden things. Modern Muslims interpret the name either way. The name is well-known from that of Muhammad's favourite daughter, who died in AD 632, probably aged 26.

Fátima The village in central Portugal that is a Roman Catholic centre of pilgrimage, with its famous shrine of Our Lady of *Fátima*, takes its name, however incongruously, from FATIMA, daughter of Muhammad, founder of Islam. The village name existed long before 1917, when the Virgin Mary is said to have appeared here to three peasant children, and is itself testimony to Portugal's Muslim heritage.

Faulkner The name originally denoted not so much a *falconer* as such, but someone who kept falcons for the lord of the manor to use.

Faust In German legend, *Faust* was the magician who sold his soul to the Devil in exchange for knowledge and power. He is based on a historical character of the same name who died in about 1540, and whose own name is either the German word for 'fist' or a form of Latin *faustus*, 'fortunate', 'lucky'.

Fauves, Les The name is that of a group of early 20th-century French painters whose work was characterized by bright colours and a direct manner. The French word *fauve* means 'wild beast', and the nickname was given to the group by the art critic Louis Vauxcelles, who on coming across a classic-style statue among their paintings at the 1905 Autumn Salon in Paris exclaimed: 'Donatello au milieu des fauves!', with reference to the famous Florentine sculptor. The Fauves are chiefly associated with Matisse.

Fawcett The name derives from a place so called, such as what is now *Facit* near Whitworth in Lancashire. The place-name itself means 'variegated slope', that is, one with brightly coloured flowers or plants on it, from Old English *fāg*, 'variegated' and *sīde*, 'slope'.

Feast of Tabernacles *See* SUKKOTH.

Feather A person of this name would originally have been a trader of down or a maker of quilts. The name could also have been a nickname for a very light person.

Featherstone A name that is not what it seems. It originates from one of the places so called, such as the village near Wolverhampton in Staffordshire. The original meaning is 'four stones', referring to the prehistoric structure known as a tetralith, having three standing stones capped with a fourth as a 'lid'. The Old English word for this was *fetherstān*, from *fether*, a

northern form of *fēower*, 'four' and *stān*, 'stone'.

February The name of the month represents Latin *Februarius mensis*, 'month of expiation'. The Roman *februa* (plural of *februum*, 'purgation') was a festival of purification held on 15 February.

Fécamp The present name of the town and port in northern France has evolved from its Roman name of *Fiscamnum*. This in turn represents Old German *fisk*, 'fish' and *hafn*, 'port', so that the name is somewhat similar to that of FISHGUARD. *Cp.* also LE HAVRE.

Felicity The name relates to the abstract quality of good luck or good fortune. It is thus not only a propitious name but literally a *felicitous* one. Its male equivalent is FELIX.

Felix The name was originally a Roman nickname, from Latin *felix*, 'lucky', 'fortunate'. *Cp.* FELICITY.

Felixstowe The name of the Suffolk port and resort appears to mean '*Felix*'s place', with Old English *stōw*, 'place' following the name of St *Felix*, the first bishop of East Anglia. However, a 13th-century record of the name has it as *Filchestou*, which refers not to Felix but to a person named *Filica*. Doubtless this earlier name became assimilated to that of the bishop in subsequent years. *See also* ST FELIX SCHOOL.

Fenella The name is the English form of the Irish name *Fionnuala*, meaning 'white-shouldered', from Irish *fionn*, 'white', 'fair' and *guala*, 'shoulder'. *Cp.* FIONA.

Fenian In Irish mythology, the *Fenians* were the legendary warriors led by Fionn mac Cumhaill whose exploits are usually assigned to the 2nd and 3rd centuries AD. In the 19th century, the name was that of the revolutionaries of American origin who campaigned for an independent Ireland. The name has become associated with Irish *fianna*, collective plural of *fian*, 'band of warriors'. *See also* FIANNA FÁIL.

Fenwick The surname comes from any of the places so called, such as the village near Stamfordham in Northumberland. Its own name means 'marsh farm', from Old English *fenn*, 'marsh' (modern English *fen*) and *wīc*, 'farm', usually specifically a dairy farm.

Ferdinand The name derives from Spanish *Ferdinando*, which itself is of Germanic origin, from either *farth*, 'journey' or *frith*, 'peace' and *nand*, 'ready'.

Fergus The name is the English form of the Gaelic name *Fearghas*, from *fear*, 'man' and *gus*, 'vigour'.

Fermanagh The Irish county has a tribal name, that of the *Fear Manach*, 'men of *Monach*', the latter being the personal name of their leader. These people came and settled here from their native Leinster after murdering the son of its king.

Fernando Po The former name (until 1973) of what is now the island of *Bioko*, in Equatorial Guinea, represents that of the Portuguese explorer *Fernão do Po*, who discovered it in about 1470. He himself had named the island *Formosa*, 'beautiful'.

Ferney-Voltaire The town of eastern France, on the shore of Lake Geneva, derives the first part of its name from the Roman personal name *Ferennus*, a form of *Ferenius*, itself perhaps a shortened form of Latin *ferentarius*, a term for a type of soldier who fought with missiles. The modern town grew up round the colony of watchmakers set up here by *Voltaire*, who lived here from 1759 to 1778. The famous French writer's name was added in 1881. His own name is generally regarded as being an anagram of *Arouet L.J.*, otherwise *Arouet le jeune*, 'Arouet the younger', from his original surname, with *u* and *j* becoming respectively *v* and *i*.

Ferranti The electrical and electronic engineering company takes its name from its founder in 1882, Sebastian Ziani de *Ferranti* (1864–1930), born in Liverpool as the son of a photographer who had come to England from the Netherlands, and who was ultimately of Italian extraction.

Ferrara The city of northern Italy is believed to derive its name from Latin *ferrarius*, 'blacksmith', itself from *ferrum*, 'iron'. However, the name has not been recorded earlier than the 8th century, and evidence for the Roman original is missing.

Ferrari The famous sports and racing car is named for Enzo *Ferrari* (1898–1988), an Italian racing car driver who set up his car manufacturing company in Modena in 1939.

Festival Hall The London concert hall, with the full name of *Royal Festival Hall*, was built on the South Bank of the Thames for the 1951 *Festival* of Britain. The Festival itself, held a century after the Great Exhibition of 1851, was designed to revive the nation after five years of postwar austerity.

Fettes College The Edinburgh public school opened in 1870 on the terms of the beneficent bequest made by Sir William *Fettes* (1750–1836), Lord Provost of Edinburgh.

Fez The city in north central Morocco has a name of uncertain origin. It may represent Arabic *fa's*, 'axe', although the sense of this is not clear. The name gave the word *fez* for the type of Turkish hat shaped like an inverted flower-pot, usually red and with a tassel on top.

Fianarantsoa The town in southeast Madagascar derives its name from Malagasy *fianàrana*, 'study', 'school' and *sòa*, 'good', implying a place where one studies what is good.

Fianna Fáil The major Irish political party was founded by Eamon De Valera as a republican party in 1926 and has an Irish name meaning 'warriors of Ireland', from *Fianna*, 'band of warriors' (*see* FENIAN) and *Fáil*, 'of Ireland', from *Fál*, an ancient name of Ireland, literally meaning 'defensive fortification' and related to Latin *vallum* and English *wall*. In 15th-century Irish poetry *Fianna Fáil* was understood as 'people of Ireland', but members of the modern political party interpret the name as 'soldiers of destiny'.

Fiat The name of the Italian car is an abbreviation of that of its manufacturing company, founded in Turin in 1899: *Fabbrica Italiana Automobili Torino* ('Turin Italian Automobile Works'). The chance association with *fiat* as a term for an official sanction is a commercial bonus.

Field A person of this name would have lived in a *field*, not as we now understand it, but as a stretch of open country cleared of trees, more like the modern South African *veld*. The name *Fielding* has the same basic meaning.

Field of the Cloth of Gold The name is that of the site near Calais in northeast France where in 1520 Francis I of France met Henry VIII of England with the aim of gaining the latter's support in opposing the Holy Roman Emperor, Charles V. His attempt was unsuccessful, but the occasion was grand enough to give the name, which alludes to the richness of the clothes and pavilions that each side displayed to impress the other. The awkwardness of the phrase results from the literal translation of the French *Camp du drap d'or*.

Fife The former Scottish county, now an administrative region, was originally an ancient kingdom, and traditionally takes its name from *Fib*, a legendary ancestor of the Picts. The exact source of the name remains uncertain.

Fifth Dimension, The The American pop group was formed in Los Angeles in 1966 as the *Versatiles*. The following year one of the members suggested they adopt the name *Fifth Dimension* to reflect the 'psychedelic' image they were keen to promote, this being one step beyond the existing 'fourth dimension' associated with supernatural phenomena. The name also referred to the number of members in the group.

Figaro The well-known French character is familiar from two plays by Beaumarchais, both of which subsequently served as the base for popular operas by Mozart and Rossini. In *Le Barbier de Séville* (1775) he is a barber, and in what is essentially its sequel, *Le Mariage de Figaro* (1781), he is a valet. His name is probably a form of Spanish *figurón*, a colloquial term for a whimsical or eccentric person. The daily French newspaper *Le Figaro*, founded in 1854, is named for the literary character.

Fiji The Pacific island colony has a name of uncertain origin. In its present form, the name probably represents that of *Viti*, the main island in the group.

Filby The surname derives from the village of this name near Great Yarmouth, in Norfolk. Its own name means '*Fili*'s farm', and is Scandinavian in origin.

Finchley The London district has a more or less straightforward name meaning 'finch wood', from Old English *finc*, 'finch' and *lēah*, 'wood'. There is not much of the original wood here now, nor even of Finchley Common, its Victorian legacy.

Findus The brand of frozen foods derives its name from a Swedish firm named '*Fruit Industries*' that was set up in the Second World War by two chocolate companies with the aim of expanding the food retail market.

Fine Gael The major Irish political party, founded in 1933, has an Irish name meaning 'race of the Gaels', from *fine*, 'tribe' and *Gael*, 'of the Gaels'.

Fine Young Cannibals The British rock group, first recording in Birmingham in 1984, adopted their name from the title of the American movie *All the Fine Young Cannibals* (1960), starring Robert Wagner and Natalie Wood.

Fingal's Cave The cave on the Scottish island of Staffa, in the Hebrides, takes its name from the legendary Irish hero *Fingal*, otherwise *Fionn mac Cumhaill*, also known as *Finn Mac Cool*, leader of the FENIANS. He is said to have built the GIANT'S CAUSEWAY in Northern Ireland, and to have lived in this cave. As it stands, *Fingal* can be interpreted as meaning 'fair stranger', from Gaelic *fionn*, 'white', 'pale' and *gall*, 'stranger', 'Gaul', 'Celt'. This would have been an Irish name for a Norse settler in Ireland. The familiar form of the warrior's name was introduced by James Macpherson in his *Fingal, an Ancient Epic Poem* (1762), which purported to be the translation of a Gaelic epic by Ossian, Fingal's son. The association with the cave has been popularized by Mendelssohn's *Fingal's Cave* overture, written in its original form in 1829 after the composer had visited the Hebrides and Staffa.

Finistère The tip of the western end of Brittany, northwest France has a name that comes from Latin *finis terrae*, 'end of the earth', otherwise the same as its Cornish counterpart, LAND'S END. The cape's Breton name, *Penn-ar-Bed*, literally 'head of the world', is similar. Cape *Finisterre*, the headland in northwest Spain, has an identical name. *Cp*. also PEMBROKE.

Finland The name of the Scandinavian country means 'land of the FINNS', *which see*.

Finn The name of the native people of FIN-LAND comes from a Germanic word *finna* or *fenna*, 'fish-scale', to which English *fin* is directly related. This is simply a translation of the Finnish *suomu*, with the same meaning, from which comes the native name of Finland, *Suomi*. The name is said to refer to the garments of fish-skin worn in early times by the Finns. However, some authorities prefer to derive the indigenous name from Finnish *suo*, 'marsh' and *maa*, 'land', referring to Finland's many lakes.

Finnmark The large county of northern Norway has a name that means 'border-land of the *Finns*', from Norwegian *finne*, 'Finn' and *mark*, 'field', 'ground'. The county borders Finland.

Fiona The name is of Gaelic origin, from *fionn*, 'white', 'fair'. It was popularized by 'Fiona Macleod', the pen-name of the Scottish romantic writer William Sharp (1855–1905) (who himself interpreted it as 'fair maid'), although he was not the first to use it.

Fiorentina The leading Italian football club was founded in *Florence* in 1926 as a merger of two existing clubs, *Libertas* and *Club Sportivo Firenze*. Its name thus means 'Florentine'.

Firestone The brand of tyre originates from the American founder of the manufacturing company in Akron, Ohio, in 1900, Harvey Samuel *Firestone* (1868–1938).

Fireworks Music The instrumental suite by Handel, also known by the fuller title of *Music for the Royal Fireworks*, was written for the fireworks display held at Green Park, London, to mark the Peace of Aix-la-Chapelle in 1749.

Firkins The name means 'son of *Firkin*', this being either an occupational name for someone who made casks and barrels (*cp.* the measure *firkin*, as a quarter of a barrel) or a person who was a heavy drinker.

Fish The name usually denoted someone who caught or sold fish, or someone who resembled a fish in some way. *Cp.* FISHER.

Fisher The name was either an occupational name, for a fisherman, or denoted some-one who lived by a fish weir, from Old English *fisc*, 'fish' and *wer*, 'weir'.

Fishguard The port and resort in southwest Wales has a Scandinavian name, from Old Norse *fiskr*, 'fish' and *garthr*, 'yard'. The original 'fish yard' here would have been for catching fish or keeping them in when caught. Scandinavian names are found for many places round the Welsh coast, and especially for its islands.

Fisons The brand of pharmaceuticals owes its name to Joseph *Fison*, who set up a business making fertilizers in East Anglia in 1847.

Fitch The name remains tantalizingly elusive in origin. It can hardly refer to a *fitch* or polecat, since this word is not recorded earlier than the 16th century. It may come from Old French *fiche*, literally 'stake', and so refer to someone who used a pointed iron implement of some kind.

Fitzgerald The name means 'son of *Gerald*' with an old Anglo-French form of what is now modern French *fils*, 'son'. Other names like this will have a similar origin, such as *Fitzpatrick*, 'son of Patrick'. But *see also* FITZROY.

Fitzroy As with FITZGERALD, the first part of the name means 'son'. The latter part represents Old French *roy*, 'king'. The name 'king's son' was traditionally given to illegitimate sons of a king, such as Henry *Fitzroy*, Duke of Richmond (1519–1536), son of Henry VIII by Elizabeth Blount, a lady in waiting to Catherine of Aragon, or Henry *Fitzroy* (1663–1690), son of Charles II by his mistress Barbara Villiers, Duchess of Cleveland. A descendant of the latter was Robert *Fitzroy* (1805–1865), captain of the *Beagle* in which Darwin made his surveying expedition to South America. The settlement of *Fitzroy* in the Falkland Islands is named for him.

Fitzwilliam College The Cambridge college was founded in 1869 and takes its name from the FITZWILLIAM MUSEUM, opposite which it stood in Trumpington Street until it was rehoused in new buildings on Huntingdon Road in 1963.

Fitzwilliam Museum Cambridge's prime art museum, in Trumpington Street, was founded in 1816 by bequest of Richard

Fitzwilliam, seventh Viscount Fitzwilliam (1745–1816).

Five Star The black British pop group, formed in 1983 as a family band, with three sisters and two brothers, took a name that related both to their number and to their aim to be stars, as well as punning on the superior rating awarded to top hotels and restaurants.

Five Towns, The The name is that given by Arnold Bennett in his fiction to the towns of the Potteries, in Staffordshire, with *Turnhill, Bursley, Hanbridge, Knype* and *Longshaw* respectively representing Tunstall, Burslem, Hanley, Stoke-on-Trent and Longton. There are actually six towns, with Fenton unrepresented. The original towns are now all part of the city of Stoke-on-Trent. Bennett's names are fairly close to the originals with the exception of *Knype*, which he seems to have based on the village of *Knypersley* near Biddulph, about five miles (8 km) north of Stoke-on-Trent.

Fixx, The The British new wave rock group originally formed in 1980 as the *Portraits*. When their line-up stabilized the following year they changed this to *The Fix*, but altered the spelling to *Fixx* when it was realized that the name could suggest a connection with drugs.

Flag Day The name is that of the annual holiday in the United States held on 14 June. It celebrates the adoption on 14 June 1777 of the Stars and Stripes as the national *flag* instead of the Grand Union Flag.

Flaminian Way The Roman road in Italy that runs from Rome to Rimini is named for the Roman general Gaius *Flaminius*, who built it in 220 BC. Its Latin name is *Via Flaminia*.

Flanagan The Irish name is a form of *Ó Flannagáin*, 'descendant of *Flannagán*, with the latter personal name derived from *flann*, 'red', 'ruddy' (of hair or complexion).

Flanders The historic region of the Low Countries, notorious as a battleground in many wars, has a Flemish name that probably represents *vlakte*, 'plain' and *wanderen*, 'to wander', implying a flat and expansive region. Today the name is found for the two Belgian provinces of East Flanders and West Flanders.

Flavia The name comes from the Roman *nomen* (clan name) *Flavius*, itself from Latin *flavus*, 'yellow', 'fair-haired'.

Fleet Street The street of central London, formerly the home of many newspaper offices, takes its name from the little river *Fleet*, now underground at the eastern end of the street, that flows into the Thames at Blackfriars. The river's own name derives from Old English *flēot*, 'flowing water', to which modern *float* and *flood* are related.

Fleetwood The Lancashire fishing port has a modern name (by British standards), from that of Sir Peter Hesketh *Fleetwood* (1801–1866), of Rossall House, now Rossall School, who founded it in the 1830s. The name is coincidentally suitable for a port, which could have arisen by a *fleet* or stream flowing out of a *wood*.

Fleetwood Mac The famous British rock group was formed in 1967 and took its name from two of its members, drummer Mick *Fleetwood* and bassist John '*Mac*' McVie.

Fleming The name is that of a person from FLANDERS, who could have originally been one of the many weavers or dyers from there who came to settle in England in medieval times. *Cp.* the adjective *Flemish*, meaning 'of Flanders'.

Flensburg The port in northern Germany derives its name from Low German *flēn*, 'mound of earth', 'sand heap' and *burg*, 'fort'.

Fletcher The name is an occupational one for a person who made arrows (from Old French *fleche*, 'arrow'). *Cp.* ARCHER, BOWMAN, BOWYER.

Flight of the Bumble Bee, The The name is that of the orchestral interlude in Rimsky-Korsakov's opera *The Tale of Tsar Saltan* (1899) in which a prince becomes a bee and stings his wicked relatives. The music suggests the erratic, wavering flight of a bee (which is frequently anything but in a beeline). *Cp.* BEE'S WEDDING.

Flinders Range The mountain range in South Australia is named for the English navigator Matthew *Flinders* (1774–1814) who explored and surveyed the coast of New South Wales in the last five years of the 18th century and circumnavigated Australia in the first four years of the 19th. It was Flinders who revived the classical name *Terra Australis* which gave that of modern AUSTRALIA.

Flint The town and former county in northeast Wales have a name that means exactly what it says, referring to the hard rock here on which Flint Castle was built.

Flock of Seagulls The British new wave rock group was formed in Liverpool in 1979 and chose a name based on the cult novel by Richard Bach, *Jonathan Livingston Seagull* (1970).

Flodden, Battle of The battle, also known as *Flodden Field*, takes its name from the hill in Northumberland where the Scots were defeated by the English in 1513 and where James IV of Scotland was killed. The hill name, first found only in records of the battle itself, may mean 'slab hill', from Old English *flōh*, 'stone slab', 'fragment' and *dūn*, 'hill'. In the longer name *Flodden Field* it is hard to say whether *Field* refers to the battlefield or is an actual part of the name, with *field* here in its medieval sense of 'open land'.

Flood The name was originally either that of a person who lived by a well or spring (Old English *flōd*) or an English form of the Welsh name LLOYD.

Floréal The month of the French revolutionary calendar, corresponding to the period 21 April to 20 May, has a name that means 'floral', 'flowery', from Latin *floreus*, 'of flowers'.

Florence The famous Italian city, capital of Tuscany, had the Roman name of *Colonia Florentia*, 'flowering colony', referring either literally to its abundance of flowers or figuratively to its 'flourishing' growth and expansion. However, the 16th-century Italian sculptor and writer Benvenuto Cellini maintained that the origin of the name lay in Latin *Fluentia*, 'flowing', relating to the location of Florence on the river Arno. The city's modern Italian name is *Firenze*, from Old Italian *Fiorenza*.

Florence The name comes from the Latin name *Florentia*, itself based on *florens*,

'blossoming', 'flowering'. It is familiar from *Florence* Nightingale, who was herself so named because she was born in FLORENCE, Italy. (Her elder sister, Frances Parthenope Nightingale, had been born in Naples, and was given her second name from one of the classical names of that city.)

Flores Sea The region of the Pacific Ocean in Indonesia is named for the island of *Flores* here, which itself derives its name from Portuguese *flores*, the plural of *flor*, 'flower', alluding to its rich flora.

Florianópolis The port in southern Brazil was founded by the Spanish in 1542 but passed to the Portuguese in 1675, who in 1700 established a convict settlement called *Desterro*, 'exile', 'banishment'. The town retained this name until 1893, when it was renamed in honour of the Brazilian president *Floriano* Peixoto (1842–1895).

Florida The American state, a prominent peninsula on the Atlantic coast, derives its name from Spanish *florida*, 'flowering', perhaps referring to its fertile vegetation, but more likely representing *Pascua florida*, literally 'flowering Easter', otherwise the Spanish name for 'Palm Sunday'. This would refer to 20 March 1513, the day when the expedition of the Spanish explorer Ponce de León discovered the peninsula.

Flow Country The area of moorland and peat bogs in northern Scotland is so named from the Scottish word *flow* meaning 'morass', 'marshland'. The word is related to, but distinct from, English *flow*.

Flower The surname could relate to modern *flower* or *flour*. If the former, it could have been a term of endearment, and *Flower* was a regular girl's name in medieval times. If the latter, it would have denoted a miller or flour merchant.

Flushing The port in the southwest Netherlands has a name that is an English corruption of *Vlissingen*, its Dutch name. This has a basic sense 'flowing', 'current' (modern Dutch *fluissen*, 'to flow strongly', related to English *flush*), referring to its location at the mouth of the West Scheldt estuary.

Flushing Meadow The American national tennis centre is located in *Flushing*, in the

Queens district of New York. The original settlement here was made in 1644 by English Puritans who had been living in FLUSHING (Vlissingen) in the Netherlands.

Foden The make of trucks and buses is named for Edward *Foden* (1841–1911), a Cheshire agricultural engineer who patented his first steam traction engine in 1880.

Foggia The Italian city has a name that is believed to come from a local dialect word for a type of grain store, and that itself derives from Latin *fovea*, 'pit', a word related to *fovere*, 'to keep warm'.

Folies-Bergère The well-known Paris music-hall, famous for its nude shows, opened in 1869 at the corner of the rue Richer and the rue Trévise, and was originally intended to have the name *Folies-Trévise*, after the latter street. However, the Duc de Trévise objected to the association of his title with the suggestive word *folies*, so the theatre instead adopted the name of the rue *Bergère*, actually some distance away. This street was itself named for a master dyer who owned property there, one Jean *Bergier*.

Folkestone The Kent town and port has a name that means either 'people's stone' or '*Folca*'s stone', the former from Old English *folc*, 'people' (modern *folk*), the latter from an Old English personal name. Either way, the *stone* would have been a meeting-point, and Folkestone is known to have been the centre of its hundred.

Fomalhaut The name of the brightest star in the constellation Piscis Austrinus derives from Arabic *fum al-ḥūt*, 'mouth of the fish'. The stars in Piscis Austrinus represent a drinking fish, with Fomalhaut at its mouth.

Fontainebleau The town of northern France has a name recorded in the 12th century as *Fontem Blahaud*, from Latin *fons*, genitive *fontis*, 'spring', 'fountain', and *Blahaud*, a personal name of Germanic origin but uncertain meaning.

Fonteney-le-Comte The historic town in western France had the Roman name *Fontanetum*, a diminutive of *fontanum*, from Latin *fons*, genitive *fontis*, 'spring' (English *fount*). The latter half of the name dates from the reign of Louis IX, in the 13th century, when the king installed a count (French *comte*) at Fontenay on its becoming the capital of Bas-Poitou.

Fonthill Abbey The ruined Gothic Revival mansion near Tisbury, Wiltshire, takes its name from the nearby villages of *Fonthill* Gifford and *Fonthill* Bishop, which in turn take their name from the *Fonthill* Brook here. The basic name derives from Old English *funta*, 'spring' (modern *fount*), while the apparent 'hill' is actually a word related to Welsh *ial*, 'fertile land'. The 'Abbey' was never a proper one, but the building was supposed to suggest one.

Foot The name would have originally been a nickname for someone with an unusual or deformed foot. No evidence has been found to suggest that the name denoted a person who lived at the foot of a hill, however.

Forbach The town in northeast France has a name of Old German origin, from *fohra*, 'picea' (a genus of spruce) and *bach*, 'stream'.

Forbes If a Scottish name, the derivation is in the place so called near Aberdeen, originating from Gaelic *forba*, 'field'. If an Irish name, it is a form of *Mac Fearbhisigh*, 'son of *Firbhsigh*', a personal name meaning 'man of prosperity'.

Forbidden City The name has been applied to two famous cities: Lhasa, Tibet, which foreigners were long forbidden to enter, and the walled section of Peking, China, that encloses the Imperial Palace. The latter translates the Chinese name *jinchéng*, but the name for Lhasa, probably based on it, was apparently given by westerners only in the 19th century.

Ford The name denoted a person who lived by a ford, or who came from a place with *ford* in its name.

Ford The famous make of car takes its name from the American engineer Henry *Ford* (1863–1947), who manufactured his first automobile in Detroit in 1896.

Forest of Dean The well-known Gloucestershire wood lies between the rivers Severn and Wye, and the *Dean* of the name is simply Old English *denu*, 'valley'.

Forest School The boys' public school in Snaresbrook, northeast Greater London, was founded as *The Forest Proprietary School* in 1834 and takes its name from its location in an open area of EPPING FOREST.

Forez The historic region of central France had the Roman name of *Forensis pagus*, 'land of Feurs', where *Feurs*, the name of the plain in the centre of the region, represents Latin *forum*, 'public place', 'market'. There may have been a trading centre here.

Forfar The Scottish town near Dundee has a Gaelic name which probably means 'ridge wood', from Old Gaelic *fothir fàire*, although it is possible the second word of the name may be Gaelic *faire*, 'watching', so that there was a sort of lookout point here. If so, it would not have been the town itself, which is on level ground, but a nearby hill, such as the Hill of Finhaven, well-known as a local viewpoint. *Forfarshire* was formerly an alternative name for the county of *Angus*, in which the town was situated.

Forman The name could denote someone who was the leader of a group, in the way that a *foreman* today is the leader of a gang of workmen. But it could also be an occupational name for a swincherd, from Old English *fōr*, 'hog', 'pig' and *mann*, 'man'.

Formica The proprietary make of laminated plastic sheet has a name that seems to suggest a connection with *formic* acid, but which was actually devised in 1913 by two young American scientists who were developing a natural resin substitute *for mica* as an insulation material for electrical wiring. The two men, Herb Faber and Dan O'Connor, founded the *Formica* Company that same year.

Formosa The former name of TAIWAN is simply the Portuguese word for 'beautiful', given the island by Portuguese explorers in the early 16th century. *See also* FERNANDO PO.

Formula One The class of motor racing is so called from the specific category in which a car competes, judged according to its engine size, weight, and fuel capacity, with *Formula One* the highest or best (and specifically applied to an engine of 1500 to 3000 cubic centimetres displacement). The word *formula* seems to have been adopted for this technical sense some time in the early 1920s. *Formula One* is also used as the name of the actual race in which cars of this class compete. The first *Formula One* World Championship was held in 1950.

Forster The name can have one of three occupational origins. It could apply to a *forester*, to a maker of scissors (from Old French *forcetier*, from *forcettes*, 'scissors'), or to a wood-worker (from Old French *fustrier*, from *fustre*, 'block of wood').

Forsyth The Scottish surname derives from the Gaelic personal name *Fearsithe*, 'man of peace'.

Fortaleza The port in northeast Brazil has a name that is simply the Portuguese word for 'fortress'.

Fort-de-France The capital of Martinique, in the French West Indies, was founded in 1640 at a time when the island had not long been settled by the French, and was given a name that indicated its status as an 'outpost'. It was originally known as *Fort-Royal*.

Forte The British hotel group was founded in 1903 as the *Hertfordshire Public House Trust Company*, its aim being to restore the standards of the old coaching inns of Britain, many of which had suffered with the coming of the railways. The company grew, and soon adopted the shorter name *Trust Houses*. In 1970 it merged with *Forte Holdings*, founded in 1935 by Sir Charles *Forte* as a catering business, and became *Trust Houses Forte*. In 1979 the name was modified slightly to *Trusthouse Forte*, usually abbreviated to *THF*. When these initials came to be regarded as too impersonal, with the full name also wrongly suggesting a financial trust, the name was changed again in 1991 to *Forte*, now representing the name of the company's chief executive, Sir Charles Forte's son Rocco *Forte* (1945–　). The surname has a coincidentally favourable association as a commercial name, suggesting a company whose *forte* is hotel management and catering.

Fortescue The name originated as a nickname for a brave person, from Old French *fort*, 'strong' and *escu*, 'shield'.

Forth The famous Scottish river has a Celtic name deriving from a root word meaning 'silent one', referring to its slow current. In the name *Firth of Forth*, applied to its estuary, *firth* is a word of Scandinavian origin, related to *fjord*. The word order here is Celtic, as for *Boat of Garten* and *Mull of Kintyre*, where the generic Gaelic word would originally have been followed by the specific name in the genitive case.

Forties The sea area off the east coast of Scotland, familiar from shipping forecasts, takes its name from a lengthy depression in the sea bed here at a depth of around *forty* fathoms.

Fort Knox The military reservation near Louisville, Kentucky that is the site of the United States Gold Bullion Depository takes its name from the American Revolutionary officer and first secretary of war, Henry *Knox* (1750–1806).

Fort Lauderdale The famous Florida city was founded in 1895 and arose round the fort that was named for Major William *Lauderdale*, leader of an expedition against the Seminole Indians in 1838.

Fortnum and Mason The high-class London provision store takes its name from William *Fortnum*, a royal footman, and his friend Hugh *Mason*, a grocer, who together in 1707 set up a grocery stall in Piccadilly, where the firm's premises remain today.

FORTRAN The high-level computer language has a name that derives from '*for*mula *tran*slation', referring to its use for mathematical and scientific purposes.

Fort Sumter The fort in South Carolina, captured by Confederate forces in 1861 in the first action of the Civil War, takes its name from the Revolutionary officer Thomas *Sumter* (1734–1832), known as the 'Carolina Gamecock'.

Fortune Theatre The London theatre in Russell Street, Covent Garden was opened in 1924 and named for the historic *Fortune Theatre* in Golden Lane, Cripplegate, to which it is said to bear some resemblance. The earlier theatre had been built in 1600, modelled on the GLOBE THEATRE, and was so named from a statue of the goddess *Fortune* that stood over the main entrance. It burned down in 1613.

Fort William The Scottish town takes its name from the *fort* here, originally built in 1655 but rebuilt in 1690 and named for the reigning monarch, *William* III.

Fort Worth The Texas city takes its name from the American general William J. *Worth* (1794–1849), hero of the Mexican War and commander of the troops in Texas at the time of its foundation as a frontier outpost in 1849.

Forty-Five, The The name is the nickname of the Jacobite rebellion of 1745 led by Charles Edward Stuart (the 'Young Pretender') in an attempt to restore the Stuarts to the throne.

Forty-Niners The name is a nickname for the prospectors who took part in the California gold rush of 1849.

Foshan The city in southeast China has a name that means 'mountain of the Buddha', from *fó*, 'Buddha' and *shān*, 'mountain'. Its former name was *Namhoi*, representing Chinese *nánhǎi*, 'southern sea'.

Fosse Way The Roman road between Lincoln and Exeter is so named since it had a *fosse* or ditch on either side.

Foster The name could be a form of FOR-STER, in any of its senses, but could also apply to a person who was a *foster* parent.

Fosters The well-known brand of Australian lager takes its name from two American brothers, W.M. and R.R. *Foster*, who in 1886 went to Australia from New York to set up a brewing business.

Fosters The familiar brand of menswear, with its many High Street branches, is named for William *Foster*, who opened a draper's shop in Pontefract, Yorkshire in 1876. The firm's former name of *Foster Brothers* was a commercial invention, since William Foster actually had no brother.

Fotheringhay The Northamptonshire village, with its ruined castle where Mary, Queen of Scots was imprisoned and executed in 1587, has a name that means 'island of *Forthhere*'s people'. 'Island' here refers to raised land among streams. The Old English personal name means 'army leader'.

Foula The Scottish island, in the Shetlands, is noted for its bird life. Its name relates precisely to this, deriving from Old Norse *fugl*, 'bird' (related to German *Vogel* and English *fowl*) and *ey*, 'island'. *Cp*. FOULNESS.

Foulness The island in Essex is noted for its wildlife, and especially for wildfowl. Its name descriptively relates to this, and comes from Old English *fugol*, 'bird' (modern English *fowl*) and *næss*, 'promontory' (*cp*. DUNGENESS, SHEERNESS). *See also* FOULA.

Foulsham The British publishing house, well known for its annual *Foulsham's Old Moore's Almanac*, takes its name from William *Foulsham*, who founded the business in 1819. He was a friend of the astrologer Edwin Raphael, and when the latter published *Raphael's Prophetic Almanac and Year Book* that year, Foulsham agreed to bring it out annually.

Fountains Abbey The famous ruined medieval abbey, a popular Yorkshire tourist attraction, has a name that refers more to springs than actual fountains. It originally applied to the springs discovered by the monks of St Mary's, York, when they began building the Cistercian monastery and abbey here in the early 12th century.

Fowler The name would originally have been a nickname for a person who resembled a bird in some way, from Old English *fugol*, 'bird' (modern *fowl*).

Fox The name originated as a nickname for a cunning person, or for someone who resembled a fox in some way, such as a person with red hair.

Foyles The famous London bookshop takes its name from the brothers William and Gilbert *Foyle*, who set up a secondhand bookselling business in 1903, moving to the firm's present address in Charing Cross Road in 1907. The dominant brother in the business was William Alfred Foyle (1885–1963), and it was his daughter, Christina Foyle, who inaugurated the firm's famous 'literary luncheons', attended by well-known personalities.

Fram The name of the ship in which the Norwegian explorer Fridtjof Nansen attempted to reach the North Pole in his expedition of 1893 is the Norwegian word for 'forward'.

France The country takes its name from the FRANKS, the Germanic people who spread from the east into Gaul in the 4th century AD.

Franche-Comté The historic region of eastern France has a name that literally translates as 'free county'. The origin lies in the *county* of Burgundy, as distinct from the *duchy* of Burgundy further west (the Burgundy of today). In 1361 the duchy escheated (reverted) to the French crown, to which it had earlier belonged, but the county remained a domain of Margaret I, widow of the Count of Flanders. Hence it was a 'free county' in the sense that it had not passed to the crown.

Francis The name derives from Late Latin *Franciscus*, 'French', and was popularized by St *Francis*, who was originally *Giovanni* but who came to be nicknamed *Francesco* because of his father's commercial connection with France. He subsequently adopted the name.

Franciscan The various orders of friars and nuns of the name trace their origins back to St *Francis* of Assisi, who founded the first such order in the early 13th century.

Francis Holland School The name is that of two London public day schools for girls, one founded in 1878, the other in 1881. The founder of both was the Rev *Francis Holland* (1828–1907), at the time minister of Quebec Chapel (later the Church of the Annunciation), near Marble Arch. The original school, now in Regent's Park, arose when the minister and his wife felt there was a need to provide a religious-based secondary education for their daughter Lucy. The second school is now in Sloane Square.

Franconia The historic duchy of Germany has a Medieval Latin name deriving from that of the FRANKS, who inhabited it from the 7th century.

Frank Although now often regarded as a pet form of FRANCIS, the name originally referred to someone who was a member of the tribe of FRANKS.

Frankenstein The Gothic novel by Mary Shelley, published in 1818, tells of a student of this name who builds a manlike creature and gives it life. His own name (sometimes wrongly taken to be that of the monster he created, which has no name in the novel) is a standard German one meaning literally 'Frankish rock', and probably deriving from a place so called, which would itself have acquired its name by reference to the FRANKS.

Frankfort The state capital of Kentucky takes its name from Stephen *Frank*, a frontiersman killed here in 1780 at a *ford* over the river Kentucky. The name of course also suggests FRANKFURT.

Frankfurt Both German cities have one and the same origin, except that *Frankfurt an der Oder*, in eastern Germany, took its name from *Frankfurt am Main*, in the west. The basic sense is 'ford of the FRANKS', meaning that the original town arose by a ford over the Main that was used by the Frankish army in the 1st century AD. *Cp.* HEREFORD.

Frankie Goes to Hollywood The controversial British pop band, formed in 1980, chose a name that is said to be based on a headline in the American magazine *Variety* about *Frank* Sinatra's plans to move from Las Vegas to Los Angeles in order to take up a film career in *Hollywood*.

Franklin The name would originally have applied to someone who was a *franklin*, the title (from Norman French *franc*, 'free') for a person who was a landholder of *free* but not noble birth. The name is fairly common among Jews, where it represents the English form of a Jewish name of similar sound but different origin.

Franklin District The northern district of the Northwest Territories, Canada, is named for the British explorer Sir John *Franklin* (1786–1847), who disappeared in the Arctic here in a search for the Northwest Passage.

Franks The name is that of the Germanic people who gave the name of FRANCE. The origin of their name is disputed. It may derive from an Old German word *franka*, 'brave' (modern English *frank*), or from a personal name *Francio* or *Francus*, perhaps related to that of PRIAM. A recent theory sees the source of the name in the Germanic word *wrang*, from *wringen*, 'to

wring', 'to wrench', so that the meaning would be 'the wrenched ones', that is, people uprooted from their original homeland. *See also* the personal name FRANK.

Franz Josef Land The archipelago in the Arctic Ocean, administratively part of Russia, was discovered by the Austrians in 1873 and named by them in honour of the Austrian emperor, *Franz Josef* I (1830–1916).

Fraser The Scottish name is of uncertain origin. It may represent the corrupt form of a Gaelic personal name.

Fraser The Canadian river is so named for the fur trader Simon *Fraser* (1776–1862), who explored the Rocky Mountains in 1806–8 and who journeyed down the river, mistakenly supposing it to be the Columbia.

Fray Bentos The familiar brand of corned beef takes its name from the port of *Fray Bentos* in western Uruguay, noted for its meat-packing. The town was founded in 1859 and has a Spanish name meaning 'Brother Benedict'.

Frederick The name is an old Germanic one, from *fred*, 'peace' and *rīc*, 'power', so denoted a warrior who gained 'peace through strength', or who was a peaceful ruler.

Free The British pop group, formed in 1968, were given their name by the rhythm 'n' blues musician Alexis Korner after his own trio of the early 1960s, *Free At Last*.

Free Church The name is now used for any Protestant or Nonconformist church that is not part of the established church, *i.e.* the Church of England in England, and that is therefore *free* from it. The term originally applied to the *Free Church* of Scotland, which seceded from the established Presbyterian church in 1843.

Free Foresters The touring cricketing team of this name was originally formed in 1856 from members in the Midlands, many of whom lived in or near the *Forest* of Arden. The team is *free* in that it is a touring side, with no regular home ground.

Freeman The name denotes a person who was born *free*, as distinct from a serf.

Freeman Hardy Willis The well-known shoe shops take their name from the directors of a footwear manufacturing company formed in Leicester in 1876, William *Freeman*, Arthur *Hardy* and Frederick *Willis*.

Freetown The capital of Sierra Leone was founded in 1787 as a haven for liberated or rescued African slaves. Hence the name.

Freiburg The city in southwest Germany was founded in 1120 by the dukes of Zähringen as a free market town. Hence its name from German *frei*, 'free' and *Burg*, 'fort', 'town'. The same dukes founded FRIBOURG in Switzerland.

Freir The god of vegetation and the harvest in Norse mythology has an Old Norse name meaning 'lord', 'nobleman'. He traditionally features as the brother of FREYA.

Fréjus The ancient town of southeast France was founded by Julius Caesar in 49 BC, hence its name, from Latin *Forum Julii*, 'market place of Julius'. *Cp.* FOREZ and FRIULI.

Fremantle The port in Western Australia was founded in 1829 and was subsequently named for Captain Charles *Fremantle* (1800–1869), the British naval officer who brought the first settlers here.

French A person with this name could either originally have come from FRANCE or have been someone who adopted French manners or fashions.

French The present form of the name of the people and language of FRANCE developed from Old English *Frencisc*, 'Frankish' (*see* FRANKS), so that the final *-ch* represents the *-ish* found more commonly in ethnic names such as *English*.

French Guiana The country of northeast South America takes its name from its original indigenous inhabitants, as does GUYANA (*which see* for the origin of their name). It has been a *French* overseas region since 1637. Its capital, CAYENNE, has a name of the same origin.

Frey *See* FREIR.

Freya The Scandinavian goddess of love, fertility and beauty has a name that derives from an Old Norse root word meaning 'noble', itself related to modern English *free*. She is very similar to FRIGG.

Friar Tuck The name of the jolly friar who joined Robin Hood and his Merry Men as their chaplain does not refer to his liking for *tuck* (good food) but is simply the surname now more common as *Tooke*. This is said to derive from a Scandinavian personal name *Tóki*, of unknown meaning.

Fribourg The town in western Switzerland has a name that represents Medieval Latin *Friburgum*, itself of Germanic origin meaning 'free fort'. It was founded by the dukes of Zähringen in 1157 as a military post to control a ford over a river. *Cp.* FREIBURG.

Frick Collection The well-known New York art gallery takes its name from the industrialist Henry Clay *Frick* (1849–1919), who bequeathed his collection to New York City together with his former Fifth Avenue mansion that still houses it.

Fricker The name is probably occupational in origin, although it is not certain what the occupation was. It could perhaps have evolved from Old English *fricca*, 'herald', 'crier', to which a final *-er* was added as in other occupational names.

Friday The sixth day of the week takes its name from FRIGG, the Germano-Scandinavian goddess of love, and was a direct adaptation of Latin *Veneris dies*, 'day of VENUS', since Frigg answered to this Roman goddess (although FREYA was actually a closer equivalent). Hence French *vendredi*, 'Friday'. The Latin name of the day was itself based on Greek *Aphrodités hēmera*, 'day of APHRODITE', as Venus in turn corresponded to that Greek goddess.

Friday Robinson Crusoe's companion and servant was so called since, in Defoe's famous novel (of 1719), he saved his master's life on a FRIDAY. Crusoe usually referred to him as 'my man Friday', which gave the term 'man Friday' for an obsequious follower, as in: 'Count von Rechberg [...] was Prince Bismarck's man Friday' (*Athenaeum*, 16 April 1887). In the mid-20th century the phrase gave 'girl Friday' as a term for a resourceful young woman assistant. The expression was popularized by the Hollywood comedy movie *His Girl Friday* (1940), in which the title role of ace reporter Hildy Johnson was played by Rosalind Russell. (The film was a remake of *The Front Page*, screened nine years previously, in which Hildy Johnson was a *male* reporter.)

Friend The name means what it says, and would have originally been a nickname for a *friendly* person, or for someone who was a relative.

Friesland The province of the northern Netherlands has a name of the same origin as that of the FRISIAN ISLANDS, *which see*.

Frigg The goddess of love who was the wife of ODIN in Germano-Scandinavian mythology derives her name from a conjectural Old German root element *frijo* meaning 'beloved', to which modern English *free* is probably related. She gave her name to FRIDAY. *Cp*. FREYA.

Frimaire The name was that of the third month in the French Revolutionary calendar, corresponding to the period from 22 November to 21 December. It derives from French *frimas*, 'hoarfrost' (related to English *rime*).

Frisian Islands The island chain of north-west Europe, off the coast of Holland, Germany and Denmark, takes its name from its inhabitants, known to the Romans as the *Frisii*. The name may derive either from Old High German *fri*, 'free' or from Old Frisian *frisiaz*, 'frizzy', referring to their curly hair, or from an Indoeuropean root word *fers* or *fars*, 'coast'. The last seems the most likely.

Friuli The historic region of northeast Italy has a name that is a much eroded form of its Roman name *Forum Julii*, 'market place of Julius', that is, Julius Caesar. *Cp*. FRÉJUS.

Frobisher The name is an occupational one, from Old French *fourbisseor*, 'furbisher', the term for someone who polished armour or put the finishing touches to it.

Frog Quartet Haydn's String Quartet in D, Op 50 No 6 (1787) is so nicknamed for the 'croaking' theme in its finale.

Fronde In French history, the name is that of the rebellious movement against Cardinal Mazarin in the 17th century. It is the French word for 'sling', since the insurgents were likened to naughty school-boys using this weapon as a 'catapult' to attack their opponents.

Frost The name was originally a nickname for a person with an 'icy' or 'cold' nature, or for a person who had white hair or a white beard.

Fructidor The month of the French Revolutionary calendar, corresponding to the period 19 August to 22 September, has a name meaning 'fruitful', from a combination of Latin *fructus*, 'fruit' and Greek *dōron*, 'gift'.

Frunze *See* BISHKEK.

Fry The name has the same origin as FREEMAN, from Old English *frīg*, a southern form of *frēo*, 'free'.

Frys The well-known brand of chocolate owes its name to the Quaker apothecary Joseph *Fry* (1728–1787), who in 1748 first made chocolate in Bristol.

Führer, Der The German title, meaning 'the leader', was given to Hitler after he became Chancellor of Germany in 1933 and turned the country from a democratic republic into the totalitarian Third Reich. *Cp*. the titles CAUDILLO, DUCE.

Fuji, Mount The famous extinct volcano in central Japan, also known as *Fujiyama*, has a name of uncertain meaning. The two Japanese ideograms (symbols) that phonetically make up the basic name can be understood as 'prosperous man', but this is not the actual meaning. A sense 'fire spitter' or 'incomparable' has been suggested. The final *yama* of the alternative name is simply the word for 'mountain'.

Fukuoka The city and port in southwest Japan has a name that means 'hill of happiness', from *fuku*, 'fortune', 'blessing', and *oka*, 'hill'.

Fukushima The Japanese city, in northern Honshu, has a name meaning 'island of happiness', from *fuku*, 'fortune', 'blessing' and *shima*, 'island'.

Fukuyama The Japanese city, in southwest Honshu, has a name that means 'mountain of happiness', from *fuku*, 'fortune', 'blessing' and *yama*, 'mountain'.

Fulham The district of London lies beside the Thames and has a name that means

'*Fulla*'s riverside meadow', with the personal name followed by Old English *hamm*, literally 'hemmed-in land', as typically land in the bend of a river. There are no waterside meadows here now, but they have modern equivalents of a kind in Bishop's Park and Hurlingham Park, both of which are in a broad bend on the north bank of the Thames.

Fuller The name is an occupational one, given to a person who dressed cloth. *Cp.* TUCKER and WALKER.

Funafuti The capital of Tuvalu has a name that may represent *futi*, 'banana', originally applied to the island as a whole, or *Futi*, the name of one of the wives of a ruler here, with *funa* added as a feminine prefix.

Furnival The name is a Norman one, either from the place called *Fournival*, near Caen, or from *Fourneville*, near Beauvais, both in northern France, and themselves perhaps based on a personal name *Furnus*.

Fushun The city in northeast China has a name that represents Chinese *fŭ*, 'to stroke', 'to comfort' and *shùn*, 'along', 'obedient'.

Fuzhou The port in southeast China has a name that means 'happy region', from *fú*, 'happiness' and *zhōu*, 'region'.

Fyffes The well-known banana company takes its name from Edward Wathen *Fyffe* (1853–1935), originally employed in the tea trade, who imported his first consignment of bananas to Britain from the Canary Islands in 1888.

Fylde The name of the region in Lancashire means 'plain', from Old English *filde*, related to modern *field*. The name is pronounced 'filed'.

G

Gabon The country of equatorial Africa takes its name from the river *Gabon* here whose estuary was discovered by the Portuguese in the late 15th century. They named it *Gabão*, from the Portuguese word for 'hood', doubtless on account of its shape.

Gaborone The capital of Botswana is named for a local Tswana chieftain, who reigned here from 1880 to 1932.

Gabriel The biblical name is that of the archangel who in the Old Testament interprets the visions of Daniel and who in the New Testament announces the forthcoming birth of John the Baptist to Zacharias and that of Jesus to the Virgin Mary. It is Hebrew in origin, from *gabhrī˘el*, 'my strength is God'.

Gabrovo The town in central Bulgaria has a name that represents Bulgarian *gabăr*, 'hornbeam', a tree once abundant here.

Gad In the Old Testament, the name is that of Jacob's sixth son, by Zilpah, Leah's maid, of the Israelite tribe descended from him, and of the territory of this tribe. It is popularly derived from the Hebrew word for either 'troop' or 'fortunate', and in the latter sense is associated with that of his brother ASHER, 'happy'. The account of Gad's birth in the Authorized Version alludes to the former meaning: 'And Leah said, A troop cometh: and she called his name Gad' (*Genesis* 30.11). The Revised Version, however, has the latter interpretation.

Gadsden Purchase In American history, the name is that of the purchase of a large area of land in what is now New Mexico and Arizona by the United States in 1853. The treaty for the sale of the land was negotiated by the army officer and diplomat James *Gadsden* (1788–1858).

Gaekwar The title, also spelled *Gaikwar*, is that of the ruler of the former native state of Baroda, India. It derives from Marathi *gāekwād*, 'guardian of the cows', from Sanskrit *gauh*, 'cow' and *vad*, 'guardian'. 'The word literally means a cow-keeper, which, although a low employment in general, has, in this noble family among the Hindoos, who venerate that animal, become a title of great importance' (James Forbes, *Oriental Memoirs*, 1813). *Cp.* GURKHA.

Gaelic The Celtic language of Scotland or Ireland is that of the *Gaels*, the people who are said to derive their name from a root word meaning 'white'. If so, there could be an association with ALBION, the historic name for Britain, which has also been interpreted in this sense. *See also* CELTIC; GAUL.

Gaeltachd The name is used for any region of Ireland where Irish is the native language, and itself represents Irish Gaelic *Gaedhealtacht*, literally 'Gaeldom'. *Cp.* GAIDHEALTACHD.

Gagauzi The language spoken on the northwest coast of the Black Sea, in Ukraine, is Turkic in origin, and is named for its speakers. Their own name represents Turkish *gagauz*, said to mean 'men with blue arrows', from Turkish *gök*, 'blue' and *ok*, 'arrow'.

Gaia The goddess of the earth in Greek mythology has a name that simply represents Greek *gē*, 'earth'.

Gaidhealtachd The name is used for any area of Scotland where Scottish Gaelic is the native language. It is itself the Scottish Gaelic word for 'Gaeldom'. *Cp.* GAELTACHD.

Gaillard Cut The name is that of the south-eastern section of the Panama Canal, *cut* through Culebra Mountain. It derives from the name of the American engineer who planned its construction, David du Bose *Gaillard* (1859–1913).

Gaitskill, Gaitskell *See* GASKELL.

Galahad As the purest and noblest knight of the Round Table in the Arthurian romances, Sir *Galahad* has a name that is probably of Celtic origin, like those of most Arthurian characters. Its precise meaning remains uncertain, however. Some have linked it with modern Welsh *cad*, 'battle'; others, less convincingly, with *gwalch*, 'hawk'. There is even a school of thought that sees a derivation in the biblical name GILEAD, although this is hardly Celtic.

Galápagos Islands The group of islands off the west coast of Ecuador, South America, takes its name from the giant land tortoises that the Spanish discovered here on landing in 1535. The Spanish word for these was *galápagos*, from a pre-Latin word *kuluppuku*, based on *kal*, 'scale'. To day there are few such tortoises left on the islands.

Galashiels The town in southeast Scotland has a name whose first part represents that of the *Gala* Water, the river on which it stands. This may itself mean 'gallows stream'. The second part of the name means 'shelters', 'huts', as for SOUTH SHIELDS, referring to temporary shelters used by shepherds in summer pastures. Galashiels has long been a centre of woollen manufacture.

Galata The port in northwest Turkey, now a district of Istanbul, derives its name from Italian *calata* or Genoese *caladda*, 'descent', 'slope'. The reference is to the location of the town on the northern shore of the Golden Horn at the foot of Mount Pera (Beyoğlu).

Galatea In Greek mythology, the name is that of the statue of a maiden sculpted by Pygmalion which was brought to life by Aphrodite in response to the prayers of its creator, who had fallen in love with it. Her name derives from Greek *gala*, genitive *galaktos*, 'milk', referring to the milk-white marble (or ivory) from which the statue had been made.

Galaţi The port on the Danube in southeast Romania may derive its name from Latin *Galatia*, although evidence for the town's Roman settlement remains uncertain. If so, it would be related to that of GALATIA, perhaps referring to its foundation by a *Gaul* (a Gaulish chief named Brennos has been mentioned).

Galatia The ancient region in central Asia Minor that was conquered by the Gauls in the 3rd century BC has a name that is directly related to that of GAUL itself, so has the same ultimate origin. In the Bible, the *Galatians* were one of the peoples to whom St Paul wrote an epistle.

Galaxy The name is an alternative one for the MILKY WAY, and the two titles are directly linked through Greek *gala*, genitive *galaktos*, 'milk' (to which, with the same meaning, Latin *lac*, genitive *lactis*, is also related).

Galbraith The Scottish name derives from Gaelic *gall*, 'stranger' and *Bhreathnach*, 'Briton', and originally applied to a person descended from a tribe of Britons who had settled in Scotland. Such people could have been Britons driven north by the Anglo-Saxon invasion, just as others had been driven across the Channel to BRITTANY. *Cp.* GALLOWAY, *and see also* GALL.

Galicia The name is a historic one for two regions, one in east central Europe, the other, smaller, in northwest Spain. The first of these may have a name that ultimately goes back to a Lithuanian word *galas*, 'end', 'peak', relating to the mountains here. The second could derive from a Celtic root word *cala*, 'water course', referring to the inhabitants of the region, who lived near the sea. But many scholars prefer to associate the name overall with that of GAUL.

Galilee The region of northern Israel, with the sea of the same name, derives its name from Hebrew *galil*, 'district'. The reference is probably to a district of pagan people, these being the foreigners who had come to settle here or who had been forcibly deported to the region.

Galileo The famous Italian mathematician and astronomer had the full name *Galileo Galilei* (1564–1642), meaning 'Galileo son of Galilei'. Both names derive from GALILEE, implying that he was the descendant of a someone who had made a pilgrimage to the Holy Land.

Gall The name derives from Gaelic *gall*, 'stranger', 'foreigner', originally given as a nickname to someone who had settled in a Gaelic region from elsewhere, such as an Anglo-Saxon or a Scandinavian.

Gallagher The Irish name is an English form of *O Gallchobhair*, 'descendant of *Gallchobhar*', a personal name that itself means 'foreign aid', from *gall*, 'foreign', 'strange' and *cabhair*, 'aid', 'help'.

Gallaher The familiar cigarette company was founded in Belfast in 1863 by Thomas *Gallaher* (1840–1927), a Northern Ireland farmer's son.

Galle The coastal town in southwest Sri Lanka takes its name from Sanskrit *galla*, 'stone', 'rock'. The town is a fortified seaport on a rocky promontory.

Gallipoli The peninsula and port of northwest Turkey, scene of a costly military campaign in the First World War, has a name that represents Greek *Kallipolis*, 'beautiful town', from *kalos*, 'beautiful' and *polis*, 'town'. This also gave the town's present Turkish name of *Gelibolu*. An identically named town and port in southeast Italy has the same origin.

Galloway The region of southwest Scotland has a tribal name, from Gaelic *Gall-Ghóidil*, 'stranger Gaels', these being the people of mixed Irish and Norse descent who settled here from the 9th century. The 'stranger' element (*gall*) is also present in the name of ARGYLL.

Galsworthy The surname comes from a place so called near Bideford in Devon, itself probably meaning 'bog myrtle slope', from Old English *gagol*, 'gale', 'bog myrtle' and *ōra*, 'slope'. This name was recorded in the Domesday Book as *Galeshore*, and has gained its present form through the influence of names ending in -*worthy*.

Galway The Irish county takes its name from its county town. The name itself means 'stony', from the Gaelic word that is now Irish *gall*, 'stone', referring to the rocky location of the place and the stony bed of the river Corrib at whose mouth it lies.

Gamages The former well-known London store took its name from Albert Walter *Gamage* (1855–1930), a glazier's son from Hereford, who with a colleague opened a draper's shop in Holborn in 1878. The flourishing department store that subsequently developed closed in 1972.

Gamaliel In the Old Testament, the name is that of a leader of the tribe of Manasseh, and in the New Testament, that of a teacher of St Paul. It derives from Hebrew *gamlī'ēl*, 'my reward is God'.

Gambia The country of East Africa takes its name from its main river, which came to be so called by Portuguese explorers in the 15th century as a corruption of its native name, *Ba-Dimma*, meaning simply 'river'.

Gambier Islands The South Pacific island group was discovered in 1797 and named in honour of the British naval commander James *Gambier*, first Baron Gambier (1756–1833).

Gamble The name originates from the Scandinavian nickname *gamall*, 'old', which was adopted in England in medieval times as a personal name.

Gandhara The historic region of India, in what is now northwest Pakistan and part of eastern Afghanistan, derives its name from its former inhabitants, whose own name comes from Sanskrit *gandha*, 'odour', 'perfume'. The ancient name is preserved in the modern one of *Kandahar*, the province of southern Afghanistan.

Gandzha The city in Azerbaijan takes its name from the river here. Its own name is of uncertain origin, despite attempts to associate it with that of the GANGES. In 1804 the town was renamed *Yelizavetpol* ('Elizabethopolis'), for the German princess Louise Maria Augusta, daughter of the Margrave of Baden-Anspach, who took the name *Elizabeth* Alexeevna on marrying the Russian tsar Alexander I in 1793. (She was then only 14, and he 16. The precocious marriage was designed to guarantee descendants for the Romanov dynasty.) In 1918 it reverted to its original name, but in 1936 was further renamed *Kirovabad*, for the Soviet Communist Party leader Sergei *Kirov* (for whom many other places were named, including what is now VYATKA).

The final -abad means 'inhabited place', 'town', as for HYDERABAD. In 1991 the city once more assumed its old name.

Ganesh The Hindu god of prophecy, usually portrayed with the head of an elephant, has a name of Sanskrit origin representing *gana-īsa*, 'lord of the multitude', referring to the lesser gods, over whom he is superior. His name is also spelled *Ganesha*.

Ganges The famous Indian river has a name that derives from Sanskrit *gangā*, meaning simply 'river'. *Cp.* India's other great river, the INDUS. *See also* GUNGA DIN.

Gangtok The city of northeast India, the capital of Sikkim state, derives its name from Tibetan *gang*, 'hill' and *tok*, 'summit', referring to its location.

Gansu The province of northwest China takes its name from Chinese *gānsù*, from *gān*, 'gentle', 'kindly' and *sù*, 'respected', 'serious'.

Ganymede The name of the beautiful youth abducted by Zeus and taken to Olympus, where he was made cupbearer to the gods, is probably pre-Greek in origin. However, to the Greeks it must have suggested *ganos*, 'beauty' and *mēdea*, meaning either 'cunning' or 'genitals'. Either way the name can be seen as a compliment to its bearer. *Cp.* MEDEA.

Gap The town of southeast France was known to the Romans as *Vapincum*, a name of obscure, perhaps Ligurian origin. The Provençal poet Frédéric Mistral claimed that the name came from *gavot*, 'Gavot', a Provençal nickname (meaning 'goitrous') for a local people who inhabited this part of the Alps. Whatever the case, it was the latter word that gave the name of the dance known as the *gavotte*.

Garda The name of the Irish police force means simply 'guard'. The full title is *Garda Síochána*, 'guardian of the peace', the latter word being the genitive of Irish *síocháin*, 'peace'. The name is pronounced approximately 'Garda Shiahana'.

Garda, Lake Italy's largest lake, in the north of the country, takes its name from the town of *Garda* here, whose own name means, as it implies, 'guard', 'watchtower'. The Roman name of the town was *Benacus*, 'two waters', as the town is at the point where the lake divides into two bays.

Gardener The name is an occupational one, meaning what it says. However, a medieval gardener would have been more concerned with growing fruit and vegetables than mowing lawns and weeding flower beds!

Gareth The name has been associated with GARY, GERAINT and GERARD, but its actual origin and meaning remain uncertain. In the Arthurian romances, the name is that of the nephew of King Arthur.

Garfield The fat ginger cat in the popular cartoons by the American artist Jim Davis first appeared in 1978. Davis gave him his grandfather's middle name.

Gargantua The bibulous giant who is a central character of Rabelais' great satire, *Gargantua and Pantagruel* (1532–64), has a name that echoes those of his mother, *Gargamelle* ('throat'), and father, *Grandgousier* ('great gullet'). All three names were taken by Rabelais from a contemporary chapbook entitled *Les Grandes et Inestimables Chronicques du geant Gargantua*. According to the narrative, *Gargantua* received his name from the exclamation *'Que grand tu as!'* ('How big you are!') made by his father at his birth:

> Ce que ouyans, les assistans dirent que vrayement il debvoit avoir par ce le nom de Gargantua, puis que telle avoit esté la premiere parolle de son pere à sa naissance, à l'imitation et exemple des anciens Hebreux. ('On hearing which, those present said that he should indeed have the name of Gargantua, as that had been the first comment of his father at his birth, in imitation and example of the ancient Hebrews.')
>
> Book I, Chapter 7.

But the origin is of course a typical piece of Rabelaisian folk etymology, and the name itself clearly means 'throat', doubtless as a direct borrowing from Spanish *garganta* in this sense.

Garlick As it implies, the name was originally that of a grower or seller of garlic, although in some cases it could have been an uncomplimentary nickname for a person who regularly ate garlic and so stank of it.

Garnett The name was originally used for a person who grew or sold *pomegranates*. The fruit was sometimes known simply as *granate* or *grenade*, but in this case the name has been based on what was originally the second half of a two-word phrase, Latin *pomum granatum* and subsequent Old French *pome grenate*, literally 'seeded fruit'.

Garonne The French river has a name that goes back to a pre-Indoeuropean root element *kar* or *gar*, meaning 'stone', 'rock'. *Cp.* CARIA.

Garrard The famous London jewellers were founded in 1735 by a goldsmith, George Wickes. They take their name, however, from Robert *Garrard* (1758–1818), also a goldsmith, who joined the firm in 1792 and who took it over in 1812.

Garrick Club The select London club was founded in 1831 by the Duke of Sussex for actors, painters and writers, and was named for the great actor, David *Garrick* (1717–1779), whose portrait by Zoffany hangs here. *Cp.* GARRICK THEATRE.

Garrick Theatre The London theatre was opened in Charing Cross Road in 1889 and was named for the famous actor David *Garrick* (1717–1779). A copy of a lost portrait of Garrick by Gainsborough hangs in the foyer. *Cp.* GARRICK CLUB.

Gary The first name derives from a surname, itself probably from a Norman personal name based on the Germanic word *gar*, 'spear' that is found in such names as GERALD and GERARD.

Gary The port in northwest Indiana, famous for its steel production, was founded in 1906 by the United States Steel Corporation and was named for the company's chairman, Judge Elbert H. *Gary* (1846–1927).

Gascoigne The name originally applied to someone from GASCONY, the French name of which is *Gascogne*.

Gascony The former province of southwest France was known to the Romans as *Vasconia*, in turn referring to the BASQUE people, whose region this is.

Gaskell The name derives from the place called *Gatesgill* near Keswick in Cumbria, itself having a Scandinavian name meaning 'goat shelter'. The name *Gaitskill* has the same origin.

Gateshead The town of northeast England has a name that literally means 'goat's head', from Old English *gāt*, 'goat' and *hēafod*, 'head', 'headland'. This may indicate that goats were formerly found on a headland here, or that a goat's head (or representation of one) was set up for some religious or totemic reason, perhaps in connection with sacrificial rites.

Gath In the Old Testament, *Gath* is one of the five cities of the Philistines, and birthplace of the giant Goliath. Its name represents Aramaic *gat*, 'press', that is, a wine-press. *Cp.* GETHSEMANE.

Gatwick The well-known airport south of London arose by a village of the name, itself meaning 'goat farm', from Old English *gāt*, 'goat' and *wīc*, 'farm'.

Gaul The historic name of France derives from that of its indigenous people, the *Gauls*, whose own name may derive from a Gaulish word *gal* or *gala* meaning 'brave', or be a form of a Celtic word meaning 'white', as (perhaps) for the *Gaels* (*see* GAELIC). Some scholars link the name with a Germanic word *walho*, 'stranger' that is related to the modern names of WALES (another Celtic land) and WALACHIA. The cockerel that is the national symbol of France was the result of a verbal association between Latin *Gallia*, 'Gaul' (or *Gallus*, 'a Gaul') and *gallus*, 'cock'. But the fighting spirit is common to both. *See also* GALATIA.

Gauloise The popular brand of French cigarettes has a name that means simply 'Gallic', referring to GAUL, the country from which France arose. The name was registered as a trademark in 1920.

Gaumont The name, familiar for cinemas, is that of the French motion picture inventor Léon Ernest *Gaumont* (1864–1946), who in 1901 developed a method of synchronizing a film projector with a gramophone. The *Gaumont* Company was founded in Britain in 1909, and was acquired in 1927 by the Gaumont-British Picture Corporation.

Gavin The name is of Celtic origin, but its meaning is uncertain. As with GALAHAD, some have associated it with Welsh *gwalch*, 'hawk'. Like Galahad, too, it is the name of a knight of the Round Table in the Arthurian romances, where it is more familiar as GAWAIN.

Gawain The knight of the Round Table in the Arthurian romances has a name that first appeared in French texts as *Gauvain*. It gave the common first name GAVIN, so has the same origin and meaning, whatever these may be. The character's most famous single adventure is told in the medieval alliterative poem *Sir Gawain and the Green Knight*, dating from the 1370s.

Gaza The historic Philistine city and modern Israeli-occupied one has a name of Arabic origin, from *'az*, 'force', 'strength', this being the name of the original fortress here. It is this city that probably gave modern English *gauze*, the silk fabric that is said to have originated there.

Gdańsk Poland's chief port, on the Baltic, has a Gothic name, from *Gutisk-anja*, 'end of the GOTHS', as the territory of these people extended to here. The former German name of the town, *Danzig*, falsely suggesting a connection with the *Danes*, is still familiar to many. *Cp* GDYNIA.

Gdynia The Polish port on the Baltic has a name of the same origin as that of GDAŃSK. Gdynia and Gdańsk are only ten miles (16 km) apart.

Gee The familiar name is of very uncertain origin. It was probably a personal name of some kind, but its meaning is unknown.

Geelong The port of southeast Australia, in Victoria, has an aboriginal name probably meaning 'marshy place'.

Geest The well-known banana company take their name from their Dutch founder, Jan van *Geest* (1906–), who came to England to set up a horticultural business in Spalding, Lincolnshire, in 1935. He began importing bananas from the Windward Islands after the Second World War.

Geffrye Museum The London museum, with a fine collection of furniture dating from the 17th century, was founded in 1715 under the bequest of Sir Robert *Geffrye* (1613–1703), Lord Mayor of London.

Gehenna In the Old Testament, the name is that of the valley below Jerusalem where children were sacrificed and idols worshipped (2 *Kings* 23.10, *Jeremiah* 19.6) and where refuse was slowly burnt. In the New Testament *Gehenna* is a place where the wicked are punished after death (*Matthew* 5.29, 20.28), otherwise *Hell*. The name represents Hebrew *gē-hinnōm*, 'valley of *Hinnom*', the latter probably being the name of the owner of the valley.

Gelderland The name, also spelled *Guelderland*, is that of a province and former duchy of the eastern Netherlands. It is Germanic in origin, from *gelwa*, 'yellow' and *haru*, 'mountain', to which *land* has been added. It relates to the sandy soil of the hills in the east and south of the region, bordering with Germany. The dukes of Gelderland had their seat at *Geldern*, in western Germany.

Gemara In Judaism, the *Gemara* is the main body of the TALMUD, which it comprises together with the MISHNA. It interprets the latter, and is regarded as being complementary to it. Hence its name, representing Aramaic *gemārā*, 'completion', from *gemār*, 'to complete'.

Gemini The constellation in the northern hemisphere contains the stars CASTOR and POLLUX, the 'heavenly twins', seen in the sky as holding hands. Its Latin name, meaning 'twins', thus relates to these two.

Gemma The name is the Italian word for 'gem', 'jewel', but has been adopted by some modern parents purely as a variation on EMMA.

Generalife The palace and gardens of the Moorish kings in Granada, Spain, as an outlying part of the Alhambra, take their name from Arabic *jannat ar-rīf*, 'garden of the bank', from *janna*, 'garden', *al*, 'the' and *rīf*, 'bank' (*cp*. RIF).

Genesis The name of the first book of the Bible represents Greek *genesis*, 'origin', 'creation', 'generation', referring to this word as it appears in the Septuagint (Greek version of the Old Testament): 'These are the *generations* of the heavens and of the earth' (*Genesis* 2.4). (A more meaningful word in modern terms here would be *origins*.) The name was thus left untranslated in both the Vulgate (Latin version) and Authorized Version. The Hebrew name of Genesis is *Berešith*, 'in the beginning', from its opening words: 'In the beginning God created the heaven and the earth' (*Genesis* 1.1).

Genesis The British rock group was originally formed as *Garden Wall* in 1965. In 1967 they were renamed *Genesis* by the pop entrepreneur Jonathan King, then at Decca Records, this being a propitious name for a group that was at the birth or beginning of its career.

Geneva The Swiss city has a name that is probably of proto-Indoeuropean origin, from *gan*, 'estuary', referring to the location of Geneva at the point where the Rhône flows from Lake Geneva. Some authorities, however, relate the name more specifically to an Indoeuropean root *gen* meaning 'bend' (hence Latin *genu* and French *genou*, 'knee'), relating to the curve of Lake Geneva at its southern end, where the city lies. *Cp.* GENOA.

Genevieve Although thought of primarily as a French name, *Genevieve* is probably a name of Germanic origin, from conjectural words *geno*, 'race', 'people' and *wefa*, 'woman', so that the meaning is 'kinswoman'. St *Genevieve* is the patron saint of Paris.

Genghis Khan The famous Mongol ruler, whose empire stretched from the Black Sea to the Pacific, was originally named *Temujin*, after a leader who had been defeated by his father, Yesugei, at the time of his birth. In about 1206, when he set out to unify the Mongol nation, Temujin changed his name to *Genghis Khan*, a title that means 'universal ruler'. *Khan* is familiar from the names or titles of other famous Mongol rulers, such as KUBLAI KHAN and *Batu Khan*, the latter being Genghis Khan's own grandson and leader of the Golden Horde. *Cp. also* AGA KHAN.

Gennesaret, Lake The name is one of those found in the Bible for the Sea of Galilee. It derives from Hebrew *gē*, 'valley' (*cp.* GEHENNA) and either *nétser*, 'branch' or *natsor*, 'to guard', 'to watch'. The former sense is referred to in the Old Testament: 'And there shall come forth a rod out of the stem of Jesse, and a Branch shall grow out of his roots' (*Isaiah* 11.1). *See also* NAZARETH.

Genoa The port of northwest Italy lies at the head of the Gulf of *Genoa* and has a name relating to this location, deriving from the Indoeuropean root word *gen*, 'curve', 'bend'. *Cp.* GENEVA.

Gentile The name, used of a person who is not Jewish, derives from the Vulgate (Latin version of the Bible), in which *gentes* (or *gentiles*), 'races', 'nations' translates the word that in the Hebrew Bible is *goyyim*. Examples occur several times in the Bible, one of the most significant being in *Genesis* 10.5: 'By these were the isles of the Gentiles divided in their lands; every one after his tongue, after their families, in their nations.' Since most non-Jews were subsequently Christians, the name later came to be equated with 'Christian' itself.

Geoffrey The familiar name has been derived from GODFREY, but may actually be a combination of the Germanic words *gavya*, 'territory' and *fridu*, 'peace', implying a peaceful ruler.

George The well-known name derives from Greek *gēorgos*, 'farmer', literally 'earth worker', from *gē*, 'earth' and *ergein*, 'to work'. It is familiar from St *George*, patron saint of England, slayer of the dragon, and from six English kings. George III gained the somewhat tautological nickname of *Farmer George*, with reference to his rustic tastes.

George Cross The high-ranking civilian award for bravery was instituted by King *George* VI in 1940 and bears a design of St *George* and the Dragon. The *George Medal*, a lesser award, has a similar design and was also instituted that year.

George Heriot's School The Edinburgh public school was founded in 1628 under the will of the goldsmith and banker *George Heriot* (1563–1624) as a school for the fatherless sons of former burgesses and freemen of Edinburgh. It was modelled on CHRIST'S HOSPITAL, London, and was itself originally known as *Heriot's Hospital*.

Georgetown The capital of Guyana was so named by the British in 1812 in honour of *George* III (1738–1820). The settlement's earlier name, given by the Dutch, had been *Stabroek*, 'stagnant pool'.

George Town The Malaysian port, the capital of Penang state, is named for *George* IV of England, in whose reign (1820–30) it was founded.

George Watson's College The Edinburgh public school takes its name from its founder, *George Watson* (d. 1723), first accountant of the Bank of Scotland. It amalgamated with George Watson's Ladies College in 1974 to form a coeducational school.

Georgia The name is familiar as that of the American state and the former Soviet republic. The state was colonized by the British in 1732 and named in honour of *George* II (1683–1760). The republic takes its name from its historic people, the *gurz*. This is a name (or word) of unknown meaning, but one that has been inextricably linked with that of St GEORGE, the country's patron saint. The Russian name of Georgia is *Gruziya*. The Georgians' own name for themselves is *kartveli*, and for their country is *sakartvelo*, 'land of Georgians'.

Georgian The term applies to architecture, furniture and decorative art in the period between 1714 and 1830, that is, during the reigns of the first four English kings named *George*.

Georgics Virgil's great poem, written in imitation of Hesiod's *Works and Days*, presents an idealized picture of the farmer's life. Hence its name, from Greek *geōrgika*, 'farming skills', 'husbandry' (literally 'earth works'). *Cp.* GEORGE.

Geraint The Welsh name is probably of Celtic origin, but its meaning is unknown. The name is that of one of the knights of the Round Table in the Arthurian romances.

Gerald The name is of Germanic origin, from *gēr*, 'spear' and *waltan*, 'to rule'. It has long been regarded as a variant of GERARD, but that name has a different origin.

Geraldine The name is a feminine form of GERALD, invented in the 16th century by the poet Henry Howard, Earl of Surrey, who wrote a sonnet to 'the Fair Geraldine', believed to have actually been Lady Elizabeth Fitz*gerald* (hence her name), daughter of the ninth Earl of Kildare.

Gerard The name is of Germanic origin, and consists of the words *gēr*, 'spear' and *hart*, 'hard', 'bold', implying a keen warrior.

Germany The precise origin of the well-known country name is still not certain. The source is generally held to lie either in Celtic words meaning 'neighbouring people' (*cp.* Old Irish *gair*, 'neighbour' and *maon*, 'people'), or else in a Germanic phrase derived from *gari*, 'spear' and *man*, 'man' (as for the personal names GERALD and GERARD). An origin in Germanic *ger-man*, 'greedy hand' or even *ger-man*, 'head man' has also been suggested. The names for Germany vary from one language to another. The French name, *Allemagne*, relates to the *Alemanni*, the race who once lived here, with their own name meaning literally 'all men', implying a single group or totality of people. The Germans' own name for their country is *Deutschland*, literally 'land of the DUTCH' (*which see* for the meaning). The Finns know Germany as *Saksa*, 'land of Saxons'. The Russian name for Germany is *Germaniya*, but for a German is *nemets*, from the Slavic root element *nem*, 'dumb', referring to a people who spoke a language that could not be understood, and that was therefore as valid for communication as no language at all.

Germinal The seventh month of the French Revolutionary calendar, corresponding to the period 22 March to 20 April, derives its name from Latin *germinare*, 'to sprout', so means 'seed time', 'month of budding'.

Germiston The city in the Transvaal south of Johannesburg, South Africa, was founded in 1887. In 1904 it was named after a farm near Glasgow, Scotland, that was the birthplace of one John Jack, a gold-mining pioneer here.

Gerontius The name derives from Greek *gerōn*, genitive *gerontos*, 'old man', and is familiar in literature as the central character in the poem by John Henry Newman, *The Dream of Gerontius* (1865), later set to music by Elgar. The poem is in the form of a monologue by a just soul on the point of death.

Gertrude Like GERALD and GERARD, the name *Gertrude* is of Germanic origin. It derives from *gēr*, 'spear' and *thrūth*, 'strength', implying an able warrior.

Geryon In Greek mythology, the name is that of the winged monster whose cattle Hercules stole as his tenth labour. It may relate in some sense to Greek *gērus*, 'voice', or *gēruō*, 'I speak', 'I shout'.

Gestapo The name of the secret state police in Nazi Germany is a shortened form of their full name, *Geheime Staatspolizei*, 'secret state police'.

Gestetner The familiar make of office equipment is named for David *Gestetner* (1854–1939), a Hungarian entrepreneur, who after a number of jobs in continental Europe came to Britain in 1879 and set up a stationery business. In 1881 he patented his best-known invention, the Cyclostyle, a pen with a sharp toothed wheel at its tip.

Gethsemane The garden in Jerusalem where Christ was betrayed on the night before his Crucifixion has a name of Aramaic origin meaning 'oil press', from *gat*, 'press' and *ŝemena*, 'oil', 'fat'. The press would have been used for extracting olive oil.

Gettysburg The name of the Pennsylvania town, famous for its national cemetery on the Civil War battlefield that was dedicated (in the *Gettysburg* Address) by Abraham Lincoln in 1863, derives from that of its founder in the 1780s, General James *Getty*.

Gezira The region of the east central Sudan between the Blue Nile and the White Nile has a name that refers to this location, from Arabic *al-jazīra*, 'the island'. *Cp.* ALGECIRAS, ALGIERS.

Ghana The country of West Africa takes its name from a tribal leader here that itself amounts simply to the royal title 'king'. The territory so named was originally much larger than present Ghana. Until 1957 the country was known as the *Gold Coast*, from the gold discovered here by Portuguese explorers in the late 15th century.

Ghats The mountain range of southern India, divided into the Eastern Ghats and Western Ghats, has a basic name that simply means 'pass', 'mountain', from Hindi *ghāṭ*.

Ghent The city and port in northwest Belgium has a name that probably derives from Celtic *condate*, 'confluence', referring to the town's location at the confluence of the rivers Lys and Scheldt.

Giant Fugue Bach's chorale prelude for organ *Wir glauben all' an einen Gott* is so nicknamed for the wide-striding notes of the pedal part, like those of a giant.

Giant's Causeway The famous promontory on the north coast of Northern Ireland, with its many basalt pillars, has a 'folk' name to match the many legends attached to it. The chief of these concerns the famous *giant* Finn mac Cool who is said to have built a bridge from the promontory across to Scotland in order to vanquish a mighty foe. It was the same hero who gave the name of FINGAL'S CAVE.

Gibbs The name means 'son of *Gibb*', this itself being a form of the medieval name *Gib*, a pet form of GILBERT.

Gibbs The familiar brand of toothpaste takes its name from Alexander *Gibb*, who set up a business as a candlemaker in London in 1768. His descendants eventually produced the well-known 'Gibbs SR' toothpaste in 1936.

Gibraltar The former British crown colony at the southern tip of Spain has an Arabic name, deriving from *jabal ṭāriq*, 'mountain of *Tariq*', from *jabal*, 'mountain' (*i.e.* the Rock of Gibraltar) and the name of a famous Berber leader who conquered the territory in 711. His own name means 'nocturnal visitor', from *ṭaraqa*, 'to come by night'.

Gibson Desert The Australian desert was discovered in 1873 by the Anglo-Australian explorer Ernest Giles. He named it for his travelling companion, Alfred *Gibson*, whom he had sent to pick up a supply of water from a previous camp but who never returned.

Gideon In the Old Testament, the name is that of the Hebrew judge who led the Israelites to victory over the Midianites. It is Hebrew in origin, from *Gidʿōn*, 'he who cuts down'. *See also* JERUBBAAL.

Gieves The famous men's outfitters owe their name to James *Gieve* (1820–1888), who in 1852 became a partner in a tailoring firm in Portsmouth that had been founded in 1785. The name is pronounced with a hard *g*.

Gilbert The name is a Germanic one, deriving from *gīsil*, 'hostage', and *beraht*, 'bright', 'famous'. A 'hostage' in the medieval sense of the word was a person, often a noble youth, handed over temporarily to an enemy as a condition for them to carry out some agreed task or deed, such as releasing an important prisoner. A famous bearer of the name was St *Gilbert* of Sempringham, the 12th-century Lincolnshire priest who was the founder of the only native English religious order, the *Gilbertines*, abolished on the Dissolution of the Monasteries.

Gilead The name is that of both a place and a person in the Old Testament: a mountainous region east of the river Jordan, and a grandson of Manasseh. It is popularly derived from Hebrew *gilʿad*, which probably contains the Aramaic root word *gal*, 'heap of stones'. The character of the name is so called since he came from the region. *Cp.* GILGAL.

Giles The name is an English form of the Latin name *Aegidius*, itself from Greek *aigidion*, 'kid', 'young goat'. St *Giles* is the patron saint of cripples.

Gilgal The Old Testament name, famous as that of the first encampment of the Israelites on entering Canaan after crossing the Jordan (*Joshua* 4.19), is Aramaic in origin meaning 'circle of stones', from *gil*, 'circle' and *gal* 'heap of stones'. Its location is uncertain, but the stones were almost certainly a sacred circle of some kind: 'And those twelve stones, which they took out of Jordan, did Joshua pitch in Gilgal' (*Joshua* 4.20). *Cp.* GALILEE, GILEAD and GOLGOTHA.

Gilgamesh The name of the semi-legendary Sumerian king is Akkadian in origin, and in its Sumerian variant, *Bil-ga-mes*, probably means 'ancestor hero'.

Gillette The well-known make of razors and razor blades takes its name from the American inventor of the first safety razor, King Camp *Gillette* (1855–1932), originally a bottle cap salesman, who patented his invention in 1910.

Gillian The name is a variant form of JULIAN, formerly a girl's name.

Gimcrack Stakes The six-furlong horse race for two-year-old colts, run annually at York since 1846, takes its name from the *Gimcrack* Club which manages racing at York. The club itself, founded in 1767, is named after a horse that once ran at York, but lost. The word *gimcrack* now means 'worthless object', but in the 18th century also meant 'fop'.

Ginn The American publishing house, specializing in educational books, takes its name from its founder, Edwin *Ginn* (1838–1914), a farmer's son who founded his business in 1867, his first publication being an edition of *The English of Shakespeare* by the Scottish literary authority George L. Craik. The name is pronounced with a hard *g*.

Gioconda, La The name is an alternative one for the MONA LISA, Leonardo da Vinci's famous portrait of a young woman with an enigmatic smile. As it stands, *La Gioconda* is Italian for 'the merry one', and the name is translated as such in other languages (such as French *La Joconde*). However, the lady is not obviously jocund (the English equivalent of the name), but gently smiling. This is because the name is probably that of the Florentine merchant Francesco del *Giocondo*, whose third wife she was. The name of the portrait thus represents her married surname, and really means 'Giocondo's wife'.

Giotto The space probe launched by the European Space Agency in 1985 to study Halley's comet was named for the Italian painter *Giotto*, who in 1305 painted a series of frescoes showing the Star of Bethlehem as a comet, two years after Halley's comet had itself appeared.

Gippsland The region of southeast Australia was so named in 1840 by the Polish explorer Count Strzelecki in honour of the British governor of New South Wales, Sir George *Gipps* (1791–1847).

Gipsy Moth The name of the yachts in which Sir Francis Chichester raced and sailed alone round the world (1966–7) was adopted from the *Gipsy Moth* aircraft in which he made a solo flight to Australia (1929).

Girl Guides The sister organization of the BOY SCOUTS, formed in 1910 by Robert

Baden-Powell and his sister Agnes in response to popular demand (from the girls), has a name that was suggested by the military guides who carried out reconnoitring. In this sense, the term *guide* is virtually synonymous with *scout*, whose duties were similar. The following passage is of interest in this respect: 'In the Indian army the name of "Guides" is given to a regiment of cavalry and infantry attached to the Punjab frontier force. It was raised [...] chiefly with the view to the men acting as scouts' (George E. Voyle and G. de Saint-Clair Stevenson, *A Military Dictionary*, 1876). Boy Scouts are now known simply as *Scouts*, and Girl Guides officially dropped the 'Girl' in 1991. Their American equivalents are *Girl Scouts*.

Girlschool The British heavy metal group, formed in 1978 as an 'all-*girl*' quartet, originated from a band started by two of their number when still at *school*. Their major hit of 1981, 'The St Valentine's Day Massacre', was recorded jointly with MOTORHEAD under the name *Headgirl*.

Gironde The name of the estuary of the rivers Garonne and Dordogne, in southwest France, is a variant on that of the GARONNE itself, so has the same meaning.

Girondist The members of the moderate republican party during the French Revolution were so named since its earliest leaders came from the GIRONDE district.

Girton College The Cambridge college, until 1977 taking women only, was founded in Hitchin in 1869 as the *College for Women*. In 1872 it moved to its present site, in the village of *Girton*, on the outskirts of Cambridge, and takes its name from it. The village name itself means 'gravel estate', from Old English *grēot*, 'gravel' (modern *grit*) and *tūn*, 'farm', 'estate'. The reference is to the gravelly soil here.

Givenchy The well-known brand of perfume is named for Hubert de *Givenchy*, who opened a fashion salon in Paris in 1951.

Giza The city in northeast Egypt, also known as *El Gîza*, has an Arabic name that itself represents Egyptian *Er-ges-ḥer*, 'beside the high', from its location next to the great pyramids.

Gladstone The Scottish name derives from a place so called near Biggar, in the former county of Lanarkshire. Its name is said to derive from Old English *gleoda*, 'kite' (the bird) and *stān*, 'stone'.

Gladwin The name was originally an Old English personal name, meaning 'joyful friend'.

Gladys The name is of Welsh origin, from *Gwladus*. The meaning of this is uncertain, although some have related it to Welsh *gwledig*, 'lord', 'prince'.

Glamis Castle The famous Scottish castle, the birthplace of Princess Margaret, has a Gaelic name representing *glamhus*, 'open land', referring to the terrain here north of Dundee where the castle was built.

Glamorgan The former county of South Wales, now divided into Mid, West and South *Glamorgan*, has a name meaning '*Morgan*'s shore', comprising Welsh *glan*, 'bank', 'shore' followed by the personal name MORGAN, probably that of a 7th-century prince of Gwent. The Welsh name of Glamorgan is *Morgannwg*, 'Morgan's territory'.

Glarus The town of east central Switzerland has a name that may derive from Latin *clarus*, 'clear', perhaps originally referring to a clearing here.

Glasgow The famous Scottish city and port has a Gaelic name that means 'green hollow', from *glas*, 'green' and *cau*, 'hollow'. This would originally have been a natural feature by the Clyde long before the settlement arose.

Glastonbury The Somerset town, famous for its pagan and mystic associations, has a name based on a Celtic word meaning 'woad', represented now by the first syllable *Glast-*. Woad is the plant yielding the blue dye with which the Britons decorated their bodies. The second part of the name, suggesting -*ton*, was in fact originally -*ing*, meaning 'people' (as in WORTHING), so that Glastonbury was the 'place of the woad people'. Old English *burh*, meaning 'fort', was then added to this. *See also* AVALON.

Glaxo The present group of pharmaceutical companies was founded as a small import-export business in New Zealand in 1873. In about 1900 its founder, Joseph Nathan, began to export dried milk from Australia. He originally wanted to name the product *Lacto*, after Latin *lac*, genitive *lactis*, 'milk'. When this proved legally unacceptable, however, he chose *Glaxo* instead, basing this on the Greek equivalent element *glakto*, from *gala*, genitive *galaktos*, 'milk' (*cp.* GALAXY).

Gleave The name derives from the former word for a sword, itself ultimately from Latin *gladius* in this sense. It would have been an occupational name for a maker or seller of swords, or a nickname for an experienced swordsman.

Glencoe The *glen* (valley) of the Scottish river *Coe*, running to Loch Leven near Ballachulish, is now associated with the notorious massacre of the Macdonalds by the Campbells and English troops that took place there in 1692. The meaning of the river's name is unknown.

Glenda The name is a modern Welsh one, combining *glân*, 'clean', 'pure' and *da*, 'good'.

Gleneagles Hotel The well-known hotel near Auchterarder, central Scotland, with its famous golf courses, takes its name from the locality here, itself meaning 'church valley'. The reference is to the *glen* of the river Ruthven and the church (Gaelic *eaglais*) that was built in it. Most Scottish places with *Glen-* are named for the river of the particular valley, but *Gleneagles* is an exception. Another is GLENROTHES.

Glenfiddich The famous blend of whisky takes its name from the distillery built in 1887 at Dufftown in *Glen Fiddich* (the valley of the small river *Fiddich*) by the Scottish distiller William Grant (1839–1923). There are seven whisky distilleries in Dufftown alone, but Glenfiddich is the only Highland distillery to bottle its own malt whisky on the spot.

Glen Grant The distillery that gave its name to the well-known blend of whisky was founded in Rothes, Scotland, in 1840 by two brothers, James and John *Grant*, the sons of a Banffshire farmer. The *Glen* of the name is the valley of the Spey, where the distillery stands.

Glenlivet The blend of whisky, properly *The* Glenlivet, takes its name from the *Glen Livet*, the valley of the *Livet* Water near Tomintoul, Scotland, where the company built the first of five distilleries in 1824. It should not be confused with other whiskies of the same name, which by law must be prefixed by a second distinguishing name, such as *Dufftown-Glenlivet* and *Braes of Glenlivet*.

Glenrothes The New Town in east central Scotland, founded in 1948, has an artificial name devised to blend in with the many *Glen* names of this part of Scotland. There is no obvious glen here, but a reference might be supposed to the river Leven, which flows past the north of the town. The second part of the name relates to the earls of *Rothes*, who have long been connected with the region and who had an estate here.

Globe Theatre The famous round wooden theatre built in 1598 by the Thames in London took its name from its shape, with its sign showing Hercules carrying the world as a *globe* on his shoulders. Another *Globe Theatre* existed in the Strand from 1868 to 1902, and a third opened in Shaftesbury Avenue in 1906 (called the *Hicks Theatre* to 1909, after the co writer and producer of its first play, Seymour *Hicks*). A new theatre that is a copy of the original is currently being built on its old Bankside site. Its first two bays opened in 1992.

Glorious Revolution The name is that of the coup of 1688 in which the Roman Catholic king James II was deposed and replaced by the Protestant king William III of Orange and his wife Mary, James's sister. It is uncertain when and where the phrase originated, but the epithet *glorious* has long been associated with a rightful monarch.

Gloucester The English cathedral city was a Roman settlement, as the final *-cester* of its name indicates, representing the Old English *ceaster* that ultimately derived from Latin *castra*, 'camp'. The first part of the name represents the town's Roman name of *Glevum*, itself deriving from a Celtic root word meaning 'bright', 'shining', and a reference to the river Severn on which Gloucester stands.

Glubbdubdrib The name of the island of sorcerers in Swift's famous novel *Gulliver's Travels* (1726) has been 'decoded' as spelling out 'Dub-bul-lin', otherwise 'Dublin', where Swift himself was born. Similarly, the 'great Island of *Luggnagg*' has been interpreted (by being read backwards) as 'Anggul', *i.e.* 'Angle-land', *i.e.* 'England'. But Swift may not actually have had anything so subtle in mind!

Glumdalclitch The name is that of the little girl (in fact a giant) who is Gulliver's 'guardian' in Swift's *Gulliver's Travels* (1726). It has been 'decoded' as meaning 'grim doll clutch', since many small girls clutch their dolls tightly. However, although Gulliver might have seemed like a doll to Glumdalclitch, the narrative hardly bears this out:

> She apprehended some Mischief would happen to me from rude vulgar Folks, who might Squeeze me to Death, or break one of my Limbs by taking me in their Hands.
>
> Book II, Chapter 2.

Glyndebourne The Elizabethan house near Lewes, Sussex, famous for its annual summer opera season, takes its name from the local *bourne* (river) called *Glynde* Reach, itself named for the nearby village of *Glynde*. This in turn probably represents an Old English unrecorded word *glind*, meaning 'fence', 'enclosure'.

Glynis This name and *Glenys* may have the same Welsh origin, from *glân*, 'clean', 'pure' and the ending *-ys* as for GLADYS.

Goa The state on the west coast of India, a former Portuguese possession, derives its name from local words *goe mat*, 'fertile land'.

Gobi The desert of eastern Asia has a name of Mongolian origin, from *gov'*, 'steppe', 'desert'. The desert's Chinese name is *Shamo*, meaning 'desert of sand', from *shā*, 'sand' and *mò*, 'desert'.

Godalming The Surrey town has a name meaning 'place of *Godhelm*'s people'. It is not known who Godhelm was but his name means literally 'God's helmet', that is, 'fighter for God'.

Godavari The river of central India has a name of uncertain origin. The second part is almost certainly Sanskrit *vāri*, 'river'.

The first part may possibly be a form of *Goth* (*see* GOTHS).

Goddard The surname was originally the personal name *Godhard*, from the Germanic words *got*, 'god' (or *gōd*, 'good') and *hart*, 'hardy', 'brave'. This name was borne by the 11th-century bishop who founded the hospice on the St *Gotthard* pass between Switzerland and Italy.

Godfrey The name is Germanic in origin, from *god*, 'god' (or possibly *gōd*, 'good') and *fridu*, 'peace'. It has long been associated with GEOFFREY, but that is a name of different origin.

Godiva The name is famous from Lady *Godiva*, who in the 11th century is said to have ridden nude through the streets of Coventry on condition that her husband, Leofric, Earl of Mercia, lift the heavy taxes he had imposed on the townsfolk. Her name is a latinized form of Old English *Godgifu*, 'God-given', or 'gift of God', from *god*, 'god' and *gifu*, 'gift'. The meaning is thus exactly the same as that of DOROTHY. GOODWOOD is so called after another lady of the name.

Godolphin and Latymer School The London public school for girls takes its name from Sir William *Godolphin* (1634–1696), who left provision in his will for the education of poor scholars. In 1856 the Charity Commission used this money to found the *Godolphin School* for boys. At the end of the 19th century it was decided to turn the school into a secondary day school for girls, who duly moved into the old premises of the boys' school in 1905. They did so with the financial support of the *Latymer* Foundation that had earlier founded LATYMER UPPER SCHOOL. Sir William was the uncle of Elizabeth *Godolphin*, founder of the GODOLPHIN SCHOOL, Salisbury.

Godolphin School The girls' public school at Salisbury, Wiltshire was founded in 1707 by Elizabeth *Godolphin*, a niece of Sir William *Godolphin*, who founded the GODOLPHIN AND LATYMER SCHOOL, London. The unusual surname is Cornish in origin, and of unknown meaning.

Godthaab The former name of NUUK, the capital of Greenland, on the southwest coast, represents Danish *Godthåb*, 'good hope', from *godt*, the neuter of *god*, 'good' and *håb*, 'hope'. The town was founded in 1721 by a Norwegian missionary, Hans Egede, and is said to be so named for the 'good hope' he entertained of converting the Eskimos here. The name may have been at least partly suggested by that of the CAPE OF GOOD HOPE, South Africa, similarly located on the southwest coast.

Godwin The name is an Old English one, from *god*, 'god' and *wine*, 'friend', so meaning 'friend of God' or 'befriended by God'.

Godwin-Austen, Mount The alternative name for K2, the second highest mountain in the world, in northern India, derives from that of the British explorer and geologist, Lieutenant-Colonel Henry *Godwin-Austen* (1834–1923), who first sighted it in 1865.

Gog and Magog In the Old Testament, *Gog* is a hostile prince, and *Magog* the land from which he comes to attack Israel (*Ezekiel* 38). In the New Testament, the names are those of two warring tribes hostile to the Church (*Revelation* 20.8). The origin of the names remains uncertain, although *Gog* may mean 'darkness', and in the Old Testament context *Magog* probably means 'land of *Gog*'. Gog's name has also been related to those of AGAG and *Gyges*, king of Lydia. The statues of Gog and Magog in the Guildhall, London, are believed to represent the legendary giants GOGMAGOG and *Corineus*. Presumably Corineus was forgotten after a time, and Gogmagog's name was split in two to give the familiar biblical names, from which it had evolved in the first place.

Gogmagog The name of the legendary British giant, killed in battle by Corineus, probably derives from the biblical characters GOG AND MAGOG. An effigy of Gogmagog cut in the chalk hills outside Cambridge gave the name of the *Gog Magog Hills* there, popularly known as 'The Gogs'. There is no trace of the figure today.

Goidelic The name for the northern group of Celtic languages in Britain, comprising Irish Gaelic, Scottish Gaelic and Manx, derives from Old Irish *Goidel*, 'Gael' (*see* GAELIC).

Golan Heights The range of hills in southwest Syria, possession of which is currently disputed between Israel and Syria, takes its name from the biblical city of *Golan* (*Deuteronomy* 4.43, *Joshua* 20.8), whose own name is of uncertain origin. It has been related to Hebrew *galgal*, 'circle', 'circuit', as for GALILEE, GILGAL and GOLGOTHA.

Golconda The ruined town and fortress in south central India, famous for its diamonds, has a name that derives from Telugu *golla*, 'shepherd' and *konda*, 'hill'.

Gold The name means what it says in one of a number of ways. It could have originally been the name of a person who worked in gold, or a nickname for someone with golden hair, or, for Jews, a purely arbitrary name with a favourable meaning. In America the Jewish name *Gold* is often a short form of one of the many compound names beginning with this word, such as *Goldberg*, *Goldstein* or *Goldstern*.

Goldberg Variations Bach's variations for harpsichord (1741) are named for the German musician and composer Johann Gottlieb *Goldberg* (1727–1756). Goldberg was then only 13, too young to have actually commissioned the work, although Bach gave him a copy.

Golden Arrow The famous train that ran between London and Paris from 1929 to 1972 originated as an exclusive Pullman service for first-class passengers, the English name having its French counterpart as *La Flèche d'Or*. In folklore, the 'Golden Arrow' was the one sought by a pair of lovers in the land of their dreams, and possibly the namers of the train intended a reference to Paris as the 'City of Lovers'. There is an allusion to the legend in the title (and story) of Mary Webb's early novel *The Golden Arrow* (1916).

Golden Gate The strait between the Pacific and San Francisco Bay, crossed by the *Golden Gate* Bridge, was so named in 1846 by the American general and explorer John Charles Frémont (1813–1890), who based the name on that of the GOLDEN HORN. The name gained added significance with the Californian gold rush of 1848. California is now nicknamed 'the Golden State'.

Golden Hind The name of the express train that runs between London and Plymouth, making its first journey in 1964, derives from that of the ship (originally the *Pelican*) in which Sir Francis Drake, a Plymouth man, made his famous journey round the world in 1577–80. Drake himself named his ship as a compliment to Sir Christopher Hatton, a financial partner in his venture, whose crest included a heraldic hind.

Golden Horde The name is that of the *horde* or tribe of Mongols who, under Batu Khan, grandson of Genghis Khan, devastated eastern Europe in the early 13th century. They were so named for the luxurious trappings of Batu's field headquarters. The English word *horde*, now meaning little more than 'crowd', 'mass', derives from this historic people, and is itself from Turkish *urdū*, 'camp', a word that also gave URDU.

Golden Horn The inlet of the Bosporus in northwest Turkey was so named for its abundance of fish, especially tunny, which are trapped here on entering from the Black Sea. *Golden* thus refers to the wealth of fish; *Horn* describes the shape of the inlet. There could also be an overall suggestion of a 'horn of plenty', or cornucopia.

Golding The name means 'son of GOLD', when this word was in use as a personal name, not a surname.

Goldsmiths' College The London University college is named for the *Goldsmiths' Company*, the City of London livery company that founded it in 1891 as a school to provide classes in art and music and to prepare students for external degrees from the University in engineering and science.

Golgotha The hill just outside Jerusalem where Jesus was crucified, also known as CALVARY, takes its name from Aramaic *golgoltā* or *gulgaltā*, 'skull', itself a borrowing from Hebrew *gulgólet* with the same meaning. The word has the root element *gal*, 'heap of stones' found also in the names of GALILEE, GILEAD and GILGAL. Despite its associations with death, strengthened by the event itself, the name is purely descriptive, referring to a round, bare hill resembling a skull.

Goliath The famous biblical giant, killed by David with a stone from a sling, is introduced in the Old Testament as 'the champion, the Philistine of Gath, Goliath by name' (1 *Samuel* 17.23), implying that his name derives from that of GATH itself. Some have similarly attempted to match his name with the actual word *giant*. But in the Hebrew Bible his name is *gŏljat*, and the relationship between that and Greek *gigas*, genitive *gigantos*, 'giant' (perhaps akin to *gē*, 'earth'), which gave the English word, is more than a little tenuous.

Golightly The name probably originated as a nickname for a messenger, someone who would 'go lightly', in the sense 'move swiftly'.

Gollancz The British publishing house takes its name from Victor *Gollancz* (1893–1967), born in London the son of a Polish Jew who ran a jewellery business. He entered publishing in 1921 and founded his own company in 1927.

Gomel The city in Byelorussia has a name of uncertain origin. It has been tentatively linked with Old Slavonic *gomila*, 'burial mound'.

Gomorrah The well-known name is that of the ancient city near the Dead Sea which, together with SODOM, was destroyed by God as a punishment for the wickedness of its inhabitants. It derives from the Hebrew root word *'ōmer*, 'sheaf', referring to its corn. Archaeological research has shown that the plain where the two cities stood was probably unusually fertile.

Gondwana The region of central north India, regarded as part of a ancient supercontinent, derives its name from the *Gond*, the people who ruled this region from the 12th to the 18th century, and Hindi *van*, 'forest'.

Gonville and Caius College See CAIUS COLLEGE.

Gonzalez, Byass The well-known brand of sherry takes the first part of its name from a Spanish wineseller, Manuel María *Gonzalez* Angel, who started his business in Jerez, the town that gave the name of sherry itself, in 1835. The second part of the name is that of his London agent, Robert Blake *Byass*, who joined him as partner in 1855.

Good As it implies, the name was originally a nickname for a good person, one who did good.

Goodchild The name was originally a nickname for either a good child (in the medieval sense: *see* the surname CHILD), or for a good person in general, or alternatively for someone who was the *godchild* of a famous person.

Good Friday The Friday before Easter, observed as a commemoration of the Crucifixion of Jesus, came to be called *Good* in the sense 'holy', and the word is not a corruption of 'God', despite the popular explanation to that effect. Similar names for holy days existed in medieval times. Christmas, for example, was called *Goodtide*, and Shrove Tuesday was also known as *Good* Tuesday. Good Friday is the holiest day of HOLY WEEK.

Goodman The name was the equivalent of a title for the master of a house or, in Scotland, for a landowner. But it could also simply be a nickname for a good person. There was also an Old English personal name *Gūthmund*, 'battle protection', which could have given the name in some cases.

Goodrich The well-known make of tyre takes its name from the American entrepreneur and former army surgeon Benjamin Franklin *Goodrich* (1841–1888), who bought the Hudson River Rubber Company in 1869 and the following year relocated it in Akron, Ohio, the 'rubber capital of the world'.

Goodwin Sands The notorious shoals in the Strait of Dover have a name that may derive from the Old English personal name corresponding to modern *Godwin*, meaning 'good friend'. The shoals could thus have been given the name in an attempt to placate any evil spirit they contained. But the reference may actually be a historic one, to Earl *Godwine* of Kent, who held the island here that was subsequently submerged to become the present sands, an event that is said to have occurred in 1097.

Goodwood The famous Sussex racecourse takes its name from nearby *Goodwood* Park, part of the estate of Goodwood House, whose own name means '*Godgifu*'s estate'. *Godgifu* was an Anglo-Saxon female name, meaning 'God-given', and was made famous by Lady GODIVA.

Goodyear The well-known tyre manufacturing company was founded in Akron, Ohio, in 1898 by the American businessmen Frank Seiberling and his brother Charles, who named it after Charles *Goodyear* (1800–1860), the discoverer of vulcanized rubber.

Gorakhpur The city of northern India derives its name from that of the GURKHAS, the people of Nepal, with Hindi *pur*, 'town', added.

Gorbals The district of Glasgow, formerly notorious for its slums, has a name of uncertain origin. It appears in a document of 1521 as *Baldis*.

Gordium The ancient city that was the capital of Phrygia is traditionally said to take its name from *Gordius*, king of Phrygia, who gave his own name to the *Gordian* knot. But he belongs to mythology, and the place-name may originate in a pre-Celtic root word *gord*, meaning 'fortified height'.

Gordon The name comes from the Scottish surname, which is itself from the village of *Gordon* near Kelso, not far from the English border. Its own name is said to mean 'spacious fort', from words to which modern Welsh *gor*, 'spacious' and *din*, 'fort' are related. But in some cases the name may represent the Norman place-name *Gourdon*, itself based on the personal name *Gordus*. As a Jewish name, *Gordon* probably refers to someone originally from GRODNO.

Gordons The familiar brand of gin is named for the Scottish businessman Alexander *Gordon*, who opened a distillery in Finsbury, London, in 1769.

Gordonstoun The well-known Scottish public school was founded in 1934 in a mansion on an extensive estate that was acquired in 1638 by the historian and privy councillor Sir Robert *Gordon* (1580–1656). Scottish *toun* means 'estate' much in the same way as Old English *tūn*, with both words related to modern *town*.

Gorgan The city of northern Iran has a name of uncertain origin. It has been popularly derived from Iranian *gorgān*, the

213

plural of *gorg*, 'wolf', allegedly for the wickedness of its inhabitants.

Gorgio The name is used by Gypsies for a non-Gypsy, and is a Romany word of unknown origin. The English form of the word is a corruption of the Spanish Romany *gacho*, and appears to have been introduced by George Borrow in his novel LAVENGRO (1851): 'But you are of the Gorgios, and I am a Romany Chal' (Chapter 17). It is very easy to be beguiled by Borrow's sometimes fanciful philology, although the title of this particular novel is the Romany word for 'philologist' itself.

Gorgon The Gorgons were the three monstrous sisters of Greek mythology, Stheno, Euryale, and Medusa, who had live snakes for hair and a look that turned the beholder into stone. Fittingly enough, their name derives from Greek *gorgos*, 'terrible'.

Gorky *See* NIZHNY NOVGOROD.

Görlitz The city of southeast Germany has a Slavic name, based on *gora*, 'mountain'. The town lies on the northern foothills of the Sudeten Mountains.

Goshen The region of ancient Egypt was the land that the Israelites occupied until the Exodus. The name may be Semitic in origin, but its meaning is unknown.

Goslar The city in north central Germany derives its name from Old High German *gôze*, 'flood' and *lar*, 'pasture'.

Gosport The Hampshire town has a name that probably means what it says, showing that in medieval times it was a 'goose port', that is, a market town (rather than a port in the modern sense) where geese were sold. Local guidebooks like to derive the name from 'God's port', referring to an occasion when a French bishop took refuge from a storm here in the 12th century. But this is folk etymology at work!

Göteborg The port in southwest Sweden has a name that means 'fort of the GOTHS', from Swedish *Got*, 'Goth' and *borg*, 'fort'. The name is also spelled *Gothenburg*. *Cp.* GDAŃSK and GDYNIA.

Gothic In its basic sense, the name relates simply to the GOTHS, the people and their language. But as applied to the well-known architectural style, represented in many European churches and cathedrals of the 12th to 16th centuries, the name has a more oblique reference. The Goths had a reputation for barbarity, and Italian art connoisseurs of the Renaissance period adopted the term 'Gothic' to describe medieval architecture, which they regarded as 'barbaric' by comparison with their own classically-inspired styles. The term later lost its derogatory sense, and is now standard for the overall period of medieval architecture, itself subdivided (in England) into Early English, Decorated and Perpendicular. As applied to literature, the term *Gothic novel* is now used of tales with a macabre or 'bloodthirsty' content. It was originally used simply in the sense 'medieval', however, after the architecture, and first occurs with this meaning in the title of Horace Walpole's novel *The Castle of Otranto: A Gothic Story* (1740). However, this had its fill of ghosts, mysterious vaults, living statues and the like, and so promoted the more popular sense of the term for later literature with such elements.

Gothic Revival The name is used for the *revival* of the GOTHIC style of architecture that was taken up in the 19th century. It is typified by the Houses of Parliament, London.

Gothic Symphony The first symphony by Havergal Brian, composed between 1919 and 1927, is so named for its 'barbaric' style and for the vast resources of players and singers needed to perform it.

Goths The Goths were an East Germanic people of Scandinavian origin who settled in the region of the Black Sea in the 2nd century AD. They are divided into two groups, the OSTROGOTHS. or eastern Goths, and the VISIGOTHS, or western Goths. Their name remains of uncertain origin. It has been variously derived from that of the Scandinavian god ODIN, from the Germanic word *got*, 'god', and from an Indoeuropean root word *gauta*, 'flowing', so that they are named after some river. They gave their names to various places, including the modern cities of GÖTEBORG, GDAŃSK and GDYNIA. *See also* GOTHIC.

Gotland The island in the Baltic Sea has a name that relates directly to the GOTHS, and it is possible that these people may have originated here. For other names relating to the Goths *cp.* GDAŃSK, GDYNIA, GÖTEBORG.

Götterdämmerung In German mythology, the name, traditionally translated 'Twilight of the Gods', is that of the ultimate destruction of the gods in a battle with the forces of evil. It is familiar as the title of the final opera in Wagner's *Ring of the Nibelung* (1876).

Göttingen The city of western Germany may have a name deriving from Germanic *got*, 'god', without necessarily being a Christian reference.

Gough The name is Celtic in origin, either as an occupational name for a smith (Gaelic *gobha*) or, in Wales, as a nickname for a red-haired person (from *coch*, 'red').

Gower In most cases the name derives from a Norman place-name such as the region north of Paris formerly known as *Gohiere*, or any of the places called *Gouy*, the latter deriving from the Roman personal name *Gaudius*. As a Welsh name, it could denote a person from the *Gower* Peninsula.

Goya The well-known brand of perfume was not named for the famous Spanish painter but has an arbitrary name, devised by the firm's founder in the 1930s. (He originally wanted *Loya*, but that suggested the name of an existing company.) The firm began its promotion with a drawing of a reclining nude, but chemists refused to display it so the company had to overprint a sort of nightdress. This debut happened to associate the name with the two famous paintings by Goya, *Naked Maya* and *Clothed Maya*, so that the makers of the perfume were able to capitalize on the artistic link after all. The name was registered in 1936.

Gracchi The two 2nd-century BC Roman politicians and reformers, Tiberius Sempronius *Gracchus* and his brother Gaius Sempronius *Gracchus*, are traditionally bracketed together under the plural name *Gracchi*. *Gracchus* was their *cognomen* or nickname, probably from Latin *gracilis*, 'slender', either in a favourable sense, 'graceful', or an unfavourable one, 'meagre', 'scant'.

Grace The name means what it says, implying that the bearer of the name is either specially favoured by God or is an embodiment of Christian grace.

Graf Spee The name of the German pocket battleship blown up by her crew after the Battle of the River Plate (1939) derives from that of the German admiral and count (*Graf*) Maximilian von *Spee* (1861–1914), who died when his own ship, the *Scharnhorst*, was sunk by the British off the Falkland Islands.

Graf Zeppelin The first airship to operate on a transatlantic passenger service (from 1928 to 1937) was named in memory of the German airship pioneer, Count (*Graf*) Ferdinand von *Zeppelin* (1838–1917). The first rigid-bodied airships constructed by him (from 1900) were also known by the name *Zeppelin*, and in the First World War came to be known by the colloquial name of *Zepps*. A second *Graf Zeppelin* airship was tested in 1938 but never exploited commercially because of the outbreak of the Second World War.

Graham The first name derives from a Scottish surname, itself from a place-name. Rather unexpectedly this is not in Scotland but GRANTHAM in Lincolnshire, which was recorded in the Domesday Book as *Grandham* and *Granham*. *See* GRANTHAM for its own meaning.

Graham Land The Antarctic peninsula that contains the region of this name was discovered by the English explorer John Biscoe in 1832, when he called it after the then First Lord of the Admiralty, Sir James *Graham* (1792–1861). The name originally applied to the whole peninsula, which was claimed by Britain. The Americans, on the other hand, called the region *Palmer Peninsula*, after their own explorer Nathaniel *Palmer* (1799–1877). In 1964 place-name committees in both Britain and America agreed to 'partition' the peninsula, so that the northern half is now *Graham Land* and the southern *Palmer Land*.

Grammy The annual American award of a gold-plated disk for outstanding achievement in the record industry, inaugurated in 1958 by the National Academy of Recording Arts and Sciences, is so named from '*gram*ophone', with an ending matching that of EMMY.

Grampians The famous Scottish mountains have a name that unfortunately remains of uncertain origin. Attempts have been made to derive it from a *Mons Graupius* mentioned here by the Roman writer Tacitus: *Agricola ad montem Graupium pervenit* ('Agricola reached Mount Graupius'). But it has been established that the mountain mentioned by Tacitus was actually Bennachie, the upland area west of Inverurie, which is not even in the Grampians. It seems likely that 16th-century antiquarians introduced the name *Grampian*, based on *Graupius* (and perhaps misreading *n* for *u*, this later becoming *m*), to replace the earlier name of *The Mounth* for the district here. This name itself derives from Gaelic *monadh*, 'hilly district'.

Granada The well-known name is that of the former kingdom and present province of Spain, and of the historic capital of both. It derives from that of a hill on which the present city stands, from Latin *granatum*, 'pomegranate', referring either to the cultivation of this fruit locally or to the fact that the city is laid out on four hills, like the fourfold sections of a pomegranate. *Cp.* GRENADA.

Granada The British commercial group, best known as the Manchester-based television company, takes its name from GRANADA, Spain. The name was chosen by the group's chairman, Sidney Bernstein, who was impressed with the city when on holiday there in the 1920s, and who was also looking for a name for the theatres owned by his company. He decided that *Granada* was the right name to convey the exotic escapism and excitement that a theatre should offer its audience.

Gran Chaco The vast plain of south central South America has a name representing Spanish *gran*, 'big' and a Quechua word meaning 'hunting land'.

Grand Canal Venice has 180 canals and the *Grand Canal* is by far the largest and most important of them, following a natural channel through the city and dividing it into two halves. The name represents Italian *Canal Grande*, literally 'main channel'.

Grand Canyon The famous ravine in the river Colorado, Arizona, was at first known in English as the *Big Canyon*, the latter word an anglicized adoption of the original Spanish *cañón*. The American Civil War veteran Major John Wesley Powell made an exploration of the canyon in 1871 and in his subsequent report changed the name from *Big Canyon* to *Grand Canyon*.

Grand Guignol The French phrase is used to denote a short but horrifying play of some kind. It originated as the name of a Paris theatre, the *Théâtre du Grand Guignol*, that staged such plays in the 19th century. *Guignol* itself is the name of a French puppet that first appeared in Lyon in the late 18th century and that more or less corresponded to Punch. Its own name was based on *guignon*, 'evil eye', 'bad luck'.

Grand Marnier The French liqueur, similar to Curaçao, is so named from its manufacturing company, *Marnier-Lapostolle,* with *Grand* here in the sense 'fine'.

Grand National The famous annual steeplechase, run at Aintree, Liverpool, was first held in 1839 as 'the Grand National Steeple Chase', implying a race that was one of the greatest and most spectacular yet organized in Britain.

Grand Rapids The Michigan city was founded in 1826 by *rapids* on the *Grand* River, whose own name was adopted from that of *La Grande Rivière*, 'the big river', given it by French explorers in the early 18th century.

Grand Remonstrance The name was given to the resolution passed by the Long Parliament in 1641 that listed the evils of government of Charles I and that demanded specific reforms. *Remonstrance* amounts to 'protest' and was already in use as a parliamentary term for a statement of grievances.

Grand Union Canal The canal in the south of England that was opened in the early 19th century to link London and the Midlands was originally so named only in its northern section, with the southern section known as the *Grand Junction Canal*. The latter was built first, and was so named for the *junction* it formed with the existing Oxford Canal and with the Thames. The former followed, and made a *union* with the Grand Junction Canal.

Grangemouth The Scottish port on the southern side of the Firth of Forth takes its name from its location at the mouth of the *Grange Burn*, a small river that is itself named after the *grange* of nearby Newbattle Abbey.

Grant The Scottish name originated as a nickname for a tall or big person, from the word that gave modern French (and English) *grand*.

Grantchester The village near Cambridge, familiar from the poems of Rupert Brooke, has a misleading name. The final *-chester* suggests that it was originally a Roman fort, like other places ending thus, such as *Winchester* or CHICHESTER. However, the *-chester* was not Old English *ceaster*, 'Roman camp', but *sæte*, 'settlers', like the final *-set* of DORSET or SOMERSET. The name thus means 'place of the settlers on the river *Granta*'. The river's own name, meaning 'fenny one', from a Celtic root element *grant*, gave the name of CAMBRIDGE itself, although there it is now the Cam. To complicate matters further, an early name of Cambridge was also *Grantchester*.

Grantham The Lincolnshire town has a name that means either '*Granta*'s village' or 'gravel village', from the conjectural Old English word *grand*, 'gravel' (to which modern *grind* is related) and *hām*, 'village'. The town's name gave the surname and first name GRAHAM.

Grants The blend of whisky takes its name from William *Grant* (1839–1923), a tailor's son who opened a distillery at Glenfiddich, Scotland, in 1886.

Grape Nuts The brand of breakfast cereal, first marketed in 1897, was so named because it has a *nutty* flavour and because its inventor, the American nutritionist Charles Post, mistakenly believed that *grape* sugar (another name for dextrose) was formed during the manufacturing process.

Grasmere The lake in the Lake District has a name that means 'grassy lake', probably referring to its grassy shores, or perhaps to the grass-like vegetation of its waters. The lake gave the name of the village of *Grasmere* here, famous as the home of Wordsworth.

Grasse The town in southeast France, famous for its manufacture of perfumes, takes its name from the Roman personal name *Crassus*, meaning 'fat'.

Grateful Dead, The The American rock group, formed in San Francisco in 1963, are said to have taken their name from an Egyptian prayer book. Eastern folklore tells of an unburied corpse who, grateful for at last being buried, helps a bridegroom successfully marry his bride and not be killed by the monster that had killed grooms before him. A similar theme is found in the apocryphal Book of *Tobit*, although there the 'groom' is a father and son, Tobit and Tobias, and the 'corpse' is an angel.

Grattan The well-known mail-order firm takes its name from *Grattan* Road, Bradford, where it opened in new premises in 1920 after moving out of cramped quarters in a jeweller's shop in Manchester Road, its place of origin in 1912. Its founder was John Fattorini, the son of the Italian immigrant to Britain Antonio Fattorini whose family had founded Empire Stores in Bradford in 1910 as another familiar mail-order business.

Graubünden The canton of eastern Switzerland derives its name from German *Grauerbund*, 'Grey League'. This was a league founded in 1395 to combat the rising power of the Hapsburgs, and was itself so named for the homespun grey cloth worn by its members. The French name of the canton is *Grisons*, the Italian *Grigioni*, and the Romansch *Grishun*, all implying 'grey'.

Graves The white or red wine of this name properly comes from the *Graves* district of Bordeaux, France, although there are also Spanish Graves wines. The place-name derives from a word related to English *gravel*, referring to the coarse sandy soil there.

Gravesend The Kent town, by the Thames, has a name that means 'end of the grove', not 'end of the grave'. It derives from Old English *grāf*, 'grove', therefore. The original grove here was probably at the east end of the town, where the Fort Gardens are today.

Gray In most cases, the name will have arisen as a nickname for a person with grey hair or a grey beard. In some instances, however, it could denote a person who originally came from *Graye* near Caen, in northern France. This place-name derives from a personal name *Gratus*, meaning 'pleasing'.

Gray's Inn The name is that of one of the four legal societies in London that together form the Inns of Court. It derives from the original building on the site, the manor house that was the London residence of Sir Reginald le *Grey*, chief justice of Chester, who died in 1308. By the end of the 14th century the house had become a lodging for lawyers.

Graz The city in southeast Austria has a name of Slavic origin, representing *gradets*, 'small fort'.

Great Barrier Reef The coral reef in the Coral Sea, off the northwest coast of Australia, is so named for the lengthy *barrier* it forms here, requiring careful negotiation by ships approaching the shore.

Great Britain The Roman name of the main island of the British Isles (present-day England, Scotland and Wales) was simply *Britannia*. When BRITTANY was settled by (and named for) Britons who had crossed the English Channel, it became necessary to distinguish the two lands. Brittany, as a younger and smaller derivative, was thus 'Little Britain', while the main land of the Britons was 'Great'. The name is first recorded in the late 13th century as *the more Brutaine*, with *Bretaygne the grete* found in the early 14th. *More* here means 'greater' (as in 'the more fool you').

Great Dane The large breed of dog was originally raised in the 17th century (or possibly earlier) for boar-hunting in Germany, *Denmark* and France. It was called *Great* by contrast with the *Lesser Dane*, a former name of the Dalmatian.

Great Dividing Range The series of mountain ranges and plateaux running from north to south in eastern Australia is so named since it *divides* the east coast territory from the outback.

Great Eastern The famous steamship, regarded as the prototype of the modern liner, was launched in 1858 and was designed for the *Eastern* Navigation Company, to ply as a passenger and cargo ship between Britain and India. In the event it was put on a New York trade route, so went west, not east.

Great Lakes The five lakes in central North America, between the United States and Canada, form the largest group of lakes in the world, and so deserve their descriptive name.

Great Salt Lake The lake in Utah is one of the largest in the United States, and its salt content is over 25%, as compared to the average 3.5% of the sea. Hence its name, referring to both its size and its salinity.

Great Slave Lake The lake in northwest Canada is so named for the *Slave* Indians who formerly lived on its western shores. Their own name is a translation of their native name, *Awokanak*, given them by the Cree Indians, who plundered and en*slaved* them. The *Slave* River flows into the lake on its southern shore.

Great War The name was formerly in use for the First World War, regarded as 'Great' by contrast with earlier wars. It had previously been used for the French Revolutionary War of 1793–5 and the Napoleonic Wars of 1803–15, which were equally 'great' for their time.

Great White Way The nickname for New York's Broadway has special reference to its bright street lights and illuminations, and is said to have been originally given in December 1901 after a heavy fall of snow. The name itself suggests a quasi-Indian origin. (*Cp.* pseudo-Indian 'big white chief'.)

Greece The country is named for its inhabitants, the *Greeks*, whose own name may derive from an Indoreuropean root element *gra*, 'venerable'. The name originally applied to the inhabitants of a much smaller territory, corresponding to just a part of Epirus, in northwest modern Greece. It then spread to a much wider area. The Ancient Greeks' own name for their country was *Hellas*, traditionally derived from *Hellen*, the mythical son of Deucalion. As in similar instances, this means that the true origin of the name is unknown.

Green The common surname was originally given to a person who liked wearing green, to someone who played the part of the 'Green Man' ('Jack in the Green'), dressed in a garland of ivy, in the May Day celebrations, or simply to someone who lived near a village green.

Green College The Oxford graduate college was founded in 1979 in the former Radcliffe Observatory by Dr and Mrs Cecil *Green* of Texas. The colour of the name is represented prominently in the college arms.

Greenland The name means what it says, 'green land', and the cold country was so named in 982 by the Norse navigator Eric the Red to attract settlers.

Green Line The London buses are so named as they run out of London into the *green* rural areas. The buses themselves are green to reflect their name, and doubtless to blend in with the countryside.

Green Park The well-known London park is named for the overall *green* of its grass and foliage, with a complete absence of flowers that might add other colours.

Green Party The political parties of this name arose in western Europe in the 1970s with the aim of preserving the natural environment (which is predominantly *green*) and its inhabitants, otherwise the planet and its people. The British Green Party was founded in 1973 as the *Ecology Party*, but subsequently abandoned this scientific name for the general and simpler one.

Greenpeace The organization was founded in Canada in 1971 to campaign for the preservation of the natural environment, of which the colour is predominantly *green*. The second half of the name relates to the organization's policy of nonviolent action to achieve its aims.

Greensleeves The well-known English tune, mentioned more than once by Shakespeare, takes its title from the ballad it accompanies. The ballad itself, first recorded in 1580, tells of an inconstant lady-love who wears *green sleeves*. It contains the lines: 'Greensleeves was all my joy, Greensleeves was my delight: Greensleeves was my heart of gold, and who but my Lady Greensleeves?'

Greenwich The name of the well-known district of London, formerly a village in Kent, means 'green port', from Old English *grēne*, 'green' and *wīc*, 'harbour', 'port'. (*Cp.* WOOLWICH.) The implication is that the landing place by the Thames was noticeably grassy. Greenwich is famous as the site of the prime meridian of longitude (0°), the basis of Greenwich Mean Time, from which the time in most other countries is calculated. In 1637 Louis XIII of France decreed that French maps should have as their own meridian the longitude that passed through *Valverde* ('green valley'), in the Canary Islands. To go one better than his father, Louis XIV decided that the meridian should pass through an observatory that he had built to the south of Paris in a place named *Vauvert* ('green valley'). It is a curious coincidence that all three places have 'green' names.

Greenwich Village The residential district of New York in the lower west side of Manhattan, famous as the home of unconventional artists and writers, originated as a genuine village in colonial times and took its name from its British counterpart in London, with *green* additionally an attractive term for a new settlement.

Gregory The name comes from the Latin name *Gregorius*, itself ultimately from Greek *gregōrein*, 'to watch'. The name, because of its origin, was understandably popular with early Christians, who bore in mind the biblical exhortation: 'Be sober, be vigilant' (1 *Peter* 5.8). The name subsequently became associated with Latin *grex*, genitive *gregis*, 'flock', to give another Christian association, that of the good shepherd.

Grenada The island state in the West Indies was discovered in 1498 by Christopher Columbus and named by him *Concepción*, for the Feast of the Immaculate *Conception*. At some stage later it was renamed for the Spanish kingdom of GRANADA.

Grenoble The name of the city in southeast France has evolved from its Roman name of *Gratianopolis*, 'city of *Gratian*', otherwise the 4th-century Roman emperor

Flavius *Gratianus*, who founded an episcopal see here. For a brief period in 1793, at the time of the French Revolution, the name of the city was changed to *Grelibre*, its *noble* having been interpreted as an aristocratic epithet.

Gresham's School The public school in Holt, Norfolk was founded in 1555 by Sir John *Gresham* (d. 1556), Lord Mayor of London, and the endowments were placed by him under the management of the Fishmongers' Company, who remain its estate trustees today and appoint its governors. The school's oldest building, the Old School House, was erected in 1870 on the site of its foundation, the former Gresham family seat in Holt market place. Most of the school's buildings are modern, however, and are out of the town centre on the Cromer road. The surname *Gresham* is itself of local origin, coming from the village of this name only six miles (10 km) from Holt, and itself meaning 'grassy homestead', from Old English *græs*, 'grassland', 'pasture' and *hām*, 'farm', 'homestead'.

Gretna Green The village in southern Scotland, famous as a former place of marriage for eloping couples, takes its name from the neighbouring village of *Gretna*. This is close enough to the English border to have a name of Old English origin, which is 'gravel hill', from *grēote*, 'gravel' and *hōh*, 'hill', 'height'.

Greycoat Hospital The state secondary school for girls in southwest central London arose from the school founded in 1695 for 40 poor boys and 40 poor girls, who wore *grey coats* or uniforms. The school was reorganized in 1874 to become a day school for girls and became a Church of England comprehensive school in 1977. Wooden figures of a boy and girl wearing their grey uniforms stand at the entrance to the remains of the original school in what is now Greycoat Place.

Griffiths The name means 'son of *Griffith*', itself representing the Welsh personal name *Gruffydd*. The meaning of this is uncertain, although the second part has been associated with *udd*, 'lord'.

Grimsby The well-known port at the mouth of the Humber has a Scandinavian name

meaning '*Grim*'s village'. *Grim*, meaning 'masked person' (who looked literally *grim*), was one of the names of the Scandinavian god Odin, and the Danes who gave the name here may have had him particularly in mind. The final *-by* of the name is Old Norse *bý*, 'village', found commonly in place-names in this part of England.

Griselda The Scottish name may derive from the Germanic words *gris*, 'grey' and *hiltja*, 'battle', perhaps suggesting a seasoned warrior. The name has become traditionally associated with 'patient Griselda', the long-suffering wife and mother in the tales by Boccaccio and Chaucer.

Grisons *See* GRAUBÜNDEN.

Grodno The city in Byelorussia has a name that simply means 'city', based on the Slavic *grad*, 'town' that lies behind such well-known names as VOLGOGRAD and BELGRADE.

Grogan The Irish name is an English form of *Ó Gruagáin*, 'descendant of *Gruagán*', this personal name deriving from *gruag*, 'hair'.

Groningen The city in the northeast Netherlands has a name based on Old German *grōni*, 'green'.

Grosvenor The name is an occupational one of Norman origin for a person who managed the arrangements for hunting on a lord's estate, from Norman French *gros*, 'great' and *veneor*, 'hunter' (*cp.* English *venison*). It is the name of one of the wealthiest families in Britain, with the title of Duke of Westminster. *Grosvenor Square*, Mayfair, is the centrepiece of the Grosvenor estate in London.

Grosvenor House Hotel The prestigious hotel in Park Lane, London, was built in 1928 on the site of the former mansion house occupied in the early 19th century by Robert GROSVENOR, second Earl Grosvenor. The *Grosvenor Hotel* by Victoria Station, however, is so named because it faces *Grosvenor Gardens*, although they themselves are equally named, if indirectly, for the original *Grosvenor* estate, whose boundary was marked by *Grosvenor* Place, extending north from Grosvenor Gardens.

Groves The name originally applied to someone who lived by a grove or thicket.

Grozny The city in southwest Russia, the Checheno-Ingush capital, arose from a Russian fortress of this name erected in 1818. The name is the standard word for 'fearful', 'awesome', but was here applied in the sense of a fort that was regarded as a threat to the enemy in the Russo-Turkish War. The Russian name of IVAN THE TERRIBLE is *Ivan Grozny*.

Gruyère The well-known pale yellow cheese, with its distinctive holes, takes its name from the Swiss town and district where it was first made. The place-name itself means 'place frequented by cranes', from Latin *grus*, 'crane'.

Guadalajara The city in central Spain derives its name from Arabic *wādī al-ḥajāra*, 'river of stones', referring to the river Henares, on which it stands. The city in Mexico of the same name was called after the historic Spanish town.

Guadalcanal The Pacific island, the largest of the Solomon Islands, was discovered in 1568 by the Spanish navigator Álvaro de Mendaña de Neira, who named it after his native town in Spain, *Guadalcanal*. Its own name is based on the Arabic *wādī*, 'river' that is found in the names of several Spanish rivers, notably GUADALQUIVIR. *Cp. also* GUADALAJARA.

Guadalquivir The name of the chief river of southern Spain is Arabic in origin, from *al-wādī al-kabīr*, 'the big river' (literally 'the-river the-big').

Guadalupe The town in southwest Spain takes its name from the Sierra de *Guadalupe*, on whose slopes it lies. The mountain's own name comes from that of the river here, itself from Arabic *wādī*, 'river' and *Lupus*, the former name of the river, meaning 'wolf'. Its 12th-century monastery, dedicated to the Virgin Mary, caused the transfer of the name to many Spanish colonial settlements, especially in Mexico. *See* GUADALUPE HIDALGO and also GUADELOUPE.

Guadalupe Hidalgo The city of central Mexico took its name from the Spanish town of GUADALUPE, with particular reference to its medieval monastery. In the 16th century the Mexican town acquired its own similar shrine when an apparition of the Virgin Mary was said to have appeared

to an Indian convert. In the 18th century a papal bull made the Virgin of Guadalupe patroness of New Spain (as Mexico was then called), and in the early 19th century she also became the patroness of the Mexican independence movement when the Mexican priest and revolutionary Miguel *Hidalgo* y Costilla took her image for his banner. He was captured and executed in 1811, and his campaign against the Spanish government marked the start of the war for Mexican independence. His name is now commemorated in that of the city.

Guadeloupe The French island territory in the Caribbean was given its name by Christopher Columbus in 1493 in honour of the monastery of Santa María de GUADALUPE, in Spain.

Guadiana The river of Spain and Portugal has a name representing Arabic *wādī*, 'river', and *Ana*, its former Roman name, of uncertain meaning.

Guam The largest of the Mariana Islands, in the Pacific, has a name that may be an alteration of that of its indigenous people, the *Chamorro*, although it is also seen as a modification of Spanish *San Juan*, 'St John', as the Spanish first explored the island on 24 June 1521, St John's Day.

Guangdong The province of southeast China, also known as *Kwangtung*, has a name that means 'vastness of the east', from Chinese *guǎng*, 'huge', 'vast' and *dōng*, 'east'. It is so named for its location to the east of the river XIJIANG. *Cp.* GUANGXI.

Guangxi The autonomous region of southern China, also known as *Kwangsi*, has a name that means 'vastness of the west', from Chinese *guǎng*, 'huge', 'vast' and *xī*, 'west'. It is so named for its location to the west of the river XIJIANG. *Cp.* GUANGDONG.

Guangzhou *See* CANTON.

Guatemala The country of Central America takes its name either from the Indian word *Quauhtemellan*, 'land of the eagle', this being a totemic bird, or possibly from another Indian word *Uhatzmalha*, 'mountain where water gushes', referring to the volcano Agua, near Guatemala City.

Gucci The prestigious brand of handbag is named for Guccio *Gucci* (1881–1953), an Italian craftsman who first set up as a saddlemaker in Florence in 1904. It was his son, Aldo Gucci, who introduced the famous handbag with its detachable gold chain.

Gudrun The wife of Sigurd in Norse mythology has a name that comprises *guth*, 'god' and *rūn*, 'secret' (English *rune*). The name is now sometimes adopted as a first name.

Guernsey The second largest of the Channel Islands has a Scandinavian name that probably means '*Grani*'s island' rather than 'green island', the traditional origin, despite its abundance of vegetation by comparison with neighbouring JERSEY. Either way, the last part of the name represents Old Norse *ey*.

Guienne The former province of southwest France, also spelled *Guyenne*, has a name that has evolved from Latin *Aquitania* (*see* AQUITAINE).

Guildford The first part of the name of the Surrey town rightly suggests 'gilded' or 'golden'. It was long supposed to refer to the golden flowers that grew by the ford over the river Wey here. It is now known, however, that the reference is to golden sand, not golden flowers. Approaching the town from the east one can even today see the golden sandy soil on the escarpment below the district known as St Catherine's, and the ford would probably have been to the south of the town in the same area, where the Pilgrims Way crosses the river.

Guinea The name of the country of western Africa originally applied to a coastal region that extended from present Senegal as far south as Gabon. It derives from Tuareg *aginaw*, 'black people'. It was this Guinea that gave the name of the *guinea*, the coin originally made out of gold from here.

Guinea-Bissau The country of West Africa has the same basic name as that of GUINEA, with the second part of the name that of its capital, *Bissau*, from the native name of the people here, the *Bijuga*. The meaning of their own name is uncertain.

Guinevere The beautiful wife of King Arthur has an appropriately descriptive name that represents the Old French form of the Welsh name *Gwenhwyfar*, from *gwen*, 'white', 'fair' and *hwyfar*, 'soft',

'smooth'. The Cornish form of this name gave the more familiar JENNIFER.

Guingamp The town in Brittany, northwest France, has a Breton name meaning 'white camp', from *gwenn*, 'white' and *kamp*, 'camp'.

Guinness The well-known brand of beer derives its name ultimately from Arthur *Guinness* (1725–1803), an Irishman who in 1756 took over a small brewery in Leixlip, Co Kildare. In 1759 he moved to a larger building in Dublin, where the company has had its headquarters ever since. The *Guinness Book of Records* was first published by the company in 1955 to provide answers to the sort of questions argued about in pubs.

Gujarat The Indian state takes its name from its people, the *Gujarati*, whose own name represents that of an ancient dynasty.

Gulf Stream The name is that of the relatively warm ocean current in the eastern part of the *Gulf* of Mexico. It was proposed in 1772 by Benjamin Franklin. Its earlier name had been *Florida Stream*.

Gulliver The name derives from Old French *goulafre*, 'glutton', so came to be given as a nickname for a greedy person. It is famous as that of Lemuel *Gulliver*, the central character of Swift's satirical novel *Gulliver's Travels* (1726). It has been suggested that Swift may have chosen the rather unusual name to suggest the *gullibility* of his hero. *Lemuel*, from the Hebrew meaning 'devoted to God', could be taken equally ironically.

Gunga Din The loyal Indian water-carrier who is the central character in Kipling's poem of the same name, in *Barrack-Room Ballads* (1892), has a name based on Hindi *gaṅgā*, 'GANGES', with *Din* representing *dīn* 'religion'. The Ganges is the sacred river of India. *Cp.* ALADDIN.

Guns N' Roses The American heavy metal group were formed in Los Angeles in 1985. Their lead singer, William Bailey, had discovered that his real surname was Rose, as his father had left home when he was still a baby and his mother had taken a second husband in L. Stephen Rose. Bailey himself then adopted the name W. Axl Rose, with *Axl* from the name of a band he had played with in Indiana. He and guitarist friend Izzy Stradlin linked up with guitarist Tracii Guns to form a group that was at first called *Rose*, then *Hollywood Rose*, then *LA Guns*. After Guns and drummer Steven Adler had been replaced by two other members, the group became *Guns N' Roses*, having rejected the names *Heads of Amazon* and *AIDS*. Their new name happens to evoke the 'flower power' movement of the 1960s, and the placing of roses in the rifle barrels of armed troops by peace protesters. At the same time, *Guns* suggests 'heavy metal'.

Gurkha The Hindu people, living mainly in Nepal and noted for their service in the Indian and British armies, take their name from Sanskrit *gauh*, 'cow' and *rakṣā*, 'guard', 'protection'. The cow in India is a sacred animal. *Cp.* GAEKWAR.

Guthrie The Scottish name derives from the place so called near Forfar, with its own name meaning 'windy place', from Gaelic *gaoth*, 'wind'. As an Irish name, *Guthrie* is an English form of *Ó Flaithimh*, 'descendant of *Flaitheamh*', this personal name meaning 'prince'.

Gutteridge The name derives from the former English personal name *Goderiche*, meaning 'good power', or *Cuterich*, meaning 'famous power'. Its present form has developed by false association with *gutter* and *ridge*.

Guy The name is of Norman origin, from the short form of a Germanic name beginning with the word *wit*, 'wide' or *witu*, 'wood'. The Germanic *w* regularly became *gu* in Norman French, hence such modern English and French doublets as *war* and *guerre*, *wasp* and *guêpe*, *wicket* and *guichet*.

Guyana The country of South America has a name that is probably of Indian origin meaning something like 'respectable', although some derive it from Guarani *guai*, 'born' and *ana*, 'kin', implying a united and interrelated race of people. Until 1966, when it gained its independence, Guyana was known as *British Guiana*.

Guy's Hospital The famous London hospital owes its name to the successful publisher and printer Thomas *Guy* (1644–1724), who had been a benefactor of St Thomas's Hospital and who founded his own hospital across the street from it in the closing years of his life.

Gwendolen The Welsh name probably comprises the words *gwen*, 'white', 'fair' and *dolen*, 'ring', 'bow', presumably applied descriptively.

Gwent The county in southeast Wales has an ancient name that is probably of pre-British (*i.e.* pre-Celtic) origin meaning something like 'place', implying a region or area that was favourable for some purpose, such as trading. The conjectural word behind the name is *venta*, seen also in the name of WINCHESTER.

Gwynedd The county in northwest Wales has a historic name representing that of *Cunedda*, a 5th-century ruler who had a kingdom here. One of his sons, Ceredig, gave the name of CARDIGAN. Cunedda's own name probably means 'good quality', from words that in modern Welsh are *cynneddf*, 'quality', 'faculty' and *dda*, 'good'.

Gymnopédies The title of the three piano pieces of this name by the French composer Erik Satie, written in 1888, is said to refer to the ancient Greek festival known as the *Gymnopaedia*, held annually at Sparta in honour of Apollo. In this, naked boys danced and performed gymnastic exercises. The word itself comprises Greek *gumnos*, 'naked' and *pais*, genitive *paidos*, 'child', 'boy'.

Győr The historic town in northwest Hungary is said to derive its name from a personal name *Jewr*. The Romans knew it as *Arabona*, from the name of the river *Rába* here, with Celtic *bona*, 'foundation', 'fort' (as for BONN). This gave the town's German name of *Raab*. The name is pronounced approximately like the first syllable of 'Germany'.

Gypsy The *Gypsies* were originally thought to have come from EGYPT, hence their name. It is now known that they originated in northwest India, migrating westward from the 9th century on. They are today scattered throughout Europe and North America. The French call the Gypsies *bohémiens* because they believed they came from BOHEMIA. *See also* I ZINGARI, TZIGANE. The Gypsies' own name for themselves is ROMANY.

H

Haarlem The city in the western Netherlands has a name that probably derives from *haar*, 'height' and *lem*, 'silt', referring to its site by the river Spaarne, which is slightly elevated by comparison with the surrounding low-lying plain. *See also* HARLEM.

Habakkuk The Old Testament prophet, with a book named for him, has a name of Hebrew origin, from *Habaqqūq*, 'embraced'.

Haberdashers' Aske's School The public day school for boys, now in Hertfordshire, was founded in 1690 on funds from an estate left in trust to the *Haberdashers' Company*, a City of London livery company, by Robert *Aske*, a liveryman of the Company.

Hachette The well-known French publishing house evolved from the bookshop opened in Paris in 1826 by Louis *Hachette* (1800–1864).

Haddon Hall The medieval manor house near Bakewell in Derbyshire takes its name from the location here in the Wye valley. The meaning is 'heath hill', from Old English *hæth*, 'heath' and *dūn*, 'hill'. The 'hill' is the rising ground to the west towards the village of Over Haddon.

Hades In Greek mythology, *Hades* was the underworld abode of the souls of the dead, the equivalent of *Hell*. The name also occurs in the Bible in much the same sense. It derives from *Hades*, the god of the dead, in Greek spelled *Aides*, a name traditionally interpreted as 'unseen', 'formless', from *a-*, 'not' and *eidō*, 'I see' or *eidos*, 'form', 'shape', to which English *idol* is related.

Hadhramaut The plateau region of the southern Arabian Peninsula, corresponding roughly to the former East Aden Protectorate, has a name that may be biblical in origin, representing that of *Hadoram*, the grandson of Eber (*Genesis* 10.26). This Hebrew name probably means 'Hadad is raised up'. The place-name has also been derived from Arabic *ahdar*, 'green' and *mawt*, 'death', but such an etymology seems unlikely, if only because in Arabic the adjective always follows the noun. It is also hard to envisage what a 'green death' could be.

Hadley The name is from any of the places so called, such as the village of *Hadley* near Wellingborough, Shropshire, or the town of *Hadleigh* in Suffolk. Most of these have a name meaning 'heathland clearing', from Old English *hæth*, 'heath' and *lēah*, 'wood', 'clearing'.

Hadrian's Wall The famous fortification, which runs across the north of England, is named for the Roman emperor *Hadrian* (or Adrian), who ordered its construction as a defence against northern tribes, and who himself visited Britain in AD 122.

Haeju The North Korean town and port has a name that means 'sea region', from Korean *hae*, 'sea' and *chu*, 'region'.

Haffner Symphony Mozart's Symphony No 35 in D major, K 385 (1782) is so named since it was intended for the *Haffner* family of Salzburg, where he lived. It should not be confused with the *Haffner* Serenade, which he composed for a marriage in the same family in 1776.

Hafnarfjördhur The town in southwest Iceland has a name that means simply 'port fjord', from Old Icelandic *hafnar*, 'port' (English *haven*) and *fjördhur*, 'fjord'.

Hagar In the Old Testament, the name is that of Sarah's servant, who bore Ishmael to Abraham. It represents Hebrew *Hāghār*, 'abandoned'. After Sarah had given birth to Isaac she persuaded Abraham to drive Hagar and her son into the wilderness (*Genesis* 16.1–16).

Hagen The city of northwest Germany has a name representing Old High German *hac* or *hago*, 'forest' (English *hedge*).

Haggai The Old Testament prophet, with a book named for him, takes his name from Hebrew *Haggai*, 'festive', implying a person born on a festival day.

Hague, The The English name of the seat of government (but not the capital) of the Netherlands is a rendering of its Dutch name *Den Haag*, itself a short form of its full name, *'s Gravenhage*. This means 'the count's hedge', referring to the woodlands and hedged enclosure here that originally surrounded the hunting lodge of the counts of Holland.

Haifa The well-known Israeli port has a name that derives from Hebrew *kef*, 'rock', 'cliff', referring to its location on the heights of Mount Carmel. The same root word (although Aramaic) lies behind the name *Cephas*, the biblical byname given Simon Peter by Jesus (*John* 1.42). (*See* PETER.)

Haig The Scottish name is of Norman origin, from one of a number of places in northern France with a name such as *Hayes*, meaning 'enclosure'. As an English name, *Haig* derives from an English place-name of the same meaning, such as *Haigh* near Manchester.

Haig The well-known brand of whisky takes its name from John *Haig*, who in 1824 built a distillery on the river Leven in Fife, Scotland.

Haileybury The Hertfordshire public school for boys takes its name from its location near Hoddesdon. The place-name itself probably derives from Old English *hēg*, 'hay' and *hlēt*, 'share', to which *burh* in the sense 'manor' was added later. The overall sense is thus 'manor by the hay allotment'.

Hainault *Hainault* Forest is a surviving part of the Royal Forest of Essex, like EPPING FOREST. Its name relates to a wood owned by a monastic community here in medieval times, and derives from Old English *hīgna*, 'household' and *holt*, 'wood'. The name subsequently gained its present spelling through a supposed association with Phi-

lippa of *Hainault*, queen of Edward III. Her title is an alternative spelling of HAINAUT, the former county in the Netherlands that is now a province of Belgium.

Hainaut The province of southwest Belgium has a name based on that of the river *Haine* that flows through it as a tributary of the Scheldt, with the final part of the name representing the Germanic element *gawja* (modern German *Gau*), 'district'. The river's own name is also of Germanic origin, from *hago*, 'forest' (*cp.* HAGEN). *See also* HAINAULT.

Haines The name may derive either from a Germanic personal name *Hagano*, meaning 'hawthorn', or from the name of the village of *Haynes* near Shefford in Bedfordshire. The village's own name may perhaps mean 'enclosure', and be related to modern English *hedge*.

Haiphong The port in northern Vietnam has a name that means 'sea room', from Vietnamese *hái*, 'sea' and *phòng*, 'room'. The reference is to the natural harbour here.

Haïti The present country occupies only a part of the Caribbean island of Hispaniola, but the name formerly applied to the island as a whole. It may represent either of two Caribbean words: *haiti*, 'mountain land', or *jhaiti*, 'nest'.

Hakodate The port in northern Japan has a name that derives from Japanese *hako*, 'box' and *tate*, 'house', 'fort'. This refers to the fort of Goryokaku, the only western-style fort in Japan, begun in 1855 as the seat of the Hakodate magistracy, which lies in the centre of the city. The fort's own name means 'government square'.

Halesowen The town near Birmingham has a name that means '*Owen*'s nooks of land', *Owen* being a Welsh prince who married a sister of Henry II and became Lord of Hales in the early 13th century. The 'nooks of land' (from Old English *halh*) are probably more in the nature of slight valleys. The same Old English word gave the name of the town of *Hale*, near Altrincham.

Halfords The chain of motor and cycle accessory stores takes its name from *Halford* Street, Leicester, where in 1902 the firm's founder, William Rushbrooke, opened a warehouse to sell bicycle parts.

Halfpenny The name arose as a nickname for a small or 'worthless' person, or perhaps in some cases was given to someone who had to pay (or collect) a regular rent of a halfpenny.

Halicarnassus The ancient Greek city, on the southwest coast of Asia Minor, has a name of pre-Hellenic origin. Its meaning is unknown. It is now *Bodrum*, in Turkey.

Halifax The capital of Nova Scotia, Canada, was founded in 1749 by the British and named in honour of George Montague Dunk, Earl of *Halifax* (1716–1771), then President of the Board of Trade. The earl took his title from the English city in Yorkshire. Its own name has long been popularly interpreted as 'holy hair', giving rise to many legends about beheaded virgin martyrs and the like. The second part of the name does indeed represent Old English *feax*, 'hair', but here it refers to long, 'hairy' grass. The first part is from Old English *halh*, 'nook', so that the overall name means 'rough grassland in a nook of land'. Halifax lies in a hilly district on the river Hebble. *Cp.* FAIRFAX.

Hall The familiar surname was originally given as a name to a person who lived near or worked at a *hall*, that is, a manor house. The commonness of the name is an indication of the important role played by the manor house in medieval times.

Halle The city of southern Germany has long been famous for its saltworks, and this is the basic meaning of its name, from a western Indoeuropean root word that gave Latin *sal*, Greek *hals*, French *sel*, German *Salz*, Russian *sol'* and English *salt* itself. *Cp.* HALLSTATT, SALZBURG.

Hallelujah Chorus The familiar musical name refers to the words of the final movement of Part 2 of Handel's *Messiah*, which centre on the exclamation 'Hallelujah' (familiar in other contexts as *Alleluia*). The word itself represents a Hebrew phrase meaning 'Praise Jehovah', or literally 'Praise Yah', from *hellēl*, 'to praise' (here in the imperative plural) and *yāh*, 'Yah'. (*See also* JEHOVAH, YAH.) The words of the chorus are based on those of *Revelation* 19.

Hallé Orchestra The British symphony orchestra, based in Manchester, is named for its founder in 1858, the Anglo-German composer and conductor Charles *Hallé* (1819–1895), who was its conductor from that year until his death.

Halliday The name means what it says, that is, *holiday* or *holy day*, and would have originally been given in connection with a religious festival, perhaps to someone born at Christmas or Easter.

Halliwell The name derives from any of the places that themselves were named for a *holy well*, such as the village of *Halwell* near Totnes in Devon, or the many villages called *Holwell* or *Holywell* in various parts of the country.

Hallmark The well-known make of greetings card takes its name from its American founder, Joyce Clyde *Hall* (1891–1982), who started a business selling postcards in Kansas City in 1910. When his whole stock was destroyed by fire in 1915, he and his brother started to produce their own cards, eventually registering their brand name in 1923.

Hallowe'en The popular festival is held on 31 October, the *even* (eve) of All*hallows*, otherwise ALL SAINTS DAY, itself celebrated on 1 November. In the Old Celtic calendar, the year began on 1 November, so that the previous day was the equivalent of the modern *New Years Eve*. The church attempted to associate the day with the following religious festival, but it remains only nominally Christian, and still retains much of its original pagan content, linked with witches and the like. In its modern form it has come to include costume dances ('witches and warlocks' and 'vicars and tarts' are 20th-century favourites), light-hearted fortune-telling, and 'trick or treat' pranks.

Hallstatt The name is that of the Austrian village where an extensive prehistoric cemetery was found in the second half of the 19th century and which in turn gave the name of a distinctive Bronze Age culture of central Europe. The name itself derives from West Indoeuropean *sal*, 'salt' (*cp.* HALLE) and German *Statt*, 'place'. Salt mines here also date from prehistoric times. Hallstatt is only about 31 miles

(50 km) from SALZBURG, also named for its salt.

Ham The name of Noah's second son is of uncertain origin and meaning. In the *Psalms* his name is associated with Egypt (for example *Psalm* 78.51), and for this reason it has been linked with an Egyptian word meaning 'black', or a Hebrew word meaning 'hot'. *See also* HAMITIC.

Hama The Syrian city, famous for its huge water wheels, has an Arabic name that ultimately derives from Phoenician *ḥamat*, 'fort'. Hama was a noted Hittite settlement.

Hamadān The city in west central Iran has a name that derives from Old Persian *Haṅgmatāna*, itself from Greek *Hagbatana*. This represents the name of the ancient Medean capital ECBATANA from which it evolved.

Hamamatsu The Japanese city has a name that relates to its location, from *hama*, 'shore', 'bank' and *matsu*, 'pine'. Hamamatsu is on the Pacific coast, halfway between Tokyo and Kyoto.

Hamburg The second half of the name of the city and port of northwest Germany almost certainly means 'fort'. The first part of the name is much more problematical. Proposed Germanic origins for it include *hamma*, 'forest', *ham*, 'gulf', and *hemnis*, 'obstacle'. Depending which of these is correct (if any), the name would thus mean 'fort of the forest', 'fort of the gulf', or 'fort by the obstacle'. The city was founded by Charlemagne in 811, and had the Medieval Latin name of *Hamburgium*.

Hamilcar Barca The 3rd-century BC Carthaginian general, famous as the father of Hannibal, had a common Punic name meaning 'great king', perhaps originally in the form *Ha-melk-art*. The middle element of this corresponds to Hebrew *melek*, 'king', seen in the biblical names MELCHIZEDEK and MOLOCH. The second word of his name is a Punic borrowing from Arabic *barq* or Hebrew *baraq*, meaning 'thunderbolt', a descriptive nickname for a military leader. It was Hamilcar Barca who is said to have given the name of BARCELONA.

Hamilton The familiar Scottish surname, borne by many aristocratic families, origi-

nated as a place-name, not that of the well-known town near Glasgow, which was founded by a Hamilton, but ultimately from the now deserted village of *Hamilton* near Leicester, whose own name means 'broken hill'. (*Cp.* HEMEL HEMPSTEAD.) The name went from England to Scotland via the 13th-century Norman knight Walter de *Hameldone*, who supported Robert the Bruce.

Hamilton The Canadian city and port, in Ontario, was originally named *Burlington Bay*, but in 1813 was renamed for George *Hamilton* (1787–1835), son of the Hon. Robert Hamilton, of Niagara, who had bought a farm here the previous year and divided it into building lots. The American city of *Hamilton*, Ohio, was named for the American politician Alexander *Hamilton* (1755–1804), and *Hamilton*, New Zealand, was named for the British naval captain John *Hamilton*, who was killed here in 1864 in a battle against the Maoris.

Hamilton Academicals The Scottish football club, based in Hamilton, near Glasgow, was formed in 1875 and took its name from *Hamilton Academy*, the secondary school which its original members attended.

Hamish The English spelling of the Scottish name represents an original *Sheumais*, the Gaelic form of JAMES.

Hamish Hamilton The British publishing house is named for its Scottish-American founder, *Hamish Hamilton* (1900–1988), who after working for other publishers launched his own business in London in 1931.

Hamitic The North African languages grouped under this name are those, such as Egyptian and Berber, spoken by the *Hamites*, the peoples supposedly descended from HAM, son of Noah.

Hamlet The name of the central character of Shakespeare's tragedy, that of the prince of Denmark, occurs in his principal source for the play, the 12th-century *Historia Danica* by the Danish chronicler Saxo Grammaticus, as *Amleth* or *Amlothi*. These Old Norse names are based on a word meaning 'home'. Shakespeare named his only son *Hamnet*, after one of his godfathers.

Hamleys The famous London toy store is named for William *Hamley*, a Cornishman who came to London in 1760 to open a small toy shop called 'Noah's Ark'. The firm has been in Regent Street since the mid-19th century, though not always at the same address.

Hammerklavier Sonata The name of Beethoven's Piano Sonata No 29 in B flat, Op 106 (1817) means simply 'Piano Sonata', *Hammerklavier* being the full German word for this instrument. *Hammer* refers to the fact that the piano had strings struck by *hammers*, unlike the harpsichord from which it developed, where the strings were plucked by quills.

Hammersmith The district of west London has a name that refers to the 'hammer smithy' once here, the 'hammer' referring to the fact that the smithy was a forge. It is not known where the original smithy was, but the location of Hammersmith on an important route into and out of London would have made it a place of importance (the equivalent of a modern motorway service station) for travellers by horse.

Hammond The name derives from one of a number of historic personal names, such as Germanic *Haimo*, 'home' or Scandinavian *Hámundr*, 'high protection'.

Hampden Park The famous Glasgow football ground, the home ground of QUEEN'S PARK Football Club, takes its name from *Hampden* Terrace nearby, itself named for the English patriot and parliamentarian John *Hampden* (1594–1653).

Hampshire The English county takes its name from SOUTHAMPTON, on which it has long been historically based, with the county designation *shire* added. Southampton was originally simply *Hampton*. The county's abbreviated name of *Hants* represents the Domesday Book spelling *Hantescire*, this itself being the Norman simplification of *Hamtunscir*, the earlier form of the name.

Hampstead The residential district of north London has in effect a residential name, meaning simply 'homestead'. In Anglo-Saxon times this would have meant a small settlement, perhaps even a single dwelling, such as a farm.

Hampton The surname comes from any of the places in England so called, including NORTHAMPTON and SOUTHAMPTON, which were both originally *Hampton*. The name usually means either 'homestead village' or 'riverside village', depending on the location. For an example of the latter, *see* HAMPTON COURT.

Hampton Court The famous palace near Kingston upon Thames takes its name from the location here, which itself probably means 'settlement in the bend', that is, of the river Thames, from Old English *hamm*, 'hemmed-in land' and *tūn*, 'farmstead', 'settlement'. *Court* in this sense denotes a manor house. The name as a whole refers to an earlier building than that of the present palace, which was built by Cardinal Wolsey in the 16th century.

Han The name of the imperial dynasty that ruled China for most of the period from 206 BC to AD 221, in Chinese *hàn*, represents that of the dynasty's founder, *Han* Kao Tsu, originally Liu Pang (256–195 BC). The word itself had no original meaning but subsequently came to mean 'person', 'man'.

Hananiah There are over a dozen characters of the name in the Old Testament. The two best known are the prophet whose prophecy regarding the imminent return of the exiles from Babylon proves to be false (*Jeremiah* 17), and one of the three companions of Daniel, together with Mishael and Azariah, who is chosen to advise King Nebuchadnezzar. (His name is changed to *Shadrach* on this appointment, just as his companions are given new names.) The name itself is related to HANNAH and represents Hebrew *Hannā-nyah*, 'Yah (*i.e.* Jehovah) has shown favour'.

Hancock The name amounts to 'Little John', and represents the name HANN with the diminutive word *cock* added. *Cp.* Alcock and *see* COX.

Hann The name usually represents the medieval form of JOHN, although in some instances it may derive from HENRY.

Hannah The biblical name, that of the mother of Samuel, represents Hebrew *Hannah*, 'favoured', implying a person who has been favoured by God, or more specifically a woman whom God has favoured with a child. Hannah was barren before God granted her gift of a son. The name gave the well-known first name ANN.

Hannibal The 3rd-century BC Carthaginian general and son of Hamilcar Barca, famous for crossing the Alps with a vast army and several elephants, has a name of Punic origin, from *hann*, 'grace' and the name of the god BAAL, so overall means 'grace of Baal'.

Hanoi The name of the Vietnamese capital means 'inside the river', from *hà*, 'river' and *nôi*, 'inside'. The city arose on a bend in the Red River.

Hanover The city in northern Germany has a name of Germanic origin meaning 'high bank', from words that correspond to modern German *hoch*, 'high' and *Ufer*, 'bank'. Hanover lies on the river Leine and the Mittelland Canal, at the point where the spurs of the Harz and Mittelgebirge mountains join to form the North German Plain.

Hansard The official verbatim report of the proceedings of the Houses of Parliament takes its name from its original printer from 1774, Luke *Hansard* (1752–1828).

Hanseatic League The name is that of the commercial group of towns formed in northern Germany in the 14th century to protect and control trade. The title derives from the Old German word *hanse*, 'guild', related to Old English *hōs*, 'company'. *See also* LUFTHANSA.

Hansel and Gretel The brother and sister of the fairy story by the brothers Grimm, familiar from Humperdinck's opera (1893), have names that are pet forms of the German names *Hans* and *Greta*, themselves respectively diminutives of *Johannes* (English JOHN) and *Margarete* (English MARGARET). Their English equivalents might thus be 'Jackie and Peggy'. The German *-el* suffix has the same 'pet' connotation that English *-ie* or *-y* has. Hansel's name is properly *Hänsel*, pronounced approximately 'Hensel'.

Hanukkah The annual eight-day Jewish festival of lights, commemorating the rededication of the Temple in Jerusalem by Ju-

das Maccabaeus in 164 BC, has a name that is the Hebrew word for 'dedication'.

Hanuman The name of the Hindu monkey god and king of Hindustan derives from Sanskrit *hanumaṅt*, 'having a jaw', from *hanu*, 'jaw'. A legend tells how soon after his birth Hanuman seized the sun, thinking it was something to eat. Indra, god of thunder, came to the rescue by striking Hanuman on the jaw with a thunderbolt. Hence his name. *See also* ANDAMAN ISLANDS.

Happy Mondays The British pop group, initially performing in Manchester in 1980, were given their name by their guitarist Mark 'Cow' Day, who adapted it from the title of the New Order hit 'Blue Monday' (1983).

Hapsburg The German princely family was founded by Albert, count of *Hapsburg* in 1153, and takes its name from that place, now a hamlet in north central Switzerland. Its own name means 'hawk fort'. The German spelling of the name, also sometimes used in English, is *Habsburg*.

Harare The capital of Zimbabwe, formerly familiar (until 1982) as SALISBURY, takes its present name from that of a village or district here, itself named for *Neharawa*, an African chieftain, whose own name means 'he who does not sleep'. His name, and that of the village, were corrupted by the first European colonists.

Harbin The city of northeast China has a name of Manchu origin meaning 'place where fish is dried'.

Hardcastle The name derives from that of *Hardcastle* Crags, near Hebden Bridge in West Yorkshire, itself probably so called since it was regarded as being *hard* to approach. There is no actual castle here.

Hardicanute The 11th-century king of Denmark and England, son of CANUTE (now usually known as *Cnut*), has a name based on that of his father, with Old Norse *harthr*, 'hardy', added. He was thus 'Canute the Bold'.

Hardwick Hall The Elizabethan mansion near Mansfield, Derbyshire, takes its name from its location. The meaning is 'herd farm', from Old English *heorde-wīc*, probably denoting the part of a manor that was devoted to livestock.

Hardy The name arose as a nickname for either a brave man or a fool*hardy* one. Unfortunately there is no way of telling which.

Hare Krishna The Hindu sect is based on worship of the god KRISHNA. *Hare* is the Hindi equivalent of 'O God', and *Hare Krishna* are the opening words of a sacred verse or mantra often chanted in public by adherents of the sect. The mantra itself is very simple, and runs: 'Hare Krishna, Hare Krishna, Krishna, Krishna, Hare, Hare', and is repeated, substituting RAMA, the name of the second most popular Hindu deity, for 'Krishna' every second verse. The formal name of the sect is the *International Society for Krishna Consciousness*.

Harewood House The 18th-century mansion near Harrogate, Yorkshire, takes its name from its location. The meaning is probably what it says, 'hare wood', implying a wood where hares are found.

Harfleur The port in northern France, important in medieval times, has a name that is a combination of Old Norse *hár*, 'high' and Old English *flēot*, 'estuary', 'inlet'. The town stands on an elevated site near Le Havre at a point where the small river Lézarde flows into the estuary of the Seine.

Hargreaves The name derives from any of the places so called, such as the village of *Hargrave* near Chester. The name itself usually means 'hare grove'.

Hari Rud The river of Afghanistan has a name deriving from Old Persian *Harawaia*, 'river rich in water', to which is added Iranian *rūd*, 'river'. Pliny cites the river name as *Arius*.

Harker The name could either derive from the place so called near Carlisle in Cumbria, perhaps itself meaning 'hart marshland', or have originated as a nickname for an eavesdropper, who liked to *hearken* to what other people were saying.

Harland The name originates from any of the places so called, now usually very minor. Their own name means either 'grey

land' (from Old English *hār*, 'grey', as modern *hoary*) or 'hare land'.

Harlech The historic North Wales town, famous for its castle, has a name that refers to the original site of the castle, and that means 'beautiful rock', from words corresponding to modern Welsh *hardd*, 'beautiful', 'handsome' and *llech*, 'slab', 'smooth rock'. Harlech Castle was built in the 13th century on the craggy hilltop here.

Harlem The district of New York, noted for its black community, was named in 1658 for the Dutch town of HAARLEM by Peter Stuyvesant, governor of the Dutch colony of New Netherland in this part of America.

Harlem Globetrotters The American basketball team, famous for their spectacular ball-handling and amusing antics, were founded in 1927 with players from HARLEM. Having no home base, however, the team became *globetrotters*, touring the United States and subsequently worldwide to promote their particular style of play.

Harlequin The name is that of the stock comic character in the *commedia dell'arte* who in the English version is the lover of Columbine. He traditionally wears patterned tights with a regular diamond motif, and has a black mask. In the *commedia dell'arte* his Italian name is *Arlecchino*, which probably itself derives from the Old French name *Herlequin* or *Hennequin*, used for a devil in medieval legends. This is perhaps of Germanic origin meaning 'Herle the king', referring to a mythical being identified with Wotan.

Harlequins The London rugby football club, formed in 1866, takes its name from the multicoloured squares of its shirts, which suggest the costume worn by HARLEQUIN.

Harley Street The London street, famous for its medical consultants and specialists, was built in the 18th century on land belonging to the Duke of Portland and inherited from his wife, formerly Lady Margaret Cavendish *Harley*.

Harlow *Harlow* New Town, designated in 1947, takes its name from the older *Harlow* here in Essex, whose own name goes back to Anglo-Saxon times. It means 'army mound', from Old English *here*, 'army' and *hlāw*, 'mound'. An 'army mound' would have been both an administrative centre and the meeting place of the local hundred. The actual site of the mound was that of the Roman temple now in Harlow Old Town immediately west of Harlow Mill station.

Harmonious Blacksmith, The The nickname for the air and variations in Handel's Harpsichord Suite No 5 in E (1720) is said to have been given with reference to the sound of a blacksmith's anvil that the opening chords of the air suggest. The name was given only after Handel's death, and there is no evidence that the composer heard the original tune sung by a blacksmith at Edgware, London, as has been claimed. *Harmonious* here has the sense 'singing tunefully' rather than 'singing in harmony'.

Harold The Old English name derives from *here*, 'army' and *weald*, 'ruler', denoting a strong military leader or warrior. The name is familiar from King *Harold*, but he did not popularize it, thanks to his losing the Battle of Hastings in 1066.

Harp The familiar brand of lager is marketed by Arthur GUINNESS Son and Company. Guinness is an Irish firm, and the harp is the traditional Irish national instrument. Hence the name of the lager.

Harpagon The name of the miser who is the central character in Molière's play *L'Avare* ('The Miser') (1668) derives from Latin *harpago*, 'grappling hook', itself from Greek *harpagē* in the same sense. The suggestion is of a greedy, rapacious person. Molière based the play on the classical comedy *Aulularia*, by Plautus, although there the miser is called *Euclio*.

Harpenden The Hertfordshire town has a name that has long been traditionally interpreted as 'harper's settlement', from Old English *hearpere*, 'harper'. But such a name would be most unusual by comparison with the topographical nature of many place-names, and it is now believed that the name actually means 'valley of the military road', from Old English *here-pæth*, 'army way' and *denu*, 'valley'. The reference is probably to Watling Street, which runs along the slight valley here. The road could well have been used by both Anglo-Saxon

and Danish armies after the Romans had originally exploited it.

Harper The name is an occupational one, for someone who played on the harp. This was an important position in a medieval baronial hall, especially in Scotland and the north of England.

Harper and Row The American publishers take their name from James *Harper* (1795–1869), who with his brother John opened a printshop in New York in 1817, and R.K. *Row*, the founder of a publishing business in 1906 with whom they merged in 1962.

Harpers Bizarre The American pop group, formed in San Francisco in 1963, chose a name that was a variant of that of the fashion magazine *Harper's Bazaar*, founded by James *Harper* and his brothers in 1850 and now represented by *Harpers & Queen*.

Harpic The familiar lavatory cleanser is named for *Har*ry *Pic*kup, the man who invented it and first sold it in London in the early 1920s. The *Harpic Manufacturing Company* was registered in 1924.

Harrap The London publishers take their name from their founder in 1910, George Godfrey *Harrap* (1866–1938), who had been in publishing himself for the previous 19 years.

Harriet The name is an English form of French *Henriette*, itself a pet feminine form of *Henri*, English HENRY. *Cp.* HARRY.

Harris The name means 'son of HARRY', as does *Harrison*.

Harrisburg The state capital of Pennsylvania was laid out in 1785 and named for John *Harris* (1727–1791), eldest son of the English settler John *Harris* who in about 1718 established a trading post here on the Susquehanna River.

Harrods The world-famous London store is named for its founder, Henry Charles *Harrod* (1800–1885), a tea merchant who opened a grocer's shop in Brompton in 1849. The business was largely built up by his son Charles, who took it over in 1861.

Harrogate The North Yorkshire town has a Scandinavian name with the basic meaning 'cairn way', from Old Norse *hǫrg*, 'heap of stones' and *gata*, 'way', 'road' (as in the modern -*gate* of northern street names such as *Briggate*, Leeds). However, *gata* had a later sense 'pasture', evolving when a particular road became a right of way for leading cattle to pastureland, and this is probably the sense here. The name thus means 'place by the road that leads to the pastureland'. The latter would have been on the nearby moorland.

Harrow The borough of northwest London, with its famous public school, has a name that represents Old English *hearg*, the word for a heathen temple. There must have been a Saxon shrine of this type here, probably on the summit of the hill (literally Harrow-on-the-Hill) where St Mary's Church stands prominently today. There has long been a Christian church on this site, and Pope Gregory the Great specifically urged Christian missionaries to convert heathen temples into places of Christian worship whenever they could.

Harry The name is a pet form of HENRY, familiar from medieval times, and occurring in Shakespeare's plays (as in 'a little touch of Harry in the night' in *Henry V*). It evolved through the French form of the name (modern *Henri*), with its nasalized vowel, which the English denasalized.

Hart The name arose as a nickname for a person who in some way resembled a hart or stag, either in appearance or behaviour.

Hartford The state capital of Connecticut, founded in 1635 by English settlers from New Towne (now Cambridge, Massachusetts), was named for HERTFORD, the birthplace of one of their number, William Stone. The spelling reflects the pronunciation of the English name.

Hartlepool The town and port on the bay of the same name near Middlesbrough has a name that actually relates to this bay, meaning 'hart island pool', since 'Hart Island' (or simply 'Hart') was the original name of the headland on which the town stands today. The reference is probably to the stags that lived on the headland, rather than to its shape. The middle -*le*- represents the original word for 'island', Old English *ēg*.

Hartley The name comes from any of the places so called, such as the village near Kirkby Stephen in Cumbria, or the one near Cranbrook in Kent. The place-name itself usually means 'hart wood', from a wood or clearing in a wood where stags lived.

Hartleys The well-known make of jam and marmalade takes its name from William Pickles *Hartley* (1846–1922), a grocer who became a jam manufacturer by accident in 1871. Hartley's local jam supplier in Colne, Lancashire failed to make his usual delivery, so that he had to make it himself. His business grew, and in 1884 he formed the company of William Hartley and Sons, moving to Aintree, Liverpool, the following year.

Harvard University America's oldest university, at Cambridge, Massachusetts, is named for the British-born Puritan minister John *Harvard* (1607–1638), who left his library and half his estate to the college founded in 1636 at 'New Towne', as Cambridge was then called. Harvard had himself been educated at Cambridge University, England.

Harvey The name is of Breton origin, from *haer*, 'battle' and *vy*, 'worthy', implying an able warrior. It was introduced to England by Bretons settling there after the Norman Conquest.

Harveys The well-known brand of sherry takes its name from John *Harvey* (1806–1879), who in 1822 joined his uncle's sherry retail business in Bristol. The company dates its foundation from 1796, although no Harvey was at that time involved in the business.

Harvill Press The British publishing firm was founded in 1946 by the Russian-born translator Manya *Har*ari (1905–1969) and her colleague Marjorie *Vill*iers, and took its name from the first halves of their surnames. In 1954 Harvill became a subsidiary of Collins, and is now an imprint of HarperCollins.

Harwich The name of the Essex town and port means 'military settlement', from Old English *here-wīc*. There was a sizeable Danish military camp here in the 9th century. *Cp.* other 'army' names such as HARLOW, HARPENDEN, HEREFORD, HERSTAL.

Harz Mountains The mountains in central Germany derive their name from Old High

German *hart*, 'forest', relating to the forests that still extend over much of the region.

Haslemere The Surrey town has a straightforward name meaning 'hazel mere', that is, a lake among hazel-trees. There is no lake here now, but there was possibly one at some time between the High Street and Derby Road.

Hastings The well-known Sussex resort has a name meaning 'place of the people of *Hæsta*', whose own name probably arose as a nickname meaning 'violent' (to which modern English *hasty* is related). The 'place' is not actually mentioned in the name, but is implied, and would have originally been much more extensive than the territory of the present town.

Hatchards The well-known bookshop in Piccadilly, London, was opened in 1797 by the publisher and bookseller John *Hatchard* (1769 1849).

Hatfield Both the Hertfordshire town and the one in South Yorkshire have a name of identical origin, meaning literally 'heath field', implying either a stretch of open land covered in heather or simply a heath.

Hathi The name of the wild elephant in Kipling's *Jungle Books* (1894, 1895) simply represents Hindustani *hāthi*, 'elephant'.

Hathor The name is that of the mother of HORUS and goddess of creation in ancient Egyptian mythology. It literally means 'mansion of *Horus*', symbolizing the goddess as bearing the god in her womb.

Hattersley The name derives from a place so called just outside Manchester. Its own name is of uncertain origin. Some derive it from Old English *hēahdēor*, 'deer' (literally 'high animal', as the deer was highly valued for game) and *lēah*, 'wood', 'clearing'.

Havana The capital of Cuba was founded in 1514 by the Spanish soldier and administrator Diego Velázquez, who named it *San Cristóbal de la Habana*. The final word of this probably represents the name of an Indian tribe, but its meaning is unknown.

Havant The name of the Hampshire town means '*Hāma*'s spring', with the Anglo-Saxon personal name followed by Old English *funta*, 'spring' (to which modern *fountain* is related).

Haverfordwest The Welsh town near Pembroke was originally known as the equivalent of 'Haverford', which means 'goat ford', referring to a ford over the Western Cleddau here where goats can cross. The name acquired medieval spellings that suggested HEREFORD, so *west* was added to distinguish the town from that city.

Havilah The name of the region mentioned in the Old Testament (*Genesis* 2.11) derives from Hebrew *hôl*, 'sand'. In *Genesis* 10.7 the name is given as that of one of the sons of Cush, and in *Genesis* 10.29 as that of one of the sons of Joktar and a grandson of Eber.

Havre, Le *See* LE HAVRE.

Hawaii The name of the Pacific group of islands, a state of the USA, represents the Polynesian name *Owhyhii*, 'place of the gods', referring to the two volcanoes Mauna Kea and Mauna Loa, regarded as the abode of the gods. Cook's name for the archipelago here was SANDWICH ISLANDS.

Hawarden The North Wales town, famous for *Hawarden* Castle, the former home of W.E. Gladstone, has a name that means 'high enclosure', from Old English *hēah*, 'high' and *worthig*, 'enclosure' (the equivalent of -*worth* in many other names). This describes the site of Hawarden, on high ground over the river Dee.

Hawke Bay The bay off the east coast of North Island, New Zealand, and the land district of *Hawke's Bay* on the island itself, were so named in 1769 by James Cook in honour of the British First Lord of the Admiralty, Edward *Hawke*, first Baron Hawke (1705–1781).

Hawkins The name means 'son of *Hawkin*'. This name in turn is a diminutive form of *Hawk*, originally a nickname for a person resembling a hawk in some way, perhaps in ferocity or greediness.

Hawley The origin of the name is in any of the places so called, such as the *Hawley* that is now the suburb of Farnborough in Hampshire, or the one near Dartford in Kent. The meaning of the place-name varies, depending on the location, and can be 'holy wood', 'hall wood' or 'clearing with a mound'.

Hawthorns, The The home ground of West Bromwich Albion football club, southeast of West Bromwich town centre, takes its name from the *Hawthorns* Hotel that formerly stood at one corner of the original pitch.

Haydn Quartets The name is that of six string quartets by Mozart: No 14 in G major, K 387 (1782), No 15 in D minor, K 421 (1783), No 16 in E flat major, K 428 (1783), No 17 in B flat major, K 458 (1784), No 18 in A major, K 464 (1785), and No 19 in C major, K 465 (1785). They are so called because he dedicated them to *Haydn*, who played the first violin when they were performed in Mozart's house, the composer himself taking the viola part.

Haydock Park The Merseyside racecourse near Wigan takes its name from the town of *Haydock* just outside which it is located.

Hayes The name comes from any of the places so called, such as the *Hayes* in Greater London that was formerly in Middlesex. These mostly have a meaning 'enclosure', from a word to which modern *hedge* is related.

Haÿ-les-Roses, L' *See* L'HAŸ-LES-ROSES.

Haymarket Theatre London's well-known theatre takes its name from its site in the *Haymarket*, where the original theatre opened in 1720. The street is so named for the market of hay and straw that was held here from the mid-17th century.

Hay-on-Wye The South Wales town takes its name from Old English *hæg*, the term for a fenced enclosure, in this case probably being an area of the forest fenced in as a hunting ground (*cp.* The HAGUE). The river name was added to distinguish this *Hay* from others.

Hayward Gallery The South Bank art gallery, London, was opened in 1968 and named for Sir Isaac James *Hayward* (1884–1976), leader of the London County Council and planner of the South Bank arts complex as a whole.

Haywards Heath The Sussex town was originally simply 'Heyworth' (actually spelled as such in a 13th-century document),

meaning 'hedged enclosure'. *Heath* was added later to give a general sense of 'heathland by a fenced enclosure'. A local legend tells how a highwayman named *Hayward* carried out robberies on the *heath*. But this is simply an attempt to make colourful fiction out of more prosaic fact.

Hazel The name originated from the tree, like other names from flowers and plants, but in this case perhaps with particular reference to its light brown nuts, rather than its blossom. This made the name suitable for a person with hazel eyes.

Head The name arose either as a nickname for someone with a distinctive head or to describe a person who lived on a hill (Old English *hēafod*, which also gave modern *head*) or at the head of a stream or valley.

Healey If English in origin, the name derives from one of the places so called, such as the various villages in Yorkshire. The name itself means 'high wood'. If Irish, however, the name derives from either *Ó hÉilidhe*, 'descendant of the claimant', or *Ó hÉalaighthe*, 'descendant of *Éalathach*', this personal name meaning 'ingenious'.

Heart of Midlothian Walter Scott's famous novel of 1818 takes its name from the former Edinburgh Tolbooth, an infamous prison that was itself so called with reference to Edinburgh as the capital of the county of Midlothian. The Scottish football club *Heart of Midlothian* took their name from a popular Edinburgh dance club which was itself named after the Tolbooth prison.

Heath The name denoted a person who lived on a heath, or who came from one of the many places with *heath* in the name, such as *Heathfield*.

Heather The name derives from the plant, which came to be associated with the *heath*. The words are really of distinct origin, however.

Heathrow The name of London's major airport derives ultimately from a *row* of cottages that stood by a *heath* here in medieval times. The heath would have been the one that later became Hounslow Heath. Heathrow was merely a hamlet down to the 20th century.

Heaven 17 The British pop group, formed in Sheffield in 1980, took their name from a group mentioned in Anthony Burgess's novel *A Clockwork Orange* (1962):

> These young devotchkas [girls] had their own like way of govoreeting [speaking]. 'The Heaven Seventeen? Luke Sterne? Goggly Gogol?'
>
> I, 4.

Burgess himself perhaps based the name on the phrase 'seventh heaven'.

Hebblethwaite The name derives from a place so called near Sedbergh in Cumbria. *Hebble* is a dialect name for a type of plank bridge. *Thwaite* is a word for a clearing (*see* THWAITES). Both words are of Scandinavian origin.

Hebe The goddess of youth and the spring, and wife of Hercules, has a name that actually represents the Greek word for 'youth', *hēbē*.

Hebei The province of northeast China, also known as *Hopeh* or *Hopei*, has a name that means 'north of the river', from Chinese *hé*, 'river' and *běi*, 'north' (*cp.* HUBEI, PEKING). The province lies to the north of the Huang Ho (Yellow River).

Hebrew The Semitic people claiming descent from Abraham, and the language they spoke, now revived as the official language of Israel, have a name that according to the Bible derives from that of *Eber*, the great-grandson of Shem (*Genesis* 10.21). His own name probably comes from Hebrew *'avor*, 'to go beyond', so that the Hebrews are 'those from beyond', that is, from the other side of the Euphrates, from where they came 'into the land of Canaan' (*Genesis* 11.31). However, the three consonants that form the Hebrew name of the Hebrews (*'br*) also appear in that of the *Arabs*, although in a different order (*'rb*), so it seems likely that the former name derives from the latter. In the Old Testament, the Hebrew language is referred to as 'the language of Canaan' (*Isaiah* 19.18) or 'the Jews' language' (*Isaiah* 36.13). Only much later, in the Prologue to *Ecclesiasticus* in the Apocrypha, does one find 'things uttered in Hebrew' (Greek *hebraisti legomena*, Latin *verba hebraica*). The New Testament mentions the language more than once, however, in the phrase 'in the Hebrew' or 'in the Hebrew tongue' (*John* 5.2, 19.13–20, *Acts* 21.40).

Hebrides The Scottish islands have a name that is of uncertain origin. The Roman name for them was *Ebudae*, and the present form of the name is due to a miscopying at some stage of the *u* as *ri*.

Hebron The city on the West Bank of the Jordan has a name that derives from Hebrew *havor*, 'to join', 'to unite'. The Arabic name of Hebron is *Al-Ḥalīl*, 'the friend', the Muslim name for Abraham (implying 'friend of God'), who according to tradition is said to be buried here. The city's ancient name was *Kirjath-arba* (*Genesis* 23.2), representing Hebrew *qiryat arba'*, 'city of the four', otherwise Greek *Tetrapolis*, perhaps with reference to four united settlements here in biblical times.

Hecate The name of the Greek goddess of the underworld has been associated with both *hekas*, 'far' and *hekaton*, 'hundred'. If the former, she can be regarded as a 'goddess from afar'. If the latter, she could be related in different ways with things that were 'hundred', such as victims on her altars, months of a king's reign, or the multiplicity (hundredfold) of something such as a harvest.

Hector The son of King Priam of Troy, killed by Achilles, has a name that probably derives from Greek *ekhein*, 'to hold', 'to check'. Hector was after all the famous war leader and 'prop of Troy'. The sense of English *hector* to mean 'bully' derives from the representation of Hector in medieval romances as a blustering character.

Hecuba The wife of King Priam of Troy, and mother of Hector and Paris, may have a name that is related to Greek *hekas*, 'far', like that of HECATE. The precise sense of such an epithet is uncertain, however.

Hefei The city of southeast China derives its name from Chinese *hé*, 'to close', 'to join' and *féi*, 'fat', 'fertile'.

Hegira The name of the flight of Muhammad from Mecca to Medina, marking the starting point of the Muslim era, is simply the Arabic word *hijrah*, meaning 'flight'.

Heidelberg The city in southwest Germany derives its name from words equivalent to modern German *Heide*, 'heath' and *Berg*, 'mountain', 'hill'. A view of the city will instantly show the aptness of the name, with its location by the river Neckar at the foot of the forested hills of Odenwald.

Heidsieck The well-known champagne takes its name from Charles-Camille *Heidsieck*, born in Reims, France, in 1822. He became a champagne shipper to this city in 1851.

Heilbronn The city of southwest Germany, on the river Neckar, has a name that means 'holy well', from words that gave modern German *heilig*, 'holy' and *Brunnen*, 'well', 'spring' (to which English *burn* and *bourne* are related). The 'holy well' is the stream that formerly emerged from under the high altar of St Kilian's Church.

Heilongjiang The province of northeast China, in Manchuria, has a name that derives from the Chinese name of the river Amur that flows through it. This is *hēilóngjiāng*, 'River of the Black Dragon', from *hēi*, 'black', *lóng*, 'dragon' and *jiāng*, 'river'.

Heineken The Dutch family of *Heineken* have been brewing beer in Amsterdam since the 16th century. The present lager company takes its name from Gerard Adriaan *Heineken*, who bought a brewery in the Dutch city in 1864, and who opened a second in Rotterdam ten years later.

Heinemann The British publishing house was founded in 1890 by the son of a naturalized German, William *Heinemann* (1863–1920), who had earlier been studying music in Germany with the aim of becoming a composer. He lacked the necessary flair, however, so turned to a career with books instead.

Heinz The famous brand name, virtually synonymous with baked beans, is that of Henry John *Heinz* (1844–1919), an American greengrocer who in 1869 formed a partnership with a friend to sell bottled vegetables, and who eventually made his name with the beans and his familiar '57 Varieties', launched in 1892.

Hejaz The provincial area of western Saudi Arabia has a name that represents Arabic *hajz*, 'obstacle', from *hajaza*, 'to separate'. The Hejaz lies between the high plains that border the Red Sea.

Hekla The active volcano in southwest Iceland has a name that is said to come from an old word meaning 'cloak', referring to the 'cloak' of mist that hides its summit.

Helen The famous classical beauty, 'Helen of Troy', had a name that may be related to the Greek word for 'sun', *hēlios*, so that the general sense is 'bright'. It is likely that the similarity between her name and the Greek word for 'Greek', *Hellēn*, is purely a coincidence. *See also* ELAINE.

Helena The state capital of Montana, founded in 1864, is probably called after a town of the same name in Minnesota, from where one of its early settlers doubtless came.

Helicon The famous Greek mountain, believed in classical times to be the home of the Muses and regarded as the source of poetic inspiration, has a straightforward descriptive name, from Greek *helix*, genitive *helikos*, 'spiral', 'twisted', 'winding', referring to its shape.

Heligoland The small island in the North Sea, also known as *Helgoland*, is said to derive its name either from Old High German *heilig*, 'holy' and *land*, 'land', with reference to an ancient shrine here, or from Old Frisian *halik*, 'steep' and *land*, 'land', alluding to its cliffs.

Heliogabalus The 3rd-century AD Roman emperor, with a reign notorious for debauchery and extravagance, had the original name of *Varius Abitus Bassianus*. He was the priest of the West Semitic sun god *Elagabalus*, however, to whom he was fanatically devoted, so that he came to be generally known by that name. Greek writers subsequently corrupted the emperor's name to *Heliogabalus* by association with *hēlios*, 'sun'. The sun god's own name means 'El (*i.e.* god) of the mountain' (*cp.* GIBRALTAR).

Heliopolis The city in ancient Egypt near the apex of the Nile delta was a centre of sun worship, as its name implies, from Greek *hēlios*, 'sun' and *polis*, 'city'. The biblical name of the city was *On* (*Ezekiel* 30.17), and it is also referred to as *Beth-*

shemesh (*Jeremiah* 43.13), where the Hebrew name, meaning 'house of the sun', is rendered in the Septuagint (Greek version of the Old Testament) as *Heliopolis*. The sun god worshipped there was Ra. *Heliopolis* was also the ancient Greek name for BAALBEK.

Hellespont The name is found in classical literature for the strait between the Aegean and the Sea of Marmara that is now known as the DARDANELLES. It represents Greek *Hellēspontos*, 'Helle's sea', with reference to *Helle*, daughter of King Athamas in Greek mythology. The story tells how Helle and her brother Phrixus fled from their father and cruel stepmother Ino by flying over the strait to Colchis on the back of the ram with the Golden Fleece. Helle fell off, however, and was drowned. The waters were thus named commemoratively for her.

Helmand The river of Afghanistan and Iran has a name that ultimately goes back to Sanskrit *setumant*, 'having a bridge', from *setu*, 'bridge' and *mant*, 'having'. In the lower reaches of its course it flows under the desert sands without surfacing, so has many points where it can be easily crossed.

Helsingborg The Swedish port lies opposite the Danish port of *Helsingør*, otherwise ELSINORE, and takes its name from it, with Swedish *borg*, 'fort', added.

Helsinki The capital of Finland was founded in 1550 by King Gustav Vasa of Sweden with the name *Helsingfors*, from *Helsing*, an Old Norwegian tribal name, and *fors*, 'waterfall'. The present name is the Finnish form of this. The city was originally on the estuary of the river Vantaa, where the waterfall was, but in 1640 moved down to its present location on a promontory in the Gulf of Finland.

Hemel Hempstead The Hertfordshire town has a name that overall means 'homestead in the broken country'. The first word represents Old English *hamol*, a term used for 'broken' land, that is, a terrain with a mixture of hills and valleys. This exactly fits the countryside to the east of the Chiltern Hills nearby. The second word is the same as the name of HAMPSTEAD, so like it means 'homestead'. The two halves

of the name gradually blended over the years to become just *Hemsted* in the mid-16th century. The original name was subsequently 'reconstructed' in its separate parts, however, and remains as such today.

Henan The province of north central China, also known as *Honan*, has a name meaning 'river of the south', from Chinese *hé*, 'river' and *nán*, 'south' (*cp.* NANKING). The province is to the south of the Huang Ho, just as HEBEI is to the north of it.

Henderson The name is Scottish in origin, and means 'son of HENRY'.

Hendon The district of Greater London grew up round St Mary's Church, which like many churches is on a hill. The name relates to this, meaning 'at the high hill', from Old English *hēah*, 'high' followed by *dūn*, 'hill'. *Cp.* HENLEY.

Hengist The 5th-century Jutish leader is said to have founded the kingdom of Kent, together with his brother *Horsa*. His name means 'horse' (Old English *hengest*), as equally, and more obviously, does that of his brother.

Hengyang The city of southeast central China has a name that derives from Chinese *héng*, 'to balance', 'to weigh' and *yáng*, 'light', 'sun'. *Cp.* ANYANG.

Henley Both *Henley*-on-Thames, in Oxfordshire, and *Henley*-in-Arden, in Warwickshire, have names that mean the same, 'high clearing', from Old English *hēah*, 'high' (as for HENDON) and *lēah*, 'clearing'. Henley-on-Thames is hardly 'high' in the accepted sense, however, so the term is probably metaphorical, meaning an important place. *See* ARDEN separately.

Henrietta The name is a Latin-style form of French *Henriette*, itself a feminine pet form of *Henri*, English HENRY.

Henry The well-known name is of Germanic origin and comprises the words *haim*, 'home' and *rīc*, 'power', 'ruler', implying an able monarch. For this reason, perhaps, it has proved popular with rulers in many countries, including no less than eight kings of England.

Hephzibah In the Old Testament, the name is that of the mother of King Manasseh of

Judah. It is Hebrew in origin, from *Hephtsī-bāh*, 'in her is my delight', alluding to a newborn daughter. The name is also used metaphorically of Jerusalem: 'Thou shalt be called Hephzibah, [...] for the Lord delighteth in thee' (*Isaiah* 62.4).

Heptameron The name is that of an unfinished collection of love tales by Margaret of Navarre, published in 1559. The stories were based on the plan (but not content) of the DECAMERON, and like it were to have consisted of 100 tales told by ten people in ten days. But her collection stopped at 72 tales, so was (posthumously) given the more appropriate title *Heptameron*, 'seven days'.

Heptateuch The name is used by biblical scholars for the first seven books of the Old Testament on account of their supposed unity, since the last two (*Joshua* and *Judges*) contain the history of the Jews in the Promised Land under the religious principles historically developed in the first five (the PENTATEUCH). The Greek name thus means 'seven books', from *hepta*, 'seven' and *teukhos*, 'book'.

Hepworth The well-known menswear chain owes its name to Joseph *Hepworth* (1834–1911), who set up as a woollen draper in Leeds in 1864 and who opened his first shops elsewhere in the early 1880s.

Hera The name of the queen of the Olympian gods and sister and wife of Zeus represents Greek *hēra*, 'lady', 'mistress', the feminine equivalent of the word that gave English *hero*.

Heracles The Greek name for HERCULES is usually interpreted as meaning 'glory of HERA', from the name of the goddess and *kleos*, 'glory'. It is thus a theophoric name, based on that of a deity.

Heraclitus The name of the 5th-century BC Greek philosopher, who held that all things are in perpetual flux, means 'famous through HERA', from the name of the Greek goddess followed by *kleitos*, 'famous'. *Cp.* HERACLES.

Herbert The name is of Germanic origin, from *heri* or *hari*, 'army' and *beorht*, 'bright', 'famous', implying a successful warrior.

Herculaneum The ancient city in southwest Italy has a name traditionally linked with that of HERCULES.

Hercules The famous classical 'he-man' hero has a name that is a Latin form of his original Greek name, HERACLES.

Herdwick The hardy breed of sheep from northwest England derives its name from the obsolete word *herdwick*, used for a pasture or sheep farm, itself from Old English *heorde-wīc*, literally 'herd farm'. (A *heorde-wīc* was the part of a manor that was used for livestock, as distinct from the *bere-wīc*, 'barley farm', which was devoted to arable farming. In other words, it was the stables and cowsheds as distinct from the barns and storehouses.) The particular breed is thought to have originated on the *herdwicks* of Furness Abbey, near Barrow-in-Furness, Cumbria.

Hereford The cathedral town on the river Wye has a name that means 'army ford', from Old English *here*, 'army' and *ford*, 'ford'. An 'army ford' was probably one where an army could cross the river without breaking formation. A Roman road crosses the Wye at Hereford, so the ford would have been there. *See also* HAVERFORDWEST.

Hereward the Wake The 11th-century Anglo-Saxon rebel, who defended the Isle of Ely against William the Conqueror, was popularly promoted by Charles Kingsley's novel of this name, published in 1866. His name is appropriate, representing Old English *here*, 'army' and *weard*, 'guard'. *Wake* means 'watchful', referring to his vigilance.

Heriot-Watt University The Edinburgh university was founded in 1966 and evolved from the former *Heriot-Watt* College that was established in 1885 and that itself grew from the Edinburgh School of Arts, founded in 1821, and the *Watt* Institution and School of Arts, established in 1852. The former was initiated from funds that had accrued from the original bequest of George *Heriot* (1563–1624), founder of GEORGE HERIOT'S SCHOOL. The latter bears the name of the famous Scottish engineer and inventor James *Watt* (1736–1819).

Herm The small island near Guernsey, in the Channel Islands, has a name that has been romantically linked with HERMES and *hermits* but whose actual origin remains obscure. Its Roman name was *Sarmia*, which evolved over the centuries to the present name.

Her Majesty's Theatre The original theatre on the present site, in the Haymarket, London, opened in 1705 as the *Queen's Theatre*, named for Queen Anne. On the death of the queen in 1714 its name was changed to the *King's Theatre*, in honour of George I. When Queen Victoria came to the throne in 1837 the name was again changed to *Her Majesty's Theatre*. It retained this name until 1901, when Edward VII acceded, and it accordingly became *His Majesty's Theatre*. It finally assumed its present name in 1952 on the accession of Queen Elizabeth II. The present theatre is actually the fourth to be built.

Herman's Hermits The British pop group was formed in Manchester in 1961 with Peter Noone as its lead singer. A member of the group, bassist Karl Green, noticed a resemblance between Noone and the character *Sherman* in the American television cartoon *The Rocky and Bullwinkle Show*, in which Rocky was a flying squirrel and Bullwinkle a moose. *Sherman* became *Herman* and the name of the group developed to the randomly alliterative *Herman and his Hermits*. This was later shortened to *Herman's Hermits*.

Hermes The name of the messenger of the gods in classical mythology is traditionally linked with Greek *herma*, 'prop', 'pillar', alluding to the role of Hermes as protector of travellers. The word came to apply in particular to a heap of stones set up to mark a boundary or crossroads, and in due course this pile was refashioned as a pillar with a bust of Hermes on top. *See also* HERMIONE.

Hermes Trismegistus The name was that given by the Greeks to the Egyptian god *Thoth*, who was credited with various works on mysticism and who closely resembled their own god HERMES. The meaning is 'thrice great Hermes', from Greek *tris*, 'three times' and *megistos*, 'greatest'. This epithet relates directly to an inscription found in a temple at Isna, near Thebes: *Djeyeuty pa aa, pa aa, pa aa*,

'Thoth the great, the great, the great'. *See also* TRISTRAM.

Hermione In Greek mythology, the name is that of the daughter of Helen and Menelaus who married Orestes, her cousin. It derives from that of HERMES, the messenger god, although the semantic link remains unclear. In modern times the name has been more readily associated with Shakespeare's *Hermione*, wife of King Leontes in *The Winter's Tale*. It is significant that Hermione is a statue that comes to life in the play, no doubt alluding to the meaning of Hermes' name as 'prop', 'support', and to the stone pillars with a bust of him on top called *hermae*.

Hermitage, The The famous Russian art museum, in St Petersburg, was founded by Catherine the Great in 1764 when she bought a collection of 225 old masters in Berlin, mostly works of the Dutch and Flemish schools. She housed them in rooms of the Winter Palace that were known as 'The Hermitage' for their secluded location. When the museum itself was built next to the Palace, and the collection was added to, the name was transferred to it. The name itself, properly that of the abode of a hermit, was similarly adopted by the Russian nobility for various country villas and summer retreats. The Russian name for the museum is *Ermitazh*, a direct untranslated borrowing from French *ermitage*.

Hermon, Mount The mountain ridge on the border between Lebanon and Syria has a Hebrew name, from *ḥermōn*, 'consecrated'. It was a sacred site in ancient times, representing the northwest limit of Israelite conquest under Moses and Joshua. Its Arabic name is *jebel esh-sheikh*, representing *jabal aṣ-ṣayḥ*, 'mountain of the chief'.

Hermopolis The ancient Egyptian city has a Greek name meaning 'city of HERMES'. The Greek god HERMES TRISMEGISTUS was identified with Thoth, worshipped here, as were the eight primeval gods of the Ogdoad (from the Greek for 'group of eight') said to have created the world. The latter gave the Egyptian name of the city, *Khmunu*, from *ḥemen*, 'eight', and this in turn gave the present Arabic name of Hermopolis, *El-Aṣmūnayn*.

Hero The priestess of Aphrodite, who killed herself when her lover Leander drowned while swimming the Hellespont, has a name that probably means something like 'dedicated to HERA'.

Herod There are several rulers of the name in the Bible, notably *Herod* the Great, king of Judaea, who ordered the Massacre of the Innocents, *Herod* Antipas, his son, tetrarch of Galilee, *Herod* Agrippa I, his grandson, also king of Judaea, and *Herod* Agrippa II, son of Herod Agrippa I. Whichever is concerned, the name derives from Greek *hērōs*, 'hero'. The second name of Herod Antipas (the Herod referred to by Jesus as 'that fox') represents Greek *Antipatros*, meaning 'in place of the father', that is, in place of Herod the Great, whose own father was actually named *Antipater*, since he in turn was in place of *his* father, also *Antipater*...

Herodias The wife (and niece) of HEROD Antipas and mother of Salome had earlier been the wife (and niece) of Herod Philip. She was also the granddaughter of Herod the Great. The family origin of her name is thus self-evident. She is remembered not so much for her name, however, as for inciting her second husband to put John the Baptist to death for denouncing her illegitimate marriage to him. *See also* SALOME.

Herstal The town of eastern Belgium has a name that derives from Old High German *hari*, 'army' and *stal*, 'place', meaning that there was a permanent encampment here.

Hertford The town on the river Lea has a name that means what it says, denoting a ford where *harts* crossed regularly or where they gathered. *Cp*. OXFORD. The name has retained the medieval spelling *hert*, itself from Old English *hēort*. *Cp*. HARTFORD.

Hertford College The Oxford college was founded in 1874 as a refoundation of the earlier *Hart Hall*. This was itself founded in 1283 in a house leased to scholars by its owner, Elias of *Hertford*.

Hertz The well-known car hire company takes its name from John Daniel *Hertz* (1879–1961), a Czech-born immigrant to America who began working as a car salesman in 1909 and who founded the famous Yellow Cab taxi company in Chicago in 1915.

Herzegovina *See* BOSNIA-HERZEGOVINA.

Hesperides The 'Islands of the Blessed' in classical mythology were thought of as being in the west (Greek *hesperos*, 'western') and have been variously identified with the Canary Islands or those of Cape Verde. The name is intimately linked with that of the *Hesperides*, the three daughters of HESPERUS who guarded the garden of golden apples on the islands.

Hesperus The alternative name of Venus, the 'Evening Star', derives from Greek *hesperos*, 'western', as it is in that part of the sky that the 'star' (actually a planet) appears.

Hesse The name of the state of central Germany goes back to *Hassi* or *Hatti*, the Roman name for a tribe who originally inhabited this region. Their own name means (as it suggests) 'hat', and is said to relate to their long hair, which was bound up on their head in a way that resembled a turban.

Hester The name is a variant form of ESTHER. They are thus really one and the same name in origin, although now usually regarded as two distinct names.

Hever Castle The famous fortified and moated Tudor house in Kent takes its name from the village of *Hever* in which it is situated. The name derives from the Old English descriptive phrase *æt thǣm hēan ȳfre*, 'at the high bank'. The village is at the tip of a spur overlooking the valley of the river Eden.

Hewitt The name can either derive from the medieval personal name *Huet*, a diminutive of HUGH, or describe a person who lived by a *hewitt*, the medieval name for a clearing cut in a wood, from a word that gave modern English *hew*.

Heythrop College The Roman Catholic theological college in London, now part of London University, takes its name from *Heythrop* House, the home of the Catholic earls of Shrewsbury near Chipping Norton in Oxfordshire, where it was originally founded as a Jesuit college in 1922.

Hezbollah The Lebanese fundamentalist Shi'ite and pro-Iranian organization, involved with the holding of western hostages in the late 1980s and early 1990s, has a name that means 'party of Allah', from Arabic *hisb*, 'party' and the Muslim name of God, ALLAH.

Hezekiah The king of Judah has a Hebrew name, from *Hizqīyāh*, 'my strength is Yah' (that is, Jehovah).

Hiawatha The famous central character of Longfellow's long poem *The Song of Hiawatha* (1855) is based on a historic figure, a legendary 15th-century chief of the Onondaga tribe of North American Indians. His name is said to mean 'he makes rivers'. *See also* MINNEHAHA.

Hibernia *See* IRELAND.

Hibernian The well-known Scottish football club, based in Edinburgh and known to its fans as *Hibs* or *Hibees*, was formed in 1875 by a group of Irishmen to raise money for Catholic charities. It therefore based its name on *Hibernia*, the Roman name of Ireland. The name was also at one time that of a rival club at Glasgow, who succeeded in luring a number of players over from Edinburgh. CELTIC football club had a similar origin, although aimed at helping poorer Catholics.

Higginbottom The name is probably a corruption of a northcountry place-name meaning 'oak tree valley', from Old English *æcen*, 'oaken' and *botm*, 'valley'.

Higgins The name means 'son of *Higgin*', a diminutive form of the name *Hick*, which in turn is a pet form of RICHARD.

High Church The movement within the Church of England that stresses continuity with the Catholic tradition is so called because it accords a *high* priority to bishops and priests, to sacraments and ritual, and generally to doctrines which distinguish the Anglican church from Nonconformist churches in England and Calvinist churches in continental Europe. The name arose in the 17th century as a derisory nickname, similar to that of TORY, but with the increasing influence of the contrasting LOW CHURCH it gradually became an acceptable title. In the 19th century the name came to be equated with that of the OXFORD MOVEMENT.

Highgate The district of Greater London has a name that means what it says, referring to a 'high gate', that is, a former tollgate here on a high section of the Great North Road as it ran uphill on its way out of London.

Highlands The northernmost mountainous region of Scotland is so named by contrast with the LOWLANDS further south. The Highlands are traditionally thought of as the 'true' Scotland, with its Celtic speech and its distinctive customs and costume.

High Wycombe The Buckinghamshire town is *High* as against nearby (and much smaller) West Wycombe, formerly an individual village but now a district of High Wycombe itself. The second word of the name represents Old English *wīcum*, the grammatical form (dative plural) of the noun *wīc*, 'farm' required after *æt*, 'at'. The name thus means 'place at the farms', with *wīc* normally used to denote an outlying farm rather than the main one. (The word gave the *-wich* of many place-names.) The present spelling has developed by association with *combe* (as for ILFRACOMBE). High Wycombe is not noticeably high, so the word here may have the metaphorical sense 'important', as for HENLEY-on-Thames.

Hilary The name can now be used for male or female. It was formerly mostly borne by men, and derives from the post-classical Latin name *Hilarius*, itself from *hilaris*, 'joyful' (hence modern English *hilarious*).

Hilda The name is of Germanic origin, based on the word *hild*, 'battle', that was normally found in longer names such as *Hildegard* ('battle protection', 'fellow combatant').

Hildesheim The city in north central Germany probably has a name that derives from the short form of a personal name such as *Hildegard*, meaning 'battle' (*cp.* HILDA), with Old High German *heim*, 'homestead'.

Hill The common name was originally used of a person who lived on or by a hill.

Hillsborough The original name of Sheffield Wednesday Football Club's ground was

241

Owlerton, northwest of Sheffield city centre. Hence the club's nickname of *The Owls*. In 1914, however, Owlerton became part of the new parliamentary constituency of *Hillsborough*, and the name of the ground was changed accordingly. The name means what it says. It was originally simply *Hills*, referring to the rising ground here. *Borough* was added subsequently.

Hi-Los The American pop group, formed in the mid-1950s, took their name from the fact that two of their members, Robert Morse and Robert Strasen, were over six feet tall, towering over the other two. The name additionally referred to the ability of Clark Burroughs, a third member, to sing high notes, reaching the G above middle C without difficulty.

Hilton The well-known hotel group is named for its American founder, Conrad Nicholson *Hilton* (1887–1979), who opened his first hotel in Cisco, Texas, in 1918.

Himachal Pradesh The state of northern India has a Hindi name, with *Himachal* another name for the HIMALAYAS, from Sanskrit *hima*, 'snow', 'winter' and *ĉal*, 'troubled', and *Pradesh* meaning 'country', 'land'. Cp. ANDHRA PRADESH.

Himalayas The vast mountain system of southern Asia has a name that ultimately represents Sanskrit *hima*, 'snow', 'winter' and *ālaya*, 'abode', 'house', itself from *ā-*, a prefix denoting a slight increase, and *laya*, 'place of rest'.

Himeji The name of the city in central Japan, in Honshu, represents Japanese *hime*, 'princess' and *-ji*, 'road', 'distance'.

Hindi The language of INDIA takes its name from *Hind*, the Hindi name of India. Cp. HINDU.

Hindu The name of the religion of INDIA derives, through Persian, from the HINDI name of the country, *Hind*.

Hindu Kush The mountain range of central Asia has an Iranian name, from *hendū koŝ*, 'killer of Indians', from *hendū*, 'Indian', 'Hindu' and *koŝtan*, 'killer'. The name was given by the Persians to a mountain pass where Indian slaves had perished in the bitter winter weather.

Hindustan The name of the general region of India north of the Deccan means 'HINDU land', from Iranian *hendū*, 'Hindu' and *ostān*, 'country'. Cp. AFGHANISTAN.

Hine The blend of brandy derives its name from Thomas *Hine* (1773–1822), a Dorset man who went to France in 1792 to complete his education and who subsequently took over a cognac company near Cognac itself in 1817.

Hinton The name derives from any of the places so called, several of them now with a distinguishing second word, such as *Hinton St George* near Crewkerne in Somerset, or *Hinton Waldrist* near Faringdon in Oxfordshire. The place-name itself can mean either 'high settlement' or 'monastery settlement'.

Hipparchus The name of the 2nd-century BC Greek astronomer has the literal meaning 'horse ruler', from Greek *hipparkhos*, representing *hippos*, 'horse' and *arkhein*, 'to rule'. The word was not only one of the bynames of Neptune but the title of a cavalry general at Athens.

Hippo The ancient city of North Africa has a name of Greek origin, from *hippōn*, 'stable' (from *hippos*, 'horse'), denoting a place where horses would be fed and watered while working at the port here. The name gave that of the modern city of BÔNE in Algeria, now called ANNABA. St Augustine of *Hippo* was bishop here.

Hippocrates The famous Greek physician, regarded as the father of medicine, has a name that literally translates as 'powerful in horse', from *hippos*, 'horse' and *kratos*, 'power'. The name implies a military leader whose horses are victorious in battle.

Hippocrene The name of the spring on Mount Helicon in Greece, held to give poetic inspiration, has the literal meaning 'horse spring', from Greek *hippos*, 'horse' and *krēnē*, 'spring'. The spring was said to have been created by a stamp of the hoof from the famous flying horse Pegasus.

Hippolyta The name of the queen of the Amazons in Greek mythology means literally 'horse releaser', from *hippos*, 'horse' and *luein*, 'to loose', 'to free'. The same origin gave the name of *Hippolytus*, Theseus' son, killed after his stepmother Phaedra falsely charged him with raping her. Both characters rode in horse-driven chariots, for which their name would be appropriate.

Hiram The name is biblical in origin, as that of the king of Tyre who supplied Solomon with materials and craftsmen for the building of the Temple. It may derive from Hebrew *Hīrām*, meaning 'noble'.

Hiroshima The Japanese city, largely destroyed by the atomic bomb dropped by the Americans in 1945, has a name that refers to its location on the delta of the river Ota in southwest Honshu, from Japanese *hiro*, 'broad', 'wide' and *shima*, 'island'.

His Master's Voice The famous record company name is that of the painting that became the company's trademark. It shows a dog listening to *his master's voice* on an old-style gramophone. The dog is Nipper, the gramophone was originally an Edison phonograph, and the painter was Nipper's owner, the professional artist Francis Barraud (d. 1924). The Gramophone Company offered to buy Barraud's painting if he would delete the phonograph and paint in their own 'Improved Gramophone'. He did so, and the picture became the company's property. They first used it and the name *His Master's Voice* on their record label in 1909. In itself, the name happens to suggest a 'masterly' recording.

Hispaniola The name of the West Indian island, divided politically into Haïti and the Dominican Republic, evolved from the original Spanish title of *la isla española*, 'the Spanish island', said to have been given it by Christopher Columbus in 1492.

Hitachi The well-known Japanese brand name, familiar from electrical and electronic products such as televisions, derives from the former fishing village (now coastal city) of *Hitachi*, northeast of Tokyo, where the company was founded in 1904 by an electrical engineer, Fusanosuka Kuhara. The place-name itself represents Japanese *hi*, 'sun', 'daytime' and the suffix *-ta* or *-tachi*, meaning 'ended'.

Hitchin The town in Hertfordshire takes its name from that of the *Hicce*, a people who lived in this region in Anglo-Saxon times. Nothing is known about them, and the name of *Hitchin* is the only record of their existence.

Hittite According to the Bible, the name of the ancient people of Anatolia is said to mean 'sons of *Heth*' (*Genesis* 22.3), Heth being the son of Canaan (*Genesis* 10.15). However, the Hittites' own name for their land was *Hatti*. Both this and the name of *Heth* are of unknown origin, despite attempts to derive the place-name from Chinese *hòutŭ*, 'god of the earth'.

HMV *See* HIS MASTER'S VOICE.

Hoare The name was originally either a nickname for a person with grey hair or a grey beard (*cp.* modern *hoary*), or related to someone who lived by a slope (Old English *ōra*).

Hobart The capital of Tasmania, Australia, was founded in 1804 and named for Robert *Hobart*, fourth Earl of Buckinghamshire (1760–1816), then secretary of state for the colonies.

Ho Chi Minh The Vietnamese statesman and president of North Vietnam (1890–1969) began life as *Nguyên Sing Cung*. At the age of ten he became *Nguyên Tât Thành*. In 1917, when in Paris, he took the name *Nguyên Ái Quôc*, meaning 'Nguyên the patriot'. (*Nguyên* itself is a fairly common family name in Vietnam.) In 1941 the Chinese named him *Hú Guãng*, based on *guãng*, 'light', and in 1942 he took the definitive name *Hô Chi Minh*, in which *Chi Minh* means 'he who enlightens'. (The second word of this relates directly to MING, the Chinese dynasty.) *Hô* was perhaps suggested by the famous Chinese inventor of paper money, *Hô Qui Ly*. The Chinese themselves render his name as *húzhimíng*.

Ho Chi Minh City The Vietnamese port, long familiar by its former name (to 1976) of SAIGON, takes its present name from the Vietnamese statesman and president of North Vietnam HO CHI MINH (1890–1969). The city's name was changed when it ceased to be capital of the Republic of Vietnam (*i.e.* South Vietnam).

Hock Tuesday The name is that of a festival formerly celebrated in Britain on the second Tuesday after Easter, when money was collected for church purposes. It ori-

243

ginally involved the capturing and tying up of men by women on the Monday, and of women by men on the Tuesday, these captives then obtaining their release by means of a payment. The origin of *Hock* remains unknown. Some have linked it with *high*, as if a 'high' holiday, while others have attempted to associate the word with the capturing custom, as the persons so seized would be held 'in *hock*', as if imprisoned. But these explanations are really little more than inspired guesswork.

Hodder and Stoughton The British publishing house takes its name from Matthew Henry *Hodder* (1830–1911) and Thomas Wilberforce *Stoughton* (born 1840), who after working for different London publishing firms set up their own business as partners in 1868.

Hodgson The name means 'son of *Hodge*', itself a pet form of ROGER. There are several names of the same origin, such as *Hodson*, *Hodges*, *Hodgkinson* and *Hotchkiss*. The last two are based on diminutive forms.

Hódmezővásárhely The city in southeast Hungary has a name that represents Hungarian *hód*, 'beaver', *mező*, 'field', *vásár*, 'fair' and *hely*, 'place', in other words 'place of the fair by the field of beavers'. The name is pronounced approximately 'hode-mazur-*varsh*-ahay', but not sounding the *r*s and with the second part as in 'mazurka'.

Hoffmann The name is of German origin, and means literally 'farm man', from German *Hof*, 'farm', 'settlement'. This is a loftier name than it might seem, denoting a farmer who owned his land instead of renting it.

Hogg The name arose as an occupational term for a swineherd. In some cases, too, it could equally have been a nickname for someone who resembled a pig in some way. This need not necessarily have implied a dirty person, as pigs were not felt to be particularly 'unclean' in medieval times.

Hogmanay The popular Scottish celebration, held on New Year's Eve, is said to derive its name from the similar French custom of *aguillanneuf*, meaning 'a gift at the new year'. Attempts to link this term with French *gui*, 'mistletoe' are the result of popular etymology, or the desire to make an apparently meaningless word meaningful. The French tradition is said to have been brought to Scotland by the Normans, but is not actually recorded before the 17th century.

Hohenzollern The German noble family of this name trace their ancestry back to the 12th century, when Friedrich I was count of *Zollern*. Hohenzollern itself is a place near Hechingen, southwest of Stuttgart. The name means 'High Zollern', the latter representing the historic place-name *Zolorin*, of unknown meaning.

Hohhot The city of northern China, also known as *Huhehot*, has a name of Mongolian origin, from *hoh*, 'blue' and *hot*, 'city'. The 'blue city' is probably so named for the dark, blue-tinged stone of its original Buddhist temples. When the Chinese settled here in the 17th century, they named the city *kāihuà*, 'return to civilization'.

Hokkaido The second largest of Japan's islands has a name that means 'north sea province', from *hoku*, 'north', *kai*, 'sea' and *dō*, 'way', 'province'. This summarizes its geographical and administrative status.

Holberg Suite Grieg's piano suite, composed in 1884 and orchestrated the following year, was written for the bicentenary of the birth of the Norwegian dramatist Ludvig *Holberg* (1684–1754), and is named for him.

Holborn The district of London has a name that means literally 'hollow bourne', that is, a stream running through a hollow or depression in the ground. The name was that of the stream itself, a tributary of the Fleet. The 'hollow' can be detected today in the form of a dip in a section of the Farringdon Road.

Holkham Hall The 18th-century house near Wells, Norfolk, takes its name from the locality. The meaning is 'homestead in a hollow', from Old English *holc*, 'hollow' and *hām*, 'homestead'. The 'hollow' may have been a lake in the park here.

Holland The precise origin of the name of the European country that is also known as the NETHERLANDS remains uncertain. It may lie either in Old Dutch *Holtland*, 'forest land' or in *Holland*, 'hollow land'. This part of the continent was certainly well wooded at one time. On the other hand, as the country's alternative name implies, the terrain here is flat, not raised. The latter explanation seems the more likely. The English district of *Holland* in Lincolnshire, which bears a physical resemblance to its continental namesake, complete with low-lying land and tulip fields, probably has a name that means 'heel land', from Old English *hōh*, 'hill-spur' and *land*, 'district', if only because early forms of the name suggest this particular origin. There are no obvious 'hills' in the accepted sense, however, and the name is said to refer to the raised salterns by the coast, as places where salt is obtained from pools of evaporated sea water.

Holland House The Jacobean mansion in Kensington, London, or what now remains of it, takes its name from Sir Henry Rich (1590–1649), created first Earl of *Holland* in 1624, who inherited it from his father-in-law, Sir Walter Cope. The original house was built in about 1606. Sir Henry's mother, Lady Penelope Rich, was the STELLA of Sir Philip Sidney's sonnets and songs entitled *Astrophel and Stella* (1582).

Hollies, The The well-known British pop group, formed in Manchester in 1962, took their name as a tribute to Buddy *Holly*, the famous American pop singer who had died in an air crash in 1959. For a similar tribute to Holly's group, the Crickets, *see* BEATLES.

Hollingsworth The name derives from one of the places now called *Hollingworth*, such as that near Glossop, Greater Manchester. The place-name itself means 'holly enclosure'.

Holloway The London district, with its women's prison, has a name that means what it says: 'hollow way'. This was a road, now a section of the A1, that ran through a valley here, between the contrastingly named Highbury and HIGHGATE.

Hollywood The famous name, that of the centre of the American cinema industry, in Los Angeles, is said to have been given in 1887 by the community's developers, a Mr and Mrs Wilcox, who doubtless adopted it

from another place so called. In most places of the name in the United States, the meaning is likely to be 'holly wood' rather than 'holy wood', as it quite often is in England.

Holmes The source of the name is in *holm*, formerly a word either for a holly tree or for an island. In the latter case the 'island' was often simply a raised area of land among streams or in a marsh. A person of the name would thus originally have lived by or at these places.

Holofernes The story of how the Assyrian general of this name came to be killed by Judith in order to save her native town is told in the Book of *Judith* in the Apocrypha. The commander's own name is traditionally explained as 'head shepherd', as if based on a word meaning 'sheep' related to the name of the FAEROES. But it is probably of Persian origin, and is of uncertain meaning. Shakespeare adopted the name for the pedantic schoolmaster in *Love's Labour's Lost* (1594). It has been suggested that he may have intended it as a near-anagram for *John Florio*, with the character himself a satirical portrait of this noted dictionary writer.

Holstein The region and former duchy of northwest Germany has a name that means '*Holt* settlers', from the place-name *Holt*, itself meaning 'wood', and *sittan*, 'to be settled', 'to be situated'. The original *Holtsetar* was then corrupted to *Holstein*, as if the second half of the name came from *Stein*, 'stone'. Holstein later united with SCHLESWIG to form SCHLESWIG-HOLSTEIN.

Holy Grail According to medieval legend, the name is that of the bowl used by Jesus at the Last Supper, in which Joseph of Arimathea received Christ's blood during the Crucifixion. Joseph is then said to have brought the cup to Glastonbury, in Britain, where it became the quest of many knights, and especially King Arthur's knights of the Round Table. It is known by the alternative name of *Sangrail* or *Sangreal*, as if from Old French *sang real*, 'true blood', but in fact it is from Old French *Saint Graal*, 'Holy Grail'. *Grail* itself may have originated from Medieval Latin *gradalis*, 'bowl', a word that is perhaps related to Greek *kratēr* (modern

English *crater*), the term for a bowl in which wine and water were mixed before being poured into cups. Some, however, have linked the word with Medieval Latin *gradale*, 'by degrees', 'by stages' (from classical Latin *gradus*, 'step'), as if applied to a dish or platter that was brought to the table at various stages in a meal. Others, on the other hand, have derived the word either from Medieval Latin *gradualis*, modern English *gradual*, as a sung portion of the Roman Catholic mass, or even from Irish *críol*, 'basket', 'casket' (English *creel*).

Holyhead The Anglesey port has a name that relates directly to the island, meaning 'holy headland'. Holyhead has a long history as a Christian centre. The actual *head* of the name is Holyhead Mountain, to the west of the town. An exactly parallel (though Celtic) name is that of PENZANCE. The Welsh name of Holyhead is *Caergybi*, '*Cybi*'s fort', from the name of the saint to whom the town's parish church is dedicated.

Holy Land The alternative name for Palestine or modern Israel, favoured by tourist companies, is of biblical origin. It has its genesis in the scene where God appears to Moses in the burning bush: 'And he said, Draw not nigh hither: put off thy shoes from off thy feet, for the place whereon thou standest is holy ground' (*Exodus* 3.5). The presence of God thus made the place where he appeared holy. Later, the name is applied for the first time to Israel: 'And the Lord shall inherit Judah his portion in the holy land' (*Zechariah* 2.12). The English name directly translates Medieval Latin *Terra Sancta*.

Holy Roman Empire The name of the complex of European territories that existed for 1000 years from the early 9th century was based on that of the Western *Roman Empire*, which had lapsed with the sack of Rome in AD 476. The title of *Roman Emperor* was revived by Pope Leo III in 800 and conferred on Charlemagne. It again lapsed after the Carolingian line died out, but was once more adopted in the coronation of Otto I the Great on Sunday 2 February 962, and existed continuously from then on. In 1157, the (new style) Roman Emperor Frederick I Barbarossa introduced the concept of *Holy* to emphasize the sacred nature of the imperial office, so that it was of equal status to the Church of Rome. The full Latin title of *Sacrum Romanorum Imperium*, however, dates only from 1254. The title *Holy Roman Emperor* was originally never in official use, and the heir to the throne was known as *Rex Romanorum*, 'king of the Romans'. After the mid-15th century the title was extended further to *Sacrum Romanorum Imperium Nationis Germanicae*, or in German, *Heiliges Römisches Reich Deutscher Nation*, 'Holy Roman Empire of the German Nation', since German lands were the chief component of the complex. The Holy Roman Empire was dissolved in 1806 when Francis II, the first emperor of Austria, finally dropped the title *Holy Roman Emperor*.

Holyroodhouse Scotland's main royal residence, in Edinburgh, was built in the mid-16th century by James IV, who based the palace on the existing guesthouse of the 13th-century *Holyrood* Abbey. The palace thus takes its name from this. The abbey's name states its dedication to the *Holy Rood*, otherwise the Holy Cross, that on which Christ was crucified.

Holy Week The name is that of the week before Easter, introduced to England by Roman Catholics as a translation of either Italian *settimana santa* or French *semaine sainte*. The older English name for this week is *Passion Week* (*see* PASSION SUNDAY).

Homburg The town of western Germany, famous for its hats of the same name, is so called from the nearby *Hohenburg* fortress, built in the 12th century but now long in ruins. Its own name means 'high fort', from words that gave modern German *hoch*, 'high' and *Burg*, 'fort'.

Home Counties The name of the counties surrounding London has *Home* in the sense 'base', 'headquarters', referring to the capital. A similar use of the word is found in the common name *Home Farm* for a farm with outlying holdings, and also in the *home ground* of a sports team.

Homer The name of the famous Greek poet, supposed author of the *Iliad* and the *Odyssey*, is of uncertain origin. It outwardly resembles the Greek word *homēros*, 'joined together', 'united' (also 'hostage'), but the precise implication of this is unclear, if in fact it can be related to the poet at all.

Homerton College The Cambridge teachers training college was founded in 1823 in *Homerton*, east London, as a college for Protestant Dissenters. It moved to Cambridge in 1894.

Honda The famous make of car and motorcycle takes its name from Soichiro *Honda* (1906–1991), a Japanese blacksmith's son who set up a business making piston rings in 1931 and who branched out into motorcycle production after the Second World War.

Honduras The republic of Central America has a name that is the Spanish word for 'depths'. The story goes that when Christopher Columbus reached this land in 1524, he and his crew noticed the unusual depth of the sea off the coast and gave thanks to God for their safe passage over such dangerous waters.

Honeycombs, The The British pop group, formed in 1963, took a name that was a punning reference both to their female drummer, Ann *'Honey'* Lantree, whom they regarded as their main 'selling point', and to the fact that she and another member of the group, Martin Murray, had previously worked together as hairdressers.

Honfleur The port in northwest France derives its name from the Germanic personal name *Hun* or *Hunn* and Old English *flēot*, 'estuary', 'inlet'. *Cp.* HARFLEUR. Honfleur and Harfleur are almost exactly opposite each other on the estuary of the Seine near Le Havre.

Hongkong The name of the British Crown Colony (until 1997) represents the Cantonese pronunciation of Chinese *xiānggǎng*, 'fragrant port', from *xiāng*, 'perfume', 'scent' and *gǎng*, 'port', 'harbour'. The reference is to the currents of Victoria Harbour, between mainland Kowloon and the island of Victoria, which are sweetened by the fresh water brought down from the estuary of the river Xijiang to the west of Hongkong.

Honiara The capital of the Solomon Islands has a name that represents *Naghoniara*,

'place of the east wind' or 'facing the trade winds', with *ala* the local word for the east or southeast trade winds. The town is on the northwest coast of the island of Guadalcanal.

Honiton Early spellings of the name of the Devon town tend to suggest that it means *'Huna's* farm' rather than 'honey farm', although the latter sense need not be entirely ruled out.

Honolulu The Hawaiian port has a native name meaning 'calm harbour', from Hawaiian *hono*, 'port', 'harbour' and *lulu*, 'calm'. The harbour is naturally sheltered here.

Honshu The largest of Japan's islands has a name that means 'main district', from *hon*, 'main', 'principal' and *shū*, 'district', 'region'. The self-explanatory reference is both geographical and administrative.

Hook The name could originally have described someone who made and sold hooks, who lived by a 'hook' of land, such as a river bend, or who had a hooked nose or a hunched back. It is virtually impossible to tell which in most instances.

Hook of Holland The name is a translation of the Dutch name of the cape on the southwest Netherlands coast, *Hoek van Holland*, meaning 'corner of Holland'. It is a 'hook' in the sense of being an angle of land, although the word in English is more usually applied to a bend in a river or corner of a hill rather than a cape or headland at sea.

Hoover The well-known make of vacuum cleaner owes its name to the American saddler William Henry *Hoover* (1849–1932), who in 1907 bought the embryo Electric Suction Sweeper Company formed by the cleaner's actual inventor, a department store floorwalker named Murray Spangler.

Hoover Dam The highest concrete dam in America, on the river Colorado at the border between Arizona and Nevada, was built in the 1930s and originally named *Boulder Dam*, for the huge rock formations in Black Canyon here. In 1947 it was renamed in honour of US president Herbert Hoover (1874–1964). It would have been named for him originally, but he was under stern criticism at the time for his refusal to provide federal funds for the unemployed, so was something of a *persona non grata*.

Hope The name does not relate to a hopeful person but originally described someone who lived in a small valley, the Old English word for which was *hop*. This is found in several place-names, such as Stanford le *Hope* in Essex, or *Worksop* ('*Weorc*'s valley') in Nottinghamshire.

Hopi The name of the North American Indian people and the language they speak derives from their own name for themselves, *Hópi*, meaning 'peaceful'.

Hopkins The name means 'son of *Hopkin*', this being a diminutive of *Hobb*, itself a pet form of ROBERT.

Horace The modern name derives from the Roman clan name *Horatius*, itself of obscure origin and meaning, although associated by some with Latin *hora*, 'hour', 'time'. It was the name of the famous 1st-century BC Roman poet who was the author of the *Ars Poetica*.

Horeb, Mount The name, an alternative one for Mount Sinai, represents Hebrew *hôrev*, 'dryness', referring to the mountain's natural aridity.

Horlicks The familiar malted drink is named for James *Horlick* (1844–1921), an English-born saddler's son who with his brother William set up a partnership in Chicago in 1873 to manufacture a baby food he had invented.

Hormuz The island in the Strait of *Hormuz*, at the entrance to the Persian Gulf, has a name that represents Greek *Harmoson* or *Harmosa*, itself probably the name of the Zoroastrian god *Ormuzd*, which in turn is a form of the name of Ahura MAZDA, the god of goodness and light.

Hornby The familiar make of model railway takes its name from Frank *Hornby* (1863–1936), a Liverpool provision merchant's son who in 1901 patented the MECCANO construction kit he had invented and who started manufacturing the kit in 1908. The electric trains followed in 1925, and the famous *Dinky Toys* in 1934.

Horniman Museum The London museum arose (in 1897) out of the collection of works of art and artefacts, gathered during his world travels, of Frederick John *Horniman* (1835–1906), son of John Horniman, founder of the well-known tea business.

Horn of Africa The name is sometimes applied to the cape of northeast Africa that is now occupied by the Somali Republic. It is so called because it is pointed, in the shape of a *horn*. It is thus distinct etymologically (and of course geographically) from CAPE HORN, even though that promontory is much more obviously horn-shaped.

Horn Signal Symphony Haydn's Symphony No 31 in D major (1765) is so nicknamed for the four horn calls that come in its slow movement.

Horsham The West Sussex town has a name that means 'horse village', showing that horses were probably bred here in Anglo-Saxon times.

Horst Wessel Song The official song of Hitler's Nazi Party took its name from the student who wrote its words, party member *Horst Wessel* (1907–1930), who was killed in the Communist quarter of Berlin. The tune dates from a pre-First World War music-hall song.

Hortense The ultimate source of the name is the Roman clan name *Hortensius*, perhaps itself related to Latin *hortus*, 'garden'.

Horus The sun god of ancient Egyptian mythology has a name representing Egyptian *Har*, probably meaning 'high' or 'far-off'. He is usually depicted with a hawk's head.

Hosea The name of the Old Testament prophet and his book is a form of JOSHUA, so like it had the meaning 'Jehovah saves' in the original Hebrew.

Hoskins The name means 'son of *Hoskin*', itself the diminutive form of a medieval personal name containing the word meaning 'god' that is now found in names such as OSBORN.

Hot Chocolate The British pop group was formed in London in 1969 by two black musicians, Jamaican-born singer Errol Brown and Trinidadian bassist Tony Wilson. Their name, given them by an agent from the Apple record company, punningly refers to their colour and their 'hot' reggae-style music.

Hotspur Harry *Hotspur* was the nickname of Sir Henry Percy (1364–1403), the English rebel who was killed when leading his army against Henry IV. The name relates to his impetuous spurring-on of his horse, which was in the event the cause of his (literal) downfall as he rode ahead of his men in a final charge at Berwick. The name is now familiar from TOTTENHAM HOTSPUR Football Club, and as the name of a comic for boys published from the 1930s to the 1980s.

Hottentot The people of southern Africa, with their unusually small stature, are said to have a name of Dutch origin that refers imitatively to the distinctive 'clicks' and other unfamiliar sounds of their language, which to a European suggested stammering or stuttering. The name is now regarded as derogatory, so that the people are known by their own name for themselves, *Khoikhoin*, meaning 'men of men'. *See also* KHOISAN.

Houghton The name comes from any of the places so called, such as *Houghton*-le-Spring in northeast England. The meaning of the place-name in most cases is 'ridge settlement', from Old English *hōh*, literally 'heel', and *tūn* (modern *town*), 'settlement'.

House It may seem strange that a person should be named after the building in which he normally lives. But in medieval times most people lived more modestly in cottages or even huts rather than houses, so the name originally denoted a person of some importance. The 'house', too, was often that of a religious community.

House of Fraser The well-known department stores take their name from Hugh *Fraser*, who opened a draper's shop in Glasgow in 1849. The effective founder of the present business, however, was his grandson, Lord Hugh Fraser (1903–1966), who brought the Scottish family business down to London in 1959.

House of Keys The lower chamber of the legislature of the Isle of Man has a name that means what it says, although the reason for the title is unclear. The Manx name for the chamber is *Yn Kiare as Feed*, 'the four and twenty', alluding to the number of its members. It is not likely that

the English name represents a version of *Kiare as*, 'four and', as has been sometimes claimed.

Houston The Texas city, famous as the site of the Manned Spacecraft Center, was founded in 1836 and named for the first president of Texas, Sam *Houston* (1793–1863).

Houyhnhnms The name of the talking horses in Swift's *Gulliver's Travels* (1726) clearly represents a horse's *whinnying*, otherwise 'talking'. Even so, one ingenious commentator claims that if the name is read backwards one can (rather tortuously) derive something like *manni voc*, suggesting Latin *manni*, 'horses' and *voces*, 'voices'. *Cp.* YAHOOS.

Hove The town and resort near Brighton in Sussex has a name that ultimately comes from Old English *hūfe*, 'hood'. This probably referred metaphorically to some natural feature here that acted as a 'hood' or shelter. It is not clear what it was. It may have been a shelter for people arriving by boat, and the Old English word may even be indirectly linked with modern *haven*.

Hovis The familiar brand of wholemeal bread was originally *Smith's Patent Germ Bread* when first marketed in 1887. In 1890 a competition was held to devise a neater name. It was won by a Mr Herbert Grime, who took the Latin words *hominis vis*, 'strength of man', and contracted them to *Hovis*. The Hovis Bread Flour Company was formed in 1898, and evolved to Hovis Limited in 1918. For many years the company spelled the name with a tilde (as *Hõvis*) to indicate that it was an abbreviation.

Howard The first name derives from the surname, well-known as that of a noble English family. It is probably of Scandinavian origin, from *hā*, 'high' and *ward*, 'guardian'.

Howe If not a form of HUGH, the name usually denoted a person who lived by a small hill or manmade barrow (Old Norse *haugr*), or who came from a place with the word in its name, such as the village of *Howe* near Norwich.

Howell If a Welsh name, the origin lies in the personal name *Hywel*, meaning 'emi-

249

nent', 'conspicuous'. If an English name, the source is probably in the small village so called near Sleaford, Lincolnshire. Its own name probably means '*Huna*'s well'.

Hradec Králové The name of the town in the northwest Czech Lands derives from words corresponding to modern Czech *hrad*, 'castle', 'fort' and *králova*, 'queen', so meaning 'royal fortress'. The town was fortified in the 14th century and was associated with Elizabeth of Poland. The German name of the town is *Königgrätz*, a part-translation, part-corruption of the Czech.

H. Samuel The well-known chain of jewellers was founded in 1821 as a clockmaking business in Liverpool by two brothers, Moses and Lewis *Samuel*. On their death, the business was continued by Moses' son. But when he outlived his father by less than two years the firm was taken over by Moses' widow, *Harriet Samuel*, and it is for her that the company came to be named.

Hsian *See* XI AN.

Hsining *See* XINING.

HTV The independent television company, serving Wales and the west of England, originated in 1967 as *Harlech* Television, taking its name from its founder and first chairman, David Ormsby Gore, Lord *Harlech* (1918–1985). His own title derives from the Welsh town of HARLECH.

Huang Hai The Chinese name of the *Yellow Sea*, an arm of the Pacific between Korea and northeast China, has the same meaning as the English name, from *huáng*, 'yellow' and *hǎi*, 'sea'. It takes its name from the colour of the silt-laden water discharged into it from many rivers, one of which, until its course was diverted in 1852, was the HUANG HO.

Huang Ho The second longest river of China, known to Europeans as *Yellow River*, has a name that means the same as the English, representing Chinese *huáng*, 'yellow' and *hé*, 'river'. The reference is to the yellow silt of its waters. It formerly flowed into the HUANG HAI, but its course was diverted in 1852 and it now enters the sea to the north.

Huascarán The extinct volcano in the Peruvian Alps, the highest peak in Peru, has a Spanish name representing that of the Inca ruler *Huáscar* (d. 1533).

Hubei The province of central China has a name that means 'north of the lake', from *hú*, 'lake' and *běi*, 'north'. The reference is to the location of the province with regard to Lake Dongting. *Cp*. HEBEI, HUNAN.

Hubert The name is Germanic in origin, from *hugu*, 'mind', 'spirit' (*cp*. HUGH) and *beraht*, 'bright', 'famous'. The name implies a person noted for his understanding and generosity.

Huddersfield The name of the Yorkshire town means '*Hudrǣd*'s open land', with the rare Anglo-Saxon personal name followed by Old English *feld*, 'open land' (modern *field*).

Hudibras The name of the central character of Samuel Butler's satire of this name, published in three parts between 1662 and 1680, is said to be based on the *Hudibras* who is the lover of Elissa in Spenser's *Faerie Queene* (1590, 1596). His own name is supposed to represent that of Sir *Hugh de Bras*, one of the Knights of the Round Table in the Arthurian romances.

Hudson The name means 'son of *Hudd*', this perhaps being a pet form of HUGH, if not associated with an earlier Old English name, such as the one that gave the name of *Huddington*, near Droitwich.

Hudson Bay The Canadian inland sea, joined to the Atlantic by Hudson Strait, takes its name from the English navigator Henry *Hudson* (d. 1611), who explored both the river, also named for him, and the bay. In Hudson Bay his crew mutinied and cast him adrift to die. His name was also preserved in that of the *Hudson's Bay Company*, the English company chartered in 1670 to trade in those parts of North America that were drained by rivers flowing into Hudson Bay.

Hué The former capital of Annam, now a port in central Vietnam, has a name that ultimately derives from Chinese *huá*, 'China' (literally 'brilliant', 'prosperous'), used as an abbreviation for *huáqiáo*, 'overseas China', that is, a term for a Chinese living outside China.

Huelgoat The town in Brittany, northwest France, has a name that represents Breton *An Uhelgoad*, 'the high wood', from *an*, 'the', *uhel*, 'high', and *goad*, a mutated form of *koad*, 'wood'. The name is pronounced approximately 'Uelgwat'.

Huelva The port in southwest Spain has a name recorded by Pliny as *Onuba*. This is probably of Punic origin, but its meaning is unknown.

Huesca The city in northeast Spain was known to the Romans as *Osca*. This may derive from the name of the OSCAN people.

Hugh The name has evolved as a short form of a longer Germanic name that contained the word *hugu*, 'mind', 'spirit'. *Cp.* HUBERT.

Hughenden Manor The late 18th-century house in Buckinghamshire, the home of Disraeli for much of his life, takes its name from the nearby small village of *Hughenden*. This means '*Hucca's* valley', but over the years the name has come to be associated with the modern personal name HUGH.

Hughes The name means 'son of HUGH'.

Hughes Hall The Cambridge college, since 1949 an institute to train women graduates as teachers, was founded in 1885 as the *Cambridge Training College for Teachers*. Its founder and first principal was Elizabeth Phillips *Hughes* (1851–1925), a Welsh-born schoolmistress who had studied moral sciences and history at Newnham College, Cambridge. She subsequently adopted the Welsh bardic name of *Merch Myrddin*, 'daughter of Carmarthen', her native town in Wales.

Huguenot The name of the French Calvinists of the 16th and 17th centuries, many of whom were forced to flee to other countries to escape persecution, derives from the Genevan dialect word *eyguenot*, ultimately from Swiss German *Eidgenoss*, 'confederation'. An *eyguenot* was a Genevan supporter of an alliance with Fribourg and Bern in order to prevent annexation by Savoy. The present spelling arose by association with the name of the Swiss magistrate who led the alliance, Bezanson *Hugues* (d. 1532).

Hull The well-known city and port lies at the confluence of the small river *Hull* with the much larger Humber, and takes its name from the former. The river's own name is probably very old, and may come from a Celtic root word meaning 'muddy'. The official name of the city is *Kingston-upon-Hull*. The first part of this refers to *King* Edward I, who exchanged lands elsewhere for the port here in 1292. A third name of Hull in the 12th and 13th centuries was *Wyke*. This probably represents Old English *wīc*, the word sometimes used for a port, as for HARWICH and IPSWICH. However, it could also derive from Old Norse *vík*, 'creek', 'inlet', as for WICK in the north of Scotland. The former seems more likely.

Human League, The The British 'electropop' band, formed in Sheffield in 1977 by two former computer operators, took their name appropriately from a science-fiction computer game.

Humber The estuarial river in the east of England probably has a name of Celtic origin, perhaps meaning 'good river', the final *-ber* representing 'river'. A 'good river' would have been one favourable for fishing and trading, although the name could equally have been a 'placatory' one designed to appease a destructive river god.

Humble Pie The British rock band, formed in London in 1969, took a name that reflected its modest beginnings by comparison with the 'pop idol' status earlier enjoyed in other groups by its founders, Peter Frampton from The Herd and Steve Marriott from The SMALL FACES.

Humphrey The name is Germanic in origin and has been popularly associated with that of the HUNS. Its actual source, however, is likely to be in the standard words *hun*, 'warrior' and *fridu*, 'peace'. The implication is of a military man who brings 'peace through strength'.

Hunan The province of southern China has a name that means 'south of the lake', from *hú*, 'lake' and *nán*, 'south'. This describes the position of the province with regard to Lake Dongting. *Cp.* HUBEI.

Hundred Years War The name was given to the series of conflicts between England

and France that in fact lasted 106 years, from 1337 to 1453.

Hungary The name of the European country does not derive from its inhabitants, as in many cases, since the indigenous name for these is MAGYAR. It may be related to the name of the Russian river *Ugra*, southwest of Moscow. Some, however, see a link between the country's name and that of the HUNS.

Hungerford The Berkshire town has a name that means what it says: 'hunger ford'. The reference would have been to a ford over the river Kennet here that led to barren ground, where crops could not easily be grown, so that people went hungry.

Hungerford Bridge The iron railway bridge over the Thames at Charing Cross, London, takes its name from the former bridge here that was built in 1841 to serve *Hungerford* market. This was a market on the north side of the Thames that originated in the gardens of the family house of Sir Edward *Hungerford* in the late 17th century. The market was demolished in 1860 to make room for Charing Cross Station.

Hungnam The port in eastern North Korea derives its name from Korean *hŭng*, 'joy' and *nam*, 'south' (*cp.* VIETNAM itself).

Huns The Asiatic peoples who dominated much of Asia and eastern Europe from the 3rd century BC, and who invaded the Roman Empire in the 4th and 5th centuries AD, have a name of Mongolian origin, meaning simply 'man'. It was the legendary brutality of these people that gave the derogatory nickname applied to the Germans in both World Wars. Ironically, it was a speech by the German emperor Wilhelm II on 27 July 1900, made to German troops at Bremerhaven about to set sail for China, that originally promoted it in this particular sense. As reported in *The Times* of 30 July that year, the speech contained the following passage:

> No quarter will be given, no prisoners will be taken. Let all who fall into your hands be at your mercy. Just as the Huns a thousand years ago, under the leadership of Etzel (Attila) gained a reputation in virtue of which they still live in historical tradition, so may the name of Germany become

known in such a manner in China that no Chinaman will ever again even dare to look askance at a German.

Hunt The name originally denoted someone who was a hunter, this being not just a huntsman in the modern sense, but anyone who caught animals or birds for food, such as a poacher. The surname *Hunter* is usually of the same origin.

Huntingdon The Cambridgeshire town and former county town of the now abolished Huntingdonshire has a name that means 'hunter's hill', that is, a hill favoured by huntsmen. The hill in question was probably the low broad one on which the town lies overlooking the river Ouse.

Huntley and Palmer The familiar brand of biscuits is named for Thomas *Huntley* (1803–1857) and George *Palmer* (1818–1897), who became partners in a bakery and confectionery business in Reading in 1841.

Hunt Quartet Mozart's String Quartet No 17 in B flat major, K 458 (1784) is so nicknamed for the 'tally-ho' motifs which introduce the first subject of its first movement.

Hurlingham Club The well-known London sports club, originally but no longer a polo club, was founded in 1869 at *Hurlingham* House, built in 1760. The house was named for its location, but the meaning of the place-name itself is uncertain. An origin in Old English *thyrelung*, literally 'piercing', referring to a gap or hollow, has been tentatively proposed. The suggestion of *hurling* in the name of a sports club is pleasant but in this case purely fortuitous.

Huron, Lake The second largest of the Great Lakes takes its name from the Indian *Huron* people, who lived on its shores. Their own name was given by French colonists in the 16th century, and represents the archaic French word *huron*, 'bristle-haired', related to modern French *hure*, 'boar's head'. The reference was probably to the Indians' headdress rather than to their natural hair.

Hussey The name has at least three possible sources. It could be of Norman origin, referring to a person who came from *Houssaye* near Rouen in northern

France, with the place-name itself meaning 'holly'; it could represent Middle English *husewif*, 'housewife', referring to a woman who was mistress of her own household; or it could have originated as a nickname for a person who wore unusual boots, from Old French *husé*, 'booted' (related to modern English *hose*). It would not have originated from *hussy* meaning 'impertinent girl', as this sense evolved too late to give a surname. (It did develop from *housewife*, however.)

Hutchins The meaning of the name is 'son of *Hutchin*', itself a diminutive form of HUGH. *Hutchinson* is of the same origin.

Hutchinson The London publisher takes its name from its founder, George Thompson *Hutchinson* (1857–1931), who set up his business in 1887 and published his first books two years later.

Hutton The name derives from any of the places so called, such as those in Yorkshire. The meaning of the name is 'ridge settlement', like HOUGHTON.

Huxley The surname comes from the village of this name near Tarporley in Cheshire. The meaning of the place-name is probably '*Hucc's* wood'.

Hvar The Croatian island, in the Adriatic, was settled by the Greeks in the 1st century BC and was known to them as *Pharos*. This name is a direct borrowing of that of the Egyptian island of PHAROS, off Alexandria, Egypt. The town of *Hvar* takes its name from the island, of which it is the capital.

Hwang Hai *See* HUANG HAI.

Hwang Ho *See* HUANG HO.

Hyacinth The girl's name derives from that of a boy. In classical mythology *Hyacinthus* was the beautiful youth loved by Apollo. At the place where Apollo accidentally killed him, a flower sprang from the blood of Hyacinthus and came to be called by his name. Hence the modern name, which like other girl's names originated in a flower. The origin of the youth's name is uncertain, however. Some have fancifully related the marks on the leaves of the flower to the early Greek letters *AI*, 'woe!', representing the cry of Hyacinthus as he fell. Others see the first two letters of his name as forming a similar cry. But that is equally fanciful, as of course the whole story is in the first place. *Hyacinth* was in fact a boy's name in many European countries, including Britain, before it was adopted for female use.

Hyades The name of the star cluster in the constellation Taurus is traditionally derived from Greek *huein*, 'to rain', since it was observed that when the cluster appeared in the sky just before sunrise in early November that was often the start of the rainy season. In Greek mythology the *Hyades* were the five daughters of Atlas and the nymphs that supplied moisture to the earth.

Hyde Park London's famous park has a name that probably derives from Old English *hīd*, 'hide', this being the area (anything between 60 and 120 acres) of the ground belonging to the manor of Ebury on which it arose. Its present area is 615 acres (249 ha).

Hyderabad The city and former state of southern central India have a name that literally means 'lion town', from Hindi *haidar*, 'lion' and Iranian *ābād*, 'inhabited place' (*cp*. ABADAN). The reference is to Ali, son-in-law of Muhammad, the founder of Islam, who took the title 'Lion'. Hyderabad was founded in 1589, however, so that the name is commemorative, and does not imply that the town dates back to the 7th century, when Ali lived. The city of *Hyderabad* in southwest Pakistan has a name of the same origin.

Hyères The town in southeast France has a name that ultimately derives from Latin *area*, 'open space' (modern English *area*).

Hyksos The name of the nomadic Asian people who controlled Egypt from 1720 to 1560 BC derives, through Greek, from Egyptian *ḥeqaŝesaut*, 'ruler of foreign lands'. The name was (wrongly) explained by Manetho, the 3rd century BC Egyptian historian, as coming from Egyptian *hyk*, 'king' and *sos*, 'shepherd'.

Hypatia The Greek philosopher, famous for her beauty and her cruel death, has a name that is derived from Greek *hupatos*, 'highest', 'best'. Her story is told in Charles Kingsley's historical novel of the same name, published in 1851.

Hyperborean In Greek mythology, the *Hyperboreans* were the people believed to live beyond the North Wind, in a permanently sunny land. Their name relates to this location, and derives from Greek *huper*, 'beyond' and *Boreas*, the god of the North Wind. His name also lies behind the French word *bourrasque*, meaning 'squall'.

Hyperion In Greek mythology *Hyperion* was a Titan, the son of Uranus and Gaia and the father of Helios, the sun, with whom he is sometimes identified. His name literally means 'going over', from Greek *huper*, 'over' and *iōn*, 'going'. This is a suitable name both for a giant, as the Titans were, and for his *alter ego* as the sun, which 'goes over' daily.

Hyrcania The ancient district of Asia, southeast of the Caspian Sea, derives its name from the Greek personal name *Hyrkanos*. This itself is of uncertain origin.

Hythe The Kent resort has a name that simply means 'landing-place'. The Old English word *hȳth* with this meaning always referred to a landing stage on a river, not on the sea, so at Hythe it would have been some short distance inland. Coastal changes have been so great here since Anglo-Saxon times, however, that it is impossible to tell where it was. For names of places in London on the Thames containing the same word (though now often well disguised), *cp.* PUTNEY, CHELSEA, LAMBETH, STEPNEY and ROTHERHITHE.

I

Ian The name is a Scottish version of JOHN, now widely used in its own right.

Ibadan The city in southwest Nigeria has a name of Arabic origin, from *'ibāda*, 'worship', deriving from *'ibād*, the plural of *'abd*, 'servant' (*i.e.* of God). Ibadan has long been an important Islamic centre.

Iberia The name of the peninsula occupied by Spain and Portugal derives from that of its inhabitants, the *Iberians*, whose own name comes from that of the river EBRO which flows through it.

Ibiza The Spanish island in the Mediterranean, as one of the Balearic Islands, has a name of Punic origin, representing *ī busim*, 'island of perfumes', from *ī*, 'island' and *busim*, 'perfumes'. The reference is to the shrubs and trees found widely over the island's mostly hilly terrain.

Ibrox Park The home ground of Glasgow Rangers football club is named after the district of Glasgow in which it was built in 1887. The name itself is said to mean 'ford of the badger', from Gaelic *àth*, 'ford' and *bruic*, genitive of *broc*, 'badger'.

Icaria The Greek island in the Aegean Sea is traditionally said to take its name from ICARUS, who according to legend drowned in the Aegean. In actual fact it may come from Pelasgian *īkar*, 'timber', referring to the island's once plentiful forestland.

Icarus In Greek mythology, *Icarus* and his father Daedalus escaped from the clutches of the Minotaur in Crete by flying with wings made from wax and feathers. When Icarus flew too near the sun, however, the wax melted, so that he fell into the Aegean Sea and was drowned. His name may have a bearing on this, since it means (according to one authority) 'dedicated to the moon'. It is probably not Greek in origin.

Icehouse The Australian rock group was originally named *Flowers* when formed in Sydney in 1980. The following year they were obliged to change this, however, in order to avoid conflict with the Scottish group *The Flowers*. They therefore took a new name from their first album, *Icehouse* (1981).

Iceland The name of the island republic of northern Europe means what it says, 'ice land', from Icelandic *ís*, 'ice' and *land*, 'land'. The name was given to the island by the Viking settler Floki, who came here in 960. The name is today something of a misnomer, since Iceland's climate is comparatively mild, with an average January temperature ranging from 0°C on the coast to −10°C in the mountains, and a corresponding July one from 11°C to 0°C. Either way, it is not noticeably 'icy'. But 1000 years ago, when it was so named, the climate may well have been different.

Iceni The name of the ancient British tribe, who in the 1st century AD rebelled against the Romans under Queen Boudicca, is of uncertain origin. Some recent scholars, however, have tentatively proposed a link with a Celtic and Indoeuropean root element *iak*, meaning 'healthy'.

Ichabod The biblical name is that of the son of Phinehas, who was born on a day of two calamitous events: first, the Ark was captured by the Philistines, then his father, mother, uncle Hophni, and grandfather, the priest Eli, all died. Hence his name, from Hebrew *Ī-ḥābhōdh*, popularly understood to mean 'without glory'. The Bible duly associates name and events: 'And she (*i.e.* his mother, on the point of death) named the child Ichabod, saying, The glory is departed from Israel: because the ark of God was taken, and because of her father in law and her husband' (1 *Samuel* 4.21).

I Ching The ancient Chinese book of divination is traditionally known in English as *Book of Changes*, a rendering of its Chinese name, *yichīng*, literally 'change classic', from *yì*, 'change' and *chīng*, 'scripture', 'classics'. The book is one of the so called 'Five Classics', or sacred books of China, that comprise the *Four Books* (the 'Great Learning', 'Doctrine of the Mean', 'Confucian Analects' and 'Works of Mencius') and the *I Ching* itself.

Icknield Way The name of the ancient British trackway, originally running from The Wash down to the south coast, has traditionally been linked with that of the ICENI tribe. But even though the Iceni had their capital at what is now Caistor St Edmund, Norfolk, in a region where the Icknield Way begins its route, any connection between the names is linguistically unproven. Until further evidence is forthcoming, therefore, the origin and meaning of the name must remain uncertain.

Ida The name is popularly linked with the Mount IDA of classical mythology. It is actually of Germanic origin, however, from a root element *īd*, meaning 'work'.

Ida, Mount The name is that of both a mountain in central Crete, formerly associated with the worship of Zeus, and of one in northwest Turkey, near the site of the ancient city of Troy. In Greek mythology it has been associated variously with the personal names IDA, *Idaea* and *Idaeus*, but it probably relates to Greek *idē*, 'timber', with reference to the forests on both mountains.

Idaho The American state has a name that is almost certainly of Indian origin, but from which language and with what meaning is uncertain. An interpretation 'fish-eaters' has been suggested, although according to some sources the sense is 'jewel of the mountains', referring to the region's natural deposits of gold and silver.

Idlewild The former name of Kennedy Airport, New York, arose as a settlers' general commendatory name for an attractive site, one that was *idyllic* in the *wilds* of nature. The airport was renamed in 1963.

Ido The artificial language was devised in 1907 as a modified form of Esperanto, and derives its name from an Esperanto suffix *-id* meaning 'derived from' (itself from a Greek suffix).

Idomeneus The mythical king of Greece who fought for the Trojans in the Trojan War has a name that may derive from *idmōn*, 'practised', 'skilled'.

Idris The Welsh name is generally held to comprise the two words *iud*, 'lord' and *rīs*, 'ardent'.

Ife The town in west central Nigeria has a long history and may derive its name from that of *Ifa*, a Yoruba god of divination. The fact that it is a holy city and that it has gold mines has led some to link its name with that of the biblical OPHIR.

Ifni The former Spanish province in southern Morocco has a name of Tuareg origin, from *isafen*, the plural of *asif*, 'water', 'river'.

Ignatius The name is a Late Latin one, from the Roman *nomen* (clan name) *Egnatius*. The meaning of this is uncertain, but it came to be associated with *ignis*, 'fire'.

Igor The well-known Russian name is Scandinavian in origin, evolving from *Ingvarr*, which itself represents *Ing*, the name of the god of fertility, and *varr*, 'careful', 'attentive'.

IJssel The river in the central Netherlands has a name that derives from a root word meaning 'water', 'river', found in many European languages, from Old English *ēa* to modern French *eau*. The river gave the name of the *IJsselmeer*, the large lake in the northwest of the country. (In Dutch, the digraph *ij* is regarded as a single letter, pronounced like English *I* or *eye*, so that when it begins a proper name it is written as a double capital.)

Île-de-France The region round Paris has come to be known as the 'island of France' for reasons that are probably both geographical and historical. Geographically, the area is more or less bounded by several rivers, many of them important, such as the Seine, Oise and Marne. Historically, the Île-de-France represents the original *Francia* from which modern France grew. And politically, of course, it is the region surrounding the capital. In this last sense the name bears some correspondence to the English HOME COUNTIES that centre on London.

Île de la Cité The 'city island' is the ship-shaped island in the Seine in the centre of Paris where the French capital arose, and where some of its most historic and important buildings remain today, such as Notre-Dame Cathedral and the Palais de Justice. In many ways the Ile de la Cité thus corresponds historically and administratively, if not geographically, to the City of London. The physical resemblance of the island to a ship is reflected in the city's Latin motto, *Fluctuat nec mergitur*, 'It tosses on the waves but does not sink'.

Ilfracombe The Devon resort has a name that means 'valley of *Ilfred*'s people', with the personal name being a West Saxon form of ALFRED. The 'valley', represented in the name by Old English *cumb*, is the one up which Ilfracombe's steep High Street runs westward from the harbour to Holy Trinity Church.

Iliad Homer's epic poem describing the siege of Troy takes its name from *Ilion*, a name of Troy that gave its more familiar Latin name of ILIUM. The final *-ad* comes from the Greek feminine suffix used to denote 'offspring', as in *dryad, naiad*, PLEIADES. Here it implies that the poem is an 'offspring' of Ilion.

Ilium The name of ancient Troy is the Latin form of the city's alternative Greek name *Ilion*, itself traditionally linked with *Ilus*, its legendary founder. *See also* ILIAD.

Ilkley The West Yorkshire town, famous from the song about Ilkley Moor, has a name that is difficult to interpret satisfactorily. The second part is almost certainly Old English *lēah*, 'wood', 'clearing'. The first part remains a mystery, and cannot be meaningfully associated with any known word or name.

Illiers-Combray The town near Chartres in northwest France was originally just *Illiers*, perhaps from a Germanic personal name *Illhari* or *Islar*. In the novels of Marcel Proust the town appears as *Combray*, and this name was officially added to the original one in 1970, so that it now bears both names. The real *Combray* is further to the north, near Caen, and it is possible that

Proust based the fictional name on that of the village of *Combres*, near Illiers.

Illingworth The name derives from the place so called that is now a district of Halifax in West Yorkshire. It means 'enclosure of *Illa*'s people'.

Illinois The American state ultimately takes its name from the Algonquian tribal name *illini*, probably meaning simply 'men', 'warriors'. The final *-ois* was added by French settlers to name the river that flows through the state.

Illyria The ancient region on the eastern coast of the Adriatic Sea has a name of uncertain origin. It may come from a root element such as *is-lo* meaning 'living' in some sense. Even the geographical extent of the historical Illyria is unknown.

Iloilo The port in the Philippines has a name that was corrupted by the Spanish from an original *Ilong-Ilong*, 'nose-shaped', referring to the winding course of the river Jaro as it enters the sea here.

Imagist The name was that of the English and American poets of the 1920s who aimed to convey clarity of expression through the use of vivid visual *images*. The prime originator of *imagisme*, as the movement was initially known, was the American poet Ezra Pound, who wrote of it: 'I should like the name "Imagisme" to retain some sort of a meaning. It stands, or I should like it to stand for hard light, clear edges' (letter of 1 August 1912).

Immaculate Conception In Christian theology, the name is that of the Roman Catholic doctrine according to which the Virgin Mary was conceived without any stain of original sin, so that she was sinless herself. The doctrine does not thus relate to the Virgin Birth of Jesus to Mary, as sometimes supposed, but to her own birth, the circumstances of which are not recorded in the Bible. (Her parents are traditionally said to be the aged couple Joachim and Anna.) The dogma of the Immaculate Conception was declared an article of faith of the Roman Catholic Church only in 1854. The term itself dates back long before this, however.

Immanuel The biblical name is the Old

Testament variant of EMMANUEL, so has the same meaning, 'God with us'.

Imogen The name is first recorded in Shakespeare for the daughter of Cymbeline. It suggests *image*, but appears to have arisen as a miscopying of an earlier name *Innogen*. This in turn suggests *innocence*, aptly enough for Shakespeare's character, but is probably of Celtic origin meaning 'girl', 'maiden', as does Irish *inghean*.

Impressionists The name is used of those French painters of the 1870s such as Monet, Renoir, Pissarro and Sisley who used the effects of natural light to create a transient *impression* of the scene they depicted. It originated from the title of the painting by Monet, *Impression: soleil levant* ('Impression: sunrise') (1872), showing the play of light on water in the harbour at Le Havre, and was at first applied derisively.

Inca The famous South American Indian people, with an empire centring on Peru, derive their name from Quechua *inka*, the regular royal title (meaning roughly 'king') of their ruler. The Incas themselves called their territory *Tawantinsuyu*, 'empire of the four districts', from *tawa*, 'four', the suffix *-ntin*, and *suyu*, 'district'.

Inchon The port in western South Korea derives its name from Korean *in*, 'virtue' and *ch'ŏn*, 'river'. Inchon is near the mouth of the Han-gang river on the Yellow Sea.

India The country takes its name from the river INDUS, now mostly flowing not through India itself but through Pakistan. The native (Hindi) name of the country is BHARAT (*which see*).

Indiana The future American state was given its Latin-style name in the mid-18th century by French settlers or developers, the reference being to the *Indian* tribes (*see* INDIANS) whose territory it was.

Indianapolis The state capital of INDIANA has a name that explicitly refers to the territory itself, with Greek *polis*, 'city' added. It was founded in 1821.

Indians As applied to the *American Indians*, the name does not of course relate to INDIA at all. It arose through the error of Christopher Columbus, who conceived the plan of sailing due west from Portugal to reach Asia, and who believed he had reached India when he had actually arrived in the WEST INDIES in 1492. If this was India, then the indigenous inhabitants must be Indians! *See also* RED INDIANS.

Indochina The name for the extensive peninsula between INDIA and CHINA was proposed for this region in the early 19th century by the Scottish poet and orientalist John Leyden, who lived and worked in India from 1803 until his premature death eight years later at the age of 35.

Indonesia The republic of southeast Asia has a name based on POLYNESIA that was designed to mean 'Indian islands' when introduced in 1884 by a German geographer. The adjective *Indonesian* was then already in use for the people.

Indra The name is that of the god of thunder and lightning in Hindu mythology, and probably derives from a root element denoting strength or fertility. He is best known from the *Rig-Veda*.

Indus The great Asian river, flowing for almost the whole length of its course south though Pakistan to the Arabian Sea, has an appropriately basic name, from Sanskrit *sindhu*, 'river'. It has bequeathed its name not only to INDIA, but to INDOCHINA, INDONESIA and, indirectly, the WEST INDIES and the American INDIANS. *See also* SIND.

Ingersoll The well-known make of watch derives from that of the American founder of the manufacturing company, Robert Hawley *Ingersoll* (1859–1928), who in 1892 set up a business producing goods such as typewriters, cameras and watches for just one dollar each. He subsequently concentrated on watches alone, and in 1896 produced the famous 'Yankee' model with the slogan 'The watch that made the dollar famous'.

Ingrid The Scandinavian name derives from a combination of *Ing*, the name of a fertility god, and *frithr*, 'fair', 'beautiful'.

Inkatha The name is that of the South African political organization originally founded in 1928 by the Zulu king Solomon but revived by Chief Gatsha Buthelezi in 1975 as a body aiming for a single state with equality for all. It derives from the *inkatha*, the Zulu word for the grass coil worn on the head by Zulu women for carrying heavy loads. As such it is regarded as a tribal emblem, its many strands giving it strength.

Inkerman, Battle of The battle was that of 1854 in the Crimean War, ten days after the Battle of BALACLAVA, in which the Russians were pushed back by the British on a ridge near Sebastopol. The name is that of the village here, itself perhaps of Turkish origin meaning 'new fortress', from *yeni*, 'new' and *kerman*, 'fort'.

Ink Spots, The The black American vocal quartet, popular in the 1930s, chose a name that punningly related both to their colour and to their 'spot', or performance as a particular item in a show or programme.

Inman The name was originally an occupational designation for an 'inn man', that is, a lodging-house keeper.

Innes The Scottish name represents that of an estate near Elgin in the former county of Morayshire, itself deriving from Gaelic *inis*, 'island' (in the sense of land between rivers or streams).

Innisfail The poetic name for Ireland derives from Irish *inis*, 'island' and *fáil*, genitive of *fál*, literally 'rampart'. The latter word came to apply to the 'rampart' of mountains that surrounds the central plain of Ireland, so is tantamount to 'Ireland' itself. *See also* FIANNA FAIL.

Inniskilling *See* ENNISKILLEN.

Innsbruck The Austrian city has a name that means '*Inn* bridge', from the name of the river here and a word that gave modern German *Brücke*, 'bridge'. The river name is of Celtic origin, coming from a root word *enos*, 'water'.

Interlaken The Swiss town and resort is situated between Lakes Brienz and Thun, a location indicated by its original name, representing Latin *inter lacus*, 'between the lakes'. The town grew up in the 12th century round an Augustinian convent. Hence this particular Latin origin.

Internationale The well-known revolutionary socialist hymn, the Soviet national anthem from the 1917 Revolution until 1944, was composed and first sung in France in 1871. Its name is an abbreviated form of French *chanson internationale*, 'international song'.

Interpol The name is the abbreviation of the *Inter*national Criminal *Po*lice Organization, which combines the police forces of over 100 countries. It was set up in Vienna in 1923 and was designed to have a short name that would itself be international, since *inter-* is a prefix standing for *interna-tional* in many languages. The syllable *pol-* often begins the word for 'police' similarly.

Intifada The word represents Arabic *inti-fāḍa*, literally 'shaking off', used for an uprising of some kind. It has come to apply in particular to the revolt of Palestinian Arabs against the Israeli occupation of the West Bank and Gaza Strip that began in 1987. The name is also used as a title for the Liberation Army of Palestine, itself actively involved in this uprising.

Intourist The Russian travel agency has a name that is a Soviet style abbreviation of Russian *inostrannyy turist*, 'foreign tourist'. The organization was founded in the Metropol Hotel, Moscow, in 1929.

Inuit The name for the Eskimo people of North America, as distinct from those of Asia, represents Eskimo *inuit*, 'people', the plural of *inuk*, 'man'. The language they speak is known as *Inuktitut*, from *inuk*, 'man' and *titut*, 'speech'.

Invalides, Les The historic building in Paris, properly *Hôtel des Invalides*, was erected in the 1670s as a home for disabled French soldiers. Hence its name. French *hôtel* here has a sense that combines those of English *hospital* and *hostel*, words to which it is itself related.

Inverness The town in northern Scotland has a name beginning with the *Inver-* found elsewhere for many other coastal towns. It represents Gaelic *inbhir*, meaning 'rivermouth', 'confluence', and corresponds to the *Aber-* found in both Scottish and Welsh names (such as ABERDEEN and ABER-YSTWYTH). *Inver-* is usually followed by the name of the river at whose mouth the town itself stands. In the case of Inverness, this is the *Ness*, of the famous Loch NESS.

INXS The Australian rock band was originally formed in 1977 as *The Farriss*

Brothers, referring to the three brothers of this name who made up half the group's complement. In 1979 the group took the new name *INXS*, pronounced 'in excess', and designed to pun on this phrase.

Io The maiden loved by Zeus, and turned by him (or Hera) into a heifer, has a name that is traditionally associated with that of another *Io*, the moon, itself derived from Greek *iō*, the root of the verb *eimi*, 'to go'. The horns of a cow or heifer were regarded by the Greeks as symbolic of the horns of the moon.

Iolanthe The name is most familiar from the title of the Gilbert and Sullivan opera, first performed in 1882. It is probably based on Latin *viola*, 'violet' and Greek *anthos*, 'flower', especially given the other classical names in the opera, which include the traditionally 'rustic' Strephon and Phyllis.

Iona A scribal error lies behind the name of the historic island off the west coast of Scotland, famous as the site of the monastery founded by St Columba in the 6th century. It was originally known simply as *I*, probably representing a Celtic word meaning 'yew tree'. This was incorporated into various forms of the name, and in a document of the early 8th century the island is named as *Ioua insula*, 'island of the yew-trees'. But the first word of this was subsequently miscopied as *Iona*, giving rise to a spurious association with the biblical prophet *Jonah*. The error went uncorrected, and remains to this day.

Ionia The name of the ancient region of Asia Minor has been popularly linked with that of *Ion*, son of Creusa and Apollo in Greek mythology. It is probably pre-Hellenic in origin, however, with a suggested source either in a word *yawane* meaning 'western' or in Sanskrit *yoni*, 'womb', 'vulva', 'yoni', referring to a 'feminine', moon-worshipping people.

Iowa The American state takes its name from the river that flows through it. The river in turn derives its name from that of an Indian tribe perhaps meaning 'sleepy ones' or 'palefaces'. The name has been recorded in a variety of spellings over the years. A French map of 1673 has it as *Ouaouiatonon*.

Iphigenia The name of the daughter of Agamemnon and Clytemnestra, taken by her father to be sacrificed to Artemis but saved by this goddess, represents Greek *iphios*, 'strong' and *genos*, 'race', so that she was 'of mighty birth'. The name is appropriate for one of royal parentage, as she was.

Ipswich The Suffolk town and port lies on the river Orwell at its confluence with the much smaller *Gipping*. The name derives from the latter, which itself takes its name from the village of *Gipping* near Newmarket. The village name in turn means 'place of *Gip*'s people'. The name of Ipswich thus comprises this personal name followed by Old English *wīc*, here meaning 'port', 'landing-place'.

Iran The name of the Middle East country can be traced back to Sanskrit *ārya*, 'ARYAN'. *See also* ARARAT. The ultimate reference is to a land of mountains.

Iraq The Arabic name of the Middle East country is *al-ʿirāq*, perhaps meaning 'the bank', with reference to the basin of the rivers Tigris and Euphrates. *Cp.* MESOPOTAMIA.

Ireland The western island and independent republic of the British Isles has a name that means 'EIRE land', the first word here being the Irish name for the country. It may itself mean 'western land', from a root word related to Gaelic *iar*, 'west', although some sources see it as a blend of Gaelic *i*, 'island' and *iarunn*, 'iron'. The Latin name of Ireland, *Hibernia*, evolved as a corruption of *Iverna*, itself representing Old Celtic *Iveriu*. This gave both the poetic name of Ireland, *Erin*, and the name for the land in other Celtic languages, such as Welsh *Iwerddon*, Breton *Iwerzhon* and Cornish *Ywerdhon*. For a different name for Ireland, *cp.* INNISFAIL.

Irene The name represents Greek *eirēnē*, 'peace'.

Irian Jaya The Indonesian province that now forms the western part of the island of New Guinea has a name of Malay origin. *Irian* is a dialect word from the island of Biak off the north coast of Irian Jaya, and has the meaning 'cloud-covered'. *Jaya* means 'victory', and replaces *Barat*, 'west', the former second word of the name.

Iris The first name can be taken as representing either the flower or the minor Greek goddess who was the messenger of the gods. The latter's name comes straight from Greek *iris*, 'rainbow'. She was so called because the rainbow was itself seen as a 'message' from the gods to man.

Irkutsk The well-known Siberian city takes its name from the river *Irkut* here in far eastern Russia. The river's name is said to be of Ainu origin and to mean 'big bend'.

Iron Butterfly The American heavy rock band, formed in San Diego, California in 1966, chose a name that imaginatively combined the contrasting concepts of 'heavy' and 'light'. Their aim was to create a music and style which would embody both these qualities simultaneously. The name itself may well have been adopted from the nickname *The Iron Butterfly* given in the 1930s to the American movie actress and singer Jeanette MacDonald and in more recent times to Imelda Marcos, forceful but flamboyant wife (now widow) of the Filipino president Ferdinand Marcos. *Cp.* IZPAPALOTL as a near-equivalent name.

Iron Maiden The British heavy metal group, formed in London in 1976, took the name of the medieval instrument of torture for that of their first song and their general theme. *Iron* reflected their heavy metal style of music, and *Maiden* perhaps punned on 'made'. There is an additional contrast of opposites in the name as a whole (iron is hard, maidens are gentle) similar to that in IRON BUTTERFLY.

Iroquois The name of the North American peoples is of Algonquian origin, from *iroqu*, said to mean either 'true snakes' or 'worse enemies'. If the latter, it distinguishes them from the SIOUX, 'lesser enemies'. The final *-ois* was added by French colonists.

Irrawaddy The chief river of Burma has a name of Sanskrit origin, ultimately from *airāvata*, the name of a sun god, who is the prototype of the elephant, produced at the churning of the ocean, and regarded as Indra's beast of burden.

Irtysh The Siberian river has a name that almost certainly has its origin in a Turkic root element *ir*, 'to flow'. The current in the upper reaches of the river is rapid and turbulent.

Irvine The Scottish name derives from either of the places *Irvine*, now the New Town in Strathclyde, or *Irving*, now the hamlet of *Irvingtown* near Gretna Green. Both are named from a river. As an English name, *Irvine* could represent the Old English personal name *Eoforwine*, literally 'boar friend'.

Isaac The well-known biblical name, that of the son of Abraham, derives from Hebrew *Yitschāq*, popularly regarded as meaning 'he will laugh', referring either to God's delight in him, to that of his father on his birth, or to his own joy. The Old Testament prefers the second of these, with Abraham laughing at the thought of an elderly couple being able to produce a son: 'Then Abraham fell upon his face, and laughed, and said in his heart, Shall a child be born to him that is an hundred years old? and shall Sarah, that is ninety years old, bear?' (*Genesis* 17.17).

Isabel The name arose as a Spanish form of ELIZABETH, refashioned with an ending that suggests *bella*, 'beautiful'. It has long been popular as a royal name, and *Isabella* has been the wife of three English medieval kings: John, Edward II and Richard II. The Spanish use the name for any member of the British royal family called Elizabeth, including the present Queen (*Isabel II de Gran Bretaña*).

Isaiah The famous Old Testament prophet, with the book named after him, has a name of Hebrew origin, *Yeŝa'yāh*, meaning 'salvation of Yah' (that is, of Jehovah).

Isauria The ancient district of south central Asia Minor has a name of uncertain origin. It has been popularly but almost certainly erroneously linked with Latin *aurum*, 'gold'.

Iscariot *See* JUDAS ISCARIOT.

Isfahan Iran's second largest city has a name that has been variously explained. The traditional origin is usually given as in Avestan *espahān*, the plural of *sepah*, 'army'. It has also been derived from *esb*, 'horse', followed by the Iranian plural ending, or from a word *hān*, 'country', 'land'. The first may be the likeliest.

Ishmael The name of the son of Abraham and Hagar in the Old Testament represents the Hebrew name *Yiŝmā'ēl*, 'God will hearken', as an angel explains to his mother, the maidservant of Abraham's barren wife Sarah: 'And the angel of the Lord said unto her, Behold, thou art with child, and shalt bear a son, and shalt call his name Ishmael; because the Lord hath heard thy affliction' (*Genesis* 16.11).

Ishtar The Babylonian and Assyrian goddess of love and war has a name that derives from Akkadian *'astar*, meaning simply 'goddess' and seen in the name of her Phoenician equivalent, ASTARTE.

Isis The Egyptian goddess of fertility, the wife and sister of Osiris, probably originated as a personification of the sky. Hence her name, which is the Greek form of her Egyptian name *Iset*, meaning 'throne', 'place'. This also hints at her role as mother of the sun-god, Horus.

Isis The name of the Thames at Oxford is said to derive from the division of *Thamesis*, a Roman name for the Thames, into *Thame* and *Isis*, the former then serving as the name of the river *Thame*, a tributary of the Thames west of Oxford, and the latter adopted for the Thames itself at Oxford, in the process becoming associated with the name of the goddess ISIS. But the whole explanation seems suspect, and the true origin of the name is probably quite different.

Iskenderun The port in southern Turkey, formerly known as *Alexandretta*, derives its name from Turkish *İskender*, 'Alexander'. It lies at or near the site of *Alexandria ad Issum*, founded to commemorate the victory of *Alexander* the Great over Darius III at Issus in 333 BC.

Islam The name of the Muslim religion is directly related to MUSLIM itself, and represents Arabic *islām*, 'surrendering', as the verbal noun of *aslama*, 'he surrendered himself' (*i.e.* to God). Hence also the related word *salaam*, the Muslim form of salutation, from Arabic *salām*, 'peace'.

Islamabad The capital of Pakistan (since 1967) has a name that means 'city of ISLAM', from Arabic *islām*, 'Islam' and Iranian *ābād*, 'inhabited place' (*cp.* HYDERABAD). The former capital was Karachi.

Isle of Dogs *See* DOGS, ISLE OF.

Isle of Wight *See* WIGHT, ISLE OF.

Isleworth The district of London lies by the Thames but has a name that is nothing to do with *isle*. It means '*Gīslhere*'s enclosure', with the Anglo-Saxon personal name (itself meaning 'army hostage') followed by Old English *worth*, 'enclosure'. *Cp.* ISLINGTON.

Islington The London borough has a name somewhat similar to that of ISLEWORTH. It means '*Gīsla*'s hill'. The *-ington* of the name is misleading, and the final *-ton* represents Old English *dūn*, 'hill' (modern *down*), not *tūn*, 'farm' (modern *town*).

Ismailia The city in northeast Egypt takes its name from *Ismail* Pasha (1830–1895), viceroy of Egypt, then khedive from 1867 to 1879. The town was founded in 1863 as a halfway station on the Suez Canal, whose construction, then in progress, had been actively encouraged by Ismail.

Isocrates The name of the 3rd-century BC Athenian orator and teacher of oratory means literally 'of equal power', 'having the same privileges', from Greek *isos*, 'same', 'equal' and *kratos*, 'power'.

Isolde The name of the beautiful princess, tragically in love with Tristram in the Arthurian romances, is probably Celtic in origin, from a root word meaning 'beautiful', as in the Welsh name *Esyllt*, meaning 'of fair aspect'.

Israel The Middle East republic, established in 1948 in the former British mandate of Palestine, takes its name from the biblical *Israel*, as the name given to Jacob when he was wrestling with God, and so as the name that was that of the land of the Hebrews, the 'children of Israel'. The Bible gives the following explanation of the personal name: 'And [the angel] said, Thy name shall be called no more Jacob, but Israel: for as a prince hast thou power with God and with men, and hast prevailed' (*Genesis* 32.28). It has been pointed out that in the original Hebrew, 'hast thou power with God' is *sarīta 'im elohīm* ('struggled with God'), letters from which form the name *Israel*. But this etymology is very contrived, like many biblical derivations, and a more likely origin for the name is in Hebrew *īš réa'el*, 'man friend of God', from *īš*, 'man', *rea'*, 'friend', 'companion' and *el*, 'god'. The name has also been linked with that of the pagan god *Isra*, to which Hebrew *el*, 'god' was added.

Israfil The name is that of the archangel who, according to the Koran, will sound the trumpet on the Day of Judgment. It relates to the biblical *seraphim*, the fiery six-winged beings seen by Isaiah in a vision, so has the same origin, from Hebrew *serāphīm*, 'fiery', in turn from a root element *srp* meaning 'to burn'. *Israfil* is thus the 'fiery angel'.

Issachar The name of the fifth son of Jacob by his wife Leah derives from Hebrew *Yis'sākār*, '(he) will pay', from the root word *sākār*, 'to give wages'. The biblical text relevant to the name runs: 'And Leah said, God hath given me my hire, because I have given my maiden to my husband: and she called his name Issachar' (*Genesis* 30.18). (Leah's 'maiden' was her servant Zilpah, who had borne Jacob his first two sons, Gad and Asher.)

Issas The *Issas* are a branch of the Somali peoples living in what was formerly the French territory of Afars and *Issas* and is now Djibouti. They take their name from the early Yemeni ruler Sheikh *Issa* ibn Ahmed, from whom they claim to be descended. His own name *Issa* is none other than the Arabic form of the name of JESUS.

Issyk-Kul The lake in Kirgizia, one of the largest mountain lakes in the world, has a name of Kirgiz origin, from *ysyk*, 'warm' and *köl*, 'lake'. The lake never freezes over in winter.

Issy-les-Moulineaux The southwest suburb of Paris has a basic name that ultimately derives from the Gaulish personal name *Iccius* or *Icisius*. The addition to the name means 'little mills', from a diminutive of Low Latin *molinum*, 'mill', modern French *moulin*.

Istanbul The famous Turkish city and former capital of the Ottoman Empire is traditionally held to derive its name from the Byzantine Greek phrase *eis tēn polin*, 'into the city', implying 'city-dwellers'. Another account sees the name as a form of *Islambul*, 'city of Islam', with the final *bul* coming from Greek *polis*, 'city'. This might seem plausible if the city's name had not existed long before it became a Muslim capital in 1453. Its original name, however, was CONSTANTINOPLE, and it is obvious that *Istanbul* has simply evolved as a form of this. Another name for the city, especially its old or historic part, is *Stambul* or *Stamboul*, familiar from Graham Greene's novel *Stamboul Train* (1932). The Russian name for the city is still *Stambul*.

Italian Concerto Bach's harpsichord work (1735) of this name is apparently so called from the fact that the composition is in three movements, like the Italian concerto grosso.

Italian Symphony Mendelssohn's Symphony No 4 in A major was begun in *Italy* and completed in 1833, although not published until 1847.

Italy The country's name is traditionally said to have evolved from that of the *Vitali*, a northern tribe whose own name is believed to be linked in some way with Latin *vitulus*, 'calf'. But the true origin may be in some Illyrian word, or in the name of a legendary but perhaps historic ruler known to the Romans as *Italus*.

Ithaca The Greek island in the Ionian Sea almost certainly has the Phoenician word *ī*, 'island' for its first part. *Cp.* IBIZA. The rest of the name, however, is of unknown origin.

Ivan The familiar Russian name is the equivalent of English JOHN.

Ivanhoe The hero of Walter Scott's novel of 1819 is Wilfred, knight of *Ivanhoe*, the latter being the place that gave his title. Scott took this from the real village of *Ivinghoe*, near Tring in Berkshire.

Ivanovo The city in western Russia is said to be named for IVAN THE TERRIBLE. However, there is no firm evidence for this, and the identification of the particular IVAN who gave his name to the original settlement here remains a mystery. In 1871 the original industrial settlement of *Ivanovo* merged with the nearby village of *Vozne-senskaya* to form the town of *Ivanovo-Voznesensk*, a name it retained until 1932, when it dropped the latter part of the name (from that of the village church, dedicated to the Ascension, Russian *Vozne-seniye*).

Ivan the Terrible The first tsar of Russia, otherwise Ivan IV (1530–1584), has gained a nickname that in English is a misrepresentation of the Russian original. This is the word *groznyy*, meaning 'awesome', so is positive, not negative and disapprobatory. It is true that many of his methods were cruel, especially his public executions, but no more so than those of his contemporaries. *See also* GROZNY.

Iveco The familiar make of truck has a name that is an abbreviation of that of its manufacturing company, the *I*ndustrial *V*ehicles *C*orporation, formed in 1975 as the commercial vehicle wing of the Italian company Fiat, based in Amsterdam.

Ivor The name is of Scandinavian origin, and comprises a combination of Old Norse *ýr*, 'yew' and *herr*, 'army'. Here 'yew' has the transferred sense 'bow' (made from yew wood), so that the name overall means 'bowman', 'archer'.

Ivory Coast The West African republic, now officially known (since 1986) by its French name of CÔTE D'IVOIRE, takes its name from the ivory first traded by Portuguese settlers here in the 16th century. They also traded in slaves, hence the more general name of SLAVE COAST for this region of West Africa.

Ivry-sur-Seine The southeast suburb of Paris derives its basic name ultimately from Gaulish *ivo*, 'yew'. The name is found elsewhere (sometimes as *Ivrey*), so that the latter part of the name distinguishes this place, on the SEINE, from others.

Ivy League The name is that of the universities on the American eastern seaboard that are generally regarded as academically and socially superior, *viz.* Harvard, Yale, Pennsylvania, Princeton, Columbia, Brown, Dartmouth and Cornell. The term originally applied to their football teams, and related

to the ancient *ivy* that grew on the walls of the universities, which are America's oldest.

Ixion The name is that of the king of Thessaly who after being helped by Zeus tried to seduce his wife Hera. By way of punishment, Zeus tied him to a perpetually revolving wheel. His name may thus relate to Greek *axōn*, 'wheel', a word that gave English *axis* and *axle*.

Izal The brand of disinfectant was first marketed in the 1890s, and the story goes that it was named anagrammatically for a certain young lady called *Liza*, the sister of the English chemist who helped produce it. But archive evidence for this origin is lacking, and the name may simply have been an advertising agent's arbitrary whim.

Izhevsk The industrial city in eastern Russia takes its name from that of the river *Izh*, on which it arose as an ironworks in 1760. The river's own name is of uncertain origin.

I Zingari The touring British cricket team, founded in 1845, took their name from the Italian for 'The Gypsies'. They have no ground of their own, so are obliged to 'wander'. The word *zingaro* for a Gypsy has been current in English since the 17th century. The cricketers may have had some specific literary reference in mind. Walter Scott uses the name more than once in *Quentin Durward* (1823), for example: 'I am a Zingaro, a Bohemian, an Egyptian, or whatever the Europeans [...] may choose to call our people' (Chapter 16). *See also* TZIGANE.

Izmir The Turkish port and city is said to derive its present name from Byzantine Greek *eis Smurnē*, 'to SMYRNA', this being its former name. But it is much more likely to be simply a corruption of *Smyrna* itself. *Cp.* the evolution of ISTANBUL from CONSTANTINOPLE.

Izpapalotl The goddess of fate in Aztec mythology has a Nahuatl name meaning 'obsidian butterfly', *obsidian* being a form of volcanic rock. The goddess was represented as a butterfly having wings edged with sharp slivers of obsidian rock (a sort of IRON BUTTERFLY, in fact).

J

Jabberwocky The name is that of the famous nonsense poem in Lewis Carroll's *Through the Looking-Glass* (1871), in which the *Jabberwock* itself is the dragon-like monster 'with eyes of flame' that is slain by the White Knight. The creature's name appears to suggest a *wock* that *jabbers*, but since the poem is a mock medieval ballad, with 'Anglo-Saxon' words invented by Carroll, one may look for a mock medieval derivation for the name itself. When a class in the Girls' Latin School, Boston, wrote to Carroll to ask permission to use the name *The Jabberwock* for their magazine, he replied as follows:

> Mr. Lewis Carroll has much pleasure in giving to the editors of the proposed magazine permission to use the title they wish for. He finds that the Anglo-Saxon word "wocer" or "wocor" signifies "offspring" or "fruit". Taking "jabber" in its ordinary acceptation of "excited and voluble discussion," this would give the meaning of "the result of much excited discussion." Whether this phrase will have any application to the projected periodical, it will be for the future historian of American literature to determine. Mr. Carroll wishes all success to the forthcoming magazine.

Martin Gardner, ed., *The Annotated Alice*, 1970.

Carroll was not entirely indulging in verbal whimsy here, since Old English *wōcer* or *wōcor* really does mean 'offspring', as he says.

Jabez In the Old Testament, the name is that of a descendant of Judah. It derives from Hebrew *Ya'bēts*, interpreted as 'he will cause sorrow', and based on *ya'zeb*, 'sorrow': 'And his mother called his name Jabez, saying, Because I bare him with sorrow' (1 *Chronicles* 4.9).

Jabneel The Palestinian town mentioned in the Old Testament, as *Jabneel* (*Joshua* 15.11) or *Jabneh* (2 *Chronicles* 26.6), has a name that respectively represents Hebrew *yavne'el*, 'God causes to be built' and *yavne*, 'he causes to be built', from *havne*, 'to cause to be built', a derivative of *bano*, 'to build'.

Jack The name was originally a pet form of JOHN, evolving through a form *Jankin*, 'little Jan'. It is also sometimes regarded as a pet form of JAMES, by association with the French equivalent of that name, *Jacques*.

Jack Daniels The well-known blend of American whiskey takes its name from *Jack Daniel* (1848–1911), born near Lynchburg, Tennessee, who before he was 20 had bought land locally on which to build the distillery that today produces his distinctive Tennessee Sour Mash Whiskey.

Jack Russell The breed of short-legged terrier is named for John *Russell* (1795–1883), the Devonshire clergyman nicknamed 'The Sporting Parson' who developed it to work in fox hunts on Exmoor. The original strain is now extinct, so that the name is today applied somewhat vaguely to various small terriers of different shapes and sizes.

Jackson The name means 'son of JACK', and is one of the commonest surnames in the English-speaking world.

Jackson The state capital of Mississippi is named in honour of Andrew *Jackson* (1767–1845), seventh president of the United States.

Jack the Ripper The nickname was given to the still unidentified murderer of a number of London prostitutes in 1888. The name is descriptive, referring to the murderer's mutilation of his victims' bodies.

Jacob Familiar in the Old Testament as the son of Isaac and Rebecca and the twin (but

265

marginally younger) brother of Esau, Jacob has a name that represents Hebrew *Yaʿakub-'ēl*, 'may God protect'. The name is traditionally linked, however, with Hebrew *āqēb*, 'heel' or the closely related word *āqāb*, 'to usurp', together implying a person who follows on the heels of another and supplants him. The biblical account of Jacob's birth alludes to the first of these: 'And after that [*i.e.* the birth of Esau] came his brother out, and his hand took hold on Esau's heel; and his name was called Jacob' (*Genesis* 25.26). Jacob subsequently persuaded Esau to part with his right to his inheritance in exchange for 'a mess of pottage' and tricked Isaac into blessing him in place of Esau, so that a later passage alludes to the second word: 'And he [*i.e.* Esau] said, Is not he rightly named Jacob? for he hath supplanted me these two times: he took away my birthright; and, behold, now he hath taken away my blessing' (*Genesis* 27.36).

Jacobean The style of architecture or furniture has a name that places it in the first quarter of the 17th century, during the reign of James I (whose name in Latin was *Jacobus*).

Jacobin The *Jacobins* were the radical movement of the French Revolution who under Robespierre overthrew the Girondists and instituted the Reign of Terror. Their name derives from Latin *Jacobus*, referring to the Dominican convent of St *Jacques* (St James) in Paris where they first met in 1789.

Jacobite The *Jacobites* were the adherents of James II (whose Latin name was *Jacobus*) after his overthrow in 1688. Hence the *Jacobite* Rebellion of 1715 led by his son James Francis Edward Stuart (the 'Old Pretender') and the later rebellion of 1745 led by *his* son, Charles Edward Stuart (the 'Young Pretender').

Jacobs The British biscuit company take their name from William Beale *Jacob*, born in Ireland in 1825, who took over his father's bakery business in Waterford when in his teens, later forming a partnership with his brother Robert as W. & R. Jacob. He introduced the familiar 'Cream Crackers' in 1885, two years after the business had been organized as a limited company.

Jacquard The name of the distinctive fabric, with its design incorporated into the weave instead of being printed on, derives from that of its creator, the French inventor Joseph Marie *Jacquard* (1752–1834).

Jacqueline The name is a feminine form of the French male name *Jacques*, itself corresponding to English JAMES and JACOB.

Jacquerie The name of the revolt of the peasants of northern France against the nobility in 1358 derives from *Jacques* (in full *Jacques Bonhomme*), the generic name for a peasant.

Jacuzzi The name of the special type of 'whirlpool bath' with underwater jets derives from that of its Italian-born American inventor, Candido *Jacuzzi* (1903–1986). He originally devised it for his young son, who suffered from rheumatoid arthritis.

Jaeger The well-known brand of knitwear takes its name from Gustav *Jaeger* (1832–1917), a German naturalist and hygienist who promoted his theory that it was healthier for people to wear clothes made of wool, from animals, than of cotton and linen, from plants. The first shop to sell such clothing opened in London in the late 1870s.

Jaffa The ancient Canaanite city, now part of the modern Israeli port of Tel Aviv-*Yafo*, has a name that represents Hebrew *yafe*, 'beautiful'. The reference is to its attractive site on a promontory overlooking the Mediterranean. The city is the JOPPA of the Bible.

Jaguar The familiar make of car first appeared in 1935, with its name chosen to evoke the sleek, speedy and powerful animal.

Jainist The name is that of a member of an ancient Hindu sect founded in the 6th century BC who hold that the material world is eternal, progressing in a series of gigantic cycles. It derives from Hindi *jaina*, 'saint' (literally 'overcomer'), referring to the great religious figures or *saints* on whose example the sect centres its belief and doctrine.

Jaipur The city of northern India has a Hindi name meaning '*Jai*'s town', with the personal name followed by *pur*, 'town'. The name is that of Sawai *Jai* Singh II, king of

Amber, who founded the city in 1727. The name *Jai* derives from Sanskrit *jaya*, 'victory'.

Jairus In the Old Testament, the name is that of the synagogue official whose 12-year-old daughter dies but is restored to life by Jesus. It derives from Hebrew *y'āïr*, 'he enlightens'. We are not told the little girl's name, unfortunately.

Jakarta The capital of Indonesia has a Malay name that is a form of its historic name *Jayakarta*. This means 'victory and prosperity' and was the name given the former city of *Sunda Kelapa* in 1527 by Prince Fatahillah, Sultan of Bantam, after he had conquered it. The name is also spelled *Djakarta*.

Jalalabad The city of eastern Afghanistan takes its name from that of the Mogul emperor *Jalal*-ud-Din Muhammad Akbar (1542–1605), who founded it in about 1560, with the last part of the name representing Iranian *ābād*, 'peopled', 'inhabited' (*cp.* FAISALABAD, HYDERABAD, and similar names). The name *Jalal* itself represents Arabic *jalāl*, 'greatness', 'glory'.

Jam, The The British new wave rock group arose in 1975 from the *jam* sessions held by two Surrey schoolboys in the music room during their lunch hour. Hence the name.

Jamaica The current form of the name of the well-known Caribbean island represents its Arawak name *Xaymaca*, meaning 'rich in springs' or 'land of springs'.

James The name is familiar in the New Testament as that of two of Christ's disciples. It derives from Late Latin *Iacomus*, a form of JACOB, so ultimately has the same origin as that name.

James Allen's Girls' School The public day school for girls in Dulwich, southeast London, was founded in 1741 by *James Allen*, master (*i.e.* headmaster) of Dulwich College.

Jameson Raid The unsuccessful attempt to topple the Boer regime in the Transvaal, South Africa, in 1895 is named for the British administrator in South Africa at that time, Sir Leander Starr *Jameson* (1853–1917).

Jane The name arose as the feminine form of JOHN, from the Old French form of that name, *Jehanne*. Despite its popularity and impeccable historic credentials, it has never become an established royal name, like its male equivalent. It has some royal representation, however, in *Jane* Seymour (1509–1537), wife of Henry VIII and mother of Edward VI, and in the tragic Lady *Jane* Grey (1537–1554), unwilling wife and queen, executed when still only 16 with her husband, Lord Guildford Dudley, on a charge of high treason. *See also* JEAN, JOAN.

Janet The name, long popular in Scotland, is a diminutive of JANE.

Janiculum The hill in Rome, across the river Tiber from the Seven Hills, derives its name from that of the Roman god JANUS.

Jan Mayen The island in the Arctic Ocean, between Greenland and Norway, takes its name from that of the Dutch navigator *Jan Mayen*, who rediscovered it in 1611 after Henry Hudson had first discovered it in 1607.

January The first month of the year had the Roman name *Januarius*, after JANUS, the god of doorways and passages. The name is appropriate for a month that is the 'doorway' to a new year.

Janus As the Roman god of doorways and passages, depicted in art with two heads facing opposite ways, *Janus* derives his name from Latin *ianus*, 'doorway', 'passage'. It was Janus who gave the name of JANUARY.

Japan The Japanese name for the oriental country is *Nippon*, from *nichi*, 'sun' and *hon*, 'origin'. The western form of the name represents the Chinese pronunciation of the two Japanese pictograms, which is *rìbĕn*, pronounced approximately 'jipen'. This has the same meaning, representing Chinese *rì*, 'sun' and *bĕn*, 'origin'. The reference is to Japan's eastern location with regard to China. Hence the familiar 'Land of the Rising Sun' as a byname of Japan.

Japan The British 'new romantic' rock group was formed in London in the early 1970s and adopted a name that reflected its members' interest in oriental music.

Japheth The name of the second son of Noah in the Old Testament comes from Hebrew *Yepheth*, 'increase', 'enlargement': 'God shall enlarge Japheth, and he shall dwell in the tents of Shem; and Canaan shall be his servant' (*Genesis* 9.27).

Jarlshof The well-known prehistoric site near Sumburgh in Shetland has an obviously Norse name, meaning 'jarl's temple', a *jarl* (related to English *earl*) being a Norse nobleman. The name is thus linguistically historic, but was actually devised for the site in modern times by Walter Scott, who visited it in 1816 and invented the name for the medieval farmhouse that features in his novel *The Pirate* (1821).

Jarrow The industrial town in northeast England has a name that relates to the tribe known as the *Gyrwe*, who once lived here. Their own name may mean 'fen people'.

Jarvis The name derives either from the Norman personal name *Gervase*, itself based on the Germanic word *geri*, 'spear', or from the name of JERVAULX ABBEY.

Jason The name of the famous classical hero, leader of the Argonauts, derives from Greek *iasthai*, 'to heal'. Greek myths tell how he was named by the kindly centaur Chiron with reference to the skills in medicine that he had taught Jason on Mount Pelion. The name has experienced a popular resurgence in the late 20th century, and has been borne by various film and television 'heroes', both real and fictional.

Jasper The name is traditionally that of one of the Magi or Three Wise Men who brought gifts to the infant Jesus. It does not appear in the Bible, however. It is said to have evolved from a Persian word meaning 'treasurer'. It is unlikely to have derived from *jasper*, the gemstone. Other forms of the name are *Caspar* and *Gaspard*.

Java The island of Indonesia has a name that represents Sanskrit *yavadvīpa*, 'island of barley', from *yava*, 'barley' and *dvīpa*, 'island'.

Jay The name arose as a nickname for someone who resembled the bird in some way, perhaps as a chatterer or a thief. The jay itself is perhaps so named from the personal name *Gaius*.

Jean The name is a medieval spelling of Old French *Jehanne*, a feminine form of the equivalent of JOHN. It is thus in the same group as JANE and JOAN.

Jedidiah In the Old Testamant, *Jedidiah* is an alternative name for King Solomon. It is Hebrew in origin, meaning 'loved by Yah', that is, by Jehovah (otherwise God): 'And he [*i.e.* David, his father] called his name Jedidiah, because of the Lord' (2 *Samuel* 12.25).

Jeep The well-known utility vehicle has a name that basically represents the abbreviation *G.P.*, as a *g*eneral *p*urpose vehicle, but that at the same time was perhaps suggested by the cartoon character Eugene the *Jeep*, a creature of resource and power devised by the American cartoonist E.C. Segar, creator of Popeye.

Jeeves The name is familiar as that of the perfect English valet in the stories by P.G. Wodehouse, and to some extent has entered the language generally. (A personal advertisement in *The Times* for 8 April 1970 ran: 'Jeeves required to attend the needs of wealthy bachelor.') In response to a request from a reader for the origin of the name, Wodehouse wrote in a letter of 20 October 1960:

> I was watching a county [cricket] match on the Cheltenham ground before the first war, and one of the Gloucestershire bowlers was called Jeeves. I suppose the name stuck in my mind, and I named Jeeves after him.
>
> quoted in Daniel Garrison, *Who's Who in Wodehouse*, 1987.

Jefferson Airplane The American rock group, formed in San Francisco in 1965, took as their name the hippie jargon expression for a paper match split at one end to act as a holder (a so-called 'roach clip') for a marijuana cigarette that has become too short be held in the fingers. The band changed their name to *Jefferson Starship* in 1974, then to just *Starship* in 1985.

Jefferson City The state capital of Missouri was founded in 1821 and named in honour of Thomas *Jefferson* (1743–1826), third president of the United States.

Jeffery The name is another, phonetically more straightforward spelling of GEOFFREY, in use from medieval times.

Jehoshaphat The name, that of a king of Judah in the Old Testament, derives from Hebrew *Yēhōsāfāt*, 'Yah (*i.e.* Jehovah) has judged'.

Jehovah The personal name of God, revealed to Moses on Mount Horeb, evolved from his original name of YAHWEH, *which see* for its meaning.

Jehovah's Witnesses The American Christian sect, who believe that the end of the world is near, and that all other churches and religions are evil, was founded in about 1879 under the name *International Bible Students*. Their current official title, however, is the *Watchtower Bible and Tract Society*. Their popular name of *Jehovah's Witnesses* relates to their belief that they have been chosen to be the *witnesses* on earth of *Jehovah God*, as ordained by him in the Old Testament.

Jehu The successor to Ahab as king of Israel has a name of Hebrew origin that probably means 'he will live'.

Jekyll The name derives from an old Celtic personal name *Iudicael*, itself comprising words meaning respectively 'lord' and 'generous'.

Jelenia Góra The city in southwest Poland has a name that means 'deer mountain', from Polish *jeleń*, 'deer' and *góra*, 'mountain'. The German name of the city, with the same meaning, is *Hirschberg*.

Jemima The biblical name is that of the eldest of Job's three beautiful daughters, and derives from Hebrew *Yemīmāh*, 'dove'.

Jena Symphony The symphony that was long attributed to Beethoven but that now is now known to be by Friedrich Witt is so named as it was discovered at *Jena*, Germany, in 1909.

Jenkins The name means 'son of *Jenkin*', the latter being a diminutive of JOHN. *Cp.* JENNINGS.

Jennifer The name represents a Cornish form of GUINEVERE, familiar from the wife

of King Arthur and lover of Lancelot in the Arthurian romances.

Jennings The name means 'son of *Jenyn*', this being a diminutive form of JOHN. *Cp.* the similar JENKINS.

Jenny The name is generally taken to be a pet form of JENNIFER, but existed as a pet form of JEAN in medieval times, so really originates there.

Jephthah The name of the judge of Israel, who sacrificed his daughter in fulfilment of a vow, is Hebrew in origin, meaning 'he opens'. This can be interpreted in different ways, although 'he' undoubtedly refers to God.

Jeremiah The name of the major prophet of Judah, with a book of the Old Testament named for him, represents Hebrew *Yirmeyāh*, 'raised up by Yah' (*i.e.* Jehovah).

Jeremy The name is an English form of the biblical name JEREMIAH.

Jerez de la Frontera The well-known Spanish town, which gave the world the word and wine *sherry*, takes its own name from *Ceres*, the Old Spanish name for a Tuscan town that was itself famous for its wines. The second part of the name refers to the former *frontier* of the Moorish territories here in southwest Spain.

Jericho The historic city of Jordan has a Hebrew name that may ultimately derive from *yaréah*, 'moon', 'month', and relate to an ancient cult of the moon practised here.

Jeroboam The name of the two kings of Israel, the second being the grandson of Jehu, is Hebrew in origin, meaning 'may the people increase'.

Jerome The name is sometimes taken as a form of JEREMY. It in fact derives from the Greek name *Hieronymos*, comprising *hieros*, 'holy', and *onoma*, 'name'.

Jersey The chief of the Channel Islands has a name that is probably Scandinavian in origin, meaning '*Geirr*'s island', with the final two letters representing Old Norse *ey*, 'island'. *Geirr* is a Norse personal name meaning 'spear'. *See also* NEW JERSEY.

Jerubbaal The Old Testament name is that given to GIDEON after he had destroyed the altar of Baal. It is Hebrew in origin, meaning 'may BAAL defend'. The popular etymology in the Bible is rather different: 'Therefore on that day he [*i.e.* Joash, Gideon's father] called him Jerubbaal, saying, Let Baal plead against him, because he hath thrown down his altar' (*Judges* 6.32).

Jerusalem The famous city that is the capital of Israel has an ancient name of uncertain origin. Cuneiform texts give it in the form *Urusalimmi*, and Egyptian hieroglyphics as *Šalam*. It is possible that *uru* means 'house', 'town', while *salim* means 'peace' (*cp.* SALEM). On the basis of this the name probably means 'town of peace'. Some authorities, however, hold that *Salem* is the name of a Semitic god, regarded as the 'patron' of the city. The standard Arabic name of Jerusalem is *al-quds*, 'the holy one'. Hence its Turkish name of *Kudüs*.

Jervaulx Abbey The ruined Cistercian monastery near Masham in North Yorkshire lies above the river *Ure* and takes its name from it. The meaning is thus 'Ure valley', with the second half of the name evolving from Old French *val*, 'valley'. *Cp.* RIEVAULX.

Jesse The name of the father of David in the Old Testament represents Hebrew *Yišay*, said to mean either 'the Lord is' or 'gift of God'.

Jessica The name appears to have been invented by Shakespeare for the daughter of Shylock in *The Merchant of Venice* (1596). He may well have based it on a biblical name. That of *Iscah*, daughter of Haran and sister of Lot (*Genesis* 11.29), has been suggested, partly through its similar form and partly because Iscah was Jewish, as Jessica was. Perhaps also significantly, Iscah was a descendant of *Salah* (*Genesis* 11.15), whose name Shakespeare may have used as a basis for that of SHYLOCK.

Jesuit The members of the Roman Catholic religious order take their name from the order's title, Society of JESUS, with the ending *-it* a form of *-ite*, as if they were 'Jesusites'. The order was founded in 1534 by the Spanish soldier Ignatius Loyola, who had been recently converted and who composed the *Spiritual Exercises* as a guide to convert people's hearts and minds to a closer following of *Jesus* Christ.

CHRISTIAN itself was of course already in use as a name for a religious group.

Jesus The name is naturally not unique to *Jesus* Christ, although for him it has special significance. *Jesus* is a Greek form of JOSHUA, so like it is of Hebrew origin and means 'Jehovah saves'. Reference to the meaning is found early in the New Testament, when an angel of the Lord tells Joseph that his wife Mary is pregnant: 'And she shall bring forth a son, and thou shalt call his name JESUS: for he shall save his people from their sins' (*Matthew* 1.21). The meaning is further underscored in Jesus's title of *Saviour*, which occurs about 30 times in the New Testament. In hymns, *Jesu* occurs as the form of the name when addressing Jesus (for example, 'Jesu, Lover of my soul'). This represents the Greek (also Latin) vocative case. The name *Jesus* is sometimes found as an ornamental abbreviation or monogram, for example on an altar cloth, in the form IHS. This represents the first two and last letters of ΙΗΣΟΥΣ, the name in Greek, but is popularly taken as the abbreviation of an appropriate Latin phrase, such as I*esus* H*ominum* S*alvator*, 'Jesus Saviour of men', or I*n* H*oc* S*igno* (*vinces*), 'in this sign (thou shalt conquer)', or I*n* H*ac* S*alus*, 'in this (cross is) salvation'.

Jesus and Mary Chain, The The Scottish rock quartet, formed in 1983, are said to have based their name on that of McGee's Club, London, where they performed some of their early hits. The club was itself named for (and owned by) their manager Alan McGee. The name has caused offence, and resulted in the group's being banned from the American equivalent of the TV show *Top of the Pops* in 1987.

Jesus College The Cambridge college was founded in 1496 on the site of the former nunnery of St Radegund by John Alcock, bishop of Ely. Its official full name has no mention of Jesus at all, and is: *The College of the most Blessed Virgin Mary, Saint John the Evangelist and the Glorious Virgin Saint Radegund*. Records show, however, that it was the founder's intention that the college title should actually be *The College of Jesus, the Blessed Virgin Mary and Saint John the Evangelist*, and when the conventual chapel of St Radegund became the college chapel, Bishop Alcock did in fact rededicate it to the *Name of Jesus*. In deference to the founder's wishes, the words *commonly called Jesus College* are therefore added to the official college title whenever it is quoted today.

Jethro In the Old Testament, the name is that of the Midianite priest who is the father of Moses's wife Zipporah. It is apparently a variant of the Hebrew name *Ithra*, also biblical (2 *Samuel* 17.25), which is said to mean 'superabundance'.

Jethro Tull The British rock group, formed in Blackpool in 1968, took as their name that of *Jethro Tull*, the 18th-century inventor of the seed drill. The name had no particular relevance to the group's music or to their own background, but simply appealed.

Jeu de Paume The Paris art museum, noted for its exhibitions of Impressionist paintings, opened in 1947 in a building that was formerly the royal tennis courts. French *jeu de paume*, literally 'game of the palm' (*i.e.* of the hand), means 'real tennis', that is, the game that was originally 'royal' tennis.

Jew The name of the Semitic people derives, through Latin and Greek, from Hebrew *yehūdīm*, the plural of *yehūdī*, the adjective formed from the personal name JUDAH, that of the fourth son of Jacob, from whom the Jews are notionally descended. *See also* JUDAEA.

Jewison Contrary to popular belief, the surname does not mean 'son of a Jew'. It ultimately derives from a female personal name that itself evolved as a diminutive of JULIAN. This was a common girl's name in medieval times, and gave the modern first name GILLIAN.

Jeyes Fluid The well-known disinfectant takes its name from John *Jeyes* (1817–1892), a Northamptonshire pharmacist's son, who evolved a new kind of disinfectant based on creosote and patented it as his 'Fluid' in London in 1877.

Jezebel The name of the infamous wife of Ahab, king of Israel, adopted as a byword for a shameless woman, derives from a Hebrew word meaning 'domination'.

Jezreel The plain in northern Israel, now known as *Esdraelon* but occurring in the Bible as 'the valley of Jezreel' (*Joshua* 17.16), has a name of Hebrew origin, from *yizrᵉel*, 'God will sow', ultimately from *zéraᶜ*, 'seed' and *el*, 'God' (*cp.* BETHEL).

Jiangsu The province of eastern China takes its name from Chinese *jiāng*, 'river' and *sū*, 'thyme'. The name is also known as *Kiangsu*.

Jiangxi The province of southeast central China, also known as *Kiangsi*, has a name meaning 'west of the river', from *jiāng*, 'river' and *xī*, 'west'. The province is west of the river XIJIANG, as opposed to GUANGXI, which is to the east.

Jidda The name of the port in western Saudi Arabia, also spelled *Jedda*, derives from Arabic *judda*, 'sign', 'landmark', referring to the city's origin as a centre for Muslims making a pilgrimage to Mecca.

Jihlava The city of the western Czech Lands takes its name from Old Czech *jihla* (modern Czech *jehla*), 'needle'. The name is that of the river on which it stands. The river's own name appears to refer to the needles of the pine forest through which it passes. The German name of the town is *Iglau*, of the same origin.

Jilin The province of northeast China, also known as *Kirin*, has a name meaning 'favour of the forest', from *jí*, 'favour', 'luck' and *lín*, 'forest'. The name is also that of a town and river port in the same province.

Jill The name is a short form of GILLIAN, with a slight respelling, as if to realign it with the many other names beginning *J*. It is familiar from the old nursery rhyme about 'Jack and Jill', and since medieval times has had a generic sense to mean 'girl', 'woman', just as *Jack* means 'boy', 'man'. In the proverb 'Every Jack must have his Jill', the sense is thus 'Every lad must have his lass'. Its older spelling of *Gill* may even have been popularly associated with that of *girl*.

Jim The name is a short form of JAMES that has been in use since medieval times.

Jingdezhen The city in southeast China has a name that represents Chinese *jīng*, 'landscape', 'view', *dé*, 'virtue' and *zhèn*, 'town'. The city is famous for its porcelain industry, and is situated at the foot of the hill called *Gaoling* (from *gāo*, 'high' and *lĭng*, 'hill'), a name that gave the word *kaolin*.

Joachim The name is represented in the Bible in its fuller form *Jehoiakim*, that of the second son of Josiah. It derives from Hebrew *Yehoyaqim*, 'Yah (*i.e.* Jehovah) will establish'. In Christian tradition, *Joachim* is the name of the father of the Virgin Mary.

Joan The name is a contraction of the Old French name *Johanne*, itself from Latin JOANNA. It was adopted in England in medieval times as a feminine equivalent of JOHN, so in this respect is exactly the same as JANE and JEAN.

Joanna The name is a Latin form of Greek *Iōanna*, the feminine equivalent of *Iōannēs*, which is itself the source of English JOHN. *See also* JOAN.

Joan of Arc The famous French heroine and saint of the 15th century takes her name not so much from her birthplace as from that of her father, Jacques *d'Arc*, who came from the estate of *Arc* near DOMRÉMY-LA-PUCELLE, where Joan may have been born and where she was probably baptized. *Arc* is a fairly common place-name in France, deriving from Latin *arcus*, 'arch', referring to an arch of a bridge.

João Pessoa The port and state capital of Paraíba in northeast Brazil was founded in 1585 by Portuguese colonists with the name of *Filipea de Nossa Senhora das Neves*, for Philip I (Philip II of Spain) and the dedication of the church to 'Our Lady of the Snows'. After further changes of name, it eventually gained its present name in 1930, for *João Pessoa*, the state president who was killed in the revolution led by Getulio Vargas, president of Brazil from that year until 1945.

Job Familiar in the Bible from the Old Testament book named for him, *Job* has a name that derives from Hebrew *iyyōbh*, 'persecuted'. This is appropriate for a man whose name is a byword for stoical patience, and who bore many grievous misfortunes, yet remained loyal to God.

Jocasta The name of the tragic figure of Greek mythology, who was first the mother of Oedipus then, through various misunderstandings, his wife and the mother of his children, remains of uncertain origin. Attempts have been made to link it to that of IO, as if somehow connected with the moon. But this is likely to be purely a chance similarity of name, with no relevant significance.

Jodhpur The name of the Indian city and former state means '*Jodha*'s town', with Hindi *pur*, 'town', added to the name of its founder in 1459, the local ruler Rāo *Jodha*. His own name means 'warrior'. Jodhpur is more familiar to English speakers as the source of the riding breeches known as *jodhpurs*, a word which purely coincidentally happens to suggest *jumpers*.

Jodrell Bank The astronomical observatory in Cheshire takes its name from its location, a *bank* or hill-slope owned by one *Jodrell*.

Joel The name is that of a minor prophet of the Old Testament with a book named for him. It represents Hebrew *Yō'ēl*, 'Yah (*i.e.* Jehovah) is God', implying that the Hebrew god Jehovah is the only one.

Johannesburg The well-known South African city was founded in 1886 and has a name that means '*Johannes*' town'. Despite its recent history, the identity of the particular *Johannes* (or *Johann*) has not been established with any certainty. The traditional contenders are *Johann* Rissik (1857–1925), principal clerk of the office of the Surveyor-General of Transvaal, and Christian *Johannes* Joubert (1834–1911), Chief of Mining and a local politician.

John The most popular of all names is Hebrew in origin, from *Yōhānān*, 'Yah (*i.e.* Jehovah) has shown favour'. The name is borne by three important biblical characters: *John* the Baptist, *John* the Apostle, and *John* the Evangelist, the latter giving his name to the fourth gospel and in Christian tradition identified with the apostle.

John Lewis The familiar department stores take their name from an identically named father and son. *John Lewis* (1836–1928) opened a draper's shop in Oxford Street, London in 1864. In 1904 he was joined in his expanding business by his elder son, *John Spedan Lewis* (1885–1963), who eventually took it over. The company is famous for the *John Lewis Partnership*, in which employers and employees alike share in the profits and responsibilities of ownership.

John Lyon School The public day school for boys in Harrow, Middlesex was founded in 1876 to provide an education for the sons of Harrow townsfolk under the statutes made by the governors of Harrow School, whose own founder in 1572 was the local yeoman *John Lyon* (1514–1592).

Johnnie Walker The well-known blend of whisky is named for the Scottish retailer *John Walker*, who set up a grocery, wines and spirits business in Kilmarnock in 1820. It is the latter year that features in the company's advertisements, with the slogan 'Johnnie Walker, born 1820, still going strong' accompanied by a picture of the founder striding out as a 'walker'.

John o'Groats The name of the extreme northeastern point of mainland Britain may derive from that of a Dutchman, *Jan de Groot*, who is said to have been a bailie to the earls of Caithness here in the 15th century. The name would originally have applied to his house.

Johns Hopkins University The university in Baltimore, Maryland, was founded in 1876 as a graduate school for men under an endowment from *Johns Hopkins* (1795–1873), a Baltimore banker.

Johnson The name means 'son of JOHN'. *Cp.* JONES.

Johnston The name may be either a form of JOHNSON or else indicate a person who came from one of the places so called in Scotland, such as *Johnstone* near Paisley in Strathclyde.

Johore The state of Malaysia, on the southern Malay Peninsula, is said to take its name from a local word meaning 'to tie', with reference to Johore Strait here, which 'ties' Malaya and Singapore island.

Jonah The name of the Hebrew prophet who was famously swallowed by a whale in the Old Testament story is not related to JOHN but derives from Hebrew *yōnāh*, 'dove'. *See also* JONAS.

Jonas The name is the Greek form of JO-NAH.

Jonathan The son of Saul and intimate friend of David in the Old Testament, *Jonathan* has a name deriving from Hebrew *Yᵉhōnāthān*, 'Yah (*i.e.* Jehovah) has given'. *Cp.* MATTHEW and NATHANIEL, which have the same meaning.

Jones The common surname, widely found in Wales, means 'son of JOHN'. *Cp.* JOHNSON.

Jönköping The city in southern Sweden takes the second part of its name from Swedish *köping*, 'trading settlement', from a word seen also in the names of CHIPPING CAMDEN and COPENHAGEN. The first part of the name is of uncertain origin. *Cp.* in eastern Sweden, NORRKÖPING and NY-KÖPING.

Joppa The familiar biblical name is that of the modern city and port of JAFFA. It is now found elsewhere in the world for places that were named specifically for this town, such as *Joppa* near Baltimore, Maryland, or *Joppa*, the district of Edinburgh in Scotland.

Jordan The Middle East kingdom is named for the river that flows through it. The river itself has a Hebrew name of disputed origin. It may represent *yarod*, 'to descend', referring to its strong current. It could also mean 'river of DAN', or derive from the Indoeuropean root words *yor*, 'year' and *dan*, 'river', implying a river that flows constantly throughout the year, without drying up. St Jerome claimed that the name referred to the river's two sources, *Jor* and *Dan*, but no source *Jor* has ever been discovered.

Joseph As the favourite son of Jacob and Rachel, and one of the 12 patriarchs of Israel, *Joseph* is an important Old Testament character. His name is Hebrew in origin, from *Yōsēph*, 'he will add', meaning that God will add other children to the one already born. In the New Testament, *Joseph* is the name of the husband of the Virgin Mary and that of Joseph of ARI-MATHEA (*which see* in connection with his name).

Josephine The name is a feminine form of JOSEPH, made by adding the French suffix *-ine* to the male name, as for *Clementine*.

Joshua In the Old Testament, the name is famous as that of the Israelite leader who took the children of Israel into the Promised Land after the death of Moses, as told in the book that bears his name. It derives from Hebrew *Yᵉhōšūʾa*, 'Yah (*i.e.* Jehovah) saves'. It was the Greek form of his name that gave that of JESUS.

Josiah The name of the last king of Judah whose story is told in the Old Testament derives from Hebrew *Yōšīyāh*, 'Yah (*i.e.* Jehovah) supports'.

Jotunheim In Norse mythology, the name of the home of the giants in the northeast of Asgard derives from Old Norse *jötunn*, 'giant' and *heimr*, 'world', 'home'. Its alternative name is UTGARD.

Journey The American middle-of-the-road band, formed in San Francisco in 1973, acquired their name as the result of a radio competition. There was presumably an intentional pun on the group's particular style of music.

Jove The popular name of the Roman god JUPITER derives from the Old Latin form of it, *Jovis*.

Joy The name represents the standard word, and was readily adopted by English Puritans in the 17th century in their wish to be 'joyful in the Lord'.

Joyce The name looks as if it should be associated with *joy* and *rejoice*, but it actually comes from a Norman male name that ultimately meant 'lord'. The same Norman name gave the modern Irish surname *Joyce*.

Joy Division The British rock band, formed in 1977, took as their name the Nazi slang term for a military brothel, as described in the novel set in a German concentration camp *House of Dolls* (1958) by 'Ka-Tzetnik 135633'. *See also* NEW ORDER.

Juan-les-Pins The French Riviera resort takes its name from the *Golfe Juan* on which it lies, with *Pins*, 'pines' added comparatively recently. The name of the gulf or bay is actually a corruption of *Gour Jouan*, an ancient name of unknown meaning. *Gour* may perhaps mean 'river'. *Gour-Juan* is also the name of another resort to the west of Juan-les-Pins.

Jubilee Line The London Underground line was built to relieve overcrowding on the heavily used BAKERLOO LINE, and was initially known as the *Fleet Line* when work began on it in 1972. In 1977, the Queen's *Jubilee* Year (the 25th anniversary of her accession), it was given its present name, and eventually opened in 1979.

Judaea The ancient region of southern Palestine takes its name from the historic kingdom of *Judah*, itself named for JUDAH, the fourth son of Jacob. The name is also spelled *Judea*. *See also* JEW.

Judah The name of the fourth son of Jacob in the Old Testament represents Hebrew *Yehūda*, from *hōde*, 'to praise', 'to confess'. Judah gave his name to the tribe that descended from him and to the southern kingdom of *Judah*, with Jerusalem as its centre, that became JUDAEA. *See also* JEW, JUDAS, JUDE.

Judas The name is a Greek form of JUDAH. It is borne in the New Testament by several characters, but is best remembered as that of JUDAS ISCARIOT. It is also familiar from the Jewish leader *Judas* Maccabaeus, who liberated Judaea from the Syrians in the 2nd century BC but who was killed in battle. (*See also* MACCABEES.) Another form of the name is JUDE.

Judas Iscariot The apostle JUDAS, notorious for betraying Jesus to his enemies for 30 pieces of silver, has a surname of much disputed origin. Proposed explanations to account for it include the following: 1. his family belonged to the *Sicarii*, the most radical Jewish group; 2. it is a corruption of Latin *sicarius*, 'murderer', 'assassin' (the origin of the name of the *Sicarii*); 3. it derives from Hebrew *'iš qᵉrijjōt*, 'man of Keriot', the latter place perhaps identifiable with the biblical *Kerioth* (*Joshua* 15.25); 4. it represents Aramaic *'išqariā'* , 'false'; 5. it derives from a Judaeo-Aramaic root element *sqr* 'to dye', so that Judas had the occupation of *dyer*.

Judas Priest The British heavy metal band, formed in Birmingham in 1973, took their name from the song by Bob Dylan 'The Ballad of Frankie Lee and Judas Priest' on his LP *John Wesley Harding* (1968). Dylan in turn took the name from the oath *Judas*

Priest used euphemistically in place of *Jesus Christ.*

Jude The name is a short form of JUDAS, adopted in the New Testament to distinguish the apostle *Judas* Thaddaeus from JUDAS ISCARIOT. In literature it is familiar as that of the central character of Thomas Hardy's novel *Jude the Obscure* (1895), a title that was perhaps itself subconsciously suggested by the name *Judas Iscariot.*

Judges The book of the Old Testament takes its name from what was essentially the title (the equivalent of *king*) of the temporary but charismatic Israelite leaders in the period between the reign of Joshua and that of Saul. English *judge* here translates the Latin *judex* of the Vulgate (Latin version of the Bible), which in turn was the word used to render Hebrew *šōphēt.* The Hebrew name of *Judges* is thus *Šōphetīm.*

Judith The name is that of the heroine of the book of the same name in the Apocrypha who saved her people from the enemy Assyrians by gaining the confidence of Holofernes, their leader, and cutting off his head as he slept. Her name derives from Hebrew *Yᵉhūdhīth,* meaning simply 'woman of JUDAEA', 'Jewess'.

Judy The name arose as a pet form of JU-DITH, and is now often regarded as a name in its own right.

Juggernaut Now familiar as a colloquial term for a large truck or lorry, the name was originally that of a huge idol of Krishna wheeled through the town of Puri in eastern India on a gigantic chariot as an object of Hindu worship. The idol's Hindi name was *Jagannath,* from Sanskrit *Jagannatha,* 'lord of the world' (a title of Vishnu, one of the three chief Hindu gods), itself comprising the words *jagat,* 'world' and *nātha,* 'lord'. The English spelling of the name seems to have been influenced by words ending in *-naut* such as *Argonaut,* the common link being the concept of transportation.

Julia The name is the feminine form of the Roman *nomen* (clan name) JULIUS.

Julian The name derives from the Late Latin name *Julianus,* itself directly related to JULIUS. For some time *Julian* was a woman's name, and is well-known as such from the 14th-century English mystic *Julian* of Norwich.

Julie The name is a French form of JULIA.

Juliet Forever linked with Romeo as 'a pair of star-crossed lovers', *Juliet* has a name that is an English spelling of Italian *Giulietta* or French *Juliette,* both of them ultimately diminutive forms of JULIA. In Shakespeare's play, Juliet is specifically named for JULY, the month in which she was born ('Lammas-eve at night', *i.e.* 31 July).

Julius Famous as the name of the great Caesar, *Julius* is a Roman *nomen* (clan name) that has engendered several other well-known names, such as JULIA, JULIAN, and JULY, but that itself remains of obstinately obscure origin. Attempts to link it with ILIUM, the Roman name of Troy, are unfortunately linguistically untenable.

July The name was originally that of the fifth month of the old Roman year, earlier known as *Quintilis,* for this ordinal number. After the death of JULIUS Caesar in 44 BC it was renamed for him and subsequently became the seventh month.

Jumbo The standard name for an elephant, or now for anything large, was popularized by a particular elephant sold by the London Zoo to the American showman P.T. Barnum in 1882 and exhibited by him. The name itself derives from Swahili *jumbe,* 'chief', and was already in use as a general term or name for a large person or animal.

June The sixth month of the year has a name that has been popularly linked with that of the goddess JUNO, and there seems little reason to doubt this origin.

Juneau The state capital of Alaska was settled in 1881 when gold was discovered here and takes its name from one of the prospectors, Joe *Juneau.* The pronunciation of the name is identical to that of the goddess JUNO, and some of the classical association may have rubbed off on the city.

Jungfrau The well-known mountain in the Swiss Alps has a German name meaning 'maiden', literally 'young woman', from *jung,* 'young' and *Frau,* 'woman'. The name may relate to the mountain's appearance, which resembles a nun in a white habit. On the other hand it could have arisen by contrast with the nearby peak named *Mönch*, 'monk'.

Junior Carlton Club The former London club was founded in 1864 to provide facilities for members waiting to gain admission to the restricted CARLTON CLUB.

Juno The name of the Roman goddess of marriage and wife of Jupiter may well be meaningfully associated with the root of Latin *juvenis*, 'young'. It is tempting to link her name with that of JUPITER himself, although the resemblance is probably coincidental.

Jupiter The name of the great Roman god who corresponds to the Greek ZEUS probably itself corresponds to its counterpart, with a form of *pater*, 'father', added. Jupiter is thus *Zeus-Pater*, and since Zeus's name means 'sky' he is thus 'Father Sky'. Moreover, Zeus's name also means 'god', otherwise 'Father God'. JOVE, his alternative name, has ultimately the same origin.

Jupiter Symphony Mozart's Symphony No 41 in C major, K 551 (1788) was said by the composer's son, Franz Xavier Wolfgang Mozart, to have been so nicknamed by the London violinist and impresario Salomon. The reason for the name is not known, but presumably a classical reference is intended, or even an astronomical one, for the planet.

Jura The mountain range of eastern France is said to derive its name from Gaulish *iuris* or *iuri*, meaning 'wooded mountain'.

The name itself is the source of the geological term *Jurassic*.

Justin The name derives from the Roman name *Justinus*, itself a form of *Justus*, meaning 'just', 'fair', as it implies.

Jute The name of the Germanic people who came from *Jutland* to invade England in the 6th century, probably means simply 'men'.

Jutland The continental region of Denmark takes its name from the JUTES, the Germanic tribe who invaded Britain in the 6th century.

Juvenal The full name of the famous Roman satirist of the 1st and 2nd centuries AD was Decimus Junius *Juvenalis*. This last name was his *cognomen* or nickname, which as it stands is Latin for 'youthful', 'juvenile'. It seems to have been given as a pun on his *nomen* (clan name), *Junius*, which itself means 'younger', 'junior'. Unfortunately very little is known about his life.

Juventus The famous Italian football club was founded in 1897 by students in Turin. Hence its name, which is the Latin word for 'youth' (in the sense of both 'young time of life' and 'young people'). Despite this, Italians have nicknamed the club *La vecchia signora*, 'the old lady'. This is because it is the older of Turin's two clubs, the other, *Torino*, having been founded in 1906 when a breakaway group from Juventus merged with another club.

Jyväskylä The city of south central Finland has a name that represents Finnish *jyvä*, 'grain' and *kylä*, 'village'.

K

Kaa The name of the snake in the story 'Kaa's Hunting' in Kipling's *Jungle Books* (1894, 1895) is one that the author made up, 'from the queer open-mouthed hiss of a big snake' (*Author's Notes on the Names in the Jungle Books*, 1937). A Hindustani word for 'snake', which Kipling might have otherwise used, is either *sãnp* or *nãg* (*cp.* KALA NAG).

Kaaba The sacred Muslim shrine in the quadrangle of the Great Mosque at Mecca is in the form of a cube-shaped building containing nothing but the pillars that support it and a number of suspended lamps. Its northeast corner, however, contains the Black Stone declared by Muhammad to have been given to Abraham by the archangel Gabriel. The name of the shrine is simply the Arabic word *ka'bah*, 'building'.

Kabardian The name of the Circassian people of the North West Caucasus derives from Russian *kabarda*, 'otter'. The Kabardians inhabit the autonomous republic of *Kabardino-Balkaria*.

Kabul The capital of Afghanistan takes its name from a river here, a tributary of the Indus. The meaning of its own name is uncertain.

Kabyle The Berber people who inhabit the eastern Atlas Mountains in Tunisia and Algeria have a name deriving from Arabic *qabīla*, 'tribe'.

Kaesŏng The city in southwest North Korea takes its name from Korean *kae*, 'to open' and *sŏng*, 'castle', 'fortress'.

Kaffir The now offensive term for a black African or, among Muslims, for a non-Muslim derives from the Arabic word *kāfir*, 'infidel', from the verb *kafara*, 'to deny', 'to refuse to believe'. The word lies behind the name *Kaffraria* for a former region of South Africa. *See also* NURISTAN.

Kagoshima The port in southwest Japan, on Kyushu, has a name that means 'fawn island', from *ka*, 'deer', *ko*, 'child', 'young', and *shima*, 'island'.

Kaiserslautern The city of western Germany takes its name from the *kaiser* (emperor) Frederick Barbarossa who built a fortress by the river *Lauter* here in the 12th century.

Kajagoogoo The British pop group, formed in 1983, appear to have a random but memorable name that nevertheless curiously suggests *Kazanjoglou*, the original surname of the American film director of Greco-Turkish descent, Elia *Kazan* (1909–).

Kalahari The desert of southern Africa has a name that derives from the local word *karri-karri* meaning simply 'desert'.

Kalamazoo The Michigan city has a name of Algonquian origin, said to mean 'he smokes' or 'boiling water'.

Kala Nag The name of the elephant in the story 'Toomai of the Elephants' in Kipling's *Jungle Books* (1894, 1895) means, as the narrative itself explains, 'black snake'. Hindustani *kāla nāg* is the phrase used for 'cobra'.

Kalashnikov The well-known Russian submachine gun or assault rifle takes its name from the Russian tank driver Mikhail *Kalashnikov* (1919–), who conceived it in 1941 when convalescing after a tank battle. The famous AK47 (so named from Russian *avtomat Kalashnikova obraztsa 1947*, 'Kalashnikov automatic 1947 model') was widely adopted after the Second World War, not only by the Soviet Army but by forces of many other countries. It has been particularly admired by terrorist organizations. In the early 1990s, Colonel Kalashnikov, now in his 70s, was still the head of the design team.

277

Kalevala The name of the Finnish national epic, also a poetic name for Finland itself, derives from that of the dwelling-place of its chief characters, and in particular that of its hero *Kaleva*. The name means 'land of heroes', from *kaleva*, 'of a hero' and the suffix *-la* meaning 'place', 'home'. The name of the epic's hero thus actually means 'hero'.

Kalgoorlie The city in Western Australia has an Aboriginal name, said to be that of a shrub that grows locally.

Kali The name of the Hindu goddess of destruction, the consort of Siva, derives from Sanskrit *kāli*, feminine of *kāla*, 'black'. It is also linked with *Kālà*, meaning 'time' (*i.e.* as destroyer), one of the names of Siva himself. It was Kali who gave the name of CALCUTTA.

Kalimantan The Indonesian name for Borneo, now applied to the Indonesian part only, represents the Malay name for the island's indigenous inhabitants, the *Kalimantan*. Their own name derives from Sanskrit *kāliman*, 'blackness', from *kāli*, 'black' and Malay *tanah*, 'country', 'land'.

Kalinin *See* TVER.

Kaliningrad The city and port in the extreme west of Russia was named commemoratively in the year of his death for the Soviet statesman Mikhail *Kalinin* (1875–1946). The city's earlier name was *Königsberg*, 'royal mountain', although there is no mountain here. The town was founded in 1255 as a fortress (*Burg* rather than *Berg*) named in honour of the German emperor Ottokar II. The resemblance of the city's Russian name to its historic German one is purely fortuitous.

Kaluga The name of the city in western Russia represents the Russian dialect word *kaluga*, 'marsh', 'swamp'.

Kama The river in the east of Russia, where it is the longest tributary of the Volga, has a name that may derive from Votyak *kam*, meaning simply 'river'.

Kama Sutra The title of the ancient Hindu text on erotic pleasure derives from Sanskrit *kāma*, 'love' and *sūtra*, literally 'thread' (to which English *sew* and *suture* are related), so overall means effectively 'rules of love'.

Kamchatka The peninsula at the eastern end of Siberia takes its name from the *Kamchadal*, the people who live here. Their own name is said to represent Koriak *konchachal*, 'men of the far end'.

Kampala The capital of Uganda is said to take its name from the type of antelope known as the *impala*. The reason for the name is uncertain.

Kampuchea The name is that given to CAMBODIA by the Khmer Rouge in 1976, and current until the pro-Vietnamese government reverted to the original name in 1989. The two names are identical in origin.

Kandahar *See* GANDHARA.

Kandy The city in central Sri Lanka has a name that derives from the Singhalese word *kandha*, 'mountain'.

Kangchenjunga The mountain in the Himalayas on the border between Nepal and Sikkim has a name representing Tibetan *kangĉendzonga*, 'the five treasures of the snows', from *kang*, 'snow', *ĉen*, 'having', *dzod*, 'treasure', and *nga*, 'five'. The reference is to the mountain's five peaks.

Kangol The familiar make of sports and safety clothing and equipment takes its name from a blend of the materials used for making the berets that were its original product in the 1930s. These were sil*k* and *ang*ora wool.

Kansas The American state takes its name from the river that flows through it, itself so called for the North American Indian *Kansa* people who lived here. Their own name is said to mean 'people of the south wind'. *See also* KANSAS CITY.

Kansas City The city in Missouri (not KANSAS) lies on the river Missouri, at the mouth of the river *Kansas*, and takes its name from the latter. The city is close to the frontier with Kansas, however, and is contiguous with *Kansas City* in that state.

Kapilavastu The town of ancient India, the birthplace of the Buddha, has a name of Sanskrit origin, from *kapila*, 'brown' and *vastu*, 'reality'.

Karachi The port and former capital of Pakistan has a name that represents that of the *Kulachi*, the Baluchi people who lived here. The meaning of their own name is uncertain.

Karaganda The city in Kazakhstan has a name that is said to derive from a Kazakh word *karakan*, the name of a type of yellow acacia that grows here.

Kara-Kalpak The Mongoloid people of Uzbekistan have a name meaning 'black kalpak', from *kara*, 'black' and *kalpak*, 'kalpak', the traditional large brimless hat that men wear in this region.

Karakoram The mountain system of north Kashmir has a name that means 'black mountains', from Turkish *kara*, 'black' and *koram*, 'mountain'.

Kara Kum The desert in Turkmenistan has a name meaning 'black sands', from Turkish *kara*, 'black' and *kum*, 'sand'. The reference is to sands that are overgrown with vegetation, as distinct from the pure white sands found in many other deserts.

Kara Sea The arm of the Arctic Ocean of the northern coast of Russia takes its name from the river that flows into it. The river's name derives from Mongolian *har*, 'black'.

Karelia The region of northeast Europe that is now part of Russia takes its name from its indigenous inhabitants, whose own name may derive from a Finnish word *karja* meaning 'herd', so that they were primarily 'herdsmen' or 'shepherds'.

Karen The name is a Danish form of CATHERINE, taken to America by Scandinavian immigrants in the early 20th century, and subsequently becoming widely popular among English speakers on both sides of the Atlantic.

Karen The name of the Thai people of Burma derives from Burmese *ka-reng*, 'wild man', implying a dirty or low-caste person. The Karen are not themselves Burmese.

Karl-Marx-Stadt *See* CHEMNITZ.

Karlovy Vary The city of the western Czech Lands has a name that means 'Charles's bath', seen more clearly in the town's German name of *Karlsbad*. The city was founded by the Holy Roman Emperor *Charles* (*Karl*) IV in the 14th century. The 'bath' is the warm thermal springs here.

Karlsruhe The city of western Germany has a name meaning 'Charles's rest', with German *Ruhe*, 'rest' following the name of the margrave *Karl* Wilhelm von Baden-Durlach, who in 1715 built a hunting lodge here on the edge of the Black Forest as a place of retreat and relaxation.

Karnak The Egyptian village on the Nile that is the site of the ancient city of Thebes has a name that is said to derive from the pre-Indoeuropean root word *kar*, 'stone'. If so, the name is probably of the same origin as that of the Breton village of *Carnac*, with its many megalithic monuments.

Karnataka The southern Indian state has a name of Tamil origin, from *karuppu*, 'black' and *nāṭu*, 'country', 'land'.

Kärnten *See* CARINTHIA.

Karoo The extensive plateau of South Africa probably derives its name from the Hottentot word *garo*, 'desert'.

Kashmir The region of southwest central Asia, divided between India and Pakistan, has a name representing Sanskrit *kāśyapa-mara*, 'land of *Kaśyapa*', the latter being the name of a Hindu god. It is the name of this historic region that gave *cashmere* as the word for the fabric made of fine wool from the goats here.

Kassel The city of western Germany was founded in the 10th century (or perhaps earlier) and takes its name from Latin *castellum*, 'fortress'.

Katanga The former name (until 1972) of SHABA, the district of southern Zaïre, is a Hausa word meaning 'ramparts', 'fortifications', referring to its former capital.

Kate The name is a short form of CATHERINE, in use from medieval times. Shakespeare has the name for two leading female characters. In *Henry V* (1598) the king woos (and wins) *Katharine*, daughter of the king of France, and soon moves from addressing her by her formal name to calling her by its friendly diminutive. In his earlier play, *The Taming of the Shrew* (1593), Petruchio makes great play with the name when first meeting *Katharina* (the 'shrew' of the title) as her potential suitor, although she herself resists the familiarity:

PETRUCHIO Good morrow, Kate; for that's your name, I hear.

KATHARINA Well you have heard, but something hard of hearing:

They call me Katharine that do talk of me.

PETRUCHIO You lie, in faith; for you are call'd plain Kate,

And bonny Kate, and sometimes Kate the curst;

But Kate, the prettiest Kate in Christenom;

Kate of Kate-Hall, my super-dainty Kate,

For dainties are all cates (*i.e.* delicacies): and therefore, Kate,

Take this of me, Kate of my consolation.

It is this play that has the famous 'Kiss me, Kate' which was adopted as the title of the Broadway musical of 1948 based on it. *See also* KISMET.

Katharevusa The name is that of the 'official' style of modern Greek, as distinct from the spoken DEMOTIC. The term deMrives from classical Greek *katharos*, 'pure', as Katharevusa is regarded as a 'purist' language.

Kathleen Mavourneen The name is the title (and that of the subject) of an 'Irish' poem by the English poet Julia Crawford (1800–1885), written in 1835, with its well-known opening lines: 'Kathleen Mavourneen! the grey dawn is breaking,/The horn of the hunter is heard on the hill'. *Mavourneen* is not Kathleen's surname but a term of endearment, representing Irish *mo mhurnín*, 'my dear one'. *Kathleen* is itself a form of the Irish name *Caitlín*. This actually represents CATHERINE, but is spelled with a final *-ín* as if having the diminutive suffix seen in the Irish origin of *Mavourneen*. *Cp.* similar names such as COLLEEN and MAUREEN.

Katmandu The capital of Nepal has a Nepalese name meaning 'wooden temples', from *kaṭh*, 'wooden' and *māṇḍū*, 'temple'. Most of the temples here are timber-built. The city's former name, until the 16th century, was *Kantipur*, 'town of beauty', from *kāṅti*, 'beauty', 'charm', and *pur*, 'town'.

Katowice The city of southern Poland has a name that derives from the Slavic root word *kot*, 'cat', probably itself the basis of a personal name. The name is pronounced approximately 'Cato*vit*sa'. From 1953 to 1956 the city was known as *Stalinogród*, 'Stalin's town'.

Kattegat The strait between Denmark and Sweden has a name that derives from Old Norse *kati*, 'boat' and *gata*, 'way', 'strait', denoting a navigable channel.

Kaunas The city of Lithuania, its provisional capital from 1920 to 1940, has a name of uncertain origin. It has been tentatively derived from Slavic *kovati*, 'to forge' (steel).

Kawasaki The Japanese city and port, between Tokyo and Yokohama, has a name that means 'river cape', from *kawa*, 'river' and *saki*, 'cape', 'promontory'. This describes its location on Tokyo Bay at the mouth of the river Tawa.

Kay The name has several possible origins. They include: 1. a person who made *keys*, from Old English *cæg*, 'key'; 2. a person who lived by a wharf, or in modern terms a *quay* (*cp.* KEW); 3. a person who resembled a jackdaw, known as a *kay* (from its call) in a northern dialect; 4. someone who was left-handed, from a Danish dialect word that was borrowed into English as *kay* or *key*. In some cases, a person with the surname *Kay* may have simply adopted the initial of a longer name, especially a foreign one, as a surname. The American actor Danny *Kaye* (1913–1987) was thus originally Daniel *Kaminsky*.

Kazakhstan The republic of west central Asia takes its name from its indigenous people, the *Kazakhs*, whose own name derives from the Turkic root word *kazak*, 'nomad'. To their name Iranian *ostān*, 'country', 'land' has been added, as for AFGHANISTAN. The Kazakhs gave the name of the familiar COSSACKS.

Kazan The city of eastern Russia has a name representing Tatar *kazan*, 'cauldron'. This refers to the strong current of the river *Kazanka* on which the town stands, now at its confluence with the Volga, but originally some 28 miles (45 km) upstream.

Kazbek, Mount The extinct volcano in the Caucasus derives its present name from the village of *Kazibegi* that grew up in the early 19th century at its foot, the village itself being named for the landowner here, Prince *Kazibeg*. The volcano is in Georgia, and its Georgian name is *mqinuli*, 'mountain of ice', from *mta*, 'mountain' and *qinuli*, 'ice'.

KB Denmark's oldest football club, founded as a rounders club in 1876, has a name composed of the initials of Danish *Kjøbenhavns Boldklub*, 'Copenhagen Football Club'.

KC and the Sunshine Band The American dance band, formed in Florida in 1973, takes its name from its founder, Harry Wayne *Casey* (1951–).

Keats Both this name and *Keating* ultimately derive from an older form of the word *kite*, originally given as a nickname for a person who was fierce or greedy, like this bird of prey.

Kedron The biblical river and ravine between Jerusalem and the Mount of Olives, mentioned in the Bible as both 'the brook Cedron' (*John* 18.1) and 'the brook Kidron' (2 *Samuel* 15.23), has a name of Hebrew origin, from *qidrōn*, itself from a root word *qador*, 'to be black'. The name of *Kedar*, the second son of Ishmael (*Genesis* 25.13), comes from the same root.

Keewatin The administrative district of the Northwest Territories of Canada has a name of Cree origin meaning 'people of the north wind'.

Keflavík The town in southwest Iceland, with its international airport, takes its name from the small bay on which it is situated. The meaning is 'bay of sticks', from Icelandic *kefla*, genitive plural of *kefli*, 'stick', 'piece of wood' and *vík*, 'bay', referring to the flotsam often encountered by fishermen here. Not far away is REYKJAVÍK, the country's capital.

Keighley The West Yorkshire town has a name that is of Old English origin meaning 'Cyhha's clearing'. The name is pronounced 'Keethly' in an attempt to preserve the original sound of Old English *h* which was something like modern Scottish *ch* in *loch*.

Keith The name derives from a Scottish surname, itself from the Celtic name of a place in East Lothian meaning 'wood'. (It is not far from the town of *Dalkeith*, whose name contains the same word.)

Keith Prowse The name of the well-known theatre ticket agency is that of two men, not one. They were Robert W. *Keith* and William *Prowse*, who formed a partnership in London in about 1800, originally to make musical instruments and publish sheet music.

Kelantan The state of northeast Malaysia has a Malay name meaning 'land of the jujube tree', from *koli*, 'jujube' and *tanah*, 'country', 'land'.

Kelloggs The familiar brand of breakfast cereal is named for William Keith *Kellogg* (1860–1951), business manager at the Battle Creek Sanitarium, Michigan, where his brother, Dr John Harvey Kellogg, was the chief surgeon and superintendent. The brothers first devised their prototype corn flakes in a nutritional experiment in 1894. Dr Kellogg began to produce them commercially, and William Keith Kellogg then took over the business to found the Battle Creek Toasted Corn Flake Company in 1906.

Kelly The Irish surname represents the original name *Ó Ceallaigh*, 'descendant of *Ceallach*', the latter name perhaps meaning 'strife'.

Kelly College The public school in Tavistock, Devon, was founded in 1877 by Admiral Benedictus Marwood *Kelly*, and retains a special naval connection today.

Kemerovo The city in southern Russia derives its name from Turkish *kemer*, 'bank', referring to its location by the river Tom.

Kemp The name was originally an occupational one for a champion jouster or wrestler, from a word that ultimately gave *champion* itself.

Kendal The town in Cumbria lies on the river *Kent* and takes its name from it, with *-dal* representing modern *dale*. It was earlier known as *Kirkby Kendal*, that is, 'village with a church in the valley of the Kent'. The second word of this was added to its original name of *Kirkby* in order to distinguish this 'village with a church' from the many others in the district, such as the towns now known as *Kirkby Lonsdale* and *Kirkby Stephen*. They, however, have retained their original name, whereas *Kendal* has dropped it, so that it now has its distinguishing addition as its sole name.

Kenilworth The Warwickshire town has a name that means '*Cynehild*'s enclosure', with the Anglo-Saxon female name (itself meaning 'royal battle') followed by Old English *worth*, 'enclosure'. It is the 12th-century castle here that is the subject of Walter Scott's novel of the same name, published in 1821.

Kennedy The Irish name is an English form of *Ó Cinnéidigh*, 'descendant of *Cinnéidigh*', the latter name meaning literally 'armoured head', from Irish *ceann*, 'head' and *éidigh*, 'armoured'. This could have referred to a warrior, wearing a helmet, but was also a nickname for someone with an ugly head.

Kenneth The name is of Gaelic origin, from an original name *Cainnech* meaning 'fair', 'beautiful'.

Kensington The district and royal borough of west central London has a name that only coincidentally suggests *king*. It actually means 'farm of *Cynesige*'s people', although it has to be said that this Anglo-Saxon personal name literally means 'royal victory', so that the kingly connection is historically represented, if indirectly.

Kensington Gore The name of the London street in KENSINGTON derives the second word of its name from Old English *gāra*, 'corner', 'point of land'. The reference is to the wedge-shaped piece of land that was originally bounded by Queen's Gate, Cromwell Road and Kensington Road. This land was known until at least the 17th century as *King's Gore*, a name that appears to have subsequently blended with that of *Kensington* itself. It is not known which king held land here. The royal connection is recorded as early as the 13th century.

Kent The county of southeast England has a very old name, dating back to at least the 1st century BC, when it is mentioned by the Greek geographer Strabo. It probably derives from a Celtic root element *cant* meaning 'border', 'edge'. This would have referred to a section of the coast here, although probably a much smaller region than that of the modern county. It may have originally been the name of what is now just the North Foreland of the Isle of Thanet. *See also* CANTERBURY.

Kent College The Methodist public school in Canterbury, founded in 1885, takes its name from its county of *Kent* (which itself gave the name of *Canterbury*). The girls' public school of the same name and foundation is at Pembury near Tunbridge Wells in Kent.

Kentucky The American state takes its name from the river that flows through it. The river's own name is believed to represent Iroquois *kentake*, 'meadow-land', although other, more colourful meanings have been suggested, such as 'land of tomorrow', 'land dark with blood' (alluding to intertribal wars) and 'land of green reeds'.

Kenwood House The 17th-century mansion on Hampstead Heath, London, takes its name from the wood here, recorded in 1543 as *Canewood*. The origin of this is obscure. The name is unlikely to be associated with *Caen* in northern France, as sometimes suggested.

Kenya The country in East Africa takes its name from Mount *Kenya*, whose own name probably means simply 'mountain'.

Kerala The state of southwest India has a name that probably derives from Tamil *keralam*, 'mountain range', referring to the Western Ghats.

Kerenhappuch The biblical name is that of the third of Job's beautiful daughters. It derives from a Hebrew phrase meaning 'horn of antimony', the latter being a metal used as a pigment in eye-paint, and intended in that sense here. The name thus implies that the bearer has beautiful eyes.

Kerguelen The archipelago in the southern Indian Ocean, comprising one large volcanic island and hundreds of small ones, takes its name from the French sailor who discovered the group in 1772, Yves Joseph de *Kerguelen* de Trémadec (1734–1797). When Cook came here in 1776 he named the largest island *Desolation Island*.

Kerman The city in southeast Iran takes its name from the *Carmani*, the historic people who inhabited the region. The origin of their own name is uncertain.

Kermanshah The city of western Iran (now *Bakhtaran*) has a name from Sanskrit *karmanśa*, representing the river here, usually known as the *Qareh Sū*. This means 'destroying a good work', from *karman*, 'work', 'karma' and *śa*, 'destroying', from *śat*, 'to destroy'. The river, a tributary of the Ganges, waters the fertile plain here but also frequently floods it.

Kerr The name, common in Scotland, originally applied to someone who lived near a *carr* or *kerr*, a dialect word for a marshy clump of bushes, from a Scandinavian word *kjarr*. The names CARR and *Keir* are variant forms of this.

Kerry The Irish county has a name of tribal origin, referring to *Ciar* and his people. Ciar appears in early legend as the son of King Fergus and Queen Maeve.

Kesteven The district of Lincolnshire, now administratively divided into North and South *Kesteven*, derives its name from an unusual combination of Celtic *cēto*, 'wood' and Old Norse *stefna*, 'meeting-place'. The mixture of languages shows that the same meeting-place must have been used by both the Danes and the Britons before them.

Keswick The name of the Cumbria town exactly corresponds with that of CHISWICK in London, so means 'cheese farm', from Old English *cēse*, 'cheese' and *wīc*, 'dairy farm'. The spelling and pronunciation of the name here, in the north of England, are due to Scandinavian influence.

Kettering The name of the Northamptonshire town has to date remained tantalizingly obscure. It is probably based on a personal name, with the final *-ing* meaning 'people of', as for a name such as READING. Unfortunately, no personal name has been traced that could have given the earliest record of the name available, *Cytringan*, in 956.

Kettner's Restaurant The well-known London restaurant, off Cambridge Circus, takes its name from Auguste *Kettner*, chef to Napoleon III, who established it in the 1860s.

Kevin The Irish name is a form of the original Gaelic name *Caoimhín*, a diminutive of Irish *caomh*, 'fair', 'beautiful'.

Kew The district of west London, famous for its Royal Botanic Gardens, is right by the Thames and has a name that relates to this location. It has evolved as a blend of two words: Old French *kai*, 'landing place' (modern English *quay*), and Old English *hōh*, 'heel'. The 'heel' is the spur of land in the bend of the Thames here.

Keynes The name denotes someone who originally came from either *Cahaignes* or *Cahaynes* in the north of France, the former near Evreux, the latter near Caen.

Kezia The biblical name is that of the second of Job's three beautiful daughters. It derives from Hebrew *Qetsi'āh*, 'cassia' (which English word is directly related to it). Cassia bark yields a spice that would have been used in biblical times.

Khabarovsk The city of eastern Russia, a port on the river Amur, was founded in 1658 by Russian Cossacks and named by them for the explorer Yerofey *Khabarov*, who reached the Amur here in 1649.

Kharkov The former Ukrainian capital is said to take its name from its Cossack founder in 1656, *Kharko*.

Khartoum The Sudanese capital has an Arabic name, from *al-hurṭūm*, a short form of *ra's al-hurṭūm*, 'end of an elephant's trunk', from *ra's*, 'head', 'end', *al*, 'the' and *hurṭūm*, 'trunk'. The name is descriptive of the narrow stretch of land between the White Nile and Blue Nile here.

Kherson *See* CHERSONESE.

Khmer Rouge The former Kampuchean (Cambodian) Communist Party took its name from the *Khmer*, the indigenous inhabitants of the country, and French *rouge*, 'red', denoting their political stance. The *Khmer* themselves are said to derive their name from a blend of *Kamba* and *Mera*, the names of their legendary ancestors (*see* CAMBODIA). The party has been in exile since 1979.

Khodzhent The town in Tajikistan is of ancient origin. In the 6th and 5th centuries BC the settlement here was known as *Cyropolis*, for *Cyrus* the Great, founder of the Persian empire. In the 4th century BC it was captured by Alexander the Great, and renamed for him as *Alexandria Eskhata*, 'Outer Alexandria'. The second word is

Greek *eskhatos*, 'furthermost', and refers to the city's location as the outermost of the places called *Alexandria* in the king's empire. By the 7th century AD the name had become *Khudzhand* or *Khodzhent*, a corrupt form of this. The city retained this name until 1936 when it was renamed *Leninabad* for Lenin, with *-abad* meaning 'inhabited place', as for FAISALABAD. In 1990 the city reverted to its original name.

Khoisan The name is used generally for the Hottentots and Bushmen of southern Africa. It derives from *Khoikhoin*, 'men of men', the name the Hottentots use for themselves, and *San*, the name the Hottentots give the Bushmen, from the root element *sa*, 'to pick', 'to collect', implying their procurement of food by gathering fruits and plants and by hunting animals. *See also* HOTTENTOT, BUSHMEN.

Khovanshchina Mussorgsky's opera of 1886 is set in Russia at the time of the accession of Peter the Great in 1682. It deals with the struggle for power between various factions of the day, and especially that between the respective followers of Prince *Khovansky* and Prince Galitsyn. The title would be better translated *The Khovansky Affair*. The Russian suffix *-shchina* is regularly used with a personal name to denote disapprobation for the person concerned. For example, *stalinshchina* means 'the abuses of Stalinism', 'the evil times of Stalin'. The opera title is pronounced approximately 'Ho*v*ansheena'.

Kia-Ora The brand of soft drinks has a name that is a traditional Maori greeting or good luck wish, literally meaning 'be well'.

Kidd The name was originally a nickname for someone who resembled a kid (a young goat) in some way, such as a frisky or capricious person. In some cases it could also have been a name for an actual goatherd, who looked after the *kids*.

Kidderminster The town near Birmingham has a name that shows it to have had an important monastery or *minster*. The first half of the name represents the Old English personal name *Cyda*. The monastery itself was founded in the 8th century on the site now occupied by All Saints Church.

Kidron *See* KEDRON.

Kiel The port of northwest Germany derives its name from Old Norse *kíll*, 'bay', 'gulf', referring to the inlet of the western Baltic on which it stands.

Kiev The Ukrainian capital, the 'mother of Russian cities', is said to take its name from a prince *Kiy* who is supposed to have founded it in the 9th century. This looks like popular legend at work, however, and the actual source of the name remains uncertain.

Kigali The capital of Rwanda takes its name from Mount *Kigali*, near which it arose in the 19th century when this territory became part of German East Africa. The mountain's name consists of the Bantu prefix *ki-* followed by Rwanda *gali*, 'broad', 'wide'.

Kildare The name of the Irish county derives from that of the town, itself meaning 'church of the oak', from Irish *cill*, 'church' and *doire*, 'oak grove' (as for LONDONDERRY). St Brigid is said to have founded a nunnery here in the 5th or 6th century in a pagan oak grove. The present St Brigid's cathedral may stand on its original site.

Kilimanjaro The famous volcano of East Africa, in Tanzania, has a Swahili name meaning 'mountain of the god of cold', from *kilima*, 'mountain' and *njaro*, 'god of cold'.

Kilkenny The Irish county takes its name from its county town, whose own name represents Irish *Cill Chainnigh*, 'church of St KENNETH'.

Killarney The Irish town and tourist resort near the lakes of the same name derives its name from Irish *Cill Airne*, 'church of the sloes'.

Killiecrankie The name of the Scottish pass where the Jacobites defeated the forces of William III in 1689 means 'wood of aspens', from Gaelic *coille creitheannich*.

Kilmarnock The Scottish town near Glasgow has a name meaning 'St *Ernan*'s church', from Gaelic *cill*, 'church' and the saint's name prefixed by *mo* and suffixed by *-oc*. Gaelic *mo* means 'my', showing a personal dedication to the name. The suffix *-oc* serves as a diminutive. Overall, therefore, the name means effectively 'church of my little Ernan'. Ernan himself was a 6th-century disciple of St Columba.

Kilpatrick If an Irish name, the original form would usually have been *Mac Giolla Phádraig*, literally 'son of the servant of St Patrick'. If a Scottish name, it would have applied to someone from a place so called, such as *Kilpatrick* on the island of Arran. The meaning of the place-name itself is 'church of St *Patrick*'.

Kim The present girl's name, now given in its own right, is strictly speaking a short form of the boy's name *Kimberley*, itself adopted from the South African town of KIMBERLEY at the time of the diamond strike there in the late 19th century. In Kipling's novel *Kim* (1901), however, the Irish boy who is the central character was originally called *Kimball*, from a surname.

Kimberley The well-known city of South Africa was founded in 1871 after diamonds were discovered here and was named for the then British secretary of state for the colonies, John Wodehouse, first Earl of *Kimberley* (1826–1902). The earl took his title from *Kimberley* near Wymondham, Norfolk, his birthplace. *See also* KIM.

King The well-known surname was originally a nickname for someone who behaved or looked like a king in some way, for example by putting on 'airs and graces'. In some cases, the name would have applied to a person who acted the part of king in a pageant. Only rarely would the name have been an occupational one for a person employed in a king's household, since he would then have been known by his particular occupation or status. (*See* for example STEWART.)

King Edward's School There are several public schools of the name. Those in Bath, Birmingham and Surrey were founded by *King* Edward VI, the first two in 1552, the latter in 1553, in which year the same king also founded *King Edward VI School* in Southampton. *King Edward VII School* at Lytham in Lancashire was opened in 1908 and named for the king then reigning. *See also* KING'S SCHOOL.

King Kong The giant ape who was the famous monster of the film named for him, released in 1933, appears himself to have a name that suggests a *king of the Kongo* (or

CONGO), the latter name being both that of the native African people and their land. The association of name is reinforced by the fact that the Kongo are forest dwellers, as are apes. On the other hand the second word of the name may simply represent a Germanic word for 'king' itself, such as Danish *konge*. Or of course there could simply be a random alliteration (as for *ding-dong, ping-pong, sing-song*).

Kings The two Old Testament books of *Kings* are so named because they recount the history of the *kings* of Israel and Judah after the death of David. The division into two books, 1 and 2 *Kings*, is arbitrary. The original Hebrew text, without vowels, took up only one volume, but the Greek translation, with vowels, occupied two scrolls. Hence 1 and 2 *Kings*.

King's College The famous Cambridge college takes its name from *King* Henry VI, who founded it in 1441 as partner to his other foundation at Eton, where the 70 foundation scholars are known as *King's Scholars*. The London University college of the same name was founded by royal charter in 1828, so that the *king* was George IV. *King's College*, the boys' public school in Taunton, Somerset, was founded in 1880 and named in memory of Alfred the Great, *King* of Wessex a thousand years earlier.

King's College School The London public day school for boys was founded in 1829 as a junior department of KING'S COLLEGE in the University of London. The Cambridge preparatory school of the name opened in 1878 to provide an education for the choirboys of *King's College* as well as generally for boys who were not choristers.

King's Cross The well-known district of north London, with its mainline railway station, takes its name from a *cross* that was erected here (moreover at a *cross*roads) as a memorial to *King* George IV after his death in 1830. It remained in place until 1845, when it was removed for the present railway terminus to be built. The earlier name of the district was *Battlebridge*, a corruption of *Bradford*, itself denoting a 'broad ford' over the former river Fleet here (*see* FLEET STREET). This old name is preserved in that of Battlebridge Road, a short street behind King's Cross station.

Kingsley School The girls' public school at Leamington, Warwickshire, takes its name from Miss Rose *Kingsley*, who founded it in 1884 together with Dr Wood, later headmaster of Harrow.

King's Lynn The name of the Norfolk town and port basically means 'king's manor in *Lynn*', the king being Henry VIII. The second word of the name is Celtic in origin and means 'pool' (like modern Welsh *llyn* and the first half of the name of LINCOLN). The 'pool' would have been the mouth of the river Ouse where the town now stands.

King's School There are no less than seven public schools of the name. That in Bruton, Somerset, was originally founded in 1519 but refounded by *King* Edward VI in 1550. Those in Canterbury, Chester, Ely and Worcester were founded by Henry VIII in 1541. *King's School*, Rochester followed a year later. *King's School*, Macclesfield was originally founded in 1502 but in 1552 was refounded by *King* Edward VI, like its Somerset namesake. *Cp.* KING EDWARD'S SCHOOL.

Kingston The capital of Jamaica was founded in 1692 and named in honour of *King* William III, who had come to the throne three years earlier.

Kingston Lacy The 17th-century (and later) house near Wimborne, Dorset, takes its name from the village here. *Kingston*, as in many identical names elsewhere, means 'king's farm', or more specifically 'royal manor', *i.e.* one owned by the king. *Lacy* represents the name of the Norman family *de Lasey*, who held the manor here in the 13th century. (*See* LACEY.) *Cp.* POLESDEN LACEY.

Kingston upon Thames The former Surrey (now Greater London) town and royal borough was a royal possession as long ago as the 9th century, when it was already a 'king's farm'. Later, its location by the Thames was added to distinguish it from the many other places called *Kingston*.

Kingswood School The Methodist public school near Bath was founded by John Wesley in 1748 and takes its name from its location on Lansdown hill outside the city. The place-name, found elsewhere in England, means what it says, denoting a wood that belonged to a king in medieval times.

King William's College The Isle of Man public school was founded in 1668 by the Bishop of Sodor and Man but did not open until 1833, when it was named for *King William* IV, the reigning monarch.

Kinks, The The British pop group, formed in London in 1963, were given their name by pop impresario Larry Page, basing it on *kinky*, a vogue word then in 'swinging London' that had a number of meanings ranging from 'sexually perverse' to 'unusually fashionable' (such as *kinky* boots).

Kinshasa The capital of Zaïre has a name that is of Bantu origin but unknown meaning. Until 1966 the city was known as *Léopoldville*, for the king of the Belgians, *Léopold* II (1835–1909).

Kirgizia The republic of central Asia takes its name from its native people, the *Kirgiz*. Their own name is said to be formed from the Turkic root words *kir*, 'steppe' and *gizmek*, 'wander', implying a nomadic race. The official indigenous name of the republic is *Kyrgyzstan*.

Kiribati The western Pacific island republic has a name that is a native pronunciation of the country's former name of *Gilbert* Islands. The islands were discovered in 1765 and were subsequently named for Thomas *Gilbert*, who arrived here in 1788 after helping to convey the first shipload of convicts to Australia. *Cp.* KIRITIMATI.

Kirikkale The town in west central Turkey derives its name from Turkish *kırk*, 'broken' and *kale*, 'fort'.

Kiritimati The island in the central Pacific, famous as the largest atoll in the world, was formerly known as *Christmas* Island, and its present name is a native form of this. The atoll was named by Captain Cook, who discovered it on 24 December 1777, *Christmas* Eve. *See also* CHRISTMAS ISLAND.

Kirk The name originally applied to someone in the north of England or Scotland who lived by a church, or who was employed in one. *Cp.* CHURCH.

Kirkcudbright The town and former county of southwest Scotland has a name meaning 'St Cuthbert's church', the saint being the 7th-century Northumbrian monk who made many missionary journeys to this part of Scotland. The word *kirk* in a name is normally Scandinavian in origin, and usually follows the saint's name, as for ORMSKIRK. The fact that the word for 'church' precedes the saint's name here suggests that it was originally not Norse *kirkja* but Gaelic *cill*, since in Gaelic names this is the normal word order.

Kirkwall The chief town and port of the Orkney Islands has a Scandinavian name meaning 'church bay', from Old Norse *kirkja*, 'church' and *vágr*, 'bay'. The church here is the 12th-century cathedral of St Magnus, while the bay is the Bay of Kirkwall. The Norse word for 'bay' gives the *Voe* found for the names of various inlets in the Orkneys and Shetlands, such as the well-known SULLOM VOE.

Kirov *See* VYATKA.

Kirovabad *See* GANDZHA.

Kirovograd The city in Ukraine was founded in 1764 near the Fort of St Elizabeth that had been built in 1754 by the empress Elizabeth Petrovna (1709–1762) to defend the southern borders of Russia from invasion by the Turks and Tatars. In 1775 it was named *Yelizavetgrad*, 'Elizabeth's town', after her. In 1924 it was renamed *Zinovievsk*, for the Soviet politician and chairman of the Comintern, Grigory *Zinoviev* (1883–1936). In 1934 it was further renamed *Kirovo* after the Communist leader Sergey *Kirov* (*see* VYATKA), assassinated that year. Two years later, on the execution of Zinoviev for alleged complicity in Kirov's murder, it was further renamed *Kirovograd*, 'city of *Kirovo*' (also implying 'Kirov's city', which would actually be *Kirovgrad*).

Kirstie The Scottish name, now used independently, originated as a pet form of *Kirstin*, itself a Scottish form of CHRISTINE.

Kishinëv The capital of Moldavia derives its name from a word of Turkic origin meaning 'winter' (modern Turkish *kış*).

Kismet The name was originally popularized in the western world by the American-born British playwright Edward Knoblock's oriental fantasy *Kismet*, first staged in 1911. Various films and musicals based on it have followed since. The name is Turkish in origin, meaning 'destiny', 'fate', and ultimately derives from Arabic *qisma*, 'portion', 'lot', from *qasama*, 'to divide'. Because of the play's romantic content, its name has popularly come to suggest an origin in *kiss me*, so that it has subsequently been confused by some with *Kiss Me Kate*, Cole Porter's musical of 1948, based on Shakespeare's *The Taming of the Shrew*. Conversely, it has been suggested that the famous words uttered by Nelson when mortally wounded at the Battle of Trafalgar were not 'Kiss me, Hardy' but 'Kismet, Hardy', *i.e.* 'Fate, Hardy'.

Kit If male, the name is a pet form of CHRISTOPHER. If female, it will ultimately derive from CATHERINE, with the *a* altered to *i*. In the latter case, it developed its own pet form *Kitty*, which by association with *kitten* became a stock name for a *cat*.

Kitakyushu The Japanese city and port, at the northern end of the island of KYUSHU, has a name that describes its location, from *kita*, 'north' and the name of the island itself.

Kitty Hawk The name is the one popularly given to the aircraft (actually called 'Flyer I') in which Orville Wright made the first powered flight in history, in 1903. It derives from that of the village in North Carolina near the hill where the flight was made. The place-name suggests that of a bird, which is doubtless why it was popularly adopted for the plane. It actually derives, however, from an Indian (Algonquian) name recorded in 1729 as *Chickahauk*. The meaning of this is uncertain. (There is no such bird as a *kitty hawk*, although there is a *kittiwake* and a *kitty wren*.)

Kiwanis The name of the North American organization of clubs for professional and businessmen, founded in Detroit in 1915 to promote community service, is said to derive from an Indian word meaning 'to make oneself known'.

Kizil Irmak The river of Turkey has a name that means 'red river', from Turkish *kızıl*, 'red' and *ırmak*, 'river'. The name refers to the red clay washed down from its source in the *Kizil Dag*, 'red mountain', in north central Anatolia.

Klagenfurt According to popular legend, the city of southern Austria is said to take its name from a mythical woman known as the *Klagefrau*, 'weeping woman', who kept the *ford* (German *Furt*) here. The actual origin of the name remains uncertain. It was recorded in the 12th century, when the town was founded, as *Chlagenvurt*.

Klaipeda The port in Lithuania, on the Baltic Sea, has a name of uncertain origin. The second part appears to derive from Lithuanian *pèda*, 'territory'. The German name of the town is *Memel*, a corruption of *Nemen*, the name of the river on which it stands.

Kleenex The well-known make of paper tissues has a name that denotes their purpose: to *clean* and to take the dirt *out* (Latin *ex*). The name was first registered in Wisconsin in 1925.

KLM The Dutch airline was formed in 1919 and has a name derived from the initials of the first three words of its full original name, *Koninklijke Luchtvaart Maatschappij voor Nederland en Kolonien*, 'Royal Airline Company for the Netherlands and Colonies'. The airline's English name is now conventionally *Royal Dutch Airlines*.

Klondike The region of northwest Canada, famous for its former rich gold deposits, takes its name from the river *Klondike* here. The river's own name is said to derive from an Indian word *throndik* meaning 'river of fish'.

Knatchbull The name originated as an occupational one for a person who *knocked bulls*, that is, slaughtered them by knocking them on the head, from a former verb *knatch* or *knetch*. There is no evidence that this verb is related to modern *knacker*, despite the association of sense.

Kneller Hall The Middlesex home of the Royal Military School of Music takes its name from the court painter Sir Godfrey *Kneller*, for whom the house was built as a country villa in the early 18th century.

Knesset The name of the parliament of Israel represents the Hebrew word *keneset*, 'gathering', 'assembly', from *kānas*, 'to gather'.

Knight The name originally applied to someone who was a servant of a *knight* or who worked in his household, rather than being an actual knight himself. It is unlikely to have had the general sense 'servant' that *knight* itself initially had (*see* KNIGHTS-BRIDGE).

Knightsbridge The name of the fashionable London district means more or less what it says, 'knights' bridge', although the 'knights' would not have been the titled noblemen of today but, in the medieval sense of the word, the servants of a baron or lord (*see* the surname KNIGHT). The name is therefore better rendered as 'bridge of the young menservants'. The 'bridge' would have been over the river Westbourne, near the site of the present Albert Gate. The original 'lowly' sense of *knight* in English still exists in continental European languages, so that modern German *Knecht*, for example, means 'farmhand', 'servant'.

Knights Castile The well-known brand of soap takes its name from John *Knight*, a Hertfordshire farmer's son who set up a soap-making business in London in 1817. His firm introduced its popular type of soap in 1919. The name is a standard one for any kind of hard soap made with olive oil and soda like that originally produced in *Castile*, Spain. The brand name happens to evoke a blend of *knights* and *castles*.

Knights Templar The name is ultimately that of the order of military crusaders founded in 1119 in Jerusalem with the aim of protecting the Holy Sepulchre and recovering Palestine from the Saracens. They were so called because their house in Jerusalem was near the site of the famous *temple* built by Solomon. The order was dissolved in 1312, and in England their headquarters, on the site of the present TEMPLE, London, passed to the crown. In 1324 it was granted to the *Knights* Hospitallers of St John. (*See* ST JOHN AMBULANCE BRIGADE.)

Knockando The blend of Scotch whisky takes its name from the site of its distillery, opened in 1898 near the river Spey west of Craigellachie. The name of the locality itself represents Gaelic *Cnoc-an-dhu*, 'little black hill'.

Knole The mansion to the east of Sevenoaks, Kent was built in the 15th century for the Archbishop of Canterbury and later became the home of the Sackville family. It derives its name from Old English *cnoll*, 'hillock' (modern *knoll*). There is no single obvious hillock here, but Knole Park is undulating and the name could apply to any of the rises. Minor places of the name are common in Kent, and are usually in the form *Knowle*, as elsewhere in England.

Knox The Scottish name originally applied to someone who lived on or near a hilltop, the Old English word for which was *cnocc*. In some cases the person could have come from a place called *Knock* with the same meaning.

Knoxville The city in Tennessee, formerly the state capital, was settled in 1786 and named in honour of General Henry *Knox* (1750–1806), hero of the American Revolution (War of American Independence). *See also* FORT KNOX.

Knutsford The Cheshire town has a name that has long been traditionally associated with King CANUTE (Cnut), and that has been interpreted as '*Cnut*'s ford'. In a sense this is correct, although the link is almost certainly not with the famous king but with another man of the same name. (The town's *Canute Place* is a modern name, replacing as recently as the mid-19th century the former *Market Place*.) It is difficult to say exactly where the ford would have been, as Knutsford has no river and is on high ground. It may have been a crossing over marshy ground by Tatton Mere, the lake that lies to the north of the town.

Kobe The Japanese city, in southern Honshu, has a name meaning 'house of god', from *kō*, 'god' and *he*, 'house'.

Koblenz The name of the city of western Germany has evolved from its Roman name of *Confluentes*, from Latin *confluens*, 'confluence'. Koblenz lies at the confluence of the Rhine and the Moselle.

Kodak The well-known make of film and camera has a name that is purely arbitrary. It was devised by the American photographic pioneer George Eastman in 1888 as an 'incisive' name that was easy to spell, to pronounce and to memorize. It has been pointed out that the name happens to suggest the click of a camera shutter, but this is a purely fortuitous bonus.

Kohinoor The large Indian diamond that has been part of the British crown jewels since 1849 has a name that represents Persian *Kōh-i-nūr*, literally 'mountain of light', from *kōh*, 'mountain' and Arabic *nūr*, 'light'.

Kolynos The make of toothpaste has a name devised from the roots of Greek words to mean 'I check disease', from *kolouō*, 'I check' and *nosos*, 'sickness', 'disease'.

Komatsu The Japanese construction equipment company takes its name from the city of *Komatsu*, in the island of Honshu, where it was founded in 1921.

Komsomol The Soviet Communist youth organization, founded in 1918, has a name that is an abbreviation formed from the first syllables of its Russian name, *Kommunisticheskiy Soyuz Molodëzhi*, 'Communist Union of Youth'. The Komsomol was disbanded in 1991.

Komsomolsk The industrial city in eastern Russia was founded in 1932 by volunteers recruited from the KOMSOMOL. Hence its name.

Kon-Tiki The name is that of the raft of balsa wood in which the Norwegian anthropologist Thor Heyerdahl sailed in 1947 from Peru to the Tuamotu islands in the South Pacific with the aim of proving that the Polynesians could have emigrated from South America. In his account of his voyage, first published in Norwegian as *Kon-Tiki Ekspedisjonen* in 1948, Heyerdahl explains how he came across the name when reading about the Inca sun-king Virakocha:

> The original name of the sun-god Virakocha, which seems to have been more used in Peru in old times, was Kon-Tiki or Illa-Tiki, which means Sun-Tiki or Illa-Tiki. Kon-Tiki was high priest and sun-king of the Incas' legendary 'white men' who had left the enormous ruins on the shores of Lake Titicaca. [...] In a battle on an island in Lake Titicaca the fair race was massacred, but Kon-Tiki himself and his closest companions escaped and later came down to the Pacific coast, whence they

finally disappeared overseas to the westward.

The Kon-Tiki Expedition, 1950.

Konya The ancient city of southwest central Turkey has a name that is a corruption of its original Greek name *Ikonion* (Latin *Iconium*). This is popularly derived from Greek *eikōn*, genitive *eikonos*, 'image', 'icon'. The reference is to the classical story telling how Prometheus made men out of mud here to replace those drowned during the Great Flood. The city was thus the first to emerge when the waters receded. The true source of the name is uncertain, however.

Kop, the The name of the terraced spectator stand at Anfield, the home ground of Liverpool Football Club, is a short form of *Spion Kop*. This was the Afrikaans name, meaning 'spy hill', 'look-out', of a hill near Ladysmith in South Africa that in 1900 was the scene of a battle in the Boer War. The Liverpool 'Kop' was built in 1906 and is said to have been so named on the suggestion of a local journalist, Ernest Edwards, sports editor of the *Liverpool Post and Echo*. The particular association with Anfield stems from the fact that Liverpool is (or was) a Lancashire club, and that the futile British assault on Spion Kop had been led by the 2nd Royal Lancaster Regiment and the 2nd Royal Lancashire Fusiliers. Similar terraces at some other football grounds are also known as 'kops'.

Kópavogur The town in southwest Iceland has a name that means 'bay of baby seals', from Icelandic *kópa*, genitive plural of *kópur*, 'young seal' and *vogur*, 'bay' (related to the *Voe* of SULLOM VOE).

Koran The sacred book of Islam has a name that represents Arabic *qurʾān*, literally 'reading', 'book'. *Cp*. its Christian counterpart, the BIBLE.

Korea The east Asian country, now divided into North Korea and South Korea, takes its name from Chinese *gāoli*, that of a dynasty founded in 918, and itself meaning 'high serenity'. The Japanese name of Korea is *chosen*, from Korean *chosŏn*, meaning 'land of morning calm', from *cho*, 'morning' and *sŏn*, 'freshness', 'calm'.

Kosciusko, Mount The mountain in New South Wales, Australia, was disovered in 1839 by the Polish explorer Paul Strzelecki and named for the famous Polish patriot Tadeusz *Kościuszko* (1746–1817), with a slight simplification of spelling. The mountain name is pronounced approximately 'Koziusko', the middle syllable as in 'bus'. The Polish surname is properly pronounced more like 'Kosh*choosh*ko'.

Kosovo The autonomous region in southern Serbia, Yugoslavia, may derive its name from Serbian *kos*, 'blackbird'.

Kota Kinabalu The Malaysian port and capital of Sabah was founded in the late 19th century and originally named *Jesselton*, for Sir Charles *Jessel*, a director of the British North Borneo Company. In 1968 it was given its present name, meaning 'fort of Kinabalu', after nearby Mount *Kinabalu*. The mountain is regarded as the spiritual home of the indigenous Dusan people, and its name is a form of their term for it, *Aki-nabalu*, 'revered place of the dead'.

KP The brand of nuts and crisps has a name formed from the initials of *K*enyon *Pro*ducts, the trading name of their original manufacturers, Kenyon, Son & Craven, of Rotherham, Yorkshire. The *KP* peanut was introduced by Simon Heller, a world authority on nuts, who acquired the firm in 1948.

Kraftwerk The German rock group, formed in Düsseldorf in 1970, chose a name that is the German word for 'power plant', referring to their electronic synthesizers and their emphasis on the role played by machines in creating music. The group's own nicknames for themselves include *Die Menschenmaschine* ('The Human Machine') and *Klangchemiker* ('Sound Chemists').

Krakatoa The volcanic island in Indonesia, between Java and Sumatra, famously erupted in 1883, destroying most of itself in the process. Its name relates to its fissile nature, from the Malay prefix *ke-* and Javanese *rekatak*, 'to split'.

Kraków The city of southern Poland is said to take its name from one *Krak*, who founded it in the 10th century or even earlier. The meaning of his name is not known.

Krasnodar The city of southwest Russia was originally named *Yekaterinodar* when founded in 1793. This means 'gift of Catherine', and was bestowed in honour of the Russian empress Catherine the Great, with *dar*, 'gift', added. When the town was taken by the Red Army in 1920, its name was changed to *Krasnodar*, from Russian *krasnyy*, 'red' and the same *dar*.

Krasnoyarsk The city in east central Russia, founded in 1628, has a name that means either 'red bank' or 'beautiful bank', Russian *krasnyy* meaning either 'red' or 'beautiful' (*see* RED SQUARE). If 'red', the reference is to the soil here. The 'bank' (Russian *yar*, a word of Turkish origin) is that of the river Yenisei where the original fort was set up in the year mentioned.

Kreisleriana Schumann's piano work, composed in 1838, consists of eight fantasies and is named for the fictional composer Johannes *Kreisler* who features in the story *Kater Murr* ('Tomcat Murr') (1820) by the German writer of fairy tales E.T.A. Hoffmann.

Kremlin The historic citadel in Moscow that is the centre of Russian government has a name that may be related to Russian *kremen'*, 'flint', indicating the material from which the original fort here was built. It remains uncertain to what extent its name and that of the CRIMEA have anything in common. The citadel is not unique to Moscow, and many other cities equally have a *Kremlin*, such as the medieval ones at Novgorod and Pskov. They are almost always on a raised site by a river. The Moscow *Kremlin* was originally known simply as *grad*, 'city', and the name *Kremlin* is not recorded before the 14th century.

Kremlin-Bicêtre The name of this southern suburb of Paris, familiar as a Métro station, is something of a curiosity. The present district dates only from 1894. The first word derives from the name of an inn here, *Au sergeant du Kremlin* ('The Kremlin Sergeant'), relating to Napoleon's invasion of Russia in 1812. The second word is traditionally held to be a distortion of the name of WINCHESTER, referring to the bishop of that city who represented the English sovereign at Paris in the 15th century during the Hundred Years War.

However, a recent authority claims that the name is actually a corruption of Old French *bissexte*, 'bissextile', a word for the extra day in a leap year (*i.e.* 29 February). This day was regarded as unlucky, so that the word came to be used of anything ill-omened. It later developed a special sense to refer to a ruined castle, or to haunted ruins, and this may well have been the original sense here.

Kreutzer Sonata Beethoven's Violin Sonata in A, Op 47 (1802) is so named because he dedicated it to the French violinist Rodolphe *Kreutzer*, who did not appreciate it and apparently never played it.

Krishna The most famous of the Hindu gods, the incarnation of VISHNU, has a name deriving from Sanskrit *kṛṣṇa*, 'black', 'dark'. Krishna's 'blackness' is probably due to his origin in southern India. His body is always dark-coloured in depictions of him and is traditionally compared to the colour of a rain cloud that brings relief from deadly heat. However, 'blackness' also conveys a sense of evil, even to a Hindu. The story of Krishna is told in the MAHABHARATA. *See also* HARE KRISHNA.

Kristiansand The port in southern Norway is named for its founder, King *Christian* (Danish *Kristian*) IV of Denmark and Norway, who built a fort here in 1641. The latter part of the name is Norwegian *sand*, 'sand'. *Cp.* KRISTIANSUND.

Kristianstad The town in southern Sweden was founded in 1614 as a Danish fortress and is named for its founder, King *Christian* (Danish *Kristian*) IV of Denmark and Norway.

Kristiansund The city and port in western Norway was incorporated as a city in 1642 and named for King *Christian* (Danish *Kristian*) IV of Denmark and Norway. The latter part of the name represents Norwegian *sund*, 'strait', 'inlet' (English *sound*). Because of the similarity between its name and that of KRISTIANSAND, it is postally known as *Kristiansund N.* (for *nord*, 'north'), while its near namesake is *Kristiansand S.* (for *sør*, 'south').

Krivoy Rog The Ukrainian city is situated in a wide bend of the river Dnieper, and it is to this that the name refers, as the Russian for 'curved horn', the latter word

291

(Russian *rog*) here more in the sense of 'headland'.

Krk The island at the head of the Adriatic Sea, in northwest Croatia, was known to the Romans as *Curicum*. The origin of the name is unknown, although attempts have been made to link it with *Kerkyra*, the Greek name of CORFU. The Italian name for the island is *Veglia*, as if meaning 'old' (*cp.* modern Italian *vegliardo*, 'very old man'), perhaps comparing the island to the town of *Krk* at its southern end. Modern Italian *veglia* means 'vigil', 'watch', however. The name is pronounced as if 'kirk'.

Kronstadt The Russian port, on an island in the Gulf of Finland, has a name of German origin meaning 'crown city', from *Krone*, 'crown' and *Stadt*, 'town'. This is a part translation, and perhaps also part corruption, of its original Swedish name *Kronslott*, 'crown castle'. The royal reference is to Peter the Great, who set up a defensive fort here in 1704 and converted it into a full fortress in 1723.

Krug The familiar champagne is named for Johann-Joseph *Krug*, a German who founded a champagne business in Reims, France in 1843.

K2 The mountain in northern India is so named as it is in the *K*arakoram Range and is the *second* highest in the world. It was also the *second* to be surveyed in this range. Its alternative name is Mount GODWIN-AUSTEN.

Kuala Lumpur The Malaysian capital has a name meaning 'mouth of the muddy river', from Malay *kuala*, 'mouth', 'estuary' and *lumpur*, 'mud'. The river so designated is the Klang.

Kublai Khan The famous 13th-century Mongol emperor of China who was the grandson of GENGHIS KHAN bore a traditional Mongol name, *Khan* being his title meaning 'ruler'. The Mongols themselves gave him the posthumous title of *Setsen Khan*, 'wise khan', while his Chinese temple name was *Shih-tzu*, 'son of a lion'. His name was widely popularized by Samuel Taylor Coleridge's poem *Kubla Khan* (1816), with its famous opening lines: 'In Xanadu did Kubla Khan/A stately pleasure-dome decree'. (*See also* XANADU.)

Ku Klux Klan The name is that of the familiar secret organization of white Southerners formed in America after the Civil War to fight Northern domination and black emancipation. It subsequently became an organization designed to promote white Protestant supremacy over blacks, Jews, Roman Catholics and essentially anyone who was not a white Protestant. The fanciful, quasi-mystic name is probably based on Greek *kuklos*, 'circle' (giving the first two words) and English *clan*.

Kuku Nor China's largest lake, in the northeast Tibetan Highlands, has a Mongolian name meaning 'blue lake', from *höh*, 'blue' and *nuur*, 'lake'. Its Chinese name of *Qinghai* has the same meaning, from *qīng*, 'blue' and *hǎi*, 'lake'.

Kumamoto The city in southwest Japan, in Kyushu, has a name that represents Japanese *kuma*, 'bear' (the animal) and *moto*, 'origin', 'foundation'.

Kumayri The town in Armenia arose as a medieval or even earlier settlement with a name of obscure origin. In 1837 a fort was built by the village that had developed, and in 1840 the settlement was raised to the status of a town and renamed *Aleksandropol* ('Alexandropolis'), for *Alexandra* (originally Charlotte), wife of Tsar Nicholas I. The final *-pol* represents Greek *polis*, 'town'. The town retained this name until 1924, when it was renamed *Leninakan*, for Lenin. The latter part of the name means 'town', as in similar names of Turkic or related origin, such as SAMARKAND and TASHKENT. In 1990 the town reverted to its original name.

Kunlun The mountain range in China, extending east from the Pamirs, has a name representing Chinese *kūnlún*. The two syllables of this have no meaning apart from the name itself.

Kuomintang The Chinese nationalist party, founded in 1911, has a name that means 'National People's Party' from Chinese *guó*, 'nation', *mín*, 'people' and *dǎng*, 'party'.

Kurds The nomadic people of Turkey, Iraq and Iran have a name that perhaps represents Iranian *kard*, 'active'. They gave the name of *Kurdistan*, 'land of the Kurds', the broad plateau and mountainous region between the Caspian Sea and the Black Sea.

Kuril Islands The chain of islands off the northeast coast of Asia has a name that is uncertain in its origin and meaning. It may derive from an Ainu word *kuri* meaning 'cloud', 'fog'. As the islands are volcanic, an origin in Russian *kurit'*, 'to smoke', has also been suggested. But the islands probably have a name from a local language rather than a mainstream one such as Russian.

Kursk The city in western Russia takes its name from the small river *Kur* here. The river's own name may derive from Finnish *kuru*, 'deep valley'.

Kuwait The state on the northwest coast of the Persian Gulf takes its name from that of its capital, which is identically named and is known in Arabic as *al-kuwait*. This represents a diminutive of *kūt*, which in the dialect of the inhabitants of southern Iraq and the eastern part of the Arabian Peninsula denotes a kind of fortress-like house surrounded by smaller houses and encircled with water, something like a medieval English manor with its outbuildings and moat.

Kuybyshev *See* SAMARA.

Kuzbass The region of western Siberia, the richest coalfield in Russia, has a name that is an abbreviation of *Kuznetskiy ugol'nyy basseyn*, 'KUZNETSK coal basin'. The reference is to the industrial town now called NOVOKUZNETSK. *Cp.* DONBASS.

Kuznetsk The name is both an existing one for a city in east central Russia and the former one of a Siberian city that was renamed NOVOKUZNETSK in order to be distinguished from it. (*See* KUZBASS.) Either way, both are long-established industrial towns, and the reference is to the forge-workers (Russian *kuznetsy*) who set up their trade in each place in the 18th century to exploit iron deposits.

Kwangju The city in southwest South Korea derives its name from Korean *kwang*, 'light', 'brightness' and *chu*, 'province'.

Kwangsi *See* GUANGXI.

Kwangtung *See* GUANGDONG.

Kyle of Lochalsh The Scottish village and port takes its name from the strait (Gaelic *caol*) that is the narrow entrance to Loch *Alsh*. The loch's own name is of uncertain meaning.

Kylie The girl's name is Australian in origin and is probably a blend of *Kyle* and *Kelly*, both originally surnames. It was popularly promoted in the late 1980s by the Australian actress and singer *Kylie* Minogue (1968–).

Kyoto The city of central Japan, on Honshu, has a name that represents Japanese *kyō*, 'capital' and *to*, also 'capital'. Its former name was *heionkyō*, 'capital of calm peace', from *hei*, 'calm', *on*, 'peace' and *kyō*, 'capital'.

Kyushu The southernmost (and westernmost) of Japan's four main islands has a name that means 'nine provinces', from *kyū*, 'nine' and *shū*, 'province', describing its former administrative division. It is now divided into seven prefectures.

Kyzyl Kum The desert in Uzbekistan and Kazakhstan has a Kazakh name meaning 'red sand', from *kyzyl*, 'red' and *küm*, 'sand' (*cp.* KIZIL IRMAK and KARA KUM). The reference is either to the reddish colour of the desert sands or to the former name, *Kzyldarya*, 'red river', of the river now called the Dzhanydarya, an estuarial channel of the SYR DARYA that flows to the east of it into the Aral Sea.

Kzyl-Orda The city of Kazakhstan has a Kazakh name meaning 'red fort' (literally 'red horde'). The designation is a Communist one. From 1853 to 1925 it was called *Perovsk*, for General *Perovsky* who commanded the troops that captured the fortified settlement here, itself founded in 1820 and originally named *Ak Mechet*, from the Turkish words for 'white mosque'. *Cp.* SIMFEROPOL.

L

Laban In the Old Testament, the father-in-law of Jacob and father of Leah and Rachel has a name of Hebrew origin, representing *Lābhān*, from *lavan*, 'white'. *Cp.* LEBANON.

Labor Day In the United States and Canada, the name is that of the public holiday, federally adopted in 1894, that is held on the first Monday in September in special recognition of working people, or *labour*. A similar holiday of the same name is held in Australia on different days in different states. *Cp.* LABOUR DAY.

Labour The British *Labour Party* was formed in 1900 from various trade unions and socialist groups with the aim of serving the interests of *labour* (in the sense of productive work and the people involved in it), and adopted its name in 1906. The name already existed for similar parties elsewhere.

Labour Day The name is that of the public holiday held in many countries in special recognition of working people, or *labour*, usually on 1 May. This particular date was probably chosen because it was on 1 May 1889 that the Second International first proposed a workers' festival for all countries. Labour Day in Britain has been marked by the May Day bank holiday (the first Monday in May) since 1978. *Cp.* LABOR DAY.

Labrador It is generally agreed that the source of the name of the northeast region of Canada is in Portuguese *lavrador*, 'labourer', although the reason for the name remains disputed. One theory claims that when the Italian-born navigator John Cabot came here in 1498 he named the land for a Portuguese sailor, João Fernandes, who had already visited the region and described it, and who was known as *o lavrador*, 'the farmer', as he had a smallholding in the Azores. Another account attributes the name to the Portuguese navigator Gaspar Côrte-Real, who reached the peninsula in 1501 and named it *Terra de lavradores*, 'land of labourers' for the people he had seen tilling the soil here.

Labyrinth In Greek mythology, the *Labyrinth* was the huge maze in Crete that Daedalus built for King Minos to house the Minotaur. The name is probably pre-Greek in origin, and its meaning is uncertain. According to Plutarch, it was based on the Lydian word *labrys* meaning 'double-headed axe', this being the royal symbol often found in palace remains in Minoan Crete. The original Labyrinth was said to have been at Knossos.

Lacedaemonia The ancient Greek name for SPARTA is certainly related to that of LACONIA, its Latin equivalent, although in what way is uncertain. It is tempting to see Greek *daimōn*, 'demon' in the name, although again the reason for such a reference is unclear.

Lacey The name is Norman in origin, indicating a person from *Lassy* near Caen, with this place-name in turn deriving from the Gaulish personal name *Lascius*. *See also* KINGSTON LACY, POLESDEN LACEY.

Lachesis *See* FATES.

Lachlan The river in southeast Australia was discovered in 1815 by the British explorer George William Evans, who named it for *Lachlan* Macquarie (1761–1824), governor of New South Wales. The name is pronounced 'Locklen'.

Laconia The ancient country of southern Greece took its name from its indigenous inhabitants. However, the origin and meaning of their own name is unfortunately unknown.

Lada The popular make of Russian car takes its name from a Russian folk word meaning 'spouse', 'beloved'.

Ladakh The region of Kashmir, mostly in India, has a name that represents Tibetan *ladag*, 'land of passes', from *la*, 'pass', 'col' and *dag*, 'pleasant', 'open'.

Ladbrokes The well-known chain of betting agents takes its name from *Ladbroke Hall*, the Warwickshire home of Harry Schwind, racehorse trainer and cofounder of the firm (with a Mr Pennington) in the 1880s. The irony of a name that outwardly suggests *lads* who go *broke* is fortunately lost on most punters.

Ladd The name was originally an occupational one for a servant, and did not have its present sense of 'boy', 'young man' until much later.

Ladies' Plate The *Ladies' Challenge Plate* is one of the leading awards at the annual Henley Royal Regatta, although it is not for women's crews, as the name seems to suggest. It was first offered in 1845 as a new challenge prize for eight-oared crews by the local *ladies* of Henley. Hence the name. The Regatta itself was established in 1839.

Ladoga, Lake The large lake in northwest Russia has a name of Finnish origin, from *aallokko*, 'sea swell', 'waves', itself from *aalto* 'wave'. The lake is noted for its squalls and storms, especially in autumn, when the waves can be nearly 20 feet (6 m) high.

Ladybird The brand of children's clothing, manufactured by Pasolds, is said to be so named because Johann Adam Päsold, an 18th-century Czech master weaver and ancestor of the firm's chairman in Britain, Eric Pasold, had had a dream in which a ladybird had revealed the secret of frame knitting.

Lady Day In the Christian calendar, the name is in alternative use for the feast (on 25 March) of the ANNUNCIATION of the Virgin Mary, that is, of *Our Lady*. The original name actually was *Our Lady Day*, and was given not just to the feast of her Annunciation but also to those of her Conception (8 December), Nativity (8 September) and ASSUMPTION (15 August).

Lady Eleanor Holles School The public day school for girls at Hampton, Middlesex, was founded in 1711 under the will of *Lady Eleanor Holles*, the unmarried daughter of John Holles, second Earl of Clare. It was originally in Cripplegate, London, and was a Church of England foundation, although it is now non-denominational.

Lady Margaret Hall The Oxford college, founded in 1878 to provide higher education for women within the traditions of the Church of England, was named for *Lady Margaret* Beaufort (1443–1509), wife of Edmund Tudor, Earl of Richmond, mother of Henry VII, and a noted patron of learning. She had herself founded CHRIST'S COLLEGE and ST JOHN'S COLLEGE, Cambridge.

Ladysmith The city in Natal, South Africa, besieged by the Boers in the Boer War, was founded in 1847 and originally named *Windsor*, after a local trader. It was renamed for *Lady Smith*, née Juana Maria de los Dolores de León, wife of Sir Harry Smith (1787–1860), governor of the Cape Colony. She also gave her name to the town of *Ladismith*, Cape Province, while her husband's name is preserved in *Harrismith*, Orange Free State, and that of his birthplace (and place of burial), Whittlesey in Cambridgeshire, in *Whittlesea*, Ciskei. The town of *Aliwal* North, Cape Province, is named for Smith's victory over the Sikhs at Aliwal, India, in 1846.

Laertes The name of the father of Odysseus is said to mean 'people-urger' from Greek *laos*, 'people' and a basic root element *er*, 'to urge on' to which Greek *ergon*, 'work' and modern English *urge* itself are ultimately related. Laertes' name appears in the Linear B tablets at Knossos as *Law-er-tas*.

Laetitia The name is the original Latin form of LETTICE, so means 'joy', 'happiness'.

Lagonda The make of car takes its name from *Lagonda* Creek, Ohio, the home of its original manufacturer, the American Wilbur Gunn, who came to England to make tricars at Staines, Middlesex. He produced his first four-wheel car in 1907.

Lagos The former capital of Nigeria was given its name by Portuguese colonists, who landed here in 1472. The coast here has many lagoons, and this prompted the settlers to name it *Lagos*, 'lakes', partly descriptively but also with reference to the harbour of *Lagos* in southern Portugal.

La Guardia Airport New York's main airport for internal flights, in northern Queens, was named for Fiorello Henry *La Guardia* (1882–1947), three times mayor of New York City, famous for his campaign of slum clearance and fight against corruption. The airport is now integrated with KENNEDY Airport.

Lahore The city in northeast Pakistan has a name that is traditionally derived from that of its legendary founder *Lo*, whose Sanskrit name was *lava*. *See also* LAOS.

Lahti The town in southern Finland was founded in 1905 on a bay of Lake Vesijärvi and was simply named with the Finnish word for 'bay'.

Lake Poets The collective literary nickname is that of the poets Wordsworth, Coleridge and Southey, who lived in and were inspired by the *Lake* District in the early 19th century.

Lakshadweep Islands The islands off the southwest coast of India, formerly more familiar as the *Laccadives*, derive their name from Sanskrit *laksa dvīpa*, 'hundred thousand islands', from *laksa*, 'hundred thousand' and *dvīpa*, 'island'. This number is a vast exaggeration, and there are in fact only 26 coral islands and reefs.

Lakshmi The Hindu goddess of wealth, fortune and beauty, wife of Vishnu, has a name that represents Sanskrit *Laksmī*, 'sign', 'portent', 'happiness'. Her other name is SRI (*which see*).

Lalage The name is classical in origin, and was used by Horace in one of his *Odes* for his beloved. It was not her real name, but was a pseudonym, from Greek *lalagein*, 'to babble', 'to prattle', presumably intended as a compliment rather than a criticism. The name is usually pronounced in three syllables with either a hard or soft *g*.

La Línea The town in southwest Spain, on the frontier with Gibraltar, has a name that is Spanish for 'the line', referring to this boundary.

Lalla Rookh The name of the Mogul emperor's daughter who is the central character of the oriental tales by Thomas Moore, published in 1817, means 'tulip face', from Hindi *lāla*, 'tulip' and *rukh*, 'face'. The reference is to a delicate complexion, with rosy cheeks.

La Mancha The plateau of central Spain, associated with the adventures of Don Quixote, has a name of Arabic origin, from *mansa*, 'dry land', from *nassa*, 'to be dry'. Rather misleadingly, modern Spanish *la mancha* means 'the spot', 'the mark'. *See also* ENGLISH CHANNEL.

Lamb The name originally applied either to a person who kept lambs or to someone who was 'meek and mild', like a lamb. In some instances the name could also represent a short form of LAMBERT.

Lambert The name derives from a Germanic personal name, comprising *lant*, 'land' and *beraht*, 'bright', 'famous', implying a noted landowner.

Lambeth The district of London, on the south bank of the Thames, has a name that relates directly to the river, meaning 'landing-place for lambs', from Old English *lamb*, 'lamb' and *hȳth*, 'landing-place'. The original word for 'landing-place' is fairly well disguised here, although it is even more so for CHELSEA and PUTNEY.

Lamborghini The well-known make of sports car takes its name from Ferruccio *Lamborghini* (1916–), an Italian manufacturer of tractors and heating equipment who in 1963 produced the first car to have his name at a specially built factory near Modena.

Lambretta The familiar make of motorscooter takes its name from *Lambrate*, the district of Milan in Italy where it was first produced in 1947.

Lamentations The book of the Old Testament, ascribed to the prophet Jeremiah, is so named as it *laments* the destruction of Jerusalem by the Babylonians in the 6th century BC. *See also* WAILING WALL.

Lamentation Symphony Haydn's Symphony No 26 in D minor (late 1760s) is so nicknamed because some of its themes suggest the plainsong chants sung in Roman Catholic churches in Holy Week.

Lamia Keats's poem of 1820 tells (or retells) one of the stories connected with the female monster of Greek mythology, half serpent and half woman, who fed on the flesh of children. Her name is traditionally derived from Greek *laimos*, 'throat', referring to the latter attribute.

Lammas The name is that of the former English harvest festival held on 1 August, when loaves of bread made from the first ripe corn were consecrated. Its derivation thus lies in Old English *hlæfmæsse*, 'loaf mass'. For Roman Catholics, the name and day are those of the *Festum Sancti Petri ad Vincula*, the feastday when the miraculous deliverance of St Peter from prison is celebrated. The calendar date for the latter coincides with the harvest festival purely by chance, and was that of the dedication of the church of S. Pietro in Vincoli ('St Peter in Chains') in Rome. (The chains that originally bound St Peter are said to be preserved in this church.)

Lampeter The town of southwest Wales has a name that represents its Welsh name of *Llanbedr*, 'St Peter's church'. Despite this dedication, Lampeter is best known for St David's College, of the University of Wales.

Lanark The Scottish town has a Celtic name that in modern terms can be seen in Welsh *llannerch*, 'glade'. This is therefore the original meaning.

Lancashire The county of northwest England takes its name from its county town of LANCASTER, as if 'Lancastershire'.

Lancaster The county town of LANCASHIRE is on the river *Lune*, and this is represented in the first half of its name. The latter half represents Old English *ceaster*, ultimately from Latin *castra*, 'camp', showing that Lancaster was a Roman encampment. The river's own name is probably Celtic in origin, meaning 'healthy one'.

Lancaster House The grand house in central London, used mainly for government conferences, was originally known as *York House*, after Frederick, Duke of *York*, who came to live here in 1807. In 1912 it was bought by Sir William Lever, the future Lord Leverhulme, who renamed it *Lancaster House* after his native county and who the following year presented it to the nation. The houses of *York* and *Lancaster* were opposed in the Wars of the Roses, and doubtless Lord Leverhulme aimed to choose a name that 'scored' for his own particular 'house'.

Lancelot The name of the famous trusted Knight of the Round Table, subsequently the lover of King Arthur's wife, Queen Guinevere, is probably of Celtic origin, like the names of most other characters in the Arthurian romances. However, through French versions of the stories it has become associated with a form of *l'ancelle*, from Latin *ancillus*, 'servant', or with Latin *lancea*, 'lance', as befits a knight.

Lancia The familiar make of car is named for its designer and manufacturer, Vincenzo *Lancia* (1881–1937), a soup merchant's son who became a racing driver and who in 1906 set up his motor business in Turin. The first car of his name was produced two years later.

Landerneau The town in Brittany, northwest France, has a name that means 'place of *Ternok*', this being the name of a local saint. Breton place-names beginning *Lan-* correspond to Cornish ones in *Lan-* (such as *Lanhydrock*, '*Hydrek*'s place') and to Welsh ones in *Llan-* (such as LLANDUDNO). The element usually denotes the site of a church, and is frequently followed by a saint's name, as here.

Landes The region of southwest France has a name that goes back to Gaulish *landa*, 'enclosure', 'land', with this word directly related both to the Welsh *llan*, 'church', that begins many Welsh place-names and to English *land* itself. *See also* LANDERNEAU.

Land-Rover The well-known four-wheel drive vehicle was first produced by the ROVER Company in 1948. Its name refers to its original purpose, which was to provide farmers with a cheap, sturdy vehicle that could travel almost everywhere over their *land*. *Cp.* RANGE ROVER.

Land's End The most westerly point of England, in Cornwall, has a self-descriptive name, although 'land' here has more the sense of 'mainland'. The name has its parallel in those of FINISTÈRE in France and PEMBROKE in Wales.

Lane The name was originally used of someone who lived in or by a lane, this being at first a narrow passage between hedges, then a narrow path of any kind, including one between houses in a town.

Langford The name denotes a person who came from one of the many places so called. The place-name means 'long ford', that is, a ford that crosses a river obliquely or that approaches it by a causeway.

Langham Hotel The well-known London hotel takes its name from its location in *Langham* Place, itself named for Sir James *Langham*, landowner here in the early 19th century. The Langham Hotel opened in 1864 but passed to the nearby BBC after the Second World War for use as offices and studios. In 1991 it once again became a hotel.

Langley The name originally applied to anyone who lived in or near a long wood or clearing, or who came from one of the many places named *Langley* with this meaning.

Languedoc The historic province of southern France has a name that represents French *langue d'oc*, 'language of *oc*', *oc* being the word for 'yes' in the south of France, as distinct from *oïl*, in the north, where they spoke the *langue d'oïl*. The word *oc* came from Latin *hoc*, 'this', while *oïl* came from *hoc ille (fecit)*, 'this he (did)'. It was the latter word that gave modern French *oui* (not the archaic verb *ouïr*, 'to hear', as sometimes stated).

Lansing The state capital of Michigan was founded in 1847 and named by settlers from the village of *Lansing*, New York, which had itself been named for the politician and lawyer John *Lansing* (1754–1829).

Lanzhou The city in northern China has a name that derives from Chinese *lán*, 'orchid' and *zhōu*, 'region'.

Laocoön In Greek mythology *Laocoön* was a priest of Apollo who warned the Trojans about the wooden horse left by the Greeks, and who was killed, with his twin sons, by two sea serpents. His name may derive from Greek *laos*, 'people' and *koinos*, 'common', 'shared', so that in some sense he was 'common to the people' or perhaps 'of the common people'.

Laodicea The name is that of several ancient Greek cities, but in particular the

one that is modern *Latakia*, the chief port of Syria. In each case the name goes back to that of *Laodice*, the 3rd-century BC Syrian queen who was the wife of Antiochus II. Her own name means literally 'people ruler', in other words amounts to 'queen'.

Laois The name of the Irish county, formerly anglicized as *Leix*, derives from the personal name *Lugaid Laigne*, that of the legendary Irish king whose descendants were granted lands here. The name is pronounced approximately 'Layish'.

Laomedon The name of the founder and ruler of Troy, who was also the father of Priam, derives from Greek *laos*, 'people' and *medōn*, 'ruler', so that he was a virtual 'king'.

Laon The town in northern France was known to the Romans as both *Laodunum* and *Lugdunum*. The latter was also the Roman name of LYON, so that both places appear to have a name of identical origin.

Laos The republic of southeast Asia derives its name from that of its legendary founder, *Lao*, whose own name may have the same origin as that of *Lo* (*see* LAHORE). The Laotians' own name for their land is *Pathet Lao*, 'country of Lao', from Pali *padesa*, itself from Sanskrit *pradeśa* (*see* ANDHRA PRADESH).

La Paz The Bolivian city, the country's seat of government (though not its capital), has a Spanish name meaning 'the peace'. This is all that remains from its original name of *Ciudad de Nuestra Señora de la Paz*, 'City of Our Lady of Peace', given it in 1548 on its foundation by the Spanish conquistador Captain Alonso de Mendoza.

Laphroaig The blend of Scotch whisky takes its name from the village on the island of Islay where its distillery opened on a farm in 1815. The name is pronounced 'Lafroig'.

Lapiths The semi-legendary, semi-historical people of Thessaly derive their name from the Pelasgian root word *lap* or *lep*, meaning 'rock'. They were thus mountain dwellers, whether in fact or fiction.

Lapland The Arctic region of northern Europe is named for its native dwellers, the *Lapps*, whose own name may go back to a root word meaning either 'solitary' or 'frontier', referring to a remote people.

Lapsang Souchong The variety of China tea, noted for its slightly smoky flavour, has a name that consists of an arbitrary commercial word followed by Chinese *xiǎo*, 'small' and *zhǒng*, 'sort'.

Laptev Sea The arm of the Arctic Ocean on the northern coast of Russia takes its name from the Russian explorer cousins Dmitri and Khariton *Laptev*, who led a lengthy Arctic expedition over the period 1739–42. The sea has borne the name only since 1913. An earlier name was *Nordenskjöld Sea*, after the Swedish Arctic explorer Nils *Nordenskjöld*, who discovered it in 1878.

Laputa The imaginary flying island inhabited by absurd scientists in Jonathan Swift's *Gulliver's Travels* (1726) has a name that was given a mock derivation by Swift himself, in the process satirizing the classical scholar Richard Bentley:

> The Word, which I interpret the *Flying* or *Floating Island*, is in the Original *Laputa*; whereof I could never learn the true Etymology. *Lap* in the old obsolete Language signifieth *High*, and *Untuh* a *Governor*; from which they say by Corruption was derived *Laputa* from *Lapuntuh*. But I do not approve of this Derivation, which seems to be a little strained. I ventured to offer to the Learned among them a Conjecture of my own, that *Laputa* was *quasi Lap outed*; *Lap* signifying properly the dancing of the Sun Beams in the Sea; and *outed* a Wing, which however I shall not obtrude, but submit to the judicious Reader.
>
> Part III, Chapter 2.

It has been suggested that the name actually represents Spanish *la puta*, 'the whore', with reference to the proverb 'Beware of the whore, who leaves the purse empty'. In the context of the novel this could be an allusion to England's impoverishment of Ireland. As Laputa itself satirizes scientists and academics, there could equally be a suggestion of Latin *putare*, 'to think', implying a 'land of thinkers'. At the same time, the name is somewhat similar to that of the novel's other famous fictional island, LILLIPUT.

La Retraite School The public day school for girls in Salisbury, Wiltshire, was founded in 1911 under the original name of *Leehurst*. In 1953 it was taken over by the nuns of *La Retraite* Roman Catholic convent, and adopted that name instead. The French name means 'the retreat', in the religious sense of the word for a place of seclusion and prayer.

Largactil The anti-depressant drug has a name that was chosen to represent French *large activité*, 'broad activity', denoting the essential feature of its main ingredient, chlorpromazine, defined by its manufacturers as the 'extreme diversity of its pharmacodynamic activities'.

Large The name originally applied to a generous person, either approvingly or ironically. It would not have been used for a 'big' or fat person, as this sense of the word developed only later.

Lark Quartet Haydn's String Quartet in D major, Op 64 No 5 (1790) is so named because of the soaring violin theme of its opening bars.

La Rochelle The port in western France had the Latin name of *Rupella* in the 10th century, from *rupes*, 'cave'. By the 12th century this had become a more meaningful *Rochella*, and so was associated with French *roche*, 'rock'.

La Sagesse Convent High School The name of the public school for girls in Newcastle upon Tyne is almost self-explanatory. It was founded in 1906 by Roman Catholic nuns from the Congregation of *La Sagesse* at Gateshead, and took the name of their convent. The school moved from Gateshead to its present location in 1912. The French name means 'the wisdom' in the sense of the holy wisdom of God.

La Scala The famous opera house in Milan was originally named *Teatro alla Scala* when opening in 1778, as it was built on the site of the former church of S. Maria *alla Scala* ('St Mary at the Stairway').

Las Palmas The port in the central Canary Islands has a straightforward descriptive name, from the Spanish for 'the palm-trees', which are plentiful here.

Las Vegas The city in Nevada, famous for its luxury hotels and casinos, has a name that is Spanish for 'the meadows'. Mormon settlers were drawn here in 1855 by the artesian wells in the dry valleys along the Old Spanish Trail.

Latakia *See* LAODICEA.

Lateran Palace The palace in Rome was the former official residence of the popes and gave its name to the ecumenical councils of the Roman Catholic church held here in medieval times. The palace earlier belonged to the ancient Roman family Plautii *Laterani* and is named for them. They themselves were named after the locality, whose own name may be related to that of LATIUM.

Latimer The name was originally an occupational one for a *latiner*, that is, for a person who kept records in Latin, which in medieval times was the regular language for official documents.

Latin The famous ancient language of Rome takes its name from its original speakers, the *Latini*, who inhabited LATIUM from the 10th century BC.

Latin America The name is used for those countries and regions of Central and South America (and also Mexico) where Spanish and Portuguese are spoken. These are Romance languages, derived from *Latin*.

Latin Quarter The area of Paris south of the Seine is noted for its educational establishments and as a centre for students and artists. In medieval times it was the site of the University of Paris where *Latin* was spoken. Hence its name. The district basically corresponds to the LEFT BANK.

Latium The ancient territory of western Italy, originally a small area southwest of Rome, may have derived its name from Latin *latus*, 'broad', 'wide', with reference to the plain of the lower Tiber here. Whatever the case, it was this territory that gave the world the word (and language) LATIN. Its historic name is preserved today in that of the much larger region of *Lazio*.

Latvia The Baltic republic is named after its people, the *Letts*, whose own name is of uncertain origin. There may well be a link between their name and that of neighbouring *Lithuania*.

Latymer Upper School The London public day school for boys takes its name from Edward *Latymer*, an official of the Crown, who in his will of 1624 made provision for the education of a small number of boys and men of Hammersmith. The boys first attended a school in Fulham, then in 1648 moved to a school specially built for them in Hammersmith, A new school was built in Hammersmith Road in 1863 and was known as *Latymer Lower School* until 1963 when it closed. *Latymer Upper School* had meanwhile been opened in 1895 to provide secondary education, and now is the sole school with the Latymer name except for GODOLPHIN AND LATYMER SCHOOL. Perhaps appropriately for an academic establishment, the name *Latymer* originally applied to a learned clerk who knew *Latin* (*see* LATIMER).

Laura The name is a feminine form of the Late Latin name *Laurus*, 'laurel'.

Laurasia The name of the ancient supercontinent, comprising what are now North America, Greenland, Europe and Asia (apart from India), derives from New Latin *Laurentia*, as a name for ancient North America, and ASIA. *Laurentia* is named for the ST LAWRENCE river.

Laurence The name ultimately derives from the Latin name *Laurentius*, 'man of *Laurentum*', this being a city of Latium, Italy, southwest of Rome. Its own name may derive from Latin *laurus*, 'laurel'.

Lausanne The Swiss city, on the northern shore of Lake Geneva, probably derives its name from Gaulish *leusa*, 'flat rock' and *onna*, 'river', although an alternative theory sees the present name as a corruption of its Roman name *Lausodunum*, meaning 'fort on the (river) *Laus*', with the river name itself meaning 'stony'. There has never been a river of any size here.

Laval University The well-known Canadian university, in Quebec, was founded in 1663 as the *Seminary of Quebec* by François *Laval* (1623–1708), the first Roman Catholic bishop in Canada. Its original function was thus as a training school for priests and a home for retired priests. Laval himself spent his final years at the Seminary, which in 1852 became a university and was named commemoratively for him.

300

Lavengro The name of the novel by George Borrow, subtitled *The Scholar, The Gypsy, The Priest* and published in 1851, is the Romany word for 'philologist'. It was the nickname given Borrow himself in his youth by Ambrose Smith, who features in the book as the Gypsy Jasper Petulengro:

'We'll no longer call you Sap-engro [Snake Master], brother,' said he, 'but rather Lav-engro, which in the language of the Gorgios meaneth Word Master'.

Chapter 17.

Lavinia In Roman mythology, the name is that of the daughter of Latinus and wife of Aeneas, and so that of the mother of the Roman people. It has been derived from the ancient city of *Lavinium*, in Latium, south of Rome, but was almost certainly devised to explain it. Her father's name had been similarly invented to explain the origin of LATIUM.

Law The surname has nothing to do with a legal occupation, but was either a short form of *Lawrence* (*see* LAURENCE) or was used for a person who lived on or near a hill, an Old English word for which was *hlāw* (*cp.* LEWES).

Lazarus The name is that of two different people in the New Testament: the brother of Martha and Mary who is raised from the dead by Jesus, and the beggar who features in the parable of Dives and *Lazarus*. The name is Hebrew in origin, from *El'āzār*, 'God has helped'.

Lazio *See* LATIUM.

Lea and Perrins The well-known make of Worcester sauce is named for its inventors in 1835, the Worcester druggist John Wheeley *Lea* (1791–1874) and the Evesham chemist William *Perrins* (1793–1867).

Leah The elder daughter of Laban and first wife of Jacob has a name that has been traditionally derived from Hebrew *le'ah*, 'gazelle'.

Leamington The Warwickshire town derives its name from the river *Lean* on which it stands, with the river's own name meaning 'elm river'. The final *-ton*, as in so many English names, represents Old English *tūn*, 'farm', 'village' (modern *town*). The full formal title of the town is *Royal Leamington Spa*, referring to its medicin-ally beneficial springs, with the regal prefix granted in 1838 by Queen Victoria, after she had visited Leamington.

Leander The hero of Greek legend who nightly swam across the Hellespont to visit his beloved Hero, but who drowned one night in a storm, has a name that means 'lion man', from Greek *leōn*, 'lion' and *anēr*, genitive *andros*, 'man'.

Leatherhead The Surrey town on the river Mole has a name of Celtic origin (not Old English, as previously thought), meaning 'grey ford', from words with counterparts in modern Welsh *llwyd*, 'grey' and *rhyd*, 'ford'. This interpretation was deduced (as recently as 1980) from a 9th-century record of the town's name as *Leodridan*.

Lebanon The Middle East country has a name of Hebrew origin, from *lavan*, 'white', referring to the snowy peaks of its many mountains. The same root word gave the name of LABAN in the Old Testament.

Le Bourget The Paris airport takes its name from the locality in which it arose, itself meaning 'little settlement', ultimately from Low Latin *burgus*, to which modern French *bourg* and English *borough* are related.

Lec The familiar make of refrigerator has an acronymic name representing the initials of its original manufacturers, the *L*ongford *E*ngineering *C*ompany, founded in Longford Road, Bognor Regis, Sussex, in 1942, and still based in that seaside town. The name fortuitously suggests 'electricity'.

Leda The name is that of the queen of Sparta in Greek mythology who was ravished by Zeus in the form of a swan and who subsequently gave birth to two eggs, from which hatched two sets of twins, respectively Helen and Hermione and Castor and Pollux. It is said to derive from a Lycian word meaning simply 'woman'.

Led Zeppelin The British heavy metal band, formed in 1968, took their name from a turn of phrase frequently used by Keith Moon, drummer of The Who, who would say of a gig that flopped, 'it went down like a lead Zeppelin' (instead of the more usual 'like a lead balloon'). Guitarist Jimmy Page liked the expression, dropped the *a* from

301

lead (either deliberately or in ignorance), and adopted the phrase as the name of the group.

Lee The familiar name originally applied to someone who lived near a meadow or wood, or in a clearing in a wood, the Old English word for which was *lēah*. *Cp.* LEES.

Lee Cooper The make of jeans is named for its manufacturer after the Second World War, Harold *Cooper*, who prefaced his own name with *Lee*, a simplified spelling of the maiden name of his wife, Daphne *Leigh*.

Leeds The well-known Yorkshire city has a name that was originally that of the region here, itself deriving from a people who lived by what is now the river Aire. The river must then have been called something like *Lāt*, itself of Celtic origin meaning 'flowing'. *Leeds* thus means 'place of the people who live by the *Lāt*'. The original river name has been preserved in the villages of *Ledsham* and *Ledston*, both by the Aire southeast of Leeds.

Leeds Castle The moated medieval castle in Kent has a name that is quite unrelated to that of the north of England city. It comes from the village of *Leeds* nearby, whose own name derives from that of the brook on which it lies, in turn representing a conjectural Old English word *hlȳde*, 'loud one'.

Leek The Staffordshire town has a name that means simply 'brook', from Old Norse *lǽkr*, to which modern English *leak* is related. The reference is to the stream that flows through the town as a tributary of the nearby river Churnet.

Lees The name originally applied to a person who lived in or near meadows, or by woods, in either case from a word ultimately deriving from Old English *lēah*, 'wood', 'clearing'. *Cp.* LEE.

Leeuwarden The first part of the name of the city in the northern Netherlands is probably a personal name in origin. The second part may mean 'hill of refuge'. The city's Frisian name is *Ljouwert*.

Leeward Islands There are three groups of islands of the name, one in the West Indies, another in the South Pacific in French Polynesia, and the third extending west-

ward from Hawaii. In each case the name implies that the islands are sheltered from the prevailing wind. In the case of the Caribbean group, this means the northeasterly trade winds, although the Leeward Islands are hardly protected from these. The description is more accurate in the original Spanish use, which applied the name *Leeward Islands* to the Greater Antilles (mainly Cuba, Jamaica, Puerto Rico and Hispaniola), and *Windward Islands* to the Lesser Antilles (the remainder, including both the present Windwards *and* Leewards).

Left Bank The name is that of the area frequented by students and artists south of the Seine in Paris, otherwise the LATIN QUARTER. The *left* bank of a river is the one lying to one's left as one faces downstream. Students of the Left Bank came to be noted for their 'progressive' intellectual views, so that the name has subconsciously come to be associated with the political *left*. The English name translates French *rive gauche*. London's cultural equivalent is the *South Bank* complex, with its theatres and concert halls.

Leghorn *See* LIVORNO.

Lego The famous make of toy building bricks has a name that was devised in the 1930s for the wooden toys manufactured by a Danish carpenter, Ole Kirk Christiansen. It represents the Danish words *leg godt*, 'play well'. It also happens to be the Latin word for 'I collect', 'I read' and Greek for 'I lay in order', 'I arrange'. In 1968 the miniature 'town' of *Legoland* was constructed entirely out of Lego bricks near the company's headquarters at Billund, Denmark.

Le Havre The port in northern France was founded by Francis I in 1517 as *Le-Havre-de-Grâce*, 'the harbour of grace', taking its name from the chapel already here called *Notre-Dame-de-Grâce*, 'Our Lady of Grace'.

Leica The internationally known make of camera takes its name from the German company that first manufactured it in 1924, the *Leitz* Optical Works, with the first two letters of '*camera*' added. The company was itself named for its founder, Ernst B. *Leitz*.

Leicester The latter half of the name of the well-known city indicates that it was a Roman station, from Old English *ceaster*, 'Roman camp'. In names of this type the first part of the name is often based on that of the river on which the place stands. In the case of Leicester, however, this is the Soar, which does not fit. The reference is thus probably to the small stream called the *Leire* that is a tributary of the Soar. Its own name, of unknown origin, then passed to the people who lived here. Leicester's name overall thus means 'Roman camp at the place of the people who lived by the Leire'.

Leicester Square The familiar London square takes its name from Robert Sidney, second Earl of *Leicester*, who acquired the land here in the first half of the 17th century.

Leiden The city of the western Netherlands, also spelled *Leyden*, has a name of Germanic origin, from *leitha*, 'canal', a word that is related to modern English *lead* (in the sense 'conduct'). Leiden is on a canal that leads to the North Sea.

Leila The name is Arabic in origin, meaning 'night', describing a dark-haired or dark-skinned person. Through literary characters of the name, such as *Leila* in Byron's *The Giaour* (1813) and Lord Lytton's novel *Leila* (1838), it has come to be regarded as the name of a typical eastern 'dusky beauty'.

Leinster The former province of eastern Ireland has a name that means 'place of the *Lagin*', these being a Celtic people who probably came to Ireland in the 3rd century BC. Their own name may relate to modern Irish *laighean*, 'spear', so that they were the 'spear folk'. The final part of the name represents Irish *tír*, 'land', as for MUNSTER and ULSTER. *See also* TYRONE.

Leipzig The city of eastern Germany has a name of Slavic origin, from *lipa*, 'lime-tree', showing that the Slavs formerly had territory extending this far west and that lime-trees were a special feature here. *Cp.* Latvia's LIEPAJA, Russia's LIPETSK and Berlin's UNTER DEN LINDEN.

Leitrim The county of Northern Ireland takes its name from the village of *Leitrim*, whose own name represents Irish *Liatroim*, 'grey ridge'.

Le Mans The city in northwest France, famous for its annual motor race, was originally named *Celmans*, a reduced form of *Cenomannis*. This was the capital of the Gallic people known as the *Cenomani*, whose own name may represent Gaulish *cen*, 'peak' and *mano*, 'man'. The initial *cel-* of *Celmans* was subsequently taken as a form of the demonstrative pronoun *celui*, which itself became confused with the definite article *le*. Hence the present form of the name. *See also* CREMONA.

Lemnos The Greek island in the north Aegean Sea has a name of Phoenician origin meaning 'white' (*cp.* LEBANON). The Phoenician sailors must have been impressed by the pale-coloured volcanic rock here.

Lemon The surname has no connection with *lemon* the fruit, as that is a word of Arabic origin. It derives from the archaic word *leman* meaning 'lover', 'sweetheart', from Old English *lēof*, 'dear', 'beloved' and *mann*, 'man'. (It occurs in Shakespeare, as in Sir Andrew Aguecheek's query to Feste in *Twelfth Night*: 'I sent thee sixpence for thy leman: hadst it?') This could either have been a nickname or a personal name, the latter usually in the form *Lefman*.

Lemuel In the Bible, *Lemuel* is a wise king and composer of proverbs (those in *Proverbs* 31.1–9, mainly about drink, are attributed to him). His name derives from Hebrew *Lemū'ēl*, 'devoted to God'. In literature the name is famous as that of *Lemuel* Gulliver, hero of Swift's *Gulliver's Travels* (1726). *See also* GULLIVER.

Lemuria The name is that given to the lost land which was believed to connect Madagascar with India and Sumatra in ancient times and which is now covered by the Indian Ocean. It derives from the *Lemures*, the people who are thought to have inhabited it. Their own name represents that of the *lemures*, the ghosts or spirits of the dead in Roman religion. At the same time the name has been linked with the *lemur*, the small animal so named because of the ghost-like appearance of its face and its nocturnal habits. Lemurs and related animals such as the maki and aye-aye are found not only in Madagascar but also in Malaysia, and the missing continent was at one time held to account for the presence of the animal in both widely separated lands. Their distribution is now usually explained, however, through the geological theory of plate tectonics.

Lena The lengthy Siberian river has a name that may represent Evenki *yelyuyon*, 'river'.

Leninabad *See* KHODZHENT.

Leninakan *See* KUMAYRI.

Leningrad *See* ST PETERSBURG.

Leningrad Symphony Shostakovich's Symphony No 7 in C major, Op 60 (1941) is so named as it was composed during the Siege of *Leningrad*.

Lennox The Scottish name derives from the place so called, now a district near Dunbarton. The place-name itself probably derives from Gaelic *leamhan*, 'elm-tree'.

Lent The period of 40 weekdays from Ash Wednesday to Easter Eve, observed by Christians as a time of penance and fasting, and commemorating the 40 days' fast of Jesus in the wilderness, takes its name from the Old English word *lencten*, 'spring', that is, the time of year when the hours of daylight *lengthen*.

Lenthéric The brand of perfume is named for the French hairdresser Guillaume *Lenthéric* (d. 1912), who in 1875 opened his salon in the Rue St Honoré, Paris, where he came to create exclusive perfumes for his fashionable clientele.

Leo The name for a lion in children's stories and elsewhere is simply the Latin word for 'lion'.

León The region and former kingdom of northwest Spain is said to derive its name from Latin *legio septima*, 'seventh legion', the military force who occupied its capital when it was a Roman encampment, with *León* representing Latin *legio*, genitive *legionis*.

Leonard The name is of Germanic origin and means 'strong lion', from *leon*, 'lion' and *hart*, 'hardy', 'strong'.

Leopold The name, of Germanic origin, means 'brave people', from *liut*, 'people' and *bald*, 'bold', 'brave'.

Lepanto The port of western Greece has an Italian name representing its original Greek name of *Epakhtos*, itself an alteration of *Naupaktos*, from Greek *naus*, 'ship' and *pēgnumi*, 'I fix', 'I make fast'. The name is coincidentally appropriate for a place that was the scene of the naval battle of 1571 in which the Turkish fleet was defeated by the fleets of the Holy League.

Le Puy The city in south central France had the Medieval Latin name of *Podium*, from Latin *podium*, 'height', itself from Greek *pous*, genitive *podos*, 'foot'. The city is named for the distinctive volcanic peaks in the locality, notably the Rocher Corneille, with its huge statue of Our Lady of France, and the Mont Aiguilhe, with the church of Saint-Michel. *Cp.* PUY-DE-DÔME.

Le Quesnoy The town in northern France, near Valenciennes, had the Medieval Latin name of *Quercetum*, from Latin *quercus*, 'oak'.

Lerwick The Shetland town has a Scandinavian name, as one would expect in this part of Scotland. It means 'mud bay', from Old Norse *leirr*, 'mud' and *vík*, 'inlet', 'bay' (as for WICK). The bay in question is Bressay Sound.

Lesbos The Greek island in the eastern Aegean Sea has a name that probably originally meant 'wooded'. It was this island that gave the term *lesbian*, from the Greek poetess Sappho who wrote of such love here in the 6th century BC.

Leslie The first name is from a Scottish surname, itself from a place-name of uncertain origin. As a girl's name, the spelling is usually *Lesley*.

Lesotho The kingdom of southern Africa takes its name from the *Sotho* who are its indigenous people. Their own name probably means 'black', 'dark-skinned'. Their name in the plural is *Basotho*, which gave the former name of Lesotho, *Basutoland*.

Letchworth The Hertfordshire town has a name ending in Old English *worth*, 'enclosure'. The first part of the name is less certain in origin, but may represent Old English *lycce*, 'locked place', so that the overall sense in some way was 'locked enclosure'.

Lethe In Greek mythology, the name is that of the river in Hades that caused forgetfulness in anyone who drank its waters. It is simply the Greek word *lēthē*, 'oblivion'.

Lettice The name evolved from the Latin name LAETITIA, 'joy', 'happiness'. Perhaps through its chance resemblance to *lettuce* it has now fallen from favour.

Letts The well-known make of diary is named for John *Letts* (1772–1851), a London stationer and printer who in 1812 published what is generally regarded as the first commercial diary, officially designated *Letts Diary of Bills Due Book and Almanack*.

Levallois-Perret The northwest suburb of Paris was formed as a town in 1867 through the merging of four separate hamlets: *Levallois*, Courcelles, *Champerret* and Villiers. The first of these represents the name of Nicolas-Eugène *Levallois* (1816–1879), who founded the village in 1846. *Champerret* takes its name from Latin *campus petrosus*, 'stony field', although it so happened that a landowner here was one Jean-Jacques *Perret*. His name was therefore chosen for the second part of the new town's name.

Levant The former name of the countries of the eastern Mediterranean derives from Old French *levant*, 'rising', that is, the land of the rising sun, otherwise the east. Inhabitants of the region were the *Levantines*. For names with an identical meaning, but in other languages, *cp.* ANATOLIA, JAPAN.

Level 42 The British pop group, formed in 1980, took their name from the cult humorous book by Douglas Adams, *The Hitch Hiker's Guide to the Galaxy* (1979), in which the answer to the question 'What is the meaning of life?' is '42'.

Leven, Loch The Scottish loch takes its name from the river that flows into it. The river's own name derives from Gaelic *leamhain*, 'elm-tree'.

Lever The name originated either as a Norman nickname for someone who resembled a hare (Old French *levre*), perhaps as a swift-footed or nervous person, or as a name for a person who lived near reeds or rushes, from Old English *lǣfer*, 'reed', 'rush'.

Levi In the Old Testament, the name is that of the third son of Jacob and Leah and the

ancestor of the priestly tribe of *Levites*. It derives from Hebrew *lēwī*, 'joined', 'associated', explained in the account of Levi's birth: 'And she conceived again, and bare a son; and said, Now this time will my husband be joined unto me, because I have born him three sons: therefore was his name called Levi' (*Genesis* 29.34).

Leviathan The biblical monster, of obscure origin, is described variously as a giant serpent (*Isaiah* 27.1), as a crocodile (*Job* 41), and generally as some kind of sea dragon. Its name derives from Hebrew *liwyātān*, itself from *lawā*, 'to writhe', 'to coil'. The name was adopted by Thomas Hobbes for his work *Leviathan* (1651) on the nature of government, with particular reference to the description of the monster as 'a king over all the children of pride' (*Job* 41.34).

Levin The Jewish surname means 'son of LEVI', otherwise '*Levite*'. The Levites were an inferior hereditary caste of priests who assisted the *kohanim* (who themselves gave the name COHEN).

Levis The world-famous make of jeans is named for *Levi* Strauss (1830–1902), a German-Jewish immigrant to America in 1850 who used tent canvas to make durable trousers for Californian goldminers. The miners called them *Levi's* after him, and the name is that still used by the manufacturing company today.

Leviticus The book of the Old Testament takes its name from the *Levitical* laws it contains, that is, those of the *Levites* (*see* LEVI and LEVIN). Its Hebrew name is *Wayigra*, 'and he called', from the book's opening words: 'And the Lord called unto Moses' (*Leviticus* 1.1).

Lewes The East Sussex town has a name that is generally regarded as representing Old English *hlǣwas*, the plural of a south of England variant of *hlāw*, 'hill', 'mound', found elsewhere in names such as *Bassetlaw*. This could refer to the South Downs here, although is more likely to relate to the many tumuli (burial mounds) in the vicinity. Recent scholarship, however, has expressed reservations about this origin. The initial *h* and final *s* of the Old English word do not appear in early records of the name, and the modern pronunciation of the name is not monosyllabic, as one would expect (*i.e.* as for *lose*), but bisyllabic. A derivation has thus been proposed in a Celtic word meaning 'slope', to which modern Welsh *llechwedd* in the same sense is related. But Celtic names are very rare in Sussex!

Lewis Whether a first name or surname, *Lewis* usually derives from the French name *Louis*, itself of Germanic origin, representing a combination of *hlūt*, 'famous' and *wig*, 'warrior'. These two same words gave the modern German name *Ludwig* and also the Scottish name *Ludovic*.

Lewisham The district of southeast London has a name meaning '*Lēofsa*'s village', with the Anglo-Saxon personal name followed by Old English *hām*, 'village' (to which modern English *hamlet* and *home* are related).

Lexington The name is that of at least two cities in the United States, one in Kentucky, the other in Massachusetts, the latter seeing the first action of the American Revolution (War of American Independence) in 1775. The Massachusetts town gave the name of all the others, and itself was named by English settlers from the Northamptonshire village of *Laxton*, near Corby, whose own name was at one time *Lexington*, '*Leaxa*'s farm'.

Leys School The Cambridge public school takes its name from the estate, *The Leys*, where it was built in 1875 and where it remains today south of the city centre. The location's own name means 'the meadows'.

Leyton Orient The well-known London football club was founded in 1881 by members of a Hackney cricket club so that they could continue playing together in the winter months. In 1888 they adopted the name *Orient* on the suggestion of a player who worked for the *Orient* Shipping Line. The name was appropriate for a club that played in East London. In 1898 they became *Clapton Orient*, adding the name of this select London suburb with the aim of gaining added respectability. In 1937 the club moved to a new ground further east in *Leyton*, and duly became *Leyton Orient* in 1946. In 1966, however, they dropped *Leyton* when the area was absorbed into the new borough of Waltham Forest.

Lhasa The capital of Tibet, known as the 'Forbidden City', has a name of Tibetan origin meaning 'city of the gods', from *lha*, 'god' and *sa*, 'city', 'land'. Its famous *Potala* Palace, former fortress of the Dalai Lamas, takes its name from that of the BUDDHA, with Tibetan *la*, 'mountain pass' added. (*Cp.* SHANGRI-LA.)

L'Haÿ-les-Roses The town in northern France derives the first part of its name from the Latin personal name *Laius*, itself from Greek *laios*, 'left' (as opposed to 'right'). The latter part of the name refers to the town's famous rose gardens. The original form of the basic name was *Lay*, but the initial *L* became detached as if to serve as the definite article ('the'), so that the name appears to mean 'the hedge'. (*Cp. La Haye* as the French name of The HAGUE.)

Lhotse The name of the Himalayan peak represents Tibetan *lhotse*, 'southern summit', from *lho*, 'south' and *tse*, 'summit', 'peak'. There are actually two peaks of the name, *Lhotse* I and *Lhotse* II. The higher, *Lhotse* I, is also known as *E1*, a designation given by the Survey of India in 1931. It is an abbreviation for *Everest 1*, as the mountain is sometimes regarded as part of the Everest massif.

Libby *See* ELIZABETH.

Libbys The familiar brand of corned beef and fruit drinks takes its name from the American brothers Arthur and Charles *Libby*, who formed a partnership in Chicago in 1868, originally to pack meat in tins.

Liberal The British *Liberal Party* evolved in the mid-19th century from the WHIG party, and was so named for its *liberal* policies that favoured progress and reform. The name was originally given to certain Whigs who were felt to be too permissive or even radical, rather in the manner of European revolutionaries. But as the word *liberal* had positive associations, the Whigs so branded were happy to adopt the name.

Liberec The city in the northwest Czech Lands has the German name of *Reichenburg*, apparently meaning 'rich town' (perhaps propitiously). The German name was pronounced by the local people as *Riberg*, and this gradually evolved to the present *Liberec*, with the first letter *R* becoming *L*.

Liberia The country of West Africa was founded in 1822 by *liberated* black American slaves, who migrated here from the New World during and after the suppression of the transatlantic slave trade. The name is appropriate for the only black African state never to have been subjected to colonial rule. *Cp.* LIBREVILLE.

Liberty The well-known make of quality fabrics and furnishings takes its name from Arthur Lazenby *Liberty* (1843–1917), a Buckinghamshire draper's son who began his own career as a draper in London at the age of 16 and who in 1876 set up business in Regent Street dealing in silks, shawls and other fashionable fabrics and garments. This was the germ of the present London store, still in Regent Street today.

Libra The constellation of the southern hemisphere takes its name from the stars that suggest the outline of a pendant balance (Latin *libra*). The name has a calendar interpretation in the corresponding sign of the zodiac, which was so called because the sun enters that sign at the time of the autumn equinox, when day and night are of equal length, and so *balance* each other.

Libreville The capital of Gabon was founded in 1849 by a group of *liberated* black slaves in what was then French Equatorial Africa. Hence the French name, which under a British administration in similar circumstances could well have been FREETOWN, like the capital of Sierra Leone (although confusion of identity would have resulted).

Librium The tranquillizer drug has a name, patented in 1960, that is said to be random but that nevertheless suggests *equilibrium* (as if for its ability to restore balance to those who are 'upset').

Libya The name of the North African country is very ancient and is known in Egyptian hieroglyphics of 2000 BC. Its meaning is obscure. Some biblical scholars regard the Old Testament mention of *Lehabim* (*Genesis* 10.13), one of the descendants of the sons of Noah, as a reference to the Libyan people, who are elsewhere referred to as 'the Lubims' (2 *Chronicles* 12.3).

Lichfield The Staffordshire town has a name meaning 'open land by the grey forest'. The first part of the name is the oldest, from Celtic words that are represented in modern Welsh by *llwyd*, 'grey' (as for LEATHERHEAD) and *coed*, 'wood' (as for BETWS-Y-COED). To the forest name was then added Old English *feld*, 'open land' (modern *field*), so that the overall name was recorded in the 8th century as *Liccedfeld*.

Lido The name of the popular island bathing beach near Venice, Italy, is simply the Italian word for 'beach', ultimately from Latin *litus*, 'shore'. As in Italian, so now in English the name has become a generic term for a fashionable beach or popular bathing place, such as the *Lido* on the Serpentine in Hyde Park, London.

Liebfraumilch The white table wine from the Rhine vineyards of western Germany takes its name, literally meaning 'virgin's milk', from the *Liebfrauenstift* convent in Worms where it was originally made. The convent's own name represents its dedication to the Virgin Mary, *Stift* meaning simply 'convent', 'foundation'. The German equivalent of English 'Our Lady' is *unsere liebe Frau*, 'our beloved lady', which in church and convent names is abbreviated to *Liebfrau(en)*. 'Virgin's milk' implies a wine that is pure in quality and white or transparent in colour.

Liechtenstein The small European principality takes its name from the princes of *Liechtenstein*, who created it in 1719 when they united the barony of Schellenberg here, already held by them, with the county of Vaduz. The family itself originated in the 12th century in the Austrian castle of *Liechtenstein* ('light stone') near Vienna.

Lieder ohne Worte *See* SONGS WITHOUT WORDS.

Liège The city and province of eastern Belgium ultimately derive their name from that of the Frankish people here called simply *leudi*, 'people'. The Late Latin name of the city developed from this as *Leodium* and eventually gave the modern name, which in its Flemish form is *Luik* and in German is *Lüttich*.

Liepaja The Latvian port, on the Baltic Sea, derives its name from Lettish *liepa*, 'lime-tree'. *Cp.* LEIPZIG and LIPETSK.

Liffey The Irish river, flowing into Dublin Bay at Dublin, has a name that has not as yet been satisfactorily explained. It cannot be meaningfully related to existing Irish words or other names.

Liguria The region of northwest Italy, on the *Ligurian* Sea, may take its name from the Celtic god *Lugus* who also gave the name of CARLISLE.

Lilian The name appears to have evolved as a pet form of ELIZABETH, although it is now associated with the *lily* flower (or with the name *Lily*).

Lilith The name is that of a Babylonian goddess of the night referred to in the Authorized Version of the Bible as a 'screech owl' and in the Revised Standard Version as a 'night monster' (*Isaiah* 34.14). In Jewish folklore the name is that of Adam's first wife, who left him to become the 'devil's dam'. It is traditionally derived from Hebrew *lyl*, 'night'. The goddess herself is generally equated with LAMIA.

Lille The city of northern France may originally have been named for a man with the Germanic name *Rizili*. Whatever the case, and whatever his name, the place-name was soon corrupted to a form such as *Lizle*, which came to be understood as the equivalent of modern French *l'île*, 'the island'. This was a perfectly appropriate name for a settlement surrounded by marshland, as was originally the case. The kind of strong fine cotton thread known as *lisle* takes its name from *Lisle*, the medieval spelling of *Lille*, where it was made.

Lilliburlero The well-known ballad and tune in mockery of the Irish Roman Catholics has a name (and refrain, *Lilliburlero Bullenala*) that is said to be a corruption of the Irish words *An lile ba léir é ba linn an lá*, 'the lily was triumphant and we won the day'. The ballad was composed at the time of the Glorious Revolution of 1688. The lily referred to is said to be the orange lily that was the symbol of the Irish supporters of William of Orange.

Lilliput The famous country of tiny inhabitants in Swift's *Gulliver's Travels* (1726) has a name apparently based on Danish *lille*, 'little' and Italian *putto*, 'child', although English *little* and Latin *putus*, 'boy' would work almost as well. Critics of the work have suggested that -*put* may equally derive from Latin *putare*, 'to think', so that the land is a 'country of little minds', or that Swift may have intended a pun on *put*, so that the country is simply 'Little-place'. *Cp.* LAPUTA and also BRAHMAPUTRA.

Lilongwe The capital of Malawi is named for the river on which it lies. The origin of the river name remains obscure.

Lima The capital of Peru has a name that is a Spanish corruption of its Quechua name *Rimak*, which itself represents the name of a god and his temple, from *rima*, 'to speak'. The allusion is to the priests of old who addressed the faithful from a place of concealment inside the statues of the gods they worshipped, something like a modern Roman Catholic priest in a confessional (if one sees this as a sort of altar). Francisco Pizarro, the Spanish conqueror of Peru, originally named the town here *Ciudad de los Reyes*, 'City of the Kings', that is, the Magi, as it had been founded on Wednesday 6 January 1535, the Feast of the Epiphany.

Limbo In the Christian religion, *Limbo* was the name of the abode of infants who died without being baptized. The name derives from Latin *limbus*, 'edge' (as the *limb* of the moon), since it was located, depending on the accounts one reads, on the edge of either Paradise or Hell.

Limburg The former duchy of western Europe, now divided into the two provinces of *Limburg*, respectively in northeast Belgium and the southeast Netherlands, takes its name from Germanic *lindo*, 'lime-tree' and *burg*, 'fortress'. This itself applied to the settlement that is now the small Belgian town of *Limbourg*, east of Liège. *Cp.* LINZ and Berlin's UNTER DENP LINDEN.

Limerick The Irish town (and also its county) has a name meaning 'bare area of ground', as represented by its Irish name of *Luimneach*, from the root word *lom*, 'bare', 'thin'. The land referred to would have originally been by the lower reaches of the river Shannon, on which the town stands. The name could also have been applied figuratively to a place that was exposed and that was thus difficult to defend.

Limoges The city of south central France, famous for its porcelain, takes its name from the original people here, the *Lemovices*, whose own name is based on Gaulish *lemo*, 'elm-tree' with Latin *vicus*, 'village' added. It was Limoges, or rather its people, who gave the name of the former French province of *Limousin*, which in turn gave the type of luxury car known as a *limousine*. The roof over the driver's seat in early models of such cars was fancifully seen as resembling a *limousine*, the distinctive cloak worn by shepherds in *Limousin*.

Limpopo The river of southeast Africa has a name that is a Portuguese (or possibly English) corruption of its local name, *Lebepe* or *Lebempe*, said to mean either 'dark river' or 'crocodile river' or even 'river of waterfalls'. The Boers called it the *Krokodil Rivier*.

Lincoln The name of the English city was recorded by Ptolemy in the 2nd century AD as *Lindon*. This represents the Celtic word for 'pool', 'lake' which has its modern counterpart in Welsh *llyn*. The reference was to the marshy lands and pools of the river Witham on which Lincoln stands, with one such pool still partly preserved as Brayford Pool. The Romans established a station for retired soldiers here, and to the latinized name of the place, *Lindum*, added *colonia*, 'colony'. The first two parts of each word have thus combined to form modern *Lincoln*. Unusually, the name never acquired the *-caster* or *-chester* found for other cities that were once Roman stations. On the other hand, early Anglo-Saxon settlers may well have understood the meaning of *colonia* and therefore regarded the addition of Old English *ceaster* as superfluous. The identically named capital of Nebraska was laid out in 1859 as *Lancaster*. When the site was selected for the capital in 1867, the year that Nebraska was itself proclaimed a state, it was renamed for Abraham *Lincoln*.

Lincoln College The Oxford college was founded in 1427 and named for its founder, Richard Fleming, bishop of *Lincoln*.

Lincoln Handicap The famous annual flat race for horses, over a one-mile course at Doncaster, was until 1965 run at *Lincoln*, hence its name.

Lincoln's Inn One of the four Inns of Court, London, *Lincoln's Inn* takes its name from Henry de Lacy, third Earl of *Lincoln* (1249–1311), whose family house it was. It was first leased out to law students as a hostelry in the mid-14th century.

Linda The popular name remains of uncertain origin. It may have evolved as a pet form of BELINDA, but some associate it with the Spanish word *linda* meaning 'pretty' or similarly with Italian *linda*, 'clean', 'neat'.

Lindisfarne The alternative name for *Holy Island*, off the Northumberland coast, derives from that of *Lindsey*, the northern region of Lincolnshire whose own name is based on that of *Lincoln* itself. To this has been added Old English *faran*, 'travellers' (modern *wayfarers*), referring to the pilgrims who at one time must have made regular journeys from Lindsey to Lindisfarne, although the distance is considerable.

Lindisfarne The British folk rock group, formed in Newcastle in the late 1960s, took their name from the island of LINDISFARNE, with its mystic associations. The island lies off the Northumberland coast only a few miles from Newcastle.

Lindsey The surname derives from either *Lindsey*, the district of Lincolnshire, itself taking its name from LINCOLN with Old English *ēg*, 'island' added, or from *Lindsey* near Hadleigh in Suffolk, a name that means '*Lelli*'s island'.

Lindt The make of Swiss chocolate is named for Rodolphe *Lindt* (1855–1909), who set up a chocolate factory in Bern in 1879.

Linguaphone The patent language-teaching system takes its name from Latin *lingua*, 'tongue', 'language' and 'gramo*phone*', as the learning method originally involved the use of gramophone records. It was launched in London in 1904 by an immigrant Russian, Jacques Roston.

Linköping The city of southern Sweden has a name that means 'flax market', from Swedish *lin*, 'flax' (modern English *linen*) and *köping*, 'market', 'trading place' (basically the same word as for CHIPPING CAMPDEN). *Cp*. JÖNKÖPING, NYKÖPING.

Linz The town and port of northern Austria probably derives its name from the Germanic word *lindo*, 'lime-tree'. *Cp*. LIMBURG and Berlin's UNTER DEN LINDEN.

Linz Symphony Mozart's Symphony No 36 in C major, K 425 (1783) is so named because it was composed and first performed in *Linz*, Austria.

Lionel The name originated as a diminutive of the Old French name *Léon*, meaning 'lion'.

Lions, Gulf of The French name of this Mediterranean bay in the south of France is singular, as *Golfe du Lion*. Whether there was one or several *lions* of any sort here is a mystery. The name is said by some to have referred to the statues of lions at one time on the coast here. Others claim that the name relates to the mistral, the strong, cold, winter wind whose roaring resembles that of lions. Both explanations seem equally fanciful, but as yet no convincing alternative has been offered in their place.

Lipari Islands The islands belonging to Italy, off northwest Sicily, are named for *Lipara*, one of their number. This in turn is said to derive either from the name of an early ruler, *Liparus*, or from Greek *liparos*, 'fat', 'rich'.

Lipetsk The city in Western Russia derives its name from the Slavic source that gave modern Russian *lipa*, 'lime-tree'. *Cp*. LEIPZIG and LIEPAJA.

Lipizzaner The breed of riding and carriage horse used by the Riding School in Vienna takes its name from the place where it was first raised, the former Austrian Imperial Stud at *Lipizza*, near Trieste.

Liptons The well-known brand of tea is named for Thomas Johnstone *Lipton* (1850–1931), born in Glasgow the son of an Irish labourer turned grocer. He opened his own grocer's shop in the same city in 1871, but did not begin selling his famous tea until 1889.

Lisa The name is one of the many pet forms of ELIZABETH, as is its sister, *Liza*.

Lisbon The name of the Portuguese capital has been traditionally traced back to that of its legendary founder, the Greek hero ULYSSES. This is popular etymology at work, however, since although the town is certainly ancient, and although early forms of its name do resemble *Ulysses*, the name is probably of Phoenician origin, whereas that of the legendary Greek is Etruscan. The original name may have actually had a meaning something like 'bay'.

Lisburn The town in Co Down, Northern Ireland, has the Irish name *Lios na gCearrbhach*, 'fort of the gamblers', referring to a site outside the town where 'outlaws' used to gamble with cards and dice. The English form of this name was *Lisnagarvey*. At some point in the 17th century the English name became *Lisburn*. The second part of this is of uncertain origin, but almost certainly represents an Irish word.

Lisieux The town of northwest France, famous for its shrine to St Theresa, derives its name from the Gaulish people who lived here, the *Lexovii*. The meaning of their own name is uncertain.

Lithuania The Baltic republic may take its name from a former name of the river Neman that flows through it. The meaning of the name is obscure. It has been associated by some with Latin *litus*, 'shore', from the location of the land by the Baltic. Others link it with the name of neighbouring *Latvia*, although that has an origin that is equally uncertain.

Little Feat The American blues and rock band was formed in Los Angeles in 1969 by Lowell George, previously guitarist with the Mothers of Invention. George recalled an incident during his early days when he had been teased about his 'little feet'. By changing the spelling slightly, he adopted the phrase for the punning name of the group.

Littlehampton The West Sussex resort was originally simply *Hampton*, or 'homestead'. It later added *Little* in order to be distinguished from SOUTHAMPTON, further along the coast, which had itself also been simply *Hampton* initially.

Little John In the stories about Robin Hood, *Little John* is the sturdy yeoman and archer. His name is thus ironic, as he is anything but little. *John* is a name commonly used to apply to any person. One account explains his name by saying that he was originally *John Little*. But this is probably a device to provide a plausible origin. His name gave the nickname that in turn produced the standard English surname *Littlejohn*.

Little Red Riding Hood The name is familiar as that of the little girl in the children's story who meets a wolf when she is visiting her sick grandmother and who then finds that her grandmother actually *is* the wolf in disguise. The story is first recorded in Charles Perrault's *Contes de ma mère l'Oye* ('Mother Goose Tales') of 1697, in which the story is called *Le Petit Chaperon Rouge*. This is the nickname given to the 'little village girl, the prettiest that was ever seen' on account of the red hood (*chaperon*) that she wears. Strictly speaking, 'riding' does not come into it, and forms no part of the story. In many European languages the girl is simply 'Little Redcap', as in German *Rotkäppchen*, Italian *Cappuccetto rosso*, Russian *Krasnaya shapochka*, and the French title quoted. But the type of large hood that she wore was originally associated with an English riding costume, and was called thus to be distinguished from other types of hood or cap. A similar concept gave the related name of the CAPUCHIN branch of the Franciscan order of friars.

Little Rock The state capital of Arkansas was given its name in 1722 by the French explorer Bernard de la Harpe, who finding two distinctive rock formations on the river Arkansas here, called the larger one *La Grande Roche* and the smaller *La Petite Roche*, as straightforward descriptive names. The 'little rock' subsequently became the base for a railway bridge, while the 'big rock', two miles away, was the site of an army post. In 1812 a trapper named William Lewis built his home at the 'little rock', and this was in essence the foundation for the present city.

Little Russian Symphony Tchaikovsky's Symphony No 2 in C major, Op 17 (1872) is so nicknamed because it contains folktunes from Ukraine, otherwise 'Little Russia'.

Littlewoods The football pools, mail order business and High Street stores all spring from the firm founded in 1923 by John Moores (1896–   ) as a football pool business in Liverpool. Because he and his co-founders did not wish their employers to know of their activity, they chose the name *Littlewood* instead of Moores, this being the original family name of one of the partners. The mail order business followed in 1932 and the chain stores in 1936.

Liverpool The famous Merseyside city and port has a name that literally means 'livered pool', that is, one that is clotted with weeds. (In medieval texts, the Red Sea was often referred to as the *livered* sea, as *Red* was understood to mean *reedy*.) The pool in question was a former creek of the Mersey that has now been filled in. The mythical creature called the *Liver bird* (pronounced to rhyme with *diver*) was invented to explain the name, and was adopted as the city's emblem.

Liverpool Street The mainline London station is named for the street near which it was built in 1862. The street is itself named for Lord *Liverpool*, Britain's prime minister from 1812 to 1827.

Living Color The American pop group originated as a 'power trio' in New York in 1984. Its members adopted their name from the announcement by NBC TV in the early days of broadcasting: 'The following program is brought to you in living color.'

Livingstone The Scottish surname derives from the place that is now the town of *Livingston* near Edinburgh. Its own name comes from that of *Levin*, who owned it in medieval times.

Livonia The former Russian province on the Baltic is said to derive its name from a word related to Estonian *liiv*, 'sand'. This would certainly suit its location.

Livorno The port of west central Italy takes its name from the *Liburni*, the people who at one time inhabited the region. Their own name is obscure in origin. The name was long familiar in English in the corrupted form *Leghorn*. This was popularly promoted by the breed of domestic fowl, for whom a name suggesting *leg* and *horn* was felt to be somehow meaningful and even descriptive. The breed was so called as it was developed in this part of Italy.

Liza *See* ELIZABETH.

Lizard, The The well-known Cornish peninsula, the southernmost point of the English mainland, has a name of Cornish origin meaning 'court (on a) height', from the conjectural words *lys*, 'court' and *ardh*, 'height'. The 'court', a local administrative centre approximating to a modern town hall, would probably have been at the present village of *Lizard* on the peninsula itself.

Ljubljana The capital of Slovenia has a name that has been popularly associated with the Slavic root word *ljub*, 'dear', as if it were a 'loved' or favourite place. But the actual origin is probably pre-Slavic, and has not been satisfactorily explained. The city's German name is *Laibach*.

Llandaff The suburb of Cardiff in Wales, famous for its ancient cathedral and bishopric, has a Welsh name meaning 'church on the *Taff*', from *llan*, 'church' and the river name. Most Welsh names beginning *Llan-* have a saint's name as the second element. *Cp.* LLANDUDNO, among others.

Llandudno The Welsh coastal resort has a name that means 'St *Tudno*'s church'. Hardly anything is known about the saint himself, who may have been active here in the 6th century. Welsh *llan*, now meaning 'church', and in place-names usually followed by a saint's name, as here, had the original sense 'enclosure', and is ultimately related to English *land*. *Cp.* LLANDAFF. *See also* LANDERNEAU, LANDES.

Llanelli The South Wales town has a name meaning 'St *Elli*'s church'. Elli was a female saint, and is said to have been a daughter of the 5th-century prince Brychan who gave the name of the BRECON BEACONS.

Llanfairpwllgwyngyllgogerychwyrndrob-wllllantysiliogogogoch The colourful Welsh name, perennially popular, is actually that of a village in Anglesey which was originally called *Llanfairpwllgwyngyll*, meaning 'St Mary's church in the hollow of

the white hazel'. The already lengthy name arose to distinguish this particular 'St Mary's church' from the very many others. In the 19th century, partly as a typical Victorian curiosity but also perhaps with the more practical aim of attracting tourists, the name was embellished by the addition of *Llandysylio*, 'St *Tysil*'s church' and *Gogo*, 'cave', the names of two neighbouring parishes, these being separated from the original name by a middle section *goger y chwyrn drobwll*, 'near the fierce whirlpool', and themselves rounded off with a final flourish of *goch*, 'red'. Mary's name appears here in its mutated form of *Fair*, from the regular form *Mair*. The name is sometimes rather crudely abbreviated to *Llanfair P.G.*

Llewellyn The familiar Welsh name originated as *Llywelyn*, of uncertain origin and meaning, but was respelled under the influence of the word *llew*, 'lion'. In Welsh history the name gained fame from the two princes of Gwynedd in North Wales *Llewelyn ap Iorwerth* and his grandson *Llewelyn ap Gruffudd*, who in the 13th century opposed the Norman barons in the south.

Lloyd The familiar Welsh name represents Welsh *llwyd*, 'grey', so was originally a nickname for a person with grey hair or for someone who often wore grey.

Lloyd's The famous London insurance market takes its name from Edward *Lloyd* (d. 1726), at whose coffee-house in Tower Street London underwriters originally carried on their business.

Lloyds Bank The High Street bank takes its name from Charles *Lloyd* (b. 1637), a Welshman from Montgomeryshire who became an ironmaster and who founded a bank in Birmingham in 1677.

Loch Ness *See* NESS, LOCH. For other loch (or lough) names *see* the second word similarly.

Lock The name has various possible origins, relating to its bearer's home, his occupation, or his appearance. It could apply to someone who lived by an enclosure (which could be locked), or to a lockmaker, or to a lock-keeper on a river, or to a person who had curly locks of hair.

Łódź The city in central Poland has a name that is identical to the standard Polish word for 'boat', as represented on the city's coat-of-arms. The meaning is appropriate enough for the town's location in a region of rivers, but the actual origin may be in a quite different word. The approximate pronunciation of the name is 'Woodge'.

Lofoten Islands The island group off the northwest coast of Norway has a name of unknown meaning, but one that has nevertheless been popularly interpreted as 'fox foot', from Norwegian *lo*, 'fox' and *fot*, 'foot'.

Logan The Scottish or Irish name derives from any of the places so called, which in turn originate in Gaelic *lagan*, 'little hollow'.

Lohengrin The name is familiar in German legend as that of the son of Parzival (Percival) who is a knight of the Holy Grail. In the medieval stories about him, his name is given as *Loherangrin*. This itself is said to derive from the name of the original character, *Lorengel*. The exact origin remains uncertain. The name has become popular through Wagner's opera *Lohengrin* (1850).

Loire The famous French river had the Roman name of *Liger*, which can perhaps be traced back to an Indoeuropean root *leg* or *lig*, meaning 'mud'. The end of the name may be related to a similar root element meaning 'river', as for ARAGON.

Loki The god of mischief and destruction in Norse mythology is said by some authorities to derive his name from Old Norse *lok*, 'end', or *ljúka*, 'to close', 'to end', to which modern English *lock* is related. This interpretation sees him as an 'eschatological' god, asssociated with the end of the world. In the *Younger Edda*, the Old Norse treatise on versification, his name is linked with *Logi*, meaning 'fire', as if he were a fire god (or devil). But this is almost certainly a folk etymology.

Lollard The *Lollards* were the followers of the radical philosopher and theologian John Wycliffe in the 14th to 16th centuries. They took their name from a Middle Dutch word meaning 'mutterer' (from *lollen*, 'to mumble') that had been earlier applied to various continental groups accused of both pious pretence ('mumbling' their prayers) and heretical views.

Lombard Street London's banking centre, in the City, takes its name from the merchants of LOMBARDY who settled here from the 12th century.

Lombardy The region of north central Italy had the Roman name of *Langobardus*. This relates to its people, the *Lombards*, a Germanic race who invaded Italy in the 6th century. Their own name may mean 'longbeards', from the Germanic words *lang*, 'long' and *bart*, 'beard'. Some authorities, however, prefer an original meaning 'long axes', from *lang* and *barta*, 'axe'. Either name is intimidating.

Lomond, Loch The well-known Scottish loch (lake) takes its name from the nearby mountain of Ben *Lomond*, whose own name derives from a Celtic word meaning 'beacon hill'.

London Despite its familiarity, the name of the capital of the United Kingdom remains tantalizingly obscure in origin. Various etymologies have been proposed over the years, with Celtic words frequently favoured, such as *lan*, 'lake' and *din*, 'fort', or, for the first half, *lon*, 'hill', *llwyn*, 'wood' or *londo*, 'wild'. This last is said to have been the name of a tribe or even a single person. However, the origin is almost certainly pre-Celtic, and the meaning so ancient that it may never be definitively known. The Canadian city of *London*, Ontario, was founded in 1826 and named for the British capital.

Londonderry The well-known city of Northern Ireland was originally (and remains today, in nationalist usage) *Derry*, representing its Irish name *Doire*, 'oak wood'. It gained its addition in the early 17th century, when James I granted a charter authorizing merchants from LONDON to make a settlement here.

Londonderry Air The attractive Irish folktune, also popularly known as 'Danny Boy', is so named as it was first recorded in 1855 by the folk-song collector Jane Ross in Limavady, Co LONDONDERRY.

London Palladium The popular London theatre off Oxford Street opened as a music-hall in 1910 on a site long connected with entertainment. Until 1934 it was known simply as the *Palladium*. The name may have been based on a misunderstanding of the classical term (*see* PALLADIUM). At the same time the theatre's first manager, Walter Gibbons, wished to outdo the other leading London music-halls of the day, the COLISEUM, *Hippodrome* and *Palace Theatre*, so chose a name that appeared to rival theirs.

London Symphonies Haydn's last 12 symphonies are so called as they were composed in the 1790s for the impresario Salomon and were first performed in *London* during Haydn's visits there that decade. *See also* LONDON SYMPHONY.

London Symphony The name is that of two noted orchestral works: Haydn's Symphony No 104 in D major (1795), the last of the LONDON SYMPHONIES, and Vaughan Williams' second symphony (1912), which incorporates evocations of London life, such as Westminster chimes, street cries and the sounds of street musicians.

Long The name originally described someone who was tall, from Old English *long* or *lang*, which had this meaning.

Long Beach The city in southwest California, on San Pedro Bay, was laid out in 1881 and originally named *Willmore City*, after its founder. It was subsequently promoted as a seaside resort and in 1888 was renamed as now for its beach, which is eight and a half miles (13.5 km) long.

Longchamp The well-known Paris racecourse is named after its location, meaning 'long field'. The name is found elsewhere in France, representing Medieval Latin *Longus Campus*, but for a racecourse is particularly appropriate.

Longford The Irish town and county has a name that could mislead. It actually represents the Irish name *An Longfort*, 'the fortress', from Irish *longphort*. Longford was formerly the site of a fortress of the O Farrells, although no trace of it remains today.

Longines The well-known make of watch takes its name from the Swiss village of *Longines*, near St Imier, where in 1867 a watch factory was opened by the watch-makers Ernest Francillon and Jacques David.

Long Island The island in New York State, containing the boroughs of Brooklyn and Queens as well as several resorts (including Coney Island), has a self-descriptive name. It is 118½ miles (190 km) in length and has a greatest width of 23 miles (37 km).

Longjumeau The town in northern France, just south of Paris, has a name that suggests 'long' and 'twin' (French *jumeau*). In fact it is a corruption of its Late Latin name *Nongemellum*, which itself originated as *Noviomagus*. This means 'new market', from Gaulish *novio*, 'new' and *mago*, 'field', 'market'. The name existed for several other Roman settlements in Europe. Some, like CHICHESTER, have acquired a quite different name. Others have retained a name that recognizably resembles the original, such as NIJMEGEN in the Netherlands.

Longleat The well-known Renaissance mansion and seat of the Marquess of Bath, in western Wiltshire, takes its name from the *long leat* or water channel that flowed here and that was flooded to form ornamental lakes when the house was built in the late 16th century.

Longman The British publishers take their name from Thomas *Longman* (1699–1755), born in Bristol but apprenticed to a London bookseller at the age of 16 and setting up his own bookselling business in 1724.

Long Parliament The name is that of the parliament summoned by Charles I in November 1640 which lasted until its forcible expulsion by Cromwell in 1653 or, by another reckoning, to its final dissolution in 1660. Either way, it was named by contrast with the earlier *Short Parliament* of April to May 1640. *Cp.* RUMP PARLIAMENT.

Longwy The town in northeast France has a name of Germanic origin, from words corresponding to Old English *lang*, 'long' and *wīc*, 'village'. In England it would have probably become *Longwich*, and was actually recorded as such in the 7th century.

Lonsdale Belt The belt awarded as a trophy to professional boxing champions takes its name from Hugh Cecil Lowther, fifth Earl of *Lonsdale* (1857–1944), who as president of the National Sporting Club presented the first such belt in 1909. The first Viscount Lonsdale, Sir John Lowther (1655–1700), took his title from the Westmorland (now Cumbria) town of *Kirkby Lonsdale*.

Lord The surname originated as a nickname for a person who resembled a lord in some way, perhaps putting on 'airs and graces'. In some instances it could also have been an occupational name for a servant in the house of a lord.

Lord's The famous London cricket ground, the headquarters of the Marylebone Cricket Club (MCC), takes its name from Thomas *Lord*, a Yorkshire cricketer who in 1787 opened the original ground on the site of what is now Dorset Square, just over half a mile (1 km) away.

Lord Wandsworth College The public school near Basingstoke in Hampshire was founded in 1912 under the will of Sydney James Stern, Baron *Wandsworth* (1845–1912), who owned a considerable amount of property in London and who had inherited the title from his father. As he was unmarried, it became extinct on his death.

Lorelei In German legend, the name is that of the siren who lives on a rock at the edge of the Rhine near Koblenz, where she lures boatmen to their death by combing her long blonde hair and singing. The name, properly that of the rock itself, regarded as a danger to shipping, means 'fairy cliff'.

Loreto The town of central Italy, famous as a place of pilgrimage, takes its name from Latin *lauretum*, 'laurel grove'. *See also* LORETTO SCHOOL.

Loretto School The Scottish public school in Musselburgh, near Edinburgh, was founded in 1827. It takes its name from a former pre-Reformation chapel and hermitage here, with the chapel dedicated to Our Lady of *Loretto*, that is, LORETO in Italy. The mansion that was later partly built on the site of the chapel was subsequently converted by the school to its use. The school itself is non-denominational, not Roman Catholic.

Lorient The port in western France, on the Bay of Biscay, was founded in 1664 by the French East India Company (*Compagnie de l'Orient*) and was named for them.

Lorna The name was apparently invented by R.D. Blackmore for the heroine of his famous novel *Lorna Doone* (1869). He seems to have based it on a word such as *forlorn*, referring to the initial kidnapping of the young child Lorna by the Doones. On the other hand, it turns out that Lorna is of noble Scottish birth, so that her name could have been taken from the Scottish place-name *Lorn* (an area of Argyll). Perhaps the true origin is in a blend of both.

Lorraine The region and former province of eastern France has a name that has evolved from its Medieval Latin name of *Lotharingia*. This itself represents *Lotharii regnum*, 'kingdom of *Lothair*'. The kingdom was created for *Lothair* II (835–869), to whom it was bequeathed by his father, *Lothair* I, the emperor who was the grandson of Charlemagne.

Los Angeles The famous Californian city was founded in 1781 on a Spanish grant and was originally named *El Pueblo de Nuestra Señora de los Ángeles*, 'the village of Our Lady of the Angels'. The name was gradually shortened to its present form, which is now even further abbreviated colloquially to *LA*.

Lot The name of Abraham's nephew in the Old Testament is traditionally derived from a Hebrew root element meaning 'to wrap', 'to cover'. His wife, name unknown, is famous for being turned into a pillar of salt when she disobeyed God's command 'look not behind thee' (*Genesis* 19.17).

Lothian The Scottish region, divided into the districts of East Lothian, Midlothian, West Lothian and Edinburgh City, has a name whose origin remains uncertain. It may be a tribal name, relating to one *Leudonus*, although nothing is known about him. *See also* HEART OF MIDLOTHIAN.

Loughborough The Leicestershire town has a name that means '*Luhhede*'s fortified place', with the Anglo-Saxon personal name followed by Old English *burh*, 'fort', often found in place-names as *-bury*.

Louis *See* LEWIS.

Louisa The name is a Latin-style feminine form of the French name *Louis* that gave English LEWIS. Its sister form *Louise* is more obviously French.

Louisiana The southern American state was named in 1682 by the French explorer Robert Cavelier, Sieur de la Salle, for *Louis* XIV of France. The name originally applied to the whole of the basin of the Mississippi as French colonial territory. *See also* LOUISIANA PURCHASE.

Louisiana Purchase The name relates to the *purchase* from Napoleon in 1803 of LOUISIANA, as the western region of the Mississippi basin, by the American president Thomas Jefferson. The land deal was the largest in American history, and doubled the size of the United States at a stroke.

Louisville The port in Kentucky was founded by the French in 1778 and given its name in 1780 in honour of *Louis* XVI of France in recognition of his aid during the American Revolution (War of American Independence).

Lourdes The town in southwest France, famous as a place of pilgrimage for the sick, takes its name from one *Luridus* or *Lordus* here in the time of Charlemagne.

Louth The Irish county takes its name from the small village of *Louth*, whose own Irish name was originally *Lughmhaigh*. The latter half of this represents Irish *magh*, 'plain', but the first part is of uncertain meaning. It does not appear to be a personal name.

Louvain The name of the town in central Belgium comes from the personal name *Lubianos*, itself meaning 'loved'. The town's Flemish name of *Leuven* and German name of *Löwen* wrongly suggest a link with *lions*.

Louvre The famous national museum and art gallery of France, in Paris, originated as a royal palace, built in 1546 in a district known in medieval times as *Louvrea*. This means 'place of wolves', ultimately from Latin *lupus*, 'wolf'.

Love The name derives either from the Old English personal name *Lufa*, meaning 'love', or from Norman French *louve*, 'she-wolf'. The latter would have served as a nickname for a brave soldier, one who defended his people or property in the way that a she-wolf would have protected her young.

Lovelace The name now suggests a fop or dandy who *loves lace*. It originated, however, as a nickname for a person who was *loveless*, in the sense that he was 'fancy free' and a philanderer. Hence the literary pun on the name in works by Cibber, Vanbrugh and Sheridan, where a woman named *Amanda* ('beloved') is the wife of a man named *Loveless*.

Lovell The name is a diminutive of LOW in its sense of 'wolf'.

Lovin' Spoonful The American folk-rock group, formed in 1965, took its name from a line in a song by bluesman John Hurt which ran: 'I love my baby by the lovin' spoonful'.

Low Like LAW, the name could apply to a person who lived on or near a hill, one Old English word for which was *hlāw*. It could also be a nickname for a short person, from a dialect word that gave modern *low*. In another sense, it could have been used as a nickname for a cunning or dangerous person, from the Norman French word *lou*, meaning 'wolf'. (Wolves were still found in Britain in medieval times.) Finally, it could have evolved as a short form of *Lawrence* (*see* LAURENCE).

Low Church The evangelical wing of the Church of England gives a *low* place doctrinally to the priesthood and sacraments, and was so nicknamed by contrast to the HIGH CHURCH, which rates them highly.

Low Countries The name is that of the *lowland* region of western Europe that includes Belgium, Luxembourg and especially the NETHERLANDS (whose own name is identical in meaning).

Löwenbräu The well-known German beer has a name meaning 'lion's brew', designed to suggest strength and quality.

Lowestoft The coastal town in Suffolk has a Scandinavian name meaning '*Hlothvér's* dwelling place', with the personal name followed by Old Danish *toft*, originally 'building site', familiar in the names of many villages and hamlets in the east of England.

Lowlands The name applies to the mostly flat region of central Scotland which is *low-lying* by contrast with the mountainous HIGHLANDS further north.

Low Sunday In the Christian calendar, the Sunday after Easter is popularly so called because it is relatively *low* in importance by contrast with the *high* festival of Easter, and thus marks a return to the normal Sunday services. The name is unlikely to derive from Latin *laudes*, 'praise', as some claim, with reference to the Latin hymn *Laudes Salvatori*, 'Praise to the Saviour', appointed for this day.

Luanda The capital of Angola takes its name from a native word meaning 'tax'. The reference is to the cowrie shells at one time gathered from the beach here by the local people to pay their dues to the king of the Congo. *See also*, in respect of the latter, KING KONG.

Luang Prabang The town in northern Laos, formerly the residence of the monarch of Laos, has a name that refers to this status, representing Laotian *muong luong*, from *muong*, 'town', 'city' and *luong*, 'great', 'royal'.

Lübeck The port in northern Germany has a name of Slavic origin, from that of the principality of the *Liubichi*, the descendants of an original prince *Liubu*, whose own name means 'beloved' (*cp*. LOUVAIN).

Lubyanka Moscow's once notorious prison takes its name from the street where it stands. The street's own name has been linked with the Pskov dialect word *lubok*, a term for a kind of bast basket or punnet, said to have been traded here by merchants from Pskov who settled in this region of Moscow in the early 16th century.

Lucas The name represents a continental European form of LUKE, so has the same meaning.

Lucas The manufacturers of lamps, batteries and other electrical equipment take their name from Joseph *Lucas* (1834–1902), a Birmingham metalworker's son, who set up a business in Birmingham selling household goods in 1860, dealing in oil and paraffin in 1869, and producing his first bicycle lamp in 1875.

Lucca The city of northern Italy has a name of Celtic origin, from the root word *luc*, 'marsh', 'damp place'. *Cp*. LUTETIA.

Lucerne The name of the well-known Swiss city, on the lake of the same name, has attracted several possible etymologies. Of the main contenders, three at least relate to the lake and see the source in different Latin words: *lucerna*, 'lamp', with reference to the phosphorescent fish in the lake, *lucius*, 'pike', from the abundance of these fish, or *lutum*, 'mud', purely descriptively. A further theory derives the name from the monastery founded in the 8th century here by St *Leodegar*. This last explanation is probably the most likely.

Lucifer The name is Latin in origin, meaning 'light-bearer' from *lux*, genitive *lucis*, 'light' and *ferre*, 'to bear'. It has, or had, two main applications. The first was as a name of the planet Venus when it appeared as a 'morning star' before dawn. The second was as the former archangel whose 'fall from grace' is referred to in the Bible: 'How art thou fallen from heaven, O Lucifer, son of the morning!' (*Isaiah* 14.12). As a result of the latter text, the name of *Lucifer* has come to be generally identified with that of *Satan*.

Lucinda The name is a form of *Lucia* (which gave modern LUCY), with the *-inda* ending found in names such as BELINDA.

Lucknow The city in northern India, the scene of a brave defence by British troops during the Indian Mutiny of 1857, derives its name from Hindi *lakhnaū*. This represents Sanskrit *lakṣmaṇavati*, from *lakṣmaṇa*, 'sign', 'mark', referring to the goddess LAKSHMI, whose own name symbolizes prosperity and happiness.

Lucozade The tonic drink has a name that suggests both its chief constituent, *glucose*, and a fruit drink such as lemon*ade*.

Lucretia The name is the feminine form of the Roman clan name *Lucretius*, itself of uncertain origin although linked by some with Latin *lucrum*, 'gain', 'profit'. It was notoriously promoted by *Lucretia* Borgia, said to have committed incest with her father and her brother Cesare and to have shared many of the evil traits ascribed to members of her family in medieval Italy. (Today, however, she is usually seen much more positively and sympathetically.)

Lucy The name goes back, through French, to the feminine form of the Roman name *Lucius*, itself probably based on Latin *lux*, genitive *lucis*, 'light'.

Lucy Cavendish College The Cambridge college was founded in 1965 to provide academic courses for women whose studies had been postponed or interrupted for any reason. It is named for Lady *Lucy Cavendish*, née Lyttelton (1841–1925), a keen advocate of education for women and an aunt and godmother to one of the college founders, Margaret Braithwaite. Lady Lucy's husband was the statesman Lord Frederick Cavendish (1836–1882), assassinated in the year of his appointment as Chief Secretary for Ireland.

Lüda The conurbation and port in northeast China, also known as *Lü-ta*, derives its name from the first part of the names of the two cities that combined to form it, LÜSHUN (formerly PORT ARTHUR) and *Talien* (DAIREN).

Luddites The name is that of the textile workers who rioted and destroyed machines as a protest against mechanization in the 1810s. They are said to have taken it from Ned *Ludd*, an 18th-century Leicestershire workman who destroyed stocking machines similarly.

Ludlow The Shropshire town stands on a hill over the river Teme, and its name relates to both these natural features. It derives from Old English *hlūd*, 'loud', describing the noisy torrent of the river, and *hlāw*, 'hill'.

Ludovic *See* LOUIS.

Lufthansa The German airline was founded in 1926 as the result of a merger of two existing companies and originally had the name *Deutsche Luft Hansa*. It ceased operations in 1945, at the close of the Second World War, but was revived as *Luftag* in 1953. The following year it reverted to its original name in slightly altered form, as *Deutsche Lufthansa*. Its general name, and that appearing on its aircraft, is simply *Lufthansa*, however. This combines German *Luft*, 'air' and *Hansa*, 'Hansa', as if the original commercial association was akin to that of the HANSEATIC LEAGUE.

Luftwaffe The name of the German Air Force literally means 'air weapon', a designation that is more explicit and concrete than the *force* or its equivalent that is found in the titles of other air forces of the world.

Lugano The town and resort on the northern shore of the lake of the same name in Switzerland traces its own name back to Gaulish *lacvanno*, 'lake dweller', these being the people who at one time lived in this region.

Lugansk The Ukrainian city arose round the iron foundry that was built in 1795 on the river *Lugan*, from which it took its name. The river's own name is of uncertain origin. In 1935 it was renamed *Voroshilovgrad*, for the Soviet military leader and statesman, Marshal Kliment *Voroshilov* (1881–1969), who engaged in revolutionary activities here. The city retained this name until 1958, when it reverted to *Lugansk* after Voroshilov's attempt to oust Khrushchev. In 1970, however, after the death of the rehabilitated Voroshilov, it again became *Voroshilovgrad*, and kept the name until 1989, when it once more reverted to its original name.

Luke The biblical name goes back to the Greek form *Loukas*, meaning 'man from *Lucania*' (a west coast region of southern Italy). Much of its popularity derives from St *Luke* the apostle, identified in readily appreciated terms as a doctor and friend of St Paul.

Lund The city of southern Sweden was founded in about 1020 by the Danish king Cnut (Canute), who is said to have named it after LONDON. But this is probably a misapprehension of its Medieval Latin name, *Londinum Gothorum*, 'Londinum of the Goths', where the main part of the name is actually of Celtic origin, perhaps meaning 'forest'.

Lundy The island at the entrance to the Bristol Channel is famous for its puffins, and its name actually means 'puffin island', from Old Norse *lundi*, 'puffin' and *ey*, 'island'.

Lüneburg The city of northwest Germany was known in the 8th century as *Liuniburg*, a name that may represent a Germanic word such as *hleuni*, 'defence' or *hleo*, 'mound', but that certainly ends in *burg*, 'fortress'.

Lunéville The city in northeast France had the Medieval Latin name of *Lienatis villa* or *Lunivilla*. The first part of this is of uncertain origin. It hardly represents French *lune*, 'moon'.

Lunn Poly The British travel agents take their name from Henry *Lunn* (1859–1939), a Methodist minister who began arranging educational and religious travel tours in 1892. In the 1960s his company merged with the *Poly*technic Touring Association, itself founded in 1888 to provide travel facilities for the students of the Regent Street Polytechnic, London.

Lupercalia The ancient Roman festival of fertility, celebrated annually on 15 February, takes its name from *Lupercus*, a Roman god of flocks. His own name presumably derived from his task of protecting flocks from *lupi*, 'wolves'. The connection with wolves was more explicitly marked in the gathering of worshippers at the *Lupercal*, the cave on the Palatine Hill where Romulus and Remus are said to have been suckled by a wolf. The ceremony existed until the 5th century AD.

Lupton The name derives from the hamlet so called near Kirkby Lonsdale in Cumbria. The place-name itself probably means '*Hluppa*'s settlement', although this Anglo-Saxon personal name is only conjectural.

Lusatia The historic region of central Europe, now mostly in southeast Germany, derives its name from that of a Slavic people, the *Lusici*, 'plain dwellers'.

Lüshun The port in northeast China, now part of the conurbation of LÜDA, derives its name from Chinese *lü*, 'traveller' and *shùn*, 'along'. Its former name was PORT ARTHUR.

Lusitania The former Roman province of the western Iberian peninsula, corresponding roughly to modern Portugal and western Spain, is named for the people who lived here, the *Lusitani*. Their own name is of uncertain origin, but has been related to the Celtic personal name *Luso* or that of the Ligurian god *Lugus* whose name lies behind that of CARLISLE and possible LYON.

Lutetia The historic name of Paris probably derives from Gaulish *luto*, 'mud', 'marsh', referring to the low-lying ground by the Seine here.

Luther The name is famous both from the 16th-century German Protestant leader Martin *Luther* and from the 20th-century black civil rights leader, named for him, Martin *Luther* King, each a martyr to his beliefs, the latter literally so. The name itself derives from Germanic *liut*, 'people' and *heri*, 'army', appropriately enough for two religious pioneers.

Luton The Bedfordshire town has a name that means 'farmstead on the *Lea*', the latter being the river on which it stands. The river's own name may mean 'bright one'. The town of *Leyton* in Greater London (formerly in Essex) has a name of exactly the same origin and meaning. It is not clear how *Luton* came by its change of vowel.

Luton Hoo The 18th-century mansion southeast of LUTON is named for that town. *Hoo* means 'spur of land', from Old English *hōh*. The same word lies behind the name of Plymouth *Hoe*, from which prominence Drake had a good view of the Armada as he finished a game of bowls. *Cp. also* SUTTON HOO.

Lutterworth The second part of the name of the Leicestershire town is the familiar Old English *worth* that means 'enclosure'. The first part of the name is harder to interpret. It may represent a former name of the river, now the Swift, on which the town stands. If so, it could have been something like *Hlūtre*, meaning 'clean one', from Old English *hlūttor*, 'clear', 'clean' (modern German *lauter*).

Lutterworth Press The British publishing house, now based in Cambridge, arose out of the Religious Tract Society, itself set up in 1799 to bring religious or 'improving' literature to poor people. In about 1932 the publishing side of the Society adopted its present name as a tribute to the famous religious reformer John Wycliffe, who had become rector of LUTTERWORTH, Leicestershire in 1374. *See also* WYCLIFFE HALL.

Luxembourg The well-known grand duchy in western Europe resembles LILLIPUT in more ways than one. Not only is it small, but its name proclaims it to be so, deriving ultimately from the Germanic words *luttila*, 'little' and *burg*, 'fort', 'castle'. The present form of the name evolved through Medieval Latin *Luciliburgum*.

Luxor The ancient town on the Nile in southern Egypt, famous for its tombs and temples, has a name that is a corruption of Arabic *al-uqṣur* or *al-quṣūr*, 'the camps', from *al*, 'the' and *quṣūr*, plural of *qaṣr*, 'camp', itself a borrowing of Latin *castrum*.

Luzon The main and largest island of the Philippines is said to derive its name from *losong*, a local word for a pestle for pounding rice. But this may simply be an attempt to find an origin in a native word that happens to resemble the name and be reasonably apt, as is often the case.

Lvov The Ukrainian city was founded in the mid-13th century by Prince Daniil Romanovich of Galicia, who is said to have named it for his son, *Lev* (Leo).

Lyall The name is Scottish, and probably derives from a Scandinavian personal name *Liulfr*, of uncertain meaning (perhaps based on *úlfr*, 'wolf').

Lyceum The original place of this name was a school and sports ground near Athens where Aristotle held discussions with his pupils in classical times. The name was taken from the temple here dedicated to Apollo *Lukeios*, the latter being a byname that appears to mean 'wolf' (Greek *lukos*) but that is actually of uncertain origin. The classical associations of the name have favoured its adoption for theatres, concert halls and the like, and it also gave the standard French word *lycée* for a type of secondary school.

Lycidas Milton took the title of his elegy on the death of his young friend Edward King, published in 1637, from the name of a shepherd in Virgil's *Eclogues*. The name itself means 'son of a wolf', from Greek *lukos*, 'wolf' and the patronymic suffix *-idas* (found also as *-ides*).

Lycra The name of the synthetic elastic fabric, used for tight-fitting garments such as underwear and swimming costumes, was patented in 1958. It is apparently of random origin. As the fabric is lightweight, however, it could conceivably derive from Greek *lukē*, conventionally transliterated *lyce*, 'light' (although in the sense 'brightness').

Lycurgus The 9th-century BC Spartan lawgiver has a Greek name that literally means 'wolf-worker', from *lukos*, 'wolf' and *ergon*, 'work'.

Lydd The name of the town near Dungeness in Kent is all that remains of the original Old English phrase *æt thāra hlithum*, 'at the slopes', referring to the slight slope on which Lydd arose above the marsh here. *Cp.* LYTHAM ST ANNE'S.

Lydia The ancient region of western Asia Minor is said to derive its name from one *Ludos* who was the ancestor of the *Lydian* people, although this is often a stock recourse for an unexplained name! The Old Testament mentions the *Ludim* as being the descendants of Ham (*Genesis* 10.13). Yet just a few verses later *Lud*, with the same basic name, is given as the son of Shem (10.22).

Lydia The name is of Greek origin and means 'woman of LYDIA'. It is found in the New Testament for a woman, 'a seller of purple' (*Acts* 16.14), who is converted by St Paul.

Lyme Regis The main name of the Dorset resort, on the English Channel, is that of the river on which it lies. This in turn is of Celtic origin, and means simply 'flood'. The second word of the name, representing the Latin for 'of the king', was added in the 13th century when Edward I declared the town a royal borough.

Lynn The name seems to be a pet form of LINDA rather than an adoption of the surname *Lynn*. It equally reflects the endings of names such as CAROLINE and EVELYN.

Lynyrd Skynyrd The American blues band, formed in Jacksonville, Florida, in 1966, based their name rather maliciously on that of *Leonard Skinner*, their high school gym teacher who had had them expelled from school for wearing their hair long. Later, when the group became a success, its members made up with their former teacher and he even introduced them at one concert.

Lyon The city in southeast central France has the Roman name of *Lugdunum*, representing its Gaulish name *Lugudunu*. The last part of this means 'fort'. The first part may derive from the name of the god *Lugus* who also lies behind the name of CARLISLE. Alternatively, it may have evolved from Gaulish *louco*, 'shining', for the waters of the rivers Rhône and Saône, which meet here, or from *lugu*, 'small'.

Lyonesse The name is that of the mythical land of the Arthurian romances, from which Sir Tristram came. It is traditionally located in southwest England, where it is now said to be submerged beneath the sea somewhere between Mount's Bay (or Land's End), Cornwall, and the Scilly Isles. The name occurs in Thomas Malory's *Le Morte D'Arthur* of the late 15th century, but in earlier Arthurian accounts is spelled *Leonais*. This is now believed to have evolved not from Cornwall but from the Celtic land of Brittany, where it probably represents the region round ST-POL-DE-LÉON. In Cornish folklore, however, the land is usually equated with a region known as *Lethowstow*, while Scotland claims an association with LOTHIAN.

Lyons The well-known brand of foods and the famous tea-shops (Lyons' Corner Houses) take their name from Joseph Nathaniel *Lyons* (1847–1917), who in 1887 became a partner of Montague Gluckstein in managing the catering arrangements for the Newcastle Jubilee Exhibition that year and who in 1894, after further catering experience, formed a company to operate restaurants and tea-shops generally.

Lyric Theatre There are two London theatres of the name, one in King Street, Hammersmith, the other in Shaftesbury Avenue, both opening in 1888. The name is a traditional one for a place of musical entertainment, and both theatres staged musical shows in the early days. The Hammersmith Lyric closed in 1966 but re-opened in a new building in 1979.

Lysaght The name is Irish, representing the original Gaelic form *Mac Giolla Iasachta*, 'son of the servant of the stranger', from *iasachta*, 'strange', 'foreign'.

Lysander The name of the famous 4th-century BC naval commander is Greek in origin, meaning 'liberator of men', from *lusis*, 'release' and *anēr*, genitive *andros*, 'man'.

Lysistrata The name of the comedy by Aristophanes is that of its central character, meaning 'disbander of armies', from Greek *lusis*, 'loosing', 'setting free' and *stratos*, 'army'. This is appropriate for the theme of the comedy, which concerns what is effectively a women's peace organization and its endeavours to bring the Peloponnesian War to an end. Lysistrata persuades the women of Athens to refuse sexual relations until this is achieved.

Lytham St Anne's The compound name of the Lancashire town and resort is the result of the amalgamation in 1922 of the two separate towns of *Lytham* and *St Anne's*. The former name means 'at the slopes', and is exactly the same in origin as that of LYDD in Kent. (The final *-ham* is thus misleading.) The latter name is that of the town's parish church, which was the first building to be erected when it began to develop in the late 19th century.

Lyttelton Theatre The second largest of the three theatres that together form the Royal National Theatre, on London's South Bank, opened in 1976 and is named for Oliver *Lyttelton*, Viscount Chandos (1893–1972), first chairman of the National Theatre Board. There were presumably specific reasons for not choosing the better-known (and more easily spelled) name of *Chandos* for the theatre, from the chairman's title.

M

Maastricht The Dutch town is on the river *Maas* or MEUSE, as the first part of its name indicates. The second half evolved from Latin *trajectus*, 'crossing', referring to the ford here in Roman times.

Mabel The present English name evolved from the Old French word *amable*, meaning 'lovely' (related to modern English *amiable*), with the first vowel *a* lost over the centuries.

Mabinogion The well-known collection of Welsh medieval tales was first translated into English in the 19th century by Lady Charlotte Guest. The name derives from the plural of Welsh *mabinog*, 'young poet', 'apprentice bard'. This word, itself from *mab*, 'boy', 'son', soon also came to refer to the actual poems and tales themselves.

Mablethorpe The Lincolnshire seaside resort has a name that means '*Malbert*'s outlying settlement', with the Norman personal name *Malbert* followed by Old Norse *thorp*, used of a settlement that was dependent on a larger place.

Macao The Portuguese overseas territory, on the south coast of China, has a name that is a Portuguese corruption of South Chinese *ama*, the name of an ancient goddess, the patron of sailors, and *ngao*, 'bay', 'port'. The official Chinese name of Macao is *Aomin*, from *ào* (pronounced *ngao* in the south), 'bay' and *mén*, 'gate'.

Macbeth The 11th-century king of Scotland who is the central character of Shakespeare's play named for him (1605) derives his own name from the Gaelic personal name *Mac Beatha*, 'son of life', implying a man of religion.

Maccabees The last two books of the Apocrypha take their name from the priestly family headed by JUDAS *Maccabaeus*. There is some uncertainty regarding its meaning, since the original Hebrew can be understood as 'hammer', 'hammerer' or 'extinguisher'. The general sense of the name is probably similar to that behind the nickname of 'Hammer of the Scots' for King Edward I of England. Judas would have thus been given the name as an honorary title with reference to his valour.

Macclesfield The name of the Cheshire town means '*Maccel*'s open land'. The open land (Old English *feld*) in question was probably at one time part of the forest that was here in the Peak District.

McCulloch The Scottish and Irish name means effectively 'son of a boar', with the main part of the name representing a personal name that was apparently based on Gaelic *cullach*, 'boar'.

Macdonald The Scottish name means 'son of DONALD'.

McDonalds The well-known fast-food restaurant chain, famous for its hamburgers, was founded in Chicago in 1955 by the milk-shake machine manufacturer Ray Croc when he took over the hamburger business run by the brothers Maurice and Richard 'Mac' *McDonald*. Considerately, he retained their name for his business, although his own would have been neater and more original for what is now a worldwide company.

Macedonia The ancient region of the Balkan Peninsula, now familiar from the independent republic formerly in Yugoslavia, has a name that is mythologically linked with that of *Macedon*, a son of the god Zeus. Its actual origin may be in Greek *makednos*, literally 'tall', referring to the raised terrain of the region. Some, however, derive the name from Illyrian *maketia*, 'cattle', referring to the pastures here. The culinary term *macedoine*, as applied to diced vegetables, is a punning reference to the heterogeneous nature of the dish, and alludes to the mixture of nationalities that inhabit Macedonia.

Macgillycuddy's Reeks The mountain range in Co Kerry, Ireland, was a place of refuge for the powerful sept (tribal branch) of the *Mac Gillicuddys*, whose descendant still bears the title *Mac Gillicuddy of the Reeks*. *Reeks* is an English word, a variant of *ricks*, and means 'ridges', 'crests'.

Macgregor The Scottish name means 'son of GREGORY'.

Machiavelli The adjective *Machiavellian* is used to mean 'cunning', 'amoral', and refers to the alleged political policies of the Florentine statesman and philosopher Niccolò *Machiavelli* (1469–1527), famous for his controversial treatise *Il Principe* (*The Prince*) (1532). Somewhat appropriately, although not actually in its explicit sexual sense, his name means 'bad penis', from Italian *malo*, 'bad' and *chiavello*, literally 'nail', 'spike'. It originated as a nickname for any notorious philanderer.

Machpela The name is that of the cave near Hebron where the patriarchs were buried (*Genesis* 23.9, 25.9), representing Hebrew *mahpela*, 'double'. Where the English Bible has 'cave of Machpelah', older versions simply have 'double cave', as follows: Vulgate (Latin), *spelunca duplex*; Septuagint (Greek), *to spēlaion to diploun*; Peshitta (Syriac) *meʿartō aʿifotō*; Targum (Aramaic) *meʿarat kafeltā*; Martin Luther (German) *zweifache Höhle*. The cave appears to have had an upper and a lower chamber, so making a pair or 'double'.

Machu Picchu The famous ruined city of the Incas in south central Peru has a name of Quechua origin, from *machu*, 'old man' and *pikchu*, 'peak'. The city stands on top of high cliffs in the Andes. The name is pronounced 'Ma-choo Peak-choo'.

Mackenzie The Scottish name means 'son of *Coinneach*', the latter being a personal name meaning 'handsome', itself based on Gaelic *cann*, 'bright'.

Mackenzie Canada's longest river, in the Northwest Territories, is named for the Scottish explorer Sir Alexander *Mackenzie* (1764–1820), who discovered and explored it in 1789. The administrative district of

Mackenzie here is named after the river, which flows through it.

Mackie The firm that manufactures WHITE HORSE whisky was founded by James Logan *Mackie* in 1883 on the Scottish island of Islay. The company name was changed to *White Horse Distillers* in 1924.

Mackinlays The well-known brand of whisky takes its name from Charles *Mackinlay* (1795–1867), who set up as a whisky merchant in Leith, near Edinburgh in 1815. In 1850 he launched his own distinct blend, the *Original Mackinlay*.

McKinley, Mount The mountain in Alaska, the highest peak in North America, was so named in 1896 by the prospector William A. Dickey in honour of William *McKinley* (1843–1901), elected president of the United States that year. The American Indian name of the mountain is *Denali*, 'the high one'.

Mackintosh The Scottish name means 'son of the chief', the last syllable of the name representing the Gaelic word *toiseach* that has its equivalent in the Irish title TAOISEACH for the prime minister of Ireland.

Mackintoshes The familiar make of toffee is named for John *Mackintosh* (1868–1920), a Derbyshire cotton spinner's son, who himself originally worked in a cotton mill but who left to join his wife in running a pastrycook's shop. The couple decided to specialize in making toffee, and after an extensive advertising campaign launched *Mackintosh's Celebrated Toffee* in 1890.

McLaren The well-known racing car, the most successful Formula One Grand Prix car of the 1980s, is named for the founder of its manufacturing company in 1966, the New Zealand racing driver Bruce *McLaren* (1937–1970), killed testing a car on the Goodwood track.

Maclean The name is both Scottish and Irish, and means 'son of the servant of JOHN', referring to the saint. The full Scottish Gaelic form of the name is *Mac Gille Eáin*, while the Irish is *Mac Giolla Eóin*. The middle word here means 'boy', 'servant', and is the origin of the Scottish *gillie* who attends or guides a sportsman when hunting or fishing.

Macleans The well-known make of tooth-paste takes its name from Alex C. *Mac-lean*, a New Zealand-born salesman for Spirella corsets in America. In 1919 he came to Britain to set up the Spirella business there but after a quarrel left the company and turned to making 'own brand' products for chemists. He first produced *Macleans Peroxide Tooth Paste* in 1930.

Macleod The Scottish name means 'son of *Leòd*', the latter being the Gaelic form of the Old Norse name *Ljótr*, meaning 'ugly'.

Macmillan The Scottish name means 'son of *Maolán*', the latter being a diminutive of the word *maol*, meaning 'bald'. The reference is to a tonsured monk, regarded as a devotee of a particular saint.

Macmillan The noted British publishing house takes its name from Daniel *Macmillan* (1813–1857), a Scottish farmer's son who worked in bookshops in London and Cambridge before setting up his own bookselling business in London in 1843. He then took over the Cambridge bookshop where he had worked, and first began publishing there in 1844.

Mâcon The city of east central France, famous for its wines, has a name that ultimately derives from the Ligurian root word *mat*, 'mountain', with the Ligurian suffix *-asco*. The present form of the name evolved from the town's Roman name of *Matisco*, genitive *Matisconis*. Mâcon lies in the valley of the Saône on the eastern edge of the Massif Central.

Macpherson The name is Scottish and means 'son of the parson'. *Cp.* PARSONS.

Macys The well-known New York department store was founded in 1858 by Rowland Hussey *Macy*, a former seaman and Boston dry goods store owner.

Madagascar The island republic off the east coast of Africa takes its name from the Somali capital MOGADISCIO. The name was first recorded in the 13th century by Marco Polo, who instead of applying it to the eastern Somali coast, where it properly belongs, took it to be the name of the island. This came about because when noting the name in the original Arabic, he translated the word *jezīra* as 'island', whereas it can actually mean either 'island' or 'peninsula'. When the Portuguese explorer Diego Dias discovered Madagascar on 10 August 1500, St Laurence's Day, he named it accordingly *São Lourenço*. The island now had two names, that given by Dias, and that recorded by Marco Polo. When the duplication was discovered in 1531 it was Marco's name that was selected. There has never been an indigenous MALAGASY name for Madagascar, only local names for different regions of the island.

Madame Tussaud's The popular London waxworks takes its name from *Madame Tussaud*, née Anne-Marie Grosholtz (1761–1850), a French wax modeller from Strasbourg who opened her London exhibition in 1802.

Madeira The group of islands in the Atlantic, west of Morocco, forms an administrative district of Portugal and takes its name from Portuguese *madeiro*, 'log', 'wood' (a word related to English *material*), since the largest island of the group is covered in trees. The river *Madeira* in Brazil, South America, is named for the island group.

Madeleine The name is the French form of the second word of the name of MARY MAGDALENE, which itself derived from the place-name MAGDALA.

Madeleine The well-known Paris church dates from 1816 and is dedicated to MARY MAGDALENE, French *Marie Madeleine*. It was originally planned by Napoleon as a temple of glory to his army. This role, however, was instead assigned to the ARC DE TRIOMPHE.

Madhya Pradesh The state of central India has a name that describes its geographical location, from Sanskrit *madhya*, 'centre', 'middle' and *prades*, 'state'. The root of the word *madhya* is the same as that of Latin *medium* and English *middle*.

Madison The state capital of Wisconsin, USA, was founded in 1836 and named commemoratively for James *Madison* (1751–1836), fourth president of the United States, who had just died. *Cp.* MADISON AVENUE, MADISON SQUARE GARDEN.

Madison Avenue The New York street, famous for its advertising offices and public relations firms, takes its name, like MADI-SON, Wisconsin, from the fourth American president, James *Madison* (1751–1836).

Madison Square Garden The well-known New York sports area, named for President James *Madison*, was originally a converted railway station (not a 'garden' as such) at *Madison Square*, used as a concert hall. In 1890 a sports arena was built on the site, devoted chiefly to boxing. The present building is the fourth of the name.

Madness The British pop group, formed in 1976, took their name from the best-known song, 'Madness', of the Jamaican political pop singer Prince Buster, first popularized when he toured Britain in 1964.

Madonna The title of the Virgin Mary derives from the Italian words *ma donna*, 'my lady', so in a way corresponds to another of her titles, *Our Lady*, only regarded more personally. The name is familiar from many portraits of Mary holding the infant Jesus (*Madonna and Child*), and has been adopted in some countries as a first name.

Madras The port and city of southeast India has a name that may derive from Sanskrit *maṇḍarāṣṭra*, 'kingdom of Manda', from *maṇḍa*, the name of a god of the underworld, and *rāṣṭra*, 'kingdom' (related to *raj*). However, some sources take the name from Arabic *madrasa*, 'school' (*i.e.* a Muslim one), from *darasa*, 'to study', or even from Portuguese *madre de Deus*, 'mother of God'. The city's former name was *Mailapur*, 'city of the peacock'.

Madrid The capital of Spain has a name of uncertain origin. Some authorities link it with the Latin word *materia*, 'materials', referring to the wood that was originally used for building here. Others prefer a derivation in Latin *matrix*, genitive *matricis*, 'river bed', with the present spelling evolving under Arabic influence. However, Madrid is not on a major river, but on the little Manzanares, and originated as a small Moorish fort on a bluff over this river, rather than by its bed. (Unusually for a country's capital, Madrid is on no major river, no important trade route, no ancient religious site. It is, however, almost exactly in the middle of the Iberian Peninsula, so in that sense is unique.)

Madura The island in Indonesia has a Sanskrit name, from *madhura*, 'gentle', 'calm', literally 'honeyed' (related to English *mead*). The reference is presumably to the climate. The same source gave the modern Indian first name *Madhur*.

Madurai The city in southern India derives its name from Sanskrit *madhura*, 'gentle', 'calm'. *Cp.* MADURA.

Maeander This is the anglicized version of the ancient Greek name of the Turkish river now known as the *Menderes*. The Greek name was linked with that of the god of the river, which in turn was interpreted as meaning 'seeking a man', from *menaōs*, 'seeking' and *anēr*, genitive *andros*, 'man'. The meaning is related to a story in which the god Maeander vowed he would sacrifice the first person to congratulate him after his storming of the Phrygian city of Pessinus. The person to do so was his son, Archelaüs. Maeander kept his vow, but then jumped in the river in remorse. The name gave the English word *meander*, since the river follows a winding course.

Maebashi The city in central Japan, in Honshu, has a name that represents Japanese *mae*, 'front' and *hashi*, 'bridge'.

Maecenas The 1st-century BC Roman statesman, patron of Horace and Virgil, has an Etruscan name of uncertain meaning.

Maelstrom The name is that of the strong tidal current in the Lofoten Islands off the northwest coast of Norway. It derives from the Old Dutch word *maelstroom*, from *malen*, 'to grind', 'to whirl round' and *stroom*, 'stream'. (Modern English *millstream* is indirectly related to this.) The word came to apply to this particular current from its appearance on early Dutch maps.

Maeve The Irish name, familiar from Irish epics as that of the semi-legendary Queen of Connacht, has the Irish form *Meadhbh* and derives from an old Celtic word meaning 'intoxicating', to which modern English *mead* is related. It can thus be best interpreted as 'she who makes drunk', 'she who inebriates', that is, by her charms. It is possible that Queen Maeve lies behind Shakespeare's Queen *Mab*, 'the fairy's midwife' in *Romeo and Juliet*.

Mafeking The South African town, since 1980 known more accurately as *Mafikeng*, has a name of Tswana origin meaning 'place of rocks', from *mafika*, the plural of *lefika*, 'rock', 'cliff'. The town is famous for its lengthy siege in the Boer War of 1899–1900.

Mafia The international criminal organization, founded in Sicily in the 15th century to oppose tyranny, derives its name from an identical Sicilian dialect word meaning 'boldness', 'swagger', probably ultimately from Arabic *mahyah*, 'boasting'.

Magadan The Russian city in eastern Siberia, on the Sea of Okhotsk, arose only in the 1930s. Despite the town's recent history, however, the origin of the name remains obscure. It may represent the personal name of an Evenki tribesman, *Magda*, who lived here at one time.

Magdala The biblical town on the west shore of the Sea of Chinnereth, mentioned in *Matthew* 15.39, is very likely the one that gave the name of MARY MAGDALENE. Its name is Hebrew in origin, from *migdal*, 'tower'. It is probably also the town of *Migdal-el* ('tower of God') mentioned in the Old Testament (*Joshua* 19.38) as one of those inherited by Nephtali. The Talmud (code of Jewish law) names the town as *migdal-nūnayyā*, 'tower of fish'. The present Hebrew name of Magdala, now in Israel, is *Migdal*, while its Arabic name is *Al-Majdal*.

Magdalena The river in Colombia, South America, was discovered by the Spanish explorer Rodrigo de Bastidas on Friday 22 July 1502, the Feast of St MARY MAGDALENE, and was named by him for this day.

Magdalen College The Oxford college was founded in 1448 by William of Waynflete, Bishop of Winchester, and takes its name from its dedication (and that of its chapel) to St MARY MAGDALENE. The name retains its medieval pronunciation of 'Maudlin'. *Cp.* MAGDALENE COLLEGE. *See also* MAGDALEN COLLEGE SCHOOL.

Magdalen College School The Oxford public school for boys was founded in 1480 by William of Waynflete, Bishop of Winchester, as a grammar school within the premises of MAGDALEN COLLEGE, his earlier foundation. The school moved out of the college premises in 1851 and settled in its present premises across the river in 1894.

Magdalene College The Cambridge college was founded by Lord Audley in 1542 and is named for St MARY MAGDALENE, to whom it and its chapel are dedicated. As for its near namesake, MAGDALEN COLLEGE, Oxford, the name is pronounced 'Maudlin'.

Magdeburg The city in eastern Germany is apparently named for a woman called *Magda*, although it is not certain who she was. She may have owned land here, or have been a local deity. Her name itself simply means 'maid', and for this reason it is equally possible that the city's name may mean 'maiden's town', alluding to an otherwise unnamed pagan goddess.

Magellan, Strait of The strait between the mainland of South America and Tierra del Fuego was discovered in November 1520 by the Portuguese navigator Ferdinand *Magellan* (Fernão de Magalhães) (1480–1521), and is named for him.

Maggie The name is one of the many pet forms of MARGARET that came to be adopted in its own right.

Maggiore, Lake The well-known lake, partly in northern Italy and partly in western Switzerland, has an Italian name meaning simply 'greatest', referring to its size by comparison with nearby Lake Como and Lake Lugano.

Maghreb The region of northwest Africa that includes Morocco, Algeria and Tunisia, and where also the *Maghreb* Desert is found, has an Arabic name, representing *maḡrib*, from *ḡarb*, 'west'.

Magi The 'three wise men' who came from the east bearing gifts for the infant Jesus have a collective name that is the plural of *magus*, the term for an astrologer or ancient magician. The word is Latin, ultimately deriving from an identical Old Persian word meaning 'magician'. It occurs in the Vulgate (the Latin version of the Bible) but not in the English Authorized Version, where it is translated 'wise men'. It does appear, however, as the title of *Simon Magus*, a sorcerer who tried to buy spiritual powers from the apostles (*Acts* 8.9–24).

Maginot Line The line of fortifications built by France to defend its border with Germany before the Second World War was named for André *Maginot* (1877–1932), French minister of war at the time when construction of the fortifications began in 1929.

Magna Carta The name of the famous charter of personal and political liberty granted by King John at Runnymede in 1215 represents the Medieval Latin words for 'great charter'. The charter was probably entitled 'great' to distinguish it from an almost contemporary lesser charter, the *Charta Forestae* or *Forest Charter*, which was granted by Henry III in 1217 and which modified the restrictive forest liberties of earlier reigns. The name is sometimes spelled *Magna Charta*.

Magnesia The ancient Greek city, in Lydia, takes its name from the *Magnēs*, the people who lived here. Their own name is of uncertain origin. The region is rich in natural minerals, and gave its name to both the *magnet* and *magnesium*. *See also* MAGNITOGORSK.

Magnitogorsk The city in west central Russia arose in 1930 by Mount *Magnitnaya* (Russian *Magnitnaya gora*), and takes its name from this. The mountain is famous for its rich magnetic iron ore.

Magnox The type of nuclear reactor, installed in Britain at Calder Hall, has a name that is properly that of the tubes of magnesium alloy in which the uranium fuel for the reactor is encased. It is an abbreviation of '*mag*nesium *no ox*idation'.

Magog *See* GOG AND MAGOG.

Magyar The name is that of the people or language of HUNGARY, and may derive from a Ugrian people, the *Magy*, whose own name means simply 'men', 'people'. *See also* UGRIAN.

Mahabharata The epic Sanskrit poem of India, telling of the rivalry between two families, derives its name from Sanskrit *mahā*, 'great' and *bhārata*, 'story'. The name is stressed on the third syllable.

Maharashtra The state of west central India has a Sanskrit name, from *mahā*, 'big', 'great' and *rāṣṭra*, 'kingdom', 'empire'. *Cp.* MADRAS.

Mahavira The name of the last Jain (saint) in the Hindu sect of Jainism represents Sanskrit *mahā*, 'great' and *vīra*, 'hero'.

Mahayana The branch of Buddhism that seeks enlightenment for all humanity has a name of Sanskrit origin, from *mahā*, 'great' and *yāna*, 'vehicle'.

Mahdi The title assumed by the Sudanese military leader Mohammed Ahmed (1843–1885) derives from Arabic *mahdīy*, 'guided one', from *madā*, 'to guide'. In Islam the title is that of a number of Muslim messiahs who are expected to convert all mankind forcibly to their faith.

Mahé The main island of the Seychelles was so named in 1742 by the French captain Lazare Picault in honour of Bertrand François *Mahé*, Comte de Bourdonnais (1699–1753), commander of the French royal navy. The Indian town of *Mahé*, on the Malabar Coast, was originally known as *Mayyali*, but this was altered to its present form in 1727 in honour of the same man when it was occupied by the French.

Mahón The capital of Minorca, in the Balearic Islands, had the Roman name *Portus Magonis*, 'port of Magon', the latter being the name of the Carthaginian general who was the brother of Hannibal. The type of salad dressing known as *mayonnaise* is said to have been named commemoratively for the French capture of *Mahón* (then called *Port-Mahon*) by the Duc de Richelieu in 1756.

Maia The eldest of the seven Pleiades in Greek mythology, the mother of Zeus by Hermes, has a name with the basic meaning 'mother', 'nurse'. The Romans had a rather obscure goddess of the same name whom they identified with her, and it was she who gave the name of the month of MAY.

Maida Vale The district of London northwest of Charing Cross was developed in the mid-19th century and is named for the Battle of *Maida* in 1806, in which the English under Sir John Stuart defeated the French. *Maida* itself is a village in Calabria, southern Italy. The *vale* of the name arose because the new houses were built at the foot of a hill called *Maida Hill*, and this was the feature that originally bore the name. From there it spread to the whole district.

Maiden Castle The prehistoric hill fort near Dorchester, Dorset, has a name that probably means 'fort that has never been taken', that is, it is a 'virgin' castle. There are other ancient hill forts of the name elsewhere in Britain.

Maidenhead The Berkshire town is on the Thames and has a name that is usually interpreted as meaning 'maidens' landing-place', the *-head* representing Old English *hȳth* (as in other names such as ROTHERHITHE). The name does not necessarily imply that young women landed their boats here. More probably it was simply a place where they regularly met. *Cp.* MAIDSTONE.

Maid Marian According to early editions of Dr Brewer's *Dictionary of Phrase and Fable*, such as that of 1894, the name of the legendary sweetheart and companion of Robin Hood is said to derive from that of a traditional character in the morris dance, a boy called *Mad Morion*, himself so named from his crazy dancing and from the fact that he wore a *morion*, or type of open helmet. But this origin seems very suspect! The morris dance connection, and the name, are more likely to be associated with *May Day* celebrations and *marriage*. And although such celebrations and dances are pagan in origin, the name may have subsequently come to be associated with that of the Virgin MARY. There has long been a subconscious link between *Mary* and *marry*, if only because the Virgin's marriage was unique. She was moreover a *maid* (in the sense 'virgin'). So Maid Marian combines the pagan and the Christian, and was effectively the original 'May queen'.

Maidstone The town in Kent has a name that probably means what it says, 'maidens' stone', implying a stone of some kind (perhaps a boundary marker) where young women and girls regularly met. But some authorities prefer an origin not in Old English *mægden*, 'maiden' but in Old English *mægth*, 'folk', 'people'. In this case the stone would have been a general assembly point, as for a moot, and the name would be similar to that of FOLKESTONE, also in Kent. Support for the latter origin lies in

the fact that Maidstone was formerly the capital of western Kent.

Main The river of central and western Germany probably has a name of Celtic origin, deriving either from *mo*, 'slow' and *enos*, 'water' or perhaps from Gaulish *magio*, 'great'. *See also* MINSK.

Maine The American state is more likely to be named for the French province of MAINE than for being marked on a map, according to some, as the *'main* land of New England'. The precise reasons for the name are uncertain, but it is known that French explorers were referring to the region west of the Kennebec River here as *Maine* before 1500, while the area to the east was *Acadie* (*see* ACADIA).

Maine The former province of western France takes its name from the river *Maine* that flows through it. The river's own name may be Gaulish in origin, from *magio*, 'big', although some sources derive the name from that of its inhabitants, the *Cenomani* (*see* LE MANS). The French refer to the province as *le Maine*, but to the river as *la Maine*.

Mainwaring The name is a Norman baronial one, deriving from an unidentified place in northern France. The place-name itself means '*Warin*'s domain', from Norman French *mesnil*, 'domain' and the personal name *Warin*, which itself gave the modern English surname WARING.

Mainz The city and port in western Germany had the Roman name of *Magontia* or *Mogontiacum*. This is said to derive from the personal name *Mogon*, that of either a local owner of territory here or of a Celtic deity.

Maisie The name is a pet form of MARGARET through its Gaelic equivalent, *Mairead*. The *r* of this name pronounced in Gaelic sounds like *z* to English speakers, but came to be written *s*, perhaps by association with DAISY.

Majorca The largest of the Balearic Islands has a name deriving from Latin *major*, 'greater'. The island's Spanish name is *Mallorca*, with the same origin. *Cp.* MINORCA.

Makhachkala The port on the Caspian Sea in southwest Russia, where it is the capital of Dagestan, takes its name from *Makhach*, the pseudonym of the Russian revolutionary leader Mahomet-Ali Dakhadayev (1882–1918), with the final part of the name representing Armenian *kala*, 'settlement', 'fortress'. Before 1922 the name of the town was *Petrovsk-Port*, for the fort said to have been built here by Peter the Great. Dakhadayev set up the local Soviet government here, but was killed in the Civil War.

Malabar The coastal region of southwest India has a name that derives from Tamil *malay*, 'mountain' (*cp*. MALAYA) and Iranian *barr*, 'continent'.

Malabo The capital of Equatorial Guinea takes its name from the local ruler who was the legitimate successor to Moka, king of the Bubi, who died in 1937.

Malacca The state of southwest Peninsular Malaysia has a name of two possible origins. It may represent Sanskrit *mahā*, 'great', and *laṅkā*, 'island' (*cp*. SRI LANKA), or on the other hand derive from Malay *melaka*, 'emblic' (an East Indian tree of the spurge family, found widely here).

Malachi The name of the last book of the Old Testament is not a personal name but a descriptive title of the anonymous prophet whose writings it contains. It represents Hebrew *malāhī*, 'my messenger', and is appropriate for the minor prophet who foretold the coming of Christ. The name is drawn from the text of the book itself: 'Behold, I will send my messenger, and he shall prepare the way before me' (*Malachi* 3.1). The title of the book should not be confused with the personal name of St *Malachy*, the 12th-century Irish prelate and reformer. This represents Irish *Máel Máedóc*, otherwise *Maolmhaodhóg*, 'devotee of St *Máedóc*'.

Málaga The well-known Spanish port and resort has a name of Phoenician origin, from *malaka*, 'queen', referring to its prime position (now in the centre of the Costa del Sol).

Malagasy The name is that of the people or language of MADAGASCAR, and derives from that of the island state itself. Madagascar was officially known as the *Malagasy Republic* from 1958 to 1975.

Malakoff The southern suburb of Paris takes its name from the Russian village of *Malakhov* in the Crimea which was captured by the French in 1855 during the Crimean War, resulting in the fall of Sebastopol. The direct source of the name was an inn named *A la Tour de Malakoff* ('The Malakoff Tower'), itself so called from its location at the foot of a tower of this name which was destroyed in 1870 during the siege of Paris.

Malawi The state of east central Africa takes its name from the *Malavi* people who are known to have inhabited the region from the 14th century. Their own name means 'flames', perhaps referring to the reflection of the rays of the rising sun in the waters of Lake Malawi. The former name of Malawi was *Nyasaland* (*see* Lake NYASA).

Malaya The western and continental part of *Malaysia*, in southeast Asia, has a name that probably derives from Tamil *malay*, 'mountain', with reference to one of the region's main geographical features. *Malaysia* has the same origin, and only coincidentally suggests *Asia*.

Malcolm The well-known Scottish name derives from the Gaelic name *Mael Coluim*, 'devotee of St *Columba*', the latter being the saint who converted much of Scotland and northern England to Christianity in the 6th century. His own name derives from the Latin word for 'dove'.

Maldives The archipelago in the Indian Ocean, southwest of Sri Lanka, has a name that may derive from Sanskrit *mālādvīpa*, 'garland of islands', from *mālā*, 'garland' and *dvīpa*, 'island'. Some prefer to see an origin, however, in Tamil *malay*, 'mountain' (*cp*. MALAYA) with the same *dvīpa*.

Mali The West African state took a name in 1960 that was that of a former empire, extinct from the 17th century. It may derive from the MALINKE, an indigenous people in this region of Africa, or come from a Mandingo (Malinke) word meaning 'hippopotamus'.

Malinke The name of the people and language of West Africa derives from the Mandingo (Mandinke) words *ma*, 'mother' and *dink*, 'child'. The overall meaning is thus 'child of the mother', alluding to the matrilineal descent of Malinke families, that is, through the female line, not the male. The term MANDINGO is still sometimes used for both people and language.

Mall, The The main thoroughfare of St James's Park, London, is named for the game of *pall-mall* formerly played here, as it had been earlier on the site of the present PALL MALL, which runs parallel to it. It was this *Mall*, as a fashionable walk bordered by trees, that gave the later general sense of the word for a similar street elsewhere and for the modern shopping *mall*.

Mallorca *See* MAJORCA.

Mallory The name developed from the Norman nickname for an unlucky person, from *malheure*, 'unhappy'. A noted bearer of the name was Sir Thomas *Malory*, who wrote *Le Morte D'Arthur* (printed 1485).

Malmaison The château near Paris, famous as the residence of the Empress Josephine, was built in 1622 on a site that already had the name, recorded in the 13th century in the Latin form *Maladomus*. The meaning is literally 'bad house', referring to a place that was originally difficult to build on.

Malmesbury The Wiltshire town has a name that means '*Mailduf*'s fort', referring to the Irish monk who founded a monastery here. (His own name means 'black prince'.) The middle *m* of the name arose through the influence of the name of St *Aldhelm*, who built a monument and chapel on the site of Mailduf's cell in the 7th century.

Malmö The Swedish port, in the south of the country, derives its name from Swedish *malm*, 'mineral' and *ö*, 'island', with reference to its geological and geographical characteristics.

Malpas The Cheshire town has a name of Norman French origin meaning literally 'bad step', that is, a place where passage was difficult. Malpas is not actually in such a place, but is on a hill over a route that at one time could have been marshy or muddy. There are other places of the name elsewhere in Britain, such as *Malpas*, the suburb of Newport, Gwent, or *Malpas*, the village near Truro, Cornwall. France also has places so named.

Malta The island republic in the Mediterranean has a name that perhaps originally goes back to a pre-Indoeuropean root element *mel*, 'high', referring to its rocks. A more picturesque origin derives the name from Greek *melitta*, a form of *melissa*, 'bee', 'honey'. Malta was at one time famous for its production of honey.

Maltravers The name is of Norman origin, and derives from a place in northern France that has not been identified. The meaning is probably 'bad crossing', from Old French *mal travers*, referring to a ford that was difficult to cross.

Malvern The well-known hills in Hereford and Worcester are near enough to the Welsh border to have a Welsh name. It means 'bare hill', from Welsh *moel*, 'bare', 'bald' and *bryn*, 'hill'. The name has passed to the town and village of *Great Malvern* and *Little Malvern*, among others, and also to the district of Great Malvern known as *Malvern Link*, where the latter word represents Old English *hlinc*, 'ridge' (as found in modern golf *links*).

Malvinas *See* FALKLAND ISLANDS.

Malvolio The humourless steward in Shakespeare's play *Twelfth Night* (1599) has a name that implies 'ill will'. It is thus a name opposite in meaning to that of *Benvolio* in Shakespeare's earlier play *Romeo and Juliet* (1594). There have been ingenious attempts to relate the steward's name to that of the code he gives in the letters 'M.O.A.I.' (II, v). They are obviously present in the name itself, but what else could they mean? Theories to account for them include the following: 1. they are an acronym for '*m*y *o*wn *a*dored *i*dol' or (more seriously) for Latin *m*are, *o*rbis, *a*er, *i*gnis ('water, earth, air, fire', the four elements regarded as constituting the universe); 2. they are a partial anagram of 'I am Olivia', linking Malvolio, in the sub-plot, to this key character in the main plot; 3. they represent egocentricity, producing English *I*, Italian *io*, 'I' and *mio* and *mia*, 'my', as well as French *moi*, 'I', 'me'; 4. they represent the name of the French writer *Montaigne*, who is said to have influenced Shakespeare.

Mamas and the Papas, The The well-known American folk-rock group, formed in New York in 1965, took its name from the two married couples who were involved in the initial stages, John and Michelle Phillips, and Cass Elliot and her first husband John Hendricks. Hendricks did not belong to the final line-up, however, which had Dennis Doherty as its fourth member.

Mameluke The *Mamelukes* were a military class, originally of Turkish slaves, who ruled in Egypt from the 13th to the 15th century and who were eventually crushed in 1811. The ultimate derivation of their name is in Arabic *mamlūk*, 'slave'. The word is also in general use to apply to a slave in Muslim countries.

Mammon The name is used in the Bible (once only) as the personification of riches and greed in the form of a false god, although in most English texts it does not appear with a capital letter: 'Ye cannot serve God and mammon' (*Matthew* 6.24). The word represents Aramaic *māmōnā*, 'wealth', 'riches'.

MAN The familiar make of truck takes its name from the initials of its German manufacturing company, the *Maschinenfabrik Augsburg-Nürnberg*, ('Augsburg-Nuremberg Motor Works'). It made its first diesel engine in the late 19th century, and started selling lorries to Britain in 1974.

Man, Isle of The name of the island of the British Isles (though not part of the United Kingdom) is Gaelic in origin, probably deriving from a root word meaning 'mountain'. It thus corresponds to modern Welsh *mynydd* in this sense, and is also cognate with Latin *mons* and so with English *mountain* itself. The reference would be to the mountainous mass that culminates in Snaefell in the centre of the island. It is probably no coincidence that *Môn*, the Welsh name of ANGLESEY, the island that lies due south of Man, is identical in origin and meaning. The Manx name of the Isle of Man is *Ellan Vannan*, where *ellan* means 'island' and *Vannan* is the mutated form of *Mannan*. Julius Caesar recorded the name as *Mona* in the 1st century BC. *See also* MANX.

Managua The capital of Nicaragua takes its name from Lake *Managua*, whose own name derives from Guarani *ama*, 'rain' and *nagua*, 'spirit', 'ghost'.

Manama The name of the capital of Bahrain is Arabic in origin, representing *al-manāma*, 'the place of rest', 'the place of dreams', from *al*, 'the' and *manāma*, 'dream', itself from the verb *nāma*, 'to sleep', 'to dream'.

Manasseh The elder son of Joseph has a name that represents Hebrew *Menaŝŝeh*, 'he who makes forget'. The meaning is alluded to in the account of Manasseh's birth: 'And Joseph called the name of the firstborn Manasseh: For God, said he, hath made me forget all my toil, and all my father's house' (*Genesis* 41.51).

Manchester The well-known city has the *-chester* that indicates it was once a Roman station, from Old English *ceaster*, ultimately from Latin *castra*, 'camp'. The Roman name of the settlement here was *Mamucium*, itself probably from the Celtic word *mamma*, 'breast', describing the rounded hill on which the Roman fort was situated. The adjective *Mancunian*, meaning 'of Manchester', seems to have arisen from a miscopying of the Roman name as *Mancunium*. *Cp.* MANSFIELD.

Manchester City The familiar football club was formed in 1887 by the amalgamation of two existing teams as *Ardwick* Football Club, after the district of Manchester where their ground was. In 1894 they became *Manchester City*.

Manchester College The Oxford college was founded in *Manchester* in 1786 as a theological college offering ministerial training mainly to Unitarian and Free Church students. It moved to Oxford in 1889, but was incorporated into the university only in 1990.

Manchester United The famous football club was formed in the 1870s as the *L and Y Railway* Football Club, so named as its players were employees of the *L*ancashire and *Y*orkshire Railway Company. In 1878 they became *Newton Heath*, after the company's main Manchester depot. In 1902, facing liquidation, the club was rescued by a local brewer and turned into *Manchester United*. *Cp.* MANCHESTER CITY.

Manchuria The region of northeast China takes its name from its indigenous people, the *Manchu*, whose own name is the Manchu word for 'pure'.

Mandalay The well-known Burmese city, the former capital, has a name that represents Sanskrit *maṇḍala*, 'circle', 'disk'. This is the same word as the *mandala* which in Hinduism and Buddhism is the circular symbol that represents the evolution and involution of the universe.

Mandarin The official language of China, spoken by about two-thirds of the population, takes its name from the *mandarins*, who were the senior officials of the bureaucracy in the Chinese Empire, and who therefore spoke 'official' Chinese. Their own title derives, through Portuguese, from Sanskrit *mantrin*, 'counsellor', itself from *mantra*, 'counsel'. The Chinese name of Mandarin is *guānhuà*, 'civil servant language'. The type of small orange called *mandarin* is so named because its colour suggests that of the robes worn by the historic *mandarins*.

Mandingo The name is that formerly used for the MALINKE people (*which see*).

Manfred The name is Germanic in origin, comprising either *man*, 'man' and *fridu*, 'peace', or *magin*, 'strength' (as for English 'might and *main*') and *fridu*. If the latter, the name equates to 'peace through strength'.

Manfred Mann The British pop group, formed in 1962, took their name from their South African-born keyboard player *Manfred Mann*, whose original name was Michael Lubowitz.

Mang The name of the bat in Kipling's *Jungle Books* (1894, 1895) is one that the author admitted to inventing. The actual Hindustani word for 'bat' is *chamgādar*.

Mangalore The port of southern India, on the Malabar Coast, has a name deriving from Sanskrit *maṅgala*, 'happiness', 'good fortune' and *pur*, 'town'. The form of the name appears to have been influenced by that of BANGALORE, which lies due east of Mangalore.

Manhattan The island that is administratively a borough of New York has a name deriving from that of the Indian people who once lived here. Their own name has been explained in a number of ways, most of them colourfully speculative, such as 'place of drunkenness' or 'place where we were cheated', referring to supposed (or actual) incidents.

Manhattan Transfer The American pop group, formed in 1969, took their name from the title of the novel by Jon Dos Passos, *Manhattan Transfer* (1925), itself describing the decadent life of New York. The novel in turn took its title from the name of the station on the Pennsylvania Railroad in New Jersey where passengers travelling between New York and points south and west had to change trains.

Manichaeism The form of dualistic religion takes its name from its founder, the Persian prophet *Manichaeus* or *Mani* (or *Manes*), who lived in the 3rd century AD. A number of fantastic etymologies have been proposed to explain his name, including an origin in *mania* or Sanskrit *mani*, 'precious jewel'. The Manichaeans themselves derived their name from Syrian *Mânî hayyâ*, 'Mani alive'.

Manila The port and capital of the Philippines has a name that represents Tagalog *may*, 'there is' and *nila*, the native name of a shrub of the indigo family.

Manipur The name of the union territory of northeast India derives from that of its people. Their own name is of uncertain origin.

Manitoba The province of western Canada takes its name from Lake *Manitoba*, itself named for one of its islands. The island's name derives from Algonquian *Manitou*, 'great spirit'.

Manley The name derives from a place so called, such as the village of *Manley* near Chester. It means 'shared wood', from Old English *mǣne*, 'common', 'public' and *lēah*, 'clearing', 'wood'. The surname has found some use as a first name, no doubt through its suggestion of *manly*.

Mann The name originated either as a nickname for a fierce or strong boy or man or for a person who was a servant. For the latter sense, *cp*. MASTERMAN.

Mannerism The name applies to the style of art or architecture that developed in

Italy in the 16th century and that broke from classical norms in its deliberate distortion of traditional forms, colours and perspectives. It was coined (as *manierismo*) by the contemporary Italian art historian Vasari in his *Lives* (1520) to refer to the *mannered* characteristics of the style.

Manners The name is Norman in origin, from the place-name *Mesnières*, now a small village near Dieppe. Its own meaning is 'residence', from Latin *manere*, 'to remain', 'to reside'. *Cp.* MENZIES.

Mannheim The city of southwest Germany probably takes its name from *Mano*, a man's name (itself meaning 'man') and *heim*, 'home'. According to some authorities, however, the first part of the name could be Celtic in origin, meaning 'stone' (as modern Welsh *maen* in this sense). The 'stone' might then have been a boundary marker of some kind. The natural boundary here would be the river Rhine, and Mannheim itself is even now close to the border between the Rhineland Palatinate and Baden-Württemberg, while itself being geographically in the latter.

Manon The operas *Manon* (1884) by Massenet and *Manon Lescaut* (1893) by Puccini are both based on the novel *Manon Lescaut* (1731) by Abbé Prévost, in which the young Chevalier des Grieux elopes with the heroine, who is about to be made a nun. Her first name is a French pet form of *Marie* (*see* MARIA). The Massenet opera title is sometimes confused with that of MIGNON, by Thomas.

Mans, Le *See* LE MANS.

Mansell The name derives either from the Old French word *mansel*, the term for an inhabitant of LE MANS, or from an identical Norman French word that denoted the occupant of a *manse*, in its original sense of a measure of land sufficient to support a single family.

Mansfield The Nottinghamshire town takes its name from the river *Maun*, on which it stands, with the second half of the name representing Old English *feld*, 'open land' (modern *field*). The river takes its name from a hill some four miles (6.5 km) away, formerly called *Mammesheud*, meaning '*Mam*'s headland'. *Mam* is not a personal name but that of the hill itself, probably deriving from the same Celtic word *mamma*, 'breast' that lies behind the name of MANCHESTER.

Mansfield College The Oxford college has its origins in the Congregational theological college that moved from Birmingham to Oxford in 1886. When in Birmingham the college was known as *Spring Hill College*, from its location, but on moving to Oxford was renamed *Mansfield College* after the *Mansfield* family who had originally founded Spring Hill College in 1838. Since 1955 the college has been a permanent private hall, similar to a full college, with students studying subjects other than theology.

Mansura The city in northeast Egypt has an Arabic name, from *al-manṣūra*, 'the victorious', referring to the battle of 1250 in which the Crusaders were defeated by the Mamelukes, with the capture of Louis IX of France. For a similar name, *see* CAIRO.

Mantua The city of northern Italy probably derives its name from that of *Mantus*, the Etruscan god of the Underworld mentioned by Dante in the *Divine Comedy* (*Inferno*, 20).

Manx The name of the people and language of the Isle of MAN is of Scandinavian origin. Hence the final *x*, which represents the *sk* of the Old Norse original *mansk*. *Cp.* modern Norwegian *norsk* for 'Norwegian' and Danish *dansk* for 'Danish'. The last native speaker of Manx died in 1974, although the tongue continues to be promoted by local linguists.

Maori The name of the indigenous people of New Zealand means 'native', 'people' in their own language.

Maples The well-known London furniture store takes its name from John *Maple* (d. 1900), who with a partner first set up business as a draper and furnisher in Tottenham Court Road in 1840.

Mappa Mundi The name is that of the famous 13th-century map of the world in Hereford Cathedral. It is Medieval Latin for 'map of the world'.

Mappin and Webb The firm of London goldsmiths, silversmiths and jewellers is named for its founder in 1870, John Newton *Mappin* (1836–1913), a Sheffield cutler's son, with a Mr *Webb* as his partner.

Maputo The capital and chief port of Mozambique takes its name from that of the river which flows into the bay on which it stands. This in turn was named for one of the sons of the local chief Nuagobe, who lived in the 18th century. Until 1976 Maputo was known as *Lourenço Marques*, after the Portuguese trader who explored the region in 1544.

Maquis The French resistance movement against German occupation in the Second World War took its name from the *maquis*, the type of scrubby woodland that grows by the coast in Mediterranean countries. The term was originally current in Corsica for the scrubland there used as a place of refuge by escaped prisoners, and the French patriotic force adopted the term because they regarded their underground activities as taking place in cover of this kind. The word derives from Italian *macchia*, 'thicket', itself from Latin *macula*, 'spot'.

Maracaibo The city and port in northwest Venezuela takes its name from Lake *Maracaibo*, itself so named by the Spanish explorer Alonso de Hojeda after the cacique (American Indian chief) that he met here in 1499.

Marais The district of Paris, to the east of the city centre, has a name referring to the *marsh* that was here in medieval times. It became the market garden of Paris, and as such gave the term for market gardening generally in France, *culture maraîchère*.

Marajó The island in northern Brazil, at the mouth of the Amazon, has a name that refers to its location, from Guarani *para*, 'river' and *jho*, 'to go out'. *Cp.* MARANHÃO.

Maranhão The state in northeast Brazil takes its name from the island on which the state capital of São Luís lies, the city being named by the French in 1612 in honour of Louis XIII (St Louis), but captured soon after by the Portuguese, who adapted the name to their own language. The island is now also called São Luís, but earlier had a name of Guarani origin, from *para*, 'river', *na*, 'parent' and *jho*, 'to go out' (*cp.* MARAJÓ), which evolved to the current *Maranhão*. The island is now more a long

peninsula between the drowned mouths of two rivers, the Mearim and the Itapicuru.

Marathon The plain in Attica, famous for the victory of the Athenians over the Persians in 490 BC, takes its name from Greek *marathron*, 'fennel', a plant that grows abundantly here. The modern sporting *marathon* takes its name from the feat of the messenger who in the year stated ran 26 miles (42 km) from Marathon to Athens to bring news of the victory. The distance he ran remains basically that of the Olympic marathon of today.

Marazion The small town and resort near Penzance, Cornwall, has a Cornish name that means 'little market', from *marghas*, 'market' and *byghan*, 'little'. The alternative name of the town is *Market Jew*, preserved in the name of *Market Jew* Street, Penzance, which leads from the Market Place in the direction of Marazion. The second word of this name represents Cornish *yow*, 'Thursday', so that there would at one time have been a 'Thursday market' as well as a 'little market', the latter presumably so called as it was the less important of the two.

Marble Arch The famous London landmark at the northwest corner of Hyde Park was originally erected in 1827 in front of Buckingham Palace, where it was intended to serve as a main gateway. As its name implies, it is made of *marble*. It is said to have been based on the Arch of Constantine before the Colosseum in Rome.

March The third month of the year was the first in the Roman republican calendar, when as *Martius* it was dedicated to the god MARS.

March The Cambridgeshire town has a name that shows it was originally a place on a boundary, from Old English *mearc*, 'boundary' (modern *mark*). However, March is not and never has been on a county boundary, so there must have been some other delimitation here. It has been suggested that March was at the western limit of the administrative region of ELY, whose own name means 'eel district'. *See also* MARCHE, MARCHES, MERCIA.

Marchant The name denotes someone who was originally a buyer and seller of goods, otherwise a *merchant*. The standard English word has restored the *er* that was present in the original Latin word *mercari*, 'to trade'.

Marche The former province of central France has a name that means 'boundary', since it was bordered by five other provinces. The Old French word *marche* that gave the name has many related words in modern English, including *mark*, *marquis*, *margrave* and *margin*. *See also* MARCHES, MERCIA.

Marches, the The name is a traditional one for the border country between England and Scotland, or England and Wales (the 'Welsh Marches'). It was adopted as a title by the earls of *March*, those of the Scottish peerage bearing the surname Dunbar or Douglas, and those of the Welsh peerage Mortimer. The name is also the English rendering of the Italian name *Le Marche*, the region of central Italy that was divided into three *marches* (border provinces) in the 10th century. The origin of the name lies in the Indoeuropean word *marg*, 'border' that has its modern equivalents in English *margin*, *mark* and *march* (in the sense used here). *See also* MARCHE, MERCIA.

Marcia The name is often regarded as a female equivalent for MARK, but it actually arose as a feminine form of MARCUS.

Marco Polo The 13th-century Venetian traveller and writer has a name of Italian origin, his first name *Marco* corresponding to MARK, his family name *Polo* to PAUL. In most reference books he is entered under his surname, but here he is entered under his first name as that is the one with which he is popularly associated in the English-speaking world.

Marcus The name is the Latin name, itself perhaps connected with the name of the god MARS, that gave modern English MARK.

Mardi Gras The name of the French equivalent to SHROVE TUESDAY, a day devoted to feasting and revelry before the start of Lent, literally means 'fat Tuesday'. The specific reference in the name is to the custom of roasting a fat ox (*boeuf gras*) during the day's celebrations.

Marduk The chief god of the Babylonians has a name that has been explained as either deriving from Sumerian *Amar-Utu*, 'calf of *Utu*', the latter being the god of the sun, or as representing the name *Mar-Duku*, 'son of *Duku*', that is, of the place where Marduk's temple was situated. His name is an element in the names of various Babylonian kings, such as *Marduk-idin-achi*, 'Marduk gave the brother' in the 12th century BC, and *Marduk-nadin-shum*, 'Marduk is giver of the name' in the 9th. The name is thought to have also given that of MORDECAI.

Margaret The familiar name ultimately goes back to an origin in Greek *margarites*, 'pearl'. It has long been a popular name among royalty, from St *Margaret* of Scotland, wife of King Malcolm Canmore in the 11th century, to Princess *Margaret*, younger sister of Queen Elizabeth in the 20th.

Margate The Kent coastal resort has a name that is usually explained as meaning 'sea gate', from Old English *mere*, 'sea' and *geat*, 'gate', 'gap'. A more precise interpretation, however, would probably be 'pool gate', referring to a gap in the cliffs here by a pool or pond that has now dried up.

Maria The name is the Latin form of MARY, still popular as a first name not only in continental Europe but among English speakers. In Roman Catholic countries it is specially associated with the Virgin Mary. It has many forms and variants, ranging from French *Marie* and its diminutive *Marion* or *Marian* to English MOLLY and POLLY. *See also* MARILYN.

Mariana Islands The islands in the West Pacific were so named (as Spanish *Islas Marianas*) in 1668 in honour of Queen *Mariana* of Austria, widow of Philip IV of Spain. The name was given by Spanish Jesuits in place of the earlier Portuguese name, *Islas dos Ladrões*, 'islands of thieves', given by Magellan (from personal experience) on his discovery of the islands in 1521.

Marianne The name is that of the female figure who came to personify the French republic after the Revolution of 1793. She is traditionally portrayed as a bust, and wears a Phrygian cap (a symbol of liberty at the time of the Revolution). The reason for the choice of this particular name is uncertain. According to one theory, her name echoes that of the Spanish Jesuit historian Juan de *Mariana* (1532–1624), who spoke in favour of the assassination of tyrant monarchs. Another authority claims that the name is a mystical representation of the French words *République démocratique et sociale*. From a religious viewpoint, the name can be seen as combining that of the Virgin *Mary* with that of her mother, St *Anne*, as does the popular French name *Anne-Marie*.

Mariánské Lázně The town in the western Czech Lands was a fashionable spa in the 18th and 19th centuries, when it had the more familiar German name of *Marienbad*. Both names have the same meaning, '*Mary*'s springs'. The thermal springs had an image of the Virgin Mary at their entrance. To many local people, however, the name was connected more readily with that of *Maria Theresa* (1717–1780), archduchess of Austria and queen of Hungary and Bohemia.

Marienbad *See* MARIÁNSKÉ LÁZNĚ.

Marillion The British rock band, formed in 1979 in Aylesbury, Buckinghamshire, had the original name *Silmarillion*, adopting this from the identically titled Tolkien novel that had been published two years earlier (as a 'prequel' to *The Hobbit*). In 1980 the group shortened their name to *Marillion*. The name of the novel itself was intended to mean 'book of the *Silmarils*', these being three exquisite jewels made of *silima*, a mysterious hard crystalline substance.

Marilyn The name is a combination of MARY and the *-lyn* that ends such names as *Carolyn* and that is itself popularly associated with the independent name LYNN.

Marina The name is sometimes regarded as a form of MARY, although it actually evolved as a feminine form of the Latin name *Marinus*. This itself has been associated with the Latin adjective *marinus*, 'of the sea', but is more likely to be ultimately derived from the name of MARS, the Roman god of war.

Mariner The name of the American space probes that explored the planets Mercury, Venus and Mars between 1962 and 1975

had the meaning 'navigator', 'seaman'. It also happens to suggest the name of MARS itself.

Mariupol The Ukrainian port, on the Sea of Azov, was founded as a Greek settlement in 1779 and named (as if 'Mariopolis') for *Maria* Petrovna (original name Sophia Dorothea), wife of the future emperor of Russia (from 1796) Paul I. In 1948 the city was renamed *Zhdanov* for the Soviet politician and Communist Party official Andrey *Zhdanov* (1896–1948). In 1989 it reverted to its original name.

Marjoribanks The name is Scottish, and is said to have been adopted in the early 16th century by a family originally called Johnston when they acquired the estate of *Ratho-Marjoribankis* in Renfrewshire. This in turn was so named because it had been granted to *Marjorie*, the daughter of Robert the Bruce, on her marriage to Walter the High Steward in 1316. The name is usually pronounced 'Marchbanks'.

Marjorie The name developed from the earlier name *Margery* that was itself a medieval form of MARGARET. The spelling was perhaps altered by association with the flowering herb *marjoram*.

Mark The English name evolved from the Latin name MARCUS, and is familiar as that of the apostle who is regarded as the author of St Mark's Gospel.

Market Bosworth *See* BOSWORTH, Battle of.

Market Harborough The Leicestershire town derives the second word of its name from Old English *hæfera*, 'oats' (as originally carried in a *haver*sack) and *beorg*, 'hill'. The name as a whole thus means 'market place on a hill where oats are grown'. The first word emphasizes the fact that the *market* here was important.

Marks and Spencer The well-known department stores are named for Michael *Marks* (1859–1907) and Thomas *Spencer* (1852–1905). Marks, a Russian Jewish immigrant to Britain, first set up a 'Penny Bazaar' in Leeds marketplace in 1884. His business grew, so that in 1894 he was joined as partner by Spencer, a cashier at one of Marks's suppliers. It was Marks's first name that gave the company its distinctive brand name of *St Michael*.

Marlboro The familiar brand name of American cigarettes is (in a modified spelling) an English aristocratic one, associated not so much directly with the town of MARLBOROUGH as with the dukes and earls who took the name of the town as their title. The most famous was the military commander John Churchill, first Duke of *Marlborough* (1650–1722), who led the British forces in the War of the Spanish Succession, winning a famous victory at Blenheim in 1704. Originally launched in the 19th century, the *Marlboro* cigarette was promoted in the 1920s as a brand specially suitable for women. In their case the association could equally have been with the Duke's wife, the famous Sarah Churchill, Duchess of *Marlborough* (1660–1744), an influential friend of royalty.

Marlborough The Wiltshire town has a name of disputed origin. It ends in Old English *beorg*, 'hill', but the first half of the name may be either a personal name or, according to some authorities, the Old English word *mēargealla*, meaning 'gentian'. This plant may have been specially grown here for medicinal purposes.

Marlborough House The mansion in Pall Mall, London, now used for Commonwealth conferences but earlier a royal residence, was built in 1711 for Sarah Churchill, Duchess of *Marlborough* (*see* MARLBORO).

Marlow The Buckinghamshire town, on the Thames, has a name deriving from Old English *mere*, 'lake' and *lāf*, 'that which is left'. In other words, it arose as a drained place by a lake. The lake itself would originally have linked up with the river here.

Marmaduke The origin of the rather aristocratic-sounding name is uncertain. It has been associated with the Celtic name *Madoc*, itself said to derive from a word related to modern Welsh *mad*, 'good'.

Marmara, Sea of The sea between the Bosporus and the Dardanelles takes its name from the island group of *Marmara*. The islands themselves derive their name from

Greek *marmaros*, 'marble', which together with granite and slate is still quarried here.

Marmite The familiar name of the yeast and vegetable extract derives from the French word *marmite*, the term for a type of large cooking pot. The proprietary name was first used in 1902.

Marne The river in northeast France derives its name from Gaulish *matra*, 'mother', probably referring to a 'mother goddess' who was believed to dwell in its waters in ancient times.

Marple The name of the town near Manchester means 'boundary stream', from Old English *gemǣre*, 'boundary' and *pyll*, 'pool', 'stream'. The stream in question is the river Goyt on which the town stands, and the boundary is the former county one between Cheshire and Derbyshire.

Marquesas Islands The islands in the South Pacific, in French Polynesia, were discovered by the Spanish explorer Álvaro de Mendaña in 1595 and named by him *Islas Marquesas*, in honour of the *Marquis* Antonio de Mendoza, Viceroy of Peru.

Marrakech The city and former capital of Morocco derives its name from a Berber word meaning 'fortified'. It came to give the name of MOROCCO itself.

Mars The Roman god of war has a name that has been variously associated with Greek *marnamai*, 'I fight', Latin *mas*, 'virility' (hence English *masculine*), and a Sanskrit root word meaning 'striker'. The planet *Mars* is named for the god, probably because its reddish-orange surface gives it a 'belligerent' appearance.

Mars The well-known *Mars Bars* take their name from Forrest *Mars*, an American confectionery manufacturer, who after a quarrel with his father came to Britain in the 1930s to set up his own company. The same man's name lies behind the coloured chocolate buttons marketed as *M & Ms*, standing for 'Mars and Mars'.

Marsala The town in Sicily has a name that is probably of Arabic origin, from *marsā-allah*, 'port of Allah' (*i.e.* of God), or possibly *marsā-ʿalī*, 'port of Ali'. The town was founded by the Arabs in the 9th century on the ruins of the ancient city of

Lilybaeum, itself founded by the Carthaginians in 397 BC.

Marseillaise The name of the French national anthem refers to its historic origin in MARSEILLE, where it was composed by the army captain Claude Rouget de Lisle in 1792 during the French Revolution and taken up to Paris by volunteer army units. Its original title was *Chant de guerre de l'armée du Rhin* ('War Song of the Rhine Army'). It was officially adopted as the national anthem in 1795, although banned more than once subsequently for its Revolutionary associations. No doubt some French people subconsciously associate the name, not inappropriately, with that of MARS, the god of war.

Marseille The famous city and port in the south of France has a name that is an alteration of its ancient Greek name *Massilia*. This is probably pre-Latin in origin, and may represent the Ligurian root word *mas*, 'spring'. In 1793, at the time of the French Revolution, Marseille was punished for its royalist views by being renamed *Ville-sans-Nom*, 'Town Without a Name' (which is nevertheless a name!). *See also* MARSEILLAISE. The *r* in the name may have come about through an association with MARS, the god of war.

Marshall The surname, occasionally used as a first name, derives from the Old French word *mareschal* that gave the ordinary word (and military rank) *marshal*. It was used in French as a title for a groom (a person who looked after horses), and is itself of Germanic origin, from *marah*, 'horse' (related to English *mare*) and *scalc*, 'servant' (related to the second half of *seneschal*). The use of the word as a personal name may have been influenced by its resemblance to the name of the god MARS.

Marshall Islands The group of islands in the West Pacific was explored in 1788 by the British naval officer, Captain John *Marshall*, and was named for him. The islands were originally discovered by the Spanish in the early 16th century.

Marston Moor, Battle of The site of the Parliamentarian victory of 1644 in the English Civil War takes its name from the nearby village of *Long Marston*, near York. The name itself means 'marsh farm', from

Old English *mersc*, 'marsh' and *tūn*, 'farm', 'settlement' (modern *town*).

Martell The familiar French brandy is named for Jean *Martell* (d. 1750), who in 1715 left his native Channel Islands to set up a brandy exporting company in France near Cognac. The company is now the second largest cognac house in the world, and remains in the hands of the Martell family.

Martha The name is of biblical origin, from Aramaic *Mārthā*, 'lady', 'mistress'. It is an appropriate name for Martha, sister of Lazarus and Mary of Bethany, who was 'cumbered with much serving' (*Luke* 10.38) when Jesus visited her, while Mary sat at his feet listening to him. For this reason the two names have come to be regarded as expressing a contrast, with *Martha* in particular associated with domestic drudgery. It is sometimes punningly linked with *martyr* in the latter sense, as in the following: 'She belonged to that noble army of Marthas who cook the dinners that the Marys gobble up to keep them going between their visions and their dreams' (Elizabeth Goudge, *Towers in the Mist*, 1938).

Martha and the Vandellas The American pop group was formed in Detroit in 1961 with *Martha* Reeves as its lead singer. The *Vandellas* were the two other members of the trio, Annette Sterling and Rosalind Ashford, named after *Van* Dyke Street, Detroit, and *Della* Reese, Reeves' favourite singer.

Martha's Vineyard The island off Cape Cod, Massachusetts, now a popular resort, was discovered by Gabriel Archer in 1602 and apparently named by him for a woman called MARTHA and for the vines he saw growing there. The name has a certain biblical allusiveness (as if a blend of *Martha* and *Naboth's vineyard*), but this may be purely coincidental.

Martin The name is Latin in origin, from *Martinus*, itself perhaps originally deriving from MARS, the name of the Roman god of war. The name was made famous by St *Martin* of Tours, who is remembered for dividing his cloak in two and giving half to a beggar. His act of doing this gave the English word *chapel*, from the sanctuary where his cloak (Latin *cappella*) was preserved as a holy relic by the Frankish kings. *See also* MARTINMAS, ST MARTIN'S.

Martini The well-known vermouth is named for its Italian manufacturers, now *Martini* and Rossi, but originally founded in Turin in 1840 as *Martini* and Sola. Rather confusingly, the cocktail known as a *Dry Martini* is named for another man of the name, one *Martini* di Taggia di Arma, head bartender at the former Knickerbocker Hotel, New York, who invented it in 1910.

Martinique The Caribbean island, administratively an overseas department of France, has a name of uncertain origin. According to one account, when Christopher Columbus approached the island in January 1493 he saw a group of women on the shore calling *'madinina!'* The meaning of this was never discovered, but the word was entered on early charts and was corrupted to *Martinique* under the influence of the name of St MARTIN.

Martinmas In the Christian church, the name is that of the feast of St MARTIN, 11 November, when fairs were formerly held and cattle slaughtered for consumption.

Marvin *See* MERVYN.

Mary The well-known name is biblical in origin, with the New Testament *Mary* a form of the older Old Testament name MIRIAM. The traditional interpretation of the name is as either 'bitter' or 'rebelliousness'. But both these seem unlikely. More probably the name evolved from the Egyptian root element *mrh* meaning 'to be fat', giving a transferred sense 'strong' or 'fertile' (or a combination of both). The name is most familiar from the Virgin *Mary*, the mother of Jesus, and worship of Mary from the earliest Christian times has made the name enduringly popular. Apart from the Virgin, other prominent women of the name in the New Testament are MARY MAGDALENE, *Mary* the sister of Martha, *Mary* the mother of James and Joseph, and *Mary* the mother of Mark. The name in any of its forms (especially Latin MARIA) has also been widely adopted by members of royal families, and is well known in British history alone from four queens: *Mary* I ('Bloody Mary') and *Mary*, Queen of Scots in the 16th century, *Mary* II (reigning with her husband William) in the 17th, and

Queen *Mary*, the Queen Mother, wife of George V and mother of George VI, in the 20th.

Maryland The original territory of the American state was granted in 1632 to George Calvert, Lord Baltimore, as a proprietary colony, and was named for Queen Henrietta *Maria*, wife of Charles I.

Marylebone The district of north central London takes its name from the stream here. This is now known as *St Mary's* stream, but was originally called TYBURN, meaning 'boundary stream'. The *burn* of this is the *-bone* of the present name, and derives from Old English *burna*, 'stream' (as for Scottish *burn*). The *-le-* of the name was probably inserted by false association with *St Mary-le-Bow* (*see* BOW BELLS). The stream's name was changed because *Tyburn* came to be unfavourably associated with the Tyburn gallows, erected at Marble Arch. It was therefore replaced by a 'good' name.

Mary Magdalene The biblical MARY cured of evil spirits by Jesus (*Luke* 8.2) is so named because she came from MAGDALA, on Lake Galilee. She has also been identified with the unnamed woman who wept in repentance for her sins and washed the feet of Jesus with her tears (*Luke* 7.38). The many paintings of her doing so gave the English word *maudlin* to mean 'foolishly tearful or sentimental'. *See also* MADELEINE, MAGDALEN COLLEGE, MAGDALENE COLLEGE, MAUDLING.

Masan The port in southeast South Korea takes its name from Chinese *mä*, 'horse' and *shān*, 'mountain'.

Maserati The famous racing car is named for five of six Italian brothers who were involved in the motor industry, Alfieri, Carlo, Bindo, Ettore and Ernesto *Maserati*, the sixth, Mario, being an artist. Alfieri (d. 1932) first developed the car in Bologna in 1924.

Maseru The capital of Lesotho, southern Africa, has a name representing Sesotho *maseru*, 'red sandstones', as a word that is the plural of *leseru*.

Mashhad The city in northeast Iran, the holy city of Shi'ite Muslims, derives its name from Iranian *maḥal*, 'palace' (*cp.* TAJ

MAHAL) and *šahādat*, 'martyr'. It was the place of martyrdom of Ali Reza, eighth Shi'ite imam, in 818.

Mason The name is the ordinary word for a person who worked in stone, itself ultimately connected with the word *make*.

Mason-Dixon Line The state boundary between Maryland and Pennsylvania, popularly regarded as the dividing line between North and South in the United States, and particularly between the free and slave states before the American Civil War, takes its name from the English astronomers who surveyed it between 1763 and 1767, Charles *Mason* and Jeremiah *Dixon*.

Masora The official text of the Hebrew Bible, as revised by the Masoretes (the school of rabbis named for it) from the 6th to the 10th centuries, has a name that represents the Hebrew word for 'tradition'. The name is sometimes spelled *Massorah*.

Massachusetts The American state takes its name from the Algonquian Indian people who originally lived here, with their own name deriving from *mass-adchu-seuck*, 'people of the big hill'. The 'big hill' was the group of hills now known as the Blue Hills. The Pilgrim Fathers founded the Plymouth Colony here in 1620, and gave the Indian name to the bay, from which it subsequently passed to the territory and state. The name was first recorded in writing (without its present final *s*) in 1614.

Massif Central The mountainous plateau of south central France has a name that refers to its location and to the linking *masses* of crystalline rocks that underlie it.

Masterman The name originated as a Scottish occupational title for a servant, someone who was his 'master's man'. The name has occasionally been adopted as a first name, as famously for the central character of Captain Marryat's novel for children *Masterman Ready* (1841), a literary title that is sometimes assumed to allude to a naval rank. (He is actually an old seaman, which compounds the confusion.)

Masuria The region of northwest Poland has a name that is of the same origin as that of MAZOVIA (*which see*).

Matabeleland The region of western Zimbabwe takes its name from the *Matabele*, the African people who live here. Their own name is a Sotho or Tswana form of *Ndebele*, itself from a Zulu word *amandebele* meaning 'those who disappear'. The Ndebele had been obliged to flee their original territory in the early 19th century, and moved north to the present Matabeleland.

Matilda The name is Germanic in origin, representing *maht*, 'might' and *hild*, 'battle', so 'mighty in battle'. Appropriately, it was the name of the wife of William the Conqueror. In its turn it gave the name MAUD.

Matlock The name of the Derbyshire town means 'assembly oak', from Old English *mæthel*, 'council', 'assembly' and *āc*, 'oak'. The reference is to a tree where a moot or Anglo-Saxon council would have been held to discuss matters of law and local administration.

Mato Grosso The state of west central Brazil takes its name from the extensive forested plateau here, with the name itself simply the Portuguese for 'dense forest', from *mato*, 'forest', 'bush' and *grosso*, 'thick', 'dense'.

Matsushita The Japanese electronics company is named for its founder in 1926, Konosuke *Matsushita* (1894–1989). The company introduced such well-known trade names as *National* and *Panasonic*.

Matsuyama The city and port in southwest Japan has a name that means 'pine mountain', from *matsu*, 'pine' and *yama*, 'mountain'.

Matterhorn The mountain on the border between Italy and Switzerland derives its name from German *Matte*, 'meadow', 'pastureland' and *Horn*, 'horn', the latter referring to the curved shape of the mountain's peak (actually the end of a ridge). The French and Italian names of the mountain, respectively *Mont Cervin*, *Monte Cervino*, derive from Italian *cervino*, 'cervine', 'deer-like', comparing the peak similarly to a deer's curved antlers.

Matthew The biblical name, familiar as that of the apostle who is regarded as the author of St Matthew's Gospel, evolved as a shortened form of the Hebrew name

Mattathiāh, 'gift of Yah', *i.e.* Jehovah, found for five Old Testament characters named *Mattithiah* and five named *Mattathias*. MATTHIAS is a name of identical origin.

Matthias The name is familiar in the New Testament as that of the disciple who was elected in place of Judas Iscariot. His name is of the same origin as that of the apostle MATTHEW, but in the English Bible differs from it so that the two can be distinguished.

Maud The name is a medieval Germanic spoken form of MATILDA, so has the same origin as that name.

Maudling The name represents a medieval spoken form of *Magdalene*, the Greek girl's name that itself derives from that of the biblical MARY MAGDALENE.

Mau Mau The name is that of the secret political society of Kikuyu tribesmen formed in 1952 to drive Europeans out of Kenya. The name itself is Kikuyu but its meaning is unknown.

Mauna Kea The extinct volcano in Hawaii has a native name meaning 'white mountain', from Hawaiian *mauna*, 'mountain' and *kea*, 'white'. Mauna Kea is the highest island mountain in the world. *Cp.* MAUNA LOA.

Mauna Loa The active volcano in Hawaii has a native name meaning 'big mountain', from Hawaiian *mauna*, 'mountain' and *loa*, 'big'. Mauna Loa is not quite as high as MAUNA KEA, however.

Maundy Thursday In the Christian calendar, the name is that of the Thursday before Easter, when the Last Supper is celebrated. The day was originally associated with the ceremony of washing the feet of poor people in commemoration of Jesus' own washing of his disciples' feet. The origin of the name lies in an Old French word based on Latin *mandatum*, 'commandment', from the Latin text of Jesus' words after his own act of washing (*John* 13.5): *Mandatum novum do vobis*, 'A new commandment I give unto you' ('that ye love one another') (*John* 13.34). The ritual of washing the feet of the poor in English churches was followed by the distribution of clothes, food or money. Today, the distribution of *Maundy money* by the sovereign to selected pensioners is normally all that remains of this ceremony, although certain churches do re-enact the washing in some form.

Maureen The name is an English form of Irish *Máirín*, which is a pet form of *Máire*, the Irish equivalent of MARY. The pet form has the Irish diminutive ending -*ín*, as in *colleen*, the English word for an Irish girl (which itself gave the name COLLEEN). *Cp. also* KATHLEEN MAVOURNEEN.

Mauretania The ancient region of North Africa takes its name from the MOORS who inhabited it. The modern republic of *Mauritania* in northwest Africa has essentially the same name.

Maurice The English name derives from the Latin name *Mauricius*, itself a form of *Maurus*, meaning 'Moor', so 'dark', 'swarthy'. MORRIS is another form of the name. *See also* MOORS.

Mauritania See MAURETANIA.

Mauritius The island and state in the Indian Ocean was discovered by the Portuguese in 1505 but occupied by the Dutch in 1598, when they named it in honour of the future Prince of Orange, *Maurice* of Nassau (1567–1625), stadholder (chief executive) of the Dutch Republic (from 1584).

Mavis The name is a relatively modern one, not recorded before the late 19th century. It probably derives from the alternative name for the song thrush.

Max The name is a shortened version of a name such as *Maximilian* or MAXWELL. The first of these derives from the Latin name *Maximilianus*, a diminutive of *Maximus*, meaning 'greatest'. Today, however, the name *Max* is popularly associated with *Mac*, itself the short form of a Scottish surname beginning *Mac-* or *Mc-*, sometimes used to address a man whose real name is unknown.

Max Factor The well-known cosmetic company is named for its founder, *Max Factor* (1877–1938), a Polish wigmaker and makeup artist who emigrated to America in 1904, setting up business in Hollywood five years later as a creator of cosmetics for the growing cinema industry.

Maxwell The Scottish surname, sometimes also used as a first name, comes from a place-name, itself meaning '*Mack*'s well', with *Mack* here a form of *Magnus*, the Latin word for 'great'.

Maxwell House The familiar brand of coffee is named for an American hotel, the prestigious *Maxwell House*, in Nashville, Tennessee, where in 1883 a coffee manufacturer, Joel Owsley Cheek, won approval for a new blend of coffee that he had devised.

May The first name has an unusually large number of pleasant associations. It is actually a pet form of MARGARET or MARY, but is also regarded as a 'month name', like APRIL or JUNE, and as a 'flower name', from the hawthorn. All these senses (name, month, flower) more or less combine in the title of *Queen of the May*, as that of a pretty girl chosen to display her charms in May Day celebrations. *See also* the name of the month MAY and MAID MARIAN.

May The fifth month of the year is named for the Roman goddess MAIA, to whom it was dedicated in the Roman republican calendar.

Maya The American Indian people of central America take their name from the peninsula of Yucatan where they originally lived. The name is said to represent the Maya word for 'not enough', 'not much', referring to their limited territory.

Mayenne The department of northwest France takes its name from the river that runs through it. The river's own name is probably pre-Indoeuropean in origin, from either a root element *med* found in river names, or from Gaulish *medio*, 'middle', denoting the location of the river between the Sarthe and the Vilaine.

Mayfair The famous district of west central London has a name that means what it says, referring to the annual summer *fair* that was formerly held here in *May*. The site of the fair was Brook Field, beside the Tyburn, where Brook Street is today. The fair was suppressed in the mid-18th century, by which time building had already begun on the site.

Mayflower The name is famous as that of the ship which brought the Pilgrim Fathers from England to America in 1620. The name had no special significance for this voyage, and the *Mayflower* did not even set sail in May. It is simply a standard ship name adopted from that of a flower, in this case one that blooms in May. The name predates the earliest record (1626) of the word *mayflower* in the *Oxford English Dictionary*.

Maynard The surname, which is sometimes adopted as a first name, itself derives from a personal name meaning 'strong and brave', from Old German *magin*, 'strength' and *hard*, 'hardy', 'brave'.

Maynard School, The The public day school for girls in Exeter, Devon, opened in 1877 under an endowment of 1658 made by the Presbyterian royalist Sir John *Maynard* (1592–1658).

Mayo The Irish county takes its name from the village of *Mayo*, whose own name means 'plain of the yew tree', as represented in its current Irish name of *Maigh Eo*. The village became important through the abbey nearby, which was founded in the 7th century and became a centre of learning.

Mayotte The island in the Indian Ocean, administered by France, has a name that is a corruption of its native name *M'Ayâta* or *Mawutu*. The meaning of this is unknown.

Mays The name is that of the rowing races held at Cambridge University between competing college crews in *May Week*. Despite its name, this week has long been in June, at the end of the academic year, but was originally in May.

Mazda The name of the Persian god of wisdom, goodness and light represents the Avestan word meaning 'wise'. His other name was *Ormazd* or *Ormuzd*. Until recently *Mazda* was regarded as a contracted form of his full name AHURA MAZDA, although it was debated whether *Mazda* should be understood as an epithet of *Ahura* (*i.e.* 'wise Ahura') or whether it was simply a noun meaning 'wisdom', so that *Ahura Mazda*'s name meant 'spirit of wisdom'. Modern orientalists are inclined to the view that *Mazda* was essentially the personification of wisdom. There has, however, been some linguistic discussion as to whether the name originated from a noun or an adjective. The difference may seem small, but implies that either *Mazda* actually *is* wisdom or that he is simply a god who is wise.

Mazda The make of car was initially named for the founder of the company that manufactures it, the Japanese engineer *Matsuda* Jujiro (b. 1875). The original name of the company had been *Toyo Kogyo* ('Oriental Industry'), but Matsuda chose the name of the Persian god MAZDA, reflecting his own family name, for his first motor car, a three-wheeled truck produced in 1931. The company became the *Mazda* Motor Corporation in 1984.

Mazovia The ancient principality of Poland, east of the Vistula, derives its name from the personal name *Mazew*, perhaps that of a man who owned territory here. The name of MASURIA has the same origin. It was Mazovia that gave the name of the *mazurka*, as this was where the dance originated.

Mbabane The capital of Swaziland derives its name from that of the river that flows through it. The river's own name is said to represent the native word *lubabe*, referring to a type of local shrub used as animal fodder.

Mc- For Scottish or Irish surnames beginning thus, see the appropriate name under *Mac-*. In each case this represents the Scottish and Irish word *mac*, meaning 'son'.

Meadowbank Thistle The Edinburgh football club was formed in 1943 as *Ferranti Thistle*, its members being employees of the FERRANTI works in the city. They originally played in public parks, but in 1969 settled at City Park (the former home of the defunct team, Edinburgh City). When they were elected to the Scottish League in 1966 they were advised to adopt a less obviously commercial name and to find a new ground. They were allowed by Edinburgh City Council to use the newly built *Meadowbank* Stadium, and adopted its name. The stadium was itself opened in 1970 on the site of a former speedway stadium in order to stage the Commonwealth Games. *Thistle* represents

the flower that is the Scottish national emblem. *Cp.* PARTICK THISTLE.

Meath The English name of the Irish county represents its Irish name *An Mhí*, 'the middle'. Meath was the fifth and final province of Ireland to be established, and the name refers to its historic location between the provinces of Ulster to the north, Connacht to the west, and Leinster in the south. This means that the territory was more extensive than today, and included what is now the county of WESTMEATH.

Mecca The city in western Saudi Arabia, the birthplace of Muhammad and the holiest city of Islam, has a name that has been traced back to a Phoenician word *maqaq* meaning 'ruined'. Some authorities, however, favour an origin in Arabic *maḥrāb*, 'sanctuary', referring to an ancient place of worship which with the rise of Islam in the 7th century became a Muslim shrine.

Meccano The well-known miniature metal construction kit was invented in 1901 by Frank Hornby, maker of the famous model railways named for him (*see* HORNBY). It was originally called *Mechanics Made Easy*, but this was abbreviated to the more manageable *Meccano* in 1907.

Mechelen The city in northern Belgium derives its name from Old High German *muhal*, 'meeting place', 'place of judgment', referring to its former status as a centre for the dispensation of justice, rather in the manner of an Anglo-Saxon moot. The traditional English form of the name is *Mechlin*. Its French name is *Malines*.

Mecklenburg The region and former state of northeast Germany derives its name from Old High German *michil*, 'big' (related to Latin *magnus* and archaic English *mickle*) and *burg*, 'fortress'.

Medan The city in Indonesia, in northeast Sumatra, has a name that is an abbreviation of Malay *medan perang*, 'field of battle', since it was in this region that there was a war between Aceh and the neighbouring kingdom of Deli.

Medea The princess of Colchis, who helped Jason obtain the Golden Fleece from her father Aeëtes, has a name that probably derives from the Greek root element *mēd* meaning 'thought', 'care' found also in English *meditate*. *See also* MEDUSA.

Medes The people of West Iranian speech, famous for destroying the Assyrian capital of Nineveh in the 7th century BC, and for later battling with (and losing to) the Persians, take their name from that of their first king, in Greek *Mēdos*.

Medina The city in western Saudi Arabia, the second most holy city in Islam (after Mecca), has a name that represents Arabic *al-madīna*, 'the city'. This is itself an abbreviated form of its full name, *madīnat an-nabiyy*, 'city of the Prophet', referring to the tomb of Muhammad here.

Mediterranean The well-known sea derives its name from Latin *Mediterraneum mare*, 'sea in the middle of the land', referring to its geographical location, virtually enclosed by Europe in the west and north, Asia in the east, and Africa in the south. Two other Roman names for it were *Mare internum*, 'inner sea', and *Mare nostrum*, 'our sea', as it lay at the heart of the Roman Empire. Many European languages translate the name literally, such as German *Mittelmeer*, modern Greek *Mesogeios* and Russian *Sredizemnoye more*. But the Turkish name of the Mediterranean is *Akdeniz*, 'white sea', as opposed to *Karadeniz*, the BLACK SEA. The Arabic names vary from *al-baḥr al-mutawassiṭ*, 'the middle sea' and *al-baḥr ar-rūm*, 'the sea of Rome' to *al-baḥr al-abyaḍ*, 'the white sea', as for the Turks.

Medusa The name of the famous Gorgon slain by Perseus represents Greek *medousa*, the feminine of *medōn*, 'ruler', 'lord'. It can therefore be understood as the equivalent of 'queen'. Some authorities, however, prefer to link it with the Greek *mēd* root meaning 'thought', alluding to her cunning. (*Cp.* MEDEA.)

Medway The river of southeast England has a Celtic name meaning literally 'mead way', referring to the colour of the water (or perhaps its sweetness) and to its current. By a coincidence (or as a result of folk etymology), the river serves as a *midway* dividing line between the *Men of Kent*, who live to the east of it, and the *Kentishmen*, who live to the west, both these being traditional names for natives of Kent.

Megan The Welsh name arose as a pet form of *Meg*, which is itself a short form of MARGARET.

Meghalaya The state of northeast India has a name that derives from Sanskrit *megha*, 'cloud' and *ālaya*, 'stay'. The region is noted for its long rainy season.

Mehitabel The biblical name, little more than mentioned briefly in a lengthy genealogy (*Genesis* 36.39), somehow caught on as a Christian name among 17th-century Puritans. Its actual Old Testament spelling is *Mehetabel*, and this represents Hebrew *Mehēytabēl*, meaning 'God does good', interpreted more personally as 'she who is helped by God'.

Mekong The river in southeast Asia has a name of Thai origin, representing *menam*, 'river' and *khong*, 'water', in other words simply 'river'. The latter half of the name is identical to that of the GANGES.

Melanesia The grouping of islands in the Pacific northeast of Australia has a name meaning 'black islands', devised from the Greek words *melas*, 'black' and *nēsos*, 'island'. The reference is to the black skin of the indigenous inhabitants. The name is only of 19th century origin, and was modelled on that of POLYNESIA.

Melanie The name derives, through the Latin name *Melania*, from the Greek word *melas*, 'black', 'dark', referring to someone with dark hair, dark eyes or dark skin. Today, however, it tends to be popularly linked either with honey, through Latin *mel*, French *miel* and the like, or with *melody*, associations that are sweet rather than swarthy.

Melbourne The port in southeast Australia, where it is the capital of Victoria and the country's second largest city, was so named in 1837 in honour of William Lamb, second Viscount *Melbourne* (1779–1848), the British prime minister. The minister's own title comes from his seat, *Melbourne Hall* in Derbyshire.

Melchior The name is traditionally that of one of the Magi (Three Wise Men) who brought gifts to the infant Jesus, although it does not occur in the Bible. It is said to mean 'king of the city', from Persian *melk*, 'king' and *qart*, 'city'. *Cp.* MELKART.

Melchizedek The name is that of the Old Testament priest-king of Salem who pronounces a blessing on Abraham. It is Hebrew in origin, representing *Malkizedeq*, 'my king is justice'. It is strictly speaking a theophoric name, based on that of a god, in this case the Semitic deity *Zedek*. The word that gave his name also lies behind that of ZADOK.

Melissa The name represents Greek *melissa*, 'bee', implying industry rather than 'honey sweet', although the Greek word is itself directly related to *meli*, 'honey'. *Cp.* DEBORAH.

Melkart In West Semitic mythology, the name is that of the tutelary god of the city of Tyre, worshipped in Phoenicia and beyond (and especially in Carthage and Damascus) as the protector of sailors. His name represents Phoenician *mlqrt*, 'king of the city'. *Cp.* MELCHIOR.

Melpomene The muse of tragedy in Greek mythology has a name that is the Greek word for 'songstress', itself from *melpomai*, 'I sing'.

Melrose The Scottish town on the river Tweed, famous for its abbey, has a French-looking name that is actually Celtic, from the root elements *mailo*, 'bare' and *ros*, 'moor'.

Melton Mowbray The Leicestershire town, famous for its pork pies and Stilton cheese, has a name with a first word that means 'middle farm' and a second word that derives from the name of the Norman owner of the manor here in the 12th century, Roger de *Moubray*, who came from *Montbray* in northern France. *See also* the surname MOWBRAY.

Melusine In French legend, the name is that of a powerful water-sprite who marries Raimond of Poitou. Her name is of uncertain meaning, but is likely to be Celtic in origin. In folklore it has been linked with that of the French house of *Lusignan*, which ruled Cyprus in medieval times.

Melville The name originated as a Scottish surname, and is familiar as the title of Henry Dundas, first Viscount *Melville* (1740–1811), who is commemorated in Melville's Monument, near Perth. His title derives from the Scottish baronial place-name *Melville*, which itself originated in northern France in one of the places called *Maleville* or *Malleville*, both meaning 'bad settlement' (for their poor sites).

Melvin The popular first name is of recent origin, and appears to be a blend of MELVILLE and MERVYN.

Memorial Day The name is that of the annual day of remembrance in the United States for all Americans killed in war. It is observed as a public holiday on the last Monday in May and was originally instituted in 1868 in memory of those killed in the American Civil War. It was formerly known as *Decoration Day*. Its British counterpart is REMEMBRANCE SUNDAY.

Memphis The ruined city in northern Egypt, famous as the capital of ancient Egypt and a centre sacred to the worship of the god Ptah, has a name that is a Greek form of its Egyptian name *Mennefer*, meaning 'his beauty', from *men*, 'his' and *nefer*, 'beauty' (*cp.* NEFERTITI). The reference is to the handsomeness of the Pharaoh Pepi I, who reigned in the 24th century BC. The American port of *Memphis*, Tennessee, was named in 1826 for the ancient Egyptian city, either to imply a place of grandeur or because its location on the Mississippi suggested that of its historic namesake on the Nile.

Menai Strait The sea channel separating Anglesey from mainland northwest Wales has a Celtic name meaning 'carrying', referring to its swift current. The original word has its equivalent in modern Welsh *men*, 'wagon', 'cart'.

Menam The river in northern Thailand derives its name from Thai *me*, 'mother' and *nam*, 'water'.

Menander The 3rd-century BC Greek comic dramatist has a name meaning literally 'abiding man', from Greek *menō*, 'I remain', 'I continue' and *anēr*, genitive *andros*, 'man'. *Cp.* MENELAUS.

Men at Work The Australian pop group, formed in Melbourne in 1979, took their name from the road sign 'DANGER MEN AT WORK', punning on the fact that they specialized in 'middle-of-the-road' music, appealing to a wide audience.

Mendips The first half of the name of the chain of hills in Somerset is Celtic in origin, relating to modern Welsh *mynydd*, 'mountain', 'hill'. The second half represents Old English *hop*, 'valley'. The name thus means literally 'hill valley', referring to the alternate hills and valleys of the ridge, which is 27 miles (42 km) long.

Menelaus The king of Sparta who was the husband of Helen in Greek mythology has a name that means either 'withstanding the people', from *menō*, 'I remain', 'I wait for' and *laos*, 'people' or 'might of the people', from *menos*, 'force', 'strength' and *laos*. His 'waiting' could be interpreted as that of the famous 'long stand' of his army before Troy. His brother AGAMEMNON has a similar name.

Mensa The name is that of the organization whose members must pass a special 'intelligence' test proving them to have a score higher than that expected for 98% of the population. The name is officially explained as deriving from the Latin word for 'table', since all its members have equal status, as if at a 'round table'. But the founders must also surely have had in mind Latin *mens*, 'mind', 'intellect'.

Mensheviks The name was that of the moderate wing of the Russian Social Democratic Party, who split from the BOLSHEVIKS in 1903. It indicates that they were a minority party, from Russian *men'she*, 'less', 'fewer'.

Menton The Mediterranean port and resort in southeast France has an ancient name deriving ultimately from a pre-Celtic root element *men* meaning 'rock'.

Menzies The Scottish surname is a form of MANNERS. The *z* is an attempt to represent a now disused letter of the English alphabet that had a sound similar to modern *y*. The name is still pronounced 'Mingiz' (similar to 'Ming is') by many Scots.

Mephistopheles The devil of medieval mythology, famous as the one to whom Faust sold his soul, has a name that first appears in the German *Faustbuch* of 1587 as *Mephostopheles*. It is now also familiar from Goethe's *Faust* (1808) in the abbreviated form *Mephisto*. Its true origin is unknown, but it has been popularly interpreted as 'hating light', *i.e.* 'liking dark', from the Greek words *mē*, 'not', *phōs*, genitive *phōtos*, 'light', and *philos*, 'loving'.

Mercedes The car that first bore this name in 1901 was originally known as a DAIMLER, after its manufacturer. The change of name was due to the influential Austrian banker and racing driver Emil Jellinek, who suggested Daimler should bring out a new model, which as a Daimler enthusiast he would then be interested in buying in quantity. Daimler did so, and named it *Mercedes* after the pseudonym adopted by Jellinek when racing. The name itself was that of Jellinek's young daughter and is from the Spanish title of the Virgin Mary, *María de las Mercedes*, 'Mary of the mercies'. For a fast car the name has a coincidental suggestion of MERCURY, the 'winged messenger' of the gods. Possibly Jellinek had this subconsciously in mind when he initially adopted it for his racing name.

Merchant Taylors' School The boys' public school in Northwood, Middlesex, was founded in 1561 by the Master, Wardens and Court of Assistants of the Worshipful Company of *Merchant Taylors*, a historic London livery company, who are still the school's governing body. The school was originally in London on a site near that of today's Cannon Street Station. In 1933 it moved out of London to its present location. *Merchant Taylors' School* in Great Crosby, near Liverpool, also a boys' public school, was founded in 1620 by John Harrison, a native of Great Crosby and a member of the same London company, who were the school's governors until 1910. The school moved to new premises in the same town in 1878. *Merchant Taylors' School* for Girls, Liverpool, is of the same foundation, and opened in 1888 in the premises vacated the previous year by the boys' school.

Mercia The Anglo-Saxon kingdom altered its precise boundaries and area several times, but broadly came to occupy the south central region of Britain, between Wales to the west, Wessex to the south, and East Anglia to the east. Its name is a latinized form of Old English *Mierce*, 'people of the border country', from *mearc*, 'border' (literally 'mark'). *Cp.* MARCHES.

Mercury The well-known Roman messenger of the gods, identified with the Greek HERMES, was originally a god of trade. Hence the origin of his name in Latin *merx*, genitive *mercis*, 'goods', 'merchandise'. His name passed to the planet *Mercury* as it was regarded in ancient times as the 'fastest' planet: it is the closest to the Sun and orbits it in only 88 days, just under a quarter of the time that the Earth takes. It was the associations of speed that gave the name of the god to the chemical element *mercury* or *quicksilver*, the only metal to remain liquid at normal temperatures, and so to move freely and rapidly.

Meredith The name is Welsh in origin, from *Maredudd*, itself based on *iudd*, 'lord' with a first half of uncertain origin. It began as a boys' name but is now sometimes given to girls, perhaps by association with the word *merry*.

Mérida The historic market town in western Spain was founded by the emperor Augustus in 25 BC and has a name that represents its original Roman name of *Augusta Emerita*, 'completed by Augustus'. The cities in Mexico and Venezuela of the same name were founded in the 16th century and named for the Spanish town, which later became the capital of Lusitania and one of the most important cities in Iberia.

Merioneth The former North Wales county has a name that is now represented by the administrative district of *Meirionnydd*. This is based on the personal name *Meirion*, that of the son (or possibly grandson) of the 5th-century ruler Cunedda, whose name lies behind that of GWYNEDD, in which the present district lies. The name as a whole thus means 'seat of Meirion'. The same name gave that of the resort of *Portmeirion*.

Merlin The name is familiar as that of the 'court wizard' to King Arthur. He first appears, as *Merlinus*, in the 12th-century *Historia Regum Britanniae* of the medieval chronicler Geoffrey of Monmouth. This tells how Merlin was born in CARMARTHEN, and his name in fact derives from the Welsh name of the town, *Caerfyrddin*. This was taken to be based on a personal name and to mean 'Myrddin's fort'. *Myrddin* was then latinized as *Merlinus*, with the *dd* becoming *l* in order to avoid a possible *Merdinus*, which would suggest an origin in Latin *merda*, 'dung'. Thus Merlin the magician was born!

Mermaid Theatre The London theatre by the Thames arose from the theatre created in 1951 by the actor Bernard Miles and his wife in the garden of their house at St John's Wood. It was named for the historic *Mermaid* Tavern, the meeting-place of the Friday Street or *Mermaid* Club, founded by Sir Walter Raleigh, whose members included such famous writers as Shakespeare, Donne, Beaumont, Fletcher and Jonson. The tavern was destroyed in the Great Fire of London (1666). The name happens to be appropriate for the theatre's present riverside site at Puddle Dock.

Mers el-Kébir The port in northwest Algeria derives its name from Arabic *al-marsā al-kabīr*, 'the big port', from *al*, 'the', *marsā*, 'port' (*cp.* MARSALA) and *kabīr*, 'big'.

Mersey The well-known river of northwest England has a name that means 'boundary river', from Old English *gemǣre*, 'boundary' (as for MARPLE) and *ēa*, 'river'. The Mersey formed the old county boundary between Cheshire and Lancashire, and originally that between the kingdoms of Mercia and Northumbria. The centuries-old historic link was broken in 1974 when the new county of Merseyside was formed.

Merthyr Tydfil The town in South Wales has a name that means '*Tydfil*'s burial place', with *merthyr* the Welsh word for 'martyr'. *Tydfil* was a female saint, said to be a daughter of Brychan, who gave his name to *Brecon* (*see* BRECON BEACONS). According to tradition she was murdered by pagans in the 5th century and buried here. The town's parish church is dedicated to her.

Merton The borough of southwest London and former Surrey town has a name that means 'farm by a pool', from Old English *mere*, 'pool', 'lake' and *tūn*, 'farm', 'village'. The pool in question was probably one in the river Wandle nearby.

Merton College The Oxford college was founded in 1264 by the prelate Walter de Merton, who himself probably came from MERTON, Surrey.

Mervyn The name is Welsh in origin, and represents *Merfyn*, itself of uncertain origin, but perhaps with the second half deriving from *myn*, 'eminent'. The name gave the popular American name *Marvin*.

Mesopotamia The region of southwest Asia, corresponding to modern Iraq, has a name of Greek origin meaning 'between the rivers', from *mesos*, 'middle' and *potamos*, 'river', referring to its location between the Tigris and the Euphrates. The name occurs in the Bible (*Genesis* 24.10), where the original Hebrew text has *aram naharáyim*, 'Syria of the two rivers'. Oxford University scholars gave the name *Mesopotamia* to a strip of land in Oxford between the river Cherwell and one of its branches, where unlike its Asian namesake it serves as a pleasant place for a shady stroll in summer by a stretch of the river that is popular for punting.

Messene The ancient Greek city in the southwest Peloponnese derives its name from Greek *mesos*, 'middle', referring to its location in *Messenia*, of which it became the capital. *See also* MESSINA.

Messiah The well-known title of Jesus is the Hebrew equivalent of CHRIST. It thus has the same meaning, from *máshiah*, 'anointed', itself from *máshah*, 'to anoint'. The title occurs as *Messias* in the Vulgate (Latin version of the Bible) and in Greek versions of the New Testament. Wycliffe left the word unaltered in his 14th-century English translation of the Bible, and it was retained in later English versions, including the Authorized Version of 1611: 'We have found the Messias' (*John* 1.41), 'I know that Messias cometh' (*John* 4.25). The present spelling of the title with a final *h* was invented by the translators of the Geneva Bible of 1560 with the aim of giving it a more 'Hebraic' look. (The translators used Hebrew forms of Greek proper names in the Old Testament for the same reason, although they kept Greek names in the New Testament.) The *h* spelling appears in the only two occurrences of the name in the Authorized Version of the Old Testament: 'Messiah the Prince' (*Daniel* 9.25) and 'After threescore and two weeks shall Messiah be cut off' (*Daniel* 9.26). 'Messiah' here is a promised deliverer of the Hebrew nation. Hence the word's adoption for Jesus, regarded as fulfilling that promise. The Revised Version of the Bible has the spelling *Messiah* in the two passages in the New Testament (1881), but has 'the anointed' in the Old Testament (1885) in place of the titles in Daniel. The word is almost always preceded by 'the', except in three of the four biblical occurrences, in poetry (where it is more of a proper name), and in the title of Handel's famous oratorio of 1742.

Messina The Sicilian port was so named in the 4th century AD by immigrants from the Greek city of MESSENE.

Metallica The American heavy metal band was formed in Los Angeles in 1981 and adopted a name that epitomized its particular type of rock music.

Metcalf The name comes from the north of England and probably means 'meat calf'. This was a term for a calf being fattened up for slaughter to provide veal, so that the name was probably applied to a slaughterman or herdsman, or was possibly a nickname for a plump person, a 'fatted calf'.

Methodism The name of the evangelical Protestant church, founded in Oxford by John Wesley in 1739, somewhat obscurely derives from the basic word *method*. It probably alludes to the fact that Wesley and his followers advocated a new *method* of religious belief and practice.

Methuen The British publishing house took its name from its founder, Algernon Methuen Marshall *Methuen* (1856–1914), a London doctor's son whose original surname was Stedman. He began his career as a schoolmaster and writer of classical textbooks, but in 1889 set up a publisher's office in London, using his second name *Methuen* because he did not wish to mix his teaching with his publishing. He abandoned teaching altogether for publishing in 1895, and in 1899 changed his own name to *Methuen*.

Methuselah The Hebrew patriarch mentioned in the Old Testament as living for 969 years has a name that represents Hebrew *Methúselah*, 'man of Shelah', the latter apparently being the name of a god corresponding to that of *Salah*, the son of Shem (*Genesis* 10.24). The name of

Methuselah became a byword for longevity, and under the influence of JERUSALEM acquired the form *Methusalem* in some literary texts. For example: 'So though my Life is short, yet may I prove/The great Methusalem of Love' (Abraham Cowley, *The Mistress, or Love Verses*, 1647).

Metropolitan Line The name of the world's first underground railway, in London, derives from that of the company, the *Metropolitan* Railway, which built the line opened in 1862 from Paddington to King's Cross. It relates to London as the capital or *metropolis*, from the Greek word meaning 'mother city'. From the London line the name came to be adopted as the standard word for an underground railway in other countries, such as the Paris *métropolitain* or *métro*, which in turn gave the Russian *metropoliten* or *metro* in Moscow. The word *Metropolitan* was already in use for the titles of other organizations that related to London as a whole, as distinct from the City of London. One of the most familiar is the *Metropolitan* Police Force, founded in 1829. A later promoter of the name was the *Metropolitan* Water Board, which operated from 1904 to 1974, when its administration passed to the Thames Water Authority, now Thames Water Utilities. *Cp.* METROPOLITAN MUSEUM OF ART.

Metropolitan Museum of Art New York's largest art museum opened in 1872 and is named for the *metropolis*, that is, in American terms, New York. The term is found in the titles of other New York institutions, such as the *Metropolitan Opera*, founded in 1883, and the *Metropolitan Hospital*, while Upton Sinclair's novel *The Metropolis* (1908) is set in New York. *Cp.* METROPOLITAN LINE.

Metz The city in northeast France takes its name from the *Mediomatrici*, the tribe whose capital it was in Roman times. Their own name derives from Gaulish *medio*, 'middle' and *Matrici*, the name of another people here among whom they lived.

Meuse The river in western Europe, rising in northeast France and flowing through Belgium and the Netherlands to the North Sea, probably derives its name from a Germanic word *mos*, 'marsh' (modern English *moss*), referring to the low-lying

ground through which it runs. *See also* MOSELLE.

Mevagissey The town near St Austell, Cornwall, takes its name from the two saints to whom its church is dedicated. The name thus means 'Meva and Issey', from Cornish *Meva hag Issey*. Nothing is known about either saint, although the latter also has a church dedicated to him in the village of *St Issey*, near Wadebridge.

Mexico The North American republic has a name that is a smoothed-down Spanish rendering of its original Nahuatl name *Metztlixihtlico*, meaning either 'in the middle of the moon' or 'in the middle of the magueys' (a type of agave plant). The country's capital, now *Mexico City*, was founded by the Aztecs in 1325 on an island in a lake that was itself called *Metztliatl*, from *metztli*, 'moon', to whom the lake was dedicated as a goddess, and *atl*, 'water'. The original name of the city before it adopted that of the island was *Tenochtitlán*, 'place of the prickly pear of stone', from Nahuatl *tetl*, 'stone' and *nuchtli*, 'prickly pear'. The fruit symbolized the heart of human victims who had been sacrificed to the sun god. *See also* NEW MEXICO.

MFI The 'do-it-yourself' furniture stores take their name from the initials of their original name, *Mullard Furniture Industries*. This was itself based on the maiden name, *Mullard*, of the wife of the firm's founder in 1964, Donald Searle.

MG The well-known make of sports car takes its initials from *Morris Garages*, this being the name of the motor repair business opened in Oxford in 1909 by William MORRIS, who is equally familiar from the car named for him.

Miami The city and resort in Florida takes its name from that of an Indian people whose own name is of uncertain origin. It may derive from Ojibwa *oumaumeg*, 'people of the peninsula'.

Micah The book of the Old Testament is named for the prophet whose prophecies it contains. His name derives from Hebrew *Mikhāh*, 'who is like?', an abbreviated form of the name *Mikhāyāh*, 'who is like Yah?' (*i.e.* Jehovah). The name thus has the same basic meaning as MICHAEL. The interrogative phrase that forms the name is found elsewhere in the Bible, typically as in 'Who is like unto thee, O Lord, among the gods?' (*Exodus* 15.11).

Michael The familiar name represents Hebrew *Mĩhã'ēl*, 'who is like God?', appropriately borne in the Bible by one of the archangels. *Cp*. MICHELANGELO.

Michaelmas The name is that of *Michaelmas Day*, 29 September, the feast day of St MICHAEL and All Angels, a special day in the Christian calendar and a quarter day in English law. The name is pronounced 'Micklemas', popularly suggesting an association with English *mickle*, 'great', as if the festival were a specially important one.

Michelangelo The Italian name is familiar as that of the famous 16th-century Florentine painter, whose full name was Michelangelo Buonarroti. It means 'MICHAEL (the) angel', referring to the archangel Michael.

Michelin The French make of motor tyre has a name representing that of two brothers, André *Michelin* (1853–1931) and Edouard *Michelin* (1859–1940), who together began manufacturing bicycle tyres in 1888.

Michigan The American state takes its name from Lake *Michigan*, itself having an Algonquian name, from *michaw*, 'big' and *guma*, 'lake'. Aptly, Lake Michigan is one of the five Great Lakes.

Micklethwaite The name derives from one of the Yorkshire places so called, their own name meaning 'big meadow', from Old Norse *mekil*, 'great' and *thveit*, 'meadow' (*cp*. THWAITES).

Micronesia The grouping of islands in the Pacific has a name formed in modern times from Greek *mikros*, 'small' and *nēsos*, 'island'. The islands in the group are generally much smaller than those in MELANESIA to the south. The name was modelled on that of the third group in the region, POLYNESIA.

Midas The legendary king of Phrygia, famous for turning to gold everything that he touched, has a name that some have related to a word *mita*, 'seed', although the relevance of this is unclear.

Middle Ages The historical period is so named as it represents the era of European history between 'ancient' and 'modern' times, or more precisely that between the fall of the Roman Empire in the 5th century and the Italian Renaissance (or fall of Constantinople) in the 15th.

Middle East The name is applied somewhat imprecisely to the countries east of the Mediterranean, from Turkey in the north to Egypt in the south, but especially including Israel and the Arab states. This was formerly known as the *Near East*, so that the original *Middle East* was the region extending eastwards from Mesopotamia to Burma, which was thus midway between the *Near East* and the *Far East*. The current sense of the name is quite recent, evolving in the Second World War, and appears to have developed by association with the name of the MEDITERRANEAN.

Middlesbrough The town and port in Cleveland has a name that means 'middle fortified place', from Old English *midleste*, 'middlemost' and *burh*, 'fort'. It is not certain in what way the fort was 'middlemost', although it may have been a halfway halting place for travellers in medieval times between St Cuthbert's monastery at Durham and St Hilda's at Whitby. On the other hand, the 'middle' could simply have been the name of a district, with the river Tees, on which Middlesbrough stands, as its northern boundary.

Middlesex The former county of southeast England has a name that means 'territory of the Middle Saxons', these being the ones between the East Saxons of ESSEX and the West Saxons of WESSEX. The original territory was considerably larger than the county, and included the whole of London. *Cp*. SUSSEX.

Middlesex Hospital The London hospital in Mortimer Street was founded in 1745 as the *Middlesex Infirmary* in Windmill Street, a short distance from its present site. It is so named because it was then in the county of MIDDLESEX.

Middleton The name derives from any of the places so called, such as the town near Manchester. The place-name usually means 'middle settlement'.

Midgard In Norse mythology, the name is that of the dwelling-place of mankind, said to be made from the eyelashes of the giant Ymir and linked by the bridge Bifrost to Asgard, home of the gods. Its name represents Old Norse *Mithgarthr*, from *mith*, 'middle' and *garthr*, 'enclosure'. *Cp*. English *garth* and *yard*, also ASGARD itself.

Midhurst The West Sussex town has a name meaning 'place amid wooded hills', from Old English *mid*, 'among', 'amid' and *hyrst*, 'wooded hill'. Midhurst is still surrounded by wooded countryside today.

Midland Bank The High Street bank was founded in Birmingham in 1836 as the *Birmingham and Midland Bank*, the latter word referring to its location in the MIDLANDS. It moved its headquarters to London in 1891 on acquiring the Central Bank of London.

Midlands The name for the central counties of England has been in use since at least the 17th century, and refers to those regions that are geographically in the *middle* of England. The name is currently familiar from the county of *West Midlands*, centred on Birmingham, and *East Midlands* Airport, near Nottingham. *See also* MIDLAND BANK.

Midlothian The former Scottish county is so named since, rather obviously, it lay between East Lothian and West Lothian. In many ways the name is synonymous with that of Edinburgh, its main city. *See* HEART OF MIDLOTHIAN, LOTHIAN.

Midrash The name is that of the ancient Jewish commentaries on the Bible, compiled between about 400 and 1200, and represents the Hebrew word for 'investigation', from *daraś*, 'to search'. In the Authorized Version of the Bible, the word is translated as 'story' (2 *Chronicles* 13.22, 24.27), but in the Revised Version as 'commentary'.

Midsomer Norton The town near Bath has a name that correctly suggests *midsummer*. The origin of the name lies in a former annual festival held here, probably on Midsummer Day (24 June), today represented by the Midsomer Norton Fair held every May. The second word of the name indicates that the place was originally a 'northern settlement' by comparison with some other place further south, although it is not known where this was. *See also* the related name SOMERSET.

Midway Islands The atoll in the central Pacific is so named for its approximate location *midway* between America and Asia.

Midwest The Midwest or *Middle West* of America is the general name for the northern states grouped around the Great Lakes, from Ohio in the east to Minnesota in the west, sometimes extending as far south and west as Nebraska. It came to be so called by contrast with the *Far West*, and is sometimes known by the alternative name of *Heartland of America*.

Mie The prefecture in the island of Honshu, Japan, has a name that means 'triple', 'threefold', from *mi*, 'three' and *-e*, 'fold'. The reference is to its administrative division.

Mignon The opera of this name by Ambroise Thomas, first performed in 1866, is based on Goethe's novel *Wilhelm Meisters Lehrjahre* (1795). In this, *Mignon* is the central character, a young Italian girl street dancer. Her name derives from the French word *mignon*, meaning 'dainty', 'sweet'. The opera is sometimes confused with MANON, which also has a young girl as its heroine.

Mikado, The The name of the popular comic opera by Gilbert and Sullivan, first performed in 1885, is the title of the emperor of Japan, from Japanese *mi-*, 'honourable' and *kado*, 'door', 'entrance'. The name is the only genuine Japanese one in the work, which is set in the town of 'Titipu' and has characters with mock-Japanese names: 'Pooh-Bah', 'Nanki-Poo', 'Yum-Yum', 'Ko-Ko', 'Pish-Tush', 'Pitti-Sing' and 'Peep-Bo'.

Milan The famous Italian city had the Roman name of *Mediolanum*, from Gaulish *medio*, 'middle' and *lanu*, 'plain', referring to its location in the broad plain of the river Po. The French village of *Meillant*, south of Bourges, has a name of the same origin, and is located at most only four miles (7 km) from the exact centre of France.

Milburn The name originated from a place-name, meaning 'mill stream', that perhaps originally was that of the village of *Milburn* near Appleby in Cumbria.

Mildmay The name literally means 'mild maiden', and was originally a nickname for an inoffensive or uncomplaining person.

Mildred The name comprises Old English *mild*, 'mild', 'gentle' and *thrȳth*, 'power', 'strength', which together have a suggestion of a 'gentle giant'. But as in many Old English names the elements combine not so much for their meaning here but to repeat elements in names of other members of a family. The 7th-century abbess *Mildred*, for example, to whom the English basically owe the name, had an elder sister named *Mildburh*, literally 'gentle dwelling-place'.

Miles The name has come to be linked with both Latin *miles*, 'soldier' and the biblical MICHAEL, perhaps through the 'militant' associations of the archangel Michael. It is probably unconnected with either, however. The Medieval Latin form of the name was *Milo*, suggesting a possible origin in Slavonic *mil*, 'dear'.

Milford Haven The town and port in southwest Wales is named for the natural harbour (*haven*) on which it stands. The first word of the name represents Old Norse *melr*, 'sand' and *fjǫrthr*, 'inlet', 'fjord'.

Militant Tendency The name is that of the radical faction that formed in the British Labour Party in the 1970s, and that aligned with the views expressed in the political journal *Militant*. The second part of the name appears to have been influenced by the French word *tendance*, meaning 'trend'. Members of the faction were banned from the Labour Party in the mid-1980s.

Military Symphony Haydn's Symphony No 100 in G major (1793) is so nicknamed for its use of 'military' (*i.e.* band) instruments, with a solo trumpet call in the second movement.

Milky Way The name for the blurred band of light that stretches across the night sky and that consists of millions of stars is a translation of Latin *via lactea*, 'milky way', describing its appearance. The Greeks knew it as *kuklos galaktikos*, 'milky circle',

and of course had a story to account for its origin. (It was the milk that spurted from the breast of the goddess Hera when she pushed the baby Heracles from her while suckling him.) *See also* GALAXY.

Miller As it suggests, the name originally applied to someone who was a miller. *Cp.* MILLS and MILLWARD.

Mill Hill School The London public school for boys was founded in *Mill Hill* in 1807 and takes its name from the locality, in the northwest of the city. A windmill must have stood on the rising ground here at some time.

Millicent The name is of Germanic origin, combining *amal*, 'hard work', 'labour' with *swinth*, 'strength', a 'tough' image not now normally associated with the name itself.

Mills As it implies, the name was originally given to someone who lived near a mill or even to a miller himself. The mill was an important rural 'factory' in medieval times, with one in almost every village. It was normally powered by water, although windmills were also quite common. *Cp.* MILLER and MILLWARD.

Mills and Boon The famous publishers of romantic fiction take their name from the two men who founded a conventional publishing business in London in 1908, Gerald *Mills* (d. 1927) and Charles *Boon* (1877–1943). They first turned to romantic fiction when light reading of this type became a popular form of escapism for women in the depressed years between the wars.

Millwall The district of London on the Isle of Dogs by the Thames is named after the mills that existed here until the 18th century. The 'wall' was a riverside embankment.

Millward The name originally applied to someone in charge of a mill, with the second half of the name similar to modern English *warden*. *See also* MILLER, MILLS.

Milton The name is a frequently found place-name, meaning 'middle settlement' (as for MILTON KEYNES, among many others).

Milton Keynes The present New Town in Buckinghamshire, designated in 1967, has retained the name of the former village here. The first word of the name means 'middle farm'. The second is that of the Norman lord of the manor here in the 13th century. He was Lucas de *Kaynes*, from *Cahagnes* near Caen in northern France.

Milwaukee The port and city of Wisconsin, on Lake Michigan, takes its name from the river at the mouth of which it is located. The river's name is Algonquian in origin, perhaps meaning 'good country', referring to its pastures.

Minas Gerais The state of eastern Brazil has a Portuguese name meaning 'general mines', referring to the gold, diamond and iron mines in the region.

Minch The *Little Minch* and the *North Minch* form a sea passage between mainland Scotland and the Hebrides. The basic name is probably Scandinavian in origin, from Old Norse *megin*, 'great' and *nes*, 'headland'. The headland in question could be either Cape Wrath on the mainland or the Butt of Lewis in the Western Isles. The name may equally have been intended to denote a passage that ran between both these headlands.

Mindanao The name of the second largest island of the Philippines is a contraction of *Magindanau*, probably meaning 'place by a lake'. Malay *danau* means 'island'.

Mindoro The mountainous island in the central Philippines has a name that is a contraction of Spanish *mina de oro*, 'gold mine'.

Minerva The name of the Roman goddess of wisdom is probably based on the root element seen in Latin *mens*, 'mind', and thus in English *mental* and *mind* itself.

Ming The Chinese dynasty extended from 1368 to 1644 and is famous for the porcelain produced during this period. Its name represents Chinese *míng*, 'clarity', 'brightness'. *Cp.* the related name of HO CHI MINH.

Minneapolis The city in MINNESOTA derives its name from the first half of the state name with the addition of Greek *polis*, 'city'.

Minnehaha The name is familiar as that of the beautiful Indian girl who marries Hiawatha in Longfellow's well-known poem. A frequently quoted couplet from the poem explains the name:

> From the waterfall he named her,
> Minnehaha, Laughing Water.

The waterfall in question is the one in the river of the same name near MINNEAPOLIS, MINNESOTA, where *minne* is undoubtedly the Sioux word for 'water'. However, the rest of the name only coincidentally suggests laughter. It actually means 'falls', so that *Minnehaha* is simply 'waterfall'. The error is not attributable to Longfellow, who simply repeated a popular etymology for the name.

Minnesota The American state takes its name from the river that flows through its southern region. The river's name itself represents Sioux *minne*, 'water' and *sota*, perhaps meaning 'cloudy', with reference to the drab colour of the water from its reflection of grey skies.

Minoan The name is that of the Bronze Age civilization of Crete first revealed by excavations at Knossos. It derives from the name of the legendary Cretan king MINOS, and was devised for the period by the British archaeologist Sir Arthur Evans in the 1890s.

Minolta The familiar make of camera has a name that is an acronym formed from the letters of '*ma*chine', '*in*strument', '*o*ptical' and '*Ta*shima'. This last was the name of a Japanese wholesale silk fabrics business, *Tashima Shoten* ('Tashima Shop'), run by the father of Kazuo *Tashima*, the founder of the *Minolta* Camera Company.

Minorca The second largest of the Balearic Islands has a name that is the Spanish word for 'lesser', 'smaller', referring to its size by comparison with MAJORCA.

Minos The legendary king of Crete has a name of uncertain origin that may be related to Greek *mēn*, 'month', perhaps reflected in the 12-monthly (*i.e.* annual) despatch to him of seven boys and seven girls to be devoured in the labyrinth by the MINOTAUR. *See also* MINOAN.

Minotaur The name of the half-bull, half-man that was kept in the labyrinth by the legendary king Minos has a name that simply means 'bull of Minos' from Greek

MINŌS, 'Minos' and *tauros*, 'bull'. It is really more of a title, and the actual name of the Minotaur was *Asterius* or *Asterion*, 'starry'. This is found for other mythological characters and was regarded as a generally propitious name, one that would bring good fortune (like a modern 'lucky star').

Minsk The capital of Byelorussia probably derives its name from the river name *Men*, perhaps at one time the name of the river Svisloch (or a section of it) on which the city stands. This would conform to the pattern of names ending *-sk* found for other Russian towns named for their rivers, such as Omsk on the Om, Tomsk on the Tom, Irkutsk on the Irkut, Tobolsk on the Tobol, and the like. The river name itself may be related to that of the German river MAIN.

Minton The well-known make of china is named for its original manufacturer, Thomas *Minton* (1765–1836), who founded his pottery in Stoke-on-Trent in 1796.

Minute Waltz The well-known piano composition by Chopin, officially his Waltz in D flat, Op 64 No 1 (1846), is so nicknamed because it is supposed to take only a minute in performance. However, many musicians feel that this would be to play the piece too fast.

Miquelon The group of islands in the French territory of St Pierre and Miquelon, off the east coast of Canada, may derive its name from that of some navigator or explorer, although the identity or even nationality of such a person is uncertain. In its present form the name is a Norman French diminutive of *Michel*, 'Michael'.

Miracle Symphony Haydn's Symphony No 96 in D major (1791) is so called from an incident said to have occurred at its first performance that year in London, when the audience rushed forward at the end to congratulate the composer, thus miraculously escaping injury from a chandelier which at that moment crashed down on their seats. In fact this incident happened during Haydn's second visit to London in 1795, after a performance of his Symphony No 102, so it is really that work which should have the name.

Miranda The name was made famous by Shakespeare for Prospero's daughter in *The Tempest* (1612). It represents Latin *miranda*, the feminine form of *mirandus*, 'fit to be wondered at', from the verb *mirari*, 'to wonder at', 'to admire'. As so often, Shakespeare plays on the name through the words of his characters. On first meeting Miranda, and without knowing her name, Ferdinand exclaims, 'O you wonder!' Later, on learning her name, he cries, 'Admir'd Miranda! Indeed, the top of admiration.' In the final scene of the play she herself begins her famous 'brave new world' speech with 'O, wonder!' *Cp.* AMANDA.

Mirande The small town in southwest France has a name that represents Occitan *Miranda*, meaning 'watch-tower', from *mirar*, 'to watch'.

Mirepoix The small cathedral town in southwest France has a name that represents Occitan *Mirapeis*, meaning 'watching the fish', from *mirar*, 'to watch' and *peis*, 'fish'. The town is on the river Hers Vif.

Miriam The name is the Old Testament form of the Hebrew name *Maryam* that gave MARY.

Mishna The compilation of Jewish oral law that forms the earlier part of the TALMUD has a name representing the Hebrew word for 'repetition', from *šānāh*, 'to repeat'. *Cp.* GEMARA.

Mission, The The British rock group was formed in 1985 on the break-up of the band *Sisters of Mercy*. They were originally billed as *The Sisterhood*, but when this was disallowed on legal grounds chose another name in the same mould. It may itself have been suggested by the popular British movie *The Mission* (1986), starring Robert De Niro.

Mississippi The American state takes its name from the well-known river, whose own name derives from words common to many Indian languages meaning 'great water'. One of the earliest records of the name is that of *Messipi* in 1666.

Missouri The American state takes its name from the familiar river, whose own name is that of an Indian people who lived near it. The meaning of their own name is unknown. The river's earlier name was *Pekitanoul*, said to mean 'muddy water'.

Mitchell The surname, sometimes in use as a first name, is a medieval version of MICHAEL, with the spelling representing an anglicized pronunciation of *Michel*, the French form of this name.

Mitchelmore The name is Scottish or Irish in origin, and originally denoted the oldest (or sometimes biggest) person named MICHAEL in a community, the last part of the name representing Gaelic *mór*, 'big'.

Mitford The name comes from the village of *Mitford* near Morpeth in Northumberland, where it means literally 'mouth ford', that is, a ford at a confluence. The novelist Nancy *Mitford* traced her ancestors back to the Sir John *Mitford* of this village, who died in the early 14th century.

Mithras The name is that of the Persian god of light, identified with the sun. His name equates to that of the Vedic god *Mitra*, and derives from Avestan *mithra*, 'friend', 'agreement' (a friend being a person who is the second party to an agreement). Mithras was himself regarded as a friend and mediator, much as Jesus Christ is in the Christian religion.

Mithridates The king of Pontus (on the Black Sea), who waged three wars against the Romans in the 1st century BC, has a name that means 'gift of MITHRAS'. His name should more accurately be *Mithradates*.

Mitsubishi The Japanese car manufacturer has a name that represents the Japanese for 'three diamonds', from *mitsu*, 'three', and *bishi*, 'diamond', this being the company's symbol of three equilaterally spaced rhombuses. The company originated from a shipping service founded in 1870.

Mizpah The name is that of various places mentioned in the Old Testament, such as the 'land of Mizpah' in the book of *Joshua*. The most familiar is the heap of stones set up by Jacob and Laban to mark the covenant between them: 'And Mizpah; for he said, The Lord watch between me and thee, when we are absent one from another' (*Genesis* 31.49). Laban's words are a popular gloss on the literal sense of the name, which represents Hebrew *mitspa*, 'lookout post', from *tsafo*, 'to look out', 'to keep watch'. The meaning of the name explains its frequency as a place-name. The name is sometimes used as a 'codeword' in communications between lovers, the sense being that of the biblical verse.

Mnemosyne In Greek mythology, the name is that of the goddess of memory and mother of the Muses by Zeus. It is the actual Greek word for 'memory'. The goddess was so named because 'before the invention of writing, *memory* was the Poet's chief gift' (H.G. Liddell and R. Scott, *Greek-English Lexicon*, 1843). (Liddell has two claims to fame. He was not only a distinguished Greek scholar and co-author of the famous Greek dictionary, but the father of Alice Liddell, for whom Lewis Carroll wrote *Alice in Wonderland*.)

Moab The ancient kingdom east of the Dead Sea has a name that is derived from that of *Moab*, son of Lot. His own name is popularly derived from Hebrew *Mō'ab*, meaning 'of the father', from *me*, a form of *min*, 'of', 'from' and *ab*, 'father': 'And the firstborn bare a son, and called his name Moab: the same is the father of the Moabites unto this day' (*Genesis* 19.37). The mother of Moab was Lot's own elder daughter, so that the birth was incestuous. Hence the significance of the name.

Mobil The familiar brand of motor oil has a name based on either English *mobile* or perhaps more likely Latin *mobilis*, 'moveable'. The name dates back to the late 19th century, and *Mobiloil* is known to have been available in England in 1899.

Mobile The name of the Alabama port is a gallicized form of an Indian name of uncertain meaning. A sense 'to paddle' has been suggested.

Mobutu Sese Seko, Lake The lake in eastern Africa, between Zaïre and Uganda, was discovered by the English explorer Samuel Baker in 1864 and named by him Lake *Albert*, after the Prince Consort. In 1973 it was renamed by President Mobutu of Zaïre after himself. The president was born in 1930 and christened *Joseph-Désiré Mobutu*. In 1972 he dropped his baptismal name and assumed his 'warrior' names to become *Mobutu-Sese-Seko-Kuku-Ngbendu-Wa-Za-Banga*, meaning 'invincible warrior cockerel who leaves no chick intact'.

Moby-Dick The name is that of the great white whale which is the central character of the novel by Herman Melville, published in 1851. The origin of the name is obscure, although Melville may have based it on the nickname of a real whale, *Mocha Dick*, which caused loss of life to whalers and damage to whaling ships in the 1830s and 1840s. An account of this whale was published in *The Knickerbocker Magazine* (1839).

Moby Grape The American rock band, formed in San Francisco in 1966, took as their name the answer to the surreal riddle, 'What's blue, large, round and lives in the sea?', with punning reference to the title of the famous Herman Melville novel MOBY-DICK.

Modena The name of the city in northern Italy has been tentatively linked with Latin *mutulus*, 'corbel' (a stone bracket in a wall), perhaps with reference to some historic incident.

Moët et Chandon The famous champagne takes its name from Claude *Moët*, who founded the business in Epernay in 1743, and his grandson's son-in-law, Comte Pierre-Gabriel *Chandon* de Briailles, who joined the company at the turn of the 19th century, and who married Mademoiselle *Moët* in 1833.

Mogadiscio The capital and chief port of Somalia has a name that is an Italian form of Arabic *maqdašū* or *muqdišū*, from the root word *qds*, 'holy'. The name is also spelled *Mogadishu*.

Modred The knight of the Round Table who rebelled against his uncle King Arthur and killed him has a name that in some accounts is spelled *Mordred*. Its Welsh form is *Medrawd* or *Medrod*, which has been explained as deriving from Welsh *meddu*, 'to own' and *rhawd*, 'course'. The exact sense of this is not clear, however.

Mogadon The drug used to treat insomnia, a proprietary preparation of nitrazepam, has an apparently arbitrary name that was patented in 1956. It nevertheless suggests a combination of Greek *mogos*, 'toil', 'trouble', 'pain' and *donax*, 'dart', 'arrow', as if a drug able to 'shoot' or kill pain and worry.

Mogul The Muslim dynasty of Indian emperors, established in 1526, derive their name from Persian *mughul*, 'Mongol' (*see* MONGOLIA), as they were descendants of Timur (Tamerlane), the 14th-century Mongol leader.

Mohammed *See* MUHAMMAD.

Mohawk The North American Indian people, who lived by the *Mohawk* river in what is now the state of New York, have a name that is related to Narraganset *Mohowaùuck*, 'they eat inanimate things', said to refer to the cannibalism that they practised. The river name came from that of the people, not the other way round, as is more common.

Mohican The name of the Indian people derives from the Algonquian word *maìngan*, 'wolf'. The tribe is now extinct: hence the famous title of Fenimore Cooper's novel *The Last of the Mohicans* (1826).

Moira The Irish and Scottish (and English) name is an English form of the Irish name *Máire*, itself the equivalent of MARY.

Moira House School The girls' public school in Eastbourne, East Sussex, was founded in Croydon in 1875 in a house already named *Moira*, apparently for the Greek goddess of fate (*see* FATES). The school moved to its present location in 1887.

Moirai This is the Greek name for the Greek goddesses of fate. *See* FATES.

Mold The town west of Chester in northeast Wales has a name that is Norman French in origin, from *mont hault*, 'high hill', with these two words blending to form the present name. The hill in question is Bailey Hill, northwest of the town, where there was a Roman fort and later a medieval castle.

Moldavia The East European republic borders on Romania and derives its name from the Romanian river *Moldovă*. The river's own name perhaps goes back to an Indoeuropean root element *mel*, 'dark', 'black'. The official indigenous name of the republic is *Moldova*.

Molesworth The surname derives from the name of the village near Thrapston in Cambridgeshire. Its original meaning is '*Mule's*

356

enclosure', *Mule* (Old English *Mūla*) being a nickname for a stubborn person.

Molineux The home ground of Wolverhampton Wanderers Football Club, in Wolverhampton, takes its name from the former nearby *Molineux* Hotel, itself named after the *Molineux* family (*see* MOLYNEUX) whose home it originally was.

Molly The name is a pet form of MARY, with an alteration of *r* to *l*. Cp. the similar association between SALLY and SARAH. The name has come to be specially associated with Ireland, although it is not Irish in origin.

Moloch The Phoenician deity worshipped in Jerusalem in the 7th century BC, to whom parents sacrificed their children, has a name that is traditionally regarded as a contemptuous form of the Semitic element *mlk* meaning 'king', as for ABIMELECH and MELCHIZEDEK. Moloch is usually identified with *Milcom*, king of the Ammonites, mentioned in the Old Testament (1 *Kings* 11.5). However, recent studies of Neopunic inscriptions dating from about 1000 BC have led Semitic scholars to deduce that the name has a different meaning, referring to the act of sacrifice itself.

Moloney The Irish name is an anglicized form of the Irish original, which could be either *Ó Maol Dhomhnaigh*, 'descendant of a devotee of the church', or *Mac Giolla Dhomhnaigh*, 'son of the servant of the church'. A 'devotee of the church' or 'servant of the church' was a priest, and the name would have applied to the illegitimate son of such a priest.

Moluccas The islands in the Malay Archipelago have a name that means 'main islands', from Malay *molok*, 'main', 'chief'. *Cp*. MOLOCH.

Molyneux The English and Irish name is Norman in origin, representing *Moulineux*, the name of a place near Rouen in northern France. The place-name itself means 'little mills'. *Cp*. ISSY-LES-MOULINEAUX.

Mombasa The port in southern Kenya was founded by the Arabs in the 11th century. They gave the settlement a name transferred from a town in Oman, itself from Arabic *mumbaṣa*, of uncertain meaning.

Monaco The well-known principality, an enclave in southeast France, has a name that is popularly derived from Greek *Monoikos*, 'solitary'. This was a byname of the god Hercules, and the place-name is said to refer to a statue of *Hercules Monoecus* that stood here in the 7th or 6th century BC. But the name is more likely to be of Ligurian origin, from *monegu*, 'rock', with this word reflected today in the adjective *Monegasque*. However, another school of thought proposes an origin in Basque *muno*, 'mountain'. Monaco is rather remote from the Basque Country, but it is known that the influence of the Basque people and language was fairly widespread in France as a whole. This last proposed origin has its counterpart in that for MONTE CARLO, Monaco's most famous town.

Monaghan The Irish county took its name from that of its county town, which itself means 'little thickets', from Irish *muineach*, 'thorns', 'thicket'.

Mona Lisa Leonardo da Vinci's famous painting of a young woman with an enigmatic smile, now in the Louvre, Paris, is believed to be a portrait of the wife of a Florentine official, Francesco del Giocondo. Hence the portrait's alternative name, *La Gioconda* (*see* GIOCONDA). *Mona Lisa* means 'Lady Lisa', with *mona* a form of *monna*, modern Italian *madonna*, 'my lady'.

Monastir The seaport town in northeast Tunisia has the Arabic name of *al-munastīr*, probably from Latin *monasterium*, 'monastery'. It is believed that a Christian monastery existed here before the advent of Islam. However, it is by no means certain that this is the origin, since texts of the 17th and 18th centuries record the name as *Munāsir* and *Manāsir*. Moreover, the inhabitants regularly pronounce the name *Mistīr*. Its ancient name was *Ruspina*, of Phoenician origin.

Mönchengladbach The city near Düsseldorf in western Germany arose round a monastery founded in the 10th century. Its name thus means 'monks' Gladbach', with the latter name meaning 'clear stream', from Old German words corresponding to modern *glatt*, 'smooth', 'clear' and *Bach*, 'stream'. The first half of the name is the same as that of MUNICH.

The stream in question is the river Niers on which the city stands.

Moncrieff The Scottish name derives from that of *Moncreiffe*, now a suburb of Perth, itself probably meaning 'tree hill', from Gaelic *monadh*, 'hill' and *craoibhe*, the genitive of *craobh*, 'tree'.

Monday The second day of the week (often popularly regarded as the first, following the weekend) is so named from its dedication to the Moon, as a translation of its Late Latin name, *lunae dies*. *Cp.* SUNDAY.

Monday Club The club of right-wing Conservatives, founded in 1961, is so named as its members originally met up for lunch on a *Monday*.

Mongolia The region and republic of central Asia takes its name from its indigenous inhabitants, the *Mongols*, whose own name derives from the Mongolian root word *mengu* or *mongu*, 'brave', 'unconquered'. *See also* MOGUL.

Monica The name is ultimately of uncertain origin, although attempts have been made to derive it from Latin *monere*, 'to warn', 'to advise' or Greek *monos*, 'sole', 'lonely'. It was the name of the mother of St Augustine, and since she was instrumental in bringing about her son's conversion to Christianity, the first of the proposed meanings here has come to be associated with her.

Monk The name was not that of an actual monk, but either a nickname for a person who resembled a monk in some way, in dress or religiosity, for example, or else an occupational name for a person who was a servant in a monastery. *Cp.* MONKHOUSE.

Monkees, The The American pop group was formed in 1966 as the result of a recruitment of four young musicians to star in a television comedy series about a pop group. Their name means what it implies, but was a specific reference to one of their number, the former child actor Mickey Dolenz. He 'played the monkey' in his film roles, and so was given a nickname that punned on *Mickey*.

Monkhouse The name was originally an occupational one for a person who lived near a 'monk house', otherwise a monastery, or who worked in one.

Monmouth The town and former county in southeast Wales takes its name from the river *Monnow*, on which it stands at the point where it merges with the Wye. The river's own name perhaps means 'fast-flowing'.

Monroe The name is Scottish, and in that land is traditionally spelled *Munro*. The original bearers of the name are said to have come to Scotland from Ireland, so that the name refers to their place of origin, by the river Roe in Co Londonderry. It is therefore explained as deriving from Irish *bun Rotha*, literally 'bottom of the Roe', that is, at the river's mouth (on Lough Foyle, north of Limavady).

Monrovia The capital of Liberia was founded in 1822 as a home for liberated slaves by the American Colonization Society, who named it after the American president James *Monroe* (1758–1831).

Mons The town in southwest Belgium derives its name from the Latin word *mons*, 'hill', 'mountain', although the terrain here is not noticeably hilly. The town's Flemish name, *Bergen*, has the same meaning.

Monsalvat The name is that of the land of the Holy Grail in medieval legend, and in particular in the 13th-century verse epic *Parzifal* by Wolfram von Eschenbach, familiar to music-lovers from Wagner's opera *Parsifal* based on it. But what does the name mean, and where is Monsalvat? The name suggests an interpretation 'mountain of salvation', from Latin *mons*, 'mountain' and *salvare*, 'to save'. If this is the case, the location may be *Montségur*, the village and ruined castle in southwest France near the border with Spain. The name of this place also suggests 'mountain of safety' (from Latin *mons securus*) and, no doubt significantly, Wagner himself specified that the setting for the first act of *Parsifal* was *Gegend im Charakter der nördlichen Gebirge des gotischen Spaniens* ('locality similar to that of the northern mountains of Gothic Spain'). However, the true meaning of *Montségur* is said to be 'sun mountain', from Basque *muno*, 'mountain' and *eguzki*, 'sun', perhaps alluding to an ancient centre of pagan sun worship.

Montacute House The Elizabethan country house near Yeovil in Somerset takes its name from the estate village of *Montacute*. This has a Norman name meaning 'pointed hill', from words that correspond to modern French *mont aigu* and that derive ultimately from Latin *mons acutus*. The name was presumably imported from one of the places called *Montaigu* in Normandy, such as that near Caen. The Domesday Book records not only the Norman name of the place, but also its Anglo-Saxon name, which in its modern form would be *Bishopstone*. *See also* MONTAGUE.

Montagnard The name means 'mountaineer', and was used for members of the French legislative assembly and National Convention who met after the Revolution of 1793 and supported its more extreme measures. They were so named because as deputies they sat on the higher seats of the assembly.

Montague The name is a Norman baronial one, brought to England by lords from *Montaigu* in northern France. The placename itself means 'pointed hill'. *Cp.* MONTACUTE HOUSE.

Montana The name of the American state is Latin in origin, meaning 'mountainous', and was proposed when the Montana Territory was organized in 1864 from a portion of the former Nebraska Territory. The Rocky Mountains occupy much of the western area of the state.

Montargis The town in north central France derives its name from Latin *mons*, genitive *montis*, 'hill' and the Gaulish personal name *Argio*. A suburb of Montargis has the name *Chalette*, from Low Latin *cataracta*, 'waterfall', 'cataract'.

Montauban The city in southwest France had the Medieval Latin name of *Mons Albanus*, apparently meaning 'white hill'.

Mont Blanc The well-known mountain peak in the Western Alps has a French name meaning 'white mount', referring to its permanent glaciers. The name is also that of the massif of which Mont Blanc is itself the highest point. Other peaks here are *Mont Maudit*, 'cursed mount', *Aiguille du Géant*, 'giant's needle', *Mont Dolent*, 'doleful mount', *Aiguille du Midi*, 'needle of noon' (as the sun is over it at noon when seen from the north), and *Aiguille Verte*, 'green needle'.

Monte Carlo The famous town in Monaco, with its casino and annual motor rally, has a name of Italian origin meaning 'Charles's mountain', from *monte*, 'mountain' and *Carlo*, 'Charles'. The town was founded in 1866 during the reign of Prince *Charles* III of Monaco (1818–1889). Monte Carlo stands on an escarpment at the foot of the Maritime Alps.

Monte Cassino The hill in central Italy is famous for its Benedictine monastery, destroyed by the Allies in the Second World War when they mistook it for a German observation post. The hill is named for *Cassino*, the town that lies below it. The town was known in Roman times as *Casinum*, a name of uncertain origin.

Montecristo The Italian island in the Tyrrhenian Sea has a name that apparently means 'Christ's mountain', the reference probably being to the medieval monastery formerly here. The name was adopted by Alexandre Dumas for the hero of his novel *The Count of Monte Cristo* (1844).

Montenegro The republic and former kingdom of Yugoslavia has an Italian name meaning 'black mountain', this being a rendering of the Serbo-Croat name *Crna Gora*. The name alludes to the general sombre colour of the region, which is mountainous and heavily forested.

Monterey The city in western California, the capital of Spain's Pacific empire from 1774 to 1825, takes its name from *Monterey* Bay here. This was named in 1603 for the Spanish colonial administrator, Viceroy of New Spain (Mexico), Gaspar de Zúñiga, Conde de *Monterrey* (1540–1606).

Montevideo The capital and chief port of Uruguay has an intriguing name that has not yet been satisfactorily explained. There are two rival popular accounts, each as improbable as the other. One claims that the explorer Magellan cried (in Portuguese) *Monte vidi eo*, 'It was I who saw the mountain', on seeing the site. The other derives the name from the wording on a chart, *monte VI de O*, 'sixth mountain from the west'. There is also a third explanation, seeing the name as a combination of Spanish *monte*, 'mountain' and Latin *video*, 'I see'. However, Spanish *monte* can mean both 'mountain' and 'hill', and whatever the meaning of the second part of the name, the first part probably refers to the hill called the *Cerro* (also meaning 'hill') that rises at the entrance to the bay on which the city stands, and that serves as a landmark when viewed from the sea.

Montgomery The surname is a Norman baronial name, itself from one of the places so called in northern France. The place-name is itself a combination of Old French *mont*, 'hill' and the Germanic name *Gomeric*, from *gūma*, 'man' and *ric*, 'power'. *See also* the Welsh place-name MONTGOMERY.

Montgomery The former Welsh county takes its name from its county town, now a village, whose own name represents that of Roger de *Montgomery*, the Norman owner of the manor here. He himself came from *Montgommery* near Caen in northern France. *See also* the surname MONTGOMERY.

Montgomery The state capital of Alabama was given its name in 1819 in commemoration of Richard *Montgomery* (1738–1775), the American Revolutionary officer and hero who was killed leading an assault on Quebec.

Montluçon The city in central France has a name that means 'mountain of *Luçon*'. The latter represents the Roman personal name *Luccius*.

Montmartre The famous artists' quarter of Paris, on a hill to the north of the city centre, had the Roman name of *Mons Martyrum*, 'martyrs' mount'. The reference was to St Denis, first bishop of Paris, beheaded in 258, and his two companions, a priest named Rusticus and a deacon named Eleutherius. The 'Christian' name replaced the earlier pagan name of *Mons Mercurii*, 'Mercury's mount'.

Montmorency The aristocratic surname is French in origin, and represents what is now the northern Paris suburb of *Montmorency*. The place-name means 'hill of *Maurentius*', after a Roman personal name.

Montparnasse The district of Paris, to the south of the Seine, adopted its name from that of *Mount Parnassus* (French *Mont Parnasse*), the mountain in Greece that was sacred to the gods. The hill formerly

here was levelled during construction of the Boulevard Montparnasse.

Montpelier The state capital of Vermont was founded in 1780 and named after the French town of MONTPELLIER, with a slight modification of spelling, in token of gratitude for French support during the War of American Independence (American Revolution). The name is pronounced 'Mant*peel*yer'.

Montpellier The city in the south of France evolved the present form of its name from its Medieval Latin name of *Mons pislerius*, representing Latin *mons*, 'mountain' and *pestellus*, a form of Late Latin *pastellus*, 'woad', used for dyeing locally. *See also* MONTPELIER.

Montreal The well-known Canadian city, in Quebec, was named *Mont Réal*, 'royal mountain' in 1534 by the French sailor and colonist Jacques Cartier in honour of Francis I of France, who had financed his expedition. Cartier's name, as it implies, was not given to the actual settlement but to the hill near the Indian town of *Hochelaga*. The present city was founded in 1642 with the name of *Ville Marie de Montréal*. This was shortened to *Montréal* in 1724. The French spelling of the name (with its accent) is frequently found today.

Montreuil The eastern suburb of Paris takes its name from Latin *monasteriolum*, 'little monastery', a diminutive of *monasterium*, 'monastery'. The former town is sometimes known as *Montreuil-sous-Bois*, 'Montreuil by the Wood' to distinguish it from other places of the same name, such as *Montreuil-sur-Mer*, 'Montreuil on Sea', the small town (not actually 'on sea' although not far off) near Boulogne. The name in all cases has the same origin. *Cp.* MONTREUX.

Montreux The town and resort in western Switzerland derives its name from Latin *monasterium*, 'monastery'. The town arose in the 9th century by a monastery on an island at the eastern end of Lake Geneva.

Mont-Saint-Michel The rocky islet off the northwest coast of France had the Latin name of *Mons Sancti Michaelis*, 'St Michael's mount'. The name was given in 709 when the abbey chapel here was dedicated to the archangel Michael. The islet and its abbey has its exact counterpart in England in the form of ST MICHAEL'S MOUNT, near Penzance, Cornwall, and in fact this island was given to Mont-St-Michel in the 11th century, but later returned to English hands.

Montserrat The island in the West Indies was discovered by Columbus in 1493 and named for the monastery of *Santa María de Montserrat* near Barcelona in Spain. The monastery itself was named for the mountain on which it stands, this in turn deriving from Catalan *mont*, 'mountain' and *serrat*, 'serrated'. The particular reference is to the mountain's jagged pinnacles, but the name is equally appropriate for the island, which has a range of serrated mountain peaks.

Monty Python's Flying Circus The famous BBC television comedy series, with its droll, deadpan humour, was broadcast from 1969 to 1974. Original proposals for a programme title were mainly random or surreal, and included *Gwen Dibley's Flying Circus*, *Vaseline Review* and *Owl Stretching Time*. The first of these was preferred, with John Cleese, one of the comedy team, suggesting *Python* in place of the first part, to which Eric Idle, another member, added *Monty*. This last name was adopted from that of a pub 'regular' that Idle knew, about whom fellow drinkers would enquire 'Monty in yet?', 'Anyone seen Monty?' and the like.

Moody The name was originally a nickname for a rash or brave person, or for someone subject to fits of anger. It does not thus mean exactly the same as 'moody' in its present sense.

Moody Blues, The The British progressive rock group, formed in Birmingham in 1964, took their name from the title of a song by the American blues singer Slim Harpo. It also alluded to the rhythm 'n' *blues* idiom that they themselves favoured.

Moomba The annual pre-Lent carnival held in Melbourne, Australia, since 1954 was so named in the (mistaken) belief that *mumba* was an Aboriginal word meaning something like 'let's have a party'. It actually means 'buttocks', 'anus'.

Moonies The colloquial name for the members of the *Unification Church* derives

from that of its founder in 1954, the Korean industrialist Sun Myung *Moon* (1920–   ). The religious sect teaches that the original purpose of creation was to set up a perfect (unified) family, in a perfect (unified) relationship with God.

Moonlight Sonata The well-known work by Beethoven, officially his Piano Sonata No 14 in C sharp minor, Op 27 No 2 (1801), derived its name from a review by the German musician Heinrich Rellstab, in which he wrote that the first movement of the piece reminded him of moonlight on Lake Lucerne. He was no doubt referring to the opening bars, for the movement as a whole is more like a funeral march than a moonlight idyll!

Moore The name denoted a person who lived in or near a moor or marsh, or who came from a place named *Moor* or its equivalent, such as the Cheshire village of *Moore* near Warrington, or the Shropshire village of *More* near Bishop's Castle. It was also a nickname for a dark-skinned person, who looked like a Moor.

Moors The Muslim people of North Africa, of mixed Arab and Berber descent, take their name either from Greek *mauros*, 'dark', referring to the colour of their skin, or Punic *mahurīm* or *mauhārīn*, 'western', referring to the geographical area of North Africa that they chiefly occupied. *Cp.* MAGHREB.

Moral Rearmament The name is that of the worldwide religious revivalist movement founded by the American evangelist Dr Frank Buchman in 1938. The intention was that individuals should *morally re-arm* in order to deepen their spiritual lives and their relationships with others. The movement was also known as *Buchmanism* or simply *MRA*. An early name in Britain for the movement was the OXFORD GROUP.

Moravia The region of the eastern Czech Lands takes its name from the river *Morava* here. The river's name in turn derives from the Germanic words *mar*, 'marsh' and *ahwa*, 'water'. There are actually two rivers of the name, one in the Czech Lands, the other in Serbia. Both are tributaries of the Danube.

Moray The former county of northeast Scotland takes its name from the ancient province that extended over a wider area here. The name means 'sea settlement', from Old Celtic words that are related to modern Welsh *môr*, 'sea' and *tref*, 'homestead', 'town'. The province gave the name of the *Moray Firth*, the great arm of the North Sea that extends inland as far as Inverness. *See also* the surname MURRAY.

Morbihan The department of northwest France, in Brittany, takes its name from *Morbihan* Bay off its coast. The name of the bay is Breton in origin, from *mor bihan*, 'little sea'.

Mordecai The name of the cousin of Esther in the Old Testament is said to derive from that of MARDUK, the chief god of ancient Babylon.

Mordred *See* MODRED.

Mordvin The Finnish people of Russia, living chiefly in the middle Volga basin, derive their name from the Votyak word *murt*, 'man'. *See also* UDMURT.

Morecambe The popular Lancashire coastal resort takes its name from *Morecambe Bay*, on which it arose. The name of the bay derives from the Celtic root elements *mori*, 'sea' and *cambi*, 'curved', these describing the bay itself (as a 'curved sea'). It has been pointed out that the name of Morecambe also happens to suggest that of other resorts, such as *Ilfracombe*, and that it even serves as a touristic promotion for a resort to which 'more come'.

Moreland The name originally applied to a person who lived on or near moorland or marshland, or who came from a place so called, such as the village of *Morland* near Appleby in Cumbria.

Morgan The name passed from a male given name to a surname, then on to a female first name. It is Welsh in origin, perhaps from words corresponding to modern Welsh *mawr*, 'great' or *môr*, 'sea' and *can*, 'bright' or *cant*, 'circle'. As a female first name Morgan probably derives from that of *Morgan le Fay*, the wicked fairy who was King Arthur's half-sister. The county of GLAMORGAN contains the name.

Morgannwg *See* GLAMORGAN.

Moriah The name is both that of the place of Isaac's sacrifice (*Genesis* 22.2) and that of the hill on which the temple of Jerusalem was built (2 *Chronicles* 3.1). With regard to the former, it is traditionally derived from Hebrew *mūr*, 'to substitute', since it was in Moriah that Abraham sacrificed a ram in place of his son. The name appears to have existed before Abraham's time, however. Moreover, the account of Isaac's sacrifice speaks of 'the land of Moriah', whereas the temple was built 'in mount Moriah'. Early biblical texts themselves render 'into the land of Moriah' differently, thus: Vulgate (Latin), *in terram visionis* ('into the land of vision'); Septuagint (Greek), *eis tēn gēn tēn hupsēlēn* ('into the high land'); Targum (Aramaic), *ŀarᶜā pūlhanā*, ('into the land of worship'); Peshitta (Syriac), *ŀarᶜō dᵉamūroyō* ('into the land of the Amorites'). So the true origin remains as yet unresolved.

Moriarty The Irish name is an English spelling of the original Irish *Muircheartach*, from *muir*, 'sea' and *ceardach*, 'skilled', otherwise an experienced sailor.

Morley The name derives from one of the places so called, such as the town of *Morley* near Leeds. The name itself means 'moorland clearing', from Old English *mōr*, 'moor', 'marsh' and *lēah*, 'wood', 'clearing'.

Mormon The name for a member of the Church of Jesus Christ of Latter-Day Saints, founded by Joseph Smith in America in 1830, derives from that of the ancient prophet *Mormon* whose prophecies Smith claims to have recorded in the *Book of Mormon*, the sect's sacred scriptures. Smith himself explained the prophet's name as deriving from English *more* and Egyptian *mon*, 'good', but this was probably an invention designed to satisfy questioners.

Morocco The name of the kingdom in northwest Africa represents the old Arabic form, *marūkus*, of the name of the country's former capital, MARRAKECH. The first recorded occurrence of the country's name in the western world is in the medieval *Nibelungenlied*, where it appears as *Marroch*. English is unusual in spelling the name with the first vowel as *o*. Most other languages have *a*, such as French *Maroc*, German *Marokko*, Spanish *Marruecos*, and so on. This probably came about through an association with the MOORS, who established themselves in Morocco and northwest Africa generally. The Arabic name for Morocco is *al-maġrib al-aqṣā*, 'the far west'. *Cp.* MAGHREB.

Morpeth The town in Northumberland, of which it is the administrative centre, has a name that literally means 'murder path', from Old English *morth*, 'murder' and *pæth*, 'path', 'way'. Doubtless the neighbourhood was at one time regarded as dangerous here. The 'murder path' itself was probably the road that became the Great North Road and that is now the A1. The name is popularly interpreted as 'moor path', which happens to be appropriate for a town that is regarded as a gateway to the moors and hills of Northumberland.

Morpheus The god of dreams in Greek and Roman mythology has a name that derives from Greek *morphē*, 'form', 'shape', referring to the figures typically seen in dreams, or remembered on waking. The god gave the name of the drug *morphine*, used as an anaesthetic and sedative.

Morphy Richards The make of electrical appliances is named for William *Morphy* (1901–1975) and Charles Frederick *Richards* (1900–1964), two electrical engineers who set up a partnership assembling electric fires in Kent in 1936.

Morris The name arose as a medieval variant of MAURICE.

Morris The well-known make of car is named for William *Morris* (1877–1963), later Lord Nuffield, the son of a Worcester draper's assistant, who set up a business as a bicycle manufacturer in Oxford in 1901 and who progressed to making motorcycles and cars, including the famous MG. He produced the first *Morris* Oxford car in 1913.

Morrison's Academy The Scottish public school was founded in Crieff, Perthshire, in 1860 with funds from the bequest of Thomas *Morrison*, an Edinburgh builder. The former separate though adjacent boys' and girls' schools set up under the endowment merged into a single school in 1979.

Mortimer The name is a Norman baronial one, representing the place-name *Mortemer* in northern France. This itself means 'dead sea', and originally described a stagnant marsh.

Morton The familiar surname derives from one of the many place-names *Morton*, most of them in the Midlands and north of England. The meaning is 'moor settlement' or 'marsh settlement', from Old English *mōr* and *tūn*, the latter eventually giving modern *town*.

Moscow The capital of Russia takes its name from the river *Moskva* on which it stands. The origin of the river name has not yet been precisely established, and there have been many hypotheses to account for it. They include the following: 1. from a root word meaning 'to wash' related to Latin *mergere* and so to English *immerse*; 2. from a Slavic word *moskva* meaning 'damp', 'marshy'; 3. from a Slavic phrase *most-kva* meaning 'bridge-water'; 4. from Finno-Ugrian words *moska* meaning 'calf' and *va* meaning 'river', so 'calf ford' (something like English OXFORD); 5. from Finno-Ugrian *mos*, 'to darken' and *ka*, 'water'. Probably the basic meaning, whatever its exact origin, was no more than 'water', as for many ancient river names.

Moselle The European river that is a tributary of the Rhine has a name that simply means 'little MEUSE', from Latin *Mosella*, the diminutive of *Mosa*, the Roman name of the Meuse.

Moses The name of the famous patriarch of the Old Testament probably derives from an Egyptian root word *mes* meaning 'son', although the Bible links it with Hebrew *mašah*, 'to draw out', specifically in the account of the finding of Moses by Pharaoh's daughter in the rushes at the riverside: 'And she called his name Moses: and she said, because I drew him out of the water' (*Exodus* 2.10). The name has always been very popular among Jews.

Moslem *See* MUSLIM.

Mosquito Coast The Caribbean coast of Honduras and Nicaragua, with its swamps and tropical rain forests, is said to be named for the biting insect, which thrives in such conditions. The name was then given by European explorers to the Indian people who inhabit this region, so that they are known as either the *Mosquito* or the *Miskito*, among other spellings.

Moss The name is a medieval form of MOSES, and for this reason is common among Jews, although also found fairly widely among Gentiles.

Moss Bros The name of the famous tailors and outfitters derives ultimately from that of Moses *Moses* (1820–1894), a Jewish bespoke tailor who set up shop in Covent Garden, London, in 1860. The *Bros* were two of his five sons, brothers George (1855–1905) and Alfred (1862–1937), who inherited the business on their father's death. Like many Jews originally named *Moses*, they anglicized their name to *Moss*.

Mosul The city of northern Iraq derives its name from Arabic *waṣala*, 'to join', 'to unite', as it arose at a point where the river Tigris was crossed by both a bridge and a ford. It was Mosul that gave the English word *muslin*, since this fabric was first produced there.

Mothering Sunday The fourth Sunday in Lent, also known as *Mother's Day* (or *Mothers' Day*), is a day when children traditionally give presents to their mothers. The alternative name is relatively recent, however, and was imported to Britain from America, where the day is marked on the second Sunday in May. In Britain, *Mothering Sunday* has been observed since at least the 17th century, and was originally a time when children visited their parents and presented their mothers with flowers and a simnel cake, the latter made from fine flour and other ingredients that were normally not used in Lent. Some authorities claim that the name is of religious origin, referring to an annual visit by the faithful to their local cathedral or *mother* church as a reminder of their baptism.

Mothers of Invention The American rock band was formed by Frank Zappa in Los Angeles in 1965. It was originally called the *Muthers*, then became the *Mothers*, then finally, in order to achieve publicity without the (intended) suggestion of an obscenity (*mothers* is a short form of *motherfuckers*), the *Mothers of Invention*, as if from the proverb 'Necessity is the mother of invention'.

Motley Crue The American heavy metal band, formed in 1981, took their name from the phrase *motley crew*, used to describe a mixed bunch of people. The name is more than apt for the members' strikingly bizarre appearance.

Motorhead The British heavy metal band were formed in 1975 by bassist Ian 'Lemmy' Kilminster after he had been sacked from the group Hawkwind, accused of taking drugs. The group's name derives from a song written by Kilminster for Hawkwind that itself represented the American slang word for a taker of amphetamine drugs, a 'speed freak'. The group's name is spelled *Motörhead* by its devotees.

Motown The first black-owned record company in America was founded in Detroit in 1959 and named after the city's nickname, *Motor Town*, given for its important automobile industry. The name became that of a distinctive type of black music, typically combining rhythm 'n' blues and pop.

Mott the Hoople The British rock group, formed in Hereford in 1968, took their name from the title of an obscure novel by Willard Manus published the previous year.

Moulin Rouge The Paris dance hall, famous for its cabaret with its regularly performed cancan, opened in the Place Blanche, Montmartre, in 1889 and took its name from that of a former dance hall and restaurant in the Avenue d'Antin (now the Avenue Franklin D. Roosevelt). Over the entrance it had a model of a *red windmill*, with moving sails and the figures of a miller at one window and his wife at another. When the sails turned, the two gave a friendly wave to each other. In the 17th century there were over 30 windmills on the heights of Montmartre, but today only two remain. One of these, the *Moulin de la Galette* ('Pancake Mill'), was built in 1662 and is famous from Renoir's painting of 1876.

Moulton The name derives from any of the places so called, such as the villages respectively near Northampton, Newmarket, or Spalding in Lincolnshire. The meaning of the place-name is in most cases 'Mule's settlement', from the Old English personal name *Mūla*, for a person resembling a mule in some way. (In a few instances, however, the place may have been named for real mules, kept for farmwork.)

Mountbatten The royal surname is a partial translation of the German name *Batten-*

berg, itself that of a place on the river Eder east of Cologne. Bearers of the original name changed it in the First World War due to anti-German feeling. The German place-name itself probably means 'hill by a water meadow'.

Mourne Mountains The mountains in southwest Northern Ireland take their name from that of the *Mughdhorna* tribe who once inhabited the region, with the people in turn named for their leader, *Mughdhorn* (literally 'ankle').

Move, The The British pop group was formed in Birmingham in 1966 by five musicians when they made a *move* from their respective bands to take on a greater challenge as a single team.

Mowbray Bearers of the name were originally Normans from the place called *Montbray* ('muddy hill') near Caen in northern France. *See also* MELTON MOWBRAY.

Mowgli The famous Indian boy raised by wolves in Kipling's *Jungle Books* (1894, 1895) is given his name by Mother Wolf, referring to his appearance as a naked 'man's cub': 'O thou Mowgli – for Mowgli the Frog I will call thee'. Kipling freely admitted that he had made the name up: 'It does not mean "frog" in any language that I know of' (*Author's Notes on the Names in the Jungle Books*, 1937). Perhaps the name of the Indian river *Hooghly* (or *Hugli*) may have partly suggested the name. The actual Hindustani word for 'frog' is *meṅdak*. So why did Kipling not choose a name based on that?

Mozambique The republic of southeast Africa has a name that is a Portuguese corruption of its Arabic name *mūsā malik*, 'Musa king', from *mūsā*, 'Musa' (the name of an early African ruler) and *malik*, 'king'.

Muhammad The founder of Islam (in 622 AD) has an Arabic name that means 'praiseworthy', 'commendable', from *ḥamida*, 'to praise'. His name is also spelled *Mohammed*, and was formerly familiar in the western world as *Mahomet*.

Muir The Scottish name originally applied to a person who lived on or near a moor or marsh. *Cp.* MOORE.

Mukden The name is that of the Chinese city now known as SHENYANG, in Manchu-

ria, where it was the capital of the Manchu dynasty from 1644 to 1912. It is Manchurian in origin, and is said to mean 'divine wind'.

Mulholland The name is an English form of the Irish name that was originally *Ó Maolchalann*, 'descendant of the devotee of *Calann*', the latter being a saint's name.

Mulhouse The city in eastern France is close enough to the German border to have a name of German origin. Its German name, *Mülhausen*, shows it to mean 'mill houses', from *Mühle*, 'mill' and *Haus*, 'house'. The town arose as a settlement by a mill on the river Ill.

Mull of Kintyre The well-known cape in western Scotland has a name that represents Gaelic *ceann*, 'head' and *tìre*, 'land' preceded by the common Scottish word *mull* to denote a promontory. The name as a whole is thus somewhat tautological, meaning 'cape of the headland'. No doubt *Mull* was added when the meaning of the Gaelic name had been forgotten. *Mull* itself may derive from the Old Norse word *múli*, meaning 'snout', and so be related to modern German *Maul* in the same sense.

Mumbai The well-known port in western India, formerly familiar as *Bombay*, has a name that is probably a shortening of *Mumbadevi*, 'goddess *Mumba*', referring to a Hindu deity worshipped here. It was apparently the Portuguese who introduced the European form of the name, which was officially superseded by the present spelling in 1990.

Mungo The Scottish name is familiar as the byname of the 6th-century saint Kentigern. Its origin is uncertain, and although it has been popularly explained as meaning 'amiable' it does not appear to correspond to any Gaelic words or elements.

Munich The well-known German city, capital of Bavaria, traces its name back to the word that gave its modern German name *München* and the German word *Mönch*, 'monk'. The town was founded by monks in the 12th century. Confusingly, the Italian name of Munich is *Monaco*. *Cp.* MÖNCHENGLADBACH, MÜNSTER.

Munro *See* MONROE.

Munster The ancient kingdom of Ireland, in the south of the country, has a name that means 'land of the Mumu people', with the tribal name followed by the Old Norse genitive ending *s* and Irish *tír*, 'land'. (*Cp.* TYRONE.)

Münster The city in northwest Germany derives its name from Latin *monasterium*, 'monastery'. *Cp.* MUNICH.

Murcia The region and ancient kingdom of southeast Spain takes its name from its capital city, itself with a name that is Arabic in origin, from *mursah*, 'fortified'.

Murdoch The Scottish name has an anglicized spelling of the original, which is *Muireadhach*, based on Gaelic *muir*, 'sea'.

Murgatroyd The name comes from Yorkshire, and represents an unidentified place-name that itself means '*Margaret*'s clearing', with the latter part of the name derived from the dialect word *royd*, 'clearing'.

Muriel The name is probably of Celtic origin, comprising words corresponding to Irish *muir*, 'sea' and *geal*, 'bright'.

Murmansk The port in northwest Russia takes its name from the coastal region of *Murman* here. This itself probably derives from the Finno-Ugrian words *mur*, 'sea' and *ma*, 'land', although some authorities see it as a corruption of *Norman*, 'northerner', as a general medieval name for a Scandinavian. The town arose in 1915 as the northern terminus of the railway that led up to the Arctic Ocean, and was originally named *Romanov-na-Murmane*, 'Romanov-on-Murman', after the Russian royal family. It was renamed two years later.

Murphy The familiar Irish name has an anglicized spelling of the original, which is *Ó Murchadha*, 'descendant of *Murchadh*'. The latter personal name means 'sea warrior', from Irish *muir* and *cadh*.

Murray The name is Scottish in origin, and is a form of the place-name MORAY.

Murray The river in southeast Australia was discovered in 1824 by the explorers W. H. Hovell and Andrew Hume, with the former originally naming it for his companion as the *Hume*. In 1830 it was renamed by the British explorer Captain Charles Sturt in honour of the Colonial Secretary of the day, Sir George *Murray* (1772–1846).

Murrayfield The famous Scottish rugby ground, the home of the national team in Edinburgh, was built on the site of the former Edinburgh Polo Ground in the 1920s, taking its name from the locality. The name means '*Murray*'s field' and is said to derive from a local 18th-century advocate, one Archibald *Murray*.

Murrumbidgee The river in southeast Australia has a name of Aboriginal origin perhaps meaning 'big water'.

Muscat The capital of Oman, a port on the Gulf of Oman, has the Arabic name of *Masqat*, said to mean 'hidden', referring to the location of the port, which is isolated from the interior of the country by a range of hills.

Musgrave The name derives from that of a village near Brough in Cumbria, itself meaning literally 'mouse grove'. This could either describe a grove infested with mice or mean the equivalent of 'Mouse's grove', from a name for a person resembling a mouse in some way.

Musical Joke, A Mozart's Divertimento in F major for two horns and strings, K 522 (1787) is so named from its deliberate parody of contemporary popular works and their performers. The original German title was *Ein musikalischer Spaß*, the latter word implying more a witty 'jest' than simply an amusing 'joke'.

Musical Offering, The The 13 works by Bach so named consist of ricercars and canons on a theme given to him for extemporization by Frederick the Great of Prussia in 1747. Bach's development and creative treatment of the theme was thus his offering to the king, as a musical dedication in kind. The German title of the work is *Das musikalische Opfer*, with the latter word implying 'offering' in the sense of 'special gift made to an important person' rather than the popular English meaning 'thing offered to be accepted or not'.

Muslim The name (also spelled *Moslem*) for a follower of the religion of Islam derives from Arabic *muslim*, 'surrendering'. This is the active participle of the verb *salama*, 'to be safe', 'to be at rest', that also gave the verbal noun (*islām*, 'submission') which lies behind ISLAM itself. *Cp.* also *salaam*, the Muslim form of salutation signifying peace, which represents Arabic *salām*, 'peace', from the same root word.

Musselburgh The Scottish town on the Firth of Forth has a name that means what it says, referring to the mussels that have made it famous for the past 800 years or more.

Mustapha The well-known Arabic name (more correctly *Muṣṭafa*) means 'chosen', 'elect', and for Muslims is familiar as an epithet of Muhammad, as *Al-Muṣṭafa*, 'the chosen one'.

Myanmar The country of southeast Asia, long familiar as *Burma*, changed the spelling of its name in 1989 to represent the Burmese original more accurately. This is *myanma*, meaning 'the strong', as applied to the Burmese people themselves.

Mycenae The ancient Greek city is traditionally said to have been founded by Perseus and named after the nymph *Mycene*.

Myfanwy The Welsh name derives from the affectionate prefix *my-* followed by a word related to *benyw*, 'woman', so means something like 'darling'.

Myra The name appears to derive from *myrrh*, but is popularly associated with MOIRA, and so with MARY, of which it happens to be an anagram.

Myrmidons The name is that of the race of people in Greek mythology who were created by Zeus from a nest of ants. It is traditionally derived from Greek *murmēx*, 'ant'.

Mysore The city in southern India has a name of Sanskrit origin, from *mahiṣūru*, 'town of buffalos', from *mahiṣa*, 'buffalo' and *uru*, 'land', 'region'.

Mývatn The lake in northeast Iceland has a name that means 'mosquito lake', from Icelandic *mý*, 'mosquito' and *vatn*, 'lake'. An exact correspondence in English would be 'midge water'.

N

Naboth The Old Testament character, notorious for refusing to hand over his vineyard to King Ahab and for consequently being stoned to death at the instigation of Queen Jezebel, has a Hebrew name that has been popularly interpreted as 'garden', 'fruitfulness'.

Nagaland The state of northeast India was established in 1964 at the request of its native people, the *Naga*. The origin of their name is disputed. Some derive it from Sanskrit *nāga*, 'snake', used as the name of a mythical creature with the body of a man as its upper half and of a snake as its lower. Others see the origin in either Hindi *nanga*, 'naked' or *naga*, 'hill', as the people are hill dwellers. But it may well be based on a word *nok* meaning simply 'people'.

Nagasaki The port in southwest Japan has a name that describes its location, from *naga*, 'long' and *saki*, 'headland', 'promontory'.

Nagorno-Karabakh The administrative region of Azerbaijan derives the first part of its name from Russian *nagornyy*, 'mountainous', 'hilly', from *na*, 'on' and *gora*, 'mountain', 'hill'. The second half of the name has been explained as deriving from Turkic words meaning 'black garden', referring to the black grapes of the vineyards here. However, this is probably an attempt to explain a name whose origin is actually uncertain.

Nagoya The Japanese city, in southern Honshu, has a name deriving from *na*, 'name', *ko*, 'old' and *ya*, 'house'. The 'old house' is the great castle built by a shogun here in 1610 for his son as the *daimyo* (local lord).

Nagpur The city of central India has a name representing Hindi *nāgpur*, from the river *Nag*, itself named for the *Naga* people (*see* NAGALAND), and *pur*, 'fort', 'town'.

Nahum The name is that of the prophet who foretold the destruction of Nineveh in the Old Testament book named for him. It represents Hebrew *Nahūm*, 'comforted', 'consoled'.

Nairn The town and resort in northeast Scotland takes its name from the river at the mouth of which it stands, with the river's own name of Celtic origin and perhaps meaning 'penetrating one'. The town gave the name of the former Scottish county of *Nairnshire*.

Nairobi The capital of Kenya has a name that represents the Swahili word for 'marsh'.

Nakhichevan The city in Azerbaijan has an ancient name recorded by Ptolemy in the 2rd century AD as *Naxouana*. This has been popularly derived from Armenian *nakh*, 'first' and *idzhevan*, 'landing', said to be that of the mountain here on which Noah's Ark came to rest after the Flood. But more realistically it probably represents the personal name *Nahich* or *Nahuch*, with the Armenian suffix *-avan*, 'settlement'.

Nakhon Pathom The town near Bangkok, Thailand, has a name meaning 'first town', from Thai *nakhom*, 'town' (*see also* BANGKOK) and *pathom*, 'first'. The town is said to have been the first to be founded in the country. Other towns in Thailand have similar names, such as *Nakhon Ratchasima*, 'frontier town of the king', *Nakhon Sawan*, 'paradise town', and *Nakhon Si Thammarat*, 'town of the good and just king'.

Nalchik The capital of Kabardino-Balkaria, southwest Russia, has a name that has been explained as deriving from a Balkarian word meaning 'little horseshoe'. The sense of this is obscure.

Namaqualand The coastal region of south-west Africa, partly in Namibia and partly in South Africa, takes its name from the Khoikhoin (Hottentot) *Nama* people who formerly inhabited it. The origin of their own name is uncertain. *Namaqua* is the plural of *Nama*.

Namibia The country of southwestern Africa derives its name from that of the Khoikhoin (Hottentot) *Nama* people who inhabit it. The origin of their own name is uncertain.

Namur The town of southern Belgium has a name of Gaulish origin, although the meaning is disputed. The derivation may be in *nemeto*, 'holy wood' (*cp.* NANTERRE), *nanto*, 'valley' (*cp.* NANTES), or possibly *nam*, 'to wind' with the suffix *-uco*, referring to a bend in the river Sambre or Meuse here.

Nanchang The city in southeast China, where it is the capital of Jiangxi province, has a name meaning 'prosperous south', from *nán*, 'south' and *chāng*, 'prosperous', 'flourishing'.

Nancy The name came to be adopted as a diminutive of ANN, but may have originally evolved from a medieval form of AGNES.

Nancy The city in northeast France had the Medieval Latin name of *Nanceiacum* or *Nantiacum*. This derives from the Gaulish personal name *Nantio*, with the Latin suffix *-acum*, 'place'.

Nanda Devi The name of the Himalayan mountain in the north of India means 'goddess of happiness', from Hindi *nanda*, 'riches', 'happiness' and *devī*, 'goddess'.

Nanga Parbat The mountain in the western Himalayas has a name meaning 'bare mountain', from Hindi *nanga*, 'naked', 'bare' and *parvat* (Punjabi *parbat*) 'mountain'.

Nanking The city of east central China, capital of Jiangsi province and former Chinese capital overall, has a name that means 'southern capital', from *nán*, 'south' and *jīng*, 'capital'. The name is applied contrastingly to that of PEKING, 'northern capital'. The city's name is now often spelled *Nanjing*. The Chinese word for 'south' has its equivalent in the second half of the name of VIETNAM. *Cp.* NANNING.

Nanning The port of southern China has a name meaning 'southern peace', from *nán*, 'south' (*cp.* NANKING) and *níng*, 'peace', 'calm'.

Nan Shan The name of the mountain range of north central China means (despite its location) 'southern mountains', from *nán*, 'south' (*cp.* NANKING) and *shān*, 'mountain'.

Nanterre The northern French town had the Roman name *Nemptum Dorum*, deriving from Gaulish *nemeto*, 'sacred wood' (*cp.* NAMUR) and *duru*, 'door', 'house', 'village'.

Nantes The city and port in western France has a name that derives ultimately from the *Namnetes* or *Nannetes*, the Gaulish tribe of the region. Their own name may come from Gaulish *nanto*, 'valley' (*cp.* NAMUR). Nantes is at the head of the Loire estuary.

Nantucket The name of the island off Massachusetts is Indian in origin but of uncertain meaning. An early map marks the island as *Natocko*.

Nantwich The Cheshire town was a former centre of the salt-mining industry, and its name, meaning 'famous saltworks', reflects this. The two halves of the name comprise Old English *named*, 'renowned' (literally 'named') and *wīc*, 'settlement', 'special place', with specific reference to the saltworks. The 'salt' sense of the latter word applies also to the Cheshire towns of *Middlewich* and NORTHWICH (the former lying midway between Northwich and Nantwich) and to DROITWICH in Hereford and Worcester.

Naomi In the Old Testament, *Naomi* is the mother-in-law of Ruth and mother of the grandfather of King David. Her name represents Hebrew *Nāʾomī*, 'my delight', 'my sweetness'.

Naphtali The name of the son of Jacob and Rachel's handmaid Bilhah is popularly derived from the Hebrew phrase meaning 'I have fought', as implied in the Old Testament: 'And Rachel said, With great wrestlings have I wrestled with my sister and I have prevailed: and she called his name Naphtali' (*Genesis* 30.8).

Naples The famous Italian city and port, in the southwest of the country, has a name of Greek origin, from *Neapolis*, 'new city', representing *neos*, 'new' and *polis*, 'city'. The city was laid out by Greek colonists in the 5th century BC according to a chequered plan, an innovation for its day. The origin of the name is preserved more precisely in the adjective *Neapolitan*.

Napoleon The Italian name is famous as that of the French emperor *Napoleon* Bonaparte, born in Corsica into a family of Italian descent. It is probably of Germanic origin, however, and may be connected with that of the NIBELUNGS. Later, it was altered by association with *Napoli*, the Italian name of NAPLES, and with Italian *leone*, 'lion'. The Russians fought Napoleon in the campaign of 1812, and were intrigued to find that in their language his name spells out as *na pole on*, 'he is on the field'.

Napoleonic Wars The name is that of the series of wars fought between France and (mainly) Britain, Prussia, Russia and Austria from 1799 to 1815, with France under the command of *Napoleon* Bonaparte. One of the major conflicts of the series was the PENINSULAR WAR. Most continental European countries regard the wars as being specifically *against* Napoleon, so that the Germans know the period as *der Kampf gegen Napoleon* ('the struggle against Napoleon'), and even the French talk of *les guerres contre Napoléon*.

Narbonne The historic city of southern France had the Roman name of *Narbona*. This was probably based on an Iberian or Aquitanian root element *nar*, simply meaning 'river', and found in many river names. The city was originally a port on the Mediterranean, but is now some distance inland.

Narcissus The name of the beautiful youth who fell in love with his own reflection in a pool and pined away is popularly regarded as giving the name of the *narcissus*. But it is almost certainly of pre-Greek origin, although the link with the flower, some species of which have narcotic properties, suggested an origin in Greek *narkē*, 'numbness'.

Narnia The name is that of the imaginary land in which the seven children's books by C.S. Lewis are set, the first being *The Lion, the Witch and the Wardrobe* (1950).

Lewis was a classical scholar, and creatures from classical mythology feature in the books (collectively known as the *Chronicles of Narnia*), so it is possible he took the name of their country from that of *Narnia*, the Roman name of the Umbrian town now known as *Narni*.

Narvik The port in the north of Norway has a name relating to the inlet at the head of which it stands. The meaning is 'narrow bay', from Old German *narwa*, 'narrow' and Old Norse *vík*, 'bay'.

Naseby, Battle of The Northamptonshire village is the site of an important Parliamentarian victory (1645) in the English Civil War. The name itself means '*Hnæf*'s village', the first part of this being an Old English personal name.

Nash The name originally applied to someone who lived by an ash tree, from Middle English *atten ash*, 'at the ash', wrongly divided as *atte nash*.

Nashville The state capital of Tennessee was founded in 1779 and named for the Revolutionary War general Francis *Nash* (1742–1777), killed in battle.

Nassau The capital of the Bahamas was laid out as a city in 1729 but the locality already had its present name in the 1690s. It was given in honour of King William III of England (1650–1702), of the house of Orange-*Nassau*, who succeeded to the throne in 1689. The royal Dutch title itself derives from what is now the German village of *Nassau*, near Koblenz, and has its own origin in a meaning 'damp land'.

Natal The southeastern province of South Africa takes its name from the port of *Natal*. This has its origin in Portuguese *Costa do Natal*, 'Christmas coast', the name given to the maritime region here by Vasco da Gama when he discovered it on Christmas Day 1497.

Natalie The name is the French form of Russian *Natalya*, itself representing Latin *natalia*, from *natalis dies*, 'birthday', especially Christ's birthday, otherwise Christmas. The name *Natalie* thus has the same ultimate origin as its male equivalent, NOEL.

Nathan In the Old Testament, the name is that of a prophet who rebuked King David for sending Uriah the Hittite to his death in battle so that he (David) could gain possession of Uriah's wife. It originates in Hebrew *Nāthān*, 'he (*i.e.* God) has given'. *Cp.* NATHANIEL.

Nathaniel The name is that of one of the apostles (sometimes identified with Bartholomew) in the New Testament. It represents Hebrew *Nethan'el*, 'God has given' (*cp.* NATHAN).

National Gallery The famous art gallery in Trafalgar Square, London, was founded in 1824 with a purchase of paintings from government funds, not through a private bequest. It is therefore *nationally* owned and financed, unlike many other galleries.

National Liberal Club The London club was established in 1882 for members of the LIBERAL Party with the great Liberal leader and prime minister William Gladstone as president. Members are still required not to undertake anti-Liberal political activities, although with the party now a shadow of its former self, the specific connection is hardly what it was.

National Trust The British organization that is concerned with the preservation of historic buildings and beautiful areas of the countryside is not so named because it is *nationally* funded, by the government, but because it operates for the benefit of the *nation*. It was founded in 1895 and has the full name *National Trust for Places of Historic Interest and Natural Beauty*.

National Westminster Bank The present High Street bank came into being in 1970 following the merger of the *National Provincial Bank* with the *Westminster Bank* and the *District Bank*. The *National Provincial Bank of England* was founded in 1833. Its name referred to its aim to be a truly *national* bank in England and Wales by the setting up of *provincial* branches, of which there were 15 by 1835. It was based in London, as was the *London and Westminster Bank*, established in 1834. The latter's name relates to its two original offices, one in Throgmorton Street, in the City of *London*, the other in Waterloo Place, in *Westminster*.

Nationwide Building Society The society was founded in 1884 and was at first named the *Co-operative Permanent Build-*

ing Society. Because of confusion with the *Co-operative Society*, however, and doubt among members of the public as to whether its services were available to everyone or not, the name was changed to the simple, less ambiguous *Nationwide* in 1970. In 1987 the society merged with the *Anglia Building Society*, founded in 1848, to form the *Nationwide Anglia*, but it dropped the latter word in 1991.

Navaho The name of the North American Indian people and their language represents the native (Tewa) name *Navahú*, meaning 'great planted fields'.

Navarre The former kingdom of southwest Europe, divided in the 16th century between Spain and France, has a name of pre-Latin origin probably based on *nava*, 'plain'.

Naxos The Greek island in the Aegean Sea is said to derive its name from that of an ancestor of the people who inhabit it. The meaning of his own name is uncertain.

Naylor The name was originally an occupational one for a person who made nails.

Nazarene The name has different applications, some of them overlapping. It can mean 'from NAZARETH', it can refer to a follower of Jesus, or be a title of Jesus himself, and it can also apply to certain groups of early Jewish Christians. As used for Jesus, the title occurs 12 times in the New Testament (notably in *Matthew* 2.23) and is traditionally taken to mean 'of NAZARETH', as that was the village where he lived in his youth. But many biblical scholars derive the name not from the town but link it with that of the *Nazarites*, the Jewish ascetics of ancient Israel mentioned in the Old Testament. Their name derives from the Hebrew word *nazīr*, 'consecrated', 'sanctified', itself from the verb *nazir*, 'to abstain', since the Nazarites were required to 'drink no wine nor strong drink' (*Judges* 13.5–7). If this interpretation is correct, and in view of the difficulties surrounding the name of *Nazareth* itself, Jesus' title of *Nazarene* could have meant 'consecrated one'.

Nazareth The town in northern Israel, famous as the home of Jesus in his youth, has a name of uncertain origin. Although it occurs several times in the New Testament (for example *Matthew* 2.23) it is not found in the Old Testament or in any contemporary rabbinical texts. The present city dates from some time after the beginning of the Christian era, and some biblical references do not square with the present site. For example, one account tells how 'all they in the synagogue' led Jesus 'unto the brow of the hill whereon their city (*i.e.* Nazareth) was built, that they might cast him down headlong' (*Luke* 4.28, 29). But the Nazareth of today, although on rising ground, is on nothing like a steep hill or mountain. Some scholars are inclined to the view that the name of the biblical Nazareth is a corruption of the name of GENNESARET, an alternative name for the Sea of Galilee, with the first syllable, representing *gē*, 'valley', perhaps deliberately dropped. Jesus of *Nazareth* should therefore perhaps really be Jesus of *Gennesaret*. *See also* NAZARENE, as one of his titles.

Nazarite *See* NAZARENE.

Nazi The name of the National Socialist German Workers' Party, founded in 1933, is an abbreviation representing the pronunciation of the first two syllables of *Nationalsozialistische*, the first word of its German name.

Ndebele *See* MATABELELAND.

N'Djamena The capital of Chad, north central Africa, has a name meaning 'resting place', perhaps alluding to a settlement where travellers could shelter from the extreme heat. The city's name until 1976 was *Fort-Lamy*, for the French soldier and explorer François *Lamy* (1858–1900), killed by Africans at Lake Chad.

Neagh, Lough The lake in Northern Ireland, the largest in the British Isles, has a name meaning '*Eochaid*'s lake'. The named man is said to have been a legendary king of Munster who drowned in the lake when it flooded in the 1st century AD. The name is pronounced 'Ney'.

Neanderthal The name for the type of primitive man derives from that of the *Neandertal*, 'valley of the (river) *Neander*', near Düsseldorf in western Germany, where the remains of such a human being were discovered in a cave in 1856. Rather curiously, the name of the river means

'new man', from Greek *neos*, 'new' and *anēr*, genitive *andros*, 'man'.

Neasden The district of northwest London has a name meaning 'nose-shaped hill', from Middle English *nese*, 'nose' and Old English *dūn*, 'hill'. It is not certain where exactly the hill in question was.

Neath The South Wales town near Swansea takes its name from the river on which it stands. The river's name is Celtic in origin and probably means 'shining one'.

Nebo, Mount The mountain in Jordan, northeast of the Dead Sea, is mentioned in the Bible as the one from which Moses viewed the Promised Land (*Deuteronomy* 34.1). The name is that of the Assyrian god *Nabu*, the god of learning and writing, also mentioned in the Bible (*Isaiah* 46.1), whose own name means 'speaker', 'announcer', from *navī*, 'prophet'. The name of this god also lies behind that of NEBUCHADNEZZAR.

Nebraska The American state takes its name from the river *Nebraska* which flows through it, with the river's name in turn deriving from an Indian word meaning 'flat', 'shallow'. The river also has the French name *Platte*, with the same meaning.

Nebuchadnezzar The well-known name of the king of Babylon who conquered and destroyed Jerusalem represents Akkadian *Nabu-kudurri-usur*, 'May Nabu protect the boundary stone'. 'Boundary stone' here refers to his line of succession. Nabu was an important Babylonian and Assyrian god (*see* NEBO). The king's name is sometimes rendered more accurately in English as *Nebuchadrezzar*. *See also* ABEDNEGO.

Neferhotep In Egyptian mythology, the name is that of the god of the moon, whose centre of worship was at Thebes. It means 'the beautiful one is satisfied'.

Nefertiti The name of the Egyptian queen who was the wife of AKHENATEN (AMENHOTEP) in the 14th century BC means 'the beautiful one cometh'. The elegant portrait bust of her, found in Middle Egypt and now in the Berlin Museum, confirms the aptness of the name.

Negev The semidesert region in southern Israel has a name representing Hebrew *negev*, 'south'.

Negro The name for a dark-skinned member of one of the native peoples of Africa, or a descendant of one, derives from Spanish or Portuguese *negro*, 'black', itself from Latin *niger* with the same meaning.

Nehemiah The name is that of the Jewish official who obtained permission from King Artaxerxes to rebuild Jerusalem after the Babylonian captivity. The account of how this was done is told in the Old Testament book named for him. His name represents Hebrew *Nehemyāh*, 'consolation of Yah', *i.e.* of Jehovah.

Neil The Scottish and Irish name derives from Gaelic *Niall*, perhaps meaning 'champion', 'conqueror'.

Nejd The flat desert region of central Saudi Arabia has a name that simply represents Arabic *najd*, 'plateau'.

Nell The name is a short form of ELEANOR, ELLEN or HELEN, with the initial *N* perhaps deriving from a combination of *mine* with the name, so that *mine Ellen*, for example, became *my Nell*. The same thing happened with EDWARD to produce the pet form *Ned*.

Nelson The name means either 'NELL's son' or 'NEIL's son'. The popularity of the British admiral Horatio *Nelson* led to the adoption of the name as a first name, and also indirectly gave the name of the town of *Nelson* in Lancashire, which developed in the early 19th century round an inn named commemoratively for the admiral after the Battle of Trafalgar in 1805.

Nelson Mass Haydn's Mass No 11 in D minor (1798) may have been written to celebrate the victory of Nelson at the Battle of Aboukir Bay (1798), although according to some authorities the work is so named because Nelson was present during its performance at Eisenstadt in 1800. Haydn himself headed his composition *Missa in angustiis* ('Mass in difficulties'), implying he had found it hard to write. It is also known as the *Imperial Mass* or *Coronation Mass*.

Nemea The valley in ancient Greece, famous for the Nemean Games, derives its name from Greek *nemos*, 'wooded pasture', 'sacred grove'.

Nemesis The name of the Greek goddess of retribution and vengeance derives from Greek *nemesaō*, 'I feel righteous anger', from *nemō*, 'I distribute'. Both words in fact apply to Nemesis, since she oversaw the fair distribution of blessings among people while venting her righteous indignation against those who had offended against the law.

Nemours The town in northern France was known to the Romans as *Nemausus*. This is the same name as that for NÎMES, and is probably of the same origin.

Nepal The kingdom in southern Asia, in the Himalayas, has a name that represents Sanskrit *nepāla*, perhaps from *nipat*, 'to fly down' (itself from *ni*, 'down' and *pat*, 'to fly') and *ālaya*, 'stay', 'house'. The reference is to villages at the foot of the many mountains here.

Neptune The Roman god of the sea has a name of uncertain origin, although some scholars have variously derived it from Greek *naō*, 'I flow', Latin *nato*, 'I swim', Latin *nauta*, 'sailor', or the Iranian word that gave modern *naphtha*, which in its natural state as petroleum is found in the sea. A further theory suggests a connection with Greek *nephelē*, 'cloud', and the name has also been linked with the root of English *potent* and *despot*. The name of the planet *Neptune*, discovered in 1846, was chosen to match that of Jupiter. In Greek mythology, Jupiter is the equivalent of Zeus, while Neptune corresponds to Poseidon, Zeus's brother. Neptune and Jupiter thus belong to the same 'family', as do Jupiter, his father Saturn, and his grandfather Uranus, all four being the names of adjacent planets.

Nergal The Babylonian god of the sun and ruler of the underworld derives his name from Akkadian *Ne-uru-gal*, 'lord of the great city', that is, of the grave.

Nerissa The name derives from the Greek word *nērēis*, 'Nereid', that is, one of the sea-nymphs said to have been the daughters of the sea-god *Nereus*.

Nero The notorious Roman emperor, alleged to have started the fire that destroyed much of Rome in AD 64, was originally known as *Lucius Domitius Ahenobarbus*. On his adoption at the age of 13 by the emperor Claudius as his son and heir, however, he assumed the name of *Nero*, a *cognomen* (nickname) in the Claudius *gens* (clan) that had been originally borne by a son of Appius Claudius Caecus the Censor. It is said to be a Sabine word meaning 'brave', 'lively'.

Nescafé *See* NESTLÉ.

Ness, Loch Famous for its putative monster, the Scottish lake derives its name from that of the river that flows from it to Inverness. The name has nothing to do with the latter town, but probably represents an Old Celtic word meaning 'roaring one'.

Nestlé The familiar brand name, associated with dairy products, chocolate and instant coffee, is that of the company's founder Henri *Nestlé* (1814–1890), born in Germany but living in Switzerland from 1843. He was originally a research chemist, but invented a new milk-based baby food in 1867 and produced it in commercial quantities when he found there was a demand for it. He sold his business to another group in 1875, but they kept the name. *Nescafé* instant coffee came on the market in 1938 as the company's first non-dairy product. Its name is a blend of *Nestlé* and French *café*, 'coffee'.

Nestor In Greek mythology, the name is that of the oldest and wisest of the Greeks in the Trojan War. It may derive from Greek *nostos*, 'travel', 'journey'.

Netherlands The English name of the west European country is a translation of its Dutch name *Nederland*, 'lower land'. The name was originally given to this part of Europe by the Austrians, who saw it as low-lying by contrast with the mountainous terrain of their own country.

Neuchâtel The town in western Switzerland has a name that corresponds exactly to that of Britain's NEWCASTLE, from French *neuf*, 'new' and *chatel*, an old form of *château*, 'castle'. The Medieval Latin name of the town, recorded in the 11th century, was *Novum Castellum*, and the 'new castle' dates from this time. The town stands on the lake of the same name. The town of *Neufchatel*, in northern France, has a name of identical origin.

Neuilly The suburb of northwest Paris has a name found elsewhere in France. It represents the personal male name *Nobilis* or *Novellius*, probably deriving from Latin *novellus*, a diminutive of *novus*, 'new'. The reference is perhaps to the owner of newly cleared land.

Neustria The western part of the kingdom of the Merovingian Franks, in what is now northern France, derives its name from Old German *Neuwestarrīhi*, 'new western kingdom', from *neu*, 'new', *westar*, 'west' and *rīhi*, 'kingdom'. It was so named in the 6th century when the former *Westarrīhi*, 'western kingdom', separated from the *Ōstarrīhi*, 'eastern kingdom' by the Rhine, was divided into *Austrasia*, 'eastern kingdom' and *Neustria*, 'western kingdom'. *See also* AUSTRIA.

Neva The river in western Russia has a name of Finnish origin, from *neva*, 'marsh', 'peat bog'. The name is a historic one for Lake LADOGA, which drains through the Neva into the Gulf of Finland. The river's name thus probably derives from that of the lake rather than referring to its marshy delta, as is sometimes proposed.

Nevada The American state has a name that is a shortened form of *Sierra Nevada*, the mountain range in eastern California, forming the western boundary of Nevada. The range was given its name, meaning 'snowy mountain chain', by Spanish explorers in memory of the identically named mountain chain in the south of Spain. The Spanish word *sierra* literally means 'saw', implying jagged peaks.

Nevers The city in central France takes its name from the river *Nièvre* on which it stands. The river's own name probably represents a basic root element *nev* meaning simply 'water', 'river'. The former province of *Nivernais* took its name from Nevers.

Neville The name was adopted from the surname, itself from a Norman personal name deriving from one of the places in Normandy called *Neuville*, 'new settlement'.

Newark The town near Nottingham, formally known as *Newark-on-Trent*, has a name meaning 'new work', referring to an Anglo-Saxon fort that was built over the former Roman one. *Cp.* NEWCASTLE.

Newark The port in New Jersey, just west of New York City, was settled by Puritans from Connecticut in 1666 and is said to have been given its name by the Rev. Abraham Pierson for his home town, NEWARK in England. However, other accounts claim that the name had a biblical interpretation, as *New Ark*, or that it was regarded as a *New Work*, a newly built settlement (like its English namesake). It may well have been a blend of two or even all three of these.

New Britain The island in the South Pacific, the largest of the Bismarck Archipelago, was given its name in 1699 by the British buccaneer William Dampier. The archipelago passed into German hands (as its name still implies) in 1884, when New Britain became *Neu-Pommern*, 'new Pomerania'. The name reverted to *New Britain* after the First World War when the territory was mandated to Australia.

New Brunswick The Canadian province was created in 1784, when it was separated off from *Nova Scotia*, and was given its name in honour of George III, of the house of Hanover, which had the alternative name of BRUNSWICK.

Newbury The Berkshire town has a name meaning 'new town', or more exactly 'new market town'. In many English place-names a final *-bury* (from Old English *burh*) means 'fort'. But Newbury arose only in the 12th century, later than most of the other places so named, so requires a different rendering of the word.

New Caledonia The island in the southwest Pacific was discovered by Captain Cook on Sunday 4 September 1774 and named by him with the Latin name of Scotland, CALEDONIA. He chose the name as a compliment to the nearby *New Hebrides* (now VANUATU), which he had named shortly before.

Newcastle The well-known Tyneside city has a name that means what it says, referring to the 'new castle' that was built here in the 11th century on the site of the former Roman fort. *Newcastle*-under-Lyme, Staffordshire, similarly had a 'new castle' in the 12th century. The second part of the name describes the town's proximity to *Lyme* Forest, formerly here, its own name meaning 'place of elms'. *Cp.* NEUCHÂTEL.

Newcastle United The famous football team was formed as *Newcastle East End* in 1882, playing on a ground at Heaton, to the east of the city. To the west, on Town Moor, played their deadly rivals, *Newcastle West End*. The latter had taken over the ground from a team called *Newcastle Rangers*. In 1892 *Newcastle East End* amalgamated with *Newcastle West End* to form *Newcastle United*, moving into the superior ground at Town Moor. This itself became known as St James' Park soon after, a name it retains today.

New College The Oxford college was founded in 1379 as *St Mary's College*, but in 1400 adopted the name *New College* to be distinguished from the university's other *St Mary's College*, now ORIEL COLLEGE. Perhaps because of its adjectival nature, the name is traditionally not shortened to the first word only, as for other colleges.

Newcombe The name was originally given to a *newcomer*, someone who had recently arrived in a place. The letter *b* in the name came about through association with *combe*, 'valley'. *Cp.* NEWMAN.

New Delhi The capital of India was inaugurated in 1912 when the British moved the capital from Calcutta to a *new* site to the south of what is now Old DELHI. The new city was completed in 1929 when the viceroy took up residence there, and it was formally opened in 1931.

Newdigate Prize The annual prize for verse, open to Oxford University students, was instituted in 1805 and named for its founder, Roger *Newdigate* (1719–1806), Member of Parliament for Oxford University.

New Edition The American vocal quintet became established as an all-male black teenage group in Boston ·in the early 1980s. They were trained by their discoverer and manager Maurice Starr as an eighties version of the Jackson Five, so were given a name to reflect this role. Their name was partly the inspiration for that of NEW KIDS ON THE BLOCK, also managed by Starr.

New England The name of the territory that now comprises the six northeastern states of America was given it in 1614 by the English captain John Smith (with his typically English name). The name turned out to be appropriate, since the first English settlement was established six years later at Plymouth, Massachusetts (one of the six states) by Puritans who had sailed from Plymouth, England. Smith, however, had given the name in a generally commemorative way for his native land, rather than for settlements that he expected his fellow countrymen to make in the future.

New Forest The south of England woodland region, mainly in Hampshire, was 'new' when it was created as a hunting preserve by William the Conqueror in the 11th century. Its name is recorded in the Domesday Book as *Nova Foresta*.

Newfoundland The island of eastern Canada has a name that means what it says, describing a land that has just been discovered. It evolved from the *new founde isle* recorded by its discoverer John Cabot in 1497, with *New founde launde* appearing in official documents as early as 1502.

New Guinea The island to the north of Australia was discovered by the Portuguese explorer Jorge de Meneses in 1526 and given its name in 1546 by the Spanish explorer I. Ortez de Aetes, from the similarity in appearance (as it seemed to him) of the indigenous people here to those of GUINEA in West Africa.

New Hall The Cambridge college was founded as a *new* undergraduate college for women in 1954. Its name is coincidentally similar to that of NEWNHAM COLLEGE, the university's only other college still solely for women.

New Hampshire The American state, in NEW ENGLAND, was given its name in 1529 by the English settler, Captain John Mason, in memory of HAMPSHIRE, his home county. The territory had been granted to Mason by Charles I.

Newhaven The East Sussex port has a name meaning 'new harbour', referring to the harbour that was built in the 16th century when the lower section of the river Ouse here was dredged and widened with the aim of improving navigation. The French port of LE HAVRE ('the harbour'), due south of Newhaven across the English Channel, was itself known by the English

as *Newhaven* for some time after its foundation in 1517.

New Ireland The South Pacific island, in the Bismarck Archipelago, was discovered by the Dutch in 1616 but not named until 1767, when the English navigator Philip Carteret arrived here. He discovered that NEW BRITAIN was not one island, as had been thought, but two, so he named the second one for IRELAND to compliment (and complement) the first.

New Jersey The American state was named in 1664 by one of the proprietors of the territory, Sir George Carteret, after his native island of JERSEY, in the Channel Islands.

New Kids On the Block The American vocal quintet were formed in Dorchester, Massachusetts, in 1984 by the music entrepreneur Maurice Starr, who sought to promote a white group as an equivalent to the black NEW EDITION whom he already managed. He originally named the five *Nynuk*, a word or acronym of disputed origin, but when they were signed up by CBS Records in 1986 the company persuaded him to give the group a more meaningful name. *New Kids on the Block* was the result, reflecting the name of the existing quintet.

Newman The name was originally given to someone who had recently arrived in a place, so that he was a 'new man'. *Cp.* NEWCOMBE, STRANGE.

Newmarket The Suffolk town, famous for its racecourse, has a name dating back to the 13th century, when the settlement had gained the right to hold a 'new market'. *Cp.* NEWBURY and *Newport*.

New Mexico The American state has a name that is an English translation of its original Spanish name, *Nuevo México*. This had been given to the territory in 1562 by the Spanish explorer Francesco de Ibarra in the hope that it would become as rich as neighbouring MEXICO.

Newnham College The Cambridge college for women was founded in 1871 in Cambridge itself but in 1875 moved to newly built premises in the village of *Newnham*, just outside the city. The name of the village, appropriately for the college at the time of its foundation, means 'new dwelling-place'.

New Order The British new wave rock group was formed in 1980 by the remaining four members of JOY DIVISION after the suicide of their lead singer, Ian Curtis. Their new name resembled their old in that it had Nazi connotations. It evoked 'the new order' (German *die neue Ordnung*) that Hitler planned for the reconstitution of Europe, and seems to have been prompted by contemporary political events, in particular the 'new order' that the Khmer Rouge aimed to impose as a Communist regime in Cambodia. At the same time, the name is generally apt for anyone making a fresh start, as the four were doing.

New Orleans The famous Louisiana port was founded by the French in 1718 and named *Nouvelle Orléans* in honour of the French regent, Philip, Duke of ORLÉANS. The name was anglicized in 1803 when Louisiana was sold by the French to the English, although the French still know it as *La Nouvelle-Orléans* (feminine, because the feminine noun *ville*, 'town' is understood).

Newport The name is familiar for at least three British towns, two of them in South Wales and the third in the Isle of Wight. The Old English word *port* meant both 'place on a river or by the sea', as now, and 'market town'. Historically the latter sense is the older, since a market town or commercial centre often arose at a place where there were ready facilities for transportation by water. All three Newports mentioned here arose as trading centres in medieval times, and all are on rivers. But *cp.* NEWPORT PAGNELL.

Newport News The port and industrial centre in Virginia is believed to derive its name from two of its original founders in about 1621, Christopher *Newport* and William *Newce*, the latter's name being altered though popular association with the word *news*.

Newport Pagnell The Buckinghamshire town arose as a 'new' town with market rights, as did NEWMARKET and NEWPORT, Isle of Wight. Like the latter, it is on a river. The second word of its name (which distinguishes it from other Newports) refers to the Norman lord of the manor here in the 12th century, Fulc *Paganel*. His own name was originally a nickname meaning 'little pagan'.

Newquay The Cornish resort derives its name from the 'new quay' that was built in the mid-15th century so that ships could anchor under the protection of its wall, which the original harbour lacked.

Newry The town in Northern Ireland near Carlingford Lough has a name that represents its Irish name *An tIúr*, 'the yew tree'. Tradition tells how St Patrick planted a yew tree at the head of the lough when he founded the monastery here in the 6th century.

New Siberian Islands The Arctic archipelago, off the north coast of Russia, takes its name from the single island of *New Siberia* here, so named in 1910 by the Russian polar explorer M.M. Gedenshtrem, who saw it, understandably enough, as an extension of SIBERIA. The Russian name of the group is *Novosibirskiye ostrova*.

New South Wales The name was that selected for the whole of the eastern coast of Australia by Captain Cook, who was here in 1770 and who saw what he took to be a resemblance between this coastline and that of South WALES. The territory named *New South Wales* then came to include all the Australian continent except Western Australia. Later, the establishment of new colonies reduced its size considerably, with South Australia formed in 1836, Victoria in 1851, Queensland in 1859 and Northern Territory in 1863.

New Testament The *New Testament* is the specifically Christian part of the Bible, as distinct from the Jewish OLD TESTAMENT. *New Testament* is the English rendering of Latin *novum testamentum* which itself translated Greek *hē kainē diathēkē*, literally 'the new covenant'. The 'new covenant' was the agreement between God and man as revealed through Jesus Christ, by comparison with the 'old covenant' revealed to the Hebrew people by Moses. It was 'new' because: 1. it involved the blood and suffering of its central figure, Christ, as against the ritual sacrifices and sprinkling of blood in the Old Testament; 2. it contained a fuller, clearer revelation of the mysteries of religion, with the additional power and grace of the Holy Spirit, than the many shadowy rites and obscure revelations of the Old Testament; 3. it proclaimed a religion for all, not simply one for a single race, the Jewish people of the Old Testament; 4. it introduced a religion that was for all time, not one that would eventually be superseded, as Judaism was by Christianity; 5. it was newly written (in the 1st and 2nd centuries AD), as distinct from the Old Testament, parts of which dated back hundreds of years. The New Testament was originally written in Greek, while the Old Testament was in Hebrew and (in part only) Aramaic.

Newton The name was originally that of a person from one of the many places so called, the place-name itself meaning 'new farm', 'new settlement'.

Newton Abbot The Devon town has a basic name that is the most common in Britain, meaning simply 'new farm', 'new village'. Many Newtons acquired an additional name to be distinguished from one another. In the case of Newton Abbot, the added word indicates that the place was given to the *abbot* of Torre Abbey (*see* TORQUAY).

New World The name for the Americas, first current in the 16th century, relates to the fact that they were discovered and colonized relatively late, by contrast with the long known *Old World* countries of Europe and Asia. The phrase predates Shakespeare's famous 'brave new world' of *The Tempest* (1612).

New World Symphony The exact title, or subtitle, of Dvořák's Symphony No 9 (formerly No 5) in E minor, Op 95 (1893) is *From the New World* (in the original Czech *Z nového světa*). The reference is generally taken to be to the Negro spiritual melodies in the work, although none is directly quoted. (One tune, however, does suggest 'Swing low, sweet chariot', and the main theme of the Largo has itself been turned into a spiritual called 'Goin' home'.) The composer intended the symphony as a sketch for a opera based on Longfellow's *The Song of Hiawatha* (1855). In the event this was never realized. *See also* NEW WORLD.

New York The state of New York was named in 1664 by the English in honour of James, Duke of *York* and Albany (1633–1701), the future James II, to whom the colony had been entrusted by his brother, Charles II. The English had captured the territory from the Dutch, whose earlier name for it had been *New Amsterdam*, for their capital.

New Zealand The independent dominion in the southeast Pacific has a name that is a partly anglicized form of the original Dutch name *Nieuw Zeeland*, 'new sea land', perhaps also with reference to the Dutch province of ZEELAND. The islands were discovered by the Dutch explorer Abel Tasman (*see* TASMANIA) in 1642, and originally named by him *Staaten Landt*, 'land of the States', with reference to the original name of the Netherlands as the *United Provinces*. The Dutch authorities changed the name, however, the following year.

Niagara The famous falls, on the border between the United States and Canada, have a name that may represent Huron or Iroquois *nee-agg-arah*, 'thundering water' but that is more likely to derive from an Iroquois word meaning 'neck of land', or more specifically 'point of land cut in two', referring not to the falls themselves but to the point where the river Niagara flows into Lake Ontario. There are two towns named *Niagara Falls* on opposite banks of the river, one in the United States at the falls, and one in Canada just below them. They are linked with each other by bridges.

Niamey The capital of Niger, in north central Africa, has a name that according to one account is said to derive from the order of an African chief to his seven slaves, '*Wa niammane*', 'stay here'. This subsequently became *Niamma*, then *Niamey*. However, this is just one of a number of legendary explanations for the name, and its true origin remains uncertain.

Nibelungs The supernatural race of dwarfs in German mythology, who guarded the treasure hoard stolen for them by Siegfried, have a name that is variously derived from that of their king, that of their hoard, that of their land, or that of the *Burgundians* who (in some accounts) they are said to represent. The meaning of the name is as obscure as its origin. Attempts have been made to relate it to German *Nebel*, 'mist' on the one hand, and Old Norse *nifl*, 'dark', on the other (*cp.* NIFLHEIM). If the latter holds, the Nibelungen (or Nibelungs) were an underworld race, as dwarfs are popularly said to be.

Nicaea The ancient city in Asia Minor is said to have been given its name in honour of *Nikaia*, wife of the 3rd-century BC Macedonian general Lysimachus, who captured it. Its present Turkish name is *İznik*, from the Greek *eis Nikian*, 'to Nicaea'.

Nicaragua The country of Central America was discovered in 1522 by the Spanish explorer Gil Gonzalez and named for *Nicarao*, the chieftain of a local tribe.

Nice The city and resort in the south of France was founded in the 3rd or 2nd century BC by Greek colonists from Massilia (now MARSEILLE) and was dedicated by them to *Nikē*, the Greek goddess of victory, in gratitude for their defeat of the Ligurians.

Nicholas The name is Greek in origin, from a combination of *nikē*, 'victory' and *laos*, 'people'. It was widely popularized by St *Nicholas*, a 4th-century bishop of Myra in Lycia, who became the patron saint of countries such as Greece and Russia and of sailors and children, among others. This last association produced the form of his name now familiar as SANTA CLAUS.

Nicholson The name means 'son of NICHOLAS'. *Cp.* NIXON.

Nicodemus The name is familiar in the Bible as that of the Pharisee who came to Jesus by night to discuss questions of faith and belief. His name represents Greek *nikē*, 'victory' and *dēmos*, 'common people', 'populace'.

Nicomedia The ancient town of Asia Minor and former capital of Bythinia was named for *Nicomedes* I (d. about 250 BC), who rebuilt it in 264 BC. His own name means 'mindful of victory', from Greek *nikē*, 'victory' (*cp.* NICE) and *mēdomai*, 'I think'. The Turkish name of the town here today is *İzmit*, from Byzantine Greek *eis Mēdeia*, 'to Nicomedia', with the abbreviated form of the name.

Nicosia The capital of Cyprus has a name based on Greek *nikē*, 'victory'.

Niflheim In Norse mythology, the name is that of the world of darkness that existed before creation. It derives from Old Norse *nifl*, 'dark' and *heimr*, 'abode'.

Nigel The name is Medieval Latin in origin, from *Nigellus*, itself a form of the equivalent of NEIL, with the spelling influenced by Latin *niger*, 'black'. Sir Walter Scott did much to popularize it with his novel *The Fortunes of Nigel* (1822).

Niger The republic of West Africa takes its name from the river here. The first Arab explorers called the river *nahr al-anhur*, 'river of rivers', translating the Tuareg name for it, *egereou n-igereouen*, with the same meaning, from *egereou*, 'big river', 'sea' and its plural, *igereouen*. It was the second part of the Tuareg name (*n-igereouen*) that probably gave the modern European name *Niger*. The present form of the name is first recorded in the writings of the Arab explorer Leo Africanus, who noted it in 1526 as *Niger*, doubtless under the influence of Latin *niger*, 'black', as if the river name could also mean 'river of the blacks'. *Cp.* NIGERIA.

Nigeria The republic of West Africa takes its name from the river NIGER, which flows through it, with the Latin 'country' suffix *-ia*.

Nightingale The name was originally given as a nickname to someone who had a good voice, whether for singing or speaking.

Nijmegen The town in the eastern Netherlands has a name that represents its Roman name of *Noviomagus*, from Gaulish *novio*, 'new' and *mago*, 'place', 'market'. There were other Roman settlements of the name in Europe. One was CHICHESTER (*which see*).

Nikolayev The Ukrainian port on the Black Sea is so named either because it was founded on 6 December 1788, the feastday of St *Nicholas* (Russian *Nikolay*), or because the first ship to be launched here (in 1790) was the 44-gun frigate *St Nicholas*, named for the patron saint of sailors.

Nikolayevsk The Russian seaport town at the mouth of the river Amur, on the east coast of Siberia, was founded as a trading post in 1852 in the reign of *Nicholas* I, and is named for him. Its full name is *Nikolayevsk-na-Amure*, 'Nikolaevsk-on-Amur', with this addition made in 1926 to distinguish it from other towns of the same name, such as *Nikolayevsk* east of the Volga, later renamed *Pugachëv*.

Nikon The well-known Japanese make of camera has a name that evolved as an abbreviation of that of the optical company founded in 1917 as *Nippon Kogaku KK*. In 1932 this company produced camera lenses named *Nikkor* and in 1948 its first 35 mm camera named *Nikon*. The company subsequently adopted this as its general commercial name, while retaining the original name for formal use.

Nikopol The Ukrainian town on the river Dnieper was founded in 1781 on the site of the village called *Nikitin Rog*, 'Nikita's horn', referring to the promontory here. Its original name was *Slavyansk*, 'Slav town', but this did not become permanent, mainly because there was a fashion for 'Greek' names in this part of Russia at the time. Doubtless under the influence of the original name the town was thus called *Nikopol*, 'victory town', from Greek *nikē*, 'victory' and *polis*, 'town', with perhaps a specific reference to *Nikē*, the Greek goddess of victory. Two other well-known towns with Greek names in Ukraine are SEBASTOPOL and SIMFEROPOL.

Nile The famous river of northeast Africa has a name that is one of the oldest in the world, going back to the Semitic root word *nahal*, 'river'. The Nile is mentioned in the Bible, but never by name. It is always referred to as 'the river' (Hebrew *yᵉ'or*), as for example: 'And it came to pass at the end of two full years, that Pharoah dreamed: and, behold, he stood by the river' (*Genesis* 41.1).

Nîmes The city in the south of France was known to the Romans as *Nemausus*, a name that ultimately goes back to Gaulish *nemo*, 'sanctuary'. NEMOURS, in the north of France, has a name of identical origin.

Nimrod The name of the famous Old Testament 'mighty hunter', noted for his prowess, probably represents Akkadian *nimru*, 'tiger'. It has traditionally been derived, however, from the root element

mrd meaning 'resist', 'revolt', so that he was 'he who stirs up the people against the lord'. *See also* NIMRUD.

Nimrod The ninth of Elgar's ENIGMA VARIATIONS is so called because it is a portrait of his friend A.J. Jaeger, and *Jaeger* is the German word for 'hunter', which the biblical NIMROD was. It is the one variation of the work that is often played separately, and is popular for its slow, moving melody.

Nimrud The ancient city in Assyria, near the present Iraqi town of Mosul, where it is a noted archaeological site, takes its name from the biblical NIMROD. *See also* NINEVEH.

Nineveh The ancient capital of Assyria, on the Tigris opposite the modern Iraqi city of Mosul, is said to derive its name from that of *Ninus*, the mythological first king of Assyria and husband of Semiramis. According to the Bible, however, Nineveh was founded in Assyria by NIMROD (*Genesis* 10.11), and 'the land of Assyria' is equated with 'the land of Nimrod' (*Micah* 5.6). This is not to suggest that the name of Nineveh actually derives from that of Nimrod, although the physical proximity of Nineveh to NIMRUD is probably relevant in accounting for the traditional origin of the city.

Niobe The daughter of Tantalus in Greek mythology, whose children were killed after she boasted about them, has a name that may represent either Greek *neos*, 'new', 'young' or Greek *nipha*, 'snow', in the latter case in the figurative sense 'snow-white', 'fair-skinned'.

Niort The town in western France was known in the 6th century as *Noiordo*, a name that represents *Novioritu*, from Gaulish *novio*, 'new' and *ritu*, 'ford'. Its later Latin name was *Nyrax*, genitive *Nyractis*.

Nirvana The British psychedelic rock group, formed in 1967, took as its name the Buddhist term for absolute blessedness. The term itself is the Sanskrit word for 'extinction', literally 'blowing out', from *nir*, 'out' and *vāti*, 'it blows'.

Niš The town in eastern Yugoslavia, in Serbia, was known to the Romans as *Naissus* and to the Greeks as *Naissos*. It takes its name from the river *Nišava*, on which it stands. The river's name is based on a Slavic root word *niz*, meaning 'lower', doubtless referring to a river at the bottom of a valley.

Nisan In the Jewish calendar, the name is that of the first month of the year according to the biblical reckoning and that of the seventh month in the civil year. It is Babylonian in origin, and of uncertain precise meaning.

Nishinomiya The city in central Japan, in Honshu, has a name that represents Japanese *nishi*, 'west' and *miya*, 'temple', 'palace', with the middle syllable *no* the sign of the genitive. The overall meaning is thus 'temple of the west'.

Nissan The well-known Japanese car manufacturers were originally a foundry, dating from 1910. They later became a motor parts firm and in 1931 absorbed Japan's first car company, *DAT*, the forerunner of DATSUN. In 1934 they became the *Nissan Motor Company*, taking this name as a short form of *Nihon Sangyo*, from Japanese *nihon*, 'Japan' and *sangyō*, 'industry'. In the early 1980s a policy decision was taken to standardize all *Datsun* cars as *Nissan*s.

Nitty Gritty Dirt Band The American country rock group was formed in 1966 as the *Illegitimate Jug Band*, punningly referring to the fact that they had no jug player. Two years later they adopted their new name, designed to be both eye-catching and to denote their 'basic' or adaptable approach to their music. For about five years from 1976 they appeared simply as the *Dirt Band*.

Nivôse The fourth month of the French Revolutionary calendar, corresponding to the period from 22 December to 20 January, had an appropriate name for this midwinter time, deriving from Latin *nivosus*, 'snowy'.

Nixon The name means 'son of *Nick*', this being a short form of NICHOLAS. *Cp.* NICHOLSON.

Nizhny Novgorod The industrial city in western Russia, east of Moscow, has a name that literally means 'Lower NOVGOROD', relating it to the ancient town of the same name northwest of Moscow. The latter became the centre of a principality in the 9th century, an event regarded as the founding of the Russian state, and for this reason was often known as *Novgorod Velikiy*, 'Novgorod the Great'. The later Novgorod (originally known also thus when founded in the 13th century) was therefore 'Lower', or less important by comparison, and was subsequently designated as such. The name does not thus refer to the geographical location of the city, although it is further south than its older namesake. In 1932 it was renamed *Gorky*, for the Russian writer Maxim *Gorky* (real name Aleksey Maximovich Peshkov) (1868–1936), who was born there. It reverted to its former name in 1990.

Njord In Norse mythology, the name is that of the god of the sea and fishing who was one of the *Vanir* and the father of *Frey* and *Freya*. It represents Old Norse *Njörthr*, a form of *northr*, 'north'.

Noah The name of the biblical character, famous for building an ark to save his family and living things from the Flood, is popularly derived from Hebrew *Nōah*, 'rest', 'comfort', as is implied in the account of his birth: 'And he (*i.e.* Lamech) called his name Noah, saying, This same shall comfort us concerning our work and the toil of our hands' (*Genesis* 5.29).

Noble The name was originally a nickname for a 'high born' person, or for someone who acted as if he was. In the manner of nicknames, it could equally be applied to an extremely poor and 'lowly' person.

Nod The biblical 'land of Nod, on the east of Eden' (*Genesis* 4.16) has a name related to Hebrew *nūd*, 'to travel', 'to wander'. The name is omitted in the Vulgate (Latin version of the Bible), which has simply 'on the east of Eden'.

Noel The name is French in origin, meaning 'Christmas', from the first word of Latin *natalis dies*, 'birthday', that is, Christ's birthday. The same word gave the familiar *Nowell* of Christmas carols. *Cp.* NATALIE.

Nogent The name is found for several towns in France, the largest including *Nogent*-sur-Marne, now an eastern suburb of Paris, and *Nogent*-le-Rotrou, southwest of Chartres. The Roman name of such places was invariably *Novientum* or *Novigentum*, representing Gaulish *novio*, 'new' with the Latin suffix *-entum*. The name thus denoted a new Gaulish settlement, and corresponded to the later French *Neuville* and *Villeneuve*.

Noirmoutier The island in the Bay of Biscay, off the west coast of France, is noted for the site of its 7th-century monastery. It was this that gave the island its name, from Latin *Nigrum Monasterium*, a corruption (suggesting 'black monastery') of *Nerium Monasterium*, from the phrase *in Herio monasterio*, 'in the monastery of Herus'. *Herus* is thus the original name of the island. Its meaning is unknown. The *Noir-* of the modern French name has translated the misleading *Nigrum* of the Latin.

Noisy-le-Grand The town east of Paris, France, derives its name ultimately from Latin *nux*, genitive *nucis*, 'nut'. This place, like others of the same name, was at one time noted for its nut trees.

Nolan The Irish name is an English spelling of the original form *Ó Nualláin*, 'descendant of *Nuallán*', this being a name derived from Irish *nuall*, literally 'shout', implying someone famous or notorious.

Nonconformist When the term first arose, in the early 17th century, it applied to any members of the Church of England who disagreed with certain of its customs and practices (such as kneeling to receive Holy Communion) and who refused to *conform* to them. Later, after the Act of Uniformity of 1662, and the expulsion from their livings of those ministers who refused to conform, the name came to apply to former members of the Church of England who, like the Methodists, had left it altogether to set up their own Protestant churches.

Nora The name developed as a short form of names such as *Eleonora* (modern ELEANOR), *Honora* and *Leonora*.

Noraid The American organization that supports the Republicans in Northern Ireland derives its name from '*Nor*thern Ireland' and '*aid*'.

Norfolk The East Anglian county is so named as it was inhabited by the 'northern folk', that is, by the northern group of East Anglian tribes, as distinct from the southern group, who inhabited what is now SUFFOLK. Both names are unusual in that they are simply the names of the people, with

no word such as *land* for their territory. *Cp.*, for example, NORTHUMBERLAND, WESTMORLAND. The port of *Norfolk*, Virginia was founded in 1618 and named for the English county.

Norman The name is of Germanic origin and means 'north man', otherwise 'Norseman', or an inhabitant of Scandinavia. The name was in use in England before the Norman Conquest of 1066, so was reinforced by its adoption among the invaders themselves.

Normandy The former province of northern France takes its name from its inhabitants, the *Normans*, themselves so called as they were descended from the Vikings or *Norsemen* ('north men'), the 10th-century Scandinavian conquerors of the region and the native French. *Cp.* NORWAY and *see also* MURMANSK.

Norns The three virgin goddesses of fate in Norse mythology have a name of Old Norse origin (*Nornir*) but uncertain meaning. Their individual names were *Urd*, 'fate' (also interpreted as 'past'), *Verdande*, 'coming into being' ('present'), and *Skuld*, 'duty' ('future'). They lived in the roots of the world tree Yggdrasil.

Norris The name denoted a person who came from the *north* in some way, either as a settler from the north, or someone who lived on the northern edge of a settlement. The origin is in Old French *norreis*, 'northerner'. In some cases the name was an occupational one for a *nurse*, that is, a wet nurse or foster mother.

Norrköping The port in southeast Sweden has a name that means (despite its location) 'northern trading place', from Swedish *norr*, 'north' and *köping*, 'trading place', 'village' (*cp.* CHIPPING CAMDEN). It is 'north' by comparison with the much smaller port of *Söderköping*, 'southern trading place' immediately south of it. *Cp.* also JÖNKÖPING, LINKÖPING, NYKÖPING.

Northallerton The North Yorkshire town has a name showing that it arose as a 'northern *Allerton*', as distinct from any other places identically named, such as the Allertons that are now districts of Bradford and Liverpool. The basic name itself means '*Ælfhere*'s farm'.

Northampton The county town was originally *Hampton* (or its Anglo-Saxon equivalent), meaning 'home farm'. It then added *north* to be distinguished from its southern namesake, SOUTHAMPTON, also originally *Hampton* (although there with a different meaning).

Northern Territory The administrative division of north central Australia has a self-explanatory name. It could well have had a more original name, however. It was annexed to South Australia in 1863, having earlier been part of New South Wales. The following year the name *Alexandra Land* was proposed for it, in honour of Princess Alexandra, and was officially adopted for a time. In the Second World War the name of *Churchill Land* was put forward, and when Queen Elizabeth visited Australia in 1954, *Elizabeth Land* was similarly suggested. But the uninspiring original name has always prevailed.

North Sea The sea between Britain and the European continent was so named by the Dutch (as *Noordzee*) by contrast with the ZUIDER ZEE ('south sea'). The Romans called it *Oceanus Germanicus*, 'German sea', and the Danes have sometimes referred to it as *Vesterhavet*, 'western sea'. The name *German Sea* was in general use in English to at least the 18th century, as in the following:

> HUMBER, a river formed by the Trent, the Ouse, and several other streams united. It divides Yorkshire from Lincolnshire, and falls into the German Sea at Holderness.
>
> *Encyclopaedia Britannica*, first edition, 1771.

Northumberland The county of northeast England derives its name from the Anglo-Saxon people who occupied *land* to the *north* of the river HUMBER. Their kingdom here from the 7th to the 9th century had the Medieval Latin name of *Northumbria*. Its territory was much larger than that of the present county and included land north of the Tweed in what is now southeast Scotland.

Northwich The town near Manchester has long been famous for its salt industry, and this is referred to by the second half of its name, which represents Old English *wīc*, 'special place'. The word similarly relates specifically to salt production in the names of DROITWICH and NANTWICH. Northwich is *north* of the latter.

Norway The Scandinavian country derives its name from Old Norse *Norrevegr*, 'northern way'. The Vikings (*Norsemen*) sailed on three main routes between Scandinavia and the rest of Europe: the 'eastern way', through the Baltic, the 'western way', across the North Sea, and the 'northern way', along the coast of what is now *Norway*. Cp. NORMANDY.

Norwich The county town of NORFOLK has a name meaning 'northern port', from Old English *north* and *wīc*. The 'port' here was the commercial one on the river Wensum. The name was originally that of the *northernmost* of four or more separate settlements, and because it was the most important (on a Roman road as well as the river) its name was gradually extended to include the others.

Nostradamus The noted 16th-century French astrologer is popularly known by a Latin form of his original name, Michel de *Nostre-Dame*. This derives from the place that was the home of his ancestors, itself named for the dedication of its church to *Our Lady*, otherwise the Virgin Mary.

Nostromo The well-known novel by Conrad, published in 1904, takes its title from the nickname of its central character, the Italian dockworkers' foreman known as *Nostromo*, 'our man' (Italian *nostr'uomo*). His real name is Gian Battista Fidanza.

Nosy Be The volcanic island off the northwest coast of Madagascar has a Malagasy name meaning 'big island', from *nòsy*, 'island' and *be*, 'big'. The name is also spelled *Nossi-Bé*.

Notre-Dame The famous medieval cathedral of Paris stands on the site of an original 6th-century church that had the same dedication to 'Our Lady', that is, to the Virgin Mary. The dedication is appropriate for a 'mother church'.

Nottingham The county town has a name meaning 'homestead of *Snot*'s people', with the initial *S* of the personal name dropped by the Normans, who found it difficult to pronounce *sn*. However, the original name (of the same man) is preserved in the eastern district of Nottingham known as *Sneinton*, 'farm of Snot's people'.

Nottingham Forest The NOTTINGHAM football club was formed in 1865 and took its name from its first ground, the *Forest* Racecourse, now *Forest* Recreation Ground. This was an open area to the northwest of the city, and was itself named after SHERWOOD FOREST, which stretches to the north of Nottingham. *Cp.* NOTTS COUNTY.

Notting Hill The district of west London has a name that probably means 'hill of the *Knottings*', referring to a family named *Knotting* who probably came from *Knotting* in Bedfordshire.

Notts County The NOTTINGHAM football club, formed in 1862 and the oldest club in the Football League, arose as a sporting club for 'county gentlemen', as the second word of their name indicates. Their first ground was in a private park next to Nottingham Castle, and they played games only among themselves until 1864, when they first challenged another team.

Nouakshott The capital of Mauritania, northwest Africa, is said to derive its name from a Berber (Zenaga) dialect phrase *in wakchodh*, 'having no ears', from *akchud*, 'ear'. This presumably refers descriptively to a local chieftain here at some time.

Nova Scotia The peninsula and province of eastern Canada has a name that is the Latin for 'New Scotland'. The territory was granted in 1621 by James I to the Scotsman Sir William Alexander, Earl of Stirling, with the conveyance including words referring to lands 'to be known as Nova Scotia, or New Scotland', and it was the Latin version of the name that (unusually) prevailed. The territory had earlier belonged to the French, under the name of ACADIA.

Novaya Zemlya The archipelago in the Arctic Ocean, off the north coast of Russia, to whom it belongs, has a Russian name meaning 'new land'. The name was given by Russian traders on the islands by contrast with the 'old' trading settlements on the mainland. On historic maps the name frequently appears as *Nova Zembla*, and in modern French is still *Nouvelle-Zemble*. The *b* represents the French attempt to pronounce the unfamiliar sound of *ml*.

Something similar happened in the evolution of the name of WIMBLEDON.

November The name of the 11th month of the year derives from Latin *novem*, 'nine', so numbered as it was formerly the ninth month from the beginning of the Roman year, in March. *Cp.* SEPTEMBER, OCTOBER, DECEMBER.

Novgorod The Russian city northwest of Moscow has a name meaning 'new town', from Russian *novyy*, 'new' and *gorod*, 'town' (*cp.* VOLGOGRAD). The city was founded in the 9th century and is one of the oldest in Russia, but was a 'new town' (by comparison with other existing towns) when it originally arose. The Varangians (Scandinavians who settled in Russia from the 8th century) knew it as *Holmgard*, 'island town', referring to its location on raised land by the river Volkhov. *See also* NIZHNY NOVGOROD.

Novial The artificial language devised by the Danish philologist Otto Jespersen in 1928 was given a name representing the first element of Latin *novus*, 'new' and the initials of '*i*nternational *a*uxiliary *l*anguage'.

Novi Sad The port on the Danube in Serbia, northeast Yugoslavia, has a Croatian name meaning 'new garden', from *nov*, 'new' and *sad*, literally 'plantation', 'garden', but here essentially 'settlement'. The town's German name of *Neusatz* has the same sense.

Novocaine The proprietary name for the drug procaine hydrochloride, used in local anaesthetics, was registered in 1905. The drug was regarded as being a more effective substitute for cocaine, so was given a name that combined elements from Latin *novus*, 'new' and '*cocaine*' itself.

Novokuznetsk The name of the city in central Russia, in Siberia, means 'new Kuznetsk'. It arose in 1617 as the village of *Kuznetsk*, so named for its iron mines, from Russian *kuznets*, 'forge worker'. When a steelworks was set up here on the river Ob in 1929, as part of the current Five Year Plan, its name was modified to *Novokuznetsk* in order to distinguish it from KUZNETSK in central Russia near Penza. From 1932 to 1961 it was known as *Stalinsk*.

Novomoskovsk The industrial city in western Russia south of Moscow has a name that means 'new MOSCOW'. Its original name was *Bobriki*, from the small river *Bobrik* on which it stands, the river's name in turn deriving from Russian *bobr*, 'beaver'. From 1934 to 1961 it was known as *Stalinogorsk*, 'Stalin's hill'. It then gained its present name, referring to its location in the *Moscow* Coal Basin.

Novorossiysk The Russian Black Sea port has a name meaning 'new Russia', from *novyy*, 'new' and *Rossiya*, 'Russia'. 'New Russia' (*Novorossiya*) was the name given to the territory here that passed from Turkey to Russia at the end of the 18th century. The town itself arose as a fortified post in 1838.

Novosibirsk The Russian city, the largest in Siberia, arose in 1894 at a crossing of the river Ob during construction of the Trans-Siberian Railway. Its original name was *Gusevka*, then from 1903 *Novonikolayevsk*, 'new Nicholas town', for Tsar *Nicholas* II, with 'new' distinguishing it from the existing NIKOLAYEVSK. In 1926 it adopted its present name, 'new Siberia', with reference to its growing industrial and commercial importance in this part of Russia. The name was chosen by local workers from a short list offered them in the newspaper *Sovetskaya Sibir'* ('Soviet Siberia'). Names proposed but rejected included: *Oktyabr'grad* ('October town'), *Ob'gorod* ('Ob town'), *Sibgrad* ('Siberia town', also alluding to the Trans-*Siberian* Railway), *Krasnosibirsk* ('Red Siberia'), *Krasnoobsk* ('Red Ob'), *Krasnograd* ('Red town') and *Krasnokuznetsk* ('Red Kuznetsk', as distinct from the Siberian town, also on the Ob, that became NOVOKUZNETSK). *Krasno-* in all these names can equally be understood as 'beautiful'.

Nowa Huta The industrial suburb of Kraków that is the centre of Poland's steel industry has a name meaning 'new foundry', from *nowa*, the feminine of *nowy*, 'new' and *huta*, 'foundry', a word borrowed from German *Hütte* with the same meaning (literally 'hut').

Nubia The ancient region of northeast Africa takes its name from its indigenous inhabitants, the *Nubians*. Their own name is said to be related to Coptic *noubti*, 'to weave', referring to the important local craft of basket-making. Some authorities, however, link the name with Nubian *nub*, 'gold', with reference to another local craft.

Nuffield College The Oxford college for graduates was founded in 1937 by William Morris, Viscount *Nuffield* (1877–1963), the famous motor manufacturer (*see* MORRIS) and founder of the *Nuffield* Foundation charitable trust in 1943. He took his title from the Oxfordshire village of *Nuffield*, near Wallingford, where he had made his home (he was born in Worcester) and where he is buried.

Nugent The name is of Norman origin, applying to someone who had come from one of the places called *Nogent* in northern France. The place-name derives from Gaulish *novio*, 'new', with the Latin ending *-entum*. This would have been used of a 'new village', so that in effect the English name *Nugent* has essentially the same origin as the name NEVILLE.

Nuits-Saint-Georges The fine French red wine takes its name from the town in Burgundy. The town is itself named from the site of its vineyards, in the nearby *côte de Nuits*, 'hill-slope of Nuits'. The latter name may ultimately derive from Latin *nauda*, 'marshy place'. It is appropriate that the town should be named for St George, whose own name means 'cultivator' (literally 'land worker').

Nuku'alofa The capital of Tonga, in the southwest Pacific, has a name, meaning 'south', that originally applied to the whole archipelago.

Nullarbor Plain The low plateau in southern Australia has no water or trees. Its name refers to the latter lack, and was artificially composed from Latin *nullus*, 'no' and *arbor*, 'tree', by the explorer Alfred Delissier.

Numbers The fourth book of the Bible is so named because it describes the two *numberings* of the tribes of Israel, both at the beginning (chapters 1–4) and at the end (chapter 26) of their wanderings. The English name translates the Greek name *Arithmoi* used in the Septuagint (Greek version of the Old Testament). The Hebrew name of the book is *Bemidbar*, 'in the wilderness', taken, as for other Old

Testament books, from the opening words: 'And the Lord spake unto Moses in the wilderness of Sinai' (*Numbers* 1.1).

Numidia The ancient country of North Africa takes its name from its native inhabitants, the *Numidians*. Their own name is a form of the word *nomad*, referring to their wandering existence. The word itself literally means 'go from one pasture to another', and ultimately derives from Greek *nomē*, 'pasture', itself from *nemō*, 'I distribute', 'I allot'.

Nuneaton The name of the Warwickshire town means 'nuns' river farm'. The original name of the place here by the small river Anker was the equivalent of ETON. In the 12th century a nunnery was founded, and *Nun-* was added to the name to distinguish it from the many other 'river farms'.

Nuremberg The city in southern Germany has a name ending in the German word for 'mountain' but with a first half that is of uncertain meaning. It has been related to the NORNS, the Norse goddesses of fate. The Medieval Latin name of the city was *Norimberga* and the present German form of the name is *Nürnberg*.

Nuristan The region of eastern Afghanistan derives its name from Afghani or Iranian *nūrestān*, 'land of light', from *nūr*, 'light' and *ostān*, 'land', 'country'. The name was introduced only in the late 19th century, when the population was forcibly converted to Islam. The former name of the region was *Kafiristan*, 'land of the KAFFIR', *i.e.* of non-Muslims.

Nursery Suite Elgar's orchestral suite of this name, composed in 1931, is so called because it was dedicated to the Duchess of York and her daughters Princess Elizabeth (the future Queen Elizabeth II), then aged five, and Princess Margaret Rose (Princess Margaret), aged one.

Nutcracker Suite Tchaikovsky's popular piece of this name originated as a ballet written to a libretto based on Alexandre Dumas' version of the story by E.T.A. Hoffmann, *Der Nussknacker und der Mäusekönig* ('The Nutcracker and the Mouse King') (1816). The ballet was first performed in 1892, and that same year the composer arranged an orchestral suite of eight numbers from it (as Op 71a). The French title of the work is also familiar, as *Casse-noisette*, but less so the original Russian, which is *Shchelkunchik*.

Nuttall The name has nothing to do with nuts but was originally an occupational name, either for a keeper of oxen, from Middle English *nowt*, 'beast', 'ox' (*cp. neat's-foot oil*, made by boiling cattle feet and bones), or for a scribe or clerk, from Middle English *notere* (modern *notary*).

Nuuk The capital of Greenland has an Eskimo name meaning 'summit'. Its former name (until 1979) was GODTHAAB.

Nyasa, Lake The lake in central Africa has a name that in a local African language means simply 'lake'. The Malawi name of the lake is Lake MALAWI. Malawi itself was formerly known as *Nyasaland*.

Nyíregyháza The town in northeast Hungary has a name meaning 'church by (or among) the birch trees', from Hungarian *nyír*, 'birch' and *egyház*, 'church'. The word for 'church' literally means 'one house', from *egy*, 'one' and *ház*, 'house', implying a place of assembly.

Nyköping The port in southeast Sweden has a name meaning 'new trading place', from Swedish *ny*, 'new' and *köping*, 'trading place', 'village' (*cp.* CHIPPING CAMDEN). There are many market towns with similar names in Sweden: compare JÖNKÖPING, LINKÖPING, NORRKÖPING. A further related name is that of COPENHAGEN. The port of *Nykøbing* in southern Denmark has a name of identical origin.

O

Oahu The island in central Hawaii is said to have a name meaning 'place of assembly'.

Oakapple Day The name is that of the annual commemoration (on 29 May) of the restoration of the monarchy in 1660. People formerly wore *oak apples* or oak leaves on this day to symbolize the oak tree at Boscobel in which Charles II hid after his defeat at the battle of Worcester (1651).

Oakham The former county town of Rutland has a name that does not refer to oaks but means '*Occa's* riverside meadow', with the Anglo-Saxon personal name followed by Old English *hamm*, 'meadow', 'riverside pasture'. The town is on a tongue of land between two streams.

Oaks, the The annual horse race for fillies held at Epsom since 1779 takes its name from an estate nearby, where the house was used as a hunting and racing box by its owner, the twelfth Earl of Derby (founder of the DERBY) in the late 18th century. The estate was originally known as *Lambert's Oaks*, after a local family.

Oaxaca The city in southern Mexico is said to have a name representing Nahuatl *Huaxaca*, meaning 'at the point of the acacia'.

Ob The river of western Siberia has a name that probably derives from the Iranian root element *āb*, 'water'. This is directly related to the word for 'water' found behind the names of many other rivers and places in Europe. *Cp.* AACHEN and AQUITAINE, for example.

Obadiah The name of the prophet and book of the Old Testament called after him derives from Hebrew *'Ōbadhyah*, 'servant of Yah', *i.e.* of Jehovah. The name is thus identical in origin and meaning to ABDULLAH.

Oban The west coast Scottish port and resort has a Gaelic name, meaning 'little bay', that refers to the small bay on which it stands.

Oberammergau The village in southwest Germany, famous for its decennial Passion Play, has a name that means 'district over the Ammer', from German *ober*, 'over', *Ammer*, a river name, and *Gau*, 'district'. The name of the river is based on the Old High German root word *am*, 'to flow'. Oberammergau is in the Alpine foothills.

Oberon The name of the king of the fairies and husband of Titania in medieval folklore is familiar from Shakespeare's *A Midsummer Night's Dream* (1595). It is a form of the name AUBERON, so like it is probably of Germanic origin, meaning 'noble bear'.

Oceania The name of the islands of the central and south Pacific was devised in 1812 by the Danish geographer Conrad Malte-Brun, basing it either on *ocean* or, more likely, on the name of the Greek Titan *Oceanus*, god of the stream believed to flow round the earth, whose own name originally gave the word *ocean*.

O-Cedar The familiar furniture polish was originally manufactured by a firm founded in Chicago in 1910. It was at first called *Wondermist* but then was renamed by the firm's founder, Charles A. Channell, allegedly as the result of the following incident:

> He had just finished polishing the bar of a public-house and the proprietor and himself were admiring the glistening surface, when a negro porter came in, and seeing the brilliant shining bar, exclaimed in his vernacular "O see dar," and so was born a name that has reverberated around the world.
>
> W.H. Beable, *Romance of Great Businesses*, Vol II, 1926.

O'Connor The name is an English spelling of the Irish name *Ó Conchobhair*, 'descendant of *Conchobhar*'. The latter name was that of a 10th-century king of Connacht from whom many people named O'Connor now claim descent. The king's own name apparently derives from Irish *cú*, 'hound' and *cobhar*, 'desiring'.

Octavia The name is Latin for 'eighth', and was sometimes given to an eighth daughter or eighth child (if female) in a large Victorian family. (An eighth male child could be correspondingly *Octavius* or *Octavian*.) In Roman history *Octavia* is famous as the wife of Mark Antony, while *Octavian* was the name of AUGUSTUS before he became emperor. The literal meaning of the name is exemplified by the famous English philanthropist *Octavia* Hill (1838–1912), who was the eighth daughter to be born to her parents.

October The tenth month of the year derives its name from Latin *octo*, 'eight'. It was formerly the eighth month of the Roman year, which began in March. *Cp.* SEPTEMBER, NOVEMBER, DECEMBER.

October Revolution The name is an alternative one for the Russian Revolution, when the Bolsheviks came to power under Lenin in November 1917. The apparently inaccurate name came about because Russia was then still on the Julian (Old Style) calendar, which differed by 13 days from the Gregorian (New Style). The Revolution thus occurred on 25 October (Old Style), corresponding to 7 November (New Style). Soviet Russia transferred to the New Style reckoning in 1918.

Oddbins The chain of wine shops has a name devised in the early 1970s from *odds-and-ends* and *bin-end*, the latter being a wine merchant's term for a small lot of wine sold off at a reduced price because it is too small to be included in a new wine list.

Odense The port in southern Denmark takes its name from that of the famous Norse god ODIN, to whom it was sacred in ancient times.

Odeon The familiar cinema name derives from those built in the 1930s by the British film distributor and cinema chain owner Oscar Deutsch (1893–1941). Deutsch chose the name not only because it directly derived from the Greek word *ōdeion*, a term for a building for musical performances, but because its first two letters represented his own initials. The first *Odeon* cinema opened in the Birmingham suburb of Perry Barr in 1930.

Odessa The Ukrainian port, on the Black Sea, was founded in 1795 by order of Catherine the Great at a time when Greek place-names were in vogue in this part of Russia. It was given a name based on that of *Odessos*, an ancient Greek colony said (on rather dubious grounds) to have been near here. The name has been popularly but erroneously linked with that of ODYSSEUS.

Odin The name of the supreme god in Norse mythology derives from the Germanic root word *odo*, perhaps meaning 'fury', referring to the poetical inspiration or shamanic ecstasy that he was believed to generate. *Cp.* Latin *vates*, 'soothsayer', 'poet'. His Anglo-Saxon counterpart was WODEN.

Odysseus The great hero of Greek mythology, known to the Romans as ULYSSES, has a name that is traditionally derived from Greek *odussaō*, 'I hate', 'I am angry', as he was subject to the wrath of the gods and in particular to that of Poseidon because he had blinded Polyphemus, Poseidon's son.

Odyssey The epic poem by Homer tells the story of the ten years of adventures of ODYSSEUS on his return journey to Ithaca after the fall of Troy and of the revenge he took on the suitors of his wife Penelope.

Oedipus The tragic figure of Greek mythology, who unwittingly killed his father and married his mother, has a name that is traditionally related to an incident in his babyhood. His father, Laius, had been warned by an oracle that any son his wife Jocasta bore him would kill him. He therefore abandoned the baby on a mountain, piercing its foot with a spike to hasten its death. As a result, the baby had a swollen foot, so that its name derives from *oideō*, 'I swell' and *pous*, 'foot'.

Oenone In Greek mythology the name is that of the Phrygian nymph loved by Paris. Her name means 'wine queen', from Greek *oinos*, 'wine'. The name can be regarded as representing the best attributes of wine (richness, fullness, sweetness, delicate flavour, and the like) rather than drunkenness or lasciviousness. It is sometimes adopted as a first name.

Offaly The name of the Irish county is an English spelling of its Irish name, *Uíbh Fhailí*, 'descendants of *Failghe*', referring to the legendary ancestor of the people who once lived here.

Offa's Dyke The lengthy entrenchment running south from Prestatyn in North Wales to Chepstow in the south takes its name from *Offa*, king of Mercia, who built it in the 8th century to mark the boundary between England and Wales. The present border only rarely coincides with the Dyke.

Ogilvie The Scottish name comes from the glen of *Ogilvie* in the Sidlaw Hills near Glamis Castle north of Dundee. The place-name is probably of Celtic origin meaning 'high hill', from words related respectively to modern Welsh *uchel* and *bryn*.

Ogyges The ancient king of Greece, the legendary ruler of Boeotia and founder of Thebes, has a name that has been related to the mythical island of *Ogygia*, identified with Calypso in Homer's *Odyssey*, and to that of *Oceanus*, the god of the ocean in which the island is located. Whatever its actual origin, it probably has a basic sense 'water', 'flood'.

O'Hara The Irish name is an English spelling of *Ó hEaghra*, meaning 'descendant of *Eaghra*'. The latter personal name is of uncertain meaning.

Ohio The American state takes its name from the river *Ohio*, with its own name derived from an Iroquois or other Indian word meaning 'beautiful'. French colonists here named the river *La Belle Rivière* similarly.

Oireachtas The name of the Irish parliament means 'assembly', from Old Irish *airech*, 'nobleman'. It is pronounced approximately '*Enctus*'.

Oise The river in the north of France had the Roman name *Isara* or *Esara*, from the pre-Celtic root element *is*, 'holy', 'sacred' and *ar*, 'water', 'river'. The name is thus of the same origin as that of the river ISÈRE.

Ojibwa The name of the North American Indian people, also spelled *Ojibway*, derives from a native word with a root meaning 'puckered', referring to the plaited or puckered moccasins that the people wear. The name is also familiar in its corrupted form CHIPPEWA.

Oka The Russian river, a tributary of the Volga, has a name of uncertain origin that has been variously derived from Gothic *aka*, 'water', 'river', Finnish *joki*, 'river' and Slavic *oko*, 'eye' (in the sense of an open expanse of water). Whatever the precise linguistic origin, it is most likely to mean simply 'water', 'river'.

Okayama The city in southwest Japan, in Honshu, has a name deriving from Japanese *oka*, 'hill' and *yama*, 'mountain'.

Okhotsk, Sea of The sea between the east coast of Siberia and the Kamchatka peninsula takes its name from the river that flows into it. The river's name has been popularly but erroneously linked with Russian *okhota*, 'hunt', but is actually from the Evenki word *okat*, meaning simply 'river'.

Okinawa The island of southwest Japan, a scene of heavy fighting in the Second World War, derives its name from Japanese *oki*, 'open sea' and *nawa*, 'cord', 'chain'. This describes the string of islands that extend into the East China Sea here.

Oklahoma The American state has an Indian name proposed in 1866 by the Rev Allen Wright, chief of the Choctaws, to designate land in what was then known simply as *Indian Territory*. It means 'red people', from Choctaw *okla*, 'people' and *humma*, 'red'.

Öland The second largest island of Sweden, in the Baltic, has a name that merely means 'island', from Swedish *ö*, 'island' and *land*, 'land'.

Old The surname means what it says, although not necessarily implying old age but distinguishing an older person from a younger with the same given name, much as today one has for example 'Old John' and 'Young John' in a family.

Old Bailey The popular name for the Central Criminal Court, London, derives from that of the street where it is located. The street name itself refers to the *old bailey* or outwork that was at one time attached to the wall of the City of London here.

Oldenburg The city and former state of northwest Germany has a name that means 'old fortress'. Medieval Latin documents record its name as both German *Aldenburg* and Slavic *Starigrad*, the latter having the same meaning.

Oldham The town near Manchester has a name meaning 'old promontory', with the second half of the name not the usual Old English *hām*, 'village' or *hamm*, 'river meadow' but Old Norse *holmr*, 'island', 'promontory'. The 'promontory' referred to is the spur at the western edge of Saddleworth Moor on which the town is situated. It may have been called 'old' simply because it was a place where people had long been living.

Old Hundredth The well-known metrical psalm tune has a name indicating that it was set to the 100th psalm in the 'old' version of the metrical psalms, that is, in the one compiled in the 16th century by Thomas Sternhold and John Hopkins, as against the later (and better-known) version by Nahum Tate and Nicholas Brady. It was first published in 1560 to the words 'All people that on earth do dwell'.

Oldsmobile The American car takes its seemingly unpropitious name from its original manufacturer, the inventor and engineer Ransom Eli *Olds* (1864–1950), who founded the *Olds* Motor Works in 1899 and two years later produced the first *Oldsmobile*, the first commercially successful American car. In 1904 he founded the Reo Motor Car Company, with a name based on his initials. *See also* REO SPEEDWAGON.

Old Testament The first part of the Bible, originally in Hebrew (and partly in Aramaic) and telling the history of the Hebrews as the chosen people of God, is so named because it historically predates the Christian era, and because the Mosaic laws and religion which it describes were succeeded by the new religion of Christianity, as revealed by Jesus Christ and set forth in the NEW TESTAMENT (*which see* for more particular differences between the two).

Old Vic The famous London theatre originally opened in 1818 as the *Royal Coburg Theatre*, so named for its royal patrons, Princess Charlotte of Wales and her husband Prince Leopold of Saxe-*Coburg*. In 1833 it was renamed the *Royal Victoria Theatre* in honour of the 14-year-old Princess *Victoria*, the future Queen Victoria. The name (which altered slightly over the years, but always included *Victoria*) was familiarly abbreviated to *the Old Vic*, and this title was generally adopted by the public and even by the theatre itself. Officially, however, it remains the *Royal Victoria*. *Cp.* YOUNG VIC.

Olga The Russian name is of Scandinavian origin, the equivalent of *Helga*, so like it means 'healthy', 'holy'. The name was taken to Russia by the Varangians (Scandinavian settlers) in the 9th century, and was promoted there by St *Olga* of Kiev, wife of Prince Igor, who came a pagan but converted to Christianity (taking the new Christian name Helen) after the murder of her husband.

Oliphant The name means 'elephant', from Middle English *olifant*, probably originally as a nickname for a large or clumsy person.

Oliver The name has long been popularly associated with *olive*, and regarded as the male equivalent of OLIVIA, but it originated as the Scandinavian name *Anleifr*, literally 'the ancestor remains'. It was made famous in French folklore by *Oliver*, the close friend and companion of Roland, both men being paladins (retainers) of Charlemagne.

Olivia The name relates to the *olive* tree and its fruit, and is sometimes specifically associated with the *olive* branch as a symbol of peace and friendship. It was popularized by Shakespeare, whose *Olivia* in *Twelfth Night* is a wealthy countess wooed by Duke Orsino. It has been pointed out that the name, if pronounced quickly, suggests 'I love you'.

Olivier Theatre The largest of the three theatres that together form the Royal National Theatre, on London's South Bank, is named for the famous actor-manager Sir

Laurence (later Lord) *Olivier* (1907–1989), first director of the National Theatre Company. It opened in 1976.

Olomouc The Czech city and former capital of Moravia has a name representing Old Czech *holy mauc*, from *holy* (modern Czech *holý*), 'bald' and *mauc*, 'rock'. The city lies on the river Morava.

Olwen The Welsh name means 'white footprints', from *ôl*, 'track', 'footprint' and *gwen*, 'white', 'fair'. A character of the name in Welsh legend caused white flowers to spring up wherever she walked.

Olympia The state capital of Washington was founded in 1851 and originally named *Smithfield*. It was subsequently renamed after the nearby *Olympic* Mountains, whose highest peak, *Olympus*, was so called in 1788 by the English traveller John Meares after the famous Greek Mount OLYMPUS.

Olympic Games The present world sporting contest arose as a revival in 1896 of the Panhellenic festival held every fourth year in honour of Zeus at *Olympia*, the plain in southern Greece that took its own name from Mount OLYMPUS.

Olympus, Mount The famous mountain in northeast Greece, believed in Greek mythology to be the home of the gods, may derive its name from an Indoeuropean root word *ulu*, 'to turn', referring to the mountain's rounded summit.

Omagh The town in Co Tyrone, Northern Ireland, has a name based on Irish *magh*, 'plain'. The initial *O-* is of obscure origin.

Omaha The city in Nebraska takes its name from the Sioux *Omaha* people formerly here. Their own name has been translated as 'those who live upstream on the river'.

Oman The sultanate in southeast Arabia has a name recorded by Pliny in the 1st century AD as *Omana*. It is said to derive from the founder of the state, *Oman* ben Ibrahim al-Khalil.

Omar Khayyám The 12th-century Persian poet, famous for his *Rubáiyát*, especially in the Victorian version by Edward Fitzgerald, had the full original name *Gheyās od-Dīn Abū ol-Fath 'Umar ebn Ebrahīm ol-Khayyāmī*. The second part of this means

'Omar son of Ibrahim the tentmaker', with *Ibrahim* the Arabic form of ABRAHAM. The name *Omar* represents Arabic *'āmir*, 'flourishing'. *Rubáiyát* is Arabic for 'quatrains', from *rubā'īy*, 'comprising four elements'.

Omsk The city in eastern Siberia stands at the confluence of the rivers Irtysh and *Om* and takes its name from the latter. The river's name is said to derive from Tatar *om*, 'calm', 'smooth'.

Onega, Lake The lake in northwest Russia, the second largest lake in Europe, has a name that has been unconvincingly linked with that of the river *Onega* to the northeast of it, flowing into the White Sea. The river's name is said to represent Finnish *Enojoki*, 'main river', from *enin*, 'most' and *joki*, 'river'.

Oneida The lake in New York State takes its name from the Indian people who formerly lived here but who then moved west to settle by Lake Ontario. Their own name represents Iroquois *onēyóte*, 'people of the standing stone'.

One Thousand Guineas The annual horse race for fillies at Newmarket was first run in 1814, when it had a winning prize of 1000 guineas (£1050). *Cp.* TWO THOUSAND GUINEAS.

Ontario The Canadian province takes its name from Lake *Ontario*, whose own name is said to represent Iroquois *oniatariio*, 'beautiful lake'.

Oonagh *See* UNA.

Open University The non-residential university, founded in 1969 and based in Milton Keynes, is so named as it is *open* to all to become students, without previous qualification. It was originally called *University of the Air*, as its students follow courses through the medium of radio and television. The *Open College*, founded in 1987 for mature students studying arts and crafts by television, has a similar name.

Ophelia Famous as the beautiful daughter of Polonius in Shakespeare's *Hamlet*, *Ophelia* has a name that derives from Greek *ōpheleia*, 'help', 'aid', 'gain'.

Ophir The biblical region, noted for its gold and precious stones (1 *Kings* 9.28, 10.10), is of uncertain location. It may have been on the southwest Arabian coast, by the Red Sea, although some scholars locate it in modern Somalia, by the Horn of Africa. Its name is also found for one of the sons of Joktar (*Genesis* 10.29). The meaning of the name is uncertain, but attempts have been to link it with those of AFRICA and the Nigerian town of IFE, among others.

Oporto The city and port in western Portugal has a name that is simply Portuguese *o porto*, 'the port'. It gave the name of PORTUGAL itself and also that of *port* wine.

Oracle The teletext service of the Independent Television Commission has a name that is an acronym of its full name, *O*ptical *R*eception of *A*nnouncements by *C*oded *L*ine *E*lectronics, at the same time punning on *oracle* in its sense of 'one who announces', 'one who says what the future will bring'. *Cp.* CEEFAX.

Oradea The city in northwest Romania has a name that is a form of the second half of its Hungarian name, *Nagyvárad*, 'big town', from *nagy*, 'big' and *város*, 'town'. The town's German name of *Grosswardein* is a part translation of the Hungarian. The city was ceded to Romania by Hungary in 1919. Until recently its Romanian name was *Oradea Mare*. This fully translates the Hungarian name, the second word being Romanian *mare*, 'big' (from Latin *magnus*).

Oradour-sur-Glane The village near Limoges in south central France, whose entire population of 642 was massacred by the German SS on 10 June 1944, derives its name from Occitan *orador*, 'oratory', from Latin *oratorium*, itself from *orare*, 'to pray'. The river *Glane* has a name that represents Gaulish *glanno*, 'bank'.

Oran The name of the port in northwest Algeria represents Arabic *wahrān*, itself the name of a medieval Berber chief deriving from Berber *iren*, 'lions'. The Romans knew the location here as either *Portus divinus*, 'divine harbour' or *Portus magnus*, 'great harbour'.

Orange The town in southeast France was known to the Romans as *Arausio*, from a pre-Indoeuropean root element *ar*, 'mountain' with the suffix *-aus*. This was subsequently corrupted to the present name. The town was the former centre of a county, then a principality, that in 1544 passed to the Dutch count of Nassau who was the future William I of *Orange* and cofounder of the United Provinces of the Netherlands. William III of *Orange* (1650–1702) became king of Great Britain and Ireland, and the title *Orange* has been that of the reigning Dutch royal family since 1815. *See also* ORANGE FREE STATE, ORANGEMAN.

Orange Free State The South African province is situated between the rivers *Orange* and Vaal and takes its name from the former. The river was given its name in 1777 by the Dutch explorer R.J. Gordon in honour of the Dutch royal house of *Orange*, itself so named for ORANGE in the south of France.

Orangeman The name is that of a member of the society founded as a secret order in Ireland in 1795 to uphold the Protestant religion, a Protestant dynasty, and general Protestant supremacy against Irish nationalists and Roman Catholics. It is named for William III (William of *Orange*) (1650–1702), the Protestant king of Great Britain and Ireland who in 1690 went to Ireland and defeated the Roman Catholic king James II in the Battle of the Boyne. The annual celebration known as *Orangeman's Day*, held on 12 July, commemorates the anniversary of this victory. Orangemen wear orange-coloured sashes, just as supporters of William III wore orange ribbons, scarfs, cockades and the like. But the name is only coincidentally the same as that of the fruit (and its colour). The English word *orange* came from France, where it had become associated with the name of the town of ORANGE, perhaps partly because oranges may have been imported through there. The ultimate origin of the word, however, is in Sanskrit *nāranga*. The initial *n* of this was subsequently confused with the French indefinite article (*un*), so was dropped.

Oratory School The Roman Catholic public school for boys near Reading, Berkshire, was founded in 1859 by Cardinal Newman. An *oratory* is a place of prayer, from Latin *oratorium*, from *orare*, 'to pray'.

Ordnance Survey The official government body for the mapping of Britain was founded in 1791 to carry out a *survey* for the purposes of making maps under the direction of the Master-General of the *Ordnance*. The latter title was that of the head of the Board of Ordnance, a government body of partly military and partly civil composition that provided all necessary stores and equipment for the army. The Ordnance Survey was set up at a time when an invasion of Britain by France was expected.

Ordzhonikidze *See* VLADIKAVKAZ.

Oregon The American state has a name of disputed origin. It may derive from Shoshonean *ogwa*, 'river' and *pe-on*, 'west', as a former Indian name of the present river Columbia.

Orël The Russian city on the river Oka southwest of Moscow has a name that happens to be the Russian word for 'eagle' but that actually derives from the small river *Orel* (now the *Orlik*) that flows into the Oka at this point. The river's own name is believed to be of Turkic origin, meaning 'bend', 'angle'.

Orenburg The city in southwest Russia, on the river Ural, takes its name from the river *Or* on which it originally stood, with German *Burg*, 'fort' applying to the fort that was built on the river in 1735 and that was given a German name in the fashion of the day. The fort was subsequently moved almost 200 miles (300 km) west from the river Or, but kept the name. The city of ORSK now stands on the original site, and so has a name of identical origin. From 1938 to 1957 Orenburg was known by the name of *Chkalov*, for the Soviet pilot Valery *Chkalov* (1904–1938), killed when testing a new fighter aircraft.

Orestes Famous in Greek mythology as the son of Agamemnon and Clytemnestra, who kills his mother and her lover Aegisthus in revenge for the murder of his father, *Orestes* has a name that appears to mean 'mountain dweller', from Greek *oros*, 'mountain'.

Oriana The beloved of Amadis in the medieval romance *Amadis of Gaul* has a name that probably derives from Latin *or-iri*, 'to rise', 'to originate'. The suggestion is of the rising sun or a rising spring or of any kind of 'birth'.

Oriel College The Oxford college was founded in 1326 and three years later settled in a house called *La Oriole*, from which it took its name. The house itself was presumably named for its *oriel* window, although this word is first recorded only in about 1440, a century later.

Orinoco The river in northern South America derives its name from Guarani *ori-noko*, 'place of paddling'.

Orion The famous giant and hunter of Greek mythology has a name traditionally derived either from *oros*, 'mountain' or *ouron*, 'urine'. The latter relates to the story that Orion was born from a bull-hide on which the Boeotian king Hyreius had urinated, having been advised by Zeus that to do so would produce the child he desired. The goddess Diana finally changed Orion into the constellation that bears his name. The Arabic name of the constellation was *al-jabbār*, 'the giant'. It is mentioned in the Bible (*Job* 9.9), where it translates the Hebrew word *kesīl*, 'mad', showing that the Israelites had little respect for the giants who were their fellow inhabitants in those days (as mentioned at various points in the Old Testament, for example *Genesis* 6.4, *Numbers* 13.33, *Deuteronomy* 2.11, 3.11).

Orissa The state in eastern India takes its name from Sanskrit *oḍradeśa*, *oḍra* being the name of a local people, and *deśa* meaning 'country'.

Orkneys The islands northeast of mainland Scotland have a name that ends in Old Norse *ey*, 'island' but that is otherwise of uncertain origin. It has been tentatively derived from a word meaning 'whale', 'sea monster', corresponding to Latin *orca* and English *orc*.

Orlando The name is the Italian version of ROLAND (*which see* for its origin).

Orléans The city in north central France was given the Roman name *Aurelianum* when it was rebuilt in the 3rd century AD, in honour of the emperor *Aurelius*, and this gave its present name. Its earlier Roman name was *Genabum*, from proto-Indoeuropean *gen*, 'bend' (in a river) and pre-Indoeuropean *apa*, 'water'. Orléans is on the river Loire. *See also* NEW ORLEANS.

Orlon The name of the patent acrylic fibre or crease-resistant fabric was patented in 1950. It appears to be based on *nylon*, with an arbitrary alteration of the first syllable.

Orly The suburb of Paris, with its international airport, has a name that ultimately derives from the Roman personal name *Aurelius*, as for ORLÉANS (although not for the emperor).

Ormond The Irish name represents an English spelling of *Ó Ruaidh*, 'descendant of *Ruadh*', with the latter personal name meaning 'red'.

Ormskirk The Lancashire town has a name meaning '*Orm*'s church', with the personal name followed by Old Norse *kirkja*, 'church' as an alteration of the earlier Old English *cirice*. It is not certain who Orm was.

Orpheus The mythological Greek lyre-player and poet has a name traditionally derived from Greek *orphnē*, 'darkness', 'night'. The reference is to his search for his wife Eurydice in Hades after her death and to his own association with nocturnal initiation ceremonies.

Orpington The former Kent town, now in Greater London, has a name meaning 'village of *Orped*'s people'. *Orped* is a personal name meaning 'active', 'strenuous', from an Old English word of obscure origin found in literature down to at least the 16th century.

Orr The name has various possible origins. If an English name, it could originally have applied to someone who lived by the shore or by a hill slope, with both these called *ōra* in Old English. (The same word lies behind the place-name *Oare*.) If a Scottish or Irish name, the origin is likely to be in the Old Norse personal name *Orri*, literally 'blackcock' (a species of grouse). Alternatively, the Scottish name could derive from the Gaelic word *odhar*, 'pale'.

Orsk The city in southwest Russia takes its name from the river *Or* on which it stands, at its confluence with the Ural. It is situated on the original site of ORENBURG, whose name thus has the same source. The latter city moved early as a fortified post to a new location some 200 miles (300

km) to the west, however, but kept the name of the river on which it first arose.

Orthodox Church The collective name is that of the Eastern Christian church that was separated from the Western church in the 11th century and that is now familiar as the Greek Orthodox and Russian Orthodox Church. The name literally means 'right opinion', from Greek *orthos*, 'right' and *doxa*, 'opinion', 'glory', and is popularly seen as contrasting the Orthodox (Eastern) faith with that of the Roman Catholic or Protestant (Western). However, the term predates this major division, and originally applied to that stem of the Eastern church which held to the 'true faith' as distinct from the various branches that developed with differing doctrines, such as the Monophysites and Nestorians. The full ancient Greek designation of the Orthodox Church is *hē hagia orthodoxos katholikē apostolikē anatolikē ekklēsia*, 'the holy, orthodox, catholic, apostolic, Eastern church'. The Greek Orthodox Church dates from the 4th century, and the Russian from the 10th.

Oruro The city in western Bolivia, South America, has an Indian name meaning 'black and white', referring to paintings of animals on rocks here.

Orvieto The name of the town in central Italy represents its Roman name *Urbs vetus*, meaning 'old town'.

Orwell The name of the tidal part of the river Gipping from Ipswich, Suffolk, to its confluence with the Stour at Harwich probably means 'shore river', based on Old English *ōra*, 'shore'.

Osaka The city and port in south Japan has a name meaning 'big hill', from *ō*, 'big' and *saka*, 'slope', 'hill'. The city lies on a river delta between mountain ranges to east and west.

Osbert The name is Old English in origin, comprising the words *ōs*, 'god' and *beorht*, 'bright', 'famous'. The overall meaning could be interpreted as 'made famous by a god'.

Osborn The surname derives from the Old Norse personal name *Ásbjorn*, from *ós*, 'god' and *bjŏrn*, 'bear'.

Osborne House The house near Cowes on the Isle of Wight, the favourite residence of Queen Victoria, who died there, has a name that may mean 'sheep stream', from Old English *ēowestre*, 'sheepfold' and *burna*, 'stream'. The first part of the name is to some extent conjectural, however. The name was recorded in the early 14th century as *Austeburn*.

Oscan The extinct language of southern Italy, and the people who spoke it, derive their name from an Oscan word meaning 'cultivator', from Latin *operari*, 'to work', 'to till the land'.

Oscar The name can be taken as English or Irish in origin. If English, it is traditionally derived from Old English *ōs*, 'god' and *gar*, 'spear'. If Irish, the source is said to lie in *os*, 'deer' and *cara*, 'friend'. It is familiar from the Irish writer and wit *Oscar* Wilde (1854–1900).

Oscar The small gold statuette awarded annually in America by the Academy of Motion Pictures and Sciences for outstanding achievement in the cinema is said to have been so named by an Academy official, who in 1931 is recorded as commenting that it reminded her of her 'Uncle Oscar'. The gentleman in question has been tentatively identified as *Oscar* Pierce, a wheat and fruit grower. The awards themselves were first made in 1928.

Osiris The name of the ancient Egyptian god, the personification of goodness and ruler of the underworld, is a Greek form of his basic name *Usir*. The origin of this is uncertain, though some scholars have connected it with the word *woser*, which would give it a meaning 'mighty one'. His name lies behind that of SERAPIS.

Oslo The name of the Norwegian capital is possibly based on Old Norwegian *os*, 'estuary', 'river-mouth', itself from Latin *os*, 'mouth', although some authorities derive it from *As*, the name of a Scandinavian god, and *Lo*, the name of the river near which the old city arose. Its Medieval Latin name was *Ansloga*. After a disastrous fire in 1624 the city was rebuilt under the new name *Christiana*, for King *Christian* IV. In 1877 this was modified to *Kristiania*. In 1924, three hundred years later, the city reverted to its original name.

Osnabrück The city in northwest Germany derives its name from Old High German *asa*, 'current' and *brugge*, 'bridge'. The town stands on the river *Hase*, itself representing the former word.

Osram The make of electric light bulb is said to take its name from a blend of *osmium* and *wolfram*, the two metals that form the basis of the filament.

Ossa The mountain in northeast Greece perhaps takes its name from a pre-Greek root element *okya* meaning 'lookout post'. This is probably related to the first syllable of Latin *oculus*, 'eye'.

Ossian The legendary Irish bard, whose poems the Scottish writer James Macpherson claimed to have translated, has a name that is an English spelling of Irish *Oisín*. This means 'fawn', 'young deer', as a diminutive of Irish *oss*, 'deer'.

Ostend The port and resort on the North Sea in northwest Belgium has a Flemish name meaning 'east end', from *oosten*, 'east' and *einde*, 'end'. The town, spelled *Oostende* in Flemish, is at the eastern end of a long beach, at the other end of which is the less well-known *Westende*.

Ostia The ancient town in west central Italy is at the mouth of the Tiber. Its name indicates its location, deriving from Latin *ostium*, 'estuary', from *os*, 'mouth'.

Ostrava The city in the eastern Czech Lands stands above the confluence of the rivers Oder and *Ostravice*, and takes its name from the latter. The river's own name derives from Czech *ostrov*, 'island'.

Ostrogoth The name is that of the eastern group of GOTHS who settled in Italy. It denotes the direction of their migration, from a Germanic root word meaning 'eastern' found also in the name of AUSTRIA. *Cp.* VISIGOTH.

Oswald The name is Old English, from *ōs*, 'god' and *weald* 'rule'. It is familiar from the 7th-century king of Northumbria St *Oswald*, who is said (on doubtful historical grounds) to have given the name of the town of OSWESTRY.

Oswestry The Shropshire town has a name meaning '*Oswald*'s tree', with the final syllable representing Old English *trēow*, 'tree'.

The name has been linked with King *Oswald* of Northumbria, but he was killed in battle in the 7th century, many years before the name of the town was first recorded (in the late 12th century), and the lengthy time gap between the names makes the historical association unlikely.

Othello The name of the 'Moor of Venice' who is the central character of Shakespeare's play (1604) appears to have been invented by the dramatist himself, as it does not appear in any of his sources. It is not actually mentioned until Act I, Scene iii, lines 48 and 49:

> Valiant Othello, we must straight employ you
> Against the general enemy Ottoman.

This may give a clue to the origin, since the OTTOMAN Empire took its name from its founder *Osman*, known to the Arabs as *Othoman* or (more accurately) *'Uthmān*. Shakespeare could then have devised an Italian-style version of this for his hero. (All the main male characters in the play have names ending in *-o*.) It could even be said that the *-ello* of the Moor's name is intended as an Italian diminutive suffix, as in *Punchinello*, the prototype of PUNCH. Ruskin claimed that the name *Othello* meant 'the careful', presumably deriving it from Greek *othomai*, 'to have a care for'.

Otranto, Strait of The strait between southern Italy and Albania takes its name from the Italian port of *Otranto*, the easternmost town in the country. Its own name evolved from the Roman name *Hydruntum*, from Late Greek *Hudranton*, 'water town', based on *hudōr*, 'water'. The ruined castle at *Otranto* was the setting for Horace Walpole's famous Gothic novel, *The Castle of Otranto* (1765).

Ottawa The Canadian capital takes its name from the river on which it stands. The river's name derives from Algonquian *adawe*, perhaps meaning 'big river', or according to some authorities 'merchant', from the name of a tribe who lived by it and who controlled local trade. The city took the name when it became the capital in 1854. It had been founded in 1827 as *Bytown*, from the name of Colonel John *By* of the Royal Engineers, whom the British government had entrusted with the construction of the Rideau Canal.

Otto Famous from the 10th-century Holy Roman Emperor *Otto* the Great, the name is based on the Old German root word *ot*, meaning 'riches', 'fortune', corresponding to the first syllable of Old English names such as EDWARD and EDWIN. *Cp.* the surname OTTOWAY.

Ottoman The name was that of the Turkish people who invaded the Near East in the 13th century and established the *Ottoman* Empire. Their name represents Turkish *Osmanlı*, after *Osman* I (1258–1326), founder of the Empire, with the suffix *-lı* meaning 'of', 'belonging to'. Osman's own name is the Turkish form of the Arabic name *'Usmān*, itself a form of *'Uthmān*, literally 'young bustard'. *See also* OTHELLO.

Ottoway The name came into English through a Norman French personal name that itself derived from Germanic words *od*, 'riches' (*cp.* OTTO) and *wid*, 'wide' (also 'wood').

Ouagadougou The capital of Burkina Faso, West Africa, is said to take its name from two different African languages, with *ouaga* meaning 'come' in one, and *dougou* meaning 'village' in the other. But this is almost certainly conjectural, and the true meaning of the name is uncertain.

Ouija The board marked with the letters of the alphabet, used at seances, takes its name from a combination of French *oui* and German *ja*, both meaning 'yes'. The name was patented in the United States in 1891, originally for a novelty toy known as a 'Talking Board'.

Oulu The city and port in western Finland has a name that means basically 'water'. Its Swedish name is *Uleåborg*, from the same name, to which *borg*, 'fort' is added. Oulu is at the mouth of the river Oulujoki (named for it) on the Gulf of Bothnia.

Oundle The Northamptonshire town has a name referring to the people who lived here. They were the 'non-sharing ones', from Old English *un-*, 'not' and *dal*, 'share' (modern *dole*). The name implies that the territory given to these people was left over after the land had been divided up and duly allocated to others elsewhere.

Ouse The well-known English river name, wherever it occurs, almost always has the same meaning, which is 'water', from a Celtic root with counterparts in Greek *hudōr* (as in *hydrant*), Gaelic *uisce* (giving English *whisky*), English *wash*, and ultimately even *water* itself. The exception is the *Ouse* in Sussex, which probably took its name from that of LEWES.

Outer Mongolia The name is that formerly used (until 1924) for the country that is now the *Mongolian People's Republic*. *Inner Mongolia* is an autonomous region of northeast China. The name of Outer Mongolia is still sometimes used as an expression of remoteness, as denoting a place felt to be 'off the map'. *Inner Mongolia* translates Chinese *nèiménggŭ*, from *nèi*, 'interior' and *ménggŭ*, 'MONGOLIA', and is a name in use since 1644. *Outer Mongolia* followed, becoming an independent republic in 1911.

OutRage The name is that of a broad-based coalition of lesbians and gay men committed to fighting homophobia through radical, non-violent, direct action. Formed in 1990 in London, the group adopted a name which puns on the notion of 'coming out'. The merging of this notion with a sense of 'rage' is intended to signal a sea-change in lesbian and gay attitudes away from the stale 'Glad to be Gay' marches of the 70s and early 80s and towards a militant campaign for the legislation of equal rights and against discriminating laws such as the notorious Clause 28 of the Local Government Act. It is thus synonymous with a new-style 'queer politics' characterized by defiance and involving media-orientated demonstrations and public protests or 'zaps'. *See also* ACT UP.

Oval, The The well-known London cricket ground, the home of Surrey County Cricket Club, has a name that simply describes its shape. The name is etymologically unpropitious for a cricket ground, as *oval* means literally 'egg-shaped', and a 'duck' (originally 'duck's egg') is a batting score of zero, so called because the scorer's '0' resembles an egg! The shape of the ground is delineated by Kennington Oval, the semi-circular street that runs round it.

Oval Office The private office of the president in the White House is a large *oval*-shaped room, designed for round-table discussions.

Ovaltine The malt food drink was launched by Dr George Wander in Bern, Switzerland in the 19th century under the name of *Ovomaltine*. This indicated its two main ingredients, eggs (from Latin *ovum*, 'egg') and *malt*, with *-ine* a standard suffix for a manufactured product. The name was shortened to *Ovaltine* when the drink was marketed in Britain.

Overijssel The province of the eastern Netherlands lies to the north of the river IJSSEL, so that its name means 'over the IJssel' (as regarded from the centre or south of the country). The name is thus on a par with names comprising *Trans-* and a river name, such as TRANSVAAL.

Ovid The famous 1st-century BC Roman poet had the full name of Publius *Ovidius* Naso. *Ovidius* was thus his *nomen*, or clan name. It appears to derive from Latin *ovis*, 'sheep', perhaps originally an affectionate nickname (something like 'little lamb') for his ultimate ancestor. *Naso* is a *cognomen* or nickname meaning 'big nose'.

Owen The name is traditionally said to be a Welsh form of the Latin name *Eugenius* which gave modern English EUGENE, so therefore has the same meaning, 'well-born'.

Oxfam The well-known charity arose from the *Ox*ford Committee for *Fam*ine Relief that was set up in OXFORD in 1942 as one of a number of such committees in Britain to aid the suffering and hardship of the civilian population, and especially children, in European countries then under the control of Germany. The present abbreviated name was adopted in 1958 when the charity was registered as a limited company. It echoes that of OXFORD itself.

Oxford The famous university city has a name that means exactly what it says, as at one time there was a regular *ford* for *oxen* over the Thames here. The location of the ford was perhaps just below Folly Bridge, south of the city centre, although some toponymists favour a siting at Hinksey Ferry, to the west. Not all places with names in *Ox-* refer to oxen, however. Oxshott and Oxted, for example, both in Surrey, have names that respectively mean '*Ocga*'s piece of land' and 'oak-tree place'.

Oxford Circus The famous central point of London is named from *Oxford Street*, which runs across it at the junction with REGENT STREET. Oxford Street is itself so named partly because it has long been the main road to OXFORD, now as the start of the A40, but also because it developed in the 18th century as part of the estate belonging to Edward Harley, Earl of *Oxford*, whose daughter gave the name of HARLEY STREET. Oxford Circus was originally known as *Regent Circus*, but the more important thoroughfare of the two eventually gave it its name instead. *Cp.* CAMBRIDGE CIRCUS.

Oxford Group The name was originally that of the worldwide movement for moral and spiritual renewal known as MORAL REARMAMENT. The movement's founder, Dr Frank Buchman, had come to Oxford in 1921 to campaign for a revival of the 'truths of simple Chistianity', and his followers became known as the *Oxford Group* for this reason. The name may have been subconsciously promoted by (and in some cases even confused with) the more familiar OXFORD MOVEMENT.

Oxford Movement The name is that of the High Church movement within the Church of England that began at OXFORD in 1833.

Cp. TRACTARIANISM. The name should not be confused with that of the OXFORD GROUP.

Oxford Symphony Haydn's Symphony No 92 in G major (1789) is so nicknamed because it was performed when the composer received the honorary degree of Doctor of Music at *Oxford* University in 1791. Haydn did not compose the work with Oxford specifically in mind, however.

Oxley The name derives from an identical place-name, such as *Oxley* that is now a district of Wolverhampton. The meaning is 'ox wood' or 'ox clearing', from Old English *oxa* and *lēah*.

Ox Minuet The minuet, long attributed to Haydn, is said to have been written by the composer for a butcher who gave him an ox in exchange. However, the piece is actually by Haydn's pupil Ignaz Xaver von Seyfried, who introduced it into his opera *Die Ochsenmenuett* (1823).

Oxo The familiar name of the beef extract, popularly available in cube form, was registered in 1899 and derives simply from *ox* with the traditional 'commercial' suffix *-o* found in many other names of the Victorian period.

P

Pacific The name was given to the world's largest and deepest ocean by the Portuguese explorer Magellan in 1520, originally as *Mar Pacífico*, 'calm sea', since he had encountered no storms on his journey of discovery from Tierra del Fuego to the Philippines.

Padang The port in western Indonesia takes its name from the nearby *Padang* Mountains, whose own name represents Malay *padang*, 'plain', 'field'.

Paddington The district of west central London, with its mainline railway terminus, has a name that means '*Padda*'s farm'. As frequently, it is not known who Padda was.

Paddington Bear The bear who features in the popular children's stories by Michael Bond was named for a small teddy bear bought by the author at a time when he and his wife were living near *Paddington* station.

Paderborn The name of the town in northwest Germany derives from the personal name *Pater* and Old German *brunn*, 'spring'.

Padma The river in India and Bangladesh has a Sanskrit name meaning 'lotus'. The same word occurs in the well-known Tibetan Buddhist mantra *om mani padme hum*, 'hail to the jewel in the lotus', as well as in the title of the *Padma Shri*, 'lotus decoration', the Indian award for distinguished service.

Padstow The Cornish town and resort has a name meaning 'St *Petroc*'s church', with the saint's name somewhat corrupted over the centuries.

Padua The city in northeast Italy probably derives its name from a Gaulish word *padi* meaning 'pine', referring to the pine forests that are found near the mouth of the river PO (from the same source).

Pagalu The island of Equatorial Guinea has a name that is a Creole form of Spanish *papá gallo*, 'father cockerel'. The cockerel was the symbol of Francisco Macías Nguema, president of Equatorial Guinea, in the presidential election campaign of 1968. He was elected, but ruled as a tyrant until 1979 when he was overthrown and executed. *Macías Nguema* was for a while the name of the Equatorial Guinea island that was originally Fernando Po but is now Bioko.

Page The name was originally an occupational one for a young servant, the forerunner of the *page*boy of today. The word itself is ultimately related to Greek *pais*, 'child', 'boy'.

Paignton The name of the Devon seaside town means '*Pæga*'s farm'. In the 18th and early 19th centuries the name was usually spelled *Paington*, and the middle *ng* seems to have been reversed by the Great Western Railway, perhaps under the influence of TEIGNMOUTH, just up the line.

Paimpol The coastal town near St Brieuc in Brittany, northwest France, derives its name from Breton *pen*, 'head', 'headland' and *poull*, 'hole', 'ditch', 'marsh'.

Pain The present English surname evolved from the Roman name *Paganus*, referring to a country dweller. The same source lies behind modern English *pagan* for a person who was a 'heathen', both in the literal sense of 'heath-dweller' and figurative sense of 'non-believer'.

Paisley The Scottish town near Glasgow has a name that basically means 'church', from a Celtic word that itself derived from Latin *basilica* (in turn from Greek *basilikos*, 'royal'). The town was given its name by the 'Scots' who came from Ireland to settle in western Scotland from the late 6th century.

Pakistan The republic in southern Asia was formed in 1947 from the predominantly Muslim parts of India and given a name that was invented in the early 1930s by a group of Muslim students at Cambridge University. It represents the initials of *P*unjab, *A*fghanistan and *K*ashmir with the common eastern place-name suffix *-stan* meaning 'country'. At the same time, the name puns on the Iranian word *pāk*, 'pure', so that Pakistan is the 'land of the pure'.

Palaiseau The town south of Paris, France, was known in the 9th century by the Medieval Latin name of *Palatiolum*. This represents Latin *palatium*, 'palace' with the diminutive suffix *-eolum*.

Palamedes The Greek mythological hero, said to have invented the game of draughts and some of the letters of the alphabet, has a name that means 'ancient cunning', from Greek *palai*, 'of old' and *mēdēa*, 'cunning', 'skill'.

Palatinate The name is that of either of the two territories in southwest Germany, Upper *Palatinate* in Bavaria and Lower *Palatinate* in Rhineland-Palatinate, Baden-Württemberg and Hesse, that were at one time ruled by the counts *palatine*. The name derives from Latin *palatinus*, 'belonging to the *Palatium*', that is, to the *palace* of the Roman emperors on the PALATINE, Rome. The title *Palatinate* (German *Pfalz*) thus originally applied to the castles here where the emperor stayed in his travels across the Holy Roman Empire. The head of such an imperial castle was known as the *count palatine* (German *Pfalzgraf*). This title later came to apply specifically to the counts palatine of the Rhine.

Palatine The name of one of the Seven Hills of Rome, traditionally the site of the first settlement of the city, represents Latin *Palatinus mons* or simply *Palatium*. Many famous Romans lived on the hill, including Hortensius, Cicero, Crassus and Mark Antony. Hortensius' house was acquired by the emperor Augustus and formed the nucleus of the group of buildings known as *palatia*, the plural of *palatium*, 'palace'. It was the latter Latin word that gave the English one. *See also* PALATINATE.

Palawan The westernmost island of the Philippines has a local (Buginese) name meaning 'gate of combat'. The island in effect serves as a barrier against the violence of the South China Sea.

Palermo The Italian city and port that is the capital of Sicily has a name that, through Latin, represents the original Greek name *Panormos*. This means 'safe anchorage', from *pan*, 'all' and *ormos*, literally 'cord', 'chain', hence 'roadstead' (chain of boats), 'anchorage'. The name implies a safe haven for all ships.

Palestine The name of the region of the Middle East that is famous as that of the biblical Holy Land means 'land of the PHILISTINES'. The name does not occur in the Bible itself, but was applied to the territory as early as the 2nd century AD by the Roman emperor Hadrian as part of the Roman Empire.

Palestrina The historic town southeast of Rome, Italy, was known to the Romans as *Praeneste* or *Praenestum*. The origin of this is uncertain. The latter part of the name is almost certainly non-Indoeuropean, and may denote a town on a river. It was this town that gave the name of the 16th-century Italian composer Giovanni Pierluigi da *Palestrina*.

Palladium The name is that of the statue of the goddess *Pallas* Athena which in Greek mythology was said to have been sent down from heaven by Zeus to protect Troy. The meaning of *Pallas* as a byname of Athena is disputed. The two traditional origins give a sense either of 'brandisher' (of weapons) from Greek *pallō*, 'I wield', 'I brandish', or of 'girl', 'maiden', from Greek *palla* (related to Latin *puella*). A late legend says that the name was that of a friend of the goddess whom she killed accidentally. *See also* LONDON PALLADIUM.

Pall Mall The famous London street, noted for its many clubs, derives its name from the game of *pall-mall* formerly played on the site where the street was laid out in the 17th century. The game was similar to croquet and was itself named, through French, from Italian *pallamaglio*, representing *palla*, 'ball' and *maglio*, 'mallet'. *See also* The MALL.

Palma The name of the popular tourist resort in Majorca, where it is the capital of the Balearic Islands, is simply the Spanish word for 'palm tree'. It is a translation of the original Phoenician name of Majorca, *tamar*, in the same sense. This word itself gave both modern Portuguese *tâmara*, 'date' and the Russian girl's name TAMARA.

Palm Beach The Florida town and luxury resort, the 'American Riviera', was settled in 1873 as *Palm City*. It received its present self-descriptive name in 1887 when it was developed as a resort.

Palmer The name originally denoted someone who had been on a pilgrimage to the Holy Land. Such people often brought back a *palm* branch as proof that they had actually made the journey.

Palmerston North The New Zealand city, in the south of North Island, was founded in 1866 and named for the famous British statesman Viscount *Palmerston* (1784–1865). The city is *North* to be distinguished from the smaller town of the same name in South Island. The Australian city of DARWIN was also formerly known as *Palmerston*.

Palmolive The familiar make of toiletries derives its name from the *palm* and *olive* oils used in the soap that was first manufactured in Milwaukee, Wisconsin, in 1898.

Palm Springs The Californian city, a popular resort, has a self-descriptive name referring to its native *palms* and its natural *springs*. It was originally known by the Spanish name *Agua Caliente*, 'hot springs'.

Palm Sunday In the Christian calendar, the Sunday before Easter is so named because it celebrates Christ's triumphal entry into Jerusalem, when the people 'took branches of palm trees, and went forth to meet him' (*John* 12.13). The ceremony was formerly widely marked in churches by the blessing, distributing and carrying in procession of palm branches, but is less widely observed today, or is confined to the 'sale' (for a voluntary offering) of small palm crosses. The Sunday is not so named in the Book of Common Prayer (where it is either the Sixth Sunday in Lent or the Sunday next before Easter) and, curiously, the biblical passage appointed to be read as the second lesson at evensong that day, describing the triumphal entry into Jerusalem, is the only one in the four gospels (*Luke*

19.28–48) that does not mention the palm branches!

Palmyra The ancient city of Syria has a name that represents the Greek male name *Palmus*. It is mentioned in the Bible under its former name of *Tadmor* (1 *Kings* 9.18, 2 *Chronicles* 8.4).

Palo Alto The Californian city near San Francisco has a Spanish name meaning 'tall tree', referring to a high redwood tree here at one time.

Palomar, Mount The mountain in southern California, site of the famous observatory of the same name, takes its name from Spanish *palomar*, literally 'dovecote', but in this case probably meaning a place frequented by doves.

Pamela The name was invented by the Elizabethan pastoral poet Sir Philip Sidney for the character (the daughter of Basilius) who is the heir to the dukedom in his famous romance *The Arcadia* (1581). He stressed the name on the second syllable and seems to have intended it to mean 'all sweet' from Greek *pan*, 'all' and *meli*, 'honey'. The name was later borrowed and made famous by Samuel Richardson for the heroine of his novel *Pamela, or Virtue Rewarded* (1740). She is a servant girl, albeit an ostentatiously virtuous one, and the use of the 'grand' classical name in her case may have been intentional. In Henry Fielding's novel *Joseph Andrews* (1742), which begins as a parody on Richardson's work, Pamela becomes the hero's sister. Fielding writes, on introducing her: 'She told me that they had a daughter of a very strange name, *Paměla* or *Puměla*; some pronounce it one way, and some the other'. Today it is always stressed on the first syllable.

Pamiers The town in the south of France derives its name from that of the ancient Syrian city of *Apameia* ad Orontem, built by the Macedonian general Seleucus Nicator in the 4th century BC and named for his wife *Apama* or *Apamē*. The name was probably brought to France by Roger II, Comte de Foix, who gave it to the fort he built here as a memorial to the First Crusade.

Pamirs The mountains of central Asia, mainly in Tajikistan, Kirgizia and China, have a name that has been explained as deriving from either Sanskrit *upa-meru*, 'near mount Meru' or Iranian *pāye-mihr*, 'foot of Mithra', that is, at the feet of the sun god. Other proposed Iranian origins include *pāye morğ*, 'foot of the bird' and *pāye marg*, 'foot of death'.

Pamphylia The name of the southern coastal region of Asia Minor is of Greek origin meaning 'all races', from *pan*, 'all' and *phulon*, 'race'. The name implies a territory inhabited by a mixture of peoples.

Pamplona The city in northern Spain has a name that is a corruption of the Roman *Pompeiopolis*, meaning 'Pompey's city'. Pamplona was founded by the Roman emperor Pompey in 68 BC.

Pan The Greek god of fields, woods, shepherds and flocks has a name that is the Greek word for 'all', implying that he was a kind of universal god, of everything and everybody. He was believed to cause sudden groundless fear: hence the modern *panic*.

Pan Am The former well-known American airline was founded in 1927 as a merger of three small existing companies, and at first transported mail between Key West, Florida, and Havana, Cuba. Its full name was *Pan American Airways*, indicating its aim to serve 'all the Americas', not just internal routes within the United States. It subsequently become a fully global airline, with the official name *Pan American World Airways*, but ceased operation in 1991.

Panama The republic of Central America has a name of Indian (Guarani) origin. It is traditionally interpreted as meaning 'place of many fish' but its true sense is uncertain. The name was at first that of the city, now *Panama City*, then that of the country (and, later, the canal).

Panasonic The brand name is one of five owned by the Japanese electronics company MATSUSHITA. It is mostly used for audio equipment, such as radios and televisions, and is designed to mean 'sounding everywhere' from Greek *pan*, 'all' and Latin *sonus*, 'sound' (or English *sonic*).

Pan Books The familiar paperback publishing company was founded in 1944 and took its name from a drawing of the god PAN by the writer and illustrator Mervyn Peake

that the artist had given to the company's founder, Alan Bott, then managing director of the Book Society, and that hung in his office at the time.

Pancake Day The name is a popular one for SHROVE TUESDAY, referring to the custom of eating (and tossing) pancakes that day as a 'final fling' before Lent.

Panchen Lama The title is that of one of the two Great Lamas of Tibet, ranking below the DALAI LAMA. The first word is a shortened form of Tibetan *paṇḍita-chen-po*, 'great learned one' (the source of modern English *pundit*).

Pandarus In Greek mythology, *Pandarus* was the leader of the Lycians, who were allies of the Trojans in their war against Greece. He broke the truce by wounding Menelaus and was eventually killed by Diomedes. His name is usually interpreted as meaning 'he who flays all', from Greek *pan*, 'all' and *derō*, 'I flay'. In medieval legend Pandarus was the name of the 'procurer' of Cressida on behalf of Troilus, and his role between them gave modern English *pander*, which originally meant 'act as a go-between in a love affair'.

P & O The well-known shipping company has the full name *Peninsular and Oriental Steam Navigation Company*. It was founded in 1837 as the *Peninsular Steam Navigation Company*, operating a steamship mail service between Britain and the Iberian *Peninsula*, that is, Spain and Portugal. This service was extended to Egypt in 1840, and the name was altered to incorporate the reference to the *Orient*, as the countries immediately to the east of the Mediterranean were then collectively known. By an apt coincidence, Latin *pando* means 'I extend', 'I fling wide'.

Pandora In Greek mythology, *Pandora* was the first woman. When given a box ('Pandora's box') that she was told not to open, she nevertheless did so out of curiosity, thereby releasing all the ills that beset the world, Hope alone remaining inside. Her name means 'all gifts', from Greek *pan* 'all' and *dōron*, 'gift', and is thus ironic.

Pankhurst The name, familiar from the English suffragette Emmeline *Pankhurst*, is traditionally derived from PENTECOST. It is more likely, however, to represent the place-name *Pinkhurst*, found in both West Sussex and Surrey, where it means 'finch wood'.

Panmunjom The name is that of the village in the demilitarized zone of Korea where peace talks were held in the early 1950s, leading to the end of the Korean War. The meaning of the name is literally 'floor gate shop', from Korean *p'an*, 'floor', 'flat', *mun*, 'gate', 'door' and *chŏm*, 'shop', 'stall'.

Pannonia The name of the former Roman province south and west of the Danube, in what is now Hungary, has been explained as deriving from Ligurian *pannus*, 'rag'. It is hard to see the significance of this, however, and it might be more meaningful to relate the name to that of the Greek god PAN.

Pantagruel The famous giant who is the son of Gargantua in Rabelais' satire *Gargantua and Pantagruel* (1532–64) has a name which the writer ascribes to the fact that his hero was born on a day of extreme drought, when the earth sweated great drops of water that were saltier than sea water. He gives the origin of the name as follows:

> Et parce que en ce propre jour nasquit Pantagruel, son pere luy imposa tel nom, car *Panta* en grec vault autant à dire comme *tout*, et *Gruel* en langue hagarene vault autant comme *alteré*. ('And because Pantagruel was born on that day, his father gave him such a name, for *Panta* in Greek means "all", and *Gruel* in Arabic means "thirsty"').
>
> Book II, Chapter 2.

But this is a partly whimsical etymology of an earlier name, that of a sea devil in medieval legend who threw salt into the mouths of drunks to stimulate their thirst. (The story occurs in the 15th-century mystery play by Simon Greban entitled *Actes des Apôtres*.) The Arabic word is bogus, and is akin to those in the 'Arabic' passage in the famous multilingual chapter (II, 9) in the same work.

Pantheon The name is that of the circular temple in Rome, built in the 1st century BC, that was dedicated to all the gods, from Greek *pan*, 'all' and *theos*, 'god'. Construction of the *Panthéon* in Paris was be-

gun in 1764, and the building was originally intended to be a church dedicated to St Genevieve, patron of Paris. It was finished only at the time of the Revolution, however, when the authorities declared it should be a resting place for great men of the past under the name of *Panthéon*. It twice subsequently reverted to being a church, but since 1885, when Victor Hugo was buried there, it has remained a non-religious shrine, despite retaining a cross on its dome.

Panurge The name is that of the famous rogue, drunkard and coward who is the companion of PANTAGRUEL in Rabelais' satire *Gargantua and Pantagruel* (1532–64). It is Greek in origin, meaning 'all-doer', from *pan*, 'all' and *ergon*, 'work'. The Greeks used *panourgos* as a term for 'rogue', implying that all the deeds done would be bad ones. Panurge first appears in the famed multilingual Chapter 9 of Book II, in which he meets Pantagruel and addresses him in 14 different languages, three of them bogus. He is usually regarded as the real hero of the story. The name *Panurge* is also an anagram of letters from the name *Pantagruel*, so that it is an appropriate 'companion' name for a character who is himself a companion of the named person.

Pan Yan The familiar brand of pickle has a name with a Chinese look but one that is not intended to have any meaning. It was chosen as the result of a competition among the employees of a London food manufacturer in 1907. (However, Chinese *pán* means 'plate' and *yán* means 'feast', so that the name may not be entirely as arbitrary as the manufacturers claim.)

Papeete The capital of French Polynesia has a name deriving from Tahitian *pape*, 'water' and *ete*, 'basket'. The overall sense is 'place where people come with baskets to get water'.

Papua The territory that is now part of Papua New Guinea, in the southwest Pacific, derives its name from its indigenous inhabitants, the *Papuans*, whose own name represents Malay *pua-pua*, 'frizzled', referring to their hair.

Pará The state of northern Brazil derives its name from Guarani *para*, 'river', referring to the Amazon and many other rivers that wind their way over the floodplain here. The name in particular applies to the navigable eastern mouth of the Amazon.

Paraclete The title of the Holy Ghost as comforter derives from Late Greek *Paraklētos*, 'advocate', from *para*, 'beside' and *kalein*, 'to call'. The Greek word is translated 'Comforter' in the English New Testament (*John* 14.26).

Paradise The alternative name of the Garden of Eden, where Adam and Eve lived before the Fall (the first sin), comes ultimately from Avestan *pairidaēza*, from *pairi*, 'around' (hence Greek *peri-* in English words such as *periscope*) and *daēza*, 'wall', 'rampart'. In other words it was a 'walled-round' place, otherwise an enclosure, or (in the original, literal sense) a 'garden', a word that itself implies an enclosed area and that is related to *yard*. The Hebrew name EDEN is translated as *paradeisos* in the Septuagint (Greek version of the Old Testament), *paradīs* in the Samaritan (Aramaic) Pentateuch, and *pardaysō* in the Peshitta (Syriac version of the Bible).

Paraguay The South American republic takes its name from the river *Paraguay*, whose own name derives from Guarani *para*, 'water', 'river' and *guay*, 'born'. This was in turn the name of a local chieftain who signed a treaty with the first Spanish explorers.

Paraíba The state of northeast Brazil takes its name from the identical river name, itself representing Guarani *para*, 'water', 'river' and *aí*, 'bad', referring to the poor natural irrigation here. There are two important rivers of the name, *Paraíba do Norte*, 'northern Paraíba' and *Paraíba do Sul*, 'southern Paraíba'.

Paramaribo The capital of Surinam has a name deriving from Guarani *para*, 'water', 'river' and *maribo*, 'inhabitants'. The city is situated at the mouth of the river Surinam.

Paraná The state of southern Brazil takes its name from the river that flows through it. The river's own name represents Guarani *para*, 'water', 'river' and *aná*, 'parent', 'union', referring to its formation by the confluence of the Rio Grande and the Paranaíba.

Parcae The name is that of the Roman goddesses of fate corresponding to the Greek *Moirai*. See FATES.

Pardoe The name arose as a nickname for a Norman whose favourite oath was *par Dieu*, 'by God'.

Paris The French capital takes its name from the *Parisii*, the Celtic people who had their capital at LUTETIA (the former name of Paris). Their own name is of uncertain origin. Proposed etymologies include the following: 1. from Celtic *par*, 'boat' and *gwys*, 'men'; 2. from Greek *baris*, 'boat'; 3. from Latin *Bar Isis*, 'son of Isis' (with *bar* an Aramaic word in origin). Paris is on the river Seine, and is also the capital of the ÎLE de France. The Greek name here is Egyptian in origin, and its 'boat' theme is reflected in the coat of arms of Paris. This shows a galley sailing over the waves under a chief (upper part of the shield) of fleurs de lys together with the Latin motto *Fluctuat nec mergitur*, 'It is buffeted but does not sink'.

Paris In Greek mythology, Paris was the prince of Troy who abducted Helen ('of Troy') from her husband Menelaus and so started the Trojan War. His name is traditionally derived from *pēra*, 'pouch', 'wallet', referring to the bag in which the shepherd Agelaüs had taken the infant Paris to his farm after he had found the child abandoned on Mount Ida.

Parish The name has nothing to do with a parish but was used either for someone who came from PARIS or, more often, for a person with the medieval name *Paris*, itself a form of PATRICK.

Paris Symphony Mozart's Symphony No 31 in D major, K 297 (1778) is so nicknamed because it was written and first performed in *Paris*.

Parjanya The name of the god of thunder clouds and rain in Hindu mythology represents the Sanskrit for 'rain cloud'.

Parker The name was an occupational one for a person who was a gamekeeper in a *park*. In medieval times this was an enclosed area where a local landowner would hunt game.

Parker Knoll The well-known make of furniture, especially chairs and settees, takes its name from those of its original manufacturers in the 1930s, the Englishman Tom *Parker* and the German Willi *Knoll*.

Parkeston Quay The suburb of Harwich, in Essex, familiar to boat passengers, takes its name from Charles H. *Parkes*, chairman of the Great Eastern Railway in the late 19th century, at a time when the railway opened a quayside terminus here to facilitate the transfer of passengers from boat to boat-train on their arrival at Harwich from the Continent.

Park Lane The name of the fashionable London street relates to the narrow *lane* that it originally was, running beside a high wall that enclosed Hyde *Park* at its eastern end.

Parma The city in northern Italy takes its name from the river *Parma* on which it stands. This in turn represents the name of the Etruscan people who lived here and who founded the town in 525 BC. The meaning of their own name is uncertain, although it has been popularly associated with Arabic *barma*, 'circle'. Parma's important food industry gave the culinary world *Parmesan* cheese.

Parmenides The 5th-century BC Greek philosopher, who held that the universe is single and unchanging, has a name that means 'survivor', 'endurer', from Greek *paramenō*, 'I stand fast', 'I survive'.

Parnassus The famous Greek mountain, sacred to Dionysus, Apollo and the muses, derives its name from a Hittite word *parna*, 'abode'.

Parr The name originated from the place now called *Parr Brow* near Manchester, with *Parr* itself meaning 'enclosure', from a word related to modern English *park*.

Parry The name is Welsh in origin, meaning 'son of HARRY', with the initial *P-* representing Welsh *ap*, 'son'. A similar name is PRICE.

Parsee The *Parsees*, who practise a Zoroastrian religion in western India, were driven out of their native PERSIA, from which they take their name, by Muslims in the 8th century AD.

Parsifal In German mythology, *Parsifal* (or *Parzival*) was the hero of a number of legends about the Holy Grail. He corresponds to PERCIVAL in the Arthurian cycle, so has a name of the same origin. His exploits are musically familiar from Wagner's opera *Parsifal* (1882).

Parsons The name originally applied to the servant or child of a priest or parson.

Parthenon The famous Greek temple on the Acropolis in Athens, where it was built in the 5th century BC, was dedicated to the goddess Athena *Parthenos*. Her byname means 'maiden', hence the name of the temple.

Parthenope In Greek mythology, *Parthenope* is a siren who drowned herself in frustration when Odysseus managed to escape the lure of the sirens' singing. Her name means 'maiden face', from Greek *parthenos*, 'maiden' (an epithet of the goddess Athena) and *ōps*, 'face'. Her body was said to have been washed ashore at the point where Naples later arose, so that the Greek colony here was allegedly named for her. (*See* FLORENCE for a modern use of the personal name.)

Parthia The country of ancient Asia has a name of Scythian origin meaning 'banished', 'exiled', referring to its original inhabitants.

Partick Thistle The Glasgow football club was formed in 1876 and takes its name from what is now the western district of the city, where many of their players lived. Their first home ground was at Kelvingrove, west of the city centre, but in 1909 they eventually settled at Firhill Park, north of the city centre. *Thistle* represents the plant that is Scotland's national emblem. *Cp.* MEADOWBANK THISTLE.

Pasadena The Californian city has a name with a complex origin. When it was founded in 1874 by Thomas B. Elliot, an Indian name was sought for it. Since there were no Indians locally, a missionary working among the Chippewa (Ojibwa) Indians was entrusted with the task of providing a name that meant 'crown of the valley', this being suitable for the chosen location. The missionary sent back four long Indian names, ending respectively in *-pa*, *-sa*, *-de*, *-na*. The founder quietly dropped the rest of the names and joined these four syllables together to make the new city's name. Perhaps appropriately, it happens to suggest Spanish *pasada*, 'passage'.

PASCAL The high-level computer language, developed as a teaching language and used for general purpose programming, was designed in the 1960s and named for the French mathematician and philosopher Blaise *Pascal* (1623–1662).

Pascoe The Cornish name arose as a diminutive of the medieval name *Pask*, denoting someone born at Easter. *Cp*. English *paschal* and *see* PASSOVER.

Pasiphaë In Greek mythology, the name of the wife of Minos and mother (by a bull) of the Minotaur is usually explained as meaning 'all-shining', from Greek *pas*, 'all' and *phainein*, 'to show', 'to shine'.

Passion Sunday In the Christian calendar, the name is that of the fifth Sunday in Lent (the second Sunday before Easter). It is so called because it begins *Passiontide*, the fortnight before Easter when church services centre on the *Passion* of Christ, that is, his sufferings before his crucifixion. The name is also sometimes applied more meaningfully to PALM SUNDAY, the Sunday before Easter, since the gospel appointed for that day (*Matthew* 27.1–54) recounts the culmination of the Passion, that is, the trial and crucifixion of Jesus. The name *Passion Week*, too, was formerly common for the week before Easter, now usually referred to as HOLY WEEK. However, the name is now normally reserved for the previous week.

Passmore The name originated as a nickname for a person who would regularly *pass* over a *moor*, either because he lived near a moor or because he knew a safe way across it.

Passover The annual Jewish festival, commemorating the exodus of the Israelites from captivity in Egypt, is so named because the destroying angel *passed over* or spared the houses of the Israelites when he slew the firstborn of the Egyptians (*Exodus* 12.23–27). The name translates Hebrew *pesah*, from *pāsah*, 'to pass over'. This word gave modern English *paschal*, referring to the Passover or to Easter (the Christian festival that superseded it), as well as the word for 'Easter'

itself in some languages, such as French *Pâques*, Italian and Spanish *Pascua*, Russian *Paskha*, Welsh *Pasg*.

Pastoral Symphony Beethoven's Symphony No 6 in F Major, Op 68 (1808) is so called because of its musical representation of various aspects of the countryside. It contains imitations of birdsong and of a storm, and its movements have allusive titles such as 'Awakening of happy feelings on arriving in the country', 'By the brook', and 'Shepherd's song: happy and thankful feelings after the storm'. The name is also that of Vaughan Williams' third symphony (1921) and of a short orchestral movement in Handel's *Messiah*. The latter relates to the 'shepherds abiding in the field' who were told of Christ's birth by an angel (*Luke* 2.8–11).

Patagonia The southernmost region of South America, in Argentina and Chile, has a name that was originally applied by European explorers to the native Tehuelche (Chonan) people who lived on the Atlantic coast here. The name is based on Spanish or Portuguese *pata*, 'paw', 'animal's foot', probably referring to the lama-skin shoes that the people wore.

Patan The town in east central Nepal derives its name from Nepalese *pāṭ*, 'linen', 'silk', from Sanskrit *paṭa*, 'cloth', 'material'. Its ancient name is *Lalitpur*, meaning 'pleasant town', from Nepalese *lalit*, 'agreeable', 'pleasant' and *pur*, 'town'.

Paterson The city in New Jersey was founded in 1791 and named for William *Paterson* (1745–1806), governor of New Jersey and one of the framers of the United States Constitution.

Pathetic Symphony The subtitle of Tchaikovsky's Symphony No 6 in B minor, Op 74 (1893), suggested by the composer's brother Modest, is *Pateticheskaya* in the original Russian, a word that means 'passionate' rather than 'pathetic'. The title frequently occurs in a French form, as *Symphonie Pathétique*, perhaps by association with Beethoven's PATHÉTIQUE SONATA.

Pathétique Sonata Beethoven's Piano Sonata No 8 in C minor, Op 13 (1797) was so named by the composer (in full as *Grande sonate pathétique*) to express its deeply emotional mood.

Patmos The Greek island in the Aegean, according to the Bible the place where St John wrote the Apocalypse (*Revelation* 1.9), was known in medieval times as *Palmosa*, apparently for its palm trees. But this is not the source of the name, which is much older than this and of uncertain meaning.

Patna The city in northeast India has a Hindi name that is an abbreviation of its former name *pāṭaliputra*, from *pāṭala*, literally 'pale red', the name of a flower of the begonia family, and *putra*, 'son'.

Patricia The name is the feminine form of PATRICK, adopted in English from Spanish or Portuguese.

Patrick The name is famous as that of the 5th-century patron saint of Ireland (although he was actually born in Britain). It derives from the Latin name *Patricius*, 'patrician', a term describing a member of the Roman aristocracy. In the case of St Patrick, the name may well have translated an earlier Celtic name, although it is not known what this was.

Patroclus In Greek mythology, *Patroclus* was the friend of Achilles who was killed in the Trojan War by Hector. His name means 'father's glory', from Greek *patēr*, 'father' and *kleos*, 'glory'. It is thus the exact counterpart of CLEOPATRA.

Patten The name was an occupational one for a person who made or sold *pattens*, that is, wooden clogs. It could equally be a nickname for someone who regularly wore them.

Patterson The name means 'son of *Pate*', this being a diminutive of PATRICK.

Pau The city in southwest France has a name that may represent the pre-Indoeuropean root word *pal*, 'mountain'. This would originally have been the name of the *Gave de Pau*, the river that flows down to and through the town from the Pyrenees nearby.

Paul The name is famous from the biblical St *Paul*, who is regarded as the cofounder (with St Peter) of the Christian church. It originated as the Roman *cognomen* (nickname) *Paulus*, 'small', which subsequently became a family name. St Paul was at first known as SAUL, and took his new name mainly to mark his dramatic conversion from Jew to Christian, but also presumably because it was close to the original.

Pauline The name evolved as the French form of *Paulina*, which was the Latin feminine form of *Paulinus*, itself a derivative of *Paulus* (the source of modern PAUL).

Pavia The town in northern Italy had the Late Latin name of *Papia*, representing a personal name. Its Roman name was *Ticinum*, of uncertain origin.

Payton A person of this name would originally have come from one of the places so called, such as what is now *Peyton* Hall in Suffolk. The place-name itself means '*Pǣga*'s settlement'.

Peacehaven The East Sussex town, now a virtual suburb of Newhaven, arose in the First World War as a 'plotland' development, as happened elsewhere at this time along the south coast. Its original name was *New Anzac-on-Sea*, given as the result of a competition ('£2,600 in prizes for a Name of a NEW SOUTH COAST RESORT', *The Times*, 10 January 1916). This was intended as tribute to ANZAC (Australian and New Zealand Army Corps) troops who were stationed locally. However, in 1917 the original planner of the plotland, Charles Neville, announced a new name, *Peacehaven*. This not only denoted a 'peaceful haven' but expressed the common wish for peace to end the war. It also matched that of nearby NEWHAVEN.

Peacock The name was originally a nickname for a person who was vain in manner or appearance, that is, who was 'proud as a peacock' in a not very complimentary sense.

Peak District The upland region of England between Manchester and Sheffield, one of Britain's original National Parks, takes its name from the *Peak*, or *High Peak*, an area of millstone grit hills east of Hayfield, Derbyshire, with Kinder Scout as the summit. *Peak* itself is thus a general name, and does not refer to any particular peak.

Pearce The name represents the medieval name *Piers*, a colloquial form of PETER. In many cases it could equally mean 'son of *Piers*', so that it has the same sense as

PEARSON. The already existing final -s of *Piers* makes it difficult to tell which of the two is the actual origin.

Pearl Harbor The inlet of the Pacific on the island of Oahu, Hawaii, the site of an American naval base attacked by the Japanese in 1941, is so named for the pearl oysters that once grew here. The name is a translation of the Hawaiian *Wai Momi*, 'pearl waters'.

Pears The well-known toilet soap takes its name from Andrew *Pears* (d. 1838), a Cornishman who opened a barber's shop in Soho, London, in 1789, and who perfected his famous 'transparent' soap there as one that would treat complexions more kindly than the many harsh soaps of his day.

Pearson The name means 'son of *Piers*', so is the equivalent of PEARCE.

Pechora The river of northwest Russia derives its name from a Slavic word meaning 'cave', related to modern Russian *peshchera* in the same sense. *Cp.* PÉCS.

Peck The name was originally occupational for a person who dealt in weights and measures, using the *peck* (a quarter of a bushel) as a dry measure for grain.

Peckham The district of south London has a name meaning 'hill village', from *pēac*, 'hill' (modern *peak*) and *hām*, 'village' (modern *hamlet*). There is no obvious hill at Peckham, but the old village is on higher ground to the west of the area now known as Telegraph Hill, with the latter's name significant in this respect. *See also* PECKHAM RYE.

Peckham Rye The area in London south of PECKHAM proper was so named for its *rithe* or stream (Old English *rīth*), now long covered over. The same word lies behind the name of RYDE, Isle of Wight.

Pécs The city in southwest Hungary has a name meaning 'cave', from a word related ultimately to Latin *specus*, 'cavity', 'hollow'. The city's former German name was *Fünfkirchen*, 'five churches'.

Peebles The Scottish town and resort south of Edinburgh has a name of Celtic origin meaning 'shelters' (as in modern Welsh *pebyll*, the plural of *pabell*, 'tent', itself related to English *pavilion*). The reference is to shepherds' huts or shielings used in summer pastures here. The Celtic plural word has gained an extra English plural *s*.

Peel The name originated as a nickname for a tall, thin person, from a Norman word derived from Latin *palus*, 'stake'. In some instances it could have applied to a person who actually lived by a staked fence, or who made such fences.

Peel The well-known Isle of Man resort has a name referring to its ancient (now ruined) castle, deriving from Middle English *pēl*, literally 'enclosure' (modern *pale*, as in 'beyond the pale'). Before the 16th century the town was known as *Holmetown*, 'island town', and this is reflected in the Manx name for Peel, which is *Port-na-Hinsey*, 'port of the island'.

Pegasus The famous winged horse of Greek mythology has a name popularly derived from Greek *pēgē*, 'spring'. He was born from the blood of Medusa, who was pregnant by Poseidon when she was killed by Perseus. The particular springs referred to are said to be those of Oceanus (the Ocean), near which she met her fate. Later, Pegasus was said to have caused various springs to appear by stamping on the ground with his hoof, the best known being the HIPPOCRENE. In actual fact, however, his name is probably of pre-Greek origin.

Peggy The name is a pet form of MARGARET, evolving as a variant of *Maggie*, with *M* becoming *P* as for MOLLY and POLLY.

Peipus The lake in Estonia and western Russia has a name that ultimately derives from Finnish *peipponen*, 'finch', or more precisely from the genitive plural of this, *peipposen*. It is thus 'finch lake'.

Pekinese The small breed of dog with the long silky hair, curled tail and wrinkled nose is so named because the original dogs were kept as imperial pets in the Summer Palace at PEKING. When the city was occupied by European expeditionary forces in 1860, some of the dogs were taken and brought back to Europe. One of them, named 'Looty', was presented to Queen Victoria. The name is also spelled *Pekingese*.

Peking The capital of China has a name that is a western approximation of BEIJING, its true Chinese name (now also officially used in the west), *which see* for its history and meaning.

Pelasgian The name is that of the pre-Hellenic people who inhabited Greece and the coasts of the Aegean before the arrival of the Bronze Age Greeks. Its origin is disputed. Theories to explain it include the following: 1) from a pre-Indoeuropean root element *pala* meaning 'rock', to which Greek *lithos*, 'stone' has been added; 2) from the biblical name *Peleg*, son of Eber, representing Hebrew *palog*, 'to share', so named 'for in his days was the earth divided' (*Genesis* 10.25); 3) from Greek *pelargos*, 'stork', itself composed of *pelos*, 'dark' and *argos*, 'white'. The first of these is supported by the fact that the Pelasgians were mountain-dwellers. The last has aptness in that Pelasgians founded several 'white cities' such as *Alba* and ARGOS. Some scholars also believe that it was their descendants who gave the name of ALBANIA. *See also* PELION.

Pelion The mountain in northeast Greece, famous in mythology as the home of the centaurs, has a name that probably goes back ultimately to the pre-Indoeuropean root element *pala*, 'rock'. *Cp.* PELASGIAN.

Peloponnese The southern peninsula of Greece has a name meaning 'island of Pelops', from *Pelopos*, genitive of *Pelops*, the name of the son of Tantalus in Greek mythology, and *nēsos*, 'island'.

Pemba The island in the Indian Ocean, off the coast of Zanzibar, has a name that is Bantu in origin but of uncertain meaning. Its Arabic name is *al-jazira al-ḥaḍrāʾ*, 'the green island'.

Pemberton The name derives from the place so called, now a district of Wigan near Manchester. The place-name itself means 'barley enclosure on the hill', from Celtic *penn*, 'hill' and two Old English words that gave the modern place-name and surname *Barton*.

Pembroke The town in southwest Wales lies on a peninsula somewhat similar to LAND'S END in Cornwall. Its name indicates this location and is its Celtic equivalent, from words corresponding to modern Welsh *pen*, 'head', 'end' and *bro*, 'region', 'land'. There seems to have been a general European 'westward ho!' drive that gave identical names to west coast headlands: not only Pembroke and Land's End in Britain, but FINISTÈRE in France and Cape Finisterre in Spain.

Pembroke College The Cambridge college was founded in 1347 by Marie de St Pol, widow of Aymer de Valence, Earl of *Pembroke*. The Oxford College of the same name was founded in 1624 by James I and was named for William Herbert, third Earl of *Pembroke*, who was then Chancellor of the University.

Penang The state of peninsular Malaysia has a Malay name, from *pinang*, 'areca' (a genus of palm tree with egg-shaped nuts).

Pendle Hill The well-known hill near Clitheroe in Lancashire, in the area known as the Forest of Pendle, has a name that is something of a curiosity, since it effectively says 'hill' three times. The first part of the name represents both Celtic *penno* (modern Welsh *pen*), 'hill' and Old English *hyll*, 'hill'. The second word, *Hill*, was then added to this when its meaning was no longer understood, just as the Anglo-Saxons must have added *their* word to the original Celtic.

Penelope In Greek mythology, *Penelope* is the faithful wife of Odysseus, loyal to him during his long absence despite continuous harassment from would-be suitors. She pretends she cannot remarry until she has woven a shroud for Laertes, Odysseus' father, but postpones doing so by unravelling every night what she weaves by day. For this reason, her name has been associated with Greek *pēnē*, 'thread'. Its precise origin, however, is uncertain.

Penguin Books The pioneering paperback company was founded in 1935 by the publisher Allen Lane and was given a name suggested by his secretary. According to Sir Allen himself the name appealed because it 'had an air of dignified flippancy and was easy to draw in black and white' (quoted in Patrick Robertson, *The Shell Book of Firsts*, 1986).

Peniel The biblical name of the place where Jacob wrestled with an angel means 'face of God', from Hebrew *penŭ* or *penī*, 'face of', old forms of *penē*, construct state (*see* BETHANY) of *panáyim*, 'face', and *el*, 'God'. The meaning is interpreted in the verse that concludes the account of Jacob's match: 'And Jacob called the name of the place Peniel: for I have seen God face to face, and my life is preserved' (*Genesis* 32.30). The name occurs elsewhere in the Bible in the form *Penuel*, for example in *Judges* 8.8,9.

Peninsular War The war was that of 1808 to 1814 in the Iberian *Peninsula*, *i.e.* in Spain and Portugal, where it was fought by British, Portuguese and Spanish forces against the French. It resulted in the defeat of the French, and was part of the NAPOLEONIC WARS. The name is first recorded during the war itself.

Penmaenmawr The North Wales coastal resort has a name meaning 'big stony headland', from Welsh *pen*, 'head', *maen*, 'stone' and *mawr*, 'big'. This is properly the name not of the town itself but of *Penmaen Mawr*, the mountain nearby.

Penn The name either applied to someone who was a shepherd, putting sheep into their *pen*, or who came from a place called *Penn* (meaning 'hill'), such as the village near Beaconsfield, Buckinghamshire, that is the supposed ancestral home of William *Penn*, founder of PENNSYLVANIA.

Pennines England's main mountain range, extending from the Peak District in the south to the Cheviot Hills in the north, has a name that is obviously based on Celtic *penno*, 'hill'. Strangely, however, no record of the name has been found earlier than the 18th century, and some toponymists came to regard it as a mock-Celtic invention by the literary forger Charles Bertram (1723–1765), who claimed to have found it in the writings of the 14th-century chronicler, Richard of Cirencester. *Cp.* APENNINES.

Pennsylvania The American state is *not* named for its founder in 1682, the English Quaker William *Penn*, as often stated, but for his father. Moreover, the name was given not by Penn but by Charles II, who had granted him the territory here the previous year. The following extract on the matter is from a letter of 14 March 1681 written by William Penn to his friend Robert Turner:

> After many waitings, watchings, solicitings, and disputes in Council, this day my country was confirmed to me under the great seal of England, with large powers and privileges, by the name of *Pennsylvania*; a name the new king would give it in honor of my father. I chose New Wales, [that] being, as this is, a pretty hilly country; but Penn being Welsh for *a head* (as Penmanmoire [modern Penmaenmawr] in Wales, and Penrith in Cumberland, and Penn in Buckinghamshire), [they] called this Pennsylvania, which is the high or head woodlands; for I proposed, when the secretary, a Welshman, refused to have it called New Wales, *Sylvania*, and they added *Penn* to it; and though I much opposed it, and went to the king to have it struck out and altered, he said it was past, and would take it upon him; nor could twenty guineas move the under-secretary to vary the name; for I feared lest it should be looked on as a vanity in me, and not as a respect in the king, as it truly was, to my father, whom he often mentions with praise.
>
> Quoted in A. Howry Espenshade, *Pennsylvania Place Names*, 1925.

William Penn was buried in England at Jordans, near the Buckinghamshire village of Penn, and many of his descendants lie buried in Penn parish church itself. His father was Admiral Sir William Penn (1621–1670), whom Charles II had wished to compliment for his success in the Anglo-Dutch Wars. *See also* the surname PENN.

Penny The surname derives from the familiar name of the coin, which had considerable value in medieval times. A person so nicknamed would thus have been regarded as wealthy.

Penrith The Cumbrian town has a Celtic name meaning 'ford by a hill', from words corresponding to modern Welsh *pen*, 'hill' and *rhyd*, 'ford'. The hill in question is Penrith Beacon, to the east of the town. The ford was probably over the river Eamont by Brougham Castle, two miles (just over 3 km) from Penrith, as this was the point where a Roman road crossed it.

Pensacola The port in Florida, with its naval air-training station, was founded by the Spanish in the late 17th century and has an Indian tribal name, said to mean 'long-haired people', from Choctaw *panshi*, 'hair' and *okla*, 'people' (as for OKLAHOMA).

Penshurst Place The fine 14th-century manor house near Tonbridge, Kent, takes its name from the village here, whose own name means *'Pefen's* hurst'. The Anglo-Saxon personal name is followed by the Old English word *hyrst*, used for a hillock or wooded hill. *Place* has been used as a word for a main dwelling-place or country house since at least the 14th century, and is found in Chaucer in this sense ('With grene trees shadwed was his place', Prologue, *Canterbury Tales, c.* 1387).

Pentagon The building near Washington DC that houses the headquarters of the American Department of Defense is so named because it is a *pentagon*, that is, it has five sides.

Pentateuch The name is used by Christian biblical scholars for the first five books of the Old Testament, which are regarded as a connected group. The meaning of the name is 'five books', from Greek *pente*, 'five' and *teukhos*, literally 'tool', 'implement', later 'book'. The equivalent Jewish name is TORAH.

Pentecost In Judaism, the name is that of the harvest festival (also known as the *Feast of Weeks*, or SHAVUOT) held on the 50th day after the second day of the Passover, commemorating the giving of the Torah (the Ten Commandments) on Mount Sinai. The period of time is based on the Old Testament: 'And ye shall count unto you from the morrow after the Sabbath [...] Even unto the morrow after the seventh sabbath shall ye number fifty days' (*Leviticus* 23.15,16). In the Christian church, *Pentecost* is the festival of *Whit Sunday*, occurring seven weeks after Easter and commemorating the descent of the Holy Ghost on the Apostles. The name represents Greek *pentēkostē*, 'fiftieth'. Christians originally celebrated the whole 50 days, regarding Pentecost as an extension of Easter, and observing it as the 'Great Forty Days' from Easter Day to Ascension Day, with a further ten-day period to Whit Sunday.

Penthesilea In Greek mythology, the name is that of the queen of the Amazons, slain by Achilles. Her name appears to be based on Greek *penthos*, 'grief', 'sorrow'.

Pentland Firth The sea strait between mainland Scotland and the Orkneys has a name meaning 'Pictland', *i.e.* 'land of the PICTS', a designation used generally by the Vikings for the north of Scotland.

Pentland Hills The Scottish chain of hills southwest of Edinburgh has a name based on Celtic *penn*, 'head', 'hill', with English *land* added. This name is thus quite different to that of the PENTLAND FIRTH.

Penuel *See* PENIEL.

Penzance The resort and port in southwest Cornwall has a Cornish name meaning 'holy headland', from *pen*, 'head', 'hill' and *sans*, 'holy' (related to English *saint*). The name refers to the old chapel of St Mary, now represented by St Mary's Parish Church, which stood on the headland at what is now the lower end of Chapel Street. *Cp.* HOLYHEAD.

Pepper The name was either an occupational one for a spicer, who dealt in *pepper*, or was a nickname for an irritable or quick-tempered person, otherwise someone who was *peppery*.

Pepsi-Cola The name of the familiar drink was devised in 1898 in North Carolina by a drugstore manager who aimed to market an elixir that relieved dys*pepsi*a. Hence the first half of the name. The drink was modelled on COCA-COLA, so was given an identical (generic) word for the second half of the name.

Pepsodent The well-known toothpaste has a name that combines Greek *pepsis*, 'digestion' (also suggesting English *peps* or *peppermint*) with Latin *dens*, genitive *dentis*, 'tooth' (similarly suggesting English *dentist*).

Pequot The North American Indian people, and their language, have a name that probably derives from Narraganset *paquatanog*, 'destroyers'.

Peraea The region of ancient Palestine derives its name ultimately from Greek *peran*, 'beyond', as the region lies beyond (*i.e.* east of) the river Jordan. The name is mentioned by the Jewish historian Josephus but does not appear in the Bible, where the Septuagint (Greek version of the Old Testament) simply has *tō peran tou Iordanou*, 'beyond the Jordan'. *Cp.* PIRAEUS, and *see also* TRANSJORDANIA.

Percheron The breed of heavy carthorse takes its name from its place of origin, the region of *Perche* in northwest France. The region's name derives ultimately from Latin *pertica*, 'pole', 'rod' (the former English *perch* as a unit of measurement), referring to the forests of the region.

Percival The name occurs in medieval legend as one of the knights in King Arthur's court, and in the French versions of the tales is spelled *Perceval*, as if meaning 'piercing the valley', an appropriate name for a valiant knight on horseback. But most names of characters in the Arthurian romances are Celtic in origin (like that of Arthur himself), so that *Percival* probably evolved as an alteration of *Peredur*, that of an Arthurian hero in the *Mabinogion*, with whom Percival has traditionally been identified. The alteration may have been influenced by the name PERCY. *Peredur* probably means 'steel spear', from words having their respective equivalents in modern Welsh *peri*, plural of *pâr*, 'spear' and *dur*, 'steel'. *Cp.* PARSIFAL, another form of the same name.

Percy The first name was adopted from the aristocratic surname, itself from a Norman personal name that originated in a place-name in northern France, such as what is now the small town of *Percy* south of Cherbourg. The French place-name derives from the Roman personal name *Persius*. *Percy* is now popularly taken to be a short form of PERCIVAL, but is at least as old as that name.

Perdita The name was invented by Shakespeare for the daughter of Leontes and Hermione in *The Winter's Tale* (1611). It means 'lost', from the feminine of Latin *perditus*, and the significance is both continually implied and explicitly referred to in the text. Hermione thus requests, after her baby daughter is abandoned on the order of Leontes:

for (*i.e.* as) the babe
Is counted lost for ever, Perdita
I prithee call't.
III, iii, 32–34.

Peregrine The name derives from the Latin name *Peregrinus*, 'stranger', 'wanderer', 'pilgrim'. English *pilgrim* itself came from the Latin word, and the name was taken up by early Christians who doubtless regarded themselves as 'travellers' on earth until they reached their true home in heaven (as later did Christian, the hero of Bunyan's *Pilgrim's Progress*).

Père-Lachaise Cemetery The famous Paris cemetery, to the north of the city centre, was opened in 1804 and is named for the Jesuit priest and confessor of Louis XIV, *Père* François de *La Chaise* (1624–1709), whose house had been formerly on the site.

Pergamum The ancient city of northwest Asia, famous as a Greek capital and centre of art and culture, has a name that may derive from Greek *purgos*, 'tower', 'fortress'. The city gave its name to *parchment*, which was invented there.

Pericles The well-known Athenian statesman, who conducted the Peloponnesian War in the 5th century BC, has a name meaning 'very glorious', from *peri*, 'round' and *kleos*, 'fame', 'glory'.

Périgord The region of southwest France, in Aquitaine, takes its name from the *Petrocorii*, the Gaulish people who once lived here. For the origin of their own name, *see* PÉRIGUEUX.

Périgueux The French city, in the Dordogne, takes its name from the *Petrocorii*, the Gaulish people who formerly inhabited the region. Their own name means 'four armies', from Gaulish *petro*, 'four' (related indirectly to Latin *quattuor*) and *corio*, 'army'. *Cp.* PÉRIGORD, the region that lies to the south of *Périgueux*.

Perm The port on the river Kama in central Russia has a name that may derive from Finnish *perämaa*, 'rear land', from *perä*, 'rear', 'back' and *maa*, 'land', 'country'. The reference would be to a town that lay further inland (to the north) on the Kama than some other place nearer its confluence with the Volga. The town was founded in 1780. In 1940 it was renamed *Molotov*, for the Soviet statesman Vyacheslav *Molotov* (1890–1986), but reverted to its former name in 1957 when Molotov fell from grace through his participation in the 'antiparty group' that attempted to depose Khrushchev.

Pernambuco The state of northeast Brazil, on the Atlantic, derives its name from Guarani *paraná*, 'big river' and either *puku*, 'wide' or possibly *mbuku*, 'arm'. The name of the state was also formerly that of its capital, RECIFE, which arose on the delta of two rivers.

Pernod The aniseed-flavoured aperitif takes its name from Henri-Louis *Pernod*, who together with his father-in-law began to produce the drink commercially in Switzerland in the late 18th century, having purchased the recipe for it from the housekeeper of its original creator, a French doctor named Pierre Ordinaire.

Perpignan The name of the historic town in the south of France ultimately derives from *Perpennio*, a Gaulish personal name.

Perrier The well-known mineral water takes its name from Louis Eugène *Perrier* (1835–1912), a French landowner's son who qualified as a doctor, specializing in arthritic diseases. In 1875 he became the director of a thermal establishment near Nîmes, and in 1894 leased mineral springs nearby to provide natural mineral water for his patients. Soon he was bottling the water and selling it in commercial quantities.

Perrin The name represents the medieval name *Perrin* which was a diminutive form of PETER.

Perry A person of this name would originally have lived near a pear-tree, Old English *pirige*.

Perry Barr The district of Birmingham has a name meaning 'pear-tree place near Barr', from Old English *pirige*, 'pear-tree' (related to modern *perry*) and the name of a hill here called *Barr*, itself simply meaning 'hill'.

Persephone In Greek mythology, *Persephone* was the daughter of Zeus and Demeter who was abducted by Hades and made his wife and queen of the underworld. Her name has been interpreted in various ways, but one of the most popular is 'bearer of death', from *pherein*, 'to bear' and *phonē*, 'murder'. This relates to her role as queen of the underworld. But she was a contradictory figure, bringing death in the winter and life in spring, and for this reason her name could equally be seen as 'destroyer of death' (*i.e.* of winter), in this case taking the first half of her name from Greek *perthō* 'I destroy' (*cp.* PERSEUS). Her Roman counterpart was PROSERPINE, which although probably a corruption of her name, is usually interpreted with quite a different meaning.

Persepolis The capital of ancient Persia has a name meaning simply 'Persian town', from Greek *Persēs*, 'a Persian' and *polis*, 'town'.

Perse School The Cambridge public school for boys was founded in 1615 under the provisions of the will of Stephen *Perse* (1548–1615), a fellow of Gonville and Caius College. The *Perse School for Girls* was founded under the same endowment in 1881.

Perseus The famous hero of Greek mythology, who slew the Gorgon Medusa and saved Andromeda from a sea monster, has a name that is traditionally interpreted as 'destroyer', from *perthō*, 'I destroy' (or even, as the future tense of this verb, *persō*, 'I shall destroy').

Persia The former name of IRAN is traditionally derived from that of *Persēs*, son of the Greek mythological hero PERSEUS and his wife Andromeda. The true source of the name, however, is more closely bound up with that of the province of *Fars* (see FARSI for the origin). It was the name of *Persia* that gave that of the *peach*, through Latin *Persicum malum*, 'Persian apple'. *See also* PARSEE. The country's name was changed to *Iran* in 1935 as being 'inappropriate for the native stock of the country and offensive to native dignity'.

Persil The familiar name of the washing powder is the French word for 'parsley'. It refers to the sprig of parsley that was the trade mark of a Frenchman named Ronchetti who discovered a method of adding bleach to soap in 1907. At the same time the name combines elements of '*per*borate' and '*sili*cate', two important ingredients of the new discovery.

Perspex The type of transparent thermoplastic that is a proprietary substitute for glass derives its name from Latin *perspicere*, 'to look through', with this verb having the form *perspexi* to mean 'I have looked through'. As for many trade names, however, the final *-ex* may have been intended to mean 'out'. The name was patented in 1935. In America, Perspex is sold under the names of *Plexiglas* and *Lucite*.

Perth The ancient Scottish town on the river Tay has a name of Pictish (pre-Celtic) origin probably meaning 'bush', 'thicket', related to modern Welsh *perth* in the same sense. *Perth*, the capital of Western Australia, was settled in 1829 and named for *Perth*shire, birthplace of the then British Colonial Secretary, Sir George Murray (1772–1846), who also gave the name of the river MURRAY.

Pertwee The name is Norman in origin, from one of the places in northern France called *Pertuis*, *Pertuy* or something similar. These derive from Old French *pertuis*, 'ravine' (now a geographical term for a narrow strait).

Peru The republic of western South America takes its name from the river *Birú* or *Perú* here, itself deriving from Guarani *piru* or *biru*, meaning simply 'water', 'river'.

Perugia The city in central Italy has a name that may be Etruscan in origin, perhaps representing *phaersu*, the name of a devil that led the souls of the dead to the underworld, with this name itself indirectly related to Latin *persona*, originally 'mask', then 'part' (in a play), 'character', 'person'. The Roman name of Perugia was *Perusia*.

Pescara The city and resort in east central Italy, on the Adriatic, takes its name from the river on which it stands. The river's own name ultimately derives from Latin *piscis*, 'fish'.

Peshawar The city in northern Pakistan stands at the eastern end of the Khyber Pass and has a name that was given it in the 16th century by the emperor Akbar. It is a corruption of its earlier Hindi name *puraśāpura* or *paraśāvara*, meaning 'front-

ier town'. Peshawar is one of the oldest cities in Pakistan and was capital of the ancient kingdom of Gandhara.

Petach Tikva The city northeast of Tel Aviv-Jaffa, Israel, derives its name from Hebrew *petah-tiqwa*, 'gate of hope', from *petah*, 'door', 'gate' and *tiqwa*, 'hope'. The allusion is to the biblical passage: 'And I will give her her vineyards from thence, and the valley of Achor for a door of hope' (*Hosea* 2.15). The city was founded in 1878 as the first village in the modern Jewish settlement of Palestine. For this reason it is also known in Hebrew as '*Em ha-Mošavot*, 'mother of villages'. It was incorporated as a city in 1937.

Peter The familiar biblical name is that of the apostle who became (with St Paul) the founder of the Christian church. It derives, through Latin, from Greek *petros*, 'stone', 'rock' (as in English *petrified*). In the New Testament, this is used as a translation of the Aramaic name *Cephas*, given by Jesus to Simon, son of Jona, to distinguish him from Simon Zelotes: 'When Jesus beheld him, he said, Thou art Simon the son of Jona: thou shalt be called Cephas, which is by interpretation, A stone' (*John* 1.42). In another gospel, Jesus comments further on the name, saying to Simon: 'And I say also unto thee, That thou art Peter, and upon this rock I will build my church' (*Matthew* 16.17). The correspondence between name and meaning is much more obvious in French, where *Pierre*, 'Peter' is exactly the same as *pierre*, 'stone'.

Peterborough The Cambridgeshire city was originally known by the Anglo-Saxon name of *Medeshampstead*, probably meaning 'homestead by the whirlpool'. This denoted the settlement that arose on the site of a monastery here in the 7th century. The monastery was destroyed by the Danes in the 9th century, but rebuilt as a Benedictine abbey in the 10th, and soon afterwards the settlement became known simply as *Burg*, 'town'. *Peter* was then added to this from the dedication of the abbey. The present cathedral, also dedicated to St Peter, was built in the 12th century on the former abbey site.

Peterborough The gossip column in the *Daily Telegraph*, long familiar as 'London Day by Day', takes its name from *Peter-*

borough Court, London, where the newspaper formerly had its offices. The court itself, off Fleet Street in the City, is named for the abbots of *Peterborough*, who had a town house here until the Dissolution of the Monasteries in 1539.

Peter Dominic The British wineshop chain takes its name from the pseudonym adopted by the firm's founder, the Scottish-born Frenchman Paul Dauthieu, who began his career as a wine waiter in Edinburgh and who opened his first wineshop in Horsham, Sussex, in 1939. He took a name that was more readily remembered by the British than his original French name.

Peterhead The Scottish fishing port near Aberdeen has a name meaning what it says, referring to the former 12th-century St *Peter*'s Kirk (church) that stood on a *head*land here. The headland was named for the church, and the town, founded in the late 16th century, for the headland.

Peterhouse Cambridge's oldest and smallest college, founded in 1284, takes its name from the church that was originally used as the college chapel, that of St *Peter* without Trumpington Gate, now known as Little St Mary's. The official name of the college is still *St Peter*'s today.

Peter Jones The well-known department store in London's Sloane Square takes its name from *Peter Jones* (1843–1905), a Welsh hatmaker's son who came to London and opened a draper's shop in Hackney in 1868.

Peterlee The New Town near Hartlepool, Co Durham, was designated in 1948 and named for a local miner and trade union leader, *Peter Lee* (d. 1935). The artificial name nevertheless happens to suggest a genuine place-name, with its second half similar to the commonly found *-ley*.

Peterloo Massacre The name is that of an incident in Manchester in 1819 in which a radical meeting was broken up by a cavalry charge, resulting in many injuries and 11 deaths. The name is a combination of St *Peter*'s Fields, the site of the incident, and Water*loo*, as the name of the famous battle that had occurred only four years before. For another name blended with that of the battle, *cp*. BAKERLOO.

Peter Pan The famous 'boy who wouldn't grow up' of the play by J.M. Barrie, first performed in 1904, was given his first name from one of the young sons of the Llewelyn Davies family, with whom Barrie was friendly, and his surname from the Greek god PAN. It has been pointed out that Barrie also knew the children of the writer Maurice Hewlett, whose play *Pan and the Young Shepherd*, published in 1898, had the opening line 'Boy, boy, wilt thou be a boy for ever?' This could have influenced Barrie's choice. Peter Llewelyn Davies grew up to be a publisher, but committed suicide, aged 63, in 1960. He had himself been named after the central character in George du Maurier's novel *Peter Ibbetson* (1891).

Peters The make of chocolate is named for Daniel *Peter* (1836–1919), a Swiss butcher's son who turned from candlemaking to chocolate manufacturing, and who produced the world's first milk chocolate in 1875.

Petersfield The name of the Hampshire town was first recorded only in the late 12th century, showing it to be a Norman 'new town'. The town took its name from what is now its parish church, dedicated to St Peter, which already existed when the borough was founded. But it is possible the church may itself have been so named from the similarity of *Peter* to an Anglo-Saxon name such as *Peohthere*, so that this may have been the name of the original owner of the *feld*, or open land here.

Peter Stuyvesant The American brand of cigarettes takes its name from *Peter Stuyvesant* (1610–1682), the Dutch governor of New Amsterdam (the future New York) who tried to resist the attempts of the British to seize the city in 1664. His farm nearby gave the name of the BOWERY.

Petra The ancient city in the south of what is now Jordan, famous for its rock-cut monuments, has a name that is the Greek word for 'rock'. Petra is the 'rose-red city – "half as old as Time"!' in the poem of 1845 by John William Burgon that bears its name, the 'rose-red' colour being that of the sandstone cliffs that surround it.

Petrodvorets The Russian town on the Gulf of Finland arose from the residence built by Peter the Great in 1704 for him to stay at during his frequent journeys from St Petersburg to the fortress then being built at Kronstadt. Hence its name, meaning 'Peter's palace', from Russian *Pëtr*, 'Peter' and *dvorets*, 'palace'. Until 1944 it was known as *Petergof*, representing German *Peterhof*, with the same sense.

Petrograd *See* ST PETERSBURG.

Petrokrepost The Russian town near St Petersburg has a name that means 'Peter's fort' from Russian *Pëtr*, 'Peter' and *krepost'*, 'fort'. It was founded in 1323 as *Oreshek*, taking this name from that of the river *Orekhov* on which it stands. In 1612 the fort was captured by the Swedes and renamed *Noteburg*, from their interpretation of the river name as 'nut' (Russian *orekh*, Swedish *nöt*), with the Swedish word for 'fort' (*borg*) added. In 1702 the fort was regained by Peter the Great and renamed in the German fashion of the day as *Schlüsselburg*, 'key fort'. The fort and town kept this name until 1944, when it was renamed in commemoration of the victory of Peter the Great in the northern war against the Swedes.

Petropavlovsk The city in Kazakhstan was founded in 1752 as the fort of St *Peter* and St *Paul*, so named from the dedication of the church within its precinct. The name thus represents those of the two saints, which in Russian are respectively *Pëtr* and *Pavel*. *Cp.* PETROPAVLOVSK-KAMCHATSKY.

Petropavlovsk-Kamchatsky The town and port in eastern Russia takes the latter part of its name from the KAMCHATKA peninsula, where it was founded in 1740 by the Danish navigator Vitus Bering. The first part of the name represents those of two of his ships, the *St Peter* and *St Paul*. The second half of the name was added in 1924 to distinguish this town from PETROPAVLOVSK.

Petrozavodsk The city in northwest Russia, where it is the capital of Karelia, has a name meaning 'Peter's factory', from Russian *Pëtr*, 'Peter' and *zavod*, 'works', 'factory'. It was founded by Peter the Great in 1703 as an ironworks to exploit the natural ore deposits here.

Pet Shop Boys, The The British pop duo, formed in London in 1981, was named by its members for friends who worked in an Ealing pet shop.

Petticoat Lane The name is familiar from the popular Sunday street market held in and around Middlesex Street in the East End of London. It was originally the sole name of the street, recorded in the early 17th century and referring to the old clothes sold there. In 1830 the street was officially renamed *Middlesex Street* as it ran along the boundary between the City of London and the former county of Middlesex. But the old name is still regularly in use, and appears on modern street plans of London.

Pettifer The name was originally a nickname, and represents Old French *pie de fer*, 'iron foot', as applied to a keen walker, or possibly to someone with an artificial leg.

Petulengro Familiar from 'Gypsy Petulengro' booths at country fairs, the name is a genuine Gypsy one, and in literature was promoted by Jasper *Petulengro*, the main Gypsy character in George Borrow's novel *Lavengro* (1851) and its sequel *The Romany Rye* (1857). In these, the character is based on the Gypsy Ambrose Smith, whom Borrow had known in his youth. Borrow allows Petulengro to explain the meaning of his name to the narrator, whom he knows as *Sapengro* ('snake-master') and whom he later renames LAVENGRO:

'Tawno Chikno take care of Jasper Petulengro!'
'Is that your name?'
'Don't you like it?'
'Very much, I never heard a sweeter; it is something like what you call me.'
'The horse-shoe master and the snake-fellow, I am the first.'

Lavengro, Chapter 17.

Petworth House The Sussex mansion, rebuilt for the Duke of Somerset in the late 17th century and famous for its art collection, its gardens, and for being the subject of paintings by Turner, takes its name from the nearby town of *Petworth*. The town has a name that means '*Pēota's* enclosure', with the Anglo-Saxon personal name followed by Old English *worth*, 'enclosure'.

Peugeot The French car takes its name from Armand *Peugeot* (1849–1915), a hardware and farm equipment manufacturer's son from near Belfort, in eastern France, who began making bicycles in the 1880s and who produced the first petrol-driven *Peugeot* car in 1890.

PG Tips The well-known brand of tea was originally known as *Digestive Tea* when it was introduced in the 1940s, since it claimed to relieve indigestion. The manufacturers were requested by the government to drop the reference to a medicinal benefit, however, so they altered the name to *Pre-Gestee*, suggesting a *tea* that could be drunk before food was di*ges*ted. This rather awkward name was soon abbreviated to *P.G.*, and *Tips* was added to refer to the tips of tea leaves that give a blend's distinctive flavour.

Phaedra The wife of Theseus in Greek mythology has a name meaning 'shining', 'bright', from *phainein*, 'to shine'.

Phaëthon In Greek mythology, the name is that of the son of Helios, the sun god. Appropriately, it means 'bright', from *phaethōn*, 'shining'.

Phaidon Press The Oxford publishing house, famous for its finely illustrated art books, was founded in Vienna in 1923 and is named after *Phaidon*, the speaker in one of Plato's dialogues who is himself named for the 4th-century BC Greek philosopher and pupil of Socrates. The Press's logo is the Greek letter *phi* (φ) that begins the name.

Pharaoh The title (rather than name) was that of the ancient Egyptian kings, and ultimately derives from Egyptian *pr-'o*, 'great house'. The final *h* of the name comes from its Hebrew form, *paraōh*.

Pharisee The name is that of the ancient Jewish sect that was opposed to the Sadducees and that taught strict observance of the traditional and written Jewish law. The ultimate origin of the name is in Aramaic *p'rishāiyā*, plural of *p'rīsh*, 'separated', *i.e.* in the sense 'separatist'.

Pharos The name of the ancient lighthouse built on a island off Alexandria, Egypt, in the 4th century BC is of unknown origin. It was adopted by many languages as a general word for a powerful light, however, so that today French *phare* and Italian *faro*

mean 'lighthouse', 'headlight'. The original lighthouse is traditionally regarded as one of the Seven Wonders of the Ancient World. *See also* HVAR.

Pheidippides The name is famous in Greek history as that of the Athenian athlete who ran to Sparta to seek help against the Persians before the Battle of Marathon. His name means (rather inappropriately) 'sparing the horses', from Greek *pheidomai*, 'I spare' and *hippos*, 'horse'.

Phi Beta Kappa In the United States, the name is that of a national honorary society to which students of high academic ability are granted membership. The society's name comprises the Greek initial letters (ΦΒΚ) of the words of its motto: *philosophia biou kubernētēs*, 'philosophy (the) guide of life'. The society was founded at the College of William and Mary, Williamsburg, Virginia, in 1776.

Philadelphia The city and port in Pennsylvania was founded in 1682 by the English Quaker William Penn. He gave it the name of the ancient city of Lydia in Asia Minor, the seat of one of the 'Seven Churches' mentioned in the Bible (*Revelation* 1.11), no doubt interpreting this as meaning 'brotherly love', from Greek *phileō*, 'I love' and *adelphos*, 'brother'. However, the biblical city was actually named for its founder in the 2nd century BC, Attalus II *Philadelphus*, king of Pergamum, whose nickname or title meant 'loving the brethren'.

Philemon In the Bible, the name is that of a Christian of Colossae whose escaped slave Onesimus came to meet Paul. The New Testament book named for him (*The Epistle of Paul to Philemon*) represents Paul's request to Philemon to forgive Onesimus for escaping. Philemon's name derives from Greek *philēma*, 'kiss', so is essentially a 'loving' name. In classical mythology it is also familiar from the elderly couple *Philemon* and Baucis, who entertain the gods Zeus and Hermes without being aware of their true identity.

Philip The well-known name, familiar from the Bible and from history (especially as that of the father of Alexander the Great), means 'lover of horses', from Greek *philein*, 'to love' and *hippos*, 'horse'. It has proved coincidentally appropriate in modern times for Prince *Philip*, Duke of Edinburgh, an accomplished equestrian.

Philip Morris The American tobacco company owes its name to an Englishman, *Philip Morris*, who in 1847 opened a cigar shop in Oxford. After his death in 1873, an import agency was set up in New York to market the products of the firm he had built up, and it was in the United States that the company's subsequent development lay.

Philippa The name is a Latin-style feminine equivalent of PHILIP. In its turn it gave the name PIPPA.

Philippi The ancient city of Macedonia, where Antony and Octavian won a victory over Brutus and Cassius in 42 BC, takes its name from king PHILIP of Macedonia, who developed and fortified it in the 4th century BC in order to control its gold mines. *See also* PHILIPPIANS.

Philippians The book of the New Testament (in full *The Epistle of Paul the Apostle to the Philippians*) represents a letter addressed to the Christian converts at PHILIPPI, Macedonia, by St Paul.

Philippines The island republic in southeast Asia was discovered by the Portuguese navigator Magellan in 1521. Its name, however, was not given by him but by the Spanish explorer Ruy López de Villalobos, who landed on the island that is now Mindanao in 1543 and named it *Filipina* in honour of the future king *Philip* II of Spain, then aged 16. Magellan's earlier name for the archipelago had been *St Lazarus Islands*, since he had made his discovery on Tuesday 17 December, the feast of St Lazarus.

Philips The well-known manufacturers of electrical and electronic products take their name from Gerard *Philips*, a Dutch engineer who started up a factory in Eindhoven in 1891 to make electric light bulbs.

Philistine The name of the non-Semitic people who inhabited the coast of southwest Palestine in ancient times is Hebrew in origin, perhaps deriving from a root word *paloŝ* meaning 'to invade'. In Assyrian inscriptions the land of the Philistines is named as *Palastu* or *Pilistu*. It was the Philistines who gave the name of PALESTINE itself. In the Septuagint (Greek version of the Old Testament) they are also named as *oi allophuloi*, 'the strangers' (literally 'of another tribe'), probably because they were not Semitic in origin. (They are also called 'uncircumcised' in the same sense.) The use of the word *philistine* to mean 'boorish' was popularized only in the 19th century, and derives not so much from the biblical people as from the German term *Philister* used by students of Jena University in the 17th century to denote non-members of the university, 'town' rather than 'gown'.

Phillimore The name derives from the Norman personal name *Filimor*, itself of Germanic origin, from *filu*, 'very' and *mari*, 'famous'. The present spelling of the name is due to its association with PHILIP.

Philomela In Greek mythology, the name is familiar as that of the Athenian princess who was raped and had her tongue cut out by her brother-in-law Tereus, and who was subsequently turned into a nightingale. Her name means literally 'lover of song', from Greek *philein*, 'to love' and *melos*, 'song'. The name was also the actual Greek word for 'nightingale', and this is popularly derived from the myth.

Philomena The name was that of an obscure 3rd-century saint but is sometimes given as a first name. It appears to mean 'strength-loving', from Greek *philein*, 'to love' and *menos*, 'strength', and is probably a female adoption of a male name *Philomenēs* in this sense.

Philosopher Symphony Haydn's Symphony No 22 in E flat major (1764) is so named for the 'thoughtful' mood of the opening Adagio.

Philpott The name suggests 'fill pot' but is actually a diminutive form of PHILIP. *Cp.* POTTS.

Phineas The name occurs in the Bible for two minor Old Testament characters (where it is spelled *Phinehas*) and is traditionally explained as deriving from Hebrew *Pīnehās*, said to mean 'serpent's mouth', that is, 'oracle'. However, it actually represents the Egyptian name *Panhsj*, meaning 'black', originally a nickname for a dark-skinned person.

Phlegethon In Greek mythology, the name is that of the river of fire in Hades. It means 'blazing', 'flaming', from Greek *phlegethein*, 'to blaze', 'to flame'.

Phnom Penh The capital of Cambodia has a name meaning 'mountain of plenty', from Cambodian *phnŏm*, 'mountain', 'hill' and *penh*, 'full'. A Cambodian tradition derives the name from a elderly rich lady called *Don Penh*, who is said to have built a shrine at this spot, so that the meaning is '*Penh*'s hill'. But this is local legend at work!

Phocaea The ancient port in Asia Minor derives its name from Greek *phōkē*, 'seal', probably referring to the monk seals that were at one time abundant in the Mediterranean.

Phoebe In Greek mythology, *Phoebe* is a Titaness who became identified with Artemis (Diana) as goddess of the moon. Her name, like that of her brother PHOEBUS, represents Greek *phoibos*, 'bright'.

Phoebus In Greek mythology, *Phoebus* is a poetic name of Apollo, the sun god, brother of PHOEBE, goddess of the moon. His name, like hers, represents Greek *phoibos*, 'bright'.

Phoenician The ancient Semitic people of northwest Syria, noted as traders, have a name that is traditionally derived from *Phoenix*, son of Agenor, king of Tyre, their legendary ancestor. More prosaically, the name could come from Greek *phoinix*, 'purple', for it was the Phoenicians who invented the purple dye. On the other hand, it would certainly be more logical to derive the word *phoinix* from the name of the people. The same Greek word is the source of the *phoenix*, the fabulous bird said to set fire to itself and rise from its own ashes every 500 years. Yet another meaning is 'date palm'. The colour purple could apply to the flames associated with the bird, but the ultimate link between Phoenicians, purple, the phoenix and the date palm has become blurred. *See also* PUNIC WARS.

Phoenix The state capital of Arizona was founded in 1867 on the ruins of an ancient Indian city. It was given a symbolic name referring to the *phoenix*, the legendary bird that arose from its own ashes (*see* PHOENICIAN).

Photostat The proprietary process (or machine) for making photographic copies of documents and the like was patented in the United States in 1911 and given a name that combined *photo* with the *-stat* found in such scientific instruments as *rheostat* and *thermostat*, where it represents Greek *statos*, 'stationary'. The process thus produced copies that were 'fixed' from the original.

Phrygia The ancient country of Asia Minor has a name that may derive either from Greek *phrugō*, 'I burn' or from Pelasgian *bher*, 'to move rapidly'. The Phrygians were noted for their impetuosity. They gave the name of the 'Phrygian bonnet', the distinctive conical cap with bent peak that was adopted as a 'cap of liberty' at the time of the French Revolution and that is worn by Marianne, the female figure who symbolizes the French republic.

Phyllis In Greek mythology, the name is that of a Thracian king's daughter who killed herself for love and was turned into an almond tree. It appropriately represents Greek *phullas*, 'leaves', 'foliage', and its meaning caused it to be traditionally adopted in pastoral poetry for a pretty country girl.

Piacenza The town in northern Italy was founded in the 3rd century BC with the Roman name of *Placentia*. This means 'caring', 'pleasing', and refers to the remnants of Scipio's army who were cared for here after the Battle of the Trebia in 218 BC.

Picardy The region of northern France takes its name from Old French *pic*, modern *pique*, 'pike', this being the weapon for which the inhabitants of Picardy were noted in historic times.

Piccadilly The famous London street derives its name from a house here in the early 17th century called (or nicknamed) *Piccadilly Hall*. This belonged to a tailor named Robert Baker who had made his fortune by selling *pickadills*, a fashionable type of wide high collar, in vogue among aristocrats of the day. The name has been further promoted by *Piccadilly Circus*, formed in 1819 by the intersection of Piccadilly with the new Regent Street, and by the *Piccadilly Line* of the London Underground, opened in 1906 as the then longest tube railway in London, from Finsbury Park in the northeast to Hammersmith in the southwest, with *Piccadilly Circus* as its central station.

Pickering The North Yorkshire town has a difficult name whose origin has not been conclusively established. It may be a tribal name, based on Old English *pīc*, 'point' (modern *pike*), so meaning something like 'place of the hill-dwellers'. Pickering lies at the foot of the North Yorkshire Moors, and the word *pike* is used for various hills in the region, such as *Pike* Hill Moss, north of Pickering Moor.

Pickford The name derives from a place-name, such as *Pickford* near Coventry in the Midlands. The place-name itself means 'pig ford'.

Pickfords The famous firm of carriers and furniture removers takes its name from Thomas *Pickford*, who started a haulage business in Burton-upon-Trent, Staffordshire in about 1662.

Picts The name of the pre-Celtic people who lived in what is now northern Scotland is said to derive from Latin *pictus*, 'painted', referring to their habit of painting or tattooing themselves. But this traditional etymology is highly suspect, and the actual source probably lies in the Picts' name for themselves. Unfortunately, we do not know what this was. However, it has been established that the initial *Pit-* of Pictish place-names in Scotland, such as PITLOCHRY, *Pitsligo* and *Pittenweem*, means 'share' (that is, share of land), so that perhaps the Picts were originally the 'share-of-land people'. *See also* PENTLAND FIRTH, POITIERS, POITOU.

Piedmont The region of northwest Italy derives its name from Old Italian *pie di monte*, 'foot of the mountain', referring to its location at the foot of the Alps.

Pied Piper of Hamelin In German legend, the name is that of the piper who was engaged to lure the rats out of the city of Hamelin by piping, so that they followed him, but who when he was not paid for his services lured away the children instead. He was *pied* because he wore a coat of contrasting colours, like the black and white plumage of a mag*pie*. The legend was popularized by Robert Browning's poem of the name, published in 1842. The character's English title is more poetic than the German, in which he is usually known as *der Rattenfänger von Hameln*, 'the ratcatcher of Hamelin', with no reference to his costume or his piping.

Pierre The state capital of South Dakota takes its name from the French fur trader *Pierre* Chouteau (1789–1865) who set up a market here in 1837 to trade with the Indians.

Pietermaritzburg The capital of Natal, South Africa, was founded in 1839 and named after the Voortrekker leaders *Pieter* Retief (1780–1838) and Gerrit *Maritz* (1798–1839), with the final *burg* meaning 'town'.

Pifco The make of electrical products such as torches and lamps has a name that is an acronym of the company's full name when it was founded in Manchester in 1900. This was the *P*rovincial *I*ncandescent *F*ittings *Co*mpany.

Piggott The name is a form of the Old French name *Picot*, a diminutive of *Pic*, meaning 'pike'. *See also* PIKE.

Pike The name can have several origins. It may initially have denoted someone who lived by a pointed hill or *pike*. As an occupational name, it could refer to a person who caught *pike*, who worked the ground with a *pick*, or who was a foot soldier armed with a *pike*. Equally, the name could evolve as a nickname for a tall, thin person, someone who was the equivalent of modern 'thin as a rake'.

Pilate *See* PONTIUS PILATE.

Pilgrims Way The ancient trackway that follows the southern slope of the North Downs in southeast England has a name that appears to refer to the *pilgrims* who journeyed along it to Canterbury in medieval times. However, the name is first recorded only in the 18th century, and although it *may* have been followed by such pilgrims, it would not have been used by them alone, if only because it existed long before their time.

Pilkington The well-known make of glassware takes its name from William *Pilk-*

ington, who with five partners founded the St Helens Crown Glass Company in St Helens, Lancashire (now Merseyside) in 1826.

Pilsen Famous for its beer, the Czech town has a name that derives from Old Czech *plz*, 'damp', 'moist'. The medieval town arose on a damp and slippery site at a point where several small rivers meet to form the Berounka. The Czech name of the town is *Plzeň*.

Pimlico The district of south London has a curious name that is said to derive from that of a local innkeeper, one Ben *Pimlico*, or from that of an inn named after him. The name is first recorded in 1630, as *Pimplico*. The region was virtually without inhabitants until the 19th century.

Pimms The well-known proprietary cocktail *Pimm's No 1* takes its name from its inventor in 1840, James *Pimm*, a London barman. The cocktail was gin-based, and for many years there were five other 'numbers' with other bases. These were *Pimm's No 2* (whisky), *Pimm's No 3* (brandy), *Pimm's No 4* (rum), *Pimm's No 5* (rye) and *Pimm's No 6* (vodka). It was *Pimm's No 1*, however, that was consistently the most popular.

Pindus The mountain range in central Greece derives its name from Greek *pidax*, 'spring', 'fountain'. A number of streams and rivers rise here.

Pine A person with this name would originally have lived by a distinctive pine tree, or in or near a pine forest.

Ping-Pong The commercial name for table tennis dates back to the late 19th century, and derives from the sound of the celluloid ball as it hits bat (*ping*) and table (*pong*). The name is still a proprietary one in the United States. In China, the game is known as *pīngpāng*.

Pingxiang The town in southeast China derives its name from Chinese *píng*, 'duckweed' and *xiāng*, 'canton', 'district'.

Pink Floyd The British psychedelic rock band, formed in London in 1965, took a name that was a tribute to the American bluesmen *Pink* Anderson (1900–1974) and *Floyd* Council (1911–1976).

Pinkie, Battle of The battle of 1547 in which the Scots were defeated by the English is named for the site near Musselburgh where it took place. The name itself means 'wedge valley', from Celtic words having a modern equivalent in Welsh *pant*, 'valley' and *cŷn*, 'wedge'.

Pinocchio The well-known wooden puppet boy in the children's book by the Italian writer Carlo Collodi (real name Carlo Lorenzini), published in 1883, has a name that is the Italian word for 'pine-seed', since the puppet is 'born' from a piece of pinewood.

Pippa The name is a contracted form of PHILIPPA. It was popularized in the 19th century by Browning's poem *Pippa Passes* (1847), where it is the name of a young Italian girl working in a silk mill. It is not an Italian name, however.

Piraeus The ancient city in southeast Greece was founded in the 5th century BC as a port for Athens. Its name is based on Greek *peran*, 'beyond'. Piraeus was formerly an island, across marshes from Athens. *Cp.* PERAEA.

Pirelli The Italian make of tyre is named for Giovanni Battista *Pirelli* (1848–1932), who founded Italy's first rubber factory in Milan in 1872 and who went on to pioneer the manufacture of electric cable in 1884 and of tyres in 1899.

Pisa The famous city in northwest Italy has an Etruscan name of uncertain meaning. A possible sense 'estuary' has been proposed, which would describe the city's location at the mouth of the river Arno.

Pishpek *See* BISHKEK.

Pisistratus The name of the 6th-century BC tyrant of Athens should more accurately be spelled *Peisistratos*, to match the original Greek. It means 'army persuader', from *peithō*, 'I persuade', 'I prevail on' and *stratos*, 'army'.

Pistoia The city in northern Italy is said to derive its name from Latin *pistor*, 'pounder', that is, one who pounds or mills grain, otherwise a baker. Some etymologists derive the word *bistoury* (a type of surgical knife) from the name, while others similarly relate *pistol* to it. The latter word, however, is now more reliably traced back to a Slavic source meaning 'pipe'.

Pitcairn Island The South Pacific island was discovered in 1767 by the English colonist Philip Carteret, and is named for Midshipman Robert *Pitcairn* (1747–1770), the sailor who first sighted it from the ship HMS *Swallow*. The name is curiously suitable for the rocky, rugged island, with its many 'pits' and 'cairns'.

Pithiviers The town in north central France was known in the 11th century as *Petuarensis Castrum* or *Pitueris Castrum*, from the Gaulish personal name *Petuario*, 'fourth' (*cp*. PÉRIGUEUX) and Latin *castrum*, 'encampment', 'castle'. The personal name derives from Gaulish *petro*, 'four', and was given to the fourth child in a family.

Pitlochry The Scottish resort near Dunkeld, famous for its festival theatre, has a Pictish name meaning 'portion of the stones', with the conjectural Pictish word *pett*, 'portion' followed by Gaelic *cloichreach*, 'stony place'. The reference is probably to stepping stones over the river Tummel, on which the town stands.

Pitt The name originally denoted a person who lived by a *pit* or hollow, or who came from a place named from the Old English word *pytt* that meant this, such as the village of *Pitt* near Winchester, Hampshire.

Pittsburgh The Pennsylvania port was founded in 1754 by French colonists and originally named *Fort Duquesne*, for the French governor of Canada (then called 'New France'), Michel-Ange *Duquesne* (1702–1778). In 1758 it was captured by the English and renamed in honour of the British statesman William *Pitt* the Elder (1708–1778).

Pius The name borne by many popes means rather more than 'pious'. It derives from Latin *pius*, which had the basic sense 'dutiful' (to gods, country, family, friends and so on), but which developed the wider senses 'holy', 'honest'. The basic sense is probably the one that most popes had in mind when adopting the name, seeing their role as dutiful to God, the Church and their fellow men.

Plaid Cymru The Welsh nationalist party, founded in 1925, has a name meaning 'party of Wales'. Its original name was *Plaid Genedlaethol Cymru*, 'national party of Wales'.

Plant A person of this name was originally either a gardener, working with plants, or else a delicate individual, like a young plant.

Plantagenet The line of English kings, from the accession of Henry II in 1154 to the death of Richard III in 1485, took a name that was the Old French phrase for 'sprig of broom', itself from Latin *planta*, 'sprig' and *genista*, 'broom'. The reference was to the crest of the kings of Anjou, since members of the Plantagenet line were descended from Geoffrey, count of Anjou (d. 1151) and his wife Matilda, daughter of Henry I. Geoffrey was said to have worn a sprig of broom in his hat.

Planxty The Irish folk group, formed in 1972, took as their name the word (not itself Irish in origin) for a type of Irish dance or dance-tune.

Plasticine The soft coloured modelling material, used mainly by children, is so named because it is *plastic* (in the sense 'malleable'), with *-ine* a common suffix for a commercial product.

Plata, La The wide estuary in South America, between Argentina and Uruguay, and formed by the rivers Uruguay and Paraná, has a name deriving from Spanish *la plata*, 'silver'. The rich deposits of silver here also gave the name of ARGENTINA. The city of *La Plata* was founded near the La Plata estuary in 1882. The river is also known by the full Spanish name of *Río de la Plata* and is often referred to in English as the *River Plate*.

Plataea The ancient village in Boeotia, the scene of the defeat of a large Persian army by the Greeks in 479 BC, derives its name from Greek *platus*, 'flat', describing the terrain where it was located south of Thebes.

Plato The famous Greek philosopher, who lived in the 4th and 5th centuries BC, has a name that is traditionally derived from Greek *platus*, 'flat', or in Plato's case 'broad-shouldered', describing his physical appearance. Unlike the Romans, the Greeks were generally given just one name.

Platt The name arose as a nickname for a thin person, from Old French *plat*, 'flat'. In some instances it could also have denoted someone who lived in a region of flat land.

Platters, The The black American pop group, formed as a 'doo-wop' vocal quartet in Los Angeles in 1953, took as their name the colloquial word for 'gramophone records'.

Player The name was originally occupational to describe an actor, musician or sportsman. It is thus coincidentally appropriate for Gary *Player*, the South African golfer.

Players The familiar brand of cigarettes takes its name from John *Player* (1839–1884), a Nottingham shopkeeper who added tobacco to his wares in the 1860s and who in 1877 bought a local tobacco manufactory so that he could make and sell blends of his own. He died of lung cancer, aged 45.

Plaza The common theatre and cinema name derives from Spanish *plaza*, as a word for a public square or *place* where people gather for entertainment.

Pleiades In Greek mythology, the name is that of the seven daughters of Atlas, who were placed in the sky as stars to save them from being pursued by Orion. Whether sisters or stars, the name has been derived from that of *Pleione*, the mother of the seven, as well as related to *plein*, 'to sail', since the rising of the stars indicated a safe time for navigation by sea. Astronomically, the *Pleiades* are a star cluster in the constellation Taurus.

Plessey The telecommunications and electronics company, founded in 1917, takes its name from the middle name, *Plessey*, of a Mr Parker who was one of the firm's original shareholders. It also happened to be the name of the small hamlet of *Plessey* near Morpeth, Northumberland, that was the birthplace of the company founder's wife.

Pleven The town in northern Bulgaria takes its name from the small river *Pleva* on which it stands. The river's name derives from a Slavic root word meaning 'to swim', 'to float', indirectly related to English *flow*.

Pliny There were two famous Roman writers of the name, uncle and nephew, re-

spectively *Pliny* the Elder, who lived in the 1st century AD, and *Pliny* the Younger, who was born in the 1st century but died in the 2nd. The full name of the former was Gaius *Plinius* Secundus, and of the latter, who was adopted by his uncle, Gaius *Plinius* Caecilius Secundus. Pliny the Elder thus passed his own *nomen* or clan name to Pliny the Younger. The name itself has been related to Greek *plinthos*, 'brick', although the original sense of this is obscure.

Ploërmel The town in Brittany, northwest France, has a name meaning '*Armel*'s parish', from Breton *plo*, 'parish' and the name of the 6th-century saint *Armel* to whom the town's parish church is dedicated. There are a number of places in Brittany with names beginning *Ple-*, *Plo-*, *Plou-* and the like. In each case this means 'parish' and is followed by a descriptive word or saint's name. Examples are *Pleubian* ('little parish'), *Pleumeur Bodou* ('big parish of the bushes'), *Pleyben* ('parish of the headland'), *Plougastel-Daoulas* ('parish of the castle of Douglas'). The Breton word is itself related to Latin *plebs*, 'people'.

Ploeşti The city in southeast Romania has a name based on the personal name *Ploaie*, itself identical to the Romanian word for 'rain'.

Plough, The The group of seven bright stars in the constellation Ursa Major is popularly so named because the stars suggest the outline of a *plough*.

Plough Monday In the Christian calendar, the name is that of the first Monday after the Epiphany (6 January), regarded as the start of the ploughing season. Prayers were formerly said in churches for a favourable ploughing, and (especially in the north and east of England) the day was marked by a procession of men and boys drawing ploughs from house to house.

Plovdiv The name of the city in southern Bulgaria is of Thracian origin, and represents *Pulpudava*, 'Philip's town', from *Pulp*, 'Philip' and *dava*, 'town'. This refers to its founder in the 4th century BC, *Philip* II, king of Macedonia. The Greeks later translated the Thracian name as *Philippopolis*. The Romans, however, called the settlement *Trimontium*, 'three hills'.

Plowman The name is occupational, but was more likely to refer to a plough*wright*, who actually made the ploughs, than to a plough*man*.

Plummer The name has three possible origins. It could refer to someone who lived by a plum-tree, to someone who dealt in feathers (from Old French *plume*), or to an actual *plumber*, meaning a person who made lead pipes (rather than repairing them, as now).

Plutarch The noted Greek biographer and philosopher, who lived in the 1st century BC, had a name meaning 'chief in riches', from *ploutos*, 'wealth', 'riches' and *arkhōn*, 'chief'.

Pluto The Greek god of the underworld has a name representing *ploutos*, 'wealth', 'riches'. The meaning is traditionally explained as referring to corn, which was the 'wealth' of the earth, sent from under the ground. But there are other more tangible 'riches' under the earth, too, such as the precious metals gold and silver, and Pluto's name must also have related to these.

Pluto The farthest known planet in the solar system, discovered in 1930, was so named for three main reasons. First, it matched the classical names of the other planets, with PLUTO, the god of the underworld, being the brother of Poseidon and Zeus, otherwise *Neptune* and *Jupiter*, whose names already existed as planets. Second, as the name of the god of the underworld, it was appropriate for the planet that was, as far as was known, the outermost, and so the most remote and in 'eternal night'. Third, the first two letters of the name represented the initials of the discoverer of the planet, the American astronomer Percival *L*owell. The name was actually chosen for the planet by an 11-year-old Oxford schoolgirl, Venetia Burney.

Plymouth The famous Devon city and port has a name that means 'place at the *mouth* of the river *Plym*'. The river derived its own name from *Plympton*, now an eastern district of Plymouth, although this is not actually on it. The river must therefore have had an earlier name. This was *Sutton*, 'southern village', from the settlement here in which the manor was held by the priory

of Plympton. (The old river name is preserved in that of *Sutton* Pool, one of Plymouth's three main harbours.) Plympton's own name means 'plum-tree village', and it probably gave the river name because the river itself formed the western boundaries of the parishes of Plympton and its southern neighbour of *Plymstock* ('outlying district of *Plympton*'). It was thus assumed that they were both named after it.

Plymouth Argyle The Plymouth football club was formed in 1886 as *Argyle* Athletic Club, apparently taking this name since members met at a house in *Argyle* Terrace, Mutley, now a northern district of Plymouth. They had no regular home ground until 1901, when they settled at Home Park, built originally for the Devonport Rugby Club. They adopted their present name in 1903 on turning professional.

Plymouth Brethren The fundamentalist religious sect was founded in Dublin in about 1827 but takes its name from PLYMOUTH, Devon, where in 1831 an assembly was held to celebrate its arrival in England.

Plymouth Rock The heavy breed of American domestic fowl takes its name from its place of origin, *Plymouth Rock*, Massachusetts, itself so named from the boulder here regarded as the landing place of the Pilgrim Fathers on their arrival from PLYMOUTH, Devon, in 1620.

Po The river in northern Italy has a name of Romano-Gaulish origin, representing *padi*, 'pines'. Pine forests were at one time abundant in the region of the river's mouth. *Cp.* PADUA.

Poco The American country-rock band, formed in Los Angeles in 1968, originally adopted the name *Pogo*, after the comic strip. The creator of the strip objected, however, so they modified the name to *Poco*, a musical term in its own right.

Podolsk The Russian city near Moscow has a name that reflects the geographical term *podol*, describing a low-lying stretch of land by a river (from *po*, 'along' and *dol*, 'valley'). Podolsk began as a village on the lower left bank of the river Pakhra before later expanding to be a town on the higher right bank. The region known as *Podolia* in western Ukraine has a name of identical origin, referring to its location on the left bank of the middle Dniester.

Pogues, The The anarchic Anglo-Irish folk-rock band, formed in 1983, had the original name *Pogue Mahone*, representing Irish *póg mo thón*, 'kiss my arse'. The BBC banned the daytime transmission of their debut single in 1984 on discovering the meaning of the name, and when that same year the record company Stiff Records offered to sign them up, they insisted the name be shortened, and so censored, to *Pogues*.

Poissy The town in northern France, west of Paris, had the Roman name of *Pinciacum*. This derives from the Latin personal name *Pincius*, with the place-name suffix *-acum*. The origin of the personal name is uncertain.

Poitiers The city in south central France takes its name from the *Pictones*, the Gaulish people who inhabited the region in historic times. Their own name is probably related to that of the PICTS. The former Roman name of the settlement was *Lemonum* or *Limonum*, from Gaulish *lemo*, 'elm'. Poitiers was the capital of POITOU.

Poitou The former province of west central France has a name of the same origin as that of its capital, POITIERS, so derives from that of the Gaulish people known as the *Pictones*.

Poland The republic of central Europe takes its name from its native people, the *Poles*, whose own name represents Polish *pole*, 'field', 'plain', as they are primarily plain-dwellers. Between the natural borders of the Baltic Sea to the north and the Sudeten and Carpathian Mountains to the south, Poland is almost entirely a lowland country, with numerous lakes and rivers. The name for Poland in some non-Indoeuropean languages is different, such as Turkish *Lehistan* and Hungarian *Lengyelország*. These derive from the personal name *Lech*, that of the legendary founder of the Polish people (and, in modern times, that also of the President of Poland from 1990, *Lech* Walesa).

Polaris The name of the Pole Star derives from Medieval Latin *stella polaris*, 'polar star'. The Pole Star itself is so called since it is slightly less than 1° from the north celestial pole. The name *Polaris* was adopted by the US Navy for a type of guided missile developed in the 1950s to be launched by submerged submarines. It was so called because it could be carried by submarines based in the Arctic *polar* regions, from where it could be launched against Russia.

Polaroid The proprietary make of 'instant' camera is named after its manufacturing company, who pioneered a method of *polarizing* a transmitted beam of light by using special thin sheets composed of long parallel molecules.

Polesden Lacey The Regency house near Dorking in Surrey takes its name from that of the earlier settlement here. The meaning is '*Pāl*'s valley', with the Anglo-Saxon personal name followed by Old English *denu*, 'valley'. It is not certain who *Lacey* was. The name looks like that of the Norman lord of the manor (*cp*. KINGSTON LACY), but it is first recorded late (only in the 16th century) and it may be a spurious addition. The name is mirrored in that of *Camilla Lacey*, a nearby country house. (*See* CAMILLA for its origin.)

Police, The The British pop trio was formed in 1977 in London by two English musicians (Sting, real name Gordon Sumner, and Andy Summers) and an American living in England (Stewart Copeland). The three aimed to make music in a modified punk style, and wanted a name that matched their mood. It was created by Copeland, who intended it as an ironic comment on his father, a important official in the CIA.

Polish Symphony Tchaikovsky's Symphony No 3 in D major, Op 29 (1875) is so nicknamed because the finale is in the rhythm of a polonaise (a Polish dance).

Pollard The name arose as a nickname for someone with a large or unusually shaped head, from *poll* in its original sense of 'head'.

Pollux The name of the famous twin brother of CASTOR in Greek mythology is the Latin form of his Greek name, POLYDEUCES.

Polly The name is a variant form of MOLLY, with *M* becoming *P* as for PEGGY from MARGARET. *Polly* has long been a traditional name for a parrot, perhaps because of the similarity between the personal name and that of the bird, or because the typical utterance of a parrot suggests the sound of the name. (The standard name of many birds comes from their cry or call, such as *crow, cuckoo, finch, owl, peewit, quail, rook, shrike*, although none of these has given a first name.)

Polly Peck The international company, familiar for its marketing of fruit and other agricultural products, took its name from the mispronunciation of *Polytechnic* by the young daughter of the firm's founder, Raymond Zelkar. The original business was in premises next door to the Regent Street Polytechnic, London. *Cp.* the name LUNN POLY.

Polperro The Cornish coastal resort near Looe has a name based on Cornish *porth*, 'harbour'. The second half of the name is probably a personal name such as *Pyre*, although its precise origin is uncertain.

Poltava The town in central Ukraine has a name based on that of a river here. The river's own name appears to mean 'along the Ltava', from Slavonic *po*, 'along' and *Ltava*, the earlier name of the river, perhaps based on the Indoeuropean element *ap*, 'water', 'river'. Poltava itself is on the river Vorskla.

Polydeuces The Greek name of POLLUX, twin brother of CASTOR in Greek mythology, appears to mean 'much sweetness', from Greek *polus*, 'much' and *deukos*, the latter word being a variant of *gleukos*, 'must', 'sweet new wine', in turn from *glukus*, 'sweet'.

Polynesia The group of Pacific islands has a name of Greek origin, meaning 'many islands', from *polus*, 'many' and *nēsos*, 'island'. The name is similar to those of the neighbouring island groups of MELANESIA and *Micronesia*. It is the oldest of the three, however, and was invented for the archipelago by the French historian and archaeologist Charles de Brosses, who introduced it in his *Histoire des navigations aux terres australes* (1756), setting out the different regions of Australasia and Polynesia.

Poly-Olbion The vast poem by Michael Drayton, published in 1612 and 1622 as a 'Chorographical Description' of England and Wales, has a name that ostensibly means 'much blessed', from the Greek prefix *poly-*, 'many', 'much' and *olbios*, 'happy', 'blessed'. However, the second half of the name may equally have been intended to suggest ALBION as a name for England or Britain.

Polyphemus The name of the cyclops who imprisoned Odysseus and his companions in his cave in Greek mythology means 'many rumours', from Greek *polus*, 'many' and *phēmē*, 'rumour', 'report'. In other words he was *famous* (in the sense 'notorious').

Pomerania The region of north central Europe, bordering on the Baltic, takes its name from Polish *pomorze*, 'coastland', literally 'l ' by the sea', from *po*, 'by', 'along' and *morze*, 'sea'. *See also* POMERANIAN.

Pomeranian The breed of toy dog takes its name from POMERANIA, where it is said to have been bred down from a large sheepdog to its present small size in the early 19th century.

Pomp and Circumstance The title of Elgar's set of five marches for orchestra, Op 39, first performed between 1901 and 1930, alludes to their royal and patriotic nature and is a quotation from Shakespeare: 'Pride, pomp, and circumstance of glorious war!' (*Othello*, III. iii). March No 1 contains the popular melody of 'Land of Hope and Glory'.

Pompeii The ancient city in Italy, famous for being buried but preserved in the eruption of Vesuvius in AD 79, has a name that probably derives from Oscan *pompe*, 'five', referring to its five districts. *See also* POMPEY.

Pompey The noted Roman general of the 1st century BC had the full name Gnaeius *Pompeius* Magnus. *Pompey* was thus his *nomen* or clan name. It probably originated from a dialect word meaning 'five', so had the same sense as modern English QUINTIN. *Cp.* POMPEII.

Pondicherry The territory of southeast India takes its name from its identically named port. This is of Tamil origin meaning 'new town', from *putu*, 'new' and *čēri*, 'village', 'town'.

Ponsonby The name derives from that of the village so called near Gosforth in Cumbria. The place-name means '*Puncun*'s settlement'.

Pontefract The West Yorkshire town, near Leeds, has a name meaning 'broken bridge', from Latin *ponte fracto*, the ablative ('locative') form of *pontus fractus*. It is surprising that the name has survived in this original form, and has not been 'smoothed' under Norman influence to *Pumfret*, as the name of the famous *Pontefract* cakes has. It is thought that the original 'broken bridge' was over a small stream here known as the Wash Dike at the point where Bubwith Bridge is today, near the present A645 road. The stream is small, but the bridge over it would have been important, giving access to the Great North Road. It is not known exactly when or under what circumstances the bridge was broken. The earliest record of the name dates from the 11th century.

Pontevedra The port in northwest Spain had the Medieval Latin name of *Pons vetus*, meaning 'old bridge'. The city has retained its ancient Roman bridge.

Pontiac The make of American car takes its name from its manufacturing company, who produced their first car, the *Oakland*, in *Pontiac*, Michigan, in 1907. The name of the city itself, adopted by the company as their trading name, came from the chief of the Ottawa Indians who led an unsuccessful rebellion against the British in the 1760s.

Pontius Pilate The 1st-century AD Roman procurator who reluctantly ordered the crucifixion of Jesus had the Latin name *Pontius Pilatus*. He belonged to a Samnite *gens* (clan) of the *Pontii*. Hence his first name. His second name is a *cognomen* or nickname. It represents Latin *pilatus*, 'armed with a javelin', from *pilum*, 'javelin', implying a regular soldier. The mountain of *Pilatus* in central Switzerland is so named from a legend that the body of Pontius Pilate lay in a former lake on it.

Pontivy The town in Brittany, northwest France, derives its name from Breton *pont*, 'bridge' and *Ivy*, the name of a local saint who founded a monastery here in the 7th century. In 1805 Napoleon built a new town to the south of the medieval town centre, so that the whole town was renamed *Napoléonville* until 1814 and again, for his nephew, Napoleon III, from 1848 to 1871.

Pont-L'Évêque The town in northern France, south of Deauville, has a name meaning 'bishop's bridge'. The name (originally Latin *Pons Episcopi*) has been recorded since the 9th century, and refers to the right of the bishop of Lisieux to collect tolls from those passing over a bridge here. The name has passed to that of a famous local cheese.

Pont Neuf The oldest bridge of Paris, over the Seine, has a name that means 'new bridge', an accurate description at the time it was built, from 1578 to 1604. For similar historic 'new' names, *cp.* NEW COLLEGE, NEW FOREST.

Pontoise The town in northern France has a name meaning 'bridge on the OISE', from its location on this river. The original bridge here dates back to at least the 4th century AD.

Pontus The ancient region of northeast Asia Minor lay by the Black Sea, as its name indicates, from Greek *pontos*, 'sea'.

Pontypool The town in South Wales near Newport has a half-Welsh, half-English name meaning 'bridge by the pool', from Welsh *pont*, 'bridge' and English *pool*. The 'pool' was probably a stretch of the river Llwyd on which the town stands.

Pontypridd The South Wales town at the confluence of the rivers Rhondda and Taff has a name that represents its original Welsh name of *Pont y Tŷ Pridd*, from *pont*, 'bridge', *y*, 'the', *tŷ*, 'house' and *pridd*, 'earth'. There must therefore have been a 'bridge by the earthen house' over the river here at some time. The word for 'house' disappeared from the name, since the two letters that comprise it were already present in the initial *pont y*, and were thus felt to be unnecessarily repeated.

Poole The Dorset town and port has a straightforward name that means what it says, referring to the 'pool' or harbour here.

Pope The name developed as a nickname for someone who resembled or behaved like the *pope* or any other high-ranking church official, or in some cases for a person who had played the part of the pope in a medieval play or pageant.

Poplar The district of east London has a name meaning what it says, referring to one or more distinctive poplar trees formerly here. The name is recorded in a document of 1327 (as *Popler*, predating the earliest record of the tree name in the *Oxford English Dictionary*, which is dated 1382).

Popocatépetl The Mexican volcano has a name of Indian (Nahuatl) origin meaning 'smoking mountain', from *popokani*, 'to smoke' and *tepetl*, 'mountain'.

Porsche The prestigious make of car takes its name from Ferdinand *Porsche* (1875–1951), an Austrian motor engineering consultant based in Stuttgart. His son Ferdinand ('Ferry') Porsche worked with him and in 1947 built the first *Porsche* cars at Gmünd, near Stuttgart.

Portadown The town in Co Armagh, Northern Ireland has a name representing Irish *Port an Dúnáin*, 'landing place of the little fort', from *port*, 'landing place' and *dúnán*, the diminutive of *dún*, 'fort'. The 'little fort' would have guarded a strategic crossing over the river Bann here.

Port Arthur The town and port in northeast China, now usually known as LÜSHUN, was founded as a British naval base in 1857 during the Anglo-French war against China. It was named for Lieutenant *Arthur*, the English naval officer who reconnoitred the site when under the command of Rear-Admiral Sir Michael Seymour.

Port-au-Prince The capital of Haiti is probably named after a ship called the *Prince* that had taken shelter in the bay here some time in the early 18th century. It is not certain whether the ship was French or English.

Port Elizabeth The South African port, in Cape Province, was so named in 1820 by the acting governor of the Cape, Sir Rufane Donkin, for his wife *Elizabeth* who had died two years previously.

Porter The name was originally an occupational one, denoting either a gatekeeper or doorkeeper (*cp.* modern French *porte*), or who carried loads for his living, like a modern *porter*.

Port Harcourt The port in southern Nigeria was founded in 1912 and named for the then British colonial secretary, Lewis *Harcourt*, first Viscount Harcourt (1863–1922).

Portia Famous from the rich heiress in love with Bassanio in Shakespeare's *The Merchant of Venice* (1596) and from the wife of Brutus in his *Julius Caesar* (1599), the name *Portia* originated as a feminine form of the Roman *nomen* (clan name) *Porcius*, apparently derived from Latin *porcus*, 'pig'. The wife of the historical Brutus on whom Shakespeare's character was based was actually named *Porcia*. No doubt Shakespeare preferred a name that suggested *portion* rather than *pork*!

Portland There are several American towns and ports of the name, which is itself self-descriptive for a port while also being adopted from the English *Portland* in Dorset, with its broad harbour between the Isle of Portland and Weymouth. The port in Maine was settled by the English in 1632, and the inland port in Oregon, which arose later, is named for it.

Port Louis The capital and chief port of Mauritius was founded in about 1736 by the French and named for *Louis* XV of France.

Port Moresby The capital of Papua New Guinea had its harbour explored in 1873 by Captain John Moresby, who named it for his father, Admiral Sir Fairfax *Moresby* (1786–1877).

Pôrto Alegre The port in southern Brazil, the chief port of the country as a whole, has a Portuguese name meaning 'joyful port', from *porto*, 'port' (*cp.* OPORTO) and *alegre*, 'joyful', 'cheerful'. The town was founded in 1742 by about 60 married couples from the Azores, and was originally known as *Pôrto dos Casais*, 'port of the couples'.

Portobello The small port in Panama, Central America, was founded in 1597 by the Spanish and took the name of the bay here, itself named in 1502 by Columbus as 'beautiful harbour'. It had considerable strategic and commercial importance, and was attacked many times by British buccaneers. As a result, its name was transferred to places in Britain. One of the best known is the *Portobello* that is now a district of Edinburgh, Scotland, on the Firth of Forth. This took its name from a house called *Portobello Hut* here in the mid-18th century, itself said to have been so named by a sailor who had been present at the capture of the Panamanian port in 1739. The name happens to be appropriate for the Scottish resort, with its extensive sands and coastal attractions.

Port of Spain The name of the capital of Trinidad is an English translation of the original name *Puerto de España*. This was given by the Spanish colonists to their new capital in 1595 after their old one had been destroyed.

Porto Novo The capital of Benin, West Africa, has a Portuguese name meaning 'new port', given when the settlement was founded in the 15th century.

Portora Royal School The public school in Enniskillen, Northern Ireland, was founded by James I in 1608 and was originally at Ballybalfour, not far from Enniskillen. In 1641 the school moved to Enniskillen itself, and made a further move in 1777 to new buildings on *Portora* Hill. The school is *Royal* because of its foundation. For many years it was in the hands of the king and the viceroy of Ireland, but since 1890 has been managed and governed under the provisions of the Irish Educational Endowments Act of 1885 and its subsequent amendments.

Port Said The city and port in northeast Egypt was founded in 1859 when the Suez Canal was begun. It was named in honour of the viceroy of Egypt, *Said* Pasha (1822–1863), who had granted a concession to the French diplomat de Lesseps for the construction of the canal. The Arabic name *Sa'īd* means 'happy', 'lucky'.

Portsmouth The well-known port and naval base in Hampshire has a name that refers to its own harbour, so means 'place at the mouth of the port'. The name thus differs from many south coast *-mouth* names,

which are usually based on the name of a river (such as BOURNEMOUTH on the Bourne, FALMOUTH on the Fal, WEYMOUTH on the Wey, and so on). The port of *Portsmouth*, Virginia, was founded in 1752 and named after the English port. It is actually a *port* at the *mouth* of the Elizabeth River, and most other American places of the name are similarly situated at river-mouths.

Port Talbot The Welsh town and port near Swansea takes its name from the *Talbot* family of nearby Margam Abbey, who inherited the abbey and the surrounding land in the mid-18th century and who sponsored the development of Port Talbot itself when docks were built here in 1836.

Portugal The republic of southwest Europe, on the Atlantic seaboard west of Spain, has a name deriving from Latin *Portus cale*, 'warm harbour', the Roman name of OPORTO. The name thus spread from the port to the whole territory. It originally referred to the fact that the harbour at Oporto was always free of ice.

Port Vale The Stoke-on-Trent football club take their name from that of the house in Longport, Burslem, in which they were formed in 1876, originally as *Burslem Port Vale*, with a ground at Limekiln Lane, Longport. (The *Vale* is the valley of Fowlea Brook here.) When the club moved to a new ground in Hanley in 1913 they dropped the initial *Burslem* from their name.

Port-Vendres The coastal town and resort near the border with Spain in southeast France derives its name from its Roman name of *Portus Veneris*, 'port of Venus'.

Poseidon The name of the Greek god of the sea is now regarded as developing from the original Doric form *Poteidan*. This means 'lord of waters' and represents *poeti*, 'lord' in the vocative case, and the adjective *daon*, 'watery', also in the vocative, itself from the Indoeuropean root element *da* or *danu* found in river names such as the DON, DNIEPER and DANUBE. In saying the name one is thus saying 'O lord of water', addressing the god who not only rules over the sea but provides the moisture necessary for fertility on land.

Post Toasties The American brand of breakfast cereal takes its name from Charles William *Post*, who first produced it in 1904. A few years earlier he had invented GRAPE NUTS.

Potiphar In the Old Testament, the name is that of the official of Pharaoh who bought Joseph as a slave. It is of Egyptian origin, and is a form of *Potiphera*, meaning 'he whom RA has given', after the Egyptian sun god.

Potomac The river of east central America was first recorded in 1608 by the English explorer John Smith as *Patawomeck*, which he took to be the name of an Indian tribe. It was later established that the name in fact means 'where goods are brought in', referring to a stretch of riverside land where Indians had set up a trading post.

Potsdam The city in east central Germany has a name that is of Slavic origin meaning 'under the oaks', from *pod*, 'under' and *dombimi*, the instrumental plural case of *domb*, 'oak'. Cp. DUBROVNIK. The town of *Potsdam* in New York State was founded in 1803 and was so called from its reddish sandstone deposits, which are similar to those of its German namesake.

Potter The name does not quite have today's sense, but originally denoted a person who made *pots*, that is, vessels for drinking and storage. Moreover, such pots could be made of metal, not simply clay.

Potters Bar The town north of London probably took its name from a man named *Potter* who kept a gate or 'bar' here in medieval times, the latter leading into Enfield Chase.

Potts The name means 'son of *Pott*', this being a short form of PHILPOTT.

Powell The name is usually of Welsh origin, meaning 'son of *Howell*', with the initial *P*-representing *ap*, denoting 'son'. If of English origin, the name is simply a variant of PAUL.

Powys The present county of central Wales was formed in 1974 and took the name of a former kingdom here. Its own name means 'provincial', and evolved from Latin *pagensis*, the adjectival form of *pagus*, 'province', 'district' (the word that gave English *pagan*). The implication is that the people who lived here were 'country folk', inhabiting open and unprotected land, unlike those who lived in regions to the north and south, where hills and valleys provided shelter.

Poznań The city in western Poland had the Medieval Latin name of *Poznani civitas*, deriving from the personal name of the original landowner here, itself apparently based on *pan*, 'lord'.

Pozzuoli The port in southwest Italy was founded by the Greeks in the 6th century BC and was known to the Romans as *Puteoli*, as which it is mentioned in the Bible (*Acts* 28.13). The name derives from either Latin *puteus*, 'pit' (French *puits*, 'well') or *putere*, 'to stink' (English *putrid*), or even a blend of both, referring to the unpleasant smell from the sulphur springs here.

Prado The famous art gallery in Madrid takes its name from Spanish *prado*, 'meadow', the parkland site where the gallery was built in the late 18th century.

Prague The Czech capital has a name that is usually interpreted as 'threshold', from a Slavic word related to Russian *porog* in this sense. But although the origin is almost certainly Slavic, it is likely to be not in this word but in one related to modern Czech *pražiti*, a term for woodland cleared by burning.

Prague Symphony Mozart's Symphony No 38 in D major, K 504 (1786) is so nicknamed because it was first performed during the composer's visit to *Prague* in 1787.

Praia The capital of Cabo Verde (Cape Verde), the island republic off the west coast of Africa, has a Portuguese name meaning simply 'beach', 'shore' (related to French *plage*).

Prairial The ninth month of the French Revolutionary calendar, corresponding to the period from 21 May to 19 June, was named 'meadow month', from French *prairie*, 'meadow'.

Prajapati The god who is the creator of all things in Hindu mythology has a name of Sanskrit origin meaning 'lord of posterity', from *prajā*, 'creature' and *pati*, 'lord'.

Prakrit The name is that of any of the vernacular Indic languages that are distinguished from SANSKRIT. It represents Sanskrit *prākrta*, 'original', literally 'done before', from *pra-*, 'before', *kr*, 'to do' and *-ta* denoting a participle.

Pratt The name arose as a nickname for a clever or cunning person from Old English *prætt*, 'trick'. (This is not the same as the modern *prat*, the colloquial term for a stupid person, which derives from the identical word meaning 'buttocks'.)

Pratt's Club The London club was founded in 1841 by William Nathaniel *Pratt*, steward to the seventh Duke of Beaufort and a former croupier at Crockford's.

Praxiteles The famous Greek sculptor, who lived in the 4th century BC, has a name meaning appropriately 'done perfectly', 'fully completed', from Greek *praxis*, 'doing', 'action' and *telos*, 'end', 'completion'.

Prefab Sprout The British new wave pop group, formed in Consett, Co Durham, in 1982 by Newcastle University student Paddy McAloon, adopted a name that McAloon had been wanting to use since he first came across it in 1973. It was actually a mishearing of the phrase 'pepper sprout' in Nancy Sinatra's country and western version of the song 'Jackson' (1967).

Premonstratensian The name is that of the religious sect founded in the 12th century by St Norbert at what is now the town of *Prémontré* in northern France. The town's own name represents its Medieval Latin name of *Praemonstratum*. This in turn probably evolved either from *pratum monstratum*, literally 'shown meadow', referring to the site said to have been pointed out by St Norbert, or perhaps more likely from *pratum monasterium*, 'monastery meadow'. On the other hand, it could equally represent *praemonstratum*, 'foreshown (place)', with St Norbert prophesying where the site would be, rather than pointing it out.

Prendergast The name is of uncertain origin, perhaps deriving from some Flemish place-name. An original *Brontegeest* has been proposed, but no place of this name is known today.

Prentice The name was originally used for an *apprentice*, a person learning a trade or craft. In this sense it was more a nickname than an occupational one.

Pre-Raphaelite The painters such as Rossetti, Holman Hunt and Millais who formed the *Pre-Raphaelite* Brotherhood in 1848 had the aim of reviving the fidelity to nature and vivid colouring that they regarded as typical of Italian painters before *Raphael*, that is, of the period before the High Renaissance in art typified by the works of Leonardo da Vinci, Michelangelo and Raphael in the 15th and 16th centuries.

Presbyterian The various Protestant churches of this name are so called because they are governed by *presbyters*, that is, lay elders, who correspond to the ordained clergy of many other churches. The word itself derives from Greek *presbuteros*, literally 'older man', from *presbus*, 'old man'.

Prestatyn The North Wales coastal resort, east of Rhyl, is near enough to England to have an English name, although the original has been altered under Welsh influence. It means 'priests' village', from Old English *prēosta-tūn*. In other words, it is exactly the same as PRESTON. But the expected *-ton* has become *-tyn*, and the stress has passed from the first syllable to the second, as is common in Welsh names (for example *Llanelli*, *Machynlleth*).

Prestel The viewdata service operated by BT (formerly British Telecom), introduced in 1978, has a name that is probably a blend of *press* (for the push-button telephone used) and '*tele*phone', at the same time suggesting *presto* for rapid information.

Prester John The legendary Christian priest and king, identified in the 14th century with the king of Ethiopia, has a name that means 'priest John', from Medieval Latin *presbyter Ioannes*.

Preston The Lancashire town near Manchester has a name found elsewhere in the country meaning 'priests' village', from Old English *prēosta-tūn*. The name does not necessarily imply that several priests lived here, but that the place was an endowment for priests who served a church somewhere else. *Cp.* PRESTATYN and PRESTONPANS.

Prestonpans The Scottish town near Musselburgh has a name meaning 'salt pans by the priests' village', with the first part of the name as for PRESTON. The priests here were those at Newbattle Abbey, who laid out salt pans by the Firth of Forth in the early 13th century.

Prestwich The name of the town near Manchester means 'priests' outlying farm', from Old English *prēosta*, 'priest' and *wīc*, 'farm', 'special place'. The farm was probably an endowment to support a religious house somewhere else, as for PRESTON. *Cp.* PRESTWICK.

Prestwick The Scottish town and port on the Firth of Clyde, with its well-known airport, has a name that is exactly the same as that of PRESTWICH in England, so like it means 'priests' outlying farm'.

Pretenders, The The British new wave rock group was formed in London in 1978 by American-born singer and guitarist Chrissie Hynde, who gave it a name that she based on The Platters' hit 'The Great Pretender' (1956).

Pretoria The administrative capital of South Africa and capital of Transvaal was founded in 1855 and takes its name from the Voortrekker leader Andries *Pretorius* (1798–1853).

Pretty As a nickname, the name was originally used not just of a handsome person, but for someone who was regarded as generally excellent.

Pretty Polly The well-known make of hosiery owes its name to a Staffordshire knitwear firm taken over in 1926 by the original manufacturers, who had set up a contract knitting business in Sutton-in-Ashfield, Nottinghamshire, in 1919. The acquired firm was itself named for the famous racehorse *Pretty Polly*, winner of several important races in the early years of the 20th century.

Pretty Things, The The British rhythm 'n' blues band, formed at Sidcup, Kent, in 1963, adopted their name from the Bo Diddley hit 'Pretty Thing' (1963).

Priam The last king of Troy in Greek mythology has a name that is almost certainly pre-Greek in origin but that has been popularly interpreted as 'chief', 'leader', from *prin*, 'before', corresponding to Latin *prius*.

Priapus The god of procreative powers in Greek mythology has a name of obscure origin. It is probably pre-Greek, but attempts have been made to link it with *priō*, 'I saw', 'I sever', referring to the pruning of fruit trees as one of his 'procreative' gardening activities.

Price The familiar name could be either Welsh or English in origin. If Welsh, it meant 'son of RHYS', with the initial *P*- standing for *ap*, denoting 'son'. As an English name, it probably meant what it implies, and was a nickname for someone regarded as being *precious* or valuable.

Priest The name originally denoted a person employed by a priest, or who was perhaps the (illegitimate) son of a priest. *Cp.* PRIESTLEY.

Priestley The name does not mean quite what it seems, but originally denoted a person from a place of this name, such as what is now *Priestley* Green near Halifax in Yorkshire. The place-name itself means 'priests' wood' or 'priests' clearing', that is, one that belonged to the church.

Primrose Day The day, 19 April, is that of the death of Benjamin Disraeli, Earl of Beaconsfield, in 1881. Two years later the *Primrose League* was formed in his memory as an association that aimed to promote the principles of Conservatism that he represented. It was named for what was said to be Disraeli's favourite flower, and the day is still observed by some in commemoration of one of Britain's best-known prime ministers.

Primrose Hill The district of north London has a self-explanatory name, referring to a hill where primroses grew. The name was first recorded in a song title of 1586: '*A Sweete and Courtly Songe of the Flowers that grow on Prymrose Hyll*'.

Prince The name arose as a nickname for a person who behaved in a princely or 'regal' manner, or who had perhaps been awarded the title *prince* in some contest.

Prince Edward Island The Canadian island province, in the Gulf of St Lawrence, was discovered by the French in 1534 and originally named *Île Saint-Jean*, 'St John's island'. This name continued in use (in its English form from 1763) until 1799, when the island was renamed in honour of *Prince Edward* Augustus (1767–1820), Duke of Kent, the fourth son of George III and future father of Queen Victoria.

Prince of Wales Island The island in northern Canada, in the Northwest Territories, was discovered in 1851 and named for the ten-year-old *Prince of Wales*, the future king Edward VII.

Prince of Wales Theatre The London theatre, in Coventry Street, opened in 1884 as the *Prince's Theatre*. This was a name transferred by its owner, the actor-manager Edgar Bruce, from that of the *Prince of Wales Theatre*, in Tottenham Street, which he had also owned and which had closed two years earlier. In 1886 the new theatre adopted the full name of the previous one, itself given in honour of Albert Edward, *Prince of Wales* (1841–1910), the future king Edward VII.

Princes Risborough The Buckinghamshire town has a basic name meaning 'brushwood hill', from Old English *hrīs*, 'brushwood' and *beorg*, 'hill'. The first word of the name relates to the Black Prince, no less, the eldest son of Edward III, who held the tenure of the place in the 14th century. The royal prefix was added to distinguish this Risborough from *Monks Risborough*, which lies immediately to the north, and which belonged to the monks at Canterbury.

Princess Astrid Coast The section of East Antarctica, a Norwegian dependency, was named for *Princess Astrid* (1905–1935), daughter of Prince Charles, brother of the king of Sweden, who married Prince Leopold of Belgium in 1926 and became Queen of the Belgians in 1934 when he was crowned king as Leopold III.

Princess Helena College The public school for girls near Hitchin, Hertfordshire, was founded in 1820. Its aim was to educate future governesses, taking as pupils the daughters of deceased Anglican clergymen and of officers who had lost their lives in the Napoleonic Wars. The school had royal support from the first, initially in the person of Princess Augusta, daughter of George III, then of George IV, who became the school's patron in 1823. *Princess Helena* (1846–1923), third daughter of Queen Victoria, became associated with the school in 1868, and in 1879 it adopted her name in her honour.

Princeton The town in New Jersey, famous for its university, was founded by Quaker settlers in 1696 and originally named *Stony Brook*, after the home of one of them. In 1723 it was renamed *Princeton* in honour of William III, *Prince* of Orange-Nassau. Until 1896 *Princeton University*, founded in 1746, was known as the *College of New Jersey*.

Prior The name originally denoted the servant of a prior (the deputy head of a monastery or abbey), or in some cases arose as a nickname for a person who behaved like this particular ecclesiastic.

Priscilla The name is biblical in origin, and occurs in the New Testament for a woman, the wife of one Aquila, with whom St Paul stayed at Corinth (*Acts* 18.2). It is a feminine diminutive of the Roman clan name *Priscius*, itself from Latin *priscus*, 'ancient' (to which English *pristine* is related).

Priština The city of southern Serbia takes its name from the river here, whose own name probably derives from Serbo-Croat *prišt*, 'ulcer', 'tumour', referring to its 'boiling'.

Pritchard The name is Welsh in origin, meaning 'son of RICHARD', with the initial *P*- representing *ap*, denoting 'son'. *Cp.* similar names such as PARRY and PRICE. The English equivalent is RICHARDS.

Privas The town in southeast France derives its name from that of *Privatus*, 3rd-century bishop and martyr.

Procol Harum The British rock band, formed in Southend, Essex, in the early 1960s, at first performed as the *Paramounts*. In 1967 they adopted their new name, said either to represent Latin *procul harum*, 'far from these things', or to have been the name of someone's cat. But the Latin phrase is dubious, since *procul* is followed by the ablative case, not the genitive!

Procrustes The infamous robber of Greek mythology, who made travellers fit his bed by stretching them or lopping off their limbs, has a name that describes his unpleasant practice, from Greek *prokrouein*, 'to hammer out', 'to stretch out'.

Procter & Gamble The manufacturers of detergents and allied products are named for their founders, William *Procter* and James *Gamble*, who first made candles and soap in Cincinnati, Ohio, in 1837. Procter was the candlemaker, and English in origin. Gamble made soap, and was Irish.

Proctor The name was originally an occupational one for a steward or court official, in particular an attorney in a spiritual (*i.e.* church) court.

Procyon The name of the brightest star in the constellation Canis Minor means literally 'before the dog', from Greek *pro-*, 'before' and *kuōn*, 'dog'. It is so called because it rises just before Sirius, the DOG STAR.

Prometheus The Titan of Greek mythology, who stole fire from Olympus to give to mankind and was punished as a result, has a name representing Greek *promēthēs*, 'cautious'. He was thus 'forethought', providing for what was to come, as distinct from his brother *Epimetheus*, who was 'afterthought', because he made plans only when it was too late.

Promised Land The biblical name refers to Canaan, which was promised by God to Abraham and his descendants as their heritage: 'And the Lord appeared unto Abram, and said, Unto thy seed will I give this land' (*Genesis* 12.7). The original Hebrew text of the Old Testament has no word corresponding to 'promise', and the title itself was taken from the New Testament, as a translation of Greek *gē tēs epaggelias*, 'land of the promise' (*Hebrews* 11.9). The name came to be used among Christians for Heaven, and more generally for any longed-for place where one may find fulfilment and contentment.

Proserpine In mythology, *Proserpine* is the Roman counterpart of PERSEPHONE, the goddess of the underworld. Her name is almost certainly a Latin adaptation of the Greek name, but has gained its own traditional derivation in Latin *proserpere*, 'to creep forth'. This is said to refer to the re-emergence of Proserpine in spring, after the winter, or to the fact that it was she, as goddess of the spring, who made the flowers 'creep forth' then.

Prospero The name occurs in Shakespeare for the Duke of Milan in *The Tempest* (1612), and is an Italian form of the Latin name *Prosperus*, itself from *prosper*, 'favourable'. To modern ears it suggests a sense 'prosperous', but this is not quite the original meaning.

Protestant The term for those members of the Western Church that are separated from the Roman Catholic Church originated in Germany with the followers of Luther who *protested* at the Diet (*i.e.* assembly) of Speyer in 1529 when it reaffirmed the edict of the Diet of Worms (1521). This had condemned Luther and the radical reforms in the Roman Catholic Church which he advocated. The specific source of the word is in the *protest* (in the Latin original, *protestatio*) that six German princes and 14 free cities addressed to the Archduke Ferdinand at the Diet, in which they defended freedom of conscience and the right of minorities.

Prothalamion The title is that of Spenser's poem written in 1596 to celebrate the double betrothal of the daughters of the Earl of Worcester, Lady Katherine and Lady Elizabeth Somerset. The poet glossed the title as 'a spousal verse', basing it on that of his earlier EPITHALAMION. The latter literally means 'upon the bridal chamber', so that *Prothalamion* can be interpreted as 'before the bridal chamber'.

Prothero The name is Welsh in origin, meaning 'son of *Rhydderch*', this being the Welsh name that was frequently anglicized to give RODERICK. The initial *P-* represents Welsh *ap*, denoting 'son'.

Provence The former province of southeast France has a name that means simply 'province'. This apparently unoriginal name came about because it was the first Roman *provincia* to be founded beyond the Alps (in the 2nd century BC). Its actual Roman name was *Gallia Transalpina*, 'Transalpine Gaul'.

Proverbs The book of the Old Testament is so named because it contains the sayings or maxims of various Israelite sages, especially those of Solomon. The name itself comes from the opening words of the book: 'The proverbs of Solomon the son of David, king of Israel' (*Proverbs* 1.1).

Providence The Rhode Island port was founded in 1636 by the English-born American clergyman Roger Williams, who named it for 'God's merciful providence to me in my distress'. Williams had been banned from Plymouth Colony for his unorthodox religious beliefs.

Provins The town in eastern France derives its name from the Latin personal name *Probus*, meaning 'excellent', 'upright'.

Proxima Centauri The name is that of the member of the triple star Alpha *Centauri*, in the constellation CENTAURUS, which is nearest (Latin *proxima*) to the Sun.

Prudence The name was adopted by Puritans in the 17th century from the standard word, denoting a 'virtue' or desirable quality (caution). It was already a (male) personal name, however, as Late Latin *Prudentius*, itself from *prudens*, 'foreseeing', 'circumspect'. In Bunyan's *Pilgrim's Progress* (1678, 1684) Prudence is one of the damsels (together with Discretion, Piety and Charity) who talks with Christian in the Palace Beautiful.

Prunella The name is an Italian-style feminine diminutive of Latin *prunum*, 'plum'. It came to be adopted as a first name only in the 19th century, when it was associated with the flower names that became fashionable then. *Prunella vulgaris* is the Latin botanical name of the plant known more widely as self-heal.

Prussia The former German state, in northern and central Germany, took its name from the *Borussi*, the Slav people who gave the name of the German football club BORUSSIA. The origin of the tribal name is uncertain.

Przemyśl The city in southeast Poland arose in about the 8th century and traditionally derives its name from its founder.

His own name means 'plan', 'stratagem' (literally 'through thought').

Pskov The city in western Russia may derive its name from that of a river, in turn perhaps based on Old Russian *ples*, 'reach', 'stretch of river from one bend to the next'. Pskov is actually on the river Velikaya ('great').

Psyche In Greek mythology, *Psyche* was the beautiful girl loved by Eros (Cupid) who became the personification of the soul. Her name thus directly represents Greek *psukhē*, 'breath', 'soul'.

Psychedelic Furs, The The British new wave pop group, formed in London in 1977, took a name that was suggested by the Velvet Underground hit 'Venus in Furs' (1967). The dated adjective *Psychedelic* lost the group bookings in the early years, and they temporarily shortened the name to *The Furs* in 1982.

Ptah In Egyptian mythology, the name is that of the major creative god whose worship was particularly associated with the city of Memphis. Its origin is uncertain, but its most probable etymology is in a root element meaning 'to sculpture'. *See also* EGYPT.

Ptolemy The famous Greek astronomer and geographer of the 2nd century AD was said to have been born at *Ptolemais* Hermiou, Egypt, so took his name from it. The city name represents that of the Macedonian Greek dynasty which ruled Egypt from the 4rd century BC until the Roman conquest in 30 BC. It derives from *ptolemos*, a form of *polemos*, 'war'.

Puck The name is familiar as that of the mischievous sprite, originally a more sinister and evil spirit, who appears in Shakespeare's *A Midsummer Night's Dream* (1595). Unfortunately his name is of obscure origin. In Old English he was *púca*. He is familiar in Irish as the hobgoblin or sprite known as a *púca*, often rendered in English as *pooka*, which suggests that his name may be Celtic in origin. But the Irish word (also Welsh *bwci*) may have been borrowed from English. In English folklore he is represented also by ROBIN GOODFELLOW.

Puebla The city of southern Mexico was founded in 1532 and named by the Spanish Franciscan Toribio de Motolinía as *Puebla de los Angeles*, 'town of the angels'. Its full name today is *Puebla de Zaragoza*, for General Ignacio *Zaragoza*, who repulsed the French here in 1862.

Puerto Rico The island commonwealth in the Caribbean has a name that is the Spanish for 'rich harbour'. It was given to the bay by Christopher Columbus when he discovered the island in 1493. His name for the island itself was *San Juan*, 'St John', since he had arrived here on Monday 24 June 1493, *St John*'s Day. The bay's name was adopted for the whole island, and the island's name is now that of its capital.

Pugh The Welsh name means 'son of HUGH', with the initial *P-* representing Welsh *ap*, 'son' (itself from *mab*).

Punch The familiar character in the children's puppet show *Punch and Judy* took his name from *Punchinello*, the Neapolitan form of the name of *Pulcinella*, a masked comic actor representing a hook-nosed, humpbacked servant in the Italian *commedia dell'arte* of the 16th to 18th century. The origin of his name is uncertain, although as it stands *pulcinella* is the diminutive of *pulcina*, the feminine of *pulcino*, 'chicken', and it is possible that a form of this word was used for a young turkeycock, whose hooked beak suggested the hooked nose of the character. No doubt the English name *Punch* was associated with the word *punch* as a dialect term for a short, fat person. (Hence the name of the thickset horse known as the Suffolk *punch*.)

Punic Wars The three wars of the 3rd and 1st centuries BC, in which Rome successfully fought Carthage to gain dominance in the Mediterranean, are named from the *Poeni*, the Latin name for the Carthaginians that itself derived from the Greek name *Phoinix*, 'PHOENICIAN'.

Punjab The former province of northwest British India, now a region divided between India and Pakistan, derives its name from Iranian *panjāb*, 'five rivers', from *panj*, 'five' and *āb*, 'water'. The five rivers in question, as tributaries of the Indus, are the Jhelum, Chenab, Ravi, Beas and Sutlej.

Punta Arenas The port in southern Chile, the southernmost city in the world, has a name that is the Spanish for 'sandy point'. The name is found elsewhere in the Spanish-speaking world, often as *Puntarenas*.

Punt e Mes The name of the Italian aperitif means 'point and a half' in the Piedmontese dialect, and is said to derive from the custom of asking customers how many 'points' of vermouth they wished to add to wine when drinking in a bar. The usual amount was one or two, so 'one and a half' was judged to be a 'happy medium'.

Purbeck The *Purbeck* Hills, in Dorset, famous for their limestone quarries, have a name that perhaps means 'bittern's beak', from Old English *pūr*, 'bittern', 'snipe' and a conjectural word *bic*, 'beak'. The reference would not be to the actual birds but to the hills, which cross the Isle of Purbeck in a shape suggesting that of a bittern's long pointed bill. It is curious that only a few miles away is *Portland Bill*, the southern point or 'beaklike' tip of the Isle of Portland.

Purification The name, short for *Purification of the Virgin Mary*, is that of the Christian festival celebrating the presentation of Christ in the temple 'when the days of her purification according to the law of Moses were accomplished' (*Luke* 2.22), that is, when Mary had completed the ritual cleansing that Jewish law required of a woman who had given birth. (A mother was regarded as unclean after bearing a son and was not allowed to touch any holy object for 40 days. She completed her purification by offering a one-year-old lamb and a pigeon or dove in the temple.) The day, popularly known as CANDLEMAS, is observed on 2 February and is now usually named by the other main event it commemorates, the *Presentation of Christ in the Temple*.

Purim The Jewish holiday celebrated on 14 Adar (in February or March) commemorates the deliverance of the Jews from the massacre planned for them by Haman (*Esther* 9). The name represents Hebrew *pūrīm*, the plural of *pūr*, 'lot', referring to the casting of lots by Haman (*Esther* 9.24).

Puritan The name, in its historic sense, applied to those Protestants who in the late 16th and 17th centuries wished to carry the Reformation further by *purifying* the Church of England of what they regarded as 'popish idolatry', that is, of the ceremonies it had inherited from the Roman Catholic Church. The name was originally a nickname of contempt, but later, doubtless through its association with *pure* and *purity*, became a name of approbation and even pride.

Purley The former Surrey town, now in Greater London, has a name meaning 'pear-tree wood', from Old English *pyrige*, 'pear-tree' and *lēah*, 'wood'. There are several other 'woodland' names nearby, such as those of Woodmansterne, Woodcote, Whyteleafe, Forestdale and Farleigh, this last meaning 'woodland clearing with ferns'. Equally, there are several individually named woods still in existence, especially to the immediate east of Purley, such as Kings Wood, Selsdon Wood, Frith Wood.

Purves The name ultimately relates to *purvey*, and arose as an occupational name for a person who was responsible for the provisions required by a monastery or manor house.

Pusan The port in South Korea derives its name from Korean *pu*, 'pot', 'cauldron' and *san*, 'mountain'. The 'pot mountain' is probably an allusion to the shape of the mountain at the foot of which the city lies.

Pushkin The Russian town near St Petersburg, a prime tourist attraction, takes its name from the famous Russian poet Alexander *Pushkin* (1799–1837), who spent six of his student years here. The earlier name of the town was *Tsarskoye Selo*, 'tsars' village', referring to the summer residence of the Russian royal family here. But this name was actually a fortuitous adaptation of the original name of the place, which was *Sarskoye Selo*, from the Finnish word *saari*, 'island', a term for land rising above the surrounding low-lying plain. In 1918, after the Russian Revolution, the 'tsarist' name was changed to *Detskoye Selo*, 'children's village', since the royal residence had been converted for use as a summer holiday camp for workers and their families. In 1937 the town was given its present name to mark the centenary of Pushkin's death.

Pusht-i-Kuh The mountain range of western Iran, near the border with Iraq, has an Iranian name meaning 'back of the mountain', from *pušt*, 'back' and *kūh*, 'mountain'. The name is also spelled *Poshtkūh*.

Putney The district of southwest London, on the south bank of the Thames, has a name meaning '*Putta*'s landing-place', with the Anglo-Saxon personal name followed by Old English *hӯth*, 'landing-place', as for ROTHERHITHE.

Puy, Le *See* LE PUY.

Puy-de-Dôme The volcanic mountain in central France, in the Auvergne, derives the first word of its name from Latin *podium*, 'height' (itself from Greek *pous*, genitive *podos*, 'foot') and *Duma*, the Gaulish name of the mountain, popularly interpreted as modern French *dôme*, 'dome'. *See also* LE PUY.

Pye The name originated either as an occupational name for a person who made and sold *pies*, or as a nickname for a talkative or thieving person, like a *pie*, that is, a magpie. If a Welsh name, the origin is more likely to be in the meaning 'son of HUGH', with the initial *P-* representing *ap*, denoting 'son'.

Pygmalion The name is that of the king in Greek mythology who fell in love with the statue of the woman he had sculpted, which in answer to his prayer to Aphrodite came to life as Galatea. His name appears to derive from Greek *pugmē*, 'fist' and *malion*, 'hair', as if meaning 'hairy fist'. The exact relevance of this is unclear, however.

Pygmy The name of the dwarf people of Equatorial Africa derives from Greek *pugmaios*, 'undersized', from *pugmē*, 'cubit' (a measure of length from the elbow to the knuckles), literally 'fist'. The Greek cubit was about 1 ft $1\frac{1}{2}$ in (34 cm), but Pygmies are at least four times taller than this.

Pyongyang The capital of North Korea derives its name from Korean *p'yŏng*, 'flat' and *yang*, 'land', describing the city's location by the river Taedong.

Pyramus The well-known lover of Thisbe in Greek legend has a name derived by some from *puramous*, the word for a cake of roasted wheat and honey that was given as a prize to the person who kept awake the longest during a night watch. But this seems too involved for Pyramus, so it might be better to seek an origin in the root word *pur*, 'fire', referring to the 'burning' love that Pyramus had for Thisbe.

Pyrenees The name of the mountain range between France and Spain is traditionally derived from that of the Greek nymph *Pyrēnē*, daughter of Bebryx, king of Narbonne. She was said to be loved by Hercules and to have been buried in the mountains. Her own name appears to derive from Greek *pur*, 'fire' and *eneon*, 'dumb', 'secret', and may have translated the name of some Celtic goddess. The resemblance of the name to Celtic *ber* or *per*, 'peak', 'summit' is probably fortuitous. In medieval times there was no single name for the range, and people living here would only know the names of local mountains and valleys.

Pyrex The patent make of heat-resistant glassware has a name that seems to suggest an origin in Greek *pur*, 'fire' and

Latin *rex*, 'king'. However, the name originated in 1915 at a time when many trade names were formed from a standard word with the regular suffix -*ex*, and the manufacturers in fact intended it to represent *pie*, since their earliest products were glass baking dishes.

Pytchley The famous hunt takes its name from the small village of *Pytchley* near Kettering, Northamptonshire, where it was founded in about 1750. The Elizabethan house in which the masters of the hunt once lived no longer exists, and the hunt kennels have long been at Brixworth, some eight miles (13 km) away. The name of the village, pronounced with a long vowel (like *pie*), means '*Peoht*'s wood'.

Pythagoras The famous Greek philosopher and mathematician, who lived in the 6th century BC, has a name explained as meaning 'persuader of the assembly', from *peithō*, 'I persuade' and *agora*, 'marketplace'. But this is to distort the first half of his name, which more obviously relates to *Pytho*, the earlier name of Delphi, or to *Pythia*, the priestess of Apollo at Delphi, who transmitted the oracles. Perhaps it is better understood, therefore, as something like 'speech of Apollo', much as *Apollodorus* means 'gift of Apollo'. Apollo himself had the byname *Pythius* because he slew the serpent or dragon *Python*.

Q

QANTAS The Australian national airline was founded in 1920 with the full name Queensland *a*nd *N*orthern *T*erritory *A*erial *S*ervices, soon abbreviated to the present acronym, pronounced 'Quontas'. The abbreviated name happens to suggest Latin *quantus*, 'how much'.

Qatar The Arabian state probably derives its name from the same Arabic root as *qaṭura*, 'to exude', from *qaṭrān*, 'tar', 'resin', and perhaps relates to the country's rich resources of petroleum and natural gas.

Qingdao The port in eastern China has a name deriving from Chinese *qīng*, 'green', 'blue' and *dǎo*, 'island', originally referring to the island in the natural harbour here.

Qinghai The province of northwest China takes its name from Chinese *qīng*, 'green', 'blue' and *hǎi*, 'sea', properly referring to the large lake here also known by the Mongolian name *Koko Nor*, of identical meaning.

Qom The city in central Iran has a name that is an Arabic abbreviation of *komendān*, the name of one of the seven villages that combined to form the present town. The meaning of this is uncertain. It may be the name of one of its original Shi'ite founders in the 8th century.

Quadragesima In the Christian calendar, the name is that of the first Sunday in Lent. It derives from Medieval Latin *quadragesima dies*, 'fortieth day', as it is (roughly) 40 days before Easter. The name was also formerly used for Lent itself, and in some languages actually gave the word for 'Lent', such as French *carême*, Italian *quaresima*, Spanish *cuaresma*, Welsh *grawys*. The 40 days represent the period spent by Jesus fasting in the wilderness. *Cp.* QUINQUAGESIMA, SEPTUAGESIMA, SEXAGESIMA.

Quaker The name is that of a member of the Society of Friends, a Christian sect, noted for their rejection of sacraments and ritual, and for their pacifist views, founded by George Fox in about 1650. It was originally a derogatory nickname, referring either to their alleged 'quaking' in ecstatic fits, or to George Fox's bidding to his followers to 'tremble at the word of the Lord'. The Friends themselves have never adopted the name, but have long ceased to regard it as derogatory. A similar name is that of the *Shakers*, the American millenarian sect formed as an offshoot of the Quakers in 1747.

Quantocks The Somerset hills have a name that was recorded in a 7th-century document as *Cantucuudu*. This represents a combination of Celtic *canto*, 'edge', 'rim' (as for KENT) and Old English *wudu*, 'wood'. The 'edge' would probably have been just one section of the hills, not the whole chain, which effectively comprises a series of ridges extending for some eight miles (13 km) between Bridgwater and Taunton.

Quartermain The name arose as a Norman nickname meaning 'four hands', from Old French *quatre*, 'four' and *main*, 'hand'. This would have been used for a person obliged to wear heavy gloves, or perhaps was given to a person who worked so fast that he seemed to have two pairs of hands.

Quasimodo In the Christian calendar, the name is sometimes used to denote LOW SUNDAY. Latin *quasi modo* means literally 'as if just now', and here represents the opening words of the Latin introit for that day: *quasi modo geniti infantes*, 'as newborn babes' (1 *Peter* 2.2). The name is familiar as that of the hunchback bell-ringer in Victor Hugo's novel *Notre-Dame de Paris* (1831). It was given him by his adoptive father, Claude Frollo, archdeacon of Notre-Dame:

> He christened his adopted child by the name of Quasimodo, either because he chose thus to commemorate the day when he had found him, or because he meant to mark by that name how incomplete and imperfectly moulded the poor little creature was. Indeed, Quasimodo, one-eyed, hump-backed, bow-legged, could hardly be considered as anything more than an *as if*.
>
> *Book IV, Chapter 2.*

Quebec The well-known Canadian province, with its identically named capital, derives its name from Algonquian *quilibek* meaning 'place where waters narrow', referring to the gradually narrowing channel of the St Lawrence, or specifically to the narrows of the river at Cape Diamond. The city was founded by the French in the early 17th century and was long in French hands, so that the name is frequently found today, especially among French-Canadians, as *Québec*, pronounced 'Kebek'.

Quechua The South American Indian people and their language (more precisely group of languages) derive their name from Quechua *k'echua*, 'plunderer', 'despoiler'.

Queen The famous British pop group was formed in London in 1970, and selected a name that was intended to reflect their professional ability and style. (It may have been a subconscious or even intentional pun on the part of the group's founder, guitarist Brian May, so that they were the 'Queen of the May'.) The implicit 'camp' overtones of the name accorded well with the flamboyant image subsequently cultivated by their lead singer, Freddie Mercury.

Queen Anne's School The girls' public school at Reading, Berkshire, was founded in London in 1698 and named for *Queen Anne*, the reigning monarch.

Queenborough The town in Kent, on the Isle of Sheppey, arose in 1367 as a chartered *borough* named for *Queen* Philippa of Hainault (1314–1369), wife of Edward III. *See also* QUEEN'S COLLEGE, Oxford.

Queen Charlotte Islands The islands of British Columbia, off the west coast of Canada, were so named in 1787 by the Englishman George Dixon for his trading vessel the *Queen Charlotte*, itself named for *Queen Charlotte* (1744–1818), wife of George III.

Queen Elizabeth's Grammar School There are two boys' public schools of the name, one in Blackburn, Lancashire, re-founded in 1567 from an earlier school established in 1509, and one in Wakefield, West Yorkshire, founded in 1591. Both were granted their Royal Charter by *Queen Elizabeth*.

Queen Elizabeth's Hospital The Bristol public school for boys was established as a BLUECOAT SCHOOL on the lines of CHRIST'S HOSPITAL according to provisions under the will of John Carr, a local merchant, in 1586. In 1590 the school was granted its Royal Charter by *Queen Elizabeth*.

Queen Margaret's School The public school for girls in York was founded in Scarborough, Yorkshire, in 1901 and named for St *Margaret* (1045–1093), sister of Edgar Atheling and *queen* of Scotland as wife of Malcolm III Canmore. The school moved to York in 1949.

Queen Maud Land The large section of Antarctica, claimed by Norway in 1939, is named for *Queen Maud* (1869–1938), daughter of Edward VII of England and wife of King Haakon VII of Norway.

Queen of the South The Scottish football club, based in Dumfries, was formed in that town in 1919 and took the town's nickname as their own name. The nickname itself contrasts Dumfries, in the south of Scotland, with Edinburgh, known as *Queen of the North* (meaning north of Britain, however, not north of Scotland).

Queen's College The Oxford college was founded in 1340 by Robert Eglesfeld, chaplain to *Queen* Philippa, wife of Edward III, and is named for her. There are two public schools of the name, both for *Queen* Victoria. That in Taunton, Somerset, originally for boys, was founded in 1843 as the *West of England Wesleyan Proprietary Grammar School* and was renamed *Queen's College* in 1887 on the occasion of the Queen's Jubilee. That in London, for girls, was founded in 1848 as the first school in the country for the higher education of women and was incorporated by Royal Charter in 1853. *Cp.* QUEENS' COLLEGE, Cambridge.

Queens' College The Cambridge college was founded in 1446 on the site of a former priory as *St Bernard's College*. Within a year Queen Margaret of Anjou, wife of Henry VI (the founder of KING'S COLLEGE) gained her husband's consent to rename and refound the college, as no Cambridge college had yet been founded by a queen of England. The college thus became *Queen Margaret's College* in 1448. Henry was then deposed by Edward IV in 1461, but Queen Elizabeth, Edward's wife, decided to continue the patronage given by her predecessor. The college is thus named for the two queens, with the apostrophe after the *s* denoting the plural possessive. *Cp.* QUEEN'S COLLEGE, Oxford.

Queen's House The Palladian mansion in Greenwich, London, designed by Inigo Jones, was begun in 1616 for Anne of Denmark, *queen* of James I. She died in 1619, however, so when it was completed in 1635 it went to Henrietta Maria (1609–1669), *queen* of Charles I, James's successor.

Queensland The Australian state was founded in 1859 when it was formed from the northern portion of the colony of New South Wales, which originally extended along the whole of the eastern Australian coast. The name *Cooksland* was at first proposed for the new state, for the famous explorer who had visited this coast in 1770. But it was the compliment to *Queen* Victoria that prevailed, especially as the name complemented that of VICTORIA, the state that had been set off from the southern portion of New South Wales eight years previously.

Queen's Park The Scottish football club, based in Glasgow, was formed in 1867 and takes its name from its first ground at *Queen's Park* Recreation Ground. The park itself is named for Mary, *Queen* of Scots, who fled south from here after the Battle of Langside in 1568. In 1873 the club moved to its present ground nearby, HAMPDEN PARK. *Cp.* QUEEN'S PARK RANGERS.

Queen's Park Rangers The famous London football club was formed in 1885 as a merger between two existing clubs and originally bore their names, as *St Jude's and Christchurch Rangers*. Two years later the club adopted its present name, since *Queen's Park* in northwest London was the district where most of the players lived. As for many parks elsewhere in England (but not necessarily Scotland!), the name honours *Queen* Victoria. QPR's actual ground is some two miles southwest of Queen's Park, in Shepherds Bush. *Cp.* QUEEN'S PARK.

Queen's School, The The Chester public school for girls was founded in 1878 and is named for *Queen* Victoria, who became the school's first patron in 1882.

Queen's Theatre The London theatre, in Shaftesbury Avenue, opened in 1907 and was named for *Queen* Alexandra (1844–1925), consort of Edward VII. There was much discussion about the choice of name. Other names for the new theatre that were considered included *Piccadilly*, *Wardour* and *Central*.

Queen's University of Belfast The Northern Ireland university was founded as *Queen's College* in 1845, when there were three Irish cities in keen rivalry to found a new college (named for *Queen* Victoria) for students not belonging to the Church of Ireland. (The two losing contenders were Cork and Galway, where the present University College in each is now a constituent college of the National University of Ireland.) Queen's College was raised to university status in 1908. *See also* ROYAL BELFAST ACADEMICAL INSTITUTION.

Queenswood The public school for girls at Hatfield, Hertfordshire, was founded in 1894 by two Methodist ministers and was given a name based on Ruskin's lecture of 1864 on the education of girls entitled 'Lilies: of the Queens' Gardens'. This complemented another lecture of his that year on the value of reading entitled 'Sesame: of Kings' Treasures'. Both lectures were published in book form the following year as *Sesame and Lilies*.

Quemoy The name of the island in Formosa Strait, off the southeast coast of China, is a western corruption of Chinese *jīnmén*, meaning 'golden gate'.

Quesnoy, Le *See* LE QUESNOY.

Quetta The city in west central Pakistan derives its name from Pashto *kwatkot*, 'fort'.

Quetzalcoatl The god of the Aztecs, usually represented as a feathered serpent, has a name that means 'brightly feathered snake' from Nahuatl *quetzalli*, 'brightly coloured tail feather' and *coatl*, 'snake'. The first part of the name is represented in that of the *quetzal*, the brightly plumed crested bird of Central and northern South America.

Quezon City The city and former capital of the Philippines was founded in 1948 and named for the Philippine (but not Filipino!) statesman Manuel Luis *Quezón* y Molín (1878–1944), the country's first president.

Quiberon The peninsula and town in Brittany, northwest France, has a name that is probably Breton in origin but that has been variously interpreted. Proposed derivations include: 1. *kêr broenn*, 'town of reeds', referring to the marshes here; 2. *gwez brain*, 'rotten trees', similarly; 3. *kebrienn*, 'chevron', referring to the shape of the peninsula; 4. *kêr brec'hagn*, 'infertile town'. But the name could also be Gaulish, perhaps from *co*, 'high', 'big' and *peroen*, 'owner', referring to the original Breton settlers who took possession of this territory in the 5th century as the people who had been driven out of Britain by the Anglo-Saxons.

Quick The name was originally either a nickname for a lively or nimble person, or was used for someone who lived by *quick* grass, that is, couch grass, or by the trees known as the *quicken* (rowan) or *quickbeam* (aspen). In some instances the named person could have lived at a dairy farm, from Old English *cū*, 'cow' and *wīc*, 'farm'.

Quimper The city in Brittany, northwest France, has the Breton name *Kemper*, deriving from *kember*, 'confluence', itself from Gaulish *comboro* with the same meaning. The city stands at the confluence of the rivers Odet and Steir. In 1793, when some places in France were renamed at the time of the Revolution, Quimper was temporarily known as *Montagne-sur-Odet*, from the *Montagnes* Noires to the northeast of the town. The smaller town of *Quimperlé*, some 30 miles (48 km) to the east, has a name of identical origin. It stands at the confluence of the Isole and the Elle.

Quinn The Irish name has an English spelling of the original *Ó Cuinn*, 'descendant of *Conn*', the latter name meaning 'leader'.

Quinquagesima In the Christian calendar, the name is that of the Sunday before Ash Wednesday, otherwise the Sunday before Lent. It derives from Medieval Latin *quinquagesima dies*, 'fiftieth day', referring to the 50 days (seven weeks) from that Sunday to Easter Day. *Cp.* QUADRAGESIMA, SEPTUAGESIMA, SEXAGESIMA.

Quintin The name derives, through French, from the Latin name *Quintinus*, itself from *Quintus*, 'fifth'. The name was sometimes used for a fifth son or fifth male child in a family, especially in Victorian times. Unlike OCTAVIAN ('eighth'), however, it had no regular feminine equivalent.

Quintin Kynaston School The state secondary school in St John's Wood, London evolved as a merger in 1969 of *Quintin* School and *Kynaston* School. Quintin School was founded in 1886 as the *Polytechnic Day School* by the philanthropist *Quintin* Hogg (1845–1903), grandfather of the Conservative Lord Chancellor, Lord Hailsham, and was subsequently named for him. Kynaston School was founded by Sir *Kynaston* Studd (1858–1944), former Lord Mayor of London and chairman of the school governors.

Quirinal The name of one of the seven hills on which ancient Rome was built derives from that of QUIRINUS, the Sabine god of war. The god's name represents that of the *Quirites*, the Sabino-Roman people who were the region's earliest inhabitants. Their name was itself popularly believed by the Romans to derive from the Sabine capital of *Cures*.

Quirinus In Roman mythology, the name was that of the god of war who came to be identified with Romulus, the supposed founder of Rome. It has traditionally been derived either from that of the Sabine capital *Cures* (*see* QUIRINAL) or from the Sabine word *quiris*, 'spear'. Recent scholars, however, have linked his name with Latin *vir*, 'man', 'citizen', or more specifically with *coviria*, 'gathering of men'. Quirinus was the god of public gatherings. Hence, after the union of the Sabines and the Romans, the designation of the Roman people on solemn occasions as *Populus Romanus Quirites* or simply *Quirites*.

Quirk The name is both Irish and Manx in origin, and represents Gaelic *Ó Cuirc*, 'descendant of *Corc*'. The latter name means 'heart'.

Quito The capital of Ecuador takes its name from that of *Quitu*, a now extinct Indian tribe. The meaning of their own name is uncertain. The city of *Quito* was founded in 1533, and until 1830 the name was also that of the country as a whole. Its similarity to the country's name in some languages, such as French *Équateur*, is purely coincidental.

Qumran The archaeological site in northwest Jordan, famous for the caves where the Dead Sea Scrolls were found in 1947, has the full name *Khirbet Qumran*. The first word of this represents Hebrew *horba*, 'ruins'. The second is the name of the river here, itself of uncertain origin.

Quorn The name of the well-known Leicestershire hunt derives from that of the village also known as *Quorndon*, near Loughborough. This means 'millstone hill', from Old English *cweorn*, 'hand mill' (modern *quern*) and *dūn*, 'hill'. The name implies that millstones were obtained locally.

R

Ra The name of the ancient Egyptian god of the sun, also spelled *Re*, actually means 'sun'. He was regarded as the creator of the world and of mankind, so that he was 'father of the gods' and 'father of kings'. The latter aspect is reflected in the name RAMESES for all kings of ancient Egypt. The name is also spelled *Re*.

Rabat The capital of Morocco has a name that represents Arabic *ar-ribāt̤*, from *al*, 'the' and *ribāt̤*, the word for a fortified monastery, in this case one to guard the frontier. The word is related to *marabout* as a term for a Muslim holy man or hermit.

Racal The well-known electronics company takes its name from the first names of two of the original partners who founded it in 1951, Sir *Ra*ymond Brown (1920–) and G. *Cal*der Cunningham.

Rachel The biblical name, that of the second wife of Jacob and mother of Joseph and Benjamin, derives from Hebrew *Rāhēl*, 'ewe'. It is sometimes spelled *Rachael* under the influence of MICHAEL.

Rackham The name derives from that of the Sussex village near Storrington, with the place-name itself meaning 'homestead by the mound', from Old English *hreac*, 'mound', 'rick' (referring to a hill here) and *hām*, 'homestead'.

Radcliffe Camera The historic Oxford library takes its name from its founder, the physician John *Radcliffe* (1652–1714), who bequeathed £40,000 for the building of the library. It was completed in 1748. *Camera* refers to its domed upper room, from Latin *camera*, 'vault', 'arched roof', itself from the Greek *kamara*, a word for anything having an arched or vaulted cover. *See also* RADCLIFFE INFIRMARY.

Radcliffe College The women's college of Harvard University, Cambridge, Massachu-setts, was founded in 1879 and named in 1894 for Ann *Radcliffe* (d. 1661), founder of the first scholarship in the original Harvard College in 1643.

Radcliffe Infirmary Oxford's famous hospital takes its name from Dr John *Radcliffe* (1652–1714), a wealthy Oxford physician who bequeathed funds for its foundation in 1761. The title *Infirmary* was adopted from the 18th century for the names of various provincial hospitals. Others include the *Royal Infirmary*, Edinburgh, and the *Royal Infirmary*, Liverpool. Some hospitals have dropped the word, however, with its suggestion of poverty and permanent disability. It is intended that the Radcliffe Infirmary, in the centre of Oxford, will eventually be replaced by the *John Radcliffe Hospital*, whose main building opened in Headington, outside the city, in 1979. *See also* RADCLIFFE CAMERA.

Radetzky March The march Op 228 (1848) by Johann Strauss the elder is named for the Austrian field-marshal Joseph *Radetzky* (1766–1858), who defeated the Sardinians at the Battle of Custoza (1848). The composition should not be confused with the RÁKÓCZI MARCH.

Radford The name derives from any of the places so called, such as *Radford* that is now a district of Nottingham. The place-name normally means 'red ford', referring to the colour of the soil.

Radio Caroline The British 'pirate' radio station, which began transmitting pop music in 1964 from a ship anchored off the east coast, was named for *Caroline* Kennedy (1957–), daughter of the recently assassinated American president John F. Kennedy (1917–1963). The station made a 'legal' return in 1992, broadcasting from a boat berthed in Dover harbour.

Radnor The Welsh administrative district that corresponds to the former *Radnorshire*, in east central Wales, has a name of English origin meaning 'red bank', from Old English *rēad*, 'red' and *ōfer*, 'bank', 'slope'. The reference is to the red loamy soil found on the hill-slopes here.

Raffles Hotel The famous Singapore hotel is named after the former British colony's founder in 1819, Sir Stamford *Raffles* (1781–1826). The hotel itself opened in 1889. The name of Raffles is found widely in Singapore, which has the *Raffles* Institute, *Raffles* Museum, and *Raffles* Library. The University of Singapore (formerly University of Malaya) was founded in 1929 as *Raffles* College. The same man discovered and gave the name of the tropical Asian plant *rafflesia*.

Ragnarok In Norse mythology, the name is that of the final destruction of the gods in a cataclysmic battle with evil, leading to the birth of a new order. The original Old Norse name was *Ragnarǫk*, from *ragna*, genitive of *reginn*, 'gods', and *rǫk*, literally 'marvels', 'fate', 'doom'. The second element soon became confused with the word *rǫkkr*, 'twilight', however, so that the name means 'twilight of the gods', otherwise the German GÖTTERDÄMMERUNG, familiar as the fourth opera in Wagner's cycle *Der Ring des Nibelungen* ('The Ring of the Nibelung') (1876).

Ragusa *See* DUBROVNIK.

Raindrop Prelude Chopin's Prelude in D flat, Op 28 No 15 (1836–9) for piano is so nicknamed because the repeated note A flat is said to suggest the sound of pattering raindrops.

Raines The name means 'son of *Raine*', this in turn usually representing the short form of the Germanic name that gave modern English RAYMOND, for example, so meaning 'counsel'. In some cases the name could have derived from Old French *Raine*, 'frog' as a nickname for a person who looked or behaved like this creature.

Rainier, Mount The name, that of the highest mountain in the state of Washington and in the Cascade Range, derives from that of the British admiral Peter *Rainier* (1742–1808). It was given the mountain in 1792 by Rainier's friend, Captain George

Vancouver (whose own name is borne by VANCOUVER).

Raith Rovers The Scottish football club, based in Kirkcaldy, Fife, was formed in 1883 and takes its name from the Laird of *Raith* and Novar, from whom its members leased one of their first grounds, Robbie's Park.

Rajasthan The state of northwest India has a Hindi name meaning 'land of kings', from Sanskrit *rāja*, 'king', 'prince' and *sthāna*, 'stay', related to Iranian *ostān*, 'land', 'country'. *Cp.* RAJPUTANA.

Rajputana The former group of princely states in northwest India, now mostly part of RAJASTHAN, derives its name from the *Rajput*, the Hindu military caste who claim descent from the Kshatriya, the original warrior caste. Their own name means 'sons of the king', from Sanskrit *rāja*, 'king' and *putra*, 'son' (*cp.* BRAHMAPUTRA).

Rákóczi March The popular national Hungarian march is named for Prince Ferenc *Rákóczi* (1676–1735), who led the Hungarian revolt of 1703–11 against Austria. Berlioz used it in *La Damnation de Faust* (1846) and Liszt based his 15th Hungarian Rhapsody for piano (1852) on it. The composition should not be confused with the RADETZKY MARCH.

Raleigh The surname derives from the identical Devon place-name, now familiar from Withycombe *Raleigh* and Colaton *Raleigh*, both near Exmouth. The name itself comes from Old English *rēad*, 'red' and *lēah*, 'wood', 'clearing'. The famous explorer Sir Walter *Raleigh* (1552–1618) came from this part of Devon.

Raleigh The state capital of North Carolina was founded in 1792, soon after the War of American Independence (American Revolution), and named for the famous English explorer and writer Sir Walter *Raleigh* (1552–1618), who had attempted to colonize this region of America.

Raleigh The well-known make of bicycle takes its name from *Raleigh* Street, Nottingham, where a small cycle business existed in the 1880s and where the *Raleigh* Cycle Company was founded in 1887. The street itself is named commemoratively for Sir Walter *Raleigh*.

Ralph The name is Norman in origin, representing the Germanic name *Radulf*, itself made up of *rād*, 'counsel' and *wulf*, 'wolf'. Its spelling with *ph* is due to classical 'improvement' in the 18th century. *Cp.* RANDOLPH.

Rama In Hindu mythology, the name is that of any of three incarnations of the god Vishnu, otherwise the heroes Bala*rama*, Parashu*rama* or RAMACHANDRA. The origin is in Sanskrit *rāma*, 'black', 'dark'.

Ramachandra The name is that of the incarnation of Vishnu in Hindu mythology who is the hero of the RAMAYANA. His name is Sanskrit, meaning 'RAMA (beautiful as the) moon'.

Ramadan The period of 30 days in the ninth month of the Muslim year, in which a strict fast is kept, has a name of Arabic origin, meaning 'hot month', from *ramiḍ*, 'dryness'.

Ramah Several cities of the name are mentioned in the Bible, for example in *Joshua* 18.25. Their origin is in Hebrew *rama*, 'hill', 'height'.

Ramat Gan The city near Tel Aviv, Israel, has a Hebrew name meaning 'hill of the garden', from *ramat*, construct state (*see* BETHANY) of *rama*, 'hill' (*see* RAMAH) and *gan*, 'orchard'.

Ramayana The Sanskrit epic poem, recounting the feats of RAMACHANDRA, has a name that means '(things) related to RAMA'.

Rambo The name of the fictional film character John *Rambo*, noted for his mindless cruelty and brutality, is probably a shortening of the colloquial American word *rambunctious*, meaning 'boisterous', 'unruly'. He was popularized worldwide by the movie *Rambo: First Blood, Part Two* (1985), but appeared earlier in the film *First Blood* (1982), based on the novel of the same name by the Canadian writer and professor of American literature David Morrell, published in 1972. He was played in both movies by the actor Sylvester Stallone, who co-wrote the script of the second film.

Rambouillet The town in northern France, famous from the Marquise de *Rambouillet*, the 18th-century French society hostess, derives its name from a personal name that is a diminutive of *Rambo*, with the final part of the name representing Gaulish *ialo*, 'clearing', 'village'.

Rameses The name, more accurately *Ramses*, is that of all kings of ancient Egypt in the first and second millennia BC, and is particularly famous from *Rameses* the Great, who reigned from 1304 to 1237. It represents Egyptian *Ra-me-su*, 'son of RA', that is, of the sun god, so that all the kings were regarded as his sons. *Cp.* POTIPHAR.

Ramsbottom The name comes from what is now the town of *Ramsbottom*, north of Manchester. The place-name itself means 'wild garlic valley', from Old English *hramsa*, 'wild garlic' (modern English *ramson*) and *bothm*, 'valley' (literally 'bottom'). *Cp.* RAMSEY.

Ramsey The Isle of Man resort has a name meaning 'river of wild garlic', from Old Norse *hramsa*, 'wild garlic' and *á*, 'river', from the stream at whose mouth the town stands. The Cambridgeshire town of *Ramsey*, near Peterborough, has a similar name, meaning 'wild garlic island', from Old English *hramsa* and *ēg*, 'island', the latter word used for dry land in marshland, appropriately for the fenland town.

Ramsgate The Kent resort has a name meaning 'raven's gap', from Old English *hræfn*, 'raven' and *geat*, 'gap' (modern *gate*). It is not certain who or what the 'raven' was. It may have been the name of a raven-shaped rock, or even a personal name. It could equally have applied to the birds themselves, which may have been frequent visitors here.

Randall The name evolved as a diminutive of the medieval given name *Rand*, itself either a short form of a Germanic name that gave modern RANDOLPH and other names, or else a name for a person who lived on the edge of a settlement or by the bank of a river, from Old English *rand*, 'edge', 'rim'. The surname *Rendall* has the same origin.

Randolph The name is of Norman origin and represents the Germanic name *Randulf*, itself comprising *rand*, 'rim', 'edge' (*i.e.* of a shield) and *wulf*, 'wolf'. The final *ph* evolved through 18th-century classical 'improvers', as for RALPH.

Randolph Hotel Oxford's well-known hotel, opened in 1866, took its name from the *Randolph* Gallery that formerly stood opposite it in Beaumont Street and that was itself named from the Rev Dr Francis *Randolph*, one of the main benefactors of the Ashmolean Museum in the 18th century.

Ranelagh Gardens The former gardens in Chelsea, London, famous as a meeting and strolling place for fashionable people, took its name from the Irish statesman Richard Jones, third Viscount and first Earl of *Ranelagh* (1636–1712), in the grounds of whose house, built in 1690, they were located. The gardens opened in 1742, some time after his death, and closed in 1804. They now form part of the grounds of Chelsea Hospital. The name is preserved in those of streets here, such as *Ranelagh* Grove and *Ranelagh* Road. The earl's own title came from *Ranelagh*, now a southern district of Dublin.

Ranfurly Shield The premier New Zealand rugby trophy, competed for annually by provincial teams, is named for Uchter John Mark Knox, fifth Earl of *Ranfurly* (1856–1933), Governor of New Zealand, who presented it to the New Zealand Rugby Football Club in 1902. The earl's title comes from *Ranfurly*, near Paisley in west central Scotland.

Range Rover The familiar cross-country and road vehicle was first produced in 1970 and was given a name based on that of the LAND-ROVER. The first word of the name indicates the ability of the vehicle to travel over a wide *range* of terrain while remaining basically suitable for road use.

Rangoon *See* YANGON.

Rank The name is familiar from three leading commercial companies. The *Rank* Organization is a large leisure group, *Rank* Xerox is noted for its copiers and office equipment, and *Ranks* Hovis Macdougall (RHM) is famous for its food products, especially bread and cakes. The name is ultimately that of Joseph *Rank* (1854–1943) a Hull miller's son who became a miller himself and won a reputation for his fine flour. His milling activity was the germ

from which sprang the RHM of today. Joseph Rank's third son was J. Arthur *Rank* (1888–1972), well known from the cinema 'man with the gong' symbol. He founded the *Rank* Organization in 1953 to unify his cinema and leisure interests, and in 1956 merged with the American Xerox Corporation to form *Rank*-Xerox.

Raper *See* ROPER.

Raphael The name is familiar as that of the angel who in the Apocrypha heals the blind, aged Tobit. He does not reveal his name, however, until the end of his mission (*Tobit* 12.15). It derives from Hebrew *Rephā'ēl*, 'God has healed'.

Ras el Khaimah The emirate, one of the seven United Arab Emirates, has an Arabic name representing *ra's*, 'head', *al*, 'the' and *hayma*, 'tent' (as for OMAR KHAYYÁM). The name is also that of the emirate's capital.

Rasht The name of the city in northwest Iran, also spelled *Resht*, derives from Iranian *reŝte*, 'thread'. The town was formerly noted for its spinning mills.

Rastafarian The name is that of the Jamaican cult whose members regard *Ras Tafari* as God. The latter name, meaning 'Chief Tafari', was that of Haile Selassie (1892–1975) from 1916 until his accession as emperor of Ethiopia in 1930. This event was seen as the fulfilment of a prophecy, and members of the cult acknowledged him as the Messiah, or incarnation of God.

Ratcliffe The name comes from any of the places so called, such as *Ratcliffe* on Soar, near Loughborough, or what is now the town of *Radcliffe* near Manchester. The place-name means 'red cliff', 'red slope', referring to the colour of the soil.

Rathbone The name is probably a form of the place-name *Radbourne*, as for the village near Derby. Its own meaning is likely to be 'reedy stream' rather than 'red stream'.

Ratisbon *See* REGENSBURG.

Ratnapura The town in southwest central Sri Lanka has a Hindi name meaning 'jewel town', from *ratna*, 'jewel' and *pura*, 'town'.

Ratners The familiar High Street jewellers take their name from Leslie *Ratner*, a

Jewish watchmender who opened a jeweller's shop in Richmond, Surrey, in 1949 and gradually built up a small chain of shops. These were taken over by his son Gerald Ratner in 1984 and expanded to the hundreds of branches that exist today. It is a curious coincidence that the Hindi word for 'jewel' is *ratna* (*see* RATNAPURA).

Rattigan This is the English form of the Irish name *Ó Reachtagáin*, 'descendant of *Reachtagán*'. The latter personal name derives from *reachtaire*, 'lawgiver', 'steward'.

Raven The name would originally have been a nickname for someone resembling a raven in some way, either because they were dark-haired or because they were notorious thieves.

Ravenna The city and port in northeast Italy has a name of Etruscan origin. Its meaning is unknown.

Rawalpindi The ancient city in northern Pakistan has an Urdu name, from Hindi *rāvalpiṇḍī*, 'village of the *Ravals*', these being a tribe of yogis (ascetics).

Rawlings The name means 'son of *Rawling*'. This represents the given name *Rawlin*, itself a diminutive of *Raw*, a variant of the medieval name that gave modern RALPH.

Rawlplug The familiar wall fixing device was invented just before the First World War and takes its name from its inventor, John *Rawlings*, who first marketed the fibre plug of today in 1919.

Ray The name has several possible origins. It could derive from Old French *rey*, 'king', given as a nickname to a 'regal'-looking person, or to someone who had played the role of king in a pageant, or won a contest of some kind. It could represent Middle English *ray*, 'roedeer', as a nickname for a timid person. Equally, it could have denoted a person who came from RYE or from a place named *Wray*, such as the Lancashire village near Kirkby Lonsdale. The latter place-name comes from Old Norse *vrá*, 'nook', 'corner'.

Raymond The name is Norman in origin, deriving from a Germanic name that comprised the words *ragin*, 'reason', 'advice' and *mund*, 'protector', suggesting an overall 'counsel for the defence'.

Razor Quartet Haydn's String Quartet in F minor, Op 55 No 2 (late 1780s) is so nicknamed from the story that the composer exclaimed 'I'd give my best quartet for a new razor' and was taken at his word by a visitor, the London music publisher John Bland.

Razumovsky Quartets Beethoven's String Quartets Op 59 Nos 1, 2 and 3 in F major, E minor and C major, (1805–6) are so named because they are dedicated to Count Andrey *Razumovsky* (1752–1836), Russian ambassador to Austria from 1801 to 1807. The ambassador was a keen musician and organizer of concerts and recitals.

Re *See* RA.

Ré, Île de The island in the Bay of Biscay, off the west coast of France, had the original Roman name of *Radis*. This subsequently became *Rhea*, by association with the Greek goddess of fertility or with the Roman vestal virgin *Rhea* Silvia who was the mother of Romulus and Remus. The meaning of the original name is uncertain.

Read The name frequently originated from Old English *rēad*, 'red' as a nickname for someone with red hair or a ruddy complexion. (*Cp.* RUFUS.) In many cases, however, it denoted a person who came from a place named *Rede* or *Reed*, such as the Suffolk village of *Rede* near Bury St Edmunds. The meaning of this name is 'roedeer headland', from Old English *rǣge*, 'female roedeer' and *hēafod*, 'headland'. The spellings of the name as *Reed* and *Reid* have the same origin.

Reader The name is an occupational one, for a 'reeder', that is, a person who thatched cottages with *reeds*. *Cp.* THATCHER.

Reading The well-known Berkshire town has a name meaning 'place of *Rēad*'s people', with the Anglo-Saxon personal name meaning 'red one'.

Reagan The name is Irish in origin, from *Ó Riagáin*, 'descendant of *Riagán*', the latter being a personal name of uncertain origin. The American president Ronald Reagan had Irish ancestry, and his great-grandfather was born in 1829 in Ballyporeen, Co Tipperary.

Rebecca The name is familiar from the Bible as that of the wife of Isaac. It is traditionally derived from Hebrew *ribhqāh*, from a root element *rbk* meaning 'to fatten' (in the sense 'feed up'), but may actually have its origin in Akkadian *rabāka*, 'to be gentle'.

Rechabite The biblical name is familiar in modern times as that of a member of the Independent Order of *Rechabites*, who are noted for being total abstainers from alcohol. Their name derives from Hebrew *Rē kābīm*, 'descendants of *Rēkāb*', otherwise the Old Testament character *Rechab*, whose son Jonadab had commanded his family: 'Ye shall drink no wine, neither ye, nor your sons for ever' (*Jeremiah* 35.6).

Recife The town and port at the easternmost point of Brazil, on the Atlantic, was originally named *Cidade de Recife* by the Portuguese in about 1535. This means 'reef town', for the reef that lies off the coast here. The city, which is partly built on an island, was formerly known as PERNAMBUCO, now the name of the state of which it is the capital.

Reckitt and Colman The familiar brand of domestic products, including such household names as Brasso and DETTOL, traces its name back to Isaac *Reckitt* (1792–1862), a Hull starch manufacturer, and Jeremiah *Colman*, a Norfolk flour miller who set up in 1814 as a mustard grinder. The two businesses, run by the men's respective descendants, eventually merged in 1938.

Red Army The name was that of the Soviet Army from 1918, following the Russian Revolution, to 1946, at the conclusion of the Second World War. The colour is symbolic of the blood shed in revolutionary uprisings, and was adopted as that of the Communist Party. It is not specifically Russian, however, and the French Second Republic of 1848, based on socialist principles, was known as the *Red Republic*, while a connotation of blood or fire for the colour red has existed since classical times. The planet MARS, for example, was named for the Roman god of war on account of its red colour. But in a Russian name *Red* may have a quite different sense: *see* RED SQUARE.

Red Cross The famous international humanitarian organization was established by the Geneva Convention of 1864. To denote its neutrality and impartiality, the organization adopted the emblem of a red cross on a white background, the colours of the Swiss flag reversed. Because the cross is a specifically Christian symbol, however, in non-Christian countries it is replaced by another, so that in Muslim states the organization is the *Red Crescent*, while in Iran it is the *Red Lion and Sun*.

Redditch The town near Birmingham has a name that could mean either 'reedy ditch' or 'red ditch', depending whether the first part of the name represents Old English *hrēod*, 'reed' or *rēad*, 'red'. A Latin text of about 1200 has the name of the place as *Rubeo Fossato*, however, which suggests that 'red ditch' is the true origin. The colour would have been that of the soil rather than of the water.

Redemptorist The full name of the Roman Catholic missionary society, founded in 1732 to work among the poor, is the Congregation of the Most Holy *Redeemer*, that is, of Christ regarded as having brought mankind *redemption*, or deliverance from sin.

Redfern The name comes from a placename, that of *Redfern* near Rochdale. Its meaning is what it says, 'red fern', referring to a place with reddish-coloured bracken.

Redhill The Surrey town, now a district of Reigate, has a name meaning 'red slope' rather than 'red hill', as early records of the name show the second half to be Old English *helde*, 'slope' rather than *hyll*, 'hill', although the general sense is much the same. There was nothing like a town here until the 19th century, with the coming of the railway. The slope is probably the modern Redstone Hill, leading east out of the town, with the name referring to the colour of its soil.

Red Indians The name is an alternative one, formerly popular but now regarded as offensive, for the INDIANS of North America. It relates, somewhat dubiously, to the supposed colour of their reddish skin (hence also the name *Redskins*, now equally offensive). One theory claims that the name originally referred to the now extinct Beothuks Indians of Newfoundland, who painted their bodies with red ochre.

Red Maids' School The Bristol public school for girls was founded in 1634 on funds bequeathed by the local merchant adventurer John Whitson (1557–1629). According to the terms of his will, 'forty poor women children, daughters of Burgesses deceased or decayed' were to 'go and be apparelled in Red Cloth'. The colour is still dominant in the school's everyday uniform. The girls wear a red jersey, red kilt and white blouse in winter and red cotton dresses in the summer. Boarders also have red cloaks, and on special occasions wear a traditional uniform of a red bonnet and white tippet and apron over red dresses.

Red River The name is that of two sizeable American rivers, one in the north, flowing into Lake Winnipeg, one in the south, a tributary of the Mississippi. In each case the reference is to the colour of the water at various points, caused by silt washed down from the red soil or rocks through which it flows. The *Red River* of northern Vietnam has a name of the same origin. It is now also known by its Vietnamese name *Song Hong* or Chinese name *Yüan Chiang*, both meaning the same.

Redruth The Cornish town has a name meaning 'red ford'. It is the second half of the name that means 'red', however, not the first. The two halves represent Cornish *rid*, 'ford' and *ruth*, 'red', with the adjective following the noun as normally in Celtic languages. There is no river at Redruth, so the ford must have been over the small stream on which Redruth Church stands to the southwest of the town.

Red Sea The well-known sea between Arabia and northeast Africa has a name that is usually translated literally in modern languages and that similarly corresponded in classical times. To the Romans it was thus *Mare rubrum* and to the Greeks either *Eruthra thalassa* or *Eruthros pontos*. The Arabic name for it is *al-bahr al-ahmar* (literally 'the sea the red') and its Amharic (Ethiopian) name is *qǎyyě bahr*. And this is to say nothing of French *Mer Rouge*, German *Rotes Meer*, Russian *Krasnoye more*, and so on. However, the sea's Hebrew

name is *yam sūf*, 'sea of reeds'. The reason for the colour *red* remains disputed. The following are some of the theories proposed: 1. it is that of the algae in its waters and along its shores; 2. it is that of the sandstone along its coasts; 3. it refers to the *Himarites*, a people here whose own name means 'red' (*cp.* ALHAMBRA); 4. 'red' means 'south', just as 'north' means 'black' (*see* BLACK SEA). This last theory is favoured by some modern scholars. At the same time, there are those who point to the similarity between the English meaning of the Hebrew name and the English name itself, so that the *Red* Sea is 'really' the *Reed* Sea. (This despite the totally different languages!)

Red Square Moscow's famous central square has a name that only coincidentally suggests an association with Communism. It was laid out in the late 15th century on a site where dwelling houses had been destroyed by fire. It was thus originally known as *Fire Square*. In the 16th century it became *Trinity Square*, from the Church of the Holy Trinity that stood where St Basil's Cathedral stands now. It soon became the political and commercial centre of the city, and gained its present name in the 17th century. The meaning is 'Beautiful Square', from Old Russian *krasnyy*, which now means 'red' (while 'beautiful' is *krasivyy*). For the Russians, therefore, 'red' is 'beautiful'. *See* RED ARMY for the specific Communist connotation of the colour.

Reed International The well-known paper company takes its name from Albert Edwin *Reed* (1846–1920), a Devon excise officer's son, who became a Somerset paper-mill manager in 1867. He went on to buy other mills and founded his own paper-making company in 1894.

Reed's School The boys' public school in Cobham, Surrey, was founded in London in 1813 by the philanthropist and Nonconformist minister Andrew *Reed* (1787–1862). It was originally a school for boys whose fathers had died, and was known as the *London Orphan Asylum*. Reed also founded the Royal Hospital and Home for Incurables at Putney, London.

Rees *See* RHYS.

Reformation The religious and political movement of 16th-century Europe is so named because it began as an attempt to *reform* the Roman Catholic Church. It resulted in the establishment of the PROTESTANT churches.

Reformation Symphony Mendelssohn's Symphony No 5 in D major, Op 107 (1832) is so named because it was written for the tercentenary of the Augsburg Confession of 1530, the statement of Protestant faith as held by the Lutheran church at the time of the REFORMATION. The first and last movements quote the 'Dresden Amen' and the Lutheran chorale *Ein' feste Burg*.

Reform Club The well-known London club was founded in 1832 as the prime club for Radicals, who supported parliamentary reform and who had been instrumental in bringing about the *Reform* Bill passed that same year. Many leading 19th-century Whigs were members. Today, however, membership is more for social than political reasons.

Regency The styles of art, architecture and literature of this name relate in England to the period from 1811 to 1820, when the Prince of Wales (later George IV) acted as *regent* during the insanity of his father, George III. In France, the equivalent name applies to the period from 1715 to 1723, when Philip, Duke of Orleans acted as *regent* during the minority of Louis XV, who succeeded to the throne when he was only five.

Regensburg The city of southeast Germany has a name meaning 'fortified town on the (river) *Regen*'. It was formerly known as *Ratisbon*, from its Roman name of *Ratisbona*, which derives from Celtic *rhath*, 'plain' and *bona*, 'foundation', 'fort'.

Regent's College The London college was established in 1984 as a private liberal arts college and centre for European studies. It takes its name from its location in REGENT'S PARK, where it occupies the buildings that belonged to BEDFORD COLLEGE before the latter's amalgamation with the Royal Holloway College.

Regent's Park The famous London park was created in 1812 by the architect John Nash for the Prince *Regent* (see REGENCY) and was named for him.

Regent Street London's well-known street was laid out by the architect John Nash over the period 1813 to 1821 as part of a scheme for the Prince *Regent* (see REGENCY). The street formed a 'royal mile' from REGENT'S PARK, also in the scheme, to the prince's house in St James's.

Reggio di Calabria The port in southern Italy, in CALABRIA, derives the main part of its name from Latin *regius*, 'royal'. Its original Roman name was *Regium Julium*, 'royal (town of) *Julius* (Caesar)'. *Cp.* REGGIO NELL'EMILIA.

Reggio nell'Emilia The city in northern Italy, in EMILIA-Romagna, had the original Roman name *Regium Lepidum*, 'royal (town of) Marcus Aemilius *Lepidus*'. *Cp.* REGGIO DI CALABRIA, from which it is differentiated by the additional name ('in Emilia'). Lepidus was the Roman statesman who supported Julius Caesar and who after the latter's death formed a triumvirate with Mark Antony and Octavian.

Regina The Canadian city, capital of Saskatchewan, was assigned its name in 1882 by the governor general, the Marquess of Lorne, in honour of his wife's mother-in-law, Queen Victoria, the latter's Latin title being *Victoria Regina*, 'Victoria, Queen'.

Reginald The source of the name lies in Latin *Reginaldus*, itself a form of *Reynold* (influenced by *regina*, 'queen'), which is Germanic in origin and derives from *ragin*, 'advice' and *wald*, 'ruler'.

Regulus The name of the brightest star in the constellation Leo derives from Latin *regulus*, 'young king', 'young prince', as a diminutive of *rex*, genitive *regis*, 'king'. Its Arabic name is *qalb al-asad*, 'heart of the lion', referring to the constellation. The name shows that the lion has long been regarded as a royal beast.

Reichstag The building in Berlin that was destroyed by fire in 1933 took its name from the legislative assembly that met there, first (from 1867) that of the North German Confederation, then (from 1871) that of the German empire, and finally (from 1919) the sovereign assembly of the Weimar republic. The name itself means 'imperial diet', from German *Reich*, 'empire' and *Tag*, 'diet', literally 'day'.

(Both German *Tag* in this sense and English *diet* derive from Latin *dies*, 'day', implying a fixed day of assembly.) *Cp.* BUNDESTAG.

Reigate The name of the Surrey town means 'doe gate', from Old English *rǣge*, 'doe' and *geat*, 'gate'. A 'doe gate' would have been an entrance to a deer park, or a gap in a fence where a doe could pass with her young.

Reilly The familiar name is the English spelling of the Irish name *Raghailleach*, whose own meaning is unknown.

Reims The cathedral city in northeast France takes its name from the *Remi*, a Gaulish people whose own name means 'dominant ones'. The name gave that of St *Remigius*, otherwise St *Rémi* or *Rémy*, the 6th-century bishop of Reims who converted Clovis, the pagan king of Gaul, to Christianity. Many French kings were subsequently crowned here. The city's name is still sometimes spelled *Rheims* by English speakers.

Reine, La Haydn's Symphony No 85 in B flat major (1785) is so nicknamed because it was admired by Marie Antoinette, *La Reine* ('the queen') of France.

Religio Medici The famous work by Sir Thomas Browne, meditating on his attitudes as a Christian and a doctor, was published in 1642 and has a Latin title meaning 'Religion of a Doctor'. A similar title is that of Dryden's religious poem *Religio Laici*, published in 1682, and meaning 'Religion of a Layman' (but actually subtitled *A Layman's Faith*).

R.E.M. The American rock group, formed in Athens, Georgia, in 1980, is said to have based its name on a random sequence of letters. However, *REM* is a recognized abbreviation for 'rapid eye movement' (the state of sleep in which dreaming takes place), and this may well have prompted the name.

Remembrance Sunday The name is that of the second Sunday in November, when (in Britain) the dead of both world wars are commemorated or *remembered*. This Sunday is the one closest to 11 November, the date of the armistice of 1918 that ended the First World War. An alternative name for the occasion, which was also formerly known as *Armistice Day*, is *Remembrance Day*.

Remington The famous make of typewriter is named for Eliphalet *Remington* (1793–1861), an American blacksmith's son who constructed a flintlock rifle in his father's forge in Utica, New York, who went on to manufacture sports guns and rifles, and who with his own son Philo Remington (1816–1889) founded a small arms factory. Philo continued his father's work after his death, expanding the business to include sewing machines in 1870 and typewriters in 1873.

Remus The name is familiar in Roman legend as that of the twin brother of ROMULUS who together with him is said to have founded Rome. The origin of his name is uncertain, but it is bound so closely with that of his brother that, like it, it may well ultimately derive from the name of ROME itself.

Rémy Martin The well-known brandy takes its name from the French wine-grower who founded the company in 1724. A document of 1738, issued in La Rochelle, authorizes a Monsieur *Rémy Martin* to replant his vineyards, showing that even at this early date there was official control of wine-growers and their business.

Renaissance The name is that of the transition period in European history from the Middle Ages to the modern world, with its revival of arts and letters. It is usually considered as beginning in Italy in the 14th century. The name is French, meaning literally 'rebirth', but translates Italian *renascenza* or more commonly *rinascimento*, in the same sense. The English use of the term dates only from the 19th century.

Renault The familiar make of French car takes its name from Louis *Renault* (1877–1944), who with his brothers Fernand and Marcel set up a motor engineering business at Billancourt, Paris, in 1898, the same year that he launched his first shaft-drive prototype voiturette.

Rendall *See* RANDALL.

Rendcomb College The boys' public school near Cirencester, Gloucestershire, was founded in 1920 and is named for *Rend-comb* Park, the Victorian country house in which it is based. The house takes its name from the village of *Rendcomb*, whose own name means '*Rend* valley', the proper name (originally *Hrinde*) being that of a stream here.

Renfrew The town in west central Scotland has a name meaning literally 'current point', from Celtic words related to modern Welsh *rhyn*, 'point' and *ffrwyd*, 'current'. Renfrew stands at the confluence of the small river Gryfe with the Clyde.

Rennes The city in northwest France takes its name from the *Redones*, the Gaulish people whose capital it was. Their own name derives from Gaulish *redo*, 'course', referring to the rivers Ille and Vilaine which meet here. The city's Roman name was *Condate*, 'confluence' (*cp.* KOBLENZ), for its location at the confluence of the rivers mentioned.

Rennies The antacid tablets take their name from John *Rennie*, a Yorkshireman who is believed to have been their original formulator. For some reason he chose France as his sole marketing area, hence the wording '*Digestif Rennie*' on the packets.

Reno The city in Nevada, famous for its liberal laws, was settled in about 1860 and subsequently named for the Virginia-born Union general Jesse Lee *Reno* (1823–1862), killed in the American Civil War.

Rentokil The name of the patent woodworm and dry rot eradication process suggests 'rent to kill'. It was originally *Entokil*, however, from Greek *entoma*, 'insects' and English *kill*, implying a process that killed insects. When application was made to register the name in the 1920s, permission was refused, as a similar name already existed. An initial *R* was therefore prefixed.

REO Speedwagon The American rock group, formed in Champaign, Illinois, in 1967, took their name from an early make of fire engine, with *REO* standing for the initials of its manufacturer, *R*ansom *E. O*lds. Olds (who also gave the name of the OLDSMOBILE) had challenged the established motor giants, such as General Motors, and the group chose the name be-

cause they, too, felt they were pitting themselves against the big names of rock. The name was also memorable, and its capital letters caught the eye on posters.

Republican Party The American political party originated in 1854 and was given a name that reflected the importance its founders attached to *republicanism*, that is, to national interest, as against sectional interest, or the rights of individual states. Many members, too, admired the form of republicanism advocated by Thomas Jefferson, founder of the *Democratic Party* (*see* DEMOCRAT). The latter party, now in 'opposition', was itself known as the *Republican Party* initially because of support for his views.

Resht *See* RASHT.

Restoration The name is used in British history for the period from 1660 to 1685 when the monarchy was *restored* in the person of Charles II after the Commonwealth of Cromwell from 1649 to 1660. The previous monarch, Charles I, had been executed in the former year.

Resurrection Symphony Mahler's Symphony No 2 in C minor (between 1888 and 1894) is so named because the finale is a setting of the *Aufersteh'n* ('Resurrection') chorale by the German poet Friedrich Klopstock (1724–1803).

Retrovir The brand name of the drug zidovudine, used in treating AIDS, is so named as it combats *retroviruses*, which cause AIDS and other infections of the immune system. Retroviruses themselves are so named not from Latin *retro-*, 'back', but from the initial letters of '*re*verse *tr*anscriptase' (plus a linking *-o-* before '*virus*'). Reverse transcriptase is an enzyme that gives a 'reverse transcription', copying RNA (ribonucleic acid) into DNA (deoxyribonucleic acid), instead of DNA into RNA, the latter being the usual flow of genetic information.

Reuben In the Old Testament, the name is that of one of the 12 sons of Jacob. It derives from Hebrew *Re'ūbēn*, 'see, a son'. The sense of this is explained in the text: 'And Leah conceived, and bare a son, and she called his name Reuben: for she said, Surely the Lord hath looked upon my affliction; now therefore my husband will love me' (*Genesis* 29.32). (Leah was 'afflicted' because her husband Jacob had been deceived into marrying her instead of his first love, her younger sister, Rachel.)

Réunion The island in the Indian Ocean, a French possession since 1642, was discovered by the Portuguese explorer Pedro de Mascareinhas in 1513, and when first occupied by the French was called by them *île Mascareigne*. In 1649 it was renamed *île Bourbon*, for the French royal house, but in 1793, at the time of the Revolution, was further renamed *Réunion* to commemorate the *reunion* of the revolutionaries from Marseille with the National Guard in Paris on 19 August 1792. Under Napoleon it was for a while known as *île Bonaparte*, then with the restoration of the monarchy in 1815 it reverted to *île Bourbon*. Finally, with the Revolution of 1848, it regained its former name *Réunion* and has retained it ever since.

Revelation The full title of the last book of the Bible is *The Revelation of St John the Divine*, implying in effect a revelation *to* St John, its purported recorder. It is so named because it *reveals* (in the sense of 'unveils') the future as far as the church and the world are concerned. The Latin-derived name translates the book's Greek name of APOCALYPSE.

Revised Standard Version The title is that of the *revision* by American scholars of the American *Standard Version* of the Bible, itself published in 1900 (New Testament) and 1901 (Old Testament). The RSV appeared in 1946 (New Testament) and 1953 (whole Bible).

Revised Version The name is that of the 19th-century *revision* of the AUTHORIZED VERSION of the Bible by British scholars. The New Testament was published in 1881 and the Old in 1885.

Revlon The noted brand of cosmetics takes its name from three American businessmen: Charles Haskell *Revson* (1906–1975), his brother Joseph, and their partner Charles R. Lachman. In 1930 Charles Revson set up a firm to make nail polish in Newark, New Jersey, and was soon joined by his brother. Charles Lachman worked with a similar company in New Rochelle, New York. They formed a partnership in 1932, adopting a name based on Charles Revson's surname with the letter *s* replaced by the initial *L* of Lachman's name.

Revolutionary Study Chopin's Etude in C minor, Op 10 No 12 (1830) for piano is so nicknamed because it is felt to express the composer's patriotic rage on learning that Warsaw had been captured by the Russians.

Reykjavík The capital of Iceland has a name meaning 'bay of smoke', from Icelandic *reykja*, 'to smoke' (related to German *rauchen* and English *reek*) and *vík*, 'bay' (as in the Scottish place-name WICK). The name alludes to the steam or vapour given off by the natural hot springs here.

Reynard The standard name for a fox derives from medieval tales and fables, in which the animal was personified thus. He is the hero in the French *Roman de Renart* of the late 12th and early 13th centuries, in which he is referred to as *Reynard le goupil*, 'Reynard the fox'. The standard French word for 'fox' was *goupil* (from Latin *vulpes*) until these popular tales appeared, as a result of which it was superseded by *renard*. The name is Germanic in origin, and comprises the words *ragin*, 'advice', 'counsel' and *hart*, 'hardy', 'brave'.

Rhaetia The Alpine province of ancient Rome takes its name from the Etruscan king *Rhaetus*, who was driven back into northern Italy by the Gauls. The meaning of his own name is unknown.

Rheims *See* REIMS.

Rhenish Symphony Schumann's Symphony No 3 in E flat major, Op 97 (1850) is so named because the fourth of its five movements was inspired by the installation of a cardinal at Cologne, which is on the river RHINE.

Rhesus In Greek mythology, the name is that of a king of Thrace. It seems to denote his belligerent nature, and to derive from Greek *rhēxis*, 'breaking', as if he was out to 'break' his enemies. His name was adopted for the *rhesus* monkey, used extensively in medical research, and giving its name in turn to the *rhesus* factor found as positive or negative antigens in human blood. It is not clear why the name of a mythical Greek king should have been adopted for a macaque monkey. The name was apparently devised for it by the French naturalist Jean-Baptiste Audebert in his *Histoire naturelle des Singes* (1799).

Rhine The famous river of central and western Europe has a name deriving from the people called the *Rheni* who lived along it. Their own name may derive from Gaulish *ren*, 'water', 'sea'.

Rhoda The name is traditionally derived from Greek *rhodon*, 'rose', although it could also be interpreted as 'woman from RHODES'.

Rhode Island The American state, in the northeast of the country (New England), was discovered in 1524 by the Italian explorer Giovanni da Verrazano, who is said to have observed (or fancied) a similarity between this island and the Greek RHODES in the Aegean. But the Dutch explorer Adriaen Block, here in 1635, named the island *Roodt Eylandt*, 'red island', for the colour of the soil, and it was probably this name that was rendered in English by 17th-century settlers, with the spelling perhaps influenced by that of the Greek island.

Rhode Island Red The breed of domestic fowl originated in the 19th century in the American state of RHODE ISLAND. *Red* refers to its brownish-red plumage, but happens to echo the literal meaning of the state name itself.

Rhodes The Greek island in the Aegean Sea, the largest in the Dodecanese, has a name that could represent Greek *rhodos*, 'rose' or *rhoia*, 'pomegranate'. Either source is plausible, since the ancient island inhabitants adopted the rose as the emblem of their sun god, and the island has many pomegranate trees. But the name may actually be pre-Greek in origin. Some biblical scholars claim that the name of *Dodanim* (*Genesis* 10.4), grandson of Japhet, should actually be *Rodanim*, referring to the inhabitants of Rhodes, with the error arising through a misreading of the Hebrew letter *resh* (*r*) as the very similar letter *daleth* (*d*). Moreover, while the Vulgate (Latin translation of the Bible) has *Dodanim*, the Septuagint (Greek translation of the Old Testament) renders the

name, with its Hebrew plural ending, as *Rhodioi*.

Rhodesia The former name (until 1979) for ZIMBABWE derives from the British colonial financier and statesman in South Africa, Cecil *Rhodes* (1853–1902). ZAMBIA is the former Northern *Rhodesia*.

Rhodope The mountain range in the Balkan Peninsula, on the border between Bulgaria and Greece, is said to take its name from the *Rhodope* of Greek mythology, the wife of Haemus, who (according to Ovid's *Metamorphoses*) was changed into a mountain here as a punishment for thinking herself more beautiful than Juno. Another name for the Balkan Mountains themselves, running across Bulgaria, is *Haemus*. This is supposed to derive from the name of her husband, who suffered an identical fate. Her name literally means 'rosy-faced', from Greek *rhodon*, 'rose' and *ōps*, 'face'. (*Cp.* LALLA ROOKH.)

Rhondda The South Wales town near Pontypridd takes its name from the river on which it stands, this itself meaning 'noisy one', from Welsh *rhoddni* (with the middle consonants transposed).

Rhône The river that flows through Switzerland and France has an ancient name perhaps deriving from a pre-Indoeuropean root element *rod*, 'to flow'. Whatever the source of the name, it is likely to be basic, and to mean nothing more subtle than 'river' at best.

Rhum *See* RUM.

Rhyl The North Wales resort has a name of mixed Welsh and English origin, with Welsh *yr*, 'the' prefixed to Old English *hyll*, 'hill'. There is hardly a hill here now in the normal sense of the word, but the ground does rise to the south of the town.

Rhys The familiar Welsh name, also spelled *Rees*, is a personal name in origin, from *Rīs*, 'ardour', implying a keen warrior. It is this name that gave the common surname PRICE.

Rialto The island in Venice, Italy, famous as a commercial centre in medieval and Renaissance times, derives its name from *Rivoalto*, a former name of VENICE, meaning 'high bank' (modern Italian *ripa alta*).

Ribble The north of England river has a name that is probably related to modern *rip*, meaning 'tearing one', and referring to the scouring action of the river current.

Ribena The familiar blackcurrant drink, first marketed in the late 1930s, takes its name from the Latin botanical term for this fruit, *Ribes nigrum*.

Rich The name could originally have been a nickname for a wealthy person, or have evolved as a short form of RICHARD. In some cases the origin is in a place-name *Reach*, meaning 'stream', as for Glynde *Reach* near GLYNDEBOURNE in Sussex.

Richard The long-popular name is Germanic in origin, representing a combination of *rīc*, 'power' and *hart*, 'hardy', 'brave'. It has been promoted as a royal name, and in particular by *Richard* I Coeur de Lion ('Lionheart') in the 12th century.

Richards The name means 'son of RICHARD', as more obviously does *Richardson*. Cp. PRITCHARD, the Welsh equivalent.

Richmond There are two English towns of the name, with the former Surrey (now Greater London) town taking the name of the North Yorkshire one. The Yorkshire town has a Norman name meaning 'strong hill', either given directly to the place, for its high location, or 'exported' from another place of the name in northern France. The Surrey town was originally known as *Sheen*, meaning 'shelters'. When Henry VII built a palace here in 1501, however, to replace the former one destroyed by fire, he renamed it *Richmond*, after his former title of Earl of *Richmond* (Yorkshire). He also doubtless regarded this as a more fitting name for a palace than one that simply meant 'shelters'. *Richmond*, the state capital of Virginia, was laid out in 1737 on what is now Church Hill by the English colonial official William Byrd, who named it for his native town of *Richmond*, Surrey, probably because he fancied a resemblance between the location of the settlement, on the James River, and his home town on the Thames. The name is found for many places in the United States, not simply as a direct transfer from one or other of the English towns, but equally for its association with nobility (the dukes and earls of *Richmond*) and for its implied popular sense of 'rich mount' (or even a 'mound of riches').

Rider The name was an occupational one for a *rider* as a mounted warrior or messenger (the forerunner of the knight).

Ridgways The well-known brand of tea takes its name from Thomas *Ridgway*, who opened a tea shop in the City of London in 1836. The company of today retains the founder's name, although the Ridgway family ceased to be involved in the business as early as 1871.

Riesengebirge The German name of the mountain range on the border between Poland and the Czech Lands means 'giant mountains', as which they are sometimes known in English. Their Czech and Polish names are respectively *Krkonoše* and *Karkonosze*, perhaps based on the name of a people who once lived here.

Rievaulx The North Yorkshire village, with its famous ruined abbey, has a name meaning '*Rye* valley', for the river here. The second half of the name represents Norman French *val*, 'valley'.

Rif The hilly coastal region in northern Morocco is also known as *Er Rif*, which more closely represents its Arabic origin, *ar-rīf*, 'the coastland'.

Riga The capital of Latvia has a name deriving either from Old Latvian *ringa*, 'curve', or Lithuanian *rīdziņa*, 'stream'. The curve would be that of the Western Dvina on which the city is situated, the 'stream' one of its tributaries.

Rigel The brightest star in the constellation Orion has a name of Arabic origin, representing *rijl*, 'foot', from the full phrase *rijl al-jawzā*, 'foot of Orion', since among the stars that form the outline of the giant Orion it was regarded as marking his left foot.

Righteous Brothers, The The American white soul duo was formed at Anaheim, California, in 1962 as the *Paramours*. When the two were nicknamed 'righteous brothers' (*i.e.* excellent performers) by black fans, however, they adopted the slang phrase for their name instead.

Rig-Veda The compilation of over 1000 ancient Hindu poems or hymns has a name representing Sanskrit *rigveda*, from *ric*, 'song of praise' and VEDA (*which see*).

Riihimäki The city in southern Finland has a name that is a combination of Finnish *riihi*, 'granary', 'loft' and *mäki*, 'hill', 'slope'.

Rijeka The city and port in northwest Croatia has changed hands many times, in particular passing back and forth between Italy and Yugoslavia. Its present name is the Croat word for 'river', corresponding to its Italian name of *Fiume* (from Latin *flumen*). The river in question is the one known in Serbo-Croat as *Rječina* and in Italian as *Fiumara* or *Eneo*.

Rijksmuseum The famous museum in Amsterdam houses the national art collection of the Netherlands. Its name amounts to 'state museum', from Dutch *rijk*, 'empire', 'kingdom', 'realm' (as German *Reich*) and *museum*, 'museum'.

Rikki-tikki-tavi The mongoose who is the central character in the story of the same name in Kipling's *Jungle Books* (1894, 1895) is so called from his 'war-cry, as he scuttled through the long grass': '*Rikk-tikk-tikki-tikki-tchk!*'. The author specified that the name should be pronounced 'Rikky-tikky-tar-vi'.

Rimini The port and resort in northeast Italy had the Roman name *Ariminum*, the origin of which is unknown.

Rin-Tin-Tin The name is that of the Alsatian (German shepherd) dog who starred in a number of Hollywood films from 1923. He was one of a litter that American airmen rescued from an abandoned German dugout in France in 1918, and was named by an American corporal after the tiny doll that French soldiers carried for luck. The name itself is something like English 'Tinker Bell'. The dog was usually known as *Rinty* for short.

Rio de Janeiro The port and former capital of Brazil has a Portuguese name meaning 'January river'. The expedition led by Amerigo Vespucci discovered the bay here on Saturday 1 *January* 1502, and gave it the name in the belief that they had entered the estuary of a large river. There is in fact no river here at all, so that the city's name is a geographical misnomer.

Rio de Oro The former Spanish protectorate in western Africa, today under Moroccan control in the Western Sahara, has a Spanish name meaning 'river of gold'. It was given by members of a Portuguese expedition here in 1436 to the inlet at what is now the principal town of Villa Cisneros, where they had found the local inhabitants trading gold dust.

Rio Grande The famous river of North America, forming a boundary between the United States and Mexico, has a Portuguese name meaning simply 'big river'. In Mexico it is known as the *Río Bravo*, 'wild river'. The name occurs elsewhere for other rivers, including two in Brazil.

Rio Muni The mainland province of Equatorial Guinea derives its name from Spanish *río*, 'river' and a local word meaning 'silence'. It is thus the 'silent river', referring to the estuary of the Utamboni, in the southwest of the country.

Ripon The North Yorkshire town has a name based on that of the people known as the *Hrype* who once inhabited this region. Nothing is known about them except their name, which also lies behind that of *Repton* in Derbyshire, presumably because some of them went there from Ripon.

Ripuarians The name for the group of Franks who lived near Cologne by the Rhine in the 4th century represents their Medieval Latin name of *Ripuarii*. This may derive from Latin *ripa*, 'bank', referring to that of the river Rhine by which they lived. The etymology of the name is disputed, however.

Rip Van Winkle The nickname for a person who is behind the times, or who sleeps a lot, is taken from the fictional character in the story of the same name by Washington Irving, published in 1819. In this, *Rip Van Winkle* is a lazy Dutch-American who meets a dwarf, drinks with him over a game of ninepins, and falls into a sleep which lasts for 20 years. When he eventually wakes up, he finds that the Revolutionary War has taken place. His name is a random Dutch-American one, and although *Van Winkle* exists as a real surname in its own right, it may have been chosen by Irving for its suggestion of *wink*.

Risorgimento The 19th-century movement for the political unification of Italy has a name that is the Italian word for 're-surgence', literally 'rising up again'.

Rita The name evolved as an independent diminutive of *Margarita*, the Spanish form of MARGARET.

Ritz The famous London hotel takes its name from its designer, the Swiss hotel-keeper César *Ritz* (1850–1918), who owned fashionable hotels in many cities of the world. The London *Ritz* opened in 1906, and the name itself became synonymous with opulence and social elegance.

Rivett The name was originally occupational for a person who worked with *rivets*, that is, as a metalworker.

Riviera Wherever it occurs, and most familiarly for the French *Riviera*, the Mediterranean coast between Cannes, France, and La Spezia, Italy, the name is the Italian word for 'shore'. Britain's best-known coast of the name is the Cornish *Riviera*, promoted largely by the Great Western Railway, whose famous 'Cornish Riviera Express' (originally simply 'Riviera Express') first ran from London to Penzance in 1904.

Riyadh The capital of Saudi Arabia (jointly, with Mecca) has a name representing Arabic *ar-riyāḍ*, 'the gardens', from *al*, 'the' and *riyāḍ*, the plural of *rawḍa*, 'garden'. The city arose round a small oasis.

Rizla The brand of cigarette paper derives its name from the paper manufactured by a Frenchman named Lacroix in 1796. From this developed so-called 'rice paper', used for rolling tobacco to make cigarettes. The full form of the name thus comprises French *riz*, 'rice', plus the first two letters of '*La*croix' followed by a small cross (French *croix*) to complete the surname.

Roanne The town in southeast central France had the Roman name of *Rodumna*. This probably derives from the Celtic (or pre-Celtic) root element *rod* meaning 'water', 'river', as for the RHÔNE. The town is on the river Loire.

Roanoke Island The island off the coast of North Carolina, famous as the site of the first attempted English settlement in America in 1585, has a name of Indian origin, said to mean 'place where white shells were found' or 'shells used for money'.

Roaring Forties The name is that of the ocean regions between *40°* and 50° latitude in the southern hemisphere, where there are gale-force *roaring* winds.

Robben Island The island off the Cape Peninsula, South Africa, used by the government as a political prison, has a Dutch name meaning 'seal island', from Dutch *robbe*, 'seal'.

Robert The name is one of the many introduced to Britain by the Normans. It derives from the Germanic name *Hrodebert*, comprising *hrōd*, 'fame' and *beraht*, 'bright'. Since the latter word implies 'famous', the two halves of the name are basically synonymous. Historically it was the name of the father of William the Conqueror as well as that of his eldest son. It is also well-known from several Scottish kings, especially *Robert* the Bruce, who gained Scotland's independence from England in the 14th century.

Robert Gordon's College The Scottish public school, in Aberdeen, was founded in 1729 by *Robert Gordon* (1665–1732), a former merchant in the Baltic, who beqeathed his property to the town council for the purposes of 'founding and supporting a hospital for educating indigent children'. His bequest was prompted by that of George Heriot for GEORGE HERIOT'S SCHOOL.

Roberts The name means 'son of ROBERT', as more obviously does *Robertson*.

Robertsons The familiar make of jam and marmalade is named for the company's founder, James *Robertson*, a Scottish grocer from Paisley, who in 1864 bought a barrel of bitter oranges that his wife used to make marmalade. The resulting preserve sold well in his shop, so that he gave up his grocer's trade and concentrated full-time on making marmalade, building a special factory for the purpose. In 1890 James Robertson opened a second factory in Droylsden, near Manchester, where the company's headquarters remain today.

Robin The name originated as a pet form of ROBERT, through the short form *Rob* and the Old French diminutive suffix *-in*. In recent years it has gained some popularity as a female name, doubtless influenced by the name of the bird.

Robin Goodfellow The name is an alternative one for PUCK, and is simply a combination of the 'friendly' name ROBIN (as for ROBIN HOOD) and the self-descriptive surname *Goodfellow*, originally a nickname for a convivial companion.

Robin Hood The legendary English outlaw is traditionally said to have lived in Sherwood Forest in the 12th and 13th centuries. His name is of disputed origin. His first name is almost certainly the familiar personal name ROBIN, used in a 'friendly' sense as it is for various people and creatures, such as ROBIN GOODFELLOW or the bird *robin redbreast* (originally known as *redbreast*, then *robin redbreast*, and now regularly *robin*). His surname is popularly explained as referring to the *hood* that he wore, or to the fact that he was *o' th' wood*. Such simple origins are attractive but unlikely, although his French equivalent is *Robin du Bois*, 'Robin of the wood'. Some scholars have linked the name with that of WODEN, the foremost Anglo-Saxon god, or with that of the Norse god *Hödr*, meaning 'warrior'. Another theory, still widely quoted, is that his full name is a corruption of that of *Robert Fitzooth*, said to have been a grandson of one Ralph Fitzooth, a Norman who came to England at the time of the Conquest. Other authorities point to the many place-names containing *Robin Hood* in the Midlands and north of England, especially those of natural features such as hills, woods, fields and even individual trees. Could he not be the personification of one or more of these? But most names of this type are not recorded early, and they almost certainly arose from the tales and ballads about him, rather than the other way round. The whole issue is further complicated by the fact that his name has been popularly associated with that of ROBIN GOODFELLOW. When all is said and done, however, his surname is likely to be the standard *Hood*, as originally applied to a maker or wearer of *hoods*, or to someone who lived in a naturally sheltered place, with a protective *hood* of some kind, such as an overhanging rock. For the names of his most familiar companions, see FRIAR TUCK, LITTLE JOHN, MAID MARIAN.

Robinson The name means 'son of ROBIN'.

Robinson College The Cambridge college was founded in 1979 by the millionaire television rental pioneer Sir David *Robinson* (1904–1987). The choice of name was not his, and he was not present for the official opening ceremony conducted by the Queen on 29 May 1981. The college was the first in the university to be founded for both men and women.

Robinsons The well-known make of 'Barley Water' is named for one Matt *Robinson*, whose firm of Robinson and Bellville had been making Robinson's 'Patent' Barley for some 40 years before they amalgamated with the firm of Keen & Son of London, who made mustard, to form Keen Robinson. In 1903 the combined firm was taken over by Colmans for the sake of its mustard, and it is the company of RECKITT AND COLMAN who market Robinson's 'Barley Water' today.

Rob Roy The hero of the Walter Scott novel of the same name, published in 1817, was based on a historical character, the Scottish freebooter and outlaw Robert MacGregor (1671–1734). He was nicknamed *Roy* for his red hair, from Gaelic *ruadh*, 'red'. (Hence the adjective following the noun, as regularly in Celtic languages.) The same word gave the common first name ROY, although this was popularly reinterpreted as representing Old French *roy*, 'king'.

Rochdale The name of the town near Manchester originated as something like *Rachedham*, from Old English *ræced*, 'building', 'hall', and *hām*, 'homestead', so that it was a 'homestead by a hall'. The name then passed to the river, as the *Rached*. Later, the river valley became known as the *Rached-dale*, which eventually gave *Rochdale*, and this became the name of the town instead of *Rachedham*. Finally, the *-dale* was dropped to give the modern river name of *Roch*. A rather involved evolution, therefore.

Rochelle, La *See* LA ROCHELLE.

459

Rochester The ancient city and port in Kent has the *-chester*, ultimately from Latin *castra*, 'camp', that shows it to have been a Roman station. The initial *Ro-* is all that remains of the accented second syllable of *Durobrivae*, its Roman name, meaning 'bridge fort', from two Celtic elements *duro*, 'fort' and *briva*, 'bridge'. The name was recorded in the Domesday Book as *Rovescestre*. The city of *Rochester* in New York State was founded in 1811 and originally named *Rochesterville*, for its founder, the pioneer Colonel Nathaniel *Rochester* (1752–1831). In 1822 the name was shortened to *Rochester*. This name was in turn adopted by the city of *Rochester*, Minnesota, in 1854.

Rockall The uninhabited island in the Atlantic, west of the Outer Hebrides, has a name that suggests it is 'all rock', which it is, but which probably derives from Old Norse *rok*, 'steam', 'stormy sea' (modern Scottish *roke*) and *kollr*, 'hill', 'top', 'bald head'.

Rocky Mountains The chief mountain system of western North America has a name which rather than being self-explanatory derives from the Indian *Assiniboine* people here, their name translating as 'rock'. The mountains are not noticeably rocky in any case.

Roderick The name is a Germanic one, deriving from *hrōd*, 'fame' (as for ROBERT) and *rīc*, 'power' (as for RICHARD). The name can also be an anglicized form of Welsh *Rhydderch*, which gave the surname PROTHERO.

Rodney The first name derives from the surname, which itself comes from a place-name, that of *Rodney* in Somerset, now represented by the village of *Rodney* Stoke near Wells. The place-name means '*Hroda*'s island', with the Anglo-Saxon personal name followed by Old English *ēg*, 'island', meaning raised land among low-lying marshes.

Rogation Days In the Christian calendar, the name is given to the days in spring on which special prayers are said that the newly sown crops may produce a good harvest. The term for such a supplication, which originally was combined with penitence and fasting, is a *rogation*, from Latin *rogare*, 'to ask'. The days concerned are the three preceding Ascension Day (which always falls on a Thursday). The Sunday before this is sometimes known as *Rogation Sunday*.

Roger The name, introduced to Britain by the Normans, means 'famous spear' and is of Germanic origin. The two halves of the name comprise *hrōd*, 'fame' and *gēr*, 'spear'.

Rogers The name means 'son of ROGER'.

Rokeby Venus The famous painting by Velázquez, showing a reclining nude admiring her reflection in a mirror held by a cherub, has the formal title *The Toilet of Venus* (1651). It is now in the National Gallery, London, but gained its familiar name from *Rokeby* Hall, Co Durham, the home of its previous owners, the Morritt family. The same country estate gave the name of Walter Scott's poem *Rokeby* (1813).

Roland Like ROBERT, RODERICK and ROGER, the name is Germanic in origin and was introduced to Britain by the Normans. Like them, too, its first part represents *hrōd*, 'fame'. Its second part is *land*, 'land', 'territory'. The name is famous in folklore as that of the knight of Charlemagne who was killed at the Battle of Roncesvalles in 778. His friendship with his fellow knight Oliver is legendary.

Rolex The prestigious make of watch has an arbitrary name with no precise meaning. The word does suggest '*roll*', however, which is appropriate for an instrument that records the passage of time ('like an ever-rolling stream').

Rolf *See* RUDOLF.

Rolleiflex The familiar make of camera is of German origin, and was a *roll*-film model at first called the *Rolleidoskop*, from German *Rolle*, 'roll' and a Greek word meaning literally 'form-viewer', from *eidos*, 'form' and *skopeein*, 'to view'. The latter also suggests the name of the manufacturers, Franke and *Heidecke*, whose original product was a stereoscopic plate camera called the *Heidoskop*. The final *-flex* denotes that the camera is a *reflex* model, that is, one in which the image is *reflected* on to a glass screen for composing and focusing. The name is often abbreviated to *Rollei*.

Rolling Stones, The The famous British rock band was formed in London in 1962 and took its name from the Muddy Waters song 'Rollin' Stone' (1950). The name is more subtle than it might appear. Intentionally or not, it evokes rock and *roll* on the one hand, and indulgence in drink and drugs (getting *stoned*) on the other, all three being mutually integrated ingredients of the 1960s pop scene. The overall name also implies a 'liberated' group, or one that travels widely, as the Rolling Stones did. Finally, it suggests a primeval quality, like that of the ROLLRIGHT STONES. The name may not have been created with all these overtones, but it certainly has them.

Rollright Stones The famous Bronze Age stone circle in Oxfordshire takes its name from the nearby village of Great *Rollright*, whose own name probably derives from the Anglo-Saxon personal name *Hrōlla* (the short form of a name such as *Hrōthlāf*) followed by a form of Old English *land-riht*, 'land rights'. The reference would be to an estate where special local rights applied.

Rolls-Royce The prestigious car takes its name from an electrical engineer, Frederick Henry *Royce* (1863–1933) and a motor enthusiast, the Hon Charles Stewart *Rolls* (1877–1910). Royce was born near Peterborough, a farmer's son. He became an experienced engineer and started making electrical components in Manchester in 1884. In 1902 he turned to manufacturing cars, and these came to the notice of Rolls, who had just set up as a motor trader in London. The two men met in 1904 and set up a partnership, with Rolls agreeing to be the sole selling agent for Royce's cars. They chose the name *Rolls-Royce* for their joint enterprise because they thought it sounded better this way round, although logically it should have been '*Royce-Rolls*'.

Romagna The region of northern Italy that is now part of EMILIA-Romagna derives its name from the *Romans*, whose territory it was.

Romania The republic of southeast Europe has a name telling of its *Roman* origin. It arose as an outpost of the Roman Empire in the early years AD when the Dacians crossed the Danube and settled here, intermingling and interbreeding with the indigenous people. The resulting meld came to be known as the *Romani*, 'people from ROME', and this gave the present country's name.

Romany The name for the Gypsies and their language is itself a Romany word (the adjective *romani*) meaning 'GYPSY', in turn from Romany *rom*, 'man', and ultimately from Sanskrit *ḍomba*, a term for a low caste of musicians. *See also* ROMANY RYE.

Romany Rye, The The title of the novel by George Borrow, published in 1857, is ROMANY for 'Gypsy gentleman', a nickname given Borrow himself in his youth by Ambrose Smith, a Norfolk Gypsy. The book is a sequel to *Lavengro* (1851), in which the term is introduced:

> 'Aukko tu pios adrey Rommanis. Here is your health in Romany, brother,' said Mr. Petulengro, who, having refilled the cup, now emptied it at a draught.
> 'Your health in Romany, brother,' said Tawno Chikno, to whom the cup came next.
> 'The Romany Rye,' said a third.
> 'The Gipsy gentleman,' exclaimed a fourth, drinking.
>
> Chapter 54.

Rome The famous city, capital of Italy and formerly of the Roman Empire, is popularly said to take its name from its legendary founder, ROMULUS. But his own name comes from that of the city, so that some other origin must be sought. The source may lie in *Ruma* or *Roma* as an earlier name for the river TIBER, itself of Etruscan origin, but possibly related to Greek *rheein*, 'to flow'. For the Cathars, the heretical Christian sect that flourished in western Europe in the 12th and 13th centuries, and who held that the material world is evil, *Roma*, the Church of Rome, was the opposite of *Amor*, the personification of Love.

Romeo The name, famous from Shakespeare's *Romeo and Juliet* (1595), is intimately linked with that of ROME. It originated in Italy as a medieval religious name for someone who had made a pilgrimage to that city. Shakespeare's ultimate source for the name was a story by the Italian writer Matteo Bandello.

Romford The former Essex town, now in Greater London, has a name meaning 'broad ford', from Old English *rūm*, 'broad' (modern 'room') and *ford*, 'ford'. The ford would have been over the river Rom here (which takes its name from the town itself).

Romney Marsh The name of the marshy area of Kent derives from the Old English descriptive phrase *æt thǽre rūman ē*, 'at the broad river'. The many streams that were formerly here must have given the impression of a single broad river.

Romsey The Hampshire town has a name meaning '*Rūm*'s island', with *Rūm* an Anglo-Saxon personal name that is short for a longer name such as *Rumbald* (modern *Rumbold*). The second half of the name represents Old English *ēg*, 'island', meaning land raised above a low-lying surrounding region, in this case the land round Romsey Abbey, away from the lower-lying river.

Romulus Although *Romulus*, with his twin brother REMUS, is traditionally regarded as the founder of ROME, his own name actually derives from that of the city. It is a diminutive, as if 'little Roman', and in some versions of the Romulus and Remus legend he is said to have been the smaller of the twins born to the goddess Rhea Silvia and suckled by a she-wolf.

Ronald The name is Scandinavian in origin, from *Rögnvaldr*, which combines Old Norse *regin*, 'advice' and *valdr*, 'ruler', implying a wise or inspired leader.

Roncesvalles The village in northern Spain, famous for the nearby pass where Charlemagne was defeated and Roland killed in AD 778, has a French name meaning 'bramble valley', from *ronce*, 'bramble', 'blackberry' and *val*, 'valley'. The Basque name of the pass is *Orreaga*, 'place of junipers', from *orre*, 'juniper' and the suffix *-aga*, 'place abounding in'. The French form of the name is *Roncevaux*.

Roneo The patent method of duplicating a document from a stencil has a name that evolved as an abbreviation of *Ro*tary *Neo*style. This itself was originally a make

of duplicating machine invented in New York in the 1890s by Augustus David Klaber, a former agent for Gestetner.

Ronettes, The The American pop trio was formed in New York in 1959 by two sisters and their female cousin. They based their name on that of one of the sisters, *Veronica* Bennett, known as *Ronnie*. Her surname may have further suggested the name, although *-ette* is a recognized feminine suffix (as for *usherette* or *drum majorette*).

Ronson The well-known make of cigarette lighter takes its name from the founder of the American manufacturing company in 1895, Louis V. *Aronson*.

Rooney The name is the English form of the Irish name *Ó Ruanaidh*, 'descendant of *Ruanaidh*', a personal name meaning 'champion'.

Root The name could originally have been a nickname for a cheerful person, from Old English *rōt*, 'glad'. Otherwise it could have denoted a player on the *rote*, a type of medieval stringed instrument, or someone who lived by a *retting* place (where flax was soaked until the stems *rotted* to yield the linen fibres).

Roper The occupational name was used for a person who made or sold *rope*. The surname *Raper* has the same origin, from a northern dialect form of the basic word.

Roquefort The village in southern France, famous for its strong-flavoured blue cheese, has an almost appropriate name, meaning 'strong rock'. The name is found elsewhere in France for places by solid rocks.

Rosa, Monte The mountain between Italy and Switzerland probably has a name that derives from the Celtic root word *ros* meaning 'mountain'. On the face of it, however, the name means 'rose mountain'.

Rosalind The name is traditionally explained as representing Latin (or Spanish) *rosa linda*, 'lovely rose'. But it is actually Germanic in origin, and comprises a blend of *hros*, 'horse' and *lind*, 'tender'. This is in fact just as complimentary, although less so in modern terms. The name was popularized by the heroine of Shakespeare's *As You Like It* (1599). *Cp.* ROSAMUND.

Rosamund The popular derivation of the name is usually given as Latin *rosa mundi*, 'rose of the world'. Like ROSALIND, however, it is really Germanic in origin, and represents a combination of *hros*, 'horse' and *mund*, 'protection'. In literature, the name is famous as that of the 12th-century legendary beauty 'Fair Rosamond', otherwise *Rosamond* Clifford, said to have been the mistress of Henry II and to have been murdered by Queen Eleanor of Aquitaine.

Roscoff The town and port in Brittany, northwest France, has a name that means 'hill of the blacksmith', from Breton *roz*, 'mound', 'hill' and *gov*, 'blacksmith'.

Roscommon The name of the town and county in Northern Ireland is an English form of its Irish name *Ros Comáin*, 'Comán's wood'. St Comán founded a monastery here in the 8th century.

Rose The name is normally related to that of the flower. However, flower names came into fashion only in the 19th century, and *Rose* was known long before this. For this reason it may have originated as the short form of a Germanic name in which it represents either *hros*, 'horse' or *hrōd*, 'fame'. *Cp.* ROSALIND and ROSAMUND.

Rosemary The name arose as one of those derived from flowers in the 19th century, and so refers to the aromatic shrub (whose own name actually means 'sea dew', from Latin *ros marinus*). The particular attraction of the name is that it seems also to combine the two individual names ROSE and MARY.

Rose Royce The American rock band was formed in 1976 and named by the former Motown producer Norman Whitfield after the British luxury car ROLLS ROYCE. Whitfield was commissioned to write the music for the comedy movie *Car Wash*, and the title song from this was the group's first hit. The band's lead singer, Gwen Dickey, later changed her name to Rose Norwalt.

Roses The familiar brand of lime juice and marmalade takes its name from Lauchlan *Rose* (d. 1885), a Scottish shipbuilder's son, who set up as a lime and lemon merchant in Leith, near Edinburgh in 1865. Rose's family not only built ships but also provisioned them, and they were aware of the importance of lime juice in combating scurvy among the sailors of the day. Lauchlan Rose patented a method of making a non-alcoholic drink from lime juice, and his resulting sales were so good that he moved his business down to London in 1875. The firm first produced lime marmalade in the 1930s.

Roses, Wars of the *See* WARS OF THE ROSES.

Rosh Hashanah The name of the festival marking the Jewish New Year represents Hebrew *rōš hašānāh*, literally 'head of the year', from *rōš*, 'head' and *haš-šānāh*, 'year'.

Rosicrucian The esoteric religious society, which specially venerates the *rose* and the *Cross* as symbols of Christ's Resurrection and Redemption, derives its name from Latin *Rosa Crucis*, 'rose of the Cross', a translation of the German name of Christian *Rosenkreuz*, its supposed founder in the 15th century.

Rosinante The name of Don Quixote's horse, now sometimes used for any poor old worn-out horse, derives from Spanish *rocín*, 'nag' and *antes*, 'before', as the horse was the foremost nag of his kind.

Roskilde The city in eastern Denmark, the country's capital from the 10th century to 1443, derives its name from Old Danish *Hroarskilde*, representing *Hroar*, the name of the king who was its legendary founder, and *kilde*, 'spring'.

Ross The place-name is found in that of the Scottish administrative district of *Ross* and Cromarty, and was formerly familiar as that of *Ross-shire*. It represents Gaelic *ros*, 'moorland', with this word also widely found in the sense 'promontory'. The region is large enough, in the central Highlands, to accommodate both senses.

Ross The personal name has several possible origins. It could have been imported to Britain by Normans from the French place called *Rots*, near Caen, with this itself perhaps meaning 'clearing'. In England and Scotland it could equally derive from any of the places called ROSS, where the meaning is often 'headland', 'promontory'. As an occupational name, it would have denoted someone who bred or kept horses, from Old English *hros*, 'horse'. As a nickname it could equally have been given to a person who was regarded as resembling a horse in some way.

Ross The noted brand of frozen foods is named for J. Carl *Ross* (1902–1986), who began his career as a barrow boy in the docks of Grimsby, Lincolnshire. He built up a business selling fish, and by the late 1950s had a trawler fleet of 66 ships that was the largest of its kind in the world.

Ross Dependency The section of Antarctica administered by New Zealand is named for the Scottish polar explorer Sir James *Ross* (1800–1862). He also gave his name to the *Ross* Sea, *Ross* Island and the *Ross* Ice Shelf here.

Rosslare The port and resort in Co Wexford, Ireland, has a name that represents Irish *Ros Láir*, 'middle headland', from *ros*, 'promontory' and *lár*, genitive *láir*, 'middle', 'centre'. The reference is to the location of the place between The Raven Point to the north and Greenore Point to the south.

Rostock The port in northeast Germany had the Medieval Latin name of *Rostochium*. This has been popularly interpreted as representing either *Rosenstadt*, 'city of roses' or *roter Stock*, 'red stick' (*cp.* BATON ROUGE). But both of these origins are highly unlikely, and the true source of the name is perhaps in Slavic *rastok*, 'place where rivers separate' (the opposite of a confluence). Rostock is at the head of the estuary of the river Warnow at the point where it divides into two.

Rostov The port in southwest Russia arose in 1761 as a fortress with a church dedicated to St Dmitry of *Rostov*, that is, of the ancient city of *Rostov* (also known as *Rostov Veliky*, 'Rostov the Great') near Yaroslavl. A settlement grew up round the fort, and in 1796 this became a town. The present city is often known as *Rostov-na-Donu* ('Rostov-on-Don') to be distinguished from its older namesake. The original name is of uncertain origin but may represent a Slavic personal name.

Rosyth The town in Fife, southeast Scotland, has a name that seems to comprise Gaelic *ros*, 'headland' and Old English *hyth*,

'landing place'. But although both words suit the topography of the place, their combination is unlikely, and the true sense of the name remains uncertain.

Rotary Club The name denotes any of the local clubs that belong to *Rotary International*, a club for professional and businessmen founded in Chicago in 1905 with the aim of promoting community service. The name *Rotary* was chosen for the association because meetings were to be held in *rotation* in members' offices.

Rotavator The proprietary name of the machine with rotating blades used for breaking up soil, especially on rough ground, is short for '*rota*ry culti*vator*'. The name was first registered in 1936. It is sometimes also spelled *Rotovator*, which slightly spoils the palindromic effect.

Rotherham The town near Sheffield takes its name from the river *Rother* here, with the final *-ham* meaning 'homestead'. The river's own name is probably of Celtic origin meaning 'main river'.

Rotherhithe The district of east London, by the Thames, has a name meaning 'landing place for cattle', from Old English *hrȳther*, 'cattle' and *hȳth*, 'landing place'. The *hithe* element is better preserved here than it is in the names of other Thames-side places such as CHELSEA, LAMBETH, PUTNEY and STEPNEY, all of which contain the Old English word. Rotherhithe was also known as *Redriff* (of the same origin) down to at least the 18th century, and occurs as such in Swift's *Gulliver's Travels* (1726): 'I left fifteen Hundred Pounds with my Wife, and fixed her in a good House at *Redriff*.' (Part I, Chapter 8.)

Rothmans The well-known brand of cigarettes is named for Louis *Rothman* (1869–1926), the son of a Jewish Ukrainian tobacco manufacturer, who emigrated to London in 1887 and bought the lease of a small shop in Fleet Street, making cigarettes by hand to sell to journalists. His reputation grew, so that he moved to new premises in fashionable Pall Mall. Hence the familiar '*Rothmans of Pall Mall*' of today. Rothman was granted a Royal Warrant by Edward VII in 1905.

Rothschild The standard English pronunciation of the name as 'Roths-child' effectively masks its true origin, which is in German *rot*, 'red' and *Schild*, 'shield'. The famous Jewish banking family took their name from that of a house marked with a *red shield* in the Jewish district of Frankfurt. Now, however, the name has been adopted by Jews elsewhere. The original pronunciation of the name, as still in German, was thus closer to 'Rote-shilt'.

Rotorua The city in central North Island, New Zealand, arose in the 1870s and takes its name from the lake on the southwest end of which it lies. The name of the lake is Maori in origin, and is said to mean 'long lake', from *roto*, 'lake' and *rua*, 'long'. The lake is actually pear-shaped, but is the largest in the group of about 20 lakes here.

Rotten Row The famous horse-riding road in London's Hyde Park has a name that is popularly (and persistently) said to be a corruption of French *route du roi*, 'road of the king', as if a royal route. It is true that the road approaches Kensington Palace, which was a royal residence from the time of William III (reigned 1689–1702). But why should the road have been given a French name? The name almost certainly means what it says, referring to the 'rotten' or soft state of the earth here. No written record of the name has been found earlier than 1781, however.

Rotterdam The port in the southwest Netherlands has a name meaning 'dam on the (river) *Rotte*', the latter being a minor tributary of the river Nieuwe Maas. *Cp.* AMSTERDAM, EDAM.

Rottweiler The breed of large, stocky and sometimes belligerent dogs is named for the German city of *Rottweil*, near Stuttgart, where it was originally a type of working dog used by Roman legions.

Roubaix The name of the city in northern France, near the border with Belgium, means 'horse stream', from Old German *hros*, 'horse' and *baki*, 'stream'. The reference would be to a stream where horses came to drink or where they crossed.

Rouen The city in northern France, on the Seine, had the Roman name *Rotomagus*. The latter half of this is Gaulish *mago*, 'field', 'market'. The first half may represent *roto*, 'town', or be the personal name *Roto*.

Roundhead The supporters of Parliament against Charles I during the English Civil War were so nicknamed from their short-cut hair. The name is first recorded in 1641, and is in essence a forerunner of that of the *skinhead* three centuries later.

Round House, The The London theatre, in Chalk Farm Road, opened in 1968 in former railway buildings. These included a *round house*, a spacious circular building in which, in the early days of the London and Birmingham Railway, a locomotive could be turned to face the opposite direction by being revolved on a special turntable. The building remained in railway use until 1869, when it became a warehouse. The theatre thus adopted its original name, which in itself at least partly suggested that of the historic GLOBE THEATRE. The Round House closed in 1983.

Round Table In medieval legend the table of King Arthur was shaped so that none of his knights had any precedence when they sat at it. The name was recorded as early as 1155. Since at least the 15th century a *Round Table* with the names of Arthur and his most famous knights has been preserved at Winchester, at present hanging in Castle Hall.

Roussillon The former province of southern France takes its name from the town of *Roussillon* that was its original capital, before Perpignan. The town had the Latin name of *Ruscino*, the origin of which is uncertain.

Routledge The British publishing house is named for George *Routledge* (1812–1888), a Cumberland bookseller who set up his own business in London in 1836. In 1843 he went into publishing, gaining a reputation for inexpensive novels. In 1911 his firm merged with that of another publishing house founded in 1877 by Charles Kegan Paul, and the combined business became familiar as *Routledge & Kegan Paul*. In 1988, however, the company reverted to the simple name *Routledge*.

Rover The familiar car has a name that was originally used for a make of tricycle produced in 1884 by a Coventry bicycle firm. The name was a straightforward one, designed to denote a machine on which the rider could *rove* the countryside and which was thus itself a *rover*. The first *Rover* car appeared in 1904. Its name was subsequently incorporated in those of the LAND-ROVER and RANGE ROVER.

Rovereto The town in northern Italy derives its name from Latin *roboretum*, 'oak grove', from *robur*, 'oak' (which lies behind English *robust*).

Rowena The name is traditionally regarded as a form of the Welsh name *Rhonwen*, comprising *rhon*, 'lance', used metaphorically to mean 'slender', and *gwen*, 'white', 'fair'. But it may be the other way round, with the Welsh name a form of an Old English name that comprises the Germanic elements *hrōd*, 'fame' and *wynn*, 'joy'.

Rowenta The electronics company, familiar for its electric irons, based its name on that of its German founder in 1884, *Robert Weintraud* (1860–1928), taking two letters from his first name and five from his surname.

Rowntrees The British firm, famous for its cocoa and chocolate, takes its name from that of a York grocer, Henry Isaac *Rowntree* (d. 1883), who in 1862 acquired a cocoa and chocolate business, with his brother, Joseph Rowntree (1836–1925), becoming a partner seven years later. The company went on to produce pastilles and gums in 1879, and in the 20th century introduced several well-known chocolate brand names, including *Black Magic* (in 1933), *Kit Kat* (1935), *Aero* (1935), *Smarties* (1937), *After Eight* (1962) and *Yorkie* (1976).

Roxana The name, famous as that of the wife of Alexander the Great, derives ultimately from Persian *Roschana*, meaning 'dawn'.

Roxburghshire The former county of Scotland, now in the Borders region, took its name from the village of *Roxburgh* near Kelso. The place-name means '*Hrōc*'s fort', and is Old English in origin. The Anglo-Saxon personal name means 'rook'.

Roxy The famous cinema name derives from that of the founder of the chain, the American radio and film entrepreneur Samuel L. *Rothafel* (1882–1936), known to his friends as *Roxy*.

Roxy Music The British rock band, formed in London in 1971, based their name on that of the ROXY cinema chain. It also, of course, suggests *rock* itself. The name was appropriate for a group whose music was electronic and 'glamorous', like that heard in the cinema.

Roy The name is of Scottish origin, and represents Gaelic *ruadh*, 'red', referring to a person with red hair (a typical Scot) or ruddy complexion. It later became associated with Old French *roy* (modern French *roi*), 'king', so was taken to be a 'royal' name. *See also* ROB ROY, RUFUS, RUSSELL.

Royal Belfast Academical Institution The Northern Ireland public day school for boys, in Belfast, was founded in 1810 and was originally a college as well as a school, with faculties of arts and medicine. On the foundation in 1845 of Queen's College, now the QUEEN'S UNIVERSITY OF BELFAST, it became a school offering grammar school courses. The school's cumbersome name is familiarly shortened locally to *Inst*.

Royal Court Theatre The well-known London theatre, in Sloane Square, was opened in 1888 as the second theatre of the name. The earlier Royal Court was also in Sloane Square but on a slightly different site. It had opened in 1870 and was originally the *New Chelsea Theatre*, then the *Belgravia*, before finally acquiring its generally prestigious third name, suggesting *royal* patronage at *court*. It closed in 1887.

Royal Festival Hall *See* FESTIVAL HALL.

Royal Free Hospital The London hospital, in Hampstead, was founded in 1828 by the surgeon William Marsden (*see* ROYAL MARSDEN HOSPITAL) with the aim of admitting patients *free* of charge. Until then, patients either made their own payment for treatment or were admitted to a particular hospital on the strength of a letter from a subscriber, who guaranteed payment. The hospital's original official name was *The London General Institution for the Gratuitous Care of Malignant Diseases*. When Queen Victoria became its patron in 1837, however, she requested that the name be simplified to *The Royal Free Hospital*.

Royal Grammar School There are three boys' public schools of the name. That in

Guildford was founded in 1509 and established by royal charter of Edward VI in 1552. That in Newcastle upon Tyne was founded in 1545 and was granted its royal charter in 1600 by Queen Elizabeth. The third, in Worcester, was founded some time before 1291 but although chartered by Queen Elizabeth in 1561 did not assume the title *Royal* until 1869, when it was granted by Queen Victoria.

Royal Holloway College The college of London University was founded to provide higher education for women by the philanthopist Thomas *Holloway* (1800–1883), popular for his patent *Holloway's Pills*. It was opened in 1886 and incorporated in the university in 1900. In 1984 it merged with BEDFORD COLLEGE to form the *Royal Holloway and Bedford New College*.

Royal Marsden Hospital The London hospital was founded in 1851 as the *Cancer Hospital (Free)* by the doctor William *Marsden* (1796–1867), who had been moved by the plight of the sick poor in Victorian London and who had earlier founded the ROYAL FREE HOSPITAL.

Royal National Theatre The well-known London theatre was founded in 1963 as the *National Theatre*, performing mainly in the Old Vic until the new theatre building was opened on the South Bank of the Thames in 1976. Its name thus indicated that it was *nationally* owned and funded, unlike most other theatres, which are privately owned. In 1988 it became the *Royal National Theatre*, a title unusually combining the privileged with the popular. *Cp.* NATIONAL GALLERY.

Royston There are two noted towns of the name, one in Hertfordshire, the other in South Yorkshire. The Hertfordshire town has a name that originated as Latin *Crux Roaisie*, meaning '*Rohesia*'s cross'. *Rohesia* is a name of Germanic origin, related to modern ROSE, but it is not known who the lady was. The 'cross' probably stood at a crossroads. This name was then eventually whittled down to *Roys*, and Middle English *toun*, 'town' (or possibly *stōn*, 'stone') was added in the 13th century. Its Yorkshire namesake has the meaning '*Hrōr*'s settlement', with a different personal name (meaning 'vigorous').

Rub-al-Khali The desert in southern Arabia has an Arabic name meaning 'quarter of the desert', from *rubʿ*, 'quarter', *al*, 'the' and *ḥālī*, 'desert'. The term 'quarter' here applies to an area of the desert that is shaped like a crescent moon, in its first *quarter*.

Rubicon The name is that of the stream in northern Italy that at one time formed the boundary between Italy and Cisalpine Gaul and that Caesar famously crossed in 49 BC, thus beginning the war with Pompey. Its origin is in Latin *rubicundus*, 'ruddy', referring to the colour of its soil.

Rudolf The name derives from the Germanic name *Hrodulf*, which comprises a blend of *hrōd*, 'fame' and *wulf*, 'wolf'. The name *Rolf* is of the same origin.

Rufus The derivation of the name is in Latin *rufus*, 'red', 'ruddy', used as a nickname for a red-haired or ruddy-complexioned person. *Cp.* ROY and RUSSELL.

Rugby The Warwickshire town, with its famous public school (which gave the name of the game), was originally *Rockbury* (or the Old English equivalent), meaning '*Hroca*'s fort'. The Danes then substituted their *bý* for the Old English *burh*, in the same sense, as sometimes happened.

Ruhr The chief coalmining and industrial region of western Germany takes its name from the river here, whose own name derives from the Indoeuropean root element *reu*, 'to rend', 'to hollow', relating to the natural channel of the river.

Ruislip The district of West London has a name probably meaning 'rushy leap', from Old English *rysc*, 'rush' and *hlȳp*, 'leap'. The reference would be to a point on the river Pin here where agile travellers could jump across, or at least where their horses could.

Rum The Scottish island, in the Hebrides, has a Gaelic name representing *rùim*, 'room', referring to its relative spaciousness by comparison with neighbouring Eigg and Muck. The name is sometimes spelled *Rhum*, although there is no etymological justification for this.

Rumania *See* ROMANIA.

Rumbelows The radio, television and electrical stores are named for Sydney Charles *Rumbelow* (1909–1974), a Hertfordshire painter's son, who opened his first radio and music shop in Hatfield in 1946.

Rumelia The name of the European division of the former Turkish (Ottoman) empire represents Turkish *Rum İli*, 'land of the Romans', from *Rum*, 'Rome' and *il*, 'land', 'country'. The name implies that the inhabitants were Byzantine Christians, not Muslims.

Rumpelstiltskin The famous dwarf in the German folktale has a name that is an English corruption of German *Rumpelstilzchen*, said to have originally meant 'wrinkled foreskin'. Related English *rumple* still means 'wrinkle', while *-skin* in the English name in fact represents the last part of the German name, where *-chen* is a diminutive. The name actually plays a central role in the tale. The king's bride rashly agrees to give the dwarf her first child if she is unable to find out what he is called. If she succeeds, she can keep the child. The king sends out messengers to collect all the unusual names they can, but they draw blanks until one of them comes across the dwarf dancing round a fire and singing 'Rumpelstiltskin is my name!' The bride thus guesses correctly, and the dwarf kills himself in a rage.

Rump Parliament The name is that of the remainder of the LONG PARLIAMENT after Thomas Pride had expelled members who were hostile to the army (*Pride's Purge*, 1648) and signed the death warrant of Charles I. The 100 or so Presbyterian royalist members left were thus the *rump*, or remnant (literally hinder part).

Runcorn The name of the Cheshire town on the Mersey means 'roomy cove', from Old English *rūm*, 'spacious', 'roomy' and *cofa*, 'bay', 'cove'. The reference is to the former spacious bay that existed between Widnes and Castle Rock.

Run DMC The American rap trio, formed in New York in 1982, took their name from the nicknames of their two lead singers, Joseph *'Run'* Simmons and Darryl *'D'* *Mc*Daniels.

Runnymede The historic meadows by the Thames near Egham, Surrey, where King John drew up the Magna Carta in 1215, has an appropriate name for the transaction, meaning 'council island meadow', from Old English *rūn*, 'secret', 'council' (modern *rune*), *ēg*, 'island' and *mǣd*, 'meadow'. The implication is that the site was already a meeting-place for royal or other assemblies.

Rupert The name is a German form of ROBERT, so like it derives from a combination of *hrōd*, 'fame' and *beraht*, 'bright', *i.e.* famous.

Rurik The Varangian (Scandinavian Viking) leader, founder of the Russian monarchy in the 9th century, has a name that is the Scandinavian equivalent of RODERICK.

Ruritania The imaginary kingdom of central Europe is the setting of several novels by Anthony Hope, especially *The Prisoner of Zenda* (1894). Hope apparently devised the name from Latin *rus*, genitive *ruris*, 'country' (as opposed to town) and a name such as LUSITANIA or MAURITANIA.

Ruse The city in northeast Bulgaria was founded by the Romans in the 1st century BC as *Sexantaprista*, 'harbour of the sixty (ships)'. The Turks built a new town on the site with the name of *Rusçuk*. The origin of this is not certain, but it was adopted by later Christian inhabitants in the form *Ruse*, interpreted as if deriving from Bulgarian *rus*, 'fair', 'beautiful'. The name is pronounced approximately 'Roosay'.

Ruskin College The Oxford college was founded in 1899 by an American student, Walter Vrooman, to provide education in the social sciences for working men. It was named for the famous artist and social reformer John *Ruskin* (1819–1900), and was known as *Ruskin Hall* until 1903.

Russell The origin of the name is in the Norman French name *Rousel*, a nickname for someone with red hair, from *rous*, 'red-haired' (modern French *roux*) with the diminutive suffix *-el*. Cp. ROY and RUFUS.

Russell obbs The familiar brand of electric coffee makers and jug kettles is named for William *Russell* (1920–), a factory machinery inspector's son, and Peter *Hobbs* (1916–), the son of an electric power supply company manager. After the

Second World War both men were employed by Morphy Richards, but left to set up their own business making electric coffee percolators in 1952.

Russell Square The well-known London square takes its name from the family name, *Russell*, of the dukes of Bedford, on whose land here it was built in the early 19th century.

Russia The long familiar name of the country that was the SOVIET UNION from 1922 to 1991 is probably Scandinavian in origin, from the Old Finnish name *Rus* given to the Varangians who entered from the north in the 9th century. Their own name probably means 'foreigners'. Many modern toponymists, however, link their name with that of the *Ruotsi*, 'rowers', the Swedish people who served as oarsmen on Viking ships. The latter source also gave *Ruotsi*, the Finnish name of Sweden.

Russian Quartets Haydn's six string quartets Op 33 (1781) are so named because they were dedicated to the Grand Duke Paul of *Russia*.

Rustle of Spring The popular piano piece by the Norwegian composer Gustav Sinding, written in 1896, is so named because it is intended to represent the awakening of nature in spring, and to evoke the sound of the breeze rustling the leaves on the trees.

Rustum The Persian national hero, familiar in the English-speaking world from Matthew Arnold's poem *Sohrab and Rustum* (1853) (Sohrab being his son), has a Farsi name that represents Old Iranian *Rotastakhm*, 'hero'.

Ruth The name is famous from the Old Testament Book of *Ruth* that tells the story of the devoted daughter-in-law of Naomi and wife of Boaz. The origin of her name is uncertain, although it is traditionally derived from Hebrew *re'ut*, 'friend'. Puritans adopting it in the 17th century associated it with the standard English word *ruth* meaning 'pity', 'sorrow' (now more familiar from its derivative of opposite meaning, *ruthless*). This particular association has been further promoted by the touching lines from Keats's *Ode to a Nightingale* (1820):

Perhaps the self-same song that found a path
Through the sad heart of Ruth, when sick for home,
She stood in tears amid the alien corn.

Ruthenia The region of eastern Europe that now forms part of Ukraine takes its name from the *Rutheni*, the Slavic people whose name is directly related to that of *Rus'*, the old name of RUSSIA.

Rutherford The Scottish name comes from the place that is now the village of *Rutherford* near Kelso, not far from the English border. The place-name means 'cattle ford', from Old English *hrȳther*, 'cattle' and *ford*, 'ford' (*cp.* ROTHERHITHE).

Rutland Britain's former smallest county has a name meaning '*Rōta*'s estate'. The personal name (meaning 'cheerful', *see* ROOT) is followed by Old English *land*, referring to a smallish, well-defined estate, unlike the large regions denoted by such names as *Cumberland* (*see* CUMBRIA) and NORTHUMBERLAND. Although no longer a county, *Rutland* is still on the map as an administrative district of Leicestershire and is famous for *Rutland Water*, Europe's largest manmade reservoir.

Ruwenzori The mountain range in central Africa, generally believed to be Ptolemy's 'Mountains of the Moon', has a native name meaning 'lord of the clouds'.

Rwanda The republic in central Africa takes its name from its people, the *Rwanda*, itself of unknown origin.

Ryan The common Irish name is a shortened form of *Mulryan*, itself an English spelling of *Ó Maoilríaghain*, 'descendant of the devotee of (St) *Ríaghan*'.

Ryazan The city in western Russia probably derives its name from the *Erzian*, a Mordvinian people, whose own name is of uncertain meaning.

Rybinsk The city in western Russia, an important port on the Volga, arose in medieval times as a fishing village, and derives its name from Russian *ryba*, 'fish'. It became a town in 1777. From 1946 to 1957 it was named *Shcherbakov* after the Soviet Communist leader Alexander *Shcherbakov* (1901–1945). It then reverted to its original name, but from 1984 to 1989 was again renamed *Andropov*, for the

Soviet president Yuri *Andropov* (1914–1984), who had worked as a Volga boatman and been a student here.

Ryde The Isle of Wight resort and port has a name that simply means 'stream', from Old English *rīth* (as for PECKHAM RYE). The stream in question is Monktonmead Brook, which flows through the town to the sea.

Ryder Cup The international golf match, played biennially between Europe (until 1979 Britain alone) and the United States, was first held in 1927 for a trophy awarded by Samuel *Ryder*, a British seed merchant.

Rye The East Sussex town and former port has a name that derives from the Old English phrase *æt thǣre īege*, 'at the island', with the initial *R-* of the name all that remains of the second word. Rye was actually built on an island in the flooded marshes here, and was one of the later CINQUE PORTS.

Ryukyu The Japanese chain of islands has a name meaning 'ball of precious stones', from *ryū*, 'precious stone', 'jewel' and *kyū*, 'ball', themselves from Chinese *liú* and *qiú* in the same sense.

Ryvita The familiar make of crispbread has a name that was devised in the 1920s from *rye* and Latin *vita*, 'life'.

Rzeszów The town in southeast Poland derives its name from Polish *rzesza*, 'state', 'empire'. The name is pronounced approximately 'Zheshoof' (the initial *zh* as the *s* in 'pleasure').

S

Saab The Swedish car has an acronymic name standing for *S*venska *A*eroplan *A*ktie*b*olaget, 'Swedish Aeroplane Company', the original manufacturing company, founded in 1937.

Saar The river of western Europe has a name that ultimately derives from the Indoeuropean root word *ser*, 'to flow'. *See also* SAARBRÜCKEN, SAARLAND.

Saarbrücken The industrial city in western Germany has a name that means 'SAAR bridge', from its location on this river.

Saarland The state of western Germany, with SAARBRÜCKEN as its capital, takes its name from its main river, the SAAR.

Saatchi & Saatchi The well-known advertising agency takes its name from its founders in 1970, the brothers of Jewish Iraqi stock, Charles *Saatchi* (1943–) and Maurice *Saatchi* (1946–).

Saba *See* SHEBA.

Sabaoth The name occurs in the Bible in the phrase 'the Lord of Sabaoth' (*Romans* 9.29), a title of God. It means 'lord of hosts', literally 'lord of armies', from Hebrew *ṣebāōth*, the plural of *ṣābā*, 'host', 'army'. A similar phrase is familiar from the *Te Deum* in the Book of Common Prayer: 'Holy, Holy, Holy: Lord God of Sabaoth'. The name is sometimes confused with SABBATH, and is even found in this sense in classic literature, as in the closing lines of Spenser's *The Faerie Queene* (1596):

For, all that moueth, doth in Change delight:
But thence-forth all shall rest eternally
With Him that is the God of Sabbaoth hight:
O that great Sabbaoth God, grant me that Sabaoths sight.

Sabbath For Jews, the *Sabbath* is the seventh day of the week, Saturday, the day on which God rested after his creation of the world (*Genesis* 2.2,3). For Christians,

it is the first day of the week, Sunday, when it commemorates Christ's Resurrection. For both it is a day of worship and rest from work. Its name derives, through Latin and Greek, from Hebrew *šabbāt*, from *šābat*, 'to rest'. The regular word for 'Saturday' derives directly from *Sabbath* in some modern languages, such as Russian *subbota*, Polish *sobota*, Hungarian *szombat*, Greek *Sabbato*, Arabic *es-sabt*. The term *the Sabbath* for 'Sunday' was found widely in English use until the 17th century.

Sabena The name of the Belgian commercial airline is formed from the initials of *S*ociété *a*nonyme *B*elge d'*E*xploitation de la *N*avigation *a*érienne, literally 'Anonymous Belgian Society for the Exploitation of Aerial Navigation'. The company was established in 1923 by SNETA (*Société Nationale pour l'Étude des Transports aériens*, 'National Society for the Study of Air Transport'), and the first *Sabena* flight was made that year when a single-engined aeroplane flew mail and goods from Brussels to Lympne, Kent, via Ostend.

Sabine The name of the ancient Oscan-speaking people of Italy and their language derives from that of their god, *Sabus*, whose own name is of unknown meaning.

Sable, Cape The name of the southernmost point of the continental United States, at the tip of Florida, and also that of the southernmost point of Nova Scotia, Canada, derives from French *sable*, 'sand'.

Sabrina The name is that of the character who, in Welsh legend, was the illegitimate daughter of King Locrine and who was drowned in the river SEVERN by order of the king's wife, Gwendolen. The name comes from the Roman name of the river, *Sabrina*. Its own origin is unknown.

Saccone and Speed The chain of wine and spirit shops takes its name from Jerome

Saccone and James *Speed*, who began as rival wine and spirit merchants in Gibraltar in the 1840s but who had formed a partnership by the close of the 19th century.

Sackville The name is Norman in origin, from *Saqueneville* near Rouen in northern France. The place-name itself means '*Sachano*'s settlement'.

Sacramento The state capital of California takes its name from the river on which it stands. The river's name was originally given in 1808 in honour of the Holy *Sacrament*.

Sacré-Coeur The distinctive Paris church was completed only in 1919 and is dedicated to the *Sacred Heart* (of Jesus). It was planned by the National Assembly in 1873 with the aim of expiating the spiritual and moral collapse of France which was felt to have led to the defeat of the French by the Prussians in 1870. It was paid for by national subscription. The full title of the church is *Basilique du Voeu de la Nation au Sacré Coeur*, 'Basilica of the National Vow to the Sacred Heart'. Its site on MONTMARTRE ('Martyrs' Mount') was deliberate. For Roman Catholics the Sacred Heart of Jesus is symbolic of his love for mankind, and devotion to it represents the reparation of sins, both against Jesus as man and against fellow men.

Sadducee The name is that of a member of an ancient Jewish sect that was opposed to the Pharisees, that denied the resurrection of the dead and the existence of angels, and that adhered solely to the written law. It is said to derive from that of the high priest ZADOK, the sect's supposed founder.

Sadie The name is a pet form of SARAH, with the *r* of the latter name becoming *d* for reasons that are not very clear. *Cp.* SALLY.

Sadler The name is an occupational one, originally given to a maker of saddles for horses.

Sadler's Wells The famous London theatre, former home of the Royal Ballet, takes its name from Thomas *Sadler*, who discovered some *wells* or natural springs on the site in 1683. He set up a pleasure garden and opened 'Sadler's Music House'. By 1718 his theatre had become known by its present name. The original wooden building was replaced by a stone-built theatre in 1765. The present theatre opened in 1931.

Saffron Walden The Essex town was originally known simply as *Walden*, meaning 'valley of the Britons', from Old English *walh*, 'foreigner', 'Briton' and *denu*, 'valley'. Later, *Saffron* was added to distinguish this Walden from the many others in the district. The addition refers to the fields of *saffron* crocus grown here from the 14th century and valued for its medicinal properties.

Safid Kuh The chain of mountains between Pakistan and Afghanistan has a name that represents Iranian *sefid kūh*, 'white mountain'.

Sagittarius The name, in English *The Archer*, is that of a large constellation in the southern hemisphere. Its outline represents the figure of a man holding a bow and arrow and aiming them at the heart of the neighbouring constellation of SCORPIUS.

Sahara The famous African desert has a name that simply means 'desert', from Arabic *ṣaḥrāʾ*, the feminine of *aṣhar*, 'fawn-coloured'.

Sahel The region of western Africa that extends from Senegal to the Sudan derives its name from Arabic *sāḥil* or *sahil*, 'bank', 'seaside'. The name is also applied to the coastal band of hills in Algeria and to the coastal plains of eastern Tunisia. *Cp.* SWAHILI.

Saigon The former name of HO CHI MINH CITY, the port in southern Vietnam, derives from that of the river on which the city stands, in Vietnamese *Sài-gòn*. The origin of this is uncertain. According to some scholars, the name is a corruption of *Ta Ngon*, meaning 'end of the dam', although this is a name more appropriate for a settlement than for an actual river. Others claim that the name means 'sandy bank'. In 1976 the city was renamed in honour of HO CHI MINH (1890–1969), president of the Communist state of North Vietnam from 1954 to his death. Saigon has had other names over the years, including *Rung Gon*, 'wood of kapok trees' and *Ben Nghe*, 'landing place of the buffaloes'. Its Chinese name is *xīgòng*.

Sainsbury The name derives from that of the village of *Saintbury* near Broadway in Gloucestershire. The place-name itself means '*Sǣwine*'s fort', from an Anglo-Saxon personal name meaning literally 'sea friend'.

Sainsburys The familiar food stores take their name from John James *Sainsbury* (1844–1928), a frame and ornament maker's son who married a dairyman's daughter and opened his first dairy shop in London in 1869. They expanded both domestically and commercially, so that by 1914 they had 12 children and 115 grocery stores in and around London.

St Agnes The southernmost of the five inhabited islands of the Scilly Isles, southwest of Cornwall, is not named for the well-known virgin martyr but has a name of Scandinavian origin, from Old Norse *hagi*, 'pasture' and *nes*, 'headland', 'promontory'. The name spread from a single headland to the whole island. *St* was then added to match the names of ST MARY'S and ST MARTIN'S, also in the group.

St Albans The Hertfordshire city takes its name from the 3rd-century martyr *St Alban*, to whom the abbey here is dedicated. The present cathedral stands on the site where St Alban was executed.

St-Amand-Montrond The town in central France derives the first part of its name from Latin *Sanctus Amandus*, 'St Amandus', the name of a 7th-century saint who was bishop of Tongeren in Belgium. His own name means 'worthy to be loved' (*cp.* AMANDA). The second part of the name refers to the nearby hill of *Mont-Rond*, 'round hill'.

St Andrews The historic Scottish town takes its name from Scotland's patron saint, *St Andrew*, whose relics were said to have been brought here in the 8th century. They were 'lost' in the 16th century, however, on the destruction of the great cathedral of St Andrew, built 200 years earlier to commemorate him.

St Anne's College The Oxford college, formerly for women only, originated in 1879 as the *Society of Oxford Home Students*, catering for those women students who still lived in private homes, as distinct from those who lived in the halls of residence of recently opened colleges such as LADY MARGARET HALL. The name was changed to *St Anne's Society* in 1942 and in 1952 the society was incorporated into the university as *St Anne's College*. The college is named for *St Anne*, the legendary mother of the Virgin Mary, and a particular patron saint of women.

St Antony's College The Oxford college was founded in 1950 for postgraduate students and for research into modern history and the social sciences. It was named for the patron saint of its founder, the French entrepreneur and oriental trader *Antonin Besse* (1877–1951).

St Austell The Cornish town takes its name from the 6th-century saint and monk to whom its parish church is dedicated.

St Bartholomew's Hospital London's oldest hospital was founded in 1123 as part of the priory that has survived as London's oldest church, *St Bartholomew the Great*, in West Smithfield. The priory's founder was Henry I's court jester, Rahere, who is said to have had a vision in which *St Bartholomew* saved him from a winged monster. Hence the dedication.

St Bernard The large breed of dogs, formerly used for rescue work in mountainous areas, is so named because the dogs were kept by monks at the hospice near the Great ST BERNARD PASS.

St Bernard Pass There are two Alpine passes of the name. One, the *Great St Bernard Pass*, lies east of Mont Blanc between Italy and Switzerland. The other, the *Little St Bernard Pass*, lies south of Mont Blanc between Italy and France. They are both named for the hospice founded in the 10th century near the Great St Bernard Pass by *St Bernard* of Menthon (923–1008).

St Brieuc The town in Brittany, northwest France is named for the 5th-century Breton saint *Brieg*, whose own name derives from Breton *bri*, 'respect'. In 1793, at the time of the French Revolution, the town was known for a time as *Port-Brieuc*.

St Catharines The city in Ontario, Canada, was established in 1790 and named for *Catharine* Askin Hamilton, first wife of Robert Hamilton, member of the first legislative council of Upper Canada. The name is frequently (but perhaps understandably) misspelled *St Catherines*.

St Catherine's College The Cambridge college was founded in 1473 and named in honour of *St Catherine* of Alexandria, a patroness of learning. The college crest is a stylized *Catherine* wheel. The Oxford college of the same name was founded in 1962 to replace the former *St Catherine's Society*. This had itself arisen as a students' social club in 1869, and took its name from its premises in a house named *St Catherine's Hall*, to which it had moved in 1874.

St Clement Danes The London church, in the Strand, is said to derive the latter part of its name from the fact that Danish settlers lie buried here. The name of the church is also familiar from the nursery rhyme ('Oranges and lemons/Say the bells of St Clement's') and was adopted by the novelist Winifred Ashton (1888–1965) for her pen name, *Clemence Dane*.

St Cloud The residential suburb of Paris is named for the 6th-century saint *Chlodoald*, son of King Clodomir, who founded a monastery here.

St Cross The Oxford college was established in 1965 as a graduate society enabling men and women to read for advanced degrees and diplomas. It took its name from its accommodation near *St Cross Church*, Holywell, itself named for the Holy Cross of Jesus.

St Denis The industrial suburb of Paris takes its name from *St Denis*, 3rd-century bishop of Paris (now its patron saint), who was beheaded on MONTMARTRE in 258 together with his companions Rusticus and Eleutherus. He is said to have afterwards walked to the present site carrying his severed head, a distance of about three miles (5 km). The capital of the French overseas region of Réunion has the same name.

St-Dié The cathedral town in northeast France had the Medieval Latin name of *Sanctus Deodatus*, for an 8th-century saint and bishop of Nevers. His own name means 'gift of God', from Latin *datus*, 'given' and *Deo*, 'by God'.

St Dunstan's College The public school for boys in Catford, southeast London, was founded in 1888 as a re-establishment of the 15th-century grammar school that originated in the parish of *St Dunstan*-in-the-East in the City of London.

St Edmund Hall The Oxford college was founded in about 1278 and is named for *St Edmund* of Abingdon (1170–1240), Archbishop of Canterbury, who is traditionally said to have lived and taught in a house on the present site. The college is the only historic hall of the name that survives in the university.

St Edmund's College The Cambridge college was founded as *St Edmund's House* in 1896 to educate Roman Catholic priests, and is named for *St Edmund*, Archbishop of Canterbury. In 1965, although remaining primarily Catholic in character, it became a graduate college of the university.

St Edmund's College The Roman Catholic public school for boys near Ware, Hertfordshire, arose from the English College founded in 1568 at Douai, France, by Cardinal Allen. This college was forcibly closed during the French Revolution and the staff and students returned to England. In 1793 the evicted students joined a school on the present site named *Old Hall Green Academy* which had itself been founded in 1685 as *Silkstead School*. The combined establishment was named after *St Edmund*, Archbishop of Canterbury, on whose feast day (20 November) the union took place. *Cp.* ST EDMUND'S SCHOOL.

St Edmund's School The public school in Canterbury was founded in 1749 on the same foundation as *St Margaret's School* for girls at Bushey, Hertfordshire, and is named for *St Edmund*, Archbishop of Canterbury. The school transferred from London to Canterbury in 1855.

St Edward's School The Oxford public school for boys was founded in 1863 by the Rev. Thomas Chamberlain, a member of the Oxford Movement and vicar of the church of St Thomas the Martyr. He presumably chose *St Edward* as the school's patron since the 10th-century king and martyr, assassinated at the age of 15 or 16, would have seemed a fitting exemplar for the pious High Church Victorian schoolboy, suffering for his faith.

St Émilion The full-bodied French red wine takes its name from that of the town near Bordeaux that is its place of origin. The town's name was recorded in Medieval Latin as *Sanctus Milionis*, after a saint of Breton origin who lived here as a hermit in the 8th century.

Saintes The historic town in western France was known to the Romans as *Mediolanum Santonum*, 'middle plain of the *Santones*', from the name of a Gaulish people. The name later became popularly associated with the word *saint*, which occurs in many French place-names. For another place of the same basic Roman name, *cp.* MILAN.

St Étienne The town in east central France was founded in the 11th century and dedicated to *St Stephen* (French *Saint-Étienne*), who according to the Bible (*Acts* 6.5) was the first Christian martyr.

St Felix School The girls' public school at Southwold, Suffolk, was founded in 1897 by Margaret Isabella Gardiner, a headmistress and science graduate who admired the life and work of the 7th-century bishop of Dunwich (near Southwold) *St Felix*. She therefore chose his name for the school, and incorporated its literal sense in the school's Latin motto, *Felix quia fortis*, 'happy because strong'. (The school officially spells out its name as *Saint Felix School*, as if to imply both 'holy' and 'happy'.) The girls are known as *Felicians*. The school is only some 30 miles (48 km) along the coast from FELIXSTOWE, also named for the saint.

St Gall The town and canton of northeast Switzerland are named for *St Gall*, a 7th-century Irish monk and hermit who was a pioneer of Christianity in Switzerland. His name means 'stranger' (*cp.* GALLOWAY).

St-Germain The suburb of western Paris has the full name of *Saint-Germain-en-Laye*. This represents its Medieval Latin name of *Sanctus Germanus in Laya*. The saint's name is that of *Germanus*, the 5th-century bishop of Auxerre who was sent to Britain to combat the heretical doctrine of Pelagianism. The last part of the name is that of the forest here, itself deriving from Old French *l'aye*, 'the hedge'.

St Gotthard The mountain range in southeast central Switzerland, and the pass that crosses it, take their name from the hospice and its chapel built here in the 11th century and dedicated to *St Gotthard* (960–1038), bishop of Hildesheim.

St Helena The volcanic island that is a British colony in the southeast Atlantic was discovered by the Portuguese explorer João da Nova on Sunday 22 May 1502, the feast of *St Helen*.

St Helens The Merseyside town takes its name from a medieval chapel-of-ease dedicated to *St Helen* that stood on the site of the present St Helen's church. The town arose only in the 17th century.

St Helier The chief town of Jersey, in the Channel Islands, derives its name from the 6th-century martyr who was Jersey's first saint. He was a Belgian monk, said to have lived in a cave above the town.

St Hilda's College The Oxford women's college was founded in 1893 by Miss Dorothea Beale, principal of Cheltenham Ladies' College. She dedicated the college to *St Hilda*, the 7th-century Abbess of Whitby, because she regarded her as the first great educator of women in England and as someone who 'laid chief stress on peace and love'.

St Hugh's College The Oxford college, formerly for women only, was founded in 1886 as *St Hugh's Hall* by Miss (later Dame) Elizabeth Wordsworth, first principal of Lady Margaret Hall. As the daughter of Christopher Wordsworth, Bishop of Lincoln, she named the college in honour of *St Hugh*, the famous 12th-century bishop of Lincoln.

St Ivel The familiar brand of dairy products takes its name from an imaginary monk said to have lived by the river *Yeo* which runs through YEOVIL in Somerset. The name of the river is identical in origin to that of the *Ivel* in Bedfordshire, and itself gave the name of the town. It was adopted as a 'saint's' name by way of an advertising gimmick by a Yeovil cheesemaking firm some time around the year 1900.

St Ives There are two noted towns of the name, one in Cambridgeshire, the other in Cornwall. The Cambridgeshire (formerly Huntingdonshire) town takes its name from *St Ivo*, whose remains were found here at the end of the 10th century. The Cornish resort is named for *St Ia*, a female saint, who according to legend was wafted across the sea from Ireland on a leaf to land here some time in the 6th or 7th century.

St James's Palace The famous London palace, long the official residence of the monarch and the scene of important court functions, takes its name from the medieval leper hospital of *St James* the Less on which it was built by Henry VIII.

St John The city in New Brunswick, Canada, takes its name from the river here, itself discovered by the French explorer Samuel de Champlain on Thursday 24 June 1604, *St John*'s Day. The town was founded in 1783 and originally named *Parr Town* after the governor of Nova Scotia, Colonel John *Parr*. It was renamed as now two years later.

St John Ambulance Brigade The well-known voluntary first aid organization, frequently in attendance at major public events, was founded in 1887 and adopted its name from that of the medieval religious nursing order, the Knights Hospitallers of *St John* of Jerusalem. The latter originated from the hospital for sick pilgrims in Jerusalem, and had its headquarters near the church of *St John* the Baptist there. *Cp.* KNIGHTS TEMPLAR.

St John's College The Cambridge college was founded in 1511 by Lady Margaret Beaufort, mother of Henry VII, and named for its site on the former Hospital of *St John*, with the First Court incorporating the old chapel of the hospital. The Oxford college of the same name was founded in 1555 to replace the earlier *St Bernard's College* founded in 1437. Its founder was Sir Thomas White, Master of the Merchant Taylors' Company, London, who dedicated it to *St John* the Baptist, the patron saint of tailors.

St Johnstone The Scottish football club, based in Perth, was formed in that city in 1884 by members of the existing *St Johnstone* Cricket Club. This had itself adopted the historic alternative name for the city, meaning *St John's town*, from the dedication of its first church to *St John* the Baptist.

St John's Wood The fashionable district of northwest London derives its name from the Knights Hospitallers of *St John*, to whom the land here was transferred from the Knights Templars when the latter were suppressed in the early 14th century. There is no trace of the *wood* now.

St Just The Cornish town takes its name from the saint to whom the parish church is dedicated, although almost nothing is known about him.

St Kilda The steep rocky island to the west of Scotland appears to have a name derived from a *St Kilda*, who is duly entered in *The Oxford Dictionary of Saints* (1978) as a 'virtually unknown saint who has given his (or her) name to the remote island to the west of the Outer Hebrides in the Atlantic Ocean'. However, the saint is a ghost, that is, he (or she) never existed! The Old Norse name of the island, *Skildar*, was misread on charts and as a result a spurious saint was born. The name actually means 'shields', and may have been intended to describe the outline of the island and its surrounding islets as seen from sea level.

St Lawrence The river that forms the boundary between the United States and Canada was explored by the French navigator Jacques Cartier in 1534 and was so named by him because he came to it on Monday 10 August that year, the feast of *St Lawrence*. The river gave its name to the gulf and to the much more modern *St Lawrence* Seaway.

St Leger The well-known annual horse race, run at Doncaster, takes its name from Colonel Barry *St Leger* (1739–1789), who founded it in 1776.

St Leonards The East Sussex resort near Hastings is named after the original parish church here, dedicated to *St Leonard*. The church was washed away by the sea in about 1430 and was replaced by another, in turn superseded in the 1830s by the present parish church, similarly dedicated. The resort of today developed soon after this date.

St-Lô The town in northwest France takes its name from *Lauto*, the 6th-century bishop of Coutances. His name is Germanic in origin.

St Louis The city and port in Missouri was founded in 1764 by the French and named for *St Louis*, otherwise King Louis IX of France (1215–1270), canonized in 1297. *Cp.* LOUISIANA.

St Lucia The Caribbean island was named by Christopher Columbus for the day on which he discovered it, Tuesday 13 December 1502, the feast of *St Lucy*, Sicilian virgin martyr.

St-Malo The French port on the English Channel is named for *St Maclovius*, 6th-century bishop of Aleth (now St Servan). His name is probably Celtic in origin and may mean 'son of (the god) Lug'. *See also* FALKLAND ISLANDS.

St Martin's The third largest of the Isles of Scilly, southwest of Cornwall, takes its name from the famous saint to whom its parish church is dedicated. The church has a small stained glass window showing St Martin cutting his cloak in half to clothe a beggar, the charitable act for which he is best remembered. St Martin is often associated with the founding of churches in remote or outlying districts, and this is appropriate for the island, which is the northernmost in the group.

St Martin's Theatre The London theatre, in West Street, off Shaftesbury Avenue, opened in 1916 and took its name from Upper *St Martin's* Lane, just round the corner from where it stands.

St Mary's The largest island of the Isles of Scilly, southwest of Cornwall, takes its name from the Virgin *Mary*, to whom the parish church at Hugh Town is dedicated. The dedication is significant for an island people, since the Virgin Mary (perhaps through the association of *Mary* and Latin *mare*, 'sea') is specially favoured by sailors. For the names of the other populated islands of the group, *see* BRYHER, ST AGNES, ST MARTIN'S, TRESCO.

St Michael The brand name of MARKS AND SPENCER was given by Simon Marks (1888–1964), chairman of the company from 1915, in honour of his father *Michael* Marks (1859–1907), who had founded the firm in 1884 and subsequently taken on Thomas Spencer as partner.

St Michael's Mount The well-known island in Mounts Bay, Cornwall, takes its name from the dedication of its chapel to the archangel *St Michael*. According to local legend, the saint appeared here some time in the 6th or 7th century. At some stage in the 11th century the mount and its chapel were given to its French namesake, MONT-SAINT-MICHEL, presumably through the similarity of the sites.

St Moritz The well-known sports centre in eastern Switzerland takes its name from the lake here, in turn named for a long-vanished 6th-century abbey dedicated to *St Maurice*, a 3rd-century soldier martyr.

St-Nazaire The port in northwest France, noted as a German submarine base in the Second World War, takes its name from *St Nazarius*, 5th-century abbot of Lérins. His name means 'Nazarene' (*see* NAZARETH).

St Neots The Cambridgeshire town near Huntingdon grew up round a 10th-century monastery dedicated to the Cornish saint *Neot*, whose relics were brought here from the village of *St Neot* near Liskeard.

St-Omer The town in northeast France takes its name from the 7th-century bishop *St Audemar*, whose own name comprises the elements *alda*, 'old' and *mar*, 'famous'.

St-Ouen The town in northern France, a suburb of Paris, derives its name from *St Audowin*, bishop of Rouen in the 7th century. His name is Germanic and means 'old friend'.

St Pancras The district of north London, with its well-known railway station, takes its name from the dedication of its parish church to *St Pancras*, a 4th-century boy martyr in Rome. His name represents Greek *pankratios*, 'all-powerful'. The cult of St Pancras is said to have been promoted in England by St Augustine.

St Paul The state capital of Minnesota takes its name from the log chapel built here in 1841 by the Canadian missionary Lucien Galtier and dedicated to *St Paul*.

St Paul's Cathedral London's famous cathedral is the fifth on the site. All its predecessors have had the same dedication, the first being founded by St Ethelbert, king of Kent, in the early 7th century. It is possible the dedication was intended to be complementary to that of ST PETER'S basilica in Rome, itself originally built in the 4th century. Some authorities, however, relate the name to Westminster Abbey, dedicated to St Peter. This was thus the 'west minster', while St Paul's was the 'east minster'.

St Paul's Girls' School The London public school for girls is on the foundation provided by Dean Colet in 1509 for ST PAUL'S SCHOOL for boys. It opened in 1904.

St Paul's School The London public school for boys was founded in 1509 by John Colet, Dean of ST PAUL'S CATHEDRAL. A grammar school had existed for many centuries in connection with the cathedral, and Colet doubtless absorbed it into his new foundation. The preparatory school for *St Paul's* has the name of *Colet Court*.

St Paul's Suite Gustav Holst's suite for string orchestra, Op 29 No 2 (1912–13), was written for the string orchestra of ST PAUL'S GIRLS' SCHOOL, London, where the composer was director of music from 1905.

St-Paul-Trois-Châteaux The town in southeast France has a misleading name that seems to mean 'three castles of St Paul'. Its Roman name, however, was *Civitas Trecastininsis*, from the Gaulish people mentioned by Pliny known as the *Tricastini*. The apparent reference to *St Paul*, too, is actually to a 4th-century local bishop named *Paul*. The origin of the Gaulish tribal name is uncertain.

St Peter Port The capital of Guernsey, in the Channel Islands, derives its name from the dedication of its parish church to *St Peter*. The addition of *Port* to the name emphasizes the long-established commercial importance of the town. The climatic conditions on Guernsey are much more favourable for dairy farming and market-gardening than on the larger Jersey, whose main business is tourism. The association that St Peter has with fishing is especially appropriate.

St Peter's The world-famous basilica in the Vatican City, Rome, stands on the site of a church originally built in the 4th century. It was also dedicated to PETER, the apostle who was the 'rock' on which Christ

founded his church and the saint who is regarded by Roman Catholics as the first pope.

St Petersburg The famous Russian city and port on the Gulf of Finland, the capital of Russia from 1712 to 1914, has a name (in Russian, *Sankt-Peterburg*) that means 'fortress of St Peter', after *Peter* the Great (and his patron saint), who founded it in 1703. In 1914 this name was felt to be too Germanic for its day, so when the capital returned to Moscow it was russified to *Petrograd*, where *grad* means 'city' (modern Russian *gorod*, as for NOVGOROD). In 1924, the year of the death of *Lenin*, it was renamed for him as *Leningrad*, but in 1991 reverted to its original name. The city and resort in Florida of the same name was founded in 1875 by John C. Williams and Peter A. Demens, who built a railway to the site in 1888. It was named for Demens' Russian birthplace, as well as for his own first name.

St Peter's College The Oxford college was founded as a private hall in 1929 as a memorial to Francis James Chavasse (1846–1928), Bishop of Liverpool. It took its name from the church of *St Peter*-le-Bailey, whose rectory formed part of its buildings. The college became a full member of the university in 1961 and the church is now the college chapel.

St Peter's School The York public school was founded in 627 by Paulinus, first bishop of York, who named it for *St Peter*, first bishop of Rome.

St Pierre The islands in the Atlantic, in the French territory of *St Pierre* and Miquelon, are named either for *St Peter* or for a navigator named *Peter* in some language, perhaps Portuguese (so originally *Pedro*). The name was recorded in 1536 as *ysles Sainct Pierre* by the French explorer Jacques Cartier.

St-Pol-de-Léon The Roman name of the town in Brittany, northwest France, was *Castellum Leonense*, 'castle of Leo', probably from a personal name. In the 6th century, the town added the name of the local bishop *Pol* (*Paul*), and this alone is represented in its Breton name, *Kastell Paol*, 'castle of Paul'. According to some authorities, it is the name of this town that gave that of LYONESSE, the mythical birth-place of Sir Tristram in Arthurian legend.

St-Quentin The town in northern France is named for *St Quintinus*, said to have been martyred here in the 3rd century. His own name means 'fifth' (*see* QUINTIN).

St-Raphaël The town in southeast France takes its name from its parish church, which is dedicated to the archangel RAPHAEL.

St Swithun's School The public school for girls in Winchester was founded in 1884 and named for *St Swithin*, who is buried in Winchester Cathedral and to whom the cathedral is itself in part dedicated.

St Thomas's Hospital The well-known London hospital, founded at Southwark in 1552, is the successor of a hospital that was originally founded as part of a priory in the 12th century and that was known as *The Hospital of St Thomas the Martyr*.

St Trinian's The fictitious girls' school in the cartoons by Ronald Searle, later featuring in a number of film comedies, has a name that was based on that of the school that Searle's own daughters attended, *St Trinnean's*, Edinburgh. The outrageous schoolgirls themselves first appeared in a cartoon by Searle in the September 1941 issue of the magazine *Lilliput*, with the caption: 'Owing to the international situation the match with St. Trinian's has been postponed'.

St-Tropez The well-known resort on the French Riviera takes its name from *St Torpes*, martyred in the 1st century at Pisa.

St Vincent The Caribbean island was given its name by Christopher Columbus, who discovered it on Monday 22 January 1498, the feast of *St Vincent* of Saragossa, 4th-century Spanish deacon and martyr.

Saipan The main island of the Marianas, in the West Pacific, has a name of Micronesian (Caroline) origin meaning 'deserted', 'uninhabited'. The original indigenous population had been removed by the Spanish, and Caroline settlers gave the island the name when they came here in the 17th century.

Sakai The port in southern Japan, in Honshu, has a name that means 'frontier'.

Sakhalin The island off the east (Siberian) coast of Russia has a name deriving from Manchu *Sahalin-Ula*, 'black river', the Manchu name for the Russian river Amur. The island lies opposite its estuary.

Sakyamuni *See* BUDDHA.

Saladin The name of the infamous enemy of the Crusaders and of Christians generally in the 12th century represents *Salāh-ad-Dīn*, 'justice of the faith', the Arabic title of the Muslim leader whose real name was Yusuf ibn-Ayyub.

Salamanca The city of western Spain, famous for the battle of 1812 in which the British under Wellington defeated the French in the Peninsular War, has a name that is of obscure origin. It is almost certainly pre-Roman. Its Roman name was *Salmantica* or *Salamantica*.

Salamis The island off the southeast coast of Greece has a name that derives from Phoenician *salām*, 'peace' (*cp.* SALEM). The former chief city of Cyprus has the same name.

Salar The name is familiar as that of the central character of Henry Williamson's story of wildlife and the countryside, *Salar the Salmon* (1935), a successor to his highly acclaimed *Tarka the Otter* (1927) (*see* TARKA). The name of the salmon means 'leaper', and derives from the Late Latin *salar*, 'trout', which gave the word *salmon* itself and which in turn comes from classical Latin *salire*, 'to leap'. The salmon is famous for its ability to leap up waterfalls when making for its spawning ground.

Sale The name was either an occupational one for a person who worked in a manor house (Middle English *sale*), or a topographical one for someone who lived by a willow-tree (Old English *salh*, Middle English *sale*) or who came from a place named for this tree, such as *Sale*, now a suburb of Manchester (*see* SALFORD).

Salem The state capital of Oregon was so named in 1840 after the city of *Salem* in Massachusetts, itself founded in 1626 and named for the biblical *Salem* (*Genesis* 14.18) of which Melchizedek was king. The name also occurs in the Bible as an

479

abbreviation for JERUSALEM: 'In Salem also is his tabernacle, and his dwelling place in Zion' (*Psalm* 76.2). The name itself represents Hebrew *šalōm*, 'peace'.

Salerno The port in southwest Italy has a name of pre-Indoeuropean origin, deriving from the root element *sala*, 'current' (of water).

Salesian The name is that of one of the religious orders founded by (or subsequently named after) the French churchman St Francis of *Sales* (1567–1622), bishop of Geneva, who was born in *Sales*, eastern France. The village itself derives its name from the Germanic *seli*, 'room', 'castle'.

Salford The town near Manchester has a name meaning 'willow-tree ford', from Old English *salh*, 'willow' (modern *sallow*). The ford was over the river Irwell. Only five miles (8 km) from Salford is the town of *Sale*. Its name also means 'willow', showing that the tree must have been abundant in this part of what was formerly Lancashire.

Salisbury The famous cathedral city in Wiltshire was known to the Romans as *Sorviodunum*, their settlement being not where the present city is but on higher ground at Old Sarum. This name is Celtic in origin, with the latter half meaning 'fort'. The sense of *Sorvio-* is obscure, however. The Anglo-Saxons apparently associated it with their word *searu*, meaning 'art', 'skill', 'armour', and substituted their equivalent *burh* for the Celtic *-dunum*. This gave the Domesday Book record of the name as *Sarisberie*. The first *r* of this later became *l* under Norman influence. The modern town arose in the 13th century, when the dry, bleak heights of Old Sarum were abandoned for the lush, fertile meadows surrounding the confluence of several rivers in the broad valley below. *Sarum* is an abbreviation of the Medieval Latin form of the town's name as *Sarisburia*, from the first syllable of this plus the conventional Latin ending *-um*. The modern city is now officially *New Sarum*, by contrast with the historic *Old Sarum*. The former name of HARARE, capital of Zimbabwe, was also *Salisbury* until 1982. It derived from Robert Gascoyne Cecil, third Marquess of *Salisbury* (1830–1903), who was prime minister of Britain at the time of the town's foundation in 1890.

Sally The name is a pet form of SARAH, adopted in its own right, with the *r* of the original name giving the *l* of the diminutive, as for *Hal* from HARRY.

Sally Line The well-known shipping line is Finnish in origin, and is based in the Åland islands (Ahvenanmaa). It was founded by Algot Johansson, and received its name in 1937 when he merged his businesses into a single concern. He gave it in honour of the Finnish author *Sally* Salminen (1906–), who came from Åland and who gained fame through her prize-winning novel *Katrina* (1936).

Salmon The name is a form of *Salomon*, more generally familiar as SOLOMON.

Salome The name is famous as that of the daughter of Queen Herodias who danced for her stepfather King Herod on his birthday and who so pleased him that, when told she could have anything she wished, she was granted the head of John the Baptist. She is not named in either biblical account of the event (*Matthew* 14.6–11, *Mark* 6.21–28) but is merely referred to as 'the daughter of Herodias'. Her name was supplied by the 2nd-century Jewish historian Josephus, and derives from Hebrew *šalōm*, 'peace'. The name does exist elsewhere in the Bible, however, and was that of one of the women who followed and served Jesus, and who stood near the cross at the time of his Crucifixion (*Mark* 15.40).

Salonika The name is an English form of THESSALONÍKI (*which see*).

Salop *See* SHROPSHIRE.

Salter The name is occupational in origin, either for a seller of *salt* or for someone who played on the *psaltery*, a former type of stringed instrument.

Salt Lake City The state capital of Utah, founded by the Mormons in 1847 as the world capital of the Mormon Church, takes its name from the *Great Salt Lake* near which it is located.

Saluki The ancient breed of hound with silky coat and feathered tail and legs derives its name from its place of origin, the town of

Saluk in what is now Yemen. It was formerly known as the Persian greyhound.

Salvador The city and port in eastern Brazil was founded in 1549 by the Portuguese and originally named *São Salvador*, 'Holy Saviour'. *Cp.* EL SALVADOR, SAN SALVADOR.

Salvation Army The well-known Christian religious and charitable body was founded by the Methodist minister William Booth in London in 1865. It was originally known as the *Christian Revival Association*, but in 1878 changed to its present name. This emphasizes its aim to bring both spiritual and bodily *salvation* to the poor and refers to its quasi-military organization, with ranks, uniforms and military-style brass bands.

Salween The river in southwest Asia, flowing through China and Burma, has a name representing Burmese *sanluin*, of uncertain origin. Its Tibetan name is *nagchu*, 'black water', from *nag*, 'black' and *chu*, 'water'.

Salyut The series of space stations launched by the Soviet Union between 1971 and 1982 was given a name meaning 'salute'. The name was intended to be complementary to that of the SOYUZ spacecraft.

Salzburg The well-known city in western Austria derives its name from German *Salz*, 'salt' and *Burg*, 'fort', 'castle'. The region here is rich in salt-mines. The Medieval Latin name of the city was *Salisburgum*.

Samantha The name, very popular and fashionable in the second half of the 20th century, is said to be a blend of the male name SAMUEL and an existing girl's name such as *Anthea*. The Greek appearance of the name has prompted some classicists to suggest a derivation in Greek *psamathōn*, 'sandy place', but this is simply a poetic fancy, alas.

Samara The city in southwest Russia, a port on the Volga, was founded in 1586 as a military defensive post and was named after the river that joins the Volga here. Its own name is of Kirgiz origin, probably meaning 'hollow one'. In 1935 the city was renamed *Kuybyshev* for the Russian Communist Party leader Valerian *Kuybyshev* (1888–1935), who escaped here in 1916 from exile in Siberia and became a Bolshevik activist while working at a local steelworks. In 1991 the city reverted to its original name.

Samaria The region of ancient Palestine and its capital derive their name from the Hebrew personal name *Shemer* (*šémer*, 'sediment'), this being the owner of the hill here which King Omri bought to build a city on (1 *Kings* 16.24).

Samaritans The name is familiar as that of the charitable organization founded in 1953 with the aim of helping people in distress or despair. It takes its name from the biblical parable of the Good *Samaritan*, an inhabitant of SAMARIA who helped a stranger when no one else would (*Luke* 10.30–37).

Samarkand The city in Uzbekistan derives its name from that of the Greek city of *Marakanda*, capital of Sogdiana, captured by Alexander the Great in 329 BC. Its own name derives from Old Persian *asmara*, 'stone', 'rock', with the addition of Sogdian *kand*, 'fort', 'town'. The city of TASHKENT has an identical meaning (and identically corresponding second element).

Sambo The offensive nickname for a black person derives not from *Samuel* but from American Spanish *zambo*, a term for a person of Negro descent that itself may be related to Bantu *nzambu*, 'monkey'.

Sambre The river of France and Belgium, a tributary of the Meuse, has a name of Gaulish origin, from *sam*, 'calm', 'peaceful'.

Sammael The spirit or demon who is the personification of evil in rabbinical demonology has a name that is traditionally derived from Hebrew *Samma'êl*, 'poison of God'.

Samoa The South Pacific islands are said to derive their name either from that of a local chieftain or from a native word meaning 'place of the *moa*', the latter being a large bird, now extinct, that may have been the totem of the indigenous people.

Samos The Greek island in the Aegean has a name representing Greek *samos*, 'dune', 'seaside hill'.

Samothrace The name of the Greek island in the Aegean means '(people of) *Samos* (from) THRACE'. The island was first populated by Carians and Thracians, then, in the 8th century BC, by settlers from Samos.

Samoyed The name of the northern people of Russia (originally from Siberia) and their languages derives from a local word *sāme-aena* or *sāme-yemne*, 'land of Saamians', *i.e.* Lapps. The people's own name for themselves is *Nenets*, 'person', 'man'. The distinctive breed of dog with dense white coat and curly tail is named for the people, who kept it as a working dog and companion. The name was at one time supposed to refer to the people's practice of cannibalism, since it was erroneously interpreted as 'self-eater', from Russian *sam*, 'self' and *yed*, the root of the verb 'to eat' (just as *samovar* means literally 'self-boiler').

Sampdoria The famous Italian football club, based in Genoa, was formed from two separate clubs, *Sampierdarense*, from the port district of *Sampierdarena* ('St Peter of the Sands'), and *Andrea Doria*, founded in 1895 and named for the Genoese admiral and statesman *Andrea Doria* (1466–1560). The two teams first merged in 1927 under the name *Dominante*, but renamed themselves *Liguria* in 1930. *Sampierdarense* then broke away again, calling themselves *Liguria* from 1937, but in 1946 once more merged with *Andrea Dorea* under the official name *Unione Calcio Sampierdarense-Doria*, popularly abbreviated to *Sampdoria*.

Samson Famous as the biblical hero whose physical strength was the cause of his own downfall, thanks to his weakness for women, Samson has a name that represents Hebrew *Šimšōn*, a diminutive of *šemeš*, 'sun'. It has been suggested that his 'sun locks', which were shorn off by Delilah, represent the rays of the sun, and that the name of DELILAH herself is based on Hebrew *lāila*, 'night', so that darkness conquers light just as night 'kills' day and death wins the final battle over life (in this pre-Christian context).

Samson Agonistes The title of Milton's blank verse tragedy, published in 1671, is Greek for 'Samson the Wrestler', referring to the biblical SAMSON. The poem deals with the final phase of Samson's life, when he has been blinded and is a prisoner of the Philistines (*Judges* 16). It is generally thought that the blind Milton was referring to himself, with Samson's destruction of the temple alluding to the collapse of the Commonwealth and the crushing of the poet's political aspirations.

Samuel The biblical name, familiar from the great judge and prophet and the two Old Testament books devoted to him, represents Hebrew *Šĕmū'ēl*, 'his name is El' (*i.e.* God). The name is popularly explained as meaning 'requested' in the account of the prophet's birth: '[Hannah] bare a son, and called his name Samuel, saying, Because I have asked him of the Lord' (1 *Samuel* 1.20). But this origin is more appropriate for SAUL than for Samuel.

San Antonio The city in southern Texas takes its name from the river on which it stands. This in turn was so named because it was discovered by Spanish explorers on Sunday 19 May 1691, the feast of *St Antony*.

Sanatogen The brand of tonic wine was patented in 1898 and was given a name based on classic roots that was presumably intended to mean 'produces health', from Latin *sanare*, 'to heal' and *generare*, 'to beget'. It was long associated with the anagrammatic name *Genatosan*, that of the firm that made it in Loughborough, Leicestershire.

Sandbach The name of the Cheshire town means 'sandy stream', from Old English *sand*, 'sand' and *bæce*, 'stream' (related to modern *beck*). Sandbach is on a small tributary of the river Wheelock.

Sandemans The well-known brand of port takes its name from George G. *Sandeman* (1765–1841), a Scottish wine trader in London who specialized in sherry and port and who shipped his first port in about 1790, the year of the first true vintage *Sandeman*.

Sandersons The superior make of wallpaper is named for Arthur *Sanderson* (1829–1882), who in 1860 set up in London as an importer of expensive French wallpapers. He first manufactured his own papers in 1879.

Sandhurst The Berkshire town, with its famous Royal Military Academy, has a straightforward descriptive name meaning 'sandy hurst', that is, a wooded hill on sandy soil. Officer cadets here will attest to the sandiness of the soil from their practical experience of it when training.

San Diego The Californian city and port was originally named *San Miguel* ('St Michael') when first sighted by Spanish explorers in 1542. In 1602 it was renamed *San Diego de Alcalá de Henares*, for the 15th-century Spanish Franciscan friar *St Didacus*.

Sandinistas The members of the left-wing revolutionary movement in Nicaragua that overthrew President Samoza in 1979 took their name from the Nicaraguan rebel general Augusto César *Sandino*, murdered in 1933.

Sandown The Isle of Wight resort has a name deriving from Old English *sand*, 'sand' and *hamm*, 'riverside land', referring to the flat ground between the upper reaches of the river Yar and the sea.

Sandra The name is a short form of ALEXANDRA, the female equivalent of ALEXANDER.

Sandringham The Norfolk village, famous for its royal residence, has a name that means 'sandy part of *Dersingham*', the latter being the name of the village immediately to the north. Its own name means 'homestead of *Dēorsige*'s people'. It is not known who this man was, but his name means 'animal victory', coincidentally appropriate for a locality noted for its game shoots.

Sandwich The Kent port, one of the original CINQUE PORTS, is now two miles (just over 3 km) from the sea as a result of changes in the coastline. Its name means 'sandy landing-place', from Old English *sand*, 'sand' and *wīc*, 'landing-place', 'port' (as for IPSWICH and other coastal places). The sand is not that of the seashore but that of the local soil, conducive for market-gardening.

Sandwich Islands The former name of HAWAII was given to the islands by Captain Cook in 1778 in honour of John Montagu, fourth Earl of SANDWICH (1718–1792), then First Lord of the Admiralty. It was this lord who gave the name of the familiar *sandwich*, from his custom of eating cold beef between slices of toast rather than leave the gambling table for a proper cooked meal.

Sandy The name is a pet form of ALEXANDER or ALEXANDRA as well as a descriptive name for a person with sandy-coloured hair.

San Francisco The famous Californian city is named for *St Francis* of Assisi. The name was originally given in 1595 to an unknown bay and vaguely to the land here by a Spanish *Franciscan* friar, Junipero Serra. A Spanish overland expedition arrived at the present bay in 1769 and gave it the already existing name. A *Franciscan* mission was then founded by the bay in October 1776, perhaps on the feast of *St Francis* itself (4 October). However, Sir *Francis* Drake had already been here in 1578 and is said to have named the bay *Port St Francis*, after his patron saint, though it is uncertain whether he entered it. In short, the name appears to have more than one Franciscan allusion.

Sanhedrin The supreme Jewish council or court derives its name, through Hebrew, from Greek *sunedrion*, 'council', literally 'seated together' from *sun-* (in English words usually *syn-*, 'together') and *hedra*, 'seat'. The corrupt form of the Greek word seems to have persisted from the belief that the final *-in* was an Aramaic plural, corresponding to the Hebrew plural *-im*. The title is more correctly rendered *Synedrion* in some academic texts. The word does not appear in the Bible, but the council is often referred to as 'the scribes and elders' or some similar phrase, for example in *Matthew* 26.57, when Christ appears before it on a charge of blasphemy, or in *Acts* 22.30 ('chief priests and all their council'), when Paul is brought before it on a charge of transgressing the Mosaic Law.

San José The capital of Costa Rica was settled by the Spanish in 1736 and originally named *Villa Nueva*, 'new town'. It was subsequently renamed for *St Joseph*, although the reason for the choice of this particular saint is uncertain.

San Juan The capital of Puerto Rico was founded in 1511 by the Spanish explorer *Juan* Ponce de León who named it for himself and his patron saint (*St John*).

Sankey The name derives from a Lancashire place-name, now best represented by *Sankey* Brook, a tributary of the Mersey. Its own name may mean 'holy river'.

San Marino The tiny republic, an enclave in Italy, takes its name from *St Marinus*, the deacon of Dalmatian origin who is said to have founded it in the early 4th century when he established a hermitage here.

San Remo The port and resort in northwest Italy was originally known as *San Romulo*, 'St Romulus', for the bishop who founded the town in the 6th century. In the 15th century the name became *San Remo*, either through confusion with the French saint's name *Rémy* (Italian *Remigio*) or more likely as a contraction of the Latin name *Sancti Romuli in Eremo*, '(church of) St Romulus in the Hermitage'.

San Salvador The capital of EL SALVADOR has a Spanish name meaning 'Holy Saviour'. The city was founded by Spanish colonists on Monday 6 August 1526, the feast of the Transfiguration of the *Saviour*. *See also* SALVADOR.

San Sebastián The port and resort in northern Spain was so named in 1603 for *St Sebastian*.

Sanskrit The ancient language of India, still in use for religious purposes, derives its name from Sanskrit *saṃskṛta*, 'perfected', literally 'put together'.

Santa Claus The legendary patron of children, widely also known as *Father Christmas*, is traditionally identified with ST NICHOLAS. His name evolved as an American modification of *Sante Klaas*, a Dutch dialect form of this. (Standard Dutch would be *Sint Klaas*.) *Cp.* German *Klaus* as a shortened form of *Nikolaus*.

Santa Cruz The city in Bolivia was founded by Spanish missionaries on Saturday 14 September 1560, the feast of the Exaltation of the *Holy Cross* (Spanish *Santa Cruz*).

Santa Fé The state capital of New Mexico was founded in 1610 by Spanish missionaries and originally named *Villa Real de la Santa Fé de San Francisco de Asis*, 'royal town of the holy faith of St Francis of Assisi'. The name was later shortened to *Santa Fé*.

Santa Isabel The former name of MALABO, capital of Equatorial Guinea, is Spanish for 'St Elizabeth' ('St Isabel'). The city was founded in 1820 by English missionaries as *Clarence City* or *Port Clarence*, so named for the Duke of *Clarence* (1765–1837), the future king William IV. In 1843, the year that she was declared of age by the Cortes, it was renamed in honour of 13-year-old Queen *Elizabeth* (*Isabella*) II of Spain (1830–1904).

Santander The port and resort in northern Spain has a name that is an alteration of Spanish *Santa Irena*, 'St Irene'. *Cp.* SANTARÉM.

Santarém The town of west central Portugal has a name that is an alteration of Portuguese *Santa Irena*, 'St Irene'. The port of the same name in northern Brazil has the same origin. *Cp.* SANTANDER.

Santiago The capital of Chile has a name that is a contraction of Spanish *Santo Iago*, 'St James'. The city was founded in 1541 by the Spanish soldier Pedro de Valdivia and was so named in honour of *St James*, a saint widely venerated in Spain. *See also* SANTIAGO DE COMPOSTELA.

Santiago de Compostela The city in northwest Spain has been a popular place of pilgrimage since the 9th century, for it is here that the shrine of the apostle St James the Great is to be found. The first word of the name is thus the Spanish for *St James*. The final word of the name is popularly explained as representing Latin *Campus Stellae*, 'field of the star', referring to the legend that the tomb containing the remains of St James was revealed by the appearance of a bright star over it. However, a more likely origin is in Latin *compos stellae*, 'possessing the star', denoting that the city holds the shrine.

Santo Domingo The capital of the DOMINICAN REPUBLIC has a Spanish name meaning 'Holy Sunday'. The name was formerly that of the island itself, given in 1697 in commemoration of the fact that the Spanish had established a colony here in 1496 on a *Sunday*. The island had actually been discovered four years previously by Christopher Columbus, who named it *la isla española*, 'the Spanish island'. This was later corrupted to HISPANIOLA, as if meaning

484

'little Spain'. Santo Domingo was known as *Ciudad Trujillo* ('Trujillo city') from 1936 to 1961, in honour of the Dominican army officer and statesman Rafael *Trujillo* de Molina (1891–1961). When his oppressive rule ended in his assassination, however, the city reverted to its former name.

Sanyo The Japanese electrical and electronics company, founded in 1947 as a firm making bicycle lamps, has a name that means 'three oceans'. This denoted the three principal oceans of the world, Pacific, Atlantic and Indian, that the company aims to span.

Saône The river of eastern France has a name that probably derives from that of a primitive Celtic or pre-Celtic river god, perhaps originally called something like *Sauc*.

São Paolo The city of western Brazil has a Portuguese name meaning 'St Paul'. The town was founded by Jesuit monks on Thursday 25 January 1554, the feast of the Conversion of *St Paul*.

São Tomé The island in the Gulf of Guinea, which with *Principe* forms a republic, has a Portuguese name meaning 'St Thomas'. It was discovered by the Portuguese on Saturday 21 December 1471, the feast of *St Thomas*.

Sappho The 6th-century BC Greek lyric poetess of the island of Lesbos has a name that on rather uncertain grounds has been based on the word for 'sapphire', Greek *sappheiros*.

Sapporo The city in northern Japan, on Hokkaido, has a name meaning 'pavilion of banknotes', from Japanese *satsu*, 'paper money' and *horo*, 'tent', 'pavilion'. It was founded in 1871 by the Japanese government as a centre for the commercial development of the island.

Saracen The name of the Arab Muslim people who opposed the Christian Crusades in medieval times perhaps ultimately derives from Arabic *šarq*, 'sunrise', referring to their eastern origin. The name was formerly associated with that of SARAH, the biblical wife of Abraham, as she was believed to be the people's ultimate ancestor.

Saragossa The city in northeast Spain has a name that is an English form of its Spanish name *Zaragoza*. This is itself a corruption, through Arabic, of its Roman name *Caesarea Augusta*, referring to the emperor *Caesar Augustus*, under whom it became a Roman colony in 27 BC.

Sarah The long-popular name occurs in the Bible as that of the wife of Abraham and mother of Isaac. It derives from Hebrew *Sārāh*, 'princess'. The biblical Sarah was originally *Sarai*, a name sometimes interpreted as 'contentious'. It was changed by God, however, to something more propitious: 'And God said unto Abraham, As for Sarai thy wife, thou shalt not call her name Sarai, but Sarah shall her name be' (*Genesis* 17.15).

Sarajevo The capital of Bosnia-Herzegovina, scene of the assassination of Archduke Francis Ferdinand in 1914, derives its name from Turkish *saray*, 'palace' (hence *seraglio* as the word for a harem). It was actually founded by the Turks in the 15th century.

Saratov The city in southwest Russia has a name of Tatar origin, from *sary*, 'yellow' and *tau*, 'mountain' (*cp.* DAGESTAN). The town was founded in 1590 on the high right bank of the river Volga, where the terrain is mountainous, and where one of the mountains, now called *Sokolovaya*, is noted for its yellowish slopes.

Sardanapalus The name of the 7th-century BC king of Assyria, famous for the palace and library he built at Nineveh, is a Greek form of his Assyrian name *Ashurbanipal* or *Assurbanipal*, '(the god) Assur creates the son'. He is mentioned in the Bible as 'the great and noble Asnappar' (*Ezra* 4.10). *See also* ASSYRIA.

Sardinia The Mediterranean island, belonging to Italy, has a name that may have originated as that of a local god or have derived from an Iberian tribe, the *Sards*, who emigrated here from northern Africa. The original form of the name is uncertain. The Phoenicians knew the island as *Ŝardan*, and this name was found on a Punic stele dating from the 7th century BC. The Roman name of the island, *Sardinia*, may have given that of the *sardine*, a fish formerly plentiful off the coast here.

Sargasso Sea The calm region of the North Atlantic is so named for the quantities of floating seaweed of the genus *Sargassum* that it contains. The name of the seaweed derives from Portuguese *sargaço*, itself perhaps from Latin *salix*, genitive *salicis*, 'willow'.

Sark The name of the fourth largest of the five main Channel Islands is of unknown origin or meaning. Recent research has shown that the island's Roman name was probably *Caesarea*, a name formerly assigned to Jersey. This is only loosely and indirectly connected with the name of Julius *Caesar*, since it developed from some early form of the island's name, such as *Sargia*, recorded in the 6th century.

Sarmatia The ancient name of the region of Europe corresponding to present-day Poland and southwest Russia derives from that of its indigenous people, the *Sarmatians*, whose own name may ultimately relate to Sanskrit *roman*, 'hair', so that they were the 'hairy ones'.

Sarpedon In Greek mythology, the name is that of the son of Zeus and king of Lycia who was killed by Patroclus while fighting for the Trojans. It is traditionally derived from Greek *harpagē*, 'seizure', 'rape', referring to his abduction of Europa. *Cp.* HARPAGON.

Sartor Resartus The title of Carlyle's well-known work, published in 1833, relates specifically to the first part, which satirically examines the importance of clothes. The Latin phrase means 'the tailor retailored'.

Saskatchewan The Canadian province takes its name from the river *Saskatchewan*, whose own name evolved from its Indian (Cree) name of *Kisiskatchewani Sipi*, 'rapid-flowing river'.

Saskatoon The city in Saskatchewan, Canada, derives its name from the Cree word *misaskwatomin*, literally 'fruit of the tree of many branches', the name of a type of serviceberry. The name was chosen for the town, a proposed temperance colony, by its founder in 1882, John H. Lake of Toronto.

Sassandra The port in the Côte d'Ivoire (former Ivory Coast), West Africa, has a name that is a contraction of Portuguese *Santo Andrea*, 'St Andrew'. The name was

given by the Portuguese explorers João de Santarém and Pero de Escobar who landed here on Thursday 30 November 1497, the feast of *St Andrew*.

Sassenach The name is a Scots term for an English person, or sometimes a Lowland Scot. It represents Gaelic *Sasunnach*, 'Saxon' (*see* SAXONY).

Satan The name of the Devil in the Christian religion derives from Hebrew *śāṭān*, 'adversary', literally 'one who plots against another' (in this case, God), from *śāṭan*, 'to oppose', 'to plot against'. In the Old Testament the Hebrew word is used to mean 'enemy' in the literal sense, and as such is usually translated 'adversary' (*e.g.* in *Numbers* 22.22, *2 Samuel* 19.22). In some of the later Old Testament books, however, the word (with the definite article in Hebrew) is used of an angelic opponent of mankind, for example in *Job* 1.6–12, 2.1–7. In the Septuagint (the Greek version of the Old Testament) the Hebrew name is translated as *diabolos*, 'slanderer', literally 'one who throws across', and it is this Greek word that gave English *devil*. In the New Testament *Satan* is presented as a more precise and 'concrete' character, the personification of evil, who reigns over darkness, opposes Jesus and the apostles, and so on. He is finally overcome by Christ, however: 'And he said unto them, I beheld Satan as lightning fall from heaven' (*Luke* 10.18).

Saturday The name of the seventh day of the week arose, through Old English, as a semi-translation of its Roman equivalent, *Saturni dies*, 'day of SATURN'. *Saturday* is also the Jewish SABBATH, but the similarity between the two names is merely coincidental.

Saturn The name is that of both the Roman god of agriculture and vegetation, corresponding to the Greek *Cronos*, and the sixth planet from the sun, the former name giving the latter. The god's name is traditionally related to the Latin root element *sat-* implying abundance, as in modern English *sated*, *satisfy* and *saturate*. More directly, it also relates to Latin *satum*, 'sown', the past participle of *serere*, 'to sow'. The name of the sixth planet was given because it relates to that of the fifth, JUPITER. In classical mythology, Cronos

(Roman counterpart *Saturn*) was the father of Zeus (Roman counterpart *Jupiter*).

Saudi Arabia The kingdom in southwest Asia was founded in 1932 by the Muslim leader Ibn *Sa'ūd* (1880–1953), and was named for him. His name derives from Arabic *sa'd*, 'good fortune', 'happiness', but it is purely a coincidence that the main part of the Arabian peninsula was known to the Romans as *Arabia Felix*, 'Arabia the fortunate'. (*See* YEMEN.) The Arabic name of *Saudi Arabia* is al-'*arabiyya as-s'aūdiyya*.

Saul The biblical name derives from Hebrew *Šā'ūl*, 'asked for', 'requested'. This is fitting for the first king of Israel, to whom Samuel, the last of the judges, yields place: 'And Samuel told all the words of the Lord unto the people that asked of him a king' (1 *Samuel* 8.10). The name is also that of PAUL before his conversion.

Saunders The name means 'son of *Sander*', this being a short form of ALEXANDER. *Sanders* and *Sanderson* are of the same origin.

Sauternes The sweet white wine takes its name from the district of *Sauternes* near Bordeaux in southern France. The district's name may derive from Celtic *sau*, 'mound' and *ternevan*, 'river bank'.

Savage The name was originally a nickname for a wild or boorish person.

Savage Club The well-known London club was founded in 1857 at the suggestion of the journalist George Augustus Sala and is named for the poet Richard *Savage* (1697–1743). The club has long had literary and artistic connections.

Savile Club The London club, noted for its literary associations, was founded in 1868 in Trafalgar Square as the *New Club*. It adopted its present name in 1891 when it moved to a house in SAVILE ROW. It is now in Brook Street.

Savile Row The London street, famous for its quality tailors, was laid out in the 1730s on the Burlington estate (*see* BURLINGTON HOUSE) and takes its name from Lady Dorothy *Savile*, daughter of William Savile, second Marquis of Halifax, and wife of the third Earl Burlington.

Saville The name is of Norman origin, from a place in northern France that is not certainly identified but that may have been *Sainville*, near Chartres. Its own name means 'Saxon settlement', from Old French *saisne*, 'Saxon' (*cp.* SASSENACH) and *ville*.

Savory The name derives from a Germanic personal name comprising the elements *saba*, of uncertain meaning, and *rīc*, 'power'.

Savoy The region of southeast France had the Roman name of *Sapaudia*, itself of uncertain meaning.

Savoy Hotel The prestigious London hotel, in the Strand, takes its name from the SAVOY THEATRE, next to which it opened in 1889.

Savoy Operas The operettas by Gilbert and Sullivan are so called because from *Iolanthe* (1882) onwards they were first produced at the SAVOY THEATRE, London, which was built specially for them by Richard D'Oyly Carte. A devotee of (or performer in) the Gilbert and Sullivan operas is sometimes known as a *Savoyard*.

Savoy Theatre The well-known London theatre, in the Strand, was built in 1881 by Richard D'Oyly Carte on ground within the precincts of the former historic *Savoy* Palace, itself built by the Thames here in the 13th century and granted by Henry III to Peter, Earl of Richmond (1203–1268), who became Count of SAVOY. *See also* SAVOY HOTEL, SAVOY OPERAS.

Sawyer The name is an occupational one for a person who made his living by sawing wood.

Saxbys The makers of Melton Mowbray pies are named for their founders, the brothers Herbert W. *Saxby* (1870–1953) and Edward E. *Saxby* (1873–1966), who opened a butcher's shop in Wellingborough, Northamptonshire in 1904 and set up a pie factory nearby in 1912.

Saxone The make of footwear originated as the name of a company formed in 1908 by way of a merger between two shoe manufacturing firms, one English, one Scottish. The name was chosen to suggest *Saxon*, with its associations of strength and ruggedness.

Saxony The region of southeast Germany takes its name from its native people, the *Saxons*, whose own name is said to derive from Old German *sahsa*, 'dagger', the weapon that they favoured. The root word also gave the Finnish name for Germany, *Saksa*. *See also* SASSENACH.

Sayer The name has a number of possible origins. It could represent a medieval personal name corresponding to the modern German first name *Siegher*, literally 'victory army'. As an occupational name it could apply to a *sawyer* or woodcutter (*cp.* SAWYER), a professional reciter or *sayer*, an *assayer* of metals (or even a taster of food), or a seller of the type of cloth known as *say*.

Scafell Pike England's highest mountain, in the Lake District, has a name of Scandinavian origin meaning 'hill with a summer pasture', from Old Norse *skáli*, 'shepherd's hut', 'shieling' and *fjall*, 'hill' (modern *fell*). The *Pike* is the mountain's *peak*. *Sca Fell* proper is a separate mountain here, with the *Pike*, named for it, some half a mile from it.

Scalextric The model racing car systems were originally named *Scalex* when first marketed in the 1950s, as the toy vehicles were made to no specific scale (that is, to '*scale x*'). In 1957 the manufacturers introduced an *electrical* system, and incorporated an element from this word into the original name accordingly.

Scandinavia The joint name for Norway, Sweden, Finland and Denmark evolved from an ancient name *Scania* (as recorded by the Romans), of uncertain meaning, with the addition of a Germanic element meaning 'island'. *See also* SCANIA.

Scania The make of road haulage vehicle has a name that is the Latin form of *Skåne*, the southernmost region of Sweden, where the original manufacturers, the English bicycle makers *Humber*, set up a small factory in Malmö in the 1890s. The first *Scania* car was built in 1901, and the following year the company produced their first truck, the forerunner of the commercial vehicles of today.

Scapa Flow The large natural anchorage in the Orkney Islands has a name that means 'sea-bay of the boat isthmus', from Old Norse *skalpr*, 'boat' (related to English *scalp*), *eith*, 'isthmus' and *flóa*, 'flood', 'bay'. The 'isthmus' is the stretch of land south of Kirkwall.

Scarborough The North Yorkshire port and resort is said to derive its name from its Norse founder, Thorgils *Skarthi*. If this is so, the name means 'Skarthi's fort'. An alternative explanation, however, takes the name from Old Norse *skarth*, 'gap', with the last part of the name being not 'fort' but 'hill' (Old Norse *berg*). This gives a meaning 'hill by a gap', which certainly suits the topography here, the 'gap' being the valley through which the present A64 road approaches the town from the south. Perhaps this second origin became popularly associated with the Norse personal name, which itself is a nickname meaning 'hare-lipped'.

Scarlett The name was originally an occupational one for a dyer or for a person who sold *scarlet* or any bright-coloured cloth.

Schaffhausen The town and canton in northern Switzerland have a German name meaning literally 'sheep house', from *Schaf*, 'sheep' and *Haus*, 'house'.

Schedar The name of the brightest star in the constellation Cassiopeia represents Arabic *ṣadr*, from the full phrase *ṣadr dhāt al-kursī*, 'breast of the seated woman'. The latter half of this gave the name of CASSIOPEIA itself.

Scheherazade In the *Arabian Nights*, the name is that of the daughter of the vizier of King Schahriyar. She marries the king, but escapes the death that was the fate of his previous wives by telling him a story which she leaves incomplete every night, so that he longs to hear the continuation the following night. Her name is a corruption of *Shahrazād*, from Persian *shahr*, 'city' and *zād*, 'person'. It has been popularized by Rimsky-Korsakov's symphonic suite *Sheherazade* (1888).

Scheldt The river of western Europe had the Roman name of *Scaldis*, perhaps ultimately deriving from a pre-Latin root element meaning 'shallow'. The river's French name is *Escaut*.

Schleswig The port and former duchy in northwest Germany takes its name from that of the bay here. The name is Old Norse in origin and means 'reedy harbour', from *sle*, 'reed' and *vík*, 'harbour', 'bay'. The latter word was subsequently understood as Old High German *wīch*, 'village', 'town', as applied to the port itself.

Schleswig-Holstein The state in northwest Germany evolved from the union in the 15th century between the separate duchies of SCHLESWIG and HOLSTEIN.

Schneider Trophy The trophy for international races between seaplanes takes its name from the Frenchman Jacques *Schneider*, who presented it in 1913.

Scholl The footcare products take their name from Dr William M. *Scholl* (1882–1968), an American shoemaker who graduated as a doctor of medicine in 1904 and who set up a business that year in Chicago as a manufacturer of orthopaedic foot appliances.

Schoolmaster Symphony Haydn's Symphony No 55 in E flat major (1774) is so nicknamed because the dotted figure in the slow movement is supposed to suggest the admonishing finger of a schoolmaster.

Schweppes The familiar brand of soft drink takes its name from Jean Jacob *Schweppe* (1740–1821), a German farmer's son who after working as a tinker and silversmith became a master jeweller in Geneva. His interest in mechanical and scientific processes led him to find a way of combining gases with water. By 1788 he was selling effervescent mineral water commercially, and two years later he set up his firm in Geneva.

Schwyz The town and canton of central Switzerland derive their name from that of a village here called *Suittes*, perhaps from Old High German *suedan*, 'to burn', referring to a region of the forest cleared by burning. It was *Schwyz* that gave the name of SWITZERLAND as a whole.

Scilly Isles The group of islands southwest of Cornwall have a name that remains of uncertain origin, largely because early records of it are unreliable and probably corrupt. One theory connects the name with that of the Roman god *Sulis*, as in the Roman name of Bath, *Aquae Sulis*, and some Romano-British remains on the islands suggest that there may have been a shrine here to him. Whatever the case, the final *-y* probably represents *ey*, the Norse word for 'island'. The letter *c* was added in the 16th or 17th century to distinguish the word from *silly*.

Scipio The name is famous from two Roman generals: Publius Cornelius *Scipio* Africanus Major, who commanded the Roman invasion of Carthage in the Second Punic War (218–201 BC), and his grandson by adoption, Publius Cornelius *Scipio* Aemilianus Africanus Minor, who commanded an army against Carthage in the last Punic War (149–146 BC). *Scipio* was their hereditary *cognomen* or nickname. It means 'stick', and was originally given to one of their ancestors, a Cornelius who acted as a 'stick' or guide to his blind father.

Scorpius The name is that of a large constellation lying between Libra and Sagittarius, so called because the outline of its brightest stars suggests that of a *scorpion*, complete with sting. Its alternative name, *Scorpio*, is familiar in astrology as that of the eighth sign of the zodiac.

Scotcade The familiar mail-order firm was founded in Britain in 1973 by an American marketeer, Bob *Scott*, with the second half of the name representing his 'shopping ar*cade*'.

Scotch Corner The well-known road junction on the A1 near Richmond, North Yorkshire, is so named because the road that branches off to the northwest here follows the established shortest route to SCOTLAND, *viz.* on the A66 to Penrith and from there on the A6 or M6 to Carlisle and Gretna Green. The Scottish border is about 60 miles (96 km) further south at its western end than it is at its eastern end (at Berwick-upon-Tweed).

Scotland The familiar northern country and former kingdom of Britain takes its name from its native inhabitants, the *Scots*. They were originally Celtic raiders from northern Ireland who crossed to settle in what was then known as CALEDONIA in the 5th and 6th centuries AD. By about the middle of the 9th century, *Caledonia* had come to be named after them as *Scotia* in Latin texts. The ultimate meaning of their name is uncertain, although some authorities link it with an Old Welsh word *ysgthru*, 'to cut', referring to the people's habit of tattooing themselves with iron points. *See also* NOVA SCOTIA.

Scotland Yard The headquarters of the Metropolitan Police Force in London, officially known as *New Scotland Yard*, take their name from their original location in Great *Scotland Yard*, off Whitehall, where part of the premises of the historic Whitehall Palace were used as lodgings for visiting kings of *Scotland* in medieval times. The Police Force, founded in 1829, moved to new premises on the Thames Embankment in 1890, and to their present premises on Broadway and Victoria Street in 1967.

Scott As it implies, the name originally indicated someone who came from SCOTLAND, especially a person who spoke Gaelic there.

Scottish Symphony Mendelssohn's Symphony No 3 in A minor, Op 56 (between 1830 and 1842) is so named because it was inspired by a visit the composer made to the royal residence of Holyroodhouse, Edinburgh. It is dedicated to Queen Victoria.

Scouse The colloquial name for a person from Liverpool, or for the dialect spoken by such a person, comes from that of the traditional Liverpool dish known as *scouse*, a type of stew made from pieces of left-over meat. Its own name is short for *lobscouse*, said to be from dialect words *lob*, 'to boil' and *scouse*, 'broth'.

Scouts *See* BOY SCOUTS.

Scrabble The popular board game, in which lettered tiles of differing scoring values are placed to form words, has a name that probably derives from *scribble-scrabble* as a phrase denoting hasty writing. It was patented in 1950.

Screech The name probably originated as a nickname for a person with a strident voice.

Scrimgeour The name originated as an occupational designation of a fencer or fencing-master, from Old French *eskermisseor*, 'fencer', related to modern English *skirmish*.

Scritti Politti The British rock group, formed in Leeds in 1977, based their name on the Italian phrase *scritti politichi*, 'political writings', altering the spelling to suggest the title of the Little Richard hit of 1956, 'Tutti frutti'.

Scrooge The name of the miserly old man in Charles Dickens's story *A Christmas Carol* (1843) appears to be based on *scrounge*, although this word, of dialect origin, was not in general use until the First World War, when it was popularized by servicemen. Dickens may have had in mind, at least subconsciously, an original dialect word such as *scringe* or *scrunge*, both meaning 'to steal'.

Scunthorpe The Humberside (formerly Lincolnshire) iron and steel manufacturing town has a Danish name, from its location inside the Danelaw. It means '*Skúma's* farm', with the Scandinavian personal name followed by Old Norse *thorp*, a term for an outlying farm depending on a larger one (like the English *-stoke* in names such as BASINGSTOKE). Most places with *thorp* in their name have remained small villages, but Scunthorpe gained its size and importance through the iron-ore deposits discovered here in the 1870s.

Scutari The former name of the Turkish town now known as *Üsküdar*, a suburb of Istanbul, derives from Latin *scutarii*, literally 'shield-makers', referring to a Roman legion created by Constantine, whose headquarters were here.

Scylla In Greek mythology, the name is that of the sea monster that devoured sailors as they made their way through the Straits of Messina. It is actually that of a group of rocks on the Italian side of the straits, and is said to derive from Sanskrit *skand*, 'to leap', 'to flow'.

Scythian The people of *Scythia*, the ancient region of Europe and Asia to the north of the Black Sea, now part of the Soviet Union, derive their name from an Indo-european root word *sku*, 'shepherd', referring to their nomadic way of life.

Seal If not a variant of SALE, the name was originally either an occupational one for a maker of *seals*) or *saddles* (from Old French *seele*) or a nickname for a plump or awkward person, who resembled a *seal*.

Sealyham The breed of short-legged wire-haired terrier derives its name from *Sealyham* House (originally *Sealy Ham*), south of Fishguard in South Wales, where it originated in the 19th century in the home of the Edwardes family.

Seamas The name, pronounced 'Shaymus', is an Irish form of JAMES.

Sean The name, usually pronounced 'Shawn' by the English but 'Shahn' by the Irish, is an Irish form of JOHN.

Searchers, The The British pop quartet was formed in Liverpool in 1961 and adopted the name of the identically titled John Wayne movie of 1956.

Searle The name is a form of the Norman personal name *Serlo*, perhaps related to Old English *searu*, 'armour' (*see* SALISBURY) and so meaning something like 'defender'.

Sears The American mail order company and department stores are named for Richard W. *Sears* (1863–1914), who set up as a watchmaker in Minneapolis in 1886. The following year he moved to Chicago and took as partner a watch assembler named Alvah C. Roebuck. In 1892 the two started their mail order business as *Sears and Roebuck*, and today's company of *Sears, Roebuck* is still based in *Sears* Tower, Chicago.

Sea Symphony Vaughan Williams' first symphony (1903–9) was set to a text from poems by Walt Whitman and was conceived as an orchestral and choral work that would develop the theme expressed by the title of Charles Villiers Stanford's *Songs of the Sea* (1905).

Seattle The well-known city and port in Washington was founded in 1853 and named for *Seatlh*, a local Indian chief.

Sebastian The name is familiar from the 3rd-century saint who was shot to death by arrows, his martyrdom being a popular subject for medieval artists. His name literally means 'man from *Sebastia*', a town in Asia Minor (now *Sivas*, Turkey), but is frequently interpreted as deriving directly from Greek *sebastos*, 'reverenced', 'august' (*cp.* SEBASTOPOL).

Sebastopol The Ukrainian port and resort, more accurately known as *Sevastopol*, was founded in 1784 and according to the fashion of the day given a Greek name, meaning 'great city', from *sebastos*, 'reverenced', 'august' and *polis*, 'city'.

Securicor The private security company, with its familiar fleet of vans, derives its name from a blend of '*security*' and '*corps*'.

Sedan The town in northeast France, the scene of several famous battles, has a name that may derive from Gaulish *setu*, 'long'.

Segal As a Jewish name, *Segal* is an abbreviated form of Hebrew *segan leviah*, 'member of the Levites'. As a non-Jewish name it is of French origin and originally denoted a grower or seller of rye (Old French *segal*, modern French *seigle*).

Segovia The city in central Spain derives its name from Celtic *sego*, 'strong', 'powerful'. The town is famous for the ALCÁZAR (*which see*), the fortified palace of the kings of Castile.

Seinäjoki The name of the town in southwest central Finland derives from a combination of Finnish *seinä*, 'wall' and *joki*, 'river'.

Seine The well-known river of northern France, on which Paris stands, had the Roman name of *Sequana*. This may have derived from Celtic *soghan*, 'calm', or from a pre-Celtic root word *sec*, meaning 'to spring', 'to gush', as a general term for flowing water.

Selby The North Yorkshire town on the river Ouse has a name meaning 'village by the willows', from Old English conjectural *sele*, 'willow copse' (related to *salh*, 'willow') and Old Norse *bý*, 'village'. The latter part of the name may well have replaced Old English *tūn*, so that the original name of Selby may have been the equivalent of *Salton*.

Selecter, The The British rock group, formed in Coventry in 1979, took their name from the title of the B-side song of their debut single 'Gangsters', written by guitarist Noel Davies.

Selene The name of the Greek goddess of the moon represents Greek *selēnē*, 'moon', itself a derivative of *selas*, 'brightness'.

Sélestat The town in northeast France had the Medieval Latin name of *Scalistatus*. This represents Old High German *sclade*, 'marshy region' and *state*, 'place'. The town's modern German name is *Schlett-stadt*.

Seleucia The name is that of several ancient cities of the Middle East, especially that of Mesopotamia on the river Tigris. They take their name from one or other of the dynasty of kings known as the *Seleucids*, whose founder was the 4th-century BC Macedonian general of Alexander the Great, *Seleucus* Nicator. Their name is popularly interpreted as 'bright', from the Greek root seen in the mythological name SELENE.

Selfridges The famous London department store takes its name from Harry Gordon *Selfridge* (1858–1947), an American mail order company manager who after taking early retirement came to London in 1906 to start up his own business. The store opened its doors in Oxford Street just three years later.

Selina The name is probably an altered form of SELENE, that of the Greek goddess of the moon.

Selkirk The town in southeast Scotland has a name meaning 'church by the hall', from Old English *sele*, 'dwelling', 'house', 'hall', and either Old English *cirice* or Old Norse *kirkja*, 'church'. The town is near enough to the English border to have an entirely English name.

Sellafield The atomic power station and nuclear processing plant in Cumbria, near the coast, derives its name from the locality. The origin of the place-name is uncertain, although the second half is presumably Old English *feld* (modern *field*), 'open land'. The first part of the name is recorded independently as *Sellagh* in the 13th century.

Sellers The name means 'son of *Seller*', the latter being an occupational name for a *saddler*, for a person employed in the *cellar* of a manor house or monastery, or for a merchant or *seller* of goods.

Sellotape The familiar brand of adhesive tape derives its name from another brand name, *Cellophane*, as it is this that provides the cellulose base film for the tape.

The initial *C* was replaced by an *S*, however, so that the name could be registered as a trade mark.

Selsey The West Sussex seaside resort, with its well-known nearby headland of *Selsey* Bill, has a name that means 'seal island'. The reference is not to an actual island but to the headland, on whose beaches seals were regularly seen. The name is one of those recorded and glossed by the Venerable Bede in his 8th-century *Ecclesiastical History of the English People*: *Selaesu quod dicitur Latine Insula uitili marini*, 'Selsey, which is called in Latin the Island of the sea calf' (*i.e.* seal).

Selwyn College The Cambridge college was founded in 1882 and named in memory of George *Selwyn* (1809–1878), one of the first bishops of New Zealand and later bishop of Lichfield. The college was modelled on Keble College, Oxford, itself similarly named in memory of a leading churchman.

Semipalatinsk The city in Kazakhstan was founded in 1718 and has a name meaning 'seven palaces', referring to some ancient ruins nearby (with 'seven' purely an arbitrary number meaning 'many').

Semiramis The name of the legendary founder of Babylon, the wife of Ninus, king of Assyria, represents Assyrian *Sammura-mat*, 'loving doves'. After her death, Semiramis is said to have turned into a mountain dove. She is particularly associated with the Hanging Gardens of Babylon, one of the Seven Wonders of the World, and in some languages these are known by her name rather than that of the city, for example French *les jardins suspendus de Sémiramis*, German *die hängenden Gärten der Semiramis*, Russian *visyachiye sady Semiramidy*.

Semite The name is a composite one for those people who speak a *Semitic* language, and includes the Jews and Arabs as well as the ancient Babylonians, Assyrians and Phoenicians. It derives from SHEM, the eldest son of Noah (*Genesis* 6.10), who is traditionally regarded as the ancestor of all Semites (*Genesis* 10).

Semple The name has two possible origins. As a Norman name, it represents a person who originally came from a place in northern France called *Saint-Paul* (from the dedication of its church). As a nickname it originally applied to a *simple* person, that is, someone who was humble and straightforward.

Semtex The type of plastic explosive takes its name from the Czech village of *Semtín*, near Pardubice, east of Prague, where it was originally manufactured, with the final *-ex* either the common commercial suffix (as in KLEENEX) or specifically standing for '*ex*plosive'.

Senate The upper chamber of the legislatures of the United States, Canada, Australia and many other countries bases its name on that of the legislative council of ancient Rome, the *senatus*, 'council of the elders', a word itself derived from Latin *senex*, 'old man'.

Seneca The name is most familiar as that of *Seneca* the Younger, the 1st-century AD Roman philosopher and statesman who was implicated in a plot to kill Nero and who committed suicide. He inherited his name from his father, known as *Seneca* the Elder, otherwise Lucius Annaeus *Seneca*. His *cognomen* (nickname) probably derives from Latin *senectus*, 'aged', the adjective of *senex*, 'old man'. The name would originally have implied wisdom and experience, not decrepitude and failing powers.

Senegal The republic in West Africa takes its name from its main river, whose own name may derive from a local African word meaning 'navigable'.

Senlac The name is that of the hill in Sussex, near Battle, that is the site of the Battle of Hastings (1066). It is a Norman-French form of an Old English name that might otherwise have been *Sandlake*. It thus means 'sandy stream'. This meaning was obviously too prosaic for some historical writers, who tried to find a more colourful origin for such an important place. The antiquarian William Camden, for example, writing in the late 16th century, described Battle as being in a district 'wherein there is a place called by a French word *sangue lac*, of the bloud there shed, which by nature of the ground seemeth after raine to wax red'. There is a grain of truth in his observation, however, for the small stream here is of chalybeate

origin, containing iron, and actually *does* run red after heavy rain. But from the iron, not blood!

Sennacherib The 7th-century BC king of Assyria, who defeated Babylon and rebuilt Nineveh, has a name that represents Akkadian *Sin-ahhe-eriba*, '(the moon god) Sin has replaced the brothers'.

Sens The cathedral city in northeast central France was known to the Romans as *Senones*, and was the capital of the Gaulish people of this name. The origin may be in Gaulish *seno*, 'old'. *Cp.* SIENA.

Seoul The name of the capital of South Korea derives from Korean *sŏul*, simply meaning 'capital'.

Sephardi The name is that of a Spanish-Portuguese Jew, as distinct from an ASHKENAZI, or German-Polish Jew. It derives from Hebrew *sepharad*, the name of a region mentioned in the Bible (*Obadiah* 20), now generally believed to be Spain, although identified by some with Sardis in Lydia. The Septuagint (Greek version of the Old Testament) renders the name as *Ephratha*, the Vulgate (Latin translation) as *Bosphorus*.

September The ninth month of the year has a name that derives from Latin *septem*, 'seven', since it was originally the seventh month in the ancient Roman calendar, which began in March. *Cp.* OCTOBER, NOVEMBER, DECEMBER, which are now similarly 'out' by two.

Septimania The ancient region of southern France, between the Pyrenees and the Rhône, derives its name from Latin *septimanus*, 'of the seventh'. The reference is to a colony of retired Roman soldiers from the *Seventh Legion*.

Septimus The name is Latin for 'seventh', and was adopted by some large Victorian families for a seventh son or a seventh child if male.

Septuagesima In the Christian calendar, the name is that of the third Sunday before Lent. It derives from Latin *septuagesima*, 'seventieth', as it is (very roughly) 70 days before Easter. It has been suggested that the names of QUADRAGESIMA and QUINQUAGESIMA prompted those of SEXAGESIMA and *Septuagesima*. Of these, *Quinquagesima* is the only one of the series that is arithmetically accurate, while *Septuagesima* is so far out (actually nine weeks, or 63 days) that some regard it as referring to the octave of Easter, rather than to Easter itself.

Septuagint The name is that of the principal Greek version of the Old Testament, including the Apocrypha, which is said to have been translated by 70 (Latin *septuaginta*) scholars. According to legend, the translation was made by 72 people in 72 days, as if six from each of the 12 tribes of Israel. Analysis has shown that the translation *was* made by a number of scholars, although almost certainly not 70. The *Pentateuch* (first five books) was probably translated in the 3rd century BC, and the rest in the 2nd century. New Testament writers, working in Greek, commonly quoted the Old Testament books from the *Septuagint*. Sometimes the Greek version differed significantly from the original Hebrew. The announcement of the impending birth of Jesus in the New Testament, 'Behold, a virgin shall be with child' (*Matthew* 1.23), quotes the Old Testament almost identically, 'Behold, a virgin shall conceive' (*Isaiah* 7.14). However, the *Septuagint* had rendered the Hebrew '*almah*, 'young woman' (of marriageable age) by Greek *parthenos*, 'virgin', an interpretation that could be regarded as bearing on the doctrine of the Virgin Birth.

Serapis The Greek-Egyptian fertility god was invented by the Ptolemies in the 3rd century BC as a combination of the popular Egyptian gods OSIRIS and APIS, and his name, in its original form *Osarapis*, is a similar blend of these two.

Serbia The constituent republic of Yugoslavia takes its name from its indigenous inhabitants, the *Serbs*, whose own name may have evolved from a Caucasian root element *ser* meaning 'man'. *See also* WEND.

Sergeant The name originally applied simply to someone who was a *servant*, but later came to apply to a person who occupied some special post as a *sergeant*, whether in the army or as a civil official.

Sergiyev Posad The Russian town northeast of Moscow is famous for its Monastery of the Holy Trinity and St Sergius, founded here in the 14th century by St Sergius of Radonezh. When the original settlement was merged with two others in 1782 it became *Sergiev Posad*, 'Sergius' quarter', from Russian *posad*, literally 'plantation', a term applied in the 18th century to a centre of commerce. In 1919 this name was shortened to *Sergiev*. In 1930 the town was renamed *Zagorsk*, after a Moscow Communist leader, but reverted to its original name in 1991.

Serket The name of the scorpion goddess of the ancient Egyptians is a short form of the phrase *serket hetyt*, meaning 'she who causes the throat to breathe'. This euphemistically implies 'she who may *stop* the throat from breathing', as a scorpion sting can cause death. The goddess is usually depicted as a lady whose head bears a scorpion with raised tail all set to sting. The name is also spelled *Selkis*.

Serpentine The artificial lake in Hyde Park, London, was formed in the 1730s by damming the small river Westbourne and was named for the latter's winding course. A text of 1754 refers to 'the serpentine river in Hyde-park'. Today the Serpentine belies its name and merely curves gently from north to east. The river itself is now mostly underground except very visibly here in Hyde Park and entirely invisibly at Sloane Square Underground station, where it crosses above the platforms in large iron pipes.

Sesame Street The popular American television programme for young children, first broadcast in 1969, was given a name that was meant to suggest adventure and excitement (from the famous 'Open sesame!' used by Ali Baba to open the door of the robbers' den) and that also evoked an urban setting.

Sessions A person with this surname is the ultimate descendant of someone from SOISSONS in northern France.

Sète The industrial town in the south of France derives its name from the pre-Indoeuropean root element *set* meaning 'mountain', referring to Mont Saint-Clair nearby. The name was spelled *Cette* from the 17th century until 1936, and a whale (Latin *cetus*) appears in the town's coat of arms as a visual pun on this.

Seth In the Bible, the name is that of Adam's third son, given to him by God after the murder of his second son Abel. His name derives from Hebrew *Šēt*, 'appointed', 'determined', and implies this replacement: 'And Adam knew his wife again; and she bare a son, and called his name Seth: for God, said she, hath appointed me another seed instead of Abel, whom Cain slew' (*Genesis* 4.25).

Seto Naikai The name is that of the sea in southwest Japan known in English as the *Inland Sea*. It literally means 'inland sea strait', from *seto*, 'strait' (itself from *se*, 'stream' and *to*, 'gate') and *Naikai*, 'inland sea' (from *nai*, 'inside' and *kai*, 'sea'). The sea lies between the islands of Honshu, Shikoku and Kyushu.

Sevastopol *See* SEBASTOPOL.

Sevenoaks The Kent town has a name that means what it says, 'seven oaks'. The number may simply have meant 'some', 'several', without being precise, although there could have been an actual group of seven oaks here in medieval times. In 1955 the local authorities planted seven young oaks (from nearby Knole Park) on a cricket ground to the east of the town centre. When six of them blew down in the autumn storms of 1987 they were replaced within a matter of weeks, so that they continue to serve as a visual representation of the town's name.

Seven Sisters The seven chalk cliffs that extend along the Sussex coast to the west of Beachy Head were given their collective name relatively recently. A document of 1588 records them as *the Seven Cliffes*. The name echoes the *Seven Sisters* of classical mythology, as the seven daughters of Atlas and Pleione, collectively forming the Pleiades. Each of the cliffs has its own individual name: Went Hill Brow, Baily's Brow, Flagstaff Point, Brass Point, Rough Brow, Short Brow, Haven Brow.

Seventh Day Adventist The name is that of the Protestant sect who hold that Christ's second coming (*see* ADVENT) is imminent but who are distinct from other Adventists in observing Saturday (the *seventh day* of the week) as the Sabbath instead of Sunday.

7-Up The popular soft drink was originally called *Howdy* when invented in Missouri in 1920. Its maker, a Mr Griggs, aimed to improve on it, and produced a drink that he called *Bib-label Lithiated Lemon-Lime Soda*. This name hardly led to ready sales, so he searched for another. After six tries (so the story goes) he came up with *7-Up*, and sales rocketed. No doubt the name was partly or even wholly suggested by the card game *seven-up*.

Seven Years War The name is that of the war of 1756 to 1763 between Britain and Prussia against France and Austria.

Severn Britain's longest river, rising in central Wales and flowing north and east before turning south to its estuary in the Bristol Channel, has an ancient name of uncertain origin. Tacitus, writing in the 2nd century AD, recorded the name as *Sabrina*. This is probably of Celtic origin, although no word or name is known that makes it meaningful. The Welsh name of the river is *Hafren*, of the same origin.

Severnaya Zemlya The archipelago in the Arctic Ocean, belonging to Russia, has a Russian name meaning 'northern land'. It was discovered in 1913 and originally named *ostrova Nikolaya II* ('Nicholas II islands'), for the tsar. It was renamed in 1926.

Severodvinsk The seaport town in northwest Russia has a name meaning 'Northern Dvina', from the river on which it is situated. From 1938 to 1957 it was known as *Molotovsk*, for the Soviet statesman Vyacheslav *Molotov*, who also gave the former name of PERM.

Seville The well-known port in southwest Spain has a name that is ultimately of Phoenician origin, from *sefela*, 'plain', 'valley'. The city is an inland port on the Guadalquivir estuary, where the terrain is low-lying.

Sèvres The type of French porcelain takes its name from its place of manufacture, the town of *Sèvres* that is now a southwest suburb of Paris. The name is that of a river, itself of pre-Indoeuropean origin, probably from root elements *sav*, 'hollow' and *ar*, 'water', 'river'. The name was recorded in the 6th century as *Savara*.

Seward The name represents either of the Anglo-Saxon personal names *Sigeweard*, meaning 'victory rule', or *Sæweald*, meaning 'sea rule'. It could also be an occupational name for a person who supervised seating arrangements at a banquet, from an Anglo-Norman verb related to modern French *asseoir*, 'to seat'.

Sexagesima In the Christian calendar, the name is that of the second Sunday before Lent, which is roughly 60 (Latin *sexaginta*) days before Easter. The name is one of a sequence that begins with QUADRAGESIMA.

Sex Pistols, The The notorious British punk band were formed in London in 1975 and were given their name by their manager Malcolm McLaren, the owner of a boutique called *Sex* in the King's Road, Chelsea. The bawdy significance of *Pistol* dates from at least Shakespeare's time, and the character of this name in *Henry IV Part II* and *Henry V* is the subject of several sexual puns and innuendos.

Sexton The name is an occupational one for a *sexton* or churchwarden, the term itself deriving from a Latin word that gave its near doublet, *sacristan*.

Seychelles The islands in the Indian Ocean were discovered by the Portuguese in 1502 and originally called *The Seven Sisters*. In 1742 they were explored by the French naval officer Lazare Picault for the governor of Mauritius, Mahé de La Bourdonnais (see MAHÉ), and named by him *La Bourdonnais*. In 1756 the islands passed to the French India Company and were renamed for the French finance minister, Jean Moreau de *Séchelles*. The spelling of the name was subsequently altered by the English, who captured the islands from the French in 1794.

Seymour The name derives from a place-name, either *Saint-Maur*-des-Fossés near Paris in northern France, or one or other of the villages called *Seamer* in North Yorkshire. The latter name means literally 'sea lake'.

Sfax The port in eastern Tunisia, the second largest town in the country (after Tunis itself), derives its name from Arabic *ṣafāqs* or *ṣafāks*. The sense of this is uncertain.

Shaanxi The province of northwest China has a name meaning 'western *Shaan*', from *shăn*, a proper name with no known meaning, and *xī*, 'west'. The name is sometimes spelled *Shenxi* to avoid confusion with that of SHANXI.

Shaba The province of southeast Zaïre has a name that is the Swahili word for 'copper', referring to the rich deposits of this metal here. The former name of the province was KATANGA.

Shadows, The The British instrumental rock group was formed in London in 1958 and was originally known as the *Drifters*. This name already existed for a black American vocal group, so in 1959 they became the *Shadows*, a name said to have been suggested in a Ruislip pub by bass player Jet Harris (perhaps to reflect his own 'dark' name).

Shadrach The name is that of one of Daniel's three young companions who were saved from Nebuchadnezzar's 'burning fiery furnace'. They originally had different names: Hananiah, Azariah and Mishael (*Daniel* 1.6) (or, in the *Benedicite* of the Book of Common Prayer, Ananias, Azarias, and Misael). According to custom, they were given new names (*Daniel* 1.7) when they became counsellors of King Nebuchadnezzar. Hananiah became *Shadrach*, Mishael became *Meshach*, and Azariah became ABEDNEGO. The meaning of these is uncertain, but they are probably deliberately distorted theophoric Akkadian names, based on that of a god.

Shaftesbury The Dorset town probably has a name that means '*Sceaft*'s fortified place'. However, the first part of the name may equally derive from Old English *sceaft*, 'shaft', 'pole', referring to a prominent post here at one time, perhaps as a boundary marker, or to the steep-sided hill on which the town stands. A source in the Anglo-Saxon personal name is more likely, however.

Shahjahanpur The city in northern India was founded in 1647 in the reign of the Mogul emperor *Shah Jahan* and was named for him, with *pur* the Sanskrit word for 'town', 'fort'. It was Shah Jahan who built the TAJ MAHAL, named for his wife. His own name, in reality an imperial title, means 'king of the world', from Persian *shāh*, 'king' and *jahān*, 'world'. His birth name was *Khurram*, 'joyous'.

Shakatak The British jazz-funk band, formed in London in 1980, adopted the name of a local boutique, presumably itself based on *shack* or *shack up*.

Shakespeare The name was originally a nickname for someone who 'shakes his spear', either as a belligerent person or (in a bawdy sense) as a lustful or lascivious one. *See also* FALSTAFF.

Shalamar The black American soul and dance trio were formed in Los Angeles in 1977 and adopted a name that is ultimately that of the famous *Shalimar* Gardens near Lahore in Pakistan.

Shalott, Lady of *See* ASTOLAT.

Sha Na Na The American rock 'n' roll revival group were formed in 1969 at Columbia University and took as their name a typical meaningless phrase repeated by a backing group. *Cp.* SHOWADDYWADDY.

Shandong The name of the province of northeast China means 'east of the mountain', from *shān*, 'mountain' and *dōng*, 'east'. The province lies to the east of the sacred mountain TAI SHAN. The silk fabric known as *shantung* gets its name from this province.

Shanghai The well-known city and port in eastern China has a name that basically means 'by the sea', from *shàng*, 'on', 'above' and *hai*, 'sea'.

Shangri-La The name is that of an imaginary pass in the Himalayas, an 'earthly paradise' in James Hilton's novel *Lost Horizon* (1933). The final part of the name is Tibetan *la*, 'mountain pass'. The first part is apparently arbitrary, but was perhaps suggested by Chinese *shàng*, 'above' or *shān*, 'mountain' and *rì*, 'sun'. *See also* CAMP DAVID.

Shangri-Las, The The American all-girl vocal pop quartet was formed in Queens, New York, in 1964 by two pairs of sisters who based their name on that of the fictional utopia of SHANGRI-LA, with the last part of the name suggesting singing.

Shanklin The Isle of Wight resort has a name meaning 'cup ridge', from Old English *scenc*, 'cup' and *hlinc*, 'ridge'. The reference is to the waterfall at Shanklin Chine, where the water was seen as falling from a drinking-cup. The 'ridge' was probably a feature of the waterfall itself, as one of the 'shelves' that caused the water to descend in a series of cascades.

Shannon Ireland's longest river probably has a name meaning something like 'old man river', from a root element related to modern Irish *sean*, 'old'. The river was doubtless believed to personify an ancient water god.

Shanxi The province of northern China has a name meaning 'west of the mountain', from *shān*, 'mountain' and *xī*, 'west'. The province lies to the west of the sacred mountain TAI SHAN. *Cp.* SHANDONG and *see also* SHAANXI.

Shap The Cumbrian town, with its famous railway height of *Shap* Summit, has a name that represents Old English *hēap*, 'heap'. The reference is to the remains of an ancient stone circle by the main road (the present A6) to the south of the town.

Shapiro The Jewish surname derives either from Hebrew *šapir*, 'fair', 'lovely' or from the German city of *Speyer* (known formerly in English as *Spires*), which had a large Jewish population in medieval times.

Sharon The name is familiar from the Bible as that of the plain in western Israel (1 *Chronicles* 5.16, *Song of Solomon* 2.1). It may derive from Hebrew *šar*, 'singer'. *Cp.* the Hebrew name of the SONG OF SOLOMON, *šīr haššīrīm*, 'song of songs'. *See also* the first name SHARON.

Sharon The popular modern name derives from the biblical place-name SHARON with specific reference to its occurrence in the passage: 'I am the rose of Sharon, and the lily of the valleys' (*Song of Solomon*, 2.1). The name seems to have been picked up in the late 19th or early 20th century as a type of flower name, and *rose of Sharon* is actually the name of two flowering shrubs: *Hypericum calycinum*, with large yellow flowers, and *Hibiscus syriacus*, with red or purple flowers. John Steinbeck's novel *The Grapes of Wrath* (1939) has Rose of Sharon ('Rosaharn') Joad as one of its main characters.

Sharp The name was originally a nickname for a keen or active person.

Sharp The make of calculators and other electronic instruments derives from the *Ever-Sharp* mechanical pencil invented in 1915 by the Japanese engineer Tokuji Hayakawa, who in 1912 set up business in a metal workshop in Tokyo. The growth and increasing sophistication of his firm and its products is typical of many Japanese enterprises: radios in 1925, televisions in 1951, microwave ovens in 1962, desk-top calculators in 1966, solar-powered calculators in 1976, voice-activated word processors in 1985.

Shatt-al-Arab The river in southeast Iraq, formed by the confluence of the Tigris and the Euphrates, has a name meaning 'river of the Arabs', from Arabic *šaṭṭ*, 'edge', 'bank', *al*, 'the' and *ʿarab*, 'Arabs'.

Shaughnessy The name is an English spelling of the Irish name *Ó Seachnasaigh*, 'descendant of *Seachnasach*', the latter being a personal name perhaps deriving from Irish *seachnach*, 'avoiding', 'elusive'.

Shaun The name is an English spelling of SEAN (properly *Seán*), the Irish form of JOHN.

Shavuot In the Jewish calendar, the name is that of the harvest festival also known as the *Feast of Weeks* or PENTECOST, celebrated 50 days after the second day of the Passover, and commemorating the giving of the Torah to the Jewish people on Mount Sinai. It represents Hebrew *šābhúʿōth*, the plural of *šābhūáʿ*, 'week'.

Shaw A person with this name would originally have lived by a *shaw*, a copse or thicket (Old English *sceaga*), or have come from one of the many places with this word in its name.

Shawnee The North American Indian people and their language, formerly living in Tennessee, take their name from Shawnee *Shaawanwaaki*, 'people of the south', from *shaawanawa*, 'south'.

Sheba The English first name is either a short form of BATHSHEBA, adopted, as in Hebrew, in its own right, or a borrowing of the place-name that lies behind the title of the queen of *Sheba* (1 *Kings* 10.1–13). The latter, also known as *Saba*, was the ancient kingdom of the *Sabeans*, a rich trading nation who inhabited the southwest corner of the Arabian peninsula, corresponding to modern Yemen. As a Hebrew personal name, *Sheba* means 'seven' or 'oath'. *See also* BEERSHEBA.

Sheen *See* RICHMOND.

Sheerness The Kent port and resort has a name meaning 'bright headland', from Old English *scīr*, 'bright', 'clear' and *næss*, 'headland'. The headland here was probably 'bright' through its low-lying, open terrain, overlooking the estuaries of the Thames and the Medway.

Sheffield The well-known South Yorkshire city has a name that means 'open land by the *Sheaf*', the latter being a small river that flows through the middle of the town to enter the larger Don here. The river's own name means 'dividing one', from Old English *scēath*, 'sheath', and it formed the boundary between Derbyshire and the former West Riding of Yorkshire. The second part of the name represents Old English *feld*, which although giving modern English *field* originally denoted an extensive region of open land, more like the South African *veld*. Elsewhere the name *Sheffield* can mean 'sheep field', as for *Sheffield Park*, the country house near Haywards Heath in East Sussex.

Sheffield United The familiar football club arose out of the *Sheffield* Cricket Club, formed in 1854. Its members began to play football a year later as *Sheffield* Football Club but did not form a permanent football team until 1889, when they became *Sheffield United* Football Club. The second word of the name refers to the union of the cricket and football teams, as seen in the name of the limited liability company that the players formed in 1899 when they turned professional: *Sheffield United Cricket and Football Club*.

Sheffield Wednesday The famous football club was formed in 1867 by members of the *Sheffield Wednesday* Cricket Club. The latter had existed since 1816 and was so called because its members played on *Wednesdays*, their weekly half-day holiday. The football club kept the name even when, like other clubs, their main day of play became Saturday.

Sheherazade *See* SCHEHERAZADE.

Sheila The name is an English spelling of the Irish name *Síle*, itself a Gaelic form of CECILY. The name gave the Australian word *sheila* as a general colloquial term for a girl or woman.

Sheldonian Theatre The well-known Oxford building was constructed in 1669 as a public place for the 'enactment of university business' and for ceremonies, such as the annual degree awards, that had previously been made in the University Church of St Mary the Virgin. The name is that of its founder, Gilbert *Sheldon* (1598–1677), Archbishop of Canterbury and Chancellor of the University (from 1667). Although concerts are held in the building, it is not a *theatre* in the popular sense of the word, but in the sense of a public hall with a central area where an audience may attend a lecture or watch a demonstration, as in a hospital's operating *theatre*.

Shell The well-known brand of petrol takes its name from a curio shop called the *Shell* Shop that had been opened in London in the early 19th century by Marcus Samuel, a Jewish dealer who specialized in selling seaside shells as ornaments. By 1830 he had built up an international trade in oriental curios and copra. His identically named son, Marcus Samuel (1853–1927), subsequently added barrelled kerosene to the cargo list, and in 1897 the business was consolidated as the *Shell* Transport and Trading Company.

Shelley The name has its origin in any of the places so called, such as the Yorkshire village near Huddersfield or the Suffolk hamlet near Hadleigh. The place-name itself derives from Old English *scylf*, 'shelf' and *lēah*, 'wood', 'clearing'. The famous poet was born into a Sussex family who took their name from the minor place now known as *Shelley Plain* near Crawley.

Shem The eldest of Noah's three sons in the Bible derives his name from a Hebrew word meaning 'name', 'renown'. He is the eponymous ancestor of the SEMITES.

Shenyang The famous walled city in northeast China has a name representing *shĕn*, the name of a river, and *yáng*, 'sun', 'male'. It was formerly known as MUKDEN (*which see*).

Sheol The biblical name for the abode of the dead, translated in various ways, is ultimately of Assyrian origin, perhaps representing *ŝa'ālu*, 'to consult the oracle' or else *ŝilu*, 'room', 'depth'.

Shepherds Bush The district of west London is more likely to have a name that relates to a family called *Shepherd* than to an actual *shepherd*, although the latter possibility need not be entirely ruled out. The family probably owned an area of bushy land here.

Sheppard The name was originally an occupational one for a shepherd, as it implies.

Sheppey, Isle of The island off the north coast of Kent has a name that means 'sheep island', showing that it was a suitable place for sheep to be kept, with its good grazing and natural boundary or 'fence'. The fact that 'island' (Old English *ēg*) is already in the name really makes the added 'Isle of' superfluous.

Shepton Mallet The Somerset town has a basic name that means 'sheep farm', from Old English *scēap*, 'sheep' and *tūn*, 'farm'. The second word of the name was added to distinguish this Shepton from others in the region, such as Shepton Montague, nine miles (14 km) away. It represents the name of the *Malet* family from Normandy, who held the manor here in the early 12th century.

Sherborne The Dorset town, with its two public schools (one for boys, one for girls), has a name that means 'bright stream', from Old English *scīr*, 'bright', 'clear' (as for *sheer* silk stockings) and *burna*, 'stream'. The reference is to the river Yeo here, which perhaps was at one time itself called the *Sherborne*. A 'bright' stream is one that has either sparkling water or white stones in its bed.

Shere Khan The name of the tiger in Kipling's *Jungle Books* (1894, 1895) represents Hindustani *sher*, 'tiger' and *khān*, 'chief', the latter word indicating this particular tiger's supremacy over the others. The author specified that the name should be pronounced 'Sheer Karn' (but he should have added 'in British English', as the two *r*s of his rendering are not sounded).

Sheriff The name was originally an occupational one for a sheriff, himself a 'shire reeve', or local administrative officer in a county.

Sherman The name was originally occupational, applying either to a sheep-shearer or (in Jewish use) to a tailor, who worked with scissors as a 'shear-man'.

Sherpa The people who live on the slopes of the Himalayas in Nepal, noted as mountaineers, have a name meaning 'eastern people', from Tibetan *śar*, 'east' and the suffix *-pa*, denoting belonging.

's Hertogenbosch The city in the southern Netherlands has a Dutch name meaning 'duke's wood', from Old Dutch *des Hertogen Bosch*, comprising *des*, 'of the', *hertogen*, genitive of *hertog*, 'duke' and *bosch* (modern Dutch *bos*), 'wood'. The duke in question is Henry I, Duke of Brabant, who had a hunting lodge nearby, and who founded the city in 1185. The Dutch artist Hieronymus *Bosch* was born here in the mid-15th century and is named for it. The French name of the city is *Bois-le-Duc*.

Sherwood Forest The famous ancient forest between Nottingham and Worksop, home of Robin Hood and his Merry Men, has a distinctive name meaning 'shire wood'. This denotes its special status, as a wood owned by the *shire* or county, either as a hunting ground or as a common pastureland. If the latter, it would have been for pigs, who would have fed on the mast (acorns) of the oaks that at one time dominated the forest.

Sheshach The name is that of a city mentioned in the Old Testament: 'And the king of Sheshach shall drink after them' (*Jeremiah* 25.26). Yet the name will not be found on any map! It is a cryptogram for the name of BABYLON. It is devised by the Hebrew cryptographic method known as *atbaš*, in which the first letter of the alphabet (*aleph*) is replaced by the last (*taw*), the second (*beth*) by the second to last (*shin*), and so on, until the last letter is replaced by the first. In English this would be the simple substitution code A = Z, B = Y, C = X, etc., so that YORK would be BLIP. Therefore in *babel*, the Hebrew

name of Babylon, the two *b*s are replaced by two *š*s (*sh* in the English spelling), the *l* becomes *h* (*ch*), while the vowels, *a* and *e*, change places, as *e* and *a*.

Shetland The northernmost group of Scottish islands has a rather difficult name. It probably derives from Old Norse *hjalt*, 'hilt' and *land*, 'land'. The 'hiltland' would thus have referred to the sword-shaped outline of the islands, or of Mainland, its largest island. The comparison would almost certainly have been made from sea level, although the outline of the island group on a map has a similar configuration. *Cp.* ST KILDA.

Shiah The branch of Islam, which regards Muhammad's cousin Ali and his successors as the true imams, derives its name from Arabic *šī'ah*, 'sect', from *šā'a*, 'to follow'. Adherents of this sect, now found mainly in Iran, are known as *Shi'ites* or *Shiites*.

Shikoku The smallest of the four main islands that comprise Japan has a name meaning 'four provinces', from Japanese *shi*, 'four' and *koku*, 'province'. The island consists of four prefectures: Ehime, Kagawa, Kōchi and Tokushima.

Shiloh The town in ancient Palestine, on the eastern slope of Mount Ephraim, is famous for being the place where the Tabernacle and the Ark of the Covenant were kept (*Joshua* 18.1). Its name, in Hebrew *šilo*, is perhaps an alteration of *šalo*, 'to be peaceful'.

Shinto The native religion of Japan has a name that means 'way of the gods', representing *shin*, from Chinese *shén*, 'gods', and *tō* for *do*, 'way', from Chinese (Mandarin) *dào* (*cp.* TAOISM). The religion incorporates the worship of several divinities, with the Japanese emperor said to be descended from the chief of these.

Shippams The familiar make of meat and fish paste takes its name from Charles *Shippam*, who in 1786 opened a grocer's shop in Chichester, Sussex. It was his son, also named Charles Shippam (1828–1897), who specialized as a pork butcher and sausage maker and who in 1892 first produced potted meat, so called as the paste was sold in earthenware pots. It was only after Shippam's death that the familiar glass jars were introduced, with the change of container completed by 1906.

Shiraz The city in southwest Iran, a Muslim cultural centre, takes its name from Elamite *šer*, 'good' and *raz*, 'grape'. There are said to be 170 different kinds of grape locally.

Shirelles, The The American all-girl vocal quartet was formed in Passaic, New Jersey, in 1957 and took a name based on that of their lead singer, *Shirley* Owens.

Shirley The first name derives from the surname, itself from a place-name meaning 'bright clearing', from Old English *scīr*, 'bright' and *lēah*, 'wood', 'clearing'. It was promoted as a girl's name by Charlotte Brontë's novel *Shirley* (1849), in which the parents of *Shirley* Keeldar had chosen the name in expectation of the birth of a son. When the child turned out to be a girl, however, they gave her the name all the same. A century later the name was widely popularized by the child film star *Shirley* Temple, who began her screen career at the age of four in 1932.

Shittim The place to the east of Jordan where the Israelites set up camp before crossing the Jordan (*Numbers* 25.1–9) has a Hebrew name meaning 'acacias', from the plural of *šittāh*, 'shittah'. *Shittim* wood was used for making the Ark of the Covenant and part of the Tabernacle.

Shiva *See* SIVA.

Sholapur The city in southwest India has a name deriving from Hindi *šolā*, 'flame' and *pur*, 'town'.

Shore The name originally applied to someone who lived either by the sea-shore or by a steep bank or slope (Old English *scora*, recorded only in place-names).

Short As it implies, the name was originally a nickname for a small person.

Showaddywaddy The British rock 'n' roll revival group, formed in 1973 as a merger of two Leicester groups, took their name from the chanted backing line ('Bop bop showaddywaddy') of the song 'Little Darlin'' recorded in 1957 by the Diamonds.

Showerings The well-known make of cider takes its name from a long-established Somerset family of shoemakers and inn-keepers. The present company was founded in 1932 by the four *Showering* brothers Herbert, Arthur, Ralph and Francis.

Shredded Wheat The name for the distinctive breakfast cereal 'cakes' was originally devised for the wheat cereal food produced in 1893 by Henry D. Perky in Denver, Colorado. His idea for the form of the cereal is said to have come from seeing fellow dyspepsia sufferers eating whole boiled wheat with milk for breakfast in a Nebraska hotel. Perky decided that the cereal would be more readily digestible if served 'shredded'. The name is common property in Britain, and does not belong to any one company.

Shrewsbury The well-known county town of SHROPSHIRE has a name that means 'fortified place by scrubland', from Old English conjectural *scrubb*, 'scrubland' and *burh*, 'fortified place'. This origin can better be seen from old records of the name, such as the 11th-century *Scrobbesbyrig*. The present spelling of the name may have developed by association with *shrew*, which was formerly pronounced to rhyme with *show*. Today, the name is still usually pronounced as if 'Shrowsbury', although some local people say 'Shroosbury'.

Shropshire The county of western England, bordering Wales, takes its name from its county town, SHREWSBURY. It is thus essentially 'Shrewsburyshire'. However, the -*bury* of the name has disappeared, and had already done so by the time of the late 11th-century Domesday Book record of the county name, as *Sciropescire*. The conventional abbreviation of the county name is *Salop*, and this was officially adopted for the county from 1974 to 1980. It represents a contraction of the Norman form of the county name. The Normans, as French speakers, found it difficult to pronounce the initial *Scr-* of *Scrobbesbyrig* (as they then knew SHREWSBURY). They therefore simplified *Sc-* to *S-* and separated *Sr-* by inserting the vowel *a*. They then substituted *l* for *r* (as they did for SALISBURY) to turn *Sarop-* into *Salop-*. The official change of name to this form was resented by many local people, and was particularly unpopular with the European Member of Parliament for Salop and Staffordshire, who discovered when attending debates in continental Europe that *Salop* was uncomfortably close to *salope*, the French abusive term meaning 'slut'. Even so, the name *Salopian* is still used for Shropshire people and for members (or past members) of *Shrewsbury* School, the boys' public school founded in 1552.

Shrove Tuesday In the Christian calendar, the day before ASH WEDNESDAY is so named because formerly people *shrove* then, or confessed their sins to a priest and obtained sacramental forgiveness in preparation for Lent. The word represents an archaic verb *shrive*, related to *scribe*, as the priest wrote a 'prescription' for penance.

Shulamite The name is applied to the beautiful bride in the *Song of Solomon*: 'Return, return, O Shulamite; return, return, that we may look upon thee. What will ye see in the Shulamite? As it were the company of two armies' (6.13). The name appears to mean something like 'she who belongs to SOLOMON'.

Shylock More has been written on the name of the Jewish usurer in Shakespeare's *The Merchant of Venice* than on any other of his characters. The playwright is generally believed to have based it on the biblical place-name SHILOH. Supporters of this theory point to the following verse: 'The sceptre shall not part from Judah, nor a lawgiver from between his feet, until Shiloh come; and unto him shall the gathering of the people be' (*Genesis* 49.10). The name here seems to denote that of the Messiah, otherwise Christ, and in Shakespeare's play Shylock is pardoned his sentence of death if he sheds one drop of Christian blood or takes more or less than his 'pound of flesh' (from the body of Antonio) on condition that he instead become a Christian, to which he agrees. Another school of thought, however, sees the origin in the name of the Old Testament character *Salah* (*Genesis* 11.12–15), one of whose progeny was *Iscah* (*Genesis* 11.29), a name that itself may have suggested that of Shylock's daughter, JESSICA. Yet another theory proposes a derivation from the standard surname *Shacklock*, itself originally an occupational name for a jailer.

Siam The former name (until 1939 and from 1945 to 1949) of THAILAND derives from Thai *sayam*. This represents Sanskrit *śyāma*, 'brown', alluding to the skin colour of the Siamese. A fuller form of the name is *sayam muang yim*, 'Siam, land of smiles', the latter words representing *muang*, 'land', 'town' and *yim*, 'smile'. The Austrian composer Franz Lehár used this name for his operetta *The Land of Smiles* (in the original German *Das Land des Lächelns*) (1923), but he was applying it to China, not Siam.

Sian *See* XI AN.

Siberia The vast eastern region of Russia has a name of disputed origin. Proposed derivations include: 1. from *Sibir*, the name of a Tatar people; 2. from Mongolian *šiver*, 'marsh'; 3. from *Siber*, the name of a legendary hound said to have emerged from the depths of Lake Baikal (a sort of 'Beast of Baikal'); 4. a form of Russian *sever*, 'north'. The name is certainly very ancient, and the explanations quoted here are in descending order of probability.

Sibiu The town in west central Romania had the Roman name of *Cibinium*, based on that of the river *Cibin* here. The river's own name is of uncertain origin, but has been associated with a root word *siba* meaning 'cornel' (a type of dogwood). The Hungarian name of the town is *Nagyszeben*, 'big Cibin'. The German name, however, is *Hermannstadt*, given by the German colonists from Saxony who refounded it in the 12th century.

Sibley The name derives from the identical medieval female name, itself a form of SIBYL.

Sibyl The name was adopted from that of various oracles or prophetesses in classical times, of which the best known was the *Sibyl* of Cumae, who guided Aeneas through the underworld. The origin of the Greek name *Sibulla* that gave the general name is unknown. The spelling *Sybil* for the first name became more popular from the second half of the 19th century, thanks to Benjamin Disraeli's novel *Sybil* (1845). *See also* the surname SIBLEY.

Sichuan The province of southwest China has a name meaning 'four rivers', from *si*, 'four' and *chuān*, 'river'. This refers to the four main tributaries of the Yangtze, which flows through the province. The name is also spelled *Szechwan*.

Sicilian Vespers The name is that of the revolt in 1282 against French rule in Sicily, in which the ringing of the vesper bells on Easter Monday was the signal to massacre and drive out the French.

Sicily The well-known island of Italy takes its name from its native inhabitants many centuries BC, the *Siceli* or *Sicani*, with the former people, according to ancient writers, driving the latter (who arrived later) to the west. The origin of their name is uncertain.

Sidcup The district of Bexley in southeast Greater London has a name that probably means 'flat-topped hill', or more literally 'seat-topped hill', from Old English *set*, 'seat' and *copp*, 'hill' (related to the famous KOP of football). The implication is that Sidcup is a place 'seated' on a hilltop. This seems difficult to envisage today, but the ground does fall away either side of Sidcup High Street, and street names such as Knoll Road testify to the elevated location of the place.

Siddhārtha Gautama *See* BUDDHA.

Sidgwick and Jackson The London publishers are named for Frank *Sidgwick* (d. 1939) and Robert Cameron *Jackson* (1882–1917), both with early publishing experience, who formed a partnership in 1908. Jackson was killed in the First World War, leaving Sidgwick devastated.

Sidi-Bel-Abbès The city in northwest Algeria has a name meaning the equivalent of 'Sir Bel Abbes', from Arabic *saydī* or *sīdī*, a title approximating to 'sir', 'my lord', and a personal name, that of the marabout (saint) *bāl-'abbās*, whose tomb is here.

Sidney The first name was adopted from the surname, itself said to derive either from a Norman settler from *Saint-Denis* in northern France or, more likely, from *Sidney* Wood near Cranleigh, Surrey, where the famous *Sidney* family were landowners before they became associated with Penshurst Place in Kent. The place-name means 'wide land by a marsh', from Old English *sīd*, 'wide' and *ēg*, 'island'.

Sidney Sussex College The Cambridge college was founded in 1596 under the will of Lady Frances *Sidney*, countess dowager of *Sussex*, who in 1589 bequeathed two-fifths of her estate to found a new college.

Sidon The chief city of ancient Phoenicia has a name that ultimately derives from that of a god, *tsīd*, with the final *-on* meaning 'belonging to', 'of'. It is now the Lebanese city of *Saïda*.

Sidony The name derives from the Latin name *Sidonia*, 'woman from SIDON', although it early became associated with Greek *sindōn*, the term for a fine kind of muslin.

Siebengebirge The hills southeast of Bonn in western Germany have a name that means 'seven hills'. There are actually about 40 wooded hills in the group, a popular tourist region.

Siege Perilous In the Arthurian romances, the name is that of the seat at the Round Table that was to be taken only by the knight destined to find the Holy Grail, and that was fatal for anyone else. The phrase is a direct rendering of French *siège périlleux*, 'perilous seat'.

Siegfried In German mythology, the name is that of the son of Sigmund who in the *Nibelungenlied* gained possession of the treasure of the Nibelungs by slaying the dragon that guarded it. His name comprises Old German *sigu*, 'victory' and *fridu*, 'peace', as if 'peace through victory'.

Siegfried Idyll The orchestral work by Wagner was composed in 1870 as a present for the 33rd birthday of his wife, Cosima. It contained motifs from his forthcoming opera *Siegfried* (1876) on which he was working when their son *Siegfried* was born in 1869.

Siegfried Line The line of fortifications built by the Germans before and during the Second World War opposite the MAGINOT LINE in France was named for SIEGFRIED, the hero of the *Nibelungenlied*. The Germans also used the name for the fortified line in France that they occupied in the First World War, although this was known to the English as the *Hindenburg Line*, after the famous German field marshal.

Siemens The make of electric lamp derives its name from that of four German brothers, famous for their contributions to the electrical and steel industries. They were Ernst Werner *Siemens* (1816–1892), Karl Wilhelm *Siemens*, later anglicized (as a British subject) as Sir Charles William Siemens (1823–1883), Friedrich *Siemens* (1826–1904), and Karl *Siemens* (1829–1906). It was the eldest brother who in 1847 founded the original firm in Berlin. The electric lighting side of the business, for which the company is best known today, was not begun until the 1870s.

Siena The walled city in central Italy is popularly said to have been named for *Senus*, son of Remus, its supposed founder. The name is more likely, however, to have originated from the *Senones*, the Gaulish people who settled here in ancient times. *Cp.* SENS.

Sierra Leone The country of West Africa has a name that as it stands means 'Lion Mountains', from Spanish *sierra*, 'mountain chain' and *león* (or Italian *leone*), 'lion'. The name was recorded in 1462 as *Serra da Leão* in this sense by the Portuguese navigator Pedro de Sintra. An earlier record of 1457, however, was made by the Venetian navigator Alvise Ca' da Mosto: '…and named this mountain Serre-Lionne, because of the great noise here from the fearful sound and claps of thunder that are always over it, constantly surrounded by storm clouds'. The name thus refers to the storms over the mountains, not to the roaring of lions (which in any case are not found in this part of Africa).

Sierra Madre The main mountain system of Mexico has a Spanish name meaning 'mother range', from *sierra*, 'mountain chain' and *madre*, 'mother'.

Sierra Nevada The mountain range in southeast Spain has a name that means simply 'snowy mountains', from *sierra*, 'mountain chain' (implying one with jagged peaks, as Spanish *sierra* literally means 'saw') and *nevada*, feminine of *nevado*, 'snowy', from *nieve*, 'snow'. The name has equal descriptive validity for the mountain chain in California. *Cp.* the name of NEVADA.

Sigurd The name is that of the hero in Norse mythology who killed the dragon Fafnir to gain the treasure of Andvari. It derives from Old Norse *sigr*, 'victory' and *vörthr*, 'guardian'. This corresponds to the German name *Siegward*, though his actual German counterpart was SIEGFRIED.

Sikh The name of the reformed Hindu sect, or a member of it, represents the Hindi word for 'disciple', from Sanskrit *śiksati*, 'he studies'.

Sikkim The state of northeast India has a name that may represent Sanskrit *śikhin*, 'summit'.

Silas The name ultimately derives from Latin *silva*, 'wood'. *Cp.* SILVANUS. In the Bible, *Silas* is a companion of Paul (*Acts* 15.40).

Silchester The village near Basingstoke, Hampshire is famous as the site of the Roman town of *Calleva Atrebatum*. The initial *Sil-* was long thought to represent Old English *siele*, 'willow-tree'. But it almost certainly derives from the initial *Cal-* of the Roman name. This is Celtic in origin, and means 'wood' (as modern Irish *coill* or Welsh *celli*). The *-chester*, as commonly elsewhere, denotes a Roman settlement. The *Atrebates* were the Celtic people whose capital was here. Their own name means simply 'dwellers', 'settlers', from a Celtic root element to which modern Welsh *tref*, 'village' is related.

Silesia The region of central Europe derives its name either from that of the river Ślęza, a tributary of the Oder (with its own name perhaps meaning 'damp'), or from that of the *Ślęz*, a mountain that is itself named from the *Silingi* or *Silingae*, a Vandalic people whose religious centre it was.

Silvanus In Roman mythology, the name is that of the god of woods, fields and flocks who corresponded to the Greek god PAN. It derives from Latin *silva*, 'wood'. *Cp.* SILVESTER.

Silverstone The famous motor-racing circuit near Towcester, Northamptonshire, takes its name from the nearby village of *Silverstone*. This has nothing to do with silver or stone, but derives from the Anglo-Saxon personal name *Sæwulf* or *Sigewulf* to which

Old English *tūn*, 'village' has been added. The modern name is thus a good example of a popular 'interpretation' of a name that had actually become meaningless.

Silvester The name is of Latin origin, meaning 'of the woods', from *silva*, 'wood'. *Cp.* SILVANUS.

Silvia The name has long been associated with Latin *silva*, 'wood', but originally perhaps had some other meaning. It was borne in Roman mythology by Rhea *Silvia*, the mother of Romulus and Remus. The usual spelling of the name in recent times has been *Sylvia*. It has doubtless been subconsciously associated by many with *silver*, so has the same associations of brightness, quality and value that the word has.

Simca The French make of car has a name that is an acronym for its manufacturers, the *Société industrielle et mécanique des constructions automobiles* ('Industrial and Mechanical Automobile Construction Company'). This was founded in 1934 by an Italian, Henri-Théodore Pigozzi, to expand his activities as a distributor of *Fiat* cars in France. The first Simcas were thus Fiats, and a distinctive Simca model was produced only in 1951.

Simeon The biblical name is borne by characters in the Old and New Testaments and is the source of the much more popular first name SIMON. It derives from Hebrew *šim'ōn*, '(God) has heard', as implied in the account of the birth of the second son of Jacob and Leah: 'And she conceived again, and bare a son; and said, because the Lord hath heard that I was hated, he hath given me this son also: and she called his name Simeon' (*Genesis* 29.33). (Jacob loved Laban's younger daughter Rachel more than Leah, his elder daughter.)

Simferopol The Ukrainian city on the Crimean peninsula was founded in the 17th century under Tatar domination and was originally known by the Turkish name of *Ak-Mechet*, 'white mosque'. The present name dates from 1783, when the Crimea became part of Russia. It is Greek in origin, as for several other places in this part of Russia that were named at this time, and means 'expedient city', from *sumpherōn*, 'useful', 'profitable' (literally 'carrying with') and *polis*, 'city'.

Simon The name is familiar from the New Testament as the original name of the apostle Peter, as that of the apostle *Simon Zelotes* ('Simon the Zealot'), as that of *Simon Magus* ('Simon the Magician'), who tried to buy miraculous powers from the disciples, and as that of *Simon* the Tanner, with whom Peter stayed in Joppa. It is the more common English form of SIMEON.

Simpkins The name means 'son of *Simkin*', the latter being a diminutive of *Sim*, in turn a short form of SIMON. *Cp.* the name SIMPSON.

Simple Minds The Scottish new wave group originated as a punk band in Glasgow in 1977 and adopted a mock self-deprecatory name based on the phrase *simple-minded*, in the sense 'stupid'.

Simple Symphony Benjamin Britten's work for string orchestra, Op 4 (1934) is so named as it was based on *simple* tunes he wrote at the age of 12. He actually composed it at 21.

Simplon The well-known Alpine pass between Switzerland and Italy has a name of uncertain origin. The Romans recorded the name in various ways, among them *Semplun*, *Sempilion*, *Sempronius* and *Scipionis*, these last two apparently assimilated to the names of Roman leaders. The ultimate origin may be in a Celtic source, although some relate the name to that of the nearby Swiss village of *Simpelen*, said to mean 'soft heights'.

Simply Red The British pop group, formed in Manchester in 1985, presumably took their name from the striking red hair of their lead singer, Mick Hucknall, perhaps with a pun on 'simply read', meaning 'easily understood'.

Simpson The name means 'son of *Sim*', the latter being a short form of SIMON. *Cp.* the name SIMPKINS.

Simpson Desert The arid region of central Australia was named as recently as 1929 by Dr Cecil Thomas Madigan, who crossed it by air that year. He gave the name in honour of Alfred Allen *Simpson* (1875–1939), president of the Royal Geographical Society of Australasia, which had financed Madigan's researches. The desert had been entered in 1845 by the English explorer Charles Sturt, namer of both the DARLING and the MURRAY rivers, but it remained nameless until the year stated.

Sinai, Mount The mountain on the peninsula of the same name, famous as the place where Moses received the Law from God (*Exodus* 19.20), is believed to derive its name from that of *Sin*, a moon god worshipped by the Sumerians, Akkadians and ancient Arabs. The mountain has several peaks, and that mentioned in the Bible is probably the one now called *Jebel Musa*, 'mountain of Moses'.

Sinbad *See* SINDBAD.

Sinclair The name is Norman in origin, deriving from a place in northern France called *Saint-Clair*, such as *St-Clair*-sur-Elle near Saint-Lô. The French places are named from the dedication of their churches to *St Clare*.

Sind The province of southeast Pakistan, formerly part of British India, takes its name from Sanskrit *sindhu*, 'river', referring to the INDUS (a name of the same origin), in whose valley it lies. *See also* INDIA itself.

Sindbad The name of *Sindbad the Sailor*, familiar from the *Arabian Nights*, means 'native of India'. *Cp.* SIND and the names of Indian towns ending in -*bad* such as ALLAHABAD, HYDERABAD. The name is frequently spelled *Sinbad*, as if associated with *sin*, perhaps through the concept of sin 'burdening' a person as the Old Man of the Sea did when he clung to Sindbad's back.

Sinead The name, pronounced 'Shinade', is an Irish form of JANET.

Sinfonia Antartica The title of Vaughan Williams' seventh symphony (1949–52) refers to the fact that it was based on music he wrote for the film *Scott of the Antarctic* (1948). The name is Italian for 'Antarctic Symphony', Italian being the supreme language of music.

Singapore The republic of southeast Asia has a name deriving from Sanskrit *siṁhapura*, 'lion town', from *siṁha*, 'lion' (*cp.* CEYLON) and *pur*, 'house', 'town'. The name is hard to explain, since lions are not found here. A Malayan legend tells how an Indian prince came here in the 7th century

and took the first animal he saw for a lion. The republic's national animal is, however, represented by two lions supporting the coat of arms of its identically named capital.

Singer The makes of sewing machine and motor car should be kept distinct, as they bear the names of different entrepreneurs. The sewing machine was patented in 1851 as an improved model of an existing type by the American businessman Isaac M. *Singer* (1811–1875). The car evolved from the *Singer* Cycle Company founded in Coventry in 1876 by the English engineer George *Singer*. They have not been manufactured since 1970, so are increasingly rarely seen on the road.

Sing Sing The state prison of New York takes its name from the earlier name of the village of *Ossining* in which it is located. The place-name itself derives from Algonquian *assin-is-ing*, 'stones-little-at', altered by folk etymology.

Sining *See* XINING.

Sinn Féin The Irish republican political movement was founded in 1905 by the Irish journalist and politician Arthur Griffith (1872–1922) with the aim of effecting the independence of Ireland from Britain and the revival of Irish culture. Its present goal is to win the political unification of Northern Ireland and the Republic. The name is Irish for 'we ourselves'. The Irish expression '*sinn féin! sinn féin!*' is traditionally used by a Irish speaker pacifying an argument, implying 'we're all one here'.

Sinŭiju The name of the port in North Korea represents Korean *sin*, 'new', *ŭi*, 'justice' and *chu*, 'province'.

Siobhan The name, pronounced 'Shivawn', is an Irish form of JANE.

Sion, Mount *See* ZION.

Sioux The North American Indian peoples and their languages have a name that is usually regarded as an abbreviated form of *Nadowessioux*, itself a French spelling of *Nadoweisiw*, 'little snake'. This name was given the Sioux by their neighbours, the Chippewa (Ojibwa). It has also been interpreted as 'lesser enemies', however, distinguishing them from the IROQUOIS, who are the 'greater enemies'. The name is found for the two cities of *Sioux City*, Iowa and *Sioux Falls*, South Dakota, both on the *Big Sioux* River about 75 miles (120 km) apart.

Sirius The name of the brightest star in the sky, otherwise known as the DOG STAR, in the constellation Canis Major, was *Seirios* in the original Greek. This represents *seirios astēr*, 'the scorching star', referring not simply to its brilliance but to the fact that it was near the sun in midsummer, the hottest time of the year, so that it seemed to add to the heat given by the sun. Hence Roman *dies caniculares*, 'dog days', to refer to the summer period, and English *dog days* similarly, to describe a period of inactivity, as in midsummer heat.

Sir William Perkins's School The girls' public school at Chertsey, Surrey, was founded in 1725 under the will of *Sir William Perkins*, a local wine merchant and chandler. His original house still exists in Windsor Street, Chertsey. The school moved to its present site, just south of the town, in 1819.

Sissinghurst The Tudor country house near Cranbrook, Kent, with its famous garden, takes its name from the village of *Sissinghurst* here. This itself means 'wooded hill of the Saxon people', so named to be distinguished from nearby *Angley*, owned by *Angles*. One would have expected the present name to be something like 'Saxinghurst', but doubtless the *x* became *ss* under Norman influence. This part of Kent has many *hurst* names. Others include *Goudhurst, Hawkhurst, Lamberhurst, Sandhurst* and *Staplehurst*, all testifying to hilly woodland.

Sistine Chapel The chapel of the pope in the Vatican at Rome, with its famous frescos by Michelangelo and others, is so named because it was built in 1473 for pope *Sixtus* IV, whose Italian name is *Sisto*.

Sisyphus The name is that of the king of Corinth in Greek mythology who was punished for his misdeeds by having to roll a heavy stone up a hill. Every time he neared the top, the stone escaped his grasp and rolled back down to the bottom, so that he had to start again. His name is usually said to be a reduplication of *sophos*,

'wise', in a form such as *si-sophos*. This serves as an intensive, so that he was 'very wise'.

Sita The name of the goddess of the plough in Vedic mythology represents the Sanskrit word for 'furrow'. According to the *Ramayana* she was born from a furrow in a ploughed field. Hence her name. She features in this epic poem as the wife of Rama, its main character.

Sittingbourne The Kent town near Gillingham has a name that means 'stream of the dwellers on the slope', with the first part of the name deriving ultimately from Old English *side*, 'slope' (literally 'side'). Sittingbourne is on the lower slope of a ridge by Milton Creek, the latter being the *bourne* of the name.

Siva The third chief Hindu god, together with Brahma and Vishnu, derives his name from Sanskrit *siva*, 'blessed', 'auspicious'. His name, pronounced 'Sheeva', is also spelled *Shiva*.

Siwalik Hills The range of foothills in northern India and Nepal, running parallel with the Himalayas, derives its name from Sanskrit *siva*, 'SIVA' and *alika*, 'brow'.

Siwash The derogatory name for a North American Indian is a Chinook jargon word derived from French *sauvage*, 'savage', 'wild'.

Sjælland The largest island of Denmark has a name meaning 'sea land', from Old Norse *sjá*, 'sea' and *land*, 'land'. *Cp.* NEW ZEALAND, ZEELAND.

Skagerrak The arm of the North Sea between Denmark and Norway takes its name from *Skagen*, a Danish port that stands on it, and Norwegian *rak*, 'race' (current of water).

Skara Brae The famous neolithic coastal settlement on Mainland, Orkney, derives its name from Old Norse *skari*, 'shore' and Scottish *brae*, 'bank' (as in Burns's 'Ye banks and braes o' bonny Doon'). A visit to the site will confirm the accuracy of the description.

Skegness The popular coastal resort in Lincolnshire has a name that means '*Skeggi*'s promontory', with the Scandinavian personal name (meaning 'bearded one') followed by Old Norse *nes*, 'headland'. There is no obvious promontory at Skegness, however, so the reference must be to the hook-like headland known as Gibraltar Point, some four miles (6 km) to the south of the town.

Skelmersdale The Lancashire town, designated a New Town in 1961, developed round a mining village. Its name means '*Skelmer*'s valley', with the Scandinavian personal name perhaps meaning 'horse shield'. The name thus differs from most *-dale* names, such as *Teesdale* and *Wensleydale*, which are named for rivers.

Sketchleys The well-known chain of dry cleaners owes its name to Alfred Hawley, who opened a dyeing works in Hinckley, Leicestershire, in 1885. For the actual dyeing he used water from the *Sketchley* brook, and adopted this name for the *Sketchley Fast Black* dyeing process that he introduced for cotton hose. In due course the name came to be given to his factory, and in 1889 Hawley first offered *Sketchley Dry Cleaning* as an adjunct to the dyeing process. The company itself remained *A. E. Hawley & Co.* until 1951, however, when eventually it too acquired the *Sketchley* name.

Skiddaw The well-known mountain in the Lake District has a name that could mean either 'ski height' or 'crag height', from Old Norse *skīth*, 'ski', 'snow-shoe' or *skýti*, 'crag' and *haugr*, 'height', 'hill'. 'Ski height' would have referred to the outline of the mountain, like a snow-shoe, not to the act of skiing down it.

Skinner The name was originally an occupational one for a person who stripped the skin from animals to be used for making garments or leather.

Skipton The North Yorkshire town has a name meaning 'sheep village', from Old English *scēap*, 'sheep' and *tūn*, 'village', but with Scandinavian spelling. The name thus exactly parallels that of SHEPTON MALLET and various other places named *Shipton* in the south of England. Skipton has long been famous for its sheep markets, and *Sheep Street* is one of its central streets.

Skoda The name of the Czech motor vehicles (more accurately *Škoda*, pronounced 'Shkoda'), is that of the engineer Emil von Škoda (1839–1900), who took over a firm making agricultural machinery in Pilsen (Plzeň) and in 1869 founded the *Škoda* Works. This subsequently developed into a famous weapons factory.

Skol The familiar brand of lager has a name that is a Danish toast, properly *skaal*, literally 'bowl', 'cup', a word related to English *scale* (as for a pair of *scales*).

Skopje The city in Macedonia has an ancient name of Illyrian or Macedonian origin and uncertain meaning. The earliest record of it, in Roman times, is as *Skupi*. The city was the native town of the Byzantine emperor Justinian I, who rebuilt it in 535 AD after an earthquake and renamed it for himself as *Prima Justiniana*, 'first (town) of Justinian'. A further earthquake devastated it in 1963.

Skye The well-known Scottish island, in the Hebrides, has a name that represents Gaelic *sgiath*, 'wing'. The reference is to the 'divided' appearance of the island from the mainland, with its two mountain masses in the north and south of the island rising as 'wings' either side of the central lower terrain.

Slade The British pop group was formed in Wolverhampton in 1964 and played under various names until adopting the random name *Ambrose Slade* in 1969, shortening this to *Slade* that same year.

Slănchev Breg Bulgaria's leading coastal resort, on the Black Sea near Burgas, has a name that translates as 'sunny coast', from *slănchev*, 'sunny', the adjective of *slăntse*, 'sun', and *breg*, 'coast', 'shore'. The resort has an average 2300 hours of sunshine a year, and up to 11 hours daily in July and August, so that the name is hardly a misnomer! The name is pronounced approximately 'Slinchev Bryag'. *Cp.* Spain's COSTA DEL SOL, an exact equivalent.

Slav The peoples of central and eastern Europe, typically Russians, Poles, Czechs and Bulgarians, derive their name either from Slavic *slava*, 'glory', 'fame' or else (and more likely) Slavic *slovo*, 'word', 'speech', implying a people who spoke a mutually understandable language, as against the Germanic races who were 'dumb' (*see* GERMANY) and so incomprehensible. The English word *slave* derives from the *Slavs*, since they were frequently held in bondage in medieval times. *See also* CZECHOSLOVAKIA, YUGOSLAVIA.

Slave Coast The coast of West Africa around the Bight of Benin is so named because it was from here that the majority of African *slaves* were deported to other countries from the 16th to the 19th century.

Slave River *See* GREAT SLAVE LAKE.

Slavonia The region of Croatia takes its name from its predominantly SLAV population. *Cp.* SLOVAKIA, SLOVENIA.

Slazenger The well-known make of sports equipment takes its name from the founder of the firm that came to manufacture it, Ralph *Slazenger* Moss (1845–1910), a Jewish tailor's son from Warrington, Lancashire. He followed in his father's footsteps but in the 1880s, when he dropped the *Moss* from his name, began specializing in sports clothes. By 1890 he and his brother partner, Albert, were already making tennis rackets, cricket bats and football boots.

Sleipnir The name of the eight-footed steed of Odin in Norse mythology represents Old Norse *Sleipnir*, 'slipping'.

Slieve Donard The highest peak of the Mourne Mountains, Northern Ireland, has a name meaning '*Donart*'s mountain', from Irish *sliabh*, 'mountain', 'upland' and the personal name, said to be that of a disciple of St Patrick who built his church on the mountain's summit.

Sligo The county in northwest Ireland takes its name from the town of *Sligo*, whose own name means 'shelly place', from Irish *slige*, 'shell'. The reference is to the stony bed of the river Garavogue that flows through the town.

Sloane Square London's fashionable square takes its name from Sir Hans *Sloane* (1660–1753), lord of the manor of Chelsea. It is this square that gave the name of *Sloane Rangers*, the vogue nickname in the 1970s and 1980s for a 'trendy' upper class young woman (later also man) from London. The name was promoted by the social commentator Peter York as a blend of *Sloane Square* and *Lone Ranger*, the latter being the popular hero of western stories and movies.

Sloper The name was originally an occupational one for a person who made *slops*, that is, loose articles of clothing such as smocks.

Slough The familiar industrial town in Berkshire has a name that means what it says, referring to the *slough* or marshy terrain formerly here. Despite the unpromising site (and name), the town has flourished and owes its development to commercial and logistical considerations: it is on a level location, it is near London, and it is on major road and rail (and formerly canal) routes.

Slovakia The state of eastern Europe was originally part of Hungary, taking its name from its predominantly SLAV population. In 1918 it united with Bohemia and Moravia to form CZECHOSLOVAKIA, but regained its independence in 1992.

Slovenia The east European republic is named for its indigenous population, the *Slovenes*, who arrived here in the 6th century and who spoke (and still speak) *Slovene*, a SLAV language closely related to Serbo-Croat.

Small As a nickname, the name originally applied to a little or slightly-built person.

Small Faces The British pop group was formed in London in 1965 and adopted a name referring to the generally small stature (under 5 ft 6 in) of its members, with *face* a jargon term for a stylish Mod of that era. *See also* The FACES.

Smart The name originated as a nickname for a quick or active person.

Smedley The name is found fairly widely in Nottinghamshire and probably originated from a place in that county, now of unknown location. The place-name itself may mean 'smooth clearing'.

Smedleys The brand of canned vegetables and fruit is named for Samuel *Smedley*, a Worcestershire fruit grower who before the First World War set up a stall in London's Covent Garden market and a depot in Wisbech, Cambridgeshire. By 1924 the company of S.W. *Smedley* & Co had started fruit-bottling in Wisbech, and canning began the following year.

Smethurst The name derives from a minor place near Manchester, itself meaning 'smooth hurst', that is, a level wooded hill.

Smethwick The name of the town near Birmingham means 'smith's place of work', from Old English *smith*, 'smith', 'metal-worker' and *wīc*, 'place' (implying one where a special activity was carried on).

Smirnoff The well-known vodka takes its name from Pierre *Smirnoff*, a Russian who set up a distillery in Moscow in the early years of the 19th century. The thriving business was nationalized as a result of the Russian Revolution in 1917, however, and the Smirnoffs fled to France.

Smith The most common of English names was originally an occupational name for a *smith*, that is, a worker in metal. Such a craftsman would have made many important implements, from horseshoes and ploughshares to swords and armour. It has been calculated that there are about 187,000 British telephone subscribers named *Smith*. The greatest concentration is (somewhat unexpectedly) in the Aberdeen area, but there is also a good representation in the Midlands and East Anglia.

Smith and Nephew The names behind the familiar home healthcare products, notably ELASTOPLAST, are those of a Hull chemist, Thomas James *Smith* (1825–1896), and his *nephew* Horatio Nelson Smith (1874–1960), whom he took as partner in 1896.

Smiths The popular brand of potato crisp originated with Frank *Smith*, a young grocer's assistant, who in 1920 set up his own business in London selling thinly sliced potatoes cooked in oil. His product was a great success, with the twopenny bags of *Smith's Potato Crisps* containing a blue twist of salt as a practical and imaginative touch. The whole process of preparing and packeting the crisps was carried out manually until 1939, when an automatic potato slicer was introduced.

Smiths, The The British pop quartet, formed in Manchester in 1982, adopted a name that suggested the anonymity its members sought.

Smithsonian Institution The national museum and institution in Washington DC was founded in 1846 on the funds of a bequest from the English chemist and mineralogist James *Smithson* (1765–1829).

Smolensk The city in western Russia has a name based on Russian *smola*, 'resin', 'tar', 'pitch', said to allude to a people who were noted for tarring their boats. Recent authorities, however, prefer to relate the name to the dark resinous soil here.

Smurfs, The The comic-strip pixie-like creatures were invented by the Belgian artist Peyo (real name Pierre Culliford), and first appeared in 1957. In the French original they were known as *les Schtroumpfs*, a word perhaps based on German *Strümpfe*, 'socks'. Their English name was doubtless based on the French name, with possibly a suggestion of *frumps* (if reversed).

Smyrna The ancient city on the west coast of Asia Minor, a centre of early Christianity, derives its name from Greek *smurna*, 'myrrh', obtained locally and exported for the manufacture of perfume and incense, as well as for medicinal use. It is now the Turkish town and port of IZMIR.

Snaefell The highest mountain on the Isle of Man has a straightforward Scandinavian name meaning 'snow mountain', from Old Norse *snær*, 'snow' and *fjall*, 'mountain'. Snaefell is often snow-capped. There is an identically named volcano in Iceland. *Cp.* the similar name of SNOWDON.

Snake River The river in the northwest United States, where it forms part of the border between Idaho and Oregon, is not named for its winding course but from the *Snake* (Shoshone) tribe of Indians who formerly lived along its banks in Idaho.

Snell The name was originally a nickname for a quick and active person, from a Middle English word related to modern German *schnell*, 'quick'.

Snow The name arose as a nickname for a very pale person or for someone with snow-white hair.

Snowdon The famous mountain, the highest in Wales, has a name meaning 'snow hill', from Old English *snāw*, 'snow' and *dūn*, 'hill'. The mountain's Welsh name is *Yr*

Wyddfa, 'the cairn place'. Many mountains have served as burial places in historic times. The general English name for the region centring on Snowdon is *Snowdonia*, with the Welsh equivalent *Eryri*, 'place of eagles'. Snowdon is not permanently snow-capped, but its heights retain snow for much of the year. *Cp.* the similar name of SNAEFELL.

Snow White The king's beautiful daughter in the familiar fairy story is so named because of her fair or white skin, implying delicacy and purity. In the German original tale collected by the brothers Grimm she is *Schneewittchen*, with the same meaning.

Snowy Mountains The mountain range in southeast Australia has a self-descriptive name, corresponding to the SIERRA NEVADA of Spain and California. The *Snowy River* rises in the mountains.

Sochi The city and Black Sea resort in southwest Russia derives its name from that of a Cherkess people. The origin of their own name is uncertain.

Society Islands The group of islands in the south Pacific was first discovered by the Portuguese in 1607. In 1767 the islands were rediscovered by the English naval officer Samuel Wallis, and two years later were visited by Cook, who named them for the Royal *Society*, the commissioners and sponsors of his expedition.

Socotra The island in the Indian Ocean, administratively part of Yemen, derives its name from Sanskrit *dvīpa sukhatara*, 'happy island', from *dvīpa*, 'island' and *sukhatara*, the comparative of *sukha*, 'pleasant', 'agreeable'.

Socrates The famous 5th-century BC Athenian philosopher has a name that has been popularly interpreted as 'strong saviour', as if a blend of *sōtēr*, 'saviour' and *kratos*, 'strength'.

Sodom The biblical city is notorious for being destroyed by God, together with Gomorrah, for its wickedness (*Genesis* 18, 19). Its name represents Hebrew *sedoma*, of uncertain meaning. The city did however give the term *sodomy*, from the form of this homosexual practice (buggery) said to have been practised by its inhabitants. (They wanted to 'know' the two angels staying with Lot, according to *Genesis* 19.5. Lot offered them his two daughters instead.) In recent literature Sodom represents male homosexuality, and Gomorrah female, at least in the works of Proust, notably in his *Sodome et Gomorrhe* (1921, 1922), the fourth section of *A la recherche du temps perdu*.

Sofia The capital of Bulgaria was given its name by the Turks in the 14th century when they converted its famous 6th-century Church of St *Sophia* into a Muslim mosque, as they had done at Constantinople (Istanbul). The city had the original name of *Serdica*, after the *Serdi*, a Thracian tribe. In the 1st century AD, it was known as *Ulpia Serdica*, in honour of the Roman emperor Marcus *Ulpius* Trajanus. In the early 9th century the city was seized by the Bulgarians, who renamed it *Sredets*, 'centre', 'middle' (doubtless partly under the influence of its earlier name). *St Sophia* is not the name of a saint but represents the 'holy wisdom' which, especially in the Eastern Church, is regarded as being incarnate in Christ and present in the Holy Spirit.

Soft Cell The British pop group, formed in Leeds in 1979, adopted a name that punned on *soft sell* as a term for selling by inducement.

Soft Machine The British avant-garde jazz-rock group was formed in Canterbury in 1966 and took their name from the identically titled novel of 1961 by William Burroughs.

Sogdiana The region of ancient central Asia takes its name from its inhabitants, the *Sogdians*, whose own name derives from Old Persian *Sughda* or *Sughada*, 'pure', 'clean'.

Soho The district of central London has a name that may well derive from the traditional hunting cry 'So-ho!', which was used in hare-hunting, just as 'Tally-ho!' was used in fox-hunting. There were fields in Soho before the region was built over in the 18th century, and it is on record that hunting took place here in the mid-16th century. The name is first found in a text of 1632 as *So Ho*.

Soissons The city in northern France is named for the *Suessiones*, the Gaulish people who inhabited the region and whose capital it was. The meaning of their own name is uncertain. *See also* the surname SESSIONS.

Sokol The Czech educational and athletic organization, noted for its influential role in public life, was founded in 1862 as a gymnastic society. Its name means 'falcon', a bird noted for its swift, powerful flight, its predatory instinct, and its use for the sport of falconry.

Solent The sea channel that separates the Isle of Wight from mainland Britain has a name of uncertain origin. A meaning 'place of cliffs', from the Phoenician (or Punic) has recently been proposed. The Roman name for the whole area here, including both the Solent and Southampton Water, was *Magnus Portus*, 'the great harbour'.

Solferino The village in north central Italy probably derives its name from an Italian dialect word meaning 'sulphur'.

Solidarity The Polish political party, which became the senior partner in a coalition government in 1989, arose in 1980 as a confederation of independent trade unions, uniting in *solidarity* against the Communist Party then in power. Its Polish name is *Solidarność*, a term ironically borrowed from socialist jargon, and originally applied to the unity of the working classes and trade union members against capitalist exploitation on a national or international basis.

Solignum The brand of wood preservative has a classical-based name derived from a blend of Greek *sōzein*, 'to save' and Latin *lignum*, 'wood'.

Solihull The industrial town near Birmingham has a name that probably means 'muddy hill', from a conjectural Old English word related to *sol*, 'mud' (modern *soil*) and *hyll*, 'hill'. The hill in question is probably the one south of St Alphege's Church, where the road runs through thick red clayey soil.

Solomon The name of the famous king of Israel, renowned for his great wisdom, derives from a form of Hebrew *ŝalōm*, 'peace'.

Solomon Islands The Pacific island state was so named in 1586 by the Spanish explorer Álvaro de Mendaña de Neira. On landing he saw natives wearing gold ornaments and believed he had discovered the legendary land of Ophir from which gold was brought to King SOLOMON (1 *Kings* 9.29).

Solway Firth The arm of the Irish Sea that extends between the coasts of Cumbria (England) and Dumfries and Galloway (Scotland) has a name meaning 'inlet of the pillar ford', from Old Norse *súl*, 'pillar', *vath*, 'ford' and *fjǫrthr*, 'firth', 'inlet'. The 'pillar' is almost certainly the Lochmaben Stone, a granite boulder that marks the end of the ford on the Scottish side, just south of Gretna Green.

Somalia The republic in northeast Africa takes its name from its indigenous people, the *Somalis*. The origin of their own name is uncertain, but the following theories have been proposed, in descending order of probability: 1. from a Cushitic word meaning 'dark', 'black', referring to the colour of their skin; 2. from a local phrase *soo mal*, meaning 'go and milk', indicating a hospitable people, who offered milk to their guests; 3. from the name of a tribal chieftain; 4. from Arabic *zāmla*, 'cattle', with reference to the many herds here.

Somerset The name of the West of England county means '*Somerton* settlers', that is, 'people who have come to live at Somerton'. The first part of the name thus represents that of the town, and the last part derives from Old English *sæte*, 'settlers'. *Somerton* itself, near Ilchester, has a name that means 'summer dwelling', referring to one by pastures that can be used only in summer, since in winter they are wet or marshy. The region round Somerton has now been drained, so that the land is dry more or less all the year round.

Somerset House The famous building in the Strand, London, stands on the site of a palace built for himself in the mid-16th century by the Duke of *Somerset*, Lord Protector of Edward VI. However, it was unfinished at his execution in 1552, when it passed to the crown. The present building dates from the late 18th century and houses mainly public offices, including the Board of Inland Revenue and the Probate and Divorce Registry. From 1990 it has also housed the Courtauld Institute Galleries.

Somerville College The Oxford women's college was founded in 1879 as a non-denominational alternative to LADY MARGARET HALL and was named for the Scottish writer on mathematics and science Mary *Somerville*, née Fairfax (1780–1872).

Somme The river in northern France derives its name from a Gaulish root element *sum* meaning 'to swim'. English *swim* is thus related.

Song of Solomon The Old Testament book, a collection of love poems spoken alternately by a man and his beloved, was not written by SOLOMON. Its author is unknown, and the name of the famous king of Israel was added later. Its remarkable assertion of female sexuality has led some authorities to claim that it may have been written by a woman. It is also known as the *Song of Songs* and *Canticle of Canticles*. It should not be confused with the apocryphal *Wisdom of Solomon*.

Songs without Words The title of the 48 piano pieces by Mendelssohn (in German, *Lieder ohne Worte*) (1830–45) refers to the fact that each is written in the style of a *song*, that is, with a distinct melody and its accompaniment. The composer gave titles to only five of the 48: the three 'Venetian Gondola Songs' (Nos 6, 12, 29), the *Duetto* (No 18), and the *Volkslied* ('Folk Song') (No 23). Two other titles, SPRING SONG (No 30) and BEE'S WEDDING (No 34), are both popular names given later.

Sony When Japan's first transistor radio was produced in 1955 by what was then the *Tokyo Tsushin Kogyo Kabushiki Kaisha* ('Tokyo communications industry joint-stock company'), the directors rightly judged that they needed a much briefer and more 'international' name for it. They had already used the name *Tape-corder* for a tape-recorder and *Soni* (from English *sonic*) for its tape. They decided to adopt the latter name for the radio, but judged that in this spelling it might be mispronounced in English as 'so nigh'. They therefore substituted a final *-y* for *-i* to produce a name that would also happen to suggest *sonny*, and so have a homely touch. (If they had actually spelled the name *Sonny*, however,

the Japanese would have pronounced this as 'Son-ny' and associated it with the word *son*, 'loss', 'damage'.) The name passed to the company itself in 1958.

Sonya The name is a Russian pet form of *Sofia*, the equivalent of SOPHIA. *See* SOFIA.

Soper The name was originally an occupational term for a person who made soap, which in its basic form was done by boiling oil or fat together with potash or soda.

Sophia The name derives from that of the mythical St *Sophia*, whose own name probably evolved as a misinterpretation of the Greek phrase *Hagia Sophia*, 'Holy Wisdom', a title of Christ, which was used for the dedication of churches and cathedrals in the Eastern Church. (*See also* SOFIA.) The name also occurs in the variant form *Sophie*.

Sophocles The great Greek dramatist of the 5th century BC has a name that means 'famed for wisdom', from *sophos*, 'wise', 'clever', and *kleos*, 'fame', 'glory'.

Sorbonne The common name for the University of Paris, although strictly speaking only its faculties of science and literature, derives from the original establishment founded as a theological college in 1253 by the scholar and cleric Robert de *Sorbon* (1201–1274).

Sorbs The name of the Slavic people who live in the rural areas of eastern Germany is of the same origin as that of the *Serbs* (*see* SERBIA). They are also known as WENDS.

Sosnowiec The name of the industrial town in southern Poland means 'gathering of pines', from *sosna*, 'pine-tree' and *wiec*, 'gathering', 'assembly'.

Sotho The black peoples of southern Africa have a Sesotho name perhaps meaning 'brown', 'black', referring to their skin colour. They gave the name of *Basutoland* (now LESOTHO), where *ba-* is the sign of the plural in Bantu languages. (*Sesotho* means 'language of the *Sotho*'.)

Soul II Soul The British reggae trio originated in a soul duo in London in 1982. Their name punningly reflected the intimate appeal of their music, and especially that of the dance events that the two musicians initially organized.

Sousse The Mediterranean port in eastern Tunisia, also known as *Susa*, was founded by the Phoenicians in the 11th century BC, and was originally known as *Hadrumetum*. When the Vandals conquered it in the 5th century AD it became *Hunericopolis*, for *Huneric*, son of the Vandal king *Genseric*. After the Byzantine invasion of the 6th century it was further renamed *Justinianopolis*, for the Byzantine emperor *Justinian* I (*see also* SKOPJE). The source of the present name is uncertain. It may be of Berber origin and relate to the names of *Marsa Susa* in Libya, also on the coast, or even the plain (and river) *Sous* in southern Morocco. A link with the biblical SUSA seems less likely.

South Africa The self-descriptive name for the republic in the southernmost part of Africa dates from 1910, when the Union of *South Africa* came into being.

Southampton The well-known city and port on the English Channel has a name that declares it to be a 'southern *Hampton*', by contrast with a 'northern *Hampton*'. The latter was NORTHAMPTON, and the two towns were linked by a north-south route in medieval times, despite the sizable distance between them. (The route was probably that through Abingdon and Oxford followed by the A34 and A43 today.) The *Hampton* of Southampton is a 'waterside farm', however, from Old English *hamm*, and *tūn*, as distinct from that of Northampton which is a 'home farm' (from *hām* and *tūn*). The location of Southampton between the rivers Itchen and Test confirms this origin. Both places were actually known as *Hampton* before adding their respective descriptives. *See also* HAMPSHIRE.

South Australia The state of south central Australia (not in fact the southernmost region of the country, which is VICTORIA) was formed as a British province under this self-descriptive name in 1836. Other names considered at the time included *Williamsland*, for King William IV, and, more realistically, *Central State*. *See also* NORTHERN TERRITORY.

Southend-on-Sea The Essex resort on the Thames estuary acquired its name from its original location at the *south end* of Prittlewell (now a district of Southend itself). The present town developed only as recently as the early 19th century.

Southern Cross The small but conspicuous constellation is so named because of its location in the *southern* hemisphere. Its four brightest stars form a *cross* whose longest arm points to the south celestial pole. There is no corresponding *Northern Cross*, although this name is sometimes used as a nickname for CYGNUS.

Southey The name derives from any of the places so called, such as *Southey* Green that is now a suburb of Sheffield. The place-name itself means 'southern enclosure'.

Southport The Merseyside coastal resort north of Liverpool has a modern name given to the development that arose round a hotel here at the end of the 18th century. It was presumably called *south* from its location on the southern shore of the Ribble estuary.

Southsea The residential and holiday district of Portsmouth, Hampshire, takes its name from the 'goodlie and warlyk castill' that Henry VIII plannned here in 1538 to be a 'south sea castle' at the entrance to Portsmouth Harbour. The *-sea* of the name rather obviously appears to refer to the location of the castle by the sea, but at the same time may have been suggested by the existing name of *Portsea*, the island on which Portsmouth is situated.

South Sea Bubble The name is that of the financial crash that occurred in 1720 after the SOUTH SEA Company had taken over the national debt in return for a monopoly of trade with the SOUTH SEAS, with consequent feverish speculation in their stocks. Investments that rapidly grow but then suddenly collapse are like a *bubble* that is blown up until it bursts.

South Seas The name is properly a general one for all seas to the *south* of the equator. Usually, however, it is taken to apply more specifically to the *South* Pacific.

South Shields The Tyneside port stands on the *south* side of the river mouth, opposite *North Shields*. The name common to both represents Middle English *schele*, 'shed', referring to the fishermen's huts that formed the nucleus of the respective settlements from which the towns grew.

Southwark The London borough to the south of the Thames has a name that means 'southern work', that is, a defensive post on the south side of the river, where it was designed as an outpost of the City of London. Early forms of the name show that it was related to that of SURREY ('southern district').

Sovetsk The city and port in the extreme west of Russia, on the border with Lithuania, was given its present name in 1946, with the aim of showing that it had passed to *Soviet* territory. It had earlier belonged to Prussia, and was known as *Tilsit*, after the river *Tilza*. The river's own name represents Lithuanian *tilszus*, 'marshy'.

Soviet Union The short name of the *Union of Soviet Socialist Republics* was first in official use in 1922 when, as a consequence of the 1917 Revolution, a *union* of socialist republics was set up with the *soviet* ('council') as the basic unit of local and national government. The name was unique for a major country in having no geographical or ethnic element in its composition. The Soviet Union was dissolved in 1991.

Soweto The complex of black townships near Johannesburg, South Africa, was given its name in 1963 as an acronym of *So*uth *We*stern *To*wnships.

Soyuz The series of Soviet spacecraft, first launched in 1967, has a name that is the Russian for 'union', referring not only to the SOVIET UNION but to the *union* made when the spacecraft docks with an already orbiting space station. *Cp.* SALYUT.

Spaghetti Junction The nickname of the motorway junction between the M1 and M6 near Birmingham, properly known as the *Gravelly Hill Interchange*, relates to its many intersecting and crisscrossing roads, underpasses and overpasses, which fancifully resemble *spaghetti*. The colloquial term *spaghetti* for such a junction predates the construction of this particular interchange, planned in the mid-1960s and opened in 1972.

Spain The familiar European country has a name of uncertain origin. It has been tentatively derived from Basque *ezpain* or *ezpañ*, 'lip', 'edge', perhaps in the sense 'bank', 'shore'. Others see an origin in Punic *span*, 'rabbit', while classicists favour a link with HESPERUS, in that it is a western land, a 'land of the setting sun'. Curiously, its latitude is identical to that of Japan, the 'land of the rising sun'.

Spalding The Lincolnshire town, famous for its tulips, has a name that means 'people of *Spald*'. The latter is not a personal name, but that of a district. It has not been located, however, and could be almost anywhere, even somewhere in continental Europe. Its meaning is unknown.

Spam The brand of tinned meat has a name that is a contraction of '*sp*iced h*am*'. It was devised in 1937 as the result of a competition when the American manufacturers were looking for a name for their newly marketed cans of luncheon meat. A name that was also proposed but eventually rejected was *Brunch*.

Spandau Ballet The British new wave group, formed in London in 1979, adopted a name that offered a contradictory image, with *Spandau* the West Berlin prison where Nazi war criminals were confined.

Spaniard The name for a native or inhabitant of SPAIN differs from most other nationalities by its ending, which originated in Old French. It is thus one of a group of designations of people with the French suffix *-ard*, such as *bastard*, *coward* and *wizard*.

Spanish Armada The name is that of the Spanish fleet sent to invade England in 1588 by Philip II of Spain. It was attacked in the English Channel by the English navy and subsequently scattered by storms and shipwrecks. *Armada* is the Spanish word for 'navy', 'fleet', literally 'armed force', from Medieval Latin *armata*. The term was already in use for a foreign navy (usually in the incorrect form *armado*) at the time when the Spanish attacked. The Spanish word (as distinct from any other) was adopted from the reputation of Spain as an aggressive naval power and land of maritime explorers from medieval times. The historic Spanish name for the *Spanish*

Armada is still, as it was before the attack, *La Armada Invencible*, 'the Invincible Armada'.

Spanish Main The name is that of the *main*land of *Spanish* America, especially the north coast of South America from the Isthmus of Panama to the mouth of the Orinoco, otherwise the seaboard of the Spanish-speaking countries of Colombia and Venezuela.

Sparks The name means 'son of *Spark*', the latter representing the Old Norse name *Sparkr*, a nickname meaning 'bright', 'lively'.

Sparta The ancient Greek city, famous for the military discipline of its inhabitants, derives its name from Greek *spartē*, a term for a cord or rope made from the shrub *spartos* (a kind of broom). The name implies that the cord was used for marking out the lines along which the city's foundations were laid.

Spartacus The 1st-century BC Thracian slave, famous for leading a revolt of gladiators against Rome, has a name that, despite his renowned qualities of leadership and bravery, only coincidentally means 'Spartan'.

Speaker The title of the chairman of the House of Commons refers not to the speeches that he or she makes (he actually speaks less than almost anyone in the chamber) but to the fact that he was originally the *spokesman* on behalf of the House to the sovereign.

Speakman The name originally applied to a *spokesman*, in the sense of a person who gave advice or acted on behalf of another.

Spear and Jackson The well-known make of handsaws and garden tools takes its name from a Sheffield steel founder and refiner, John *Spear* (d. 1851), and his partner from 1830, Samuel *Jackson*.

Spencer The name was originally an occupational one for a person who worked in the pantry of a manor house or monastery, from which food was *dispensed*. *Cp.* SPENDER.

Spender The name was an occupational one for a steward or a person in charge of the supply of provisions in a manor house or monastery, that is, the person who *dispensed* them (literally weighed them out).

Sphinx In Greek mythology the *Sphinx* was a monster with a woman's head and a lion's body who asked travellers a riddle and killed them when they could not answer. Her name derives from Greek *sphingein*, 'to throttle', as her usual method of killing was by strangulation.

Spica The name of the brightest star in the constellation Virgo is the Latin word for 'ear of corn'. *Virgo*, The Virgin, was regarded by ancient astrologers as symbolizing the earth and a bountiful harvest. In the constellation Virgo she is represented as holding an ear of corn in her left hand and a palm leaf in her right.

Spicer The name was an occupational one for someone who sold spices, which in medieval times would have implied a person who was a cross between a modern grocer and a druggist.

Spiller The name was originally either occupational, denoting a tumbler or jester, from Middle English *spillen*, 'to play', 'to sport', or else a nickname for a wasteful person, who *spoiled* or *spilled* materials or products.

Spillers The well-known pet food manufacturers take their name from Joel *Spiller* (1804–1853), a Somerset ironmonger's son who set up as a corn dealer in 1829. He and a partner built a corn mill and by the time the partner retired in 1864 the firm was making ship's biscuits. However, it was only in the 1930s that the company's pet foods became prominent.

Spirella The brand of corsetry has a name based on *spiral*. It originally referred to a new type of stay invented around 1900 by an American engineer, Marcus Beeman. Concerned that existing corsets had no flexible support, he devised one by bending a piece of wire into a series of 'S' shapes. His '*Spirella* Flexible Stay' was subsequently incorporated into the corset itself.

Spirit The original name of the American rock group, formed in Los Angeles in 1966, was *Spirits Rebellious*, adopted from the title of a book by Kahlil Gibran. In 1967 the name was shortened to *Spirit*.

Spitalfields The district of east central London has a name that can be understood as 'hospital fields'. The land here belonged to the priory of St Mary Spital, founded in 1197. The word *spital* or *spittle* was formerly current in English for a 'low-grade' hospital or hospice, catering for beggars and the poor.

Spithead The roadstead off the entrance to Portsmouth Harbour takes its name from a sandbank on the Hampshire coast called *Spit Sand*, now built over and represented by the strip of land that runs from Haslar Royal Naval Hospital to HMS *Dolphin*. This name was extended to the whole of the roadstead, seen as running from the *head* or end of Spit Sand.

Spitsbergen The Norwegian Arctic archipelago has a Dutch name, meaning 'mountain point', from *spits*, 'points' and *bergen*, 'mountains'. The name was given by the Dutch explorer Willem Barents who came here in 1596. An earlier name for the archipelago was *Grumant*, from the Swedish *Grönland*, 'green land', intended just as ironically (or naively optimistically) as for GREENLAND. An alternative name for the island group is *Svalbard*, from Norwegian *sval*, 'cool', 'cold' and *bård*, 'shore'.

Split The port and resort in Croatia has a name that evolved from its Roman name of *Spalatum*. This itself comes from Latin *palatium*, 'palace'. The emperor Diocletian built a grand palace here in the 4th century AD in what was then the port of *Salona*. In the 7th century, after the sacking of Salona by the Avars, the inhabitants built a new town on the ruins of the palace, using its remaining walls and pillars as foundations. Hence the name of the modern town.

Split Enz The New Zealand pop group was formed in Auckland in 1972 as *Split Ends*, punning on the term for hair that has split. In 1975 they moved to Australia and adopted an original spelling for the name.

Spokane The city in Washington has a name of Indian (Salish) origin, said to derive from *spo-kan-ee*, 'sun'. This may itself have been the personal name of a chief, passing from him to the tribe, then to the river where they lived, then from the river to the present city.

Spooky Tooth The British progressive rock group was formed in 1967 with a randomly surreal or 'psychedelic' name.

Spooner The name is occupational, and originally applied to a person who covered roofs with *spoons*, or wooden shingles. Later, the name could be have been used of a person who made wooden or horn *spoons* in the modern sense.

Sporades The two groups of Greek islands in the Aegean are widely scattered and have a name that reflects this, from Greek *sporas*, genitive *sporados*, literally 'disseminated'. The same Greek word gave modern English *spore* and *sporadic*.

Springboks The name is applied to amateur athletes in South Africa who represent their country in international sport. As a collective name it denotes a national South African sports team or touring side. It derives from the *springbok* or springbuck, the graceful antelope that is the country's emblemic animal and that is famous for its athletic leaps into the air (known as 'pronking') when startled or playing.

Springfield The state capital of Illinois arose round a log cabin erected here in 1818 and took its name from nearby *Spring* Creek. The name could be regarded as generally propitious for a new, burgeoning settlement, and has pleasant rural associations, as for a 'garden city'. *Springfield*, Massachusetts, however, was founded in 1635 by the English settler William Pynchon and named for his birthplace, the Essex village of *Springfield*, now a suburb of Chelmsford.

Spring Song The name of Mendelssohn's SONGS WITHOUT WORDS No 30 (Op 62) in A major (1844) was not given the piece by the composer. It is simply a generally romantic evocation.

Spring Symphony Benjamin Britten's choral work of this name, Op 44 (1949), is a setting of poems by Elizabethan and Romantic writers and was given an appropriately pastoral name.

Spurn Head The headland at the end of the long spit of land on the north side of the mouth of the Humber has a name referring to its contour, like that of a *spur*.

Squeeze The British rock group was formed in London in 1974 and took their name from the title of a Velvet Underground album, released two years previously.

Sredna Gora The name of the mountain range in Bulgaria means 'middle mountain'. It describes not only the location of the range across the centre of the country, but also its position between the Balkans to the north and the Rhodope Mountains to the south.

Sri The name, also spelled *Shri*, is that of LAKSHMI, the Hindu goddess of prosperity and wife of Vishnu. It is the Sanskrit word for 'beauty', 'holiness', and hence is an honorary title used when addressing or speaking of a distinguished Hindu: 'My cousin, Shri Ramram Seth, is a great seer' (Salman Rushdie, *Midnight's Children*, 1981).

Sri Lanka The island republic, formerly familiar as CEYLON, has a name that represents Sanskrit *śrī*, 'happiness', 'holiness' and *laṅkā*, 'island'. It is thus effectively 'island of the blessed'. *See also* SRI and *cp.* SRINAGAR.

Srinagar The city in northern India has a name meaning 'city of happiness', from Hindi *śrī*, 'fortune', 'happiness' and *nagar*, 'town'.

Stacey The female name was originally a male name which had evolved as a pet form of EUSTACE. It later came to be regarded as a diminutive of ANASTASIA. Its popularity in the latter half of the 20th century probably arose from its similarity to TRACY. The spelling *Stacy* is fairly common.

Staffa The Scottish island in the Inner Hebrides, famous for its columns of basaltic rock, has a name that refers to this distinctive feature. It means 'pillar island', from Old Norse *stafr*, 'pillar' (related to English *staff*) and *ey*, 'island'.

Stafford The county town of Staffordshire has a name that means 'landing-place ford', from Old English *stæth*, 'landing-place' (modern *staithe*) and *ford*, 'ford'. Stafford is on the Sow, and doubtless the ford was located at the limit of navigation on this river, which was thus a landing-place.

Stainer The name was occupational originally, referring to a dyer, especially one preparing *stained* glass rather than fabrics.

Staines The Surrey town, on the Thames, has a name meaning simply 'stone', from Old English *stān*, to which a misleading plural *s* has been added. The 'stone' in question was probably a natural glacial boulder here, rather than a Roman milestone, as sometimes popularly explained.

Stalingrad The former name of VOLGOGRAD is a reminder that there were many Soviet towns and cities formerly named for *Stalin*, almost all of them reverting to their former name on his fall from grace in 1961. Others include (present name in brackets): *Stalino* (DONETSK), *Stalinsk* (NOVO-KUZNETSK), *Stalinabad* (DUSHANBE), *Stalinogorsk* (NOVOMOSKOVSK). Similar reversions were made for towns in other East European countries, such as *Stalinogród*, Poland, now KATOWICE, and *Sztálinváros*, Hungary, now DUNAÚJVÁROS. The name is best preserved in that of the historic Battle of *Stalingrad* (1942–3), a major turning point in the Second World War, when the unsuccessful German assault on the city led to the start of a successful Soviet counteroffensive.

Stalky The name of one of the central characters in Kipling's novel *Stalky & Co.* (1899) is the nickname of the schoolboy Arthur Corkran. It is introduced (and explained) in the author's earlier story 'Stalky':

> 'It isn't stalky enough for me.'
> 'Stalky,' in the school vocabulary, meant clever, well-considered, and wily, as applied to a plan of action; and stalkiness was the one value Corkran toiled after.
> *Windsor Magazine*, September 1898.

Stamford The historic Lincolnshire town, on the river Welland in the southwest of the county, has a name meaning simply 'stone ford'. This implies a ford where stones had been laid on the river bed for ease of crossing. Ermine Street passed through Stamford, and other long-established roads converged here, with the famous Great North Road passing through the town (and over the Town Bridge) until relatively recently. The original 'stone ford' was probably sited where the two footbridges,

George Bridge and Lammas Bridge, today cross the river and its accompanying mill-stream about 200 yards west of the Town Bridge. This was not where Ermine Street crossed, however, and the former Roman road ran over about half a mile upstream, on a route now followed (on the northern side) by the streets named Water Furlong and Roman Bank. The city of *Stamford*, Connecticut, now a residential suburb of New York, was founded in 1641 and named for its English counterpart.

Stamford Bridge, Battle of The battle of 1066, in which King Harold of England defeated his brother Tostig and King Harald Hardrada of Norway, takes its name from the village near York where it was fought. The village name refers to a former *stone ford* over the river Derwent that was replaced by a *bridge* well before the date of the battle. Medieval Latin and French names for the village such as *Pons belli* and *Punt de la Bataille* refer to the battle itself and can be understood as *Battlebridge*. See also STAMFORD.

Standish The name originally applied to someone from *Standish*, now a town near Wigan. Its name means 'stone pasture'.

Stanford The name was used of a person from any place called *Stanford*, such as the Kent village near Hythe or what is now the town of *Stanford* le Hope in Essex. The meaning is 'stone ford'. *See also* STAMFORD.

Stanley The first name was adopted from the surname, itself a borrowing of a place-name meaning 'stone clearing', from Old English *stān*, 'stone' and *lēah*, 'wood', 'clearing'.

Stanley The capital of the Falkland Islands was so named in 1844 for the English colonial secretary Edward *Stanley*, fourteenth Earl of Derby (1799–1869), styled 'Lord Stanley' until 1851. It was Stanley himself who ordered the transfer of the main settlement on the islands from Port Louis to Stanley, although the name was given not by him but by Major-General Richard Moody, lieutenant-governor and vice-admiral of the Falkland Islands.

Stanley Cup The North American ice hockey award, made annually at the end of the season in the National Hockey League, was inaugurated in 1917 and named for Frederick Arthur *Stanley*, sixteenth Earl of Derby (1841–1908), former governor-general of Canada.

Stansted The well-known airport takes its name from the nearby village of *Stansted*, near Bishop's Stortford, Essex. The village's name means 'stone place', from Old English *stān*, 'stone' and *stede*, 'place'. There was probably a prominent stone building here at some time.

Stapleton The name derives from one of the places so called, such as the Leicestershire village near Hinckley or the Shropshire village near Shrewsbury. The place-name derives from Old English *stapol*, 'post' and *tūn*, 'settlement', often denoting a place by a boundary post or meeting post, or even one raised above ground on supporting posts.

Star and Garter Home The home for disabled ex-servicemen on Richmond Hill, Surrey, takes its name from an inn here in the 18th century. The inn was built on a site leased from the Earl of Dysart who was a Member of the Most Noble Order of the *Garter*. The name thus refers to this award, which has a *star* as part of its insignia. The inn name is found elsewhere in Britain.

Star Chamber The former English civil and criminal court, created in 1487 but abolished in 1641, was so named from the *star*-shaped ceiling decoration of the room in the Palace of Westminster where it was held.

Stasi The name of the feared former East German political police is an abbreviated form of *Staatssicherheitsdienst*, 'State Security Service'. The name was popularized in the West by spy novels, such as Len Deighton's *Berlin Game* (1983). Germans usually preferred the abbreviation *SSD* for the organization.

State Express The make of cigarettes takes its name from the Empire *State Express*, the fast train that formerly ran from Buffalo to New York City (the latter in New York State, the *Empire State*). The name was given by Albert Levy, founder of the manufacturing company, Ardath. He noticed when travelling on this train that the engine number was 999, a numerical combination that suggested other tobacco brand names, one of the best known now being *Three Fives*.

Stavropol The city in southwest Russia was founded as a fortress in 1777 and given a Greek name meaning 'cross city', from *stauros*, 'cross' and *polis*, 'city'. The name was probably adopted from that of another, earlier *Stavropol*, now the city of TOGLIATTI on the Volga. From 1935 to 1943 the present city of the name was known as *Voroshilovsk*, after the Soviet statesman Kliment *Voroshilov* (1881–1969).

Steel The name arose either as an occupational name for a foundry worker, or as a nickname for a person regarded as being specially tough or 'durable', like steel.

Steeleye Span The British folk-rock group was formed in 1969 with the aim of adapting and updating folk music of the 17th and 18th centuries for modern electric instruments. Their name was adopted from the character in the traditional Lincolnshire ballad 'Horkston Grange'.

Steely Dan The American pop group, formed in Los Angeles in 1972 and famous for its cryptic lyrics, took as its name that of a steam-powered dildo in the surreal novel by William Burroughs, *The Naked Lunch* (1959).

Steinway The well-known make of piano derives its name from the German cabinet-maker Heinrich Engelhard *Steinweg* (1797–1871), who built his first piano (of the type known as 'square piano') near Hanover in 1836. In 1850 his family emigrated to America, and he part-anglicized his name to Henry E. *Steinway*. He produced his first grand piano in 1856, and the first modern upright in 1862.

Stella The name represents Latin *stella*, 'star'. It was popularized (and probably introduced) by the 16th-century poet and courtier Sir Philip Sidney, who used it for his sequence of sonnets and songs *Astrophel and Stella* (1582). This tells of the unhappy love of *Astrophel* ('lover of a star') for *Stella* ('star'). Astrophel was Sidney himself, while clues in various sonnets (*e.g.* No 37, 'Hath no misfortune, but that Rich she is') have led to the identification of Stella as Lady Penelope Rich, wife of Lord Rich and mistress of Lord Mountjoy.

Stepanakert The town in Azerbaijan, where it is the capital of the Nagorno-Karabakh Autonomous Region, was so named in 1923 for the Georgian Communist leader *Stepan* Shaumyan (1878–1918), who engaged in revolutionary activities in the Caucasus but who was shot after the Revolution by counterrevolutionary forces. The final part of the name is Armenian *kert*, 'town'. The town's earlier name was *Khankendy*, 'town of the khan'.

Stephen The biblical name is familiar as that of the first Christian martyr (*Acts* 6.7). His name is Greek in origin, from *stephanos*, 'crown', 'garland'. The death of Stephen in many ways reflects that of Jesus, and the feast of St Stephen is on 26 December, the day after Christmas Day, Christ's own festival.

Stephenson The straightforward name means 'son of STEPHEN', as does its variant form, *Stephens*.

Stepney The district of east London, north of the Thames, has a name meaning 'Stybba's landing-place', with the Anglo-Saxon personal name followed by Old English *hȳth*, 'landing-place', as better preserved in the name of ROTHERHITHE.

Steppenwolf The American heavy metal band, formed in California in 1967, took its name from the central character of the identically titled novel of 1927 by the German writer Herman Hesse. The name reflected the fact that the group's founder and lead singer, John Kay (original name Joachim Krauledat), was German by birth.

Stettin *See* SZCZECIN.

Stevenage The Hertfordshire town has a name meaning '(place at) the firm oak', from Old English *stīth*, 'stiff', 'strong' and *āc*, 'oak'. There must have been a sturdy oak tree here at one time. The original *th* was 'eased' to *v* in much in the same way that *bother* in Cockney speech produced *bovver*.

Stewart The name originated from the occupation of *steward* in a manor or royal household. Its French spelling, STUART, is commonly used as a first name.

Stewart Island The third largest island of New Zealand (after North Island and South Island), in the south of the country, takes its name from the whaler Captain William *Stewart*, who visited it in 1809 and proved that it was an island, not a peninsula, as James Cook had earlier supposed.

Still The name originally applied either to a calm and placid person (*cp.* modern German *still*, 'quiet'), or to someone who lived near a fish-trap in a river (Middle English *still*).

Stilton The familiar strong cheese, made either as blue Stilton or white Stilton, takes its name from the village of *Stilton* near Peterborough, Cambridgeshire (formerly Huntingdonshire), where it was distributed from the Bell Inn, on Ermine Street (now the A1). It was not made here, however, but in Leicestershire. The village has a name meaning 'stile farm', from Old English *stigel*, 'stile' and *tūn*, 'farm'. The stile may have been one that led onto (or from) Ermine Street.

Stirling The historic Scottish town, located above the river Forth, has a name that has never been satisfactorily explained. It may have derived from a former name of the Forth. Gaelic *sruth*, 'river', 'stream' has been mentioned in this connection.

Stirling Albion The Scottish football club, based in Stirling, was formed in that town in 1945 and took its name from the *Albion* trucks that served as the club's original spectator stands. Stirling had had an earlier club, *King's Park*, but this disbanded in the Second World War. *Cp.* ALBION ROVERS.

Stockholm The capital of Sweden has a name that combines Swedish *stäk*, 'bay' or *stock*, 'stake', 'pole' and *holm*, 'island'. The overall sense is thus 'island in the bay' or 'island on poles', the latter implying a settlement built by a landmark or over the remains of some earlier foundation.

Stockport The town near Manchester has a name found elsewhere in the country, meaning 'market-place', from Old English *stoc*, 'place' (often implying a place dependent on another) and *port*, 'market', 'town'.

Stockton-on-Tees The Teesside town has a name meaning 'farm place', from Old English *stoc*, 'place' (often implying a place dependent on another) and *tūn*, 'farm'. The

name is a common one, and frequently has distinguishing additions, as here.

Stoke-on-Trent The well-known Staffordshire city has a basic name meaning simply 'place', from Old English *stoc*, here implying a place that is dependent on another.

Stoke Poges The Buckinghamshire village, popularly associated with Gray's *Elegy Written in a Country Churchyard* (1751), has a basic name meaning 'place', from Old English *stoc*, implying a place that was dependent on another. The second word, serving as a distinguishing addition, derives from the Norman family of *le Pugeis*, who held the manor here in the 13th century.

Stokes The name means 'son of *Stoke*', the latter being a name for a person who came from any of the places so called, such as STOKE-ON-TRENT or STOKE POGES.

Stonar School The girls' public school near Melksham, Wiltshire, was founded at *Stonar* near Sandwich, Kent, in 1921. On the outbreak of the Second World War it moved to its present location, keeping its original name.

Stone The name originally denoted a person who worked with stone as well as someone who lived on stony ground or by a stone structure of some kind, such as a monument or boundary marker.

Stonehenge The famous ancient earthwork and stone circle on Salisbury Plain has a name meaning essentially 'hanging stones'. The reference is almost certainly to the top horizontal lintel stones in each trilithon (group of three stones), which are supported by or 'hang' on the two uprights. Another school of thought, however, claims that the trilithons are so named as they resemble a type of gallows, a 'stone hanging place'.

Stone Roses, The The British 'psychopunk' rock group, formed in Manchester in 1980, originally performed as *The Patrol*. In 1983 they changed their name to *English Rose*. The following year, on a tour to Sweden, they adopted their present name, blending *Rose* with the name of their favourite pop group, the ROLLING STONES. The name is in the 'self-contradictory' tradition exemplified earlier by bands such as IRON BUTTERFLY.

Stormont The Northern Ireland parliament building in Belfast takes its name from the district here. The name probably derives from Irish *starr*, 'projection' and *muineach*, 'back', 'hill'. Stormont is some five miles (8 km) east of the city centre at the foot of what could be seen as a 'projecting hill' to the north of it.

Stornaway The port and chief town of the Scottish island of Lewis has a name that probably means 'steerage bay', from Old Norse *stjǫrn*, 'steerage', 'rudder' (English *stern*) and *vágr*, 'bay'. The precise sense of this is not clear, but it may have denoted a harbour where special care was needed when manoeuvring.

Stott The name was originally a nickname for a person who resembled a steer or bullock (Middle English *stott*) or who kept such animals.

Stour There are several rivers of the name up and down the country, including the Great *Stour* and Little *Stour* in Kent. Wherever it occurs, the name derives from a conjectural Celtic root element *stur*, meaning 'strong', referring to the force of the current.

Stourbridge The town near Birmingham takes its name from the river STOUR on which it stands. The original 'bridge' of the name may have been where the present High Street crosses the river to the north of the town centre. The river is bridged again in the east of the town by Stamford Street, suggesting that there was once a stone ford there also (*see* STAMFORD).

Stourhead The famous Wiltshire Palladian mansion, with its fine gardens, takes its name from the river STOUR, which rises or has its *head* near here.

Stowe School The public school for boys near Buckingham was founded in 1923 in *Stowe* House, the seat of the dukes of Buckingham and Chandos. The house is named for its locality, whose own name derives from Old English *stōw*. This basically means 'place', but here, as widely elsewhere, probably meant 'holy place', 'place of religious assembly'.

Stowmarket The Suffolk town was originally known simply as *Stow*. This represents Old English *stōw*, 'place', which often implied a place of assembly, whether for administrative or religious purposes. When the town came to be associated with its market, the latter half of the name was added, and this is first recorded in a text of the mid-13th century.

Strabo The noted Greek geographer and historian of the 1st centuries BC and AD has a name that means 'cross-eyed', from Greek *strabizein*, 'to squint'. There is no evidence that he himself was so afflicted.

Strachan The Scottish surname derives from a village of the name near Banchory in the former Kincardineshire. The place-name itself may mean 'foal valley', from Gaelic *srath*, 'valley' and *eachan*, 'foal' (literally 'little horse').

Strand The familiar London street was originally a medieval bridle path along the *strand* or shore of the river Thames, which was much broader than now until it was confined by embankments in the 19th century.

Strange The name was originally a nickname for a *stranger*, a person new to an area. *Cp.* NEWMAN.

Strangeways The district of Manchester, known for its prison, has a name that literally means 'strong washing', from Old English *strang*, 'strong' and *wæsc*, 'washing'. The reference is to the location of the place on a tongue of land between two rivers, where it was formerly subject to flooding from the rivers' strong currents. The present form of the name is an attempt to make it meaningful.

Stranglers, The The British rock band, formed in the village of Chiddingfold near Guildford, Surrey, in 1974, were originally known as the *Guildford Stranglers*, presumably modelled on a name such as the *Boston Strangler*. They shortened the name subsequently.

Stranraer The port and resort in Dumfries and Galloway, southwest Scotland, has a name that literally means 'fat peninsula', from Gaelic *sròn*, 'peninsula' and *reamhar*, 'fat', 'plump'. The name seems to refer to the broad peninsula at the northern end of the Rinns of Galloway, to the west of the town.

Strasbourg The city in northeast France has a Germanic name meaning 'fortress on the street', from Old German *straza*, 'street' (modern German *Straße*) and *burg*, 'fort'. The town arose by an important route that led from the Rhine here westward over the Vosges Mountains. *Cp.* STRATFORD.

Stratfield Saye The country house near Basingstoke, Hampshire, the seat of the Dukes of Wellington, takes its name from the village here. The first word of the name means 'open land by the Roman road', *i.e.* the one from Silchester to London, from Old English *strǣt*, 'Roman road' (modern *street*) and *feld*, 'open land' (modern *field*). The second word represents the name of the Norman family *de Say*, who held the manor here in the 13th century.

Stratford Virtually everywhere that this name occurs in Britain it means 'ford by a Roman road', from Old English *strǣt*, 'road' (a word borrowed from Latin *via strata*, 'paved way', and giving modern *street*), and *ford*, 'ford'. A good map will often show the course of the Roman road in question. In the case of *Stratford*-on-Avon, it ran between Alcester and Tiddington over the Avon. At *Stratford* in northeast London it ran from London to Colchester and crossed the Lea.

Strathclyde The well-known area and administrative region of western Scotland has a name that means 'valley of the CLYDE', from Gaelic *srath*, denoting a broad valley, and the river name. *Cp.* STRATHMORE.

Strathmore The name is that of the extensive valley that basically separates the Highlands of Scotland, to the north, from the Central Lowlands, to the south. It means 'great valley', from Gaelic *srath*, 'valley' and *mór*, 'great'.

Stratton The name derives from any of the places so called, many of them in the south of England, and nearly all meaning 'settlement by the Roman road' (*cp.* STRATFORD). *Stratton* in Cornwall, however, has Cornish *stras*, 'valley' as the first part of its name.

Strawbs, The The British folk-rock group, formed in 1967, originally called themselves the *Strawberry Hill Boys*, as their members were from that region of London. They shortened the name soon after.

Streatham The district of south London has a name meaning 'homestead by a Roman road', from Old English *strǣt*, 'road' and *hām*, 'homestead'. The Roman road here ran along the course now followed by Streatham High Road (the present A23).

Stromboli The famous island with its volcano in the Tyrrhenian Sea derives its name from Greek *strongulos*, 'round', referring to its shape.

Strong The name was originally a nickname for a strong man, or in some cases, ironically, for a noticeably weak one.

Struwwelpeter The collection of cautionary tales for children by the German writer Heinrich Hoffmann, first published in 1845, is named for the first character to appear in the book, the disobedient little boy usually known in English as 'Shock-headed Peter'. German *Struwwel* or *Struwel*, meaning 'shaggy', 'unkempt', is indirectly related to English *strew*.

Stuart The name is a French spelling of the surname STEWART. It was introduced to Scotland in the 16th century by Mary *Stuart*, Queen of Scots, who had been brought up in France.

Sturmey-Archer The well-known make of bicycle gears is named for Henry *Sturmey* and James *Archer*. In the closing years of the 19th century, both men had independently evolved a three-speed gear for bicycles as an improvement on the existing two-speed gear. Frank Bowden, founder of the Raleigh Cycle Company, realized the commercial potential of a combination of the two types, and after consultation with Archer took out a patent for the first *Sturmey-Archer* three-speed gear in 1902.

Stuttgart The industrial city in western Germany derives its name from Old High German *Stutengarten*, 'mares' garden', from *Stute*, 'mare' and *Garten*, 'garden'. The reference is to the *stud* farm or horse breeding establishment set up here in the 10th century by one of the dukes of Württemberg.

Styria The province of southeast Austria has the German name of *Steiermark*. This derives from the town of *Steyr*, whose name means 'stream', 'current', and Old High German *marcha*, 'territory', 'march' (as for the MARCHES).

Styx In Greek mythology, the name is that of the river in Hades over which Charon ferried the souls of the dead. It derives from Greek *stux*, 'hateful', 'horrible'.

Subaru The Japanese car has the Japanese name of the Pleiades cluster of stars in the constellation Taurus. The cluster's six brightest stars (named individually for the daughters of Atlas in Greek mythology) represent the six companies which merged in 1953 to form Fuji Heavy Industries, who produced the first *Subaru* car in 1958.

Subbuteo The patent game of table football was invented in the 1940s by Peter Adolph, who wanted to manufacture it under the name *The Hobby*, both for the type of falcon and, punningly, in the sense 'pastime'. The name could not be registered, however, as it was purely descriptive. Instead, he took the Latin ornithological name of the bird, *Falco subbuteo subbuteo*, and adopted the second (or third) word of this instead. It does at least suggest *boot*.

Succoth *See* SUKKOTH.

Such The name derives from Old French *suche*, 'tree stump' (related to modern English *stock*), and originally denoted a person who lived by a tree stump or someone who was noticeably stout and stocky.

Suchard The well-known make of chocolate owes its name to Philippe *Suchard* (1797–1884), who began his career in 1815 when he was apprenticed to his brother, a confectioner in Bern, Switzerland. In 1825 he started his own confectionery business in Neuchâtel, and soon after opened a chocolate factory, one of the first in Switzerland.

Sucre The constitutional capital of Bolivia (with the government residing at La Paz) takes its name from the Venezuelan-born South American liberator Antonio José de *Sucre* (1795–1830), Bolivia's first president.

Sudan The republic of northeast Africa has a name of Arabic origin, from *balad as-sūdān*, 'land of the blacks', comprising *balad*, 'land', 'country', *al*, 'the' (here *as* before *s*), and *sūdān*, the plural of *aswad*, 'black'. The name was originally given by Arab travellers to what is now Nubia.

Sudetenland The mountainous region of northern and northwest Czechoslovakia derives its name from the *Sudeten* Mountains here. Their name is an ancient one, mentioned by Ptolemy in the 2nd century, but its meaning is obscure. It may be of Illyrian origin.

Suetonius The 2nd-century AD Roman historian had the full name Gaius *Suetonius* Tranquillus. His *nomen* or clan name probably derives from Latin *suetus*, 'customary', 'familiar', referring to an ancestor of his who was noted for his regular habits or dress.

Suez The Egyptian port takes its name from Arabic *as-suways*, 'the beginning', referring to its location at the northern end of the Red Sea and now also of the canal that bears its name.

Suffolk The county of East Anglia takes its name from the 'south folk', the southern group of East Anglian peoples, whose name, as for their neighbours, the 'north folk' of NORFOLK, became a place-name without the addition of any 'territory' word such as *land*.

Sufi The name for the adherent of a Muslim mystical sect, mainly in Iran, derives from Arabic *sūfiy*, '(man) of wool'. The reference is probably to the rough woollen garments originally worn by the ascetics as a token of their disregard for material comforts, rather in the manner of a Christian penitent's hair shirt.

Sukhe Bator The town in northern Mongolia, founded in 1940, has a name (in Mongolian *Sühbaatar*) representing that of the Mongolian revolutionary hero Damdiny *Sukhe Bator* (1893–1923). His original name was *Sukhe*, literally 'axe' (Mongolian *süh*). *Bator*, meaning 'hero' (Mongolian *baatar*), was added as an honorary title for his bravery against Chinese bandits early in his military career. He died in ULAN BATOR, the Mongolian capital, also named for him.

Sukhumi The port and resort in Georgia has a name given it by the Turks when they captured the town in 1455. They called it *Suhumkale*, with *kale* meaning 'fort' and the first part of the name of less certain origin. It has been said to comprise Turkish *su*, 'water' and *kum*, 'sand', but this may be an attempt to explain its earlier Georgian name of *Tskhumi*, meaning 'hot'. It was founded as a Greek colony in the 7th century BC as *Dioscurias*, so named for the DIOSCURI, otherwise Castor and Pollux.

Sukkoth The name of the Jewish harvest festival, also called the *Feast of Tabernacles*, represents Hebrew *sukkōth*, the plural of *sukkāh*, 'booth', 'tabernacle'. The feast commemorates the *tabernacles* (temporary shelters) used by the Jews in their wandering in the wilderness.

Sulawesi The island in eastern Indonesia has a Malay name, from *sula*, 'spear', 'lance' and *besi*, 'iron', referring to the weapon favoured by its inhabitants. It was formerly (and still is sometimes) known as *Celebes*.

Sullivan The name is an English spelling of the Irish name Ó *Súileabháin*, 'descendant of *Súileabhán*'. The latter name means 'little dark-eyed person', from Irish *súil*, 'eye', *dubh*, 'dark', 'black', and the diminutive suffix *-án*.

Sullom Voe The inlet in the Shetland Islands, Scotland, with its important oil terminal, derives its name from Old Norse *súla*, 'gannet' (*cp.* English *solan* goose) and *vágr*, 'bay'.

Sumatra The mountainous island in western Indonesia has a name that may derive from Sanskrit *samudradvīpa*, 'ocean island', from *samudra*, 'ocean' and *dvīpa*, 'island'.

Sumer The region of southern Babylonia, famous for its ancient civilization, has a name that probably derives from the mythical ancestor of the people who lived here.

Summers The name means 'son of *Summer*', the latter usually being a nickname for a warm-hearted and 'sunny' person, but also a variant spelling of Middle English *sumner* (a 'summoner' of people to court) or *sumpter* (the driver of a pack animal, Old French *sommetier*).

Sumy The name of the Ukrainian city has been popularly derived from Russian *suma*, 'bag', referring to three hunters' bags said to have been found when the original fort

was built here in 1653. The city's coat of arms in fact displays three such bags. But the town stands on the river *Suma*, and almost certainly takes its name from it. The meaning of the river's name is unknown.

Sunday The name of the first day of the week derives, through Old English, from Latin *dies solis*, 'day of the sun', itself a translation of Greek *hēmera hēliou*. German has a similar name, *Sonntag*, but understandably many languages have a religious name for the day, especially in Roman Catholic countries. French *dimanche* thus derives from Latin *dies dominicus*, 'day of the Lord', as do Spanish *domingo* and Italian *domenica*. Russian *voskresen'ye* means 'Resurrection'. However, although of pagan origin, *Sunday* is a not inappropriate name for a day devoted to worship of a God named as 'Sun of righteousness' (*Malachi* 4.2), described as a 'sun and shield' (*Psalm* 84.11), and hymned as 'Sun of my soul' (John Keble, 1827). In other words the Germanic pagan name has been readily granted a Christian interpretation, as happened with EASTER.

Sunderland The port in northeast England has a name that literally means 'sundered land', that is, territory that was at one time separated from a main estate. The term probably had a technical sense, perhaps indicating private land set off from common land.

Sungari The chief river of Manchuria, northeast China, derives its name from Manchurian *Sungari ula*, 'river of milk', based on *sun*, 'milk'. The reference is to its white waters. Its Chinese name is *sōnghuājiāng*, 'pine flower river', from *sōng*, 'pine tree', *huā*, 'flower' and *jiāng*, 'river'. This gives its alternative western name of *Songhua*.

Sunni The name is that of one of the two main branches of orthodox Islam (the other being SHIAH), and refers to those believers who acknowledge the authority of the *Sunnah*, the body of Islamic law that is based on the words and deeds of Muhammad. The name represents Arabic *sunnah*, 'form', 'way', 'rule'.

Suomi *See* FINN.

Super Bowl In American football, the name is that of the final of the National Football League championship, contested annually from 1967, with a play-off (from 1970) between the winners of the two sections of the League, the National Conference and the American Conference. The name is based on that of the *Rose Bowl*, the football stadium in Pasadena, California, where a match is played every New Year's Day between rival college teams at the conclusion of the local Tournament of Roses festival. *Super* refers to the superior status of the contest, *Bowl* to the shape of the football stadium.

Superior, Lake The westernmost of the five Great Lakes of North America has a name that is a direct translation of its original French name, *Lac Supérieur*. It means 'upper lake', and refers to its geographical location with regard to Lake Huron, which is further south. At the same time its mean surface elevation above sea level is slightly higher (at 600 ft, or 180 m) than that of Lake Huron or Lake Michigan (579 ft, or 176 m). It is therefore 'upper' in this sense also.

Supertramp The British rock group, formed in London in 1969, adopted their name from the book by W.H. Davies, *Autobiography of a Super-tramp* (1908).

Supremes, The The American female vocal trio was formed in Detroit in 1959 as the *Primettes* in order to support the *Primes*, a male group that later became the *Temptations*. In 1960 the group changed its name to the *Supremes*.

Surabaya The port in Java, Indonesia, has a Malay name comprising *sura*, 'hero' and *baya*, 'danger', meaning 'brave in the face of danger'. The reference is to the resistance offered by its inhabitants to invading or attacking forces (not least during Indonesia's struggle for independence after the Second World War).

Surinam The republic in northeast South America takes its name from the river here. The meaning of the river's name is uncertain.

Surprise Symphony Haydn's Symphony No 94 in G major (1791) is so nicknamed from the sudden loud drumbeat in the slow movement. The German name of the work is *Sinfonie mit dem Paukenschlag*, 'Symphony with the drumstroke'.

Surrey The familiar southern county of England has a name meaning 'southern district', from Old English *sūther*, 'southerly' and the conjectural *gē*, 'district' (also found in the names of DUNGENESS and ELY). The name applied to the district inhabited by the Saxons of the middle Thames valley. North of the river were the 'Middle Saxons' of MIDDLESEX, between the 'East Saxons' of ESSEX and the 'West Saxons' of WESSEX. South of the river a new, distinctive name was needed for the Saxons here, and this was it. South of them again were the 'South Saxons' of SUSSEX.

Susa The ancient city north of the Persian Gulf, where it was the capital of Elam and the Persian Empire, probably derives its name from an Old Persian root element identical to that in Hebrew *šôšanna*, 'lily' (which gave the first name SUSAN). The city's name in the Bible is *Shushan* (*Esther* 1.2 and throughout that book). The modern name of the city now in southwest Iran is *Shush*. See also SOUSSE.

Susan The long-popular name arose as an English spelling of *Susanna*, itself deriving from Hebrew *šôšanna*, 'lily' (and in modern Hebrew also 'rose'). *Susanna* is familiar from the Apocrypha as the name of the beautiful wife of Joachim who was condemned to death on a false charge of adultery but who was saved by Daniel. She gave her name to *The History of Susanna*, the book that tells her story.

Susquehanna The river in the eastern United States has an Indian name meaning 'winding water', describing its meandering course.

Sussex The well-known county of southern England, administratively divided into *East Sussex* and *West Sussex*, has a name meaning 'South Saxons'. *Cp.* ESSEX, MIDDLESEX, WESSEX, and *see also* SURREY.

Sutherland The former county of northern Scotland has a name that, rather surprisingly, means 'southern territory', from Old Norse *súthr*, 'south' and *land*, 'land', 'territory'. But the name was given by the Vikings, and to the Norsemen, who settled in Orkney and Shetland, this was indeed the 'southern territory', on the Scottish mainland. Equally, the Vikings named the Hebrides as the *Suthreyar*, 'southern islands', as they were also south of Orkney and Shetland. This latter name gave modern *Sodor*, familiar from the episcopal title *Sodor and Man*, since this bishop's jurisdiction extends to the Hebrides.

Sutton The town to the south of central London, formerly in Surrey, has a name found widely in England, meaning 'southern farm', from Old English *sūth*, 'south' and *tūn*, 'farm'. It usually implies that there is a 'northern farm', or at least some place to the south of which the named place lies. In this case, Sutton is south of Acton ('oak farm').

Sutton Hoo The site of a 7th-century ship burial near Woodbridge, Suffolk, has a name that means 'southern farm by the spur of land', from Old English *sūth*, 'south' and *hām*, 'farm' (*cp.* SUTTON) and *hōh*, 'spur of land' (*cp.* LUTON HOO). The reference is not to the tumuli where the ships were buried but to a natural rise in the ground here.

Suzhou The city in eastern China has a name that represents Chinese *sū*, 'thyme' and *zhōu*, 'region'.

Suzuki The make of Japanese motorcycle takes its name from Michio *Suzuki*, the Japanese engineer who in 1909 founded the company that first produced them in 1952.

Svalbard *See* SPITSBERGEN.

Svengali The name is famous (or infamous) as that of the sinister musician and hypnotist of George du Maurier's best-selling novel *Trilby* (1894). He is a Hungarian Jew, although his name is hardly Hungarian or Jewish. It was doubtless regarded by du Maurier as being vaguely central European. The first half of the name suggests *swine*, which has closely related equivalents in Germanic and Slavic languages. The second half evokes *gall* (in its sense of 'venom', 'poison'). The name came to be used generally for a person who exerted an evil influence over another.

Sverdlovsk *See* YEKATERINBURG.

Swabia The region and former duchy of southwest Germany takes its name from its original inhabitants, the *Suebi*, a Germanic people whose own name derives from Old German *swēba*, 'free', 'independent'. *Cp.* SWEDEN.

Swahili The language of east and central Africa, and the people who speak it, take their name from Arabic *sawāhil*, the plural of *sahil*, 'coast'. The language is thus spoken by the 'coast dwellers'. *Cp.* SAHEL.

Swan The name was either a nickname for a pure or excellent person (like the bird the swan was deemed to be) or was an occupational name for a *swain*, a servant or attendant.

Swansea The South Wales town and port has a Scandinavian name meaning '*Sveinn*'s sea (place)', with the personal name (meaning 'boy', 'servant', like English *swain*) followed by Old Norse *sær*, 'sea'. The town lies at the mouth of the river Tawe, as its Welsh name of *Abertawe* indicates.

Swan Theatre The theatre that opened in Stratford-on-Avon in 1986 as a new auditorium for the Royal Shakespeare Company was given a name that is a tribute both to Shakespeare himself, as the *Swan of Avon*, and to the Elizabethan *Swan Theatre* in London, which Shakespeare knew well. The Stratford theatre was built in a style resembling that of a playhouse of Shakespeare's day.

Swaziland The kingdom in southern Africa takes its name from that used by the Zulus to refer to its indigenous inhabitants, the *Swazi*. The people's own name for themselves is *Swati*, from *Mswati*, the name of a 16th-century king. His name in turn perhaps means 'stick', 'rod'.

Sweden The familiar Scandinavian country takes its name from its original inhabitants, the *Suebi*, whose own name probably derives from Old German *swēba*, 'free', although a source in *geswion*, 'kinsman' has also been proposed.

Sweet The name, common in the West of England, was originally a nickname for someone who was popular, that is, who was *sweet* in the sense of being agreeable.

Swinburne The name derives from that of Great or Little *Swinburne* in Northumberland, near Hexham, where the place-name itself means 'pig stream', referring to a place on a stream where pigs regularly drank or were driven across.

Swindon The industrial town in the north of Wiltshire has a name that means 'pig hill', or more poetically (and literally) 'swine down'. The hill here, on which Old Swindon stands, was used as a pasture for swine.

Swinging Blue Jeans, The The British pop group were formed in Liverpool in 1958 and were originally known as the *Bluegenes*, a name punning on *blue jeans*, then at the height of fashion. In 1963, following sponsorship by a jeans manufacturer, they adopted the more commercial name of *Swinging Blue Jeans*.

Swingle Singers, The The American vocal group, formed in the late 1950s with the aim of improving its members' sightreading through the wordless singing of classical music such as Bach fugues, was named for its founder, Ward L. *Swingle* (1927–   ).

Swiss Cottage The district of northwest London takes its name from a former inn here, built in the early 19th century in the style of an Alpine chalet. It was originally called the *Swiss Tavern*, but the name was later changed to *Swiss Cottage*, perhaps because the inn had been built on the site of a former tollkeeper's cottage. The building was reconstructed in 1965.

Switch The commercial debit card, used to make a purchase or pay for a service, has a name that refers to the process by which the amount debited is *switched* from the cardholder's account to that of the retailer or service provider. At the same time, *switch* also suggests a computerized program instruction and even resembles *swipe*, the action of running the card through the electronic 'reader'.

Switzerland The name of the small mountainous republic of west central Europe derives from that of one of its cantons, SCHWYZ, which in 1291 united with the cantons of Uri and Unterwalden to form the nucleus of the Swiss Confederation. The country's names in its four different languages are respectively French *Suisse*, German *Schweiz*, Italian *Svizzera* and Romansch *Svizra*. To avoid apparent partiality, it uses none of these on its stamps but instead prints its Latin name of *Helvetia*, from the *Helvetii*, the people who were conquered by the Romans here. The origin of their own name is unknown.

Sybil *See* SIBYL.

Sydney The capital of New South Wales, Australia, the largest city in Australia and the first British settlement, was founded in 1788 and named for the British home secretary, Thomas Townshend, first Viscount *Sydney* (1733–1800).

Syene *See* ASWAN.

Sylvia *See* SILVIA.

Symonds Yat The popular beauty spot on the river Wye north of Monmouth has a name meaning '*Sigemund*'s gap', with the Anglo-Saxon personal name followed by Old English *geat*, 'gap' (modern *gate*). The 'gap' is a pass through the hills here. The site is a strategic one, on the English-Welsh border.

Symphonia Domestica Richard Strauss's orchestral work, Op 53 (1902–3), is so named ('Domestic Symphony') because it aims to depict a day in the life of the composer's family. Individual themes represent Strauss himself, his wife Pauline, and their baby son.

Symphonie Fantastique Berlioz's symphony of this name, Op 14 (1830), is an extravagant Romantic composition designed to evoke nightmarish devilry. Hence its title, which in full is *Symphonie fantastique (épisode de la vie d'un artiste)*, 'Fantastic symphony (episode in the life of an artist)'. Its five movements have individual titles: *Rêveries, passions* ('Dreams, passions'), *Un bal* ('A ball'), *Scène aux champs* ('Scene in the fields'), *Marche au supplice* ('March to the scaffold'), and *Songe d'une nuit du Sabbat* ('Witches' Sabbath').

Symphony of a Thousand Mahler's Symphony No 8 in E flat major (1906) is so (misleadingly) nicknamed because of the huge number of singers and players needed to perform it. More than 1000 people took part in the first performance in 1910, but the work can easily be performed with fewer. The composer himself did not approve of the name.

Symphony of Psalms Stravinsky's composition for chorus and orchestra (1930) is so named because it is based on the Latin text of *Psalms* 38, 39 and 150.

Syon House The 18th-century house by the Thames in west London, opposite the Royal Botanic Gardens at Kew, takes its name from a former monastery here, founded in the 15th century. It was officially known as the Monastery of the Holy Saviour and St Brigid, to which 'of ZION' was added for reasons that are not very clear. This latter word then came to be regarded as the actual name of the monastery, and persisted after it was suppressed in the 16th century.

Syracuse The port in southwest Italy, in Sicily, has a name of pre-Hellenic origin, perhaps representing Phoenician *seraĥ*, 'to feel ill', since the town was founded by the Greeks in the 8th century BC in a swampy area at the mouth of the river Anapo. The city in New York State was so named in 1825 by its first postmaster, who had read of the Sicilian port and felt that its location was similar to that of the New York town, which was also near a marsh. He was doubtless also attracted by the classical prestige that attached to the name.

Syr Darya The river in Kazakhstan, Kirgizia and Uzbekistan has a name meaning 'secret river', from Uzbek *sir*, 'secret', 'mystery' and *dario*, 'river'. The name implies a respect for the power of the river as a 'living being'.

Syria The republic of west Asia has a name that has been popularly linked with that of ASSYRIA. There are no good grounds for this association, however, although the precise source of the name remains uncertain. It appears in Babylonian hieroglyphs dating from about 4000 BC in the form *Suri*.

Szczecin The port in northwest Poland derives its name from Polish *szczotka*, 'brush', presumably alluding to the thick grass that originally grew here, although it may have been a personal nickname of some kind. The city's German name is *Stettin*. The name is pronounced approximately 'Shchechin'.

Szechwan *See* SICHUAN.

Szeged The industrial city in southern Hungary perhaps derives its name from Hungarian *szeg*, 'angle', referring to the bend in the river Tisza on which it stands. The name is pronounced 'Se-ged'.

Székesfehérvár The name of the city in west central Hungary represents Hungarian *székes*, 'royal residence' (from *szék*, 'seat'), *fehér*, 'white' and *vár*, 'fort'. This translates its former Latin name of *Alba regalis*, and is in turn reflected in the city's German name of *Stuhlweissenburg*. In the 10th century the town was chosen by Stephen I, king of Hungary, as capital of the Hungarian kingdom, which it remained until the 16th century. The approximate pronunciation of the name is '*Say*-kesh-fair-var'.

Szombathely The city in western Hungary has a name meaning 'Saturday place', from Hungarian *szombat*, 'Saturday' (literally 'sabbath') and *hely*, 'place'. A Saturday fair and market was regularly held here. The name is pronounced approximately '*Som*-but-hay'.

T

Tabitha The name is found in the New Testament for a young Christian woman: 'Now there was at Joppa a certain disciple named Tabitha, which by interpretation is called Dorcas: this woman was full of good works and almsdeeds which she did' (*Acts* 9.36). Her name represents Aramaic *Tabhītha*, 'doe', 'roe'. *Dorcas* is the Greek equivalent, from *dorkas*, 'antelope', 'gazelle', said to be so called for its large bright eyes (Greek *dedorka*, perfect tense of *derkomai*, 'I look', 'I see'). Because of the similarity between *Tabitha* and *tabby*, the name became a favourite one for cats, and has been popularly promoted as such by *Tabitha* Twitchett, the cat in the children's stories by Beatrix Potter.

Table Mountain The famous mountain in southwest South Africa, overlooking Cape Town, takes its name from the 'tablecloth' that sometimes appears over it, as a flat, white cloud which seems to hang down over the mountain's steep sides.

Tabor, Mount The mountain in northern Israel, traditionally regarded as the place where the Transfiguration occurred, probably derives its name from Hebrew *ṭabbūr*, 'navel', implying that it was the 'centre of the world'. The phrase 'navel of the earth' is found in original versions of the Bible, respectively as Hebrew *ṭabbūr haárets*, Greek *omphalos tēs gēs*, and Latin *umbilicus terrae*, but this is often wrongly translated in modern texts, so that the English Authorized Version, for example, has 'middle of the land' (*Judges* 9.37) or 'midst of the land' (*Ezekiel* 38.12).

Tabriz The ancient city in northwest Iran probably derives its name from Greek *Tauros* (*see* TAURUS), although some sources see its origin in Iranian *taprīz*, 'causing heat', with reference to the thermal springs here.

Tacitus The full name of the 1st-century BC Roman historian was Publius (or according to some sources Gaius) Cornelius *Tacitus*. *Tacitus* was thus his *cognomen* or nickname. Nothing is known of the writer's parentage, but one of his ancestors must have been so nicknamed for his *taciturn* nature, from Latin *tacitus*, 'silent', 'not speaking'.

Tadcaster The North Yorkshire town near York has a name that means '*Tata*'s Roman station', with the Anglo-Saxon personal name followed by the fairly frequent *-caster* that represents Old English *ceaster*, related to Latin *castra*, 'camp'. It is not known who *Tata* was. His name may have arisen as a nickname from Old English *tāde*, 'toad'.

Taegu The city in southeast South Korea has a name meaning 'big hill', from Korean *tae*, 'big' and *ku*, 'hill'. *Cp.* TAEJON.

Taejon The name of the city in western South Korea means 'big field', from Korean *tae*, 'big' and *chŏn*, 'field'. *Cp.* TAEGU.

Tagalog The name of the people of the Philippines, and that of their language, means 'native to the river', from Tagalog *tagá*, 'native to' and *ilog*, 'river'. The people live in and round Manila, and the river is the Pasig, which effectively divides the city into two.

Taganrog The port on the Sea of Azov in southwest Russia takes its name from Tatar (now also Russian) *tagan*, 'trivet' and Russian *rog*, 'horn', the latter in the sense 'promontory'. The city is on a raised rocky cape, and the name seems to imply that a signal fire or beacon was set up here on a large iron tripod at some time.

Taggart The Scottish name represents an English form of Gaelic *Mac an t-Sagairt*, 'son of the priest', from *sagart*, 'priest'. Priests were forbidden to marry from the

12th century, but several of them did so nevertheless.

Tagus The river of Spain and Portugal has a name that may ultimately derive from Phoenician *dag*, 'fish'. Some authorities, however, link the name with that of the Philistine god DAGON, whose own name is of Hebrew origin and means literally 'little fish'.

Tahiti The well-known South Pacific island takes its name from Tahitian *Otahiti*, perhaps representing Polynesian *Hiti-nui*, from *iti*, 'little' and *nui*, 'island', referring not so much to the island itself, which is the largest in French Polynesia, but to one or other of its extinct volcanos. It was discovered by the Portuguese explorer Fernandez de Queiros in 1606 and originally named *Sagittaria*, for the arrows (Latin *sagitta*) carried by the natives. In 1767 the English naval officer Captain Samuel Wallis claimed it under the name of *King George III Island*. The following year, however, the French navigator Louis Antoine de Bougainville made a rival claim under the name of *Nouvelle-Cythère*, 'New Cythera' (the Greek island where Aphrodite was worshipped). But the native name prevailed.

Taichung The city of west central Taiwan has a name that means 'middle Taiwan', from Chinese *tái*, a short form of TAIWAN itself, and *zhōng*, 'middle'. This describes its location both geographically and with regard to TAINAN and TAIPEI. The name is now frequently spelled *Taizhong*.

Taimyr Peninsula The large peninsula in northern Siberia, between the Kara Sea and the Laptev Sea, may have a name that derives from Tungus *taymur*, 'abundant', 'rich', referring to the plentiful fish of its rivers.

Tainan The city in southwest Taiwan has a name that means simply 'southern Taiwan', from Chinese *tái*, a short form of TAIWAN, and *nán*, 'south'. *Cp*. TAICHUNG, TAIPEI.

Taipei The name of the capital of Taiwan means 'northern Taiwan', from Chinese *tái*, a short form of TAIWAN itself, and *běi*, 'north'. The name is now often spelled *Taibei*. *Cp*. TAINAN.

Taiping The name is that of an adherent of the rebellion in China in the mid-19th century which aimed to overthrow the Manchu dynasty but which was suppressed with the help of foreign aid (notably that of General Gordon) in 1864. It represents Chinese *tài*, 'great' and *píng*, 'peace'.

Tai Shan The sacred mountain in Shantung province, northeast China, has a name that means 'peaceful mountain', from Chinese *tài*, 'peaceful' and *shān*, 'mountain'.

Taiwan The island off the southeast coast of mainland China has a name that means 'terrace bay', from Chinese *tái*, 'terrace' and *wān*, 'bay'. The reference is to the terrain of the island, which slopes down to the sea in a series of 'terraces' of alternating plateaux and hills. Its former name was *Formosa*, Portuguese for 'beautiful', so described by Portuguese explorers here in 1590 for its striking scenery.

Tajikistan The republic of south central Asia takes its name from its indigenous people, the *Tajiks*, with a suffix representing Iranian *ōstan*, 'country', 'land'. The people derive their name from Sanskrit *tājika*, 'Persian', a word that originally distinguished Arabs from Turks, and that itself represents the name of the *Tay*, an Arab tribe.

Taj Mahal The famous mausoleum in Agra, central India, was built in 1632 (completed 1643) by the emperor Shah Jahan in memory of his favourite wife (of three), Arjumand Banu Begam (1592–1631). She was known as *Mumtāz Maḥal*, 'exalted one of the palace', and the name of the building is a corruption of this.

Takamatsu The port in southwest Japan has a name meaning 'high pines', from *taka*, 'high' and *matsu*, 'pine-tree'.

Talbot The name is of disputed origin. It probably derives from a Germanic personal name comprising *tal*, 'to destroy' and *bod*, 'message', so that its overall sense was something like 'messenger of death'. The name is that of of a Norman family said to have brought the type of hound known as *talbot* to England, but the reason for the transfer of their name to the dog is unknown. The breed is now extinct. An individual dog named *Talbot* is mentioned in Chaucer's *Canterbury Tales*: 'Colle oure dogge, and Talbot and Gerland' (*Nun's Priest's Tale*, c. 1386).

Taliesin The 6th-century semi-legendary Welsh bard, the supposed author of the *Book of Taliesin*, a series of 12 heroic poems, has a name that means 'shining brow', from Welsh *tâl*, 'brow' and *iesin*, 'shining'. He is said to be buried at *Bedd Taliesin*, 'Taliesin's grave', near the hamlet of *Tre Taliesin*, 'Taliesin's village', north of Aberystwyth.

Talitha The first name is taken from Aramaic words quoted in the New Testament account of the restoration to life of Jairus's 12-year-old daughter by Jesus: 'And he took the damsel by the hand, and said unto her: Talitha cumi; which is, being interpreted, Damsel, I say unto thee, arise' (*Mark* 5.41). The word thus means 'little girl', and has been adopted as if it were the young lady's name, although this is not actually mentioned. The similar biblical name TABITHA may also have prompted the word's adoption for first name use.

Talking Heads The American new wave rock group, formed in New York in 1975, took their name from the idiomatic phrase used of television presenters, who appear on the screen as 'talking heads'. The term is similarly used for the participants in a televised discussion programme. The group had earlier considered such names as *The Portable Crushers* and *The Vague Dots*.

Tallahassee The state capital of Florida has an Indian name meaning 'old town', from Creek *talwa*, 'town' and *hasi*, 'old'.

Tallinn The capital of Estonia has a name deriving from Old Estonian *Tan-linn*, 'Danish fort', from *dan* (modern Estonian *taani*), 'Danish' and *linn*, 'fort', 'castle'. The city was founded by the Danish king Valdemar II in 1219. Its former name (until 1917) was *Reval*, from Old Danish *rev*, 'sandbank'.

Talmud The fundamental code of Jewish civil and canon law derives its name from Hebrew *talmūd*, literally 'instruction', from *lāmad*, 'to learn'. The Talmud comprises the MISHNA and the GEMARA.

Tamara The name is Russian in origin, and probably arose as a feminine form of the biblical name *Tamar*, that of the daughter-in-law of Judah (*Genesis* 38.6), of a daughter of King David, the 'fair sister' of Absalom (2 *Samuel* 13.1), and of the 'woman of a fair countenance' who was a daughter of Absalom himself (2 *Samuel* 14.27). The name represents Hebrew *tāmar*, 'date-palm', perhaps implying fecundity.

Tambov The city in western Russia takes its name from the small river on which it stands. The river's own name is said to represent Mordvinian *tombaks*, 'marshy'.

Tamburlaine *See* TAMERLANE.

Tamerlane The 14th-century Mongol ruler of Samarkand, popularly known as *Tamburlaine*, derives his name from a European corruption of his Turkic name *Timur Lenk*, 'Timur the lame', a title of contempt used by his Persian enemies. The name *Timur* represents a Turkic word (modern Turkish *demir*) meaning 'iron'. *Cp.* TEMIRTAU.

Tamil The people of southern India and Sri Lanka and their language take their name from that of the *Damila*, a warrior people mentioned in ancient Buddhist texts. The name is ultimately of obscure origin. *See also* DRAVIDIAN, TAMIL TIGERS.

Tamil Nadu The state of southeast India has a Tamil name meaning 'Tamil land', from *tamil*, 'TAMIL' and *nātu*, 'land', 'country'.

Tamil Tigers The name is popularly used for the extremist party known formally as the *Liberation Tigers of Tamil Eelam*, a TAMIL militant organization formed in 1976 with the aim of achieving an independent Tamil state in Sri Lanka. By the time of the party's legal recognition in 1989 Tamils formed about 18% of the country's predominantly Singhalese population. The name is coincidentally similar to that of the *Tammany tiger*, the symbol of TAMMANY HALL.

Tamla Motown The name is a compound one for two originally distinct American record labels, *Tamla* and *Motown*, launched in 1959, and subsequently applied to the distinctive black rhythm 'n' blues and soul music that they popularized. *Motown Records* was set up first, and named from the firm's origins in Detroit, known as '*Motor Town*' from its important automobile industry. *Tamla* followed a month later. The name intended for the label was *Tammy*, after the Debbie Reynolds hit in the film *Tammy and the Bachelor* (1957). This name was not legally acceptable, however, so *Tamla* was substituted for it instead.

Tammany Hall In American politics, the name is in popular use for the central organization of the Democratic Party in New York county. The organization was founded as a benevolent society in 1789, and took its title from a pre-Revolutionary association named for *Tamanend*, a wise and kindly Delaware Indian chief, whose own name means 'the affable'.

Tammuz In the Jewish calendar, the name is that of the fourth month of the year according to the biblical reckoning, and the tenth month of the civil year, falling between June and July. It takes its name from *Tammuz*, that of the ancient Mesopotamian fertility god whose death was solemnized in this month. His own name probably evolved from the Akkadian form *Tammuzi*, itself based on Sumerian *Damu-zid*, 'true son' (literally 'flawless offspring').

Tampax The make of sanitary tampons derives its name from a blend of *tampon* and a phonetic spelling of *packs*, the latter referring both to the function of the product and to the *packs* in which it is sold. The tampons were first marketed in 1936 and were named by their American inventor, Earle C. Haas.

Tampere The name of the city in southwest Finland is a Finnish form of Swedish *Tammerfors*, itself a translation of Finnish *Tammerkoski*, from the name of the rapids on which the town was founded in 1775. Finnish *koski* and Swedish *fors* both mean 'waterfall', 'rapids'. The first part of the name is of uncertain origin. It may represent a personal name or derive from Finnish *tammi*, 'oak'.

Tamworth The Staffordshire town near Birmingham takes its name from the river *Tame* on which it lies, with the second part of the name representing Old English *worthig*, 'enclosure'. The river name is almost certainly related to that of the THAMES.

Tancred The name is that of the Norman hero of the First Crusade in the late 11th century, the subject of Torquato Tasso's *Jerusalem Delivered* (1580). It is Germanic in origin, from *dank*, 'thought' and *rāt*, 'counsel'.

Tanganyika The former state in eastern Africa took its name from Lake *Tanganyika*, now between TANZANIA and Zaïre. Its own name was explained by the English explorer Sir Richard Burton, who discovered it in 1858, as deriving from *kou tanganyika*, 'to join', in the sense that it was a place where waters met. But Stanley, in Africa in 1871, derived it from *tonga*, 'island' (*cp.* TONGA) and *hika*, 'flat'.

Tangier The port in northern Morocco is said to take its name from the mythical goddess *Tingis*, daughter of the giant Atlas. But an origin in a Semitic word *tigisis*, 'harbour' is perhaps more realistic.

Tangshan The city in northwest China has a name representing Chinese *táng*, 'Tang' (the dynasty that reigned from the 7th to the 10th century) and *shān*, 'mountain'.

Tanner The name was originally an occupational one for a tanner of skins.

Tannhäuser The name is that of a 13th-century German minnesinger popularly identified with a legendary knight who seeks absolution from the pope after years spent in revelry with Venus. It means 'pine-forest dweller', from Old German words related to modern *Tanne*, 'silver fir' and *Haus*, 'house'. The name and legend were widely promoted by Wagner's opera of 1845.

Tannoy The patent public address system had its origins in 1922, when an English engineer produced a chemical rectifier to simplify the charging process for a lead-acid accumulator that powered radio receivers. The two different metals he used for the rectifier were *tantalum* and a lead *alloy*, and the resulting commercial name for the materials evolved as a blend (a verbal alloy) of both these words.

Tantalus In Greek mythology, the name is that of the father of Pelops who was punished for his misdeeds by having to stand in water that receded as he tried to drink it and under fruit that was withdrawn as he reached for it. It is probably based on Greek *tantalon*, 'balance', 'pair of scales'. This could refer to his legendary greed and be interpreted in one of two ways: either the more he has, the more he wants, or (more likely) the more he wants, the less he will get. Either way, his name gave the standard English verb *tantalize*.

Tantra In Hinduism and Buddhism, the name is that of the sacred books that contain a dialogue between the god Siva and his wife. It represents Sanskrit *tantra*, 'weave', 'loom', implying 'groundwork', 'underlying doctrine'.

Tanzania The republic of eastern Africa was formed in 1964 as a union of TANGANYIKA and ZANZIBAR. Its name combines equal elements of these two names (with suffix *-ia*) and is designed to represent that union.

Taoiseach The title of the prime minister of Ireland is the Irish word meaning 'leader'. It is pronounced approximately '*tee*shach', with final *-ch* as in Scottish *loch*.

Taoism The popular Chinese system of religion and philosophy derives its name from Chinese *dào*, 'road', 'way', implying the right or correct way. *Cp.* SHINTO.

Tapiola The tone-poem by Sibelius, Op 112 (1926) is dedicated to *Tapio*, the Finnish god of forests.

Taranto The port in southeast Italy may derive its name from Illyrian *darandos*, 'oak', referring to the abundance of these trees here at one time. Some authorities, however, see an origin in an Indoeuropean root element *ter* or *tor*, 'current'.

Tarawa The capital of Kiribati has a name that perhaps represents I-Kiribati (Gilbertese) *te*, 'the' and *rawa*, 'run', referring to a channel through a reef.

Tarbuck The name derives from a place so called, now *Tarbock* Green near Halewood, Merseyside. Its own name means 'thorn brook', from Old English *thorn*, 'thorn bush' and *brōc*, 'brook'. The *r* of *brōc* has disappeared, having been 'swallowed' by the *r* of *thorn*.

Tărgovishte The city in south central Bulgaria has a name that represents Bulgarian *tărgovets*, 'merchant', from *tărg*, 'market' (*cp.* TRIESTE and TURKU). Its former name was *Eski-Djumaïa*, from Turkish *eski*, 'old' and *cuma* (pronounced 'juma'), 'Friday', referring to a regular Friday market.

Tarka The otter who is the central character of the moving tale by Henry Williamson, published in 1927, has a name that according to the author was one traditionally used for an otter by the folk of Exmoor, Devon, where the story is set, and which means 'Little Water Wandering' or 'Wandering as Water'. If this is so, the name is doubtless related to *otter* itself, which in turn is a word that is ultimately related to English *water*. *Cp.* SALAR.

Tarmac The well-known type of road surface has a name based on *macadam*, the term for the compressed layers of small broken stones that was the invention of the Scottish engineer and surveyor of roads John Loudon *McAdam* (1756–1836). The present name evolved in 1902, after the accidental discovery that *tar* mixed with slag of this type made a smooth and relatively dustless road surface.

Tarn The river of southwest France may take its name from the Indoeuropean root element *tar*, 'current', although some scholars derive it from Gaulish *taran*, 'thunder' (which word gave the name of the Gaulish god of thunder, *Taranis*).

Tărnovo The town in northern Bulgaria probably derives its name from Bulgarian *tărn*, 'thorn', although an origin in a Thracian word *dru*, 'to flow' has also been suggested, referring to the river Yantra that runs through the town. The official name of the town is *Veliko Tărnovo*, 'Great Tărnovo'.

Tarquin The name is familiar from two early but semi-legendary kings of Rome, respectively *Tarquinius Priscus* ('the old') and *Tarquinius Superbus* ('the proud'). Their name is probably Etruscan in origin, and of uncertain meaning.

Tarshish The ancient port mentioned in the Old Testament (1 *Kings* 10.22) has a name representing Hebrew *taršîš*, 'chrysolite', a yellowish-green mineral used as a gemstone. It is not certain where Tarshish was. It may have been a Phoenician colony in Sardinia or Spain.

Tarragona The port in northeast Spain, one of the richest in the Roman Empire, was known to the Romans themselves as *Tarraco*. This may relate to the *Taruscans*, the people whom some regard as having founded the French town of *Tarascon* (*see* TARTARIN OF TARASCON), and whose own name may relate to that of the *Etruscans* (*see* ETRURIA).

Tarsus The city in southeast Turkey, famous as the biblical birthplace of St Paul, has a name of Phoenician origin but uncertain meaning. It is not related to the name of TARSHISH.

Tartar *See* TATAR.

Tartarin of Tarascon The name is that of the comic, boastful hero of three stories by the French writer Alphonse Daudet, beginning with *Tartarin de Tarascon* (1872) itself. He is a caricature of a typical teller of tall stories from the south of France, where *Tarascon* is a small Provençal town. *Tartarin* is an established French name meaning 'little *Tatar*', implying a wild or outrageous person.

Tartarus The name of the abyss under Hades in Greek mythology, or that of the underworld itself, may simply be a meaningless 'bugaboo' word, designed to suggest something fearful. It was probably this name that gave the spelling *Tartar* for the more correct TATAR.

Tartu The city of Estonia probably derives its present name from that of *Tar*, an ancient Estonian god. Its previous name (from the 11th century until 1918) was *Dorpat*. The origin of this is uncertain, but theories to explain it include the following: 1. Estonian name, meaning 'fortress of *Tar*' (as above); 2. Finnish name, from *tarpatto*, '(place of) aurochs' (species of wild bull, now extinct); 3. eastern in origin, from root elements meaning 'bull idol', from a word meaning 'bull' related to Hebrew *tōr*, Phoenician *ṭōr*, Greek *tauros*, Latin *taurus* and a Turkic word meaning 'idol', related to Turkish *put*. The city was founded in 1013 with the Russian name *Yuriev*, that of its founder, the Grand

Prince of Kiev Yaroslav the Wise, whose baptismal name was *Yury*, 'George'.

Tartuffe The odious hypocrite who is the central character of Molière's comedy *Le Tartuffe* (1664) is said to have been based on a similar character named *Tartufo* in an Italian comedy. His own name is the Italian word for 'truffle'. The allusion is to a product which, like the concealed intention of a hypocrite, lies hidden below the surface.

Tarzan The famous jungle hero was created by the American writer Edgar Rice Burroughs in 1912. He originated fictionally as John Clayton, Lord Greystoke, a British peer's son (at first called by Burroughs Lord Bloomstoke) who had been abandoned as an orphan in the African jungle, where he was brought up by apes. His name means 'white skin', and derives from the so-called Mangani language that Burroughs invented for his tribe of anthropoid apes. In this, *tar* means 'white' and *zan* means 'skin'. Tarzan is given the name by his foster-mother, Kala, the ape. Burroughs compiled his first 'Dictionary of Mangani' in 1939, feeling that he had given enough information on it 'to permit bright boys to carry on a conversation or a correspondence'. In the same fictional language, Burroughs names the Moon as *Goro*, from *go*, 'black' and *ro*, 'flower', that is, a 'flower in the darkness'. Burroughs himself pronounced his hero's name as *Tar-zan*, in two distinct syllables. The name has now become generic for any real or apparent 'he-man'. In the 1970s the media adopted it as a nickname for the prominent Conservative politician Michael Heseltine, not only generally for his tallness and blond hair but specifically from an incident in 1976 when he is alleged to have waved the mace aloft in the House of Commons in order to protect it.

Tashkent The capital of Uzbekistan has a name that represents Sogdian *taš*, 'stone' and *kand*, 'fort', 'town'.

Tasmania The island to the south of mainland Australia, and that country's smallest state, was so named in 1853 for the Dutch navigator Abel Janszoon *Tasman* (1603–1659), who discovered it in 1643. He himself named the island *Van Diemen's Land*, for Anthony *van Diemen*

(1593–1645), Dutch governor-general of the Dutch East Indian colonies.

Tatar The name is that of the Mongoloid people who under Genghis Khan set up a powerful state in Asia from the 13th century. It probably derives from a native word meaning simply 'people', but has been long been associated with TARTARUS, resulting in the common variant spelling of *Tartar*.

Tate and Lyle The well-known sugar manufacturers takes their name from Henry *Tate* (1819–1899) and Abram *Lyle* (1820–1891), who each developed independent businesses as sugar refiners in London and Scotland respectively. Their firms merged only in 1921, and despite their almost parallel careers it seems unlikely that the two men ever met. It was Tate who gave the name of London's TATE GALLERY.

Tate Gallery The famous London art gallery was built in 1897 on funds donated by the sugar refiner Sir Henry *Tate* (*see* TATE AND LYLE), with Sir Henry also offering the nation his own collection of paintings and sculptures.

Tatiana The Russian name, familiar from *Tatiana* Larina, the heroine of Pushkin's verse novel *Eugene Onegin* (1823–31) and Tchaikovsky's opera of 1879 based on it, probably developed as a feminine form of the Roman family name *Tatius*, whose meaning is unknown. The name was borne by various early Eastern Orthodox saints, however, and for them some authorities prefer an origin in Greek *tattō*, the Attic form of *tassō*, 'I arrange', 'I put in order', implying a personal orderliness and discipline.

Tatra Mountains The mountain range between Czechoslovakia and Poland ultimately derives its name from Greek *terthron*, 'end', 'extremity'.

Tattersall's The well-known firm of racehorse auctioneers was founded in 1766 by the horseman Richard *Tattersall* (1724–1795), and is named for him. It was originally based in London but in 1939 moved to Newmarket.

Taunton The county town of Somerset takes its name from the river *Tone* on which it stands. The river's name probably means 'roaring one', from a Celtic root element *tan*. The final *-ton* means, as frequently, 'farm', 'settlement'.

Taurus The zodiacal constellation in the northern hemisphere has a Latin name meaning 'bull'. An outline of a bull's head, with horns, is depicted by the constellation's most prominent stars, with the animal's face formed by the HYADES and its glittering eye by its brightest star, ALDEBARAN.

Taurus Mountains The mountain range in southern Turkey probably derives its name from the Celtic root element *tauro*, related to English *tor* and meaning simply 'hill', 'mountain'. Understandably, the Greeks took the name to represent *tauros*, 'bull'.

Tavistock The Devon town, on the edge of Dartmoor, takes its name from the river on which it is situated, the *Tavy*. This name may well be related to that of the THAMES, so have the same origin and meaning. The second half of the town's name derives from Old English *stoc*, often denoting a secondary settlement, one dependent on another. In the case of Tavistock, this may have been *Mary Tavy* and *Peter Tavy*, now two villages on either side of the river, but originally one settlement known simply as *Tavy*. The villages are so named from the respective dedications of their churches to St *Mary* and St *Peter*.

Tay Scotland's longest river has a name that may mean 'strong one' or 'silent one', from a conjectural Celtic name *Tausos*. The river in turn gave the names of *Loch Tay*, the Fife town of *Tayport*, and the administrative region of *Tayside*.

Taylor The widely-found name was originally an occupational one for a tailor, as it implies.

Taylor Institution The Oxford University modern languages centre was established in 1845 with a bequest from Sir Robert *Taylor* (1714–1788) for 'a foundation for the teaching and improving the European languages'. The reason for the bequest was not known and was disputed. Hence the delay in the actual founding of the *Taylorian*, as it is popularly known.

Tbilisi The capital of Georgia derives its name from Georgian *tbili*, 'warm', alluding to the natural warm springs here. The city was long familiar as *Tiflis*, a Turkish corruption of the original name.

TCP The proprietary brand of antiseptic has a name that is perhaps an abbreviation of an original chemical constituent, the most likely being *t*richloro*p*henylmethyliodisalicyl. However, some sources claim that the name comprises the initials of the chemist who invented the product, *T*heodore *C*adwallader *P*arry.

Teachers The brand of whisky takes its name from William *Teacher* (1811–1876), a Scottish tailor who acquired a grocery business in Glasgow in 1836 and became a wine and spirit merchant, blending his own whisky and selling it in a chain of 'dram shops'.

Teardrop Explodes, The The British new wave rock group, formed in Liverpool in 1978, took their name from a caption in the science fiction comic *Marvel*.

Tears for Fears The British new wave pop group, formed in 1981, took their name from Arthur Janov's book on primal therapy, *Prisoners of Pain*, in which the sufferer is told how to confront worries and causes of anxiety and abolish them by shedding 'tears for fears'.

Technicolor The colour cinematography process has a name that is a contraction of *technical color*. It dates from 1917, when the *Technicolor* Motion Picture Corporation of Boston, Massachusetts, founded two years earlier, produced the first film using a patent two-colour process. The first *Technicolor* film using a three-colour process was the Disney cartoon *Flowers and Trees* (1932). The spelling of *color* attests to the American origin of the name.

Teddington The name of what is now a district of Richmond on the Thames west of central London means 'farm of *Tudda*'s people'. It is thus a name similar to that of PADDINGTON, among others.

Tees The well-known river of the north of England has a name that is probably of Celtic origin, perhaps meaning 'boiling one', 'seething one', alluding to its many waterfalls and rapids and its strong current.

Teflon The patent non-stick coating used for cooking vessels derives its name from a contraction of the name of the thermoplastic material used to make it, poly*tetrafluoro*ethyl*ene*.

Tegucigalpa The capital of Honduras takes its name from Indian words meaning 'silver mountain', alluding to the nearby silver mines.

Teheran The name of the capital of Iran probably means simply 'flat', 'level', 'lower', referring to the location of the city in the foothills of the Elburz Mountains.

Tehuantepec, Isthmus of The name of the narrowest part of southern Mexico represents Nahuatl *tecuani*, 'beast (of prey)', probably denoting some totemic animal, and *tepetl*, 'mountain'. *Cp.* POPOCATÉPETL.

Teignmouth The Devon seaside resort takes its name from the river *Teign*, at whose *mouth* it lies. The river's name is almost certainly Celtic in origin, and probably means simply 'river'.

Tel Aviv The well-known city and port in western Israel was founded in 1909 and given the name of a Babylonian city mentioned in the Bible: 'Then I came to them of the captivity at Tel-abib, that dwelt by the river of Chebar, and I sat where they sat, and remained there astonished among them seven days' (*Ezekiel* 3.15). The reference is to a colony of deported Jews, one of whom is Ezekiel himself. The biblical city has a Hebrew name meaning 'spring hill', from *tel*, 'hill' and *avīv*, 'spring' (the season). The latter was the former name of the month of Nisan in the Jewish calendar: 'This day came ye out in the month Abib' (*Exodus* 13.4). The official name of the Israeli city is Tel Aviv-JAFFA, since it incorporated the latter city in 1950.

Telemachus The son of Odysseus and Penelope in Greek mythology has a name that means 'fighter from afar', from Greek *tēle*, 'far' and *makhē*, 'battle', 'fight'. This could be taken to refer to his 'fighting from afar' on behalf of his father, who was engaged in the Trojan war many miles from his native Ithaca. Another son of Odysseus was named *Telegonus*, 'born far off', referring to his birth on the island of Aeaea, also a long way from home.

Telford The Shropshire New Town, designated in 1963, is one of the few New Towns in Britain to have a new name. It derives from that of the Scottish civil engineer Thomas *Telford* (1757–1834), who was appointed surveyor of Shropshire in 1786 and who is famous for designing the Caledonian Canal in Scotland and the suspension bridge from mainland Wales to Anglesey over the Menai Strait. His own name happens to suggest a place-name. It has nothing to do with *ford*, however, but is Norman French, meaning 'iron cutter', from words that gave modern French *taille*, 'cut' and *fer*, 'iron'. This chances to be appropriate for a man who was a noted engineer.

Temirtau The town in Kazakhstan has a name that means 'mountain of iron', from Kazakh *temir*, 'iron' (*cp*. TAMERLANE) and *tau*, 'mountain'. The reference is not to an actual mountain but to the huge iron works here, set up in the Second World War. The town arose in 1934 and was originally known as *Samarkandsky*.

Temple The name was frequently given to a person who worked at or lived in one of the houses ('temples') held by the KNIGHTS TEMPLAR. In some cases the named person could have been a foundling baptized at the TEMPLE CHURCH, London. As a Scottish name, the origin was frequently in the place-name *Temple*, a village south of Edinburgh that was the local headquarters of the *Knights Templar*.

Temple, The The name is a composite one for the two great inns of court in London, the Inner and Middle *Temple*, that serve as a law school and that call candidates to the bar. They are so named since they stand on the site of the headquarters of the KNIGHTS TEMPLAR.

Temple Church The famous 12th-century London church, with its round nave, is so named as it serves the inns of court in the TEMPLE. It was modelled on the Church of the Holy Sepulchre in Jerusalem, the sacred object of protection of the KNIGHTS TEMPLAR.

Tenby The Welsh seaside resort near Pembroke has a name that is identical to that of DENBIGH, although in a spelling apparently influenced by the Vikings. It thus means the same: 'little fort', from Welsh *din*, 'fort' and *bych*, 'little'. The fort in question stood on Castle Hill, the rocky headland where the ruins of Tenby castle are today.

10cc The British pop group, formed in Manchester in 1972, were so named by the pop producer Jonathan King with reference to the average male semen ejaculation of 9cc, implying that the musicians were 'better than average'.

Tenerife The Spanish island off the northwest coast of Africa, the largest of the Canary Islands, takes its name from its volcano, now known as *Pico de Tenerife*. This represents a former native name *Chinerfe*. The meaning of the name is uncertain, but 'white mountain' has been proposed. Its Roman name was *Nivaria*, 'snowy'.

Tennant The name originally applied to a farmer who was the *tenant* of a local lord of the manor, paying him by rent or by service. This was the standard system in medieval feudal England, in which all land ultimately belonged to the king.

Tennessee The American state takes its name from the river, a tributary of the Ohio, that rises in it and flows southwest from it into Alabama. Its own name represents Cherokee *Tanasi* (or some similar spelling), probably meaning simply 'river'.

Tenterden The town in Kent near Ashford has a name meaning 'swine pasture for the Thanet people'. The last part of the name represents Old English *denn*, 'woodland pasture', especially a pasture for pigs. The first part of the name represents that of the Isle of THANET. A portion of land at Tenterden must have been granted to a community of people from there.

10,000 Maniacs The American new wave group was formed in Jamestown, New York, in 1981. Their name resulted from an apparent mishearing of the title of a B-movie horror film, *12,000 Maniacs*.

Ten Years After The British progressive rock group was formed in Nottingham in 1965 as *The Jaybirds*. The following year they changed their name to *Ten Years After*, a reference to the founding of rock 'n' roll in 1956. The name is one of several patterned on Dumas' historical novel *Twenty Years After* (1845). This was set in Paris in 1645 and was a sequel to *The Three Musketeers* (1844), describing events there 20 years earlier.

Teplice The city in Czechoslovakia, northwest of Prague, has a name deriving from Czech *teplý*, 'warm', 'hot'. The town is a health resort with warm springs. Its German name is *Teplitz*.

Terence The name is historically familiar from the 2nd-century BC Roman comic dramatist, whose full name was Publius *Terentius* Afer. As his *nomen* or clan name, it may have derived from Latin *terere*, 'to rub', 'to wear out', from some original application as a nickname. As a modern English name it is usually regarded as the 'full' form of TERRY, although that is strictly speaking a name of quite different origin.

Teresa *See* THERESA.

Ternopol The Ukrainian town has a name of Greek appearance, such as STAVROPOL or SEBASTOPOL. It is probably not Greek at all, however, but represents Russian *tërn*, 'blackthorn', 'sloe' and *pole*, 'field'. If this is so, the original fort round which the town grew was built in the mid-16th century on a plain where many blackthorn bushes grew.

Terpsichore The muse of the dance and choral song in Greek mythology has a name meaning 'delighting in the dance', from Greek *terpein*, 'to delight' and *khoros*, 'dance'.

Territorial Army The British standing reserve army was originally created in 1907 and was so named because it was organized on a *territorial* or local basis. Its members soon came to be aptly nicknamed the *Terriers* (as distinct from the *Tommies* who were in the regular army).

Terry The modern name, in use by both men and women, is commonly regarded as a pet form of TERENCE or THERESA. In medieval times, however, it was a distinct name of Germanic origin, corresponding to the modern German name *Dietrich* (which itself gave English DEREK). This comprises words meaning respectively 'people', 'tribe' (*cp.* TEUTON) and 'power' (*cp.* RICHARD).

Terrys The brand of chocolate takes its name from Joseph *Terry* (1793–1850), a York apothecary who by the 1840s was running a confectionery distribution business in his native city. The firm he founded was continued by his sons, but did not start making chocolate until 1886.

Tertullian The full name of the 2nd-century BC Carthaginian theologian was Quintus Septimius Florens *Tertullianus*. This *agnomen*, or second *cognomen* (nickname), is traditionally interpreted as meaning 'very ancient', literally 'thrice of the earth', from Latin *ter*, 'three times' and a form of *tellus*, 'earth'. As such, it is directly related to the name *Tullius* (*see* TULLY).

Terylene The make of synthetic polyester fibre or fabric is based on *tere*phthalic acid and eth*ylene* glycol, and takes its name from elements of both these chemicals.

Tesco The name of the familiar High Street foodmarket derives from the first two letters of the surname of the company's founder, Sir John *Co*hen (1898–1979), and the initials of *T. E.* Stockwell, Jack Cohen's tea supplier when he set up as a London street trader in the 1920s.

Tessa The name is generally seen as being a pet form of THERESA, although it may actually be of different origin. In 19th-century literature and music the name is treated as if Italian, so that in both George Eliot's novel *Romola* (1862) and the Gilbert and Sullivan opera *The Gondoliers* (1889) *Tessa* is a *contadina*, or peasant girl. Italians would associate the name with *tessere*, 'to weave'.

Tetley The well-known brand of tea takes its name from two brothers, Joseph *Tetley* (1811–1889) and Edward *Tetley* (b. 1816), who in 1837 set up a partnership as tea dealers in Huddersfield. In 1856 they moved to London to take advantage of the expanding tea trade there. The firm they founded was the first to market tea-bags (in 1952) for home retail consumption.

Teuton The ancient Germanic people, originally from Jutland, have a name that means simply 'people', from a word *theud* to which are related both English DUTCH and German *Deutsch*, 'German'.

Tewkesbury The Gloucestershire town has a name that means '*Tēodec*'s fort', with the Anglo-Saxon personal name followed by Old English *burh*, 'fortified place'.

Texas The southern American state is said to derive its name from an Indian word *techas*, meaning 'friends', 'allies'. The story goes that in 1690 a Spanish monk named Damian was greeted on his arrival here with cries of *techas! techas!* as a form of greeting.

Thackeray The name derives from that of the former village of *Thackray* west of Harrogate, North Yorkshire, where it is now submerged in Fewston Reservoir. Its name means 'reedy corner', from Old Norse *thak*, 'thatching', 'reeds' and *rá*, 'corner'.

Thaddeus In the New Testament, the name is that of one of the apostles: 'Lebbæus, whose surname was Thaddæus' (*Matthew* 10.3). It is traditionally said to be a form of the Greek name that became English THEODORE.

Thailand The kingdom in southeast Asia takes its name from its indigenous population, the *Thais*. Their name means 'free people', from Thai *tha*, 'to be free'. Their own name for their country is *prathesthay*, 'land of free men', with *prathes* meaning 'land', 'country'.

Thalia The name of the muse of comedy and pastoral poetry in Greek mythology derives from Greek *thallein*, 'to bloom', 'to flourish'.

Thame The Oxfordshire town near Aylesbury takes its name from the river on which it stands. The river's name in turn is directly related to that of the THAMES, so has the same origin and meaning.

Thames Britain's best-known river, on which London stands, has a name that probably derives from a Celtic root element meaning either simply 'river' or else more specifically 'dark one'. Toponymists are still disputing which of these origins is the more likely. The 'dark' school point to words in other languages that have this meaning, such as Sanskrit *tamisra*, 'darkness', Latin *tenebrae*, 'shades', 'shadows', Irish *teimhe*, 'darkness', Russian *ten*', 'shadow' and *tëmnyy*, 'dark', and so on. On the other hand, the frequency of the many related river names in Britain suggests that a meaning 'river' is more likely. They include the following: *Taff* (*see* LLANDAFF), *Tamar* (Cornwall/Devon), *Tame* (*see* TAMWORTH), *Tavy* (*see* TAVISTOCK), *Teviot* (Scotland).

Thames and Hudson The British publishing house, noted for its books on art, was founded in 1949 in London and New York simultaneously with the aim of finding readers on both sides of the Atlantic. Its name reflects its Anglo-American origin, as the THAMES and the HUDSON are the rivers on which the two cities respectively stand.

Thanet, Isle of The easternmost peninsula of Kent has an ancient name, known to the Romans as *Ranatis* or *Tanatus*. The origin is in a Celtic root element *Tan* meaning 'bright', 'fire', related to modern Welsh *tân*, 'fire'. A 'fire' reference may have been to a beacon here; a 'bright' reference to the exposed location of the region, with the North Sea on one side and the English Channel on the other. If the latter is correct, the name of *Thanet* mirrors that of SHEERNESS, on the north coast of Kent. Thanet was a true island until at least the 16th century, and in the first edition of the *Encyclopaedia Britannica* (1771) is described as 'a little island of east Kent, formed by the branches of the Stour and the sea'.

Thanksgiving Day The annual national holiday, celebrated on the fourth Thursday of November in the United States and the second Monday of October in Canada, is a day of *thanskgiving* to God for the harvest and for other blessings of the past year. It originated in 1621, when William Bradford, governor of the Massachusetts Bay colony, invited local Indians to join the Pilgrim Fathers for a three-day festival of games and feasting in gratitude for the natural bounty of the season. Its nearest British equivalent, although on nothing like the same national scale, is the *Harvest Festival*, held as a special service of thanksgiving in many churches in late September or early October.

Thatched House Lodge The house in Richmond Park, Surrey, since 1963 the home of Princess Alexandra and her husband, was built in the 1670s as a *lodge* for two keepers of the park. It was then redesigned and enlarged, and in 1771 given its present name, for its high-pitched *thatched* roof.

Thatcher The name, as it implies, was originally an occupational one for a thatcher, a craftsman who covered roofs with straw.

The, The The British pop group, formed in London in 1980, took a name that parodied the many rock group names beginning *The*.

Theatre Royal There are three London theatres of the name. The *Theatre Royal*, Drury Lane, was founded in 1663 under letters patent granted by Charles II. The *Theatre Royal*, Haymarket, better known as COVENT GARDEN, was given its name as a courtesy title by virtue of a patent for performances in the summer only granted by George III in 1776. The *Theatre Royal*, Stratford East, opened in 1884, adopting a name that by then had become virtually generic for any theatre. The local newspaper, *The Stratford Express*, commented on the occasion as follows:

> The so-called Theatre Royal, Stratford has been opened this week. We are not aware of any solid ground for the adoption of the 'Royal' title and if this is a prophecy it is rather a hardy one. If it is used to give an impression that the management desires to give only good plays and make the theatre really desirable to Stratford, we hail the promise with pleasure.

The following is a list of noted theatres outside London that had or have the name *Theatre Royal*. The town name alone is given in most cases, with the year of the theatre's opening or adoption of the name. Except where stated, all 18th-century theatres were granted the name by royal patent of George III (reigned 1760–1820). A different name means that the royal name was temporarily adopted within the years given. ADELPHI THEATRE, London (1829–67), Astley's Amphitheatre, London (1862–72), Bath (1768), Brighton (1866), Bristol (1778), Bury St Edmunds (1845), Exeter (1st *c.* 1828, closed 1885; 2nd 1886, closed 1887; 3rd 1889, closed 1962), John Street Theatre, New York (1775–81, during the American Revolution), Lincoln (1893), Manchester (1775), Newcastle upon Tyne (1788), Norwich (1768), Nottingham (*c.* 1760), Windsor (1778, but only by virtue of being in a royal town), York (1769).

Thebes There are two ancient cities of the name, one in Egypt, the other in Greece. The Egyptian city, on the site of the present LUXOR and at various times the country's capital, derives its name from Semitic *teba*, 'chest', 'box'. Its Egyptian name was *Wāset*, from the sacred *was* or sceptre. It was also *Nīt* or *Nīūt*, meaning 'city' (*i.e.* of the god Amon). This name gave its biblical name of *No* (*Jeremiah* 46.25). At one time its Greek name was *Diopolis*, 'city of Zeus'. It gave its name to its Greek namesake, the chief city of Boeotia, founded by the Phoenician Cadmos but destroyed in the 4th century BC by Alexander the Great.

Thelma The name seems to have been introduced, if not actually invented, by the popular writer Marie Corelli for the heroine of her novel *Thelma, Princess of Norway* (1887). Despite the character's nationality, however, the name is not Scandinavian, and it may have been designed to represent Greek *thelēma*, 'wish', 'will'.

Themistocles The famous 5th-century BC Athenian statesman has a name that means 'glory of *Themis*', from the name of the Greek goddess of justice, itself meaning 'law', 'right', and *kleos*, 'glory'.

Theobald The name is of Germanic origin, representing a combination of *theud*, 'people', 'tribe' and *bald*, 'bold', 'brave'. The first part of the name has been influenced by the many names beginning *Theo-* meaning 'God'. *Cp.* THEODORE.

Theocritus The name of the Greek poet of the 3rd century BC means 'divine judge', from *theos*, 'god' and *kritēs*, 'judge'.

Theodore The name means 'gift of God', from Greek *theos*, 'god' and *dōron*, 'gift'. It corresponds exactly to the feminine name DOROTHY, with the two elements reversed. Its direct feminine equivalent is *Theodora*. The name *Theodosia* is similar in meaning, from *theos* and *dōsis*, 'giving'. The surname *Theodosius* is of the same origin. *Crockford's Clerical Directory* for 1971–72 lists three Anglican priests of the name, a father and his two sons.

Theophilus The name is familiar from the New Testament for the addressee of *St Luke's gospel* ('most excellent Theophilus') and the *Acts of the Apostles* ('The former treatise have I made, O Theophilus'). It represents a combination of Greek *theos*, 'god' and *philos*, 'friend', so was a patently appropriate name for the early Christians, who could interpret it as either 'friend of God' or 'befriended by God'.

Theophrastus The 3rd-century BC Greek philosopher has a name that means 'divine guide', from *theos*, 'god' and *phrastēr*, 'teller', 'informer'.

Theresa The name is of uncertain or at best problematic origin. There are two competing theories to account for it. One derives the name from the Greek island of *Thera*, said to have been the birthplace in the 5th century of St *Theresa*, wife of St Paulinus, bishop of Nola. The other takes the name from Greek *therizein*, 'to reap', 'to harvest', perhaps denoting fecundity. The name was made famous by two later saints, one Spanish, the other French, respectively St *Teresa* of Ávila (1515–1582) and St *Thérèse* of Lisieux (1873–1897). The Spanish saint popularized the spelling of the name as *Teresa*.

Thermidor The 11th month of the French republican calendar, corresponding to the period from 20 July to 18 August, has a name meaning 'gift of heat', from Greek *thermē*, 'heat' and *dōron*, 'gift'.

Thermopylae The narrow mountain pass in ancient Greece, scene of a famous battle of 480 BC in which the Greeks fought (and lost to) the Persians, has a name that means 'hot gates', from Greek *thermos*, 'hot' and *pulai*, the plural of *pulē*, 'gate', 'door'. The reference is to the hot sulphur springs here.

Thermos The well-known make of vacuum flask has a name that is a straight adoption of the Greek word *thermos*, 'hot'. The name has been legally generic for any make of vacuum flask in the United States since 1963, but in Britain remains a registered trade mark.

Theseus The name of the famous hero of Attica in Greek mythology is traditionally interpreted as 'orderer', 'settler', from

tithenai, 'to place', the source of modern English *thesis*. *Cp.* THETIS.

Thespis The 6th-century BC Greek poet, famed for introducing the first actor into plays (instead of the earlier choruses), has a name that derives directly from Greek *thespis*, 'inspired', 'wonderful'. It was *Thespis* who gave the English term *thespian* for an actor.

Thessalonians The two books of the New Testament, with the full title *The First (Second) Epistle of Paul the Apostle to the Thessalonians*, contain the addresses of St Paul to the Christian community he had founded in THESSALONÍKI.

Thessaloníki The well-known port in northeast Greece, familiar under its Latin name of *Thessalonica* and its shorter English name of *Salonika*, was founded in 316 BC by the Macedonian king Cassander who named it for his wife *Thessaloníkē*, sister of Alexander the Great. Her own name means 'victory of THESSALY', from Greek *Thessalia*, 'Thessaly' and *nikē*, 'victory'.

Thessaly The region of east central Greece has a name of Illyrian origin but unknown meaning.

Thetford The Norfolk town, at the confluence of the rivers Thet and Little Ouse, has a name that means 'people's ford', from Old English *thēod*, 'people', 'tribe' and *ford*, 'ford'. The reference was probably to a public ford or to an important and frequently used one. The ford itself would probably have been over the Little Ouse rather than the Thet, and may have been just below the present Bridge Street, where the river divides into two, thus affording narrower channels to cross. The *Thet* takes its name from that of *Thetford* itself.

Thetis The name of the mother of Achilles in Greek mythology is usually interpreted as meaning 'placer', 'setter', from *tithenai*, 'to lay down'. *Cp.* THESEUS.

Thingvellir The historic site in southwest Iceland, the meeting place of the *Althing* (parliament) from the 10th to the 18th century, takes its name from *thing*, 'assembly' and *vella*, 'to well', 'to gush', referring to the geysers nearby. The Republic of Iceland was proclaimed here in

1944. *Cp.* the TYNWALD, the parliament of the Isle of Man.

Thin Lizzy The Irish heavy metal group, formed in Dublin in 1969, adopted a name that was an adaptation of *Tin Lizzy*, a colloquial name for an old car.

Third World The countries of Africa, Asia and Latin America are often commonly so designated, originally by contrast with the 'First World', or western bloc (non-Communist) countries, and 'Second World', or eastern (Communist) countries, headed respectively by the United States and the (former) Soviet Union.

Thirty Years War The name is that of the major conflict between many countries of central Europe that lasted from 1618 to 1648 and that resulted in the collapse of large areas of Germany.

Thistlethwaite The name derives from that of a parish of Lancaster, Lancashire. The place-name means 'thistle meadow'. *Cp.* THWAITES.

Thomas The name is familiar from the New Testament as that of one of the disciples: 'Thomas, which is called Didymus' (*John* 11.16), also known as 'doubting Thomas', since he did not believe in the resurrection of Jesus until he had physical proof. His name represents Aramaic *Te'ōma*, 'twin', and this is also the meaning of his alternative name *Didymus*, from Greek *didumos*, literally 'double'.

Thomas à Kempis The 15th-century German monk took his name from his birthplace, now *Kempen* near Cologne. His original surname was *Hummerken* or *Hemerken*. He spent most of his life in Holland.

Thomas Aquinas *See* AQUINAS.

Thomas Cup The international badminton trophy, awarded every three years, was donated in 1939 by Sir George *Thomas* (1881–1972), former All England Badminton Champion and president of the International Badminton Federation.

Thompson The name means 'son of THOMAS', with the added *p* reflecting the pronunciation. The spelling *Thomson* is common in Scotland.

Thompson Twins, The The British new wave rock group, formed in Sheffield in 1977, took their name from the characters in the *Tintin* cartoons by Hergé. The group started out with four members, none named Thompson.

Thomson Holidays The well-known travel agents take their name from the famous newspaper magnate Roy Herbert *Thomson*, first Baron Thomson of Fleet (1894–1976), who launched the firm in 1971.

Thor The name of the Norse god of thunder derives from Old Norse *thōrr*, actually meaning 'thunder'. *See also* THURSDAY.

Thorn *See* TORUŃ.

Thorn EMI The familiar electrical and record company takes the first part of its name from Jules *Thorn* (1899–1980), an Austrian born gas engineer who came to Britain and set up in 1926 as a distributor of electric lamps and radio valves. The second part of the name represents the initials of *Electrical* and *Musical Industries*, the company taken over by *Thorn* Electrical Industries (as it became) in 1979.

Thornton The common surname derives from the equally common place-name meaning 'thorn enclosure', from Old English *thorn*, 'thorn bush' and *tūn*, 'enclosure', 'settlement'.

Thorpe The name comes from any of the places named *Thorpe* or ending in -*thorpe*, such as Cow*thorpe*, Ravens*thorpe* or *Thorpe* Willoughby, all in Yorkshire. The derivation is Old Norse *thorp*, 'hamlet', 'village'.

Thorshavn The capital of the Faeroe Islands has a name meaning 'THOR's port', from the name of the Norse god of thunder and Faeroese *havn*, 'harbour', 'port'.

Thoth The name of the god of wisdom, reckoning and learning in Egyptian mythology is a Greek form of the ancient Egyptian name *Djeheuty*, based on a root word meaning simply 'god'. *See also* HERMES TRISMEGISTUS.

Thousand Guineas The annual horse race for fillies at Newmarket was first run in 1814 and is named for the prize awarded to the winner (with an original value of £1050). Its full name of *One Thousand Guineas* distinguishes it from the TWO THOUSAND GUINEAS.

Thousand Islands The name is that of a group of about 1500 islands in the St Lawrence River on the border between the United States and Canada.

Thrace The ancient country in the eastern Balkan Peninsula derives its name from its native inhabitants. the *Thracians*. Their own name may represent Semitic *raqiwa*, 'firmament'. *See also* TRACY.

Threadneedle Street The well-known street in the City of London, the site of the Bank of England, has a name that has been explained as deriving from the *three needles* that were the sign of the needle-makers' company. But although *Three needle Street* is recorded for it in 1598, *Thred-needle-street* is found in 1616, and it seems likely the latter is the true origin. The name could have applied to a narrow street or to one where children played the game of 'thread the needle', passing under one another's raised arms. On the other hand, it has to be admitted that the needle-makers' sign is more commercially appropriate for the region that became London's business and financial centre.

Three Dog Night The American pop group, formed in 1968, took their name from a colourful Australian expression referring to a very cold night in the outback, when a sleeper needs the company of three dogs to keep warm.

3M The brand of adhesive tape and related products is an abbreviated form of the American maker's original name, the *M*innesota *M*ining and *M*anufacturing Company, founded in Two Harbors, Minnesota in 1902 with the aim of mining corundum.

Thrower The name was occupational, describing a person who *threw* silk, that is, made silk thread from raw silk. In later medieval times the name also applied to a potter, who *threw* clay.

Thucydides The famous 5th-century BC Athenian historian has a name (in the original Greek *Thoukudidēs*) that probably derives from some earlier personal name of obscure form and meaning.

Thule Famous as the region that ancient geographers believed to be the northernmost land in the world, *ultima Thule*, 'the final Thule', has a name that may derive from Greek *tholos*, 'mud', 'slime' or possibly *tēle*, 'far'. Other theories take it from a Celtic word *thuai*, 'north', or from *Thulus*, the name of a legendary king. It is not certain where *Thule* actually was. It may have been Iceland or one of the Shetland Islands. The United States Air Force base of the name in northwest Greenland was set up as a Danish trading post in 1910.

Thummim *See* URIM.

Thuringia The region of southern Germany takes its name from its indigenous inhabitants, the *Thoringi* or *Thuringi*, whose own name may relate to the Indoeuropean root element *dur*, 'current'.

Thursday The fifth day of the week has a name that means 'THOR's day', from its dedication to the Germanic god of thunder.

Thurso The Scottish town and port near Wick takes its name from the river at the mouth of which it stands. The river's own name may mean 'bull river', from a Celtic root element related to Greek *tauros* and Latin *taurus* with Old Norse *á*, 'river' added. This would describe a river that 'roars' and that is 'headstrong', like a bull.

Thwaites The name originally applied to a person who lived by a *thwaite*, a clearing or meadow, or who came from a place with this word (Old Norse *thveit*) in its name, such as Mickle*thwaite* ('big meadow') near Wigton in Cumbria.

Tia Maria The brand of coffee-flavoured liqueur has a Spanish name that literally means 'Aunt Mary'. The story goes that a Spanish servant girl in Jamaica married a British army officer some time in the 17th century and subsequently passed an ancient family recipe for a cordial down to her children. The drink was named for her, and when the recipe came to light some 300 years later, it was adapted to make the present liqueur. Compare the name of the sherry *Tio Pepe*, from the Spanish equivalent of 'Uncle Joe'.

Tiananmen Square The central square of Peking (Beijing) derives its name from that of the *Tiananmen*, 'Gate of Heavenly Peace', from Chinese *tiān*, 'heaven', *ān*, 'peace' and *mén*, 'gate'.

Tianjin The city in northeast China derives its name from Chinese *tiān*, 'heaven', 'day' and *jīn*, 'ford'. The city is on the river Hai Ho. The name is also spelled *Tientsin*.

Tian Shan The great mountain range of central Asia, crossing the border between Russia and China, has a name meaning 'heavenly mountain', from Chinese *tiān*, 'heaven', 'day' (*cp*. TIANANMEN SQUARE) and *shān*, 'mountain'.

Tiber The name of the famous river on which Rome stands traditionally derives from that of *Tiberinus*, a king of Alba Longa who was drowned in it. But its true source is more likely to be in the Celtic root element *dubr*, 'water' that lies behind the name of DOVER, among other places.

Tiberias, Lake The alternative name for the Sea of Galilee derives from that of the Roman emperor *Tiberius*, for whom it was named in 26 AD by Herod Antipas. The emperor's own name represents that of the river TIBER.

Tibesti The mountain range in northwest Chad, in the central Sahara, takes its name from that of a Berber people here. It is said to mean 'bird', referring either to their 'cheeping' or whistling voices, or to their rapid running.

Tibet The Tibetans' name for their country, an autonomous region of northwest China, is *bod* or *bodyul*, literally '*Bod* land', with the people's name of uncertain meaning. This was eventually corrupted, under Chinese then subsequently Arab influence, to *Tibet*. The Chinese name of Tibet is *xī-zàng*, 'treasure of the west'.

Tientsin *See* TIANJIN.

Tierra del Fuego The archipelago at the southern extremity of South America has a Spanish name meaning 'land of fire'. The Portuguese navigator Ferdinand Magellan discovered the region in 1520, and he named it for the many fires he saw burning here, either as camp fires on the land or as navigational lights on boats.

Tiffany The name represents the regular medieval English form of Greek *Theophania*, 'EPIPHANY'. As such, it was a suitable name for girls born on or around this Christian festival (6 January). The original Greek name has the literal sense 'divine manifestation' or 'appearing of God', from *theos*, 'god' and *phainein*, 'to show'. The name has been popularly promoted in modern times by the famous New York jewellers, TIFFANY'S, largely through the film *Breakfast at Tiffany's* (1961) starring Audrey Hepburn as the main character, the call girl Holly Golightly.

Tiffany's The fashionable New York department store takes its name from Charles L. *Tiffany* (1812–1902), who went to New York from Connecticut in 1837 and with a partner opened a fancy goods store on Lower Broadway. In 1848 he began manufacturing the jewellery for which the store became famous.

Tiflis *See* TBILISI.

Tigris The well-known river of southwest Asia has a name that derives from Old Persian *Tigrā*, 'arrow', referring to its rapid current. Its Sumerian name, *Tigrušu*, was similar, from *tig*, 'spear', *ru*, 'to conquer', 'to overthrow', and *usu*, 'to capture', 'to catch'. It was thus the 'river running with a conquering spear'.

Tilburg The city in the southern Netherlands takes its name from Dutch *Til*, a pet form of the personal name *Theodulus*, and *burg*, 'castle', so that it is basically a 'fortified city dedicated to St Theodulus'. The saint's name is Greek in origin, meaning 'slave of God', from *theos*, 'God' and *doulos*, 'slave'.

Tilbury The Essex town and passenger port, on the estuary of the Thames, has a name that means '*Tila*'s fort', with the Anglo-Saxon personal name followed by Old English *burh*, 'fortified place'.

Tiler The name was originally occupational, applied to a tiler. In medieval times his work would have involved tiling floors and pavements more than roofs.

Timbuktu The town in central Mali, famous as a Muslim centre and for its legendary remoteness, derives its name from a Tuareg word meaning 'old', 'ancient'. It was founded in the 5th century of the Hegira in the Muslim calendar, *i.e.* in about 1100. The former popular spelling of the name was *Timbuctoo*.

Times, The The well-known newspaper was the brainchild of John Walter, a 45-year-old bankrupted Lloyds underwriter turned printer, who in May 1784 wrote to his patron, Benjamin Franklin, then the American minister in Paris, 'I am going to publish a Newspaper'. On 1 January 1785 he duly produced the first issue of *The Daily Universal Register*. It comprised four hand-printed pages and sold for 2½ pence. Its circulation gradually rose, and for issue No 940, appearing on 1 January 1788, Walter changed its cumbersome title to *The Times*, as which it has remained ever since. The word *times* here relates to the current period with regard to its prevailing conditions, as in such phrases as 'up with the times' or 'behind the times'.

Times Square The famous New York square, formed by the intersection of Broadway, 42nd Street and Seventh Avenue, takes its name from the building here that formerly housed the offices of the *New York Times* and that still transmits news on its display of electric lights.

Timişoara The city in western Romania has a name meaning 'fort on the *Temes*', with the river name followed by Romanian *vár*, 'fort'. The river has a name (pronounced 'Temesh') that is probably related to that of the THAMES, *which see* for a consideration of its origin.

Timor The island in Indonesia, in the Malay Archipelago, has a name that represents Malay *timur*, 'east', referring to its geographical location to the east of Java and Sumatra. The former Portuguese province of *East Timor*, annexed by Indonesia in 1975, thus had the native name of *Timor Timur*.

Timotei The brand of shampoo, launched in Sweden in 1975, takes its name from the Finnish word for *timothy* grass, grown for hay and pasture. The shampoo does not actually contain the grass, but its name was felt to be appropriate for a cosmetic product that has associations of 'country freshness'. The grass itself is named for *Timothy* Hanson, who brought it to colonial Carolina in the early 18th century.

Timothy The name is that of a companion of St Paul in the New Testament. It is Greek in origin, from *timē*, 'price', 'worth', 'honour', and *theos*, 'god', so has a Christian interpretation 'honouring God' or 'honoured

by God'. Paul refers to *Timothy* as 'my own son in the faith' (1 *Timothy* 1.2).

Tina The first name, popular from the 1960s, originated as a short form of a name such as *Christina*. It perhaps also came to be subconsciously associated with *teenager*.

Tintagel The Cornish village near Camelford, famous for its castle, the legendary stronghold of king Arthur, has a name that probably derives from Cornish *din*, 'fort' and *tagell*, 'throat', 'constriction'. This would refer to the ruins of the castle on the peninsula known as Tintagel Island and the rocky gorge that separates it from the mainland.

Tintern Abbey The ruined medieval abbey by the river Wye near Chepstow in South Wales has a name that means 'king's fort'. The origin is in Celtic words related to modern Welsh *dinas*, 'fort' and *teyrn*, 'monarch', 'sovereign'.

Tintin The boy detective in the children's cartoon books by 'Hergé' (real name Georges Rémi) first appeared in the Belgian newspaper *Le Vingtième Siècle* in 1929. His name is a near meaningless French pet name that might be rendered in English as 'Tinker'. It is odd that his un-English name was not given an appropriate equivalent in the English versions of the books, in which the dog *Milou* appears as 'Snowy', for example, and the twin plain-clothes policemen *Dupont et Dupond* become 'Thomson and Thompson'. In the German editions, Tintin is *Tim*.

Tiplady The name arose as a nickname for a 'ladykiller', a man who scored a sexual success with a woman of higher rank than himself. The variant form *Toplady* also exists.

Tipperary The familiar Irish town, in the county of the same name, has a name that is an English spelling of its Irish name. This is *Tiobraid Árann*, 'well of the *Ara*', the latter being the river on which the town stands. The river's own name is that of the territory here, and means 'ridged place', literally 'kidney', as for the ARAN Islands.

Tirana The capital of Albania has a name

that is probably related to those of TUS-CANY and the TYRRHENIAN Sea.

Tiruchchirappalli The city in southern India, formerly familiar as *Trichinopoly*, has a name that is of Malayalam origin meaning 'town of the sacred rock', from *tiru*, 'holy', *sita*, 'rock' and *palli*, 'town'. The city is famous for its rock fortress. The conventional English form *Trichinopoly* looks like an attempt to give the name a Greek origin, as if from *Trikhinopolis*. This, if it meant anything, would mean 'city of hair'. (Such a sense is not as bizarre as it might seem: *see* HALIFAX, for example.)

Tisiphone The name is that of one of the three Furies in Greek mythology, and means 'avenging murder', from *tisis*, 'penalty', 'punishment' and *phonē*, 'murder'. The main role of the Furies was to avenge the murder of members of a family by punishing the murderer or murderers. They drove Orestes and Alcmeon insane, for example, for murdering their respective mothers.

Tissot The make of Swiss watch is named for Charles-Félicien *Tissot* (1804–1873) and his son and partner Charles-Émile *Tissot* (1830–1910), who in 1853 founded a watchmaking business near La-Chaux-de-Fonds, not far from the border with France.

Titan The name of the family of giant gods in Greek mythology, the offspring of Gaia and Uranus, is of disputed origin. It is almost certainly pre-Greek and may simply mean 'god'.

Titania The name of the queen of the fairies in Shakespeare's *A Midsummer Night's Dream* (1595) was adopted from Ovid's *Metamorphoses*, in which it is a byname given to Diana, Circe and other goddesses as descendants of the TITANS.

Titicaca, Lake The lake between Peru and Bolivia, in South America, has a name derived by some from Indian (Quechua) *titi*, 'lead' (the metal) and *kaka*, 'mountain chain', and by others from an Aymara word meaning 'rock of the jaguar', referring to its shape.

Titmus The name was originally a nickname for a small or petite person, from *titmouse*, the small songbird.

Titograd The city in southern Yugoslavia, where it is the capital of Montenegro, was so named in 1948 for the Yugoslav president, Marshal *Tito* (1892–1980), with *grad* meaning 'town'. Its former name was *Podgorica*, meaning 'under the mountain', from Serbian *pod*, 'under' and *gora*, 'mountain'.

Titus In the New Testament, *Titus* is a companion of St Paul, with a book named for him as the recipient of one of Paul's letters. His name is Roman in origin, and may derive from Latin *titulus*, 'title (of honour)', implying a person who is specially respected.

Tiverton The Devon town near Exeter has a name meaning 'farm at the double ford', referring to its location at the confluence of the Exe and its tributary, the Loman. The origin is in Old English *twi-*, 'two', *ford*, 'ford' and *tūn*, 'farm'. A 'double ford' is either one with two tracks or two consecutive fords over different rivers (or two branches of a single river). The latter is probably the sense here. *Twerton*, now a western district of Bath, has a name of identical origin, and one that as recently as the 19th century was marked on maps as *Twiverton*. In its case the 'double ford' is over the river Avon, which divides into two there.

Tivoli The town in central Italy, a summer resort in Roman times, has a name of Illyrian origin but uncertain meaning. It has been linked with Albanian *timbi*, 'rock'. Its reputation as a resort caused the name to be adopted for the famous *Tivoli* amusement gardens in Copenhagen.

Tlemcen The city in northwest Algeria has a name that derives from a Berber word meaning 'springs'.

Toamasina The port in eastern Madagascar is said to have a name that derives from Malagasy *tòa*, 'how' and *màsina*, 'salt'. An unlikely tale tells how King Radama I saw the sea for the first time here and, having tasted the water, exclaimed, 'how salty it is!'

Tobago The name of the island in the West Indies, part of the republic of Trinidad and Tobago, was given it by Christopher Columbus. He took it from Haitian *tambaku*, 'pipe', from the strange habit the islanders had of igniting the dried cut leaves of the *tobacco* plant in a pipe and inhaling the toxic fumes.

Tobermory The Scottish resort and port on the island of Mull has a name that means 'St *Mary*'s well', from Gaelic *tiobar*, 'well' and *Moire*, 'Mary'. The well in question is by the ruins of the old chapel to the west of the present town, which was itself founded only in the 18th century by the British Fisheries Society.

Tobias The name is borne by various biblical characters but has come to be specially associated with the story of *Tobias* and the Angel, told in the book of *Tobit* in the Apocrypha. It derives from Hebrew *Tōbhīyāh*, 'Yah is good', *i.e.* 'Jehovah is my well-being'. *Tobit* is the father of *Tobias*, and there seems little doubt that the names are directly related. The most popular name to evolve from that of the biblical character, however, is TOBY (*which see*).

Toblerone The distinctive triangular-shaped chocolates take their name from Charles *Tobler* (1830–1905), a Swiss confectioner from Appenzell, who opened a chocolate shop in Bern in 1868. The final *-one* of the name is the Italian augmentative suffix, indicating a large size. (*Cp. minestrone* soup, which has a name meaning 'large helping'.)

Tobruk The famous Libyan port, a scene of severe fighting in the Second World War, has a name that is a corruption of its original Greek name *Antipurgos*, 'opposite the tower', from *anti*, 'opposite' and *purgos*, 'tower'. The bay here was sheltered from the wind by an island on which a tower stood.

Toby The name is familiar as that of the dog in the Punch and Judy puppet show. The dog may have been so called from a real dog of the name used in the performances at some period. Whether this is so or not, the original dog's name almost certainly derives from that of TOBIAS in the biblical story of 'Tobias and the Angel' in the apocryphal book of *Tobit*, in which the angel is Tobias' travelling companion on a journey to Ecbatana: 'So they went forth both, and the young man's dog went with them' (*Tobit*, 5.16). The story of the two men and their dog was formerly a rival puppet play to that of Punch and Judy.

Toc H The society formed after the First World War with the aim of encouraging Christian fellowship takes its name from the obsolete signalling code for the letters *T* and *H*. These are the initials of *Talbot House*, the society's original headquarters in Poperinghe, Belgium, opened in 1915 as a welfare centre for British troops. The house itself was named commemoratively for Gilbert *Talbot*, brother of the society's founder, Neville *Talbot*. Other letters in the same alphabet were *Ack* (A), *Beer* (B), *Don* (D), *Emma* (M), *Pip* (P) and *Vic* (V). Hence the *ack-ack* or *anti-aircraft* gun of the Second World War.

Todd The name was originally a nickname for a person who resembled a fox in some way, either in appearance (perhaps with pointed features or red hair) or character (such as cunning). The word *tod* for a fox was fairly common in medieval England, but is now found only as a dialect name, or in Scottish use. The same word occurs in the surname *Todhunter*, originally also a nickname, but in this case for a hunter of foxes.

Togliatti The city in western Russia was founded in 1738 as a fortified post on the Volga with the Greek name of STAVROPOL. This means 'city of the cross', and was given to mark the 'christening' (conversion to Christianity) of the Buddhist Kalmuck prince, Peter Taisha, together with some of his compatriots. (The equation between 'cross' and 'christening' is more readily apparent in Russian than in English, as the words for each, respectively *krest* and *kreshcheniye*, are directly related.) In the mid-1950s the site was flooded during construction of the huge V.I. Lenin dam and hydroelectric station, and the town was moved to a higher location. In 1964 it was renamed for the Italian Communist leader Palmiro *Togliatti* (1893–1964).

Togo The republic of western Africa was so named in 1884 by the German explorer Gustav Nachtigal. He adopted it from that of a small coastal village where he had signed a treaty with the indigenous people. The original name of the village, now called *Togoville*, is said to have been *Miayi To Godo*, 'we shall go beyond the hill', although it probably derives more readily from nearby Lake *Togo*, whose own name represents *to*, 'water' and *go*, 'edge', 'shore'.

Tokyo The capital of Japan has a name meaning 'eastern capital', from *tō*, 'east' and *kyō*, 'capital'. It was so named by contrast with KYOTO, the former capital, to the west of it.

Toledo The famous city in central Spain derives its name ultimately from Celtic *tol*, 'hill', 'rise'. The town is situated on a rugged promontory overlooking the river Tagus.

Toliary The port in southwest Madagascar has the Malagasy name of *Tòleara*. Its origin is traditionally explained as follows. A foreign traveller in Madagascar asked a native in a canoe where he was going to land. The man thought he was being asked where there was a mooring place, and replied '*tòly eròa*', 'the moorage there'. This was then corrupted to *Tòleara*.

Tomkins The name means 'son of *Tomkin*', itself a diminutive of THOMAS. *Tompkins* and *Tomkinson* are of the same origin.

Tomsk The city in central Russia takes its name from the river *Tom* on which it lies. The river's own name is of uncertain origin, but may mean simply 'river' or possibly more specifically 'dark one'. It is related to that of the THAMES.

Tonbridge The well-known town in Kent, on the river Medway, has a name that means 'village bridge', from Old English *tūn*, 'village' (modern *town*) and *brycg*, 'bridge'. The reference is to a bridge that led to the original village here from some other part of the manor. *Cp.* TUNBRIDGE WELLS.

Tonga The well-known island kingdom in the southwest Pacific has a name of local origin said to mean either 'island' or 'holy'. It was discovered in 1616 by Dutch explorers. When Captain Cook came here in 1773 he named the archipelago *Friendly Islands*, from the welcome given him by the natives.

Tonkin The former state of northern French Indochina, now a region of northern Vietnam, has a name meaning 'eastern capital', from Vietnamese *dông*, 'east' and *kinh*, 'capital'. The name properly applies to HANOI.

Tonle Sap The lake in west central Cambodia has a name that means 'big lake of fresh water', from Cambodian *tonle*, 'large lake' and *sap*, 'fresh', 'not salt'.

Tonton Macoute The name of the private army of death squads formed by President Duvalier ('Papa Doc') in Haiti in the 1950s is Haitian Creole in origin, but of uncertain meaning. According to some accounts it relates to a legendary evil figure in Haitian voodoo culture who is said to take his victims away when they misbehave. It therefore may mean something like 'bogeyman'.

Tony The name is a short form of ANTHONY, now sometimes given independently. In America it is often associated with the colloquial word *tony* meaning 'fashionable' (*i.e.* having good *tone*). *See also* the theatre award TONY.

Tony The award made annually in the United States since 1947 by the League of New York Theaters for outstanding achievement in some aspect of the theatre takes its name from *Tony*, the pet name of the American actress and producer *Antoinette* Perry (1888–1946).

Tootal The well-known make of menswear is named for Edward *Tootal* (1799–1873), who became a partner in a textile business in Manchester in 1842. Although he gave his name to the company, he was thus not its founder.

Tooting The district of Wandsworth, London, has a name that means '(place of) *Tōta*'s people'. *Tooting Bec* here takes the latter part of its name from the Norman abbey of *Bec*-Hellouin, holders of the manor in medieval times.

Topeka The state capital of Kansas derives its name from a Sioux word said to mean 'a good place to dig potatoes'.

Toplady *See* TIPLADY.

Torah The Jewish name for the PENTATEUCH or for the whole body of Jewish teaching in general derives from the Hebrew word for 'precept', from *yārāh*, 'to instruct'.

Toronto The well-known Canadian city, capital of Ontario, takes its name from an Indian village which was recorded as *Tarantou* on a map of 1656. This is said to derive either from Iroquois *Toron-to-hen*, 'wood in the water', or from a Huron word *Deondo*, 'meeting-place'. The present city was founded in 1793 when Governor John Graves Simcoe moved the capital from Newark (now Niagara) to Toronto Bay and renamed it *York*, in honour of the Duke of *York*, son of George III. It reverted to its original name in 1834.

Torpids The Lent (spring) rowing races at Oxford University, between competing college crews, were originally held between the second crews of the colleges. These were slower than the first or main crews, so were by comparison 'torpid' or relatively sluggish. The races were first held in about 1827.

Torquay The popular Devon coastal resort has a name that means 'Torre quay'. The *quay* here was built in medieval times by monks from nearby *Torre* Abbey, with the abbey itself named after the hill (Old English *torr*, modern *tor*) at the foot of which it lay.

Torrens, Lake The lake in South Australia was discovered in 1839 and named for the English economist, Colonel Robert *Torrens* (1780–1864), one of the founders of the colony of South Australia in 1834.

Torres Strait The strait between Australia and New Guinea was so named in 1769 in memory of the Spanish navigator Luis Váez de *Torres* who discovered it in 1606 when he sailed round New Guinea. At the time he did not realize it was a strait, as he was unaware of the existence of Australia.

Toruń The city in northern Poland was founded by the Teutonic Knights in 1231 and named after *Toron*, the name given by the Crusaders to the Palestinian town of *Tibnin*, one of the principal fiefs of the kingdom of Jerusalem. The city's German name is *Thorn*.

Tory The name was originally applied to Irish guerrillas or outlaws who attacked English settlers from the early 17th century, and derives from a conjectural Irish word *tóraighe*, 'pursuer', implicit in *tóraigheachd*, 'pursuit', from *tóir*, 'to pursue'. The name then came to be used, insultingly at first, of royalists who opposed the exclusion of James, Duke of York, from the royal

succession. Finally, in the 1830s, the successors to the anti-exclusionists, noted for their conservative views, gave birth to the present CONSERVATIVE Party, for whom the name remains today in colloquial and journalistic use.

Toshiba The make of electrical and electronic appliances has a name that is a contraction of the full title of the Japanese manufacturers, the *Tokyo Shiba*ura Electric Company. Shibaura is the region of Tokyo where the company has its headquarters.

Totnes The Devon town at the head of the tidal estuary of the river Dart has a name that means '*Totta*'s headland', referring to the promontory (Old English *næss*) on which the ruins of the medieval castle stand.

Toto The American rock group, formed in Los Angeles in 1978, took a name that was partly a simplification of the real name, Robert *Toteaux*, of lead singer Bobby Kimball, and partly an adoption of the name of the dog in the film *The Wizard of Oz* (1939).

Tottenham The district of Haringey, London, has a name meaning '*Totta*'s village'. *Cp.* TOTNES. *See also* TOTTENHAM COURT ROAD.

Tottenham Court Road The well-known street of west central London originally led to the former manor of *Tottenhale* Court, whose own name means '*Totta*'s corner of land'. The manor house was located near the present Euston Station. Its name became confused with that of TOTTENHAM, further to the north, and subsequently became identical. It is not certain that the *Totta* referred to in each name was one and the same man. Had it not been for *Tottenham*, the name of the street today could well have been something like *Totnal Court Road*.

Tottenham Hotspur The famous London football club was formed in 1882. It was originally known simply as *Hotspur*, taking this name from the fiery Harry HOTSPUR as he appears in Shakespeare's *Richard II* and *Henry IV, Part One*, in which he himself represents the historic Sir Henry Percy (1364–1403), son of the Earl of Northumberland. The name was appropriate because not only was 'spirit' a desirable quality for a football team, but because the Percy family were landowners in the Tottenham district at the time of the club's formation. The team added *Tottenham* to their name in 1885, and the following year set up their headquarters in Tottenham High Road, in the building that later became the offices of White Hart Lane.

Toul The town in northeast France had the Roman name of *Tullum*, deriving from Celtic *tol*, 'hill', 'mountain'.

Toulon The port in southeast France ultimately derives its name from either Celtic *tol*, 'height' or Ligurian *tol* or *tel*, 'spring'. *Cp.* TOULOUSE. In 1793, at the time of the French Revolution, the city was renamed *Port-de-la-Montagne*, 'mountain harbour', referring to the nearby Faron Mountains.

Toulouse The city in southern France had the Roman name of *Tolosa*, probably deriving from Celtic *tol*, 'hill', 'height'. The latter would be the Pyrenean foothills nearby.

Touraine *See* TOURS.

Tourcoing The town in northeast France had the Medieval Latin name of *Thorcunium*. This derives from the Germanic personal name *Thorkun*.

Tournai The city of western Belgium is said to take its name from the Roman personal name *Turnus*, that of a legendary king or leader here.

Tours The town in west central France takes its name from the *Turones*, the Gaulish people who once inhabited the region. Their own name may derive from Celtic *tur*, 'water'. They also gave their name to *Touraine*, the former province of which *Tours* was the capital.

Towcester The town near Northampton takes its name from the river *Tove* on which it stands, with the *-cester* referring to the Roman station (Old English *ceaster*) that was here on Watling Street. The river's name means 'slow one', referring to its winding course.

Tower Hamlets The borough to the east of the City of London has a name that means what it says. It refers to the many former *hamlets* here next to the *Tower* of London and under its jurisdiction. At one time there were as many as 20 such hamlets, but they all gradually merged and unified.

Tower of London The present famous London fortress is clearly much more than just a tower. It takes its name from the stone *tower* that William the Conqueror had built to replace the original temporary fort he had raised soon after the Battle of Hastings in 1066. It is today represented by the *White Tower* that stands at the heart of the fortress. The name is curiously casual when one compares it to the equivalent in other capitals, such as the *Bastille* in Paris or the *Kremlin* in Moscow. Nor did it evolve to include the word *castle*, as found for many other medieval fortresses.

Townley The name is that of a place, the location of *Townley* near Burnley in Lancashire. It means 'settlement by the wood' or 'settlement in the clearing', from Old English *tūn*, 'enclosure', 'settlement' (modern *town*) and *lēah*, 'wood', 'clearing'.

Townsend The name originally applied to someone who lived at the far *end* of a village (Old English *tūn*, 'settlement'), or who came from one of the many places so called.

Toyama The city in central Japan, in Honshu, derives its name from Japanese *to*, 'to be rich', 'to be in good health' and *yama*, 'mountain'.

Toynbee Hall The social service centre in London's East End was founded in 1884 and named for the social philosopher Arnold *Toynbee*, who had died the previous year.

Toyota The make of Japanese car takes its name from the engineer Sakichi *Toyoda* (1894–1952), who in 1929 turned over to his son, Kiichiro *Toyoda*, the proceeds from the sale to a British firm of the patent for an automatic loom he had invented. The son was building a car at the time, so used the funds to further his business. The family were superstitious, however, so in the late 1930s changed the name of the motor company that had developed to *Toyota*. This needed only eight strokes of the pen to write, as against ten for *Toyoda*. Eight is a lucky number for the Japanese.

Toy Symphony The little classical symphony, popular with school orchestras, is so named because it includes parts for a variety of toy instruments, such as cuckoo, trumpet, drum and rattle. It was at one time believed to be by Haydn, but it is now thought to be either by Mozart's father, Leopold Mozart (1719–1787), or by Haydn's younger brother, Michael Haydn (1737–1806).

T'Pau The British rock group, formed in London in 1986, was given its name by its lead singer Carol Decker, a fan of the cult American science fiction television series *Star Trek*. In this, *T'Pau* is the name of a high priestess of the planet Vulcan, played by Celia Lovsky in the episode 'Amok Time'.

Trabzon The port in northeast Turkey, formerly usually known as *Trebizond*, is said to derive its name from Greek *trapeza*, 'table', referring to the shape of the nearby mountain, which has a flat summit. *Cp.* TABLE MOUNTAIN.

Tractarianism The name is an alternative one for the High Church Anglican OXFORD MOVEMENT. It arose from the series of *tracts*, entitled *Tracts for the Times*, that were published from 1833 to 1841 to express the views of the movement.

Tracy The first name originated from the surname. This is itself of Norman origin, from one of the places in the north of France called *Tracy*, such as *Tracy*-le-Mont near Compiègne or *Tracy*-Bocage near Caen. The French place-name comes from the Roman personal name *Thracius*, 'man of THRACE'. The name was popularized by the character *Tracy* Lord played by Grace Kelly in the film *High Society* (1956). It has a suggestion of *tracery*, an unrelated word which nevertheless evokes a desirable delicacy and artistry.

Trafalgar, Battle of The famous naval battle of 1805, in which the French and Spanish fleets were defeated by the English under Nelson, takes its name from the cape of southwest Spain off which it was fought. The cape has an Arabic name, which could represent either *ṭaraf al-ǧarb*, 'end of the west', or *ṭaraf al-aǧarr*, 'end of the column', from *ṭaraf*, 'end', 'edge' and either *ǧarb*, 'west' (*cp.* MAGHREB) or *aǧarr*,

'column', 'pillar'. If the latter, the reference would be to the *Pillars of Hercules*, the two promontories at the eastern end of the Strait of Gibraltar, which according to legend were built by Hercules.

Trafalgar Square London's best-known square was laid out over the period 1829 to 1841 and was named for Nelson's famous victory at the Battle of TRAFALGAR (1805). Nelson himself is commemorated in the *Nelson* Column which dominates the square. It was erected in 1842.

Tragic Symphony Schubert's Symphony No 4 in C minor (1816) was so named by the 19-year-old composer himself, presumably because he felt that the work reflected the unhappy end of his first love affair at this time. The same name was originally given by Mahler to his Symphony No 6 in A major (1904), whose music is deeply pessimistic and full of dark premonitions.

Trajan The famous Roman emperor of the 1st and 2nd centuries AD had the full name of Marcus Ulpius *Traianus*. His inherited *cognomen* (nickname) is a form of *Troianus*, 'of TROY'.

Tralee The Irish town in Co Kerry, at the head of *Tralee* Bay, has a name that means 'strand of the *Lee*', referring to the river that runs into the sea just south of the town. The present name is thus an English spelling of the Irish name, *Trá Lí*, with the first word of this representing Irish *traigh*, 'strand', 'beach'.

Tranmere The district of Birkenhead, Merseyside, has a Scandinavian name meaning 'cranes' sandbank', from Old Norse *trani*, 'crane' (the wading bird) and *melr*, 'sandbank'. Cranes must have frequented the sands that were here by the Mersey at one time.

Transcaucasia The region now represented by Armenia, Azerbaijan and Georgia, south of the CAUCASUS Mountains, has a name meaning 'across the *Caucasus*', from Latin *trans*, 'that side of', 'over' and the name of the mountains. *Cp.* TRANSKEI, TRANSVAAL, TRANSYLVANIA.

Transjordania The name (also *Transjordan*) was in use for what is now the Middle Eastern kingdom of JORDAN from 1921 to 1949. It means 'beyond the

Jordan', as the greater part of the country's territory lies east of this river.

Transkei The Bantu homeland in Cape Province, South Africa, has a name that means 'that side of the *Kei*', from Latin *trans*, 'over', 'across' and *Kei*, the name of the river (usually known as the *Great Kei*) across which it lies from CISKEI, the Bantu homeland that is south of it, 'this side of the Kei'. The name was probably patterned on that of TRANSVAAL.

Transvaal The province of South Africa has a name that means 'beyond the *Vaal*', from Latin *trans*, 'across' and the name of the river VAAL. The reference is to the location of the province to the north of the river, as distinct from Orange Free State, to the south.

Transylvania The historic region of central and northwest Romania has a name that means 'beyond the forest', from Medieval Latin *trans*, 'across' and *sylva*, 'wood', 'forest'. The region is shut in by the Carpathian Mountains to the north and east, the Transylvanian Alps to the south, and Bihor Mountains to the west, the latter being thickly wooded. The German name of the region is *Siebenbürgen*, 'seven forts'. Its Hungarian name is *Erdély*, from *erdő*, 'forest'.

Trappist The branch of the Cistercian order of monks takes its name from its place of origin in 1664, the abbey of La *Trappe*, at Soligny-La-Trappe in northwest France. The place-name itself derives from French *trappe*, 'trap', denoting a place where animals or birds were caught.

Travellers' Club The London club was founded in 1819 as a place of rendezvous for gentlemen who had travelled in a direct line not less than 500 miles (804 km) from London (and outside Britain). In Europe this meant at least as far as Marseille, Venice, Berlin and Copenhagen, but not Paris, Brussels or Frankfurt. Today members are no longer necessarily travellers, however.

Travers The name was originally used of a person who lived by a river crossing, whether a ford or a bridge, or who collected the tolls at such a crossing. The origin is in Old French *travers*, 'passage', 'crossing' (which gave English *traverse*).

Trebilcock The name is Cornish in origin, deriving from the place so called in the parish of Roche, near St Austell. Many Cornish names beginning *Tre-* ('homestead', 'settlement') are followed by a personal name, often that of a local saint. Here, however, the rest of the name appears to represent the word that is now *pillicock*, a term of endearment amounting to 'darling'. Perhaps, in the Celtic manner, this was applied to a particular saint. *Cp.* KILMARNOCK, for example.

Trebizond *See* TRABZON.

Trebor The brand of confectionery has a name that is a reversal of the first name ROBERT. It was taken from *Trebor* Villas, a small row of terraced houses in east London where the firm had its beginnings in about 1910. One of the five founders was himself named *Robert Robertson*, so the name seemed doubly appropriate.

Trefusis The name is Cornish, representing that of a place in the parish of Mylor north of Falmouth. Its own origin lies in Cornish *tre*, 'homestead', 'settlement' and some other word (or name) of uncertain origin.

Trent The name of the well-known Midlands river means literally 'path', from a Celtic root element *sento* related to modern Welsh *hynt*, 'way', Latin *semita*, 'footpath' and French *sentier*, 'path'. The reference is to a river that makes 'paths' off its course, that is, it is liable to flooding. The *Trent* is famous for its spring tides ('neaps') and for its tidal bore ('eagre'). It floods only rarely today because it has been contained by embankments, but at one time it could well have flooded frequently as a result of these tides.

Trent College The boys' public school at Long Eaton, near Nottingham, was founded in 1866 and is so named because it overlooks the valley of the river TRENT.

Trento The name of the city in northern Italy has evolved from its Roman name of *Tridentum*, from Latin *tres*, 'three' and *dens*, 'tooth', referring to a triple-peaked mountain nearby. Hence the adjective *Tridentine* to refer to the city or to the Council of *Trent*, the council of the Roman Catholic Church held here in the mid-16th century to reaffirm traditional Catholic beliefs in the face of rising Protestantism.

Trenton The state capital of New Jersey has a name that represents *Trent's town*, for William *Trent*, the Philadelphia merchant who laid out the town in 1714.

Tresco The second largest of the Isles of Scilly, off mainland Cornwall, has a Cornish name meaning 'elder-tree farm', from *tre*, 'farm' and *scawen*, 'elder'. This was originally not the name of the whole island but of a farm where Tresco Abbey now is.

Trevor The first name derives from the Welsh surname, which itself is from a place-name meaning 'big village' (Welsh *tref*, 'settlement' and a form of *mawr*, 'big'). One such place is the village of *Trevor* on the North Wales coast south of Caernarfon.

T. Rex The British pop duo, formed in 1967, took the original name *Tyrannosaurus Rex*, from the scientific name for a species of dinosaur. The name was shortened to *T. Rex* in 1970.

Tri-ang The well-known toy brand name relates to the fact that the company was founded in 1919 by *three* brothers: W.I., Walter and A.E. Lines. There is also a pun in the name, since a *triangle* is a figure made up of *three lines*.

Trichinopoly *See* TIRUCHCHIRAPPALLI.

Trier The city in western Germany was the capital of the Celtic people known as the *Trevires*, and is named for them. Their own name may represent Celtic *tre*, 'across' (*cp*. Latin *trans*) and *wer*, 'crossing', referring to a crossing-place on the river Moselle here. The French name of the city is *Trèves*.

Trieste The famous port in northwest Italy has a Venetian name meaning 'trade', 'market', derived from Illyrian *terga* and related to Swedish and Russian *torg*, 'place', 'market-place'. Trieste has long been an important trading place and transit port. *Cp*. TÂRGOVISHTE and TURKU.

Trimurti The triad of the three chief gods of later Hinduism, consisting of Brahma the Creator, Vishnu the Sustainer, and Siva the Destroyer, has a composite name meaning 'three forms', from Sanskrit *tri*, 'three' and *mūrti*, 'form'.

Tring The Hertfordshire town near Berkhamsted has a name that means 'tree-covered hillside', from Old English *trēow*, 'tree' and *hangra*, 'wooded hillside' (modern *hanger* in such names as *Oakhanger*). The reference is to the town's location among hills and beech woods. The present name is a much 'smoothed-down' version of the original, which in the 13th century was recorded as *Trehangre*.

Trinidad The well-known island in the West Indies, now part of the republic of Trinidad and Tobago, has a Spanish name meaning 'Trinity'. It was discovered by Christopher Columbus in 1498 and was so named by him either because he arrived on *Trinity* Sunday (that year 10 June) or more likely because three mountain peaks symbolically suggested the Holy *Trinity*.

Trinity College The name is familiar from three university colleges in the British Isles. The oldest is the Cambridge college, endowed by Henry VIII in 1546 when he united two existing colleges, Michaelhouse (founded in 1323) and King's Hall (founded in 1336) to create a new college that would rival his earlier foundation of CHRIST CHURCH, Oxford. The precise reason for the dedication is uncertain, although there is evidence that King's Hall was already dedicated to the Trinity. It is also likely that Henry would have avoided a dedication to a saint in the sensitive world of the Reformation. (*Christ Church* was similarly dedicated to the Godhead, and not to a saint.) Oxford's college of the name was founded in 1555 on the site of the monastic Durham College, whose chapel was dedicated to the Holy *Trinity*. The third college is that of Dublin University, founded in 1590 as 'The College of the Most Holy and and Undivided *Trinity* of Queen Elizabeth'. No other colleges were founded, so that *Trinity College*, Dublin *is* Dublin University. The reason for the dedication to the Holy Trinity remains uncertain: it may have been the personal choice of Elizabeth herself. *Cp*. TRINITY HALL.

Trinity Hall The Cambridge college was founded in 1350 by the bishop of Norwich and was given the same dedication, to the Holy *Trinity*, as that of Norwich Cathedral. Many Oxford and Cambridge colleges now called *College* were originally called *Hall*.

(Strictly speaking, *hall* referred to the buildings of the establishment, and *college* to the people who lived there.) *Trinity Hall* did not change to *College*, however, as TRINITY COLLEGE already existed.

Trinity House The authority that controls lighthouses and buoys round the British coast is officially known as the Corporation of *Trinity House*. It was founded in 1512 as an association for piloting ships and takes its name from its headquarters, *Trinity House*, London. The authority is rededicated to the Church of England annually, and its name reflects the former frequent invocation of the Holy *Trinity* as a guide and protector of sailors.

Trinity Sunday In the Christian calendar, the name is that of the Sunday after Whit Sunday, dedicated to the Holy *Trinity*. Unlike the other major festivals, such as Christmas and Easter, *Trinity Sunday* has no season of preparation. It is also the only Christian festival to be dedicated to all three persons of the *Trinity*, as if gathering up at the end of the Christian year the previous festivals, which commemorate either Christ as the Second Person (Christmas, Easter, Ascension) or the Holy Spirit as the Third Person (Whit Sunday).

Triple Alliance The name is given to three historic pacts, each between three countries: 1. that of 1668, between England, Sweden and the Netherlands against France; 2. that of 1717, between France, the Netherlands and Britain against Spain; 3. that of 1882 (until 1914), between Germany, Austria-Hungary and Italy against the three countries agreed in the TRIPLE ENTENTE.

Triple Entente The name is applied to the understanding (*entente*) between Britain, France and Russia that developed between 1894 and 1907 to counterbalance the TRIPLE ALLIANCE of 1882 between Germany, Austria-Hungary and Italy. The term is French in origin,

Triplex The patent make of safety glass originated in 1909 when a type of non-shattering glass was produced by means of a 'sandwich' of celluloid in between two sheets of standard glass. The three layers gave the name of the product, from Latin *triplex*, 'three-fold', 'triple'.

Tripoli There are two famous ancient cities of the name. One is the capital and chief port of Libya, the other is a major town and port in Lebanon. Both names represent Greek *Tripolis*, from *treis*, 'three' and *polis*, 'town', since each place originally comprised three distinct cities. In Libya the three were Oea (surviving as the present Tripoli), Leptis Magna and Sabratha. In Lebanon they were Sidon, Tyre and Aradus. The Arabic name of the Libyan Tripoli is *ṭarābulus al-ġarb*, 'western Tripoli', and of that in Lebanon *ṭarābulus aš-šām*, 'Syrian Tripoli'. *See also* TRIPOLITANIA.

Tripolitania The name is that of the region of northwest Libya that centres on modern TRIPOLI and that arose as a Phoenician colony in the 7th century BC. It was under Italian rule from 1912 until the Second World War.

Tripura The state in northeast India has a Hindi name meaning 'three towns', from *tri*, 'three' and *pur*, 'town'.

Trismegistus *See* HERMES TRISMEGISTUS.

Tristan da Cunha The group of four islands in the South Atlantic, annexed by Britain in 1816, takes its name from that of *Tristan da Cunha* (1460–1540), the Portuguese admiral who discovered the islands in 1506 while on a passage to India.

Tristram The name is that of one of the Knights of the Round Table in the stories about King Arthur. It is of uncertain origin, but may derive from a Celtic word *drest* or *drust* meaning 'noise' (modern Welsh *trwst*). Through the tragic love story of *Tristram* and Isolde the name became associated with Latin *tristis* or French *triste*, 'sad'. In literature the name is familiar from Laurence Sterne's novel *Tristram Shandy* (1767), in which it is that of the central character. (Book IV tells how he was given it by mistake instead of *Trismegistus*.) *Tristan* is a French form of the name.

Triton In Greek mythology, the name is that of the sea god who is the son of Poseidon and Amphitrite. His name is sometimes popularly misassociated with the three-pronged *trident* held by Neptune, the

Roman sea god who is the equivalent of *Poseidon*. The origin of his name is obscure, however, and is probably pre-Greek. It may be related to that of his mother, *Amphitrite*, itself popularly interpreted as 'corroder', from Greek *amphi-*, 'round' and *truō*, 'I wear out'.

Trivandrum The city in southern India, where it is the capital of Kerala, derives its name as a contracted alteration of Malayalam *tiru vanantapuraṁ*, 'town sacred to Ananta'.

Trocadero The name goes back to the fortified site near Cadiz, Spain, that was the stronghold of the Constitutionalists in the revolution of 1820 and that fell to a French expeditionary force in 1823. An ornate palace of the same name was built commemoratively on the right bank of the Seine, Paris, as part of the International Exhibition of 1878. The two curving wings of this *Trocadéro* were incorporated into the Palais de Chaillot that was in turn built on the site in 1937 as a museum complex. The name was similarly taken up elsewhere in Europe for popular public places. One was the *Trocadero* Palace of Varieties, familiarly known as 'the Troc', which opened as a music hall in London in 1882 on the corner of the future Shaftesbury Avenue and Great Windmill Street. It is now a shopping, restaurant and exhibition centre. The original Spanish name means 'place of barter', from *trocar*, 'to barter', 'to exchange'.

Trojan War The famous war of Greek mythology was that fought by the Greeks against the *Trojans* (the inhabitants of ancient TROY) to avenge the abduction of Helen ('of Troy'), the most beautiful woman in the world, from her husband Menelaus by Paris, son of the *Trojan* king. It lasted ten years and ended in the sack of *Troy*. Although featuring as a mythological event, the war probably had a historical basis, and it is known that Mycenean Greece fought a foreign power in the mid-13th century BC.

Tromsø The port in northern Norway takes its name from *Troms*, the department of which it is the capital, and Danish *ø*, 'island' (the Norwegian equivalent would be *øy*). The meaning of the department name is uncertain. It originally applied to the sea current between the island on which the town is situated and the Norwegian mainland.

Trondheim The port in central Norway, the country's capital until the 14th century, takes its name from *Throndr*, that of the fjord (now *Trondheim Fjord*) on which it lies, and Old Norwegian *heimr*, 'house', 'town'. Cp. ARNHEM. The historic name of the fjord may be related to that of THOR, the Norse god of thunder, or to Old Norwegian *thōrr*, 'thunder' itself.

Trossachs, The The scenic area of central Scotland between Lochs Atray and Katrine has a name that means 'transverse hills'. It is said to be a Gaelic borrowing of the Welsh name *Trawsfynydd*, itself meaning 'cross mountain'. The reference is to the hills that divide the two lochs.

Trout Quintet Schubert's Piano Quintet in A major (1819) is so nicknamed because the fourth of its five movements is a set of variations on the tune of his song *Die Forelle* ('The Trout') (1817).

Trouville-sur-Mer The port and resort on the English Channel in northwest France derives its name from the Scandinavian personal name *Thorulfr*, with Latin *villa*, 'settlement'. The personal name is a combination of Old Norse *thor*, 'bravery' and *úlfr*, 'wolf'.

Trowbridge The Wiltshire town has a name that means 'tree bridge', from Old English *trēow*, 'tree' and *brycg*, 'bridge'. A 'tree bridge' is a simple wooden bridge fashioned from tree trunks. In the case of *Trowbridge* the bridge in question was probably one across the small river Biss to the west of the town centre. In the Domesday Book, the name of the town appears in the curiously corrupt form *Straburg*. The clerk who copied the name may have confused it with a name such as STRATFORD, and taken a form of Old English *brycg* to be *burg*, 'fortified place' (familiar as the final *-bury* of many names).

Troy The famous ancient city of Asia Minor traditionally derives its name from that of *Tros*, the legendary king of Phrygia who founded it. His own name comes from an Indoeuropean root word *treu* or *trou* meaning 'to be strong' and related to modern English *true*. There were actually nine cities of the name, each built on the ruins of its predecessor. The seventh was the site of the historic TROJAN WAR.

Troyes The city in northeast France had the Roman name of *Civitas Tricassium*, indicating that it was the capital of the Celtic people known as the *Tricasses*. The meaning of their name is uncertain. The present form of the name evolved from this, with a spelling perhaps influenced by that of the famous TROY of ancient Greece. Modern French *Troyen* can mean equally 'inhabitant of Troyes' or 'Trojan'.

Trucial States The former name (to 1971) of the United Arab Emirates denoted the maritime *truce* that was originally agreed in 1820 between the British government and the Arab sheikhdoms that make up the present country. The adjective *trucial* is found only with reference to this particular *truce*.

Truman The name means what it says, and was originally a nickname for a trustworthy person, a *true man*.

Truman The well-known brand of beer ultimately takes its name from Joseph *Truman*, who set up as a brewer in London in 1666. It was his grandson, Sir Benjamin *Truman*, who effectively formed the company that remains today as the only major brewery still active in central London.

Truro The county town of Cornwall has a difficult name. Its first part perhaps represents Cornish *try*, meaning 'three'. This could relate in some way to the two (rather than three) rivers on which the town stands. The second part of the name remains obscure. The earliest record of the name is *Triueru*, in the late 12th century.

Tsu The seaport city in southern Honshu, Japan, has a name that is simply the Japanese word for 'port'. Compare *tsunami* as the term for a large and destructive sea wave, from *tsu*, 'port' and *nami*, 'wave'.

Tsushima The group of five small islands beween Japan and South Korea, the scene of a Russian naval defeat by Japan in 1905, takes its name from Japanese *tsui*, 'pair', 'couple' and *ma*, 'horse', from the

supposed resemblance of two of them to a pair of horses.

Tswana The Negroid people of BOTSWANA, itself named for them, have a name that is said to be a Bantu word meaning 'like', 'similar', referring to a group of the people who had remained behind after an emigration. If so, the name emphasizes the identity of the two groups rather than their difference, as is more usual in ethnic names.

Tuamotu The archipelago in French Polynesia, in the south Pacific, has an indigenous name meaning 'far islands', related to Tahitian *motu*, 'island'.

Tuareg The name of the nomadic Berber people of the Sahara and their dialect is Arabic in origin and has been derived from *ṭārq*, 'night thief'. But more probably the name represents that of *Targa*, the Berber name of the region of Libya known as *Fezzan*. The meaning of this is uncertain.

Tübingen The town in southwest Germany had the medieval name of *Twingia* or *Tuwingen*, deriving from Middle High German *twing*, 'district', 'jurisdiction'.

Tucker The name was formerly an occupational one for a fuller, that is, someone who made cloth heavier or more compact by beating and pressing and perhaps originally 'teasing' it. English *tuck* in this sense derives from Old English *tucian*, 'to torment'.

Tudor The name is familiar as that of the English royal house that ruled from 1485 to 1603 and that was descended from the Welsh squire Owen *Tudor* (Owain *Tudur*) (d. 1461). His own name is a Welsh form of THEODORE, so like it means 'gift of God'.

Tudor Hall School The girls' public school near Banbury, Oxfordshire, was founded in the village of Forest Hill, near Oxford, in 1850. In 1946 it moved to its present location, and is so named because its buildings include a 17th-century manor house in the TUDOR style.

Tuesday The third day of the week takes its name from *Tiw*, the Germanic god of war and the sky, identified with the Roman god MARS.

Tuileries The former royal residence in Paris, begun in 1564 by Catherine de' Medici but finally destroyed in 1882, derives its name from the tile-works (French *tuileries*) on which it was built. The *Tuileries* Gardens are now a park on the original site.

Tula The name of the city south of Moscow in Russia is said to derive from a Baltic word *tula*, 'settlement', 'colony'.

Tullamore The county town of Offaly, in central Ireland, has a name that means 'big hill', from Irish *tulach*, 'hill' and *mór*, 'big'. The town arose only in the 18th century, so that the name would have originally been simply that of a hill. The hill in question is the prominent one to the east of the town on which St Catherine's church now stands.

Tully The name was generally used in English until the early 19th century for the famous Roman writer Marcus *Tullius* CICERO.

Tunbridge Wells The well-known Kent town arose round the springs (*wells*) discovered here in the 17th century, and takes its name from nearby TONBRIDGE, five miles (8 km) away. The name thus means 'springs near Tonbridge'. The difference of vowel now distinguishes the two towns. (Tonbridge was *Tunbridge* in the early 17th century, with the spelling reflecting the pronunciation of the name. With the development of Tunbridge Wells, however, it reverted to its earlier spelling with *o*.)

Tunis The capital of TUNISIA has an ancient name that some relate to that of the Phoenician goddess *Tanith*. The meaning of her own name is uncertain.

Tunisia The republic in northern Africa takes its name from that of its capital, TUNIS. In some languages the names for country and capital are identical, for example Spanish *Túnez*, Russian *Tunis*.

Tupi The name of the South American Indian people and their language is of disputed origin and meaning. Theories to explain it include the following: 1. from *tuva*, 'father' or *tupa*, 'god' with added *ipi*, 'origin', 'ancestor'; 2. from *tupi*, 'walkers'; 3. from *tu'upi*, 'best land'; 4. from *Tupi*, the name of an Indian chief or god. The last of these may actually be the most likely.

Tupperware The name of the familiar plastic houseware is based on that of Earl S. *Tupper* (1907–1983), an American chemist from New Hampshire who opened a factory in Massachusetts in 1937 and began producing the distinctive food and drink containers in 1942. Tupper himself introduced the system of 'Tupperware parties' in private houses as a means of selling his products to potential purchasers.

Turanian The name of the peoples who inhabited ancient Turkestan is said to derive from that of *Tur*, a mythical hero.

Turin The well-known city in northwest Italy had the Roman name *Augusta Taurinorum*, referring to the *Taurini*, the Ligurian tribe whose capital it was. Their own name may derive from Celtic *tauro*, 'mountain' or *tur*, 'water'. The civic authorities have interpreted it as 'bull' (Latin *taurus*, Italian *toro*), and the city's canting coat of arms depicts a splendidly belligerent bull.

Turkestan The region of central Asia, divided into West Turkestan (Kirgizia, Tajikistan, Turkmenistan, Uzbekistan and southern Kazakhstan) and East Turkestan (a region of northwest China), has a name that means 'land of *Turks*', from Iranian *tork*, 'Turk' and *ostān*, 'land', 'country'. *See also* TURKEY and TURKMENISTAN.

Turkey The name of the well-known country, partly in Europe and partly in Asia, derives from that of its indigenous people, the *Turks*. Their own name may mean 'strong', 'powerful'. The bird *turkey* was so named in error, even double error. The word was originally used for the African guinea fowl (from GUINEA) which was imported to Europe through *Turkey* and was thought to come from that country. The modern (American) turkey, as eaten at Thanksgiving and Christmas, was wrongly identified as a species of African guinea fowl, so was given the same name.

Turkmenistan The republic of south central Asia has a name that means 'land of the *Turkmen*', from *Turkmen* and Iranian *ostān*, 'land', 'country'. The people's own name means 'Turk-like', from Iranian *tork*, 'Turk' and *māndan*, 'to be like', 'to resemble'.

Turku The city and port in southwest Finland derives its name from Swedish *torg*, 'market-place'. *Cp.* TĂRGOVISHTE and TRIESTE. The Swedish name of the city is *Åbo*, from Swedish *å*, 'river' and *bo*, 'to inhabit' (related to the final *-by* in many English place-names).

Turner The common name was originally occupational, for a *turner*, a person who made small objects of wood or some other material by *turning* them on a lathe.

Tuscany The well-known region of central Italy takes its name from the *Etruscans* (*see* ETRURIA), its historic inhabitants.

Tutankhamen The name is famous as that of the Egyptian boy king of the second millennium BC, the son of AMENHOTEP, whose tomb at Luxor revealed a wealth of rare artefacts on its discovery in 1922. It means 'living image of AMON', the Egyptian god of life and fertility. The king's original name was *Tutankhaten*, 'living image of ATEN', the disk of the sun that was worshipped as the sole god in the reign of AKHENATEN.

Tuvalu The archipelagian republic, in the southwest Pacific, consists of nine coral islands. Its name, however, means 'eight standing together', from Tuvaluan *tū*, 'to stand up' and *valu*, 'eight'. This is because on one of the islands, Nui, the native language is not Tuvaluan but I-Kiribati (Gilbertese). The group originally formed part of the *Gilbert and Ellice* Islands, named for Thomas *Gilbert*, who gave the modern name of KIRIBATI (*which see*) and Alexander *Ellice*, head of a Canadian shipping company and owner of the ship *Rebecca* on board which the American merchant De Peyster visited the islands in 1819. *Tuvalu* gained its present indigenous name in 1978 on achieving independence.

Tver The city in western Russia, a port on the Volga, is of ancient origin and has a name that probably means 'fortress', from a word related to modern Russian *tvërdyy*, 'firm', 'solid'. In 1931 it was renamed *Kalinin*, for the Soviet titular head of state Mikhail *Kalinin* (1875–1946), who was born near here. (*Cp.* KALININGRAD). In 1991 it reverted to its historic name.

TVR The British make of car takes its name from letters in the first name of the manufacturing company's founder in the early 1950s, *Trevor* Wilkinson.

Tweed The well-known river on the Scottish–English border has a name that may mean 'strong one', referring to its current, from a Celtic root element related to Sanskrit *tavás*, 'powerful'.

Twelfth Night The name is that of the evening of 5 January, the *twelfth night* after Christmas and the eve of the Epiphany, when various festive customs were observed at one time. Epiphany itself, on 6 January, was formerly known as *Twelfth Day*, and was regarded as the end of the Christmas celebrations.

Twentieth Century Fox The well-known American film production company arose from a merger in 1935 between the *Fox* Film Corporation, founded in 1915 by the Hungarian-born film director William *Fox* (1879–1952), and *Twentieth Century* Pictures, founded in 1933 by the Russian-born director Joseph Schenck (1878–1961).

Twerton *See* TIVERTON.

Twickenham The familiar district of Greater London, on the Thames, has a name that could mean either '*Twicca*'s riverside land' or 'riverside land at the confluence'. The final part of the name is almost certainly Old English *hamm*, 'riverside land', referring to land in the bend of a river. This fits the location of Twickenham. If the second meaning is correct, deriving from a conjectural Old English word *twicca*, 'confluence', based on *twi-*, 'two', the reference could be to the point where the small river Crane flows into the Thames.

Twinings The well-known tea company, still in family hands, takes its name from Thomas *Twining* (1675–1741), who after serving an apprenticeship in the weaving trade set up a coffee house in London in 1706. In order to attract new custom, he began to serve tea as a 'sideline'. His reputation as a tea merchant and blender spread, and in 1716 he opened one of London's first combined tea and coffee houses.

Two Thousand Guineas The famous annual horse race held annually at Newmarket since 1809 takes its name from the prize originally awarded to the winner, with a value of £2100. *Cp.* THOUSAND GUINEAS.

Twyford The familiar make of bathroom furniture takes its name from Josiah *Twyford* (1640–1729), a Stoke-on-Trent potter who specialized in making red and white stoneware. By the end of the 19th century the firm he had founded was producing wash basins and lavatory units and exporting them to many parts of the world. One of the most popular makes of pedestal closet was the *Unitas*, so named as it was all in one piece, and this, influenced by the existing word *taz*, meaning 'basin', came to give the standard Russian word *unitaz* for a lavatory pan (toilet bowl).

Tyburn The notorious place of public execution in west central London (at the junction of Oxford Street and Edgware Road) takes its name from the *Tyburn* brook, whose own name means 'boundary stream', from Old English *tēo*, 'boundary' and *burna*, 'stream'. *See also* MARYLEBONE.

Tyne The well-known river of northeast England has a name of Celtic origin meaning simply 'water', 'river'. The river gave its name to the county of *Tyne and Wear*, to the town and resort of *Tynemouth*, and to the general urban and industrial region of *Tyneside*.

Tynwald The name of the parliament of the Isle of Man derives from Old Norse *thingvollr*, from *thing*, 'assembly' and *vollr*, 'field'. The actual 'assembly field' is at *Tynwald* Hill, in the west of the island. In 1979 celebrations were held to mark the millennium of the *Tynwald* as the oldest continuous assembly in the world. *Cp.* THINGVELLIR, the site of the Icelandic parliament.

Typhoo The well-known brand of tea has a name that was invented in 1863 by a Birmingham grocer, John Sumner. He is said to have intended it to suggest the *typhoon* that is the tropical storm of the China seas, while at the same time alliterating it with both *tips* and *tea*. It could in fact represent Chinese *tàifū*, 'great man', a term used in parts of northern China for a doctor, as if the tea had medicinal or at any rate restorative properties.

Tyre The ancient Phoenician port, now a market town in southern Lebanon, derives its name from Phoenician *tsor*, 'stone', 'rock'. Its current Arabic name is *Sur*, of the same origin.

Tyrol The mountainous province of western Austria derives its name from the castle of *Tyrol*, near Merano. Its own name, that of its locality, probably comes ultimately from Celtic *tir*, 'land'. *Cp.* the name of the Northern Ireland county of TYRONE.

Tyrone The county of Northern Ireland has a name that is the English form of the Irish name *Tír Eoghain*, '*Eoghan*'s land'. The reference is to *Eoghan* (*Owen*), the semi-legendary ruler whose descendants are said to have been the owners of the territory. *Cp.* LEINSTER, MUNSTER and ULSTER.

Tyrrell The name, found in both England and Ireland, is of uncertain origin but may have originally been a nickname for a stubborn person, from Old French *tirel*, related to modern French *tirer*, 'to pull', a term for an animal that pulled on the reins.

Tyrrhenian The sea that is an arm of the Mediterranean between Italy and the islands of Corsica and Sardinia had the Greek name *Turrhēnos*. This may be a Greek form of the name of the *Etruscans* (*see* ETRURIA), or perhaps derives from *turris*, 'tower', a word also Etruscan in origin.

Tyumen The port in central Russia, on the river Tura, has a name of Tatar origin meaning 'ten thousand', from *tyu*, 'ten' and *men*, 'thousand'. The reference may be to the ten thousand soldiers that the khan had in his army, or to the number of his subjects. The town is one of the oldest in Siberia, and was founded in 1586 on the site of the Tatar settlement of *Chingi-Tura*, 'town of Chingis' (*i.e. Chingis khan*, otherwise GENGHIS KHAN), itself dating back to the 14th century.

Tzigane The name is an alternative one for a GYPSY, especially a Hungarian one. It comes from Old Bulgarian *atsiganin*, itself from Byzantine Greek *tsiganos*, a form of *atsigganos*, popularly pronounced *athigganos*. This means 'not touching', from the privative prefix ('not') *a-* and *thigganō*, 'I touch'. The name denotes exclusivity, and originally applied to a Manichaean sect, regarded as magicians, who had emigrated from Phrygia to Byzantium. The name *Tzi-*

gane also has its forms in other languages to mean *Gypsy* either specifically (of a certain country) or generally, such as French *Gitan*, 'Spanish gypsy', German *Zigeuner*, Italian *zingaro*, Russian *tsygan*, Hungarian *cigány*. The English spelling *Tsigane* is sometimes found. *See also* I ZINGARI.

U

Ubangi The river in central Africa derives its name from Bantu *u*, 'land', 'country' and *bangi*, 'rapid', referring to the current of the river and the territory through which it flows.

UB40 The British rock group, formed in Birmingham in 1978, took as their name the government designation for the standard *u*nemployment *b*enefit form, used euphemistically of an unemployed person. The group's early songs were noted for their political and social comment.

Udaipur The city in northwest India has a name of Hindi origin, from *uday*, 'rising', 'birth', 'growth' and *pur*, 'town'.

Udmurt The Finno-Ugrian people of western Russia have a name that represents Votyak *ud*, a tribal name of uncertain meaning, and *murt*, 'person', 'man'. *Cp.* MORDVIN.

Ufa The city in western Russia, the capital of Bashkiria, takes its name from the river on which it stands. The river's own name may derive from a basic Indoeuropean root element *ap* meaning simply 'water', 'river'.

Uffizi The famous art gallery in Florence, Italy, arose from the building planned in 1559 by Giorgio Vasari on the orders of Cosimo de' Medici to house the offices (Italian *uffizi*) of the government judiciary. After the death of Cosimo in 1574, the building was expanded to house the art treasures of the Medici collection.

UFO The British heavy metal band, formed in 1969, took as their name the standard abbreviation for an *u*nidentified *f*lying *ob*ject.

Uganda The republic in eastern Africa derives its name from Swahili *u*, 'land', 'country' and *Ganda*, the name of its indigenous people. Their own name is of uncertain origin.

Ugarit The ancient Syrian city-state, which gave the name of the extinct Semitic language *Ugaritic*, derives its name from Sumerian *ugāru*, 'field'. The name is not mentioned in the Bible. The present name of the city is *Ras Shamra*, representing Arabic *ra's šamra*, 'headland of fennel'.

Ugrian The name of the East European peoples and their languages, represented among others by the Voguls, Ostyaks and Magyars, derives from Old Russian *Ugre*, 'Hungarians'. *See also* HUNGARY, MAGYAR.

Uhu The brand of adhesive is manufactured by a German firm who have their headquarters in the Black Forest, the haunt of the eagle owl. The German word for the bird is *Uhu*, from its cry, and this was adopted for the commercial name.

Uigur The Mongoloid people of northwest China and east and west Turkestan derive their name from Uigur *uiğur*, a dynasty name that comes from that of the people's first patriarch *Oğas* or *Oğus*. His own name is based on *oğ*, 'great'.

Ukraine The central European republic has a name that represents Old Russian *oukraina*, 'border country', from *ou*, 'by', 'at' and *kray*, 'region'. The territory was so called because it was the border land or 'frontier zone' of medieval Russia at the time of the Tatar invasion in the 13th century. The name is thus equivalent to that of the MARCHES. An alternative name for Ukraine from the 14th century was *Little Russia*, so called by contrast with *Great Russia*, after the medieval principality here had become separated from 'mainstream' tsarist Russia as a consequence of the Mongol invasion.

Ulan Bator The capital of Mongolia has a name that in Mongolian is *Ulaan-Baatar*, meaning '(town of the) red hero', from *ulaan*, 'red' and *baatar*, 'hero'. The city was so named in 1924 in honour of SUKHE BATOR, who led revolutionary activities here from 1919 and who died here. The town was founded in 1639 as the migratory (from 1778 settled) capital of the Lamaist church in Mongolia under the name of *Urga*, representing Mongolian *Orgoo*, 'headquarters', 'palace'. In 1706 it was re-named *Iȟ-ȟureheh*, 'great monastery' and in 1911 *Niislel-ȟureheh*, 'capital monastery'.

Ulan-Ude The city in southeast Russia, the capital of the Buryat Autonomous Republic, has a name that represents Mongolian *Ulaan-Ude* or *Ulaan-üd*, from *ulaan*, 'red' and *üüd*, the name of the river *Uda* on which it stands. Until 1934 it was known as *Verkhneudinsk*, 'upper *Uda*', so named not because it stands on the upper reaches of the river (it is actually at its mouth) but to be distinguished from the town of *Nizhneudinsk*, 'lower *Uda*', on another river *Uda* over 400 miles (660 km) to the northwest near Irkutsk. The river name is probably derived from a tribal name of unknown meaning.

Ullswater The second largest lake in the Lake District has a name that means '*Ulf*'s water'. It is thus based on a personal name, as is that of the district's largest lake, WINDERMERE. *Ulf* is a Scandinavian personal name meaning 'wolf'.

Ulm The city in southwest Germany has a name of Celtic origin probably meaning 'marsh'.

Ulster The name of the former kingdom and province of northern Ireland, now used as a colloquial name for Northern Ireland itself, means 'place of the *Ulaidh*', this being the name of the people who inhabited the region, itself associated with Irish *ulaidh*, 'tomb'. The second part of the name represents the Old Norse genitive ending -*s* followed by Irish *tír*, 'district', as for TYRONE. *Cp.* LEINSTER and MUNSTER.

Ultravox The British new wave rock group, formed in London in 1973, went through a variety of names before settling on *Ultravox* in 1976. Through classical connections, the name literally suggests 'beyond the voice', or at any rate a superior singing style. It was also probably linked with that of the group's founder and lead singer, John *Foxx* (real name Dennis Leigh).

Ulyanovsk The city in western Russia, on the Volga, was the birthplace of Lenin (whose surname was *Ulyanov*) and was named for him in 1924 after his death that year. The city's original name was *Simbirsk*, from a Chuvash phrase meaning 'mountain of winds'.

Ulysses The famous name of the mythological hero is a Latin form, much altered, of his original Greek name ODYSSEUS. It is not certain how the name came to be changed in this way. An intermediate Etruscan form may have produced an alteration of *d* to *l*.

Umbria The mountainous region of central Italy takes its name from its original inhabitants, the *Umbri*. They themselves derive their name from that of the river *Umbro* (Italian *Ombrone*), whose own name probably comes from Greek *ombros*, 'shower', 'rain', or more generally 'water'. This origin has engendered a legend tracing the people back to the days of the biblical Flood.

Umbriel The name is that of the 'dusky melancholy sprite' in Pope's poem *The Rape of the Lock* (1712). It was probably based by the poet on Latin *umbra*, 'shade', with -*iel* as in ARIEL, GABRIEL or URIEL. In astronomy the name is that of one of the five satellites of the planet Uranus.

Una The name is usually taken to be the feminine form of Latin *unus*, 'one', implying uniqueness. But it is also an Irish name, perhaps derived from *uan*, 'lamb', and often spelled *Oonagh*. The *Una* of Spenser's *The Faerie Queene* (1590, 1596) clearly has a name that means 'one', since she typifies the singleness of true religion. The *Una* who is one of the two main child characters (with Dan) in Kipling's novels *Puck of Pook's Hill* (1906) and its sequel *Rewards and Fairies* (1910), however, almost certainly has the Irish form of the name, although she is actually English.

Underhill The name originally applied to someone who lived *under* a *hill*, that is, at the foot of one, or who came from a place so called. *Cp.* UNDERWOOD.

Underwood The name was originally used for a person who lived *under* a *wood*, that is, on the edge of one, or who came from a place so called, such as the Nottinghamshire village of *Underwood* near Eastwood. *Cp.* UNDERHILL.

Unfinished Symphony Schubert's Symphony No 8 in B minor (1822) is so named because it contains only the first two movements instead of the full complement of four, although there are sketches for a scherzo that would have been the third. It is not known why the composer did not complete the work. He may have abandoned it because he lacked inspiration for the last two movements, or simply have put it aside and forgotten about it.

Unilever The well-known manufacturer of food products and detergents has a name that from 1930 has united that of three companies: NV Margarine *Unie*, Margarine *Union* and *Lever* Brothers. The first two of these were respectively the Dutch and British branches of the Dutch company Van den Berghs and Jurgens. *Lever* Brothers was founded in 1885 by William Hesketh *Lever* (1851–1925), later Viscount Leverhulme, and his brother James Darcy *Lever*.

Union of Soviet Socialist Republics *See* SOVIET UNION.

Unitarian The name is that of a Christian church or sect which rejects the doctrine of the Trinity and which holds that God is *one* being.

United States of America The full official name of the country usually known simply as AMERICA came into being during the discussions that led to the Declaration of Independence of 1776. The name *America* is in fact very wide-ranging, and can (with qualification) be applied to the whole of the American continent, including North, Central and South America. For this reason, various proposals have been made over the years for a more precise name for the United States and its inhabitants. One of the best known is *Usona*, an acronym of *United States of North America*, apparently suggested by the English writer Samuel Butler (1835–1902). However, this name has been adopted only in Esperanto, in which the country is called *Usono* and an inhabitant is *Usonano*. It seems strange that the familiar abbreviated name *USA* has not been enlisted for this purpose, as it is a readily pronounceable acronym.

University College There are two noted colleges of the name. *University College*, Oxford, was founded in 1249 and is the university's oldest college. Its name testifies to this unique status. *University College*, London, was founded in 1826 and was similarly the university's first college, so that its name also indicates its chronological priority.

University College School The public day school for boys in London was founded in 1830 as a school for UNIVERSITY COLLEGE, London. It moved to its present site in Hampstead in 1907.

Unst The most northerly of the Shetland Islands has a Scandinavian name meaning 'abode of eagles', from Old Norse *orn*, 'eagle' and *vist*, 'dwelling'.

Unter den Linden The main street of the former East Berlin, extending from the city centre to the Brandenburg Gate, has a name that means 'under the limes'. The trees were cut down at the time of the 1936 Olympic Games.

Unterwalden The canton of central Switzerland has a German name meaning 'under the forests', so called because it lies below the forest slopes of the Bernese Oberland. It is divided into the two demicantons of *Nidwald* and *Obwald*, respectively 'lower forests' and 'upper forests', the former bordering Lake Lucerne below the latter, to the south.

Unwin The name derives from the Anglo-Saxon personal name *Hūnwine*, comprising the two words *hūn*, 'bearcub' and *wine*, 'friend'. This name later became associated (or confused) with the quite different Old English word *unwine*, 'enemy' (literally 'un-friend'), giving a new and basically opposite interpretation.

Upanayana The Hindu initiation ceremony, undergone by Brahman boys between the ages of eight and 16, has a name of Sanskrit origin meaning 'leading towards', from *upa*, 'towards', 'near' and *nayana*, 'leading', 'bringing'. After a ritual bath, the boy is 'led towards' his guru (personal guide) and invested with a sacred thread and other garments.

Upanishad The ancient sacred books of Hinduism take their name from Sanskrit *upanisad*, from *upa*, 'near', 'towards', *ni*, 'down' and *sīdai*, 'he sits'. The overall meaning is thus 'a sitting down near', implying a confidential communication, as when one person sits down at the feet of another.

Uppingham The name of the Leicestershire town means 'homestead of the upland people', referring to a tribe who lived on a hilly site here, and who may have had a lookout point for a possible enemy on Castle Hill, west of the present town centre.

Uppsala The name of the historic city in east central Sweden means 'upper *Sala*', from Swedish *upp*, 'up', 'above' and the name of a former village here.

Ur The legendary ancient city of Sumer has a name that derives from Sumerian *uru*, meaning simply 'city'. In the Bible, the city is always referred to as 'Ur of the Chaldees' (*Genesis* 11.28 and elsewhere). Its present name is *Tell Muqayyar*, from Arabic *tall muqayyar*, 'tarry hill', 'hill covered in tar'.

Urals The mountain system of western Russia, forming the natural boundary between Europe and Asia, has a name that is said to represent Vogul *urala*, 'mountain peak', from *ur*, 'mountain' and *ala*, 'summit', 'roof'. Some sources take the origin from Tatar *ural*, 'frontier', 'boundary', however. The range gave the name of the river *Ural* that rises in its southern part.

Uranus The seventh planet from the sun was named for the Greek god who personified the sky and whose own name represents Greek *ouranos*, 'sky', 'heaven'. The name is appropriate for the seventh planet, since in mythology Uranus was the father of Cronos, the Titan whose Roman counterpart was *Mercury*, the name of the sixth planet. Cronos in turn was the father of Zeus, otherwise *Jupiter*, the fifth planet. The three successive planets thus have 'family' names linking son with father and grandfather.

Urban The name is familiar as that of eight popes, from the 3rd to the 17th century, the first being a saint. It means 'city-dweller', from Latin *urbanus*, the adjective from *urbs*, 'city'. For the popes this would have meant Rome, *the* city in the Roman world and, as still, in the Roman Catholic Church.

Urdu The official language of Pakistan, also spoken in India, has a name meaning '(language of the) camp', from Hindi *(zabān) urdū*. The latter word is directly related to English *horde* (*see* GOLDEN HORDE).

Uri The canton of central Switzerland traditionally links its name with Latin *urus*, 'aurochs' (a type of wild ox, now extinct), and this animal appears on its coat of arms. There may be some obscure reference to a totemic animal.

Uriah The name is found in the Old Testament for a warrior ('Uriah the Hittite') who was killed in battle by order of King David so that the king could marry his wife, Bathsheba, after he had made her pregnant (2 *Samuel* 11). His name derives from Hebrew *Ūrīyāh*, 'my light is Yah', *i.e.* Jehovah. The name has become unpopular through its association with Dickens's obsequious clerk *Uriah* Heep in *David Copperfield* (1850), and perhaps also through its suggestion of *urine*. *Cp.* URIEL.

Uriah Heep The British heavy metal group, formed in 1969, took their name from the Dickens character (*see* URIAH). The band's first LP was entitled *Very 'Eavy, Very 'Umble* (1970), echoing Uriah Heep's remark in the novel, 'We are so very 'umble'.

Uriel The name is that of two Old Testament characters mentioned in genealogies as well as that of one of the four chief angels in Jewish apocryphal writings. It represents Hebrew *Ūrī'ēl*, 'my light is God'. *Cp.* URIAH.

Urim and Thummim The names are those of two objects mentioned in the Old Testament: 'And thou shalt put in the breastplate of judgment the Urim and the Thummim' (*Exodus* 28.30). It is not known exactly what the objects were, but they apparently served as oracles, and were carried as such in or on the breastplate of the high priest. The names are usually translated respectively as 'light' (from Hebrew *urim*, the intensive plural of *ōr*) and 'integrity' (from Hebrew *thummīm*, plural of *tōm*). In the Septuagint (Greek version of the Old Testament) they were rendered *dēlōsis kai alētheia*, literally 'pointing out and truth'. In the Latin Vulgate this became *doctrina et veritas*, and in early English versions of the Bible *doctrine and truth*. Martin Luther, on the other hand, translated the words into German as *Licht und Recht*, which led Miles Coverdale, in his English translation of 1535, to render them as *light and perfectness*. In the Great Bible of 1539, however, and in later English versions, as the Authorized of 1611, the names are left untranslated.

Urquhart The Scottish name derives from one of the places so called, such as the present parish of *Urquhart* and Glenmoriston on Loch Ness. The place-name itself is Gaelic in origin and said to mean 'by the thicket'.

Ursula The name is a Medieval Latin diminutive of *ursa*, 'she-bear'. It was borne by a 4th-century saint said to have been martyred in Cologne together with a number of companions. (Later legends put their number at 11,000, but this was due to a misinterpretation of the Latin abbreviation *XI MV*, representing *undecim martyres virgines*, '11 virgin martyrs', as *undecim milia virgines*, '11,000 virgins'.)

Ursuline The Roman Catholic order of nuns was founded in 1537 at Brescia, Italy, and named for St URSULA, patron saint of the order's founder, St Angela Merici.

Uruguay The South American republic takes its name from the river *Uruguay* that forms its western boundary. The river name is said to derive from that of an Indian tribe who lived along its banks, with their own name perhaps representing *uru*, 'bird' and *guay*, 'tail', referring to some long-tailed bird that was their totem.

USA *See* UNITED STATES OF AMERICA.

Ushant The name of the island off the tip of Brittany, northwest France, derives from Gaulish *ux*, 'high' and the superlative suffix *-isamo*, related to Latin *-issimus*. The overall sense is thus 'very high'. The island is rocky, but not noticeably elevated. Its French name is *Ouessant*, perhaps influenced by *ouest*, 'west'.

Usher The name was originally an occupational one for a janitor or door-keeper, or for a court official, the precursor of the modern court *usher*.

Usk The town in South Wales near Pontypool takes its name from the river on which it stands. The river's own name probably means 'fish river', from a Celtic word related to Latin *piscis*, 'fish' and to the English word itself. Some authorities, however, bracket this river name with those of the *Axe* and *Exe* (on which EXETER lies), where the basic meaning is simply 'water', from a Celtic word related to Latin *aqua* and even indirectly to the modern English word.

US Open The major world golf tournament, held annually since 1895 under supervision of the United States Golf Association, is *open* to both amateur and professional players. Hence the name.

Ústí nad Labem The city and port in the northwest Czech Lands takes its name from Czech *ústí*, 'estuary', *nad*, 'on' and *Labe*, the name of the river ELBE, at the mouth of which it lies. The city's German name is *Aussig*, a corruption of this, perhaps influenced by the standard word *Aussicht*, 'outlook', 'view'. The city's medieval castle is situated on a precipitous crag over the river.

Utah The American state has a name of Indian origin, variously explained as meaning 'high up', 'tall men', 'mountain dwellers' or at any rate someone or something 'lofty'. The state is in the Rocky Mountains.

Utgard The name of the land of the giants in Norse mythology means 'outer enclosure', from *út*, 'out' and *garthr*, 'enclosure'. The name is also used as an alternative for JÖTUNHEIM, 'realm of the giants', although this name is sometimes applied to a larger region of which *Utgard* is only a part.

Uther Pendragon In the Arthurian cycle, the name is that of the king of Britain who was the father of Arthur. *Pendragon* means literally 'chief dragon', *i.e.* 'foremost leader', from Celtic words related to Welsh *pen*, 'head', 'chief' and *draig*, 'dragon'. *Uther* is a name of disputed origin. It may be related to Welsh *uthr*, 'wonderful', 'terrible'.

Utica The ancient city on the north coast of Africa, near Carthage, has a name of Phoenician origin probably meaning 'old'.

Utopia The name for an ideally perfect place or society was coined in 1516 by Sir Thomas More for the title of his book that described an imaginary island with such a society. It is usually translated as 'no place', from Greek *ou*, 'not' and *topos*, 'place'. The first part of the name can also be regarded, however, as representing Greek *eu*, 'good', referring to the ideal nature of the place, and More himself plays on the two names *Utopia* and *Eutopia* in the introduction to his book, which was originally written in Latin. *Cp.* EREWHON.

Utrecht The city in the central Netherlands derives its name from Old German *ūt*, 'out', 'outside', and the name of the Roman settlement here, *Trajectum castrum*, 'fort by the ford', from Latin *trajectus*, 'river crossing'. The present name originally applied to the town that arose below this settlement. The river here is the Oude Rijn (Old Rhine), a tributary of the Lek.

Utsunomiya The city in central Honshu, Japan, derives its name from *u*, 'roof', 'house', 'sky', *tsu*, 'capital', *no*, the genitive (possessive) particle, and *miya*, 'Shinto temple'. The overall sense thus refers to an administrative capital that arose round a Shinto temple.

Uttar Pradesh The state in northern India has a Hindi name, from *uttar*, 'north' and *prades*, 'state'. *Cp.* ANDHRA PRADESH.

Uttoxeter The Staffordshire town has a name that superficially resembles that of EXETER, suggesting it could also contain the Old English *ceaster* that denotes a former Roman settlement. But the Domesday Book has the name as *Wottocshede*, showing that this is not the origin. The name thus means '*Wuttuc*'s heath', with the Anglo-Saxon personal name followed by a conjectural Old English word *hæddre*, 'heather', 'heath'.

U2 The Irish pop band, formed in Dublin in 1977, chose a name that was intended to suggest 'you too' to its audience and that was at the same time, for a neo-punk group, strikingly different from familiar punk band names such as the *Sex Pistols* and the *Clash*.

Uusikaupunki The seaport town in southwest Finland, founded in 1617, has a name that means 'new town', from Finnish *uusi*, 'new' and *kaupunki*, 'town'. Its Swedish name of *Nystad* has the same meaning. The name is pronounced approximately 'Oosi-*cow*-punky'.

Uusimaa The name of the province of southern Finland means 'new land', from Finnish *uusi*, 'new' and *maa*, 'land'. Its Swedish name of *Nyland* has the same meaning. The approximate pronunciation of the name is '*Oo*-sima'.

Uxbridge The former Middlesex town west of London has a name that means 'bridge of the *Wixan* (people)'. The tribal name probably means something like 'village people', from a word related to the *-wich* of many English place-names. The original bridge would have been over the river Colne here.

Uzbekistan The republic of southeast central Asia takes its name from its indigenous people, the *Uzbeks*, together with Iranian *ostān*, 'country'. The people are said to derive their name from *Uzbek* or *Öz Beg* (1282–1341), a Mongol khan of the Golden Horde who, although a Muslim, encouraged Christianity in his domain. They were thus formed as a race relatively late.

V

Vaal The South African river, forming the southern border of TRANSVAAL, derives its name from Afrikaans *vaal*, 'pale', referring to the muddy colour of the waters when the river is in full spate.

Vaasa The port in western Finland takes its name from that of the *Vasa* dynasty of Swedish kings who ruled from 1523 to 1818. The town was granted the privilege of bearing their name by Charles IX of Sweden on its foundation in 1606. The dynasty's own name derives from that of the family estate in Uppland, near Uppsala.

Vaduz The capital of Liechtenstein has a name that represents Old German *Valdutsch*, itself from Latin *vallis*, 'valley' and Old German *Dutsch*, 'German'. The city is in the valley of the Rhine.

Vaisey The name was originally a nickname for a cheerful or happy person, from a form of Norman French *enveisié*, 'playful', related to modern English *vice* and ultimately to Latin *vitium*, 'fault', 'flaw', but later 'pleasure'. The name frequently occurs in the spelling *Veasey* or *Veazey*.

Valais The canton of southern Switzerland, known as *Wallis* in German, *Vallese* in Italian and *Vallais* in Romansch, derives its name from Latin *vallis*, 'valley'. The valley concerned is that of the upper Rhône.

Valdivia The port in southern Chile was founded in 1552 by the Spanish conquistador Pedro de *Valdivia* (1497–1553), who also founded Santiago and Concepción.

Valence The name of the town in southeast France ultimately derives from the Roman personal name *Valentius*, itself from Latin *valens*, 'healthy', 'strong'. *Cp.* VALENTINE.

Valencia The port in eastern Spain, the capital of the former province of the same name, was known to the Romans as *Valentia Edetanorum*, 'fort of the *Edetani*', from Low Latin *valentia*, 'strength', a derivative of Latin *valere*, 'to be strong', 'to be healthy'. The *Edetani* were a Tarraconese people from the Roman province in northeast Spain that gave the name of modern TARRAGON.

Valenciennes The town in northern France probably takes its name from that of the 4th-century Roman emperor *Valentinian* I, who ruled at the time of its foundation. The town's canting coat of arms features swans, however, as if the name derived from French *val de cygnes*, 'valley of swans'.

Valentia The island off the southwest coast of Ireland has a name that represents the original Irish *Béal Inse*, 'estuary of the island', referring to the sound that separates the island from the mainland. The present form of the name appears to have been influenced by the Spanish place-name VALENCIA, and the two are pronounced identically by the English.

Valentine The first name derives from the Latin personal name *Valentinus̃*, itself a derivative of *valens*, 'healthy', 'strong', from the verb *valere*, 'to be healthy'. It was the 3rd-century St *Valentine* whose name came to be associated with the *valentine* as a card declaring one's love or affection for someone. The association came about accidentally, since his feast day was on 14 February, the date of an existing pagan fertility festival. In a way, however, his name is appropriate for the occasion, since it implies a wish of 'good health', as regularly made at other times. *Cp.* VALERIE.

Valerian The 3rd-century AD Roman emperor had the full name Publius Licinius *Valerianus*. His *cognomen* or nickname means 'belonging to the *Valerius* clan', so like that name ultimately means 'healthy', 'strong'.

Valerie The name is in a sense the feminine equivalent of VALENTINE. It derives from the Roman name *Valeria*, itself a feminine form of the *nomen* or clan name *Valerius*, from Latin *valere*, 'to be well', 'to be strong'.

Valetta The capital of Malta takes its name from Jean Parizot de la *Valette* (1494–1568), the French general and Grand Master of the Order of Malta who founded the city in 1566.

Valhalla The name is familiar from Norse mythology as that of the great hall of Odin where warriors who die in battle live for ever as heroes. It derives from Old Norse *valr*, 'the slain' and *höll*, 'hall'. *See also* VALKYRIE.

Valium The proprietary name for the tranquillizer drug diazepam is said to be of arbitrary origin, but it may have been suggested by Latin *validum*, 'strong', 'powerful'. It was patented in the United States in 1961.

Valkyrie In Norse mythology, the name is that of one of the beautiful maidens who served Odin and rode over the battlefields to claim the dead heroes and take them to VALHALLA. It represents Old Norse *valr*, 'the slain' and *köri*, 'to choose'.

Valladolid The city in northwest Spain has a name that is probably of Arabic origin, from *balad ūlīd*, 'town of *Ulid*', although it is not known who Ulid was. Some authorities, however, prefer a derivation from Spanish *valle*, 'valley' and *Olid*, said to be the name of the city's founder. Others again propose a source in Medieval Latin *Vallisoletum*, 'valley of olive trees'.

Valmiki The name of the reputed author of the Sanskrit epic poem *Ramayana* derives from the Sanskrit word for 'ant'. He appears in the poem as one of its heroes, and is said to derive his name from an incident in his early life. As a youth he was a robber, but in sorrow for his evildoing underwent an act of self-imposed penance, standing motionless on one spot for many years until he was covered by an anthill.

Valois The historic region of northern France had the Medieval Latin name of *pagus Vadensis*, perhaps deriving from *vadus*, 'ford', presumably at some point over the river Oise. The *d* of the name then became *l* by association with Latin *vallis*, 'valley', equally that of the Oise. The place-name gave the name of the French royal dynasty that ruled from 1328 to 1589.

Valparaiso The port in central Chile has a name that means 'valley of paradise', from Spanish *valle*, 'valley' and *paraíso*, 'paradise'. The name refers to the city's scenically striking site, on mountain slopes above a broad bay, discovered in 1536 by the Spanish conquistador Juan de Saavedra.

Van, Lake The lake in eastern Turkey is named for the nearby town of *Van*, whose own name was recorded by Ptolemy in the 2nd century AD as *Bouana*. It ultimately represents Iranian *hāne*, 'settlement'.

Vancouver The well-known island and city in southwest Canada take their name from the English navigator George *Vancouver* (1757–1798), who sailed with Cook on his second and third voyages and who as a midshipman in the Royal Navy explored the Pacific coast here in 1792.

Vandals The notorious Germanic people, who raided Roman provinces in the 3rd and 4th centuries AD, take their name from Old German *wandjan*, 'to wander'. They gave their name to the term *vandal* for a person who destroys anything valuable or beautiful. The English word dates only from the 17th century.

Van der Hum It is not known who invented the tangerine-flavoured liqueur produced in South Africa. For this reason it was given a name modelled on a typical Afrikaans surname such as *Van der Post* or *Van der Stel* but actually meaning *Van der Um*, a sort of equivalent of 'Whatsisname'.

Vanessa The popular name was invented by Jonathan Swift for the heroine of his poem *Cadenus and Vanessa*, written in 1713 but published only after his death in 1726. In this, he himself is *Cadenus* (an anagram of Latin *decanus*, 'dean', his title as Dean of St Patrick's Cathedral, Dublin), while *Vanessa* is his close friend Esther Vanhomrigh. The name is formed from the first syllable of her (Dutch) surname and the first syllable of her first name, while also serving as the feminine suffix *-essa* found in such words as *contessa*. Swift was a great inventor of words and names, as witness LAPUTA and LILLIPUT in *Gulliver's Travels* (1726). *See also* STELLA.

Van Heusen The well-known make of shirts takes its name from John Manning *Van Heusen*, who founded the company in Boston, Massachusetts, in 1925.

Vanir In Norse mythology, the name is that of the race of gods, often engaged in combat with the AESIR, who were most prominently represented by *Njord* and his son and daughter *Freir* and *Freya*. It derives from that of the fertility god *Vanr*, whose own name is of uncertain origin.

Vanity Fair The name relates to the social life of a community or to the world in general, implying its more frivolous or trivial aspects. It was popularized by the title of Thackeray's novel, published in 1848. It actually originates, however, from Bunyan's *Pilgrim's Progress*:

> The name of that Town is Vanity; and at the town there is a Fair kept, called Vanity-Fair. It [...] beareth the name of Vanity-Fair, because the Town where 'tis kept is lighter than Vanity.
>
> Part I, 1678.

Vannes The town in Brittany, northwest France, was the capital of the Gaulish people known as the *Veneti*, and takes its name from them. Their own name may derive from Gaulish *vindo*, 'white', although some scholars prefer an origin in Indoeuropean *venis*, 'friend' or in pre-Indoeuropean *van*, 'marsh'.

Vanuatu The island republic in the West Pacific takes its name from native (Bislama) words meaning 'our land'. Until 1980 the islands were known as the *New Hebrides*, so named by Captain Cook in 1774 for the HEBRIDES, off the west coast of mainland Scotland.

Varanasi The city in northeast India. formerly familiar as *Benares*, has a name of Sanskrit origin deriving from the two rivers *Varana* and *Asi*, tributaries of the Ganges, on which the city lies.

Varangian The Scandinavian people who invaded and settled parts of Russia from the 8th century are said to derive their name from Old Norse *váringr*, 'bound by a pledge', from *vár*, 'pledge', related to modern German *wahr*, 'true'.

Varna The port in northeast Bulgaria is said to derive its name from the Slavic root word *vran* or *vrana*, 'black' (literally 'the colour of a crow'), perhaps with reference to the location of the city on the Black Sea. Bulgarian toponymists, on the other hand, tend to favour an origin in the Indoeuropean element *vara*, 'water'. The town was founded in the 6th century BC under the name of *Odessos*. From 1949 to 1956 it was known as *Stalin*.

Varsity Match The annual rugby football match at Twickenham between Oxford and Cambridge Universities was first played in 1872 and is properly known as the *University Rugby Match*. It takes its name from the colloquial word for *university* that arose in the 19th century as an affected form of the 17th-century abbreviation *versity*.

Varuna The name is that of the ancient sky god of Hinduism who later became the god of the waters and the giver of rain. It is probably based on a Sanskrit root element *vr* meaning 'cover', 'embrace', itself related to the name of the Greek god URANUS.

Vaseline The proprietary name for the brand of petroleum jelly is said to derive from a blend of German *Wasser*, 'water' and Greek *elaion*, 'oil' with the commercial suffix *-ine*. This, like the substance itself, was the invention in 1872 of the American chemist Robert A. Chesebrough, who believed that petroleum was produced by the decomposition of water in the earth.

Vassar College The women's college in Poughkeepsie, New York, is named for its founder in 1861, the British-born merchant Matthew *Vassar* (1792–1868).

Västerås The city in central Sweden, the country's largest inland port, has a name that means 'western river mouth', from *väster*, 'west', *å*, 'river' and *os*, 'mouth'. (For the latter, *cp*. AARHUS.) The town stands at the point where the river Svartån flows into Lake Mälaren.

Vatican The famous palace of the popes in Rome takes its name from the hill on which it stands. Its own name represents Latin *mons vaticinia*, 'hill of prophecies', from *vates*, 'prophet'. (*Cp.* English *vatic.*) The palace in turn gave the name of *Vatican City* as the world's only remaining papal state.

Vaucluse The department of southeast France has a name that ultimately represents its Roman name, *Vallis Clusa*, 'closed valley'. The valley in question is that of the Rhône (in the north) and the Durance (in the south), which is bounded on the eastern side by steeply rising mountains.

Vaud The canton of southwest Switzerland derives its name from its original inhabitants, referred to as *walho*, 'stranger' by their neighbours. *Cp.* WALES.

Vaudeville Theatre The London theatre in the Strand was built in 1870 with a name already in existence for theatres elsewhere in Europe, such as the Paris *Théâtre du Vaudeville* which opened in 1792. The name is that of *vaudeville* itself, as a term for music hall or variety, popularly said to derive from French *Vau de Vire* or 'valley of the Vire' in Normandy where folksongs were sung in the 15th century, or from *voix de ville*, 'town voice'. It seems likely, however, that the word is actually a corruption, influenced by *ville*, 'town', of French *vaudevire*, 'topical song', from French *vauder*, a form of *voûter*, and *virer*, both meaning 'to turn'. The sense is of a song 'turned' for the occasion.

Vaughan The name is either a diminutive of Welsh *Baugh*, itself meaning 'short', 'little', as a form of Welsh *bach*, or else an anglicization of an Irish name such as *Ó Mocháin*, 'descendant of *Mochán*', the latter personal name being a diminutive of Irish *moch*, 'early', 'timely'.

Vauxhall The district of Lambeth, London, has a name that means '*Vaux*'s hall', referring to the manor that was held by *Vaux*, otherwise *Falkes* de Bréauté, in the 13th century. The Norman owner had a personal name of Germanic origin meaning 'falcon'. He came from *Bréauté*, a village near Le Havre in northern France. *Vauxhall* had a famous pleasure garden from the 17th to the 19th century, and its name was adopted for similar resorts elsewhere. One of these was at the Russian town of Pavlovsk, near St Petersburg,

where its proximity to the railway station gave what came to be the standard Russian word for 'railway station', *vokzal*. The adoption of the English name was eased through the existing word *zal*, meaning 'hall', 'room', especially a public one, such as a dance hall or waiting room.

Vauxhall The make of car, long associated with its manufacturer's headquarters in Luton, was originally produced in 1903 in VAUXHALL, London, in a factory that had developed on the site of the *Vauxhall* Ironworks, founded in 1857.

Veasey, Veazey *See* VAISEY..

Veda The name for the sacred books of Hinduism represents the Sanskrit word for 'knowledge', from *veda*, 'I know'. The oldest and most important book is the RIG-VEDA.

Vedda The aboriginal people of Sri Lanka have a name of Dravidian origin meaning 'hunter'.

Vega The name of the brightest star in the constellation Lyra derives from Arabic *wāqiʿ*, 'falling', from the verb *waqaʿa*, 'to fall'. This is an abbreviated form of its full name *an-nasr al-wāqiʿ*, 'the falling eagle', as opposed to ALTAIR, 'the flying eagle', the brightest star in the constellation Aquila.

Velcro The patent type of fabric fastener derives its name from the first syllables of the French words *velours croché*, 'hooked velvet'. The fastener, invented in Switzerland in the late 1950s, consists of two imitation velvet strips made of nylon. A number of tiny hooks on one of these engage in a corresponding number of small loops on the other when the two are pressed together and conversely disengage when the strips are pulled apart.

Velvet Underground, The The American avant-garde rock band, formed in 1965, adopted their name from the title of a pornographic paperback by Michael Leigh seen (or read) by Lou Reed, the group's lead singer and lyricist.

Venables The name is Norman, originating from a place near Rouen in northern France, itself with a name perhaps deriving from Latin *venari*, 'to hunt'.

Vendée The department of western France takes its name from the river here. The river's own name may derive from Gaulish *vindo*, 'white'. *Cp.* VANNES.

Vendémiaire The name of the first month of the French Revolutionary calendar, corresponding to the period from 23 September to 22 October, means 'grape harvest', from Latin *vindemia*, 'vintage', ultimately from *vinum*, 'wine' and *demere*, 'to take away'.

Veneto *See* VENICE.

Venezuela The South American republic has a name that is a Spanish diminutive of *Venecia*, 'VENICE'. The region was so named by sailors who came here with Columbus in 1499 and saw by Lake Maracaibo an Indian village built on piles or stakes. This reminded them of Venice. London's *Little Venice* has a name that is an exact equivalent, although in this case the inspiration came from the district's canal, not its buildings. (It was compared to Venice by the poets Byron and Browning, although the present name appears not to have come into general use until after the Second World War.)

Venice The Italian city takes its name from the historic inhabitants of the region, the *Veneti*, whose own name may mean 'white' (*see* VANNES, VENDÉE). The same people gave the name of *Veneto*, the region of northeast Italy, of which *Venice* is the capital. The city has borne the name only since the 13th century. Earlier it was known as *Rivoalto*, 'raised shore', which gave the name of the modern RIALTO. A word of similar meaning lies behind that of the LIDO.

Vent-Axia The make of air-extraction unit is so named because it has an *axial* fan (one rotating on an axis, and not moving to and fro in the traditional manner) that provides *vent*ilation.

Ventimiglia The name of the town in northwest Italy appears to mean 'twenty miles'. It is actually a corruption, however, of the Roman name *Album Intimelium* or *Albintimilium*, from the name of a Ligurian tribe. The original meaning is unknown.

Ventnor The Isle of Wight seaside resort is believed to have derived its name from a local family called *Vintner*, who owned a farm here in or before the early 17th century.

Ventôse The sixth month of the French Revolutionary calendar, corresponding to the period from 20 February to 21 March, has a name meaning 'windy', from Latin *ventosus*, 'full of wind', a derivative of *ventus*, 'wind'.

Venture Scout The name replaced that of the *Rover Scout* in 1966 for a member of the senior branch of *Scouts* (*see* BOY SCOUTS), aged 16 to 20. From 1976, when GIRL GUIDES were admitted to the branch, the name has applied to both sexes. The name itself implies a person undertaking a pioneering enterprise, while also suggesting an involvement in an *adventure* (perhaps that of going out into the world).

Venus The name of the Roman goddess of love derives from Latin *venus*, genitive *veneris*, 'charm', 'love', 'sexual love' (hence English *venereal*). The second planet from the sun is so named because *Venus* was the Roman goddess who corresponds to the Greek *Aphrodite*, the latter being the name given it by Aristotle. The planet was originally wrongly identified by the Greeks as a 'Morning Star' and an 'Evening Star', named respectively *Phosphoros* ('light bearer') and *Hesperos* ('evening one'). It was Pythagoras who proposed that the two 'stars' were actually one and the same celestial body. The name of the goddess of love is very fitting for the planet that is the brightest in the sky and that has long been regarded as the most beautiful.

Venusberg The mountain in eastern Germany contains the cave in which, according to medieval legend, the goddess VENUS held her court.

Veracruz The port in eastern Mexico has a Spanish name meaning 'true cross', referring to the original one on which Christ was crucified. The town was founded in Holy Week 1519 by the Spanish conquistador Hernán Cortés and originally named by him *Villa rica de la Vera Cruz*, 'rich town of the True Cross'.

Vercingetorix The name is that of the famous Gallic chieftain and hero who led a major rebellion in Gaul against Roman rule in the 1st century BC but who was captured and executed by Caesar. His name has been interpreted as 'man who is chief of a hundred heads', from Gaulish words related to modern Irish *fear*, 'man', *ceann*, 'head', *céad*, 'hundred', and *ré*, 'king', 'chief'.

Verde, Cape The name of the westernmost cape of Africa derives from Portuguese *Cabo Verde*, 'green cape'. The cape must have been so named for its greenness or comparative fertility by contrast with the surrounding barren sands of the desert and the coast. The cape gave the name of the island republic of *Cape Verde* or (officially from 1986) *Cabo Verde*.

Verdun The town in northeast France, notorious for the longest and fiercest battle of the First World War, had the Roman name *Virodunum*, meaning '*Vero*'s fort', with the Gaulish personal name followed by *dunu*, 'fort'.

Vereeniging The city in Transvaal, South Africa, arose in 1882 on the discovery of coal here and takes its name from the Afrikaans title of the mining company, *De Zuid-Afrikaansche en Oranje Vrijstaatsche Kolen- en Mineralen-Mijn Vereeniging*, 'The South African and Orange Free State Coal and Mineral Mines Association'. The name is usually pronounced 'Fe*r*eeniking'.

Vergil *See* VIRGIL.

Verkhoyansk The Russian town in eastern Siberia has a name meaning 'upper *Yana*', from Russian *verkh*, 'height' and a river name of uncertain origin. The town is at the confluence of two rivers that form the *Yana*.

Vermont The American state has a French name that means 'green mountain'. However, the standard French form of the name would be *Mont Vert*, suggesting that the present name was promoted by an English settler who deliberately or ignorantly reversed the words of the French original. The mountains in question lie to the east of Lake Champlain, where their covering of coniferous forests keeps them green all the year round.

Vernon The name is Norman, and derives from any of the places so called in the north of France, such as the town on the Seine west of Paris. The town's name itself is Gaulish in origin and means 'place of elders'.

Vernons The well-known football pool firm takes its name from its founder, *Vernon* Sangster (1899–1986), who set up his business in Liverpool in 1926.

Verona The original Celtic name of the city in northern Italy was *Vernomago*, from *verno*, 'elder tree' and *mago*, 'field'.

Veronica The name is a corrupt form of BERENICE, influenced by the Church Latin expression *vera icon*, 'true image' (of which it is an anagram), to refer to a miraculous portrait of Christ that was capable of healing. The phrase is associated in particular with the name of St *Veronica*, said to have offered Christ a cloth to wipe the blood and sweat from his face as he carried his cross to Calvary and to have found a 'true image' of his face imprinted on it afterwards. However, she was probably invented to account for this derivation. The name has also been traditionally applied to the unnamed woman 'diseased with an issue of blood' (*Matthew* 9.20) who was healed by Jesus when she touched his garment.

Versailles The famous French city and royal residence near Paris has a name that remains of disputed origin. Proposed etymologies include the following: 1. from Latin *versus*, 'slope' with a suffix *-alia*; 2. from Latin *versum*, 'turned' and *alae*, 'wings', with reference to a former windmill here; 3. from Medieval Latin *versagium*, a legal term for a type of tax on forests; 4. from Old French *val de Gallie*, 'valley of Gaul'. Only the first of these is regarded as anything like plausible.

Vertumnus The Roman god of gardens, orchards and seasonal change derives his name from Latin *vertere*, 'to turn'.

Vespasian The Roman emperor of the 1st century AD had the full name Titus Flavius Sabinus *Vespasianus*. His *agnomen* or extra name derived from his mother, *Vespasia* Polla, whose own name is apparently a form of the Greek name *Aspasia*, meaning 'welcome', 'well-pleasing'.

Vesta The Roman goddess of the hearth and its fire has a name that derives from that of the Greek goddess *Hestia* to whom she corresponded. Greek *hestia* means simply 'hearth'. A perpetual flame in the temple of *Vesta* was kept burning by the *vestal* virgins, the select number of virgin priestesses whose lives were dedicated to her and her sacred fire.

Vestmannaeyjar The group of islands off the south coast of Iceland has a name meaning 'islands of the western men', from Icelandic *vestan*, 'west', *mann*, 'man' and *eyjar*, the plural of *ey*, 'island'.

Vesuvius The well-known volcano in southwest Italy has a name that may ultimately derive from a pre-Celtic root element *ves* meaning simply 'mountain'. Some authorities, however, prefer a source in Oscan *fesf*, 'smoke', 'steam', referring to the actual volcano rather than the mountain.

Veterans Day The name is that of the American equivalent of REMEMBRANCE SUNDAY, when the dead of both world wars and specifically American wars such as the Korean War are commemorated. It is held on 11 November (or the nearest weekday, if this is a Saturday or Sunday) and is a public holiday. *Veteran* here has its American sense to refer to a former member of the armed services.

Veuve Clicquot The familiar type of champagne takes its name from the firm of bankers and wine merchants established in Reims, France, in 1794 by François *Clicquot* (d. 1805) and his wife Marie *Clicquot* (1777–1866), the daughter of Baron Ponsardin. On the early death of her husband, Mme Clicquot, aged 28, carried on the business. It was she who added *Veuve* ('widow') to the house name, apparently implying that she was something of a 'merry widow'. Hence the colloquial English name *the Widow* for *Veuve Clicquot* champagne and even for champagne generally. The full official name of the firm is now *Veuve Clicquot Ponsardin*.

Via Dolorosa The name, Latin for 'sorrowful way', originally applied to the route followed by Christ in Jerusalem from the place of his sentencing in Pilate's judgment hall to the place of his crucifixion at Calvary. It is marked by the 14 'Stations of the Cross' and is traditionally still followed by Franciscan monks every Friday. The phrase has come to be used for any difficult or distressing time or experience. The name itself is probably based on those of famous Roman routes in Italy, such as the *Via Appia* (*see* APPIAN WAY) or *Via Sacra*, the 'sacred way' leading from the Roman Forum to Velia.

Vicenza The city in northeast Italy had the Roman name of *Vicetia* or *Vicentia*. The origin of this is uncertain.

Vichy The familiar name of the town and spa in central France may represent Latin *vicus calidus*, 'warm settlement', referring to its hot springs.

Vickers The name originally denoted the son or servant of a *vicar*, so is more or less in the same category as PARSONS.

Vicks The proprietary name of the brand of vapour rub is named for Dr Joshua *Vick*. He was the owner of the drugstore in Selma, North Carolina, where the preparation's inventor, his chemist son-in-law Lunsford Richardson, began his career. The product itself was first marketed in the 1890s as 'Richardson's Croup and Pneumonia Cure Salve'.

Victor The name derives from Latin *victor*, 'conqueror'. Early Christians adopted the name symbolically with reference to Christ's *victory* over sin and death. *Cp.* VICTORIA.

Victoria. The name is Latin for 'victory'. It was made widely known to English speakers by Queen *Victoria* (1819–1901), who was herself given it for her mother, Mary Louise *Victoria*, daughter of the duke of Saxe-Coburg. It was not popularly adopted, however, until almost the mid-20th century.

Victoria The state in southeast Australia was created as a separate territory from New South Wales in 1851 and named for Queen *Victoria* (1819–1901). The queen came to the throne in 1837 and gave her name to many places, small and large, in and beyond the British Empire of her day. Natural objects named for her include the *Victoria* Falls, on the Zambezi in Zambia, the Great *Victoria* Desert in southeast Australia, Lake *Victoria*, in East Africa, Mount *Victoria*, in Papua New Guinea, and *Victoria* Island in the Canadian Arctic.

Towns and cities named *Victoria* include the capital of British Columbia, Canada, the capital of the Seychelles, and the capital of Hong Kong. *Victoria*, the district of southwest central London, with its railway terminus, takes its name from *Victoria* Street, built in the 1850s and 1860s and named similarly for Queen *Victoria*. The London Underground *Victoria Line* was opened in 1968 and named for the station.

Victoria and Albert Museum The famous London museum and art gallery was opened in Cromwell Road by Queen *Victoria* in 1857 as a new venue for the combined Museum of Ornamental Art at Marlborough House and School of Design at Somerset House and was named for her and her husband Prince *Albert*.

Victoria College The public school for boys in Jersey, Channel Islands, was founded in commemoration of a visit of Queen *Victoria* to the island. It opened in 1852.

Victoria Day The name is that of the Canadian national holiday held on the Monday before 24 May to commemorate the birthday of Queen *Victoria*.

Vienna The capital of Austria had the Roman name of *Vindobona*, representing Celtic *vindo*, 'white' (*see* VANNES) and *bona*, 'foundation', 'fort' (*cp*. BONN). The first part of this doubtless referred not to the fort but to the small river *Wien* which joins the Danube here.

Vienne The department of western France takes its name from the river that flows through it, with the river's own name perhaps based on an Indoeuropean root element *veg*, 'damp'. The source is not the same as that of VIENNA, as evidenced by 6th-century records of the river name as *Vingenna* and *Vigenna*.

Vientiane The capital of Laos has a Laotian name meaning 'town of sandalwood', from *vieng*, 'fortification', 'town' and *chăn*, 'sandalwood'. The spelling arose under French influence.

Vietcong The name was used in the Vietnam War (1959–76) for the Communist-led guerrilla force of South Vietnam. It represents Vietnamese *Việt-Nam công-san*, 'Vietnamese Communists'.

Vietminh The name applied to the Vietnamese independence movement led by Ho Chi Minh that first fought the Japanese, then the French, in the period from 1941 to 1954. It derives from the first and last elements of the full Vietnamese title *Việt-Nam Dôc-Lâp Dông-Minh*, 'Vietnamese Independence League'.

Vietnam The southeast Asian republic, divided from 1954 to 1976 into Communist North *Vietnam* and non-Communist South *Vietnam*, has the Vietnamese name *Việt-Nam*, from *Việt*, the name of a former principality of southern China, and *nam*, 'south'.

Vigo The port in southwest Spain, famous as the site of the British and Dutch victory of 1702 over the French and Spanish, derives its name from Latin *vicus*, 'settlement', 'village', from a root word that gave the *-wich* in such English place-names as NORWICH and GREENWICH.

Vijayanagar The name of the capital of the former Hindu kingdom in southern India means 'town of victory', from Sanskrit *vijaya*, 'victory' and *nagara*, 'town'. The city was the centre of Hindu resistance against Muslim invaders until it was destroyed in 1565.

Viking The name is famous as that of the Scandinavian warriors who raided and often settled in territories (such as Britain) of northwest Europe from the 8th to the 11th centuries. Two rival etymologies have been proposed for the name. One derives it from Old Norse *vík*, 'bay', 'creek', referring either to the Norwegian fjords from which the raiders came or to the creeks in which they landed to carry out their plundering. The other links it with Old English *wīc*, 'dwelling', 'camp', with reference to the encampments that they set up in the territories where they landed. The form of the name has given a false association with English *king*, as if the Vikings were the 'masters of the sea'.

Vileda The brand of cleaning cloth is German in origin and has a name designed to represent German *wie Leder*, 'like leather'. This refers to the manufacturer's principal product, a synthetic chamois cleaning cloth which is claimed to clean like real chamois leather.

Village People, The The American rock group, formed in New York in 1977, took their name from that of Greenwich *Village*, the artistic and 'Bohemian' district of New York noted in recent years for its gay community. The latter association provided the inspiration for the six American male stereotypes who were represented in the group: a cowboy, an Indian chief, a policeman, a biker, a GI and a construction worker.

Villefranche The name is found for several places in France, notably the towns of *Villefranche*-sur-Saône, near Lyon, and *Villefranche*-de-Rouergue, near Rodez. The meaning is 'free town', denoting a town or urban centre founded by a lord and granted special tax exemptions with the aim of attracting residents.

Villeneuve There are various French places of the name, notably *Villeneuve*-sur-Lot in southwest France. The meaning is 'new town', corresponding to the name *Neuville*, also frequently found. The name is hardly original but serves a straightforward descriptive purpose. *Newton*, its English equivalent, is the most common place-name in Britain.

Villiers The name is of Norman origin, and was borne by a person who came from one of the many places called *Villiers* or *Villars* or *Villers* in northern France, such as *Villiers*-Adam northwest of Paris. The place-name itself denotes an outlying farm or dependent settlement, and ultimately derives from Latin *villa*, 'village'.

Vilnius The capital of Lithuania takes its name from the river *Vilija* on which it stands, with the river name itself representing Lithuanian *vilnis*, 'wave'. This derives from an Indoeuropean root element that also gave Latin *volvere*, 'to roll' and English *well*, as in 'to well up'.

Viminal The name is that of one of the seven hills on which Rome was built. It derives from Latin *viminalis*, 'making withies', from *vimen*, 'wand', 'osier', referring to a withy grove on the hill.

Vimto The brand of sparkling soft drink was originally known as *Vimtonic*, implying a *tonic* that gave its drinker *vim* or energy. The name was subsequently shortened as now.

Vincennes The town that is now an eastern suburb of Paris probably takes its name from the Gaulish personal name *Vilicus*, of uncertain meaning.

Vincent The name ultimately derives from Latin *vincere*, 'to conquer', so that it is essentially identical in origin to VICTOR. It has been made familiar through various saints, especially the French Roman Catholic priest who founded two charitable orders, St *Vincent* de Paul (1581–1660).

Vine The name originally applied to a person who lived near a vineyard or who worked in one. Viniculture was much more common in England than it is now, as witness the place-name *Winyard*, 'vineyard' found in the south of England, for example *Winyard* Mill, near Malmesbury, Wiltshire.

Vinland The name is famous as that of the stretch of the east coast of North America that Leif Ericson and other Vikings discovered in the early 11th century. The meaning is 'vine land', perhaps referring to the wild grapes that grew here. It has been suggested, however, that the 'grapes' found by the Vikings were actually cranberries.

Vinnitsa The Ukrainian city has a Ukrainian name meaning 'distillery', from *vino*, 'wine'. The city is the centre of a major agricultural region.

Viola The name derives from the Latin *viola*, 'violet', although in modern English it has come to be associated more specifically not with this flower but with the larger *viola*, a type of pansy.

Violet The name, now out of favour, derives from that of the flower, itself so named for its colour. *See also* VIOLA.

Virago The publishing firm, founded in 1973 with the aim of promoting books that highlight aspects of women's lives, has a name adopted from *virago*, a word that now means 'noisy, domineering woman' or 'shrew', but that originally meant 'heroic woman'. The founders also chose the name because they 'knew it would shock a little' (Adrianne Blue, 'Virago Modern Classics – Bedtime Reading for a Lifetime', *Ms*, April 1984, pp. 27–30).

Virgil The full name of the 1st-century BC Roman poet was Publius *Vergilius* Maro.

His *nomen* or inherited clan name is of uncertain origin but became associated with *virgo*, 'maiden' or *virga*, 'stick', which led to the change in spelling.

Virgin The familiar commercial name, associated exclusively with Richard Branson and popularized by *Virgin* records and record shops and more recently by *Virgin* Atlantic Airlines, originally applied to the mail-order pop record business set up by Branson in 1969. He gave it the name to indicate the *virgin* field he had discovered for a new type of commercial activity. Branson founded the airline company in 1984.

Virginia The name evolved as a feminine form of the Latin name *Virginius* or *Verginius*, a clan name probably related to *Vergilius* (*see* VIRGIL). Like it, however, it has been associated with *virgo*, genitive *virginis*, 'maiden', and it came to be associated in literature with a particular Roman maiden, the daughter of one Lucius *Verginius*, who was stabbed to death by her father to save her from the unwelcome attentions (in modern terms, sexual harassment) of the decemvir Appius Claudius. From the 16th century, the name became associated with Queen Elizabeth, the '*Virgin* Queen', and with the American state of *Virginia* named for her. The first child born in America to English parents was *Virginia* Dare (born 1587) of Roanoke Island (now in North Carolina).

Virginia The American state, the site of the first permanent English settlement in North America (at Jamestown in 1607), is named for Queen Elizabeth (1533–1603), the '*Virgin* Queen'. The first (unsuccessful) attempt at colonization was made in 1584 at Roanoke Island, and there is documentary evidence that the name was given that year by Elizabeth herself. If so, she may have intended it to refer to the newly claimed 'virgin land' as much as to her own actual (or claimed) virginity. *See also* the first name VIRGINIA.

Virginia Water The residential district near Staines, Surrey, takes its name from that of the artificial lake constructed here in the mid-18th century by the Duke of Cumberland. He gave his enterprise a 'pioneering' name adopted (perhaps with tongue in cheek) from that of the American state of VIRGINIA. He may also have seen the freshly created lake as 'virgin water', on an analogy with 'virgin earth'.

Virgin Islands The islands in the West Indies, distinguished as the British Virgin Islands in the east and the Virgin Islands of the United States in the west, were discovered and named by Christopher Columbus in 1493. The name refers either to the fact that he made his discovery on St Ursula's day, Monday 21 October, so that the name refers to the eleven thousand *virgins* who were her legendary companions, or to the supposed resemblance of the chain of islands to a procession of nuns or virgins, perhaps even these particular ones.

Virgo The name of the zodiacal constellation on the celestial equator represents the Latin for 'maiden', 'virgin'. The maiden in question is usually identified as DEMETER, the Greek goddess of the harvest, and the constellation's brightest star, Spica, represents the ear of corn (the meaning of its Latin name) that she holds in her left hand.

Virgo The surname is of uncertain origin. It appears to represent Latin *virgo*, 'maiden', 'virgin', so may have been a nickname for someone who was shy or modest, or who had played the part of the *Virgin* Mary in a medieval mystery play.

Virol The formerly familiar malt tonic food was so named for two reasons. First, because it suggested Latin *vir*, 'man' and *oleum*, 'oil' (it was widely promoted for children: '*Virol* – Growing Boys Need It'), second, because it was initially produced in the London factory that made BOVRIL, of which name *Virol* is a partial anagram.

Visby The port in southeast Sweden has a name ending in the *-by*, meaning 'settlement', that is found fairly widely in eastern England, for example in GRIMSBY or WHITBY. The first part of the name is of uncertain origin. It may mean 'holy', referring to a heathen cult practised here, or else represent Old Norse *vithr*, 'wood'. The Swedish pronunciation is approximately 'Veez-bu', with the second vowel as a lengthened *u* in French *tu*.

Vishnu In Hinduism, the name is that of one of the three gods in the TRIMURTI. He is known as 'the Sustainer', and his name represents Sanskrit *viṣṇu*, 'pervading everywhere', from *viş*, 'to penetrate', 'to pervade'.

Visigoth The name is that of the western group of GOTHS, who set up a kingdom in present-day Spain and southern France from the 5th to the 8th century. Their name probably means 'western Goths', by contrast with the OSTROGOTHS or 'eastern Goths'.

Vistula Poland's chief river has a name that perhaps ultimately derives from an Indoeuropean root element *veik*, 'to flow' or *viso*, 'water'. *Cp.* WESER. The Polish name of the river is *Wisła*, while the Germans know it as the *Weichsel*, perhaps through an association with the identical word meaning 'morello' (a variety of small dark cherry).

Vitebsk The city in Byelorussia takes its name from the river *Vit'ba* on which it is situated. The river's own name is believed to derive from a local word meaning 'marsh', 'wet place'.

Vitry There are several places of the name in France, with their origin usually in the Roman personal name *Victorius*. The two best-known towns are *Vitry*-sur-Seine, southeast of Paris, and *Vitry*-le-François, in the Champagne region southeast of Reims. The latter is named for *Francis* I, who founded it in 1545 to replace the earlier *Vitry*-en-Perthois, burned by the Imperialists (the soldiers of the German emperor).

Vivian The name derives from the Latin name *Vivianus*, itself probably from *vivus*, 'alive'. *See also* VIVIENNE.

Vivienne The feminine form of VIVIAN has followed the modern French spelling in recent times, rather than the Old French form *Vivien*. Even so, both are still found, and *Vivian* also occasionally still occurs in female use. It is familiar from literature as the name of the mistress of Merlin, the 'Lady of the Lake' in the Arthurian romances. For her, however, the name may well have been of Celtic origin, as for most of the characters in the stories about King Arthur.

Viyella The type of patent woven cloth was originally manufactured in a factory in the *Via Gellia*, near Matlock, Derbyshire. This name, a mock Latin one for a mock Roman road, was pronounced 'Vi Jella' by local residents, and influenced the final form of the commercial name, which was adopted from its place of origin. The place-name itself was actually based on that of the *Gell* family of Hopton Hall, Wirksworth, who are said to have built the road in the late 18th century.

Vlachs *See* WALACHIA.

Vladikavkaz The city in southwest Russia, where it is the capital of North Ossetia, was founded in 1784 as a military fortress. Its name means 'possessing the CAUCASUS', from the root of Russian *vladet'*, 'to possess' and *Kavkaz*, 'Caucasus'. The fort was designed to protect the Georgian Military Highway, one of the key routes over the Caucasus. The name was invented by the soldier and statesman Grigory Potëmkin, lover and favourite of Catherine the Great. In 1931 the city was renamed *Ordzhonikidze*, for the Georgian Communist leader and revolutionary Grigory *Ordzhonikidze* (1886–1937), who in the years immediately following the Revolution led the defence of the town against counterrevolutionaries and who played a leading role in bringing Georgia under Soviet rule. The city reverted to its former name in 1990. The name of VLADIVOSTOK was based on that of *Vladikavkaz*.

Vladimir The Russian name is popularly interpreted as either 'possessor of the world' or 'possessor of peace' (both equally propitious), from words related to modern Russian *vladet'*, 'to possess' and *mir*, 'world', 'peace'. However, its original form was *Vladimer* or *Volodimer*, suggesting that it may be a borrowing of the Germanic name *Waldemar*, from Old German *waltan*, 'to rule' and *māri*, 'famous', together implying a 'famous ruler'. The name is best known from St *Vladimir* (956–1015), the Grand Prince of Kiev who was the first Russian ruler to accept Christianity and who imposed it on the provinces of Kiev and Novgorod. It was his great-grandson who founded and gave the name of the city of VLADIMIR. The name is properly stressed on the second syllable, 'Vla*di*mir'.

Vladimir The city in western Russia was founded in 1108 by the Grand Prince of Kiev, *Vladimir* Monomakh (1053–1125) (so nicknamed as his mother was the daughter of the Byzantine emperor Constantine *Monomachus*, 'fighter in single combat').

Vladivostok The port in the extreme southeast of Russia was founded as a military post in 1860 and given a name based on that of VLADIKAVKAZ. It means 'possessor of the east', from the root of Russian *vladet'*, 'to possess', and *vostok*, 'east'.

Vltava The river in the Czech Lands has a name of Germanic origin, from *Wilthahwa*, 'wild water', comprising *wilth*, 'wild' and *ahwa*, 'water'. The reference is to the strong current. The German name of the river is *Moldau*, a corruption of an original variant form *Voltava*.

Vodafone The commercial name of the cellular telephone system introduced by Racal in the mid-1980s derives from a blend of '*vo*ice', '*da*ta' and a respelled 'tele*phone*'.

Vogul The people of western Siberia and northeast Europe are said to derive their name from Zyrian *va*, 'water' and *kul'*, 'devil'.

Vojvodina The region of northern Serbia has a name that means 'land of the *voivode*', this being originally the title of an army leader but subsequently that of the governor of a province.

Volapük The name of the artificial language, based on existing major European languages, represents Volapük *vol*, 'world', a form of English *world*, *-a-*, added for euphony, and *pük*, 'speech', based on English *speak*. It was invented in 1880 by the German linguist Johann Schleyer (who apparently could not bring himself to jettison his native German umlaut).

Volga Russia's famous river has a name that has so far defied any precise or conclusive interpretation. It probably derives from a root element meaning simply 'wet', 'damp', related to modern Russian *vlaga*, 'moisture'.

Volgograd The city in southwest Russia, a port on the river VOLGA, has a name that means simply that, 'Volga town', the final *-grad* found in Slavic names such as BELGRADE. It was founded in 1589 and until 1925 was known as *Tsaritsyn*, from Turkish *sarışın*, 'yellowish', referring to the colour of the water. Inevitably, the name came to be associated with *tsar*. From 1925 to 1961 it was STALINGRAD, a name complementary to that of *Leningrad* (now ST PETERSBURG).

Volkswagen The well-known make of car has a German name meaning 'people's car'. The car's main manufacturing company was set up on the orders of Hitler in 1937 as the *Gesellschaft zur Vorbereitung des deutschen Volkswagens*, 'Company for the development of the German people's car'. Hitler, who himself always had a Mercedes, had planned the car on first coming to power in 1933, and had specified a 'car for the people' that was to be air-cooled and to cost less than 1000 marks (then about £50). The first Volkswagens appeared in 1936, and were designed by Ferdinand PORSCHE.

Vologda The city in northwest Russia takes its name from the river on which it lies. This in turn is of Finno-Ugrian origin meaning 'white', as for modern Finnish *valkea*, Estonian *valge* and Hungarian *világ*.

Volsci The warlike people of ancient Latium, suppressed by the Romans in the 5th and 4th centuries BC, may derive their name from a word related to Gaulish *volca*, 'rapid', 'swift'.

Volta The chief river of Ghana, West Africa, was originally named *Rio da Volta* by Portuguese explorers here in the 15th century. This means 'river of return' or 'river of the bend', either because it marked the point where their expedition turned back, or with reference to the many bends in its lower reaches. Burkina Faso was known as *Upper Volta* until 1984.

Volta Redonda The city in southeast Brazil, founded in 1941, stands in a broad bend of the river Paraíba. Hence its name, which is Portuguese for 'complete curve'.

Volvic The small town in central France is noted for its springs, and has given the commercial name of a brand of mineral water. The name itself probably derives from a pre-Latin root word *vol* meaning 'mountain', together with Latin *vicus*, 'settlement'. However, it could also represent a Roman personal name *Volovicus*.

Volvo The Swedish make of car has a name that is the Latin for 'I roll'. This originally applied not to the car but to a subsidiary of the ball-bearing company, SKF, that employed the two engineers who were the car's original designers. The first *Volvo* made its test run, from Stockholm to Göteborg, in 1926.

Vono The patent type of bedding takes its name from that of the *Vaughan* family who founded the business in about 1920.

Voronezh The city in western Russia is named for the river on which it lies. The river's own name means 'black', from a Slavic word related to modern Russian *voron*, 'crow'.

Voroshilovgrad *See* LUGANSK.

Voroshilovsk *See* STAVROPOL.

Vorticism The art and literary movement, based on Cubism and Futurism, was initiated in 1914 by the artist and novelist Wyndham Lewis with the aggressive force of the machine age as its main inspiration. Its name refers to the *vortices* or 'nodes' of modern life that were thought to generate ideas which could be expressed in artistic or literary form.

Vortigern The name of the legendary 5th-century king of Britain is a corrupt form of the Celtic name *Gwrtheyrn* meaning 'hero king', from root words corresponding to Welsh *gwron*, 'hero' and *teyrn*, 'king'.

Vosges The mountain range in eastern France has a name of Celtic origin, perhaps representing *vos*, 'peak' or else deriving from the name of a Celtic god.

Votyak The Finnish people, inhabiting a region in Russia between the Volga and the Urals, have a name that is a form of *Vyatka*, that of the river here. This probably derives from Votyak *vu*, 'water'. The people are also known as the UDMURT.

Vouvray The dry white wine takes its name from the small French town of *Vouvray* in the Loire valley, where it is produced. The town's name derives from Gaulish *vobero*, 'ravine'.

Vulcan The name of the Roman god of fire is believed to derive from that of an identical Cretan god called *Welkhanos*, itself perhaps related, albeit indirectly, to Latin *ignis*, 'fire'. It was Vulcan who gave the word *volcano*, since the internal rumblings of the mountain were believed to be caused by the noise of his forges in action.

Vulgar Latin The name is used of those dialects of Latin that were spoken by the uneducated classes of Rome and neighbouring provinces, as distinct from 'correct' classical Latin. The first word derives from Latin *vulgaris*, 'of the multitude', from *vulgus*, 'the common people'. Vulgar Latin is also known as *Low Latin*.

Vulgate The name is that of the 4th-century Latin version of the Bible that St Jerome produced by translating from the original languages and by revising an earlier Latin text that had been based on Greek. The term did not come into use until the 13th century, and represents Medieval Latin *Vulgata*, a short form of Late Latin *vulgata editio*, 'popular version', from Latin *vulgare*, 'to popularize', itself from *vulgus*, 'the common people'. *Cp.* VULGAR LATIN.

Vyatka The city in western Russia, of medieval origin, is named for the river on which it lies. The river's own name is probably related to that of the VOTYAK people of this region. In 1934 the town was renamed *Kirov*, for the Soviet Communist Party leader Sergei *Kirov* (1886–1934), who was born near here, and who also gave his name to *Kirovabad* (modern GANDZHA), among other places. In 1991 the city reverted to its original name.

Vyborg The port in northwest Russia, on the Gulf of Finland, has a name of Swedish origin meaning 'holy fort', from *vi*, 'holy' and *borg*, 'fort'. The name originally applied to the Swedish fortress built here in 1293. The city passed to Russia in 1710.

W

Waddell The name derives from the Scottish village of Stow of *Wedale* (now just Stow), on Gala Water, near Edinburgh. The origin of the place-name itself is uncertain, although the second half appears to represent *dale* ('valley'). The name is usually pronounced like *waddle* in Scotland, but is stressed on the second syllable elsewhere, presumably to avoid association with this word.

Wafd The Egyptian nationalist political party, founded in 1923 and dissolved in 1953 (although reconstituted as the *New Wafd* in 1978), takes its name from Arabic *wafd*, 'arrival', 'deputation'. Its full Arabic name is *al-wafd al-miṣrī*, 'the Egyptian delegation'. *See also* EGYPT.

Wagga Wagga The city in New South Wales, Australia, has an Aboriginal name said to mean '(place of) many crows'. The repeated word denotes the plural, and the word itself probably derives from the bird's cry.

Waghorn The name is said to have been an occupational one for a hornblower, who *wagged* (or brandished) his *horn*. But as this analysis suggests, the origin could well have been in a bawdy nickname for a lascivious or sexually promiscuous person. *Cp.* WAGSTAFF and *see also* SHAKESPEARE.

Wagram The village in northeast Austria, famous as the scene of the defeat of the Austrians by Napoleon in 1809, derives its name from Middle High German *wâch-rein*, 'sloping bank'.

Wagstaff The name may have originated as an occupational designation for an official who carried a staff. On the other hand it could equally have been a bawdy nickname for someone who *wagged* his *staff*, or who was sexually promiscuous. *Cp.* WAGHORN and *see also* SHAKESPEARE.

Waikiki The resort area in Hawaii, a suburb of Honolulu, has a Hawaiian name said to mean 'gushing water'.

Wailing Wall The wall in Jerusalem, the only surviving remnant of the Second Temple, sacred to Jews as a place of pilgrimage, is so named for the lamentations made here by Jews for the destruction of the Temple and for the prayers they offer for its restoration. The name is an unofficial one that probably originated with European tourists who witnessed the mournful vigils of Jews here and regarded the scene as an exotic spectacle. The Jewish name for the site translates as *Western Wall*.

Wainwright The name was originally an occupational one for a maker of wains or carts. The sense is thus very close to that of CARTWRIGHT.

Waite The name was an occupational one for a watchman. Compare the term *waits* for carol singers, so called as they originated from the musicians who sounded the *watch* by playing wind instruments at stated times.

Waitrose The well-known foodmarket chain takes its name from Wallace Wyndham *Waite* (1881–1971) and Arthur *Rose* (1881–1949), two London grocery store assistants, who with a third colleague, David Taylor, opened their own shop in 1906. Taylor left soon after, and Waite and Rose combined their names to trade jointly as *Waitrose*. By the start of the First World War they owned 25 stores, a figure that by the end of the 1980s had almost quadrupled.

Wakayama The city in southern Japan, a port on Honshu, derives its name from Japanese *wa*, 'peace', 'harmony', *ka*, 'song', 'singing' and *yama*, 'mountain'.

Wakefield The county town of West Yorkshire has a name that basically means what it says, referring to the *wake* or local festivities that were held on the *field* here. Many towns in the north of England still have an annual *wake* or holiday when factories and schools close for one or two weeks. The word itself derives from Old English *wacu*, 'watch', 'wake'. Wakefield would have been an ideal site for such festivities, with its *field* being the open land between the river Calder in the south and the extensive wood of Outwood in the north.

Wake Island The atoll in the north central Pacific, claimed by the United States in 1898, takes its name from the English navigator William *Wake*, who visited it in 1796.

Walachia The former principality of southeast Europe, now part of Romania, takes its name from its indigenous people, the Walachians or *Vlachs*, otherwise the Romanians proper, who claimed to be descendants of the ancient Romans. They were so named by their Slav neighbours, who regarded them as 'strangers' or 'foreigners', and who designated them by a Slavic form of the Germanic word *walho* that essentially also gave the name of WALES and the WALLOONS. *See also* ROMANIA.

Walcheren The island in the estuary of the river Scheldt, in the southeast Netherlands, derives its name from Old German *walho*, 'stranger', referring to its original inhabitants, who were not Germanic in origin. *Cp.* WALES.

Walden The name derives from any of the places so called, such as SAFFRON WALDEN in Essex. The place-name itself means 'valley of foreigners', denoting a colony of 'Ancient Britons'.

Waldorf-Astoria New York's famous de luxe hotel takes its name from John Jacob *Astor* (1864–1912), who originally built it as the *Astoria*. In the Great Depression of 1929 the hotel was expanded and added the title of the Astor family, *Waldorf*, adopted by William Waldorf Astor (1848–1919), created Baron Astor of Hever Castle in 1916. He was the great-grandson of the American financier John Jacob Astor (1763–1848), born at *Walldorf* near Heidelberg, western Germany. The London *Waldorf* Hotel, built in 1906, took the same name. The New York hotel gave the name of *Waldorf* salad, first prepared here.

Waldstein Sonata Beethoven's Piano Sonata No 21 in C, Op 53 (1803–4) is so named because the composer dedicated it to his patron, Count Ferdinand von *Waldstein* (1762–1823).

Wales The principality in western Britain derives its name from Old English *walh*, 'stranger', 'foreigner', 'Celt'. The term was applied by the Anglo-Saxon settlers in Britain to the 'native' Celts, who were alien to them in many ways, speaking a different language and with different traditions and social customs. The *wal*nut is called a 'foreign' nut for the same reason: it was an Asian import to Britain. Other place-names based on the same word, whether in Old English or some other Germanic language, include the following: CORNWALL, SAFFRON WALDEN, WALACHIA, WALCHEREN, WALLASEY, WALTON-ON-THAMES. *See also* GAUL, WALLOON and the surname WALLACE. The Welsh themselves call their land *Cymru*, from *Cymry*, 'Welsh', literally 'compatriots', 'fellow countrymen'.

Walker The name was originally an occupational one for a fuller, that is, for a person who fulled (beat or pressed) cloth by treading on it or *walking* over it. *See also* FULLER.

Walkers The familiar make of potato crisps is named for Henry *Walker*, a Nottinghamshire pork butcher who took over a butchery business in Leicester in the 1880s. Further shops were opened, but the firm did not begin to make potato crisps until 1949.

Walkman The make of personal stereo, first marketed in the west by Sony in 1979, is so named as it can be operated as a mobile receiver, while its user is *walking*.

Wallabies The international rugby football team of Australia, formed in the early 20th century, takes its name from the small species of kangaroo that is one of the country's national emblems.

Wallace The name originally applied to a Celt, that is, a Welshman or Scotsman in England or in a predominantly English-speaking part of Britain. It comes from Old English *walh*, 'stranger', 'foreigner', found in such place-names as CORNWALL, SAFFRON WALDEN and WALES.

Wallace Arnold The firm of coach operators takes its name from *Wallace* Cunningham and *Arnold* Crowe, who ran a charabanc business in Leeds before the First World War. The present company dates from 1926, when the owner of a Leeds haulage firm bought the original concern.

Wallace Collection London's famous art gallery takes its name from the noted collector Sir Richard *Wallace* (1818–1890), who left all his property to his widow. She in turn left it to the nation on condition it be kept in central London. Sir Richard's collection was based on that formed by his father and grandfather, the Marquesses of Hertford, and the collection remains in Hertford House, the family home in Manchester Square.

Wallachia *See* WALACHIA.

Wallasey The Merseyside town takes its name from that of the region at the tip of the Wirral peninsula, which became an island at high tide and was cut off from the rest of the peninsula. The region was known as 'island of the *Welsh*', from Old English *wala*, genitive plural of *walh*, 'Welshman' (*see* WALES) and *ēg*, 'island'. The Welsh would not have had far to go to settle here.

Wallingford The name of the Oxfordshire town means 'ford of *Wealh*'s people', the ford itself being over the Thames. The personal name means 'foreigner', 'stranger', as for WALES, and probably means that its bearer was a Briton, not an Anglo-Saxon.

Wallis and Futuna Islands The French island territory in the southwest Pacific takes its name from the English explorer Samuel *Wallis* (1728–1795) who discovered the archipelago in 1767. *Futuna* is the native name of one of the islands, and is of disputed origin.

Walloon The people who live mostly in southern Belgium and northeast France derive their name from the Germanic word *walhon*, meaning 'stranger'. They are French speakers, unlike their Flemish neighbours who speak a Germanic language.

Walls The well-known make of ice cream ultimately takes its name from Richard *Wall* (1775–1836), a London pork butcher, whose business became *Thomas Wall & Son* in 1870 when his grandson, Thomas Wall (1846–1930), completed his apprenticeship. Thomas Wall was the real architect of the present company, which first produced ice cream in 1922.

Wallsend The town east of Newcastle upon Tyne has a name that indicates its location at the *end* of Hadrian's *Wall*. There was a Roman camp here named *Segedunum*, meaning 'strong fort'.

Wall Street The narrow street in Lower Manhattan, New York, regarded as the centre of the American financial world, takes its name from the stockade or *wall* that was built here by Dutch colonists in 1653 to defend the city from attacks by Indians.

Walpole The name denotes a person from a place so called, either the village near Halesworth, Suffolk, or that near King's Lynn, Norfolk. The place-name itself means either 'pool by a wall' or 'pool of the strangers', *i.e.* of the Britons (in an Anglo-Saxon territory). Sir Robert *Walpole* was born at Houghton Hall, Norfolk, a little over 20 miles (32 km) from the village of *Walpole*.

Walpurgis Night The name is that of the eve of 1 May, believed in German folklore to be the night of a witches' sabbath on the Brocken, in the Harz Mountains. The name is a part translation of German *Walpurgisnacht*, 'Walpurga's eve', referring to the 8th-century English abbess and saint, one of whose feast days is 1 May.

Walter The name is Germanic in origin, from a combination of *wald*, 'rule' and *heri*, 'army', implying overall a military leader.

Walthamstow The district of north London at first sight appears to have a name related to that of *Waltham* Abbey or to some other place called *Waltham* (meaning 'homestead by a wood'). However, a document of about 1067 records the name as *Wilcumestouue*, showing that this was not the origin. It actually means '*Wilcume*'s place', the personal name being that of the abbess here. Its own derivation is in Old English *wilcuma*, 'guest' (modern English *welcome*), implying that the abbess and her religious house would have welcomed guests. She presumably adopted a name that was meaningful in this respect.

Walton-on-Thames The Surrey town, on the Thames, has a name found elsewhere that means 'village of the strangers', from Old English *walh*, 'stranger' and *tūn*, 'village'. The reference is to a settlement of Britons, not Anglo-Saxons. Not all places named *Walton* have this meaning, however, and many mean 'village by a wood', with the first element representing Old English *weald*. *See* WEALD.

Walvis Bay The port in Namibia, southwest Africa, has a name representing Afrikaans *Walvisbaai*, from *walvis*, 'whale' (literally 'whale-fish') and *baai*, 'bay'. The port is an exclave of South Africa and has been a noted whaling centre in the past.

Wanderer Fantasia Schubert's Fantasia in C major for piano (1822) is sometimes so called because the Adagio section is a set of variations on a passage from his song *Der Wanderer* (1816).

Wandering Jew, The The name is that of the legendary Jew who, according to medieval folklore, is condemned to roam the world for ever because he mocked Christ on the day of the Crucifixion. In some languages he is known as the *Everlasting Jew*, for example German *der ewige Jude*, Russian *Vechnyy zhid*.

Wandsworth The borough of south London has a name that means '*Wændel*'s enclosure', with the same personal name (but not the same person) as found for WELLINGBOROUGH and WENSLEYDALE. The river *Wandle* here took its name from that of the borough.

Wang The well-known make of computers and electronic instruments takes its name from the Chinese-born engineer An *Wang* (1920–1990), who went to America in 1945 to study applied physics at Harvard and who in 1951 founded *Wang* Laboratories in Boston, Massachusetts.

Wansdyke The ancient earthwork that runs across much of southern England was probably constructed for defensive purposes. It takes its name from WODEN, the famous Anglo-Saxon god of war, who was supposed to have actually built the embankment or who was believed to 'preside' over it.

Wantage The Oxfordshire town takes its name from the stream that flows through it as a tributary of the river Ock. Its own name means 'diminishing one', from Old English *wanian*, 'to lessen' (modern *wane*). The *-age* of the name was thus originally *-ing*.

Wanxian The inland port in central China, on the Yangtze, has a name that derives from Chinese *wàn*, 'ten thousand' and *xiàn*, 'district'.

Wapping The district of east central London has a name meaning '(place of) *Wæppa*'s people'. The Anglo-Saxon personal name probably meant 'weapon', either because its bearer was a skilled swordsman or because he was sexually proficient. (*Cp.* Shakespeare's bawdy pun on the word in the first scene of *Romeo and Juliet*.)

War The American Latin rock band, formed in Long Beach, California, in 1959, chose a name that was designed to be in sharp contrast to the many 'peace' names and preoccupations then current, and that was thus memorable.

Ward The name was originally occupational, denoting a watchman or *guard* (the latter word directly related to it).

Waring The name represents the Norman personal name *Warin*, itself of Germanic origin and meaning 'guard'. *See also* MAINWARING, WARNER.

Warminster The Wiltshire town near Trowbridge has a name that refers to its former *monastery* on the river *Were* here. The river's own name probably derives from Old English *wōrian*, 'to wander'.

Warne The name originally applied to a person from *Warne* near Tavistock, Devon. The place-name itself is said to derive from Old English *wagian*, 'to shake', 'to wag' and *fen*, 'bog', 'marsh', denoting a 'quaking marsh'.

Warner The name represents a Germanic personal name comprising the elements *warin*, 'guard' (*see* WARING) and *heri*, 'army'. In some instances, however, it could be a form of *Warrener*, denoting a person who lived by or worked in a *warren*, or game reserve.

Warner Brothers The American film production company was founded in 1923 by four exhibitor *brothers*: Harry Morris *Warner* (original surname Eichelbaum) (1881–1958), Albert *Warner* (1884–1967), Samuel Louis *Warner* (1887–1927) and Jack Leonard *Warner* (1892–1978). After two takeovers, the company is now named *Warner Communications*.

War of American Independence The name is that of the conflict that followed the revolt of the North American colonies against British rule in the late 18th century, and that lasted from 1775 to 1783. The war resulted in the independent United States of America. The conflict is also known as the *American War of Independence* and the *American Revolution*, the latter title being the preferred one in the United States itself.

War of the Austrian Succession The name is that of the war of 1740 to 1748 between Austria, Britain and the Netherlands against Prussia, France and Spain in support of the rightful *succession* of Maria Theresa to the Austrian throne, as against the territorial claims of Prussia. *Cp.* WAR OF THE SPANISH SUCCESSION.

War of the Spanish Succession The war of this name was fought from 1701 to 1714 between Austria, Britain, Prussia and the Netherlands against France, Spain and Bavaria over the disputed *succession* to the Spanish throne. On the death of the childless Spanish king Charles II in 1700, Louis XIV of France had his 16-year-old grandson proclaimed king of Spain as Philip V in defiance of a partition treaty of 1700 under which the throne should have passed to Archduke Charles of Austria (later the Holy Roman Emperor Charles VI). Philip was eventually recognized as king, thus founding the Spanish branch of the Bourbon dynasty.

Warrington The Cheshire town has a name that means 'weir farm', referring to a farm that must have been by a weir on the river Mersey here. The first part of the name represents the conjectural Old English word *wæring*, a derivative of *wer*, 'weir'.

Warsaw The name of Poland's capital has not been definitively explained. It may have derived from *Warsz*, the personal name of an original landowner here, so that the meaning is 'territory of Warsz'.

Warsaw Concerto The Rachmaninov-style concerto for piano and orchestra by Richard Addinsell was written for the film *Dangerous Moonlight* (1941), in which a Polish pianist escapes from the Nazis and loses his memory after flying in the Battle of Britain. The name is obviously derived from that of WARSAW, the Polish capital, but may have been subconsciously suggested by the *war*time theme of the film.

Wars of the Roses The name is that of the civil war in England from 1455 to 1485 that centred on the struggle for the throne between the house of York, whose symbol was a white rose, and the house of Lancaster, whose badge was a red rose. The name was apparently introduced by Sir Walter Scott in his novel *Anne of Geierstein* (1829), where he refers to the 'wars of the White and Red Roses'. The popular origin of the emblems themselves is re-enacted by Shakespeare in *Henry VI, Part I* (1597) (II, iv), when the plucking of a white rose in the Temple Garden, London, by Richard Plantagenet, Duke of York, and of a red rose by John Beaufort, Earl of Somerset, establishes the rivalry between the two houses.

Warwick The well-known town has a name that means 'weir buildings', referring to a weir or dam on the river Avon here. The first half of the name derives from the same Old English word seen in WARRINGTON.

Wash, The The large shallow inlet of the North Sea on the east coast of England was originally known as *The Washes*, referring to the sandbanks here that were alternately covered and exposed or 'washed' by the sea, so forming two fords across the region between Lincolnshire and Norfolk. The name occurs in Shakespeare's *King*

585

John (1596), where Philip the Bastard says of the loss of King John's treasure:

half my power this night

Passing these flats, are taken by the tide; These Lincoln washes have devoured them.

Washington The New Town in Tyne and Wear, which gave the name of George WASHINGTON and so that of the American state and capital, has a name that means 'settlement of *Wassa*'s people', with the Anglo-Saxon personal name apparently comprising Old English *wāth*, 'hunt' and *sige*, 'victory'.

Washington Both the state in northwest America and the city (*Washington* DC) that is the capital of the United States derive their name from George *Washington* (1732–1799), first president of the United States. The capital was founded in 1791 and the state organized in 1853. Washington's ancestors took their name from what is now the New Town of WASHINGTON, Tyne and Wear.

Was (Not Was) The American pop duo, who released their first album in Detroit in 1981, selected a name that punned on their performing names, Don and David *Was*. They were not related, and David *Was* was not *Was*. He was David *Weiss*, while his fellow musician was Don Fagenson.

Waterford The city and port in southeast Ireland has a name of Scandinavian origin meaning 'wether inlet', from Old Norse *vethr*, 'wether' (an uncastrated ram) and *fjǫrthr*, 'inlet', 'fjord'. The town arose at the point on the river Suir where wethers were loaded onto boats for transportation to other ports. The Irish name of the city is *Port Láirge*, 'port of the haunch', referring to the contour of the river bank here.

Watergate The American political scandal of 1972, which led to the resignation of President Nixon, took its name from the office-apartment hotel complex in Washington DC that housed the national headquarters of the Democratic Party and that was secretly raided that year by people connected with the Republican administration. After slum clearance in the Foggy Bottom district of Washington, southwest of the White House, the Watergate buildings were erected in the mid-1960s at the point where a former *water gate* (channel) led to the river Potomac.

Waterloo The district of southwest central London, with its famous railway station, takes its name from the original *Waterloo* Bridge, which was opened by the Prince Regent in 1817 on the second anniversary of the Battle of WATERLOO. Construction on the bridge actually began in 1811, four years before the battle, and its original planned name was *Strand Bridge*. An Act of Parliament of 1816 changed the name to *Waterloo Bridge*, however, since 'the said bridge when completed will be a work of great stability and magnificence, and such works are adapted to transmit to posterity the remembrance of great and glorious achievements'.

Waterloo, Battle of The famous battle of 1815, in which the British and Prussian forces under Wellington and Blücher routed the French under Napoleon, took its name from the village (now town) in central Belgium near where it took place. The village's own name derives from Flemish *water*, 'water' and *loo*, 'sacred wood'. *See also* WATERLOO.

Waterloo Cup The name of the principal greyhound race in England, held at Altcar, near Formby, Merseyside, derives from that of the *Waterloo* Hotel nearby, whose owner founded it in 1936. The name is also that of the trophy awarded to the winner of the *Waterloo* Handicap, an annual bowls contest held at the *Waterloo* Hotel, Blackpool. The two hotels would both have been named commemoratively for the British victory at the Battle of WATERLOO.

Waterman The name is occupational in origin, denoting either a person who was the servant of a man named WALTER or who was a boatman or water-carrier. In some cases it could have applied to a person who lived by a river or other stretch of water.

Waterman The well-known make of pen takes its name from Lewis E. *Waterman* (1837–1901), an American insurance salesman who in 1884 invented a new type of fountain pen with an improved flow of ink and who that same year first made and sold such pens in a small shop in New York.

Water Music Handel's instrumental suites (of uncertain composition date) are so named because they were written for a royal procession on the river Thames. Six of the suites have been popularized by Hamilton Harty's orchestral arrangement of 1922.

Watford The Hertfordshire town north of London has a name that means 'hunter's ford', from Old English *wāth*, 'hunting' and *ford*, 'ford'. The reference is to a ford over the river Colne where hunters would have crossed. The name of the *Watford Gap* is of the same origin, *Watford* in this case being a village near Daventry, while the *Gap* is the break in the hills known as the Northamptonshire Uplands. (The location is worthy of a nobler name. Strategically sited in the very heart of England, it has long been a major transport channel, taking Watling Street and the Grand Union Canal in the past and now holding two important rail and road routes. The latter are familiar as the M1 motorway, with its famous service station, and as the A5 road.)

Watling Street The famous Roman military road, running from southeast England to north Wales, takes its name from St Albans, to which it led from London, that is, from the town's earlier name of *Wællingaceaster* ('Watlingchester'), derived from the tribe known as the *Wæclings*.

Watney The well-known brew of beer takes its name from James *Watney* (1800–1884), a Surrey clergyman's son who began his career as a miller but who in 1837 took a share in an existing brewery in Pimlico, London.

Waugh The name is of uncertain origin. It may well derive from Old English *walh*, 'foreign', denoting a Briton in Anglo-Saxon territory. It is still found chiefly in southern Scotland and northern England.

Waverley Walter Scott is said to have taken the title of his first novel, published in 1814, in which it is that of the hero, Edward *Waverley*, from *Waverley* Abbey near Farnham, Surrey.

Wayland Smith The *smith* of the elves in European folklore has the Icelandic name of *Volunthr*, the Scandinavian name of *Völundr*, and the German name of *Wieland*. In Old English he was *Wēland*. In Anglo-Saxon legend he is associated with the megalithic tomb known as *Wayland's Smithy* or *Wayland Smith's Cave* near Ashbury in Oxfordshire (formerly Berkshire). The origin of the name, despite wide documentation, remains uncertain.

Weald, The The region of southeast England between the North Downs and the South Downs has a name that represents Old English *wald*, 'forest', or more precisely the Kentish dialect form of this, *weald*. The name came to denote a specifically upland forest, although the forests that were once here have now largely disappeared. Another form of the word gave the name of the *Wolds*, the range of chalk hills in northeast England that comprises the Yorkshire *Wolds* in the north and the Lincolnshire *Wolds* in the south. The word is probably related to *wild*, but not actually to *wood*, which has a different derivation. The original form of the Old English word was reintroduced in the 16th century by the antiquarian William Lambarde:

> Nowe then we are come to the Weald of Kent, which (after the common opinion of men of our time) is conteined within very streight and narrowe limits, notwithstanding that in times paste, it was reputed of suche exceeding bignesse, that it was thought to extend into Sussex, Surrey, and Hamshyre.
>
> *A Perambulation of Kent*, 1576.

Weathermen The American revolutionary group, active in the 1970s, took their name from a line in a song by Bob Dylan:

> You don't need a weatherman
> To know which way the wind blows.
> 'Subterranean Homesick Blues', 1965.

Weaver The name was originally either occupational for a *weaver* or denoted someone who lived by the river *Weaver* in Cheshire. The river's name means 'winding one'. *Cp.* WEBB.

Webb Both this name and *Webster* were originally occupational, denoting a weaver, the Old English word for which was *webba*. *Webster* more precisely derives from Old English *webbestre*, the feminine of *webba*, with reference to a female weaver (*cp.* *spinster* as initially a female *spinner*). By the time the surname developed, however,

587

the original occupational term was obsolete.

Websters The familiar 'Yorkshire Bitter' beer is named for Samuel *Webster* (1813–1872), a Halifax-born brewer who took over a small business near his home town in 1838.

Weddell Sea The arm of the South Atlantic, in the Antarctic, takes its name from the English sealer and explorer James *Weddell* (1787–1834) who in 1823 penetrated farther south here than anyone before him. Weddell himself called the sea *George IV Sea*, and this name remained in use until 1900, when it was decided that the sea should be more fittingly named for the man who had discovered it.

Wedge Fugue Bach's fugue in E minor for organ (between 1727 and 1731) is so nicknamed from the melodic shape of the theme, which begins with notes that alternate in gradually increasing intervals.

Wedgwood The name probably derives from a place so called, although it has not been identified. The place-name itself means 'wych wood'.

Wednesday The fourth day of the week takes its name from the Anglo-Saxon god of war WODEN, corresponding to the Roman god *Mercury*. Hence *mercredi* as the French name of this day.

Wee Frees The name arose as a derogatory nickname for those members of the Free Church of Scotland who refused to merge with the United Presbyterian Church to form the United Free Church in 1900 when the majority of its members did so.

Wehrmacht The name of the German armed services in the Second World War translates as 'defence force', from German *Wehr*, 'defence' and *Macht*, 'force'.

Weidenfeld and Nicolson The London publishing house was founded in 1948 by Arthur George *Weidenfeld* (1919–), now Baron Weidenfeld, an Austrian-born Jew who came to Britain before the Second World War, and Nigel *Nicolson* (1917–), son of the writers Harold Nicolson and Victoria Sackville-West.

Weihai The port in northeast China has a name that means 'majestic sea', from *wēi*, 'majestic', 'imposing' and *hǎi*, 'sea'. The city is also known as *Weihaiwei*, where the added element represents *wèi*, 'to defend', 'to protect'.

Weimar The city in southern Germany, a noted cultural centre, derives its name from Old High German *win*, 'meadow', 'pasture' and *mari*, 'lake', 'spring'.

Weimaraner The breed of hunting dog originated as a sporting dog at the court of WEIMAR in the 19th century. Hence its name.

Weisshorn The mountain in the Swiss Alps has a German name meaning 'white horn', from *weiß*, 'white' and *Horn*, 'horn', 'peak'.

Welbeck College The army educational college near Worksop, Nottinghamshire, takes its name from its location at *Welbeck* Abbey, a mansion that gradually evolved from a 12th-century Premonstratensian priory. The name itself derives from a combination of Old English *wella* (modern English *well*) and Old Norse *bekkr* (modern *beck*), both meaning 'stream'. The Danes must have added the second part of the name when the original Anglo-Saxon word was no longer meaningful.

Welkom The gold-mining town in central South Africa arose in 1948 on a farm of the name, which is Afrikaans for 'welcome'. Gold had already been discovered here, so that the name was a propitious one for the *welcome* wealth that would result.

Wellcome The well-known proprietary make of pharmaceuticals takes its name from Sir Henry S. *Wellcome* (1853–1936), an American farmer's son from Wisconsin who qualified as a pharmacist and who in 1880 set up a partnership in Britain with a fellow American, Silas M. Burroughs. The firm they founded became the *Wellcome* Foundation in 1924, and on his death Sir Henry bequeathed all the company shares to trustees (the *Wellcome* Trust) to fund research in medicine and related subjects.

Wellingborough The Northamptonshire town has a name that means 'fortified place of *Wændel*'s people', with the personal name the same as that for WANDSWORTH and WENSLEYDALE.

Wellington There are two towns of the name in England, respectively in Shropshire and Somerset. The source of the name is still disputed. A formerly favoured meaning was 'farm by the grove of the shrine', from Old English *wēoh*, 'idol', 'shrine', referring to a heathen temple, *lēah*, 'wood', 'clearing' and *tūn*, 'farm'. But for various topological and linguistic reasons this has now been generally rejected. It was the Somerset town that gave the title of the famous duke.

Wellington The capital of New Zealand was founded in 1840 and named for the Duke of WELLINGTON (1769–1852). The name honoured not so much the duke's famous victory at Waterloo as the generous aid he gave to the New Zealand Company, whose colonizing members had arrived the previous year with the task of finding a suitable site for their new settlement. The city replaced Auckland as the country's capital in 1865.

Wellington College The boys' public school in Crowthorne, Berkshire, was founded by public subscription in 1853 to provide education for the sons of deceased army officers, and was named in commemoration of the Duke of *Wellington*, who had died the previous year. It should not be confused with *Wellington School*, which was founded in 1841 and which takes its name from its location in the Somerset town of WELLINGTON.

Wells The Somerset city has a self-explanatory name, referring to the natural springs or wells that have long existed here, and that are now to be found near the east end of the cathedral.

Well-Tempered Clavier, The The name was that given by Bach to his collection of 48 Preludes and Fugues for keyboard in all the major and minor keys. *Tempered* means 'tuned', and is a somewhat ambiguous rendering of the original German title, *Das Wohltemperierte Klavier*. The composition was designed to explore (and exploit) the potentials of a newly established tuning procedure which for the first time made all the keys of the clavier equally usable. A colloquial name for the work is *the 48*.

Welshpool The town in eastern Wales west of Shrewsbury has a name that means what it says, referring to a *pool* (in the river Severn) that is on the *Welsh* side of the border, not the English.

Welwyn Garden City The New Town in Hertfordshire, designated in 1948, takes its name from the old town of *Welwyn* that lies immediately to the north of it. Its own name means '(place) at the willows', from the dative plural of Old English *welig*, 'willow-tree'. The willows that gave the name would have grown beside the small river Mimram that flows through the town. The New Town is the only one in Britain to incorporate the title *Garden City* in its name. The term itself, and the concept, is an American export to Britain, where it first arose with the foundation in 1899 of the *Garden City* Association (now the Town and Country Planning Association). The first actual Garden City was created at Letchworth in 1903, although it was more a suburb than a new town, and the title was not adopted for the town as a whole.

Wembley The district of northwest London, famous for its football stadium, has a name that means '*Wemba*'s clearing', with the personal name followed by Old English *lēah*, 'clearing'.

Wemyss The Scottish name derives from a place so called, such as East or West *Wemyss* in Fife near Kirkcaldy. The meaning is 'caves', with an English plural -*s* added to Gaelic *uaim*, 'cave'.

Wend The name is that of the Slavic people who settled in east central Europe in early medieval times but who were conquered by Germanic invaders. It is of uncertain origin, but has been linked with the Indo-european root element *vindo*, 'white', and the names of the Latvian towns of *Ventspils* (German *Windau*) and *Cēsis* (German *Wenden*). Their alternative name is SORB.

Wendover The Buckinghamshire town takes its name from the stream that flows through it. The stream's own name is of Celtic origin and means 'white water', from words to which modern Welsh *gwyn*, 'white' and *dwfr*, 'water' are related. The soil here is chalky.

Wendy The name was invented by J.M. Barrie for the 'little mother', *Wendy* Darling, in his play *Peter Pan* (1904), based on the nickname, *my wendy*, given him by a small child acquaintance, Margaret Henley. (She was the daughter of the poet and editor W.E. Henley, and is the 'Reddy' in Barrie's novel *Sentimental Tommie* (1896). She died in 1894, aged only five.) The name was widely promoted by this play, and was borne by various well-known actresses, such as Dame *Wendy* Hiller and *Wendy* Barrie, both born in 1912. (The latter's original name was Marguerite Wendy Jenkins. Barrie was her godfather, and she adopted her stage surname from him. She was given her middle name specifically for the girl in his play.) Barrie's use of the name for his character may have been partly influenced by existing similar names such as *Wanda* or GWENDOLEN.

Wendy Wool The patent brand of wool is manufactured by the West Yorkshire company of Carter & Parker, whose founder, Arthur Carter, was a friend of J.M. Barrie, the author of *Peter Pan* (1904). He asked the writer if he could adopt the name WENDY (*which see*) for his hand-knitted yarns in place of the rather uninteresting existing name 'Paragon'. Barrie agreed, on condition that a royalty (now lapsed) should be paid to the Great Ormond Street Hospital for Sick Children, London.

Wensleydale. The North Yorkshire valley does not take its name from the '*Wensley*' for there is no such river. Instead, it derives from the village of *Wensley* at its lower end. The village name means '*Wændel*'s clearing', with the same personal name as for WANDSWORTH and WELLINGBOROUGH. The valley's actual river is the Ure.

Wentworth The name comes from one of the places so called, such as the village of *Wentworth* near Rotherham, South Yorkshire. The place-name itself means '*Wintra*'s enclosure', with the Anglo-Saxon personal name deriving from the word for 'winter'. *Wentworth* in Surrey, however, famous for its golf course, takes its name from *Wentworth* House, owned by Elizabeth *Wentworth*, so here the surname gave the place-name, in a reversal of the usual process.

Wenzhou The port in southeast China derives its name from Chinese *wēn*, 'mild', 'temperate' and *zhōu*, 'region'.

Weser The name of the river in northwest Germany ultimately derives from the Indoeuropean root elements *veik*, 'to flow' and *aha*, 'water'.

Wesley The surname derives from any of the places so called, usually as *Westleigh* or *Westley*. The place-name means 'western wood'.

Wessex The name of the Anglo-Saxon kingdom in south and southwest England, the most powerful in the country, shows that it was the territory of the *West Saxons*, as distinct from the South Saxons of SUSSEX and the East Saxons of ESSEX. It applied to too large an area to become a county name, however, as the other two did. It was revived by Thomas Hardy for his novels and stories set mainly in and around Dorset. In the preface to *Far From the Madding Crowd* (1874) he explains how he decided to reintroduce the name:

> It was in the chapters of *Far From the Madding Crowd*, as they appeared month by month in a popular magazine, that I first ventured to adopt the word 'Wessex' from the pages of early history, and give it a fictitious significance as the existing name of the district once included in that extinct kingdom. [...] Finding that the area of a single county did not afford a canvas large enough for this purpose, and that there were objections to an invented name, I disinterred the old one.

West The name originally applied to a person who lived to the *west* of a settlement, or to someone who had come from the *west* to live in a place further east. Similar origins gave the surnames *East*, *North* and *South*.

West Bromwich Albion The famous Birmingham football club was originally called *West Bromwich Strollers* when formed in 1879. The name referred to the fact that the team were never certain at which of two grounds they would be playing, so were 'strolling players'. In 1881 they became *West Bromwich Albion*, adopting the new name from the district of *Albion*, to the west of West Bromwich town centre, where some of the players lived. The district itself appears to have taken its name from a local ironworks.

(*Albion Station* appears on a one-inch Ordnance Survey map of 1877.)

Westbury The Wiltshire town at the foot of Salisbury Plain has a name that means 'western fort', from Old English *west* and *burh*. The fort in question is the Iron Age camp on the hill above the town, where there is a spectacular white horse cut out of the chalk on the hillside. This camp was doubtless regarded as being the 'westernmost' of any others on Salisbury Plain.

West End The name of the fashionable region of London, with its parks, theatres and shops, has always implicitly been contrasted with the poorer *East End*, with its former densely populated housing and cluster of docks. *West End* has thus meant wealth, leisure and space, and *East End* poverty, manual labour and cramped quarters. There are always local factors to explain why a city's fashionable district should extend in one direction or another. In the case of London, it was largely the existence of the docks that concentrated the working classes to the east of the city centre, so that the wealthy laid out their lands and mansions towards the rural west, away from the noisy docks and squalid tenements and the unwholesome waters of the Thames. In many cases, however, the location of a town's superior district can be determined by the weather. England has a prevailing southwesterly wind, and until modern 'smokeless zones' were introduced, the smoke from houses and factories would have blown from west to east, making a town's *west end* more favourable for residential and leisure purposes than the eastern quarter.

West Indies The Caribbean islands were discovered by Columbus in 1492 and are so named because he believed he had reached INDIA and the east by a western route, as planned. The name came into use in the 16th century when the real, 'east' India was discovered. Hence, with reference to the latter, the name of the famous British *East India* Company.

Westmeath The name of the Irish county indicates its geographical location with regard to that of MEATH. It was created in 1542, after the other county.

Westminster The famous London borough, synonymous with the Houses of Parliament, takes its name from its equally well-known abbey, which was built in the 13th century on the site of an earlier *monastery* that lay to the *west* of the City of London. The original name of the district here was *Thorney*, 'thorn island', the island itself being the land between the Tyburn and the Thames. This former name is preserved in that of *Thorney* Street, running to the rear of Thames House between Horseferry Road and Millbank.

Westmorland The former county of northwest England has a name that means what it says, referring to the people who lived on the *west moorland*, that is, on the moors to the west of the Pennines. The name originally applied only to the barony of Appleby, in the north of the county. From there, it extended to the whole region. Appleby, the former county town, is still sometimes known as *Appleby-in-Westmorland* today, partly to be distinguished from other places of the name ('apple-tree farm'), partly to preserve the historic county name.

Weston The surname derives from any of the places so called, their own name usually meaning 'western enclosure'.

Westonbirt The girls' public school near Tetbury, Gloucestershire, was founded in 1928 in the country house of the same name, part of the large estate of the royal equerry to Queen Alexandra, Colonel Sir George Holford (1860–1926). The house takes its name from the nearby hamlet of *Weston Birt*, so named as a settlement to the *west* of Tetbury with a manor held by the Norman family of *Le Bret* ('the Breton').

Westphalia The former province of northwest Prussia has a name that means 'western *Phalia*', to distinguish it from the defunct *Ostphalia*, 'eastern *Phalia*' that lay the other side of the river Weser. The basic part of the name derives from Old High German *falaho*, 'plain dweller'. *Westphalia* is now part of the state of North Rhine-Westphalia (German *Nordrhein-Westfalen*).

West Point The military reservation in New York State that is the headquarters of the United States Military Academy takes its

591

name from its location on a headland on the *west* bank of the river Hudson, where it was established in 1802. There had been a military post at the strategic site here since 1778.

Wetherby The West Yorkshire town has a name of Scandinavian origin meaning 'wether farm', denoting a farm where wethers (castrated rams) were bred.

Wet Wet Wet The Scottish rock group, formed in Glasgow in 1982, took their name from a line in the Scritti Politti song 'Getting, Having and Holding'.

Wexford The county of southeast Ireland takes the name from its main town, whose own name is of part-Scandinavian origin and means 'inlet by the sandbank', from Old Irish *escir*, 'ridge' and Old Norse *fjǫrthr*, 'inlet', 'fjord'. The town lies at the mouth of the river Slaney. The Irish name of the town is *Loch Garman*, referring to a pool at the mouth of the Slaney, whose earlier name here was *Garma*, from Irish *garma*, 'headland'.

Weybridge The fashionable residential town in Surrey obviously takes its name from the river *Wey* on which it stands. The river's own name is of Indoeuropean origin and means 'conveyor', 'moving one'. The original bridge of the name may have been where Bridge Road crosses the river today.

Weymouth The Dorset seaside town stands at the mouth of the river *Wey*, as its name implies. The river has a name that means 'moving one', and that is thus of the same origin as the *Wey* at WEYBRIDGE and as the WYE.

Wham! The British pop vocal duo, formed in London in 1981, chose a name that was designed to have 'impact' and that reflected their racy image.

Wheeler The name was originally occupational, used for a person who made wheels, either for vehicles or for some manufacturing process, such as spinning.

Whig The name of the political party that opposed the succession to the throne of James, Duke of York, in 1679 on the grounds that he was a Catholic derives from a shortened form of *whiggamore*. This was a nickname for one of the group of

Scottish rebels who in 1648 joined in an attack on Edinburgh in what was known as the *Whiggamore* Raid. The name itself probably derives from Scottish *whig*, 'to urge' and *more*, a form of *mare*. It was the Whigs who provided the nucleus of what became the LIBERAL Party in the 19th century.

Whipsnade The Bedfordshire village, famous for its zoo at *Whipsnade* Park, has a name meaning '*Wibba*'s portion', with the personal name followed by Old English *snæd*, implying something detached or cut off (compare German *schneiden*, 'to cut'). The reference is to a piece of woodland that had been apportioned in this way.

Whitbread The name was originally used for a baker of fine bread, that is, either *white* bread or *wheat* bread.

Whitbread The well-known brew of beer is named for Samuel *Whitbread* (1720–1796), who set up a brewery with a partner in London in 1742. The chairman of the company from 1984 to 1992, Samuel *Whitbread* (1937–), is the great-great-great-great-grandson of the founder, and is named after him.

Whitby The North Yorkshire resort and port has a Scandinavian name that means '*Hvíti*'s village'. The personal name means 'white', probably referring to a white-haired or pale-faced person. *Cp.* the English surname WHITE.

White The surname was originally a nickname for a person with white hair or a pale face.

White City The district of west London was so named for the *white*-stuccoed buildings erected here in 1908 for the Franco-British Exhibition. The name has its equivalents for various places in continental Europe, notably BELGOROD, Ukraine, and BELGRADE, the capital of Yugoslavia. However, the village of Andelot-*Blancheville* in eastern France derives the second half of its name from *Blanche* de Navarre, Countess of Champagne. It adopted her name in 1220, having earlier been simply *Villa Nova*, 'new village'.

Whitehall The name that is synonymous with Britain's centre of government in London derives from that of the street that runs from Trafalgar Square to the Houses of Parliament. It is named after the former *Whitehall* Palace here, of which only the Banqueting House survives. The palace itself, destroyed by fire in the late 17th century, was probably so named for the light colour of the stonework of the new buildings added to the original York House by Henry VIII in the 16th century.

Whitehorse The capital of the Yukon Territory, Canada, takes its name from the nearby *Whitehorse* Rapids, themselves so called since the falling water suggests the flying mane of a white horse.

White Horse The well-known blend of whisky takes its name from the *White Horse* Inn, Edinburgh, where it was originally sold. The inn itself, in Canongate, is said to have been named after the *white horse* ridden by Mary Queen of Scots from her palace at Holyroodhouse to Edinburgh Castle. The whisky was originally known as *Mackie's*, after the family that produced it, and was given the name *White Horse* by the company chairman, Sir Peter Mackie (1855–1924), in the late 1880s.

White House The official residence of the president of the United States, in Washington DC, was built in 1792 and was so named because its *white*-grey sandstone contrasted with the red brick of other buildings nearby. After it was burned by the British in 1814 it was actually painted white to hide its scars. The name was subsequently adopted for other presidential residences, such as Little *White House*, at Warm Springs, Colorado, where Franklin D. Roosevelt died, or Western *White House*, at San Clemente, California, where President Nixon had a home.

White Russia *See* BYELORUSSIA.

White's Club London's oldest and grandest club evolved in 1693 from *White's Chocolate House*, which stood on the site of the present BOODLE'S Club. The chocolate house had been founded by an Italian named Francesco *Bianco* (d. 1711), known in English as Francis *White*.

White Sea The inlet of the Arctic Ocean, on the northwest coast of Russia, is probably so named either for its frequent snow and ice, or for the colour of its water, which reflects these. But some toponymists see the name as a 'colour name', indicating the west, just as the BLACK SEA can be regarded as lying to the north, and the RED SEA to the south. The White Sea is in fact the westernmost inlet on the extensive northern coastline of Russia. *Cp.* also BYELORUSSIA.

Whitesnake The British heavy metal group was formed in 1978 by the Deep Purple vocalist David Coverdale after the demise of the latter band. He named the new group after the set of rock ballads that he had released the previous year as a solo LP.

Whiteways The familiar brand of cider is named for Henry *Whiteway* (1853–1932), a Devon farmer's son, whose family, like those of most Devon farmers, regularly made their own cider. Henry took to producing it commercially, however, building a factory for the purpose near the railway line at Whimple, near Exeter. His firm became a private company in 1904 and went public in 1934 as *Whiteways Cyder*, retaining the old spelling of the word.

Whitgift School The boys' public school in Croydon, Surrey, was founded in 1598 by the Archbishop of Canterbury, John *Whitgift* (1530–1604). Five of its governors are still appointed by the Archbishop today.

Whitstable The Kent coastal resort has a name meaning 'white post', from Old English *hwīt*, 'white' and *stapol*, 'post' (modern *staple*). The original 'white post' may have been a marker at the meeting-place of the local hundred, or have indicated a landing-place on the beach.

Whit Sunday In the Christian calendar, the seventh Sunday after Easter, otherwise known as PENTECOST, commemorates the descent of the Holy Spirit on the apostles 50 days after the first Easter (*Acts* 2.1–4). The name means *white Sunday*, probably with reference to the custom whereby the newly baptized wore white at Pentecost. The first part of the name was sometimes taken to represent *wit*, referring to the wisdom conferred by the Holy Ghost on the day of Pentecost. The colour *white* is presumably symbolic of cleansing and purity. Oddly, the liturgical colour for Whitsunday itself is red.

Whittaker The name derives from a place so called, such as *Whitacre* ('white acre') near Coleshill in Warwickshire, or *Wheatacre* ('wheat acre') near Lowestoft in Norfolk.

Who, The The famous British rock band, formed in London in 1962, played under a number of names until settling for the *High Numbers* in 1964. Later that year they changed this name to *The Who*, lest it be thought that their posters were advertising a bingo session. The new name was one that they had used earlier. Their manager Kit Lambert later commented:

> It was a gimmick name – journalists could write articles called 'The Why of the Who' and people had to go through a boring ritual of question and answer. 'Have you heard the Who?' 'The Who?' 'The Who.' It was an invitation to corniness and we were in a corny world.
>
> quoted in Irwin Stambler, *The Encyclopedia of Pop, Rock & Soul*, 1989.

W H Smith The familiar chain of newsagents, stationers and booksellers was founded by Henry Walton Smith, a London Custom House official, who in 1792 opened a newsagent's shop in Mayfair and set up a 'newswalk', the equivalent of a modern paper round. Sadly, he died that same year, aged 54, but not before his wife had given birth to a son, William Henry Smith. William's mother kept the business going, and after her own death, in 1816, William took it over, together with his elder brother, Henry Edward Smith. William became the dominant partner, and when the partnership dissolved in 1828, he continued the business alone, as a wholesale newsagents and stationers. In 1846 his identically named son joined him on reaching the age of 21, and the firm of W.H. Smith & Son was created. It was the younger William Henry who set up the well-known W.H. Smith railway bookstalls, the first of which opened at Euston Station in 1848.

Wick The fishing port near the tip of northeastern Scotland has a name that means simply 'bay', from Old Norse *vík*. The reference is to *Wick* Bay, on which the town stands.

Wicklow The eastern county of Ireland takes its name from the town so called,

with the town's name of Scandinavian origin meaning 'vikings' meadow'. The name thus evolved from a combination of Old Norse *víkingr*, 'viking' and *ló*, 'meadow' (to which English *lea* is related).

Widnes The Cheshire town by the Mersey has a self-descriptive name meaning 'wide ness', that is, denoting the rounded headland on which it lies.

Wiesbaden The city and spa resort in western Germany has a name that derives from Old High German *wisa*, 'meadow', 'pasture' (modern German *Wiese*) and *bada*, 'to bathe', the latter referring to the famous hot springs here, noted since Roman times.

Wigan The well-known town near Manchester has a name that is simply a personal name, without any addition such as 'farm' or 'village'. The name is of Celtic origin. Attempts have been gallantly made to link the name with Old English *wig*, 'war' in a romantic bid to associate the town with King Arthur.

Wight, Isle of The name of the well-known island off the south coast of mainland Britain has been the subject of much speculation, from the fanciful *white* (supposedly relating to its chalk cliffs) to the more realistic Latin *vectis*, 'lever', as if it were an island that had been 'levered' out of the water. It is true that its Roman name was indeed *Vectis*. But recent research has shown that the name is probably Celtic in origin, and that it relates to modern Welsh *gwaith*, 'work', 'time'. It probably thus meant something like 'division', and referred to the way in which the waters of the Solent divide when approached from Southampton Water, so that a ship will have to decide which course to follow: whether to sail east or west to reach the English Channel.

Wightman Cup The annual tennis competition between women's teams from the United States and Britain takes its name from the trophy donated in 1923 by Hazel *Wightman*, née Hotchkiss (1886–1974), a former American tennis champion of the early 20th century.

Wigmore The name comes from the village of *Wigmore* near Leominster, Hereford and Worcester. Its original meaning is 'moving marsh', from Old English *wicga*, 'insect', 'beetle' (as in modern *earwig*) and *mōr*, 'marsh' (modern *moor*).

Wigmore Hall The London concert hall was opened in 1901 in *Wigmore* Street, itself built in the first half of the 18th century and named after one of the titles, Baron WIGMORE of Herefordshire, of the ground landlord, Edward Harley, second Earl of Oxford, whose daughter, Margaret Cavendish Harley, gave the name of HARLEY STREET.

Wilberforce The name originally denoted someone from the village of *Wilberfoss* near Stamford Bridge, Humberside. The place-name means '*Wilburh*'s ditch', with the female personal name itself comprising Old English *wil*, 'will', 'desire' and *burh*, 'fort'.

Wilberforce University The university near Xenia, Ohio, was founded in 1856 as an institution of the African Methodist Episcopal Church and was named for William *Wilberforce* (1759–1833), the British politician and philanthropist who brought about the abolition of the slave trade.

Wilcocks The name means 'son of *Wilcock*', this being a pet form of *Will* (itself a diminutive of WILLIAM). The 'pet' application of the name, so that it has an overtone of endearment, is indicated by the addition of the suffix *-cock*, applied to a boy or young man. *See* COX in this respect.

Wilfred The name is Germanic in origin, and contains the elements *wil*, 'will', 'desire' and *fred*, 'peace', so as a whole implies a peacelover. The name is frequently spelled *Wilfrid*.

Wilhelmshaven The port and resort in northwest Germany was founded in 1853 as a naval base and named in 1869 for the German emperor *Wilhelm* I (1797–1888), with *haven* a Low German form of *Hafen*, 'port'.

Wilkes Land The region in Antarctica, to the south of Australia, takes its name from the American naval officer and explorer Charles *Wilkes* (1798–1877), who discovered the coast here in his expedition of 1838 to 1842.

Wilkins The familiar brand of jam and marmalade owes its name to Arthur Charles *Wilkin* (1835–1913), an Essex farmer's son, who took over his father's farm at Tiptree, near Colchester in the mid-1860s and started growing fruit. In 1883 he abandoned traditional farming and took to making jam with the strawberries and other fruit that he grew, and in 1885 he set up a company to expand the business.

Wilkinson Both this name and *Wilkins* mean 'son of *Will*'. The latter name is a pet form of WILLIAM. *Cp.* WILLIAMS.

Wilkinson Sword The well-known make of razor blades and gardening tools takes its name from James *Wilkinson*, a London gunmaker's apprentice, who rose to be partner and who inherited the business in 1805. His son, Henry Wilkinson, took over the firm in 1825 and added *swords* to the guns. In 1887 the business, now known as *Wilkinson & Son*, was renamed *Wilkinson Sword* to emphasize the company's new speciality. Razor blades were first made in the 1920s.

Willemstad The capital of the Netherlands Antilles, in the Caribbean, has a name meaning '*William*'s town', given in honour of *William* (Dutch *Willem*) the Silent (1533–1584), prince of Orange and count of Nassau, the first stadholder of the United Provinces of the Netherlands.

William The name is one of the most popular Germanic names to be introduced to Britain by the Normans. Its origin lies in a combination of *wil*, 'will', 'desire' and *helm*, literally 'helmet', implying protection or defence. The overall sense is thus 'desiring defence'. The origin can be clearly seen in its current German equivalent, *Wilhelm*. The present English form of the name arose through French influence. The fact that it was borne by *William* the Conqueror himself does not seem to have adversely affected its popularity. It has been a favourite royal name ever since, through four English kings down to Prince *William* of Gloucester (1941–1972) and Prince *William* of Wales (1982–), son of Prince Charles and the Princess of Wales.

William and Mary, College of The state university in Williamsburg, Virginia, was founded in 1693 and named for King *William* and Queen *Mary* of England who gave it its charter. It is the second oldest institution of higher learning in the United States.

William Hill The name behind the familiar betting firm is that of *William Hill* (1903–1971), a Birmingham coach painter's son who became fascinated by betting and horseracing and who started his own business as a bookmaker. Despite the risks, and some substantial losses, his enterprise gradually grew, so that in 1939 he formed a private company with headquarters in Park Lane, London. William Hill opened his first betting shops in 1966.

William Hulme's Grammar School The public school in Manchester was founded in 1887 by the Hulme Trust, the educational charity that was set up under the will of the philanthropist *William Hulme* (1631–1691).

Williams The name means 'son of *Will*', this being a pet form of WILLIAM. *Williamson* is a name of identical origin, as is WILSON.

Williams The British racing-car company takes its name from its founder in 1969, Frank *Williams* (1942–). Since 1978 the team has been one of the most successful in Grand Prix racing.

Williamsburg The city and former state capital of Virginia was settled in 1633 and originally named *Middle Plantation*. On becoming the capital in 1699 it was renamed in honour of *William* III (1650–1702).

Willoughby The name derives from any of the places so called, such as the village near Alford, Lincolnshire. The place-name means 'willow-tree farm'.

Wills The well-known tobacco company of W.D. & H.O. Wills has a name representing those of the brothers William Day *Wills* (1797–1865) and Henry Overton *Wills* (1800–1871), the sons of another Henry Overton *Wills* (1761–1826) who was a partner in a Bristol tobacco business. The small family business produced their first popular 'Woodbine' cigarettes in 1888, and by the end of the century had become the biggest tobacco manufacturers in Britain.

Wilson The familiar surname means 'son of *Will*', this being a pet form of WILLIAM. *Cp.* WILLIAMS.

Wiltshire The southern county of England takes its name from the town of *Wilton*, north of Salisbury, on which it was at one time dependent. The town's name in turn comes from that of the river *Wylye* on which it lies. The river's name, finally, is of Celtic origin and derives from a word related to modern English *guile* and *wily*. It refers to a river that is 'tricky' in the sense that it floods unpredictably.

Wimbledon The well-known district of south London has a name that means '*Wynnman*'s hill'. The final -*don* represents Old English *dūn*, 'hill'. The first part of the present name has altered somewhat from the original under Norman influence. The Normans found *Wynnman* difficult to pronounce. They therefore dropped the *nn*, changed the final *n* to *l*, then inserted a *b* after the *m* to make it easier to 'glide' from *m* to *l*.

Wimpey The well-known construction company, Britain's largest builders of private homes, was founded in 1880 by George *Wimpey* (1855–1913). He set up as a stonemason in his native Hammersmith, London and by the end of the century had gained high repute for his building work, including the construction of Hammersmith Town Hall in 1896.

Wimpy The popular hamburgers and restaurants originated in the 1930s from a Chicago grill bar, and took their name from J. Wellington *Wimpy*, a hamburger-loving character in a 'Popeye' cartoon strip. The familiar Wimpy Bars first opened in Britain in the mid-1950s and were soon selling *Wimpyburgers*.

Wincarnis The brand of tonic wine was originally known as *Liebig's Extract of Meat and Malt Wine* when it was first produced in the 1880s. After the First World War, the *meat* and *wine* elements were extracted from this to produce the new name *Wincarnis*, as a blend of Latin *vinum*, 'wine' and *caro*, genitive *carnis*, 'flesh', 'meat', as if it were 'wine of meat', or blood.

Winchester The ancient cathedral city and former capital of Wessex has a name whose -chester declares it to have been a Roman settlement, from Old English *ceaster*, ultimately from Latin *castra*, 'camp'. The initial *Win-* is of Celtic or even pre-Celtic origin and probably meant simply 'place', implying the most important location in a district. It is represented in the city's Roman name, which was *Venta Belgarum*, '*Venta* of the *Belgae*', the people whose name gave that of BELGIUM. *Cp.* GWENT, which is of basically identical origin.

Windermere The largest lake in the Lake District has a name that means '*Vinand*'s lake', with the Swedish personal name (a rarity in English place-names) followed by Old English *mere*, 'lake'.

Windhoek The capital of Namibia, southwest Africa, has an Afrikaans name meaning literally 'wind corner'. It can hardly serve as a descriptive name, since winds are rare here. The name was originally promoted in the 19th century by the Hottentot chief Jonker Afrikaner, and it may well derive from the South African village of *Winterhoek*, in the Cape, where he spent his childhood. The village is itself named for the nearby *Winterhoek* Mountains, called 'winter corner' from the fact that the highest peaks are snow-covered in winter.

Windsor The famous Berkshire town on the Thames has a name that means 'windlass shore', from Old English *windels*, 'windlass' and *ōra*, 'bank', 'shore'. This probably referred to a mechanism used to assist carts up the muddy hill from the river's edge rather than for actually hauling boats out of the water. The 'shore' is thus not the river bank, but a slope higher up. Support for this interpretation is provided by the Dorset village of the same name (actually *Broadwindsor*) near Beaminster, where the river is so small that it is not even navigable, and where the 'windlass' would have been used for carts, not boats. The original winding mechanism in Windsor may have been set up at or near the point where River Street runs down to the Thames today. The city of *Windsor* on the Detroit River in Ontario, Canada, was settled as *The Ferry* soon after 1701 and was then known as *Richmond* before acquiring its present name, for its English counterpart, in 1836.

Windsor The name is familiar as the surname of the present British royal family, who adopted it in 1917 in deference to anti-German sentiment in place of the German name *Wettin*. It was taken for its specific association with the royal residence at WINDSOR Castle, while at the same time being somewhat similar to the German name that it replaced. The name had long existed before this, however, as a standard British surname, itself either from the Berkshire town or from another place so called, such as Broad*windsor* near Beaminster, Dorset.

Windward Islands The group of islands in the southeast West Indies are so named from the fact that they lie in the path of the northeast trade winds.

Winifred The English name is of Welsh origin, and represents an original *Gwenfrewi*. This combines Welsh *gwen*, 'white', 'fair', 'holy' and *frewi*, 'reconciliation', but gained its present form through association with Old English *wynn*, 'joy' and *frith*, 'peace'.

Winnie-the-Pooh The famous bear who is the hero of the children's stories by A.A. Milne had his origin in a toy bear that belonged to the author's son, Christopher Robin Milne. The bear was named *Winnie* after an American black bear cub in the London Zoo. *Pooh* was a name transferred from a swan that the little boy had encountered on an early holiday.

Winnipeg The capital of Manitoba, Canada, takes its name from Lake *Winnipeg*, itself from the Indian (Cree) word *win-nipi* meaning 'dirty water'. The city was founded in 1738 and was known successively as *Fort Rouge*, *Fort Douglas* and *Fort Garry* before gaining its present name in 1873.

Winston The name derives either from an Old English personal name comprising the words *wynn*, 'joy' (as in modern *winsome*) and *stān*, 'stone', or else from a place of the name, such as the village of *Winston* near Barnard Castle, Co Durham. The name is also current as a first name. One of its best-known bearers was Sir *Winston* Churchill, who was given it from the maiden name of the mother of his identically named and titled ancestor, Sir *Winston* Churchill (1620–1688), Sarah *Winston*. The name has always been regularly used in his family, and is currently borne by his grandson, the Member of Parliament *Winston* Churchill (1940–   ).

Winterthur The present name of the town in northeast central Switzerland has evolved (as if meaning 'winter gate') from its Roman name of *Vitudurum*. This is probably from a Celtic personal name *Vitu* or *Vetu* and Gaulish *duru*, 'fort'.

Wirral The peninsula between the estuaries of the Mersey and the Dee has a name that has been explained as deriving from Old English *wīr*, 'bog-myrtle' and *halh*, 'nook', 'corner'. But this interpretation poses certain problems. First, the peninsula is hardly a 'nook'. Second, bog-myrtle, as its name implies, grows in damp locations, yet the Wirral is mostly a high, dry ridge. The name may therefore have some other origin. It has not been finally determined what this is.

Wisbech The Cambridgeshire town has a name that means literally 'Ouse back'. *Ouse* is the river of this name. The 'back' (Old English *bæc*) is the low ridge on which the town stands. Yet Wisbech is on the Nene! The apparent anomaly is explained by the fact that the Ouse did indeed once flow to Wisbech, but has since altered its course, as fenland rivers are liable to do.

Wisconsin The American state takes its name from the river that flows through it as a tributary of the Mississippi. The river's own name is Indian (Ojibwa) in origin, perhaps meaning either 'gathering place of the waters' or simply 'long river'.

Witwatersrand The name of the rocky ridge in northeast South Africa is Afrikaans in origin, meaning 'ridge of white water', from *wit*, 'white', *water*, 'water' and *rand*, 'ridge', 'bank'. The reference is to the watershed between the rivers Vaal and Limpopo. The region is famous for its gold mines, and came to be colloquially referred to as *The Rand*. This was in turn adopted to give the name of South Africa's currency, which replaced the pound in 1961.

Woburn Abbey The well-known 18th-century country house in Bedfordshire, with its large park, takes its name from the nearby village of *Woburn*, whose own name derives from that of the stream here, and means 'crooked stream', from Old English *wōh*, 'crooked' and *burna*, 'stream'.

Woden The name of the Anglo-Saxon god of war and wisdom, whose Norse counterpart was ODIN, derives ultimately from an Indo-european root word, implying poetical inspiration, that is seen in Latin *vates*, 'prophet' and that is related to the name of the VEDA. The god gave the name of WEDNESDAY and also that of the ancient defensive structure in southern England known as WANSDYKE.

Wogan The Irish name was imported from Wales, where it was originally a personal name, *Gwgan*, that itself originated as a nickname, ultimately from *gwg*, 'frown', 'scowl'.

Woking The name of the Surrey town means '(territory of) *Wocc*'s people'. The same people gave their name to the smaller town of *Wokingham*, Berkshire, only about 15 miles (24 km) from Woking.

Wolds *See* WEALD.

Wolfson College There are two university colleges of the name, one in Oxford and the other in Cambridge. The Cambridge college was founded for graduates in 1965 as *University College*. As its buildings were erected largely at the expense of the *Wolfson* Foundation, however, its name was changed to *Wolfson College*. Its Oxford counterpart underwent a similar name change. When founded similarly for graduate students in 1966, it was originally known as *Iffley College*, from its proposed site at Court Place, Iffley, some two miles from the city centre. A larger site then became available in Oxford itself, and the *Wolfson* and Ford Foundations made a grant, as at Cambridge, for the erection of its buildings. The college thereupon changed its name. The foundation itself was set up by in 1955 by the businessman and financier Sir Isaac *Wolfson* (1897–1991), chairman of Great Universal Stores.

Wollongong The city in New South Wales, Australia, has a name of Aboriginal origin but uncertain meaning. It is popularly explained as representing the exclamation *nwoolyarngungli*, 'see, the monster comes', made by Aborigines as an expression of fear and surprise on first seeing a ship in full sail.

Wolsey The brand of knitwear evolved from the Leicester hosiery and underwear firm of Robert Walker & Sons, itself founded as a cottage industry in 1755. In 1920 the firm merged with one of its competitors, W. Tyler & Co, and the resulting public company was registered under the name of *Wolsey*. The company had two of its factories near the remains of Leicester Abbey, where Cardinal *Wolsey* was buried, and his name was felt to have good local historical associations. It also suggested *wool*!

Wolsey Hall The Oxford establishment, familiar for its correspondence courses, was founded in Cirencester in 1894. It moved to Oxford in 1907 where it occupied a building already known as *Wolsey Hall* from its location on the site of the memorial garden of Christ Church, the college founded by Cardinal *Wolsey*.

Wolverhampton The well-known town near Birmingham has a name that means '*Wulfrūn*'s high farm', with the second half of the name not the same as in HAMPTON COURT but representing Old English *hēan*, the dative of *hēah*, 'high' and *tūn*, 'farm'. The personal name (literally meaning 'wolf counsel') is that of the lady to whom the manor here was given in the late 10th century. The civic authorities are clearly proud of her, for the town has both a *Wulfruna* Street and a *Wulfrun* Shopping Centre.

Wolverhampton Wanderers The famous football club was formed in *Wolverhampton* in 1877 as an amalgamation of two existing teams, St Luke's, Blakenhall, and *The Wanderers*, the latter having a name frequently adopted by players who had no fixed home ground of their own. The club's nickname of *Wolves* is appropriate not only for a fierce football 'pack' but in a sense historically, in that Wolverhampton itself took its name from a lady named *Wulfrūn*, 'wolf counsel'.

Wood The common surname was originally used for a person who lived in or near a wood, or who was a woodcutter or forester. In some cases it derives from Old English *wōd*, 'mad', so was a nickname for a crazy or eccentric person. Most names beginning with *Wood-* are to do with an actual wood, however, or derive from a place-name beginning thus, for example *Woodburn* ('stream in a wood'), *Woodfield*, *Woodgate*, *Woodhouse* ('house by or in a wood'), *Woodrow* ('row of cottages near a wood'), *Woodward* ('wood ward', otherwise a forester).

Woolwich The London district on the south bank of the Thames has a name that means 'wool place', with the second half of the name deriving from Old English *wīc* used to denote a special type of farm or place. In this instance, it would have been a place where wool was loaded onto or unloaded from boats on the Thames.

Woolworths The well-known High Street store takes its name from Franklin Winfield *Woolworth* (1852–1919), an American farmer's son from New York State who began to earn a living as an apprentice clerk in a corner store. In 1879 he set up his own retail business in Utica, New York, calling it 'The Great Five-Cent Store', as everything sold at this cheap price. His first venture failed, because of the store's unfavourable location, but he opened a second store at Lancaster, Pennsylvania, selling a wider range of goods, still all for five cents or less. He then introduced a ten-cent range of goods and opened further stores. Finally in 1880 he opened a store in Scranton, Pennsylvania, putting the firm's name over it in gold letters on a red background: F.W. WOOLWORTH Co. That was the founding of the chain proper. Frank Woolworth opened his first British store in Liverpool in 1909. For some years the stores sold 'own brand' products under the name *Winfield*, from Woolworth's middle name.

Woomera The town in South Australia, the site of the Long Range Weapons Establishment, has a name that derives from an aboriginal word meaning (appropriately enough) 'throwing stick'. It is not related to the word *boomerang*, as sometimes supposed.

Worcester The well-known cathedral city was a Roman encampment, as can be told by the *-cester* that represents Old English *ceaster*, 'Roman camp'. The first part of the name probably derives from that of the *Weogoran*, the people who were 'dwellers by the winding river', as the Celtic name means. Worcester is on the Severn, but this was not necessarily the river referred to. The tribal name also lies behind that of *Wyre* Forest, the woodlands north of Worcester on the Shropshire border.

Worcester College The Oxford college was founded in 1283 as a school for Benedictine monks under the name of *Gloucester College*, so called as the monks came from St Peter's Abbey, *Gloucester*. After the dissolution of the monasteries in 1540, the college was refounded in 1560 as *Gloucester Hall*. Through a successful claim for funds from a bequest from Sir Thomas Cookes (d. 1701), a *Worcester*shire baronet who wished to found a new college at Oxford, Gloucester Hall ceased to exist, and in 1714 *Worcester College* came into being in its place.

Wordsworth The name derives from that of the small hamlet of *Wadsworth* near Halifax, West Yorkshire, itself meaning '*Wæddi*'s enclosure'. The surname *Wadsworth* thus has the same origin.

Workington The Cumbrian port on the Solway Firth has a name that means 'estate of *Weorc*'s people'. The personal name is also found in the name of WORKSOP.

Worksop The town near Nottingham has a name meaning '*Weorc*'s valley', with the Anglo-Saxon personal name (found also for WORKINGTON) followed by Old English *hop*, 'valley'. It is not certain which particular valley was so called.

Worms The city in southwest Germany, famous for the Diet of *Worms* of 1521, in which Luther defended his doctrines, derives its name from a Celtic original *Borbetomago*, representing the personal name *Borbeto* and *mago*, 'field'.

Wormwood Scrubs The familiar prison in west London has an unpleasant-seeming name with a scarcely more pleasant meaning, although *wormwood* is not actually involved. The first part of the name refers to a wood that was infested with snakes. The original form of the name was *Wormholt*, from Old English *wyrm*, 'snake'

(modern *worm*) and *holt*, 'wood'. But this must have been misheard or miscopied to produce *Wormwood*, by association with the plant. The second word of the name refers to the scrubland that was here at one time, and that doubtless also served as a home for the snakes.

Worth The name was originally used of a person from any of the many places so called. The place-name itself comes from the identical Old English word that means simply 'enclosure', 'settlement'.

Worthing The well-known Sussex seaside resort has a name that means '(place of) *Wurth*'s people'.

Worthington The familiar type of beer is named for William *Worthington* (1722–1800), born near Atherstone, Leicestershire, who set up a brewing business in Burton-upon-Trent in 1744. By the end of the 19th century it had grown to be one of the largest in Britain, and although merging with BASS in 1927 continues to operate independently.

Wounded Knee The site on the Oglala Sioux Reservation, South Dakota, the scene of a confrontation between the United States Army and American Indians in 1890, has a name translated from the Sioux, originally referring to a Sioux who had been wounded in the knee here.

Wrekin, The The rocky hill near Wellington, Shropshire, has a name of uncertain origin. It may well be Celtic and identical to that found in the name of the nearby *Wroxeter*, whose second element evolved from Old English *ceaster*, 'Roman camp' (Latin *castra*). The Roman name of Wroxeter was *Viroconium*, and this presumably applied originally to The Wrekin itself, since it has an ancient hill-fort on its summit and would have been the obvious site for a military encampment.

Wrexham The Welsh town near Chester has an English name meaning '*Wryhtel*'s pasture', with the personal name (meaning 'workman', and related to modern English *wright*) followed by Old English *hamm*, 'riverside land'. There is no obvious river at Wrexham now, but there clearly was once, as witness the names of such streets in the town as Watery Road, Brook Street and Rivulet Road.

Wrigglesworth The name derives from the original medieval name of a small place near Leeds now known as *Woodlesford*. This itself probably means 'ford by the thicket', from Old English *wrīd*, 'bush', 'thicket' and *ford*, 'ford'. It is not clear why *-ford* changed to *-worth*, which normally means 'enclosure' (*see* WORTH).

Wright The name is a common occupational one for a maker of objects from wood or some other material. It is ultimately related to modern English *work*.

Wrocław The city in southwest Poland has a name of exactly the same origin as that of BRATISLAVA, Slovakia, so represents that of the identical Slav people. The name is pronounced approximately 'Vrotswaf'. The German name of the city is *Breslau*.

Wuhan The city of southeast China was formed in 1950 by the union of Wuchang, Hanyang and Hankou, and derives its name from the first elements of these, respectively *wŭ*, 'military' and *hàn*, for the HAN dynasty.

Wuppertal The city in western Germany has a name that means '*Wupper* valley', with the river deriving its name from a German word related to modern *wippeln*, 'to hop', 'to skip'. The name was given to the conurbation formed in 1929 from five existing towns.

Württemberg The former state of southern Germany derives its name from that of a town that arose round a castle. The castle derives the latter part of its name from *berg*, 'mountain'. The first part of the name may represent an ancient word denoting a rounded object, here referring to the shape of the hill.

Würzburg The city in south central Germany derives its name from words corresponding to modern German *Wurzel*, 'root' and *Burg*, 'fort'.

Wuthering Heights The title of the famous novel by Emily Brontë, published in 1847, is the name of the moorland house that is the home of the central figure, Heathcliff. The book itself explains the origin:

'Wuthering' being a significant provincial adjective, descriptive of the atmospheric tumult to which its station is exposed, in stormy weather. Pure, bracing ventilation they must have up there, at all times, indeed.

Chapter 1.

Wyatt The surname has evolved from the Old English personal name *Wīgheard*, comprising *wīg*, 'war' and *heard*, 'hardy', 'brave'. *Cp.* WYMAN.

Wychwood School The Oxford public school for girls was jointly founded in 1897 by Miss Batty, a schoolmistress, and Miss Lee, her former pupil, a lecturer in English to women students, and was named for *Wychwood* Forest, near Miss Lee's home at Leafield, northwest of Oxford.

Wycliffe Hall The Oxford theological college, noted for its evangelical tradition, was founded in 1877 and named for the religious reformer and Bible translator John *Wycliffe* (or *Wyclif*) (1330–1384). *See also* LUTTERWORTH PRESS.

Wye There are several rivers of the name in England, the best known being the one that rises in Wales and that flows through Hereford, Ross-on-Wye, Monmouth and Chepstow to enter the Severn. Its name is Celtic in origin and means 'conveyor', 'moving one', from a word that is ultimately related to English *way*. The river *Wey* has a name of identical origin. *See* WEYBRIDGE.

Wykehamist The name for a pupil or former pupil of Winchester College, the boys' public school, derives from that of the school's founder in 1382, the chancellor of England and bishop of Winchester, William of *Wykeham* (1324–1404). He took his name from his birthplace, *Wickham*, near Fareham, Hampshire. The similarity between the names *Wykeham* and *Winchester* is thus coincidental.

Wyman The name represents the Anglo-Saxon personal name *Wīgmund*, consisting of Old English *wīg*, 'war' and *mund*, 'protection'.

Wyndham's Theatre The London theatre, in Charing Cross Road, was built in 1899 by the then manager of the Criterion Theatre, Charles *Wyndham* (1837–1919).

Wyoming The American state has a name of Indian (Delaware) origin, representing *maugh-wau-wame*, 'broad meadows'.

X, Y, Z

X The American punk rock band, formed in Los Angeles in 1977, took a deliberately cryptic name which nevertheless reflected the stage name, *Exene* Cervenka, of the group's lead singer, Christine Cervenka.

Xanadu The well-known name is a corruption of that of *Shang-tu*, the historic city founded by Kublai Khan in 1256 as his summer residence at what is now the site of the present town of Tolun in Inner Mongolia, northern China. The Chinese name means 'imperial capital', from *shàng*, 'upper', 'imperial' (*cp.* SHANGHAI) and *dū*, 'capital'. The name was popularized by Coleridge's poem *Kubla Khan* (1816), with its opening lines: 'In Xanadu did Kubla Khan/A stately pleasure-dome decree'. The poem was inspired by Samuel Purchas's *Purchas his Pilgrimage* (1613), which contains the following sentence:

> In Xamdu did Cublai Can build a stately Palace, encompassing sixteene miles of plaine ground with a wall, wherein are fertile Meddowes, pleasant Springs, delightfull Streames, and all sorts of beasts of chase and game, and in the middest thereof a sumptuous house of pleasure.

Xanthippe The name of the wife of Socrates derives from Greek *xanthos*, 'yellow', 'sorrel' and *hippos*, 'horse'.

Xavier The name of the Spanish missionary St Francis *Xavier* (1506–1552), a founder of the Jesuit society, derives from the family castle of *Xavier*, Navarre, where he was born. This name is in turn a corruption of Basque *Etchaberri*, meaning 'new house'.

Xenophon The name of the famous Greek general and historian of the 5th and 4th centuries BC means 'foreign voice', from *xenos*, 'foreign', 'strange' and *phōnē*, 'voice'. The implication is of a person who can understand foreign languages. There

are other Greek philosophers with similar names, such as *Xenocrates* ('foreign power') and *Xenophanes* ('foreign appearance'), respectively of the 4th and 6th centuries BC.

Xerox The familiar patent photocopying process is *xerographic*, that is, it does not use liquids or chemical developers but a dry electrically charged plate or cylinder. The name thus derives from the same source as this term, which is Greek *xēros*, 'dry'. *Xerography* was invented by the American lawyer Chester F. Carlson in 1948, and the trade name *Xerox* was registered in 1952, although it was already in use as early as 1949.

Xerxes The name is famous as that of the 5th-century BC king of Persia who led a vast army against Greece, winning a victory at Thermopylae but losing at Salamis and Plataea. It represents Persian *Khshayarsha*, 'great king'. He is the biblical *Ahasuerus* of the Old Testament (*Ezra* 4.6, *Daniel* 9.1, *Esther* throughout).

Xhosa The people of southern Africa and their language have a name that is said to mean 'angry people'.

Xi An The city in central China, the capital of Shaanxi province, has a name that represents Chinese *xī*, 'west' and *ān*, 'peaceful'. The name is also rendered *Hsian* or *Sian*.

Xiangtan The city in south central China has a name that represents *xiāng*, the former name of HUNAN, and *tán*, 'gulf'.

Xijiang The river of southern China has a name that means 'western river', from *xī*, 'west' and *jiāng*, 'river'. The river forms the approximate boundary between the autonomous region of GUANGXI to the west and the province of GUANGDONG to the east.

Ximenes The name is the traditional European one for the famous Spanish inquisitor Francisco *Jiménez* de Cisneros (1436–1517). His native name is of uncertain origin, although it has been seen by some as a derivative of SIMON.

Xining The city in western China, the capital of Qinghai province, has a name that represents Chinese *xī*, 'west' and *níng*, 'peaceful', 'happy'. The name also appears as *Hsining* or *Sining*.

Xinjiang The autonomous region of northwest China takes its name from *xīn*, 'new' and *jiāng*, 'frontier'. It is also known as *Xinjiang Uygur*, referring to the fact that it was set up in 1955 for the *Uygur* ethnic minority.

Xmas The familiar short name of CHRISTMAS arose from the use of the letter *X* to mean CHRIST, where it stands for the first letter of His Greek name, *XPICTOΣ*. The letter itself happens also to suggest the *cross* on which Christ was crucified.

XTC The British new wave band, formed in Swindon in 1977, took a name that appeared to suggest *ecstasy* while also hinting at the initials of the group's drummer, *T*erry *C*hambers. The name predates that of the hallucinogenic drug *Ecstasy*, first made as a designer drug in the United States in 1984.

Yablonovy Mountains The Siberian mountain range has a name that on the face of it appears to derive from Russian *yablonya*, 'apple tree'. But the name is in fact an alteration of a Buryat original name *Yableni daba*, 'foot crossing', referring to a path over the mountains.

Yah The name is a conventional abbreviation of YAHWEH, the Hebrew form of the name of God more widely known as JEHOVAH. It is found as a component of many biblical names, several of which have become standard first names. It lies behind JOHN and JOSHUA (and therefore JESUS), and frequently forms the final element of names, such as AZARIAH, ELIJAH, HEZEKIAH, ISAIAH, JEDIDIAH, JEREMIAH, JOSIAH, *Mattithiah* (*see* MATTHEW), NEHEMIAH, OBADIAH, *Tobiah* (*see* TOBIAS), URIAH, ZACHARIAS, ZEDEKIAH, ZEPHANIAH. It is also the final syllable of *hallelujah* or *alleluia*, 'praise Jehovah'.

Yahoos The name of the brutish creatures resembling human beings in Swift's novel *Gulliver's Travels* (1726) fairly straightforwardly suggests the two exclamations of disgust, *yah!* and *ugh!* However, some critics of the work see the name as a form of *whinny*, and therefore related to that of the HOUYHNHNMS, the clean and noble talking horses who are essentially their opposites.

Yahweh The unpronounceable Hebrew name of God, later familiar as *Jehovah*, was originally written *YHWH*. According to the Old Testament, God revealed his name to Moses on Mount Horeb when Moses asked him by what name he should be known: 'And Moses said unto God, Behold, when I come unto the children of Israel, and shall say unto them, The God of your fathers hath sent me unto you; and they shall say unto me, What is his name? what shall I say unto them? And God said unto Moses, I AM THAT I AM: and he said, Thus shalt thou say unto the children of Israel, I AM hath sent me unto you' (*Exodus* 3.13–14). Later, God says to Moses: 'And I appeared unto Abraham, unto Isaac, and unto Jacob, by the name of God Almighty, but by my name JEHOVAH was I not known to them' (6.3). Finally God revealed his name to Moses: 'And the Lord descended in the cloud, and stood with him there, and proclaimed the name of the Lord' (34.5). The ten commandments forbade that God's name should be spoken 'in vain' (*Exodus* 20.7; *Deuteronomy* 5.11). The so called Tetragrammaton ('four letters') *YHWH* was thus for long spoken almost inaudibly only once a year by the Jewish high priest, at the Feast of the Purification. The pronunciation used was *Yahweh*, made by inserting the random vowels *u* and *e* into the Tetragrammaton. From about the 3rd century BC, however, the name was not allowed to be spoken at all, and where it occurred in texts it was replaced by the Hebrew word *Adonai*, 'lord' (*cp*. ADONIS), or by ELOHIM, another name of God. As a result of this, when in the 7th century AD the Masoretes (Jewish biblical scholars) came to compile the Hebrew text of the Old Testament, they inserted the vowels of *Adonai* or *Elohim* into the Tetragrammaton *YHWH*, so that it read *YeHoWaH*, otherwise (in its Latin form) *Jehovah*. The meaning of the original Tetragrammaton is uncertain, but many scholars believe that the sense may be something like 'he brings into being whatever is', based on Hebrew *hāwāh*, 'to be'. The name *YHWH* occurs about 7000 times in the Hebrew Bible; it appears (as *Jehovah*) only four times in the English Authorized Version, where it is usually translated as 'the LORD' (in capitals), or in certain cases, 'GOD'. The conventional abbreviated form of the name *Yahweh* is YAH, *which see* for examples of personal names containing it. There may well be some false association in the popular consciousness between *Jehovah* and JOVE, the poetic name of JUPITER. Such a link could even have been promoted by literary writers, as in the following lines from Pope's *The Universal Prayer* (1738):

> Father of All! in ev'ry Age,
> In ev'ry Clime ador'd
> By Saint, by Savage, and by Sage,
> Jehovah, Jove, or Lord!

Yakut The name of the Turkic people who inhabit a region of northeast Siberia is said to derive from Yakut or Evenki *yekot*, the plural of *yeko*, 'stranger'. They gave their name to the capital city of their region, *Yakutsk*.

Yakutsk *See* YAKUT.

Yale The well-known type of lock takes its name from Linus *Yale* (1821–1868), the American engineer who was himself the son of a lockmaker and who in 1868 founded the *Yale* Lock Manufacturing Company at Stamford, Connecticut. His important invention was that of the compact cylinder pin-tumbler lock, based on the pin-tumbler mechanism of the ancient Egyptians. Linus Yale was ultimately related to Elihu Yale who gave his name to YALE UNIVERSITY.

Yale University The third oldest American university, now at New Haven, Connecticut, was founded in 1701 at Saybrook, Connecticut as the *Collegiate School*. In 1714 and 1718 the English colonial administrator Elihu *Yale* (1649–1721) made gifts of books and goods to the college, and in the latter year it changed its name in his honour.

Yalta The Ukrainian port and resort, in the Crimea, has a name that was recorded in the 12th century as *Djalita*. This is said to represent modern Greek *gialos*, 'shore', a word that evolved from classical Greek *ialtos*, 'sent', 'despatched'. The Greeks are said to have settled on the coast here when driven from the northern and central Crimea by the Turks.

Yamaha The well-known make of motorcycle and electronic organ takes its name from the Japanese engineer Konosuke *Yamaha* (1851–1916), who began his career as a clockmaker. In 1887 he was called on to repair an organ owned by a school in Hamamatsu, and that year constructed a harmonium of his own. His expertise led to the foundation of a flourishing organ-building company. Only in 1955, some time after his death, did it diversify into the manufacture of motorcycles.

Yamoussoukro The capital of the Côte d'Ivoire (former Ivory Coast), West Africa, derives its name from that of *Yamoussou*, its founder, and the local (Baule) word *kro*, 'village'. The town replaced Abidjan as capital in 1983.

Yangon The capital of Myanmar (formerly Burma) was known as *Rangoon* until 1989, when the name was respelled in a manner more faithful to the original. This is in Burmese *yangun*, 'peaceful', 'end of conflict'. The name was given the city in 1756, when Alaungpaya, king of Burma, captured it from the Mons, who had known it as *Dagon*. This name itself derives from Burmese *takun*, 'tree-trunk'. The traditional focal point of the city is the gold-covered *Shwe Dagon* pagoda, the centre of Burmese religious life.

Yangtze China's best-known and longest river, also known as *Yangtze Kiang*, derives its name from *yáng*, 'abundant', 'prosperous' and *zĭ*, 'son', 'child', with *Kiang* representing *jiāng*, 'river'. Its alternative Chinese name is *Chang Jiang*, from *cháng*, 'long' and *jiāng*, 'river'. Its former European name was *Blue River*, apparently given by Jesuit missionaries to distinguish it from the HUANG HO or *Yellow River*.

Yankee The colloquial or derogatory name for an American probably arose from an Indian corruption of the word *English*, or its

French equivalent, *Anglais*. The name seems to have been first applied by the English themselves to the rebel colonists of New England, then by Southerners to Northerners, then finally to any American.

Yaoundé The capital of Cameroon, West Africa, represents the native name of the *Ewondo* people, whose own name is of uncertain origin.

Yardbirds, The The influential British rock band, formed in Kingston upon Thames, in 1963, presumably took their name as a tribute to the American jazzman Charlie Parker (1920–1955), nicknamed *Yardbird*.

Yardley The name derives from any of the places so called, such as *Yardley* that is now a district of Birmingham. The place-name means 'clearing of sticks', from Old English *gerd*, 'pole', 'stick' (modern *yard* as a unit of measurement) and *lēah*, 'wood', 'clearing'. The reference is to a forest site where timber could be obtained.

Yarmouth There are two English towns of the name. The Norfolk port is named from the river on which it stands, the *Yare*, or more precisely from *Gerne*, an earlier form of the river's name, which itself is of Celtic origin and probably means 'babble', 'shout', referring to its noisy current. The Isle of Wight town is also on a river *Yare* but is not named for it. Its name represents Old English *ēar*, 'gravel' and *mūtha*, 'mouth', referring to the gravelly estuary of the river on which it lies. In both cases the river takes its present name from that of the town.

Yaroslavl The historic city in western Russia, northeast of Moscow, takes its name from the Grand Prince of Kiev, *Yaroslav* the Wise (978–1054), who founded it in 1026.

Yasodharapura The name of the capital of ancient Cambodia derives from Sanskrit *yaśodhara*, 'retaining fame' (from *yaśas*, 'fame', 'glory' and *dhara*, 'supporting', 'possessing') and *pura*, 'town'.

Yazd The city in central Iran has a name representing Iranian *yazdān*, 'god', 'light'. The name is also spelled *Yezd*.

Yazilikaya The name of the Hittite monument in eastern Turkey derives from Turkish *yazılı*, 'written', 'inscribed' and

kaya, 'rock'. The monument is famous for its carvings of human figures and is of considerable archaeological significance.

Yazoo The British pop duo, formed in 1982, took their name from an early blues record label, itself perhaps named for the *Yazoo* River, Mississippi, or for the *Yazoo* Indians after whom the river is itself named. In America the duo were obliged to shorten their name to *Yaz* to avoid confusion with an identically named small record company.

Yekaterinburg The city in western Russia was founded in 1722 as a fortified settlement and was named after the future empress of Russia *Catherine* I (1684–1727), wife of Peter the Great, with *burg* the Germanic word for 'fort', as was then fashionable for Russian towns. (*Cp.* ST PETERSBURG, named after Peter himself.) Ironically, it was in this city, with its tsarist name, that the Russian tsar Nicholas II and his family were executed by the Bolsheviks in 1918. In 1924 the city was renamed *Sverdlovsk*, for Yakov *Sverdlov* (1885–1919), the Russian Communist Party official who had engaged in revolutionary activities in the Urals here. In 1991 the city reverted to its original name.

Yellowknife The capital of the Northwest Territories, Canada, on Great Slave Lake, takes its name from a local tribe of American Indians who used tools made from yellow copper. The town arose in 1934 after the discovery of gold here, and became the capital in 1970.

Yellow River *See* HUANG HO.

Yellow Sea *See* HUANG HAI.

Yellowstone National Park The oldest and largest national park in the United States, mostly in Wyoming, takes its name from the river *Yellowstone*. This is an English translation of its earlier French name, *Roche Jaune*, in turn a translation of its Indian name *nissi-a-dazi*, 'river of yellow stones'.

Yemen The republic in southwest Arabia, on the Red Sea, derives its name from Arabic *al-yaman*, 'the right', from *al*, 'the' and *yamīn*, 'right' (as opposed to 'left'), itself from *yumn*, 'happiness'. In the Arabic world, the right has always been regarded as the happy or fortunate side, as against the left, which is unfortunate or unlucky. A similar notion exists in many European languages. The Romans divided ancient Arabia into three parts: *Arabia Felix*, 'happy Arabia', otherwise modern Yemen, which is relatively damp and fertile, *Arabia Deserta*, 'desert Arabia', otherwise the northern part of the peninsula, between Syria and Mesopotamia, which is dry and infertile, and *Arabia Petraea*, 'rocky Arabia', otherwise the Sinai Peninsula (not part of modern Arabia), where the terrain is rocky and stony. Yemen is also 'right' or to the east from the point of view of a Muslim in Egypt facing Mecca, just as Syria is 'left', or to the west. The two separate republics of North Yemen (Yemen Arab Republic), formed in 1962, and South Yemen (People's Democratic Republic of Yemen), formed in 1967, were united as a single state in 1990.

Yenisei The river in central Siberia is believed to derive its name from local words *Ientaiea* or *Iondessi* meaning simply 'big river'.

Yeovil The Somerset town takes its name from the river on which it stands. The river is now called the *Yeo*, but was earlier known as the *Gifle*. This not only gave the present name of the town but is identical in origin to the name of the river *Ivel* in Bedfordshire, also formerly recorded as *Gifle*. The derivation of the name is in a Celtic root element *gablo* meaning 'forked' (*cp.* modern Welsh *gafl*, 'fork', 'stride'). *See also* the commercial name ST IVEL.

Yerevan The capital of Armenia has a very old name that is of uncertain origin. It is probably that of a people who once inhabited this region. Attempts to link the name with that of Mount ARARAT are not very convincing, although the famous mountain is barely 30 miles (48 km) away.

Yes The British rock band, formed in London in 1968, selected a name that was a general positive affirmation of their aim to succeed as a 'supergroup'.

Yeşil Irmak The river in northern Turkey has a name that means 'green river', from Turkish *yeşil*, 'green' and *ırmak*, 'river'.

Yes Tor The well-known hill on Dartmoor, Devon, has a name that means 'eagle's hill', from Old English *earn*, 'eagle' with a possessive *s* and *torr*, 'hill' (*cp.* TORQUAY).

Yeti The alternative name for the ABOMINABLE SNOWMAN derives from Tibetan *yeh-teh*, 'little manlike animal', its native Sherpa name.

Yezd *See* YAZD.

Y-front The proprietary make of men's underwear derives its name from the inverted *Y*-shaped seaming on the *front* of the underpants. The name was registered in 1953.

Yggdrasil In Norse mythology, the name is that of the 'world tree', the ash tree that was believed to overshadow the whole world, binding earth, heaven and hell together with its roots and branches. Its name is thought to mean 'Uggr's horse', from *Uggr*, a name of the god ODIN, and *drasill*, 'horse'. The god's name probably derives from *yggr* or *uggr*, 'frightful'. This origin is linked to the account of the fearful 'shamanic' initiation of Odin, who was suspended for nine days from the tree, transfixed to it by a spear. The name may also relate to the journeyings of Odin from one world to another.

Yichang The port in south central China has a name deriving from Chinese *yí*, 'suitable', 'proper' and *chāng*, 'shining', 'prosperous'. The name also occurs in the forms *Ichang* or *I-ch'ang*.

Yiddish The name for the language spoken as a vernacular by Jews in Europe, historically a dialect of Old German, derives from German *jüdisch*, the adjective of *Jude*, 'JEW'.

Yinchuan The city in north central China has a name that means 'silver river', from *yín*, 'silver' and *chuān*, 'river'. This despite the fact that it is actually on the Yellow River (*see* HUANG HO).

Yogi Bear The popular bear in the American television cartoons first appeared on the screen in 1958 and is said to have been named for the baseball champion Lawrence 'Yogi' Berra (1925–), elected American League Most Valuable Player in 1951, 1954 and 1955.

Yokohama The port in central Japan, on Tokyo Bay, has a name that denotes its location, from *yoko*, 'coast' and *hama*, 'shore', 'beach'.

Yom Kippur The annual Jewish holiday, celebrated as a day of fasting and known in English as the *Day of Atonement*, derives its name from Hebrew *yōm*, 'day' and *kippūr*, 'atonement'. It is held on the tenth day of Tishri (in September or October), the first month of the Jewish year, and ends the ten days of penitence that follow the Jewish New Year.

Yorick The name is that of the (deceased) king's jester whose skull the grave-diggers find when digging Ophelia's grave in Shakespeare's *Hamlet* (1600). It is probably a form of *Jorck*, the Danish equivalent of GEORGE. As this name means literally 'earth worker' it is punningly appropriate for the buried jester. Laurence Sterne used the name for the 'lively, witty, sensible, and heedless parson' in *Tristram Shandy* (1759–67) and himself adopted it as a pseudonym in *A Sentimental Journey* (1768).

York The famous North Yorkshire city has a name that has undergone several changes of form and interpretation. Ptolemy recorded it in the 2nd century AD as *Eborakon*. This represents a Celtic personal name *Eburos*, which probably meant 'yew man', from a word from which modern *yew* is itself indirectly derived. The name doubtless referred to the estate of yew trees owned by its bearer. This meaning was lost on the Anglo-Saxons, who took it to represent Old English *eofor*, 'wild boar', and who added *wīc*, 'dwelling place' so that the settlement was *Eoforwic*, as if 'boar farm'. The Vikings then came here, and in turn took the *wīc* of the name to be Old Norse *vík*, 'bay', although this was hardly suitable for an inland town. The first part of the name was similarly meaningless to them, so they gradually smoothed and reduced it until it became simply the first three letters of *York*, with the final *k* all that is left today of their *vík*. *See also* the first names IVOR, YVONNE. The 10th-century Viking name *Jorvik* has been preserved in that of the *Jorvik* Viking Centre, the museum of Viking artefacts opened in 1984 on an important archaeological site in the city.

York, Cape The northernmost point of Australia, in Queensland, was so named by Captain Cook in 1770 'in honour of his late Royal Highness, the Duke of York'. This was Edward Augustus, Duke of *York* and Albany (1739–1767), a brother of George III.

Yosemite National Park The national park in central California takes its name from a former local tribe of Indians here, whose own name means 'grizzly bear'. The name is pronounced 'Yo*sem*iti', in four syllables.

Young The name originally applied to the younger of two bearers of a given name, typically a son, for purposes of distinction. The usage was thus similar to that still pertaining for identically named father and son today as (say) John Smith, Sr and John Smith, Jr, especially in the United States. In medieval times, the father would have been similarly distinguished by a name that marked him as the elder and that gave the modern surnames ELDER and *Old*.

Youngbloods, The The American folk-rock group, formed in Boston in 1965, took their name from their lead singer, Jesse Colin *Young* (real name Perry Miller).

Young Vic The name is familiar today as that of the London theatre founded in 1970 near the OLD VIC with the aim of producing good drama played by adult actors for *young* people. An earlier theatre group of the name had been founded in 1945 with similar aims as part of the *Old Vic* Drama School.

Ypres The town in western Belgium, the scene of many battles in the First World War, derives its name ultimately from Gaulish *ivo*, 'yew'. Its Flemish name is *Ieper*, but to the British 'Tommy' it was colloquially 'Wipers'.

Ys The name is that of the legendary city said to have been submerged by the sea off the coast of Brittany, northwest France, in the 4th or 5th century. Its Breton name is *Kêr-Iz*, 'low town', from *kêr*, 'town' and *is*, 'low'. The city and its legend formed the basis of the opera by Lalo *Le Roi d'Ys* (1888), and it also inspired one of Debussy's best-known piano compositions, *La Cathédrale engloutie* ('The submerged cathedral') (1910).

Yucatán The Mexican state is said to take its name from a local word meaning 'massacre', from *yuka*, 'to kill' and *yetá*, 'many'. It was perhaps on the peninsula here that the Maya were exterminated. According to another account, Spanish explorers asked native people what the name of the region was and received the reply *yucatän*, 'I don't understand'.

Yugoslavia The republic in southeast Europe has a name that means 'southern Slavs', from Serbo-Croat *jug*, 'south' and SLAV. *Cp.* SLOVENIA. The name *Yugoslavia* has existed officially only since 1929. The earlier name, given in 1918 when the country was formed on the collapse of Austria-Hungary, was *Kingdom of the Serbs, Croats and Slovenes*, or in Serbo-Croat, *Kraljevina Serba, Hrvata i Slovenaca*.

Yukon The territory of northwest Canada takes its name from the river *Yukon*, whose own name represents Indian *yukun-ah*, 'big river'.

Yule The alternative name of CHRISTMAS derives from Old English *gēol*, the name of a pagan feast lasting 12 days, itself of unknown origin.

Yunnan The province of southwest China has a name meaning 'cloudy south', from Chinese *yún*, 'cloud' and *nán*, 'south'. The region here is noted for its high rainfall.

Yvelines The department of northern France, in the region of Paris, takes its name from a former forest here, known to the Romans as *Aequalina silva*. The first word of this gave the current name, recorded in the 13th century as *Yvelina*. The ultimate origin is probably in a Celtic root word meaning 'water', 'stream'.

Yvonne The popular name is a French feminine pet form of *Yves*, itself of Germanic origin, meaning 'yew'. *Cp.* IVOR.

Zaandam The former town in the northern Netherlands derives its name from the river *Zaan* here. The river's own name represents Old Dutch *saden*, 'marshland' and *dam*, 'dam'. In 1974 it became part of ZAANSTAD.

Zaanstad The port in the western Netherlands, immediately north of Amsterdam, was formed in 1974 as a merger of seven existing towns and villages, and took a name based on that of the river *Zaan* that already formed part of the names of four of them: ZAANDAM, Koog a/d *Zaan*, *Zaandijk* and *Westzaan*. Dutch *stad*, 'town' was added to the river name.

Zacchaeus The name of the rich man who climbed a sycamore tree to see Jesus (*Luke* 19.1–10) represents Hebrew *Zakkai*, 'innocent', 'justified'.

Zacharias The name of the father of John the Baptist in the New Testament derives from Hebrew *Zēkharyah*, 'Yah (*i.e.* Jehovah) has remembered'. This is also the origin of the name of the prophet *Zechariah*, for whom a book of the Old Testament is named.

Zadok The name of the chief priest of King David in the Old Testament derives from Hebrew *Tsādhōq*, 'righteous', 'just', from a word that lies behind that of MELCHIZEDEK. *See also* SADDUCEE.

Zagorsk *See* SERGIYEV POSAD.

Zagreb The capital of Croatia has a name that means 'beyond the bank', from Old Croat *za*, 'beyond' and *grebom*, the instrumental case (required after this preposition) of *greb*, 'bank', 'embankment'.

Zaïre The republic in south central Africa derives its name from an earlier and still alternative name of the river CONGO. The river's name represents Kikongo *nzai*, a dialect form of *nazdi*, 'river'. Earlier names of the country include *Congo Free State* (1885–1908), *Belgian Congo* (1908–1960), and *Democratic Republic of the Congo* (1960–71). *Cp.* ZAMBEZI, ZAMBIA.

Zambezi The river of central and eastern Africa, the fourth longest in the continent, has a name that derives from the same basic root word, *za*, 'river' that gave the name of ZAÏRE.

Zambia The republic in central Africa takes its name from the river ZAMBEZI that forms much of its southern frontier.

Zamora The city in northwest central Spain has a name that is probably of Arabic origin, from *zamurrud*, 'emerald', referring to the exploitation of this gemstone by Arabs here from the 8th century.

Zanzibar The island off the east coast of Africa, in the Indian Ocean, has a name that derives from *Zengi* or *Zengj*, the name of a local people, itself meaning 'black', and Arabic *barr*, 'coast', 'shore'.

Zaporozhye The Ukrainian city, on the river Dnieper, has a name that means 'beyond the rapids', from Russian *za*, 'beyond' and *porog*, 'rapids', literally 'threshold' (*cp.* PRAGUE). There are no rapids here now, but there were before the construction of the Dneproges dam in 1932. The town has borne this name only from 1921. Its earlier name was *Aleksandrovsk*, after the Russian general *Aleksandr* Golitsyn (1718–1783), who commanded an army that was stationed in southern Ukraine at the time when the town was founded in 1770.

Zaragoza *See* SARAGOSSA.

Zarathustra The name is the Avestan form of that of the Persian prophet ZOROASTER (*which see*).

Zebedee The name of the father of the disciples James and John, seen by Jesus in a fishing boat on the Sea of Galilee (*Matthew* 4.21), derives from Hebrew *Zebhadhyāhu*, 'Yah (*i.e.* Jehovah) has given'. The name also occurs as *Zebadiah*, found for several characters in the Old Testament.

Zebulun The name of the sixth son of Jacob, born to him by Leah, is interpreted in the Old Testament as deriving from Hebrew *zebed*, 'present': 'And Leah said, God hath endued me with a good dowry; now will my husband dwell with me, because I have born him six sons: and she called his name Zebulun' (*Genesis* 30.20). It is more likely, however, to represent Hebrew *zābal*, 'to remain', 'to stay', from *zebūl*, 'house', 'temple'.

Zechariah *See* ZACHARIAS.

Zedekiah The Old Testament name, that of the last king of Judah, derives from Hebrew *Tsidhqīyāhu*, 'Yah (*i.e.* Jehovah) is just' or 'justice of Yah'.

Zeebrugge The coastal town in northwest Belgium is linked by canal with BRUGES and is the port for that city. Its name indicates this connection, meaning literally 'sea Bruges', from Flemish *zee*, 'sea' and *Brugge*, 'Bruges'.

Zeeland The province of the southwest Netherlands has a name meaning 'sea land', from Dutch *zee*, 'sea' and *land*, 'land'. *Cp.* SJÆLLAND and ZUIDER ZEE and *see also* NEW ZEALAND.

Zen The name is familiar as the Japanese school of Buddhism which holds that the truth lies not in scriptures but in people's own hearts, if they will only try to find it by meditation and self-mastery. It derives from Chinese *chán*, itself from Pali *jhāna*, ultimately from Sanskrit *dhyāna*, representing *dhyayati*, 'he thinks'.

Zend The name is either short for the ZEND-AVESTA or is specifically that of the commentary on it that forms an integral part of it.

Zend-Avesta The name is that of the sacred writings of the Parsees, collected into their present form in the 4th century AD and comprising the AVESTA (liturgical books for the priests) with the *Zend* that is the commentary on it and that forms part of the whole work. *Zend* derives from Persian *zand*, 'commentary, 'exposition'. *See also* ZOROASTER.

Zeno The name of the Greek philosopher of the 5th century BC developed as a short form of a longer name such as *Zenorodoros* that was based on the name of the great god ZEUS.

Zenobia The Greek name of the 3rd-century queen of Palmyra means 'life of ZEUS', from *Zēn-*, a stem form of *Zeus*, and *bios*, 'life'.

Zephaniah The biblical prophet, with a book of the Old Testament named for him, derives his name from Hebrew *Tsephanyāh*, 'Yah (*i.e.* Jehovah) has hidden'.

Zeppelin *See* GRAF ZEPPELIN.

Zermatt The well-known village and resort in southern Switzerland derives its name from German *zur Matte*, 'at the pasture'. *Cp.* MATTERHORN.

Zerubbabel The Old Testament character, appointed governor of Judah by the Persians, was born in BABYLON. Hence his name, which derives from Akkadian *Zer-Babili*, 'seed of Babylon'.

Zeus The name of the supreme god of the ancient Greeks, whose Roman counterpart was JUPITER (*which see*), means 'god', 'sky', 'day', related to Sanskrit *deva*, Greek *theos*, Latin *deus*, French *dieu*, 'god', to Sanskrit *dyaus*, 'sky' and to Latin *dies*, 'day'. The equation between the three is not hard to follow, with the denominator of 'light' common to all.

Zhangjiakou The city in northeast China takes its name from *zhāng*, 'leaf', *jīa*, 'house' and *kŏu*, 'mouth'.

Zhdanov *See* MARIUPOL.

Zhengzhou The city in east central China, the capital of Henan province, has a name that represents Chinese *zhèng*, 'solemn' and *zhōu*, 'region'.

Zielona Góra The city in west central Poland has a name that means 'green hill', seen more readily in its German name, *Grünberg*. The town actually lies in a hollow of the hills.

Zimbabwe The republic in southeast Africa takes its name from a famous archaeological site, a ruined fortification near Masvingo, in the southeast of the country, whose own name represents Bantu *zimba we bahwe*, 'houses of stones', from *zimba*, the plural of *imba*, 'house' and *bahwe*, 'stones'. The country was formerly known as *Southern Rhodesia* (until 1964) and *Rhodesia* (1964–79).

Zion The name is that of the hill on which the city of Jerusalem stands, hence a name of Jerusalem itself, thus also a name for Jerusalem as the city of God, a name for the ancient Israelites, whose centre of worship it was, a name for Israel, as the national home of the Jews, and ultimately also a name for Christianity and the Christian world, as evolving from Judaism. In short, the name expands in significance, influence and scope like the diaspora itself. Its ultimate origin, however, is in the place-name of the hill, representing Hebrew *tsīyōn*. Unfortunately, the origin and meaning of this remain obscure. The name also occurs in the spelling *Sion* (*see also* SYON HOUSE).

Zlatoust The town in west central Russia arose in 1754 round the steel and iron works here. It takes its name from its

church, dedicated to St John CHRYSOSTOM, Russian *Ioann Zlatoust*.

Zoë The name derives from the Greek word *zōē*, 'life'. It was a name popular with the early Christians, who connected it with their new hope of eternal life.

Zoroaster The name is that of the Persian prophet of the 7th and 6th centuries BC who founded the dualistic religion *Zoroastrianism*, set out in the sacred writings of the ZEND-AVESTA. It evolved as a Greek form of his original Avestan (Old Iranian) name, which was *Zarathustra* (more precisely *Zarathushtra*), interpreted as '(he of the) old camels', from Avestan *zarant*, 'old' and *uštra*, 'camel'.

Zorro The black-masked and caped master swordsman, a type of Mexican Robin Hood, first appeared in the story by Johnston McCulley, *The Curse of Capistrano* (1919). This was made into a popular film, *The Mark of Zorro* (1920), in which he was played by Douglas Fairbanks. Further films followed. His nickname is Spanish for 'fox', both in the literal sense and as 'wily person'. His real name is Don Diego de la Vega.

Zug The canton of north central Switzerland takes its name from that of a lake here, with the lake's own name perhaps representing Celtic *tug*, 'roof', referring to its lofty location, at an altitude of 1368 feet (417 m).

Zuider Zee The former inlet of the North Sea in the north coast of the Netherlands has a name that means 'southern sea'. The apparent anomaly is due to the fact that the name contrasts with that of the NORTH SEA itself, and perhaps also the *Ostsee*, 'eastern sea', the German name for the Baltic. The inlet was cut off from the sea by a dam in 1932.

Zulu The name of the people of southeast Africa, and that of their language, is of uncertain origin and meaning. It is said by some authorities to mean 'sky'.

Zürich The canton of northeast Switzerland and its capital have a name that ultimately derives from the Celtic root element *dur*, 'water', referring to the location of the city on Lake *Zürich*.